Twentieth-Century Literary Criticism

Guide to Gale Literary Criticism Series

For criticism on	Consult these Gale series
Authors now living or who died after December 31, 1959	*CONTEMPORARY LITERARY CRITICISM (CLC)*
Authors who died between 1900 and 1959	*TWENTIETH-CENTURY LITERARY CRITICISM (TCLC)*
Authors who died between 1800 and 1899	*NINETEENTH-CENTURY LITERATURE CRITICISM (NCLC)*
Authors who died between 1400 and 1799	*LITERATURE CRITICISM FROM 1400 TO 1800 (LC)* *SHAKESPEAREAN CRITICISM (SC)*
Authors who died before 1400	*CLASSICAL AND MEDIEVAL LITERATURE CRITICISM (CMLC)*
Authors of books for children and young adults	*CHILDREN'S LITERATURE REVIEW (CLR)*
Dramatists	*DRAMA CRITICISM (DC)*
Poets	*POETRY CRITICISM (PC)*
Short story writers	*SHORT STORY CRITICISM (SSC)*
Black writers of the past two hundred years	*BLACK LITERATURE CRITICISM (BLC)*
Hispanic writers of the late nineteenth and twentieth centuries	*HISPANIC LITERATURE CRITICISM (HLC)*
Native North American writers and orators of the eighteenth, nineteenth, and twentieth centuries	*NATIVE NORTH AMERICAN LITERATURE (NNAL)*
Major authors from the Renaissance to the present	*WORLD LITERATURE CRITICISM, 1500 TO THE PRESENT (WLC)*

ISSN 0276-8178

R

Volume 84

Twentieth-Century Literary Criticism

**Criticism of the
Works of Novelists, Poets, Playwrights,
Short Story Writers, and Other Creative Writers
Who Lived between 1900 and 1960,
from the First Published Critical
Appraisals to Current Evaluations**

Jennifer Baise
Editor

Thomas Ligotti
Associate Editor

The Gale Group

DETROIT • SAN FRANCISCO • LONDON • BOSTON • WOODBRIDGE, CT

STAFF

Jennifer Baise, *Editor*

Thomas Ligotti, *Associate Editor*

Maria Franklin, *Interim Permissions Manager*
Kimberly F. Smilay, *Permissions Specialist*
Kelly A. Quin, *Permissions Associate*
Sandy Gore, *Permissions Assistant*

Victoria B. Cariappa, *Research Manager*
Michele P. LaMeau, Andrew Guy Malonis, Barbara McNeil, Gary J. Oudersluys, Maureen Richards, *Research Specialists*
Tamara C. Nott, Tracie A. Richardson, Cheryl L. Warnock, *Research Associates*
Corrine Stocker, *Research Assistant*

Mary Beth Trimper, *Production Director*
Deborah L. Milliken, *Production Assistant*

Christine O'Bryan, *Desktop Publisher*
Randy Bassett, *Image Database Supervisor*
Robert Duncan, Michael Logusz, *Imaging Specialists*
Pamela Reed, *Imaging Coordinator*

Library of Congress Catalog Card Number 76-46132
ISBN 0-7876-2742-9
ISSN 0276-8178

Printed in the United States of America
10 9 8 7 6 5 4 3 2 1

Contents

Preface   vii

Acknowledgments   xi

Preface

Since its inception more than fifteen years ago, *Twentieth-Century Literary Criticism* has been purchased and used by nearly 10,000 school, public, and college or university libraries. *TCLC* has covered more than 500 authors, representing 58 nationalities, and over 25,000 titles. No other reference source has surveyed the critical response to twentieth-century authors and literature as thoroughly as *TCLC*. In the words of one reviewer, "there is nothing comparable available." *TCLC* "is a gold mine of information—dates, pseudonyms, biographical information, and criticism from books and periodicals—which many libraries would have difficulty assembling on their own."

Scope of the Series

TCLC is designed to serve as an introduction to authors who died between 1900 and 1960 and to the most significant interpretations of these author's works. The great poets, novelists, short story writers, playwrights, and philosophers of this period are frequently studied in high school and college literature courses. In organizing and reprinting the vast amount of critical material written on these authors, *TCLC* helps students develop valuable insight into literary history, promotes a better understanding of the texts, and sparks ideas for papers and assignments. Each entry in *TCLC* presents a comprehensive survey of an author's career or an individual work of literature and provides the user with a multiplicity of interpretations and assessments. Such variety allows students to pursue their own interests; furthermore, it fosters an awareness that literature is dynamic and responsive to many different opinions.

Every fourth volume of *TCLC* is devoted to literary topics. These topic entries widen the focus of the series from individual authors to such broader subjects as literary movements, prominent themes in twentieth-century literature, literary reaction to political and historical events, significant eras in literary history, prominent literary anniversaries, and the literatures of cultures that are often overlooked by English-speaking readers.

TCLC is designed as a companion series to Gale's *Contemporary Literary Criticism,* which reprints commentary on authors now living or who have died since 1960. Because of the different periods under consideration, there is no duplication of material between *CLC* and *TCLC*. For additional information about *CLC* and Gale's other criticism titles, users should consult the Guide to Gale Literary Criticism Series preceding the title page in this volume.

Coverage

Each volume of *TCLC* is carefully compiled to present:

- criticism of authors, or literary topics, representing a variety of genres and nationalities

- both major and lesser-known writers and literary works of the period

- 6-12 authors or 3-6 topics per volume

- individual entries that survey critical response to each author's work or each topic in literary history, including early criticism to reflect initial reactions; later criticism to represent any rise or decline in reputation; and current retrospective analyses.

Organization of This Book

An author entry consists of the following elements: author heading, biographical and critical introduction, list of principal works, reprints of criticism (each preceded by an annotation and a bibliographic citation), and a bibliography of further reading.

- The **Author Heading** consists of the name under which the author most commonly wrote, followed by birth and death dates. If an author wrote consistently under a pseudonym, the pseudonym will be listed in the author heading and the real name given in parentheses on the first line of the biographical and critical introduction. Also located at the beginning of the introduction to the author entry are any name variations under which an author wrote, including transliterated forms for authors whose languages use nonroman alphabets.

- The **Biographical and Critical Introduction** outlines the author's life and career, as well as the critical issues surrounding his or her work. References to past volumes of *TCLC* are provided at the beginning of the introduction. Additional sources of information in other biographical and critical reference series published by Gale, including *Short Story Criticism, Children's Literature Review, Contemporary Authors, Dictionary of Literary Biography,* and *Something about the Author,* are listed in a box at the end of the entry.

- Some *TCLC* entries include **Portraits** of the author. Entries also may contain reproductions of materials pertinent to an author's career, including manuscript pages, title pages, dust jackets, letters, and drawings, as well as photographs of important people, places, and events in an author's life.

- The **List of Principal Works** is chronological by date of first book publication and identifies the genre of each work. In the case of foreign authors with both foreign-language publications and English translations, the title and date of the first English-language edition are given in brackets. Unless otherwise indicated, dramas are dated by first performance, not first publication.

- Critical essays are prefaced by **Annotations** providing the reader with information about both the critic and the criticism that follows. Included are the critic's reputation, individual approach to literary criticism, and particular expertise in an author's works. Also noted are the relative importance of a work of criticism, the scope of the essay, and the growth of critical controversy or changes in critical trends regarding an author. In some cases, these annotations cross-reference essays by critics who discuss each other's commentary.

- A complete **Bibliographic Citation** designed to facilitate location of the original essay or book precedes each piece of criticism.

- Criticism is arranged chronologically in each author entry to provide a perspective on changes in critical evaluation over the years. All titles of works by the author featured in the entry are printed in boldface type to enable the user to easily locate discussion of particular works. Also for purposes of easier identification, the critic's name and the publication date of the essay are given at the beginning of each piece of criticism. Unsigned criticism is preceded by the title of the journal in which it appeared. Some of the essays in *TCLC* also contain translated material. Unless otherwise noted, translations in brackets are by the editors; translations in parentheses or continuous with the text are by the critic. Publication information (such as footnotes or page and line references to specific editions of works) have been deleted at the editor's discretion to provide smoother reading of the text.

- An annotated list of **Further Reading** appearing at the end of each author entry suggests secondary sources on the author. In some cases it includes essays for which the editors could not obtain reprint rights.

Cumulative Indexes

- Each volume of *TCLC* contains a cumulative **Author Index** listing all authors who have appeared in Gale's Literary Criticism Series, along with cross references to such biographical series as *Contemporary Authors* and *Dictionary of Literary Biography.* For readers' convenience, a complete list of Gale titles included appears on the first page of the author index. Useful for locating authors within the various series, this index is particularly valuable for those authors who are identified by a certain period but who, because of their death dates, are placed in another, or for those authors whose careers span two periods. For example, F. Scott Fitzgerald is found in *TCLC,* yet a writer often associated with him, Ernest Hemingway, is found in *CLC.*

- Each *TCLC* volume includes a cumulative **Nationality Index** which lists all authors who have appeared in *TCLC* volumes, arranged alphabetically under their respective nationalities, as well as Topics volume entries devoted to particular national literatures.

- Each new volume in Gale's Literary Criticism Series includes a cumulative **Topic Index,** which lists all literary topics treated in *NCLC, TCLC, LC 1400-1800,* and the *CLC* yearbook.

- Each new volume of *TCLC,* with the exception of the Topics volumes, includes a **Title Index** listing the titles of all literary works discussed in the volume. In response to numerous suggestions from librarians, Gale has also produced a **Special Paperbound Edition** of the *TCLC* title index. This annual cumulation lists all titles discussed in the series since its inception and is issued with the first volume of *TCLC* published each year. Additional copies of the index are available on request. Librarians and patrons will welcome this separate index; it saves shelf space, is easy to use, and is recyclable upon receipt of the following year's cumulation. Titles discussed in the Topics volume entries are not included *TCLC* cumulative index.

Citing Twentieth-Century Literary Criticism

When writing papers, students who quote directly from any volume in Gale's literary Criticism Series may use the following general forms to footnote reprinted criticism. The first example pertains to materials drawn from periodicals, the second to material reprinted from books.

[1]William H. Slavick, "Going to School to DuBose Heyward," *The Harlem Renaissance Re-examined,* (AMS Press, 1987); reprinted in *Twentieth-Century Literary Criticism,* Vol. 59, ed. Jennifer Gariepy (Detroit: Gale Research, 1995), pp. 94-105.

[2]George Orwell, "Reflections on Gandhi," *Partisan Review,* 6 (Winter 1949), pp. 85-92; reprinted in *Twentieth-Century Literary Criticism,* Vol. 59, ed. Jennifer Gariepy (Detroit: Gale Research, 1995), pp. 40-3.

Suggestions Are Welcome

In response to suggestions, several features have been added to *TCLC* since the series began, including annotations to critical essays, a cumulative index to authors in all Gale literary criticism series, entries devoted to criticism on a single work by a major author, more extensive illustrations, and a title index listing all literary works discussed in the series since its inception.

Readers who wish to suggest authors or topics to appear in future volumes, or who have other suggestions, are cordially invited to write the editors.

Acknowledgments

The editors wish to thank the copyright holders of the excerpted criticism included in this volume and the permissions managers of many book and magazine publishing companies for assisting us in securing reproduction rights. We are also grateful to the staffs of the Detroit Public Library, the Library of Congress, the University of Detroit Mercy Library, Wayne State University Purdy/Kresge Library Complex, and the University of Michigan Libraries for making their resources available to us. Following is a list of the copyright holders who have granted us permission to reproduce material in this volume of *TCLC*. Every effort has been made to trace copyright, but if omissions have been made, please let us know.

PHOTOGRAPHS AND ILLUSTRATIONS APPEARING IN *TCLC*, VOLUME 84, WERE RECEIVED FROM THE FOLLOWING SOURCES:

Susan B. Anthony

1820-1906

(Full name Susan Brownell Anthony) American suffragist, lecturer, and nonfiction writer.

INTRODUCTION

Anthony was one of the most influential figures in the early campaign for women's rights in the United States. Devoted to a number of social causes, including the anti-slavery movement, she spent most of her adult life delivering lectures around the country and testifying at congressional hearings on the importance of an amendment to the Constitution granting voting rights to American women. The resulting amendment, not ratified until 1920, is known as the "Susan B. Anthony Amendment."

Biographical Information

Born to Daniel Anthony and Lucy Read of Adams, Massachusetts, Anthony became impressed at any early age with the value of women's rights to property and self-government. Both of her parents believed in the causes of abolition and temperance. Her father, a devout Quaker who never permitted his wife to socialize or wear the colorful dresses she liked, speculated in the textile industry until his business failed. Deeply in debt, the family was forced to auction off all of its belongings, including her mother's personal property. This incident convinced Anthony that women should be granted the right to own property and to be financially autonomous. Anthony was first schooled at home by her father and later at the Friends' Seminary in Philadelphia, which she left in 1839 to become a teacher in Canajoharie, New York. She was active in the temperance movement through the early 1850s, and she campaigned against slavery until 1863; however, in 1853 Anthony was outraged at finding that the women at a world temperance convention were refused the right to serve as delegates or to speak openly. From then on, she applied her activism to the cause of women's rights. Around this time, Anthony was introduced to Elizabeth Cady Stanton by Amelia Bloomer, the editor of the temperance journal *Lily*. While Anthony had not yet begun to focus on women's subordinate role throughout society but instead had only touched on the abuse of women as the result of male alcoholism, Stanton was already committed to changing policy and social standards regarding women. The women forged a lifelong professional partnership and friendship. Anthony began her women's rights work by campaigning for several years for women's property rights in the state of New York; her efforts were rewarded in 1860 with the passage of a law ensuring property rights for married women. In 1868 An-

thony founded with Stanton and Parker Pillsbury the *Revolution,* a feminist newspaper that by 1870 had incurred $10,000 debt; Anthony spent the next six years lecturing around the country to pay her creditors. The next year Anthony and Stanton founded the National Women's Loyal League. Anthony had been lecturing in the eastern United States for several years, and in the early 1870s she traveled to the West, where she introduced her ideas in rural communities as well as large cities. In 1872 she was arrested for voting in Rochester, New York, in the national election. The judge at her trial waived the jury's decision and found her guilty, fining her $100 and the cost of prosecution. Enraged by the injustice of her trial, Anthony ignored the judge's demand that she remain silent and delivered a spontaneous speech in which she refused to recognize all laws in the country that did not grant her basic rights of citizenship. Hoping to avoid further sensationalism and embarrassment, the judge did not enforce the penalties, and Anthony was free to leave without taking her case to a higher court. In the 1880s Anthony toured Europe and began to organize what would become the International Council of Women. The group officially convened in

1902; Anthony considered it her greatest achievement. Throughout the 1890s Anthony campaigned against suffrage initiatives designed to exclude people based on class, race, and education level. She continued to travel and lecture until her death at age eighty-six in 1906. In 1979 Anthony was the first woman to appear on a U.S. minted coin, the Susan B. Anthony dollar.

Major Works

In the 1880s Anthony realized that she and her coworkers in the women's rights movement needed to produce a written legacy detailing their work for future generations of feminists, and she did not want to leave the job to male historians. Instead, Anthony enlisted Stanton and Matilda Joslyn Gage to begin work on the *History of Woman Suffrage.* Anthony wrote and published the first three volumes with Stanton and Gage. The fourth she wrote with Ida Husted Harper, who also wrote, with Anthony's full cooperation, a three-volume *Life and Work of Susan B. Anthony.* Two more volumes of the *History,* written after Anthony's death, were published in 1922. More than anything, Anthony was known for her rigorous lecture tours around the United States and Europe, which she continued until her death. Although she was not known as a dynamic orator, she was able to hold her audiences' attention because of the passion with which she delivered her message. It is generally to her speeches that contemporary feminists, orators, and rhetoricians turn when examining Anthony's considerable influence on modern culture and politics.

PRINCIPAL WORKS

History of Woman Suffrage [with Matilda Joslyn Gage, Elizabeth Cady Stanton, and Ida Husted Harper]. 4 vols. (nonfiction) 1881-1903
Elizabeth Cady Stanton, Susan B. Anthony: Correspondence, Writings, Speeches [edited by Ellen Carl Dubois] (letters, essays, and speeches) 1981; revised 1992
Failure Is Impossible: Susan B. Anthony in Her Own Words [edited by Lynne Sherr] (nonfiction) 1995

CRITICISM

Mortimer Brewster Smith (essay date 1934)

SOURCE: "Susan B. Anthony," in *Evangels of Reform,* Round Table Press, Inc., 1934, pp. 132-55.

[*In the following essay, Smith traces the history of Anthony's interest in women's rights.*]

In the vast company of agitators who preached their social and political Utopias in the America of the last half of the nineteenth century it is difficult to find one who was entirely free from some mental abberation or psychological abnormality or whose passion for reform was not merely another expression of that deep-grained Puritanism that has been the most salient feature of the American character. Susan Brownell Anthony, woman's suffrage advocate, was a happy exception. Miss Anthony possessed the fierce determination and conviction common to the reforming species but she had also a large amount of common sense and humour and a normal human outlook on life that makes her stand out as a unique figure among American reformers. What is most impressive about her half century of agitation for the political enfranchisement of women is the complete sanity of her nature and the reasonableness of her arguments and demands. Women have won such a complete victory in all fields of human endeavor it is hard to believe that only a few short years ago the moderate demands of Susan B. Anthony aroused in her countrymen an intensity of bitter feeling unequalled in the record of American reform save in the case of [William Lloyd] Garrison. The denunciation and ridicule heaped upon her head would have intimidated and discouraged a stout-hearted man. As in the case of Mary Wollstonecraft, her eighteenth century predecessor in the fight for freedom for her sex, all the vile names imaginative man could muster were applied to her, but she had besides this violent experiences that Mary never knew.

But as in the progress of all beneficent reforms this was only a temporary phase. Susan went through the usual cycle: first, calumny and ridicule; then respectful attention; finally, honor and acceptance. When she died in 1906, at the ripe old age of eighty-six, she was generally accepted as one of the great figures of her time and although the goal of all her life's work—votes for women—was not to be realized until fourteen years later, the progress toward women's freedom had made immense strides since she started to do battle.

At the time of the first woman's rights convention held at Seneca Falls, New York, in 1848, the legal and spiritual status of woman in society was very low indeed. Under the English common law, in force generally throughout the United States, a married woman was entirely subordinate to her husband, who, in the words of Blackstone, "may choose and govern the domicile, select her associates, separate her from her relatives, restrain her religious and personal freedom, compel her to cohabit with him, correct her faults by mild means, and, if necessary, chastise her with moderation, as though she was his apprentice or child."

Teaching and domestic service were almost the only occupations open to women; their property rights were very seriously limited; their children, in case of divorce, belonged exclusively to the father. The dogma of the inferiority of women was almost universally accepted as an irrevocable truth not only supported by the evidence of nature but decreed by the express stipulations of Holy Scripture.

These conditions and this viewpoint changed so rapidly that two years after the death of Miss Anthony, at the sixtieth anniversary of the Seneca Falls Convention, the following report of progress could be made: "When that first convention met, one college in the United States admitted women; now hundreds do so. Then there was not a single woman physician or ordained minister or lawyer; now there are 77,000 women physicians and surgeons, 3,000 ordained ministers and 1,000 lawyers. Then only a few poorly paid employments were open to women; now they are in more than three hundred occupations and comprise 80 per cent of our school teachers. . . . Then a married woman in most of our States could not control her own person, property or earnings; now in most of them these laws have been largely repealed, and it is only in regard to the ballot that the fiction of woman's perpetual minority is kept up."

Today women not only have the ballot but conditions have changed to such an extent that they own, according to a recent estimate, forty per cent of the wealth of the United States. The major part of the credit for this victory must surely go to Susan B. Anthony, who, in the face of heartbreaking discouragement and persecution, devoted all her time and tremendous energies and even her meagre personal fortune to the fight for freedom for women.

II

In the lives of most of Miss Anthony's contemporaries in the struggle for women's independence it is not difficult to surmise the psychological impulsion that thrust them into the battle. For example, Julia Ward Howe's interest in woman's suffrage during the latter part of her life was the result of resentment against the dominance over her of two men, her father and her husband, a resentment her "genteel" breeding prevented her from exhibiting while they were still alive. Anna Howard Shaw's devotion to the same cause had its basis in the bitter experiences of her childhood when her mother was forced to suffer the hardships of poverty and illness through the incompetence of a loving but thoughtless father who became the image in Anna's mind of masculine injustice. And Frances Willard's pious efforts in behalf of downtrodden womanhood can be traced in large part to her humiliating defeat at the hands of her former suitor, Mr. Fowler, which gave impetus to her determination to show the world "what a woman can do."

It is not as easy to find an underlying psychological reason for Miss Anthony's desire to achieve independence for women. Her relations with the men in her life—the men of her family, that is, for there was never a suitor for her hand whom she considered with any seriousness—were ideal and had nothing in them which could possibly have been the basis for her revolt against masculine domination. Unlike other rebellious women

of her time, she had not only the respect but the hearty support of her father and brothers. The father, Daniel Anthony, a New England Quaker with astonishingly liberal ideas for a man of the time, had a passionate interest in abolition, women's rights, and other reforms of the day. The answer, then, to the question of what compelled Susan to devote her life to the fight for equality for her sex must be sought in her own nature and mental makeup. Judged by the standards of her time, if not by those of the present, she undoubtedly possessed strong masculine traits—and when those traits were confronted by the prevailing notions of how women should act and think and what their position in the world should be, the reaction was revolt and open rebellion. Her nature demanded a more satisfying self-expression than was to be found in the usual feminine round of dish-washing, mending, and housecleaning. The difference between Susan and the other women of the time who yearned for freedom was that she had the courage boldly to take her freedom in defiance of man-made traditions and convictions. And in this she possessed the first prerequisite of the reformer—the willingness to stand out against the whole world if need be for the sake of an idea.

Her first step in her program of revolt against the conventions of the period was to enter the teaching profession, which was a somewhat daring thing to do at a time when women were not expected to engage in work that actually brought remuneration in money. The Anthony family had migrated from Adams, Massachusetts, where Susan was born, to Battensville, New York, where Daniel, the father, conducted a thriving cotton manufacturing business, but by 1840 the depression of the time had seriously affected his trade and what Susan was able to contribute to the family coffers from her earnings as a teacher was welcome indeed. In 1843 she secured, through the influence of her uncle, a wealthy citizen of Canajoharie, New York, the position of head of the "female" department of the academy of that town, and here she soon established herself as a brilliant and forceful teacher, loved by her pupils and even surreptitiously respected by the male members of the community who could not quite reconcile themselves to the fact that here was a woman equal in mental stature to any man and superior to most.

At this time Susan was not a beautiful woman but she certainly was a striking one, tall and broad shouldered, with a splendid head, forceful features, and brilliant blue eyes. Her masculinity of mind did not prevent her from having a passionate desire for fine clothes or from enjoying parties and dances; and she was attractive enough to receive proposals of marriage from several of the local swains. But the prospect of domestic bliss did not seem to hold any attraction for her and before long the delights of teaching young ladies how to read and write and spell also began to pale. Feeling that she was made for sterner tasks than these she determined to find some work in which she could employ the tremendous energies she felt rising up within her soul. In despair over the continued monotony and inaction of her life she even suggested to her father that she would like to join the men who were trekking over the continent to the newly discovered gold fields in California. She found some outlet for her desire to engage in social work in making temperance speeches but in 1849 she definitely deserted Canajoharie and the teaching profession and returned to Rochester, to which city Daniel had removed his family in 1845.

While Susan had been imparting the rudiments of knowledge to her pupils in the "female" department, momentous happenings were going on in the outside world. In July, 1848, Elizabeth Cady Stanton and Lucretia Mott had called a "women's rights" convention at Seneca Falls and had drawn up a "declaration of sentiments" modeled on the Declaration of Independence, in which the grievances of women against man's domination were detailed at length and a clarion call made to the women to do battle for their rights and privileges as human beings. In a few weeks a second convention, attended by great throngs and stirring up much enthusiasm as well as much antagonism, was held in Rochester. Susan came home for a holiday to find the Anthony household aroused to a high pitch of excitement over this convention; her father and mother and sister Mary had all attended and signed the resolution demanding equal suffrage. Susan was impressed but was not yet convinced that the fight for woman's suffrage should take precedence over the causes of temperance and abolition of slavery. Her conversion to the cause in which she was to labor for the rest of her life came a short time later and was the result of meeting Elizabeth Cady Stanton, the organizer of the Seneca Falls Convention, and one of the great women of the nineteenth century.

The efforts of these two women—Miss Anthony and Mrs. Stanton—in behalf of woman's suffrage were so closely allied for over half a century it is impossible to tell the story of one without mention of the other. They were such fast friends and fought together with such unanimity of attack that for the country at large the women's rights movement was represented in their persons. In 1878 Theodore Tilton said that he knew of "no two more pertinacious incendiaries in the whole country . . . in fact, this noise-making twain are the two sticks of a drum for keeping up what Daniel Webster called the 'rub-a-dub of agitation.'" The differences between the two women were striking. Mrs. Stanton was the more cultured, having had the advantage of an education obtained at Emma Willard's famous seminary in Troy; and she had a polished and literary style of speaking and writing that was very effective. Susan's education had been less thorough and her public speaking was marked by a blunt factual presentation of her case rather than by oratorical polish. Mrs. Stanton was inclined to be lazy and not always willing to sacrifice the luxuries of life in the stern battle for reform; Susan, on the other hand, had an immense physical vitality, could endure any hardships, and would expend her energies prodigiously. During their long friendship Susan was constantly prodding Mrs. Stanton into action, on one occasion shaming her into leaving off a comfortable vacation in England to come home and make a speech at a convention, and locking her in a hotel room until the speech was written. Of the two, Mrs. Stanton was perhaps the more imaginative, Susan, the better qualified to put the plans into action. "You stir up Susan," said Mrs. Stanton's husband, "and she stirs up the world."

When Susan had once discovered what she wanted to do in the world she applied herself to the task with a vigor and force and fierce determination one would be tempted to call fanaticism if that word did not have a connotation impossible to apply to one so basically sane and realistic in her conception of how women were to attain their rights. For over half a century she worked indefatigably, traveling from coast to coast and spreading her propaganda everywhere, never taking a vacation or a salary and apparently never feeling either fatigue or discouragement. The work was chiefly that of organization and propaganda and for this sort of thing she seemed to have a perfect genius. Besides speaking, and writing thousands of letters every year by hand, she appeared before state legislatures and Congress on every possible occasion to present the claims of women, managed an equal rights journal, organized working women's clubs, and was one of the authors of a massive history of woman's suffrage in several volumes, publication of which was made possible by Miss Anthony contributing $20,000 left her as a legacy.

That all this agitation should be received with unfriendliness by a public always resentful of new ideas was inevitable; what is surprising, considered from the vantage point of the present when Miss Anthony's ideas have won such a triumphant victory, is that the resentment took such bitter and violent forms. Throughout her reforming career, especially in its earlier years, she was subjected to a degree of verbal abuse and vilification equaled today only by such patriots as the Daughters of the American Revolution when speaking of the Russian Bolsheviki. The clergy, of course, branded her "atheist"; others called her "hermaphrodite" and "unsexed monster" as well as the less violent terms of "old maid" and "hen"; the New York *World* referred to her as "lean, cadaverous, and intellectual, with the proportions of a file and the voice of a hurdy-gurdy." A newspaper of Seattle, anxious no doubt, like newspapers of today, to find some new bugaboo to expose, pounced on Susan and declared: "She is a revolutionist, aiming at nothing less than the breaking up of the very foundations of society, and the overthrow of every social institution organized for the protection of the sanctity of the altar, the family circle and the legitimacy of our offspring, recognizing no religion but self-worship, no God but human reason, no motive to action but lust."

At her public meetings Susan met with all kinds of violence and indignities. Besides the usual cat-calls and hisses, very often knives and pistols were in evidence; and if no physical violence was ever visited upon her it was solely because she was a woman. She was, at least, burned in effigy by angry mobs on more than one occasion.

But Susan was too courageous and utterly unafraid to fear what these mobs could do to her. What saddened her was that respectable people who pretended to be champions of freedom gave her no encouragement and very often put obstacles in her way. She soon came to learn that she could expect very little help from the so-called liberals of Boston—they were polite but distinctly frigid. Wendell Phillips, one of the great liberal gods of the time and supposedly a friend of woman's suffrage, deserted the cause entirely after the Civil War on the grounds that it was the "Negro's hour" and suggested that Susan devote herself to securing the ballot for the black man before she tried to get it for women.

This insistence on the part of Phillips and other abolitionists that votes for the Negro should take precedence over votes for women aroused Susan's ire, for she and Mrs. Stanton had helped organize the Equal Rights Association, in which Phillips was a leading light, with the understanding that its aims were to agitate for complete enfranchisement, not only for the Negro but for the women of the country as well. No one save Garrison himself had worked more tirelessly for emancipation of the Negro than Susan but she felt that if there was to be a question of whether woman or the Negro should have the vote first, woman should take precedence for she was far better qualified to vote than the black man who had hardly emerged from the ignorance and superstition in which he had lived for centuries.

Susan finally succeeded in bringing about the dissolution of the Equal Rights Association and founded in its place the National Woman Suffrage Association which concentrated entirely on securing votes for women. The Boston conservatives countered this action by organizing the rival American Woman Suffrage Association with Henry Ward Beecher as president and Lucy Stone as chairman of the executive board. For twenty years the two societies went their separate ways, the National Association, headed by Mrs. Stanton and Susan, concentrating on a constitutional amendment, and the American Association under the guidance of Lucy Stone, seeking to win the vote by action of the separate states. In 1889 there was a reconciliation and the two bodies united as the National American Woman Suffrage Association which was headed by Mrs. Stanton until 1892. From that time until 1900 Miss Anthony held the presidency and was succeeded by Mrs. Carrie Chapman Catt.

It was not only the disloyalty of men that Susan had to contend with—at times even the women active in the cause seemed renegade, although the fact was that most of them had children and homes to look after to say nothing of husbands who thought they ought to stay at home. Even Mrs. Stanton, loyal as she was, could not always be depended on for she, too, had a household to care for; and even when she had the time the ease-loving Elizabeth did not relish the hardships of campaigning. Only Susan, of all the women identified with the cause, devoted her entire time to the work—and at times it seemed that she was a lone figure fighting against the whole world.

There was never an individual better equipped to wage such a battle. Not only was she free of all family encumbrances but she possessed the strength of body and determination of mind needed to endure the terrific physical strain incident to traveling in those days of the stagecoach and crude trains. In the *History of Woman Suffrage* she relates vividly how she slept in dirty beds in small-town hotels, sometimes kept awake all night by persistent tormentors; ate poorly-cooked food; held meetings in country schoolhouses, barns and sawmills, with boards for seats and lanterns hung around for lights; and rode half frozen in stage coaches through prairie snow storms. Through whatever hardships she kept always in mind the goal toward which she was working, and plodded on. With Garrison she could say: "I am in earnest—I will not equivocate—I will not retreat a single inch—and I will be heard!"

III

As a reformer Miss Anthony had an unusually realistic political sense and rarely made mistakes of judgment. Even her sensational arrest and trial for illegal voting which seemed to some of the more conservative suffrage workers to be prejudicial to the cause was a carefully thought out strategic move calculated to force public interest in the claims of women. In November, 1872, Susan read in a Rochester paper that all voters should register for the coming presidential election and determined to test the Fourteenth Amendment to the Constitution which declared any person born or naturalized in the United States a citizen. She and several other women persuaded the election inspectors to accept their registrations. On election day she cast her vote and two weeks later was arrested for illegal voting. At the trial she defended her position with vehemence but was sentenced by the judge, who had refused to permit a jury to sit in the case, to pay a fine of one hundred dollars and the costs of the prosecution.

"May it please your honor," declared Susan, "I will never pay a penny of your unjust penalty." It is perhaps needless to say that she never did.

Occasionally she made mistakes in her zeal for the advancement of women but most of them occurred when she was young enough to overcome them. Thus in the 1850's she tried to assert her independence by adopting the Bloomer costume invented by Elizabeth Smith Miller, cousin of Elizabeth Cady Stanton, and made famous by Mrs. Amelia Bloomer, editor of the *Lily,* a reform journal of the period. Susan abandoned it after two years, unable to bear the constant ridicule and laughter it aroused when she appeared in public.

Her judgment of people was unusually keen and she rarely permitted the innumerable freaks of the reform movements of the time to use the suffrage association for the advancement of their pet idiocies. An exception was her association with George Francis Train and Victoria Woodhull, two of the most romantic and almost mythical figures of nineteenth century America. She met Mr. Train shortly after the Civil War when she and Mrs. Stanton were campaigning for a suffrage amendment in Kansas and found unexpected support from this eccentric Irish adventurer who had managed, in his travels all over the world, to accumulate a vast fortune and a reputation for sartorial elegance. With the Hutchinson family, a famous quartet of singers and the Rev. Olympia Brown, one of the few women preachers of the day, he became a member of Miss Anthony's band; and in the prairie towns of Kansas, appearing before audiences of cowboys, ranchers, gamblers, and their wives and daughters, he was a huge sensation with his immaculate evening dress and lavender gloves, his Irish wit and royal manner. After the campaign was over he offered to finance a suffrage magazine to be known as the *Revolution* with Susan as its proprietor and Mrs. Stanton its editor. The magazine was duly launched but on the day of its first issue George Francis suddenly departed for England, assuring Susan that his mission was to secure new subscribers and contributors. A few days later she heard with dismay that he had been arrested in Dublin for aiding the Fenians and had been sentenced to life imprisonment. The sentence was later changed to deportation but the cause of women's rights had heard the last of the gallant Mr. Train. The magazine struggled along for two years and then folded up, leaving debts of ten thousand dollars which Susan assumed and paid, over a period of years, from the proceeds of her lectures.

When Victoria Woodhull offered her services to the cause of woman's suffrage Susan did not object but she soon learned to her sorrow that the beautiful Victoria, who had been a spiritualistic medium, a highly successful stock broker, and was to become a candidate for the presidency of the United States, aimed to use the suffrage association for the furtherance of her own ambitious plans. When Susan awoke to the real character of this wily adventuress she acted promptly, decisively, and to good effect. At a suffrage convention held in Steinway Hall in New York in 1872, Mrs. Woodhull tried to insinuate herself into the program by marching onto the platform and attempting to make a speech. Before she could say a word Susan jumped in front of her, reminded the audience that Mrs. Woodhull was not a member of the association and declared: "Nothing this person can say will be recorded in the minutes." And with that she declared the meeting adjourned, rushed from the platform and turned out the lights. As far as Susan and the cause of woman's suffrage was concerned that was the end of Victoria Woodhull although she was to bob up again in sensational fashion to lay bare the amours of the pious Henry Ward Beecher.

When Susan encountered opposition from eminent men of the day (which was practically all the time) she was more than capable of defending her position and very often cast her male opponent in a very sorry light. One of the best known of these encounters was with the redoubtable editor of the New York *Tribune,* Horace Greeley, supposedly a friend of women's rights but whose real sentiments were perhaps more adequately reflected in his famous remark regarding Margaret Fuller, that she would have been better off with a couple of bouncing babies on her knee instead of dabbling in masculine affairs.

Mr. Greeley was presiding at a suffrage meeting and became piqued at Miss Anthony's insistence that the franchise be immediately extended to include women.

"Miss Anthony," he finally asked impatiently, "you are aware that the ballot and the bullet go together? If you vote are you also prepared to fight?"

"Certainly, Mr. Greeley," replied Susan with exasperating promptness. "Just as you fought in the late war—at the point of a goose-quill."

Mr. Greeley did not soon forget Susan's little triumph and told her and Mrs. Stanton that he would have his revenge. This consisted in keeping the names of the two suffrage leaders out of the *Tribune* as much as it was possible to do so, and in ruling that Elizabeth was always to be referred to in print as Mrs. Henry B. Stanton, a rule that stayed in force for a number of years after Horace's death.

At a later period in her career she became involved in a dispute with Grover Cleveland, then ex-President, who had written an article in the *Ladies Home Journal* in which he attacked women's clubs and took a few sideswipes at woman's suffrage. Susan called it "pure folde-rol" and refused to discuss it seriously but added, somewhat maliciously, that "Grover Cleveland was about the last person to talk about the sanctity of the home and woman's sphere." Mr. Cleveland retaliated by a second attack in the same magazine to which Susan replied that "he isn't worth bothering about. If he had said one new thing, given one new idea, there might have been a chance for argument, but no—just hash, hash, hash of the same old kind!" The newspapers seized avidly on this incident and treated it with a facetiousness that did not add to the dignity of the portly ex-President. A widely circulated cartoon of the time depicted Mr. Cleveland on the run with a manuscript in his hand entitled, "What I Know About Women's Clubs" being pursued by Miss Anthony with raised umbrella ready to descend on his head. Out of the affair also came this bit of popular doggerel:

> Susan B.
> Anthony, she
> Took quite a fall out of Grover C.

One of the striking things about Miss Anthony was the constancy with which she devoted her efforts to woman's suffrage to the exclusion of all other reforms. She had early abandoned temperance work for that of women's rights and thereafter steadfastly refused to dabble in any other. In the later years of her life her ire was often aroused by recent converts to the suffrage movement who tried to use the clubs and state associations as channels of agitation for various laws designed to control the individual's private life by legislative coercion.

More than once her exasperation with her good friend Frances Willard, one of the most persistent advocates of prohibitory laws, found an outlet in very caustic comment. In 1896 Susan was campaigning in California for a suffrage amendment and had extracted a promise from Miss Willard that her Woman's Christian Temperance Union would remain out of it. She had also requested Mrs. Stanton, who dabbled in free thought and liked to ride the churches, not to circulate anti-Bible literature in the State. "What I want," wrote Susan, "is for men to vote 'yes' on the suffrage amendment, and I don't ask whether they make wine on the ranches or believe that Christ made it at the wedding feast. . . . So don't load me down with Bible, social purity, temperance or any other arguments under the sun but just those for woman's right to have her opinion counted at the ballot box."

Miss Willard and the white-ribbon sisters stayed out of the campaign but publicly announced that when the amendment was carried they intended to launch a second campaign to persuade the enfranchised women of California to use their votes to destroy the liquor traffic. This announcement produced a natural panic among the men, who decided that if women were going to use the vote to dictate their personal habits it were better that women remained in their "enslaved" state; and the amendment, which Susan had been reasonably sure of winning, was lost. Her annoyance at these tactics was great and when Miss Willard wrote to her shortly afterward asking that she join in protesting against "yellow journalism" and the Corbett-Fitzsimmons prizefight she took the opportunity to tell her what she thought about them.

"Don't you see," she wrote, "that if women ever get the right to vote it must be through the consent of not only the moral and decent men of the nation, but also through that of the other kind? Is it not perfectly idiotic of us to be telling the latter class that the first thing we shall do with our ballots will be to knock them out of their pet pleasures and vices? If you think it wise to keep on sticking pins into the men you will have to go on doing it. I certainly shall not be one of your helpers in that particular line of work."

Even if she had not early determined to devote herself exclusively to suffrage it is doubtful if she could ever have taken temperance or the other "moral reforms" of the century very seriously for she did not have that deep conviction of sin that in Miss Willard and many other reformers of the day took the form of a passionate desire to bring everybody to an acceptance of Christian morality in its narrowest forms. Susan counted herself a Christian, but as a liberal Quakeress who regularly at-

tended Mr. Gannett's Unitarian church in Rochester her religious views were far from evangelical and permitted a tolerance toward the weaknesses of human nature that Miss Willard's sterner faith must have considered distressingly loose.

How shocked the pious Frances must have been when she was told that Susan, at the World's Fair in Chicago in 1893, opposed all the churches of the city by advocating the Sunday opening of the exposition! When an incredulous parson asked her if she would even allow the Wild West show to be open on the Sabbath Susan replied: "Of course I would," and added that in her opinion one could "learn more from Buffalo Bill than from listening to an intolerant sermon." And what must Frances have thought when Colonel Cody, delighted at Susan's remark, sent her a box for the show which she attended in company with several friends? When the Colonel rode directly to her box, removed his hat, and made a sweeping bow, and Susan rose and gracefully returned the bow, the applause was tumultuous.

IV

As advancing age came upon the century, and upon Susan, the attitude of the public that had for so long vilified, ridiculed and persecuted her, changed to admiration and respect, but she was not much the happier for it. She was too shrewd an old warrior not to comprehend that this reversal of public opinion was not necessarily an acceptance of woman's suffrage; when she was affectionately referred to as "Aunt Susan," and the newspapers printed glowing tributes to her courage and ability, and she was received as a distinguished guest at the White House, she knew that it was only evidence of the natural human admiration for a "game old sport" whose head was bloody but unbowed after years of constant warfare against tremendous odds. In old age she stood upon a platform in a large American city, and as she gazed around her at the cheering audience and the flowers that surrounded her on all sides, said: "Time brings strange changes. In this very city that has pelted me with roses I have been pelted with rotten eggs for saying the very things I have said tonight." In her heart there must have been a nostalgic ache for the rotten eggs for she was never so happy or so effective as when opposition put her on her mettle and aroused her zest for battle. Not being one of those reformers content to rest on his laurels when he has won celebrity and public admiration, this new respect and devotion could mean little to her until woman's suffrage, to which she had devoted all her labors with fanatical constancy for over half a century, should become an actuality.

In 1900 she relinquished the presidency of the National American Woman Suffrage Association and turned the reins over to Mrs. Catt and Anna Howard Shaw, both ladies with decided talents, but with ideas of method that were somewhat different from Susan's. Miss Shaw was a pious and chubby little Methodist preacher with little of Miss Anthony's boldness or daring, and Mrs.

Catt was a representative of the new type of suffrage worker then coming into prominence, cultured and eminently refined in her methods of agitation, to whom the mere thought of rotten eggs and cat-calls and hisses was abhorrent. Between them they succeeded in making the suffrage cause conservative, respectable and quite harmless. Contrary to Miss Anthony's advice they concentrated on State action, seeking to win the franchise by the infinitely slow process of converting each State separately rather than winning it by national amendment to the Constitution. Susan might be getting old but she was still political realist enough to know that great reforms were not accomplished by vote of the common people but by intelligent minorities able to bring influence to bear on the law makers. She knew that only by gaining the support of one of the dominant political parties could national suffrage be achieved.

The soundness of her advice was borne out by the progress of the movement after her death. The National Association, dominated by Miss Shaw and Mrs. Catt, continued to try to win the vote by amendments to State constitutions through popular vote, and met with the scant success Susan had predicted. It was not until a group of women headed by Miss Alice Paul, in schism from the National Association, descended on Washington and applied the militant methods of lobbying and picketing that the vote for women was finally won. During the two terms of Woodrow Wilson's administration these women worked valiantly, bringing tremendous pressure to bear on Congress and the President, fighting with a militancy that would have delighted the heart of Susan B. Anthony had she lived to witness it. President Wilson and Congress finally bowed to the inevitable and on May 21st, 1919, the suffrage amendment was voted on and passed by the required two-thirds majority. Thus did the women of America, one hundred years after the birth of Susan B. Anthony and seventy-one years after the Seneca Falls Convention, finally enter into that beatific state of enfranchisement that had lured Susan on through her long life like the pot of gold at the foot of the rainbow.

In old age there was no slackening of that enormous energy and enthusiasm that had enabled her to fight on through years of discouragement, hardships, and ridicule. At the age of seventy-nine she attended the convocation of the International Council of Women in London, delivered a brilliant speech in her clear and still powerful voice; was feted by the Lord Bishop of London at a garden party; given a tea by the American Ambassador and his wife; entertained by the nobility everywhere; and as the crowning honor was received by Queen Victoria, only a year older than Susan but already feeble and infirm—Victoria, whose whole life had been devoted to the exaltation of the tenets of bourgeois English morality, not the least of which was that "woman's place is in the home."

When she was eighty-four she attended the meeting of the International Council again, this time in Berlin, and succeeded in winning the organization, composed chiefly of women's cultural clubs from all over the world, to support of woman's suffrage. On her way home she stopped off in London and visited Annie Besant, another pioneer battler in the cause of women's rights, who had put her active reforming days behind her and was now nourishing her soul on the esoteric mysteries of theosophy. Mrs. Besant, heir to the mantle of the inspired Mme. Blavatsky, seemed uninterested in worldly affairs and talked incessantly of the secrets of the mahatmas.

Susan, with her Yankee mistrust of the mystical, could stand it no longer and finally asked in her bluntest manner: "Annie, why don't you make that aura of yours do its gallivanting in this world, looking up the needs of the oppressed, and investigating the causes of present wrongs? Then you could tell us what to do about it all."

And when Mrs. Besant, in answer to Susan's inquiry as to what Annie's friend of past years, Charles Bradlaugh, was doing in the other world, replied that he was hovering near the earth unable to "get away from his mundane interests," Susan cried out, "Well! that's the most sensible thing I've heard yet about the other world. It encourages me."

Back in America again she plunged into the work of completing the fund for establishing co-education in the University of Rochester, in her home town. With only a day in which to work before the time limit expired she frantically collected $6,000 and at the last moment had to pledge her life insurance of $2,000 to complete the fund. The following night she was stricken with a slight stroke of apoplexy from which she never completely recovered. Her last public appearance was in 1906 at a great celebration in the city of Washington in honor of her eighty-sixth birthday. Against the doctor's orders she rose from a sick-bed to attend, saying, "the hammer may as well fall one time as another now. I am going." Even at this advanced age, and while she was literally dying on her feet, she could still summon up that fighting spirit that made her famous. When President Roosevelt's letter eulogizing her work was read she sprang to her feet and exclaimed with all her old fire: "One word from President Roosevelt in his message would be worth a thousand eulogies to Susan B. Anthony. When will men learn that what we ask is not praise, but justice?"

It was her last stand for the cause for in Washington she contracted a severe cold and in a month she was dead.

At her death newspapers all over the country that had attacked her consistently year in and year out printed column after column of praise and eulogy; statesmen who had turned a deaf ear to all her pleadings publicly expressed their grief; clergymen who had called her all the vile names that only clergymen can think up praised her as a saint among women and offered up prayers to heaven for the rest of her soul. Everywhere there was the realization that a great figure had passed on, one of the last representatives of that young and robust America that was fast becoming only a memory.

Elaine E. McDavitt (essay date 1944)

SOURCE: "Susan B. Anthony, Reformer and Speaker," in *The Quarterly Journal of Speech,* Vol. XXX, No. 1, February, 1944, pp. 173-80.

[*In the following essay, McDavitt considers major events of Anthony's career as a reformer, including her public speaking and media reaction to her.*]

The Nineteenth Amendment to the Constitution, enacted in August, 1920, reads as follows:

> The right of citizens of the United States to vote shall not be denied or abridged by the United States or by any state on account of sex.

It seems ironical that this act, realizing the hopes and dreams of Susan B. Anthony,[1] who had dedicated over fifty years to the emancipation and enfranchisement of women, was not passed until fourteen years after her death.

Like many another great reformer in history, Susan B. Anthony did not live to see the fruition of her work, but she did achieve recognition during her lifetime as a pioneer woman reformer and speaker. We shall here follow—briefly—her career, inquire into the forces that influenced her in that career, observe some of her characteristics as a speaker, and survey the reactions of the contemporary press.

I

CAREER

Mathilda J. Gage in *A History of Woman Suffrage* has said: "The prolonged slavery of woman is the darkest page in human history." For centuries, woman was regarded with little more consideration than a slave. In her father's house she learned to cook and sew, and do his bidding. Because she was trained to believe that marriage was the only suitable end of woman's life, at an early age she acquired a new master in the person of a husband to whom she bore children and for whom she kept a house, seldom venturing into the world beyond that house, never venturing to offer an opinion on the legal, economic, or social activities of her time.

If she did not marry, she became a kind of menial in the home of a male relative, a thing of pity, unwanted and unrespected. If she had to earn a living, dressmaking, teaching, or taking in boarders were the only means available to her. Her earnings in these capacities were meagre, and her position was negligible.

In America, women's rights had been championed as early as Revolutionary days when Abigail Adams had beseeched her husband, John Adams, to make a place for women in the Constitution of the United States. In 1828 Frances Wright dared to address a meeting in Cincinnati. The decade of the 1830's witnessed the first appearances on the public platform of such women as Lucretia Mott and Angelina Grimké in behalf of the abolition of slavery. By 1832 their development as public speakers had focused attention upon the question of whether women were to be allowed on the platform.

Ten years later women were hired as reform agents, and traveled about the country giving speeches. Although their activities were encouraged by William Lloyd Garrison, William Ellery Channing and Wendell Phillips, the approval of these liberals did not quiet the fierce vituperations of certain newspapers and pulpits, which believed firmly that women's place was in the home.

Certain women resented this attitude. They began to resent, too, the laws that did not permit women to hold property, the refusal of universities to admit women to candidacies for degrees, and the low salaries that women teachers received while performing the same duties as men.

In 1840, a World's Anti-Slavery Convention was held in London. Women delegates from the United States, including Elizabeth Cady Stanton and Lucretia Mott, were refused admittance to the floor of the auditorium and were relegated to the balcony. In the conversation of these women delegates as they returned to their hotel that evening, the first seeds of a woman's suffrage movement were planted.

The first meeting in its behalf was held in the home of Elizabeth Cady Stanton in Seneca Falls, New York, in July, 1848. After two days it adjourned to meet in Rochester on August 2. Susan Anthony did not attend this convention, but her father, mother, and sister Mary were present and signed the declaration demanding equal rights for women. Their enthusiasm for the cause and for its leader, Elizabeth Cady Stanton, had a pronounced effect on Susan.

She was affected also by the restlessness and fervor of the time. More than eighty thousand men had gone to California in search of gold; telegraphs and railroads were being rapidly constructed; and the slavery question was acquiring greater significance. It was not surprising that the narrow confines of the schoolroom should seem like prison walls to an educated, public-spirited young woman, and that she should become absorbed with the thought, "What service can I render humanity; what can I do to help right the wrongs of society?"

She first sought the answer in work for the Temperance movement and then in the Antislavery movement, through which she at last met Elizabeth Cady Stanton in 1851. Mrs. Stanton was immediately charmed by the tall, shy Quaker girl, and here began a friendship and association that lasted for many years. Susan B. Anthony had found her life's work and had begun her career in public life.

In April, 1852, the Sons of Temperance invited the Daughters of Temperance to send delegates to a convention at Albany. Susan Anthony's credentials as a delegate from Rochester were accepted, but when she rose to speak, she was informed by the presiding officer that "the sisters were not invited there to speak but to listen and learn." Miss Anthony and three other delegates left the hall. On the advice of Lydia Mott they held a meeting of their own and organized the Woman's State Temperance Convention.

At the first meeting Susan Anthony was expected to present the opening address as well as to preside. Shy and reluctant, she was persuaded to do so by Elizabeth Cady Stanton, who said:

> I will gladly do all in my power to help you. Come and stay with me, and I will write the best lecture I can for you. I have no doubt a little practice will make you an admirable speaker. Dress loosely, take a great deal of exercise, be particular about your diet, and sleep enough. The body has great influence on the mind. In your meetings, if attacked, be cool and good-natured, for if you are simple and truth loving, no sophistry can confound you.

Susan Anthony gratefully accepted the offer. Thus began a collaboration which these two women continued for many years. By the application of Elizabeth Cady Stanton's facile style to Susan Anthony's arguments and statistics, there resulted speeches that were able representations of the cause of woman's rights.

Susan Anthony attended her first Woman's Rights Convention on September 8, 1852. From that time until her death in 1906, she was a devoted and ardent champion of this cause. When, at this meeting, Mrs. Smith, fashionable Bostonian elaborately dressed in a low-necked gown, was nominated for president, Susan Anthony spoke out boldly and said that nobody so dressed should represent the earnest, hard-working women of the country for whom they were demanding equal rights. She won her point, and Lucretia Mott was made president. Susan Anthony had dared to say what others had only dared to think.

Since the days when she had presided over the school room during her fifteen years as a teacher, she had been familiar with the injustices meted out to the women in that profession. In August, 1853, she attended a teachers' convention at Rochester. Over five hundred teachers were in attendance; at least two-thirds of them were women. For two days Susan Anthony sat there, and not one of the women dared to speak. Toward the close of the second day's sessions the subject under consideration was "Why the profession of teacher is not as much respected as that of lawyer, doctor or minister." After two hours she could bear it no longer. When she rose

and said, "Mr. President," a bombshell would not have created greater emotion. For the first time in all history a woman's voice was heard in a teachers' convention. The question of whether she should be heard precipitated a debate that lasted half an hour. She stood the entire time, fearing to lose the floor if she sat down. At last, given permission to speak, she said:

> It seems to me you fail to comprehend the cause of which you complain. Do you not see that so long as society says woman has not brains enough to be a doctor, lawyer, or minister, but has plenty to be a teacher, every man of you who condescends to teach, tacitly admits before all Israel and the sun that he has no more brains than a woman?

She had intended to say also that the only way to place teaching on a level with other professions was either to admit women to them or to exclude them from teaching, but her trembling limbs would no longer sustain her.

During the next few years she developed more confidence in her ability to appear before the public. She journeyed from town to town to organize associations, to make financial arrangements, and to engage halls for meetings; and she spoke briefly on programs with other performers. To present a resolution or make a five-minute speech became an easy thing, but a request to speak for an hour before a teachers' association in August, 1856, on "Coeducation" kept Miss Anthony awake for many nights. Elizabeth Cady Stanton, coming to the rescue, said, "Come here and I will do what I can to help you with your address if you will hold the baby and make the pudding." She kept her promise. When the address was completed Susan Anthony felt that in order to prove the absolute equality of women with men she ought to present this as an oration instead of reading it as an essay. She paced up and down for hours trying to commit the speech to memory, but all in vain. It was impossible for her, then or later, ever to memorize exact words. For this reason most of her speeches were given from notes, never being presented twice in quite the same way. Although Elizabeth Cady Stanton continued to be of assistance to her in the preparation of some speeches, there were no more carefully worded orations to memorize.

Conventions were abandoned during the Civil War years, and Susan became a leading force in the war work of an organization known as the Woman's National Loyal League. After the war she was influential in uniting the Anti-Slavery Society with the Woman's Right Society, a merger known as the American Equal Rights Association, for, with the abolition of slavery, the prime object of both organizations became universal suffrage. However, when the Fourteenth Amendment enfranchised Negro men, this organization was ended, and the American Woman's Suffrage Association was formed on May 14, 1870.

In 1872 Susan Anthony and fourteen other woman suffragists, supported by some of the ablest Constitutional lawyers in the country, claimed the right to vote under the Fourteenth and Fifteenth Amendments to the Constitution, which did not mention sex in awarding the privileges of franchise. Consequently, on November 1, 1872, these women cast their first votes and were immediately served warrants. In the interesting and significant trial, which dragged out for a year, Susan Anthony stood her ground. The trial was, in a measure, a farce, for Judge Hunt ignored the right of every citizen to a trial by jury when he "demanded" a verdict of "guilty." But the trial of Susan Anthony had lifted the question of woman suffrage from one of grievance to one of Constitutional law. It had been proved that further legislation was needed to secure equal rights for women.

Opportunity to earn much-needed money for her campaign came to her in an offer from the Redpath Lyceum Bureau, which, by 1870, had become a marked feature of literary life. In the decade of the 1870's she spoke in all parts of the country under both the Redpath auspices and those of the Slayton Lyceum Bureau. Her speeches, **"Woman Wants Bread, Not the Ballot,"** and **"Social Purity,"** established her at last as a speaker as well as a reformer.

By 1880 her hard work on the lecture platform was beginning to show results. More and more supporters were gathering to her cause, and great satisfaction came in February, 1887, twenty years after she had made her first Kansas campaign, when municipal suffrage was conferred on the women of Kansas. A second triumph came in 1890 when Wyoming was admitted into the Union with franchise for women, despite a long and bitter struggle. In 1893 suffrage was granted to the women of Colorado. More progress was made in 1895 when Utah was admitted, without controversy, with the same provision Wyoming had exacted five years before.

That complete suffrage was not attained in a greater number of states was a source of disappointment to Susan Anthony in her last years, yet she must have found encouragement in the legal, educational, and industrial gains that women enjoyed as a result of her devotion of fifty years to their cause. The influence of women increased in every direction, the number of women in colleges approached that of men, the number of girls in the high schools exceeded that of boys, women under liberal laws acquired property, and others enjoyed financial independence. The American Woman's Suffrage Association, which she founded with a handful of women and nursed through years of weakness and poverty, had expanded into a great organization with affiliated branches in nearly every state. Women of all classes, creeds, and interests had entered the movement for franchise.

Her last message to a convention of women suffragists concluded with these words: "The fight must not cease; you must see that it does not stop!" To Anna Howard Shaw, her devoted friend and disciple, Susan Anthony passed the torch. And Anna Howard Shaw carried on the work as she had promised at Susan Anthony's bed-side during the long hours before the latter's death on March 13, 1906.

II

BACKGROUND INFLUENCES

A study of the ancestry, home, and childhood of Susan B. Anthony reveals the significance of these influences in her development as a reformer and a speaker.

On her father's side she was descended from English stock that had first migrated to America in 1634, and eventually settled in the village of Adams in the Berkshire Hills of Massachusetts. Her father's family were Quakers, faithful upholders of the tenets of that church. Daniel Anthony, father of Susan, received an education through the efforts of his mother and returned to his local village to teach school. Among his pupils was Lucy Reade, whom he married in 1817.

Lucy Reade, mother of Susan, was also descended of English stock. Her father, Daniel Reade, fought in the Revolutionary War and was a member of the Massachusetts legislature. The Reades were firm Baptists until Daniel became interested in the teachings of John Murray, founder of the Universalist faith. Reade was one of the first persons in his vicinity to disbelieve in a literal hell. Although his wife "wore out the skin on her knees," praying for the salvation of his soul, he remained firm in his Universalist beliefs until his death at eighty-four. Because of her father's unorthodox beliefs, Lucy was brought up in a liberal manner; she was given singing lessons, allowed to attend parties and dances, and to wear pretty clothes.

When Daniel Anthony married Lucy Reade, the Quakers threatened to read Daniel out of meeting. However, a dispensation was finally made, and Lucy learned to love the religion of the Friends, but she never became a member of the church; declaring she was not good enough.

Susan B. Anthony, the second of eight children, was born on February 15, 1820. Like other girls of her generation, she was brought up to cook and sew and care for the house and younger children, but she was more fortunate than most of these "other girls"; she was sent to school, for the Quakers believed in equal education of men and women.

First, she attended an old-fashioned district school. Later, her father operated a private school in a room in his brick store, employed the best teachers and admitted only those children whom he wished to associate with his own. When she was fifteen, Susan, herself, taught the younger children during the summer months.

When she was eighteen, Susan was sent to a boarding school near Philadelphia, where Deborah Moulson had opened a "Seminary for Females." The announcement said, "The inculcations of the Principles of Humility, Morality, and a love of Virtue will receive particular attention." Susan must have been greatly influenced by the austere Deborah, who was said to have been a cultured and estimable woman but to have represented the spirit of that age toward childhood, liberally administering reproof and as conscientiously withholding praise.

During this year Susan wrote many letters to her family, but each letter that she wrote had to be copied on a slate and then censored, corrected, and recopied before it could be sent. A letter was often five or six days in preparation, and no opportunity was given for developing a facile style. In later years she attributed the stilted style in which she wrote her speeches to these laborious letters she was forced to write in school. In order to escape from this artificial method of writing, she cultivated extemporaneous speaking, using only a brief outline.

Her antipathy to drink was probably acquired at an early age. Her father kept a store where he sold intoxicating liquors; but, when he saw a man frozen to death by the side of the road, with a nearby tell-tale jug, he determined to sell no more liquor. He also became interested in the Temperance movement, a movement which Susan supported firmly when she grew up.

Her interest in reform movements became intensified in 1845. While teaching in Canajoharie, she became absorbed in the Temperance movement, and while visiting at her parents' home in Rochester, her attention was turned to the Anti-Slavery movement, an issue of controversy in the Quaker church, which finally caused Daniel Anthony, a firm believer in Abolition, to transfer his loyalty to the Unitarian church.

Finally, as the beliefs and ideals which heredity and environment had sowed in her heart and soul increasingly cried for opportunity in expression and action, school teaching became tedious and monotonous to her. Inevitably, therefore, she left this work in which she had been successful for fifteen years and in 1852 embarked upon a career as spokesman for several reform movements, a career in which she was backed by her father, financially and spiritually. In her subsequent activities it is possible to see the Quakerism of the Anthonys, who had believed in temperance, education, and adherence to uprighteous living, the liberalism and tolerance of her Universalist grandfather, Daniel Reade, and the sound ideals of morals and virtue of the austere Deborah. Perhaps the greatest influence in all she was and in all she did was her father, Daniel Anthony, who had sent her to school, encouraged her in her activities as a teacher, impressed her with the evils of drink and with the importance of adherence to beliefs of right, and who finally gave her the unwavering courage to pursue her work in reform.

III

SOME CHARACTERISTICS AS A SPEAKER

Susan Anthony was a tall, slim woman with an abundance of brown hair, that turned silver gray in her later years. She always wore it parted in the middle and drawn tightly back, covering the upper portion of her ears. Her grey-blue eyes were keen and bright behind her gold-rimmed spectacles. Except for a few months when other suffragists persuaded her to wear the Bloomer costume, her dress was always much the same—black silk or satin with a touch of lace around the neck and sleeves. The only color she ever wore in public was a shawl of red silk crepe edged with a long heavy-knotted fringe. This shawl became a kind of battle flag for the suffrage movement. One time she appeared without it in Washington, D.C., and the reporters who were present sent her a note, saying, "No red shawl, no report." She laughed and sent to her hotel for it.

For the audiences, composed of men and women of varying backgrounds and beliefs, Susan Anthony had one message. Whatever the subject of her address may have been, the fundamental purpose of the speech was always the same. From the time she became associated with the cause of Woman's Rights, it was always paramount in her thoughts. This sincere devotion to her beliefs, which so colored her personality, was largely responsible for her success in lifting the "cause" to a plane of universal respect. Through sheer devotion to this cause Susan Anthony won the admiration of all classes of people. Through her understanding of the problems of the women of her day she won for herself warm affection.

Mrs. Harper has said of her, "She struck her blows straight from the shoulder, called things by their right names, was absolutely fearless, accepted no compromises, was never silenced, never deceived, never turned aside from her purpose."

Her speech on **"Social Purity,"** illustrates these factors. Men and women of the late nineteenth century may have been shocked to hear her call a spade a spade, but the wealth of statistical material, coupled with innumerable examples of the social evils to which women of the period were being submitted, could not have failed to hold the audiences and must have sent them home with much to ponder over.

Although she was never melodramatic or sentimental to the point of being maudlin, her power as a speaker was enhanced by her use of example and statistical material which had an emotional appeal for her listeners. Women were moved by the stories of the sufferings of other women who had been subjugated throughout the ages. Men were impressed by her amazing mass of statistics.

Newspapers and contemporary critics alike never ceased to praise her use of logic. In an editorial which appeared the day after her death, the *Rochester Democrat and Chronicle* said:

> Miss Anthony was a wonderfully persuasive public speaker. She was in no sense declamatory. She did not deal in rhetoric or the flowers of fancy.

Her speech was as direct, as clearcut, and as convincing as an axiom. Her logic admitted no refutation, granting her premises. She not only herself saw the connection but had the power of making others see it and in the fewest possible words.

IV

REACTIONS OF THE CONTEMPORARY PRESS

The press notices concerning Susan Anthony's earliest appearances were usually derogatory. This reaction was probably inevitable in view of the disapproval of the causes for which she spoke and of antipathy to women speakers in general, but it must also be remembered that she was at first shy and self conscious and completely without training or experience as a public speaker.

In one of these early newspaper accounts she was assailed as "a maiden lady who claimed to understand the problems of a married woman." In another, her voice was compared to a hurdy-gurdy, and in appearance she was said to be "lean and cadaverous . . . with the proportions of a file." Other early newspapers, however, admitted that her enunciation was clear and distinct, her style earnest and impressive, and her arguments strong and stimulating.

Time, and perhaps her development as a speaker, modified these comments. The large audiences she attracted during her years with the Redpath Lyceum Bureau indicated not only the softening of public opinion toward the work for woman suffrage but also a definite improvement in her ability as a speaker. When she spoke in Cincinnati on February 12, 1889, the *Commercial Gazette* carried the following comment:

> . . . if she did not succeed in gaining many proselytes to her well-known views regarding woman's emancipation, she certainly reaped the reward of presenting the arguments in an interesting and logical manner. Every neatly turned point was received with applause and that good natured laughter that carries with it not a little of the element of conviction.

At the time of her death newspapers from New York to California recognized her accomplishments. Countless references were made to her work for temperance, abolition of slavery, and women's rights. Many paid tribute to the improved position of woman in society. Some held hope for eventual enfranchisement and prophesied that Susan's dream would some day be realized.

The day after her death Dorothy Dix wrote the following for the *New York Evening Journal:*

> She [Susan B. Anthony] found the woman, who attempted to speak in public, no matter how eloquent, or how sincere, or how important the message she had to bring, hissed and mobbed and lampooned. She leaves vast audiences listening to woman orators and applauding them to the echo.

The story of Susan Anthony's activities in the movement of reform demonstrates her development as a reformer and a speaker. The contrast between the position of women in society at the beginning of her work and their position at the time of her death in 1906 is indicative of her successful attainment of a foremost position among pioneer women—a position attained largely through her work as a speaker for reform. It does not seem presumptuous to conclude that her name will be remembered at least as long as the Nineteenth Amendment to the Constitution survives.

NOTES

[1] The most valuable treatment of her life is Ida H. Harper's *Life and Works of Susan B. Anthony* (Volumes I, II, Indianapolis, 1898; Volume III, 1908). The first two volumes, completed during Miss Anthony's lifetime, present an exhaustive study of her activities as well as innumerable press reactions to her public appearances. The third volume, completed after her death in 1906, contains a collection of eulogies that appeared in leading newspapers.

Doris Yoakam Twichell (essay date 1955)

SOURCE: "Susan B. Anthony," in *A History and Criticism of American Public Address,* edited by Marie Kathryn Hochmuth, Russell & Russell, 1955, pp. 97-130.

[*In the following essay, Twichell analyzes Anthony's effectiveness as a public speaker.*]

In view of the fact that Susan B. Anthony was not acclaimed by friends, critics, and contemporary press as a public speaker of the outstanding ability of such women as Lucy Stone, Elizabeth Cady Stanton, Anna E. Dickinson, and Anna Howard Shaw, it may seem strange to find her name listed as a woman representative in a volume on American public address. She was, however, one of the most prominent among women in American history, and as such her career upon the public platform is a subject worthy of study. But just what was her standing as a public speaker? How effective was she? The first step in answering these questions is a brief review of her life and work.

The circumstances of Susan B. Anthony's birth undoubtedly conditioned her future. The daughter of Daniel and Lucy Anthony, Quakers, she was taught the doctrines of the Society of Friends. These doctrines emphasized equality of the sexes and encouraged women to participate in spiritual and temporal matters.[1] As a citizen of New York State in the early nineteenth century she was subjected to the reform spirit which was evidenced in the many organized movements for social and economic improvement.

The question of whether Susan would follow the predilections of her environment was soon resolved. As a child she was precocious.[2] She learned to read at four, and before long demanded to be taught such aspects of arithmetic as "long division," then regarded as unnecessary for girls. She was influenced greatly by her father, a man considered radical among the Quakers, and a reformer whose ideas encompassed improvement in housing for the workers in his factory, and no trade with slaveholders.

A reversal in family fortunes taught Susan to face realities and to shoulder serious responsibilities. In order to earn her own living and to help the family recover from the financial crisis, she turned to teaching, filling positions first in New Rochelle and then near Hardscrabble, New York. For a while she served as governess for a family near Fort Edwards, New York, and here she found the opportunity to read current periodicals and to take more and more interest in national politics.

As principal of the girls' department of the Canajoharie Academy in Canajoharie, New York, a position she accepted in 1846, she gained influence and the reputation of being both a very able teacher and a popular young woman. She dropped the Quaker plain speech, the Quaker garments, and, until she found them too dull, participated in social events, going to parties, the theater, and the circus.[3] In this community she conquered the obstacles of the local teaching profession. She saw her father reinstated in a salaried position, and she came to lead for the only brief time in her career, a life of self-interest and moderate luxury. Soon she found this insufficient, deadening, boring.

THE REFORMER

Susan B. Anthony began her work for reform while teaching in Canajoharie. She joined a local woman's organization called the Daughters of Temperance and soon became its secretary. On March 1, 1849, as speaker of the evening at a village supper sponsored by the Daughters, she gave her first public speech, reading from manuscript to a two-hundred person audience a plea for support of the temperance movement. Her appeal was directed especially to the women for, as she said, "In my humble opinion, all that is needed to produce a complete Temperance and Social reform in this age of Moral Suasion, is for our Sex to cast their United influences into the balance."[4] She concluded:

> Ladies! there is no Neutral position for us to assume. If we sustain not this noble enterprise, both by precept and example, then is our influence on the side of Intemperance. If we say we love the Cause, and then sit down at our ease, surely does our action speak the lie. And now permit me once more to beg of you to lend your aid to this great Cause, the Cause of God and all Mankind.[5]

It was inevitable that soon Susan Anthony should develop into a full-fledged reformer. Upon her return to the family farm near Rochester, New York, in 1850, she listened to the discussion of leading events and issues that took place at Sunday dinners when her father was at home, and the Anthony farm, a favorite meeting place of liberal-spirited men and women, had as guests such prominent reformers as [William Lloyd] Garrison, [Parker] Pillsbury, [Wendell] Phillips, [William Ellery] Channing, and Frederick Douglass.

Susan read. She attended reform meetings. She longed to take a more active part in the two great reforms of temperance and antislavery which were absorbing public attention at the time. Her mother gave her sympathy. And her father encouraged her, giving her financial backing when necessary and moral support upon all occasions.

Having brought her credentials from the Canajoharie temperance organization she was soon at work in Rochester. In 1851 she began to demonstrate unusual executive ability in organizing a number of temperance societies in towns close to Rochester, and in raising funds through a series of local suppers and festivals. In 1852 and 1853 she was among the women temperance workers who disturbed temperance meetings in Albany, Syracuse, and New York City by attempting to speak and take part in the proceedings. She was prominent in the women's meetings held immediately upon the opposition of the general conventions.[6]

Susan Anthony undertook arrangements for the temperance convention held in Rochester on April 20, 1852, at which five hundred women assembled and formed the first Woman's State Temperance Society. She opened this meeting, reading the Call which urged women to initiate "associated Action" to protect their interests and those of society at large which "too long had been invaded and destroyed by legalized intemperance."[7]

With three other women she traveled throughout New York State during the summer of 1852, holding meetings, organizing temperance societies, and trying to rouse women to come out of seclusion and work for temperance.[8] And by 1854 she had increased her sphere of labor to the point that she was receiving such notices as the one listed in *The Liberator* on April 14th, announcing her appearance before the "Marion Temperance Society" of Baltimore.

After hearing her speak in Canajoharie, New York, in 1854, and upon learning that she was being urged to return there to teach, her uncle Read emphatically stated, "No, some one ought to go around and set the people thinking about the laws and it is Susan's work to do this."[9]

During the 1850s she joined the ranks of the abolitionists. She attended meetings and was converted to the radical sentiments of the Garrisonites. In April of 1851 she helped sponsor a meeting in Rochester conducted by Stephen and Abby Kelley Foster, among the most fearless and persecuted of the antislavery leaders.[10] As a result of this meeting she accompanied them for a week on their tour of meetings in adjoining counties and was urged by them to go actively into this reform.[11]

By 1854 she was urging the importance of bringing antislavery papers before the people at the Pennsylvania Anti-Slavery Convention.[12]

She served as general agent for the National Anti-Slavery Society for New York State in 1856 and 1857, and according to Parker Pillsbury, proved very able in planning meetings, marking out routes, and keeping three companies of speakers constantly employed.[13]

Her name appeared frequently in the "Announcement of Meetings" section of *The Liberator* for the next few years. She was advertised as holding meetings with such abolitionists as Aaron M. Powell, William Wells Brown, Parker Pillsbury, Marius R. Robinson, and Wendell Phillips.[14]

During the Civil War her work for antislavery continued. She planned and attended conventions, and took as her sole theme in 1862 "Emancipation the duty of the government."[15] Another of her activities was administrative work in the Woman's Loyal League. She and Elizabeth Cady Stanton called a mass meeting for May 14, 1863, in Dr. Cheever's church in New York City, and the league was formed. Its special purpose was to awaken public sentiment through writing and speaking, and to secure signatures to a petition to Congress demanding a Federal amendment abolishing slavery in the United States. Miss Anthony was able to say that by August, 1864, "nearly 400,000 signatures to petitions for emancipation were secured and Charles Sumner and Henry Wilson wrote us repeatedly that these petitions formed the bulwark of their demand for congressional action to abolish slavery."[16]

From shortly after the Civil War until her death on March 13, 1906, Susan B. Anthony's chief purpose was to elevate the social and economic condition of women. She was well qualified to assume leadership of the woman suffrage movement, for her activities during the first decade of her reform work had included a great deal of effort for woman's rights. She had first become aware of discrimination against women when, as a teacher, she had seen the variance in salaries paid to men and women, and the docile manner in which women accepted their inferior condition. In 1852, while canvassing for temperance, she happened into a teachers' convention in Elmira, New York. Here she determined to demand for women all the privileges then claimed by men.[17] At the State Teachers' Convention in Rochester in 1853, she fought for the privilege of speaking. By 1856 she was an invited speaker at the convention in Troy. Her subject was **"Educating the Sexes Together,"** a speech she also gave upon several other occasions.[18] In 1859 she submitted to the convention in Poughkeepsie a report of the committee upon **"Declamation and Discussion for Girls,"** and advocated the teaching of these subjects.[19]

Susan Anthony encouraged New York women teachers to fight their own battles. She argued for equal pay for equal services, and she advocated improvements in methods of teaching and in the sanitary conditions of school buildings.[20] By 1860 she was encouraged to see that there was no further need to urge the women to take part in meetings. She had succeeded in arousing them to demand justice and to become aware of their opportunities and responsibilities.[21]

Enthusiasm for the woman's rights movement manifested itself among the members of Susan's own family. She came home for a vacation in July, 1848, and found that her father, mother, and sister Mary had just attended the first Woman's Rights Convention in Seneca Falls, had signed a declaration demanding equal rights, and were enthusiastic over the subject and the leaders who had taken part in the convention. In 1849 she read Lucretia Mott's "Discourse on Woman," which explained the equality intended for women as shown by careful reading of the Scripture, justified the reasons why women needed and wanted to enlarge their sphere, defined the inequality of existing laws, and pleaded for encouragement and aid in elevating women to their rightful place as responsible citizens.[22] In 1850 her consciousness was fully awakened by reading the favorable account of the Worcester, Massachusetts, Woman's Rights Convention which appeared in the *New York Tribune*. The next year she met Elizabeth Cady Stanton, who was to become her lifelong friend and colleague.[23]

Susan B. Anthony's active work for woman's rights began at a convention in Syracuse, New York, in September of 1852. By 1854 she was acting as general agent for the state association whose program included holding a series of conventions in all of the counties and chief cities of the state in order to enlighten the people on the actual claims of the movement. The state association also prepared petitions to present to the state legislature to secure property and other rights for women.[24] In 1860 she was a prominent participant in the New York state convention in Albany. In October of that year she was invited to make a speech representing women at the Fair of the Union Agricultural Society in Dundee, New York.[25]

After the Civil War all of Miss Anthony's energies were devoted to the battle for the rights of women. By this time she was so convinced that a constitutional amendment was the only method, and that full suffrage for women was the only guarantee of equality that she never deviated from direct agitation to secure these ends.[26] She objected to the word "male" in the Fourteenth Amendment, and sought to add the word "sex" to the Fifteenth. She agitated for a constitutional amendment that would give suffrage to citizens without discrimination based on sex. She tried to educate the people of the United States to understand the rights of women and to act for women's enfranchisement.

One of her chief activities was that of organizing and supervising woman suffrage associations. She was a leader in the organization of the National Woman Suffrage Association in 1869, attended its yearly conventions with the exception of two, from the first one held in Washington, D.C., in 1869, through the 1906 convention, a month before her death. She held such offices as treasurer, secretary, and vice-president frequently, and was national president from 1892 until 1900. Yearly she served on such committees as the finance, the executive, the business, or the resolutions. She aided in the formation and encouraged the work of local and state woman suffrage groups throughout the United States. An article appearing in "Photographs of Our Agitators" in *The Hearth and Home* of January 22, 1870, said:

> She is the Bismarck; she plans the campaigns, provides the munitions of war, organizes the raw recruits, sets the squadrons in the field. Indeed, in presence of a timid lieutenant, she sometimes heads the charge; but she is most effective as the directing generalissimo. . . . She presides over the treasury, she cuts the Gordian knots, and when the uncontrollables get by the ears at the conventions, she is the one who straightway drags them asunder and turns chaos to order again. In every dilemma, she is unanimously summoned.

Work for suffrage reform resulted in Miss Anthony's speaking before audiences all over the United States. She made her first tour through Missouri, Illinois, Wisconsin, and Ohio in 1869, traveling with Elizabeth Cady Stanton, and holding meetings that were felt to have valuable results in rousing women who had been absorbed in war work to renew their efforts in their own behalf as citizens.[27] Throughout her career she appeared at state conventions, attending them from Maine to Oregon and from Minnesota to Louisiana.

When state constitutions were under revision or when state legislatures were considering woman suffrage bills, she was usually on the scene and in the midst of the campaigns. She was prominent in state canvasses not only in her own State of New York, but in Kansas, Michigan, Colorado, Nebraska, Indiana, South Dakota, California, and others.[28]

She presented the woman suffrage question to legislative groups, both state and national. She spoke to such legislative groups as those in Nebraska in 1871, New Hampshire in 1881, Indiana and New York in 1897. She appeared before congressional committees yearly, usually in hearings occurring during or after the national woman suffrage convention in January or February. She and Mrs. Stanton gave the arguments on woman suffrage before the first congressional hearing granted on the question on January 26, 1869,[29] and she presided at the hearing in 1904 in her frequent role as chairman, introducing the other women speakers, and making the closing address.[30]

Susan B. Anthony attended political conventions and endeavored to enlist the aid of political parties for woman suffrage. In addition to the Republican national conventions from 1872 to 1892, she attended Democratic conventions, National Prohibition conventions, National Liberal conventions, Greenback Labor conventions and others.

Trips to Europe were included in her journeys. In 1888 she presided over eight of the sixteen sessions of the International Council of Women, and she again appeared at the International Women's Conferences in 1899, 1902, and 1904. Her chief interest in traveling abroad was not in sight-seeing but in meeting reformers, in studying social conditions, and in furthering international organization among women.

In her program to educate the public she appeared at many general meetings and conventions and asked for resolutions supporting woman suffrage. She spoke at meetings of the South Dakota Farmers' Alliance in 1889 and 1890, the Ladies' Library Association in Ann Arbor, Michigan, in 1889, the American Federation of Labor in Indianapolis in 1899, and the Bricklayers' and Masons' International Union, Rochester, New York, in 1900. She talked to Negro audiences from Rochester to San Francisco to New Orleans. She appeared before student groups in high schools, teachers' colleges, and universities. On the long list of her appearances were those at the Woman's College of Brown University, the University of Nevada, San Jose Normal School, Atlanta University, Tuskegee Institute, and many others.[31]

Miss Anthony went on lecture tours, appearing alone or with other speakers, lecturing under private auspices, under sponsorship of a bureau, and sometimes under her own arrangement. In 1867 she and Elizabeth Cady Stanton undertook a lecture tour in company with George Train, and spoke in towns from Kansas to New York City. In 1870 she substituted for Mrs. Stanton for a month while the latter was ill, and proved so acceptable to the New York Lyceum Bureau that she was engaged by it, and spoke in Pennsylvania, Ohio, Indiana, Illinois and Michigan. From 1870 to 1876 she accepted all the lecturing dates she possibly could in order to earn money for paying the debt incurred by *The Revolution,* a woman's rights paper she ran from 1868 until it succumbed financially in 1870. She spoke for the Star Course in 1870, and the Dime Lecture Course in 1875 and 1876. She lectured under contract with the Slayton Lyceum Bureau in 1876, 1877, 1885, and 1888.

In reviewing her work for an article appearing in the *Chautauqua Assembly Herald* on August 9, 1892, Miss Anthony said that between 1870 and 1880 she spoke in public on the subject of woman suffrage on an average of nearly two hundred nights each year. From Seattle, Washington, she wrote on November 4, 1871, "I have traveled 1,800 miles in fifty-six days, spoken forty-two nights and many days. . . . "[32] In the Michigan campaign of 1874 she spoke in thirty-five places in forty days and also took three days out to attend the Illinois Woman Suffrage Convention in Chicago.[33] She told the audience at the National Woman Suffrage Convention in May, 1879, that she had already spoken in 140 places that year, and said that if there were a man in the house who had gone through that amount of physical endurance she would like to see him.[34] On a "brief lecture tour" in 1893, and at the age of seventy-three, she made nine evening addresses, attended several receptions, and traveled more than a thousand miles in twelve days. In response to a question asked her in 1897 regarding the extent of her work, she said:

> It would be hard to find a city in the northern and western States in which I have not lectured, and I have spoken in many of the southern cities. I have been on the platform over forty-five years and it would be impossible to tell how many lectures I have delivered; they probably would average from seventy-five to one hundred every year.[35]

When in Washington she talked with individual congressmen, seeing them both at the Capitol and in their homes. She interviewed Presidents Grant, Johnson, Arthur, McKinley, and Theodore Roosevelt. She accepted invitations to dinners and receptions when she saw the opportunity of influencing prominent people for woman suffrage. She called herself a lobbyist without the two necessary requisites—she neither accepted money nor had any to pay out.

Throughout her whole career Susan carried on a voluminous correspondence, and wrote letters to everyone from the most modest housewife to the most prominent politician. By way of illustration, there were nine hundred letters from all parts of the world addressed to her on her seventy-seventh birthday, and she spent three months of 1897 answering these.[36] Her letters were full of concrete and hopeful suggestions.

The records of her experiences, which came to fill thirty-three volumes of old ledgers, and her daily journal aided in the writing of *The History of Woman Suffrage.* She spent years helping to write, finance, and publish the first four volumes of this work. And she aided Ida Harper in the writing of the first two volumes of her biography, which in itself is a partial history of the suffrage movement.

She published tracts and wrote articles, drafted resolutions and circulated petitions. She urged women to read suffrage pamphlets and the equal rights papers, and she passed out literature at the end of her lectures.[37] At a meeting in Huron, South Dakota, in 1889, for example, she presented the Beadle County Suffrage Association with a gift of three volumes of the *History,* and she left a basket full of suffrage literature at the door. The literature disappeared so quickly that the leaders felt that ten times as much could have been used purposefully at the close of the meeting.[38]

Knowing the value of the press, Miss Anthony was cordial to newspaper reporters. She was eager to get as much as possible about woman suffrage into the papers, and personally she had an admiration for the faithful and industrious people who earned their living at newspaper work. She ordered a thousand copies of a Sunday edition during the 1883 national convention when she learned that the paper was going to give space to the convention, and she announced in the meeting that she would send to the address of any friend in the audience a copy free of charge.[39]

She believed that her own paper, *The Revolution,* exerted a tremendous influence for woman's rights in its short lifetime. When the paper could no longer continue because it was too expensive to run and too radical in its sentiments to be very popular, she gave it up with reluctance, and felt that the indebtedness of $10,000 which she personally assumed was not too big a price to pay for the good it had done.

In trying to demonstrate woman's rights she followed practical leads. In one attempt to verify the belief that women had the right to vote under the Fourteenth and Fifteenth Amendments she stood as the test case when she and fifteen other women were arrested for trying to vote in Rochester in 1872.[40] She lectured in her defense before the trial in 1873, and was still describing the events in 1899.

Susan Anthony insisted that women should be represented at the National Centennial Celebration in Philadelphia on July 4, 1876, in spite of the refusal of the committee in charge. Leading a small group of women to the platform during the ceremony, she presented to the chairman a "Woman's Declaration of Rights," and thus inscribed women's activities as a part of the program of that momentous occasion.[41]

THE INDIVIDUAL

At the time of her death in 1906, Susan B. Anthony was acclaimed one of the most remarkable women of her age. Obituary notices praised her as a reformer, crusader, and woman.[42] Thirty-nine years after her death her home was declared a shrine and preparations were made for its restoration. A question at once arises in the mind of the reader. What were the qualities for which this woman gained fame?

First, there was her consecration to her cause. She probably gave more time and thought to the specific issue of woman suffrage than any other person. To it she devoted most of the years of her long life. Other suffragists married and had families, and Susan had ample opportunity to do this, but she was not interested in a personal life; she was interested in helping all women toward better living. Other women leaders followed professions in addition to their suffrage work. Susan hewed so closely to her single purpose that the responsibility for care of her home and even for the selection of her clothes was largely delegated to her sister Mary, without whom she said she could not have pursued her public career. Her concentration on her work earned for her such titles as "The Apostle of Woman's Rights," "The High Priestess of Woman's Suffrage," and the "Napoleon," "the Moses," and the "Sir Galahad" of the movement. "What Gladstone has been to the home rule," said the Albany, New York, *Evening Journal* of March 14, 1894, "Miss Anthony has been to woman suffrage."

She was always available, and no task was too great. If a speaker fell ill or was unable to reach a meeting, Susan filled in. If a suffragist could not complete the arrangements for a convention, or finish writing a report, Susan completed the job. If a suffrage campaign needed someone to advertise meetings, distribute tracts, see to the personal comforts of the workers, and attend to the drudgery behind the scenes, Miss Anthony would take care of it all. This was well exemplified in 1867 in Kansas when she managed the campaign from Lawrence, while Elizabeth Cady Stanton and others stumped the state and received the publicity.[43]

As an unmarried woman she could legally assume debts for an organization that a married woman could not undertake, and this she sometimes did. When the Woman's Loyal League had overspent its treasury by $5,000 in 1863, Secretary Anthony assumed the responsibility, devised and executed means for paying it. Her undertaking of the $10,000 debt incurred in the publishing of *The Revolution,* when she could have declared bankruptcy, brought her widespread respect and was considered a good lesson in proving woman's pecuniary independence.[44]

She solicited contributions from every possible source, but accepted money for her own expenses only when absolutely necessary. She used personal bequests for the Woman Suffrage Association, and friends finally had to arrange an annuity for her so that she would not use the lump sum for the movement. In order to help the women of Michigan with their 1874 campaign she gave up lecture offers which would have helped materially to lessen the debt on *The Revolution.* She was the only speaker in the South Dakota campaign in 1890 who refused pay for her services. And in 1896 she donated her services to the California campaign, where her speeches even at twenty-five dollars an appearance would have contributed over $3,000 to the suffrage cause, not including parlor and club addresses.[45]

She did not fail an engagement, no matter what the risk or expense. In announcing her availability as a lecturer in 1877, the Slayton Bureau praised her dependability by stressing that she could lecture every night, that she did not object to night rides between appointments, and that "nothing but an Act of God" would prevent her from fulfilling an engagement.[46]

Anna Howard Shaw, who traveled seven thousand miles and gave twenty lectures during a two-week period in 1892, sometimes had trouble keeping up with her energetic friend. She liked to tell of a night during a meeting of the Woman's International Council in Chicago in 1888 when Miss Anthony, after a busy day but still "as fresh and full of enthusiasm as a young girl," came into Miss Shaw's room to talk the night away. Miss Anthony then continued with the next day's convention program with no sleep and with little attention to food.[47]

Of the women leaders, only Clara Barton and Frances Willard paid as little attention to physical needs. Susan believed in living a simple life and in eating simple foods. Her favorite exercise was long walks, and she liked to walk before bedtime, talking over issues with an accompanying friend who might have to hurry to keep up with her.

She was seldom ill, and then stayed in bed only as long as she was forced to do so, being up and on her way before friends could admonish her that she needed more time for recuperation. After an apoplectic stroke in 1900 she was warned by her physician to take care of herself, and particularly to avoid crowds and the cold. She decided to "die in the harness" and ignored his admonitions. Always rebellious against physical limitations, she attended public meetings until a month before her death.

Susan B. Anthony's physical appearance was distinctive. She was tall, slim, "Patrician-like," with strong features frequently called Grecian, firm set mouth, straight nose, and ample forehead. She had dark hair which turned a becoming gray, and deep-set gray-blue eyes which were keen and bright. Her carriage was erect, and she walked with a firm tread; she kept her toes straight ahead, and she was straight as an arrow. The *Washington Star* said of her in 1889:

> She is one of the remarkable women of the world. In appearance she has not grown a day older in the past ten years. Her manner has none of the excitement of an enthusiast; never discouraged by disappointment, she keeps calmly at work, and she could give points in political organization and management to some of the best male politicians in the land. Her face is strong and intellectual, but full of womanly gentleness. Her gold spectacles give her a motherly rather than a severe expression, and a stranger would see nothing incongruous in her doing knitting or fancy-work.[48]

Many pen-and-ink sketches of her appear in her Scrapbooks.[49] On the whole they seem to be very solemn. But they uphold the statement of the *St. Louis Daily Globe-Democrat* of May 7, 1879, that she commanded attention anywhere at a glance. Of the many pictures appearing in the three volumes of the Harper biography, and on the walls of the Anthony home in Rochester, the majority seem sad. The one taken when she was forty-eight years of age is one of the most appealing.[50]

Susan Anthony was an individualist. She had courage to uphold her convictions and she followed the course she thought right regardless of the beliefs of others. At a time when divorce was scarcely countenanced, she staunchly defended it, and emphasized women's need for the right to divorce. She argued that the World's Fair should be kept open on Sundays, and answered local clergymen by saying that young men might learn more at the Fair than at some of the churches in Chicago. She was tolerant of Carrie Nation because she felt that women had no legitimate means of enforcing their wills, although she emphasized that the hatchet was a barbarian weapon and that the ballot is the weapon of the civilized.

In conventions she fought to keep the aims and goals of the woman suffrage organization unfettered. For example, she opposed all efforts to pass resolutions concerning the reinterpretation of the Bible from woman's point of view, contending that contests on account of religious theories only set back the hands on the dial of suffrage reform.[51] She opposed such resolutions as one which proposed to place the National Woman Suffrage Association on record as abhorring "free loveism," stating that such a resolution had no place in a woman's convention because it might imply that some of the members were in favor of free love.[52] In the smallest of issues she was persistent, as in her argument that women should follow the dictates of etiquette and address audiences as "Gentlemen and Ladies."[53] As a reporter of the 1894 national suffrage convention wrote in *The Chicago Journal* of February 20th:

> Susan B. Anthony is one of the most remarkable products of this century. She is not a successful writer; she is not a great speaker, although a most effective one; but she has a better quality than genius. She is the soul of honesty; she possesses the gift of clear discrimination—of seeing the main point—and of never-wavering loyalty to the issue at hand. . . .

Miss Anthony had a youthfulness of spirit which remained with her even in her old age. Upon receiving an invitation to attend the Buffalo Bill show at the Chicago World's Fair in 1893, she took a group of women with her and entered wholeheartedly into the spirit of the occasion. At seventy-eight she attended her first football game and felt that she had spent "a pleasurable and profitable afternoon."[54] In 1900 a Chicago reporter commented that it was hard to believe that she was eighty years of age, and added:

> Talking with her and realizing how closely her fingers are upon the pulse of the world, that fact is still harder of belief. Her mantle in the movement for equal suffrage has fallen to younger shoulders, but her heart and life are in the work.[55]

Miss Anthony's greatest attribute, according to Carrie Chapman Catt, who assumed presidency of the national organization in 1900, was "her utter unselfishness and lack of self-consciousness."[56] If complimented by a chairman introducing her to an audience, Susan would remark that she preferred to have her obituaries spoken after her demise, and that now it was time to get down to the important business at hand.[57] She asked the guests at her fiftieth birthday reception to join her in demanding congressional and legislative action on woman suffrage if they wished to honor her personally.[58] She could only express gratitude for the improvement in public opinion toward the woman's movement when she was feted in Portland, Oregon, in 1905.[59] And when informed at one meeting that she was joining in with the applause for herself she continued to clap, and insisted that the praise was really intended for the cause.[60]

Her chief bias was that woman suffrage was the cure-all for social evils. As early in her career as 1852 she evidenced this tendency in a letter written to Amelia Bloomer on June 28th, saying,

> Oh! if women would but speak out—if they would but rise *en-masse,* and demand that their interests be truthfully represented in our legislative halls, then would man no longer inflict upon us, and upon society, the vile curse of the liquor traffic.[61]

She was a deeply religious woman, a Quaker turned liberal, and she attended the Unitarian church in Rochester as regularly as her travels would permit. But she considered that her true religion lay in her work. Work was a panacea for physical, mental, and spiritual ills and a refuge in time of sorrow.

Although Lucretia Mott might be said to be the "soul of the woman's rights movements," and Mrs. Stanton the "swift, keen intelligence," Grace Greenwood, a writer and correspondent, emphasized that Miss Anthony, "alert, aggressive and indefatigable," was its "nervous energy, its propulsive force."[62] And the *Boston Globe* commented in 1881,

> The young women of the day may well feel that it is she who *has made life possible* to them; who has trodden the thorny paths and, by her unwearied devotion, has opened to them the professions and higher applied industries; nor is this detracting from those who now share with her the labor and the glory. Each and all recognize the individual devotion, the purity and singleness of purpose that so eminently distinguish Miss Anthony.[63]

One can give but a glimpse of the praise bestowed upon Susan B. Anthony by both contemporary and present-day writers. Criticism and ridicule were heaped upon her as a strong-minded woman and a creature so masculine as to step outside the confines of woman's sphere, but the censure was because of the inacceptable quality of her cause to those who upheld tradition, and not because of the individual.[64]

THE SPEAKER AND HER SPEECHES

In spite of the wealth of material concerning the personality and accomplishments of Miss Anthony, one does not easily gain a picture of her ability as a public speaker. Testimonials from her friends were no doubt influenced by personal contact. Newspaper accounts during the early years of her career emphasized the subject of woman's rights and all its implications in a world of confusion, politics, and reform, and briefly mentioned that another reformer was presenting nonconformist ideas. Later, when she had become nationally known as a woman suffragist, press accounts were so taken with her sterling qualities that they often failed to mention audience reactions or her speaking style. With the spreading of her fame the discussion of suffrage issues expanded until newspaper accounts such as those reporting her California tour in 1896 filled many columns. Few of them, however, discussed her manner of speaking. An analysis of forty-two newspaper articles selected at random and covering a variety of occasions between 1869 and 1895 reveals thirty-eight résumés of subject content, seventeen descriptions of the personality of the speaker, and ten comments on speaking style.

Miss Anthony frequently appeared on the platform as one of a group of speakers, a custom popular in days when travel was not easy, and when an evening's listening was happily extended to three to five hours. She must have profited not only from practice but from listening to other speakers with whom she appeared, including Henry Ward Beecher, Wendell Phillips, Robert G. Ingersoll, Ralph Waldo Emerson, and William Lloyd Garrison.

There is little doubt that her speaking was influenced by the people with whom she worked. In the 1850's she shared audiences with such excellent women speakers as Amelia Bloomer, Antoinette Brown Blackwell, and Ernestine L. Rose. In later years she traveled extensively with Dr. Anna Howard Shaw, famous minister, physician, and public speaker.

She was aided and directed by Elizabeth Cady Stanton, with whom she worked closely for the majority of the years of her career, and whose excellence in speech composition and brilliance in conversation were widely acclaimed. Miss Anthony often attested that Mrs. Stanton was the intellectual center of the woman suffrage movement, while she herself was merely its hands and feet. Dr. Shaw insisted:

> . . . [The] two women worked marvelously together, for Mrs. Stanton was a master of words and could write and speak to perfection of the things Susan B. Anthony saw and felt but could not herself express.[65]

Amelia Bloomer said in an article written for Chicago's *New Era* in November, 1885:

> . . . without the push of Miss Anthony, Mrs. Stanton would probably never have gone abroad into active work or achieved half she has done; and without the brain of Mrs. Stanton, Miss Anthony would never have been so largely known to the world by name and deeds. They helped and strengthened each other, and together they have accomplished great things for humanity.

Susan Anthony did not consider herself an effective speaker. She began to speak in public when she could find no one else who would or could do it. She continued to speak because the public platform was the most accessible as well as the most popular medium of education and entertainment of the time. In 1870 she said that "so soon as cultivated women come up and are ready to do the speaking, I shall fall back. My work is that of subsoil plowing. . . ."[66] She told a newspaper reporter in 1896:

> I never could think up points, and I can't write a speech out. I must have an audience to inspire me. When I am before a house filled with people I can speak, but to save my life I couldn't write a speech.[67]

And after what she considered an evening's failure before an audience in Geneva, New York, in March, 1899, she stated:

> I always feel my incapacity to give a "set" address—I can when in the best condition make a few remarks, but a sustained speech was, is and always will be an imposibility. Alas, that the friends will forever press me into a position where I must attempt it.[68]

The value of her existing speeches may be questioned. Before 1858 she tried to memorize or to speak from prepared manuscripts and these samples seem stilted and labored. For the rest of her career she spoke from notes or completely extemporaneously. Reports of these speeches are given in résumé or abridged synopsis, and frequently in third person. Probably the complete speeches have lost much of their flavor for they are, at least in part, the result of attempts by Miss Anthony or a confederate to write out the addresses from memory after their delivery.[69]

The most reliable part of Susan B. Anthony's role as a public speaker was the consistency of her purpose and subject matter. If she were lecturing on temperance, she would also show how much more weighty would be the influence of women if they had the ballot. And a suffrage lecture sometimes included appeals to women to take higher standards for temperance reform. Her purpose in her long speeches, which usually ran from one and a half to two hours, was to stimulate thought and actuate change for social improvement.[70]

Frequently she described unhappy existing social conditions, presented solutions, and made appeals for action. Sometimes she traced the history of the franchise and established need for further reform. She often talked of the importance of the ballot and of the necessity for every citizen to possess the right to vote. She described the degradation of women and demonstrated their need of the ballot for the protection of their persons and interests. And as time went on she chronicled the legal and professional gains of women during the nineteenth century, pointed out that enfranchisement was inevitable, and appealed for continued work for woman suffrage.[71]

The available samples of her speeches are filled with words and phrases that had emotional meaning for the people of her time. Appearing frequently are the expressions: "Resistance to tyrants is obedience to God"; "The price of liberty is eternal vigilance"; "Truth will prevail"; "Taxation and representation are inseparable"; and "Governments derive their just powers from the consent of the governed." The ballot she referred to as "a shield," "a symbol of equality," "a weapon," and "the right protective of all other rights." The black reality of the "upas of disfranchisement," "woman's slavery," "oppression" and "degradation" was lined with the silver hope of "justice," "equality," "freedom," "democracy," and "enfranchisement." The words "peer" and "citizen" were often used.

Miss Anthony spoke to the reason of her listeners and upheld her issues with facts, figures, and examples.[72] Her recorded speeches are crowded with statistics and direct quotations from authorities, law, and history. A good memory enabled her to give her speeches on **"Constitutional Argument"** and **"The New Situation,"** both composed largely of legal and constitutional references, with the aid of only a few notes.[73]

In **"Constitutional Argument,"**[74] a good example of the repletion of her information, she first stated that she stood before her audience under indictment for the alleged crime of having voted in the last presidential election, and said that it was her work of the evening to prove that in voting she exercised her rights as a citizen. She then proceeded to analyze the Declaration of Rights, the Constitution, and laws discriminatory to women. She quoted authorities including President Grant, Chief Justice Daniels, Attorney General Bates, Charles Sumner, and others. She defined citizenship and discussed its implications. She established by syllogistic reasoning the right of women to vote under existing statutes. She concluded with a statement that upon the proof given in her address she and the women of the National Woman Suffrage Association intended to vote and to demonstrate their rights. She asked support of their program.

The *Daily Nebraska State Journal* of January 8, 1887, in reviewing the previous evening's address in Lincoln, stated that Miss Anthony spoke "evidently from inexhaustible resources of knowledge upon her subject. Her auditors followed her with the closest attention and her logical address shows her to possess a most statesmanlike insight into the affairs of the nation and society." And a report in the Terre Haute, Indiana, *Express* of February 12, 1879, concerning a recent lecture given in that city attested that "There are not half of our public men who are nearly so well posted in the political affairs of our country as she, or who, knowing them, can frame them so solidly in argument."[75]

Susan B. Anthony excelled in argument. She stated issues and defended them, making frequent use of the rhetorical question, sarcasm, and "withering invective." The recorded speeches show logical reasoning, with many "therefores," and "if-this-is-true-then-that-is-bound-to-be-so." She put her basic premises succinctly, pointed to generally entrenched beliefs, and emphasized the new ideas that must necessarily be accepted.

In her address on **"Social Purity,"**[76] first given during the spring of 1875, she insisted that the efforts of man had been insufficient to suppress the evils of intemperance. Man's legislative attempts have proved equally ineffective. Women's prayers and petitions had been futile. The solution to the problem pointed toward enfranchisement of women. She further remarked:

> . . . the tap-root of our social upas lies deep down at the very foundation of society. It is woman's dependence. It is woman's subjection. Hence, the first and only efficient work must be to emancipate woman from her enslavement. The wife must no longer echo the poet Milton's ideal Eve, when she adoringly said to Adam "God, thy law; thou, mine!" She must feel herself accountable to God alone for every act, fearing and obeying no man, save where his will is in line with her own highest idea of divine law.[77]

How could anyone doubt the power of the ballot? If, for one example, the 18,000 Chicago women, with the tens of thousands they represented, had been able to go to the ballot box at the next election, was there any doubt that respect rather than ridicule would have been shown them by the members of the Common Council, when they had presented their petition to retain the Sunday Liquor Law in that city? She insisted that it was futile for women to hope to battle successfully against the evils of society until they were armed with weapons equal to those of the enemy—votes and money:

> Archimedes said, 'Give to me a fulcrum on which to plant my lever, and I will move the world.' And I say, give to woman the ballot, the political fulcrum, on which to plant her moral lever, and she will lift the world into a nobler and purer atmosphere.[78]

To the audience of the Universalist convention held in Rochester in 1901 she said, among other things:

> I want you women to realize what a power you might be if you were enfranchised. Women constitute three-fourths of the church membership and for that reason ministers have small influence in politics. The Catholic priesthood commands considerable respect from politicians because of the large number of men in its congregations, but the Protestant ministers are not respected by them any more than are the women who compose their congregations. The same is true of the schools—three fourths of the teachers are women—and thus churches, schools and homes are all practically disfranchised.[79]

She often spoke of the injustice of allowing any class of people to have control over another. Cruelty and unfairness resulted from allowing the rich to rule the poor, the white to rule the black. Women undoubtedly would be just as unfair as men, had they been at the controls at the beginning of nations and governments. She asserted in her lecture **"Woman Wants Bread, Not the Ballot,"**[80] given many times between 1870 and 1890:

> . . . there never was, there never can be, a monopoly so fraught with injustice, tyranny and degradation as this monopoly of sex, of all men over all women. Therefore I not only agree with Abraham Lincoln that, 'No man is good enough to govern another man without his consent;' but I say also that no man is. good enough to govern a woman without her consent, and still further, that all men combined in government are not good enough to govern all women without their consent. There might have been some plausible excuse for the rich governing the poor, the educated governing the ignorant, the Saxon governing the African; but there can be none for making the husband the ruler of the wife, the brother of the sister, the man of the woman, his peer in birth, in education, in social position, in all that stands for the best and highest in humanity.[81]

It was no wonder that the "white male" class was cruel to the Negro, she said in her address on **"Reconstruction,"**[82] for men could not be trusted:

> . . . [They cannot be trusted] even to legislate for their own mothers, sisters, wives and daughters. The cruel statutes in nearly all the States, both slave and free, give ample proof. In scarcely a State has a married woman the legal right to the control of her person, to the earning of her hands or brain, to the guardianship of her children, to sue or be sued, or to testify in the courts, and by these laws have suffered wrongs and outrages second only to those of chattel slavery.[83]

If any lawyer doubted the legal inequality of women, she emphasized to audiences during the spring of 1873, she would remind him that the Common Law of England prevailed in every state but two except where the legislatures had enacted special laws annulling it.[84]

In her closing address at the 1884 National Woman Suffrage Convention she commented:

> . . . the reason men are so slow in conceding political equality to women is because they cannot believe that women suffer the humiliation of disfranchisement as they would. A dear and noble friend, one who aided our work most efficiently in the early days, said to me, "Why do you say the 'emancipation of women?'" I replied, "Because women are political slaves!" Is it not strange that men think that what to them would be degradation, slavery, is to women elevation, liberty?[85]

How could taxation without representation be any less humiliating to women of the nineteenth century than it was to the Fathers of our country a century earlier?

The suffragists did not oppose men, she insisted; they opposed the statute books.

She argued for correct interpretation of standing statutes. If women were considered to be "persons," they had a right to vote under the constitutional amendments. Even the popular contention that our laws were written with the masculine pronoun, which in itself excluded women from voting, was disproved by the decision of the Supreme Court in the case of *Silver v. Ladd* in 1868, in which it was said that the term "single man" embraced that of "unmarried woman." Moreover, if women were excluded from voting by masculine pronouns, why were they not also exempted from taxation?

That the members of her audiences were believers in good government she took for granted. In order to insure good government there must necessarily be good citizens, and if there was a need to improve the caliber of the voting populace, she told Joseph T. Alling's Sunday school class in Rochester in September, 1899, it was obvious that the best way to do it was to add the vote of women.[86] To improve society, one must have rights and powers, she argued in 1901 at the national suffrage convention held in Minneapolis:

> I am a full and firm believer in the revelation that it is through women the race is to be redeemed. For this reason I ask for her immediate and unconditional emancipation from all political, industrial, social and religious subjection. It is said, "Men are what their mothers made them," but I say that to hold mothers responsible for the characters of their sons while denying to them any control over the sons' lives is worse than mockery, it is cruelty. Responsibilities grow out of rights and powers. Therefore before mothers can rightfully be held responsible for the vices and crimes, for the general demoralization of society, they must possess all possible rights and powers to control the conditions and circumstances of their own and their children's lives.[87]

Speaking to the convention of the Bricklayers' and Masons' International Union in Rochester in 1900, she said:

> Women should vote for the sake of the home. By working to give your wives and daughters the ballot you would be working to double the representation of the home in government; for the lowest men—the men who make up the slum vote, the floating vote, the vote that can be bought by anyone for any measure—these men seldom have homes and women in them whose votes could be added to theirs. It is the honest, hard-working men, with homes and families, those who have done most to build up this country and who are the bone and sinew sustaining it today, who have most to gain from women's getting the ballot. But the best argument of all is justice—the sister should have the same rights as her brother, the wife as her husband, the mother as her son. . . .[88]

At times Miss Anthony's speeches seem very argumentative. Those available for reading appeal often to the sense of duty. Some of them seem to assert and demand rather than to persuade. The reader cannot help occasionally asking "Why?" and "What for?" and wondering if audience prejudices could accede to demands without more appeal to sentiment.

"The Demand for Party Recognition"[89] is a speech that prompts such a query. After a good introduction by which Miss Anthony established a bond between herself and the audience in talking about their common work, she went on to a detailed chronicle of past events, of women's work during the war, in previous suffrage campaigns and during political elections. She used negative suggestion in asking if the unhappy events of the past were going to be repeated in the impending campaign, and threatened to disown women who supported the Republican party unless it had a plank for woman suffrage. To a present-day reader the speech seems harsh. Yet a resolution for the support of woman suffrage which was the conclusion of the talk elicited unanimous approval.

She had a habit of calling for a show of hands from her audiences concerning their approval of her contentions and of woman suffrage, and usually she found approval.[90]

In writing about a debate between Miss Anthony and Professor E. C. Hewitt at the State Normal School in Bloomington, Illinois, in March, 1870, Emily L. Boynton observed that in spite of the popular professor's quick repartee and wit in condemning woman suffrage, Miss Anthony carried the honors of the day and won the applause of the audience.[91] A member of the Detroit audience of more than five hundred who heard her refute Rev. J. B. Fulton's speech upholding woman's sphere felt that "if cheering of the audience is any indication she must have been gratified at her success in demolishing his arguments."[92]

The general organization of the available speeches is good, although for the sake of clarity in supporting details she might profitably have rearranged subordinate ideas and changed expressions from passive to active voice.

The introductions to her speeches were brief, often a statement of fact that was thought-provoking or unusual. A clear statement of the purpose of the address followed immediately. In introducing **"Constitutional Argument,"** for example, she said:

> Friends and Fellow Citizens: I stand before you under indictment for the alleged crime of having voted at the last presidential election, without having a lawful right to vote. It shall be my work this evening to prove to you that in thus doing, I not only committed no crime, but instead simply exercised my citizen's right, guaranteed to me and all United States citizens by the National Constitution beyond the power of any State to deny.[93]

In **"Woman Wants Bread, Not the Ballot,"** she began:

> My purpose tonight is to demonstrate the great historical fact that disfranchisement is not only political degradation, but also moral, social, educational and industrial degradation. . . .[94]

In opening the meeting of the International Council of Women in Washington, D. C., in 1888, she stated:

> Forty years ago women had no place anywhere except in their homes; no pecuniary independence, no purpose in life save that which came through marriage. From a condition, as many of you can remember, in which no woman thought of earning her bread by any other means than sewing, teaching, cooking or factory work, in these later years the way has been opened to every avenue of industry, to every profession, whereby woman today stands almost the peer of man in her opportunities for financial independence.[95]

The conclusions of her speeches were equally brief and usually forceful. Upon the formation of the Woman's Loyal League in May, 1863, she concluded her speech asking for cooperation by saying,

> And now, women of the North, I ask you to rise up with earnest, honest purpose, and go forward in the way of right, fearlessly, as independent human beings, responsible to God alone for the discharge of every duty, for the faithful use of every gift the good Father has given you. Forget conventionalisms; forget what the world will say, whether you are in your place or out of your place; think your best thoughts, speak your best words, do your best works, looking to your own conscience for approval.[96]

She ended a speech, **"Social Purity,"** by observing,

> Two great necessities forced this nation to extend justice and equality to the Negro:
>
> First, Military necessity, which compelled the abolition of the crime and curse of slavery, before the rebellion could be overcome.
>
> Second, Political necessity, which required the enfranchisement of the newly-freed men, before the work of reconstruction could begin.
>
> The third is now pressing, Moral necessity—to emancipate woman, before Social Purity, the nation's safeguard, ever can be established.[97]

Her closing words to a Baltimore audience in 1894 were:

> Women of Maryland, that is what the negro got out of it. Cannot we get the same? We've never had any flag, never had any country. Let us get both. Only prejudice stands in the way. Education, reason, judgment has nothing to do with the opposition. It's only prejudice.
>
> There is an old saying that if you give a woman an inch she'll take an ell.
>
> Women of Maryland—we've got the inch.[98]

Press reports often remarked that she spoke "more concisely" than the average speaker and that she did not put much ornamentation into her speeches.[99] Her metaphors included homely phrases. She noted that money was "the wood and water of the engine" of reform. Again, she remarked that the woman suffragist organization would gladly do the work if people would only give generously to "oil the machinery." Her illustrations were simple stories of actual experiences faced by herself and others. In telling of the need for woman's enfranchisement, she narrated the story of the failure of the Collar Laundry Women's Union in Troy, New York, in its attempt to improve working conditions. In describing woman's ineffectiveness before the law, she quoted the case of the farmer's wife who could not testify that her false teeth were unsatisfactory when an uncooperative dentist brought suit against her husband for their payment.

In analyzing Miss Anthony's speaking style, May Wright Sewall, a suffragist speaker in her own right, wrote for *Our Herald* from Indianapolis, February 12, 1884:

> I am inclined to think that in the days when her own style was forming, the gravity and seriousness of the objects for which she spoke so impressed her that ornament seemed incongruous to her honest mind. Perhaps unconsciously she set rhetorical decoration aside as fit only for poetry, romances and critical essays, and the habits of "plain, unvarnished" speech remain, although she has the readiest admiration for the witty, poetical, or polished sentence of another.

Susan B. Anthony's appearance upon the platform was one of modesty, calmness, and dignity. She came forward with an "easy grace which none are so capable of assuming as those who for years have stood night after night before the footlights."[100] She stood quietly behind or beside the speaker's stand, moved around very little and made few gestures. At times she leaned forward toward her audience as if to try to bridge the distance between it and the platform.

Her contemporary biographer insisted that she was one of the most perfectly dressed women on the platform, although her tastes were very plain and simple. She usually dressed in black silk or satin, and relieved the severity of the color with a collar of rose point lace, a stomacher of white lace, a gold neck chain and pendant, or a delicate bit of jewelry such as a cameo brooch or an agate pin. She delighted her friends at a meeting in Portland, Oregon, by wearing a pink bow at her throat and a narrow pink ribbon in her hair to go with her gray silk dress. In later years she sometimes added a soft white shawl or a red crepe shawl to her costume. And on very special occasions she wore a garnet velvet dress that received widespread praise.

She always wore her hair plainly, brushed back smoothly over her ears and arranged in a knot at her neck. The Baltimore *Sun* of February 14, 1894, noted that her hair had "the same simple, old-fashioned twist that she has given to it for years and years." The paper hastened to add that she was a progressive woman in other ways than politics for the women in her audience had quickly

noticed that her "puffed sleeves and wide sloping skirt were respectively as big and broad and sloping as that of the most devoted disciple of Dame Fashion."

She believed that the appearance of the woman suffragists should attract no special attention to itself, and for this reason she gave up wearing the Bloomer dress after a few months. She tolerated but could not approve of the platform ostentation of such women as Elizabeth Oakes Smith and Victoria Woodhull.

The factor in Susan Anthony's delivery most frequently appraised by contemporary reports was her voice. She could be heard easily even in very large halls. The report of her first woman's rights convention by the Syracuse, New York, *Journal* of September 10, 1852, said that "Miss Anthony has a capital voice and deserves to be made clerk of the Assembly." During one appearance in New Orleans in March of 1885, *The Daily Picayune* remarked that "her voice was full, musical and sonorous." On January 22, 1895, *The Picayune* emphasized that her voice was "singularly sweet and clear." And during the International Council of Women held in London in 1899, Ida Harper remarked:

> . . . at nearly 80 years of age, her voice still has the best carrying quality of any of the fine voices which have been heard during the meetings. Even in these large halls, filled with thousands of people, she has been able to reach the farthest corner without apparent effort.[101]

Many felt that much of her effectiveness in speaking stemmed from the fact that she could be understood. Her utterance was rapid, and she made few pauses, but so good was her articulation that the attentive listener did not lose a word. She especially "enforced her remarks by the inflections of her voice."[102]

She was complimented for her "emphatic earnestness," and for making addresses "full of fire and prophecy." But she was also accused of being so serious as to seem solemn and so earnest as almost to become tearful.

Susan B. Anthony's audiences were usually large, numbering over three thousand at such meetings as the one in Framingham, Massachusetts, on July 4, 1862, and those of the women suffrage meetings in New York State during the summer of 1903. In 1874 her meetings throughout the state of Michigan were crowded and as many as a thousand people were unable to gain admission. The national woman suffrage meetings practically always filled whatever building they used.

Her audiences included prominent reformers, the interested, the apathetic, and the hostile. In increasing numbers were women predominant, including enthusiastic suffragists, those sincerely interested in learning about the reform and those merely curious. Newspaper comments emphasized that the woman suffrage conventions were composed of women of refinement and culture, of standing and position in society. Miss Anthony spoke especially highly of her audiences in the West, commenting on the fine pioneer character of the people and on the fact that they came many hard miles in wagons and buggies, crowding into lecture halls with enthusiasm for knowledge of the suffrage cause.

The hardships and obstacles she faced in speaking before the public were similar to those experienced by other reformers.[103] She spoke in churches, schoolhouses, wigwams, saloons, pool rooms, polling booths, out-of-doors, and on train platforms. She cheerfully endured the hardships and discomforts common to itinerant lecturers during the nineteenth century. There were disturbances created by adults and annoyances from crying babies. She experienced the difficulties common during the critical days of the antislavery movement in the 1850's and early 1860's, which meant speaking above hisses, shoutings, and booings, and which might mean hurrying out stage doors when meetings were broken up by mobs.[104] The opposition toward antislavery carried over into antagonism toward woman's rights and the women's meetings were also disturbed. But because she began her work in the 1850's, she did not have to go through the severe demonstrations endured by such reformers as Frances Wright in the 1830's, and Abby Kelley Foster and Ernestine L. Rose in the 1840's. By the mid-nineteenth century audiences had recovered at least a little from the initial shock of seeing women on the American public platform. And by 1871 the days of the novelty of hearing women speak were said to be over. Advice was given to young ladies at this time not to enter the profession of lecturing unless they had "brains and ability, culture and fitting preparation," because audiences in the hamlet as well as in the city were awake and critical.[105]

Miss Anthony faced formidable opposition throughout her career. Her propaganda was radical and it hit the defenders of the *status quo*. Opposing her were many of her own sex, and the ministry, press, and political figures in great numbers. She was accused of trying to break up the American home, of preaching doctrines which were calculated to degrade and debauch society, of being a shrew and a revolutionist.[106]

To offset the opposition and to cheer her along her way, she found friends throughout the nation who opened their homes and their hearts to her. And as her fame grew she became more and more an honored personage. During the 1897 national suffrage convention in Des Moines, Iowa, many men in the audience left when she had finished speaking, having come only to listen to her.[107] In 1896 she walked ankle-deep in roses upon California platforms.

As a participant in meetings and conventions Susan B. Anthony assumed a stellar role. As chairman she presided with what the *Washington Chronicle* of January 28, 1883, called "inspiring dignity." In reporting the suffrage convention of 1890 the *Washington Star* remarked:

> She does not make much noise with her gavel, nor does she have to use it often, but she manages to keep the organization over which she presides in a state of order that puts to shame many a convention of the other sex. Business is transacted in proper shape, and every important measure receives its due share of attention. . . . If any of those who have not attended the meetings of the association are of the opinion that serious breaches of parliamentary usage are committed through ignorance or with intent, they are laboring under a decided delusion.[108]

She insisted that speakers be heard and saw to it that freedom of speech was upheld. She kept meetings informal, but directed the discussion so that it progressed toward a goal. In general, she seemed a genial, lively leader. In telling of the events of the woman's meeting in New York, the *World* of April 21, 1888, emphasized that "if ever there was a gay-hearted, good-natured woman it is certainly Miss Anthony." And the *Sentinel* report of her appearance in Indianapolis meetings in 1899 observed that "Miss Anthony has a delightful smile, the smile and laugh of real enjoyment; her love of fun bubbles all through her talk. She will pause in the most serious conversation to laugh at a joke and her sense of humor is very keen."[109]

She did a good deal of oral reading of reports, resolutions, letters, and other papers. In 1852 she read a letter from Mrs. Stanton in "a most emphatic manner." Instead of giving a set speech at the session honoring Mrs. Stanton's eightieth birthday in 1895, she paid an eloquent tribute to the "Pioneers," and then read the most important of the one hundred telegrams of congratulation. The New York *Sun* commented that "in ordinary hands this task would have been dull enough, but Miss Anthony enlivened it with her wit and cleverness and made a success of it."[110]

Her introductions of speakers were brief and colorful, bright and spicy. Audiences liked them. When introducing Kate Field, who was known to have opposing views on the suffrage question, at the 1894 national convention, Miss Anthony said, "Now Friends, here is Kate Field, who has been talking all these years against woman suffrage. She wants to tell you of the faith that is in her."[111]

She introduced Henry Blackwell, husband of Lucy Stone, at the 1900 national convention by saying,

> Here is a man who has the virtue of having stood by the woman's cause for nearly fifty years. I can remember him when his hair was not white, and when he was following up our conventions assiduously because a bright, little, red-cheeked woman attracted him. She attracted him so strongly that he still works for woman suffrage, and will do so as long as he lives, not only because of her who was always so true and faithful to the cause—Lucy Stone—but also because he has a daughter, a worthy representative of the twain who were made one."[112]

In 1902 she remarked, "He [is] the husband of Lucy Stone; I don't think he can quite represent her but he will do the best he can."[113]

Susan B. Anthony was adept at thinking quickly on her feet. She could make quick responses to speakers from the audience, and she seemed to know the right thing to say at the right moment. There was singing at the close of the 1883 national convention. Miss Couzins and Mrs. Shattuck sang the stanzas of the "Star-Spangled Banner," and Mr. Wilson of the Foundry M.E. Church, led the audience in the chorus. Miss Anthony quipped that the audience could see how much better it was to have a man help, even in singing. The quip "brought down the house."[114]

During a discussion on the divorce question in 1860, a minister thought he could stop her with "You are not married, you have no business to be discussing marriage." "Well, Mr. Mayo," she replied, "You are not a slave, suppose you quit lecturing on slavery."[115]

In the question period that followed Mrs. Stanton's address at a committee hearing of the legislature in Albany in 1867, Mr. Greeley asked, "Miss Anthony, you know the ballot and the bullet go together. If you vote, are you ready to fight?" Instantly she rejoined with "Yes, Mr. Greeley, just as you fought in the late war—at the point of a goose-quill."[116]

In a lively session following lectures given by Susan and George Francis Train to an audience in Rahway, New Jersey, on January 6, 1868, a prominent visitor from Kansas addressed the speakers saying, "You did a good work in Kansas, Miss Anthony, but you should not charge the Republican *party* as opposing woman's suffrage. It was only individual Republicans." Miss Anthony answered promptly:

> The reverse of that is true. It was only individuals who helped us. Your State Committee declared themselves neutral, and then sent out, as agents, all the prominent anti-female suffrage men and not one prominent advocate of the Cause in the whole State.[117]

Mr. Train immediately changed the subject of the discussion.

During the South Dakota suffrage campaign of 1890 an intoxicated man kept interrupting speeches with loud remarks. Several men cried, "Put him out!" "No, gentlemen," said Miss Anthony, "he is a product of man's government, and I want you to see what sort you make."[118]

When someone quietly reminded her that the national suffrage convention of 1896 had started without the opening prayer, she said without the slightest confusion:

> Now, Friends, you all know I am a Quaker. We give thanks in silence. I do not think the heart of anyone here has been fuller of silent thankfulness

than mine, but I should not have remembered to have the meeting formally opened with prayer if somebody had not reminded me. The Rev. Anna Howard Shaw will offer prayer.[119]

Clearly, Miss Anthony had presence of mind and general affability in the handling of audiences. As the *History of Woman Suffrage* emphasizes,

> Miss Anthony seldom made a stated address either in opening or closing, but throughout the entire convention kept up a running fire of quaint, piquant, original and characteristic observations which delighted the audience and gave a distinctive attraction to the meetings. It was impossible to keep a record of these and they would lose their zest and appropriateness if separated from the circumstances which called them forth. They cannot be transmitted to future generations, but the thousands who heard them during the fifty years of her itinerary will preserve them among their delightful memories. Perfectly at home on the platform, she would indulge in the same informality of remarks which others use in private conversation, but always with a quick wit, a fine satire and a keen discrimination. Words of praise or criticism were given with equal impartiality, and accepted with a grace which would have been impossible had the giver been any other than the recognized Mentor of them all. Her wonderful power of reminiscence never failed, and she had always some personal recollection of every speaker or of her parents or other relatives. She kept the audience in continuous good-humor and furnished a variety to the program of which the newspaper reporters joyfully availed themselves.[120]

CONCLUSION

For more than a half-century Susan B. Anthony appeared upon the public platform to promote the cause of woman's emancipation. People thronged to hear her speak, and went away filled with admiration for the speaker. And yet a careful study of her life, work, and speeches reveals no satisfactorily clear picture of her speaking ability. Careful, detailed reports found about other women speakers are lacking for Miss Anthony.

Contemporary reports gave other women speakers approbation by calling them "orators," "popular lecturers," and "noted female talkers." They devoted paragraphs to method of delivery, style, and elocution, and described the women as being "eloquent," "persuasive," and "silver-tongued." Susan was referred to as a worker, an organizer, and a reformer, and was said to speak plainly. During a lecture tour from Kansas to New York in 1867, she was accompanied by Elizabeth Cady Stanton and George Francis Train. The Louisville, Kentucky, *Journal* of November 28th observed simply that Miss Anthony had been before the public for years and always had won "the applause of the multitudes in whose cause she has been a standing champion." The same article noted that Mrs. Stanton was "one of the greatest and noblest women of our country," who "addresses all her audiences with the most thrilling power and effect." Mr. Train was said to be an orator in his own peculiar way, having "dashing eloquence, resistless humor and fertility of resource." The views of the three speakers were equally radical and outspoken.

In discussing the National Woman Suffrage Convention of 1899, the *Washington Post* of January 22nd especially commended the address made by Mrs. Lillie Devereux Blake which captivated the large audience, and added that the lady in question occupied an enviable place among her sex upon the lecture platform. She elicited continuous applause on this evening as "she threw her shafts of wit and satire with electrical rapidity." The meeting was closed by a short and interesting talk by Miss Anthony "in her own inimitable style" and the audience dispersed.

In 1871 popular lady lecturers were compared. Mrs. Elizabeth Cady Stanton was considered the most dignified, Mrs. Mary Livermore the most eloquent, Mrs. Lillie Devereux Blake the wittiest, Miss Anna Dickinson the fieriest, Miss Kate Field the spiciest, Miss Olive Logan the jolliest, and Miss Lillian Edgarton the handsomest of the lecturers. Miss Anthony was not mentioned.[121]

An article on "Platform Honors," appearing in the same paper on April 13, 1871, stated that "we have yet no one more logical than Mrs. Stanton, more earnest than Miss Anthony and more persuasive and clear-headed than Lucy Stone." Among the newer speakers "Anna Dickinson stands always first and foremost for eloquence and fire. Miss Field, Miss Logan, and others are distinguished in different ways. . . ."

A report of the Fort Wayne, Indiana, *Daily Sentinel* of February 26, 1873, which was fringed with disapproval of the woman's rights movement, insisted that "Susan B. Anthony has not the dash and sparkle of Anna Dickinson, nor the pleasing oratorical grandeur of Cady Stanton. She does not thrill an audience like Mrs. Livermore with the humorous and pathetic. . . ."

And the *Boston Herald* of February 17, 1890, in describing noted "female talkers" remarked that it was a distinct loss to the platform when Anna Dickinson left it. She and Mary Livermore were the most magnetic of the women speakers of the day. Kate Field, with her exquisite pronunciation, fine humor and wit, brought the drawing room to the audience. Lucy Stone and Julia Ward Howe had choice of language that was wonderful to hear. Elizabeth Cady Stanton's "well rounded periods" were "those of the orator rather than of the talker." And Susan Anthony, "the kindliest soul that ever lived" had "few graces of oratory," but could "strike out from the shoulder in a most vigorous fashion," was never unpleasantly assertive, and spoke as if she were talking to a room full of friends and not to an audience.

In his article on "Great Orators and the Lyceum," J. B. Pond noted that Elizabeth Cady Stanton was usually

ranked higher in the list of woman suffragists than Miss Anthony, although the latter had done more work. He emphasized that Mrs. Stanton was unquestionably the ablest orator and the most scholarly woman in the movement.[122]

Of the younger speakers, Dr. Anna Howard Shaw was considered beyond question to be the "leading woman orator" of her generation.[123] When they reviewed the history of suffrage reform, Carrie Chapman Catt and Nettie Rogers Shuler explained that while Susan Anthony was the "greatest souled woman" of the movement, it was Dr. Shaw who was the "master orator," and who "stood unchallenged throughout her career as the greatest orator among women the world has ever known."[124]

There is no doubt that Miss Anthony was a master of group discussion and of impromptu speaking. She probably would have become a famous woman even if she had not appeared upon the platform as a lecturer, just as did Dorothea Dix who was not a public speaker but gained renown as a reformer in the treatment of the insane.[125]

An obituary notice in the *Des Moines Register and Leader* of March 15, 1906, concluded:

> Miss Anthony was not an orator, but her addresses did more for the advancement of woman than those of any dozen women of her time. She said the things that needed to be said at the particular time in which she was speaking. Not every man who listened to her was converted, but every man who heard her realized that she knew her business and was making a formidable appeal. The net outcome of her work and of her example it would be difficult to estimate. The status of woman has changed more in the three-quarters of a century of her active labors than it had in the nineteen centuries that preceded. In the field of mechanical invention there has been nothing to astonish the world which compares with the change in the thought of the world with regard to woman's capacities and woman's sphere. . . .

Susan B. Anthony was an effective public speaker, but probably not a great one. Perhaps the anonymous clipping found in her Scrapbook for 1890 gives the most adequate conclusion.[126] This article depicts her appearance before an audience in Aberdeen, South Dakota, on an evening when Anna Howard Shaw was unable to fill the engagement, and declares:

> . . . those who were disappointed at missing the rhetoric of Dr. Shaw were well satisfied to listen to a social talk from the old campaigner. Miss Anthony is no orator; in fact it is difficult, in listening to her, to conceive that she has stood upon the platform thousands of times in the past fifty years.
>
> Judged critically she is angular in gesture and uncouth in phraseology. But when you remember who she is—that you are listening to a woman who has fought a noble and successful battle for

half a century in behalf of her sex—that her intelligence is as keen as her persistence is laudable, you cease to criticize the orator and remember only the woman.

Enigmatic as Susan B. Anthony's power as a public speaker may remain, one thing is certain. She was a classic example of the importance of the individual in public speaking.

NOTES

[1] Auguste Jorns, *The Quakers as Pioneers in Social Work* (New York: The Macmillan Co., 1931), p. 42.

[2] Rheta C. Dorr, *Susan B. Anthony* (New York: Frederick A. Stokes Co., 1928), pp. 12-13.

[3] *Ibid.,* p. 34.

[4] Ida H. Harper, *The Life and Work of Susan B. Anthony* (3 vols.; Indianapolis: Hollenbeck Press, 1898-1908), I, 53.

[5] *Ibid.,* I, 53. Cf. also Harriett E. Grim, "Susan B. Anthony, Exponent of Freedom" (Ph.D. thesis, University of Wisconsin, 1938), III, Appendix, pp. 10-16, for a slightly different version of the same speech. Both are copied from the original.

[6] Cf. *The Liberator* (Boston), July 9, 1852, May 20, September 9 and 16, 1853; *The Lily* (Seneca Falls, New York), July, 1852, pp. 60-61; *The Una* (Providence, Rhode Island), June, 1853, pp. 73-75; September, 1853, p. 131; October, 1853, p. 154.

[7] Harper, *op. cit.,* I, 68.

[8] Elizabeth C. Stanton *et. al.,* eds., *The History of Woman Suffrage* (Rochester, New York: Charles Mann, 1887), I, 488-89.

[9] Harper, *op. cit.,* I, 121.

[10] Blake McKelvey, "Susan B. Anthony," *Rochester History,* VII (April, 1945), 6.

[11] Harper, *op. cit.,* I, 63.

[12] *The Liberator,* November 3, 1854.

[13] Harper, *op. cit.,* I, 157.

[14] Cf. *The Liberator,* January 23 and April 10, 1857; January 27, February 24, and March 2, 1860.

[15] Harper, *op. cit.,* I, 222.

[16] Susan B. Anthony, "Woman's Half Century of Evolution," *North American Review,* CLXXV (December, 1902), 806-7.

[17] Harper, *op. cit.,* I, 71-72.

[18] Cf. *National Anti-Slavery Standard* (New York), February 6, 1858.

[19] *The Daily Press* (Poughkeepsie, New York), August 4, 1859.

[20] Stanton *et al., op. cit.,* I, 513.

[21] Nanette B. Paul, *The Great Woman Statesman* (New York: Hogan-Paulus Corp., 1925), p. 17.

[22] Anna D. Hallowell, *James and Lucretia Mott, Life and Letters* (Boston: Houghton, Mifflin & Co., 1884), pp. 487-506.

[23] Anthony, *op. cit.,* p. 806.

[24] Stanton *et al., op. cit.,* I, 619, 856.

[25] Cf. *The Liberator,* March 2, 1860; Susan B. Anthony Scrapbooks (33 vols.; Rare Book Room, Library of Congress), I, 123.

[26] Cf. Stanton *et al., op. cit.,* II, 91-151.

[27] Stanton *et al., op. cit.,* II, 367.

[28] *Ibid.,* Vols. I-IV.

[29] Harper, *op. cit.,* I, 313-14.

[30] Elizabeth C. Stanton *et al.,* eds., *The History of Woman Suffrage* (New York: J. J. Little & Ives Co., 1922), V, 110.

[31] Cf. Harper, *op. cit.,* Vols. I-III; Susan B. Anthony Scrapbooks.

[32] Harper, *op. cit.,* I, 400.

[33] *Ibid.,* I, 459.

[34] *St. Louis Globe-Democrat,* May 8, 1879.

[35] Harper, *op. cit.,* II, 925.

[36] McKelvey, *op. cit.,* p. 20.

[37] Cf. *The Revolution* (New York), January 6, 1870, for a typical list of woman suffrage reading material.

[38] *Daily Huronite* (Huron, South Dakota), November 14, 1889.

[39] Stanton *et. al., op. cit.,* III, 259.

[40] Cf. Anonymous, *An Account of the Proceedings on the Trial of Susan B. Anthony . . .* pp. 1-150.

[41] Stanton, *op. cit.,* III, 944-45.

[42] Around two hundred obituary notices were placed in the appendix of Volume III of the Harper biography. The achievements she made possible for women during her career were discussed in the majority of these. Her consecration to her cause was stressed. Mention of her ability as a public speaker appeared in less than twenty of these notices.

[43] Stanton *et. al., op. cit.,* II, 253-54.

[44] Cf. May Wright Sewall in *Our Herald,* in Scrapbooks (1884), VII, 344-49.

[45] Cf. Harper, *op. cit.,* I, 459; II, 694-95, 892.

[46] *Ibid.,* I, 486-87.

[47] Anna Howard Shaw, *The Story of a Pioneer* (New York: Harper Brothers, 1915), pp. 189-90.

[48] Cited in Harper, *op. cit.,* II, 660.

[49] Cf. Susan B. Anthony Scrapbooks (1893), Vol. XVI; (1894), Vol. XVII.

[50] Harper, *op. cit.,* I, 302.

[51] Cf. Stanton *et. al., op. cit.,* IV, 263-64.

[52] *Ibid.,* II, 389-90.

[53] *Ibid.,* II, 384, 388. Cf. also Scrapbooks (1874), Vol. V.

[54] *Chicago Democrat and Chronicle,* November 20, 1898.

[55] *Chicago Tribune,* June 25, 1900.

[56] Stanton, *et. al., op. cit.,* V, 40-41.

[57] *The Revolution,* January 27, 1870.

[58] Harper, *op. cit.,* I, 342.

[59] *Ibid.,* III, 1365.

[60] Shaw, *op. cit.,* p. 208.

[61] *The Lily,* July, 1852, p. 59.

[62] Stanton *et. al., op. cit.,* II, 361-62.

[63] Cited in Harper, *op. cit.,* II, 534.

[64] Cf. *The New York Tribune,* in Scrapbooks, (1871), III, 336; *New York Herald,* May 15, 1874.

[65] Shaw, *op. cit.,* p. 240.

[66] *The Revolution,* February 24, 1870.

[67] *Rochester Democrat and Chronicle* (Rochester, New York), February 4, 1896.

[68] Harper, *op. cit.,* III, 1126.

[69] In telling of the 1876 Illinois Woman Suffrage Convention, Elizabeth Boynton Harbert commented: " . . . I wish to emphasize the great loss to women in the fact that as Miss Anthony's speeches were never written, but came with thrilling effect from her patriotic soul, scarce any record of them remains, other than the intangible memories of her grateful countrywomen." Cf. Stanton *et. al., op. cit.,* III, 580.

[70] Cf. *The Detroit Free Press,* November 30, 1889; *The Sentinel* (Indianapolis, Indiana), December 11, 1878.

[71] In selecting sixteen speaking situations at random from 1875 to 1900 it was found that thirteen dealt with the theme of the progress of women, two with the history of the franchise, and one with constitutional argument.

[72] Cf. *New York Democrat,* May 13, 1871; *The Commercial Gazette* (Cincinnati), February 11, 1889.

[73] Cf. Grim, *op. cit.,* pp. 441, 468-69; also, Harper, *op. cit.,* I, 380.

[74] Cf. Harper, *op. cit.,* II, 977-92.

[75] This lecture was given under the auspices of the Young Men's Occidental Literary Club, of which Eugene V. Debs was president and one of the founders.

[76] Cf. Harper, *op. cit.,* II, 1004-12.

[77] *Ibid.,* II, 1011.

[78] *Ibid.,* II, 1012.

[79] *Rochester Democrat and Chronicle* (Rochester, New York), July 12, 1901.

[80] Cf. Harper, *op. cit.,* II, 997-1003.

[81] *Ibid.,* II, 1000-1001.

[82] Delivered in Ottumwa, Kansas, July 4, 1865; Cf. Harper, *op. cit.,* II, 960-67.

[83] *Ibid.,* II, 965.

[84] *Ibid.,* II, 989.

[85] Elizabeth C. Stanton *et al.,* eds., *The History of Woman Suffrage* (Indianapolis: The Hollenbeck Press, 1902), IV, 27.

[86] Harper, *op. cit.,* III, 1148-49.

[87] Stanton *et al., op. cit.,* V, 4-5.

[88] Harper, *op. cit.,* III, 1161-62.

[89] Delivered in Kansas City, Kansas, May 4, 1894. Cf. Harper, *op. cit.,* II, 1015-21.

[90] Cf. *The Daily Republican* (East Saginaw, Michigan), October 30, 1874; *The Chronicle* (Muskegon, Michigan), October 8, 1874; *St. Louis Globe-Democrat,* May 11, 1879; *Rochester Morning Herald* (Rochester, New York), December 29, 1882.

[91] *The Revolution,* March 31, 1870.

[92] *Ibid.,* December 16, 1869.

[93] Harper, *op. cit.,* II, 977.

[94] *Ibid.,* II, 997.

[95] Stanton *et al., op. cit.,* IV, 133.

[96] *Ibid.,* II, 57-58.

[97] Harper, *op. cit.,* II, 1012.

[98] *The Sun* (Baltimore, Maryland), February 14, 1894.

[99] Cf. *Daily Oregonian* (Portland, Oregon), September 9, 1871; *The Evening Post* (Toledo, Ohio), November 18, 1884; *New York World,* November 5, 1899.

[100] *Labor Advocate* (Shelbyville, Illinois), April 14, 1886.

[101] Harper, *op. cit.,* III, 1138.

[102] Cf. Scrapbooks (1885), Vol. VIII; *Detroit Free Press,* November 30, 1889; *Los Angeles Evening Express,* June 13, 1895.

[103] Cf. William Norwood Brigance (ed.), *A History and Criticism of American Public Address* (New York: McGraw-Hill Book Company, Inc., 1943), I, 153-92.

[104] Cf. *Evening Telegraph* (Utica, New York), April 28, 1853; January 15, 1861.

[105] *The Revolution,* April 13, 1871.

[106] Cf. Scrapbooks (1867), II, 60; (1882), VI, 373; *The Revolution,* November 18, 1869; *Detroit Free Press,* December 10, 1869; *Union and Advertiser* (Rochester, New York), May 8, 1873.

[107] Stanton *et al., op. cit.,* IV, 270.

[108] *Washington Star* (Washington, D.C.), February, 1890, cited in Stanton *et al., op. cit.,* IV, 173.

[109] Cited in Harper, *op. cit.,* III, 1154.

[110] *Ibid.,* II, 848.

[111] Stanton *et. al., op. cit.,* IV, 235.

[112] *Ibid.,* IV, 357.

[113] *Ibid.,* V, 33.

[114] *Ibid.,* III, 260.

[115] Harper, *op. cit.,* I, 196.

[116] *Ibid.,* I, 278.

[117] *The Revolution,* January 8, 1868.

[118] Harper, *op. cit.,* III, 693.

[119] Stanton *et al., op. cit.,* IV, 252-53.

[120] *Ibid.,* IV, 238.

[121] *The Revolution,* March 30, 1871.

[122] James B. Pond, "Great Orators and the Lyceum," *The Cosmopolitan,* XXI (July, 1896), 247-56.

[123] Stanton *et al., op. cit.,* IV, 149.

[124] Carrie Chapman Catt and Nettie Rogers Shuler, *Woman Suffrage and Politics* (New York: Charles Scribner's Sons, 1926), pp. 260, 268.

Isidore Starr (essay date 1956)

SOURCE: "Susan B. Anthony," in *Great American Liberals,* edited by Gabriel Richard Mason, Starr King Press, 1956, pp. 99-108.

[*In the following essay, Starr discusses Anthony's liberal political reform theories.*]

There is a sentence in our Constitution which reads: "The right of citizens of the United States to vote shall not be denied or abridged by the United States or by any State *on account of sex.*"

These words cast a long shadow. And as we peer into their historic past we discern the dominating image of Miss Susan B. Anthony, a great American, who died almost half a century ago, but whose spirit still lives in the liberal institutions of American political life.

The liberal analyzes and questions the status quo, the habit-patterns which cake society. Critical of *what is,* he is always searching, thinking and fighting for *what ought to be.* He doesn't want society stood on its head; he wants society reformed so that all men and women may be partners in the adventure of living together and creating a better world.

Such a liberal—and such a woman—was Susan Brownell Anthony. She loved liberty, equality, and social justice for all people. Her devotion to humanity transcended class, color, race, religion, and sex. And most important of all, she was endowed with a remarkable mind of her own—a factor which was to prove most disturbing to the society in which she lived.

When Susan was quite young she heard her teacher say: "The girls of the nineteenth century must behave precisely as the girls have behaved in all the other centuries. . . . The sanctity of tradition must be always upheld." But Susan asked herself "why?" and she concluded that not all traditions were best for society. This began the great tug of war.

What were the designs that entered into the pattern of her liberalism? What led her to spend the eighty-six years of her life in a Spartan-like devotion to studying and seeking to solve the burning issues of her time—temperance, slavery, and women's rights?

Her closest friend, Elizabeth Cady Stanton, had this to say about her: "In ancient Greece she would have been a Stoic; in the era of the Reformation, a Calvinist; in King Charles' time, a Puritan; but in this nineteenth century, by the very laws of her being, she is a reformer." Perhaps this is as good an explanation as any. She was born with that mystical and unique spark which separates the reformer from the conformer.

The first thirty years of Susan's life constituted one of the most unusual periods in our history—the Age of Jacksonian Democracy. It was an era distinguished for its idealistic ferment, its intellectual unrest, and its quest for social justice. All this struck a responsive chord in Susan, and it generated in her the need for participating in the upsurging humanitarianism of her time.

Unquestionably her unusual parents played a dominant role in keeping the flame of liberalism alive. The father was an independent, one might even say a rebellious Quaker, and the mother was a very sensitive Baptist. Together they created a home atmosphere characterized by moral zeal and respect for individual freedom, even for women. Their Rochester home became the meeting place of such distinguished crusaders as William Lloyd Garrison, Wendell Phillips, and Frederick Douglass. Susan got to know these men personally, and the spark with which she was born was nurtured by their friendship.

Perhaps all these influences—the inner self, the parents, and the example of important men—help to explain why she consecrated her life to reform and why she found in the woman suffrage movement an outlet for her emotions, her religious beliefs, and her social philosophy.

Teaching in the public schools of Rochester, New York, she received $8 a month as compared with the $25 and $30 which men were paid for the same type of work. This vexed her particularly because on one occasion she was given a job in a country school where the previous teacher, a man, had been literally forced out of the

classroom by as rowdy a group of teacher-baiting students as any harassed instructor ever faced. Where the man had failed, Susan succeeded. This gentle Quaker girl picked out the leader of the louts, rolled up her sleeves, selected a sturdy birch rod, and—as her closest friend described the incident—resorted to the *argumentum ad hominem* by demonstrating the *a posteriori* method of reasoning. For this achievement she won the highest accolade that man could confer on woman. Said one of the males in the community: "By gosh, this woman's got the nerve of a man," and that was true.

She never lacked this nerve throughout her life. It was during her fifteen years as a successful teacher that she demanded equal pay for equal work for all teachers. She became an important figure at meetings of the New York State Teachers Association, where she kept offering petitions and resolutions demanding for women all the privileges enjoyed by men. In addition, she fought discrimination against Negro teachers and children in the public schools. She was also interested in coeducation and equality for both sexes in all schools, colleges, and universities.

It was at the age of thirty that Miss Anthony began really publicly to advocate her ideas of reform. The issue was "Demon Rum."

Among the customs which the colonists had imported from England was that of tippling; the Americans almost immediately improved on this practice by inventing a native whiskey and applejack. In a world characterized by Puritanical restrictions on gaiety, recreation was eagerly sought, and very often found, in drink. To the evil of the saloon was added the amazing capacity of the nineteenth-century male for liquor. It was not unusual for two bottles of wine per guest to be considered mere appetizers to the real liquid refreshment.

The victims of drunkenness were not only men but their wives and children as well. The temperance movement, aware of the crimes and sufferings resulting from the use of liquor, sought to stop its sale.

Miss Anthony, as a delegate to a meeting held by the Sons of Temperance in Albany, tried to gain the floor and speak on a motion, but she was quickly informed that sisters were there to be seen, to listen and to learn, but not to be heard. She replied, in her characteristic fashion, by helping to organize the Women's State Temperance Society of New York, the first of its kind.

But the opposition to women's participation in public affairs was overwhelming, and at times, even violent. Susan became increasingly convinced that only through equal rights could women develop into effective workers for social betterment.

Her work in the temperance movement paved her way as a reformer in the anti-slavery crusade. In the 1850s Miss Anthony worked for the American Anti-Slavery

Society. This was not surprising, as the reformers of this period were involved both in the temperance and in the anti-slavery movements. However, she took the radical abolitionist stand and campaigned under the banner, "No union with slaveholders!" It took great courage in those days—as it takes today—to espouse an unpopular cause, and, as was to be expected, she met the usual fate. There were the howling hooligans and the rambunctious rowdies; there were jeers, groans, rotten eggs, and burning effigies. But she stood her ground like a man!

After the Civil War Miss Anthony was one of the first to advocate Negro suffrage. At the same time she fought to have included in the Fourteenth Amendment a provision giving the vote to women as well as to male Negroes. When this Amendment as passed introduced into the Constitution for the first time the word "male," she exploded and refused to go along with those who believed that this should be the Negro's hour. She wanted the word "male" dropped, for she felt that in this way both Negroes and women would win the right to vote. With this defeat came the resolve to dedicate her life to the one reform which could give women the same sense of dignity possessed by men—the right to vote and thereby to determine their political, economic, and social status.

Susan B. Anthony was what one might call a fine figure of a woman, with a face "lighted with the spiritual beauty which life-long devotion to high purpose often imparts." One of her marriage proposals came from a rich dairy farmer, who appraised her as one who could do a good job milking his sixty cows.

She had several offers of matrimony, but she refused to marry and become a man's legalized servant. Her argument was that she could not consent that the man she loved, described in the Constitution as a white, male, native-born, American citizen, possessed of the right of self-government, eligible to the office of President of the great Republic, should unite his destinies in marriage with a political slave and pariah. "No, no," she exclaimed, "when I am crowned with all the rights, privileges, and immunities of a citizen, I may give some consideration to these special problems; but until then I must concentrate all my energies on the enfranchisement of my own sex."

It is interesting to note what was the legal relationship between the sexes in the mid-nineteenth century. Certainly, for women, especially the sensitive ones, many of the practices of this period seemed the offspring of social prejudice and bigotry. In general, most educational institutions were closed to them; few means of gainful employment were available; their earnings and their property belonged to their husbands; and fathers legally controlled the destinies of their children. In short, it seemed that woman was virtually the property of her male relations.

One of the most important reasons for this general acceptance of female inferiority was the fact that American law was based on the English common law. The impressive figure of Sir William Blackstone, conservative British jurist, hovered over our lawyers and lawmakers. For Blackstone, a woman civilly married was a woman civilly dead, a principle which was stated in the American law of the time as follows: "In marriage, man and woman become one, and that one is the husband."

This Quaker girl, who had never before used the ballot, believed that only through the achievement of the most important of democratic weapons—political suffrage—could woman wipe out her disabilities and gain for herself the dignified place to which she was rightfully entitled.

The half-century during which Susan B. Anthony was in the forefront of the fight for woman suffrage represents a case study of a great liberal in action. It shows how an extraordinary personality can by persistent pressure leave an indelible impression on that slow-moving mass that we call society.

First, she used her remarkable physical endurance to travel all over our country educating all she met with the importance of her cause. Here is a brief note from her diary on the last day of 1871:

> Left Medicine Bow at noon, went through deep snow cuts ten feet in length. . . . Reached Laramie at ten P.M. Thus closes 1871, a year full of hard work, six months east, six months west of the Rocky Mountains; 171 lectures, 13,000 miles of travel; gross receipts, $4,318, paid on debts $2,271. Nothing ahead but to plod on.

Barns, lyceums, lumber wagons, open air gatherings, even saloons were the platforms and forums for her views. And so also were the fashionable gatherings at Saratoga Springs. Twice she traveled to Europe—the second time at the age of eighty-four to attend the International Congresses of Women in London and in Berlin.

No personal sacrifice was too great, no discomfort too difficult for her cause. Susan B. Anthony traveled so that she could carry the message of woman suffrage everywhere. Lecturing five and six times a week when the occasion demanded, often substituting for speakers who failed to appear, she never hesitated to face an audience—even those dominated by that lunatic fringe which vents its spleen with hisses, overripe tomatoes, and vile and obscene clamor. Late in life, she couldn't help reminiscing before a large and enthusiastic audience: "Time brings strange changes. In this very city that has pelted me with roses I have been pelted with rotten eggs for saying the very things that I have said tonight."

Susan B. Anthony became a familiar figure at legislative committee hearings. In New York she pleaded for liberalization of the laws relating to a married woman's earnings and the guardianship of her children. In Washington she fought year after year for the greatest prize of all—an amendment to the Constitution. She kept trying to get woman suffrage planks into the Democratic and Republican platforms—but all she obtained were "splinters."

She set aside time for correspondence with influential people, and for the publication over a period of two years of a weekly journal, *The Revolution*. Many a complacent citizen must have been regularly ruffled by the defiant tone and slogan of this periodical which proclaimed: "Men, their rights and nothing more; Women, their rights and nothing less!"

But that was not all. Miss Anthony found it necessary to write *A History of Woman Suffrage* to summarize the achievements as well as the unfinished business of this great movement. Together with Elizabeth Cady Stanton and Mathilda Joslyn Gage she started a multi-volume repository of all the significant data which would help to educate and to enlighten the public.

All this work was significant and impressive. But we have not as yet touched upon her greatest activity—that which must serve as an object lesson to all liberals.

There comes a time in every great reform movement when the days seem very dark, the obstacles too numerous, the defeats most discouraging. There comes a time when the prima donnas in the campaign—the superb speakers and the gifted writers—having played their parts, leave the stage. There comes a time when a reform movement hovers on the brink of history's limbo. At this point in the movement to enfranchise women, Susan B. Anthony made her greatest contribution. Talk about reform was complemented with action for political change.

Marshaling every available weapon at her command, she attacked at all points: state legislatures, territorial governments, and Congress. She did not let anyone forget the ideal for which she was fighting—an amendment to the Constitution.

But there always remained the innumerable and endless minute details—the stubborn facts that have to be faced and handled to keep a movement alive from day to day. She was not only a great organizer, master tactician and leader; she was also the director of daily activities. Money had to be raised, speakers mobilized, conventions arranged, petitions signed, resolutions presented to the proper agencies. All this she did—with others when possible, alone when necessary.

Her superb skill in planning and managing was best seen in the creation of associations which became focal centers of widespread activity. When the Sons of Temperance seemed inadequate, she created the Woman's State Temperance Society of New York. Then came the American Equal Rights Association, followed by the National Woman Suffrage Association which was formed to secure an amendment to the Federal Constitution. In 1890 the more radical wing of the movement, led by Susan B. Anthony and Elizabeth Cady Stanton, merged with the more conservative group, which had advocated

state action as the better solution. The newly organized National American Woman Suffrage Association honored Miss Anthony with the presidency from 1892 to 1900, at which time she voluntarily retired.

Anyone who dedicates himself—or herself—to a public cause must be prepared for the entire spectrum of critical appraisal. Anyone who deals in public controversy knows that the very taking of a positive stand evokes the mixed chorus of applause, derogation, and belittlement.

Susan B. Anthony, during her long life, did much that aroused such sharp differences of opinion. Consider the following two incidents.

In the 1850's Amelia Bloomer and others, including Miss Anthony, introduced a new note in women's fashions: the famous Bloomer costume of short skirt and Turkish trousers. Designed to "sensationalize the men out of their fossilized prejudices," it produced results which any man could foresee, but which the feminists never anticipated. That the men were at once attracted was inevitable, but their attention most certainly was not drawn to the intellectual issues involved. One year of this bifurcated costume was enough for Miss Anthony and she abandoned it with this comment: "I found it a physical comfort but a mental crucifixion. The attention of my audience was fixed upon my clothes instead of my words. I learned the lesson then that to be successful a person must attempt but one reform."

The second incident is the important story behind the seemingly impersonal judicial note: *United States v. Susan B. Anthony*. Believing that the Fourteenth Amendment entitled women to the right to vote, Miss Anthony registered with fifteen other women and voted in the presidential election of 1872. Arrested for illegal voting, she was released on bail. While awaiting trial, she undertook a series of public lectures to educate every potential juror on the issues of the case. When the Attorney General succeeded in gaining a change of venue, she began a second campaign of juror education. However, the judge refused to give the case to the jury, delivered an opinion reportedly written before the trial had taken place, and directed the jury to bring in a verdict of guilty. The fine of $100 she simply refused to pay and it was never paid. Her philosophy in matters of this sort was stated with startling and disconcerting simplicity. She was *willing to sacrifice* her personal liberty to protect "enslaved women."

By 1906—the last year of Susan B. Anthony's life—she could look back on many successes and satisfactions. Four states had granted woman suffrage; women were being received on equal terms with men in colleges, industry, business, and the professions. The old legal disabilities against married women were being wiped off the statute books, and marriage was now a social contract between two equal partners. She could see that the legal and social revolution which she had led for more than half a century had produced substantial results. It had helped to liberate man as well as woman. But the dream was unfulfilled; the constitutional amendment had eluded her.

In her last speech on her eighty-sixth birthday she said: "What I ask is not praise, but justice." She was accorded both. From the most ridiculed and maligned of women, she became the most honored and respected. There is historic justice in the greatest of her triumphs. One hundred years after her birth the Nineteenth Amendment, giving women the right to vote, was ratified.

David K. Boynick (essay date 1959)

SOURCE: "Exponent of Woman's Rights: Susan B. Anthony," in *Women Who Led the Way: Eight Pioneers for Equal Rights,* Thomas Y. Crowell Company, 1959, pp. 27-58.

[*In the following essay, Boynick discusses Anthony's experiences as a political figure.*]

Her name is Susan Brownell Anthony and she looks out upon the world from a monument in the National Capitol in Washington. Washington is a good place for her to be. Things happen there.

Things like the adoption of the Nineteenth Amendment to the Constitution—the Susan B. Anthony Amendment, it was called—which gave women the vote in 1920.

Like President Franklin D. Roosevelt's appointment of Frances Perkins to be Secretary of Labor—the first woman Cabinet officer.

Or like the announcement of the Department of Labor two decades later that women had demonstrated they could do any work men could, because women were engaged in all 446 occupations listed by the Bureau of Census.

Susan B. Anthony fought for these advances. For more than a half century she fought. She was the leader, the voice, the inspiration of the woman's rights movement.

She was thirty-three when she made her first talk for woman's rights, a tall, straight-backed schoolteacher with luxurious brown hair and warm blue eyes. She made it in the summer of 1853 in the city of Rochester, New York.

Susan Anthony was participating at the time in the annual convention of the New York State Teachers Association. It was an odd kind of participation by present-day standards, for she was just listening and observing. But that is what society then expected of a woman at a public gathering—that is, when she was permitted to attend at all.

Women made up two-thirds of the membership of the Association, but until Susan spoke not one had ever opened her mouth at a convention except to yawn or whisper a remark to another woman.

The men, the minority, did all the speaking and voting.

For two days Susan had sat on a hard chair, struggling to contain a rising anger while man after man spoke complainingly of the poor salaries paid teachers. Her fingernails dug into her palms in vexation. Couldn't these men see the why and the wherefore of this? How could they be so blind?

A man who had been speaking for twenty minutes without saying anything new spread his coattails and sat down, and the presiding officer scanned the hall for other men who wished to speak. Apparently there were none. He was about to utter the words closing the discussion when she jumped to her feet.

"Mr. President," she said.

The presiding officer, Charles Davies, professor of mathematics at the United States Military Academy, regarded her blankly. "What will the lady have?" he asked.

"The lady," she said in a voice which emerged firm despite her inner quavering, "wishes to speak to the question under discussion."

Susan Anthony heard mutters of protest, snickers and a hiss of "shame." Susan looked straight ahead at the presiding officer in military uniform, reading the indecision in his face.

Davies tapped with his gavel for silence. The delegates would have to rule on this astonishing request. "What is the pleasure of the convention?" he asked.

A debate began. It lasted for a half hour; all the speakers were men. At length Davies put the issue to vote and by a narrow margin—with only men voting—Susan Anthony was given the floor.

She turned so as to face rows of chairs where the men were seated, clasping her hands together to hide their trembling. She spoke in a rich contralto voice.

"For two days you have deplored the fact that the profession of teacher is not so highly respected as that of lawyer, doctor, or minister. It seems to me that you fail to comprehend the cause of the disrespect of which you complain.

"Do you not see"—a note of anger entered her voice— "that so long as society says that a woman has not brains enough to be a lawyer, doctor, or minister but has plenty to be a teacher, every one of you who condescends to teach admits before Israel and the sun that he has no more brains than a woman?"

She sank to her chair. The convention sat hushed. Only the scratching of the secretary's pen racing to catch up with her words could be heard. At length a male teacher moved that the convention be recessed for the day. The men seemed to greet the motion with relief and voted it approval.

Susan Anthony walked to the door. Women went to join her, to express thanks for her remarks. But some women drew aside their skirts and turned their backs at her approach.

That evening Susan and a newly gained supporter, a Mrs. Northrop, worked on a resolution which would pledge the New York State Teachers Association to recognize "the rights of female teachers to share in all the privileges and deliberations of this body."

The next morning Mrs. Northrop, clutching Susan by the hand, asked for the floor. Recognized by the chairman, she read the resolution. The majority of women voted for it, and some men. The resolution carried.

It was Susan Anthony's first small victory.

She was born February 15, 1820, in Adams, Massachusetts, a pleasant village of white-painted dwellings tucked away in the Berkshire hills.

Many of the inhabitants of Adams were Quakers, and her father, Daniel Anthony, was himself a member of the Society of Friends. This was important in the upbringing of the child, for the Society of Friends was the first religious sect to extend equality to its women members.

When Susan was old enough to go to Quaker meeting she heard women express their views in public discussion and vote. She even saw her father's mother, Mrs. Hannah Anthony, sit on the high seat as an elder of the meeting.

To most men this was further evidence that the Quakers, with their drab garments and "thee and thou" speech, were a queer lot. By their standards Daniel was even queerer.

He believed that women were the equals of men in brains and ability. Daniel, the owner of a small cotton mill, raised four daughters and two sons. He raised them as equals. In his eyes the girls were different from the boys—different, not inferior.

Susan, the second eldest of the Anthony children, was her father's favorite. The tall, intelligent Quaker loved to hold her in his arms before bedtime and observe her eyes grow round with wonder as he told of dangerous exploration in the West, of the wonders of scientific discovery, of exciting developments in manufacture.

The child imagined herself playing starring roles in these wonderful tales, not knowing that in real life such were reserved for the male sex.

Like other girls, Susan was raised with the outlook that she would marry and have children. Her mother trained her well in household tasks, teaching her to cook and preserve food, to keep a spotless house, to spin and weave, to cut and sew clothes. As a woman Susan was a model housekeeper and an excellent cook whose dishes were the delight of her friends.

Susan's mother was not a happy woman. A non-Quaker, Lucy Read Anthony before her marriage was a happy, laughing girl, the belle of Adams. In marrying a Friend, she was compelled to put away her gay dresses and attire herself in the mud-colored clothes of Quaker women; to give up singing and dancing, which she loved.

Lucy Anthony's personality changed after her marriage. She became withdrawn and anxious. She spoke little.

As a child, Susan loved and pitied her mother. Sensing Lucy's hunger for the pretty things she once possessed, the child would save money given her by her father and grandparents and buy for her mother a bit of embroidery, a delicate cup and saucer, or a string of beads.

But often Susan was outspokenly critical of Mrs. Anthony. Once Lucy reprimanded her for staying at Grandmother Read's for supper, when the same supper was awaiting her at home. Susan replied saucily, "Why, Grandmother's potato peelings are better than your boiled dinners."

Another incident involving Mrs. Anthony left Susan with an anger which endured for years.

When Susan was nearly four she was sent with her elder sister Guelma to Grandmother Anthony's to stay during the birth of Lucy's fourth child. The two little girls remained six weeks with their grandmother and during this time they had whooping cough and learned to read.

Susan raced home at the end of the visit and excitedly told her mother that she could read—"real words in books!" Lucy, whose baby had been born dead, didn't hear a word. Shocked, she stared at Susan's eyes which had turned in toward her nose during the illness, and wrung her hands in anguish. Lucy acted as if having crossed eyes was a disgrace.

In time Susan's left eye corrected itself and her right became almost normal. But she remained convinced all her life that her eyes were markedly crossed, causing strangers to stare. As a woman she refused for many years to pose for full view portraits; she believed that they would show up her crossed eyes.

Daniel gave his daughters a good education in a time when women were not permitted to enter college. Susan and Guelma attended village school in Adams. When Susan was six the family moved to Battenville, New York, some forty miles to the northwest, where Daniel had acquired a larger mill. In Battenville he established a small private school which his children attended. In their early teens Susan and Guelma had a private tutor and later they studied at a Quaker finishing school near Philadelphia.

Daniel also taught his children himself. By word and example he instructed them in a simple religion and a way of life.

He taught them to love God. And one shows his love of God, he would say, by loving humanity. This he translated to mean working, speaking, sacrificing for human betterment.

His creed led him into many reform movements. He was a tireless worker against slavery and a force in the temperance movement. Himself a liberal employer, he spoke for good wages and working conditions for workers.

"Tolerate not evil against humanity," he would tell his children. "And when thee is powerless to do anything else, speak with vigor. Protest!"

Susan was five when she witnessed her first demonstration of protest.

As a Quaker Daniel was opposed to war and did not want to pay taxes to a government which upheld force of arms as an instrument of state policy. However, he could not escape paying his taxes so he resorted to a formula which would express his feelings about the matter.

He took Susan by the hand one day and walked with her to the home of the tax collector. There he laid his purse on the table and said, "I shall not voluntarily pay these taxes. But if thee wants to steal from my purse thou can do so." Gravely the tax collector counted out the money due the government and returned Daniel his purse.

Daniel taught his children well.

Before the Civil War broke out his son Jacob went to Kansas and enlisted in the antislavery guerrilla band of John Brown, taking part in the historical raid on Osawatomie.

His other son, Daniel Read, followed his younger brother to Kansas to fight and stayed on to become a reform-minded newspaper publisher and mayor of Leavenworth.

His daughters Guelma, Hannah, and Mary became abolitionists, worked for temperance and joined the Woman's Rights Movement when it was formed.

And Susan—Susan was her father's best pupil.

At eighteen she was a happy, eager girl, her body slim and athletic. Her features were pleasing, showing the promise of later handsomeness. She had her fair share of boy friends, with whom she went on picnics and buggy rides. In her diary she jotted many notes about the boys who were her friends:

"Job Whipple and William Norton called here last night and made quite a little visit. I had very good times . . . I awoke this morning a little after midnight and went to the window and saw the constellation Libra and some others, which so filled my mind with the beauty of the stars that I could not get to sleep."

Another note tells that "R. Wilson" sent her "a piece of poetry on love."

Susan was convinced, however, that she was homely—and cross-eyed—and one item in her diary reveals her belief that she could not compete with physical attractiveness for a boy's attention.

"Job is at Marie Wilson's," she wrote. "May he know that he has found in me a spirit congenial to his own and not suffer the glare of beauty to attract both eye and heart."

The pleasant secure life at home ended suddenly for Susan in 1838. Daniel Anthony, who had stretched his credit to the utmost to expand his Battenville business, was forced into bankruptcy in the worst economic depression the young nation had ever experienced.

Creditors seized everything—the Battenville mill, the family home, furniture, silverware, household utensils and linens. Many of the things were Lucy's, the gifts of her parents, but these were taken too. Under the law a wife owned nothing. Everything she had was her husband's and could be seized in payment for his debts.

It became imperative that the two oldest children, Guelma and Susan, go to work to support themselves and help their father. They found employment as teachers, Guelma near home and Susan at a girls' boarding school in New Rochelle, New York.

In growing up, Susan had perceived that the world's treatment of women was different from what she was used to at home and in Quaker meeting. She proceeded now to learn by experience how great that difference was.

She spent the greater part of the next fifteen years as a teacher. At the outset she was better equipped through education than most teachers of her time, men and women. Then while teaching she studied hard to improve herself, to become expert in subjects neglected in her own schooling.

Susan taught in a half-dozen schools, public and private. Her first position paid $2 a week, minus $1 a week for board. The most she ever earned was $3, out of which $1 weekly was taken for board. This summit of earnings was achieved at Canajoharie Academy, in Canajoharie, New York, where she was employed as headmistress of the girls' department. It was a much-sought-after position.

As the years passed it angered her more and more. Not the money—money never meant much to her. But money paid in salary was a measure of worth, and her greatest worth was $3 week. A male teacher was paid three times as much.

She had a strong need to progress. She believed she was able and she yearned to undertake tasks worthy of her ability. But there was no opportunity for a woman of ability, she learned. A woman could be a teacher, a governess, a seamstress, a servant, a factory hand, a barmaid—little else.

Ever since leaving Battenville Susan had taken a small part in reform, chiefly in work against slavery and strong drink. At Canajoharie, where she went at the age of twenty-six, she became more active.

She joined the Canajoharie Daughters of Temperance and was elected president. She planned various activities, got them approved by the members and then directed their execution. They were usually successful. The organization achieved a local influence.

The work gratified her. She was achieving, finding an outlet for ideas and energies, progressing—and in doing these things she was also helping people. An exciting purpose began to form in her mind—to make a career in reform.

Susan discussed it in letters to her family. Her father approved heartily. He urged her to come home to live, and offered financial help because she could not expect to earn a living in reform. Daniel, who had suffered several setbacks in his struggle to reestablish himself, had at this time a good position with an insurance company in Rochester, New York.

Susan was teaching in Canajoharie when the first Woman's Rights convention was held in Seneca Falls, New York, on July 19 and 20, 1848. She read about it in the Canajoharie newspaper which reported that sixty-eight women and thirty-two men had signed their names to a Declaration of Woman's Rights demanding for women free education, equality of opportunity in industry and the professions, free speech, the right to take part in public affairs and the right to vote.

Reading, she nodded her head in approval. This was excellent! Yet she did not feel moved to join the new Woman's Rights Movement. It was more important, she reasoned, to give her services to the abolitionist and temperance causes. Nearly five years were to elapse before she changed her mind, or rather narrow-minded men changed it for her.

In the fall of 1849 she began carrying out her plan for a reform career. She went to Rochester to live in the family's new home. She taught school for a while in the Rochester area but gradually ceased this work to give all her time to reform, particularly to temperance.

She found in Rochester a small Daughters of Temperance group and breathed vitality into it. Then she traveled about the nearby towns and villages, speaking to women about the need to curb the sale of liquor and organizing them in lodges of the Daughters of Temperance.

She was content. She felt she had found her place in life.

While she was organizing the women, she worked to obtain official recognition of the Daughters by the men's organization, the Sons of Temperance. Such recognition, she hoped, would be followed by a union of the two organizations.

She reasoned that without the men the women could not be very effective. Their lodges were few and women had no money of their own to give to organizing activities. More important, legislators paid little heed to the women's lodges because their members could not vote.

In time Susan established a state-wide organization of women's temperance groups but the men refused to recognize them. In her efforts to obtain this recognition Susan was several times harshly rebuffed.

These rebuffs prompted her to reexamine her decision to work for temperance and the abolition of slavery, and not for woman's rights. Was she making a mistake? Did women have to win all their own rights before they could work usefully in reform?

In her work for temperance Susan often collaborated with the leaders of the woman's rights movement—Mrs. Elizabeth Cady Stanton, Mrs. Lucretia Mott, pretty Lucy Stone. They sought to convince her that the answer to her questions was "yes." But they weren't successful until Susan had had a few more experiences with the men's temperance organization. The most humiliating of these occurred at Syracuse, New York.

A state convention of the New York State Sons of Temperance was scheduled to be held in Syracuse and the local lodge, as sponsor of the gathering, invited the women's state organization to send delegates. Susan and Mrs. Amelia Bloomer were appointed.

On their arrival in Syracuse the two women were met by a clergyman who said he had been delegated to inform them that the convention had rescinded the invitation of the Syracuse lodge. Susan and Mrs. Bloomer told the spokesman that they had come to Syracuse by invitation to attend the convention and attend they would. But they never bargained for the violent attack which was provoked by their entrance into the convention hall.

The two women were ordered by the chairman to leave. They were hooted at, jeered at. One man arose and declared that no business would be transacted until "these creatures, a hybrid species, half-man and half-woman, belonging to neither sex, are put out."

The women departed, trembling with wrath and shock. A short time later plump Mrs. Stanton said to Susan, "Do you see now?" Susan answered sadly, "My eyes are open. I see at last."

The Susan Anthony who began working for woman's rights was at thirty-three a poised and mature woman, well-read, well-informed.

She dressed in quiet good taste, being especially fond of a dress of gray silk with pale blue ribbons. Such a dress was frowned on by the Quakers but ever since her Canajoharie days Susan had been disregarding the Friends' severe rules of dress and deportment. At Canajoharie she had dropped the singular speech of the Quakers—the "thee" speech—and even learned to dance.

Stately, with a handsomely shaped head over which her thick brown hair was tightly drawn, she attracted all eyes at gatherings. Her expression was warm and friendly, her generous mouth usually curved in a smile. Men seeing her for the first time whispered that here was "a fine figure of a woman."

The only one who did not believe this was Susan herself. She thought of herself as an unattractive woman with crossed eyes. She persisted in this view of herself even though a number of men asked her to marry them.

She turned down all the men who proposed, always finding a reason to justify herself. One well-to-do widower, who said she reminded him of his first wife, pursued her at great length. Giggling, Susan told her friends that she wouldn't marry him because she "didn't intend to become a second."

To the woman's rights movement Susan brought a great gift. This was a talent for organizing and leading, developed in several years' work for temperance. To her, weaknesses of the movement were quickly apparent.

Talking with Mrs. Stanton, who became her dearest friend, she stressed that it wasn't enough to give speeches and write leaflets about woman's rights. The movement needed a permanent functioning organization. It needed members by the thousands and the way to get them was to go where women were to be found, in their own homes. And it needed, she declared, a program of immediate action which would attract members and give them tasks to do.

Mrs. Stanton approved of Susan's ideas and her intention of carrying them out. In the fall of 1853, following her first talk for woman's rights at the teachers convention in Rochester, Susan began to work.

Paying her own expenses with funds provided by her father, she set out on a tour of western New York State. She called on housewives in the towns and villages and told them about the movement and its Declaration of Rights.

She made many converts and organized them in groups. A large number of women, however, became angry or scornful when Susan explained her mission and ordered her from their homes. Some said cuttingly that they didn't need laws to give them rights—*they* had husbands to look after them.

En route home on a jolting soot-coated train, Susan thought long about further steps in her organizational campaign and developed a plan. There would be a state convention of the local groups which would prepare a demand for woman's rights to be submitted to the State Legislature.

With Susan attending to all the preparations, a well-attended convention was held in Rochester. Her proposal for an approach to the Legislature was approved, and she was elected unanimously to organize the project.

From among the new members Susan appointed a number of aides. Then during the winter of 1853-54 Susan and these women trudged from house to house collecting signatures to petitions requesting that married women be granted the right to their own earnings and property, to enter into contracts, to sue and be sued, to be equal guardians with their husbands of minor children, and to vote.

Ten thousand signatures were obtained and two bills embodying the intent of the petitions were introduced before the Legislature in Albany. In both the Assembly and the Senate, the bills and petitions were ridiculed and attacked. Typical were the words of Assemblyman Burnett:

> Are we going to give the least countenance to claims so preposterous, disgraceful, and criminal? Are we to put the stamp of truth upon the libel here set forth that men and women in their matrimonial relations are to be equal? We *know* that God created man as the representative of the race.

Both houses rejected the bills by overwhelming majorities. The women sitting in the galleries were discouraged. Not Susan. Grimly she told the legislators in the corridors, "We will be back. We will be back again and again until the laws are enacted giving women their due rights."

She had the tenacity of a bulldog. During the spring, summer, and fall she worked at organizing more groups and collecting signatures to the petitions. To climax her campaign she determined to give lectures in as many of the State's sixty counties as possible.

With her father guaranteeing payment, she went into debt for several thousand handbills advertising her lectures and sent them out to sheriffs and postmasters with letters asking that the handbills be prominently displayed.

Then with fifty dollars in cash and a carpetbag bulging with petitions she left Rochester by train on Christmas Day, 1854, on the start of her tour.

In her diary Susan recorded her experiences during the coldest and snowiest New York winter in ten years. In some towns she had well-attended meetings and her appeals for contributions met a good response. In other towns she was refused the use of church or schoolhouse to talk about the "detestable woman's doctrine." When this occurred she visited women in their homes, then traveled on to the next town by sleigh.

In the town of Olean she was able to hold a meeting only because the owner of the hotel offered his dining room. She noted that a young minister signed her petition, then hastily crossed off his name when a wealthy parishioner threatened to leave his church.

She stopped working in February to go to Albany with an armload of petitions to the Legislature. But none of the members of the Legislature would introduce a woman's rights bill. She wouldn't quit, but went off to the freezing Lake George and Schroon Lake districts for more meetings and signatures to be used the following year.

Often when snowstorms slowed her passage from one town to another she went hungry. Her hands and feet became frostbitten. Each night in a cold village inn she would soak them in cold water. Her back began to ache; the pain became agonizing and she had to bite her lips to keep from groaning. But she plodded on.

The first of May Susan returned home, thin as a lath, her body one whole ache. But triumphant. She had lectured and obtained signatures in fifty-four counties. She had collected $2,367, spent $2,291 and had $76 remaining.

Her father urged her to keep the surplus and buy herself some new dresses, for she was still wearing the clothes purchased in Canajoharie. "No," she said, "that will be for next year's campaign."

The next year's campaign didn't move the legislators, nor the one after that. Seven times Susan and her woman's righters went before the Legislature. On their seventh appearance they were successful. In March of 1860 the Legislature adopted a bill giving married women the right to their own earnings and property, to sue and be sued, to enter into contracts, and to be equal guardians with their husbands of their minor children.

It was the first break in the thousand-year-old English common law restricting the rights of women. The credit belonged mostly to Susan Anthony.

Soon the Civil War began. Daniel Anthony, convinced that only through war could slavery be eliminated, voted for the first time, casting a ballot for Abraham Lincoln. Before the war was over he was dead, a victim of what the doctors termed "neuralgia of the stomach."

Susan grieved over the death of her father, but while she grieved she worked. With Mrs. Stanton she organized the Woman's National Loyal League which rallied women in support of the Union, emancipation of the slaves, and woman's rights.

The war over, Susan returned to woman's rights work, proclaiming, "Still another form of slavery remains to be disposed of."

Her reputation grew and reached to every corner of the land. She was much in demand as a lecturer. Supporting herself by her fees, she traveled throughout the country, speaking on woman's rights.

In a year it was not unusual for her to speak in two hundred communities strung from the Atlantic to the Pacific. The physical strain of travel, particularly in the sparsely settled Middle and Far West, was terrific.

In order to reach her destinations on schedule she often had to take trains at all hours of the night. Sometimes the only train available was a freight and she rode squeezed in with bags of flour, cases of shoes, tools, and rifles. Many times she had to ride cross-country for twenty-five or thirty miles in a lumber wagon or an open buggy in snow and rain.

On the western frontiers she slept in dirty, unheated rooms, often the only woman in crude inns where men drank and reveled throughout the night at the bar. For weeks at a time she lived on a diet of soggy bread and dried meat.

Only one frontier hardship she found intolerable—the bedbug. Once in Kansas she went four days and nights without sleep "because our tormentors were so active." Even though she plucked thousands of bedbugs from her hair and the seams of her clothing, enough remained undetected to cover every square inch of her body with bites.

She won thousands of women to her cause, and many men. But no woman in the history of America was more savagely attacked, scorned, and slandered for her ideas.

Drunken men threatened her with guns. Men made hideous effigies of her and burned them. Once acid was thrown at her—fortunately it burned only her garments.

The newspaper *Syracuse Star* described her as "a brawling woman and an atheist," and the *New York World* said, "Susan Anthony is lean, cadaverous, and intellectual, with the proportions of a file and the voice of a hurdy-gurdy."

In a piece of doggerel which became popular in the saloons she was depicted as usually half-clad, immoral, and smoking a big black cigar. She was accused of advocating polygamy and "free love."

She learned to endure the lies and attacks in silence. Sometimes, however, she was stung into a reply. An instance of this occurred at a convention of the New York State Teachers Association as she was leaving the meeting hall after making a brief talk. A teacher, a man of about fifty-five, detained her and said, "That was a magnificent statement, Miss Anthony. But I must tell you that I would rather see my wife or daughter in her coffin than hear her speaking as you did, before a public assembly."

Susan's eyes flashed in anger for a moment. Then she said quietly, "Sir, I wonder if the ladies of your family agree with you that their deaths are to be preferred to speaking for dignity and opportunity."

On another occasion the target of her retort was Horace Greeley, the famous newspaper publisher and editor. Susan was urging a committee of the New York State Legislature to approve a proposal giving women the vote when the round-faced Greeley, the committee chairman, interrupted her.

"Miss Anthony," he drawled, "you are aware that the ballot and the bullet go together. If you vote are you also prepared to fight?"

She answered sweetly, "Certainly, Mr. Greeley. Just as you fought in the Civil War—at the point of a goose quill."

Increasingly the woman's rights forces began to stress the ballot, suffrage, as their key demand. Women would gain their full rights only when they were enfranchised, the leaders of the movement declared.

Susan and the other leaders repeatedly urged Congress to initiate a Constitutional amendment spelling out the right of women to vote. Simultaneously many of the women began to support a theory that under the Fourteenth Amendment, adopted to confer the ballot on Negroes, women were already entitled to the ballot. These women emphasized that in the Fourteenth Amendment Congress for the first time defined a citizen as any person born or naturalized in the United States. The amendment made no mention of sex.

Susan was not among the first to adopt this theory but once she adopted it she decided to act. The result was one of the most daring political coups in American history.

On November 1, 1872, Susan appeared at a shoemaker's shop on West Street in Rochester at the head of fifteen women. The shop was the polling headquarters for the city's eighth ward. Susan informed the dumbfounded election inspectors, "We are here to be enrolled as voters."

When the inspectors declared that "women can't vote—it's illegal" she produced from a capacious pocketbook a copy of the United States Constitution and challenged the men to prove it. Uneasily the inspectors enrolled all sixteen women, among them Susan's sisters, Miss Mary Anthony, Mrs. Guelma Anthony McLean, and Mrs. Hannah Anthony Mosher.

Four days later, Election Day, the same sixteen women returned to the shoemaker's shop and voted after Susan had once more disposed of the inspectors' objections.

The Anthony coup was reported in the newspapers of the land in heavy black type. At the same time newspapers published angry editorials demanding the arrest and imprisonment of Susan B. Anthony and her associates as law-breakers.

If Miss Anthony got away with it, the editorials emphasized, she would by a single pencil mark on her ballot have enfranchised every woman in America.

The administration of President Ulysses S. Grant in Washington appreciated the danger and determined on the prosecution of the Rochester women.

On Thanksgiving Day a United States marshal in top hat rang the bell of the Anthony home in Rochester. Susan came to the door and the marshal, flushed with embarrassment, produced a warrant for Susan's arrest.

The marshal said that to spare herself embarrassment Miss Anthony could go to the courthouse without him, but she said, "Oh dear, no. I much prefer to be taken, handcuffed if possible."

The officer indignantly refused to supply handcuffs but he did escort Susan to the courthouse where she found waiting the fifteen other culprits and an attorney she had engaged in anticipation of trouble. Her attorney was Henry B. Selden, a scholarly veteran of the courts who had agreed to act for her after some twenty other lawyers had turned her down.

Presented before an elections commissioner, all sixteen women pleaded not guilty to a charge of voting illegally in a national election and were ordered held in $500 bail each.

Fifteen put up bail. Susan refused and demanded her release on a writ of habeas corpus. A hearing on her request was subsequently held in the federal court in Albany and it was turned down. In Albany her bail was increased to $1,000. Once more she refused to provide bail.

The militant Quakeress would have been remanded to jail pending the start of her trial had not Selden put up bail without her knowledge. "I could not see a lady go to jail," he apologized to Susan.

The trial of the sixteen women was set for the summer of 1873 in Rochester. Susan decided that inasmuch as she had instigated the voting it was only proper that she should pay all the costs of the trial. However, on her return to Rochester from the Albany hearing she had exactly $13 in the bank. Although many woman's rights groups adopted resolutions praising the courage of the Rochester voters, not one donated as much as a dollar for the expense of the trial.

Susan decided to go on a lecture tour. By this means she would raise money and utilize the great national interest in the trial to educate men and women about woman's rights.

She toured the Midwest, speaking on the subject **"Is It a Crime for a United States Citizen to Vote?"** Everywhere she was heard by large and enthusiastic audiences. The tour was a success.

But Susan was fifty-three now and the strain of constant travel, added to the tension caused by the forthcoming trial, exhausted her. Midway through her talk in Fort Wayne, Indiana, one night she collapsed.

A doctor summoned to treat her at the home of a friend in Fort Wayne instructed Susan sternly to return home at once for a long rest. She took his advice to the extent of going home, arriving with $218 left over after paying travel expenses. Of this she gave Selden $215.

She rested for a brief period—rested her body, that is. Her mind worked energetically. The trial would be held in Rochester, the seat of Monroe County. Thus all the jurors would have to be residents of the county. Good! She would lecture throughout the county and inform everyone within reach of her voice of the issues.

She set out on this new tour. Speaking on 29 nights in one month, she covered every one of Monroe County's post-office districts. After each talk she asked her audience to vote on whether she had broken the law. By large majorities the people voted that she had not broken the law and many men came forward to pledge that if they were chosen to serve on the jury they would vote to acquit her.

The government, meanwhile, was making its own preparations for the trial. United States Senator Roscoe Conkling, President Grant's right hand man and Republican boss of New York State, was appointed to direct the government's behind-the-scenes strategy.

The first development of this strategy was a decision to try only Susan B. Anthony, the "Woman Napoleon," as the newspapers called her.

The government wanted a conviction in the case to smash the threat that women would be enfranchised and Conkling believed it would be easier to convict the detested Anthony woman than a group of sixteen women, most of them housewives whose names had never appeared in the newspapers.

A second development was a request made of the court by the prosecutor to transfer Susan Anthony's trial from Monroe County to adjoining Ontario County. The request was made, the prosecutor said, because Miss Anthony by her marathon lecture series had "corrupted" the citizens of Monroe County.

The request was granted and a trial date of June 17 was set for the little town of Canandaigua. But before the trial could begin Susan "corrupted" the citizens of Ontario County too. In three weeks she spoke in twenty-one districts of the county and Mrs. Matilda Gage, another woman's rights leader, in sixteen.

The case of the government versus Susan B. Anthony opened on a pleasant June day to the tolling of a bell in the Canandaigua courthouse. To Susan it appeared to be tolling a warning.

Judge Nathan Hall, known as a severe but fair-minded jurist, was to have presided at her trial; but in his place sat another man. In the courthouse, packed with members of the woman's movement, notables, and newspaper reporters, it was whispered that Judge Hall had "refused to take orders."

The prim, thin-lipped man in black broadcloth seated on the bench was the Honorable Ward Hunt, Associate Justice of the United States Supreme Court. The reporters scribbled furiously. A Justice of the Supreme Court assigned to try a case in the Circuit Court.

The politically wise in the courtroom, and Susan, too, were sure that they knew the explanation for the assignment of Justice Hunt. The government intended to make certain that Susan Anthony was found guilty. Judge Hunt only recently had been appointed to the High Court through the influence of his friend Senator Conkling, and this was his first trial. He naturally felt under strong obligation to the man who had managed his appointment it was thought.

The trial which all America was watching was brief. It required only two days.

The prosecuting attorney outlined the case against the defendant. Then Attorney Selden asked that his client be summoned to the stand to testify in her defense.

Judge Hunt turned down the request. The defendant, he explained, was not competent to testify—she was a woman.

As Selden protested and Susan bit her lips in anger, Judge Hunt added suavely that he would act for the defendant by reading the testimony she gave at her hearing. This he proceeded to do.

All the evidence had now been submitted in this mockery of a trial. The prosecutor made a brief, almost careless, summation. And Selden delivered a lengthy and passionate defense. Except for one further action the trial was over. It came now from Judge Hunt.

He drew from his pocket a sheet of paper, unfolded it and began to read. It was a charge to the jury and, hearing it, Susan shot to her feet in angry agitation.

Judge Hunt declared that Susan had voted illegally and was not protected by the Constitution against the consequences of her act. Then he told the jury with slow deliberation:

" . . . the result must be a verdict on your part of guilty, and I therefore direct that you find a verdict of guilty."

The outraged Selden protested that by directing the jury to submit a finding of guilty Judge Hunt was acting with serious irregularity. Ignoring him, Judge Hunt impatiently instructed the clerk of the court, "Take the verdict." The clerk mumbled:

"Gentlemen of the jury, hearken to your verdict as the court has recorded it. You say you find the defendant guilty of the offense whereof she stands indicted, and so say you all."

The jurymen had not said anything of the kind, but merely sat in embarrassed silence while the words were put in their mouths.

After the clerk had recited his formula and entered the verdict Judge Hunt said, "Gentlemen of the jury, you are discharged."

The trial was over.

Susan Anthony appeared in court again the next day to receive sentence. Her anger was under control and to those in the courtroom, aware that they were onlookers in a great moment in history, she appeared calm and poised. Selden bit his nails anxiously. He knew that his client could be fined $500 and sentenced to prison for three years.

Judge Hunt rapped the court to order, then ordered the defendant to rise. Now that the trial was over he felt that he could permit her to say a few words. "Has the prisoner anything to say why sentence should not be pronounced?" he asked.

Susan, gagged during the trial, hadn't dreamed that she would be permitted to speak at this time, hadn't prepared anything. But as a veteran of twenty years on the lecture platform she was ready.

Her voice rang out in the courtroom.

"Yes, Your Honor, I have many things to say, for in your ordered verdict of guilty you have trampled underfoot every vital principle of our government. My natural rights, my civil rights, my political rights are all ignored. Robbed of the fundamental privilege of citizenship, I am degraded from the status of citizen to that of subject; and not only myself individually but all of my sex are by Your Honor's verdict doomed to political subjection."

Judge Hunt realized his mistake. Every word uttered by the stately woman in black silk was being taken down by the reporters and would be spread before the eyes of the nation. He interrupted her, "The court cannot listen to a—"

Her trained speaker's voice rose above his, uttering facts, arguments:

" . . . all my prosecutors, from the eighth ward corner grocer politician who entered the complaint, to the United States marshal, commissioner, district attorney, district judge, Your Honor on the bench, not one is my peer, but each and all my political sovereigns. And had Your Honor submitted my case to the jury, as was

clearly your duty, even then I should have had just cause for protest, for not one of these men was my peer; but native or foreign, white or black, rich or poor, educated or ignorant, awake or asleep, sober or drunk, each and every man of them was my political superior."

"The prisoner," the Judge shouted, "will sit down!"

She ignored him, continued. Unable to cope with her, Judge Hunt was goaded into making a defense. "The prisoner," he shouted, "has been tried according to established forms of law."

Like the lash of a whip came her retort, "Yes, Your Honor, but by forms of law made by men, interpreted by men, administered by men, in favor of men—and against women."

She resumed, ignoring the rapping of Judge Hunt's gavel, with her impassioned words ripping to shreds the case against her. She finished by saying that, failing to get justice or even a trial by jury, "I ask not leniency at your hands, but to take the full rigors of the law."

Judge Hunt, glaring with anger, pronounced sentence— a fine of $100 and court costs.

Again she was on her feet to declare, "I shall never pay a dollar of your unjust penalty."

And she never did. Nor did she go to prison for her refusal, because Judge Hunt in imposing sentence had deliberately refrained from adding the customary formula that the prisoner be sent to jail until the fine was paid.

Had he done this Susan Anthony would have gone to jail and could have taken her case directly to the Supreme Court on a writ of habeas corpus.

The years passed and every year Susan Anthony gave 365 days to the cause of woman's advancement. And women were advancing. In time four states enacted legislation giving them the vote. Women and girls were entering college in increasing numbers; new colleges for women were being founded.

When she was in New York City Susan was fond of rising early and visiting the business sections to observe women and girls going to work in stores, in offices, occasionally even in professional surroundings.

To millions of women the erect Quakeress with the whitening hair was the symbol of the new progress. Many prayed for her, but when one woman confessed this to Susan she became angry. "Pray with your hands and feet," she said. "I like prayers that take the form of work."

She was even angrier when she learned that some women had taken to calling her "Saint Anthony." "What rubbish!" she snapped.

Men, too, recognized her unselfish devotion and by the thousands they swung to support of her ideas and goals. All America began to appreciate that she was one of the greatest Americans of the nation's history.

Her name became an inspiration throughout the world. Dramatic evidence of this was given in Chicago in 1893 at the World's Congress of Representative Women, the first such conclave in history. Twenty-seven nations were represented in the Chicago Art Palace.

Only ten thousand people could be seated at a time, but all one hundred and fifty thousand who passed through the gates pleaded to speak to, to touch, or at least to see the woman who had inspired them, Susan B. Anthony.

And when she was introduced to speak, men and women climbed on their chairs, threw hats, gloves, and handkerchiefs in the air and cheered for ten minutes before she said a word.

After a half century of work for woman's rights she was, as poor as when she began. Every cent she earned, every cent given to her, she used for her work, keeping only a pittance for living expenses. After her trial in Canandaigua men and women sent her money, from twenty-five-cent pieces to one gift of $62, adding up to about $1,000. She gave it all to the cause.

For several years she was the editor of a woman's rights magazine. It failed, and there were debts of $10,000. Susan told the creditors that she would pay every cent due them. It took her six years but she paid every debt. Virtually every newspaper in the land applauded her. Typical was the editorial comment in the Buffalo Express:

"She has paid her debts like a man. Like a man? Not so. Not one man in a thousand but would have 'laid down' and settled at ten or twenty cents on the dollar."

As the twentieth century neared, the movement laid greater and greater emphasis on an amendment to the Constitution which would give women the right to vote. Susan, in addition to lecturing and serving as president or other executive officer of the movement, worked vigorously to win over congressmen and presidents to support such an amendment.

With work, she told the younger women coming into the movement—it was now called the National American Suffrage Association—the amendment was sure to be adopted.

In 1900, aged eighty, she stepped down as president of the Association "because I want to see the organization in the hands of those who are to have its management in the future."

Almost to the last hour of her life, Susan worked for the cause of women.

Beginning about 1901, she gave considerable time to a campaign to induce the University of Rochester in the city where she lived to open its doors to women. In time the University's board of trustees agreed to do this if a sufficient endowment for women students were raised.

Susan saw to the appointment of a committee to solicit funds and went off to an International Suffrage Congress in Germany. Tired and ailing, she returned home to learn that her brother Daniel was dying in Kansas. Off to Kansas sped the eighty-five-year-old woman and her younger sister Mary to bid a last farewell to Daniel.

Returning once more to Rochester, Susan had a visitor, the woman secretary of the fund raising committee. This woman told her that the fund was $8,000 short of the quota and the stipulated time limit would expire the next afternoon.

Not even pausing to change her clothes, the old war horse went into action. Mary Anthony had written into her will a bequest of $2,000 to the University if women were admitted. "Mary, you have to give me that money now," Susan said.

Mary gave her the money and Susan began calling on merchants, bankers, industrialists, working until evening. All turned her down.

Still $6,000 short, she started out the next morning. The pastor of a church gave her $2,000. Friends made pledges. At three o'clock, still lacking $2,000, Susan made a desperation visit to a man she knew to be sympathetic to her cause although in modest circumstances. To her relief he pledged the final $2,000.

Her old heart pounding furiously, she raced to a meeting of the University board of trustees and announced completion of the endowment fund.

The chairman examined the names and pledges on her list and told her regretfully that the last pledge could not be accepted. The chairman did not believe that the man who made it had $2,000.

Susan sat stunned for a moment. "I must think," she told herself. "I must think." Then, inspired, she stood up. "I will pledge my life insurance for $2,000," she said. "Will you accept it?"

Her pledge was accepted. She had won another victory for women, but at a high cost.

Three days later Mary found her unconscious in bed. Doctors said she had suffered a stroke and would never be fully well again. Another stroke was certain to follow but this might be deferred if she stopped all activity and lived as a semi-invalid.

This Susan refused to do when she had improved sufficiently to leave her sickbed. "The hammer may as well fall one time as another," she said.

Accompanied by a nurse, she began to attend meetings, to lecture occasionally. In March of 1906 she went to her last woman's rights meeting, a celebration of her 86th birthday in Washington. There she gave a brief talk ending with the words—the last she spoke on a public platform—"Failure is impossible."

The trip was too much for her enfeebled body. On her return home she fell ill and succumbed a few days later. The announcement of her death in the Rochester Quaker Journal was of a simplicity in keeping with the way she had lived:

"13th 3rd mo. 1906. Susan Brownell Anthony died this morning in the 87th year of her life at her home 17 Madison Street at 12:40 o'clock. Pneumonia the cause."

Lynne Masel-Walters (essay date 1976)

SOURCE: "Their Rights and Nothing More: A History of *The Revolution,* 1868-70," in *Journalism Quarterly,* Vol. 53, No. 2, Summer, 1976, pp. 242-51.

[*In the following essay, Masel-Walters presents a history of the* Revolution, *the feminist newspaper published by Anthony and Elizabeth Cady Stanton.*]

> Men, their rights and nothing more; Women, their rights and nothing less.

Such was the goal of suffragists Elizabeth Cady Stanton and Susan B. Anthony and of *The Revolution,* the newspaper they published from 1868-1870. Though a just aim, it was distant because, in the 19th century, women had few rights, least of all the right to vote. But neither the suffragists nor their publication lived to see their goal realized. Despite this failure, *The Revolution* had an important place in the history of suffrage journalism and the feminist struggle. The first major national publication concerned with feminine equality, *The Revolution* championed not only voting rights but women's rights in general. It was also the most loyal to the cause. During the "Negro's hour," when the woman's struggle was forgotten or postponed, *The Revolution* continued fighting for the female. But the fight it prompted was not just external. *The Revolution* also served as a catalyst for a split that affected the suffrage movement for 30 years. But what was *The Revolution?* Who were the personalities that shaped it? How did it relate to contemporary events? What issues filled its pages? And what was its impact?

The Revolution was a child of turbulent times, for the years 1868 to 1870 were filled with disturbing changes in American life. The Civil War was over, but its wounds were not healed. Intraparty political warfare between conservative and radical Republicans was bitter; the few surviving Democrats were hardly a factor. The revered Lincoln was dead, his successor facing impeachment. And, although legally emancipated, the former slave was not yet free.[1]

Elsewhere other profound changes were occurring. The American city was beginning to emerge. Built by immigrants from foreign lands and domestic farms, the city wrought an upheaval disturbing to believers in the ideal of the yeoman farmer.[2] These dissidents formed splinter political parties to protect their interests against those of the growing urban centers.[3]

Different in form and number than earlier cities, the urban center was both the mother and child of other dislocations in American society.[4] The foreigner and the factory provided increased workers and work places. Thus, business boomed. Greed led to savage business and industrial competition and to the rise of monopolistic combines.[5] Too much was happening too fast and it was difficult for Americans to keep hold of the turbulent, changing world.

The woman suffrage movement in 1868 was in nearly as much disarray as the country. Before the Civil War, women had almost succeeded in winning the vote. But sectional strife brought an abrupt end to suffrage agitation as feminists joined the war effort. They formed a Woman's Loyalty League and collected 400,000 signatures on a petition calling for immediate emancipation of the slave. The League also conducted a propaganda campaign that convinced many Northerners the war was a crusade to regenerate society.[6]

This propaganda worked against women, for, when the war was over. Americans snubbed female rights and focused attention on black equality. This was true of the former champions of woman suffrage. Horace Greeley, Gerrit Smith, Wendell Phillips and others told women to stand aside.[7] Republicans, Abolitionists, and even some women believed that this was the "Negro's hour." Black enfranchisement was a party measure, a political necessity and the culmination of the anti-slavery struggle. Knowing this, imbued with the politicians' idea of one reform at a time, and trained in self-sacrifice, most women gave up their claim to enfranchisement.[8]

Not all women did. Elizabeth Cady Stanton and Susan B. Anthony, founders and leaders of the woman's rights movement, remained stalwart, campaigning throughout the country for the woman's vote. One of those campaigns was in Kansas. That state, in 1868, was holding a double referendum. One resolution proposed to remove the word "white" from the voters' qualifications; the other to remove the word "male." Stanton and Anthony stumped that state for the passage of the latter referendum.[9]

Their resolution lost, but the Kansas campaign brought the two women together with George Francis Train. A Copperhead, an eccentric, a millionaire financier, a proponent of the Fenian Revolution, Turkish baths and the water cure, Train lately had become interested in the woman's cause. Enthusiastically, he joined the Kansas campaign of Stanton and Anthony. Train's fancy clothes and oratory charmed his audiences. His desire to help the female's cause, when nobody else would, charmed the two suffrage leaders.[10]

Their affection for Train grew when, near the end of the Kansas tour, he offered Anthony money to start a woman suffrage newspaper. Speaking one night in Junction City, Train announced:

> When Miss Anthony gets back to New York, she is going to start a suffrage paper. Its name is to be *The Revolution;* its motto "Men, their rights and nothing more; women, their rights and nothing less." Let everybody subscribe for it![11]

Train's offer thrilled Stanton and Anthony. For years they had wanted to start a suffrage newspaper but had never found the money. The Equal Rights Association often had talked of raising funds for such an organ, but never translated its words into action.[12] The Hovey Fund, established to further universal suffrage, also was asked to finance a woman's publication. However, the Fund was deeply committed to the black cause, directing all its money to the *Antislavery Standard.*[13] This irritated the woman suffragists, since slavery had already been abolished. Complained Stanton, " . . . for the noble women who have labored 34 years to lift the black man to their own level, there is broader work to-day than to exhalt him *above* their own heads."[14]

To accomplish this "broader work," Stanton and Anthony accepted Train's offer despite his eccentric background. The women returned to New York and began *The Revolution,* joined in their endeavor by Parker Pillsbury. Like Stanton, Pillsbury was a prolific and courageous writer. He was a good friend of the suffragists. An experienced journalist and reformer, Pillsbury had worked on the *Antislavery Standard.* But, thinking the journal was doing too little for woman suffrage, Pillsbury left the *Standard* and gladly joined the staff of *The Revolution.*[15]

Aided by other stalwart suffragists, Stanton, Anthony and Pillsbury published the first weekly issue of *The Revolution* on Jan. 8, 1868. The 10,000 copies of the 16-page newspaper were sent throughout the country under the frank of James Brooks, Democratic congressman from New York. Announcing itself the organ of the National Party of New America, *The Revolution* said it was devoted to principle, not policy; suffrage, irrespective of color or sex; equal pay for equal work; the eight-hour day; abolition of party despotism; the regeneration of American society; and "Down with politicians, up with people."[16]

The publication also stood for the financial policies of George Francis Train. As part of the agreement for funding *The Revolution,* Train and David Mellis, financial editor of the New York *World,* were to be given the space they desired to express their opinions on financial and other matters.[17] They used the publication's back pages to espouse the Credit Mobilier and Credit Foncier Systems, greenback currency, unrestricted immigration, and penny ocean postage. Mellis also contributed a racy column of Wall Street gossip.[18]

The first issue of *The Revolution* received mixed reviews. The *Daily Times* of Troy (New York) said the woman's paper was "readable, well-edited and instructive." Although *The Revolution's* ideas were impracticable, the *Daily Times* continued, "its beautiful mechanical execution renders the appearance very attractive."[19] The Cambridge, (Massachusetts) *Press* called *The Revolution* a "great fact," while the Chicago *Times* praised the publication as a "readable sheet, well printed and well written, bold and independent."[20] The Providence (Rhode Island) *Press* said that the editors of *The Revolution* "have an irrepressible spirit, and if they do not produce a revolution it will be the first time that justice and freedom persistently set forth fail of accomplishing a grand result."[21]

Other newspapers were less laudatory. The New York *Times* said that *The Revolution* was a victim of illogical thinking and that its motto was "meaningless and foolish."[22] The New York Sunday *Atlas* and the Rochester (New York) *Evening* complained that the woman's publication "smacks very strongly of Train."[23] The New York *World* gave the newspaper and its proprietress a back-handed compliment:

> If she [Anthony] were a confiding miss of 'sweet sixteen' instead of the strong-minded woman that she is, . . . we suspect (such is the infirmity or perversity of 'those odious men') that she would make more conquests than she can reasonably expect to do with the intellectual blaze and brilliancy of this week's *Revolution.* . . . [24]

Horace Greeley's New York *Tribune* and Wendell Phillips' *Antislavery Standard* did more than criticize *The Revolution;* they ignored it. The latter would not even accept a paid advertisement of the paper.[25] Since the men and their newspapers previously had been friends of the woman's movement, this silence deeply distressed Stanton and Anthony.[26] They admitted this to their readers. Along with other newspaper reviews of *The Revolution,* they printed "*Antislavery Standard: _____*"[27]

The treatment of *The Revolution* by Greeley and Phillips was indicative of more conservative suffragists' reaction to the publication and its sponsors. There were many reasons for this hostility. The newspaper's name was too inflammatory. The association with Democrats and Copperheads was deplorable. And the affiliation with Train, a Negrophobe, and Mellis was unpardonable.[28] In a letter to Anthony, William Lloyd Garrison said that she and Stanton had "taken leave of good sense" to join with that "crack-brained harlequin and semi-lunatic, George Francis Train."[29] Lucy Stone, the Boston suffrage leader, also was infuriated by the Stanton-Anthony acceptance of Train. "Susan Anthony can be scarcely less crazy than he is," she exploded.[30]

Anthony did not let her financial "angel" go undefended. While admitting that Train had some extravagences and ideosyncracies, she noted that he was willing to devote time and money to the woman's cause when no other man was. "It seems to me," she said, "it would be right and wise to accept aid from the devil himself, provided that he did not tempt us to lower our standard."[31]

The quarrel between Stanton and Anthony and the more conservative suffragists climaxed at the 1869 Equal Rights Association Convention. There, Frederick Douglass, a leading Negro exponent of enfranchisement for his race, successfully lobbied for a resolution supporting the 15th amendment to the United States Constitution. This put the woman's movement in the position of backing a suffrage amendment excluding their sex. It was too much for Stanton and Anthony.[32] They summoned a group of women to the offices of *The Revolution* where they formed the National Woman Suffrage Association (NWSA). Although this group included several prominent women, Stanton and Anthony were given relatively free rein in the NWSA's affairs. With *The Revolution* at their command, the two women seemed well equipped to plan special campaigns and to act quickly when the occasion demanded it.[33]

Not everyone was pleased with the Stanton-Anthony leadership of the NWSA. William Lloyd Garrison, Wendell Phillips, Stephen and Abby Kelly Foster, and others believed that the two women had presumed too much in claiming to speak for all woman's movements and against the priority of Negro suffrage.[34] The bitterness between the two factions was exacerbated by *The Revolution*'s ruthless criticism of those who disagreed with its policies:[35]

> Their life boat is wrecked on the shoals; for they
> left the roadway of principle, shipped a cargo of
> expediency, and got their bottom barnacled with
> party fossils. Their estate is bankrupt; for they
> threw overboard their capital of conscience, con-
> sistency and courage.[36]

The result of this rancor was the formation of a rival group, the American Woman Suffrage Association (AWSA). Formed by Lucy Stone and headquartered in Boston, the AWSA appealed to conservative suffragists. This group attracted a large membership despite the fact that it virtually was ignored by *The Revolution.*[37]

Some suffragists remained loyal to Stanton, Anthony and *The Revolution.* Lydia Maria Childe called herself an "unswerving friend." Paulina Wright Davis, editor of another suffrage newspaper, *Una,* gave the editors a generous sum of money. Phoebe and Alice Cary wrote for the paper and volunteered for office service.[38] But Elizabeth Phelps was perhaps the greatest contributor. A rich and practical New York philanthropist, Phelps believed that there should be a rallying place in the city for women and their organizations. For this purpose, she bought a large elegant house and christened it the Woman's Bureau.[39] Its rooms were rented solely to women's clubs and to enterprises conducted by women. *The Revolution* occupied the first floor. When moving in, Anthony had warned Phelps that the newspaper's

presence might adversely affect the popularity of the Woman's Bureau. She was right; the more conservative women and groups refused to use the house. And, after a year, Phelps abandoned the project, leaving *The Revolution* to find new quarters.[40]

The end of the Woman's Bureau was not the end of *The Revolution.* It was alive and as spicy as ever. Concerned with everything that affected the nation's women, the newspaper covered female rights, financial matters, the political situation and the achievement of women in all phases of life.

Of course, *The Revolution*'s primary interest was female enfranchisement. "Our pathway is straight to the ballot box, with no variableness nor shadow of turning," wrote Anthony.[41] This pathway was strewn with constitutional road-blocks. Thus, one of the major functions of *The Revolution* was to hammer away at the 14th and 15th amendments which gave the vote to the Negro but ignored women. The 15th amendment at best, said an editorial in *The Revolution,* was a trick of a "corrupt and unprincipled . . . school of politicians . . . to save themselves and their party . . ."[42]

Because this amendment was "invidious to their sex," *The Revolution*'s editors proposed a 16th amendment to the Constitution. This based the right of suffrage on citizenship which "all citizens of the United States, whether native or naturalized, shall enjoy . . . equally without any distinction or discrimination whatever founded on sex."[43] In line with their 16th amendment, *The Revolution* promoted "educated suffrage."[44] Since blacks in America were generally illiterate, educated suffrage favored voting women over voting Negroes. An editorial by Stanton explained:

> When I protest against . . . giving Jonathan,
> Patrick, and Sambo, and Hans, and Yang-Tang
> the power . . . to make the civil and moral codes for
> proud Saxon women, I am as sacredly defending
> human rights . . . as if I were straining every
> nerve to boost two million ignorant black men
> into legislators, judges and jurors.[45]

The Revolution did more than complain about suffrage; it actively promoted the vote. The newspaper publicized suffrage meetings and lectures on woman's rights held throughout the country. It also reported the progress of the NWSA and solicited signatures for a woman suffrage petition to be sent to Congress.[46] And it constantly refuted the religious, political, social and economic arguments against female enfranchisement.

Opponents of woman suffrage, for example, claimed that God and the Bible decreed that women were inferior to men. Did not God create Eve after he created Adam? Did not the Apostle Paul tell the wife to "obey" her husband? *The Revolution,* while not disputing God and the Bible, disputed religious interpretations that placed women in a position of inequality. Eve may have been second, the publication stated, but she was not secondary. And Paul was bound to the customs of the East, inapplicable to the America of 1869.[47]

Several other arguments were raised against suffrage and each was attacked by *The Revolution*. Political participation was expected to "unsex women," harm their delicate constitutions, bring them into dangerous contact with political "riff-raff" and destroy the home and family. A favorite cry of the anti-suffragists was "What about the babies?" They insisted that enfranchised women would be too involved with politics to bother to have children. Those children who were born would be left to fend for themselves while their mothers were working in campaigns. The New York Sunday *Times* went so far with this argument as to suggest that the feminist "Don Quixotes" abandon suffrage work and return to their housework, obviously left in a "neglected condition."[48]

In answer to this, Stanton said that politics had not harmed her seven babies and would not harm other children. Voting would take a woman out of the house for only a short time and would certainly not replace the household in her affections. Then too, once enfranchised, women could vote in legislation that would protect the home and family.[49]

The vote was not only the woman's right for which *The Revolution* fought. There was little freedom for the female of 1868. Her property belonged to her father before she married, and her husband after. She had no legal control over her own children. And the large majority of schools and non-menial occupations were closed to her.[50] "Bereft of their rights, education, and the wherewithal to be independent," said *The Revolution,* women were forced to prostitute themselves on the street and in marriage. The newspaper was against both forms of prostitution, especially the legal one.[51] Stanton and Anthony were not opposed to marriage, but only to the institution as it then existed. Once wed, they claimed, a woman was essentially the property of her husband. She was treated like a brood sow, used by her spouse to "satiate his filthy lusts" and worked like a scullery maid.[52] Only when women were the political equals of men, only when they had full control over their own persons could marriage be changed into an enriching, enobling, joyful experience.[53]

Championing the right to women to any type of work or education, *The Revolution* trumpeted the accomplishments of females. The editors printed portraits of women clerks, jurors, physicians, postmasters, inventors and missionaries.[54] Women of historical importance were also praised.[55] No female deed seemed too small to merit the publication's attention. "Two women in Iowa," one story ran, "killed a wild deer with a fire shovel."[56]

Partly because of Train's involvement and partly because the editors felt that women should know about money, the newspaper contained much financial information. While Train participated in the publication, articles on these matters reflected his interests. But these same interests soon took him away from New York. On the day of *The Revolution*'s debut, Train announced that he was going to England to promote business and engage European writers and subscribers for the newspaper. He did neither. Shortly after arriving in England, Train was arrested, ostensibly for not paying a $600 debt, but probably for his outspoken support of the Fenian movement.[57] Train insisted that *The Revolution* had contributed to his downfall. British agents, reading the inflammatory name of the newspapers he carried, confiscated them as incriminating evidence.[58]

Although incarcerated in Dublin for over a year, Train did not sever his connection with *The Revolution.* He kept up a lively correspondence, published in the newspaper which propounded his financial views and narrated his experiences in prison.[59] But, when Train returned to the United States, this contribution ceased. In May 1869, *The Revolution* published a letter from Train stating he would no longer write for the publication and asking that his name not be mentioned in its pages. He noted that this move might bring the paper subscribers who had previously refused to support the publication because of his involvement.[60] Despite this possibility, Stanton was sorry to see Train go. "He takes with him," she wrote, "the sincere thanks of those who know what he has done in the cause of women, and of those who appreciate what a power *The Revolution* has already been in raising the public thought to the importance of the speedy enfranchisement of women."[61]

The departure of Train did not signal the end of *The Revolution*'s financial department. Now edited by a "cultivated and clear-sighted woman," the department still supported some of Train's economic policies,[62] such as "greenbacks forever," labor unions, expanded currency and free trade.[63] However, by the middle of 1869, the editors' interest in the financial department dwindled to a report on the "money market," advertisements and an occasional reprint from another newspaper.[64]

Besides woman's rights and financial matters, Stanton and Anthony were also concerned with the turbulent political situation in the United States. This was reflected in *The Revolution*. The editors believed that corruption had infiltrated all levels of government. State and federal legislators, the paper said, were so corrupt that they did not even adhere to the honor that prevails among thieves.[65] Civil service reform and the laundering of government, certainties if women were given the vote, were necessary to prevent the country from being stolen away from its citizens.[66]

Most of the evil, the editors claimed, rose to the top. The political parties, especially the Republicans who had forsaken the woman's cause in favor of the Negro's, were "the most corrupt and dangerous" organizations to have "ruled this nation from the foundation of the government."[67] Although President Johnson deserved to be impeached, politicians suffering from a lack of "moral courage and integrity" hesitated to do so. Other political leaders were also treated roughly by *The Revolution*. Schuyler Colfax was considered deficient because he was unmarried and Ulysses S. Grant was called the "staggering general."[68] Some politicians, like Benjamin Wade, who supported woman suffrage, were given more favorable coverage by *The Revolution*.[69]

This corruption was, to Stanton and Anthony, proof that men were incapable of running democratic government. Women voters were needed to clean up the system. "The man idea of government," ran an editorial, "is the sword, the gallows, the whip, and toe of the boot, long prayers before breakfast and supperless to bed. Against all this woman is working to usher in a new day of love, peace, equality and mercy."[70]

Economic and social issues always had concerned the editors of *The Revolution*. Their newspaper allowed them to champion causes which, although indisputedly connected with the crusade for woman's freedom, generally were ignored, even by other suffragists. One of these was the plight of the lower-class working woman. Thus, *The Revolution* called attention to women's substandard wages, demanded equal pay for equal work and an eight-hour day, supported unions and strikes, and called for an end to child labor. Only by the enactment of these reforms could women be freed from economic bondage and move toward equality with men.[71]

The Revolution also supported the cause of other downtrodden individuals. Attempting to help the poor, the editors exposed the filthy conditions in the alms-houses, jails and prisons.[72] In its pages was the story of the wretched life in the tenement districts and a denunciation of slum landlords who thrived off poverty.[73] The Indians' predicament was also publicized in *The Revolution*, which excoriated the "sane and sensible Christians" who either condoned or participated in the extermination of native Americans.[74] And one poor immigrant girl, accused of killing her newborn child, actually was saved from the gallows by *The Revolution*'s money and publicity.[75]

Though all these positions were liberal for their time, *The Revolution*'s concern with prostitution and abortion was considered radical. Abortion (delicately called "infanticide" by the editors) was, of course, deplored. But it was recognized as a product of bad conditions rather than of bad women. These conditions would be improved once the female had a more healthful life, an education and enfranchisement. The same cure was suggested for prostitution.[76] But, until that evil could be eliminated, *The Revolution* said that prostitutes and their houses should be registered and regulated and that special hospitals be built to treat the diseases of the profession.[77]

The Revolution was not all suffrage and suffering. It printed poems, book reviews and fictional stories. Publishing some of the finest American feminists and

woman writers of the day—Anna Dickenson, Lucretia Mott, Matilda Joslyn Gage, Eleanor Kirk, Olive Logan and Lillie Devereaux Blake—the journal had a fine literary reputation. Well-known European women also contributed to the foreign correspondence section of every issue.[78]

Out to save the world, *The Revolution* could not save itself. The publication was never financially solvent. There were few subscribers—about 3,000—because of the newspaper's reputation for radicalism and the fact that women had not been sufficiently aroused to support a publication of their own.[79] There were not enough advertisers; the circulation was too small and composed of women who did not, as yet, make major purchasing decisions. Also, *The Revolution* reached few homes not already covered by the liberal New York *Tribune* or *Independent*.[80] The subscription price of $2, and later $3, per year was not sufficient to support a weekly paper.

There was simply not enough money. *The Revolution*, printed on the best paper by high-salaried typesetters, was expensive to run, and Stanton and Anthony had neither the resources nor business acumen to run it.[81] Train's promise of constant support was never kept. Contributions, although frequent and welcome, were not enough. But the spinster Anthony, whose child *The Revolution* had become, was determined to keep the newspaper alive. She "worked like a whole plantation of slaves," giving lectures, soliciting contributions, finding supporters and pouring every available cent into the publication. Anthony's family, who could ill afford it,[82] even loaned her several thousand dollars.

A plan to save *The Revolution* was formulated in 1869. A stock company was to be established by several wealthy women, on a basis of $50,000, to relieve Anthony of all financial responsibility, making her simply the business manager. Isabella Beecher Hooker was anxious to keep the publication in print. She and her sister, Harriet Beecher Stowe, said they would give *The Revolution* their personal and financial support and the support of their large circle of friends. There was one condition attached: the editors must change the name of the paper to "*The True Republic*, or something equally satisfactory."[83] Anthony did not want to comply, but she consulted with other newspaper editors and Stanton on the sagacity of the change. The newspapermen said that such a move was generally fatal to a publication.[84] But, more importantly, Stanton considered it a great mistake. "A journal called *Rosebud*," she said, "might answer for those who came with kid gloves and perfumes to lay immortal wreaths on the monuments others have built; but for us . . . there is no name like *REVOLUTION!*"[85] Thus, the stock and the Beecher plans fell through and *The Revolution* received no contributions. It struggled into 1870 on its own.

The death blow to *The Revolution* was delivered by Stanton's and Anthony's old Boston rivals. Led by Lucy Stone and her husband Henry Blackwell, the group founded its own newspaper in 1870. Their *Woman's Journal* was placed on a sound financial basis from the very beginning. Not dependent on a temperamental "angel," it was a real business conducted in the best Boston tradition of trusteeships, annuity systems, family trusts and sound funding.[86] Mary A. Livermore, publisher of the *Agitator,* another suffrage newspaper, was persuaded by Stone to merge her work with the *Woman's Journal* and come to Boston to serve as its editor. This new publication had not only Boston money and Livermore experience, but also a greater audience. Being more conservative than its New York sister, the *Woman's Journal* attracted those who were in favor of woman's rights but could not accept the wide ranging radical reforms proposed by *The Revolution.*[87]

Faced with financial difficulties and the stronger *Journal, The Revolution* could not survive long. Theodore Tilton, a stalwart friend of the newspaper and a liberal journalist himself, encouraged Laura Curtis Bullard to take *The Revolution* off the editors' tired hands. A wealthy suffragist possessed of some literary ability, Bullard bought the publication in June, 1870 for the nominal sum of one dollar. Anthony assumed sole responsibility for the paper's debt of $10,000.[88] Stanton had seven children to care for; Anthony had only *The Revolution.* Thus, the spinster was crushed by the loss of the publication. Signing the transfer, she said in her diary, was "like signing my own death warrant." And, to a friend she wrote, "I feel a great calm sadness like that of a mother binding out a dear child she could not support."[89]

Bullard's *Journal,* which she published for 18 months, was *The Revolution* in name only. Hers was an inoffensive literary and social journal, adding such new features as the "Children's Corner," "Houshold" (sic), recipes and fashions. Political material was still published, but it was nearly lost amidst "kitchen and parlor" news.[90]

Sold to the New York *Christian Enquirer* in 1872, *The Revolution* disappeared even in name. It was such a short life for such a lively publication. But it was not a life without meaning. The newspaper made a considerable contribution to the nation's women and to the suffrage movement and its press. *The Revolution* championed many unpopular causes in the area of woman's and human rights. It brought attention to the plight of the immigrant, the poor and the lower-class working woman. It promoted the professional, political, cultural, financial and educational advancement of the female and discussed prostitution, abortion and illegitimacy with a sympathy few other publications evidenced. The paper also served the movement by its stalwart insistence on woman suffrage in the "Negro's hour." *The Revolution* publicized and propagandized enfranchisement and kept it in the forefront of public attention. At a time when the country was in turmoil, the movement divided, and the cause confused, *The Revolution* carried on the idea of woman's full and equal participation in all phases of American life.[91]

But, perhaps the greatest contribution of *The Revolution* was not to its present, but to its future. The newspaper set down for the first time in a major national forum arguments for women's equality that are still being used. And it began a century-long tradition of women's political journalism. *The Revolution* inspired the establishment of several contemporaneous suffrage publications, including the *Woman's Tribune* and the *Agitator.* Mary Livermore, editor of the latter, said she intended her paper to be "nothing more or less than the twin sister of *The Revolution,* whose mission is to turn everything inside out."[92] The Stanton-Anthony paper also prompted the creation of the *Woman's Journal,* the most important suffrage publication, that was to run until 1932. Today we find a child, a great-granddaughter, of *The Revolution* in *Ms.*

Even in her own time, Susan B. Anthony realized the importance of the contribution she, Elizabeth Cady Stanton, and *The Revolution* had made to suffrage journalism. In a letter to a friend, she said,

> None but the good Father can ever begin to know the terrible struggle of those years. I am not complaining, for mine is but the fate of almost every originator or pioneer who has ever opened up a way. I have the joy of knowing that I showed it to be possible to publish an out-and-out woman's paper, and taught other women to enter in to reap where I have sown.[93]

NOTES

[1] Kenneth Stampp. *The Era of Reconstruction* (New York: Knopf, 1965), passim.

[2] Blake McKelvey, *The Urbanization of America* (New Brunswick, New Jersey: Rutgers University Press, 1963), p. 63.

[3] Russell Nye, *Midwestern Progressive Politics, 1870-1950* (East Lansing: Michigan State College Press, 1951), p. 54.

[4] C.N. Glabb and Theodore Brown, *An Urban History of America* (New York: McMillan and Company, 1967), p. 10.

[5] Nye, *op. cit.,* p. 14.

[6] Andrew Sinclair, *The Better Half: The Emancipation of the American Woman* (New York: Harper and Row, 1965), p. 182.

[7] *The Revolution,* Jan. 15, 1868, p. 24.

[8] Susan B. Anthony, Elizabeth Cady Stanton, Matilda Joslyn Gage, *History of Woman Suffrage,* V. 2, (New York: Arno Press, 1969), p. 302.

[9] Sinclair, *op. cit.,* p. 180.

[10] Alma Lutz *Created Equal: A Biography of Elizabeth Cady Stanton, 1815-1902* (New York: John Day Company, 1940), p. 152.

[11] *Ibid.*, p. 153.

[12] Ida Husted Harper, *Life and Work of Susan B. Anthony, V. 1* (New York: Arno Press, 1898), p. 360.

[13] Lutz, *op. cit.*, p. 154.

[14] *The Revolution,* Jan. 8, 1868, p. 10.

[15] Lutz, *op. cit.*, p. 157. *The Post Express,* Rochester, N.Y., July 9, 1898, in scrapbook, Susan B. Anthony papers, Box 6, Library of Congress. Pillsbury remained with *The Revolution* until 1870 when he returned to the ministry he had abandoned in favor of anti-slavery work. He then served as pastor in several western towns. Pillsbury's work with *The Revolution* is difficult to assess as he and it were overshadowed by Stanton and Anthony and their important contributions to American feminism. Peering behind the shadow, Katherine Anthony described the journalistic division of authority at *The Revolution* by noting that Pillsbury wrote the leaders or lead editorials, Stanton, the articles and items, and Anthony's "drive underlay and underwrote the expenses." Katherine Anthony, *Susan B. Anthony: Her Personal History and Her Era* (New York: Doubleday and Company), p. 215.

[16] Lutz, *op. cit.*, p. 157.

[17] Harper, *op. cit.*, p. 295.

[18] *The Revolution,* Jan. 8, 1868, pp. 13-16.

[19] Lutz, *op. cit.*, p. 159.

[20] The Chicago *Times,* Jan. 15, 1868, p. 4. *The Revolution,* Jan. 22, 1868, p. 33.

[21] *The Revolution,* Feb. 19, 1868, p. 101.

[22] The New York *Times,* Jan. 12, 1868, p. 4.

[23] *The Revolution,* Jan. 29, 1868, p. 51.

[24] Stanton et al., *op. cit.*, p. 344.

[25] Katherine Anthony, *op. cit.*, p. 216.

[26] Lutz, *op. cit.*, p. 159.

[27] *Ibid.*

[28] *The Revolution,* Jan. 15, 1868, p. 20.

[29] Katherine Anthony, *op. cit.*, p. 217.

[30] Olivia Coolidge, *Woman's Rights: The Suffrage Movement in America, 1848-1920* (New York: Dutton and Company, 1966), p. 54.

[31] Theodore Stanton and Harriot Stanton Blatch, *Elizabeth Cady Stanton, V. 2* (New York: The New York Times Press, 1968), pp. 119-20.

[32] *Ibid.*, p. 54.

[33] Lutz, *op. cit.*, pp. 157-8.

[34] Coolidge, *op. cit.*, p. 55, Lutz *op. cit.*, pp. 179-80.

[35] Elizabeth Cady Stanton, letter to Wendell Phillips, June 20, 1869, Scrapbook 1860-1869. Elizabeth Cady Stanton papers, Box 2, Library of Congress.

[36] *The Revolution,* Jan. 22, 1868, p. 35.

[37] Lutz, *op. cit.*, p. 188.

[38] Katherine Anthony, *op. cit.*, p. 225.

[39] Harper, *op. cit.*, p. 320.

[40] Lutz, *op. cit.*, p. 165.

[41] Stanton and Blatch, *op. cit.*, p. 120.

[42] *The Revolution,* July 22, 1869, p. 40.

[43] Stanton et al., *op. cit.*, p. 333.

[44] *The Revolution,* April 23, 1868, p. 249.

[45] *The Revolution,* March 18, 1869.

[46] *The Revolution,* Nov. 18, 1869, passim.

[47] *The Revolution,* Sept. 16, 1869, p. 168. Stanton's desire to reinterpret the Bible to make it more favorable to female emancipation led her to publish the *Woman's Bible* in two sections in 1895 and 1898.

[48] Harper, *op. cit.*, pp. 295-6.

[49] *The Revolution,* March 31, 1870, p. 197.

[50] *The Revolution,* June 11, 1868, p. 364.

[51] *The Revolution,* Oct. 28, 1869, p. 260.

[52] *The Revolution,* May 20, 1869, pp. 310-11. *The Revolution,* April 9, 1868, p. 214.

[53] *The Revolution,* July 8, 1869, p. 3.

[54] *The Revolution,* April 30, 1868, p. 277.

[55] *The Revolution,* July 22, 1868, p. 36.

[56] *The Revolution,* Feb. 4, 1869, p. 91.

[57] Harper, *op. cit.*, pp. 298-9. *The Revolution,* Aug. 27, 1868, pp. 118-19.

[58] Katherine Anthony, *op. cit.,* p. 220.

[59] *Ibid.*

[60] *The Revolution,* May 8, 1869, p. 279.

[61] Lutz, *op. cit.,* pp. 164-5.

[62] *The Revolution,* Jan. 7, 1869, p. 8.

[63] *The Revolution,* Feb. 17, 1870. p. 233.

[64] *Ibid.*

[65] *The Revolution,* May 21, 1868, p. 312.

[66] *The Revolution,* Dec. 2, 1869, p. 345.

[67] *The Revolution,* May 14, 1868, p. 291.

[68] *The Revolution,* Feb. 19, 1868, p. 104. *The Revolution,* Feb. 26, 1868, p. 123.

[69] *The Revolution,* Feb. 19, 1868, p. 104.

[70] *The Revolution,* March 10, 1870, p. 152.

[71] Lutz, *op. cit.,* p. 161. Elinor Rice Hays, *Morning Star: A Biography of Lucy Stone, 1818-1893* (New York: Harcourt, Brace and World, 1961), p. 199.

[72] *The Revolution,* Nov. 18, 1869, passim. *The Revolution,* April 1, 1868, p. 200.

[73] *The Revolution,* Feb. 3, 1870, p. 52.

[74] *The Revolution,* April 22, 1869, p. 251.

[75] *The Revolution,* Nov. 19, 1868, p. 312.

[76] *The Revolution,* Feb. 5, 1868, p. 64.

[77] *The Revolution,* April 9, 1869, p. 216.

[78] Lutz, *op. cit.,* pp. 165-6.

[79] *Ibid.,* p. 189.

[80] *Ibid.*

[81] Susan B. Anthony, diary, 1870. Susan B. Anthony papers, box 2, Library of Congress. Harper, *op. cit.,* p. 254.

[82] *Ibid.,* p. 254.

[83] *Ibid.,* p. 256.

[84] *Ibid.,* p. 358.

[85] Lutz, *op. cit.,* pp. 189-90.

[86] Hays, *op. cit.,* p. 201.

[87] Harper, *op. cit.,* p. 360.

[88] *Democrat and Chronicle.* March 18, 1906, scrapbook, 1905-6, Susan B. Anthony papers, box 6, Library of Congress, Susan B. Anthony, diary, Aug. 20, 1870, Susan B. Anthony papers, box 3, Library of Congress.

[89] Katherine Anthony, *op. cit.,* pp. 243-4. Susan B. Anthony, diary, June 20, 1870, Susan B. Anthony papers, box 3, Library of Congress.

[90] *The Revolution,* June 2, 1870, passim.

[91] Katherine Anthony, *op. cit.,* p. 228.

[92] *Ibid.*

[93] Stanton, et al., *op. cit.,* p. 373.

Karlyn Kohrs Campbell (essay date 1982)

SOURCE: "Contemporary Rhetorical Criticism: Genres, Analogs, and Susan B. Anthony," in *The Jensen Lectures: Contemporary Communication Studies,* edited by John I. Sisco, University of South Florida, 1982, pp. 117-30.

[*In the following essay, originally presented as a lecture at the University of South Florida's Department of Communication, Campbell uses an Aristotelian theory of rhetoric to analyze Anthony's style of forensic lecture.*]

Edwin Black's *Rhetorical Criticism: A Study in Method* was a milestone because the early history of rhetorical criticism ended with its publication. Prior to 1965, relatively little criticism had been written, and what had been published generally followed the precepts of what Black termed "neo-Aristotelian" methodology.[1] After 1965, criticisms proliferated, and critics used many perspectives, including approaches based on discourse groupings or genres, a form of criticism Black encouraged by describing two broad rhetorical genres—exhortation and argumentation—in the final chapters of his book.

More recently, some of the possibilities of a generic perspective were explored in the essays published in 1978 as *Form and Genre: Shaping Rhetorical Action,* and that exploration has continued in our journals. This lecture is a partial reassessment of generic theory and criticism in 1982. More specifically, it is an attempt to clarify two aspects of generic theory. First, I shall explore the relationship between generic and analogic analysis to argue that the analog is derivative of and contingent upon a generic judgment. Second, I shall argue that the notion of genre [Kathleen H.] Jamieson and I have developed[2] is Aristotelian in origin and conception. I shall illustrate these claims through an analysis of a 19th century forensic address.

GENRES AND ANALOGS

Lawrence Rosenfield described the analog shortly after Black's book appeared and before interest in genres proliferated. As he recognized, there are many similarities between analogic and generic approaches to criticism. Both rest on comparison and both explore similarities and differences. However, despite the chronology of publication, the analog is a relatively limited subspecies of generic analysis, and understanding this relationship enables rhetorical scholars to apply insights developed from generic theory and criticism to claims about the analog.

"The Anatomy of Critical Discourse" was the first in a series of essays in which Rosenfield introduced and illustrated the analog as a mode of critical analysis. In this first essay, Rosenfield laid down a series of presuppositions for rhetorical criticism: the critic is an appreciative spectator and expert commentator; all criticism appraises; a critical essay is a piece of forensic reasoning; and evaluative norms for rhetoric cannot be expressed as general propositions. From these premises three conclusions were drawn: 1) comparison is an essential part of the critical act; 2) in making comparisons, critics can choose the model modality (comparing a discourse to an abstract norm or prototype—a genre), the analog modality (comparing two actual discourses), or the touchstone (comparing two actual discourses, one of which serves as a model or prototype—an ideal generic exemplar—for the other); and 3) the analog is the preferable modality because a) it focuses on an actual discourse rather than on a prototype and b) through its use the critic can derive new categories and precepts.[3]

I shall take issue with the last conclusion to argue that an analogic comparison presupposes a prior comparison based on a generic model or prototype and that, relative to genres, represented by models or touchstones, the analog is a less significant critical modality. Appropriately, I shall begin by testing the analog through an analogy.

In criticism, the model or genre and the analog are analogous, respectively, to ratings and rankings in forensic competition. If a judge awards a "superior" rating to, say, an extemporaneous speech, the rating says that the speech has met fully all the requirements of that form. Theoretically, this is a judgment that can be made of a single speech in isolation, because it compares an actual speech to a prototype or norm. In an actual competition, if a judge rates two extemporaneous speeches as "superior" but only one can be declared the winner, then the judge must rank and compare the two actual speeches in a process that parallels an analogic judgment. Clearly, the rating is more fundamental; it can render an analogic judgment unnecessary, but it must be made first if a subsequent analogic judgment is to be possible.[4]

In this first essay, Rosenfield made broad claims for the analog: "Theoretically, the possibilities of analysis are infinite. Why not compare messages across cultures . . . or across genres? Why not juxtapose various rhetorical forms. . . . Or why not contrast totally different rhetorical objects?"[5] By contrast, the claims made in his analogic criticisms are more modest. Regarding analogic comparison of speeches by Nixon and Truman, he writes: "The generic resemblance of the two speeches (both may be classified as mass-media apologia) invites what may be called analog criticism."[6] Put differently, analogic comparison is appropriate because a prior judgment based on a model or genre reveals the essential similarity of the two acts.

Similarly, in a critique comparing the rhetorical postures of George Wallace and Patrick Henry, Rosenfield describes Wallace as "the *archetypal* anti-aggressor rhetorician" who is "a replica of America's *prototype* anti-aggressor rhetorician, Patrick Henry."[7] Clearly, a comparison based on a model or genre has been made, or Henry serves as a generic touchstone for Wallace. Later, when essential differences between Henry and Wallace emerge, Rosenfield comments that: "The analog with Patrick Henry breaks down here,"[8] implying that the analog is dependent in every detail on generic similarity. Consequently, analogic comparisons have limited application. At most, they can serve to refine intrageneric distinctions or to define subsepecies of a particular genre.[9]

In addition, the claim that the analog can be used to derive new categories and precepts is not supported by these criticisms. Despite Rosenfield's perceptive analysis of the *apologiae* of Nixon and Truman, his general conclusions have limited theoretical power: the mass media apologia is part of a short clash, and it employs invective, locates facts in the middle third of the speech, and reassembles old arguments; the better apologia fulfills its task but is appropriately forgettable.[10] Similarly, he writes that anti-aggressor rhetoricians incorporate stylistic deformities and symptoms of inferential disorder; they provoke visceral responses in responsible citizens but have little impact on the actual issues at hand; we can expect them to reappear.[11] There are insightful comments about Wallace's rhetoric in this critique, but they appear after the analog, as a mode of critical reasoning, has been abandoned.

The limited character of the analog is worth noting because it has been misinterpreted and overrated. The analog is *not* a technique for discovering genres nor does it provide evidence for a generic claim. An inductive approach to genre, illustrated by Hart's work on doctrinaire rhetoric,[12] requires surveying many rhetorical acts; generic claims drawn from the analogic comparison of two acts are generalizations from too few cases.[13] Deductively, a generic claim can be made from an analogic comparison only if one discourse is taken as a touchstone for the other, a procedure illustrated in Windt's essay comparing the rhetoric of the ancient Cynics with that of the contemporary Yippies in order to delineate the characteristics of the diatribe.[14] Windt treats the rhetoric of the Cynics as a touchstone, and the essay is an elegant generic analysis that reveals the synthesis that is the generic diatribe—a fusion arising out of the context, the ideology, the purposes, and the character of the rhetors. Windt's essay is additional evidence that analogic comparison presupposes generic resemblance.

Because the analog presupposes a genre, analogic comparison functions to draw intrageneric distinctions, and it is a critical mode whose value rests on the theoretical and analytical power of the generic claim. The central issue is the generic claim itself.

ARISTOTELIAN GENRES REVISITED

As rhetorical scholars know, the concept of genres begins with Aristotle. What I wish to clarify is that contemporary views of genre are also Aristotelian.

In his *Art of Rhetoric,* Aristotle described three rhetorical genres: the forensic rhetoric of the law courts, the epideictic rhetoric of public, ceremonial occasions, and the deliberative rhetoric of the legislature. Each was defined in terms of the kind of decision required of its audience.[15] Forensic rhetoric occurred in the courtroom and treated questions of past fact. Its central issue was justice; its lines of argument were accusation and defense; its style was less polished than epideictic but more polished than deliberative; enthymemes were more suitable for it; and it was thought to pose a lesser challenge to the rhetor: "Once you have a starting point [the law]," wrote Aristotle, "you can prove anything with comparative ease" (1418a.22-25). Epideictic rhetoric occurred on ceremonial occasions and treated questions of present fact; the issue was praise and blame or honor and dishonor. Its style was the most polished or literary; amplification was common. Deliberative rhetoric occurred in legislative assemblies and treated questions of policy or future fact. Its central issue was expediency (practicality and benefits); its subjects were war, national defense, commerce, and other statutes; examples were most suitable to it; its style was the least polished; it posed the greatest challenge to the rhetor. In other words, Aristotle defined genres in relation to issues, lines of argument, occasion, strategies, and style. He also recognized that these genres were not discrete, that some forms might appear in more than one genre or that more than one purpose might be combined in a single rhetorical act.[16]

In a similar way, Jamieson and I have described genres as formed out of situational, substantive, and stylistic elements. The situation generates certain requirements and creates specific expectations in the audience. For instance, the eulogistic situation includes the fact of death and, implicitly, the fact of mortality of all audience members. The situation may label an act, such as inaugurals or Fourth of July speeches, and generate expectations associated with the label or with our past experience of rhetorical action on such occasions.

Substantive elements are issues, the central questions that have to be addressed. Aristotle focused on expediency in deliberation, justice in forensic address, and honor in epideictic rhetoric. As critics we ask, what must the rhetor do? In our most recent essay on hybrid genres, Jamieson and I have argued that when an ascendant Vice President takes office on the death of a President, there are three issues: 1) the eulogistic need to reknit a community sundered by the death of its leader; 2) investiture—establishing the ascendant Vice President's right to take office and asking us to legitimize him; and 3) the deliberative need to indicate the philosophy, tone, and direction of the new administration. Situational factors modify these issues, e.g. if it is wartime, as in the case of Truman, if the ascendant Vice President is unusually inept rhetorically, as in the case of Andrew Johnson, or if the President was assassinated for a political cause, the situation faced by Theodore Roosevelt.[17]

Stylistic elements focus attention on the resources available to rhetors to meet situational expectations and substantive demands. These include choices of persona, tone, purpose, structure, supporting materials, target audience, and strategies. These are some of the forms that appear in various genres.[18] A rhetor may elect to speak as a soldier, prophet, or father. A rhetor may strike a sarcastic attitude or speak emotionally and dramatically as a peer. A rhetor may develop ideas topically, in a chronological narrative, or in a problem-solution structure. The rhetor may emphasize dramatic examples, such as the anecdotes of President Ronald Reagan, or support ideas with authoritative statements that interpret data or with statistics that demonstrate scope and typicality. The rhetor may address an elite group or the whole citizenry. The rhetor may personify the issue, use allusions to develop powerful associations, or make alien experience concrete and vivid in figurative language. What generic analysis compels critics to ask is whether or not these choices are appropriate for the situation, issue, and audience, how various choices are or are not integrated into a coherent, artistic whole, and how particular choices limit the rhetor in articulating what is suitable for the issue, audience, and occasion. Generic criticism forces critics to view invention as a dynamic process by which rhetors adapt to constraints and exploit available resources.

An Aristotelian view of genre enables critics to explain rhetorical invention as a dynamic process generated by the interplay of situational, substantive, and stylistic elements. Generic analysis also allows critics to view rhetorical acts as unique responses to specific situations and as members of classes of discourses responding in similar ways to similar demands. Generic analysis acknowledges the centrality of comparison in rhetorical criticism, for it is comparison that permits critics to perceive forms and to make evaluations. To illustrate the power of generic analysis and to illustrate the relationship of genre to analog, I shall turn back the pages of history to 1872, the historic year in which Susan B. Anthony was arrested for the crime of voting.

ANTHONY IN BEHALF OF HERSELF

Efforts to obtain woman suffrage began in a formal sense with the Seneca Falls, New York, convention in 1848. This agitation was interrupted by the Civil War when all the energies of suffragists were directed to the war effort and the abolition of slavery. Women expected that their wartime contributions would be rewarded with suffrage, and the passage of the 14th and 15th amendments were a cruel blow because, given their passage, only a federal amendment could enfranchise American women. However, some feminists, particularly St. Louis lawyer Francis Minor and his wife, Virginia, began to argue that because they defined citizenship and guaranteed a citizen's right to vote, the 14th and 15th amendments perforce enfranchised women. If women were citizens, and they seemed to be included in the definition in the 14th amendment, and if citizens had the right to vote, as both amendments affirmed, then women had the right to vote, or so went the argument.[19]

Women sought to claim this right through the courts, and in such an attempt, Susan B. Anthony voted in Rochester, New York, in the 1872 election. She was promptly arrested and indicted on the criminal charge of violating the federal law passed in 1870 to prevent former rebels from voting. Since she could not speak in court as either a lawyer or a witness, Anthony took her case to the people, and between her indictment in November 1872 and her trial in June 1873, she spoke more than forty times to those citizens from whom a panel of jurors would be drawn to try her case. Her speech was called, **"Is it a crime for a U.S. citizen to vote?"**[20] Although the speech was never presented in a courtroom or delivered by a lawyer to an actual jury, hers was a forensic situation and her speech evinces the substantive and stylistic qualities of forensic rhetoric. In fact, unless we acknowledge its genre, we cannot understand Anthony's invention.

Anthony's words make sense only as forensic rhetoric. Her speech is laden with evidence, chiefly authority evidence, drawn from the Declaration of Independence, statements of the founding fathers, the U.S. and N.Y. State constitutions, court cases, and judicial opinions. Its arguments are deductive, examining the implications of principles, laws, and basic values. It is tightly structured, but like many legal briefs, it explores all possible arguments for the defendant's position. Anthony attacks by refuting opposing arguments. Her style is polished, but not literary, and her speech asks the audience to reinterpret existing law. As is evident, these characteristics are those Aristotle identified as defining forensic rhetoric.

Categorizing Anthony's speech as forensic rhetoric allows us to compare it to other great forensic addresses, such as those of Lord Thomas Erskine, Clarence Darrow, Daniel Webster, and the unusual forensic masterpieces, such as Lincoln's Cooper Union address and Martin Luther King's "Letter from Birmingham Jail."[21]

As a result, we can test our classification of the speech against what critics have recognized as the characteristics of great forensic addresses: 1) an appeal to the audience to make new law based on reinterpreting existing law or on an appeal to equity or to a higher, unwritten law; 2) enthymemic arguments grounded in basic cultural values; 3) stylistic adaptations that make evidence and argument comprehensible to lay audiences; 4) development through a systematic, coherent structure; and 5) the synthesis of logical, emotional, and characterological appeals into a unified and cogent plea.[22]

Like many other forensic orators, such as Antigone or King or Lincoln, Anthony finds herself in a situation in which the written law, treated literally, affirms her guilt. Specifically, legislators who passed the 14th and 15th amendments never intended to enfranchise women. However, unlike those who appeal to a higher law, such as Antigone and King, but like Erskine, Lincoln, and Darrow, Anthony argues that, whatever the law may have meant originally or state literally, interpreted properly it can only mean that her cause is just—that women have a citizen's right to vote. Hence, like other great forensic orators, she asks her audience to transcend narrow forensic decisions to become legislators who act deliberatively by reinterpreting the law; in this case, by interpreting the law in light of the fundamental principles of democratic, republican government: natural rights, government as a mechanism to protect natural rights, and government resting on the consent of the governed.

It is somewhat misleading to speak of Anthony as adapting to her audience. By her choices, she casts her hearers in the role of jurors and creates her audience in the forensic image. Jurors are not the typical lay audience. The nature of the decision they make is such that jurors listen attentively to large amounts of evidence and argument and weigh competing claims to make complex, significant, and difficult decisions. As jurors, audiences tolerate, even applaud, large amounts of evidence and complex, detailed argument, because they know that without them they cannot make just decisions. Through explanation, presentation of evidence, and clearly developed arguments, Anthony transforms her audience into jurors able to make a complex legal decision. She provides them with citations from the relevant written law, judicial opinions, legal interpretations, and historical precedents, and then asks them to judge.

Organization is a primary mode of adaptation. By contemporary public address standards, this is a long speech (between one and two hours would be needed to deliver it); however, it is a length still quite usual for summations or final arguments in contemporary trials. The speech is structured deductively to demonstrate that citizenship entails the franchise. That claim unifies all the arguments. It is also structured to answer questions that would arise logically in the minds of members of the audience. To establish her basic premises, she begins with the Declaration of Independence. She next looks at the alleged exclusion of women from voting in the N.Y. Constitution, turns to the U.S. Constitution to determine if such an exclusion is warranted by it, examines whether or not the male pronouns in laws have any significance and demonstrates that both in general application and as determined by the U.S. Supreme Court, they function generically. She then moves to the definition of citizenship in the fourteenth amendment, and, finally, she argues that if all other arguments are denied that women are enfranchised by the fifteenth amendment. This final argument as well as the ways in which Anthony synthesizes the modes of proof define the unique elements of this situation and this speech.

Unlike other women who sued for the right to register and vote and, hence, found themselves in court as plaintiffs,[23] Anthony was a defendant indicted for having exercised a citizen's right to vote. As a defendant, she was at a strategic and moral advantage. She was not attacking the federal government but protecting herself from its attack on her. In Anthony's words: "But, friends, when . . . I went to the ballot-box, last November, and exercised my citizen's right to vote, the courts did not wait for me to appeal to them—they appealed to me, and indicted me on the charge of having voted illegally" (635). She who had fought so energetically for the abolition of slavery was being tried for violating a law intended to prevent former slaveholders and their supporters from voting. She was defending herself on the hustings because she could defend herself nowhere else. By law, no woman could practice law, and the judge who heard this case declared Anthony, as a woman, incompetent to testify in her own behalf. She is in the unusual position of pleading her case to the public because she cannot plead her case in the courtroom.

Interestingly enough, Anthony's situation is nearly identical to the situation that held in the law courts of ancient Athens. In Athenian courts there were no professional pleaders; parties to law suits had to plead in their own behalf. Similarly, Athenian juries were very large; hundreds of citizens were drawn by lot to hear cases. Socrates, for example, is supposed to have addressed his apology to some six hundred of his fellow citizens.[24] In Athens as in nineteenth-century America, no woman could plead for herself either as counsel or witness; Anthony, however, could plead her case to her fellow citizens despite the legal disadvantages under which she labored.

Anthony's speech is unique historically and rhetorically. Historically, it can be distinguished from other efforts to argue that the newly ratified amendments enfranchised women, because of Anthony's unusual treatment of the fifteenth amendment which reads: "The citizen's right to vote shall not be denied by the United States, nor any State thereof; on account of race, color, or previous condition of servitude." In her final and most audacious argument, Anthony says: "I will prove to you that the class of citizens for which I now plead, and to which I belong, may be, and are, by all the principles of our

Government, and many laws of the States, included under the term 'previous condition of servitude'" (642). Using legal evidence and deductive argument, she demonstrates that, in law, woman's status is or has been identical to that of the slave: "'A person who is robbed of the proceeds of his labor; a person who is subject to the will of another'" (642). She continues in what is the most impassioned and bitter section of the speech:

> By the law of Georgia, South Carolina, and all the States of the South, the negro [sic] had no right to the custody and control of his person. He belonged to his master. If he was disobedient, the master had the right to use correction. If the negro didn't like the correction, and attempted to run away, the master had a right to use coercion to bring him back. By the law of every State in this Union to-day [sic], North as well as South, the married woman has no right to the custody and control of her person. The wife belongs to her husband; and if she refuses obedience to his will, he may use moderate correction, and if she doesn't like his moderate correction, and attempts to leave his "bed and board," the husband may use moderate coercion to bring her back. The little word "moderate," you see, is the saving clause for the wife, and would doubtless be overstepped should her offended husband administer his correction with the "cat-o'-nine-tails," or accomplish his coercion with blood-hounds [sic]" (642).

This is the woman-slave analogy in deadly earnest, and it is a powerful comparison in a strongly abolitionist area not long after the Civil War.

As this argument illustrates, her case is clearest in regard to married women who had had no identity in law apart from their husbands. But she extends her claim to include all women in a section that illustrates her consistent return to the basic values underlying all her arguments:

> Women are taxed without representation, governed without their consent, tried, convicted, and punished without a jury of their peers. And is all this tyrannny any less humiliating and degrading to women under our democratic-republican government today than it was to men under their aristocratic, monarchical government one hundred years ago? There is not an utterance of old John Adams, John Hancock, or Patrick Henry, but finds a living response in the soul of every intelligent, patriotic woman of the nation (644).

No other feminist, male or female, argued in this way from the fifteenth amendment or found this means to wed woman suffrage to the larger issues of woman's legal and economic rights. Historically this argument reaffirms the link between abolitionism and feminism, and it reflects one important strand of early feminism that viewed suffrage as only one part of the larger struggle for woman's rights.

Anthony's speech is distinctive substantively. It is also unique in another rhetorical way. Because she is a woman speaking in behalf of herself, she synthesizes the modes of proof in a particularly vivid and effective way. Because she is a woman accused of the crime of voting, an act that is a crime *only* because she is a woman, no argument can remain wholly abstract or theoretical. All arguments inevitably confront the question, is it a crime for *this* woman to vote? If the audience is to deny her plea, it must deny her: she embodies and personifies the issue. She enacts her claim: her speech is the ultimate proof of her right to vote. The synthesis of the modes of proof in her person is illustrated by her discussion of whether or not male pronouns function generically to include women. She says:

> In the law of May 31, 1870, the 19th section of which I am charged with having violated; not only are all the pronouns masculine, but everybody knows that this particular section was intended expressly to hinder the rebels from voting. It reads:
>
> "If any person shall knowingly vote without his having a lawful right, etc."
>
> Precisely so with all the papers served on me— the U.S. Marshall's warrant, the bail-bond, the petition for habeas corpus, the bill of indictment— not one of them had a feminine pronoun printed on it; but, to make them applicable to me, the Clerk of the Court made a little carat at the left of "he" and placed an "s" over it, thus making she out of he. Then the letters "is" were scratched out, the little carat placed under the "er" over, to make her out of his, and I insist that if government officials may thus manipulate the pronouns to tax, fine, imprison, and hang women, women may take the same liberty with them to secure to themselves their right to a voice in the government (636-637).

This is not only a strong argument for logical consistency, but an illustration of how abstract issues become concrete and personal, inevitably giving each logical question an emotional dimension and a characterological context.

Because of these unusual dimensions of Anthony's situation and speech, we may be able to glimpse through it the special drama of the Athenian law courts in which defendants spoke in behalf of themselves and in which citizen-jurors tested the case against the pleader and compared the legal principle to its concrete application. Anthony's speech enables us to experience the power of enactment both as a mode of argumentation and a form of evidence.

Was Anthony successful? The evidence suggests that she was. After her speeches in every postal district of Monroe, the county in which Rochester is located, the prosecutor applied for and was granted a change of venue to Canandaigua in neighboring Ontario county on the grounds that, because of her speeches, the case for the plaintiff could not receive a fair hearing. In the twenty-two days between the change of venue and her trial, Anthony spoke twenty-one times, and, with the

help of Matilda Joslyn Gage,[25] she reached citizens in every postal district in Ontario county. To prevent Anthony from making these arguments in the courtroom, the judge declared her incompetent to testify in her own behalf. The judge did not permit the jury in this criminal case to deliberate or to vote and directed a verdict of guilty. To prevent her case from becoming a *cause célèbre,* the judge fined her only $100 and court costs, a sentence that outraged the prosecutor. When she publicly and defiantly declared in court after sentencing— "May it please your honor, I shall never pay a dollar of your unjust penalty" (689)—no effort was made to enforce the sentence. When the election inspectors who had allowed her to register and vote were tried, found guilty, and fined, they refused to pay and went to jail. However, a presidential pardon was forthcoming. Unfortunately, because of the misplaced chivalry of her lawyer and the judge's refusal to enforce her sentence, a different case went to the U.S. Supreme Court, and in 1875 *Minor v. Happersett* closed forever the judical route to woman suffrage.[26]

Generic analysis enables us to understand the forensic requirements that informed Anthony's choice of argument, evidence, structure, and appeal. Comparison of Anthony's speech with recognized forensic masterpieces illustrates how her speech resembles these works and in what ways it is unique. Finally, historical comparisons permit us to see how Anthony's speech differed from other appeals for woman suffrage based on the fourteenth and fifteenth amendments and to recognize the unusual situation confronted by a woman defending herself against a criminal charge in the nineteenth century. This process deepens appreciation of the forensic genre and creates new understanding of the nature of forensic rhetoric as it existed in the law courts of ancient Athens.

Rhetorical criticism necessitates comparison, and contemporary rhetorical criticism, whether generic or analogic, acknowledges the centrality of comparison in perceiving the nature of a discourse and in evaluating it. I have argued that generic judgments are fundamental and that analogic judgments, where suitable, follow from them. I have argued that generic analysis is Aristotelian, reflecting Aristotle's dynamic view of rhetorical invention as a response to the demands of situations and issues and the expectations of audiences.

Contemporary rhetorical criticism has moved a considerable distance since 1965. As I survey critical scholarship between then and now, I conclude that critics had to free themselves from the shackles of a narrow neo-Aristotelianism in order to reinvent an Aristotelian perspective capable of functioning as a generative theoretical and critical tool. Both generic and analogic studies have been important contributions to that process.

NOTES

[1] Edwin Black, *Rhetorical Criticism: A Study in Method* (New York: Macmillan, 1965).

[2] See "Form and Genre in Rhetorical Criticism: An Introduction," in *Form and Genre: Shaping Rhetorical Action* ed. Karlyn Kohrs Campbell and Kathleen Hall Jamieson (Falls Church, Va.: Speech Communication Association, 1978), 9-32; Kathleen M. Jamieson, "Generic Constraints and the Rhetorical Situation," *Philosophy & Rhetoric,* 6 (Summer 1973), 162-70; Kathleen M. Jamieson, "Antecedent Genre as Rhetorical Constraint," *Quarterly Journal of Speech,* 61 (December 1975), 406-15; Kathleen H. Jamieson and Karlyn Kohrs Campbell, "Rhetorical Hybrids: Fusions of Generic Elements," *Quarterly Journal of Speech,* 68 (May 1982), 146-57.

[3] Lawrence W. Rosenfield, "The Anatomy of Critical Discourse," *Speech Monographs,* 35 (March 1968), 50-69.

[4] The evaluative function of genres is described by John Cawelti, *Adventure, Mystery, and Romance* (Chicago: University of Chicago Press, 1976), p. 7.

[5] Rosenfield, p. 68.

[6] Lawrence W. Rosenfield, "A Case Study in Speech Criticism: The Nixon-Truman Analog," *Speech Monographs,* 35 (November 1968), p. 435.

[7] Lawrence W. Rosenfield, "George Wallace Plays Rosemary's Baby," *Quarterly Journal of Speech,* 55 (February 1969), p. 36, emphasis added.

[8] Rosenfield, "George Wallace," p. 41.

[9] See, for example, James W. Chesebro and Caroline D. Hamsher, "The Concession Speech: The MacArthur-Agnew Analog," *Speaker and Gavel,* 11 (January 1974), 39-51.

[10] Rosenfield, "A Case Study," pp. 449, 450.

[11] Rosenfield, "George Wallace," pp. 40, 44.

[12] Roderick P. Hart, "The Rhetoric of the True Believer," *Speech Monographs,* 38 (November 1971), 249-61.

[13] This problem is illustrated in James Measell, "A Comparative Study of Prime Minister William Pitt and President Abraham Lincoln on Suspension of Habeas Corpus," in *Form and Genre,* pp. 87-102.

[14] Theodore Otto Windt, Jr., "The Diatribe: Last Resort for Protest," *Quarterly Journal of Speech,* 58 (February 1972), 1-14.

[15] Aristotle, *Rhetoric,* trans. W. Rhys Roberts (New York: Modern Library, 1954), I. 3-10. Subsequent citations are in the text.

[16] For example, Aristotle writes that "to praise a man is in one respect akin to urging a course of action. The suggestions which would be made in the latter case become encomiums when differently expressed" (1367b.36-1368a.2).

[17] Kathleen H. Jamieson and Karlyn Kohrs Campbell, "Rhetorical Hybrids."

[18] For a more detailed description of these forms, see Karlyn Kohrs Campbell, *The Rhetorical Act* (Belmont, CA: Wadsworth, 1982), chapter 2. The relationship between genres and forms is discussed by Northrop Frye, *Anatomy of Criticism: Four Essays* (Princeton University Press, 1957), pp. 95-115.

[19] The history of arguments for woman suffrage based on the fourteenth and fifteenth amendments is traced in the *History of Woman Suffrage, II, 1861-1876,* ed. Elizabeth Cady Stanton, Susan B. Anthony, and Matilda Joslyn Gage (New York: Fowler and Wells, 1882), pp. 407-599. The argumentative history begins with the resolutions introduced to the Missouri State Suffrage association by Francis Minor supported by the opening address of Virginia Minor, president of the association. These were printed in *The Revolution* and 10,000 extra copies of this issue were published and sent to supporters throughout the country and placed on the desk of every member of Congress (411). The next major event was the address of Victoria Claflin Woodhull, 11 January 1871, to the House Judiciary Committee and a speech in support of her memorial by attorney A. G. Riddle. Although rejected by congressional committees, William Loughridge and Benjamin Butler penned a forceful minority report citing legal and constitutional bases for the views expressed in the memorial. Mrs. Isabella Beecher Hooker spoke before the Senate Judiciary Committee. As lawyers for the plaintiffs in a suit by seventy women in the District of Columbia in 1871 seeking the right to register and vote, Albert G. Riddle and Francis Miller made speeches arguing that the fourteenth and fifteenth amendments enfranchised women.

[20] The text of the speech cited here is found in *History of Woman Suffrage,* II, pp. 630-647. Subsequent references are in the text. This text may also be found in Ida Husted Harper, *The Life and Work of Susan B. Anthony,* II (Indianapolis: The Hollenbeck Press, 1898), pp. 977-92. A slightly variant text is found in *An Account of the Proceedings on the Trial of Susan B. Anthony* (Rochester, N.Y.: Daily Democrat and Chronicle Book Print, 1874), pp. 151-78.

[21] It is not universally agreed that these are forensic addresses. Michael C. Leff and G. P. Mohrmann, "Lincoln at Cooper Union: A Rhetorical Analysis of the Text," *Quarterly Journal of Speech,* 60 (October 1974), 346-58, treat Lincoln's speech as a political campaign oration. Richard P. Fulkerson, "The Public Letter as a Rhetorical Form: Structure, Logic, and Style in King's 'Letter from Birmingham Jail,'" *Quarterly Journal of Speech,* 65 (April 1979), 121-36, treats King's essay as a public letter.

[22] The qualities of outstanding forensic addresses are drawn from the following analyses: Carroll C. Arnold, "Lord Thomas Erskine: Modern Advocate," *Quarterly Journal of Speech,* 44 (February 1958), 17-30; John W. Black, "Rufus Choate," in *A History and Criticism of*

American Public Address, I, ed. William Norwood Brigance (1943; rpt. New York: Russell and Russell, 1960), 434-58; William Norwood Brigance, "Jeremiah S. Black," *ibid.,* I, pp. 459-82; Wilbur S. Howell and Hoyt H. Hudson, "Daniel Webster," in *A History and Criticism of American Public Address,* II, ed. William Norwood Brigance (1943; rpt. New York: Russell and Russell, 1960), 665-734; Martin Maloney, "Clarence Darrow," *A History and Criticism of American Public Address,* III, ed. Marie Kathryn Hochmuth (New York: Longmans, Green, and Co., 1955), 262-312; Martin Maloney, "The Forensic Speaking of Clarence Darrow," *Speech Monographs,* 14 (1947), 111-26; Glen E. Mills, "Misconceptions Concerning Daniel Webster," *Quarterly Journal of Speech,* 29 (December 1943), 423-28; Glen E. Mills, "Webster's Principles of Rhetoric," *Speech Monographs,* 9 (1942), 124-40; Akira Sanbonmatsu, "Darrow and Rorke's Use of Burkeian Identification Strategies in *New York vs. Gitlow,*" *Communication Monographs,* 38 (March 1971), 36-48.

[23] The history of women's efforts to obtain suffrage through the courts is found in *History of Women Suffrage,* II, pp. 586-627.

[24] According to available sources, Socrates was convicted, probably by a vote of 280 to 220. See A. E. Taylor, "Socrates," *Encyclopedia Britannica,* 20 (Chicago: William Benton, 1966), p. 917. In the Greek law court or *dikasterion,* "the accuser spoke first, and the accused afterwards. If either party was a minor, a woman, or a noncitizen, the speech was made by the nearest adult male relative or patron; but otherwise each party had to speak for himself, unless clearly incapable, though he might deliver a speech written for him by a professional speechwriter, and he might call on friends to speak too in his support. . . . Women, children, and slaves could not appear in court as witnesses." (*The Oxford Classical Dictionary,* 2d ed., ed. N. G. L. Hammond and H. H. Scullard [Oxford: Clarendon Press, 1970], p. 343.)

[25] A text of Matilda Joslyn Gage's speech is found in *An Account of the Proceedings on the Trial of Susan B. Anthony,* 179-205.

[26] See *History of Woman Suffrage,* II, p. 714 for a report of the presidential pardon. The details of *Minor v. Happersett* and excerpts from the majority opinion are found on pp. 715-34.

FURTHER READING

Biography

Anthony, Katharine. *Susan B. Anthony: Her Personal History and Her Era.* Garden City, N.Y.: Doubleday, 1954, 521 p.
   Biography focusing on Anthony's personal life.

Barry, Kathleen. *Susan B. Anthony: A Biography of a Singular Feminist.* New York: New York University Press, 1988, 426 p.
   Traces Anthony's sustaining influence on the modern feminist movement.

Dorr, Rheta Childe. *Susan B. Anthony: The Woman Who Changed the Mind of a Nation.* New York: Frederick A. Stokes, 1928, 366 p.
   Focuses on the social and political environment in which Anthony lived and worked.

Harper, Ida Husted. *The Life and Work of Susan B. Anthony,* 3 vols. Indianapolis: Hollenbeck Press, 1898-1908, 1633 p.
   Standard biography, much of which was written and published during Anthony's lifetime.

Lutz, Alma. *Susan B. Anthony: Rebel, Crusader, Humanitarian.* Boston: Beacon Press, 1959, 340 p.
   Uses Anthony's letters and diaries to explore her devotion to the pursuit of civil rights.

Criticism

Burke, Ronald K., ed. "White American Females." In *American Public Discourse: A Multicultural Perspective,* pp. 253-313. Lanham, Maryland: University Press of America, 1992.
   Contains an excerpt from Anthony's speech at the Select Committee on Woman Suffrage, United States Senate.

Cottler, Joseph. "Susan Brownell Anthony vs. The United States," in *Champions of Democracy,* pp. 103-26. Boston: Little, Brown, 1936.
   Provides a history of Anthony's entrance into the realm of women's rights.

Edwards, G. Thomas. *Sowing the Good Seeds: The Northwest Suffrage Campaigns of Susan B. Anthony.* Portland: Oregon Historical Society Press, 1990, 355 p.
   Covers Anthony's lecture and campaign tour of the American Northwest beginning in 1871.

Merriam, Allen H. "Susan B. Anthony." In *American Orators before 1900: Critical Studies and Sources,* edited by Bernard K. Duffy and Halford R. Ryan, pp. 28-34. New York: Greenwood Press, 1987.
   Analyzes Anthony's influence and popularity as a public orator; includes a bibliography of primary and secondary sources related to Anthony's lectures.

Mitchell, Catherine C. "Historiography on the Woman's Rights Press." In *Outsiders in 19th-Century Press History: Multicultural Perspectives,* edited by Frankie Hutton and Barbara Straus Reed, pp. 159-67. Ohio: Bowling Green University Popular Press, 1995.
   Examines the place of feminist publications, and the *Revolution* in particular, in the struggle for both women's rights and civil rights for African Americans.

Untermeyer, Louis. "Susan B. Anthony." In *Makers of the Modern World,* pp. 60-65. New York: Simon and Schuster, 1955.
    Names Anthony as one of the most influential thinkers of the twentieth century.

The following sources published by Gale Research contain additional coverage of Anthony's life and career: *Contemporary Authors,* Vols. 89-92, 134.

Ernst Barlach

1870-1938

German playwright, novelist, autobiographer, and sculptor.

INTRODUCTION

Barlach, one of the most acclaimed sculptors of Germany's Weimar Republic, also achieved critical praise as an expressionist playwright. Focused largely on the human search for greater meaning beyond the mundane concerns of everyday life, Barlach's plays feature protagonists, usually of the bourgeois social class, who reach an impasse in their lives and, realizing the grotesque and absurd nature of daily existence, commit themselves to finding spiritual meaning. Although Barlach continues to be regarded as one of the most significant German expressionist artists in the variety of genres and media in which he worked, his artistic output was censured by the Nazis as degenerate art, and his liberal use of grotesque and absurd imagery and verbal wordplay often made audiences less than fully receptive to his plays.

Biographical Information

Barlach was born in the small northern German town of Wedel in 1870 to Luise Vollert and Georg Barlach, a village doctor. Barlach's mother was committed to a psychiatric institution in 1883; shortly after her release his father died of pneumonia, which left the already struggling family with no income. In 1888 Barlach graduated from the Realschule in Schöneberg and enrolled in the Hamburg School for Applied Arts. After finishing there, Barlach entered the Dresden Art Academy, concentrating in sculpture. He graduated in 1895 and for the next eleven years moved between Paris, Hamburg, Berlin, and Wedel, searching for a sense of purpose in his life. Sinking into a deep depression and unhappy with the work he produced, Barlach considered suicide. But in 1906 two events occurred to give him the direction he had searched for: he traveled to Russia, where he found artistic inspiration in the landscape and the peasants he encountered, and he fathered an illegitimate son, whose custody he sued for and won. The two experiences together brought Barlach to an emotional turning point that resulted in his first successful sculptures, as well as a contract with a prominent Berlin art dealer and publisher, and his first play, *Der tote Tag* (*The Dead Day*). Although Barlach began writing the play in 1907, it remained unpublished until 1912 and unproduced until 1919. *Der tote Tag* was praised by reviewers, including the German novelist Thomas Mann, but audiences were confused by it, and it had short runs in the three theatres in which it played. In 1909 Barlach's sculptures won him the Villa Romana Prize,

which enabled him to work in Florence, Italy. When he returned to Germany the next year, he settled in Güstrow, a small town in the north, and began a period of immense productivity. In addition to producing some of his best-known sculptures, Barlach began writing more, including prose fragments, the beginning of his unfinished novel *Seespeck*, and another play, *Der arme Vetter* (*The Poor Relation*). The first production of the play in 1919 was not wholly successful; Barlach himself was dissatisfied with the director's choice of sets and the lack of authenticity in the characterizations. Later productions, however, achieved what Barlach had intended, and the play went on to win the admiration of critics and audiences throughout Germany. At the beginning of World War I, Barlach volunteered at a children's daycare center in Güstrow. In 1915 he was drafted into the German army reserves and ordered to enter basic training camp in Sonderburg. Disillusioned with the war and out of place in the military, Barlach turned to some of his friends in the artistic community, who successfully petitioned to have him discharged. In 1917 Barlach began work on his third play, *Die echten Sedemunds* (*The Genuine Sedemunds*), which was published in 1920 and performed for the first time in 1921. Like *Der arme Vetter*, *Die echten Sedemunds* was a failure in its first productions, largely because of staging and directing problems; Barlach attended a performance in Berlin and was sufficiently disgusted to heckle along with the rest of the audience. In 1919 Barlach accepted an invitation to join the distinguished Prussian Academy but turned down professorships offered to him in Dresden and Berlin. The next year his mother, who had lived with Barlach since 1910 and helped care for his young son, drowned herself. Later that year Barlach began work on another play, *Der Findling* (*The Foundling*). The only attempt to perform the play was made in 1928; even Barlach was not sure the work could be staged because of its abstract, metaphysical subject matter. *Die Sündflut* (*The Flood*), written in 1923 and published and performed in 1924, won the prestigious Kleist Prize and proved to be the most accessible of all Barlach's plays. In 1925 Barlach was made an honorary member of the Munich Academy of Arts. The same year he met the sculptor Marga Böhmer, with whom he lived the rest of his life. In 1925 Barlach wrote another highly successful and critically acclaimed play, *Der blaue Boll* (*The Blue Boll*). While neither of Barlach's last two plays, *Der Graf von Ratzeburg* (*Count von Ratzeburg*) and *Die gute Zeit* (*The Good Time*), were successful, he continued to garner praise for his sculpture and woodcuts. Between 1927 and 1933 he was commissioned to create war memorials in numerous cities throughout Germany. But his pacifist political stance and depictions of the suffering of the poor and dispossessed soon raised the ire of militant right-wing organizations, and he was forced by public pressure to withdraw from some of his projects. Although Barlach protested openly and was presented with the highest honor given to German civilians, the Pour le Mérite, he continued to threaten the standards of the Nazi Party, which came to power in Germany in 1933. Soon after the Nazis rose to power, productions of Barlach's plays and commissions of his artwork were canceled. In 1937 he was labeled a "degenerate artist" by the Nazis, and much of his publicly-held art was confiscated or destroyed. Nevertheless, Barlach continued to produce sculptures and wrote fragments of a novel, *Der gestohlene Mond* (*The Stolen Moon*), until his death in Rostock in 1938.

Major Works

In *Der tote Tag* Barlach sought to express elements of the emotional crisis he had experienced prior to 1906. Highly symbolic and dark in tone, the play concerns a nameless son's attempt to remove himself from his mother's tight grip and prove himself in the world. He is helped in his aims by a god-like father, who never appears in the play but who sends the son signs to aid him. Barlach set up the mother and son as polar opposites, with the mother symbolizing suffocating darkness and oppression and the son symbolizing freedom and light. Their world is populated by numerous mythic figures, gnomes, animals, and spirits, who variously help or hinder them in their respective quests. Finally, to

prevent her son from gaining his independence from her, the mother kills the magical steed sent to him by the father. When her son discovers what she has done, she stabs herself to death. Unable ultimately to break away from his mother, the son commits suicide rather than live without her. *Der arme Vetter* begins with the attempted suicide of the protagonist, Hans Iver, on Easter Sunday. He is taken to a nearby inn to recover and there meets with the indifference and scorn of the inhabitants. Only one, Lena Isenbarn, shows Hans any compassion. In the end, Hans dies of his wound. In the play Barlach contrasts the base, materialistic, vulgar existence of the people at the inn with Hans's desire for a higher consciousness that can only come with his death. *Die echten Sedemunds*, which is based on the seventh chapter of Barlach's unfinished novel *Seespeck*, is a black comedy with grotesque elements. It takes place in a small northern German town and concerns the affairs of the Sedemund family. The young son Gerhard is lured home by his father, who wants him committed to an asylum. Instead, Gerhard and his friend Grude trick the father into confessing his part in his wife's death. In the meantime, a rumor that a lion is loose upsets life in the town and exposes the corruption and pretension of the townspeople. Finally, Gerhard voluntarily retreats to the madhouse, leaving his father and the townspeople less petty and debauched, but facing a grim and uncertain future himself. *Der Findling* is one of Barlach's most problematic plays. Resembling a medieval passion play, *Der Findling* uses extremely grotesque imagery to demonstrate the corruption of a materialistic, apocalyptic society. In order to bring about a spiritual conversion, the characters are subjected to an *Ekelkur,* a cure through disgust, in which they are forced to eat the dead body of their slain leader in order to realize their own depravity. Only two characters refuse to turn to cannibalism and instead adopt the ugly, diseased child of Mother and Father Sorrow, which turns into a beautiful infant when they hold it. In the end this action, not the *Ekelkur,* saves the community. Barlach wrote *Der Findling* in a difficult dramatic verse that most critics find obscures the meaning of the play and makes it almost impossible to perform. *Die Sündflut* is based on chapters six and seven of the biblical book of Genesis, which presents the story of Noah and the ark. But Barlach added a character of his own creation, Calan, who opposes Noah's unquestioning belief in a perfect God. Rather, Calan sees God and the world as imperfect and in need of correction. Although he does not have unwavering faith and he commits acts of cruelty to others, Calan is presented as ultimately far more compassionate and worthy of admiration than Noah because he recognizes the need for improvement. In his most acclaimed play, *Der blaue Boll*, Barlach returned to the more realistic setting of a small north German town in which Squire Boll leads a life of gluttony and debauchery. He meets the wife of a swineherd, Grete, who offers herself to him in exchange for poison with which to release her children from the cruelty of life. Tempted by her but distressed by her plans to kill her children, Boll overcomes his physical urges for the first time and enters into a life of struggling to better himself. Grete, too, sees the error of her drive to annihilate life and returns to her family to search for an acceptable integration of body and soul.

Critical Reception

·While Barlach's sculptures and woodcuts are undisputedly considered major contributions to German expressionist art, there is no critical consensus on his plays. Most of them have been occasionally revived and performed, but with varied levels of success. Early productions may have suffered from the abstract expressionist directorial conventions popular at the time Barlach was writing; although critics frequently praised Barlach's handling of his themes, audiences seldom understood early productions. Nonetheless, Barlach is admired for his use of grotesque humor and innovative language as well as for his attempts to balance realism with symbolism and the haunting quality of his characters' search for redemption in a brutal, materialistic world.

PRINCIPAL WORKS

Der tote Tag (drama) 1912 [first publication]
Der arme Vetter (drama) 1919 [first publication]
Die echten Sedemunds (drama) 1920
Die Sündflut (drama) 1924
Der blaue Boll (drama) 1926
Der Findling (drama) 1928
Ein selbsterzähltes Leben [*A Self-Told Life*] (autobiography) 1928
Die gute Zeit (drama) 1929
Der gestohlene Mond (unfinished novel) 1948
Seespeck (unfinished novel) 1948
Der Graf von Ratzeburg (drama) 1952
Das dichterische Werk. 3 vols. (collected works) 1956-59
Two Acts from The Flood*; A Letter on Kandinsky; Eight Sculptures; Brecht; Notes on the Barlach Exhibition* (drama, letters, and nonfiction) 1960
Three Plays [translated by Alex Page] (drama) 1964
Die Briefe I: 1888-1938. 2 vols. (letters) 1968-69

CRITICISM

J. W. McFarlane (essay date 1954)

SOURCE: "Plasticity in Language: Some Notes on the Prose Style of Ernst Barlach," in *The Modern Language Review*, Vol. XLIX, No. 4, October, 1954, pp. 451-60.

[*In the following essay, McFarlane discusses Barlach's ability to move easily between verbal and visual communication in his writing and sculpture.*]

As a young man of nineteen, Ernst Barlach had no hesitation in arranging the representational—or, as he called them, the 'counterfeiting'—arts in a strict order of precedence, a hierarchy of values that moreover survived the brash self-certainty of youth and guided him throughout his life:

> Als Bildhauer muss mir von den drei Arten, auf welche man das Leben und Treiben der Menschen abkonterfeit, der Plastik, dem Malen und Zeichnen und der Erzählung, die erste natürlich am geläufigsten und liebsten sein. . . . Nun kann mir aber die Plastik nicht ganz genügen, deshalb zeichne ich, und weil mir auch das nicht ganz genügt, schreibe ich.[1]

In that art which meant most to him, he lived to see his work officially rewarded by one generation with the *Pour le mérite* and officially vilified by the next as 'decadent'; and it is regrettable that even today the international reputation he deserves so abundantly should be clouded by the wholly irrelevant criticism that his sculpture is somehow 'ostisch' or 'russisch'. His drawings and sketches, some of which lived a brief public life in 1936, being published, issued, impounded and destroyed within a cycle of a few months, had to wait until 1948 before appearing again in volume form to confirm to a wider public his stature as a draughtsman.[2] His distinction as a writer, which in spite of the place of literature in his scheme of values is by no means inferior to that which he achieved in other fields, has until recently derived mainly from his dramatic work, from the seven major dramas completed between the years 1912 and 1930; and of the quality of this part of his achievement it says much that a responsible English critic should have considered T. S. Eliot's *The Family Reunion* 'reminiscent' of Barlach.[3] Among the papers left behind at his death in 1938, however, there were found not only two almost completed dramas and a number of shorter prose works but also two novels. They had belonged respectively to the early and late years of his creative life: *Seespeck,* begun in the winter of 1912/13, interrupted at the beginning of the war and never completely worked out; and *Der gestohlene Mond,* complete in itself, but planned as part of a larger narrative design, and written for the most part in 1936 and 1937.[4] They contribute substantially, by the fascination and audacity of their prose style if for no other reason, to Barlach's already considerable reputation as a writer.

We do not need the sanction of some new and heavy aesthetic theory to assume an influence from Barlach the sculptor on Barlach the novelist; it is sufficient to note that he was himself conscious of bringing to the problems of language an artistic sensibility trained and developed in plastic art. Esteeming sculpture above painting as a 'healthier' art unhampered by those devices that are necessary to reduce a three dimensional world to a two dimensional surface, and preferring both of these arts to the 'counterfeiting' of life in words, which too often retained the hard edge of the prefabricated symbol, he was, like his hero Seespeck, for ever alert for an opportunity to replace words where possible by what he considered a better medium:

> [Seespeck behielt] immer in Auge, dass man eben mit Worten seine Gefühle ausmünzt, und [war] bereit, alle Symbole fahren zu lassen, wenn man etwas Besseres als Worte finden sollte, um Empfangenes zum Eigentum zu machen.[5]

This conviction that, in contrast to the precision and delicacy of clay, wood and bronze, language tends to communicate only in approximations constituted a challenge—a challenge that stimulated him to invest his words wherever possible with those qualities of simplicity and directness that he felt were inherent in his sculpture: 'Ich weiss nur', he wrote in 1921, 'dass die Sehnsucht in mir lebt, die einfache Linie meiner Plastik und die Simpelheit des Gefühls in meinen Holzarbeiten zu gewinnen, um das auszusprechen, was ich nur im Drama sagen kann.'[6] And yet the demands made on him as a *dramatist* were, he asserted, light compared with those on the novelist; a dramatist could throw off rough-hewn blocks and achieve some success thereby, but the novelist must completely conquer and subdue his material, must shape it to his purposes without ever letting it appear forced or strained—in short: 'Der Erzähler muss ziselieren.'[7]

There were of course compensations in the use of verbal symbols, particularly in that they offered a wider range to make up for their comparative lack of precision, giving to the writer the power to probe into those corners of life where the sculptor cannot reach. Consequently Barlach considered the visual and the literary arts to be complementary rather than substitutional; the one could never adequately replace the other, but neither were they in any sense completely divorced from each other. Indeed, Barlach seems to have been able to turn easily from one to the other without any real break in continuity, and his editor has remarked that the manuscript of *Seespeck* is in many places quite obviously by a hand still trembling from long hours with mallet and chisel.[8]

To recognize in these novels a highly idiosyncratic prose style and to designate the qualities of that style as 'plastic' is in itself—even when we know Barlach's confessed approach to the problems of language—merely to state a problem rather than offer immediate enlightenment. 'Durchaus nicht jede bildartige Vergleichung von Dichtung mit bildender Kunst . . . gilt mir schon für wechselseitige Erhellung', wrote Oskar Walzel;[9] and the warning is timely. Nobody would wish to deny to Rilke, for example, his conviction that certain passages in Baudelaire seemed 'not to have been written but moulded', that certain lines were like reliefs, and certain sonnets like columns with interlaced capitals bearing the burden of the thought; and few would wish to banish entirely 'tone' from painting or 'colour' from music; but to accept synaesthetic fancies as the basis for a critical (in the sense of 'non-poetic') comparison of the arts is to initiate a futile exercise in metaphor.[10] If the term 'plastic' is to have any meaning other than a

purely private one in this present context, it must be sustained by reference to specific and analysable qualities in the prose that might legitimately be supposed to derive from a specialized attitude to language; it invites a demonstration that certain elements in the choice and arrangement of words may be properly ascribed to a distinctive 'manière de voir' trained in the disciplines of sculptural art.

It will be suggested that Barlach's preoccupation with the visual and tactual has influenced his prose at all levels except the merely referential. This saving clause—'except the merely referential'—needs perhaps a special emphasis, since some critics in comparing the arts have admitted to their arguments phrases that bear if they do not invite a dangerous interpretation. 'Tatsächlich trifft für die Musik zu,' wrote Walzel, 'was er [Lessing] von der Dichtkunst sagt. Die Dichtkunst bietet mehr als bloss artikulierte Töne in einem zeitlichen Nacheinander. Sie weckt durch den Inhalt des Wortes Vorstellungen. Was als Eindruck von der bildenden Kunst dem Auge geboten wird, was ebenso dem Ohr in der Musik als Eindruck ersteht, all das kann als Vorstellung durch die Dichtkunst erzeugt werden.'[11] It is the implied suggestion of emulation, of judging language by its powers of inventory, that must be resisted; to grant 'plasticity' to a work of literature for treating a similar *theme* to that of a piece of sculpture, say 'Adam' or 'The Unknown Political Prisoner' is admissible, possibly, but facile; one looks for 'plasticity' or 'musicality' of language elsewhere than in the mere transcribing in detail of all that which is offered to the eye in sculpture or the ear in music.

The question of the content or theme of Barlach's novels raises matters of no little subtlety; for, to take one of the novels as an example, we find on examination that *Seespeck* is and yet is not 'about' sculpture. This work—which, like *Der gestohlene Mond,* has sub-strata of personal experience and is obviously packed with allusive reference that must not detain us here—is at once a suppressed 'Künstlerroman' and a modified 'Entwicklungsroman', but without the orthodoxy of either: we are aware of a tension between the artistically disposed hero and the bourgeois world around him, but only as a subdued accompaniment carrying with it no immediate threat of tragic dissonance; we also follow a process of development through experience, not however of the whole character but of the artist's creative eye. And linking the two themes in equilibrium, we have the central thread of Seespeck's search—the search for a place or community to which he can 'belong' and which, once found, will allow him to find himself. We meet the hero in a state of disharmony with society, confused and irresolute. He is living in that state of impressionable inertia that Keats has called Negative Capability, an enduring mood of uncertainty, mystery and doubt from which all fretful reaching after fact and reason is absent. Strangers whom he meets, friends whom he visits appear out of sympathy with him; and he comes to feel that a period of quiet living in his native town of Wedel may bring its own healing solution. The care with which Seespeck implements his decision not to appear 'different' in the eyes of his fellow citizens removes the threat of tragedy that has been implicit up to this point. Wishing to mix and observe without attracting unwelcome attention, he puts on the anonymity of an ordinary tradesman, rents a shop and stocks his windows with agricultural implements—a subterfuge that protects his privacy, explains his occasional absences, and eases his entry into the society of the town.[12] And with this suppression of the latent 'Künstlertragödie' there is full scope for the 'Entwicklungsroman' to take shape.

The hero—and we have excellent reasons for assuming the equation Seespeck=Barlach[13]—thereupon contrives an environment in which he can observe and record unmolested, where he can educate his eyes, the 'Fangorgan' of his soul, in the true perception of life's mysteries, training them to penetrate beyond the mere surface realities. As children, Seespeck muses, we were aware of the ghosts that lurked behind everyday things—'man ging leise, halb furchtsam, halb neugierig daran vorbei und wagte doch nicht, hinter sich zu schauen' (p. 31). As we grow older, our perception of these mysteries is deadened; but it is the task of the artist to strip the things about him of their encrustations of conventionality, to look behind the mask. This is the high purpose to which Seespeck dedicates himself: 'Ohne Freunde erlaubte er seinen Augen, im Versteck der Einsamkeit, Freundschaft mit aller Dinglichkeit, mit jeder Farbe und Form, und das Licht der Welt wurde eigentlich erst in diesen trübhellen Tagen zum Bruder seiner Seele' (p. 97). It is his eye and not his mind that is held captive when, for example, he witnesses an argument between two of his friends: 'Ja, er wusste ihren Worten oft gar nicht zu folgen, oder vielmehr ihm wurden die Augenerlebnisse zu so viel grösseren Wichtigkeiten, dass er dem Vorrücken oder dem Weichen der Handlung durch die verschiedensten Räume des Geistes keine Aufmerksamkeit gönnen konnte' (p. 152). He disciplines himself until he seems to see with 'circle' eyes, from all sides at once, and the visual quality of things and events is felt so intensely that the rest of his mind is often seemingly paralysed.

The result is that *Seespeck* is not a novel 'about' sculpture in the referential sense—indeed the author conceals Seespeck's real activities from the reader with the same care as the latter hides them from his fellows—and yet it is conducted throughout from a sculptor's perspective. We have therefore reached the paradox that the content of the novel is built up from those elements of life that a sculptor has found enthralling and irresistible, but that these elements are amenable to expression only in verbal and not in plastic symbols. This novel certainly does not attempt to reproduce in mass detail the world of material things; but neither, on the other hand, is it limited to or even concerned with themes that might just as well have been treated sculpturally; rather it presents, through the perspective of a trained manner of seeing, and by the idiosyncratic selection of detail, an interpre-

tation of our world. For this theme, Barlach has created a correlating style, consistent within itself.

Nowhere in this novel is the sense of the sculptor more apparent than in the author's handling of space and time. It is helpful to assume, without necessarily defining, a kind of dimensional norm for works of narrative literature, a norm which might be imagined as a fictional space-time world with a reasonable balance of dimensions, with the possible admission of time as the more persistent element appropriate to a time art.[14] A writer, by a deliberate or intuitive choice and arrangement of words, can modify this norm until it shows a strong emphasis on temporal form on the one hand or spatial form on the other; in the former case his work may then appear to show close affinity with music,[15] in the latter with sculpture.

The novel form, as Edwin Muir has pointed out, can never dispense with time altogether; but although never annihilated as it often seems to be in plastic art—and indeed to attempt to eliminate it from a novel completely would be to make it conspicuous and significant by its very absence—it can be reduced in importance to a point where it is accepted merely as an accompaniment to life, like a clock ticking away with its face to the wall. The function of time in *Seespeck* is best indicated in negative terms by saying that time is not *exploited*, that the structure of the novel shows none of the obsession with time that is such a feature of the novels of this century. Perhaps the most characteristic device of the modern novelist for lending depth to character and giving tension to plot has been that of manipulating time; cut and flash-back, the measuring of one incident by another widely different in time, were seen to give a new significance to narrative cause and effect; this device Barlach almost completely ignores here. In *Seespeck* there is not more than a handful of fixed chronological reference points, giving just sufficient rigidity to the temporal form to prevent it being entirely amorphous; and even then, as though to depreciate still further their significance as time checks, Barlach mainly singles out holidays or festival days: 'am Buss- und Bettag in November' (p. 47); 'so kam Weihnachten heran' (p. 81); 'Wedel feierte sein Sedanfest' (p. 111); 'der Herbstmarkt unterbrach noch einmal den Winterschlaf, zu dem sich Wedel vorläufig bis Weihnachten angeschickt hatte' (p. 116); 'am Geburtstag des Kaisers' (p. 122). Time makes no immediate contribution to the solution of Seespeck's problems, brings no sharp conflicts; either it slips past him: 'Er lag im Gebüsch über dem Strom und liess die Zeit willing ziehend und saugend verrinnen' (p. 104); or else he follows an unhurried course through it: 'Und darum schlängelte er sich so leidlich durch einige Jahre hindurch' (p. 126).[16] Even on those rare occasions when the time references become more explicit, the matter of accuracy is subordinate to this theme of time's leisurely progress: 'Wie sich nun die Zeit vorwärts schob, von März in den April und dann in den Mai hinein . . .' (p. 98). The separate incidents in the novel are thus linked by a minimum of causality; the educative process is a leap rather than a chain of incident, an accumulation of events rather than a consequential development.

This indifference to time would itself be less conspicuous were it not that the spatial settings are so carefully differentiated. Never on any occasion in this novel is the reader left in doubt as to the exact locale, for Barlach disposes with extreme care his characters against the North German background, leaving nothing vague, scrupulously attending to the town, the street, the house and the room, specifying the precise bend in the river or the particular side of the road, often verifying by repeated cross-reference: 'Seine Wohnstube dehnte sich in seiner Anschauung bis Uetersen nordwärts, bis Buxtehude südwärts, bis Nömberg westwärts und bis Gr.-Bostel ostwärts' (p. 83)—a 'fix' in space accurate to a few yards. It must not be supposed that this careful placing of site is a crude attempt to lend an air of verisimilitude to the narrative, to make it more 'real' in the sense that Baedeker is real; nor is it, on the other hand, a facile means of provoking a ready-made emotional response—a response that attaches to such place names as, say, Weimar or Oberammergau, with their overtones of meaning. Rather this precision when dealing with the world of space is revelatory of the mental pattern of the author, one item among many in a complex style.[17]

With the wider context once established, Barlach attends carefully to the more immediate environment. His motives, whether he was conscious of them or not, no doubt were similar to those of Poe, who wrote in his *Philosophy of Composition:* 'It has always appeared to me that a close *circumscription of space* [his italics] is absolutely necessary to the effect of insulated incident. . . . It has an indisputable moral power in keeping concentrated the attention.'[18] As a sculptor working chiefly in wood on figures designed for indoor exhibition—often for display either in artificial light or, in the case of his cathedral monuments, in rather special lighting conditions—Barlach was acutely sensitive to the intensification of effect that can come with confined space and with the calculated play of light and shade. It cannot be merely coincidental that, at those points in his novel where the tension between characters is at its most pronounced, the scene should be strictly and severely confined—the inside of a coach, a ship's cabin, a rowing boat, the landing of a tiny flat—carefully and conscientiously recorded to convey an impression of spatial concentration; and that conversely where the tension is slack, the spatial concentration should also be reduced. That the exact source and degree of illumination was also important to him as a device for augmenting tension will perhaps become evident in the short analysis below.

Additionally remarkable in this fictional world of predominating space is the frequent translation of time's progress into spatial or alternatively chiaroscopic terms. The lapse of time during a journey, for example, is conveyed obliquely by reference to the geographical point reached rather than directly by the clock; the day's rhythm is measured by the degree of light and shadow in the sky, or the year's rhythm by the extent of the hours of darkness—'zu einer Jahreszeit wo die dunklen Nachtstunden schon eine kleine Schar ausmachen' (p. 109), as it is put in one case.

When furnishing his rigorously defined space with figures, Barlach reveals a highly developed sense for pose and gesture as outer signs of inner emotion. Orthodox technique in the novel is to throw a heavy burden on facial expression: the trembling lip, the tear-filled eye, the flushed cheek, all are signs common in the novel which the reader can readily interpret in terms of the appropriate emotion. But in plastic art, the sculptor has limits imposed on him by his material; stone or bronze, marble or wood will rarely allow him to reproduce the infinite subtlety of facial expression, and the features are his prime concern usually only when grotesque; rather he is in most cases compelled to achieve his communication by an emphasis on gesture and pose—a tilt of the head, a disposition of the limbs, a curve of the spine. This is reflected in Barlach's prose. Whereas grotesque and distorted facial expression does play a significant part in the narrative of *Seespeck,* as will be seen below, the main stress is on bodily attitude. Terror drains no blood from the hero's face, but compels him to an involuntary gesture: 'Darüber erschrak Seespeck und wehrte heftig ab und streckte die Hände aus, als schöbe er eine widrige Möglichkeit vom Leibe' (p. 60). Inattention, which in another's work might have been conveyed by reference, say, to 'glazed eyes', here forms itself into a studied pose: 'Eixner hatte sich in seinem Stuhl zurückgelehnt und liess die Fäuste zwischen die Beine hängen, wie zwei Schaufeln eines riesigen Maulwurfs anzusehen, er hörte nicht zu und sah irgendwo gegen die Wand . . .' (p. 34). And indifference brings its own postural correlative: 'Aber Eixner, der die Frage noch viel mehr verabscheute, ballte seine Fäuste in der Hosentasche und tat mit einem herrschaftlichen Langstrecken des Leibes vom Kopf an der Sofalehne bis zu den Zehen unter dem Tisch das ganze unbequeme Thema vornehm ab' (p. 61).

The extension of this device from a single figure to a group of figures is a natural step; and by a careful adjustment of the spatial interval between two or more figures in sympathy with their mood, thrusting their faces close together at times of high passion or opposing them across a corridor of excited spectators at moments of mounting suspense, Barlach conveys something of that electric energy that can cross the gap between two carefully juxtaposed forms. He seems to acknowledge, however, that it is a device rarely successful in isolation, and he therefore employs it in most cases to reinforce the more usual narrative techniques—the clash of temperament and personality through the medium of conversation—for building up tension.

There is no surprise in the realization that much of Barlach's imagery is derived from visual sources, and visual imagery in itself is not such a conspicuously rare phenomenon that its presence should call for special attention. We should in any case expect an author with his background to stress in his descriptions of persons the anatomical aspects of the human form (pp. 33 f.), or to discover architectural qualities (p. 190), or to visualize in terms of a sculptor's materials (p. 134); and an awareness of the hidden anatomical structure, of the curves and folds, the interlocking planes and balanced masses of the human body permeates many of his images. One special type, however, impresses the reader as being more than usually persistent, and that is the description of distortions, abnormalities or incongruities of space or vision to convey an impression of mental confusion; as when a perplexed Seespeck sees from the *rear* door of the vehicle the church tower of the town he is approaching: 'Der Kirchturm rückte langsam näher, aber Seespeck fiel es nicht ein, darüber nachzudenken, wie man aus der Hintertür eines Omnibusses nach etwas schauen und doch immer näher herankommen kann' (p. 46). Such impressions accompany the hero constantly in his bewilderment.

A brief analysis of the opening chapter of *Seespeck* may show not only how tightly these and similar devices can be woven into the texture of a narrative, but also how this concentration of qualities which we have called 'plastic' gives a peculiar force to Barlach's prose. The hero's malaise, his mood of mental confusion, his lack of harmony with the world and with other men is conveyed in characteristic terms in both the opening and closing sentences to this chapter. We meet him in a state in which the usually reliable co-ordinates of value by which he had been accustomed to measure himself and the things he saw seem to one part of his mind strangely unstable, 'als fasste ihn für die ganze Zeit ein Schwindel, weil er in einen Spiegel hineinschaute, in dem sich alles bewegte, was draussen sonst ruhig lag und stand'; and when we leave him at the end of the chapter, the apparent spatial illogicalities of his subjective world still haunt him: 'Jetzt . . . kam es ihm vor, als ginge er an einer langen Planke entlang und fände nirgends einen Ausgang, die Planke aber hatte er im Verdacht, dass sie im Kreise liefe und er mit ihr. Wie er aber hineingekommen, war ein Geheimnis.'

However dimensionally erratic this world seems to the hero, the actual narrative world created by Barlach nevertheless has a rigorously logical structure in space; and there is, at these two levels of interpretation, a strong and effective contrast. Already in the opening sentence, this contrast between precise environmental space and the mental aberrations in the hero's sense of space makes an immediate impact:

> Als Seespeck nicht lange danach in der Gegend von Wilsede in einer Postkutsche durch die Lüneburger Heide auf Buxtehude zu fuhr, weil er am Tage darauf in Hamburg sein musste, sass er mehrere Stunden in eines Mannes Gesellschaft, der seinen gewöhnlichen Zustand so sehr verkehrte, dass es ihm zu Mute war, als stände er ohne Halt auf einer hohen Leiter oder als fasste ihn für die ganze Zeit ein Schwindel. . . .

Time, it may be noticed incidentally, is a constituent part of this world, but its significance is small; present time is left virtually unrelated to time past except as an inevitable sequel; the 'nicht lange danach' is left without further explanation, an imprecise bearing on some undivulged point in time; the (narrative) present is merely an expanse of 'mehrere Stunden', a day to be followed by other days without perceptible urgency or tedium. The spatial orientation, however, is seen from the first to be precisely defined: two figures, Seespeck and 'the man', set in the confined space of a coach, the position and course of which is given in respect of urban district and rural area, destinations immediate and ultimate. These two figures are subsequently composed into a group and close attention is given to their position relative to each other, to the nature and source of the illumination and, at least in part, to bodily attitude: the man, 'auf dessen Gesicht vom Licht der Bocklaterne ein Rückwärtsstrahl fiel', was sitting in one of the corner seats; 'Seespeck selbst sass in der schräg gegenüber liegenden Ecke am effenen Türfenster und liess vor diesem noch am Seitenfenster sein Profil gegen den Himmel abschatten.' The result is an intensification, highly idiosyncratic in its nature, of the mood initiated in the opening lines.

The following day, Seespeck meets the same fellow traveller on a boat—characteristically 'eins der kleinsten Boote in der Gegend'—at Buxtehude, and the rest of the chapter covers the progress of the boat up the Elbe to Hamburg. From this point on, indications of time are translated without exception into terms of light and darkness or space: 'es wurde fast dunkel', 'bei zunehmender Dunkelheit', 'in der Dämmerung', 'indem stiess das Boot in Neumühle an die Landungsbrücke', and finally by an indication of the boat's arrival in Hamburg. It is a *gesture* that leads to recognition and brings the two travellers together again; Seespeck, knowing that the other could not have seen his face clearly in the coach, is surprised when greeted and is told in answer to his astonished questions: 'Sie tragen eine Krawatte, die ewig verrutscht, und daran fingern Sie fortwährend und wissen es vielleicht selbst nicht.' They retire to the cramped passengers' room, where they meet a drunken baker; and from this initial situation, Barlach develops the triangular tension linking these three chance acquaintances.

The relationship between Seespeck's two companions is Barlach's first concern and by communicating something of their grotesque facial expressions and their posturings, he creates an emotional meaning that is all the more remarkable for depending so little on recorded conversation. The first attitude is struck by the baker, who bars their way and offers his hand in a drunken gesture of friendship; this is countered by the photographer (as we shall call him) who turns his back, sits down and leaves the baker standing there in a 'frozen' gesture with outstretched hand. The baker answers this rebuff by singing an offensive song—a noise that presents itself to Seespeck in visual terms: 'Es war das gesungene Porträt des Bäckers, wie er etwa befreit von der Schwere seines fleischigen Überflusses, aber doch als Riese und Ungetüm leicht tänzelnd, mühelos hüpfend in grotesker Gewandtheit seiner Unförmlichkeit spottend durch Wald und Heide striche.'[19] To this the photographer responds by adopting a carefully studied attitude:

> Schliesslich drehte er sich doch um, stützte die Ellenbogen auf die Knie, duckte sich beobachtend zusammen und liess den Rauch seiner Zigarre an dem zusammengekniffenen einen Auge vorbei, vor den hochgezogenen Brauen vorweg, die heftig gerunzelte Stirn verschleiernd, mit schiefer Kopfhaltung aufsteigen. Er fasste das singende Ungetüm von Bäcker ins Auge, er sog sich fest an ihn, er schnitt in ihn hinein mit der gelassenen Sachlichkeit eines Operateurs.

Whereupon the baker retaliates with an insulting grimace:

> Seespeck ward angst und bange. Aber da sah er schon, wie des Bäckers Gesicht, wie aus einer Dunstwolke auftauchend, sich dem andern zuwandte und wie ein Grinsen, dessen Deutung nicht versucht werden kann, dieses Gesicht überzog und wie seine dicke Zunge zwischen seinen Lippen aus verborgener Höhle hervor auf den Betrachter zielte.

And the two figures fuse into a single unity:

> Der Bäcker, schnitt seine Grimasse, und der andre parierte diese Hiebe, die in ihrer Scheusslichkeit, wie Entleerungen von Unrat, schlimmer als Fausthiebe oder Schimpf-worte waren, mit der geräuschlosen Tätigkeit seiner Augen. . . .

Thus, by a sculptural device of juxtaposing two figures in meaningful attitude in space, an atmosphere is created that has an immediate relevance to Seespeck's mood of unease; it is sustained by the subsequent variations of facial contortion, 'immer neue Erfindungen in der Ausschüttung von inneren Zuständen', that the baker produces and is further augmented by the quality of the lighting: 'Es war so dunkel geworden, dass die Fettleibigkeit des stummen, rasenden Bäckers zur Gespensthaftigkeit wurde.' The termination of this episode, which has taken place in utter silence and made its appeal solely to Seespeck's visual sense, is equally the inspiration of a sculptor; Seespeck, for whom the suspense has become intolerable, calls for the lamp to be lit and as the quality of a sculpted figure varies with different illumination, so the baker assumes a new personality in the light: 'Der Bäcker, der in der Dämmerung lebendig geworden war, starb unter der Lampe ab.'

Later, a crowd of newly embarked passengers both restores the baker's drunken confidence and offers an opportunity for the author to exploit new spatial patterns to meet the changed situation; the newcomers now become an integral part of the grouping and influence the relative position of the two men. Once again the tension is built up partly on significant positioning: 'Man hatte tatsächlich zwischen dem Bäcker und dem "Hemis" [the photographer] eine hohle Gasse geschaffen, und so sassen sie sich nun im Gedränge gegenüber'; and this once more resolves itself into a tighter grouping, in which the baker seizes the hand of the other, 'während sich sogleich der freie Raum hinter ihm wieder füllte und die Leute dicht hinter ihm drängten, so dass er mit dem Bäcker Hand in Hand gefangen war'. Thus the torment of the photographer continues. Even those among the onlookers who turn away with embarrassment still apparently cannot escape the implications of space: '(Sie) orientierten sich über den Gang des Schiffes'!

It is sufficient to add that similar narrative devices, too numerous to catalogue in detail here, characterize the remaining pages of this chapter in which the other two sides of this triangular relationship are developed; and to note that crowd grouping, gesture of a provocative kind and further facial contortion play a prominent part.

The example of Poe showed how at least some of the characteristics of such a style might have been planned in advance; and it is not impossible that Barlach worked to a prepared blueprint; but it is extremely doubtful. One feels rather that a very special imaginative power, carefully nurtured and trained in the pursuit of sculpture, had been assimilated into his general consciousness, had—to speak with Rilke—turned to blood within him; and what we experience in this prose is the intuitive response of this imaginative power to the challenge of a different medium.

NOTES
[1] Letter to Friedrich Düsel, 15 and 16 June 1889, in Ernst Barlach, *Aus seinen Briefen,* ed. Friedrich Dross (Munich, 1947), pp. 16-17.

[2] Ernst Barlach, *Zeichnungen.* Mit einer Einführung von Paul Fechter (Munich, 1948).

[3] R. Hinton Thomas, 'German Expressionism and the Contemporary English Stage', *German Perspectives* (Cambridge, 1940), p. 35.

[4] Both novels have been edited by Friedrich Dross (Berlin and Frankfurt/Main, Suhrkamp Verlag, 1948).

[5] *Seespeck,* p. 124.

[6] *Aus seinen Briefen,* p. 53.

[7] Ibid. p. 62.

[8] *Der gestohlene Mond,* Nachwort, p. 269.

[9] *Gehalt und Gestalt in Kunstwerk des Dichters* (Berlin, 1930), p. 273.

[10] To equate 'a certain radiating beauty' in Rilke's verse with the 'luminosity' of Rodin's sculpture is doubtless

of value, but only as *persuasive* and not as *demonstrative* criticism (cf. G. Craig Houston, 'Rilke and Rodin', *German Studies,* Oxford, 1938, p. 263).

[11] *Gehalt und Gestalt,* p. 271.

[12] The inevitable consequences to the artist of neglecting these precautions are hinted at in *Der gestohlene Mond,* where Barlach makes an obviously personal if brief appearance in his narrative as the neighbour of one of the more important characters: 'Nebenan unter demselben Dach dieser Gehäuse dunkelte ein Pferdestall, der sonst an einen Viehhändler, jetzt an einen Mann mit einem Totengräbergesicht vermietet war, der sich seit kurzem am Ort befand . . . und sich beruflich mit Bildschnitzerei abgab. . . . Wenn er auch hin und wieder einige unnützige Wortklapperei für den Hausbesitzer, einen Mehlhändler . . . abfallen liess, so galt er doch für sonderlich, und manche nannten ihn hochnäsig. Auswärtige Zeitungen schrieben in auswärtig-hochtrabendem Ton über ihn und auswärtige Exemplare einer absonderlichen Sorte von Zeitgenossen besuchten ihn' (pp. 182-3).

[13] Cf. letter to Karl Barlach, 12 December 1935: 'Neulich las ich die Kapitel meines "unvollendeten" Seespeck-Romans aus den Jahren 1912, 13, 14 wieder durch. . . . Eine quasi fremde Hand blätterte die Seiten meines, d.h Seespecks, Lebens um . . .' (*Aus den Briefen,* p. 88). See also 'Mein Leben in Wedel ist wesentlich gezeichnet in dem Kapitel der "Wedeler Tage", meines unfertig gebliebenen Seespeck-Romans' (*Ein selbsterzähltes Leben,* erweiterte Neuausgabe, Munich, 1948, p. 39).

[14] The nearest formal statement that I can find of the aesthetic pattern that seems to be assumed by this remark is this: 'If we were to adopt the four-dimensional world of space-time, we could classify the arts more accurately on the basis of their principal dimension, allowing always for the symbolic inference of the other dimensions. Architecture and sculpture use three-dimensional space and suggest time symbolically and psychologically. Painting employs a two-dimensional surface suggesting depth through perspective and time through symbols and motional attitudes. . . . Literature employs the flow of the time dimension through a sequence of images and concepts, suggesting the four dimensions of space-time through verbal symbolism. The novel may thus be conceived as symbol-drama unfolding in the time dimension but including all dimensions through symbolism. . . .' William Fleming, 'The newer concepts of time and their relation to the temporal arts', *Journal of Aesthetics and Art Criticism,* IV (1945), 101-6.

[15] The intricate time pattern in Thomas Mann's *Dr Faustus* may be taken as an example; and in this case, it is of course obvious that its 'musicality' (in this present restricted sense) of style is linked quite unambiguously with a plot that has music as its content. It may also be that Lessing's famous analysis of Homer in the *Laokoön* should be regarded as a demonstration of this one possible, rather than the only proper, function of language.

[16] The same attitude to time is revealed in Barlach's autobiography in respect of his childhood: 'Ich glitt durch die Tage und weidete durch die Jahre hin, die Augenblicke sogen sich voll Zeitlosigkeit und häuften sich zu Schichten und Gruppen, die unzusammenhängend mit dem Organismus des Schul- und Hauskinderdaseins das Leben im Rhythmus voranführten' (*Ein selbsterzähltes Leben,* ed. cit. p. 18); and in his image of time's action as a slow, imperceptible process of maturing: 'Ich trieb mich umher, hing wie ein frischer Schinken und räucherte an in der langsam garmachenden Zeit . . .' (ibid. p. 37).

[17] Friedrich Dross stresses the psychological implications of space for Barlach, and interprets the latter's visit to Russia in 1906 as a search for space: 'Was ihn im Osten überfiel . . . das war zunächst nichts als das Geschenk des Raumes—aussen wie innen—an einen, der aus der bedrängtesten Raumnot quetschender Enge—aussen wie innen—kam und der bis dahin nicht gewusst hatte, wie viel Raum er brauchte—aussen wie innen—, wie mörderisch ihm also die Raumnot seines bisherigen Daseins den Lebensatem abgewürgt hatte' (*Aus den Briefen,* Introduction, p. 7).

[18] It is worth noticing, however, that Barlach in contrast to Poe does not interpose himself between his spatial descriptions and the reader. In *The Pit and the Pendulum,* where such description is used to augment the natural tension of the situation, Poe interprets for us the hero's emotional reactions to the confined space: 'The whole circuit of the walls did not exceed twenty-five yards. For some minutes this fact occasioned me a world of vain trouble; vain indeed—for what could be of less importance, under the terrible circumstances which environed me, than the mere dimensions of my dungeon. But my soul took a wild interest in trifles. . . .' In Barlach, no such direct interpretation is attempted and we are allowed our own unconscious reactions.

[19] Barlach himself confessed to frequent synaesthesia of this kind: 'Musik setzt sich bei mir oft unmittelbar in Bildvorstellung um . . .' (*Aus seinen Briefen,* p. 73).

Edson M. Chick (essay date 1958)

SOURCE: "Diction in Barlach's *Sündflut,*" in *The Germanic Review,* Vol. XXXIII, No. 4, December, 1958, pp. 243-50.

[*In the following essay, Chick examines the use Barlach makes of linguistic patterns and plays on words in* Sündflut.]

In 1924 Barlach won the *Kleistpreis* for his drama *Die Sündflut.* Yet to the present time little has been done to show why it deserved this recognition. To be sure, Barlach's literary significance has been acknowledged and at least once denied in several articles and literary histories,[1] but the divergence of opinion as well as the general nature of the criticism demonstrate the need for something more specific.

During his lifetime Barlach had sufficient occasion to complain of misunderstanding and misinterpretation. He comments, for example, in a conversation: "Da lesen schon die Pfarrer und die Leserinnen meine *Sündflut* mit verteilten Rollen. Der ich doch nichts anderes im Schilde führte als nachzuweisen, dass die alte Fabel schlechterdings absurd ist."[2] The pastors and ladies were quite appropriately reading aloud this play which was written more for the ear than for the eye, but their motivation was absurd in the light of the play's content. Barlach was even more dismayed by what happened to this and other plays on the stage. Audiences were apparently unprepared for what they were to see;[3] and what was worse, directors of the 1920's, steeped in expressionistic dramaturgy, produced his plays in an inappropriate stylization. "Filmtempo und Expression, damit will ich nichts zu tun haben, . . . und der Grundton des Hauptsächlichen Geschrei und Monumental-Stilbums" (*Briefe*, p. 104).

Barlach's language, like his plays, is admittedly highly stylized,[4] but not in the direction of extravagance as the theater directors seemed to assume. He aimed rather at rough simplicity. Consequently he was an outsider among his expressionist contemporaries and exposed to misunderstanding for the very reason of his simplicity. Otto Mann calls Barlach "der sprachgewaltigste Expressionist"[5] because his diction is so remote from expressionistic hyperbole and intellectualized stylization. Mann has other illuminating things to say on the subject but then drops it to comment at length on the dramatist's dangerous tendency to play the prophet and preach the Barlachian way to redemption. One wonders whether this remarkable diction is something to be admired and described for its own sake or whether under scrutiny it might not help us understand and appreciate the dramatic entities Barlach wrote. Among other critics Hans Schwerte alone[6] has recognized the importance of Barlach's language and has opened the way for further work in this direction.

In his *Nachwort* to the collected dramas[7] Klaus Lazarowicz claims no more than to discuss Barlach's symbolism in the broadest sense of the word. Lazarowicz passes quickly over the issue of diction by remarking on Barlach's mistrust of the word and saying that "Der Dichter strebt über das Wort hinaus zum Bild" (p. 583). This position is misleading if taken at face value, for Lazarowicz must recognize, as do O. Mann and Schwerte, that words and their sounds constitute the fibre of Barlach's literary work.

The question is still open as to what relevance Barlach's "Sprachgewalt" has in the totality of any one drama. If, and this would seem unlikely, he is striving to overcome language or just to propagate a new way to redemption, why then would Barlach take such pains in composition as he describes in the following passage from a letter:

"Ich kämpfe oft tagelang mit einem einzigen Wort, dreh einen Satz von drei Worten endlos hin und her und muss oft verzichten, weil ich kein Wort mit der nötigen Silbenzahl finde, es gibt das Wort nicht, sollte es aber geben. Die Meinung, der Gedanke, der Vorgang an sich ist völlig wertlos."[8]

Die Sündflut is well suited for analysis on the basis of diction because it is at least as good as any other play by Barlach, because it shows his virtuosity with language, and because the spoken word is one of its central problems. In fact, the essence of the whole drama and of Barlach's worldview can best be extracted from observation of his language here. The striking use of alliteration, repetition, parallelism, and the plays on words clearly have more than decorative function.

Otto Mann suggests that alliteration is a "Stilprinzip" (*Expressionismus*, p. 308) in Barlach's plays, but he neglects to draw the consequences of this statement. It is indeed a style principle and is used in quite appropriate ways. For example, it gives a remarkable aggressive vigor to Calan's speech to the Beggar-Lord after Calan, Noah's antagonist, has had the shepherd's hands cut off in order to put Noah and his God to the test. "Aber die Hände habe ich abgeschlagen und annageln lassen—ich, Calan, ein Kind des Gottes, der mir die Kraft gegeben hat, kein Knecht zu sein" (p. 346). The first unit of the passage, up to the dash, is held together by the *a* assonance and alliteration but is itself split rhythmically in two by the *ich*. Because of the alliteration the first unit must be read with heavy stress on the initial syllables. Thus the *ich* receives redoubled emphasis since it is totally isolated and, in its position just before another accented syllable, must be made to stand out. The *ich*, clearly the key word now, is repeated at the beginning of the second unit with the same emphasis for the same reasons. The effect of the second unit is then one of dynamic, explosive emphasis with the rapid-fire repetition of initial consonants *k* and *g*, which re-echo in the same words and others throughout the play.

Not self-assertion but the sound of violence and disaster is suggested in the following speech by the servant Chus as he tells how Calan's herds have been dispersed: "Ein zorniger Flug grosser Hornisse stiess auf die Kamele, stürzte ihnen Stiche über Nüstern und Augen, über Beine und Bäuche, bohrte ihnen Gift in Ohren und After . . ." (p. 324). The alliterative pattern of *s, st, b,* and *o* and *a* vowels accentuates the choppy rhythm. The formulary character of the short word groups with two strong, often alliterative, accented syllables is reminiscent of the Old High German *Zauberspruch*.

Barlach also uses sound to recapture the ecstasy of an overpowering emotional experience as in Awah's speech beginning with: "Ich sehe, wie es klingt, ich höre, wie es schwingt, das Ende wiegt den Anfang in den Armen" (p. 363). The whole passage echoes the rocking of the flood waves; " . . . es spielen Wort und Welle." Although it is constructed on much the same pattern as

Chus' speech, it gets its sing-song, cyclical quality from a lengthening of the word groups by adjectives and from the use of end rhyme. On the other hand, similar means may be used to describe a terrifying experience like that of Noah's son Japhet (p. 340) when the angels flew by "im Gewand wie fliessendes Geflecht von Sonnenstrahlen, zwei redende Riesen mit Gerinne und Gehetz und Gekeuch und Gehusch von Flügeln aus Luft hinter sich an den Fersen." These are not playful words but hard ones which must be read with uninterrupted, breathless haste. They are intended to reproduce the original force which was so strong that Japhet says, "dass ich zwischen ihren Worten wie von Mühlsteinen geschroten bin" (p. 340).

No less expressive in its explosive rage and disgust is the leper's vituperation of the Lord with its two long strings of alliterative words closed off by the vicious sounds of *Krallen* and *kratzen:* "Glaubst du, dass er ein einziges Mal mit Essen überschlägt, weil all das menschliche Elend mit seinem Brand und seiner Bitterkeit in seinem behäbigen Bauch beisst und die Krallen der Gebete seinen Magen wund kratzen?" (p. 380)

It should be noted here that, although these speeches are well calculated to fit the situation, the words and sounds have an existence independent of the speakers. Awah and Japhet display an unrealistic eloquence considering their emotional states. Also Noah's speeches are often larded with *l* sounds (e.g. " . . . als ob die Fettigkeit des Landes in linder leiser Lust zerflösse" [p. 325]). Yet when he gives an order for meat to be brought to the Beggar-Lord and demands "des Lammes leckerstes Lendenstück" (p. 348), Calan interrupts and adds: " . . . für einen alten Lügner und Lumpen, der längst im Grabe faulen müsste."

The use of verbal and tonal devices extends beyond what has already been pointed out as the most telling of Barlach's linguistic artifices. He has certain formulary, alliterative phrases repeated like leitmotifs with variations and by various characters through the whole drama. Thus he plays on the tonal memory of the listener and on the large scale of associations which these words and sounds eventually evoke. Such a formula is *Freude, Friede, Freiheit.* It is originally and basically part of Noah's vocabulary. He uses it twice in II, 2 after the angels have visited his camp and he has missed seeing them. Noah moans and blames his sons for his own failure: "[Ich] liess mich von euren blasigen Worten umwinden und von euren harzigen Händen halten—und so gingen Freude, Friede, Freiheit" (p. 340). Noah's whole life seems to hang on the prospect of, or longing for, these three things, but he never finds them. They prove to be chimaerical ideals which eventually rot away and crumble under the repeated assault of Calan's, or Barlach's, "Fragen und Forschen" (p. 324).

To tighten the association Noah repeats the words a third time out of mistaken pity for Calan: "Armer, grässlicher Calan, wo ist Friede, Freude, Freiheit für dich zu finden?" (p. 344). Calan indicates that the

phrase means little to him, and by the end of the play the words are emptied of their original meaning for the audience as well. The process begins when they are linked by alliteration with "Fleisch und Verderben" (p. 357). To be sure, flesh and corruption, in the person of "die dicke" Zebid, constitute at first in Noah's eyes a threat to his pious peace. Yet within a short time Noah defends Zebid before the Lord for the sake of peace and joy: "Kann sie dafür, dass ihre Speise Frass war und feistes Verderben ansetzte?" (p. 360). To keep peace in the family at all costs Noah is traveling against the Lord's will to fetch this epitome of corruption into his own household. He is aware of the dangerous ambiguity and vagueness in his *Friede, Freude, Freiheit,* but his weak acquiescence to his sons' wishes indicates what actual meaning the words have. It is significant that Japhet is the last to mouth the phrase,—this time in its adjective form: "frei, froh und friedlich" (p. 365)—and that he directs it to Zebid, with the result that *Friede, Freude, Freiheit* become entangled not only with *Frass* and *feistes Verderben* but also with the object of Japhet's longing since the play's beginning: "eine Frau mit festem Fleisch" (p. 326) and the whole crude sensuality of Japhet and Zebid. Noah's concept of freedom, "die ganze schöne Freiheit" (p. 379), is also laid bare in all its shallowness by Ham who thinks of it as license to dominate the earth.

This long development may be seen in miniature in Part II (p. 326) where the loss of verbal meaning, along with the collapse of proper family relationships, is shown primarily through plays on words. As usual Noah's sons are concerned with the problem presented by their sexual urges. Noah begins: "Es bekümmert mich, dass ihr unzufrieden seid," whereupon Sem and Japhet gloss the speech as if Noah were not there at all. Sem: "Ei ja, es bekümmert ihn . . . Er will gottgefällige Töchter, als ob es nicht vielmehr darauf ankäme, was für Frauen wir haben wollten." And then Japhet: "Mich bekümmert sein Kummer, aber darum sollen unsere Kinder nicht kümmerlich geraten. Ich will eine Frau mit festem Fleisch . . . gottgefällig, nein, gottgefällig sind sie nicht, die da auf der anderen Flussseite, aber mir genügt es, dass sie mir gefallen." Noah's piety and fatherly concern suffer two blows, one from his sons' scorn and the other from their toying with his words which opens them to question as to their essential and experiential meaning. Even Japhet's sincerity is doubtful when he talks about children. They are at best secondary to the pleasure of a wife with firm flesh.

Barlach's penetrating assault on words can also lead in the direction of positive clarity as in the instance of the words *Herr, Knecht, Vater, Sohn,* and *Kind.* In fact, the structure of **Die Sündflut** is reflected best in the interplay of the words and concepts dealing with the relationships between lord and servant, father and son. The development begins in the opening scene when the angel refers to Noah as "dein Knecht und dein Kind" (p. 322) and the Lord's reply echoes, "mein Knecht und mein Kind." The apparent solidity and propriety of the juxtaposition is promptly shaken by Calan, who says of his servant, Chus: "ja, er könnte mein Sohn sein, wenn er nicht mein Knecht wäre" (p. 325). For Calan then servitude and sonhood are mutually exclusive, and his "Fragen und Forschen" are trained on the question of what is the proper father-son (God-man) relationship (p. 324). Noah's servile piety is unthinkable and degrading in Calan's eyes, and Barlach proceeds to illustrate the weakness of all Noah represents by laying bare his relationships to his family and his God.

As head of his family Noah proves to be neither father nor lord. Actually he is the slave of his sons, his wife, and of his own senses. His caution and fear of physical servitude under Calan (p. 373) preclude the possibility of spiritual freedom. Noah is also neither a good son nor a good servant of his God. When they stand face to face (p. 346), Noah can recognize only his *former* father: "Ich bin verwirrt, du bist doch einst mein Vater gewesen." And the Beggar-Lord replies: "Du warst einst mein Sohn." Their connection seems all but dissolved. It is supported by a vague memory of the past, by the Lord's plaintive pleading for obedience, and by Noah's cautious anxiety lest he make a false step. It takes much wheedling, promises of reward, and a childish refusal to eat (p. 349) for the Lord to convince Noah that he should build an ark. And once this is accomplished, He has to remind Noah that He is hungry (p. 351). Noah's God is no better father and lord than His one "Knecht und Kind".

These words have a different sound when they come from Calan's mouth. The conviction that he is a "Gotteskind" (p. 344) governs his action through the whole play, the search for his God-father, or for "der Eine". The search nears its end with a radical reversal of roles; Calan is transformed from lord to servant and beggar and suddenly becomes aware of his true relationship to Chus. At the end of Part IV he says: "Komm, Chus, mein Kind" (p. 367), and "Komm, Kind, komm, Chus" (p. 368). From this point on through V, 3 the already familiar words are dinned into our ears reaching a crescendo in the following exchange (p. 372):

> Calan: . . . Chus, mein Kind.
>
> Zebid: Dein Kind? Dein Knecht.
>
> Calan: Ein Herr hat Knechte, ein Bettelmann nicht.

Yet in the concluding scenes after Calan says pointedly to Noah: "Ich . . . will sterben, wie es dem Sohn ansteht, der kein Knecht seines Vaters ist" (p. 377), it is as if the words have lost their sense and importance. In union with a voiceless and formless God Calan has entered a relationship inexpressible in familial terms. Such talk is left to Noah and his sons.

Barlach's technique is then one of stress and overstress. His manipulation of *Knecht* and *Kind* is analogous to his alliterative devices as it is to Calan's "Fragen und Forschen." Stress, repetition, and the cumulative force of sound build up anticipation and intensity in single passages and in the play as a whole up to the end, even after Calan claims he has given up his "Plappern über Gott" (p. 370). The alliteration is reminiscent of Old High German *Stabreim* just as the vocabulary and syntax remind one of Luther, but neither is used out of love for tradition. This would be like the vain attempt of Noah and his God to return to a dead past. Rather, Barlach and Calan are pushing ahead toward something new. The diction is conservative in a revolutionary way. Barlach is well aware that his modern audience will notice the linguistic roughness and distortion resulting from the search for alliteration and that the general effect will be unlikely to please.[9]

As we have seen, *Die Sündflut* offers much evidence of Barlach's aforementioned struggle with words themselves. He works primarily with simple words of one or two syllables like *Hand, Fleisch, Schwert, Frass, Friede,* etc. which he then repeats over and over with heavy emphasis. This everyday vocabulary becomes disturbing by its very simplicity. Through repetition and stress the words are gradually isolated and stripped of their usual associations. Eventually they become exhausted of meaning and dissolve, or, as Barlach says of the word *Gott* in a letter (*Aus seinen Briefen,* p. 40): "nimmt man es häufig auf die Zunge, so macht man daraus ein Backpflaumenmus." For instance, the hand, a central word and image, is reduced near the end to fingers which are finally literally eaten away to nothing. The general effect is quite different from that achieved by other linguistically radical writers of this century. Barlach is not concerned with nuances or stylized beauty. What results from his manipulation of words is something grotesque bordering on the absurd. Twice in his letters he maintains that *Die Sündflut* is full of humor (*Briefe,* pp. 121, 142) and that theater directors have failed to note this. The reason is probably that Barlach's humor is of a special kind and more like the "groteske Genialität" (*Aus seinen Briefen,* p. 28) that he admires in Alfred Kubin and others and that does not necessarily excite laughter. His aim is to discomfort or disconcert the listener.

The rebellion of the word against itself is indeed a grotesque prospect. Barlach's language works to expose itself as meaningless. Thus Lazarowicz' comment ("über das Wort hinaus zum Bild") would be corroborated were it not for the fact that the process of exposure is repeated without ceasing. It is Barlach's "gesegneter Fluch"[10] that he, like Wau in *Der gestohlene Mond,* is condemned to go on making words despite the realization that they are worthless when measured against the divine. Wau says in conversation with his alter ego: "Worte . . . sind der Abfall seiner [God's] Grösse, der Unwert seines Wertes, und wo ich aufhöre zu sein, da hat auch das Wort sein selbiges Ende. Was bleibt mir, als durch meinen Unwert seinen Wert zu erweisen? Darum, immer Worte gemacht, viele und frische, es kann nicht genug werden der strömenden Töne . . ." (p. 340).

The strident theological argument between Calan and Noah suffers the same fate as the individual words. It was misunderstood by the pastor and his circle because they failed to see that Barlach had chosen the insoluble problem of evil as his debate topic and did not intend to formulate an answer to it. Actually the argument becomes quite confused when, for instance, Noah finds himself defending the position of his impious opponent before the Lord. It is an argument with words, and although it underlies the main conflict, it proves unimportant in itself when at the end Calan gives up his chattering and then in his physical blindness has his mystical vision.

In Barlach's thinking words are to being as surface is to space (*Briefe,* pp. 156-157, 178, 182). Ordinary human perception cannot take in the endless spaces of the universe; we see the stars as if they were all on one surface and cannot distinguish the variations in depth. Yet, to apply this idea to the play, with words as with the woodcarver's chisel it is possible to chip out a series of small surfaces and to create thereby a three-dimensional whole. Thus Barlach concentrates attention on certain phrases, concepts, and images and builds the pressure up to what he would call the crystallization point (the word "Kristallisierung" occurs repeatedly in his letters) where one must step back and view the construction in its spatial dimensions as "kristallisierte festgeformte Gestaltung" (*Briefe,* p. 136). In *Die Sündflut* this point comes at the end of Part IV and coincides with Calan's fall and new awareness. Calan is transformed from wealthy master to beggar and father. His sensual, physical self ("Beschaffenheit")[11] loses its former glory and becomes identified with the hunchbacked leper. He no longer dines in spendor but is food for vermin. But according to a letter to Edzard Schaper (*Briefe,* p. 136) it was the discovery in Russia (1906) of the fruitful tension between limitless space and crystallized form ("stilisiertes Menschentum") which led Barlach to make his first significant plastic works. And so here Calan's new awareness of himself and the world around him is followed immediately by blindness and the revelation that God has neither flesh nor form. This sudden change is particularly forceful because Barlach's diction has succeeded in evoking the full physicality of things and senses with an intensity so strong that they and even Calan's self crumble under the force.

Barlach is not simply negating the world as a "schlechtgelüfteter Engpass" (*Aus seinen Briefen,* p. 64). His statement is that only through sharpened awareness of the world, bad as it may be, can one attain the ultimate vision. It is important that only Calan and Awah, in her passive, naïve way, are completely open to sense experience. Observation of the imagery dealing with eyes and sight, ears and hearing will show that Noah is continually afraid of his senses and what they tell him. It is characteristic of him that he fails to see things and that he often puts his hands over his ears. He is frightened by the sound of his own words and by the temptation his eyes offer him. His attitude is summed up by his treatment of the leper; he repeatedly shoos him away. It is

precisely this caution which deafens and blinds him to the presence of the divine. Calan, on the other hand, is always testing, listening, looking, and asking to be shown.

The central idea of the play is contained in Calan's investigations and the discovery of the true nature of his "Beschaffenheit." This is, so to speak, his descent into hell. His experience is like Barlach's; he is "ganz hart und unmittelbar am Verwesen" but finds that total despair can lead to highest certainty (*Briefe,* pp. 71, 178). Noah and his sons succeed in avoiding the issue and remain prisoners of the flesh. Calan goes on to the ultimate station where he is lashed to the leper. Then, with eyes and flesh gnawed away and freed from the tyranny of the senses, he finds through this experience of his own body total acceptance and a perception of God as a luminous presence.

NOTES

[1] For the denial see Helmut Krapp, "Der allegorische Dialog," *Akzente* (1954), pp. 210-219. Hans Schwerte then corrects and refutes Krapp's arguments in "Über Barlachs Sprache," ibid., pp. 219-225.

[2] *Barlach im Gespräch,* abgezeichnet von Friedrich Schult (Insel-Verlag, 1948), p. 17.

[3] *Ernst Barlach: Leben und Werk in seinen Briefen,* ed. Friedrich Dross, (München, 1952), p. 142. Hereafter cited as *Briefe.*

[4] cf. Barlach's comments on "stilisiertes Menschentum" in *Briefe,* p. 61.

[5] *Expressionismus,* eds. Friedmann and Mann (Heidelberg, 1956), p. 340.

[6] *op. cit.,* see note 1.

[7] *Ernst Barlach: Die Dramen* (München, 1956)—further references will be made by page number.

[8] *Ernst Barlach: Aus seinen Briefen,* ed. Friedrich Dross (München, 1947), p. 62.

[9] cf. Wolfgang Kayser: *Kleine deutsche Versschule,* 4. erweiterte Auflage (Bern, 1954), pp. 95-96.

[10] Ernst Barlach: *Der gestohlene Mond* (Frankfurt, 1948), pp. 136-137.

[11] See p. 366: "Wer hat meiner Beschaffenheit befohlen, sich wie Aussatz an mich zu setzen . . . ?"

Edson M. Chick (essay date 1959)

SOURCE: "Comic and Grotesque Elements in Ernst Barlach," in *The Modern Language Quarterly,* Vol. 20, No. 1, March, 1959, pp. 173-80.

[In the following essay, Chick discusses Barlach's pre-occupation with grotesque humor.]

Wolfgang Kayser's *Das Groteske: Seine Gestaltung in Malerei und Dichtung,*[1] to which this article is heavily in debt, makes only passing reference to Ernst Barlach the graphic artist, and leaves Barlach the dramatist unmentioned. Yet to judge only by the repeated use of the word *grotesk* in Paul Fechter's *Ernst Barlach,*[2] one need not look far in any direction to find grotesque elements. From the ridiculous, disgusting, early drawing entitled "Liebespaar"[3]—two, fat, smirking, walrus-like figures reclining on bulbous pillows that seem a part of their bodies, the male fondling the female's breast while she looks at him with dull expectancy—to the more horrifying "Gott Bauch" in *Die Wandlungen Gottes* (1922); from the eating of the horse in *Der Tote Tag* (1912) to cannibalism in *Der Findling* (1922) and the "Teufelsküche" scene in *Der blaue Boll* (1926), they are there, a dominant characteristic of Barlach's work.

His letters, too, betray a preoccupation with grotesque humor from as early as 1895 in a homesick letter from Paris with its remarks on "der siegreiche deutsche Geist": "Wahrlich nicht die Schönheit und Lieblichkeit ist unsere Stärke, unsere Kraft, eher das Gegenteil, die Hässlichkeit, dämonische Leidenschaft und die groteske Genialität der Grösse, vor allem der Humor mit seinem Heer von originellen Gestalten."[4] And later (1928) to say, "Es ist ein Berg Humor in der Sündflut . . . ,"[5] is to confess a view of humor which practically identifies it with the grotesque.

There is, therefore, as little need for cataloging instances and episodes to prove the existence of grotesqueness here as there is to argue that in the dramas it works with a doubled potency through both visual and auditory senses. Rather it will suffice, for now anyway, to be eclectic, to look at one play and a few sections of other works and thus arrive at some conclusions about what makes them grotesque and about the importance of the grotesque in Barlach's poetic world.[6]

Of all Barlach's plays *Die echten Sedemunds* (1920)[7] is most like traditional comedy. It has many of the archaic ritualistic traits of Attic comedy described by F. M. Cornford.[8] It is full of personal invective and references to the human digestive and reproductive systems. It also has near the conclusion something like a marriage procession (Kômos) as well as a battle between a new and an old king (Sedemunds junior and senior) and a near miraculous rejuvenation of the latter. The play ends with the prospect of a marriage between Sedemund senior and a secondary female figure. Besides this, there are the comical, or farcical, results of the false rumor that a lion has escaped from the menagerie; respected riflemen at the "Schützenfest" are allowed to boast of their bravery and then later are helpless to hide their cowardice when they think the lion nearby.

There is comedy, too, in the language: Uncle Waldemar's speech defect, which makes his pretentious way of speaking even more ridiculous; dialect; and the murdering of the German language by foreigners (for example, the name of the lion is changed from Cäsar to Schesar and finally through misunderstanding to Scheisser).[9] In general, what Barlach makes laughable is the weakness of the flesh; the play shows persons embarrassed by their instinct of fear or, in Bergson's words, "the soul *tantalised* by the needs of the body."[10]

The color and confusion of the "Schützenfest" and the large number of equally colorful characters give the play that fullness and concreteness which comic presentation needs to fill the soul with sensuousness and, to quote further from Jean Paul,[11] "mit jenem Dithyrambus sie entflammen, welcher die im Hohlspiegel eckig und lang auseinandergehende Sinnenwelt gegen die Idee aufrichtet und sie ihr entgegenhält." But there is something more unsettling in Barlach's concern with body and senses than simply the distortion of Jean Paul's concave mirror. And there is more to the comedy in *Die echten Sedemunds* than our appreciation of what Bergson calls a person embarrassed by his body.

The play begins not with the carnival atmosphere of the "Schützenfest," but rather with the somber meeting of two apprentices. One carries a funeral wreath; the other carries a child's coffin, but does not know where to deliver it. We are told immediately that hard by the new "Schützenhaus" lies the old graveyard and that some unspecified person is to be buried this day. Then, too, there are the two undertakers, Gierhahn and Ehrbahn, as well as pallbearers and a hearse driver who suddenly cuts the ears off his horses. These figures and situations, while potentially comic, have also a morbid aspect of equal force.

Nor are all the scenes laid in the "Schützengarten." The crucial one (V. Bild), where young Sedemund accuses his father of killing his mother, takes place before the ancestral tomb in the old churchyard. It begins with a bit of farce, when Gierhahn and Ehrbahn think they have the lion cornered, but ends on a morbid note so that a spectator wonders: "Ich weiss nicht, war es lustig oder traurig" (*Die Dramen*, p. 238). There is the same comic-uncanny ambiguity about the Kômos-like procession from the church to the cemetery. It begins "halb als Karnevalzug, halb als Leichenparade" (p. 248). The marchers are "Höllenbraten" and "Höllenbrüder" (p. 250), and they are led by a hurdy-gurdy man. Finally, the play closes with a happy couple dancing "gerade über die Gräber hin, mitten zwischen dem Grauen durch" (p. 265).

This, then, is one thing Barlach adds to the "humoristische Sinnlichkeit" suggested by Jean Paul: he keeps his audience aware of the dark side of sensuality, of death and decay. His characters are not simply embarrassed by the needs of their bodies; they are also uncomfortably conscious of the corrupt nature of the flesh. To judge by their figures of speech, they are obsessed by the stomach in particular. One maintains that all life is "ein Fressprozess, ein Verwandlungs- und Verdauungswunder" (p. 222). And when he sees the mangy pelt of the lion people had feared would eat them, Sedemund senior comes to the conclusion that "Fressen und gefressen werden scheint auf gewisse Art dasselbe zu sein" (p. 251). Even the old man's rejuvenation is described as a digestive process: "der Löwe beisst dich. Der gute Löwe verwandelt dich als Frass in sich" (p. 245).

The process, however, is not always so smooth. The diet of lion with its moral implications gives some people indigestion, and, according to old Sedemund, even Christ would be unable to stomach knowledge of Sedemund family affairs. "Er wird sich brechen über uns und sich beschmutzen" (p. 245), he says, pointing to a statue of the Savior. Actually only Sedemund senior and the supposedly insane Grude enjoy this consumption and transformation, and not all the eating at the "Schützenfest" is so cosmic or metaphysical. The second and third scenes take place in the garden where many people are dining and drinking. Here, for instance, the miserable tailor Mankmoos satisfies his hunger with "Eierrühr" while his child goes hungry.

Barlach seems to find the bar or restaurant a convenient background for comic-grotesque scenes in many of his other works as well. *Der arme Vetter* (1918)[12] has one where, to be sure, no lion is lurking in a graveyard nearby. Instead, a dense fog has closed in around the inn at Lüttenbargen, and a young suicide, not yet dead, is the center of attention and ridicule. The "Wirtsstube" is full of people waiting for the boat to leave, and the stage directions call for "tobendes Verlangen . . . nach Speise und Trank" (p. 143). The master of ceremonies is grotesquely costumed as Frau Venus and surrounded by his court. His wit is predominantly scatological, but it ranges over the whole anatomy. He defends it and his drunkenness with the words: "Mein Humor ist kein Miesekätzchen . . . ich muss etwas Feuchtes in der Nase haben" (p. 149).

A member of the audience accommodates by blowing his nose and offering the handkerchief then to Frau Venus saying, "Wollen Sie auch mal?" (p. 149). He then cannot understand everyone's disgust: "Mir rätselhaft—ist doch einerlei Humor." He is wrong about this, for his is only one of the several kinds of humor here which might well be distinguished by the varying admixtures of disgust. Disgust is the most important word in this scene, disgust aroused by the wet handkerchief, by the grotesque dummy called "der schöne Emil," and in general by the flesh and its appetites. The dummy and, in fact, everything that goes on here is part of what Frau Venus calls an "Ekelkur" (p. 147), and it is disgust with the flesh and this world that has driven young Iver to suicide.

Cannibalism, too, can be a cure. Iver looks at the hungry crowd and says: "dabei komme ich mir vor wie unter Kannibalen, sehen Sie nur, wie er mich mit den Augen anbeisst, sie alle fressen ein Stück von mir, saufen mein

Blut—vielleicht bin ich ihnen doch ein Tropfen gutes Gift" (p. 152). Cannibalism would seem the grotesque motif without parallel. Barlach often presents scenes of gluttony to revolt the viewer, but his most immediately affecting passages are those that deal with the eating of human flesh. To be sure, the eating of the symbolic horse in *Der tote Tag* and the references to cannibalism on a cosmic plane in *Der arme Vetter* and *Sedemunds* ("fressen und gefressen werden") are little more than suggestive. Yet it is quite real in *Der Findling,* where the bloody remains are displayed on the stage. In all cases it is a reminder of bestiality in men and arouses a total moral and instinctive revulsion. It excites what Michel, in his definition of disgust, calls "der panische Schrecken des . . . Leibes, eine Empfindung, die schon an und für sich eine Erniedrigung des Geistes bedeutet" (*Das Teuflische,* p. 67).

Another and even better example of the tavern scene and this kind of disgust, practically unrelieved, is found in the first chapter of the novel fragment *Seespeck.*[13] Here our laughter, if any, is compulsive and uncomfortable, as when one laughs at deformity or insanity. The episode has sufficient comic ingredients, but in part because of the point of view the finished product has almost no humor; it evokes disgust and terror. The fat, slovenly baker (another Frau Venus) who commands our attention has an evil quality about him, for this obscene mountain of flesh is not in the least embarrassed by the needs of his body. In fact, although he has long since satisfied his appetite, he continues to consume beer and cookies soaked in the same, befouling his front with the wet crumbs from his slobbering mouth. In the subterranean atmosphere of the ship's bar his audience grows, and he drinks and dunks with renewed delight as if saying: "Wenn ihr nur wüsstet, was für ein Ekel ich bin" (p. 17).

The baker is the incarnation of disgust. To make him even more oppressive, he is unpredictable and always on the attack. His most telling weapons are self-degradation and a total lack of shame. His actions reveal an extreme distortion and negation of human dignity, "Offenbarungen der Verblödung und der Selbstzerstückelung, der Verunehrung und Ableugnung alles Heiligen und überhaupt des menschlich Würdigen, Graden, Ganzen. Und das Schlimme schien, dass . . . die Entwürdigung mit Prahlerei gesalzen wurde" (p. 15). Yet, for all the bragging, the baker's gestures are sometimes like those of a condemned man, telling in pantomime of all his pain and guilt.

But the baker is not the only one condemned. He has selected a victim, the blank-faced Hemis,[14] a figure as grotesque as the baker but for quite different reasons. Hemis' behavior is cool and his face as rigid as a mask except for the eyes which are mobile and seem to absorb everything. At first he has nothing but scorn for his opponent; but his insatiable eyes undo him, and he becomes helpless, hypnotized by what revolts him. The baker seizes his advantage and degrades him, as Frau

Venus did Iver, before the others, who occasionally find the spectacle repugnant. In his weakness and abject terror Hemis seems to the onlooker Seespeck the personification of "Lebensangst,"[15] a man of fifty years who has avoided all strong emotional experience. With his sensitivity and anxiety he is not only the perfect victim, but also the direct opposite of the baker.

Seespeck, too, is imprisoned here in the cabin by his own disgusted fascination; he has stayed on against his better judgment. Finally, he tries to rescue poor Hemis, but he finds himself suddenly face to face with the monster. On being subjected to the same degrading treatment, he makes a surprise attack and kicks the baker in the belly, "dass er dem fetten Ungetüm sein Leibliches schmerzlich zu Gefühl brachte" (p. 22). This unreasoned act corresponds to what Barlach tries to accomplish here and elsewhere, namely, to make the reader or spectator painfully aware of his corporeal nature.

Like the kick, most of the action in the episode is sudden and unexpected, and the effect is unsettling. The entire episode is seen through Seespeck's eyes, and as he becomes enthralled by the disgusting spectacle, so does the reader. To make matters worse, his vision is disturbed by a hangover, so that even before he meets the baker the process of alienation and disruption has begun. His usual condition is so perverted "dass es ihm zu Mute war, als stände er ohne Halt auf einer hohen Leiter oder als fasste ihn . . . ein Schwindel, weil er in einen Spiegel schaute, in dem sich alles bewegte, was sonst ruhig lag und stand" (p. 9).

Jean Paul's concave mirror reflected but a mild caricature of the world of the senses. Its grotesque counterpart, Seespeck's mirror, reflects a world in dissolution and affects him with dizziness and nausea, which are aggravated by the ship's rocking and by the baker, to the point of extreme disgust, "der panische Schrecken des . . . Leibes" (Michel). Also because of his own excesses of the night before, Seespeck suffers, like Hemis, under a hypersensitivity, so that things become magnified far out of proportion. The awareness that his tie keeps slipping down distresses him painfully; when the baker sticks out his tongue and Hemis responds with a stare, we have not a childish situation but rather a deadly serious duel.

All this makes the effect of the scene grotesque rather than comic, for with a change in perspective the baker might well have been a clown rather than a monster. Comedy, says Bergson repeatedly, must not arouse our feelings; but in the first chapter of *Seespeck,* as elsewhere in Barlach, the aim is precisely to arouse the reader's feelings. The crowds in Barlach's barrooms may be able to laugh in detachment at the spectacle of the baker or Frau Venus, but the reader is made to feel discomfort. To excite this feeling Barlach lets loose in long periods a flood of words like *Scheusslichkeit, Kot, Ersticken, erwürgen, stinkende Blasen aus dem Sumpf, boshaft, unheimlich,* and so forth, until the episode comes to an arbitrary end with the boat's docking. Yet even with the tension eased, the narrator adds another image of distortion to the great accumulation: as the baker walks off, "sein Schatten äffte es ihm nach und übertrieb alles in die Breite und Dicke" (p. 29). This is, however, only a weak reverberation of what has gone before. In spewing forth his disgust in hyperboles piled one on another with little obvious sense of proportion, it seems as if Barlach has exhausted the powers of exaggeration in himself and the language.

Barlach employs language and sound for grotesque purposes just as he does other features of style. In later works he uses words in a more artful way than he does in *Seespeck,*[16] thus achieving what is really a more direct effect on the mind and senses. Certain phrases, words, and sounds are stressed, repeated, and piled up, like the impressions of the baker, to give the language a cumulative, oppressive force. This is not Bergson's comic, Jack-in-the-box kind of repetition where words are repressed and repeatedly spring up anew (*Comedy,* p. 107). It is rather an insistent, pounding repetition. Like the hard stress in the frequent alliterative passages of his plays, it disturbs rather than delights with its rude forcing of language and syntax. The constant accentuation of little words like *Bauch* and *Frass* seems at first to give them real substance. But in the end they suffer the same semantic exhaustion as do repeated abstractions like *Würde* and *Gerechtigkeit.*

Thus the grotesque extremes of sensuality (the baker) and cool abstraction (Hemis) show up again here. The recurrent stress on the sensuous element, or meat, of certain words makes them finally sound absurd, as when the "Chor der Rache" in *Der arme Vetter* picks up the phrase "Geh du—ich nicht," and changes it to a string of nonsense syllables by singing to the tune of "Krambambuli": "Geduichnicht—gedaichnicht—gedaichnicht—gedu—geda—geda—ich nicht" (*Die Dramen,* p. 147). On the other hand, repetition of abstract words with varying, often contradictory connotations renders them equally meaningless.

But this is not all. Barlach's works are not just nightmarish, cold grotesques, nor do they show the same cynicism about language as do the productions of today's French theater of alienation exemplified by Eugene Ionesco. They have a religious warmth and make a paradoxical statement of faith. Granting that words are worthless for knowing in the ordinary sense, Barlach thinks that they nevertheless have an unlimited potential and that to use them properly is something like an act of reverence. He writes in a letter to Pastor Zimmermann (1932):

> Sehen Sie, man will "wissen" und verlangt nach dem Wort, aber das Wort ist untauglich, bestenfalls eine Krücke für die, denen das Humpeln genügt. Und dennoch ist im Wort etwas, was direkt ins Innerste dringt, wo es aus dem Lautersten, der absoluten Wahrheit kommt. . . . Das Nichts am Wortmässigen mag wohl noch ans Absolute

grenzen—Zahl, Ton, reine Form sind Heger der Geheimnisse. . . . (*Leben und Werk in seinen Briefen,* p. 178)

Similarly Barlach's works do more than show us the grotesque extremes of sensuality and "Lebensangst." Characters at the extreme ends of the scale—the baker and Hemis, the fat Zebid and Noah *(Sündflut),* Otto Prunkhorst and Grete Grüntal *(Der blaue Boll)*—are caught by their obsessions in this lower phase of existence which Barlach calls a "schlechtgelüfteter Engpass" *(Aus seinen Briefen,* p. 64). But they usually are foils for thoughtful sensualists like Seespeck, Calan *(Sündflut),* and Boll, who are ready to risk transformation ("Werden") and elevation out of this phase. Because they are aware of the grotesque dissonances in themselves and this world and because they do not run away, they are transformed. They have appetites but are not gluttonous, nor are they afraid of being eaten. Calan's vision of divine being comes only after he has stayed behind the Ark and vermin have gnawed away his flesh and eyes. These central figures are strong and have a sense of humor. Their vision has distance. *Der Findling* is the least appealing of all Barlach's plays because, with the exception of the final pages, the disgust and horror are unrelieved, the diction and action chaotic, and there is no strong central figure. The disgust is so overpowering that the "Ekelkur" and epiphany at the end seem quite arbitrary.

In prose and drama Barlach is, therefore, working to the end Paul Fechter describes in respect to his graphic and plastic work:

> sein immer wiederkehrendes Ringen nämlich mit dem Geist der Schwere, sein Versuch ihn so weit zu besiegen, dass es gelingt, den Menschen wenigstens im Bilde von der Erde zu lösen, ihn in den Zustand des Schwebens, des Aufsteigens aus dem Bereich des Chtonischen in die reineren Lüfte zu bringen. (*Ernst Barlach,* pp. 50-51)

And he accomplishes this through the grotesque which is, in Friedrich Dürrenmatt's words, "ein sinnliches Paradox, die Gestalt nämlich einer Ungestalt, das Gesicht einer gesichtslosen Welt."[17] Baudelaire points to the same paradox when he says that, whereas laughter caused by comedy is the expression of man's superiority over man, laughter caused by the grotesque is the expression of the idea of man's superiority over nature.[18]

NOTES

[1] Wolfgang Kayser, *Das Groteske: Seine Gestaltung in Malerei und Dichtung* (Oldenburg/Hamburg, 1957).

[2] Paul Fechter, *Ernst Barlach* (Gütersloh, 1957).

[3] Wilhelm Michel, *Das Teuflische und das Groteske in der Kunst* (München, 1919), p. 21.

[4] Ernst Barlach, *Aus seinen Briefen,* ed. Friedrich Dross (München, 1947), p. 28.

[5] Ernst Barlach, *Leben und Werk in seinen Briefen,* ed. Friedrich Dross (München, 1952), p. 142.

[6] In his final chapter Kayser contents himself with an attempt at a "Wesensbestimmung" or phenomenological definition of the term *grotesque,* with the help of a few characteristic motifs, and comes to the conclusion that it involves a playing with the absurd and is itself the attempt "das Dämonische in der Welt zu bannen und zu beschwören" (p. 202). Beyond this, one can say that good grotesque literature appears in times of transition, is morally serious and even mystical. It seeks to delight and instruct by means of horror, disgust, the diabolic, estrangement, and the incongruity which appears in the contradiction between new conditions or content and old forms. In modern literature a serious concern with the body and the biological underlies the grotesque mode and emerges in the shape of fanatic purity and/or obsession with filth and decay. The latter definition relies in part on Kayser and the following discussions of the term: Kenneth Burke, *Attitudes toward History* (New York, 1937), pp. 49 ff. and 73 ff.; and William Van O'Connor, "The Grotesque in Modern American Fiction," *College English,* XX (1959), 342-46.

[7] A drama of unmasking and the conflict between generations. During a "Schützenfest" in a small town someone spreads a rumor that the lion—actually dead—has escaped. In the resulting terror and confusion the masks of false respectability worn by the first citizens begin to fall. Young Sedemund, whose father wants to send him to an insane asylum, confronts his father and forces him to confess publicly that he has in effect caused his mother's suicide by tricking her into a false confession of infidelity. The elder Sedemund later shows that he had good reasons for doing this to his self-righteous wife and in the course of the action proves to be more of a man than his son, who finally goes—by now a sobered reformer—voluntarily to the asylum. He does this so that the distressing disclosures can be blamed on his insanity and everything can return to normal.

[8] F. M. Cornford, *Origin of Attic Comedy* (London, 1914), pp. 8, 57, 84 ff.

[9] Ernst Barlach, *Die Dramen* (München, 1956), p. 201.

[10] Henri Bergson, "Laughter," *Comedy,* Doubleday Anchor Books A 87 (Garden City, N. Y., 1956), p. 93.

[11] Jean Paul, *Vorschule der Aesthetik,* Erste Abtheilung, 35.

[12] This dream revolves around the figure of Hans Iver, who on a Sunday outing has shot himself out of despair and disgust with this world and his own "Selbstsein." The real action, however, takes place in the souls of two other individuals, Siebenmark and Fräulein Isenbarn. Through Iver they arrive at a clear understanding of themselves and the fact that their marriage would be impossible; it would be a surrender to the godless,

purely sensual world represented by the demonic festivities at the inn where the crowd and the many characters gather.

[13] Ernst Barlach, *Seespeck* (Berlin, 1948).

[14] The name is read Hannis in *Die Prosa,* I (München, 1958).

[15] Cf. Kayser: "Es geht beim Grotesken nicht um Todesfurcht, sondern um Lebensangst" (p. 199).

[16] Barlach stopped work on *Seespeck* in 1916.

[17] Friedrich Dürrenmatt, *Theaterprobleme* (Zürich, 1955), p. 48.

[18] Charles Baudelaire, "On the Essence of Laughter," *Mirror of Art: Critical Studies,* trans. and ed. by Jonathan Mayne, Doubleday Anchor Books A 84 (Garden City, N.Y., 1956), p. 143.

Alfred Werner (essay date 1962)

SOURCE: "Ernst Barlach," in *The Kenyon Review,* Vol. XXIV, No. 4, Autumn, 1962, pp. 627-43.

[*In the following essay, Werner presents an overview of Barlach's reputation as an artist and writer.*]

The veneration of the sculptor and printmaker Ernst Barlach (1870-1938) in Central Europe has, so far, not spread much beyond the German-speaking nations. Britain's Art Council brought a large number of his works in 1961 from Germany (primarily Hamburg) to London, where they were viewed with respect rather than admiration. For one thing, there is in Barlach nothing of the non-figurative trend that has finally achieved a vogue in London. This trend was repugnant to Barlach. In a letter of 1911, to the publisher Reinhold Piper, he wrote:

> . . . my artistic language is the human figure or the object through which or in which man lives, suffers, rejoices, feels, thinks. . . . The things that arrest my attention are what a human being has suffered and is able to endure, his greatness, his concerns. . . .

He stressed the need for compassion, complained that he could not feel it in Kandinsky's "dots, specks, lines and smudges."

Nonfiguration is still considered the panacea in most artistic circles. Freedom of expression, even to a point of anarchy and confusion, is now another favored solution. Today, that aspect of German expressionism which seems to anticipate the unruliness of abstract-expressionism, action-painting, and tachism is quite acceptable in art circles. Significantly, the "expressionist" Rodin has been discovered recently, and a connection found between his gesticulating melodramas and Alexander Calder's free-swinging mobiles. A British reviewer of the Barlach show even asserted:

> Never . . . do his sculptural expressions of compassion and rage transport one to the heights Rodin could reach in his transformations of humanity. The eye appraises the postures and compact formalization of Barlach's figures without immediately identifying them with his universal message.

The recent brave attempt of New York's St. Etienne Gallery to reacquaint people here with Barlach's work[1]—no Barlachs have been shown here publicly since 1956—also met with misunderstanding by professional viewers. A *New York Times* critic dismissed him as a mere imitator of Gothic sculpture, though he liked the drawings ("The interaction between the artist and the paper gives many of his drawings a powerful sense of life"). But there were also positive voices, both in England and the U.S. In London's *Listener,* Nikolaus Pevsner declared: "If, for reasons of the violent but imprecise impacts of the abstract artists of today, those who care for art in this country have lost their appreciation of Van Gogh's *Potato Eaters* and consequently are unable to appreciate Barlach's *Beggars*—in that case I can only say goodbye." In the *Christian Science Monitor,* Dorothy Adlow explained: "His figures would be accepted and reckoned with more appreciatively in the Middle Ages when technique and style served ideas, and there was no straining for effect."

It ought to be possible to respond both to the block-like, firm, and often rather restrained "old-fashioned" pieces in bronze or wood by Barlach and to the latest neo-Dada transformations of iron sheets and bars into carriers of emotion. I believe that Barlach, though a confessed admirer of Gothic church art, in his simplifications and abbreviations was a thoroughly modern man, just as his religiosity, unlike that of the medieval carvers, was not bound to any dogma. It is also an error to link him too strongly with Emil Nolde and other expressionists, as is often done, for the leaders of *Expressionismus,* in their ardent desire to make visible the invisible, sometimes purposely violated the classic rules of composition and ignored the proper balance between the formal and the expressive. By contrast, Barlach's work proves, if such proof is necessary, that impulse can very well go along with discipline, eloquence with restraint.

Perhaps Americans will avail themselves of the opportunity to have a second, or third, look at Barlach this coming winter when no fewer than 150 of his works, assembled by the Smithsonian Institution, will be shown from coast to coast in a number of museums. Unfortunately, this exhibition will suffer from a considerable deficiency—not a single piece of wood will be on view. The lenders, German museums and private collectors, were, with some justification, unwilling to expose the fragile wood sculptures to the hazards of a year's travel. Yet Barlach was basically a carver. He needed the resistance as well as the warmth of wood to develop his plastic thought slowly. While he often made bronze versions of his wood pieces, in such versions the directness, the immediacy of appeal, is frequently lost.

To get a complete idea of Barlach's plastic oeuvre, one must travel through his native country, visit the museums, stand before the floating "Angel of Death" (the war memorial) in the Antonites Church in Cologne, and the *"Geistkaempfer"* ("Warrior of the Soul") outside the Nikolai Church in Kiel. A large *Barlach-Haus* has recently opened in Jenisch Park, a few miles west of downtown Hamburg. There can be viewed to full advantage the comprehensive collection of Germany's late cigarette king, Hermann Fuerchtegott Reemtsma, who continued to stand by his ostracized and ailing friend Barlach after the Nazis came to power. Less easy to reach are the treasures of the Ernst Barlach *Gedenkstaette* in Ratzeburg, a very old island town near Lübeck, where the artist's son Nikolaus is curator of the house in which his father spent part of his childhood (in the town cemetery, Ernst Barlach, his father, and grandfather are buried).

Out of bounds for most Western tourists is the city of Güstrow, 60 miles east of Lübeck, for it is in East Germany. Barlach scholars of the West are not permitted into this city where the artist lived and worked from 1910 until his death twenty-eight years later, and where his works are divided between his reconstructed studio and the *Gertrudenkapelle*. I was unable to obtain the books and catalogues prepared in Eastern, Communist-dominated Germany, but I have learned from *Art under a Dictatorship,* by Hellmut Lehmann-Haupt, that opinion as to the merits of Barlach is sharply divided there. Some years ago, when a Barlach exhibition was opened in East Berlin's German Academy of Art, Academy President Arnold Zweig, hailing the sculptor as a victim of Nazi terror, was joined by several East German papers in the praise of the artist and man. Yet the *Taegliche Rundschau,* which echoed the Soviet point of view, attacked Barlach's work for expressing "the anti-democratic tendencies of one section of the German intelligentsia." According to Lehmann-Haupt, the newspaper went on to say:

> His aesthetic theories served to justify the creations of a considerable number of artists who succumbed defenselessly to the anti-humanist tendencies of Imperialism. . . . His art is mystical in content, anti-realistic in its form. It is strongly dominated by anti-democratic tendencies and is an example of the crisis of ugliness in art.

German attitudes to Barlach offer, indeed, a bewildering example of a nation unaware of its great responsibility to true genius. For a short time only did Barlach enjoy fame and a modicum of financial security. When he was sixty, a large retrospective exhibition of his work was opened at the Prussian Academy of Art. Hitler was already *ante portas* when the same academy awarded him the *Pour le Mérite* medal. A few weeks later Barlach

was a doomed man. As early as April 1933 he wrote to his friend, the publisher Reinhold Piper, in Munich:

> These stirring times don't agree with us. My little boat is sinking fast. . . . I wear no nationalist get-up, sport no patriotic style, noise upsets me— instead of cheering, the louder the "Heils" roar, instead of raising my arm in Roman attitudes, the more I pull my hat down over my eyes. . . . There's only one thing I'm afraid of—getting softened-up and half-hearted, being fitted in.

It is unnecessary to relate in detail the six years of humiliation and torture that were in store for him. The reactionaries who, from the mid-'20s onward, had attacked his art for its expressionist and magical qualities—features insufferable to the Communists as well— were in power. Close to 400 of his works were removed from museums and galleries, and the war memorials he had fashioned for several cities were removed and, in some cases, destroyed (Barlach had committed the sin of telling the onlooker that war was something tragic, something terrible, rather than a happy hunting excursion). *"Das Wiedersehen"*—two gaunt figures (Christ and Apostle John) touching each other gently—was included in Munich's "Degenerate Art" exhibition. There were no commissions (with the exception of the work he continued to do for his friend Reemtsma) and finally he was forbidden to execute any work whatever. Fellow-townsmen cut him on the street; hoodlums smashed the windows of his studio. He was urged by friends to emigrate. A foreign artist, who came to Güstrow on a mission to get him out of the cursed land, found him in a state of frantic anxiety, feeling himself constantly watched and spied upon by his enemies. By August 1938 Barlach was so desperate that he was ready to forsake the country to which he was so intimately linked. Yet body and mind had been strained too much. On October 24 he was dead. Ostensibly, he died what is called a "natural death," yet there can be no doubt that years of relentless persecution had aggravated his malady, a heart ailment, and hastened his end.

A few courageous people, some themselves personae non gratae, gathered in Güstrow to bid farewell to the body; among these was Käthe Kollwitz, who drew his deathbed portrait. The only German newspaper that dared publish an appreciative obituary notice was the *Frankfurter Zeitung* that had somehow managed to retain a bit of independence. In a small magazine, Theodor Heuss, the future president of the Bonn Republic, tried to give a true picture of the deceased. But the majority of necrologies were hostile. The Elite Guard organ, *Das Schwarze Korps,* sternly rejected Barlach as an un-German, Slavic, unbalanced artist whose figures were reminiscent of unstable lunatics!

In the Bonn Republic he is now revered as a saint, even among the artists who came to the fore after 1945 and who in the international convention twist inert material into fantastic shapes that are additions to, rather than reminders of, the visible world. Far from being dismissed as passé, Barlach is acknowledged as Germany's first modern sculptor, as one who broke with the official style when the country was dominated by pompous Bismarckian art. As Alfred Hentzen, director of Hamburg's *Kunsthalle,* put it, Barlach's significance in modern German sculpture consists primarily in "the discovery of completely simple, elementary means and in the absolute honesty of the deeply-felt, new sensuous content." Others see him as a maverick *sui generis* who stood between modern industrial life and the turmoil of the Middle Ages, without belonging to either era, and whose work reminds one of medieval music in dimly lit cathedrals at one moment and of the horrors of the twentieth century at the next. Barlach, who was born the son of a country doctor in Wedel, a small town on the Lower Elbe, did, of course, go through the mill of rigid and unimaginative academic instruction that, around 1890, prevailed in art schools all over the world. His first teacher in Hamburg, a Dane and a pupil of Thorwaldsen, soon advised him to give up art since he would never create anything worthwhile. In Paris, he studied for some months at the Académie Julian, but became dissatisfied with what he later described as "miserable, monotonous accuracies, states of a miserable, monotonous nakedness of male and female, offerings so lacking in consolation that I could not understand why one should go to the trouble. . . ."

He returned to Germany and settled in Berlin.

His early work, done in the spirit of the ornamental *Jugendstil,* is not very original, rarely reproduced, and even more infrequently exhibited. Barlach did not find his true manner, fully expressive of his own self, before he was thirty-seven. Artistic experiences helped to free him. He must have seen the exhibition of Cézanne and Van Gogh in Berlin after 1900. In any event, his mature figures have the solid position and stolid look characteristic of Cézanne's monumental card players, the pensive "Boy in a Red Vest," or the proto-cubist portraits of Gustave Geoffrey and of Madame Cézanne. Spiritually, however, Barlach's works are more closely related to Van Gogh's pathos and fervor (in his letters, Barlach quotes Carlyle and Nietzsche, mentions Bach and Beethoven, but, apart from the rejection of Kandinsky, avoids references to any art except his own artistic struggle).

The profound vision, the "Damascus," was a two-month stay in Russia. Earlier, the young poet, Rainer Maria Rilke, had gone to Russia, to be impressed for the remainder of his life by an Easter celebration in a church in Moscow. To a friend Rilke wrote: "I believe that Russia will give me the words for those religious depths of my nature that have been striving to enter into my work since I was a child." Barlach, who visited a brother employed as an engineer at Kharkov, had deep and transfiguring visual experiences. Both the poet and the sculptor had traveled eastward in a mood of spiritual dissatisfaction, hoping to find solace in a milieu that had been made immensely popular by Tolstoy's narra-

tives. Seeing, on the steppe, the short, squat, round-headed, flat-faced beggars, monks, pilgrims, and peasant women who, to a large extent, were to become his principal subject matter for the three decades to follow, Barlach exclaimed, *"Donnerwetter, da sitzen Bronzen!"* ("Damn it, these are sitting bronzes!"). He was never to forget these moujiks untainted by any veneer of civilization, monumental in their immobility, set against the immensity of the steppe always waiting, but not knowing for whom or for what. He brought back landscape sketches that, in their melancholy starkness, are reminiscent of Van Gogh's production at Nuenen. More important, he found himself, opened for himself a road away from contemporary materialism and rationalism toward a new and higher metaphysics.

The Nazis were to object violently to Barlach's "Slavic" types, which were diametrically opposed to the so-called Nordic ideal of beauty. For Barlach these pre-1914 Russians epitomized all the misery of the human race and its desires for salvation. He himself expressed it in saying:

> I found in Russia this amazing unity of inward and outward being, this symbolic quality: this is what we human beings are, at bottom all beggars and *problematische Existenzen* . . . it shines out of the Slav, where others hide it.

After his return to Germany, he began the series of Russian beggars and wanderers that was to become very popular—more popular than his later, more spiritual, more mystical work, done after 1910. For a while a bit of genre art still tinged the productions of 1907-10, even though Barlach kept naturalistic details to a minimum. Although the master was entirely unaware of the cubism of this period that strove to transform natural shapes into geometric or stereometric elements, his figures, too, are composed of subtle, well-balanced combinations of spheres and cubes. The cerebral chill of so much cubist sculpture is absent. Take the "Beggar Woman" of 1907: with her bent back, hooded face, and hands extended in a beseeching gesture, she expresses graphically the humiliation of anyone requesting charity. A tragic beauty hovers over this work that is so free from all sentimentalizing, so deeply personal—and, at the same time, so broadly symbolic. Two decades later he produced the "Singing Man," who reclines on the ground, oblivious to anything but his song, his eyes closed to shut out any possible disturbing influence. A formal analysis *à la* Woelfflin would point out the clever architecture of slanting planes, but might miss the humanity in which this piece is drenched. One is reminded of Barlach's stern warning: "Whosoever concerns himself with aesthetics for its own sake, does something much akin to a sin against the Holy Spirit." The most famous of Barlach's smaller pieces is, perhaps, "The Avenger" (1914)—mind and body of this sword-wielding man are involved in one swift, brutal movement. As a correspondent of the *Christian Science Monitor,* writing from Berlin in 1929, so aptly put it: "It is not the representation of the world of form that Barlach seeks: it is the evidence of the inner man."

Work, work, and more work—in these words Barlach's life can be encompassed. At thirty-nine he made the last of his few journeys outside Germany—to Florence. Thereafter he settled in Güstrow, where his mother made a home for him and his out-of-wedlock son. Thanks to avant-garde dealers in Berlin, first Paul Cassirer and then Alfred Flechtheim, who supplied him with funds, and thanks to commissions for large monuments that he received from several city governments, Barlach was not required to engage personally in selling his own work—which would have been a difficult task for this shy, unaggressive, almost misanthropic man. Now and then he would pay a brief visit to Berlin—an unforgettable figure: a small thin man, wrapped in an old brown havelock, his somber, lean face surrounded by a short beard. He had large, earnest eyes, with dark, hollow pouches underneath, and a melancholy, severe mouth beneath a small moustache. Those who recall him describe him as a curious mixture of a simple craftsman and a fantastic creature to whom a role in one of his surrealist dramas might easily be assigned.

For an American, unfamiliar with Barlach's North German background and Gothic as well as Russian sources of inspiration, it may require some time to feel at home in this world of what appear to be bizarre and grotesque gestures, to appreciate Barlach's heavy seriousness, sometimes turned into grim, macabre humor. Yet it is impossible to remain unimpressed by this artist's stupendous ability to express fundamental human traits by the simplest means, to give voice to the essence of things rather than to depict their superficial features, and, at the same time, to exploit to the fullest the intrinsic possibilities of the materials. Slowly, one becomes accustomed to his mysticism combined with biblical simplicity, to his demoniacal passion and tortured introspection, much of which is rooted in the fog-ridden, eerie atmosphere of the Holstein region which nurtured his youth.

In one of his many letters, Barlach maintained that the true face within all matter is not revealed if the artist does not show his *own* face. Of course, he did not refer to the features that we know from his photographs, nor even to the unforgettable transfigurations he had drawn with charcoal or with lithographic crayon. He had in mind the *inner* face, the distillation of his fervent personality that sought a path to perfection neither through religion nor through machinery. Barlach urges us to strive for perfection. For Barlach, form cannot be divorced from content—the technical and aesthetic qualities have the same insoluble relationships to the emotional core as has man's body to his mind.

For in those heavy and squat, and sometimes attenuated and ascetically lean, monolithic pieces we have authentic sculpture: solid, stout, self-contained objects, direct in deportment, firm to the grasp, devoid of all unnecessary detail, often static in appearance, yet always overflowing with inner movement, what the artist called the "crystallization of the human form." Whatever medium this versatile man employed, he summarized the factual data in so bold a manner as to come, now and then, close to abstraction, without ever losing communication with the beholder. Nearly always, the body is concealed under loose clothing, so that the burden of expression is placed on face and hands. He even went so far as to conceal under a thick cloak the whole figure, except for a pair of bony hands.

For his very large work—such as the aforementioned "Warrior of the Soul" at Kiel (an angel with an uplifted sword who treads upon a rapacious animal) or the floating figure commemorating the war dead—bronze was essential. Yet his most personal works are the smaller figures in wood. He was the very opposite of Rodin, who was essentially a modeler. Though he was in Paris when Rodin was at the height of his fame, Rodin's impressionist passion for light and shade, and, in particular, the play of light over the rippling surfaces of shaped metal, did not appeal to the young German (who accepted only the "Balzac"). For Rodin, who often gave birth to things which grew quickly between his fingers without any premeditation, clay was the proper medium. Barlach, however, who was slow and philosophical, preferred the arduous, time-consuming method of cutting directly into wood. Wood was perfectly suited to his unsuave, unurbane, rustic personality; he knew its character and limitations, never camouflaged its surface, never disguised its color, respecting its texture and grain, and exploring all its potentialities. Completely oblivious of the necessity of food and sleep, as though he were driven by a demonic force, he would doggedly hammer away at the block for days and nights, betraying a robust strength unexpected in that short, slight, and slender man. He would choose a block whose shape fitted his idea, sometimes a pillar, and at other times a cube, visualizing the dormant statue in the primitive shape. Unlike others, he did not have first to knead his vision in clay; instead, he was able to carve the wood without any major preparation, throwing himself into the work with the frenzy of one totally obsessed by a single idea. Also, he did not require a professional model—he did not want his shapes to be too "real," to allow photographic realism to separate his creation from his emotion.

In his treatment of wood, he is reminiscent of the Gothic carvers. He attacked the material with thousands of hammer blows, chipping off tiny bits of wood passionately, yet also patiently, until the desired image emerged with all the required clarity and sharpness. Whereas academic sculptors would polish the surface as carefully as possible, Barlach never concealed the marks of his tools, all the facets, all the countless little planes indicative of the work's organic growth under his knowing hands. Through this homogeneous method of "chip carving" he endowed the forms with an extraordinary pulsation of life, with a vibrating quality lacking in the work of more timid men who sought to vivify their creations by trying carefully to duplicate the actual textures of skin, hair, or garment.

Due to their rhythmic articulation and flowing lines, his sculptures have a singing quality, even though his work—diametrically opposed to baroque sculpture—is essentially restrained and self-contained, "motionless" in the sense that it does not try to advance beyond the natural shape of the block. In this, Barlach was closer to archaic sculpture of all nations, to African art, and, most of all, to the images adorning medieval cathedrals, than he was to the effervescence of a Rodin. And while the egomaniac Rodin, when he wanted to be monumental, became imperial to the point of being impervious, Barlach, even in his larger works, remained "democratic," never forgetting that what he was giving was a perishable man's work, subjected to the whims of fate.

One might, perhaps, turn to his letters to learn the deepest things about his work, to watch him grow, to note how clearly aware he was from the start of the aesthetic aims he had set himself. Only nineteen, he was already able to write that sculpture was his main vocation. He added: "I do not represent what I, myself, see from this or that angle, but rather, what is the Real and True; this I have to extract from what I see before me." He is not interested in perspective, foreshortening, lengthening, and "other tricks." He is opposed to reliefs because they lap over into the sphere of painting (he thus echoed the words of Michelangelo, who maintained that sculpture became worse the closer it approached painting).

A very significant letter was written in 1911, shortly after he had withdrawn to Güstrow. After stating that it was impossible for him to represent the mystical, uncanny being that was man in the usual naturalistic style, he continued:

> I feel that the outward appearance of man presents only a mask, and I attempted to look behind the mask. How, then, am I bound by the details of the mask? I know, of course, that the mask has grown organically from the thing that is basic; hence, I depend upon the mask after all. I have to find ways of representing what I feel and sense rather than what I see. Yet I must use what I see as a means to representation.

Finally, a letter which he wrote in 1926, after he had become one of the most celebrated artistic figures in the Weimar Republic. In this letter, he referred to the struggle that was the essence of his creative life, and underlined the stubbornness of his own character:

> I can create nothing except what is akin to my own self, my personality. Whatever I, as opposed to my personality, consider as limiting, as narrow, as determined, as cursed by mortality can all be ignored, I suppose, since I want to point out that I am searching for my true self in dark unconscious depths. It is probably sufficient today that I consider my "self" different from my "personality."

> All my works are merely parts of that unknown darkness—parts created to speak and act; hence, I cannot object when I hear it said that my

sculpture is nothing but an intermediate step between the Whence and Whereto.

But though Moses, Christ, the Lord hovering over the waters occupy central positions in his plastic and graphic works, he refused to be called a God-seeker, saying that he comprehended only that God was "incomprehensible."

Though his graphic work consists of more than 200 prints, they are less widely known than his sculptures. Some of these lithographs and woodcuts illustrated Barlach's own poetic plays, while others decorated new special editions of works by other poets. Käthe Kollwitz fervently admired him as a printmaker. In a diary entry of June 25, 1920, she writes of a show in Berlin: "I saw something that bowled me over: Barlach's woodcuts." (It was his example that made her turn to this medium.) These are characterized by the same rugged strength that we admire in his sculptures, the same bold, massive forms permeated with passion. Although he has left us numerous lithographs, the more resisting wood was better suited to his nature. "The woodcut," he wrote in a letter, "demands complete avowal, an unequivocal precipitation of what one really means. It dictates a certain universal expression and rejects an amiable or easy solution." Indeed, Barlach is often more convincing, aesthetically, in the medium of the woodcut than in anything else he produced. Intuitively he knew that a metaphysical message should be presented like a piece of writing, in black and white, to avoid distortion by the impact of color. While the medium imposes certain limitations upon the artist, it also allows great emotional tensions through the contrasts between heavy blacks and stark whites; it affords severity and clarity through a direct and simple statement. Notable, in particular, are the twenty woodcuts to "Walpurgis Night" (a scene in the second part of Goethe's *Faust*), the ten woodcuts to Schiller's "Ode to Joy" (the poem which Beethoven used in his Ninth Symphony), and the eight woodcuts, "The Manifestations of God" (published in an album without text). In his autobiography, Barlach speaks of the astounding realization that came over him:

> That you may dare without reserve to give out your very own—the innermost as well as the outermost, the gesture of blessing or the blast of wrath—since expression of everything is possible, whether it be a hellish paradise or a heavenly hell.

While many of his drawings merely served as preliminary studies for prints or three-dimensional works, he very often used pencil, black chalk, charcoal, or pen for creations that have an independent life of their own. As a matter of record, he had already a modicum of success as a draftsman, as a contributor of cartoons to *Fliegende Blaetter, Jugend,* and *Simplicissimus* before his sculptural talent was discovered and encouraged by the dealer Cassirer. Even though the work done prior to the Russian journey somewhat lacks originality, one cannot help being impressed by the devastating power of observation. Klinger, Klimt, Schiele, the early Pascin, and the early Kubin come to mind, as one admires young Barlach's draftsmanship that could express itself spontaneously in a maze of loose and scratchy scribbles, upon an ordinary sized sheet of paper, capable of blending tragedy with humor, the terrifying with sardonic laughter, physical ruthlessness with metaphysical implications. As he grew older, he needed fewer and fewer lines to capture the evanescent world of man in flashes of revelation, using the boldest perspective, abbreviation, for his excursions into the no man's land between the conscious and the unconscious, between the visible and the invisible, between waking and dreaming. Also, he often used the graphic media for portraiture (whereas there are only six or seven sculptured portrait heads), and especially for mercilessly frank and revealing self-portraits.

Those familiar with the German language can understand that among the new generation that has grown up since Barlach's death there are some who claim him to have been even bolder as a writer than as a plastic artist. There are three volumes of literary work (volume one, the plays; volumes two and three, prose). There can be no doubt that he was able to express himself verbally as powerfully as he was able to extract the maximum of value and wisdom from a piece of "dead wood." Among his prose writings one finds a lengthy autobiographical sketch, ending with the year 1910 when the financial arrangement he had made with the dealer Paul Cassirer allowed him to pursue his path without compromise. In these 50 pages, his gift for penetrating self-analysis and his subtle sense of humor are conspicuous. There are two large unfinished novels, and numerous short essays. Among these latter, the Russian travel observations are most valuable, for they throw light upon visual and emotional experiences that were to give to the world a new Barlach.

Barlach wrote eight plays. Thomas Mann admired them, and Barlach was even awarded the much-coveted Kleist Prize for one, *Die Suendflut (The Flood).* But while they were produced on the stages of Weimar Germany, they never played to full houses. Unlike the dramatic work of Toller, Werfel, Hasenclever, Von Unruh, and other expressionists, they avoided the favorite political or social topics of an era that seethed with revolutionary ferment. There is little action, and the dramatis personae seem to grope blindly for a path under the veiled skies and in the brooding mists of a spooky atmosphere. "Barlach's characters resemble figures carved in wood," wrote the celebrated critic Arthur Eloesser; "they are like anonymous sufferers in some tragedy of humanity, and go muffled in their sorrows as though in a heavy mantle laid upon their shoulders by fate."

Today, they might turn out to be the right fare for the off-Broadway theatre that has successfully staged works by Ionesco, Beckett, Albee, and others who, like Barlach, write plays which are fraught with symbolic significance and which skillfully fuse tragedy with humor, the real with an unreal world.[2] Barlach's work differs, however,

from the drama of the 1960s in that it is concerned with religion (though not with any of the revealed religions). Realistic though the setting may be—in *Der arme Vetter (The Poor Cousin)* the scenes are the heath, the banks of the Elbe, and a tavern outside the city of Hamburg—and although some of the people talk a Lower German dialect, the author's concern is with the timeless issues, with the triumph of the spirit over materialism.

"It is strange that man does not want to learn that his father is God," ends his first drama, *Der Tote Tag (The Dead Day),* in which a mother vainly tries to keep her son from maturing to manhood, from finding his estranged father who, as it becomes clear at the end, is the Spirit, is God. The *Arme Vetter* is a tormented dreamer who, by committing suicide, awakens another person to a more spiritual life. In *Die Echten Sedemunds (The True Sedemunds),* the philistine inhabitants of a small town are mercilessly revealed in all their apathy to the higher values. In *Der Findling (The Foundling),* a miracle turns an ugly little creature through the healing powers of love into a radiantly beautiful child. In *Die Suendflut (The Flood),* God Himself, in the guise of a beggar, wanders through the vice-ridden world, and in *Der Blaue Boll (The Blue Boll),* the wealthy, pleasure-seeking country squire Boll, through shattering experiences, gains a new insight into the true meaning of life.

Those who read his plays—unfortunately, all that is available in English translation is part of *The Flood* (*Massachusetts Review,* Spring 1960)—will wish to read his letters as well. Several hundred of them are gathered in the large volume titled *Ernst Barlach: Leben und Werk in seinen Briefen,* yet only nineteen are now available in English (they are contained in the anthology *Art and Artist,* issued by The University of California Press in 1956). They are informal, for they were not written with publication in mind, yet they contain nothing trivial, they reveal a person with Tolstoyan concepts of morality, and with a sense of plastic responsibility akin to that of Michelangelo. They mirror his spiritual development and also his rise and fall within his native country. He was sixty-eight, and already very ill, when he informed his brother Hans that, after his major works in Magdeburg, Lübeck, Kiel, and Güstrow had been removed, his War Memorial in Hamburg was about to be sacrificed as well. Yet he ends the letter in a proud and defiant tone: "I am not in the least repentant or reformed."

Earlier, complaining about his enemies, the Nazis and Stahlhelmers, he had written to his publisher, Reinhold Piper: "I am determined to stand up against this; they shall not triumph. . . ." He was ostracized for moral rather than political reasons—a dictator wants artists to create and promote illusions, and he refused. In the Third Reich, there was no room for epitomes of real men and women, old, blind, crippled, ailing, terrorstricken, suffering from loneliness or from doubt. But there was also no need for a man like Barlach, who saw the same people as the lower rungs on the ladder to perfection, as "poor cousins" of the ideal man that slumbered in his own soul. The pain which he suffered toward the end of his life was, I suppose, relieved to some extent by the knowledge that what he had created was good, whatever his enemies might say, and also by the stoicism that had always sustained him. In the last entry of a personal diary, jotted beneath a newspaper photograph of a gigantic reclining Buddha, these significant and revealing words were found: "The voice of a world immeasurably remote from here and now . . . entry into the realm of silence, praise of timeless, everpresent life. . . ."

NOTES

[1] The show (March-April 1962) included thirty-four sculptures and forty drawings, all borrowed from American private collections.

[2] Martin Esslin mentions Barlach's plays as interesting precursors of the "Theatre of the Absurd."

Edson M. Chick (essay date 1963)

SOURCE: "Ernst Barlach and the Theater," in *The German Quarterly*, Vol. XXXVI, No. 1, January, 1963, pp. 39-51.

[*In the following essay, Chick outines Barlach's difficulties in the German theater.*]

A more accurate title to this study might have been "Barlach versus the Theater" or better "The Theater versus Barlach," for there was almost never any proper reciprocal relationship between them.[1] In his lifetime (1870-1938) there was, to put it mildly, misunderstanding on both sides, and since the war some of the tension has lived on in the attitudes of theater people and critics.

The question whether Barlach's dramas deserve a place in the repertoire of major theaters or are best played occasionally on a studio or student stage has still to be answered, and can be answered only in practise. The most an article like this can do is to sketch the stage history of the four best plays and draw theoretical conclusions about reasons for theatrical success or failure.

The so-called Barlach renaissance in leading German theaters during the early and middle 1950's has miscarried; and in general the attempts in recent years to recapture his work for the stage have led to *succès d'estime* and short runs. During Barlach's lifetime and even during the theatrical golden age of the 1920s it was little different. In those years many reviewers recognized him as the strongest dramatist of the age. Others thought quite the opposite; Alfred Kerr, who judged each work by theatrical and subjective criteria, classified him among the "Versagerchen der Nachkriegszeit" cowering in convulsive impotence and full of hot air.[2]

Barlach's personal experience and his utterances on the topic offer a good picture in miniature of the tangled problem. Probably no dramatist has ever felt more mistreated and misunderstood by directors and audiences; and few have done less to correct the situation. He betrays his uneasiness in a letter written in 1919 dealing with the imminent première of his first published drama, *Der tote Tag*: "Dass meine Überzeughtheit sich auf Andere überträgt, ist eine Aufgabe, die der Darstellung obliegt, es fragt sich aber, ob sich, was mich bewegte, überhaupt übertragen lässt. Denn der Zuschauer, der Fremde, soll weit entgegen kommen und wieviele Menschen mögen den Dingen da überhaupt ein Interesse entgegen tragen wollen."[3] Thus before his first première Barlach is moved by doubts about the dramaturgical adequacy of his play and, more important, about the alien spectator, who, he fears, will not try to understand the play.

Later, once his reputation as a writer was made, he ceased to worry about the problems of communication and placed the blame for poor reception of his work on directors and a recalcitrant audience. Unlike Bertolt Brecht he took no measures to intrigue or activate his audience, nor did he consider making revisions for dramaturgical reasons. In another letter, written also in 1919, he speaks of his disinclination even to adapt dramas in progress to the requirements of the stage: "Bin doch zu wenig bühnenkundig und überhaupt zu wenig auf Theater erpicht, um aus der Aufführung etwas für mich zu entnehmen oder zu gewinnen."[4]

Barlach accepted, even affirmed and sharpened, his alienation from the theater and contented himself with occasional caustic comments from his isolation in Güstrow. Even the possibility that Max Reinhardt might produce *Die echten Sedemunds* in Berlin failed to excite him if one is to believe the letter to Karl Barlach written on July 10, 1920: "Schliesslich ist diese Schlusssensation für mich ein Ende, das schon kaum mehr zur Arbeit gehört, wie ein bisschen 'Scheinleben nach dem Tode', ein bisschen Gespenstern und Spöken eines verstorbenen Freundes."[5]

On a few occasions, however, Barlach let himself be involved in the staging of one or another of his plays. In each instance he soon regretted it and finally withdrew altogether. He could not block all avenues of approach but did his best to discourage attempts to get his advice. In 1926, for example, Edzard Schaper, then manager of the Stuttgart Landestheater, came to Güstrow to discuss Barlach's latest play, *Der blaue Boll*. Stuttgart was to be the scene of the première as it had been two years earlier for *Die Sündflut*. Apprised of the visit's purpose, Barlach asked whether Schaper had read the play. Schaper admitted he hadn't. Thereupon Barlach bought him a copy and abandoned him in Güstrow's Hotel Erbgrossherzog for the rest of the day. That evening they met again, and Barlach asked if he had read the play. Schaper replied that he had read and understood everything. "Vorzüglich, dann brauchen wir ja nicht mehr darüber zu reden," said Barlach. Schaper then had to content himself with an extended social evening over grog in the Erbgrossherzog.[6]

Schaper was not the first to suffer such brusque treatment and was perhaps aware that theater people had become scapegoats for Barlach's dismay at the fate of his dramas on the stage. To be sure, the alien audience remained unchanged as Barlach indicates in a letter (1927) dealing with productions of his *Sündflut*: "Alles ohne Nachhaltigkeit, die Leute fühlen sich durch die Zumutung an soviel Denkerei beleidigt" (*Briefe II,* p. 142). The letter then waxes hotter and reveals the real sore point: "Und obendrein, welcher Teufel reitet die Theaterleiter, dass sie aus meinen Dramen nur Oratorien und Mysterien machen wollen statt unterhaltende Stücke!" Barlach does not stop with directors but goes on in the succeeding lines to vent his rage on costume and stage designers who seemingly aim to make his plays as boring as possible—in most cases by basing their designs on his sculpture and drawings. Barlach was convinced with good reason that his plastic and dramatic work were separate entities and could not be synthesized without destroying the effect of each.

This letter is but one of several similar utterances preserved from the decade of the 'twenties. In them one incident stands out: it is the first important production of a Barlach play in the theater capital, Leopold Jessner's staging of *Die echten Sedemunds* in the Berlin Staatstheater, first performed on April 1, 1921. In 1921 Jessner was out to discover new dramatists for the steps of his abstract stage. Zuckmayer and Barlach were two of his finds, but neither was well received. Jessner visited Güstrow to discuss plans for the production, and Barlach, despite himself, was enthusiastic about the visit and the prospect of a good professional treatment of his drama. He wrote to Reinhold Piper: "Gestern war der Intendant des Staatstheaters in Berlin hier, es geht nun mit den Sedemunds wirklich los und zwar mit allen Schikanen . . . Es ist entschieden abenteuerlich, einem Menschen gegenüberzusitzen, der die innerlichen Phasen so intensiv durchlebt hat, die man an sich selbst durchgeprobt hat . . ." (*Briefe II,* p. 102).

Yet as time for the première came closer, Barlach became more hesitant. A glance at Jessner's sketches convinced him that the production would conform more to the director's "meisterlicher Stilwillen" than to the spirit of the text. In fact, he foresees a clash between his play—"ein gelegentlicher Bummelschnack"—and the strait jacket which Jessner was imposing on it—"zwischen streng stilisierten Wänden" (*Briefe II,* pp. 103-104). The epithet "stylized" must be understood in a pejorative sense; it appears with variations like "Monumental-Stilbums" (*Briefe II,* p. 104) in nearly all of Barlach's diatribes against the theater.[7] Small wonder that he had to be dragged against his will to see the second performance of *Die echten Sedemunds* and that this was to be his first and last viewing of one of his dramas on the stage.

The whole affair—the quarrel with the usher about seats, the whistling in the audience, the confrontation with Jessner at the end, and the bad reviews—must have been a traumatic experience for someone not hardened to the ways of the theater. Barlach recounted it repeatedly in letters and conversations. Stripped of embellishments the references are all much like the account recorded by Friedrich Schult (*Barlach im Gespräch,* Insel-Verlag, 1948, p. 17): "Ich war, bei der gänzlich verfehlten Stilisierung, die den breiten Atem meines Stückes platterdings verstellte, in einer schrecklichen Lage. Als Jessner mich fragte, wie mir das Ganze denn gefallen habe, musste ich ihm antworten: Was ich hier gesehen habe, hat nichts mehr mit mir zu tun!" On leaving the theater Barlach commented to his companion that, had he been a paying spectator, he would perhaps have been the loudest whistler (*Briefe I,* p. 53).

The newspaper reviews proved Barlach's judgement correct, but the majority did this indirectly by rejecting the text—Barlach writes of "fast einhellige Ablehnung und teilweise Verhöhnung" (*Briefe II,* p. 116)—and by praising the stage technique. Most critics viewed the performance as Jessner's triumph over an impossible text unfit for the stage. Alfred Kerr pulls no punches in his review: "Jessner schrieb letztens das Werk. Etwa so, wie der geniale Koch aus dem Lederstück ein Schnitzel mit Garnierung und holden Tunken macht. Barlach gab das Leder, Jessner die Kochkunst."[8] Other less splenetic critics like Erwin Jacobsohn, Herbert Ihering, and Julius Bab came closer to Barlach's viewpoint. Bab writes: "Aber das Ganze der Aufführung blieb in einem naturlosen, starr durchgehaltenen Marionettenstil hinter der dichterischen Grösse des Textes zurück."[9]

The whistling spectators and the mocking reviews aroused a resentment in Barlach that found expression in his mockery of theater people. In 1928 he described Jessner's reaction to his comment ("Ja, mein Stück erkenne ich nicht wieder!") on the performance: "Jessner sah mich gross an, und da fiel mir erst ein, dass er wohl grosse Töööne von mir erwartet hatte, grosse Töööne über seine fabelhafte Inszenierungskunst. Natürlich macht man sich so bei Theaterleuten nicht gerade beliebt."[10]

The destinies of Barlach dramas on the stage fall into no distinct pattern, nor can the frequency or infrequency of their inclusion in the repertoires of German theaters be easily explained. One might ask, for instance, why *Die echten Sedemunds,* a play with several roles attractive to actors, with more humor and stage potential than most contemporary pieces, should have been produced altogether four times from its première in Hamburg (March 23, 1921) to the politically reckless Altona *mise en scène* of 1935, whose run was cut short after five performances on orders from Berlin. None of these four productions was performed on more than five evenings.

The first three in the early 1920s were much alike in their strict stylization and expressionistic abstraction.

The consensus is that they failed either because they were inadequate or because they worked against the text, trying to make a tasty cutlet from the piece of leather. Kurt Eggers-Kestner, however, who directed the play at the Altona Stadttheater in 1935, set out to do everything according to Barlach's dictates. He writes in retrospect: "Barlach hatte unser Unternehmen dieses Mal mit Sorge verfolgt. Die *Sedemunds* waren bei der Berliner Uraufführung etwas anderes geworden als er gemeint hatte und hatten Widerspruch geweckt. Wir waren brav und folgten dem Gedanken und Wort. Der Bühnenbildner Karl Gröning hatte sogar für die Echtheit des Friedhofes das Altonaer Gartenbauamt in Bewegung gesetzt. Als der 'echte Grude' zum Schluss zwischen den Gräbern hintanzte, konnte niemand in Zweifel darüber sein, was das zu bedeuten habe."[11]

The results would seem to prove the rightness of Barlach's ideas on staging. As one critic wrote of Eggers-Kestner's production of *Der blaue Boll* in 1934, he made Barlach's dream come true. Most astounding, when one recalls the critical reactions to earlier performances, is the quality of the reviews. They not only show appreciation for the work on the stage but reveal a thorough understanding of Barlach's peculiar style. The play was a revelation, particularly to viewers like Ihering, who had seen the opposite extreme in Jessner's Berlin production. The disappearance of expressionistic plays and performances from the stage, whether in response to Nazi edict or to a change in taste, had prepared the way for a new appreciation of Barlach. But it was too late, for he had been blacklisted.

The great discovery the critics made in 1935 was that *Die echten Sedemunds* was full of concrete, sensual reality in its characters, action, and—most important—in its language. Ihering (*Berliner Börsen-Kurier,* May 20, 1935) recalls the 1921 performance: "Es bleibt eine Tat, obgleich in der expressionistischen Periode des deutschen Theaters die Schwächen des Werkes gespielt wurden: die Rhetorik und nicht die Figuren. Ringende Gedanken wurden wie feste Formeln, verwühlte Erkenntnisse wie überschaubare Resultate gegeben. Das Wunder dieser Dichtung aber, die verkrochene Kleinstadtwelt in ihrer bösen und elementaren Kraft, in ihrem teuflischen und wieder närrischen Humor erschien wie ein stilistisches Experiment."

Eggers-Kestner's contrasting accomplishment is appraised by Bruno E. Werner in a review (*Deutsche Allgemeine Zeitung,* May 20, 1935) which belongs among the very best interpretations of Barlach to be found anywhere: "Er hatte richtig erkannt . . . , dass es darauf ankommt, reale, wirkliche Menschen hier sichtbar zu machen und dass nichts falscher ist, als Barlachsche Stücke von A bis Z in eine Traumatmosphäre zu tauchen. Denn das unterscheidet Barlach vom Expressionismus, dass er handfeste Realität in der vertrauten, heimatlichen, niederdeutschen Atmosphäre hinstellt, und dass diese Realität nur zuweilen transparent wird, so dass man hinter ihr—aber nie ohne sie—die grossen metaphysischen Gewalten eines unmittelbaren Seelenraumes erkennt." If anything, Werner continues, Eggers-Kestner did not go far enough in this direction. "Denn das Stück kann nur dann vom Zuschauer verstanden werden, wenn bei den Gestalten jede Abstraktion und Stilisierung vermieden wird, jeder nur karikaturistische Zug, wenn wir hier wirklich niederdeutsche Kleinstädter sehen und keinerlei Übersetzung ins Theaterhafte (im gleichen Augenblick versteht nämlich der Zuschauer die Gestalten nicht mehr und versucht, hinter allen ihren Worten einen verborgenen Sinn zu suchen . . .)."

These remarks apply not only to *Die echten Sedemunds* but also to Barlach's three other great dramas: *Der arme Vetter* (1918), *Die Sündflut* (1924), and *Der blaue Boll* (1926). Werner tells how Barlach should be played and explains why directors, critics, audiences, and scholars have failed to understand the dramas. A few false accents or one mistaken role interpretation, not to mention rigid stylization, suffice seriously to distort any one of them.

The melancholy stage history of *Die Sündflut* during the 1920s is a case in point. Barlach received the Kleistpreis for this drama in 1924. Yet despite this recognition most directors felt that it deserved a good deal of editing for the theater. Of Barlach's pieces *Die Sündflut* has been most popular among directors—it was produced twenty times before the hiatus of the Nazi years—and least popular with audiences. Even the Berlin production (1925) under Jürgen Fehling, noted as the finest Barlach interpreter, was dropped from the repertoire after four performances. Many others were withdrawn immediately after the première. Audiences gave either perfunctory applause or, on occasion, none at all. One reviewer attributes this silence to the religious awe inspired by the play, but evidence points to confusion and disappointment as a better explanation.

The reasons for directors' enthusiasm coincide with those for the audiences' rejection. *Die Sündflut,* with its agonized questions about God and His responsibility for evil, offered a chance to set off some rhetorical fireworks. It was repeatedly transformed into a discussion piece in pathetic, high-expressionistic style. The text was shortened and simplified in such a way that its total stage effect was often the opposite of Barlach's intention. The comic-grotesque scenes about Noah's troubled family life were omitted in order to accentuate the theological dispute between him and Calan; and the role of fat Zebid—her evil presence on the Ark means the whole effort is doomed to failure—was in some cases (Fehling and others) cut completely. Noah was often played according to the Bible as a venerable patriarch, and Calan as a villainous "Gewaltmensch." Stage designs were usually abstract, and actors were dressed to resemble Barlach's sculpture.

This experimenting and shortening, in effect, emasculated the play. In 1925 Alfred Kerr had occasion to publish another "Verriss" with phrases like "reiner

Dilettantismus" and "masslose Langweiligkeit." He comes to the same conclusion in favor of the director as he did four years earlier: "Die Aufführung unter Fehling war gekonnter als das scheintiefe Missdrama."[12]

As recently as 1954 in the Darmstadt production *Die Sündflut* suffered the same distortion. Egon Vietta, manager of the Landestheater set the tone by interpreting the play as a reflection of Heidegger's philosophy; and Gustav Rudolf Sellner followed with a performance running counter to the text. The reviews indicate that it amounted to an unconscious parody of earlier productions. The characters were "nur Figurinen mit Spruchbändern auf kahler Fläche" (Review signed "R. B." in the *Stuttgarter Zeitung,* March 15, 1954). About the contradiction between the text and the style of production R. B. then asks, "Warum diese Geometrie in einem so ungeometrischen Stück? Hat man den Mut zu einem Realismus verloren, der auch gleichnishaft sein könnte?" According to Heinz Beckmann (*Rheinischer Merkur,* March 15, 1954) the stage setting was "nichts als eine abstrakte Verlegenheit mit ernstem Bart sozusagen." Sellner's production again makes a "Missdrama" of *Die Sündflut* by obscuring its humor, ambiguity, and humanity. The worst distortion was in the characterization of Noah; instead of a timid, vacillating man, he appears as a sympathetic, pious Christian (Beckmann).

Since the war *Die Sündflut* has in general experienced more success and longer runs. In 1946 it was performed twenty times by the company of the Hamburg Schauspielhaus for reasons, however, which have more to do with the mood of the times than with the quality of the production. The audience understood little ("g.z." in the *Hamburger Allgemeine,* October 8, 1946); but the play seemed to say something about collective guilt, and the effort was thought of as expiation or "Wiedergutmachung" for Nazi sins against Barlach and the world.

Finally, the Hannover Landestheater presented the play twenty-five times in 1952, a remarkable run for any Barlach drama, particularly in a smaller theater. To judge from the few available reports the *mise en scène* conformed to Barlach's own ideas. The director, Jöns Andersson, avoided any hint of pathos and emphasized the humorous passages by making Noah somewhat like a North German peasant.

A compilation of the theater's many crimes and few justices against Barlach would be repetitive and fruitless. Nevertheless, a brief reference to the stage history of *Der arme Vetter* belongs here, if only to demonstrate again the irrational pattern of failure and success. For unlike the other three great plays it found its best stage interpretation early. Jürgen Fehling directed the drama at the Berlin Staatstheater in 1923, and this, its third, production has never since been surpassed. The run of eighteen performances is astounding after Jessner's *Sedemunds* and after the poor reception of *Der arme Vetter* in Hamburg and Halle (Saale) where the first and only performance was played before a near empty house.

The fourteen productions in German theaters between 1923 and 1933 were received with even less applause than was *Die Sündflut.* One can only guess at the reasons, for even directors who refrained from radical stylizing (e.g. the Karlsruhe production of 1925) saw their audiences leave in silence.

Fehling's success may be laid in part to an alert audience and good reviewers. However, it was mainly the combination of the finest German actors and Fehling's faithful, lively interpretation which made the difference. Barlach's plays make demands which cannot be satisfied by every theater. Fehling had the proper ingredients and knew how to put them together. This time he cut almost nothing so that the performance lasted nearly four hours. He did not oversimplify the subtle relationships between the three main figures, and he gave the indispensable secondary roles their due. Most important, he struck the proper combination of reality and irreality, foreground and background which Ihering tries to describe as follows: "Die Menschen, Ausdruck dieser brauenden Atmosphäre . . . und diese Atmosphäre wieder schaffend, real im Boden der Landschaft wurzelnd und an die Sterne reichend . . . verweben sich, durchdringen sich und finden ihr geheimnistiefes Ziel in der Beziehung zwischen Siebenmark . . . seiner Braut, . . . und Hans Iver, einer Beziehung, die ein erotisches Spiel in das letzte Gleichnis hinaufhebt, . . . wo Irdisches sich am Himmlischen sublimiert und Himmlisches am Irdischen erst sichtbar wird. *Der arme Vetter* ist das adligste, männlichste Drama unserer Tage."[13] Siegfried Jacobsohn is more specific about Fehling's accomplishment: "Der Brodem der Gegend bedrückt dir förmlich die Brust. Aus der Wirklichkeit aber steigt die Unwirklichkeit des Spökenkiekers Ernst Barlach auf—dank Fehlings Mangel an Röhren–und Druckwerk, seinem Verzicht auf alle modischen Mätzchen, seinem Respekt vor der Sache, seinem Gefühl für die Schwerelosigkeit des Details und seinem Vergnügen an den belebenden musikalischen Einlagen."[14]

Two years later Fehling made bad mistakes in his direction of *Die Sündflut* but more than made up for it with his production in 1930/31 of *Der blaue Boll,* which has an atmosphere much like that of *Der arme Vetter.* His *Boll* was the second of the total of three to be produced before the war. By the late 1920s Barlach's growing reputation as a bad risk had probably discouraged even larger theaters from further experiments with his work. The première of *Der blaue Boll* in 1926 at the Stuttgart Landestheater promised no better reception for this than for any earlier drama. It was a *succès d'estime* at best, and the performance was repeated only twice. One reviewer ambiguously called it surprisingly good; another thought it amateurish and a painful experience.

Fehling's Berlin performance had the advantage of a director, a set designer (Rochus Gliese), and a cast, all of whom were excellent craftsmen and had the experience of two Barlach productions behind them. Willy Haas's comment: "Es war ein ungeheurer Eindruck . . .

Das Herz schlägt mir heute noch schneller, wenn ich an diesen Theaterabend denke,"[15] echoes the reviews of the time. One calls *Der blaue Boll* not only great literature but the best play to appear on the Berlin stage in ten years.[16] Thanks to the unsparing efforts of Jürgen Fehling the drama remained in the repertoire through 28 performances. Like one of those sudden mystical revelations Barlach mentions, this production gave a startling insight into the stage potential of his work.

Three years later Fehling's example was heeded by Eggers-Kestner in his staging of *Boll* in Altona. Like Fehling he spared neither expense nor time; and thus the performance was termed "die wichtigste Aufführung, die in dieser Spielzeit auf die Gross-Hamburger Bühnen gekommen ist."[17]

The upward course of Barlach's stage fortunes in the years from 1930 to 1935 tempts one to speculate on what might have happened if Hitler had not become Reichskanzler. If there ever was a Barlach stage style, it was perfected by Fehling and Eggers-Kestner in those years. But their accomplishment did not carry over to the postwar era. Since 1945 three major productions of *Der blaue Boll* have failed to further the cause of a Barlach renaissance for reasons indicated in the discussion of *Die Sündflut,* namely the tendency to play it in expressionistic stylization and to overemphasize its metaphysical passages. "Mit dieser vergeistigten Auffassung des Gutsbesitzers Boll schoss das ganze Drama sofort wie eine Stichflamme davon, aufwärts zum Kirchturm, ehe es noch recht begonnen hatte," writes Heinz Beckmann of the Essen production (*Rheinischer Merkur,* December 12, 1953).

Beckmann's review is entitled "Blauer Boll—zu früh oder zu spät?", a legitimate question which brings to mind parallels between the 1920s and the 1950s. The question might be reformulated: Will Barlach win his audience again as he did earlier after a decade of grudging acceptance? At all events, in the 'twenties as in the 'fifties audiences and directors had no organ for Barlach's matter-of-fact yet deceptive realism. The understandable choice of the German theater to start again from the basis of its achievements of the 1920s has only proven again that Barlach cannot be played à la mode.

These remarks apply to matters of diction as well as of stage technique. Eggers-Kestner's production of *Die echten Sedemunds* brought critics to the recognition that the merit of the play rests, like all great literature, on its language. Wolf Schramm says of Eggers-Kestner in the *Hamburger Anzeiger* (May 20, 1935): "Er gab es ganz *vom Wort aus* und ganz für das Wort," and Ihering writes of the text: "Ernst Barlach gibt der Sprache . . . ihre Sinnlichkeit zurück" (*Berliner Börsen-Kurier,* May 20, 1935). And finally, Günther Mann presents on this occasion an unequalled description of the power and essence of Barlach's language: "Die Barlach'sche Wortwelt kann letzlich gar nicht 'gefallen': man wird von ihr *be*fallen, gestossen, gleichsam metaphysisch

angerempelt—ohne dass man zunächst recht weiss, um was es eigentlich geht. Es ist, als ob das Alltägliche des Tuns und Sagens der Barlach'schen Gestalten birst: mit einem Schlage schimmert eine andere wesentlichere Welt durch, *momenthaft*—aber sie hat uns betroffen, sie macht uns betroffen."[18]

In the ensuing quarter century no production of a Barlach play has placed the same stress on diction or received such glowing reviews. Striking stage effects have obscured the power of his language or have distracted attention from inadequate delivery of lines. Geometrical sets, exotic costumes, choreographically prescribed gestures, in short all the tricks of the stage trade have only hurt Barlach's reputation as a writer for the theater. For it is his diction which places him above his contemporaries. Paul Fechter writes in this regard: "Barlach ist es, der fast als einziger nach Wedekind die Auseinandersetzung des Dramas mit dem Wort als Material wie als grundlegendes Formelement und damit das Problem der Erneuerung des inneren dramatischen Bau- und Formstoffs weiter vorgetrieben hat."[19]

Barlach was aware, and so were Fehling and Eggers-Kestner, that unless his lines were spoken in a natural, unpretentious way and unless the *mise en scène* were straightforward and realistic, his play would shoot off toward the stars and never return. He wrote his best pieces in such a way that there would be a fine balance between reality and metaphor. Ideally the director should maintain the balance in every aspect of his production: language, gesture, and stage design. If he succeeds, the audience will have the experience described by Günther Mann: "Fühlte man sich zu Beginn des Stückes tappend wie in einem mysteriösen Dämmerzustand, so wird man am Ende zurückblickend gewahr, dass man keineswegs in einem wunderlichen Labyrinth mit unwirklichen Menschen und Worten herumgeführt und dass man sehr sinnvoll zu einem Ziel geführt worden ist."[20]

The stylistic prejudices of directors, audiences, and critics lost their rigidity in the late 1920s. Their eyes were opened to new possibilities, perhaps by the power of Brecht's revolutionary productions. Around 1930 a second look at Barlach's work brought a new understanding for its peculiar use of contrast and ambiguity, which makes it both difficult and great. Expressionist fashion had made the plays seem vague and immature because it revealed only a congenial fraction of what they contained. Under Fehling and Eggers-Kestner the whole of Barlach came to view to the delight and astonishment of audiences and reviewers.

With Barlach then it is all or nothing, and the theater of the 1950s has found it hard to satisfy his rigorous demands. The fulfillment of the following optimistic prophesy by Bruno E. Werner (*Deutsche Allgemeine Zeitung,* May 20, 1935) has yet to come: "Vermutlich wird man eines Tages Barlach gerade so zwanglos verstehen, wie man heute Kleist versteht. Die Regisseure werden dann nicht mehr unter dem Eindruck Strindbergs, Wedekinds und des Expressionismus Barlach inszenieren, sondern im Sinne Barlachs und aus dem Geist einer neuen Zeit, in der irdische Realitäten und metaphysischer Bezug keine Gegensätze mehr sind. Die Zuschauer werden dann nicht nur respektvoll tüchtig applaudieren, . . . sondern sie werden hier über die . . . Komik lachen, vom Grauen gepackt werden . . . , und etwas von jener grossen seelischen Verwandlung dieser Komödie [*Sedemunds*], die aus tiefster religiöser Erschütterung kommt, wird sie herzhaft befreiend anwehen wie ein kühler Wind."

NOTES

1 This article owes a large debt to the critical and collecting efforts of others, particularly to Dietrich Fleischhauer, whose "Barlach auf der Bühne, eine Inszenierungsgeschichte" (Diss., Köln, 1955, Typescript) is full of valuable details and statistics. Also I would like to express my gratitude to all connected with the Fulbright program for the research grant which made this paper possible.

2 Alfred Kerr, "Aussichten der Sprechbühne," *Neue Rundschau*, XXXVIII, vol. I (1927), p. 68.

3 *Zehn unveröffentlichte Briefe Ernst Barlachs an Prof. Dr. Karl Weimann*, ed. Anneliese und Hans Harmsen, Barlach Gesellschaft Gabe zum 2. January 1961.

4 *Ernst Barlach, Leben und Werk in seinen Briefen*, ed. Friedrich Dross (München, 1952), p. 95; referred to hereafter as *Briefe II*.

5 *Ernst Barlach, aus seinen Briefen*, ed. Friedrich Dross (München, 1947), p. 49; referred to hereafter as *Briefe I*.

6 Karl Barlach, *Mein Vetter Ernst Barlach* (Bremen, 1960), p. 63-64.

7 In the following vehement excerpt from an unpublished letter quoted here from Fleischhauer's "Barlach auf der Bühne," (Diss., Köln, 1955, p. 12) he gives his reasons: "Himmel, ist das nicht wahr, dass vor einem schematischen [stilisierten] Bühnenbild der agierende, feuerspeiende, Schritte zu Boden stampfende Mensch ein Pfürzlein ist?"

8 Alfred Kerr, "Rückschau, Vorschau," *Neue Rundschau*, XXXII (1921), p. 960.

9 Julius Bab, *Das Theater der Gegenwart* (Leipzig, 1928), p. 184.

10 Reinhard Piper, *Nachmittag, Erinnerungen eines Verlegers* (München, 1950), p. 160.

11 Typescript dated Berlin-Grunewald, Oktober, 1954, and signed: Eggers-Kestner; in the files of the Barlach Archiv, Hamburg.

12 Photo copy of a newspaper review found in the Barlach Archiv. Probably *Berliner Tageblatt*, April 5 or 6, 1925.

13 Herbert Ihering, *Von Reinhardt bis Brecht*, Vol. I (Berlin, 1958), p. 319.

14 *Die Weltbühne. Der Schaubühne XIX. Jahr* (1925?), p. 642.

15 Willy Haas, *Die literarische Welt* (München, 1957), p. 147.

16 Photo copy of a review by Wilhelm Westecker dated December 8, 1930; to be found in the Barlach Archiv.

17 Friedrich-Carl Kobbe in the *Hamburger Nachrichten*, March 27, 1934.

18 Review in *Die Kommenden*, Neue Folge, June 20, 1935.

19 Paul Fechter, *Das europäische Drama*, Vol. II (Mannheim, 1957), p. 539.

20 loc. cit.

Alfred Werner   (essay date 1963)

SOURCE: "The Late Glory of Ernst Barlach (1870-1938)," in *The South Atlantic Quarterly*, Vol. LXII, 1963, pp. 377-86.

[*In the following essay, Werner assesses Barlach's sculptures and reputation as an artist.*]

In the year 1888, when young Ernst Barlach entered the School of Applied Arts in Hamburg, beginning what was to be a fifty-year stretch of religious devotion to art, sculpture was at a very low ebb in Germany and, for that matter, all over Europe. In Berlin, all lucrative commissions went to Reinhold Begas who, with his disciples, created huge monuments that combine theatricality of pose with a slavish imitation of nature, including the most faithful treatment of banal accessories. There were, however, trends among the younger artists and patrons of art to replace the era's false pathos, blended with a passion for photographic verisimilitude, by an art that would once more allow its creator to make full use of his wisdom and imagination. Twelve years earlier, one of the pioneers of the new aesthetics, the philosopher and art patron, Conrad Fiedler, in his essay, *On Judging Works of Visual Art*, had attacked the official art in Bismarck's Reich. He struck out fearlessly: "Because a work of art is a product of man it must be explained and judged differently from a product of nature." He upheld the "creative power of the artist," stressed the "emotional forces" and urged painters and sculptors to be free to create real, imaginative, and autonomous art.

Fiedler's closest friends were the painter Hans von Merées and the sculptor Adolf von Hildebrand. Flattening figures, suppressing background vistas, and altogether relying on bold rhythmical simplifications, Van Marées had no market, and few admirers, in Germany. To his patron, Fiedler, the painter wrote from Rome: "I would call that man a born artist whose soul nature has from the very beginning been endowed with an ideal, and for whom this ideal replaces the truth. . . ." Von Hildebrand also sought the "ideal" in an era of triumphant naturalism. In his book, *The Problem of Form,* he looked for what he called the "unchangeable laws of art," maintaining that an artist's unawareness of them would lead to his incapacity to understand his proper relationship to nature. His work as a sculptor is a considerable improvement over the output of Begas and his school, for his portraits and nudes are characterized by the quietness and calmness, the simplification and condensation often so sadly lacking in the Bismarckian and Wilhelminian art. Von Hildebrand was capable of terse summarizing, of neglecting all that is merely subsidiary, and of producing an expressive silhouette. In a period in which many a sculptor confined himself to the execution of the cartoon or, at most, the plaster model, Von Hildebrand felt that in order to obtain the effects inherent in the material the sculptor must work directly upon the stone or bronze.

If the principles of these three innovators were known to Barlach's teachers, first in Hamburg, and thereafter at the Academy in Dresden, they were hardly the men to recommend them to their students. Young Barlach loathed his professors, yet the sculpture he did in his early years was little better than what they were doing. His development toward originality was very slow. Michelangelo was only twenty-five when he carved one of his greatest master-pieces, the gigantic "David"; Rodin made the revolutionary "Man with the Broken Nose" at twenty-four. Barlach's "Freudenschrei" ("Joy of Pleasure") which the twenty-four-year-old Dresden Academy graduate modeled from clay, is a delicate statue of a nude youth that could have been fashioned after Hellenistic models by any gifted young man in any European country in the mid-nineties.

From the decade to follow little remains to prove originality on the part of the struggling German sculptor. In Paris, where he lived in 1895-1896, studying briefly at the Académie Julian, he did not open his eyes to the greatness of Rodin (about that time, Rodin was working at his monument for Balzac, the only work by his hand which the mature Barlach, in his autobiography, later singled out for praise). Intellectually he had recognized that the Greeks' and the French academicians' notion of beauty and charm were not for him. In a letter to his friend Duesel, he extolled ugliness, demoniacal passion, grotesque geniality, and, above all, humor with its "host of original characters." Only in his scathing drawings, among them cartoons for satirical weeklies, did Barlach achieve the originality that presages his future work, but not in his early sculptures.

Little need be said about the commercial work Barlach did in that decade, including the huge bronze "Neptune" he did for the administration building of the Hamburg-America Line (at the beginning of World War I, it was melted down for the making of ammunition). For, were they not included in the *catalogue raisonée,* one would scarcely guess that these immature knick-knacks of all shapes and sizes were the work of the same man who, a few years later, would create "Panic Fright," "The Solitary One," "Man Drawing a Sword," "Man Walking," and other pieces that have their lasting place in the history of German sculpture.

More interesting is the work he did in 1903 and 1904, when, more or less isolated, he lived in his native town of Wedel, some miles west of Hamburg, doing some ceramic work for the Mutz factory in Altona, among them plaques and small decorative pieces. Barlach, like several other outstanding artists—among them Ernst Ludwig Kirchner and Vassily Kandinsky—went through a short period of *Jugendstil* prior to finding, once and for all, his own appropriate style. *Jugendstil,* more generally known as *Art Nouveau,* until recently was regarded, not as the legitimate style of a period, but as the expression of an era that had no taste at all. Today, however, one is no longer blind to the aesthetic merits of *Jugendstil,* whose arabesques and other undulating lines did help, as Gabriele Muenter, Kandinsky's friend, commented, "to destroy the old naturalism." Barlach's small pieces, among them a bowl with a triton and a "Cleopatra," demonstrates his inventiveness. About the "Cleopatra," which was included in an *Art Nouveau* show of New York's Museum of Modern Art, Peter Selz writes in the catalogue:

> with its typical Art Nouveau kidney shape, [it] is a sensuous nude completely surrounded by a sweeping cloak in which the busy movement of its delicate ripples opposes the smooth surface of the figure. These early decorative Art Nouveau sculptures, however, bear little resemblance to the monumental carvings of archetypes for which Barlach is remembered and which began after his trip to Russia in 1906.

It is perfectly true that a brief journey through Russia (August 2 to September 27, 1906) was even more important to Barlach than were the travels in the South Seas to Gauguin and Nolde. For these two had produced significant work before their arrival in the tropics, whereas Barlach, by his own admission, had done nothing very important before his return from Russia. He himself stressed the fact that the human implications derived from the trip were far-reaching: "I found in Russia this amazing unity of inward and outward being, this symbolic quality: this is what we human beings are, at bottom all beggars and *problematische Existenzen* . . . it shines out of the Slav, where others hide it."

On the steppe, seeing the short, squat, roundheaded, flatfaced beggars, monks, pilgrims, and peasant women who, to a large extent, were to become his principal subject matter for the next three decades, Barlach exclaimed, "Donnerwetter, da sitzen Bronzen" ("damn it, these are sitting bronzes"). He was never to forget these mouzhiks, untouched by any veneer of civilization, monumental in their immobility, set against the immensity of the steppe, always waiting, but not knowing for whom or for what. Yet it would be exaggerated to consider the Barlach of the post-Russian period as an entirely new person. The future Barlach was already there, before he embarked upon the train that carried him eastward; the new experience merely brought to the surface all the forces that were in him, breaking the form of conventionality, opening up new channels of communication with fellow men. If, until the "Russian Beggar Woman with Bowl," a small ceramic of 1906, the Expressionist poet, singing, in the plastic medium, of man's woe, does not quite come to the fore, we have proof of Barlach's deep humanity in numerous letters, some of them dating as far back as 1888, and in a batch of early drawings, free, loose, outspoken, that herald the coming of the Expressionist.

After the Russian journey begins the long row of wood sculptures, commencing with the "Shepherd in Storm"—soon after its birth in 1908 to become the first Barlach to enter a public collection (the Kunsthalle in Bremen). In particular, Barlach liked to work on large blocks of wood, streaked and washed by the rain, as opposed to the slick, perfect pieces preferred by nineteenth-century masters. Wood as a medium would have been out of the question for an impatient man like Rodin who loved clay because it allowed the children of his imagination to grow quickly, without any pre-meditation. Barlach, slow, contemplative, philosophical, did not mind the arduous, time-consuming method of cutting directly into wood.

Wood was perfectly suited to his unsuave, unurbane, rustic personality; he knew its character and limitations, never camouflaged its surface, never disguised its color, respecting its texture and grain, and exploring all its potentialities. Completely oblivious of the necessity for food and sleep, as though he were driven by a demonic force, he would doggedly hammer away at the block for days and nights, betraying a robust strength unexpected in so short and slender a man. He would choose a block whose shape fitted his idea, sometimes a pillar, and at other times a cube, visualizing the dormant statue in the primitive shape. Unlike the other sculptors, he did not require a professional model: he did not want his shapes to be too "real," to allow photographic realism to separate his creation from his emotion.

In his treatment of wood, he is reminiscent of the Gothic carvers. He attacked the material with thousands of hammer blows, chipping off tiny bits of wood passionately, yet also patiently, until the desired image emerged with all the required clarity and sharpness. Whereas academic sculptors would polish the surface as carefully as possible, Barlach never concealed the marks of his tools, all the facets, all the countless little planes indica-

tive of the work's organic growth under his knowing hands. Through this homogenous method of "chip carving" he endowed the forms with an extraordinary pulsation of life, with a vibrating quality lacking in the work of more timid men who sought to vivify their creations by trying carefully to duplicate the actual textures of skin, hair, or garment.

Of course, the differences in texture distinguish Barlach's bronzes from his pieces in wood, and the different media demand different approaches by the artist. Nonetheless, while many a subject by Barlach exists in versions in both media, the work usually yields differences to the touch of the hand rather than to the perception of the eye. For the basic principle is the same in both cases. His sculpture, more so than that of his compatriots of the same generation, such as Kolbe or Sintenis, was based on a logical, abstract architectonics reminiscent of the tenets of Cubism. Guillaume Apollinaire, at a point when formlessness was rampant, hailed the importance of geometry as being to the plastic arts what grammar is to the writer. Adolf von Hildebrand, who was born decades before him, might have said the same. Barlach, without having any connection with Cubist sculptors, knew how to combine cubes, spheres, and stereometrical bodies into aesthetically satisfactory figures. While he made use of the artist's freedom to exaggerate, abbreviate, elongate, and "distort," he held sacred the requirement of unchallengeable form. Like an architect, he constructed his piece so that, perfectly balanced, it would stand firmly, with one part of the construction supplementing and supporting the other. Like a good craftsman, he made pieces designed for homes pleasant to the touch and easy to handle. What distinguishes even his smallest and least ambitious pieces is the task the artist had set himself.

Vitality to him was more important than "beauty." Whatever he did, he wished to produce valid symbols, with the power to move the souls of men, rather than to give replicas of nature. Barlach would have gladly adopted Dante's magnificent definition of sculpture as being "visible speech"—sentences formed to utter anguish, defiance, or hope.

After his return to Germany, he began the series of Russian beggars and wanderers that was to become very popular—more popular than his later, more spiritual, more mystical work, done after 1910. For a while a bit of genre art still tinged the productions of 1907-1910, even though Barlach kept naturalistic details to a minimum. Although the master was not in any way close to the Cubism of this period that strove to transform natural shapes into geometric or stereometric elements, his figures, too, are composed of subtle, well-balanced combinations of spheres and cubes. The cerebral chill of so much Cubist sculpture is absent. Take the "Beggar Woman" of 1907: with her bent back, hooded face, and hands extended in a beseeching gesture, she expresses graphically the humiliation of anyone requesting charity. A tragic beauty hovers over this work that is so free from all sentimentalizing, so deeply personal while, at the same time, it is broadly symbolic. Two decades later he produced the "Singing Man," who reclines on the ground, oblivious to anything but his song, his eyes closed to shut out any possible disturbing influence. A formal analysis à la Woelfflin would point out the clever architecture of slanting planes, but might miss the humanity in which this piece is drenched. One is reminded of Barlach's stern warning: "Whosoever concerns himself with aesthetics for its own sake, does something much akin to a sin against the Holy Spirit." The most famous of Barlach's smaller pieces is, perhaps, "The Avenger" (1914)—mind and body of this sword-wielding man is involved in one swift, brutal movement. As a correspondent of the *Christian Science Monitor,* writing from Berlin in 1929, so aptly put it: "It is not the representation of the world of form that Barlach seeks: it is the evidence of the inner man."

From the viewpoint of certain fanatical exponents of non-figurative art, Barlach's work is somewhat antiquated and "old-fashioned" because the master, whatever he produced, always used a clearly recognizable human figure as carrier of the expression he sought. The same people, to whom it would not occur to so dismiss Michelangelo, or even Rodin, actually regard Barlach as anachronistic because, though a coeval of Kandinsky, Mondrian, and Brancusi, he continued the age-old tradition of the figure sculptor that began with an anonymous prehistoric carver's Venus of Willendorf. What Barlach thought of Mondrian or Brancusi is not known. But we have a long letter addressed to his friend, the publisher Reinhard Piper, that deals with Kandinsky's book, just published, in 1911, and entitled, *Concerning the Spiritual in Art.* Having looked at the illustrations, Barlach feels that the "dots, specks, lines, and smudges" can neither shake his soul, nor be of use for communication with fellow men. He does not go so far as to deny the validity of Kandinsky's theories or creations, even though he finds them unacceptable to himself. "Compassion" is the term that seems most important to him. "I have to be able to feel pity . . . my artistic language is the human figure or the object through which or in which man lives, suffers, rejoices, feels, thinks. . . . Man and his gesture tell enough."

Barlach died in 1938, many years before the abstract or near-abstract comprised four-fifths of the new objects in exhibitions throughout the Western world. Were he still alive, he might have expressed himself like his much younger friend, Gerhard Marcks, who, in 1958, wrote to his colleague, Renée Sintenis, in resignation:

> We have seen so many changes in sculptural fashions and now, at last, it has passed us by. But in so doing, it has freed us from many burdens; now, in the nature of things, we can travel lightly, along the road we have chosen. . . . Isn't it a joy to stand aside from the hurly-burly of the day?

Barlach held with Sophocles that, while there are many wonderful things in nature, the most wonderful of all is man. In Goethe's writings, he may have come across the poet's definition of the aim of sculpture to be "to render the dignity of man within the compass of the human form," and, if he did, he certainly agreed. Had Barlach lived to half a century after Kandinsky's book and the first, not entirely convincing experiments with Pure Abstraction, he might have admitted that some very beautiful things have been created by the later Kandinsky and by his numerous followers, but he would have insisted, nonetheless, that in many cases the deliberate exclusion of the human figure had led to impoverishment. At the same time, he would have been pleased to find followers among his "grand-children" in the realm of the plastic arts, among them his ardent American champion, Leonard Baskin.

Barlach has at times been charged with being a mere imitator of Gothic sculpture. Barlach gladly admitted his fascination with the wooden sculptures at the museums in Kiel and Schwerin, the Bordesholm Altar of Master Brueggemann and, in Guestrow, the city where he spent the last half of his life, the Apostles fashioned by the Luebeck carver, Claus Berg. Yet his approach to the wood is totally different. There is commotion and unrest in the work of the Gothic masters, produced by vehement gestures and the rich and often dramatic undulations in garments, created by a succession of peaks and valleys, and abrupt switches from strong light to dark shadows. Barlach, however, completely avoids these pictorial effects that, in the lesser masters of the late Middle Ages, often tend to undermine the sculptural massiveness. His manner of "chip carving" and his rigid simplifications cause the light to spread more or less evenly over the object. In his treatment of face, body, and garment, he is far less naturalistic than the late medieval German carvers.

A work of his does not suggest concentration on a small detail, since every part is essentially linked with the adjoining one and, through it, with the total structure. There is no separate gesture—all is a horizontal, vertical, or diagonal design meaningful from top to bottom, enveloped by sharp lines and contours, monumental even in a piece only seven or eight inches high. Though a larger piece may consist of two or more pieces of wood joined together, the impression is always that of a solid block cut out of a big tree. Heavily, the figure stands, sits, or lies on the base that is always included in the concept of the original composition. The necks are short, and in most cases the arms cling tightly to the body. There is always movement, yet it is, with the exception of a few pieces, such as "The Avenger" and "The Sword-drawing Man," an inner movement of planes rather than an actual gesture of the body. His disposition restrains him from showing his figures in violent action; in the main, movement is produced by the dynamic interplay of plane surfaces rather than by kinetic illusionism. As a rule, he created single figures. Where there are two, they are not separated by any distance, but rather knit to one another by the composition: the mother who holds her child tightly against her own body, or, in the "Pieta," another standing mother who carries her dead soldier son across her body horizontally (thus, the image of a cross is created); the Christ who embraces the Apostle St. Thomas ("Das Wiedersehen"); the two men who, side by side, lean backward as they look up in fright at an apparition in the sky ("Panic Fright"); the monks united by the open book on their knees; and the six figures, tightly compressed into one group, in the war memorial of Magdeburg.

While, upon close inspection, it is difficult, if not impossible to mistake a Barlach for a medieval work, it is true that his preference for the wood medium clearly links him with the Gothic past. Wood, in modern times, was the medium of folk artists in the mountains of Norway or Bavaria, or the deep forests of Africa, while the professional artists had a choice between marble and bronze. As a matter of fact, when Barlach, after his Russian journey, for the first time turned to wood, he did so without any prior training. The only ones who were familiar with the qualities and peculiarities of wood were the craftsmen making furniture or household utensils. Before him, Gauguin, fascinated by the handicrafts of the South Sea islanders, had carved a few pieces in wood. Among Barlach's fellow expressionists, wood was used by Ernst Ludwig Kirchner, whose "Dancer with Raised Leg" suggests a primitive ritual dance. Ewald Mataré is another German who used wood, and so is the much younger Karl Hartung.

Regrettably, no wood sculptures are included in the current (1963) Barlach show, circulated by the Smithsonian Institution. Since wood is most fragile, collectors as well as museums are often reluctant to loan wood sculptures for what they expect to be extended trips. The Smithsonian Institution managed to borrow no fewer than thirty-five sculptures in porcelain and bronze, and, in addition, a number of fascinating drawings and prints. It remains to be seen whether this show, organized by Germany's Barlach Society, will succeed in making the U.S.A. "Barlach-conscious." But even if it should make a few sensitive individuals understand the aesthetic and humanistic goals of the strange and in some ways tragic recluse of Guestrow, without succeeding in converting the multitudes, the efforts of the sponsors in Hamburg and in Washington will not have been wasted.

Brian Keith-Smith   (essay date 1964)

SOURCE: "Ernst Barlach," in *German Men of Letters,* Vol. III: Twelve Literary Essays, edited by Alex Natan, Philadelphia/Dufour Editions, 1964, pp. 55-81.

[*In the following essay, Keith-Smith surveys Barlach's life and works.*]

Anyone thinking of writing an essay on Ernst Barlach soon realises that there are a number of special problems to be faced which on the one hand draw him on into the core of Barlach's artistry, and on the other hand continually rebuff him. Barlach's facility to express himself in sculpture, woodcuts, lithographs, dramas and prose works shows how closely these creatures of his are bound to their creator. The detailed care of his style in all media bears witness to a continual grappling with problems of communication. The complexity of details of construction and yet overall simplicity of his work shows he perceived different levels of consciousness both in the individual and in the group. The attention paid to light effects, to positioning of his characters, and in particular to subtle descriptions of relationships—whether human or spatial—show his preoccupation with man's need to find the truth, or as he would term this—"It" or the "Other". The almost complete lack of interest in time categories except to deepen man's knowledge of himself perhaps discloses an unhurried patience and spiritual freedom in him—so contrary to much of the superficial evidence of his life. The constant intrusion of a streak of humour seems to underline his individuality—yet his whole condition he so often considers as a state of banishment. And finally his forever changing points of departure, viewpoints, perspectives and way of looking at things would seem to suggest a dilettante at work—yet Barlach the master can concentrate his imagination into such detailed plastic terms, that his mature works need the minimum of cut and line to bring out their full meaning and power of suggestion. The variety of his works, even though they all bear the signature of his creative spirit, make any attempt at a conclusive essay written from one point of view irrelevant and out of the question. All one can do is to open up vistas which may help to lead to a better understanding of this complex artistic personality, about whom so much has been written in German and so little in English, and whose works—however obscure they may seem to be—never fail to reawaken one's intrigue and enjoyment.

Barlach's early life is narrated in his autobiography, *Ein Selbsterzähltes Leben,* written in 1927. Born in Wedel in 1870, son of a practising family doctor, into a family whose previous generations back to the seventeenth century had been local tailors, doctors or pastors, he drifted into being a sculptor because there was nothing else he particularly wanted to do. In Hamburg, 1889-91, he spent much time sketching passers-by in the street instead of limiting himself to the strict academic training of the Gewerbeschule. Already he was searching for a personal style, already he witnessed the aimless rush of city life. The next four years he was encouraged by his teacher Robert Diez at the Dresdner Akademie to explore his own way, and when his student friend Carl Garbers left for Paris he joined him. Paris for Barlach meant the opportunity to see and sketch a more cosmopolitan society, to visit the Louvre for weeks on end, to be impressed by the timeless monumentality of Egyptian and Korean art, and to indulge in experiments to become a writer. Sketching nude models at the Akademie Julien only resulted for him, as he put it, in:

"ausgezogene Männekens und entfederte Gänslein."[1]

Barlach's works hardly include a single naked body—not only because that would have otherwise been irrelevant to what he has to say through art form, but also because he was primarily an artist of the face and head. Much of his work until about 1906 was directly influenced by, if not a conscious imitation of, the current *art nouveau,* a fashion through which he had to find his own way. Yet even at this stage Barlach could laugh at his own limitations and products of Kitsch—for instance in the lines he wrote on a photograph of a ceramic of a self-portrait:

> Dieses ist, herrjeh,
> Barlachs Selbsporträt!
> In Thon gebrannt und dann glasiert
> Und mit einem Vers verziert.
> Er schüttelt, vor Erwartung stumm,
> Seinen Würfelbecher um,
> Die Würfel, die beim Wiederrollen
> Sein Lebensschicksal entscheiden sollen.
> Er würfelt um keinen kleinen Gewinn:
> Um ein "Leben" (nach seinem Sinn).[2]

In Hamburg and Altona, Barlach and Garbers worked together and produced a prize-winning design for the Hamburger Rathausmarkt. This was eventually transferred to another architect—the first of many occasions on which Barlach was to be harshly treated. He left for Berlin in 1900 where he lived later on several occasions for a few weeks at a time, and of which his first impressions were to be repeated on every subsequent visit. Life in an industrialised city meant hell for him, and seemed even more so in contrast with the years 1901-04 spent in Wedel. These years, apparently wasted, are related in outline in his novel *Seespeck*; but at this time he learnt to observe and understand human life unblemished by the more flagrant materialism of the modern city, and he learnt to appreciate the quiet harmonies of a natural and agrarian landscape. His year as a teacher at the Fachschule für Keramik at Höhr was upset by suspect heart trouble. In spite of writing a much used textbook, *Figürliches Zeichen,* he was unhappy and unsuccessful. In 1906 while working in Berlin, an illegitimate son, Klaus, was born, and for three years he conducted long legal wrangles to adopt him, spending all his savings and earnings in the process. Later he was to remark that all his works up to 1906 he could forget with pleasure as lacking in aim and as expressions of "Romantik und Gefühlsschwögerei"[3]—but this was for a very different reason.

For two months in 1906 Barlach went on a trip to Russia to visit relatives working there. His impressions of this visit vary considerably from the ecstatic statements in his *Russisches Tagebuch* in which he says he there discovered his sense of perspective, proportion and form, to denials in later letters of any lasting formative influence from this period on his later work. The visit was a culmination of a search for form almost brought to its end during the unfortunately poorly documented years at Wedel, a search still lacking a final decisive experience to bring full self-assurance to Barlach's artistry. The special conditions in which Russians lived and their way of life made him forcibly realise how closely man and landscape can complement each other. Man set in rather than against nature is the background of most of his works, and Barlach applied this as a most important principle of his artistic activity. The grain of a block of wood, its texture and malleability, are all allowed to express their qualities as integral parts of his sculptures. The forces acting in one direction in a soul—fear or elation for instance—are re-expressed in the work of art by a use of shapes and planes to their best advantage; and so we find the covered head and the stooping shoulders of a downtrodden beggar, and the leaping ebullience in all directions at once of the limbs and head of a woman in ecstasy. The central point of gravity or focus of many of Barlach's figures lies outside them—perhaps at a great distance (as with the Stargazer), or sometimes so closely bound up with them (as with the floating Güstrow angel) that "Innen ist wie Aussen, Aussen wie Innen".[4] Barlach became so sharply aware of this through the Russian people and landscape, that they seemed to him sculptures in themselves. He plunged into this sea of forms, but as he pointed out in a letter to Boris Pines on January 26, 1926, it would be wrong to think that he recognised these forms as specifically Russian:

> Meine innerliche Bereitschaft, meine mir gegebene Verfassung brachte ich mit—denn das Alles war auch in mir und das Alles ist wohl enorm russisch, aber auch enorm deutsch und europäisch und allmenschlich.[5]

Barlach saw after his visit to Russia that man is an imperfect experiment of nature; he took upon himself as an artist man's suffering condition, and by expressing man's dormant possibilities, attempted to redeem him. Suffering now meant for him discord in nature, alive as he was now to man's cosmological rather than social position.

Back in Berlin, Barlach's financial position was solved by the publisher Paul Cassirer who offered to finance his work and buy all his future products. In spite of never knowing when and if Cassirer would close this arrangement, Barlach had cause to be thankful for many years for this help. Without it, he once said, he would have remained a scribbler for the periodical *Simplizissimus*. In 1909 he won a prize for a year's study in Florence, where he appreciated the brightness of the light and the easy-going Italian life, but felt out of place, lonely and ill at ease. He longed to be back in his Northern climate and landscape. In spite of this, the most formative influence he underwent in Italy was the beginning of a life-long friendship with the poet Theodor Däubler—so utterly different, with his Southern temperament, from himself.

> Däubler ist der Bewohner einer anderen Welt, eines anderen Sterns, der aus einem unerfindlichen Grunde hierher zu uns geraten. Hier wird er notwendig zu einem Ungetüm.[6]

He tried to sum up his views on Däubler in *Diaro Däubler* (1912-14), and used this material in the last two chapters of *Seespeck.* Barlach was attracted by Däubler as a Columbus to a new world of the spirit outreaching man's normal limits, as a physical giant, as a world changer, as a man who stood with one foot firmly in myth. Yet he also found in him something of a Hochstapler (fraud) attempting to by-pass the normal categories of experience in trying to reach out to a non-representational use of language. Barlach comments:

> Schliesslich soll das menschliche Auge, das Ohr, der Sinn befriedigt werden, angeregt, da kann ich keine Welt, die nicht existiert, formen, da muss ich mich mit verständlichen Zeichen ausdrücken.[7]

Däubler is a Devil leading him away from all that is human; and Däubler is a God making man doubt his position and setting him back on a way towards the true unity of nature, from the centre of which man is shown to be an outcast. As Däubler jolts man out of his egocentricity, so Barlach can see him as a second Christ figure, and Seespeck see him as a mirror to the world. In *Seespeck* Däubler speaks and challenges Barlach's mind:

> "Sie klopfen an die Tür einer Wirklichkeit, aber zum Unterschied von andern Leuten wohne ich nicht innerhalb, sondern ausserhalb meiner vier Wände. Ich bin überall zu Hause, alles ist 'Ich'."[8]

Däubler teaches Barlach that "being" cannot be characterised, only its locus can be established:

> "Sein ist etwas anderes als Ich-Sein. Das bewusste Ich, Herr Doktor, ist der Klavierspieler, aber das Sein ist die Musik. . . . denn Sie machen die Maske zum Wesen zum Ding an sich und das Wesen zum Nichts am Ding."[9]

Barlach settled down in 1910 at Güstrow with his mother and Klaus. Here he wrote the *Güstrower Tagebuch* (1914-17), recording his changing outlook on life and his outer and inner life at the time. At first he looked on war as a blessing to lift man out of his everyday meaningless activity and to inspire him with a supra-personal purpose. But he also saw, especially in the sorrow of women, the cruel side of war, which he crystallises in one of his few important works of the time—the figure of the *Berserker.* He feared the national pride that would follow a German victory, yet could equate the beating of his heart with a national pulse eager to defend the cultural values misunderstood so badly by the Americans and others. Owing to his weak heart he had to remain a non-combatant, but was called up for two months' training as a recruit in December 1915. In almost every entry he registers frustration at not being able to help in the war-effort. He helps to run a Kinderhort (nursery home), and outbursts of anger are tempered by occasional realisations of his good fortune at being away from the trenches so vividly described in letters from his friends. He claims he writes to be able to revoke his feelings later, even to make use of the diary in *Seespeck*; but for weeks on end all the entries start with news headlines, and their tone suggests a child trying to exteriorise himself, to find and formulate his values. Even the "paar Tröpchen Ewigkeit"[10] that seep through to him in a Christmas carol service, even the typically Barlachesque pranks of Klaus and the daily reading with him of classic works of literature, even the stubbornness of his ailing mother, do not seem to provide him with a solid trust in his own individuality. He shows a continual need for contact with eternal truths, for his Ich to have:

> stärkstes und höchstes Leben und doch eine Erstarrung.[11]

The war made him more responsive to the call of a level of consciousness free from the demands of the individual ego. How pathetic and how revealing of his struggle is his call into that unexplored region.

> Die Zeit will Form bekommen, also bilde die Zeit! Schaffe Rat, guter Geist, schenk mir in Linien, was ich ahne, sende mir eine Kahn, damit ich auf den Ozean schiffen kann, da ich sehe![12]

In spite of the flagging of his creative energy during the war, Barlach's understanding of his place in nature and his descriptions of nature become more and more emphatic and effective. He experiences a form of return to the first "mystical" experiences of his childhood and approaches these now with a form of active memory described as:

> Beten heisst bei mir, das Wahre, nein, das Unaussprechliche erkennen, nicht betteln, nicht quasseln, nicht beschwatzen—nein, wissen: so ist es also—heiling sien.[13]

(With this in mind we are hardly surprised to find the features of the figure *Der Asket* or *Der Beter* [1925] resemble Barlach's own.) Barlach leads on to attack images of Christ given "modern" qualities such as tidy hair or academic honours, and he admires the Roman Catholic Church for its insistence on keeping man at a respectful distance from God. To feel in complete union with God meant for Barlach death of the individual or the devaluation of God in human terms—a "Vergötterung". Barlach is indeed a seeker after God, but he hesitates to name him, for that would be the first step towards explaining him, to limiting the myth. He seeks continuous dialogue with the Creator, in which "das zarte Versilbern aller Dinge"[14] helps him to pray.

> Da Gott ist, so ist er anders als wir: ohne Erinnern, Wissen Urteilen. Wissen kann ichs nicht, sehen nicht, hören nicht, also nicht glauben letzten Endes. Aber etwas muss ich glauben können, das besteht. Das ist die Lust, der Trieb, das Muss, das Wünschen—da ist Gott.[15]

God's position but not his character can be found and continually recorded. Barlach approaches God humbly and ceaselessly, for he can never say "my God", as he can no more explain his own existence than he can God's. He in fact refers to occasions on which God spurns him, to others on which God goads his desire to enfigure whatever he sees in things.

By 1919 Barlach had become well known in Germany, and he received various commissions to construct war memorials—many of which he carried out, but always with the emphasis on man's suffering through war and the message of peace. He rejected any form of patriotism and strongly resisted attempts by vested interests such as war veteran societies to make him produce works glorifying the patriotic killer instinct. A decade was to follow in which Barlach was more widely honoured than any of his contemporary artists. In 1919 he became a member of the Akademie der Künste in Berlin and was offered a professorship which he turned down. He preferred to bring up Klaus in Güstrow and to work there in the peace of his own studio. In 1920 his mother, after a few days in a rest home for mental defectives, committed suicide by drowning—an event which left a deep scar on his soul for months, even years, to come. In 1924 he won the Kleist prize for **Der Arme Vetter.** In 1925 he became honorary member of the Munich Academy of Arts. In 1933 he received the highest possible award— Ritter der Friedensklasse des Ordens pour le mérite. Even as late as 1936 he was elected honorary member of the Wiener Sezession and of the Viennese academy of plastic arts. His dramas were performed and remained on the theatrical repertoires in at least eight large towns. His sculptures were exhibited at a time when he was producing work after work. These were mainly his most famous and most characteristic figures for the most part in wood, the end products of many preparatory models in plaster and in clay, e.g. *Moses* (1918-19); 1910 *Die verhüllte Bettlerin, Die gemarterte Menschheit;* 1920 *Der Flüchtling, Tanzende Alte, Mutter Erde;* 1921 *Stehende Bäuerin, Lesende Mönche, Der Mann mit dem Mantel;* 1923 *Das Grauen, Weinende Frau, Zwei Schlafende;* 1924 *Der Wartende;* 1925 *Der Asket, Der Träumer;* 1926 *Das Wiedersehen, Die gefesselte Hexe;* 1927 *Güstrower Ehrenmal;* 1928 *Der Geistkämpfer;* and 1930 *Der singende Mann.* These may be called the "typical Barlach" together with most of the important woodcuts, four dramas, the autobiography, and the beginnings of **Der Graf von Ratzeburg.** The story of the gradually encroaching bans on Barlach's works from any public gallery, theatre or church, and the steady whittling down of his security so as to force him to emigrate before he became too awkward a figure for the Nazis to have speaking out against them at the slightest opportunity—for instance in the *Rundfunkrede* of 1932—is one of gathering inhumanity and growing despair. This is best told in the tone and contents of his letters, many of which have already been published, but far more of which are still not available. Individual acts of mockery and sabotage are well known, such as the removal of the *Güstrower Engel,* the defacing and later removal of the *Kieler Geistkämpfer,* the inclusion of his *Das Wiedersehen* in the notorious exhibition "Entartete Kunst" in 1937. The parallel story of Barlach's struggle to express his pity and faith in a better time to come through such works as the **Fries der Lauschenden,** as a

memorial to Beethoven, and the three completed figures of the "Gemeinschaft der Heiligen" *Frau im Wind, Der Bettler* and *Der Sänger* for the St. Katharinenkirche in Lübeck, through the pathos and humanity of the *Magdeburger Ehrenmal* and through the portrayal of suffering in so many figures such as *Das Jahr 1937* is one best left to the figures themselves. These are the works that have attracted so many "Barlach-Verehrer",[16] and it is only in a sense of respectful recognition of masterly genius and talent expressed as a reaction to the brutality of the Third Reich that one can approach them. It would perhaps be wise to apply to them Guido K. Brand's remark in general about Barlach when he said:

> "Nirgends schweigt man so tief, als wenn man von Barlach spricht."[17]

The silence which grew around Barlach during the Thirties was one forced upon him by continual disappointments. There can be little doubt that the frequent bouts of illness that afflicted him during the last four or five years of his life were accentuated by growing fears for the welfare of his friends and family, and more generally for the local and European spirit to which he bore such eloquent witness. Castigated as a Jew by the Nazis, Barlach's works of art were still popular enough with their leaders for him to be allowed to die peacefully in a Rostock clinic in October 1938.

Barlach's woodcuts and illustrations are for many people his most revealing works, for these show both his virtuosity as a craftsman and the difficulties he experienced in adapting himself to enfigure the visions of other geniuses. In the woodcuts especially his individuality is clearly scored, as in these the material he uses becomes a way of recreating himself into plastic form rather than a means of interpreting the world outside him. There are also a number of incomplete models in various materials for most of the major sculptures— most of them exercises in which he worked out proportions for each subject—these too seem to be the remainder as it were of the sum of creative processes being worked out by his imagination. In his plastic art Barlach seeks to encompass and contour the inner essence of a character or event which corresponds to the response of his own imagination. For this reason perhaps, but also because of the weird effects which they produce, the woodcuts to Kleist's *Michael Kohlhaas* and the drawings for a *Nibelungen* cycle are a failure. Barlach's imagination which ironically enough was forever seeking to escape its own bounds, was incapable of completely identifying itself actively to anyone else's. His plastic art is the expression, sometimes the triumphal lay, sometimes the spectral elegy of the brotherhood that Barlach the artist found between Barlach the man and the real or fictional things in the world about him. Seespeck is carrying out this creative process when Barlach writes of him:

> Was an menschlichen Wesen vorkam, das holte er sich mit den Augen wie mit dem geistigen Fangorgan an seine Seele.[18]

And Barlach writes of himself:

> Ich fange eine Chiffre mit den Augen auf, und sie wird im Dunkeln meines Ich übersetzt und dort verarbeitet.[19]

Barlach's struggle for mastery over his material, so frequently referred to in his letters and other writings, is particularly obvious in his woodcuts and drawings. Thus the first set of thirteen lithographs to the essay *Steppenfahrt* never appeared separately, possibly because they lack interesting subject-matter, their main emphasis being on the contourless wavy shaping of figures into the landscape. In the twenty drawings on the theme *Kriegszeit* Barlach never escapes the patriotic purpose for which they were created. The hard restrictions of line found in the first set of woodcuts in 1919 for Reinhard von Walter's poem *Der Kopf* contrast strongly with the flexibility of line arrangement in the *Steppenfahrt* lithographs. Far more effective is the attention to detail and the use of light and shadow brought out as a function for the contrasts of black and white in this medium seen in the twenty woodcuts to *Der Findling* (1921), where grotesque and serious elements are found in the same cutting. Detailed characterisation of separate elements—sometimes particular parts of one body—reveals a growing facility in picking out minor details which yet do not disturb the overall effect of the whole scene. This can be seen as a stage in Barlach's way to his later ability in all his media to portray a double-sidedness in his creatures. *Der Findling* was the last of his own works that Barlach felt the need to illustrate, and it may be found that the later works are more completely pictorial in themselves, or at least that Barlach felt they were. The earlier twenty-seven lithographs to *Der Tote Tag* are an attempt to situate the events of the drama in a mythological setting, which might be said to be underdrawn in the actual play or at least not sufficiently enfigured or explained. This is also the aim of the drawings to *Der Arme Vetter* where the mythological patterns are made clear in both dialogue and drawings. The twenty woodcuts to Goethe's *Walpurgisnacht* reflect Barlach's deep and lasting interest in *Faust,* and it is hardly surprising that they embody his interpretation of the central figures. Faust looks remarkably like a Siegfried or a Hamlet accompanied by a shadowy and equally tormented Mephistopheles. Gretchen represents statuesquely particular lines from the scene. Minor and more gruesome figures allow Barlach to exploit his imagination almost at times to caricature. In 1923 Barlach again turned to Goethe, producing thirty-five drawings to join those of other artists in a volume of illustrations to Goethe's poems. Here Barlach prefers those poems where the demonic or supernatural elements play a leading part, some developing new visions in his mind others eliciting somewhat conventional responses from his imagination. The mysterious power of the woman creating stone from water in *Legende* forcibly links through the drawing Goethe's idea and Barlach's ceaseless preoccupation with the theme of form evolving out of chaos, shape out of shapelessness. On the other hand Barlach has nothing to add with his illustration to *Erlkönig. Der Zauberlehrling* becomes a farce and *Die Wandelnde Glocke* an exquisite humorous comment on Goethe's poem. With all the successful drawings Barlach has managed to probe behind the everyday, and has plumbed the depths of myth where individual mask returns to archetypal face, where man is set in space rather than time. This is also seen in the not entirely successful nine woodcuts to Schiller's *Lied an die Freude* (1927), where closed-eyed figures forget their individualities in rapt self-forgetfulness in an individuation into the cosmos about them. The greatest achievement of all Barlach's woodcuts are the seven of *Die Wandlungen Gottes* (1922). The relatively large areas of black and white in the Creator's robes in *Der erste Tag,* framed by receding billows in the dark chaos around his form-giving hands, have all disappeared in *Der siebente Tag* where a tired but pleased Creator views the order and purpose of his creation from a rock seat of the same shaped texture it would seem as the Creator's robes and even the valley below. The Creator's achievement is clear—he has moulded the forces of chaos with his energy into a harmony where creator and creature are one. The other five give proof of Barlach's imaginative powers over perspective, and his visions of God set in the panoramas of horror and peace. In these Barlach all but overcomes with increasing freedom the rectangular limitations of woodcut design.

Barlach's first attempts to write drama date from the years at Wedel with a fragment that is as yet unpublished. His first completed drama *Der Tote Tag* (1919) was originally called *Blutgeschrei* and deals with the problem of an over-possessive mother whose son waits for the divine horse to carry him away into a separate life of his own. The drama opens out from a family conflict in the naturalist manner into a *Weltanschauungsdrama* whose tension is sprung on the guilt of the son's doubt in the interest of a God-Father. The mother kills the horse, and the son is doomed to stumble blindly through his life—his hope having gone and his day of redemption being dead. Finally the mother and then the son commit suicide.

Der arme Vetter (1918) examines the effect of Hans Iver, whose insight into the true motives in human life has led him to despair and attempted suicide, on other people, especially Frl. Isenbarn. Her fiancé, Siebenmark, a philistine but aware of a purpose behind things and events, remains cut off from all true human contact because of his inability to accept his own and other people's idiosyncrasies and faults. Siebenmark's egoism and Iver's humility throw each other into sharp relief, so much so, that the sensitive and innocent Frl. Isenbarn watches herself turn towards Iver, until on his second and successful suicide attempt, she kisses his dead body and leaves her fiancé forever. Through this act Siebenmark achieves clearer insight into himself and his responsibilities towards others. Barlach also includes a tavern scene in which a grotesque figure of a young man dressed up as Frau Venus represents the unthankful world that the poor cousin Iver has come to redeem. Iver loses faith in the innate goodness of man once again and is obliged to accuse Siebenmark of looking for his own image in his fiancée. In their different ways Iver and Siebenmark are made aware of their inability to accept the independence of a Du figure—for Iver turns Siebenmark into a symbol of all mankind, and Siebenmark can scarcely comprehend Iver's accusations. Only in Frl. Isenbarn does the unasked for presence of God inform her instinct and responses to life.

Die echten Sedemunds (1920) in which a lion—symbol of a corrupt society's conscience—is supposed to have escaped is paralleled in the final chapter of *Seespeck* (*Der Löw ist Los*) where surrealist symbol contains the drama's plot and its hidden meaning. The escaping lion may also be taken as a cipher for young Sedemund cutting loose from the restrictions of family tradition, and more generally as the individual breaking free from the demands of his human condition. Young Sedemund sets out to alter the state of a society based on false values, but is at first also subject to them. He lays bare the dependence of his family on the example of their forebears who could let a wife be driven to suicide and a son of the house be sent to an asylum rather than allow any doubt attach itself to the honour of the family name. Young Sedemund spreads the rumour that a lion has escaped, and this exposes ridiculous human failings in a series of minor episodes. Gradually the major sins of the past are drawn out by fear of the lion's retribution, and it is not until Onkel Waldemar (modelled on Barlach's first drawing teacher in Hamburg?) recognises in young Sedemund the true progressive spirit of the family, that the lion is dead.

The mystery play *Der Findling* (1922) foresees in hideous detail some of the horrors of the Second World War, and seeks a way of hope for a suffering humanity that has cast out its gods and is fleeing continuously from the political upheavals caused by one despot after another. An unwanted adopted child is saved from death by a stone breaker who through his care is eventually accepted as a saviour. After the cannibalism of the first part, the figure of Elise, daughter of Kummer, and ashamed of the despair and bestial conditions of her parents, shines out with full belief in the power of grace even in the midst of misery. Thomas the puppeteer is changed through her example from a good-for-nothing into a Thomas Dogood. Elise, blessed with a faith activating others to seek and cultivate the merciful and hopeful qualities of the human soul, turns the foundling into a saviour figure for them; and at least for Thomas she becomes a new Mary, a new Mother of God. Man is shown to find redemption only by recognising the example of others as an encouragement to overcome the turning towards bestiality of his own self. The first step in this is seen to be to forget one's past by first being ashamed of it, and then by building a hopeful future on a new Ich.

The main underlying theme to *Die Sündflut* (1924) is that of various understandings of and attitudes towards the nature of God. In an important letter to Arthur Kracke referring to this (February 4, 1930) Barlach would seem to give his ultimate answer to this problem:

> Ich ergreife, nein, mich ergreift in besten Stunden die Vorstellung der Entpersönlichung, des Aufgehens im Höheren, ich nenne es das Glück der Selbstüberwindung, in dem das volle Bewusstsein des Ichs enthalten und erhalten bleibt. Unpersönlichkeit, d.h. Unbegrenztheit muss das Wesen dessen sein, den ich nur noch ungern "Gott" nenne.[20]

Forgetting one's past is now seen as not a sufficient basis to overcoming one's self. There must also be a fear of God—and in *Die Sündflut* Noah is found by an angel to be the only human to still have this. Even after the heaviest tribulations Noah is ready to prepare a sacrifice and recognise his God in the beggar crawling outside his tent. Calan, the rival shepherd, a tempter and embodiment of evil and set actively and proudly against God, brings Noah a beautiful girl Awah as a present to gain his favour. Noah is finally persuaded in spite of Calan's cynicism to go into the hills and build an ark against the coming flood. Awah's statement:

> Die Welt ist winziger als Nichts, und Gott ist Alles—ich sehe nichts als Gott. . . . Gott ist die grosse Stille, ich höre Gott,[21]

is later modified by Sem, one of Noah's sons, who sees God peeping through chinks from behind everything. This explains for him a God who can allow all his creatures except those in the ark to perish. Noah and his sons prevent Calan from taking over the ark and leave him in chains to face the rising waters, but with a plea to accept God who may then set him free. None of the many interpretations of this play seem entirely satisfactory; for any claim that Noah is not Barlach's ideal man as he turns against his neighbour and therefore becomes the symbol of irresponsibility, does not accord with Barlach's own further comments in the letter already quoted. For by judging Noah by "human" standards we may thereby idealise God in this play into a form of perfect man. Noah is only justified in his action if we accept all human actions as part of God's purpose and forget—as Barlach asks us to do—all categories of good and evil. Calan clearly is through human eyes an evil character if only for his inhuman cruelty—yet we may not interpret his fate as a just reward unless we attribute to Noah the role of God's executioner. Nor is it easy to maintain that Barlach is pointing a moral that God exists as avenger for one man and redeemer for another. Barlach is certainly destroying man as he puts it in this letter "als Ding für sich".[22] Calan after a night out in the storm and mud, and when the rats have gnawed out his once proud eyes, has become to his pleasure and pride "keine Gestalt mehr . . . nur noch Glut und Abgrund in Gott",[23] and yet he sees

> den anderen Gott, von dem es heissen soll, die Welt ist gross, und Gott ist winziger als Nichts—

ein Pünktchen, ein Glimmen, und Alles fängt in ihm an, und Alles hört in ihm auf. Er ist ohne Gestalt und Stimme.[24]

Noah still trusts in a God to lead him past the flood and its threat of annihilation. Either could be equally wrong in his certainty, but the play ends with the sound of the approaching flood, and Barlach gives no answer.

Der blaue Boll (1926) tells the story of a man who overcomes the limitations of his self and becomes a higher being. A wealthy landowner by inheritance rather than by choice, Boll has learnt to become over-ridingly self-confident and stands like a tower overlooking his fellow men. He has theoretically and forcibly overcome the temptations of the flesh, but in a scene set in the church tower, Boll is faced with the temptation of helping Grete who has given birth to three children and who has thus set three souls into the limitations of their human bodies, and who now wants to poison them and set their souls free once more. Boll has repeatedly torn himself to pieces in an effort to overcome the demands of his flesh by denying its power, but his trust in these is brought back when Grete helps him up after a fit of vertigo, and he is humiliated by the old clock maker. Boll agrees to bring the poison for Grete that evening in exchange for her love. For the whole day he is plagued with guilt, but as he will not accept that Boll has to shoulder any responsibility, he goes to fetch the poison. He changes his mind and meets Grete at the rendezvous without the poison. She mocks him and, aided by the devil Elias, leaves him to himself. Herr the stranger and Boll's wife help Boll most towards accepting responsibility for Grete, whose character also evolves after a vision of hell she has in Elias' tavern. Boll's former pride and Grete's former witchlike qualities—both growing out of dissatisfaction with their human lot—have attracted, repulsed and finally destroyed each other against a background of less complex and less extreme characters whose everyday acceptance of their fate serves as a foil and example to Boll and Grete. Boll—formerly so ready to consider suicide rather than accept the conditions of a human society—has overcome his earlier position—

Boll muss? Muss? Also—will ich![25]

Barlach's last two plays *Die gute Zeit* (1929) and the unfinished *Der Graf von Ratzeburg* are martyr dramas that look forward to the theatre of the absurd. Celestine is too close to the "Other" in her vision of the "gute Zeit" that is at variance with Atlas' system of "Absolute Versicherung",[26] and she is crucified as a herald of the time to come, as a proof of the anxiety of the time now. As she puts it:

Himmel, ja du hast recht, o, wie recht du hast, wir sind eins mit der Zeit, eins mit der guten, eins mit der bösen, und wie wir, so sind die Zeiten und die Zeiten sind wie wir. . . . Alles und Alles ist gut und reine Güte, wenn ich gut bin, und alles ist gut und reine Güte, wenn keine Angst

das Böse ruft—nur still, nur still, nur das Böse nicht gerufen, nur nicht ins Böse kommen mit der Angst, die allein das Böse bringt.[27]

Heinrich, Graf von Ratzeburg, overthrown, enslaved, humiliated into a lowly search for God and for his own true self, is eventually murdered ironically for apparently the wrong motives. In his struggles, in his constant preoccupation to keep on the right way, and in the fragmentary record that we have of him, Heinrich embodies perhaps the Pascalian aspect of Barlach's nature. The complex language and plot of this play make any interpretation of it as yet unviable—it may well remain the most puzzling of all Barlach's works.

Barlach's carefully chiselled style and highly poetic language often directly evoke both the ideas and the effects he requires in a particular context; and there are many passages, sentences or phrases into which he compresses a whole variety of stylistic devices, and which only reveal their intricate and sensitively chosen details on closer analysis. Thus the ending to Chapter 2 of *Seespeck* describing the "allerlei Krauses"[28] of Seespeck's dream:

Bei alledem hatte Seespeck Zeit, aus dem Hinterfenster herauszuschauen auf einen steilen Dorfkirchturm, gegen den sich die niedersteigende Chaussee grade herabrollte und hinter dem rechts und links die Ostsee sich verbreitete. Ganz oben stand eine gnadenlose Sonne der Kirchturm rückte langsam näher, aber Seespeck fiel es nicht ein, darüber nachzudenken, wie man aus der Hintertür eines Omnibusses nach etwas schauen und doch immer näher herankommen kann.[29]

In these two sentences there are frequent changes of perspective. Thus Seespeck, the subject in the third person (we look *at* him) who looks *out* of the rear window of a bus which we learn is moving because the objects which he watches appear to be moving, looks out *at* a church tower, *towards* which the avenue rolls, and *behind* which the Baltic stretches *to* the left and right. We look *up* at the sun, *at* the church slowly appearing to come closer. The church tower becomes in its turn a sort of starting point for further changes in perspective, the avenue and the Baltic only being fixed in relation to it. We note at first that the town is Dorfkirchturm and later just a Kirchturm, as if it is no longer seen within the confines of a village, but as the only object filling the narrow rear window of a bus. The horizontal plane of view in which we have noticed the avenue (clearly setting us at a distance from the church) and the sea behind it on either side of the church, now gives way to a vertical plane of view, the church tower filling it. There is nothing to say if the sun is right overhead the church or just "ganz oben"—the connection with the church is left for us to fill in (just as with Barlach's sculptures where their doublesidedness of character depends on the particular light in which they stand and on the viewpoint of the spectator). Moreover there is looseness of syntactical connection in the last phrase. Is the church coming nearer to the bus, or the bus to the church? Has there in fact been another change of subjects? Are we witnessing a parallel phenomenon to that of seeing wheels apparently change direction when they move fast enough? The final clauses saying that it did not occur to Seespeck to reflect on this optical illusion makes out of this sense of vertigo a form of normal experience. Seespeck's non-observance of this is shown to be abnormal. Barlach has purposely built up the sensations of this developing vertigo as if we were watching through Seespeck's eyes. But Seespeck is never aware of them—he is the passive object of a series of sensations which attain no meaning because he is not actively registering them. The underlying tension of his situation at the time is brought out here by stylistic effect. A still closer analysis shows that the objects of the verbal forms are simply places in a field of perspective, except for "Zeit" which Seespeck has but does not use. Similarity the subjects are merely viewpoints. The verbs are either directional or negative—only one has any permanency, "stand". Both this and the non-verbal adjectives refer to sun and tower, and even "steilen" and "gnadenlose" emphasise direction. It is typical that for Barlach sun and church tower seem finally to be the only points of reference around which the rest of the landscape revolves or moves. Seespeck cannot find his own position in relationship to these and remains part of a shifting, uncentred field of perspectives.

Clearly much of the linguistic value of this piece would be lost in translation and one would like to feel that Barlach has succeeded here by the standard he himself set in a letter to his cousin Karl:

> "Ich Kämpfte oft tagelang mit einem einzigen Wort, suche nach einem Satz von drei Worten endlos hin und her und muss oft verzichten, weil ich kein Wort mit der nötigen Silbenzahl finde, es gibt das Wort nicht, sollte es aber geben . . . Das Unerhörte kann nur mit unerhörten Worten erzählt werden, aber die unerhörten Worte werden plötzlich zu falschen Worten, denn das Selbstverständliche, das im Unhörbaren liegt und das man zwingen will, damit das Ergebnis befriedigt und hingenommen werden muss, das Selbstverständliche bedingt wieder das schlichteste Wort, die Aufgabe ist: zwingen und nicht bezwungen scheinen."[30]

But when Barlach chooses to introduce elements of playful irony or puns, his style becomes an appeal to the emotions or to a less sophisticated sense of humour than he is sometimes capable of. Barlach's sense of humour is one which does not always have such a direct appeal because it often also gives an extra dimension to what is normally felt to be grim. Thus the humorous treatment of Calan and minor figures in *Der Findling* which turns into the grotesque and at times the loathsome. Sometimes he appears to be using humour as a defence against despair, and he always seems to give it some further function than just being the expression of a writer brimful of play, a natural outburst of spontaneous fun for its own sake. It is a place where he can lose

himself, but it is also a place where he never entirely loses sight of man's true condition. Thus the following untranslatable passage from *Güstrower Tagebuch* (August 8, 1915) describing soldiers at Güstrow:

> Da tauchen aus lackiertem Dämmer treumichelhaft gedachte, in der Tat wie zierbengelige, von der dämlichen Backfischleutnants-idealität parfümierte Helden und treten in Beziehung zu irgendwelchen Nino-Nana—oder aber Elfriede-Mimihaften Treugretchen. Die einsame Wacht in finstrer Mitternacht flötet der Stöckelschuhelegantität ein Ständchen.

There is a far more serious problem when Barlach's language trying to express the essence of existence hiding behind the veil of human activity and humanly developed forms and modes of description, chooses to recreate the secret, unknown—perhaps unknowable—essence of things by using a series of abstract phrases, rhyme schemes or alliterative linguistic associations. Barlach's language in such instances fails to become a connecting line from the human world of expression to the essence of existence, and remains a line parallel to it. Thus in *Der Graf von Ratzeburg*:

> Das war die Lust, die lüstern ist nach der letzten Lust, und die letzte Lust ist die Gemeinschaft des Gehorsams mit seinem Widerspruch.[31]

We are left wondering, even in the context, whether the alliterations and plays on words can be any more than a revelation of Barlach's own struggle with a medium whose usefulness he continually questions, and which he sums up in his letters of October 18, 1932 and December 3, 1932 to two priests. To express any absolute concept outside the range of our senses the word, although it is something "was direkt ins Innerste dringt, wo es aus dem Lautersten, der absoluten Wahrheit kommt",[32] is nothing but "ein elender Notbehelf, ein schäbiges Werkzeug".[33] It is because he attempts to use language as a means to express the quality of an event as well as its causes and consequences, that Barlach's style develops at times too much associative meaning. It would be possible to show that all Barlach's creatures contain their own, or rather their creator's interpretation, and are aware of being in a way that reaches out beyond their own limitations as characters. This develops to such a pitch that by the time Barlach writes *Der Graf von Ratzeburg* nearly all concepts are examined, broadened out, and in the process made almost impossible to put successfully on the stage. The concrete explanatory image, powerful in its first direct statement, is examined for its universal quality, and in doing this Barlach at times opens up a level of consciousness, at times even dialogue, below or at least removed from the episodic story of his characters' lives. Thus, to take but one example, Offerus in *Der Graf von Ratzeburg* asks:

> Und ist Warten nicht ein Mantel, durchlöchert mit Gehorsam und von der traurigen Farbe der Untertänigkeit, ohne Ehre und Ansehen zu tragen?[34]

To appreciate the significance of this remark for the characters involved, one is forced to answer yes, to allow some of Offerus' limitations to become one's own. Only then does this visionary language hold the attention, only when we are prepared to overcome all the inherited logical, sensory or spiritual categories and forget ourselves can we follow Barlach's admittedly powerful but also all-demanding use of language. This is why one can only be "Barlach-Verehrer"[16] or accept him as a writer bound down to a personal vision, who can only speak to those who accept his own Weltanschauung. Occasionally, as with Boll, a character is shown as an outsider to this and can develop a personality of his own, but most of Barlach's creatures represent no more than a special stage or feature of a suffering humanity.

Barlach's unfinished Geisterroman *Reise des Humors und des Beobachtungsgeistes* sets an important pattern for much of his later characterisation—especially with Wau and Wahl in *Der gestohlene Mond.* For the dependence of the allegorical Humor on the equally allegorical Beobachtungsgeist not only suggests the interplay of two sides of Barlach's own character as an artist, but is also an early recognition of a basic theme in his work—that an individual is most clearly apprehended through his dialogue with another. The parallel to Jean Paul's Walt and Vult in *Flegeljahre* has often been made—though Barlach's debt to Jean Paul has not yet been fully examined. Written in Paris, this first attempt at a major prose work is buoyant with the humour and scepsis of a young writer experimenting with ideas and devices and pushing them to their extreme. The topsy-turvy world of the Louvre at night when the statues become alive is taken perhaps a little too far to hold the reader's fascination. The allegorical Klub der deutschen Ideen whose members include such as Kunstsinn, Ideale, Pessimismus, Autoritätenglaube,[35] etc. could well be a modern baroque-type conceit, but Barlach becomes intrigued with this, and develops the theme for its own sake. There are signs of a keen sense of fun and an eye for detail, for example in the description of a discarded newspaper on a draughty corner at night:

> Da sie gerade bei einer Querstrasse waren, so winkte das Zeitungsblatt dem Winde, ihm über die Strasse in den nächsten Rinnstein zu helfen. Denn da war eine Laterne, die sich gern von solchen Geschichten unterhalten liess, und als (sich) langsam vorwärts wälzte, fuhr es fort, einen Satz Unflat nach dem andern zu berichten. Nun waren sie bei der Laterne angelangt, und alle Lichtstrahlen versammelten sich neugierig um das Zeitungsblatt.[36]

But both the content and the dilettante approach of this work show Barlach at this time to be no more than a Schillerian "Phantast".

Barlach started to write *Seespeck* in January 1913, left it to one side in August 1914, and finally gave it up as a fragment in October 1916. The opening atmosphere is an epic counterpart to that of *Der arme Vetter* showing the environs of Hamburg and the inhabitants of the Lower Elbe. Seespeck is as much Barlach as Werther is Goethe in that the episode and attitudes are those of a recent past psychologically extended into a more universal significance. Yet the carefully constructed literary motivation and psychological interest in Seespeck as an aimless character in the opening scenes breaks down more and more into the realistic chronicle of Barlach-Seespeck in Wedel. The characters become portraits of locals instead of the author's creatures, until Theodor Däubler appears and speaks and becomes the focal point of Barlach's interest. And the last chapter *Der Löw Ist Los* becomes the epic pronouncement of the plot of *Die Echten Sedemunds,* written in a highly imaginative surrealistic language that breaks down conventional plot development in a frenzy of perspective and shifting action. The style and content of the beginning of this work underline Seespeck's lack of a centre of gravity, and by extension Barlach's. Most of the action is told through Seespeck's consciousness and Barlach's imagination. Barlach seems at times to be exploring through Seespeck the possible developments of events that might have taken place—such as the scene with Grete's family at the end of which Seespeck says to himself:

> Eine Schwiegermutter hast du nun, Seespeck, aber keine Braut, das ist dir recht, denn das passt zu dir.[37]

And there are many passages where Barlach seems to write within a tradition—such as Goethe's or Storm's anthropomorphic use of nature, or Joseph Conrad's descriptions of seafaring families. Much of this novel however seems to be a vessel into which Barlach poured the themes and problems that interested him, for example the effects of light, sufferings as a touchstone for the conscience, beauty as an enfiguration of the Weltseele, the difference of a person seen through the eyes of different people, the similarity in kind of the sinful and the sacred, the prodigal son, the Doppelgängertum of Seespeck's existence, and men caged in their own way of life (Menschentum). *Seespeck* is interesting and artistically valid only in its parts; its rambling diversity of styles deny it as a serious work of art; but through it Barlach can be seen working out a way to mastery over the novel form.

Der gestohlene Mond (April 1936-November 1937) is also considered by some critics as unfinished. As this work includes most of the maturer aspects of his Weltanschauung, it can be seen as Barlach's central work. It is also—notoriously—his most difficult. The two main characters Wau and Wahl are functions for an interplay of self-consciousness in which each reveals the other. Wau, even though not an artist, perhaps stands for Barlach himself, for he is described intimately from within, whereas all the other characters are portrayed from without. The love-hate relationship between Wau and Wahl is developed into the major interest of the work. Wau, being an entirely passive character, wishes to blend himself into an uneventful existence, and so there is no question of this being a Bildungsroman. His experience of the relativity and random encounter with culture in his life leads him to doubt the concept of personality and to have no faith in God. He can see no basis to a better existence and needs to control a Mein-Welt as a "Prüfstein des Anderen".[38] But only a constant preoccupation with death symbolised by the moon can bring him closer to the "Other", for the moon is to earth as death is to life. Wau, to form his character, needs the catalyst Wahl who warns him against subtle speculations with dilettante ideas and word plays in which he has been brought up. At times Barlach as narrator pokes fun at the seriousness of this situation where one man struggles spiritually with the other to avoid being philistine, to achieve a feeling of distance from the demands of the everyday and society. Wahl is selfish—a foil to Wau's lack of belief in any principle. Wahl is an opportunist and parasite feeding off Wau's weakness in needing continual support for his state of being an outsider which he realises after a violent dream. Wau is even haunted by Wahl's features, so demanding does Wahl become. The unsuccessful attempt of Wau's wife Henny to come back to him, makes him realise that his power over himself gradually ebbs away when he thinks back to the past when he gave himself completely to her. The broken record image of the dream and the broken marriage of the present both ironically lead to a fusion of Wau's person, for Wau's present is patterned by incursions from the past. Barlach uses time as formulated in a fragment to *Seespeck*:

> die Zeit ist ein Gummiband und lässt sich unendlich zerren, schliesslich aber schnellt sie einmal zusammen, und es ist alles beim alten.[39]

Wau in his cups envies Wahl's certainty that his world of appearances is the true world of reality, and tries to induce a state of intoxication in which he can convince himself of what he knows to be true, resulting in his first "mystical" experience:

> Es war ein Schatten dagestanden, der von ihm selbst ausging, durch die Wolken stiess, den Mond verdeckte, die Sonne trübte und in den Weltenraum unabsehbar heineinragte, ja ihn erfüllte, denn es blieb kein Raum zwischen den Gestalten der Körper und Sterngruppen war, überall waren sie von dem Schatten, der von ihm ausging, verhüllt und in ihm geborgen.[40]

A vision of a giant pulse-beat high over the sun follows and Wau hardly knows if it is an extension of his own. This Märchenwelt in which Barlach's style closely parallels with its long sentences the idea of letting a genie out of a bottle is suddenly punctuated by the direct contact of a living person Friedrich Schult. This is either a Stilbruch or an emphatic assertion that the traditional separation of the imaginary and the everyday is false. Certainly in the chaining together of Wau and Wahl in an ever tightening lock of characters the same device is used to uncover deeper levels of consciousness. In ful-

filling each other's existence Barlach can turn the style describing these two from third person narrative to third person conversation to a direct Ich-Du dialogue. The way is open for each to educate the other's spirit, yet planning not to lose face, they prepare for a long spiritual struggle for mastery over the other man. The situation is repeated in the relationship between Wau and Henny, who speaks to him in words reminiscent of the central dramatic idea in Sartre's *Huis Clos*:

> Besinnen wir uns darauf, dass wir nichts für uns sind, immer nur das Gute und Böse für jemand anders, wie er für uns—ach, diese Gegenseitigkeit die uns aufhebt, die uns zu nichts macht . . . und doch . . . [41]

With Wau Barlach allows this to be extended into two voices—Harut and Marut who discuss in his mind the issue of love and hate. A third unidentified voice closes their conversation, proof perhaps that Barlach wishes to allow for the inexplicable intrusion of God, but probably merely a device to close a section neatly. Wau becomes more and more aware of the insidious presence of Wahl in his own mind, but Barlach is careful not to let the novel burst its bounds at any place, and alternately examines Wau at such close quarters that his individuality disappears in the common humanity he has with others, and then steps back and looks at him through the eyes of another and minor character conditioned by accepting the appearance of Wau as his true self. This is perhaps a key to open up a way into the centre of this confused and confusing novel. Once again individual sections stand out for their expressivity, but this time they fit more obviously and intriguingly into the pattern of the whole. Here more perhaps than anywhere else in his works Barlach makes the reader open his eyes in many different ways to look at things, characters and events stereometrically as it were. *Der gestohlene Mond* may be seen as a workshop in which Barlach repeated the many preparatory sketches for his major sculptures in epic form. It reproduces the processes which have to take place before an artist can achieve what Barlach did in his sculptures in particular—the principle of reduction. Seen in this light, it is a tragic statement of the lack of a Du figure in Barlach's own life, perhaps even a surrogate for one.

W. Gielow's bibliography—*Ernst Barlach Literatur-Verzeichnis* (twenty-seven pages) published privately in Munich, 1954, seems now to be unobtainable. The Select Bibliography below can only include a representative list of recent monographs and articles on Barlach together with the main and popular recent editions of his work. The Ernst Barlach Gesellschaft in Hamburg has published restricted annual Barlach rarities and an occasional critical work. Dr. Friedrich Schult now lives in Barlach's Güstrow home and has made it the centre of Barlach scholarship and research, where nearly all of the major manuscripts and some of the sculptures are housed.

Any evaluation of Barlach's position as a twentieth-century artist and writer is bound to evoke a contrary opinion—for not only are his products depersonalised (they are never complete summations of the single moment or of the individual character), but they also display a doublesidedness that is often apparently a paradox in itself. An understanding of this would be essential before one could pass judgement on Barlach's creatures— even to one's own satisfaction. None of them represent complete unity between the self and the other, between the mortal individual with his own characteristics and the undefinable infinity of God. Barlach is at his greatest when he captures in a figure or character the tension between these two poles. The relaxed and carefree in his laughing statues achieve their striking effect because of the presence of lines marking previous grief or stress. The human frame is shown complete in itself but fleeting possessor of a super-human attribute. When this is allowed to fill out the whole of the human frame so that the frame is forgotten—as in the often complicated speech of Boll or the Graf von Ratzeburg for example— Barlach becomes less convincing. It might be shown that where he tries to embrace all the possibilities of one moment, where he is drawn into an ecstatic state which demands full lyrical expression, he fails. Where on the other hand he remains a conscious yet humble craftsman, where he is still alive to the tension involved in dialogue, and when he actively chooses to include this as the main focus of our perspective on to his creatures, he convinces. This is borne out in his use of language— for when his word-plays confirm the double levels of a situation, rather than create them from without, his language vibrates with the pulse of a vital experience. Barlach's humour is never so pungent as when it confirms rather than spotlights. Barlach's characterisation is at its most compelling when it frames a character's limits, and at its worst when it is a hook for endless chains of possible development. Barlach remains an enigma because he himself was constantly and consciously preoccupied with the enigma of human life. To call him a mystic is to misunderstand much of his art and life. To label him an Expressionist is to attribute to him a certainty of attitude that does not belong to an artist whose creatures bear witness to the continuous quest of their creator. Barlach had two outstanding physical features—deep, dark, enquiring eyes, and rugged, supple, tense hands. In these two features with their attributes lay the essentials of his vision and his limitations. His work records their constant interplay, and perhaps only when we can keep that in the forefront of our minds should we begin to evaluate Barlach.

TRANSLATIONS

[1] Undressed little men and plucked little geese.

[2] This is, dear me, a Barlach self-portrait! Baked in clay and then glazed and embellished with a verse. He shakes, dumb with anticipation his dice-shaker, those dice, which when they roll again shall decide his fate. He's not dicing just for a small win, but for a "life"— as he thinks it.

[3] Romanticism and bombast of his feelings.

[4] The inner world is as the outer, the outer as the inner.

[5] My inner readiness, my own constitution I took with me—for all that was also in me, and all that is indeed terribly Russian, but also terribly German and European and universally human.

[6] Däubler is the inhabitant of another world, of another star, who has come to us from an unfathomable distance. Here he necessarily becomes a monster.

[7] In the last resort the human eye, ear and senses should be gratified, excited, for I cannot form a world that does not exist, and I must express myself with comprehensible ciphers.

[8] You are knocking on a door to reality, but unlike other people I do not live inside but outside my four walls. I am at home everywhere, everything is I.

[9] Being is something other than I—being (my existence). The conscious I, Doctor, is the piano player, but being is the music . . . for you make the mask into the essence of the thing: into the thing in itself, and you make the essence into the non-thing.

[10] Few drops of eternity.

[11] The strongest and highest life and yet a numbness.

[12] Time wants to have form, so give shape to time! Dear spirit give me counsel, present to me in lines what I but vaguely feel, send me a boat so that I can push out on to the ocean, that I may see!

[13] Prayer does not mean for me being aware of truth— no I mean the inexpressible—neither begging, nor blabbering, nor prattling—no, it means knowing: this is how it is: being holy.

[14] The tender silveriness of all things (i.e. their ore-like quality or essence).

[15] Because God is, therefore he is different from ourselves and has no memory, knowledge or judgement as we understand them. I can neither know it nor see it, nor hear it, and so in the last resort nor believe it. But I must be able to believe in something, that is tangible. That is desire, compulsion, necessity, whim—for there is God.

[16] Barlach worshippers.

[17] Never does one remain so deeply silent as when speaking about Barlach.

[18] Whatever became apparent to him in human beings, that he grasped to himself with his eyes as he did to his soul with his spiritual catcher.

[19] I catch up a cipher with my eyes, and in the darkness of my self it is there translated and worked over.

[20] I seize upon, no it seizes me, in my best moments the idea of depersonalisation, of transference to the higher, I call it: the happiness of overcoming the self in which full self-consciousness remains and persists. Impersonality, i.e. illimitability must be the essence of that which I still only hesitatingly call "God".

[21] The world is less than nothing, and God is everything—I see nothing but God. . . . God is the great stillness, I hear God.

[22] As a thing in himself.

[23] No longer a figure and still only a glow and abyss in God.

[24] The other God, of whom it is said, the world is great and God is less than nothing—a little point, a glimmer, and everything begins in him and everything ends in him. He has neither figure nor voice.

[25] Boll must? Must? Very well then I shall wish it!

[26] Absolute Insurance.

[27] Heavens yes how right you are, oh how right you are, we are one with time, one with the good, one with the bad, and just as we so are the times, and times are as we. . . . Everything yes everything is good and pure goodness when I am good, and everything is good and pure goodness when no anxiety is there to call up evil—just be quiet, just be quiet, just don't call up evil, just don't fall into evil through anxiety, which alone brings evil.

[28] All sorts of muddled effects.

[29] With all this, Seespeck had time to look out of the rear window on to a steep-sloping village church tower, towards which the descending road rolled straight down, and behind which right and left the Baltic spread itself out. Straight above stood a merciless sun, the church tower backed slowly nearer, but it did not occur to Seespeck to reflect as to how one can look at something from out of the rear door of an omnibus and yet be always coming closer.

[30] I often fought for days with a single word looking for a sentence of three words endlessly back and forth and often having to give up because I cannot find a word with the necessary number of syllables, there just is no such word, but there ought to be one. . . . The unheard of can only be narrated with unheard of words, but the unheard words suddenly become false words, for the self-evident that is to be found in the unhearable and that one wants to pull out so that the effect is taken joyfully and completely, the self-evident again demands the simplest word, our task is to compel and not to seem to be compelled.

[31] That was enjoyment lurking after the last lust, and the last lust is the community of obedience with its opposite.

[32] That reaches right to the innermost where it comes from the purest, the absolute truth.

[33] A wretched implement, a rough tool.

[34] And is waiting not a cloak holed with obedience and with the drab colour of submission, without bearing honour and standing?

[35] Sense for art, ideals, pessimist, belief in authorities.

[36] As they were just by a crossing, the paper nodded to the wind to help him over the street into the next gutter. For there was a lamp that liked being entertained by such stories, and as it waltzed slowly forward, it went on giving out one sentence of rubbish after another. Now they had arrived at the lamp, and all the lamp beams gathered round the paper inquisitively.

[37] Now Seespeck you have a mother-in-law but no fiancée, and that is just as it should be, for it suits you.

[38] Touchstone of the "Other".

[39] Time is a rubber band and lets itself be stretched endlessly, but finally it snaps quickly together and everything is back where it all started.

[40] There was a shadow that had stood up, eeking out of himself, piercing through the clouds, covering the moon, darkening the sun, towering up as far as the eye could see into space, yes filling space, for there remained no space between the figures of the bodies and star clusters—everywhere they were veiled and hidden by the shadow that went out from him.

[41] Let us remember that we are nothing for ourselves, but always only good or evil for someone else, just as they are for us—ah, this opposedness that raises us up, that turns us to nothing . . . and yet. . . .

SELECT BIBLIOGRAPHY

Ernst Barlach. *Das Plastische Werk.* Bearbeitet von Friedrich Schult. Hauswedell Vlg., Hamburg, 1960.

————*Das Graphische Werk.* Bearbeitet von Friedrich Schult. Hauswedell Vlg., Hamburg, 1958.

————*Plastik.* Einführung von Wolf Stubbe. Mit 100 Bildtafeln und Fotos von Friedrich Hewicker. Piper Vlg., Munich, 1959.

————*Zeichnungen,* Einführung von Wolf Stubbe. Mit 100 Bildtafeln und Fotos von Friedrich Hewicker. Piper Vlg., Munich, 1961.

————*Die Wandlungen Gottes. 7 Holzschnitte.* (Nachdruck) Chr. Kaiser Vlg., Munich, 1954.

————*Die Dramen.* In Gemeinschaft mit Friedrich Dross hsg. von Klaus. Lararowicz mit einem Nachwort. Piper Vlg., Munich, 1956.

————*Die Prosa I.* Hsg. von Friedrich Dross und Friedrich Schult. Piper Vlg., Munich, 1958.

————*Die Prosa II.* Hsg. von Friedrich Dross mit einem Nachwort von Walter Muschg. Piper Vlg., Munich, 1959.

————*Spiegel des Unendlichen.* Auswahl aus dem dichterischen Gesamtwerk.

Die Bücher der Neunzehn. Piper Vlg., Munich, 1960. Die *Sündflut* (1959).

————*Zwischen Himmel und Erde* (45 Zeichnungen 1958).

————*Aus seinen Briefen* (1958): Piperbücherei. Piper Vlg., Munich.

————*Der Arme Vetter.* Reclam Vlg., Leipzig, 1959.

————*Der Tote Tag, Der Arme Vetter.* Deutcher Taschenbuch Vlg., Munich (September 1963).

————*Leben und Werk in seinen Briefen.* Mit 25 Bildern. Hsg. von Friedrich Dross. Piper Vlg., Munich, 1952.

————*Frühe und späte Briefe.* Hsg. von Paul Schurek und Hugo Sieker. Classen Vlg., Hamburg, 1962.

Karl Barlach. *Mein Vetter Ernst Barlach.* Heye Vlg., Bremen, 1960.

Karl Dietrich Carls. *Ernst Barlach. Das plastische, graphische und dichterische Werk.* Rembrandt Vlg., Berlin, 1931, 1958.

Helmut Dohle. *Das Problem Barlach. Probleme, Charaktere seiner Dramen.* Czwikltzer Vlg., Cologne, 1957.

Paul Fechter. *Ernst Barlach.* Mohn Vlg., Gütersloh, 1957.

Willi Flemming. *Ernst Barlach. Wesen und Werk.* Dalp Taschenbuch. Francke Vlg., Berne, 1958.

Hans Franck. *Ernst Barlach. Leben und Werk.* Kreuz Vlg., Stuttgart, 1961.

Friedrich Schult. *Barlach im Gespräch.* Aufzeichnungen. Wiesbaden, 1948.

Paul Schurek. *Begegnungen mit Ernst Barlach.* List Bücherei, List Vlg., Munich, 1959.

Heinz Schweizer. *Ernst Barlachs Roman* Der Gestohlene Mond. Francke Vlg., Berne, 1959.

————*Zugang zu Ernst Barlach. Einführung in sein künstlerisches und dichterisches Schaffen.* Beiträge von M. Gosebruch, K. Lazarowicz, H Seiler. Vandenhoeck and Ruprecht Vlg., Göttingen, 1961.

Hanns Braun. *Das Vermächtnis Ernst Barlachs.* Hochland, 1961 (53) (2), pp. 129-39.

Klaus Bremer. *Barlach und die Bühne.* Akzente, 1954, (3), pp. 226-33.

Helmut Krapp. *Der allegorische Dialog.* Akzente, 1954 (3), pp. 210-9.

Karl Markus Michel. *Sprachgewalt oder Gewalt an der Sprach: Der Dramatiker Barlach.* Frankfurter Heft, 1960 (15), pp. 549-53.

Walter Muschg. *Ernst Barlachs Briefe. Die Zerstörung der deutschen Literatur.* List Vlg., Munich, 1961, pp. 66-86.

Hans Schwerte. *Über Barlachs Sprache.* Akzente, 1954 (3), pp. 219-25.

Gottfried Sello. *Ernst Barlach als Illustrator.* Philobiblon, 1960 (4), pp. 199-230 (with 22 illustrations).

Alex Page (essay date 1964)

SOURCE: An introduction to *Three Plays by Ernst Barlach,* translated by Alex Page, The University of Minnesota Press, 1964, pp. 3-25.

[*In the following essay, Page offers an overview of Barlach's career and provides brief analyses of his major plays.*]

Ernst Barlach's fame as a sculptor of the first rank is well established throughout the Western world. His writings, however, especially his dramas, have suffered relative neglect in all countries but Germany, where they were staged soon after they appeared. The first performances usually evoked sharp reactions, were widely discussed, and exerted important influences on younger playwrights. His best-known play, **The Flood,** won the coveted Kleist prize in 1924. Since the war there has hardly been a year that has not seen a new production of one of the plays, and a number have become part of the national repertoire. Studies of them have proliferated in Germany. It is now commonly acknowledged by the German theatergoing public and by readers, critics, and scholars that Barlach's dramatic works provide a major achievement of the German theater of the second and third decades of this century and that his intimate connection with the German Expressionist movement endows them with an added historical interest. But his literary reputation abroad has lagged. The difficulty of his highly individual language is perhaps one reason; another, the unusual nature of his ideas and themes. The three plays here translated [in *Three Plays by Ernst Barlach*], *The Flood, The Genuine Sedemunds,* and *The Blue Boll,* are from his middle period, about 1918 to 1924; they were chosen because they afford a somewhat more direct introduction to his dramatic techniques and the world of his ideas, but it is not easy to decide which are his best.

Ernst Barlach was born in 1870 at Wedel in northern Germany to a middle-class family that could trace its settlement in that region back to the seventeenth century. He was the oldest of four children. As a young boy he often accompanied his father, a doctor, on his rounds and learned something of the hardy peasant humor and of the fortitude with which pain and suffering were met. He was an unusually sensitive child. In the very first pages of his *A Self-Told Life* he attributes his "melancholy nature" to his grandmother and alludes to an early awareness of "something other" beyond himself, a notion that became central to his work: "My brother [and I] . . . sensed around us a number of remarkable things to which it became necessary to pay attention, things which one could neither see nor hear but which were certainly real. 'It' could arrive or not, we agreed, as we lay in bed in daylight summer evenings—'you look at the room, I'll watch the wall,' because we soon realized that 'it' could also enter through the walls."[1]

His father died when he was fourteen. After some training in art schools in Hamburg and Dresden, he spent the years 1895-97 in Paris, his time there divided among drawing "the reality of the streets," visits to the Louvre, and his first sustained efforts at writing a prose fantasy. The first exhibition of his graphic works took place in Berlin in 1900. A few years later he traveled with his brothers Hans and Nikolaus to Russia, a journey that became a turning point in his artistic career. The figures of Russia's poor, especially the beggars and vagrants, seen against the endless steppes and humble settlements overwhelmed him as truths he had long felt; they gave him "symbols for the human condition in all its nakedness between heaven and earth." Upon his return an "unheard of" realization struck him: "You may dare to attempt fearlessly all that is yours, that which is on the very outside, and that which is deepest within, the attitude of piety, the disfigurement of rage, because for everything there is expressive form, just as either or both were embodied in Russia."[2]

At this time he also began to work on his first drama, *The Dead Day,* which has certain autobiographical elements. He won custody of his son Nikolaus, the offspring of an unhappy liaison. In 1909 he made the last of his major journeys, this one to Florence, as the recipient of the Villa Romana fellowship; there he met the Expressionist poet Theodor Däubler with whom he formed a warm, lifelong friendship. Upon his return he chose Güstrow, a small town east of Lübeck, as his residence, and there he spent the rest of his life, in semiseclusion. In the meantime his first sculptures were becoming known. The following year he met Paul

Cassirer, a well-known art dealer and later a publisher, entering into a contract with him that assured a regular income. He was soon recognized by such Expressionists as Lehmbruck, Kirchner, Trakl, Sorge, and Kollwitz as their leader and their honored master, although he kept himself aloof from the manifestoes, pronouncements, and intrigues that characterized much of the day-to-day progress of the movement. But his letters to his friends and family provide an extraordinary collection of insights and commentary upon art, his own and others', and upon the major preoccupations of the times—quite apart from revealing a deeply concerned, passionate, and magnificently humanistic temperament; these letters have as high an artistic and critical value as, say, the letters of Keats. The following two decades, especially the twenties, proved to be Barlach's most productive and creative period, the years of his major sculptures and of all his dramas, of two novels and much else besides. One glimpses his ever-youthful Faustian cast of mind in the following letter, written when he was sixty-two: "I crave ever higher vantage points. . . . Clinging to safeguarded possessions seems to me pathetic. One must dare to take the chance of heedlessness."[3]

With the coming to power of the National Socialists in 1933 Barlach found himself in growing official disfavor. His famous war memorials, all of them anti-war, were removed one by one; his sculptures, woodcuts, and drawings were withdrawn from the museums and sent back to his studio, if they were not destroyed; and finally even his favorite work, the bronze angel hanging in Güstrow Cathedral, was taken down—the hardest blow of all. He was beset by financial worries and by rapidly declining health, but he continued to work until his last months. His final note was to his brother Hans, written while he lay on his death-bed in a Rostock clinic in 1938; he asked him not to visit him because he feared his brother himself was incapacitated by influenza: "You would only have an uncomfortable visit since I am of course in no state for conversation. . . . I hope for an early and complete recovery."[4] He died three weeks later, at the age of sixty-eight, and was buried in Ratzeburg amid the eulogies of his many friends.

The Flood (1924) is essentially a long dialogue between two men who hold very different views of God. Noah joyfully submits to a God who "is everything and the world nothing," while Calan sees him as "a glimmering spark . . . who creates and his creation creates him anew," yet a God to whom he too can express gratitude. The dialogue gains its energy from the attempt to understand evil—random, man-made, and even divinely-sanctioned evil. Barlach's invention of Calan as the great taunter of Noah, as the one who glows with independence and freedom gained by an enormous assertion of selfhood, serves to render the biblical account highly dramatic, if not tragic. But to regard the play as a dialogue between these two figures no doubt reduces it too much: their views are not only stated and restated with increasing elaboration but are also embodied in their characters and in their relations to their offspring. An insistent question that occupies Barlach in most of his dramas is how much a son *owes* to his father, how much the son's life is fated and determined, and by how much the son may surpass him, the crucial relation between God and man serving as a paradigm for that between a human parent and his children. Throughout his life, most forcefully in his woodcuts, Barlach showed an intense concern for the Moses theme, Moses as a lawgiver (a father), and as having brought man's relation to God to a kind of perfection. Noah sees himself as a true son of his God; he has unbounded faith in him, a nearly total submissiveness, a belief that whatever happens must be God's will. His own sons, however, are a wrangling, self-seeking threesome who are not going to maintain the closeness to, and the immediate apprehension of, God that are Noah's outstanding gifts. But the sons are not evil or bad: merely "average." Barlach leaves no doubt that Noah's great obedience to God can become a ready cover behind which all sorts of dubious traits find shelter: lust, indecisiveness, the toleration of cruelty to innocents, and acquiescence in expediency especially where his sons are concerned. Perhaps because of the stirrings of his own desires for Awah, he cannot refuse Japheth's insistent demands for "fat Zebid," a coarse, hypersexed, heathen woman. Noah will not kill, but neither will he show mercy when it may prevent suffering and death. To regard oneself as the executor of God's will, Barlach says, can become an act of pride resembling that of the openly proud, skeptical, self-assertive Calan. Frequently enough Noah cuts a decidedly ridiculous figure. Keenly disappointed by the manner in which various directors presented Noah on the stage and by the critics' interpretations of him, Barlach wrote: "I thought of Noah as a substantial landowner who is rather easy on himself, with a hardly noticeable paunch, walks with a stick and has his little failing,—a trifle condescending in his affability. . . ."[5]

In contrast to Noah, Calan is a free spirit, with absolute faith in his own abilities and strength and the right they give him to order his life and the lives of those dependent upon him. Barlach spares no effort to impress us with his masterliness, his generosity, his integrity. Being free, he can forgo Noah's uneasy wavering between two sets of standards. More than Noah, he is able to feel the widespread misery of mankind. He commands from his servant Chus (who is perhaps his natural son) a loyalty and a love which none of Noah's sons evinces for his father. So too does one feel the depth of Calan's love for Awah; and his giving her up to Noah in fulfillment of a vow, and Noah's subsequent passing her on to Japheth for wife, rankle more than he consciously realizes—these deeds provide in part the energy for teasing, taunting, and testing Noah's faith in his God, although the argument takes place on a far more rational level. Calan's intelligence drives him to understand, and by understanding to vanquish, the last threat to the exercise of the self in all its finality. He fails, but his vision before his gruesome demise is of a God whose demand of man is not that he submit but that he develop his potentialities to the fullest, a God, as it were, who

wishes his creation well in its "becoming," its flourishing, instead of keeping a tight, capricious control over it.

Barlach vigorously denied that in Calan he had presented the spirit of nihilism. He explained that he saw in him an instance of "a dissolution into something higher . . . in which the full consciousness of the self is contained and retained." And he goes on to say, as much about himself as Calan, that the latter "envisions a God who has no more shape. By this he releases his self—that self that has reached the utmost of its possibilities, that has become so ripe as to join a higher community. With that, man is destroyed as a thing in himself. I have often maintained that the greatest fortune is to transcend oneself, the temporary attainment of a state beyond the everyday. Everyone feels it at times. Give man a high ideal and he is relieved (if he is seized by the ideal) of the suffering of the self, of his limited individuality."[6] For that reason, Calan's defeat is only partial. He knows that Awah carries his child, and if the sojourners in the Ark survive the catastrophe so will his seed. And that holds for Zebid, who has sullenly consented to become Japheth's wife in Awah's place. Both will reassert Calan's spirit after the flood: one, his tender, openhearted, perceptive side; the other, sensuous, aggressive, and brutal.

Barlach has not in any philosophical or theological terms pretended to offer a solution to the problem of evil. He comes closest to it by having Noah's God admit to a blunder, but then he says in the letter earlier referred to that "the Noahs need a Heavenly God Jehovah, who is as much their creation as they his. . . . I would even believe that he is a fact, but no more than a first-rate Lear-like master—a helper and rather irresponsible. Evil has a deeper source."[7] In the end Barlach is less concerned with God than with the noble and ignoble elements warring in the individual. His play attempts to trace their genesis.

If the struggle in man's innermost being is the recurrent concern of **The Flood,** its achievement lies in the working out of the theme, in the details, and in the secondary characters. God, for example, as he appears in several guises (especially in that of a beggar), conveys a sense both of immense power and of cross-grained irascibility. His power is made vivid by two angels who in their role of a marmoreal divine chorus are like overconscientious servants deploring their master's peccadilloes. In a moving scene between Noah, who has been apprised of God's imminent arrival, and God, who comes as an old beggar claiming by and by to be Noah's long-dead real parent, the relations between the two are most sensitively explored: Noah's great expectancy, mingled with an old man's near-senile testiness, is only partially fulfilled, since he is never sure of the beggar's identity; but the elation and excitement he feels give proof that on a deeper level he has recognized his nondescript visitor. He then takes on the role of son both to a father and to his God. The same beggar changes visibly before our eyes from a ragged, persecuted, pathetic figure to one of force and authority that earns even Calan's respect.

The ways of perceiving God are by no means confined to those of Noah and Calan; indeed, almost every character sooner or later is given an opportunity to show his own way. It is here that Barlach's dramatic inventiveness has fullest rein. Awah apprehends God (and the angels) most directly and most sensuously in a kind of ecstasy; we believe her when she laughs in pure joy at the presence of God or when later, at the approach of the rainstorm, she intones half-deliriously "the eternal song": "I can see it ring, I can hear it swing, the end cradles the beginning in her arms." Her adoration is a child's pure delight and an unaffected pleasure in taking delight—she sees God in an explosive beauty suddenly enveloping her. It is the "sturdy Shem" who understands her and wishes to make her his wife. He claims to have difficulty explaining his vision of God, but he actually does very well: "He hides behind everything, and everything has narrow chinks, through which he shines. . . . I see him often through the chinks, it's so strangely, sudden, it opens, it's gone, not a trace of a joint to be found. . . ." And the mutilated shepherd, who has served as Calan's sacrifice, may be the humblest of them all: "The word [God] is too big for my mouth. I understand that he is not to be understood, that is all my knowledge of him." A senselessly abused victim, the shepherd nevertheless is guided by a profound optimism—"Where cheer is speaking, there I will remain," he says, even though flood waters and frenzied animals are closing in. These various views are less an attempt to define the deity than to characterize the people who hold them.

One participant in this drama remains, whose connection to the plot is more tenuous and whose view of God is by far the most negative. The hunchbacked leper seems after all to be the incarnation of a mistake: ugly and diseased in body and soul, he is a universal outcast, a purposeless existence. His sole cry is an unremitting curse of God and his injustice. More than a mistake, he screams—a demonstration of God's ill-will. He is the Thersites of *The Flood*. In his blind fury he strikes God, again disguised as a beggar. The shepherd says of the leper: "He curses his God who gave him everything: leprous sores, a deformed body—and a heart," and Calan adds: "He has a right to curse." It is significant that he shares Calan's fate, indeed, is yoked to him in the last climactic scenes and partly consumed by ravening beasts. His final act is to impersonate Calan in order to deceive Noah—he meets his fate as he has lived, wholly unconverted despite his sufferings. One can see him as the underside of Calan's gigantic self-assertiveness and selfhood; like Calan, he also taunts Noah for using "God's will" to his own purposes. While he is wholly reprehensible, the magnitude of his protest, his clamorous insistence that his case too be heard and "explained," are reminders that Noah's God is guilty of inflicting pointless suffering. The sternness and aloofness of the angelic chorus, as well as their exaggerated allegiance to God, are counterbalanced by the leper as

another chorus-figure with his strident, unceasing imprecations. His claims undercut all the others' more benign concepts of God, including Calan's.

Gratuitous cruelty, cruelty by neglect, and cruelty according to design—these merge into a theme that has risen to acute prominence in our time; in a German artist like Barlach, known for his kindliness and personal warmth, it is particularly revealing. In this drama of manifold cruelties, Barlach uses every means to achieve verisimilitude in his characters and setting. His portrayal of biblical life as stark, nomadic, governed by uneasy alliances, but chiefly by might, is impressive; and the attendant cruelty is no doubt meant to be, in part, an expression of that life. But Calan's maiming of the shepherd has a special quality. Ostensibly a test of Noah and Noah's God, it is really the act of a superman who takes for granted the right to dispose of others' lives, even for the sake of an experiment. Later Calan comes to realize that the shepherd's "drops of blood have swelled to seas and drowned my herds and my dominions" and that he can "taste what came from my deeds." He even rejects Noah's God because he is "a violent God, as I was violent." The play does not then sanction the experiment, but one feels that its full meaning is lost in Calan's final grand formulation of God. For however idealistic and powerful that is, however magnificent, the selfhood he sees his God wishing on him clearly excludes any concern (compassion, pity, mercy) toward his fellow creatures. It is as though Calan had been right in theory but had merely been guilty of a tactical mistake.

Noah's refusal, on the other hand, to challenge the mutilation with anything other than words, his genial acceptance of everything as God's will, gives license to an equal, or possibly greater (because more covert, better rationalized), cruelty. His callous abandonment of Calan and the leper to the beasts is the chief evidence of this. Nevertheless, the play grudgingly admits that Noah acts "correctly"; he has at least the good sense to take all precautions to survive, however dubious a victory that is—equally dubious as would be a world peopled only by Calans. And on a somewhat lower scale, the leper's cruelty toward the shepherd, Chus's role as loyal executioner to Calan, even the thoughtless passing of Awah from man to man—all these instances of man's inhumanity to man evoke the wistful admission that cruelty is the very fabric of this life. A certain mystery envelops the maimed and martyred shepherd: his unshakable faith, his humility, his beauty (compared by Awah with God's), his uncertain fate in the flood are perhaps meant to prefigure the new teachings of Christ, a wholly unselfish, transcendent love that otherwise is not found in the events of the play.

"Was it sad or funny?" a character in *The Genuine Sedemunds* (1920) asks after a grotesque scene in front of a family mausoleum. The two Sedemund brothers have come to lay a wreath in memory of Old Sedemund's wife but are prevented by Young Sedemund's embittered denunciations and exposés. The play is both sad and funny, with perhaps a greater emphasis on the latter, as the mad, mixed-up doings in a charivari world lead to a searching treatment of what the title implies: the genuine versus the false. With the dexterity and intrepidity of a Prospero, Barlach moves from one strange and febrile locale to another while alluding to even stranger ones: fairgrounds, a beergarden, an insane asylum, a graveyard, a make-believe hell, a chapel, and a graveside encounter with the dead; and populates them with grotesques: a madman, a wheelchair cripple, a debauchee, an ascetic, a pettifogger, ghosts, and bogeymen. There is much macabre humor, and there are at least eight corpses playing their grisly parts. Again, as in _The Flood,_ we meet gratuitous violence, but now a horse is the victim. What begins as naturalism rises to hysteria as if one were trapped in the fair's fun-house. It is perhaps Barlach's most Expressionistic play, though with his distaste for easy categorization he would have protested strongly against such a label.

What brings these many diverse elements together is a recently deceased lion. His death is kept a secret by Grude who has been given a day off from the insane asylum to attend a funeral, and who manages to hoax everyone into trying to recapture the lion supposedly at large. The lion gains important meanings as the play progresses and as Grude's prank reveals the disparities between the genuine and the false. As a matter of fact, the play is full of paradoxes: a madman who is saner than all the officially sane citizens; Sabina, a "wheelchair-saint," who plans a seduction; Old Sedemund, a connoisseur of debaucheries, the only one recognizing a deity; Young Sedemund, the leader of a vastly ambitious program for improving man, committing himself to the asylum; the daemonic lion as an agent of good. One soon discovers that the title of the play is ironic and that there is far less of the genuine than its opposite to be found.

The lion stands for a reminder of aliveness, "a savage's conscience," a timeclock ticking away that says there is something more vital and more dangerous than the blandness of mere everyday existence. But the "good lion's" ferociousness can overpower one: "He opens wide his jaws inside you and eats you up, skin and all, and makes you a part of his majesty." In one sense, as the organ-grinder remarks, we are all equal before him, but in another, we dare not take the chance to discover, through him, where our true realities lie. Old Sedemund is determined to "defeat the lion"; it is doubtful whether, at the end of the play, he has succeeded for anyone but himself; for Young Sedemund's final accusation against his father is that the "lion's gullet howl[ing] wrath upon us" makes mockery of the genuineness of the Sedemunds. As in _The Flood_ Calan sees his salvation in a transcendence of himself, and as _The Blue Boll_ expounds the perilous but rewarding road to becoming, so too in this play the lion serves to exacerbate man's knowledge of himself and compels him to take a stand.

The brilliance of the play does not lie, however, in the depiction of this humanistic-theological theme, but rather in its now strident, now ironic attack against man's shams, pretensions, and self-deceptions—the not genuine in him, or, better, his disingenuousness. There is a veritable catalogue of sins: Uncle Waldemar's perjuries, the militiamen's cowardice, Greedycock's foisting off his illegitimate child on another, Grude's disregard for his wife, Old Sedemund's dissipations and his demand upon his dying wife for a false confession of an imaginary offense, a confession that led to her suicide. At one point, Old Sedemund, bristling at being taken as the arch-practitioner of vices, proves that while all the good citizens profess only the highest principles of morality, in practice they complaisantly accept in their neighbors and in themselves both heinous and petty crimes—"everyone," he cries, "shall be nailed to the cross." A more general indictment is made of official immorality that bestows a decoration on an ineffective, bedraggled person like Mankmoos and also sanctions the corruption of "our institutions," of "things as they are": cutting corners here and there, blinking at child-trade, giving preferred treatment to "our most eminent citizens."

It is less clear whether Barlach means to attack Young Sedemund's Utopian organization; his Adamism sets out to discover what in man requires improvement and finds it in man's need to sacrifice himself on the altar of an ideal—"giving makes grace." (Barlach wrote in a letter: "Give man a high ideal and he is relieved . . . of the suffering of the self. . . ."[8]) But then the ascetic puritanical Young Sedemund finds himself so much at odds with his world that he retreats to the insane asylum, as though to take Grude's place, while the latter, possibly restored and a father-to-be, dances merrily with his wife over the graves of the dead to a future that is nonetheless unlikely to be an improvement on the past. In such a compromised world no one acquits himself with honor. It may be that Young Sedemund comes closest to it, for he has at least the most optimistic vision even though he lacks the drive and the practical sense to make it actual. "I do think," he says, "in the end everything in the universe harmonizes into a delicious feast for the ears," but he quickly goes on to talk of those, like his Uncle Waldemar, who are no more than cosmic musical rests. He behaves with great tact toward Sabina and Mrs. Grude and rises to intense indignation toward his demagogic uncle and rationalizing father. But that kind of sanity, Barlach seems to maintain, is wasted on this world. And as Old Sedemund demonstrates in the scene in the abandoned chapel, this world is a literal hell: again in a prankish mood, he has no difficulty persuading the bystanders to accept the role of hell-brothers and follow him in a mock parade through that hell.

In 1921 Barlach witnessed a production of _The Genuine Sedemunds_ in Berlin. He complained in a letter to his friend Reinhard Piper that only the secondary characters like the organ-grinder, Sabina, and Mankmoos succeed in holding the stage. He added that with a cinematic pace and Expressionistic techniques "I don't want to have anything to do."[9] It is not difficult to argue that the success of the play lies exactly in the bright and varied spectacle, in a wry, Till Eulenspiegel, topsy-turvy humor. That a made-up lion should act as a catalyst in revealing the more genuine motivations and values is the final irony, and a cruel one: only fear can finally unmask the latent violence and sources of scurrility, and fear hovers not far beneath the plausibly smug surface. Those who are proof against that fear (like Young Sedemund) make a pathetically heroic stand against the shams but cannot begin to vanquish them, only withdraw into the fastness of an asylum.

In *The Blue Boll* (1926) two unhappy, life-weary people meet and by a series of mistakes and seeming accidents stumble upon the fresh beginning of a better life. Each emerges from his crisis shaken by a searing experience of the human plight. Kurt Boll, a well-to-do land-owner, sees his coddled, easygoing life as suddenly pointless, unsatisfying, trivial, and belabored by hollow truisms of those who surround him with love, as his wife does, or with respect, as the mayor and townspeople of Sternberg do. He is given to fits of temper in which his face turns blue—hence the blue Boll. Grete Greendale, again, is so hysterically obsessed and repelled by the physical, by "flesh," that she has left her husband and escaped to Sternberg. There she tries to obtain poison in order to liberate her children from that abominated flesh into pure spirit. A beautiful girl, she numbly admits that she is a witch, nor does she see anything wrong with that. Boll is attracted by her otherworldly pallor and evident despondency. Both are half-people, both find themselves caught sliding toward death, Boll toying with suicide, Grete planning the murder of her children. The drama's success lies in the gradual, hardly perceptible changes that both experience. "All kinds of things come to pass unnoticed in the dark of a person's inner life," the mayor asserts in his most important speech. These changes seem right and inevitable once they have taken place. And, though similar in effect, they are characteristically different for the two.

Boll moves from a contemptuous dismissal of all possibilities of human transcendence to a sympathy for Grete's plight. After failing to procure poison for her through a mischance or because he has second thoughts (the play does not make clear which), he must submit to her repeated taunts of being a weak, vacillating person who "does now this, now that." The self-confessed devil Elias offers to make him whole by giving him a "hellish charge," thereby accepting him in the league of those who adhere to the principle that "each is nearest to himself." Boll has chafed under that very formulation of life, one of egotistical indifference. Rather, an uncomplicated sympathy for another—Grete—takes root in him and is nurtured by the Gentleman until it reaches more and more people, like Woodfresser and Otto Pompmaster. Life to Boll is no longer a sterile, static entity but a process of becoming in which individuality

may well be lost but something indefinite yet far greater gained. Barlach was well aware of the difficulties his readers might encounter with such a semi-mystical becoming. He said in one of his letters: "It is the inconceivable magnificence of the happening which I believe is forever hidden; one cannot touch it with one's finger, never understand its purpose. Sometimes experience seems to me to point to the absorption of the individual in the superindividual (but then what is that?) as a redemption and dissolution of all human creatures."[10] And Barlach wonders if an analysis of human motivation can dramatize this becoming. Nevertheless in *The Blue Boll* he shows the psychological effect of it by Boll's altered cast of mind after he has tied himself to something outside of, and greater than, himself. It is then that courage returns, then that he gains an effortless candor toward others, a lucidity and openness, all of which contrast sharply with his earlier vagaries, his crabbed compulsion to torment, attack, and befuddle people, his macabre imaginings. The play opens with Boll admiring the church steeple enveloped in mist—a somewhat sinister, threatening image. At the end, he understands with perfect clarity both the power and the limitations of an imposing woodcarving of an apostle he has never before noticed. He has undergone a test, namely the need to face, to deal with, to accept a parallel change in Grete. His becoming, the recognition that such becoming is not compulsion but a voluntary turning of the will, has been both subtly and convincingly demonstrated.

Grete Greendale's hallucinations are more actual than Boll's fantasies: visualizing the spirit literally choked by flesh, she is determined to set it free. Her test comes as she "witnesses" her children's treatment in hell. In two brilliantly conceived scenes in Elias's Devil's Kitchen she discovers that, since one's afterlife has been determined by the tenor of *this* life, death, far from being a simple release, can hold greater terrors and degradations than does "being in the flesh." The coals of the Devil's Kitchen "burn where needed, they destroy nothing but what is spoilt," Doris, the innkeeper's wife, assures her. What the mysterious Gentleman accomplishes in helping Boll to his becoming, Doris does for Grete. Doris is a type of stolid earth-mother, who assuages Grete's feverish obsession and turns her from her contemplated deed. She relieves her of feelings of guilt by giving her a sense of at-oneness with large and more pervasive and benign forces heretofore unsuspected. Grete, too, moves from self-induced terror to calmness and dignity as she recognizes her responsibilities toward her children.

Most material in the change is the Gentleman, in whom some characters discern God, and others Satan; he is treated with disdain and contempt by Otto Pompmaster and with comradely courtesy by Boll. When accused of clothing himself in mystifications he concedes that he is indeed "a faint and meek reflection of the infinite . . . a weak, hardly discernible adumbration of God." Yet he does have some of the best lines in the play. In an obvious reference to Goethe's *Faust* (taking an anti-Mephistophelian point of view) he says: "There isn't a spot you could spit on where something doesn't hover waiting to be thrust into existence, waiting to leave its cocoon." But again there is something Mephistophelian in his provoking Boll to undergo his last and most crucial test, that is, the temptation to achieve his becoming by suicide. It is apparent that the Gentleman is hardly meant to embody either good or evil, in the usual terms, but that he is an agency of the divine: he has a hand in those changes that lead to a fuller existence, a becoming of "shoots sprouting into blades." But the individual must have started on that path of his own will. The becoming he metes out to Otto Pompmaster is sudden death. Otto's rigidity, his tirade in favor of irresponsibility except in marriage (he takes an incredibly mechanical view of it), his refusal to step in any sense beyond his confined existence, do indeed signify virtual death.

The Gentleman is one of those strange, mythic, and yet quite plausible figures that reappear in many of Barlach's dramas. The less ceremoniously he is played the better, Barlach thought, and "the more unimportant-harmless his doings are represented the more forceful will be the presentation of the happening, the 'becoming,' which is intended as a dark force in the background controlling the action."[11] In a strange way, his mission is to tell man: submit! But the submission must be voluntary, a fully conscious commitment to becoming—"I must" changes to "I want," the wanting expressed as a total allegiance to the growing force within one. Though his is a negative commitment, Elias expresses it best: "What Elias does, he must do, and what Elias must do, he wants to do."

The secondary characters provide more than a setting and a humorous undertone to the major themes. While people like Woodfresser, the mayor, and Virgin reflect the atmosphere of small-town life—Sternberg is certainly Güstrow—they also give subtle support to the central theme. Virgin the watchmaker is a dour character, unpleasant to the point of nastiness, who provokes the antipathy not only of Boll but of the reader. Yet it turns out that he is the "local correspondent" of the Gentleman and in that capacity forces Boll into taking his first responsible step toward Grete. This stern taskmaster signifies the arduousness of Boll's later becoming, his very name suggesting the purity of that ideal process. The pertinacious Woodfresser who first alerts the town to a strange visitation—a shoe attached to "Satan's hindquarters" left to him for repair has disappeared—is rather easily swayed "now this way, now that": he jumps to quick conclusions. Though he readily accepts the Gentleman as God, Woodfresser's becoming is nevertheless a maudlin affair.

On the other hand, Boll's wife makes a genuine if tentative start of her own. Upon first meeting her, she impresses us as the epitome of smugness and egotism—she is dead certain that whatever she does not under-stand cannot possibly exist. Gradually she comes to realize that to allow her husband to carry out his immediate obligations toward Grete is a means of restoring his health and restoring him permanently to herself. In this metamorphosis the Gentleman has also played a part, but it is Boll who tells her that harder tasks are ahead: "The honey of humility can help you in your sour toil to a sweet becoming." Becoming is sour toil and tough business, by no means a pure act of grace. There are two other characters that never appear on stage but are presented as vividly as any. The pompous but goodhearted Baron Ravenclaw was the first to humble Boll, yet to no effect. The encounter between Boll and Ravenclaw, related by Virgin, is meant to give a foretaste of the changes in store for Boll. And there are only three things we know about Bertha, the wife of doomed Otto Pompmaster: that she invariably goes to bed at the same early hour, that she has extraordinarily fine teeth, and that she forbids the company assembled at the Golden Ball to drink coffee—but these details are enough to show her to us as a sister of Martha Boll, smug, obsessed with meaningless routine, but far less likely to break out of her circumscribed existence.

Bertha, together with nearly all the other characters, reminds us that the play converges upon large moral issues: the possibilities open to man in achieving self-fulfillment. This intense moral concern holds for the first two plays of Barlach, as indeed for all of them. Critics were quick to draw attention to one of the ancestors of his dramas, the miracle or mystery play, although Barlach himself rejected any such connections. The conflict between two generations in *The Genuine Sedemunds* recedes before the much larger attempt to define abstract genuineness, and in *The Flood* it is one kind of God pitted against another, signifying the choices that man must come to terms with. Even if they do not rest on traditional antitheses of good and evil, his plays nevertheless have the ring of a mystery play about them: moral forces brought to the human level, "made flesh," yet leading back, always, to the more than human.

To recapitulate, the major concerns of the plays collected here are these: the relation between a child and parent (or man and God), the limitations and reductions that are characteristic of man's physical existence, the perversions man has instituted to render that existence even more depraved, man's need for and path to self-transcendence, and the ideals by which that transcendence may be brought about. Barlach's remaining five plays touch on closely related questions. Their major themes are sketched here briefly to give an idea of his dramatic works as a whole.

In *The Dead Day* (1912), Barlach's first drama, which has the austere setting and nameless mythic figures of a Nordic saga, the fate of a son's commitment to life is explored. He is a weak son dominated by a brutal, earthbound mother, a son who fails partly through his own uncertainties and is partly prevented from riding away into sunnier worlds on a stallion provided by his spiritually freer, more positive, but blind father. On the side of the mother are enlisted malefic ghosts and gnomes who join to exploit the father's blindness. Her attempt to poison her son leads to both his death and hers. *The Poor Cousin* (1918), set in an innocuous vacation spot near Hamburg, begins with the attempted suicide of Hans Iver and ends with its consummation—nothing he or anyone else can think of saves him from his despair. This play looks forward to *The Genuine Sedemunds,* published two years later. Here too, threatened or actual violence rips the masks off innocent bystanders who would rather have left things as they were but who are now pushed into lacerating self-confrontations. In only one person is there a clear change for the better. In *The Foundling* (1922) Barlach creates even more bleakness: a devastated post-war countryside with a fleeing, suffering humanity and opportunists exploiting the disorganization. A man who is known as the red emperor is nominally in charge; cannibalism prevails. Isolated clusters of refugees appear, each more suspicious and terrified than the last. A crippled foundling, symbol of these twilight times, awakens the sympathy of one of the passing wretches and by divine grace is transformed into a beautiful child, a savior. The effect of an individual assuming wholly unselfish responsibility for another, reenacted in more familiar surroundings in *The Blue Boll,* is to create a path, the dramatist asserts, to God. Another who purposefully sets out on a search for God is the title figure of *The Baron of Ratzeburg* (1951), a quasi-historical drama posthumously discovered and never wholly finished by Barlach. Dissatisfied like Boll with the meaningless, trivial complications of life and its injustices, the baron joins a pilgrimage in search of a more human existence, in search of God. He endures great suffering and is taken into slavery. Encounters with a hermit and later with Moses reveal to him that serving God is not a command but a privilege that man torturously earns for himself. His return home causes only resentment; he becomes a source of complications. But he is able to save his illegitimate and unappreciative son's life by sacrificing his own. "I have no God, but God has me," he cries near his death. His companion in these painful journeys is Offerus, in search of the "highest master" whom he finds temporarily in Marut, a Calan-figure, but a more fiercely uncompromising, utterly ruthless destroyer than Calan. Barlach's last completed play was *The Good Time* (1929), which deals with an ideal society on a Mediterranean island in which all physical and spiritual complaints have been resolved, a society in which everyone carries "absolute insurance." The members think of themselves as godlike, but the "good time" is hollow: it cannot be had in this life. The heroine finds fulfillment in giving her life for that of a stranger.

Barlach often complained that his dramas were interpreted too "metaphysically," that critics and directors fell to subtilizing the meanings at the expense of the entertainment. And it is true that his dramatic resourcefulness results in brisk scenes full of surprises, in lyrical scenes and somber ones. He is a master of evoking many moods. As he said—and demonstrated: "I believe one is entitled to demand of the drama all or nothing, wherever it is a matter of expressing absolutely and radically a fundamental feeling."[12] But at the same time his unusual language, his metaphoric daring invariably give the impression that more is meant than said and that he invites each reader to grasp that meaning in his own way. Serious critics have come forward with substantially different interpretations of the same plays, attesting more to their vitality and richness than to their obscurity. Barlach wrote: "People want to 'know' and ask for the word, but the word is useless, at best a crutch for those who are satisfied to limp along. And nevertheless there is something in the word that presses into the innermost being when it comes from the loudest, that is, the absolute, truth. But each understands it differently, he hears that which becomes understandable to him, or rather, he becomes conscious of it according to his part in the whole."[13] This explains his unceasing innovations with language. His diction often shoots from abstract to concrete; he devises new word formations, and familiar words acquire so many and such specialized meanings that the reader feels he is in the midst of a new language. The multiplying uses of "lion" as a symbol and image in *The Genuine Sedemunds,* or of "power" in *The Flood,* or of "must" in *The Blue Boll* are examples. Now he has Calan describe God as a spark, now Old Sedemund pictures his soul as an invisible point. Along with such verbal daring goes his predilection for puns and for occasional euphuistic antitheses, and also his strategic use of several North German dialects, always assigned to characters of limited imagination but of common sense. These last are likely to have revealing names. If all these devices account for the flexibility of his style, they simultaneously invite ambiguities. Finally, one must mention his experiments with syntactic innovations: run-on sentences, purposely indefinite pronomial references, ellipses, and many others. They in turn produce the effect of a nervous breathlessness, of sudden ranges of emotional intensity, and give us the feeling of momentarily witnessing the birth of fateful issues. One is constantly amazed at the reserves available to Barlach: he appears to have said all that can be said but then pushes further—and takes the reader with him.

It is as though he dealt with language as with a block of cherrywood that he must destroy in order to create from it. Such a twofold attitude perhaps explains the fruition of his "double talent," his being driven now to the plastic arts, now to literature to convey and justify the fullness of his vision. It also explains the poetic quality of his dramas even when he chose the most ordinary small-town locales for them. (And, one may add, it explains the difficulties of his translator.) No great ingenuity is needed to show that the major theme of his plays—the striving toward a magnificent reality beyond and above the casual day-to-day existence—is beautifully exemplified by his language, his style.

All of his plays, especially the three printed here, have scenes and characters that cannot be described as other than grotesque. Instances are the leper's tirade in *The Flood* (Part V, Scenes 3 and 4), Old Sedemund's processions through hell (Scene 6), or the visitation of three cadavers in *The Blue Boll* (Scene 6). In *The Poor Cousin* there is a kind of witches' sabbath around a man called "Lady Venus" and a straw doll. These grotesque scenes usually take place toward the latter parts of the plays. With Barlach's humor at its most cutting and macabre, with the tone rising to a feverish pitch, these scenes form a kind of climax—man strutting in his material depravity, all flesh, all dross, and only remotely human. The grotesque is followed by scenes unusually sober and clear, as though catharsis has taken place, as though the attempt can *now* be made to formulate the constituents of transcendence.

It is tempting to speculate whether the grotesque is what Barlach failed to get into his sculpture and hardly into his graphic art, and whether he was therefore drawn to the stage to present it there in all its gaudiness, violence, even repulsiveness. Most of his sculptures embody individual man, ecstatic or expectant, caught in earthly forces and struggling with the here and now while longing for some supernatural event, suffused with intimations of a superhuman vision that will release him. The grotesque, which dwells on the precarious earthly entanglements, finds its visual form only in caricature, and caricature has always appeared inimical to the sculptor's art. It follows that one might regard the grotesqueries so prevalent in his dramas as a complement to the rest of his work, and, conversely, as the means of freeing him to endow his sculptures with that purity of solitude and that concentration with which they listen to a different drummer. He wrote in one of his letters: "Remember—matters being what they are—that it looks hopeless for us, so you must save yourselves, at least in spirit, to a worthier state, since after all you cannot all destroy yourselves."[14] The destructive element in his plays, to oversimplify, is embodied in the grotesque; that element must be purged before the truly human can find its grandeur in the more than human.

But it is that very shriek of grotesqueness that connects him with other Expressionist playwrights of his time. Indeed, it may be of value briefly to point out the additional links between his plays and theirs. Hand in hand with the grotesque goes the tone of the visionary, the prophet on the last verge of time exhorting man. This heightened tone that in Barlach and others frequently becomes incantatory, alternating with a falsetto, is not unusual in an Expressionistic dramatist who like Sorge attempted to "stage" a fugue-like music with strategic repetitions of themes and phrases. Furthermore, in much of the drama of the period one grows uncomfortably aware that the characters fail to communicate—as though they were just talking past one another. We find this in Barlach, and we find it in the dramas of Hans Jahnn, for example. Barlach shares the others' lack of interest in analyzing character and in justifying motives psychologically, nor is he concerned with the punctilious plotting of the well-made play. But, like those dramatists,

Barlach is always aching to proclaim a dire need for reform, a new faith, with the same vigor with which Sternheim, for instance, asserted a universal nihilism.

Fundamentally, Barlach's plays are like the Expressionists' in that they are plays of ideas rather than character, but he was at great pains to delineate the *effect* of those ideas on his protagonists. Since they are apocalyptic ideas that demand nothing less than the reconstitution of man—best shown in Young Sedemund's Adamism, or at least the rediscovery of his true nature and true destiny—there is an urgency about this kind of drama that often veers toward exaggeration and in lesser playwrights to rodomontade. He partakes of the widespread desire to tear down the façade of nineteenth- and early twentieth-century optimism, behind which he too discerns a deep, despairing melancholia or else a defeated incomprehensibility of life. What Walter Sokel calls the "daemonization of everyday reality" took the form in Barlach of the grotesque, in Toller of the elevation of the machine to an archfiend, and in Kafka of the suspiciously casual manner of narration. But Barlach stands apart from the other Expressionists by adhering to a personally-conceived Christian drama of redemption, returning neither with Kokoschka to myth nor with Kaiser to clever reinterpretations of history. The movement in his plays is from a secularized, lost, misguided condition of man, encumbered by original sin, in which man often suffers unbeknown to himself, to a point at which a savior appears or salvation seems at least possible. But he demands a sacrifice. His first drama concludes with the line: "Strange that man does not want to learn that his father is God," and in his last, *The Good Time,* the heroine accepts her death with the realization that "her guilt is canceled." If Barlach's is the only truly religious attitude in the drama of the period, he shares the others' garrulous optimism in the possibilities of a new beginning. The youthfulness of the movement— some critics have called it a late flowering of romanticism—also re-echoes in his plays.

Moreover, he shares a pervasive desire to experiment with the potentialities of the stage and thus to disassociate himself from the naturalistic tradition. Herein the entire group was much influenced by Strindberg's late "dream plays." In addition to his attempt to refashion the language, Barlach paid close attention to visual presentation: lighting, long silences that call for pantomime (as in Hasenclever's dramas), quick shifts of scenes, the representation of great natural disasters on the stage, and so on. But even the more realistic settings, in, for example, *The Genuine Sedemunds* and *The Blue Boll,* afford visual shocks: the wooden figure of Christ in the first and the carved apostle in the second are meant to come briefly alive.

Barlach's prose presents the translator with a peculiar challenge—more, I think, than with any other modern author must he exercise the function of critic and interpreter while fulfilling the humbler role of translator.

Barlach's attempts to push language beyond its limits create vexing problems. Uneasy compromises were necessary. As is well known, English is less hospitable than German to abstract key words like "becoming." But there was no choice. Or again, it was impossible to reproduce with any fidelity the North German dialects for which Barlach had such a sharp ear and which provide a good deal of the humor in *The Genuine Sedemunds* and *The Blue Boll,* although I have tried to come close with American idioms and colloquialisms. Perhaps the loss of some of his puns and his frequent alliterations is less serious.

I have taken a number of liberties. Whenever I could, I found English equivalents for German names, both of persons and of places; I simplified Barlach's syntax chiefly by reducing the number of run-on sentences in order to adapt them to more natural English prose rhythms; and I also simplified his punctuation, especially the exuberant use of dots, dashes, and exclamation marks. I well realize that my practice must strike the connoisseur of pure Expressionist prose with all its syntactic and typographical intoxication as somewhat adulterated wine. But I felt that a more sober presentation would allow the reader unfamiliar with Barlach to gain a clearer view of what is most essential in his plays.

NOTES

[1] Ernst Barlach, *Das Dichterische Werk,* Friedrich Dross, ed. (Munich, 1958), II, 15. This and all subsequent quotations are my translations.

[2] *Ibid.,* II, 55.

[3] Ernst Barlach, *Aus Seinen Briefen* (Munich, 1947), pp. 76-77.

[4] Ernst Barlach, *Leben und Werk in Seinen Briefen,* Friedrich Dross, ed. (Munich, 1952), p. 252.

[5] *Ibid.,* p. 121.

[6] *Ibid.,* pp. 156-57.

[7] *Ibid.*

[8] *Ibid.*

[9] *Ibid.,* p. 104.

[10] *Ibid.,* p. 177.

[11] *Ibid.,* p. 137.

[12] *Aus Seinen Briefen,* p. 47.

[13] *Leben und Werk,* p. 178.

[14] *Aus Seinen Briefen,* p. 48.

E. M. Chick (essay date 1965)

SOURCE: *"Der Blaue Boll* and the Problem of Vision in Barlach," in *The Germanic Review,* Vol. XL, No. 1, January, 1965, pp. 31-40.

[In the following essay, Chick assesses Barlach's literary stature and value.]

The accepted image of Ernst Barlach as an eccentric, probably profound, but heavy and obscure playwright needs correction. Articles such as "'Der blaue Boll' and the New Man"[1] and Herbert Meier's *Der verborgene Gott: Studien zu den Dramen Ernst Barlachs* (Nürnberg: Glock und Lutz, 1963) may do justice to the philosophical side of the plays, but they neglect the critical question of artistic merit. Is *Der blaue Boll* (1926) a good play? Or better: Is it good literature?

When reduced to a bare ideological pronouncement—e.g., "Er [a quote from the play which allegedly contains its essence] bestätigt den transzendentalen Imperativ, widerruft die tragische 'Exkarnation' und wiederholt das Gesetz, nach dem das immanente Selbst der Grund des transzendenten ist" (Meier, p. 120)—*Boll* sounds trite and pompous. When its characters are reduced to allegorical skeletons—Boll = Everyman—, the drama is unlikely to attract new readers. What needs to be known is that it is not just another late expressionist play about the New Man. It is, rather, an intricate, vivid, lively work of art and Barlach's best play.

To gain some insight into its workings, one must first recognize that Barlach is too much of an artist to be treated as a mediocre *Dichterdenker*—one of that peculiarly German tribe of lay philosophers and mystics. The kernel of what *Boll* has to say is to be found not in simplistic generalities like "Werden vollzieht sich unzeitig"[2] but in the theatrical events or "Bilder," in the intense visible representation of people, things, and actions.

By examining the two interrelated themes and complexes of imagery at the drama's core, one can discover its coherence and fine aesthetic balance. The first might be called the alimentary vision. It finds expression in grotesque-comic references to flesh, teeth, mouth, food, and the digestive process. The second, more subtly presented but more important, is the optical vision and has to do with visual perception, light, and eyes. These two strands are woven together to form a contrapuntal design through the play's seven "Bilder."

Upon close reading it becomes clear that Barlach is trying to dramatize the experience Geoffrey H. Hartmann—*The Unmediated Vision* (New Haven, 1954), pp. 128-129—discerns in poems and poets of the nineteenth and twentieth centuries: "The mind, therefore, being most keenly aware through the dominant eye of that which is the cause of perception, pure representation will, at base, be the urge to construct that ideal system of symbols which relieves consciousness of the eyes' oppression but assures it of the eyes' luminosity." We will see that Barlach provides such a set of symbols in the final "Bild" of **Boll** where the issues of flesh and eye are resolved. The discussion of this crucial episode, however, requires a few preliminary comments.

The drama's basic figure is the confrontation and mixture of opposites. This takes place repeatedly in the action; it can be seen in individual characters as well as in the mingling of realistic, supernatural, comic, and serious elements. Apostolic Community and "gemütliche Teufelsküche" (415) face each other across a narrow street. Manor house and piggery, church and seduction are brought together in the first "Bild." The apoplectic Squire Boll and Grete Grüntal, the swineherd's wife, meet here and join in a common aim: to do away with flesh and, it seems, to indulge it too. He wants to jump from the tower; she will poison her children and hints at favors she will grant if Boll procures the poison. The remainder of the play shows, first, how Boll helps restore her to sanity and acceptance of her life and, second, how she returns the favor. Grete's transformation is visceral; Boll's too has to do with his body but is sublimated and presented finally in visual and spiritual terms. Grete is helped through her crisis by the strangely angelic devil Elias. Boll is helped by "ein Herr," who, though hobbled by a "Teufelsbein," is taken by some to be *the* Lord.[3] As in all Barlach's good plays, it is a matter here of relative proportion and emphasis rather than clear distinction.

In the shifts of proportion and emphasis lies Barlach's mastery. Through the entire play Boll hangs between two existences. We hear indirectly of the old Squire Boll. Of the new we see but a few inchoate signs. Of character development in the usual sense there is little evidence. For the play does not concern the new or the old Boll but rather the complicated circumstances surrounding his inner awakening and the subtle shift of perspective which reveals to him the way out of his dilemma. Of all Barlach's dramas, **Der blaue Boll** is at once the subtlest and the most vivid. It is so well rounded that it offers no easy handholds for interpretation.

The scenes, or "Bilder," contain sharply outlined visual effects, on which the characters' comments invite us to speculate. Their words, in accordance with Barlach's conviction that the word is at best a crutch for those satisfied to limp,[4] only complement the play of light, spatial relationships, and eyes. They lend the action an air of mystery and metaphysical import. In fact, one might read **Boll** as a mystery play by forcing the events into a pattern of death, descent into hell, resurrection, and crass comic interludes. For Barlach is generous with material suggestive of the supernatural. Yet he is also careful to keep things in a state of suspension by counterbalancing these flashes of transcendence with reminders that his characters and action are all too human. For example, the fantasies in the sixth "Bild" may be interpreted as an apocalyptic vision of suffering sinners in hell or as a delirious dream in the mind of a drunken woman. Like the Herr at the end, Barlach seems to warn us against too much speculation on Weltanschauung with a "Mehr ist vom Übel" (455).

Consequently, instead of extrapolating from the Herr's discursive remarks on becoming, we will consider the dramatic event in the seventh "Bild." It is a repetition, in altered form, of the events in each of the preceding scenes, and it has to do with eyes, vision, and flesh—Barlach's lifelong preoccupations.

The setting is inside the church which has figured in all but two scenes. The scenery is sparse to the point of abstraction; we see one pillar, one window, one bench, and an apostle carved in wood. The morning sun shines on the apostle. Present are only Boll and Grete, the swineherd's wife, whom he has brought here to sleep it off before she returns—a new woman—to husband and children. In the course of conversation about events of the night before Grete is distracted by the statue, and the following exchange begins (446):

> GRETE *sieht zwischen der Figur des Apostels und Boll hin und her, lacht:* Was der auch aussieht, wie ihr beide ausseht! Die Sonne scheint ihm ins Gesicht und er hat seine Glotzaugen weit auf—sucht er Läuse, oder was hat er in seinem Vollbart zu grabbeln?
>
> BOLL: Der? Ja, der! Sieh, jetzt scheint sie mir auch aufs Gesicht, und nun wächst ein schattiger Boll an der Wand, der Heilige aus Holz und mein Schatten stehen sich gegenüber, und man kanns gut absehen, von welcher Art Fleisch sie fallen. Er war ja auch einmal im Fleisch, und ich bins noch—sieh dirs an, Grete.
>
> GRETE: Er macht den Mund zu und seine Augen blinkern.
>
> BOLL: Glühen, glühen—und meine?
>
> GRETE: Deine—ach, blauer Boll, das ist nicht dein bester Putz. Da klappen Luken über zusammen, Luken, dass man sich schämen sollte, daheraus zu sehen. Sonst, die Augen sind richtige Augen, aber sie haben sich in dicke Walnussschalen verkrochen. Er hat einen Mund, aber er macht ihn zu.
>
> BOLL: . . . und meiner?
>
> GRETE: Dein Mund? Boll, deiner ist nicht schlecht, gut zum Gähnen und Zähnezeigen und zum Besorgen von allerlei Unrat für die Zähne. Aber deine Zähne sind sehr gut, die können ihr Teil beschicken—er, sieh hin, was für hohle Backen, da ist kein Platz mehr für Zähne, die Kammer hat dünne Wände und leere Betten. Vielleicht glühen seine Augen darum, weil er keine Zähne hat und nach was anderem ausschauen kann als nach Fleisch.

The silent but eloquent apostle dominates the entire scene. Eyes, teeth, and shadows speak louder than words.

Boll is driven to despair by the juxtaposition of his shadow and the "Petermännchen" (446), and speaks in vague abstractions that hint strongly at intended suicide (447-448). Then suddenly—perhaps he has moved his head a bit—Grete again drops the thread of conversation and notes: "Wenn die Sonne in deine Augen scheint, glühen sie besser als dem seine, das seh ich genau, wenn ich gut hinseh" (448). And Boll replies: "Was Wunder—kann er was anderes mit seinen Augen anfangen als lässt sie sehen—ich aber sehe selbst und seh dich sitzen und höre dich die Wahrheit reden, und siehst aus deinen Augen wie eine heile gesunde Frau." The dialog ends when Boll repeats the leitmotiv: "Jeder ist sich selbst der Nächste."

The rest of the scene tells of Cousin Otto's death (a comic reflection of Boll's becoming) and of Frau Boll's act of humility. Also, even though Boll continues to speak of suicide and seems about to follow the Herr's suggestion that he do it now, his point of view has already changed. He confronts the apostle with new self-assurance and says: "Seht, Kinder, den alten Griesgram—vorhin, da wollte ich bange werden vor seiner hölzernen Grandezza, aber jetzt steh ich mit seltsamer Pomadigkeit vor ihm. Dir kann ich die Zähne zeigen . . ." (452). It only remains for the Herr to force Boll to an overt decision against suicide as too primitive a mode of becoming.

One wonders why Barlach resorts to this intricate play of light, eyes, and shadow if he aims only to show the resolution of the conflict between body and spirit[5] or between free will and necessity. Reference to similar passages and parallels in other works will suggest what meanings should be attached to these images. For instance, the wooden apostle or "Petermännchen" has its counterpart in the Gothic Christ figure which dominates the crucial sixth "Bild" of *Die echten Sedemunds* (1920). This in turn is related to the gigantic crucifix Barlach saw in the church at Güstrow. He writes in 1912 of "die Kirche am Markt, wo . . . das riesenhafte Kruzifix ist aus der mittelalterlichen Zeit, wo die Menschen sich selbst und ihr Dasein mythischer begriffen. . . . nun steht er wieder da wie eine Hieroglyphe und predigt, dass es noch anderes gibt als Fleisch und Bein."[6] For Barlach the dramatist, on the other hand, the statue is a hieroglyph in a system of symbols, and the reader is struck when, in *Der arme Vetter* (1918), Siebenmark mentions the word "Petermännchen"—later "Stehaufmännchen"—in a situation like Boll's. Siebenmark admits his inability to emulate Hans Iver, the saintly suicide, and says sarcastically: "Mir fehlt der Abglanz vom Jenseits, das ist es! Ich weiss von keiner Seite Kratzfüsse vor Petermännchen im Seelenschein anzubringen" (162).

As usual in Barlach's finished works, the unambiguous statement of a letter or prose sketch is repeated with an ironic, even irreverent twist, perhaps to preserve the aesthetic equilibrium. Christ and his apostle are associated with tumbler dolls (roly-polys) just as a deep sounding bit of metaphysical speculation reappears in a novel as a product of confused thinking.[7]

Siebenmark and Boll have a good deal more in common. They discover the full meaning of "Jeder ist sich selbst der Nächste." Both may bow initially to the toothless, ascetic spirituality of their respective "Petermännchen," and each may come close to suicide in his extremity; yet each undergoes a change—largely a change in perspective—and begins a new existence.[8] Also, neither denies his selfhood; and neither gives up material things.

The dramatic event is more clearly outlined in *Boll* than in the earlier play. For Boll dominates the action, and the metamorphoses of Otto and Grete are obviously intended as reflective variants of his. The pattern is set by Grete's turn overnight from insane disgust with flesh to acceptance of her life in the piggery. Similarly, in "Bild" VII, Boll ceases to see himself solely as a shadow in this vale of misery and is set free to begin again. The dramatic events of earlier scenes prepare for this; each is rehearsal for the crisis.

The first "Bild" brings together the issues of perception—mist and blurred perspective (387)—, selfhood, and flesh—"Weg mit Fleisch" (388). Boll passes through a period of vacillation and disgust with himself but emerges from the fog of confusion with the decision to follow Grete into the church tower (401). In II he again despairs and loses direction (397, 398) but regains perspective with a scornful glance from the tower down upon the town and with the assumption of responsibility for Grete.

And so Boll continues through the stations of his trial to the final scene. Here he is brought to the brink of suicide by the sight of his shadow on the wall. The sunlight paints this simple picture of Boll's inescapable carnal condition (447) with merciless precision. But then the rays of the sun unexpectedly reveal to Grete the glow, or luminosity, of his eyes. In other words, from one point of view the sunlight reduces Boll to an ugly black mark or "ein schwarzes, schweres Stück Nacht" (433) as he pictures his body falling from the tower. Without the resonant response from Grete he cannot see what the direct rays of the sun do to him and his eyes. They illuminate and bring forth his share, however small, in divinity, the dignity of the human body and particularly of the eye, which is more than an organ of vision. Boll's new way of looking at things is thus the result of an indirect, symbolic perception that takes place when his eyes meet Grete's. In *Boll* and elsewhere Barlach tries to show that human values are revealed only when one sees rays from the beyond reflected and refracted in others.[9]

To justify such emphasis on this single event in *Boll* and to give further content to the concepts "new man" and "conversion," we need to look at some other works. The most appropriate would be *Die Sündflut* (1924), the immediate predecessor of *Boll*. On the surface the two are not alike. The final scene of *Die Sündflut* is dark, violent, crass, and grotesque. Calan, Boll's counterpart, plans suicide; he is made painfully aware of his carnal condition as Noah's sons, fearful of his strength, lash him to a leper and leave him to be devoured by vermin and drowned in the Flood; and he experiences a luminous epiphany (383).

Epiphanous visions are not granted all Barlach heroes. For example, the son in *Der tote Tag* (1912) never emerges from his state of suspension between two existences—childhood and manhood, in oversimplified terms. He longs to see what the sun can see without going blind (twice on p. 24), but he is trapped by the fog of his own incapacity to act or create (85). His last day, too, hangs dead between heaven and earth (54), and the sun never breaks through. He recognizes only his own lack of perception and kills himself. He says of his walk through the mist: "Mit offenen Augen ging ich und konnte sehen, wie blind ich war, denn das war eine Blindheit, die nicht von den Augen kommt, sondern die andere, die schlimmste, die macht, dass die Augen nicht sehen" (72).

The novel fragment *Der gestohlene Mond* (written 1936/1937 and published posthumously) stops short of the ultimate vision. In a passage which lurks behind the actions and thoughts of Wau, the central figure, through the remainder of the book we read of the "gnadenloses Erkennen"[10] he derives from the following momentary apparition:

> Es war ein Schatten dagestanden, der von ihm selbst ausging, durch die Wolken stiess, den Mond verdeckte, die Sonne trübte und in den Weltenraum unabsehbar hineinragte, ja ihn erfüllte. . . . Und es war sein Schatten, das erkannte er am Schritt. . . . Er hatte während der Nichtzeit seines Schauens noch Eins wahrgenommen: die Abschattung eines Körpers in der Unendlichkeit des Raums, eine Gestalt wie [die] der Sonne in seltsamer Verzogenheit der Form, glühend, aber wie mit Dunst getrübt, die sich seltsam regte und wie im Krampf zitterte—weit, weit hinten, hoch über die Sonne hinaus.

> *(Die Prosa, II, 483)*

The perception is merciless because the luminous shape (the cosmic enlargement of his heart) remains cloaked in haze. Wau has no vis-à-vis like Grete. Similarly, the attempt to articulate the experience and to infuse it with religious meaning is halted just as the crucial word is about to be uttered. Wau and Wahl, his alter ego, speak as one spirit: "Der Geist aus dem Mund des Zweiten verstieg sich weiter: 'Denn ob der Schatten deiner ist oder du der Schatten seiner, es kommt nur darauf an, dass ein Sein ist und eine Durchdringung der Weltweite mit . . . '-Mit?' fragte es. 'Mit . . . darauf besinne dich, ehe du etwas darüber sagst. Halt an und verstumme.'"[11] Both are ashamed of their speculative excesses and agree never to speak of such things again.

Barlach's earlier, autobiographical novel *Seespeck* (written 1913/1914) also treats again and again of shadows. It is a better aid to the understanding of *Boll* VII because, though the author never released it for publication, it is at least a full torso and, as in *Boll*, the cosmic overtones are muted. Like the play, *Seespeck* is constructed as a series of rounded episodes, or stations, leading ultimately to a new mode of vision and a new life. Seespeck, suspended in a pointless, rootless existence, is at first disconcerted by visual experiences such as the sight of the monstrous baker and his shadow; and he, too, finds himself caught and isolated at the outset. "Jetzt . . . kam es ihm vor, als ginge er an einer langen Planke entlang und fände nirgends einen Ausgang, die Planke aber hatte er im Verdacht, dass sie im Kreise liefe und er mit ihr."[12] In this peculiar limbo he is easily transported outside himself by fleeting sense impressions such as the three notes of a music box or a glimpse of a girl walking down the street. But this is just further evidence of Seespeck's confusion (*Die Prosa*, I, 406) and leads him only deeper into despondency. Right after the revery inspired by the music box he meets an attractive prostitute and suffers an odd defeat. When she fails to show a trace of hardness or indecency, he flees in disarray and disgust at himself. She lets him out of her sight like "einen kühlen, grauen, formlosen Schatten" (358). His nausea and anxiety reach panic proportions when he thinks he sees the baker ("die Vision des Bäckers"), a sharp reminder of his own condition.

This confrontation with the prostitute is one of a series of episodes in which Seespeck is betrayed and trapped by his eyes. "Und es wurde dem guten Seespeck in seinem Busen oftmals bange bei all diesen Blickerlebnissen. Was sollte es heissen, wenn er sich gestehen musste, dass seine Augen oder seine Sinne dicht an die äusserste Grenze gekommen schienen, wo bei seinem weiteren Vordringen das blanke nackte Sein ohne Schein und Schleier sich zeigen musste?" (405).

Repeatedly the object of his observation changes its aspect like a pictorial illusion that reverses itself as one stares at it; and he finds that his hungry eyes have made him a slave to naked hideousness (379). For instance, at the end of Chapter II he looks through the rear window of a coach and sees a church tower approaching; or with a slight change in point of view Seespeck and his two friends on a walk become "ein paar auf geheimen Wink und Nötigung trampelnde Puppen im Ungewissen zwischen dem wahren und gespiegelten Sternenhimmel auf einer papierdünnen, haltlosen Mitte" (375).

Each of the first four chapters ends with such an event, as if to prove to Seespeck that he is looking at things the wrong way.[13] A simple optical phenomenon, the image of a candle flame inverted and projected onto a wall by a lens, at the end of Chapter III forces Seespeck, as if his stomach were turned, to abandon his friends (382-383). These attacks of vertigo and nausea are not simply physical. They are accompanied by guilt feelings of unspecified nature and by Seespeck's conviction that he has become a shadow (387), which he regards as emblematic of his own disgrace (437).

The turning point, when the heap of experiences suddenly crystallizes into true perception, comes in the second of two Däubler chapters (VI). Seespeck believes he has found "ein Stück oder mehr von meinem Doppelgänger" (457) in the person of Däubler. The latter, like Grete and the apostle in *Boll,* catalyzes the ultimate vision. And again a subtle change in lighting is the final cause. Seespeck, in his customary shadowy capacity, sits as spectator and outsider while Däubler and the Doctor conduct a deep philosophical discussion on "dem Heil und der Zukunft der Welt" (466). The argument between the two—the latter a liberal bourgeois hedonist, the former a high priest or prophet of otherworldliness—treats of familiar issues: personality, ego, shadow, and light.[14] But Seespeck does not listen. Their phrases, like those on becoming in *Boll,* are simply an accompaniment to his visual experiences. As usual he is overpowered, but then we read the following: ". . . und doch war es am Ende Seespecks alter Freund, das trübe Licht des Herbstnachmittags, das ihm des Doktors oder Doktors oder Däublers Übermenschenhaftigkeit zur freundlichen Brüderlichkeit umfärbte. Er war nicht geringer als sie, fühlte er . . . Es durchfuhr ihn zu wünschen, seinerseits etwas zu können, das diesem Ausströmen jener beiden gleichkäme . . . Ganz wenig, ganz bescheiden, aber für immer gültig, etwas Ganzes . . . 'Nichts als Ich, aber das ohne Sprung und Fehler, das Ich, das alles in sich birgt,' so leuchtete es einen Augenblick in ihm auf" (466-467).

The momentary inner gleam leads Seespeck in the next and last chapter to the potter's workshop in Güstrow and a new career as an artist. As in Boll, the change is slight. He knows that he will never escape from himself, that "Jeder ist sich selbst der Nächste," but he refuses to take refuge in the old shadow existence. Instead, he represents himself to his prospective neighbors "mit seltener Pomadigkeit" as the most isolated of humans—a professional executioner. This is the vivid, comic extension of the decision inspired by the new look at Däubler and the Doctor. The change of light, then, does two things. It reduces Däubler to human proportions and raises Seespeck's self-esteem. This is essentially the same event which takes place in *Boll* VII, where Boll looks at the apostle not with disrespect but at least on even terms.

The precise nature of Seespeck's metamorphosis is not clearly articulated. For conceptual language, at least as far as Barlach is concerned, cannot tell us what happens here. Both Boll and Seespeck finally discover and accept their position in the logically contradictory but creative center between two poles represented by the Doctor and Däubler, or the devil Elias and the Herr. We have to do here with the paradox of simultaneous surrender and intensification of the ego. The new Boll can scoff at the apostle and then kneel before him without inner contradiction. Again and again in his letters and in his artistic endeavor Barlach tries to communicate this experience. He writes with reference to Calan in *Die Sündflut*: "Ich ergriefe, nein, mich ergreift in besten Stunden die Vorstellung der Entpersönlichung, des Aufgehens im Höheren, ich nenne es: das Glück der Selbstüberwindung,

in dem das volle Bewusstsein des Ichs enthalten und erhalten bleibt."[15]

Seespeck and all the kindred figures in Barlach's works (Siebenmark, Calan, Boll) feel at the outset that they live on the brink of physical corruption and yearn to escape this vale of tears. Yet each learns that he belongs here and that to escape into blindness, death, or other-worldliness is wrong. They keep their eyes open and their senses alert. In the end the eye becomes a source of light, not just an organ of vision; merciless perception of reality becomes creative vision; and the ego is transformed from shadow to radiant wholeness.

Through reference to Barlach's writings over many years and by suggesting a certain distribution of emphasis, the foregoing remarks are intended to illuminate the suggestive but not self-explanatory final scene in *Der blaue Boll* and to offer clues for reading the Barlachian system of hieroglyphs wherever they may appear. The following exemplary quote should now be less arcane: "Das Wesen des Seins ist dunkel, weil wir Augen haben, mit denen wir es erkennen wollen, gut nur, dass Schauen ist, das alles Erkennen überflüssig macht."[16]

NOTES

[1] I. W. Lucas, "'Der blaue Boll' and the New Man," *GLL,* XVI (1963), 238-247.

[2] Ernst Barlach, *Die Dramen* (München, 1956), p. 455. This is the source of all citations from the plays and is referred to hereafter by page number.

[3] Boll senses this Mephisiophelean element in the Herr's speech: "Ich möchte Ihren Absichten förderlich und dienstlich sein," and calls him "ein ausgelernter Satan" (454).

[4] Ernst Barlach, *Leben und Werk in seinen Briefen,* ed. Friedrich Dross (München, 1952), p. 178.

[5] Lucas, p. 242.

[6] Ernst Barlach, *Frühe und späte Briefe,* eds. Paul Schurek and Hugo Sieker (Hamburg, 1962), p. 82.

[7] Compare the passages on "augenscheinlich gemachte Weltseele" in *Die Prosa* (München, 1958), I, 334, 406.

[8] Cf. my "Ernst Barlach's 'Der arme Vetter': A Study," *MLR,* LVII (1962), 373-384.

[9] *Die Prosa,* I, 334. See also the article cited in note 8.

[10] *Die Prosa* (München, 1959), II, 482.

[11] Ibid., 504. The ellipses are Barlach's.

[12] *Die Prosa,* I, 355-356.

13 For a discerning discussion of space and vision in *Seespeck* see J. W. McFarlane, "Plasticity in Language: Some Notes on the Prose Style of Ernst Barlach," *MLR,* XLIX (1954), 451-460.

14 This assumes that the six loose pages found in Book 2 of the manuscript contain at least the essence of their dialog. See *Die Prosa,* I, 501-504.

15 *Leben und Werk in seinen Briefen,* p. 156. See also pp. 73, 78, 89; and Ernst Barlach, *Aus seinen Briefen,* ed. Friedrich Dross (München, 1949), p. 59.

16 *Frühe und späte Briefe,* p. 96.

Edson M. Chick (essay date 1967)

SOURCE: "The End Is the Beginning," in *Ernst Barlach,* Twayne Publishers, Inc., 1967, pp. 30-50.

[*In the following essay, Chick analyzes the ways in which* Der arme Vetter *is the pivotal play in Barlach's oeuvre, dealing as it does with failure and disappointment.*]

Der arme Vetter appeared in 1918, and like almost all of Barlach's plays, it is transitional and treats the themes of phase and change. Yet it merits special attention because it also marks a transition in Barlach's style. It signals the end of the old and the beginning of the new. Consequently it offers even more problems of interpretation than his other dramas. No single explanation can be tailored to fit the whole. We have the impression that one element discounts the next and feel the ground drop away from under our feet. There is only one certainty: metamorphosis. All three main characters are radically transformed, two because they yearn to be, and the third in spite of himself.

The pivotal position of *Der arme Vetter,* Barlach's second play, becomes clearer when we call to mind his first, *Der tote Tag* (1912). The former is a drama of success; the latter, of frustration and family failure. Mother, Son (they have no other names) and Kule, the supposed father, all fail in their duties to each other, and each fails himself at the crucial moment.

I *DER TOTE TAG*

This is literally Barlach's most obscure piece. Kule is blind, Mother prefers the dark, and once outside the house, Son cannot see for fog and because the sun does not shine. The stage directions specify gloom for two thirds of the play, namely Acts II, IV, and V.

The whole drama is based on a visual metaphor. Adolescent Son with his great but undeveloped capacity to see seeks to break away from Mother in order to create for the world a better visage ("Gesicht").[1] Blind Kule encourages him in this effort where he himself has failed. Kule's eyes were once eager and hungry too, but one day when the crowd of images and impressions became too large, they simply refused to function. He says, "You see, my eyes were two spiders, they sat in the web of their sockets and trapped the images of the world that fell in, trapped them and enjoyed their sweetness and delight. But the more images came, the greater was the number of those juicy with bitterness and larded with horror. Finally, since my eyes could no longer tolerate such bitternesses, they weaved the entrance closed, sat there inside, and preferred to starve and die."[2]

Opposed to Kule and Son's yearning to grow, see, and do stands Mother, a creature of darkness. As the play opens, she is seen emerging from the cellar into the great hall that serves as the scene for the entire action. In this allegory, Mother stands for the dark, dreams, static security, and the forces of blood and flesh.

Son stuggles, in effect, to escape from the womb and enter the masculine world of light, intellect, and change. But it is a stillbirth. And the day on which he had hoped to emerge "hangs dead between heaven and earth."[3] Son is akin to the expressionist hero so common in plays of the 1910's and 1920's: The New Man. But he never becomes a man.

The audience sees nothing but an undifferentiated half-dark hall peopled with three undifferentiated human characters and three spirits, one of whom is invisible. Likewise, Son never sees anything outside the house. Nor can he even use his hands effectively.

The play ends as first Mother and then Son commit suicide. Thereupon Kule and the invisible Steissbart depart carrying with them a message for the world. Steissbart, whose name might be rendered "Rumpbeard," pronounces this message: "All men have their best blood from an invisible father . . . but it is odd that mankind will not learn that its father is God."[4] These are weighty words to come from such a source, and we may well ask if they are to be taken seriously.

II *DER ARME VETTER*

Barlach finished *Der arme Vetter* in 1912, the year in which *Der tote Tag* was published. He had begun work on it some time around 1909. In 1911 it bore the provisional title "The Easter People" ("Die Osterleute"), and he referred to it as a dramatic monstrosity, perhaps never to be completed.[5] He let it lie until, in 1917, his publisher and agent, Paul Cassirer, insisted on printing it. Barlach surrendered the manuscript, and the drama appeared in 1918. In the following year a new edition with lithographs by the author came out, and the Hamburg Kammerspiele gave it its premier performance on March 19, 1919.

The audience and the theater critics were excited by it though not unanimous in praise or condemnation. One critic left the theater "bored and discouraged," and another found the play "convincing and powerful." A newspaper review describes the spectators' reactions as follows: "The drama remained obscure to a great part of the audience. The angry ones giggled, grumbled, and raised a racket. But finally the good spirit of humanity prevailed."[6] In a letter to his cousin, Barlach tells of his amazement at the response: "I must say, I'm a little astonished that they don't take these events more calmly, the work seems weightier than I could have dreamt."[7]

The drama is not Barlach's best, but it is indeed heavily freighted. It merits close attention as a drama in itself and, because it comes at a crucial point in his literary career, as a document which reveals something of his development as a writer. In his sculpture, Barlach had long since moved beyond the two-dimensional, curvilinear intricacies of *Jugendstil*. Yet his only published drama was *Der tote Tag*, that ponderous bit of neo-romantic gloom, which enjoyed little success except, to Barlach's dismay, among psychoanalysts.[8]

Der arme Vetter takes place on an Easter Sunday along the upper Elbe. Of the twelve scenes, 1, 2, and 8 to 11 are set on the sandy heath near the river; the rest in one room or another of a small inn. The most striking outward distinctions from *Der tote Tag* lie in this realistic contemporary milieu and the colorful North German types such as Captain Pickenpack of the steamer "Primus" and customs guard Sieg. Barlach is striving here, he says in a letter, for the most genuine possible milieu to serve as a contrasting surface for the inner events which emerge and explode.[9] The world of this play is thus altogether different from the flat undifferentiated one of *Der tote Tag*.

III SELF-INTERPRETATION

According to one recent study, Barlach provided his dramas with explanatory "concluding commentaries."[10] Our discussion will, therefore, begin with a summary of the twelfth and final scene in order to see how much these commentaries explain and how they should be read. In this scene, Fräulein Isenbarn is forced to choose between allegiance to the corpse of the suicide Hans Iver and marriage to her worldly fiancé, Siebenmark. The following summary will give some inkling of the obstacles that lie in the way of easy interpretation.

In the barn of the inn at Lüttenbargen, Fräulein Isenbarn and Siebenmark stand before the body of Iver, who has finally succeeded in committing suicide. At first Fräulein Isenbarn refuses to speak. Siebenmark taunts her by hitting the corpse and telling it to rise again. He wants some light shed on the situation, for Iver has died and let his light go out at the worst time. Siebenmark executes a little dance around the body, screaming blasphemies like the following, which alludes to the Resurrection: "Tumbler doll ('Stehaufmännchen'), reconsider!"[11] The only response is from Fräulein Isenbarn who, rather than throw more light on things, speaks in paradoxes. It seems to her as if Iver had murdered Siebenmark; and as if she too had died. At this point,

and without apparent motivation, she whispers to Siebenmark that she consents to sleep with him that night, and later to marry him. In the meantime, however, she insists on defining their relationship once and for all, "so to speak for eternity."[12]

Siebenmark promises to "take her at her word" with regard to the sleeping arrangements and the wedding, and she replies ambiguously, "Do it—it has nothing more to do with me."[13] The second "it" means not just that the whole matter no longer affects her but also that the *word* by which he takes her has lost its meaning. In a last vain attempt to find clarity, Siebenmark then embraces her. However, he cannot keep his tongue in check, and the word "Endlich" slips out. Thereupon Fräulein Isenbarn takes him at his word and echoes "Endlich!" Spoken by Siebenmark, the word is "finally." Spoken by Fräulein Isenbarn with scorn, it assumes a religious coloring and should be read "finite" as opposed to "infinite." The repetition leads to more vexing plays on words, to Fräulein Isenbarn's "concluding commentary" (below), and to her expression of loyalty to the dead Iver.

Even though she has renounced language and the finite world, she tries to explain herself. With verbal reference to the foregoing, she says, "I sense a beginning, finally ('endlich') a beginning!" and in response to Siebenmark's request for clarification she delivers the following speech:

> Must one descend into the grave to get away? No, there exists a mixture of beginning and end, clamped together. You can scoff at the end, you see it, and you don't like it, you have an interest in it, but the beginning, leave that alone, that is my property alone, that beginning which one experiences waking and sleeping at the same time, like a child on its first day. One can't tell right from left, but one is in the midst of things. In this new existence, one is immersed in something natural and self-evident, but now one has to learn to see, crawl, walk, and, after that, all the rest. God, what will come of all this![14]

Siebenmark can now only try to draw her away to their room, where he thinks they can be reasonable, and where life is. She, however, scoffs at his "full, foaming life" and goes back to kiss the corpse.[15] In disgust Siebenmark decides to challenge her and insists that she choose between him and Iver. With ecstatic haste she chooses the corpse, raises the lantern to light its face, and the flame is quenched leaving the stage dark.

This is not the end, however. After a time the stage is once more illuminated by the light of day, and two secondary characters, Voss and Engholm, enter, apparently returning from a funeral. We never learn whose funeral it is. The two men speak about the events in the play as if they were long past and hard to recall. They speculate on what has happened to Fräulein Isenbarn. All they have to go on is a cryptic note from her saying, "It's no longer me." She then contradicts herself by signing it with her full name, underneath which stands the designation "Maidservant of a great lord."[16] The two men begin a dispute over how this figure of speech should be construed and go off to debate the issue and a second one, namely whether they themselves are real or figurative ghosts, over a glass of grog.

Far from being a second, all-encompassing "concluding commentary," this little postlude has the effect of negating, or at least beclouding, what seemed a fairly reasonable resolution to a play which has no clearly visible human conflicts to be resolved. It leaves the audience somewhat in the position of Siebenmark, with his yearning to go somewhere else where one can be reasonable. In this connection, one understands the feelings of Barlach's autobiographical character Seespeck in the novel of the same name. Warm from rowing across the river, he gazes at the winter sky and mutters, "The cold magnificence of this Orion-night clothes the mechanism of the ultraintelligible, but whoever looks and wonders, for him looking and wondering and even he himself become unintelligible.—But tonight I intend to drink grog."[17]

This is the trouble with Barlach's "concluding commentaries" or self-interpretations; under close inspection they elude one's grasp and lead to a kind of self-alienation. None of them is nearly as reliable or satisfying as a glass of grog. The end of *Der arme Vetter* is left open, and the final episode is not really a commentary but a dissolution, or questioning, of foregoing commentaries. The word "dissolution" is appropriate because authoritative-sounding statements made in the course of the drama are regularly dipped, as it were, in a caustic solution, in which they lose all substance. It is no accident that Voss, in scene 1, pointedly describes himself as a manufacturer of caustic soda.

The postlude brings home the inadequacy of words and metaphors to describe rationally what happens within Fräulein Isenbarn or Siebenmark on this Easter Sunday. Not only is the religious issue obscured, but even the true-to-life milieu—the inn, the rough and ready north-German types—turns ghostlike. Voss and Engholm threaten to become intangible and unintelligible to themselves. They are not quite sure how long ago it all happened; the temporal perspective is more blurred than in Fräulein Isenbarn's speech which mixes end and beginning; and one has the feeling that the funeral they come from could well have been their own.[18] The last concrete interpretation is offered by Engholm, who proposes the naïve theory that Fräulein Isenbarn has become a nun.

The sequential pattern of a serious remark from a seemingly venerable source followed by a platitudinous or downright scatological one to discount it fits many dialogues and whole scenes in *Der arme Vetter.* Attempts at illumination and clarification lead inevitably to new obscurity and riddles. For example, when Iver asks Voss, "Haben Sie etwas auf dem Gewissen?" Voss replies, "Auf wem? Der Gewisse dient mir zum Sitzen."[19] Also, Iver's imitation of Christ's passion is ridiculed so effectively in scene 6 that he is led to admit falsely that his suicide attempt was a hoax.

The greatest failing of Barlach criticism, and particulary criticism of *Der arme Vetter,* his been to neglect the ambiguities. Thus it has made the play appear to be a mystically vague, rather simple-minded piece. It pronounces Iver a martyred saint, Fräulein Isenbarn an angel, and Siebenmark a hopeless philistine. The play is not so simple. There is something of the werewolf in Iver; Fräulein Isenbarn, as the iron in her name and several allusions in the text imply, is as much Valkyrie as angel; and though not as obviously as in the case of other central figures like Calan (*Die Sündflut*) and Squire Boll, Siebenmark is the play's hero.[20]

Despite the persistent ambiguity and undercutting, *Der arme Vetter* is not a cynical or nihilistic work. The purposeful ambiguity is a device for Barlach's peculiar brand of alienation. It is not superimposed by dramaturgical technique but is rather built into the language, atmosphere, and structure. Although he may be masked as a lewd, drunken veterinarian dressed up as Frau Venus and leading the wild festivities in the bar at the inn, there is a God in Barlach's play. For all its grotesquery, the play is serious and carries a religious message, of which the grotesque is an essential ingredient.

The outer action is uncomplicated. An engaged couple, Fräulein Isenbarn and Siebenmark, make an excursion to the upper Elbe on Easter Sunday. We see them first alone on the open heath, and their conversation betrays the fact that all is not well. They are becoming estranged. Hans Iver, a very distraught young man, crosses their path briefly and then runs on. They themselves move away, and Frau Keferstein, a lascivious woman, appears, followed soon by Seaman Bolz. She welcomes his rude advances even though she has never laid eyes on him before; and they set off to find privacy in the dunes. In the course of his wanderings, Iver observes them as they lie together. At the end of scene 2, as Frau Keferstein and Bolz are taking leave of each other, they hear a gunshot. Iver has shot himself in the chest. They carry him to the inn at Lüttenbargen.

The remaining scenes take place in and around the inn. A crowd of excursionists, including Bolz, Frau Keferstein, Siebenmark, and Fräulein Isenbarn, fills the bar. They are waiting for the steamer "Primus" to take them back to the city. As they drink and converse, they hear Iver knocking on the floor above. Apparently he has not wounded himself severely.

The knocking draws attention away from the colorful action in the foreground. Fräulein Isenbarn responds to this call, or warning, from above, and as the play proceeds, she concerns herself more and more with Iver. Siebenmark, on the other hand, is at first interested only in his fiancée and his immediate business plans. He wants to get back to the city for an important appointment. She wants to stay and help Iver.

Both the surface and subsurface actions reach their critical point in a wild tavern scene (6) where the master of ceremonies is a man dressed as Frau Venus. Everyone is present, including Iver and Captain Pickenpack of the "Primus." The scene ends when Siebenmark recklessly decides to forfeit his financial future and stay at the inn with Fräulein Isenbarn until Monday. His reasons are obscure. Does he fear that he is going to lose his fiancée? Or does he feel obliged to help Iver?

At all events, Siebenmark is beginning to see things with different eyes and becomes more and more aware as the play continues. He tries to force Fräulein Isenbarn to make a decision about their relationship, saying, "We've got to come to a conclusion sometime."[21] But she repulses him with the reply, "But it will be simply an end and never a new beginning." He gives up and leaves to look after Iver, who is now walking about at night on the heath. When they meet, Siebenmark offers him money, in effect a bribe to get him away from Fräulein Isenbarn and also to salve his own conscience. But it is not quite as easy to evade responsibility or to avoid confronting one's own nature. Iver refuses the money and strikes back by demonstrating to Siebenmark how he is trapped in his own selfish ego.

Siebenmark is dismayed and maddened by this revelation about himself. In two scenes on the heath he rants and raves at his inability to overcome, and see beyond, his old nature. For him there is to be no dramatic end and new beginning. Iver, on the other hand, as if demonstrating one way of doing this, completes his suicide in scene 11. The events of the twelfth and final scene we have already recounted.

IV INFINITES OF TIME AND SPACE

The key to the understanding of Barlach's drama is clearly not to be found in the "concluding commentaries" but rather, as will be demonstrated, in the change in modes of temporal and spatial perception which takes place in the course of the action. The crucial issue for Barlach, at this time and throughout his career, is the problem of gaining perspective on two kinds of infinity. These are, temporarily speaking, total lack of time and eternity; and spatially speaking, the endless minutiae of this earth and limitless space. In *Der arme Vetter,* Iver has no time and feels overwhelmed by the things about him; and Fräulein Isenbarn hovers in the vastnesses of eternity and infinity. It is Siebenmark's task to try to assert himself as a human being against the two extremes. But first he must be shocked into real awareness.

Fräulein Isenbarn's concluding comments on end and beginning in scene 12 are the culmination of a series of remarks, more by others than herself, on time and time-consciousness. The issue is raised in scene 1 and immediately involves the concomitant themes of space and the relationship between surface and depth. The question raised is whether this is a particular Easter Sunday on the Elbe, an occasion to enjoy life, or Easter *sub specie aeternitatis,* the day of resurrection, not confined to a particular time or place.

When the play opens, Siebenmark speaks of this Easter as a "langweiliger Peter" ("dull Peter") and a thing of the past.[22] But Fräulein Isenbarn says she is going for a walk with Easter; she is still in the midst of the day. Thus she is irritated by Siebenmark's repeated reference to his watch. He keeps consulting it because he is pre-occupied with the lateness of the hour and worried about making it to Lüttenbargen in time to catch the boat to the city. He has business to do there, and time is, for him, money.

Early in the scene, Iver, who has not yet put the bullet in his breast, comes rushing by. Siebenmark asks him for confirmation of the time and gets the obscure answer, "Yes, yes, high time."[23] They finally do agree on the precise time; it is 4:05. Siebenmark is relieved that the day has two more hours to live. Iver then asks directions to the inn at Lüttenbargen. Siebenmark obliges, but Iver rushes off in the wrong direction, saying, in answer to admonitions, that he cannot go along with them because he has no time; all ways are right, one must simply keep moving. Siebenmark lets him go, remarking, "He is in more of a rush than we."

This is only the beginning of the assault on Siebenmark's and the audience's naïve views of time and space. Heretofore his watch and his sense of direction have been his best defense in his struggle to give his life secure temporal and spatial limits. The difference in this regard between Siebenmark and Fräulein Isenbarn is brought out in the similes ("Gleichnisse") each has agreed to devise to describe the sound of water outside a ship's hull.[24] For Fräulein Isenbarn the hull is of no consequence; it is "like the moving and rushing of the blood in the veins of that greater life about us in which we float." Here, too, she is in the midst of things. But for Siebenmark the sound is "like the din of that unfathomable, eternally perverse absurdity in which we have to grope our way." In Siebenmark's simile the hull is all-important; it is like the walls he has constructed around his life to make it secure. "Thus I can illuminate my life like a room," he says, introducing the lantern motif, which assumes such importance as the play continues.

But listening to repetition of phrases and ideas such as "no time," "high time," and "he's in a hurry," which are sometimes intended seriously, sometimes in crude jest—"show him the way to the toilet, he's in a hurry" and once even in Low German dialect: "Ick hew keen Tid" ("I have no time")—confused by talk of directions like "northsouth" and "rightleft and leftright," Siebenmark loses his grasp on the rational co-ordinates of his "Lebensraum."[25] Thus, in the short scenes near the end, he moves in the dark aimlessly back and forth on the open heath along the river and talks about a new time-consciousness. He says, for example, to Customs Guard Sieg, "For a sleepy dormouse an hour can have a hundred years in its belly—I want to go on sleeping."[26] This is Siebenmark's moment of darkest despair, confusion, and disgust. And it is his closest approach to the moments of mystical illumination of which Iver and Fräulein Isenbarn speak.

Siebenmark never quite makes it up and over to that higher phase of existence, that state of ectasy beyond the bounds of this world. His failure is complete when he takes hold of the lantern—the one that goes out in the next and final scene and the same metaphorical light he used to drive the shadows from his life-room—and examines the body of Iver, who has finally died of a hemorrhage. From this point on he may be a wiser man, but the earth has him again. He returns to the inn. His grotesque dance and blasphemous talk of resurrection in the last scene are not, however, just further evidence of the crudity and obtuseness he showed before. They are gestures of despair at having failed to see the true light and the mystical vision which other Barlach figures enjoy at comparable times. Siebenmark points to the dead Iver and says, "If he would only make his light glow, now is the time, but he has cloaked himself in darkness at the wrong time."[27]

Iver may have obscured his light at an inopportune time, but Siebenmark has at least the visual capacity to see that marriage to Fräulein Isenbarn under her conditions will be no marriage, for she is already dead. Casting a dark shadow of doubt over the validity of her alleged resurrection and new life, he says to her in his last important speech, "You have played a Valkyrie scene, bravo! You want to rise from this dead life to the higher death—Mrs. Siebenmark sacrifices herself to Siebenmark. She is letting herself be buried in Siebenmark in order to rise again in Iver. Those are merely hysterical fits. You have the choice between the two of us."[28] This speech is a fine example of how carefully and consistently Barlach makes it impossible for us to find final answers in even the most authoritative-sounding statements; for the audience must now have serious second thoughts regarding Fräulein Isenbarn's impressive speech about end and beginning. Indeed, on thinking back one recalls the peculiarly morbid eroticism in her attachment to Iver's corpse; and in retrospect her speeches do have the ring of hysteria.

Further doubts about Fräulein Isenbarn's role arise when one considers that she is only the third most important character. Granted, she is indispensable in the triangular situation; but in effect she is only the prize in the obscure, subsurface struggle between Iver and Siebenmark. She is an undramatic, rather passive figure; and, to judge by her speeches and actions in scene 1, she has already decided in favor of Iver. In fact, she seems scarcely to belong to this world. Her ecstatic choice of the "higher death" is simply the final, overt affirmation of the completed act, of the effortless, painless "resurrection," which she accomplishes with somnambular ease.

Iver, on the other hand, is situated at the opposite extreme. Whereas Fräulein Isenbarn stands outside time from the beginning, he is caught in it like a rat in a trap. He races frantically back and forth, a man with no time and for whom it is always high time. He is possessed by the most intense time-anxiety and agoraphobia. Like the doomed mouse in Franz Kafka's "Little Fable," he is engaged in a flight forward through the world, hoping to find the end simply by running on. Iver feels himself trapped while standing on the open heath. In scene 1 he points round about and says, "You know—I've lost my way, or I've been stuck into this hole here because of some stupidity."[29] By the hole—a synonym for "badly ventilated narrow pass"[30]—Iver means, of course, his disgusting, confining environment and, foremost, his own earthly self, his "Beschaffenheit," to use Barlach's word. He retches at the sight of others eating and drinking, for example, but the nausea is more acute when he accidentally looks at himself in the mirror while brushing his teeth. A man with a morbid sensitivity and conscience of cosmic proportions, he has no choice but to cut the Gordian knot and erase himself like a smudge from the pure face of eternity.[31]

Just before his death he stands in the dunes holding the ubiquitous lantern aloft so that it obscures the view of the stars and says, "It can't be denied, before my eyes this lantern is brighter than Sirius, an oil lamp outshines it. Everyone must simply see for himself how he can keep this selfish smudge pot from extinguishing all the celestial lights."[32] He sets the lamp down, crawls off into the bushes, and the flame goes out on the empty stage. This allegorizing tendency, seen here in the use of an eloquent object, is strong throughout the play, particularly in Iver's speeches. When he speaks of going home, of losing his way, or of his father, one must assume a double meaning. The abstract, or conceptual, element outweighs the concrete. In the end he himself becomes a ghostly abstraction.

Iver's end is a death and disfiguration, a grotesque parody on the mystery of Easter. Far from being the son, he is the "impoverished relation of a great lord."[33] That is, the family relationship is at best distant and obscure. His dying is simply the extinction of a "selfish smudge pot," a gloomy, hopeless event, an escape from the tyranny of his eyes with no compensating luminous vision. All he has seen throughout the play have been reflections of his own disgusting self.

Mirrors are important for Iver, and they are specified as properties in the sparse stage directions of two scenes.[34] Like the lamp, they are intended as eloquent, allegorical objects. Siebenmark, in conversation with customs guard Sieg, is the last to talk about mirrors. He says, "And now comes the craziest thing, even though others are really different from Siegs, you don't see anything but Siegs in the world—what can one do but run away, like a lap dog that barks into a mirror and a wolf howls back at him?"[35] Iver and Fräulein Isenbarn have thus finally made Siebenmark aware that the walls of his well-lit, secure life-room have been lined with mirrors and that he was not planning to marry his fiancée but rather himself in her.

In fact, if one looks for the basic structural principle of this play, it turns out to be one of repetitive and reflexive reference: in the vexing, horizontal mirror relationships between the characters, in the aimless shuttling back and forth from right to left and back again, in the repetition of the same ideas and phrases by various characters, and in the pronominal leitmotif "I-you-we-us."[36] Most of these reflections are thrown back in distorted form from the concave mirror of the grotesque, as when the wolf howls back at the lap dog, or the invisible "Chorus of Vengeance" in scene 6 reduces simple speeches to a string of nonsense syllables by repeating them in a crude musical setting.

Iver and Fräulein Isenbarn set themselves free, albeit in different ways, from this nightmarish funhouse or maze. Siebenmark is driven to the brink of suicide because he has absorbed Iver's horror of surface reality. Outwardly it is the discovery of Iver's corpse on the shore (scene 11) which saves him by distracting him from himself. He returns to his former condition despite his panic disgust with his bestial cur of a self. This is an obscure resolution, scarcely a victory. Yet it is the only significant one in the play. For it should now be clear that Siebenmark is Barlach's central and representative human character. He is the unifying focal point of the reflections.

V MIRROR AND CRYSTAL

The figure of the mirror is distinctly symbolic of the human condition. It has far more content than Iver's abstractions. Siebenmark's path of initiation leads to the recognition of its true nature and his own. At first he is unaware that he is looking into mirrors and enjoys his unconscious narcissistic self-contemplation. After the climactic scene in the bar of the inn (scene 6), he finds that he has never seen, nor can ever see, anything but his own image. At this point the wolf howls back at the lap dog from the mirror, and the mirror has suddenly changed to an image of self-alienation. Siebenmark leaves the supposed security of the inn when it is brought home to him that he is living in a solipsistic world peopled by two-dimensional, intangible, dead Siebenmarks.

The unifying pattern of action in the whole play is that of Siebenmark's repeated attempts to break out of his world and his repeated frustration. Each time he tries to win Fräulein Isenbarn for his wife or bedfellow and to help Iver in the only way he knows how—by giving him money—he is rebuffed. The irony of the conclusion is that when Fräulein Isenbarn offers her earthly self to him, he understandably refuses. The conditions of the bargain offer no prospect of human contact. The new Siebenmark is not satisfied with earthly love alone.

Like other Barlach figures such as Squire Boll and Wau (*Der gestohlene Mond*), Siebenmark is at the outset a self-satisfied "Bürger" whose eyes are gradually opened to a new perspective on himself and the world. The

following passage by a kindred protestant mystic, Jakob Böhme (1575-1624), describes aptly his situation at the end of the drama: "You have in your soul two eyes, they are set back to back; one looks into eternity, and the other looks back into nature and keeps moving in its own direction and seeks to satisfy its desires, and makes one mirror after the other: therefore let that one go, that's as it should be; God wants it that way."[37]

The play's greatest failing is that the supporting characters attract more attention than Siebenmark, and the dissatisfaction of many reviewers may be traced to the predominance given to the role of Iver. In *Der blaue Boll*, Barlach distributes the emphasis differently so that secondary figures like Grete Grüntal, who combines traits of Iver and Fräulein Isenbarn, are clearly subsidiary. Yet, in *Der arme Vetter* Siebenmark has as much right as Iver to be considered the title figure. The lines from which the title is taken—"In my misery as impoverished relation of a great lord"—apply in fact to Siebenmark.[38] He is the naïve central character, the Everyman of the allegorical tradition; and his two guides through the ordeal, his Virgil and Beatrice, are Iver and Fräulein Isenbarn. The parallel is not as far-fetched as it might seem, for it is Fräulein Isenbarn who, to be sure without specific intent, points the way out of the slough of despond into which Iver has led him.

Her guidance is quite passive and unconscious. Her presence alone indicates to Siebenmark that one need not always look at things as Iver does, that the soul has another eye which can be trained on infinity. In scene 1 she tries to describe her Easter experience thus: "I feel, as I often have—but altogether differently today, as if there were in my soul a great confluence of things from many distances, as if something gleaming and mighty, that had been lost, is finding its way toward me again, as if something quite old and alien is becoming quite new and familiar again. Really, as if one were rising from the dead."[39]

The significant point here is that she is neither looking into a mirror nor up at the cold stars. She is not looking at all; she simply catches, like a prism or crystal, whatever it is that gleams and streams from afar. Free from tyranny of eyes focused on what Böhme calls nature, she has become a crystal to reflect and refract rays from the infinite. Thus she can mail the note saying "It's no longer me" and sign it with her full name, for she is blessed with that ideal orientation, "an orientation, whereby the ego remains conscious, that uncompleted operation which takes place when the ego becomes absorbed into essences without losing its own essence, transforms the world into itself, and transforms itself into the world . . ."[40] In other words, she is not exposed to the danger Seespeck sees in the contemplation of the stars, namely alienation from one's own vision and self.[41]

Iver, on the other hand, like Kule in *Der tote Tag*, is the slave of his eyes and does suffer this estrangement. Just before his death he turns from the "selfish smudge pot" of his earthly existence to the cool magnificence of the limitless universe and is destroyed by what Barlach elsewhere terms "the violent force of space perception."[42] His eyes have always been absorbing, drinking in sights and light; in the author's terms, he lacks the capacity for refracting and reflecting the drenching that comes from God's eyes.[43] He is like the others who become ghosts in the fog around the inn at Lüttenbargen.

What Siebenmark and the audience are supposed to realize is that we need figures like Fräulein Isenbarn, "images, to which we can cling with our souls, like telescopes, in whose lenses the rays of infinity are gathered together. Only in the fact that they are given to us, that they come near to us, that we let ourselves be deceived by them—only in this does their grace and mercy consist."[44] Such images help bring together surface and infinity, time and eternity, personality and un-personality, end and beginning.[45]

Barlach, the artist and moralist, pictures the ultimate human values as sounds or rays of light issuing from somewhere in infinity. "They are manifestations of the universal soul," he writes, "made known and audible in individual physicality and humanity. Thus they provide the imperceptible with its peculiar kind of perceptibility; they transfer some of their corporeality to the incorporeal and help it to find life in the light; they are, therefore, the mirrors which capture the rays as they rush by so that they attract my eyes' attention."[46] He then adds a counterbalancing statement which gives to the individual inherent values, color, and life that enable him to assert himself against the infinite: "But now isn't the mystery of this physicality and humanity equally great? This act of mirroring the infinite, albeit in minute, most insignificant things? Everyone reflects back a small ray, doesn't he? And toward them others reflect the infinite, and they absorb it and weave it into something tangible and visible."

Fräulein Isenbarn belongs to the instruments in the first part of this quotation. Only Siebenmark is receptive to the reflections of others. He has normal vision, so to speak, and is spared "the violent force of space perception" which destroys Iver. For Siebenmark does not look toward the Gorgon's head of the infinite absolute but rather at its reflection and refraction in "individual physicality and humanity."

From what has been shown so far, it should be clear that Barlach's *Der arme Vetter* is best explained in terms of perspective, and that to explain it on the basis of "concluding commentaries" and apparent self-interpretation is risky. As further evidence of this and as a contribution to the study of Barlach's artistic development, the following section will outline parallels between events of the play and the reorientation of his own vision.

VI "A TRIP TO THE STEPPES"

In the years prior to his epoch-making tour of Russia in 1906, Barlach worked with the false perspective of Iver

and the unenlightened Siebenmark. That is, he was obsessed by Iver's temporal and spatial anxieties and, at the same time, like Siebenmark, devoted to the full foaming life. It was the Russian trip, he writes, that gave him his new way of looking at things: "A two months' trip to Russia in 1906 is probably what gave me the concept of limitlessness. . . . A limitlessness in which humanity could assert itself only as a crystallized, firmly formed configuration, if one wanted to hold on to humanity at all."[47]

The process of change can be shown by a glance at some of Barlach's early prose sketches. Until 1906 his muse was the **"Witch of the Hours" ("Stundenhexe"),** the title of a prose study written about 1895. His awe and terror at the passage of time emerge repeatedly in these early years. In their "flight from ominous questions about life" his thoughts race back and forth between past and future.[48] These thoughts also oscillate in a confusing way between the categories of time and space; in 1903 he wrote, "I look at space and fancy in merry moments that I behold time in person, God's housekeeper, standing there in the sky."[49] Also, his concept of crystallization betrays the same enthralment by time; a thin, toothless ex-convict, who managed to avoid death longer than his contemporaries, appears to Barlach for a moment as if he embodied a piece of life, "the shell of time, crystallized."[50] This is a far cry from Fräulein Isenbarn.

Before as well as after 1906, Barlach was occupied with the problem of how to bring earth and sky ("Himmel und die Welt")[51] into meaningful relationship, but he could not have been further from the concepts of limitlessness and firm crystalline form than he is in a small landscape description of 1896-97 entitled **"Around the Birches Weaves the Spring, and Even the Elder Feels its Spell,"** a piece inspired by the vitalist philosophy of the time and full of voluptuous *Jugendstil* motifs.[52] In it the countryside is heavy, damp, almost soppy, and from it there is no transition to the sky. Even chimney smoke, however much it may yearn to rise, is rejected by the moist air and falls on the meadows. The same may be said of the visual perspective; it has no depth and never gets off the ground. The sky is lost from view as attention is drawn to objects on the earth, all seen from close up. Waddling, bowlegged geese pick at things; the path winds and nestles "cozily" ("gemütlich") among the alders in the organic, decorative style of those years. The reader is shown little nervous buds on the branches and is finally asked to imagine the presence of thousands of seeds under the ground, still asleep and dreaming but harkening upward to live and blossom. Thus the landscape dissolves to become an amorphous source of life.

The spell of the **"Witch of the Hours"** is broken for the first time on Barlach's Russian tour as described in his **"Russian Diary"** (1906 and after). She is replaced by a great cosmic clock whose pendulum moves slowly from east to west with the sun.[53] In this regard and in others, the trip results in a rebirth of feeling and a new naïveté like that described by Fräulein Isenbarn.[54]

Yet at the outset the problem is far from solved. The danger of losing oneself in the endless minutiae of the foreground, as happened to Iver and in the sketch on spring, still exists. Barlach is well aware of this danger and states at the beginning the aim of his observations in Russia. It is to bring foreground and background into relationship with each other. A representative occasion when the foreground vexatiously intrudes to obscure the background—and thus the essential view—takes place on the Vistula Bridge in Warsaw. Barlach writes: "If, for example, while driving over the bridge our wagon had not collided with another one, and if, as the two coachmen quarreled and the sounds whistled about our ears like whiplashes, the grotesque silhouettes had not been carved into the picture, then one could present a perfectly gently etched sheet showing the flat shore of a river moving through endless lowlands."[55] The flat silhouettes of the grotesque quarrel, comparable to some of Barlach's early two-dimensional drawings, effectively obscure the view into the limitless distance.

Later in the diary he turns his attention away from the grotesqueries and misery of folk life and focuses on the distance, though not on the sky. The distance as the distinct idea of infinity he finds to be the essence of all that is Russian in his experience.[56] What his eye learns to fix itself on are the sharp, firm lines of the hills on the horizon. The first time this happens in the diary, his glance follows the horizon to where it culminates in a mountain monastery. Continuing a long musical metaphor begun earlier, he writes of the monastery:

> Bald and weighty, it detaches its contours as if from the profane past of charm and joy which has borne it up this far, by which it has been intensified and raised to the heights like a roof, which can then let all the heavens spread themselves out over it naturally and harmoniously. And with four towers and golden pinnacles its mood dies away [klingt aus]. As if pious instinct had built nests up there, fitted together like cellular tissue, as if the sacred joy of the landscape had suddenly been transformed from its upward striving into the triumph of fulfilment. A swarm of roofs, the monastery gleams in the sun and leaves the wretched start of its climb, the village at the foot of the beginning rise, far behind in obscure insignificance.[57]

Thus the landscape finds its fulfilment in the coming together of heaven and earth, in the monastery which partakes of both; for it is the transfiguration of what Barlach calls the hard crystal of the horizon.[58]

A few pages later a similar landscape, but lacking a cloister, is turned into a religious allegory as Barlach writes of "the figure of the steppe as soul."[59] Having found the crystallization point in the landscape, Barlach now translates the idea into human terms, putting the individual in the place of the monastery. The individual is the seeing man, the viewer. He stands, as it were, between the "process" of two infinities: Iver's chaotic earth and Fräulein Isenbarn's heavenly calm of eternity. The viewer, however, assumes a position analogous to

Siebenmark's. He is aware of both infinities and finds himself, so to speak, at the junction of the two where, to repeat Barlach's words, under great pressure from both sides, humanity ("das Menschliche") can assert itself as firmly formed crystalline configuration.[60]

This conception of the human situation between heaven and earth clarifies somewhat the apparent confusion between the roles the devil and God play in Barlach's dramas and answers the question of how the grotesque satanic figure of Frau Venus in *Der arme Vetter* can justifiably call himself an "allerwertester Herrgottsvadder" (most esteemed Lord God Daddy). For Barlach writes (about 1914) in notes to a play called "The Day of Judgment" ("Der jüngste Tag") which he never completed: "The Devil becomes a god: for he makes man into a crystal of contradiction, of the igniting and intersection of two very different things, of struggle for struggle's sake, of fulfilment that ceases to be because it exists. *Devil and God are one. Therefore one is two.*"[61] Thus though the two are one at the horizon point, so to speak, they must not be reconciled. In Barlach's formulation of the Faustian principle—that static fulfilment is death—dissonance is important, for harmony and unity make distinctions impossible and lead to morbid paralysis.

At the end of the notes to "The Last Judgment" we read: "Everything is one. But in order that it feel itself as one, it must be infinite. But if I am to feel, I must be able to make distinctions. If there is to be such a thing as All-One, then each and every thing must be different. God and devil must not become reconciled. Devil as depth, God as height, only depth and height together make a whole, etc."

Thus Barlach's concepts of horizon and crystallinity turn out to be a peculiarly human paradox, both fixed and in motion. In the landscape it is the apparently fixed but actually movable horizon. In his sculpture it is the rigid contour within which the lines express dynamic tension and motion. In *Der arme Vetter* it is the repetitive symmetry of repeated sally and rebuff, constant shifting from sensual to conceptual language and back again, the alternating stress on the two infinities of heaven and earth, beneath which, however, Siebenmark's ordeal proceeds with restless movement on a course of dialectical intensification.

The end of the drama is left open, and the movement, one suspects, continues like that of the great bird of prey described at the end of the Russian diary: "It is the storm's son, fatherly restlessness dwells in him, and his yearning, too, breeds in far distances. He searches and storms after it. But it keeps retreating before him, and the distance keeps feeding his fierce desire, and his soul swells with eternal yearning."[62]

Finally, the concept of crystallization and the conclusions about the trio of main figures in *Der arme Vetter* may be applied to the problem of where to place Barlach in the literary history of this century. For the sake of convenience he is usually classified as an Expressionist. Yet if, as Peter Szondi maintains, the Expressionists consciously view man as an abstraction, then Barlach must be considered apart and ahead of the movement.[63] The heroes of his best works—Siebenmark, old Sedemund, Squire Boll, Wau—are great because they preserve and intensify their distinct individuality. Barlach views man as firm crystalline configuration, as the crystal of the contradiction between his views of endless minutiae in the foreground and limitless space.

NOTES

[1] *Dramen*, pp. 18, 24. Parts of this chapter have appeared in *Modern Language Review*, LVII (1962), 373-84, and are here reprinted by permission of the Modern Humanities Research Association and the General Editor.

[2] *Dramen*, pp. 23-24.

[3] *Ibid.*, p. 54.

[4] *Ibid.*, p. 95.

[5] *Briefe*, II, 58, 63.

[6] *General-Anzeiger für Hamburg-Altona*, March 21, 1919.

[7] *Briefe*, I, 47.

[8] *Briefe*, II, 83 ff.; cf. also Chapter Six, p. 107.

[9] *Ibid.*, p. 94.

[10] Horst Wagner's interpretation of *Die Sündflut* (*The Flood*) in Benno von Wiese, ed., *Das deutsche Drama*, 2nd ed. (Düsseldorf, 1960), II, 348.

[11] *Dramen*, p. 177.

[12] *Ibid.*, p. 179.

[13] *Ibid.*, p. 180.

[14] *Ibid.*, p. 181.

[15] *Ibid.*, p. 182.

[16] *Ibid.*, p. 183.

[17] *Prosa*, I, 408.

[18] In 1902 the steamer *Primus* went down on the Elbe with 112 passengers aboard. In *Der arme Vetter*, the crowd from the inn leaves to board a ship with the same name. Voss, Enghohm, and the three central characters stay behind. Although there is no evidence for it in the play itself, the funeral might have been that of the drowned passengers.

[19] *Dramen*, p. 104. A play on words. "Do you have something on your conscience ('auf dem Gewissen')?" "On what? That certain [part of the body] ('Der Gewisse') I use to sit on."

[20] A number of critics have commented on the name Hans Iver. The first was Hans Harbeck—"Hans Iver," *Der Freihafen, Blätter der Hamburger Kammerspiele*, I (1919), Heft 6, pp. 93-95. He notes, as do the others, that the name is almost identical with that of Hans Iwer, the werewolf in a poem by Klaus Groth which bears the name as its title—Klaus Groth, *Quickborn, Volksleben in plattdeutschen Gedichten ditmarscher Mundart*, ed. K. Müllenhoff, 6th ed. (Hamburg, 1856), pp. 139-41. Klaus Groth was Barlach's favorite dialect poet, and there is little doubt that the poem is the source of the name. Harbeck explains the connection between the poem and the drama on the basis of a footnote (p. 139) by the editor Müllenhoff on local werewolf superstition. Müllenhoff writes: "According to popular belief, a werewolf, i.e., a person who goes around as a wolf at times—which is considered evil magic but also an incurable affliction—must assume his natural form again as soon as he is recognized and called by his right name, and is then doomed to die. . . ." Far easier than trying, as Harbeck does, to show that Fräulein Isenbarn calls Iver by his right name and releases him from his curse is to note that Iver, with his tendency to see himself reflected in others, accuses them of being wolves and of sucking his blood (*Dramen*, pp. 152-53).

[21] *Ibid.*, p. 161.

[22] *Ibid.*, p. 99.

[23] *Ibid.*, p. 101.

[24] *Ibid.*, p. 108.

[25] *Ibid.*, pp. 149, 114, 112 f., 173.

[26] *Ibid.*, p. 173.

[27] *Ibid.*, p. 177.

[28] *Ibid.*, p. 182.

[29] *Ibid.*, p. 105.

[30] *Briefe*, I, 64.

[31] Cf. *Briefe*, I, 47.

[32] *Dramen*, p. 173.

[33] *Ibid.*, p. 128.

[34] *Ibid.*, pp. 132, 140, 144, 156, 172.

[35] *Ibid.*, p. 172.

[36] *Ibid.,* p. 182.

[37] *Vierzig Fragen von der Seele* (1620), Frage 12.

[38] *Dramen,* p. 128.

[39] *Ibid.,* p. 100.

[40] *Ibid.,* p. 183; *Briefe,* I, 59.

[41] See above, p. 35.

[42] *Briefe,* II, 156.

[43] *Prosa,* II, 289.

[44] *Prosa,* I, 327.

[45] *Briefe,* II, 156.

[46] *Prosa,* I, 334.

[47] *Briefe,* II, 136.

[48] "Dr. Eisenbart" (1899) in *Prosa,* I, 170-73.

[49] *Ibid.,* p. 212.

[50] *Ibid.,* p. 213.

[51] *Ibid.,* p. 204 f., 210.

[52] *Ibid.,* p. 103-4; cf. Goethe's *Faust,* lines 3845-46.

[53] *Ibid.,* p. 242.

[54] *Ibid.,* p. 241.

[55] *Ibid.,* p. 242-43.

[56] *Ibid.,* p. 241.

[57] *Ibid.,* p. 268.

[58] *Ibid.,* p. 271.

[59] *Ibid.,* p. 273.

[60] *Briefe,* II, 136.

[61] *Prosa,* II, 380.

[62] *Prosa,* I, 288.

[63] *Theorie des modernen Dramas* (Frankfurt, 1959), p. 92.

Bernard R. Anderson (essay date 1968)

SOURCE: "The Grotesque in Barlach's Works: Towards an Understanding of his World," in *Essays on German Literature: In Honour of G. Joyce Hallamore,* edited by Michael S. Batts and Marketa Goetz Stankiewicz, University of Toronto Press, 1968, pp. 62-95.

[*In the following essay, Anderson attempts to reassess Barlach's depiction of the grotesque in his plays.*]

The term "grotesque" appears but rarely in the writings of the sculptor-playwright Ernst Barlach. It must also be noted at the outset that very little investigation has been made of grotesquery in Barlach's works or of its origin and place within his Weltanschauung, despite the great bulk of Barlach criticism in recent years. To be sure, some of his works have been loosely described as "grotesque," but in fact, no major critic dealing specifically with the phenomenon of the grotesque has cited examples from Barlach's works either in the formation of, or as support for his thesis. However, despite all this there is good reason not only for designating as "grotesque" some of the characters which he created and situations which he depicted, but also for seeing the origin of his artistic creativity in his capacity to experience and appreciate the manifestations of the grotesque in his life. This of course does not call for a reappraisal or redefinition of the grotesque as such. Indeed, an attempt of this sort would not only be presumptuous at this stage (some excellent studies have already been made of the phenomenon) but also unnecessary, for much of Barlach's work would easily qualify as grotesque on the basis of almost any of the available studies. However, the inclusion of some of the best of Barlach within the designated limits of the term would not only give the concept added depth, but would go a long way toward resolving some of the problems connected with its use.

Although there still exists a fairly wide variance of opinion as to exactly what it is which makes an object or a situation grotesque, i.e., how the phenomenon should be formally defined—or, indeed, whether it *can* be "formally" defined—there is relatively clear agreement in the selection of examples *of* the grotesque. Many of the difficulties associated with a deductive approach to the subject can therefore be avoided by relying more upon the critics' discussion of examples of the grotesque than upon their often dubious attempts to extract a common denominator and so reduce the phenomenon to a formula.

Some attempts have been made to deal with the grotesque in purely aesthetic or formal terms, but the resulting definitions do not appear viable. In *Deutsche Lyrik der Moderne,* Clemens Heselhaus resists the inclusion of any question of content when he defines the grotesque as the appearance of the heterogeneous in unexpected combinations: "Vielleicht ist eine inhaltliche Bestimmung nicht möglich, weil das Groteske nach der jeweiligen Gesellschaftslage eine andere Funktion und andere Inhalte hat. Wohl aber gibt es eine formale Bestimmung des Grotesken als die überraschende Zusammenfügung des Heterogenen. . . . In der Vermischung der Bereiche, Ordnungen, Stile besteht als wesentlich die Erscheinung des Grotesken."[1] However, Reinhold Grimm speaks for many when in his study of the grotesque in the works of Dürrenmatt, he refers to Heselhaus' attempt at definition, expressing full appreciation of the difficulties to be encountered in any attempt to define the grotesque other than "formally" but doubting the usefulness of any definition which does not attempt to do so. The grotesque in Dürrenmatt's world, as in that of many other writers, he argues, cannot be dealt with adequately without reference to what he calls the demonic element. He contends: "In Wahrheit umfa sst das Groteske bei Dürrenmatt—und wir dürfen mit Fug und Recht vermuten: das Groteske überhaupt—sowohl das Farcenhafte wie das Dämonische, und in seinen besten Gestaltungen geht das eine ununterscheidbar ins andere über. . . . Angst und Grauen vor dem Spuk der Welt mischen sich fortwährend mit dem unbändigen Drang, dieselbe Welt zu foppen und zum Narren zu halten. . . ."[2] Without a doubt a consensus of those investigating the phenomenon would bear out Grimm's objection. Even the otherwise formal discussion of the grotesque by George Santayana is summed up in terms which leave the door open to the irrational, for he defines the grotesque as "the half-formed, the perplexed, and the suggestively monstrous."[3] It would appear that there is but little chance of survival for a definition which does not somehow take into account that element of man's irrational fear which lurks beneath the surface (John Ruskin called it "divine fear"), that element of irrational insecurity which, at its best, the grotesque has the power to lay so terribly bare.

John Ruskin's discussion of the grotesque in *The Stones of Venice* appears to be essential to both the conception and the formulation of Lee B. Jennings' original and ingenious definition in his book, *The Ludicrous Demon: Aspects of the Grotesque in German Post-Romantic Prose*. With original research carried out quite independently of Wolfgang Kayser, Jennings arrives at a tempting if perhaps deceptively simple definition. "The grotesque," he asserts, "is the demonic made trivial."[4] Ruskin had observed that in almost all cases the grotesque was composed of two elements, one ludicrous, the other fearful.[5] However, Jennings, seeing the essential dynamic of the grotesque not in the combination, but rather in the precarious balance of the two, views any excess of one or the other as a weakening of the grotesque effect, and as a degeneration into either the bizarre (droll, fantastic) or the terrible (gruesome, weird).[6] He refers to Dürer's representation of the devil and to the Gothic gargoyles, in which "the great profusion of claws, beaks, horns and so on, serves as much to diminish the elemental menace of the figure as to emphasize it, and the characteristic bestial leer of the face expresses idiotic clownishness as well as demonic malevolence."[7] The degree of dynamic tension between these two aspects determines the power of the grotesque. To the extent to which the fearful element becomes ominous and threatens to dominate, it must be disarmed and

made trivial by the ludicrous. The playful tendency in man, of which Ruskin spoke, is hereby made a mechanism for preserving the stability and well-being of the mind from the disruptive forces which threaten to destroy it. Here, in the "undisturbed functioning of the disarming mechanism and the preservation of the balance between the fearsome and ludicrous aspects," Jennings sees the "basis of the unity of the concept 'grotesque'."[8]

One will not doubt the usefulness of Jennings' study, but one can hardly refrain from asking (Jennings himself has his moment of doubt)[9] whether such a category, for all its usefulness and ingenuity, should not be given a name other than "grotesque." If this precarious balance between the fearful and the ludicrous is indeed essential, much of that which has become stock-in-trade of the grotesque, such as the tortured souls which Dante depicts in the *Inferno* as trees, must be discarded. Jennings is willing to do so, but others are not. There also appears to be an inconsistency in his requiring that the grotesque should function as a disarming mechanism, for many of the examples he cites (such as late Gothic sculpture) were works of art created, by his own admission, with a newly acquired confidence, in which the bogey has already been subdued.[10] The original effect of such grotesques would seem to be the playful invocation rather than the disarming of the supernatural. The artist was motivated by his fascination for the subject rather than by his instinct for self-preservation.

But there is yet another problem here: the term "demonic." Although its inclusion within the definition should satisfy many who are unhappy with a purely "formal" definition, its usefulness is deceptive, for the term may be defined in any number of ways and is subject to constant abuse and misuse. We are in effect back where we started. The ambiguity inherent in the word "grotesque" has been transferred to "demonic," and a real solution is as far away as ever.

Of the many attempts in our century to come to terms with the phenomenon of the grotesque, one of the most perceptive, considering its pioneering position, is the dissertation by Ernst Schweizer, *Das Groteske und das Drama Frank Wedekinds* (Tübingen, 1932), a work to which even Wolfgang Kayser acknowledges a great indebtedness.[11] Using an essentially deductive, historical approach, although he does not limit himself to that, Schweizer describes the four distinguishing characteristics of the grotesque as: 1) "Die Steigerung," 2) "Das Verlassen des Lebensgesetzlichen," 3) "Die innere Dissonanz," 4) "Die Negativität."[12] The first of these, intensification, he considers the most essential, including within the scope of the term "Steigerung" abnormal diminution as well as excessive enlargement. Essential here is that the laws of nature have been overstepped and an incursion has been made into the realm of the fantastic and unreal. "Die Aufhebung des Naturgesetzlichen, des Organisch-Gegebenen ist unbedingt notwendig, um die Bezeichnung grotesk mit Recht zu verwenden."[13] Any occurrence whatsoever which appears in nature may be bizarre, he argues, but never grotesque. Not only is the natural, external order to be abandoned, but extreme distortion on every level, causing an inner dissonance, is required. Schweizer here chooses the hunchback Quasimodo, Victor Hugo's bell-ringer of Notre Dame, as the classic example of a figure who seems to have been created at cross-purposes with himself. With reference to the last of his four points, negativity, Schweizer denies the possibility of gracing the grotesque with a positive sign. He is willing to grant to it "eine gewisse pathetische Grösse," but the grotesque and any desirable characteristics are poles apart. "Das Hässliche, Böse, Gemeine, Greuliche, Grauenhafte, Grässliche, Ungeheuerliche, Dämonische, Scheussliche, Bestialische, Unmenschliche, die Dissonanz—das ist Mutter und Nährboden des Grotesken. Die Nachtseiten des Lebens sind das grosse Gebiet, in dem das Groteske emporschiesst und sich übersteigert."[14]

In his dissertation Schweizer seems to have attempted to arrive at a "formal" definition. The first two and possibly even the first three of his points approach a definition which allows for but a nominal degree of subjectivity on the part of the observer. But as Grimm has indicated (and as Kayser clearly demonstrates in his own attempt at a definition), the three points fail to exhaust the range of what they seek to define. Nor does the additional requirement that the grotesque be negatively oriented correct the matter, for this in itself is open to dispute. Throughout his consideration of the grotesque two factors have served as norms for Schweizer: man, and associated with him, his normal, everyday reality. The perpetuation of the world which man has constructed for himself and the preservation in that world of man as he is are assumed to be the highest good, and everything else is judged in relation to these two imperatives. As a consequence of this normalization, Schweizer sees the grotesque as a product of a nihilistic tendency within the artist: "Das Groteske kennt keinen Zweck, sondern entspringt einer negativen Grundbestimmung. . . . Sein Wesen liegt tief begründet in der Weltauflösung des Menschen bezw. des Künstlers, dessen Ausdrucksform das Groteske ist."[15] In our consideration of the grotesque in Barlach our attention will centre largely around this very problem of "Weltauflösung" and negativity. As will be seen, in Barlach's world Schweizer's norms do not apply, for Barlach aligns himself not with the human but with that which surpasses puerile man in his mundane world. As a result, the dissolution of man's world may well be regarded as having purpose and as being a step upwards, and not necessarily a plunge into chaos.

The treatment of the grotesque which has enjoyed the widest acceptance and which shows the greatest promise of becoming definitive is that of Wolfgang Kayser. In his book, *Das Groteske, seine Gestaltung in der Dichtung und Malerei,* Kayser very neatly reduces the first three of Schweizer's demands to one, and what he therewith gains in elegance he gains also in general applicability.

"Das Groteske," he asserts, "ist die entfremdete Welt." And he continues:

> Dazu gehört, dass, was uns vertraut und heimisch war, sich plötzlich als fremd und unheimlich enthüllt. Es ist unsere Welt, die sich verwandelt hat. . . . Das Grauen überfällt uns so stark, weil es eben unsere Welt ist, deren Verlässlichkeit sich als Schein erweist. Zugleich spüren wir, dass wir in dieser verwandelten Welt nicht zu leben vermöchten. Es geht beim Grotesken nicht um Todesfurcht, sondern um Lebensangst. Zur Struktur des Grotesken gehört, dass die Kategorien unserer Weltorientierung versagen.[16]

For Kayser, Schweizer's "Steigerung" and "Verlassen des Lebensgesetzlichen" are but means to this end (of creating "die entfremdete Welt") and his "innere Dissonanz" is but a symptom of it. However, Kayser's inclusion of the element of surprise is new: "Die Plötzlichkeit, die Überraschung gehört wesentlich zum Grotesken."[17] This element was one of Santayana's original requirements and remains one of the chief impediments to a purely "formal" definition.

Kayser's remaining three points are concerned with the origin and content of the grotesque, and it is here that he probes most deeply but also opens himself to attack. Heselhaus appears to regard Kayser's question, "Wer aber bewirkt die Entfremdung der Welt, wer kündigt sich in der bedrohlichen Hintergründigkeit an?"[18] as little more than semantical nonsense, and the very posing of it as an unnecessary demonizing of the concept.[19] But for Kayser the question is meaningful *because* it has no answer, and in a sense, the question itself is meant to be an invocation of the unknown. A consideration of these elements, he contends, is unavoidable in any thorough treatment of the phenomenon, for the grotesque is in fact "die Gestaltung des 'Es'," "ein Spiel mit dem Absurden," "der Versuch, das Dämonische in der Welt zu bannen und zu beschwören."[20] It is unfortunate that Kayser and other critics have found it necessary to introduce into their definitions such relative indeterminants as the terms "das Es," "das Absurde," and "das Dämonische." We will have more to say in an attempt at clarification of these terms during our consideration of the grotesque in some of the works of Ernst Barlach.

Some of Barlach's earliest experiences involved encounters with the mystical "Es" of which Kayser speaks: " . . . jenes 'spukhafte' Es, das Amann als die dritte Bedeutung des Impersonalen (neben der psychologischen em es freut mich—und der kosmischen—es regnet, es blitzt) bestimmt hat."[21] In his autobiography, *Ein selbsterzähltes Leben,* Barlach describes his experiences as a child with mystical forces beyond his ken. Appearing unpredictably as if through the fissures in the masonry of creation, that which Barlach himself later designates as a supernatural and quite indescribable "Es" became an integral part of the world of the young boy.

> Mein Bruder Hans half mir bei dieser Aufgabe, so gut er konnte [he wrote], wir schmarotzten am

Frischen so gut wie am Faulen, spürten aber um uns herum manches Bedenkliche, auf das acht-zugeben nötig wurde, Dinge, die man nicht sehen und nicht hören konnte und die doch gewiss wirk-lich waren. "Es" kann kommen oder nicht, mach-ten wir uns aus, als wir am taghellen Sommera-bend im Bett lagen—"sieh du nach der Stuben-seite, ich will die Wand bewachen," denn wir wussten bald, dass "Es" auch durch Wände kam. [I, 15][22]

The same mystical insight came to him as a youth with the impact of a sudden revelation or, as he later termed it, a glimpse through the cracks or chinks in the fabric of the world:

Beim Streifen durchs Fuchsholz aber fiel mir die Binde von den Augen, und ein Wesensteil des Waldes schlüpfte in einem ahnungslos gekom-menen Nu durch die Lichtlöcher zu mir herein, die erste von ähnlichen Überwältigungen in dieser Zeit meines neunten bis zwölften Jahres, das Bewusstwerden eines Dinges, eines Wirklichen ohne Darstellbarkeit—oder wenn ich es hätte sagen müssen, wie das Zwinkern eines wohlbekannten Auges durch den Spalt des maigrünen Buchen-blätterhimmels. [I, 20]

It should be noted that such experiences were not trau-matic to the young Barlach, concerned as he was with the absorption of whatever was offered him of the super-fluity of nature. There was as yet no "Grübeln," no at-tempt to dwell upon or analyse the ultimate significance of that which was so freely offered and so joyously re-ceived. Even at the age of twenty-four Barlach could write in much the same glowing terms to his friend Friedrich Düsel of the depersonalization experienced while watching Hauptmann's *Hanneles Himmelfahrt* on stage: " . . . Ich fühle mich wie ein Geist, der die irdische Hülle mit seiner Schwere und Umständlichkeit abgestreift hat und umherschwirrt auf freien Schwingen, schwebt, wo es Liebe und Glück und Poesie und 'Mond-dämmer' und 'Bergeshöhen' gibt" (Br., II [Feb. 26, 1894], 36).

However, as Barlach dwelt upon the vision of something higher, the lower region to which he found himself bound became increasingly intolerable. Each new glimpse through the chinks increased the desire to escape his narrow confines; each new vision of something higher increased the "Panik vor dem So-Sein," as he termed it, and robbed his normal, everyday experiences of much of their worth and reality. However, Barlach was not the man to escape entirely through these chinks and lose himself to the world. Throughout his life he was con-tinually concerned with the problems of imperfect man in an imperfect world. On the contrary, he grew to find of artistic interest only that aspect of man which grew out of the misery of the times and so displayed some elemental contact with the eternal. This determination to perceive and represent artistically the incursions of the supernatural or eternal into the mundane world would not have found such grotesque expression had the panic been less acute.

This incapacity or unwillingness to treat himself or the world and its inhabitants with detached irony is also to be seen in his artistic treatment of divinity. Throughout his life Barlach nurtured a faith in the ultimate mean-ingfulness of man in his universe; and although he sel-dom gave rein to speculation about it, he also fostered a belief in higher spheres of existence. "Ich glaube ja," he wrote in 1916, "dass seit Anbeginn schon höhere Reiche gebaut und gediehen sind als das Erdenreich des Menschen. Es gibt natürlich göttliche Existenz gegen die menschliche gesehen. . . . sollte der menschlich geistig-leibliche Organismus das Letzte und Höchste sein?" (Br., II [May 20, 1916], 88). It is therefore not surprising that in Barlach's world mankind came to occupy a relatively low position in the scale of creation. Also his perception of a divine component in the world prevented him from fostering a value system in which the human element alone was normative. Yet when Barlach envisaged a higher reality than that of earth, he peopled it with deities coldly superior to man and little concerned with him. The higher existence he envisaged was not an extension of man's familiar world, now purified. On the contrary, it was non-human, threaten-ing, and hostile to man.

Among other things, it is this—from a human stand-point—questionable nature and role of the divine in Barlach's world which makes his works so problematic. The dichotomous nature of man, aware as he sometimes is of the higher, yet bound to the lower and temporal, is one of Barlach's favourite themes. In his sculpture this dichotomy is quite obvious. The massive garments which envelop his figures weigh down upon them and bind them to the earth from which they would otherwise escape in ecstasy, rage, forgetfulness, prayer, or some other means of depersonalization. Among his circle of acquaintances, Barlach describes some who seemed to suffer unduly under the massive weight of the flesh. These Barlach regarded as belonging to some higher form of life, as originating from some higher sphere of existence. As the earthly incarnations of one of these higher forms of existence, Barlach considered his friends Theodor Däubler and Albert Kollmann, with whom he was long acquainted and to whom he often referred in his works, both by name and under the guise of other characters. Of a manuscript dealing with the two, the editor of Barlach's collected works, Friedrich Dross, writes: "Auf dem Titelschild ursprünglich nur die Aufschrift: *Der hohe Herr;* darüber nachträglich in kleinerer Schrift: ***Diario Däubler/Konto Kollmann. . . .***" Especially in consideration of Barlach's use of the term "hoher Herr" in his drama, ***Der arme Vetter,*** this nota-tion indicates the position the two men held symboli-cally in the artist's mind. But Barlach himself is even more explicit. In the autumn of 1915 he wrote: "Ich weiss oder ahne nur dies, das ich ohnehin wusste: die Sünder und Unseligen sind ebenso gute Heilige, wie die Heiligen selbst, da ist kein Unterschied, wir sind Verfluchte, Verbannte, Sträflinge im Leben—Däubler, dem gebürt ein hoher Rang, er ist wie ein Grossfürst in Ungnade, seine Fürstlichkeit schaut überall durch die Nähte seiner

Kleider" (Br., II [Sept. 23, 1915], 78). And shortly thereafter: "Ich meine es . . . bitterenst, wenn ich meinen Freund, den Dichter Däubler für einen verirrten Herrn aus einer höheren Existenzform, aus übermenschlichem Bereich halte" (Br., II [April 23, 1916], 86). But Barlach did not see in Däubler the conventional divine virtues of love and compassion. On the contrary, he is "ein gnadenlos Herabschauender. In seinem Blick, bei aller Milde und Versöhntheit, liegt kein Verbrüderungsanerbieten. . . . Er schaut drein wie . . . ein gewaltiger, ungetümlicher Wanderpoet. Der leidet an sich selbst und an der Welt wie ein verbannter Gott. Er schaut drein wie ein Gesandter eines barbarischen Kaisers" (II, 371). This Däubler is not superhuman in the normal sense, as an extension of the human, but supra-human, "übermenschlich" in Nietzsche's sense, belonging to a different species in the galaxy of creation. Kollmann lacks Däubler's corporal majesty, but not his royal disdain: "Sein Her- und Absender, sein Abgott ist eine Fiktion, seine Idee, sein Gott, er selbst. . . . Er ist unerbittlich, unbarmherzig; Abwesenheit aller Weichheit ist sein Hauptmanko, denn sein freundlichstes Lächeln hat etwas Schabendes, Abblätterndes. Aber dann . . . hebt er den Stein auf und deckt ekelhafte Gänge und lichtscheues Gewürm auf in dem Andern" (II, 387-88).

In *Diario Däubler* Barlach seeks also to trace the origin of man's fear of the divine and his apparent incapacity to endure it. He speaks of that element of the unknown in man which, although godly in the highest Barlachian sense, man fears and despises for its inhumanity, for its "over-humanity":

> Die Turmvorkirche St. Marien in Stralsund, das Turminnere als Vor- und Sonderkirche eines übergöttlichen Gottes ohne Dogma und Konvention, bloss Gefühl der Gewalt, der Höhe, des Ungeheuerseins, kein Verhältnis zum Menschen wie drinnen mit Chor, Schiff und dem ganzen Herkommen—hier vorne nur ein Bekenntnis des Unbegreiflichen, nicht des Menschenvaters, sondern des Unmenschlichen, den doch auch der Mensch in sich ahnt, den er aber nicht verehrt, sondern gegen den er sich bäumt wie in Verachtung als Entgelt für Verachtung, fürs Über-Sein. [II, 373]

But with Barlach the anger is usually directed not against the higher, but against the earthly which falls so short of the divine. For example, in *Der tote Tag,* the son replies to Kule's remark that many men have "Götterwesen an sich": "Man muss sie totschlagen, dass der Gott in ihnen nicht vorher zu Schanden·wird" (p. 35). And indeed, this was to be the theme of the drama which followed, for the young Barlach knew no easy resignation. "Es brennt den Einen mehr als den Andern," he wrote, "es sind Naturen, die nicht darüber wegkommen, dass sie in der Falle stecken, sie wollen heraus und müssen tun, was Ivo [Iver] tut. Es gibt unter gewissen Umständen keinen Trost, man lehnt ihn mit Empörung ab und spuckt auf versöhnende Geschenke des Daseins. 'Wenn es einen Gott gäbe, wer könnte es ertragen, keiner zu sein!' so ähnlich spricht einmal

Nietzsche. Da ist viel Wahres drin" (Br., I [spring 1919], 47). Nor could he suppress the consciousness of his vision and then dismiss it in a kind of Orwellian "doublethink" as he allowed some of his characters to do. In the contortions of a tormented humanity he found expression and partial relief for this mounting panic, as many of his sculptures of the late 1910's and early 1920's demonstrate. Even in the early 1930's he wrote of the "Berserker" awakening continually within him (Br., II, 195). As late as during the last year of his life he testified again to this same, omnipresent panic which he could not quite conceal: "In *'dieser'* Zeit habe ich wohl immer gelebt. Die Zeit der gequälten Unschuld, der Hexen, der Ekstatiker und was Sie nennen, war schon und hat nur krassere Farben angenommen.—Die Panik vor dem So-Sein hat mir von jeher zugehört, selbst in den sogenannten paar glücklichen Jahren, die nur den Leuten als solche erschienen sind" (Br., II [Apr. 24, 1938], 245). This "Panik vor dem So-Sein" can be observed in all of Barlach's works in varying forms and intensity, and is the immediate source of most of his grotesque expression. Whenever the panic could no longer be borne, fear and desperation broke forth from within, resulting in tortured and seemingly distorted images.

Stubborn doubt and an equally persistent "Schicksalsgläubigkeit" were Barlach's constant companions. Accordingly, periods of relative peace and calm were followed closely by disgust with life and despair about the human animal. When the vision was most immediate, the panic was greatest. Thus it is not surprising that the drama *Der arme Vetter* was written in conjunction with the Däubler experience, and that both of these were followed by a period of relative calm in which Barlach appeared almost content to accept man, despite his limitations, as a reflection of the divine. As Barlach then viewed it, the eternal had no less mystery than before, but it was less immediate to him, he was less engaged, and the panic associated with such immediacy and engagement was thereby lessened. Man and his world were then to be accepted as reflections of the eternal. As he was to explain in one of his letters:

> Ich bin wie ein Verliebter, der wohl den Schöpfer verehren möchte, aber da Augen und Nerven, die ganze bewusste Fähigkeit zur Verehrung und Dankbarkeit geneigt sind, so halte ich mich mit meiner Dankbarkeit ans Geschöpf, in dem mir ein sichtbares Zeichen, wie es zum Sakrament gehört, gegeben ist. Da brauchts kein Grübeln, man muss glauben, und so ist man seiner selbst ledig . . . das Bewusstsein darf und muss vergehen, ich bin entlassen wie ein halfterloses Pferd auf der Weide der Unendlichkeit. . . . Dass einmal die Sielen wieder aufgelegt werden, kann mich nicht hindern zu wissen, es war ein Lichtblitz Jenseits, das "Ich" war unpersönlich, unbegrenzt gewesen und ist doch geblieben, nicht zersprengt. [Br., II (Sept. 23, 1915), 78]

However, there were times when all his faith, whatever its origin, threatened to peel off as a veneer, revealing chaos underneath. Such an instance was the death of his mother in 1921. In a letter written at the time to his close friend, the publisher Piper, the whole impact of the return of his doubts manifests itself in a succession of grotesque imagery unusual in his correspondence. He writes:

> Das Grab ist mir ein gräulicher Ort, will ich gestehen, alle mühsam zusammengeklaubte Philosophie fällt mir manchmal (nicht etwa bloss beim "Grabe") wie ein Kartenhaus ein, und das bohrende "Warum" und "Wozu" fällt von frischem ohne Maulkorb und mit höllisch blanken Zähnen über mich her.—Die Unheimlichkeit dieser ganzen Veranstaltung ist ein bitterböses Wissen; nehmen wir fromm an es gäbe einen Sinn, so weiss man's doch nicht genau, und man krümmt sich unter dem Fluch durch die Jahre hindurch ins Grab hinein. . . . Welche Pfuscherei—wundern Sie sich nicht wenn ich gläubig werde und mir diese Existenz nur als Strafanstalt, Verstossung, Hölle, Degradierung usw. versinnbildlichen kann? Dabei bin ich wirklich zur Heiterkeit entschlossen, denn es wäre ja dann möglich, irgendwo eine Welt des Friedens anzuneh-men. . . . [Br., II (June, 1921), 105-6]

This same element of hope and the resolve to live for some higher realm is unmistakable in almost all of Barlach's works. But so is the emptiness and chaos which threaten if the will should lapse.

Barlach's language, Hellmut Krapp contends, does not try "eine dramatische Welt als Totalität zu gestalten, sondern möchte die Realien der Bilder und des Figurenspiels ins Gleichnis umprägen. . . ."[23] This tendency to use metaphor to express the otherwise inexpressible mystical element resulted in many grotesque comparisons, as his descriptions of his friends Theodor Däubler and Albert Kollmann demonstrate. Of Däubler he writes: "Er stürmt durch die Strassen der Städte und saugt sie aus wie ein Vampyr: Schönheitsblut. . . . Er sieht eine einzige Walpurgisnacht" (II, 369). Or again: "Im Paletot ist er wie ausgestopft; wenn er übern Markt in Wismar zum Häuschen schreitet, übers holprige Pflaster stampft und durch den Schlitz des dunklen Überrocks das Jackett gelblich blitzt—man muss an eines Affen fatales Gesäss denken, der, ohne dass ers weiss, nach hinten und von hinten über ihn grinst" (II, 372). Or again: " . . . Sein Auge hat viele Jahre hindurch als Wildauge gedient, wenn er im Dschungel grosser Städte mit Übeln aller Art verfolgt wurde. Er hat das Auge des Rehs und des Bibers, ja der Ratte, die durch Löcher schlüpft und unterirdisch vor Hunger im Holz nagt" (II, 369-70). Such intermingling of the human and the non-human realms has long been recognized as grotesque. Or Däubler might lose all human form and become transformed into some object: "Wie er den Turm [of the Georgskirche in Wismar] vom Scheitel bis zur Sohle mit den Augen mass und mit den schwarzen Seitenschrägen wie mit Keilen sein Inneres aufsprengte und sich zum Turm weitete!" (II, 372).

Such imaginative use of language appears at first to be merely playful distortion, but Barlach seldom lost himself in play without attempting something more serious. Referring to his own attempt to describe the enigmatic phenomenon of Däubler, Barlach queries: "Aber was geht das uns an." But the reply to his own question reveals his intent and justifies his use of grotesqueness: "Wir finden Behagen im kleinlichen Humor am komischen Miss verhältnis, durch dessen Spalte wir wohl seine Herrlichkeit spüren" (II, 377).

Albert Kollmann is described in less trancendental metaphors, but the combination of animal and human features is just as grotesque.

> "Ist sein Kopf ein Fuchskopf? Wenigstens hat er die Überlaufenheit, das ewige Aufmerken, Spannen, Wenden, Lauschen, Einstellen der Augen, Drehen des Lauschers, Verfolgen, Kombinieren, Verachten des Dummen und Groben. Er schnappt nach Leckerdingen (im Geiste). . . . Wölfe haben so diese Überaugen, diesen festen Form- oder Farbenpunkt, durch den die Miene das Grausame, Erschreckende, Faszinierende bekommt, Feindliches ankündet, mit Bellen und Beissen droht. . . . Und sein Mund! . . . Ein Marderloch, ein Iltisschlupf; da drin fährt das geschäftige Tier von Zunge blitzschnell auf und ab, spitzt heraus und lässt das Lächeln wie ein Huschen und Schwenken eines schnellen Schweifes einen Schattenblitz übers Gesicht werfen." [II, 386-87]

These grotesque metaphorical descriptions were written around 1912, and have stylistically much in common with the metaphors of Barlach's early plays in which an overlapping of the human and the animal realms is used to similar effect. "Traumgedanken sind schleimige Würmer, blinde Wühler im Geheimen der Seele," says Steissbart in **Der tote Tag.** "Die letzen sich bei Nachtzeiten und tummeln sich nach ihrer Art bei offenen Türen der Seele" (p. 13). Barlach's next play, **Der arme Vetter,** is equally rich in such metaphorical description. One character remarks: "Bei unserem Kapitän fängt der Humor im Bauch an, mit dem Schwanz zu wedeln . . ." (p. 144). Other metaphors are of a similar nature. Frau Keferstein tells Iver: " . . . Der Mauseschwanz hüpft in Ihrem Kopfe und rührt alles durch einander" (p. 132). Elsewhere, the "lady" herself is described as having "unterm Bauch als Gewissen eine zahnlose Laus" (p. 133). In Barlach's next play, old Sedemund counters his son's implied criticism of his behaviour with the remark: "Nenne mich lasterhaft: Gott selbst hat lästerlich geliebt, als er die Welt mit ihren Greulen gestaltete und ihre Schönheit schuf. . . . Er wieherte donnernd wie ein geiler Hengst dabei" (p. 257). In **Die gute Zeit** the moon is called "eine Blase, voll zum platzen," and is represented as a giant male sexual organ about to erupt and cover the earth with its seed (p. 492). Grotesque metaphors such as these, and many others, were the basic elements of Barlach's expressive language. " . . . Die Sonderbarkeiten, an denen meine Seele hängt," he wrote in 1899 in early recognition of the grotesqueness of his stock of images, "lass ich lieber in ihren urwüchsigen Miss gestalten, wo sie gewachsen sind, für die Salonspalten vom Publikum gelesener Zeitschriften taugen sie nicht" (Br., II [March 15, 1899], 41).

It becomes evident that Barlach was much less concerned with the average man in the everyday world than with that which could be manifested through him. "Gerade das Vulgäre, das Allgemein-Menschliche, die Urgefühle aus der Rasse, das sind die grossen, die ewigen. Was der Mensch gelitten hat und leiden kann, seine Grösse, seine Angelegenheiten (inklusive Mythos und Zukunftstraum), dabei bin ich engagiert" (Br., II [Dec. 28, 1911], 65). It is not surprising therefore that much of Barlach's work appears rough and unpolished since the writer was concerned much more with the truthfulness of his creations than with their aesthetics: " . . . Meine Gestalten sind gut, wenn sie echt sind; schlecht, wenn sie aus der Spekulation kommen; sie reden aus sich, nicht aus mir, und so sind sie verständlich oder unverständlich—je nach der Empfänglichkeit des Betrachters" (Br., II [Oct. 18, 1932), 176). Although he acknowledged the effort spent in wrestling with nature to attain his particular type of "stilisiertes Menschentum," to his mind, the finished product, if successful, was a creation of nature. "Ich lebe mit den Gestalten jahrelang so, dass sie mir so unpsychologisch vorkommen, wie uns das Leben um uns. Sie handeln so, weil sie müssen, die Natur schafft es, nicht die Überlegung oder Konstruktion. Ich fühle nicht, dass ich schreibe, dichte, schaffe, sondern ich schreibe nieder, was geschieht, was ich erfahrend wahrnehme. Ich wäre versucht, beteurend zu sagen: es war in Wirklichkeit so" (Br., I [Feb. 10, 1918], 42). His poetic world was then felt to be a true projection of the world in which he lived, of the world as he saw it. The artist here was not the sovereign bystander, but was an artist because he was more human than his fellows and suffered longer and more deeply than they. As he wrote in 1933 after a lifetime of preoccupation with the problem: "Gerade, weil er gedrängt ist, ganz und gar sein Menschentum durchlebt, durchleidet, oft mit der Verschärfung, tiefer leiden zu können, schwerer leiden zu müssen, ist der Künstler, was er ist" (Br., II [Feb. 12, 1933], 186). Barlach's world had no room for decadence. Art served him cathartically as it did Goethe, for whom artistic creation was but part of one great confession. "Du hast Recht", he wrote to his cousin Karl concerning his own creative process, "ich habe das alles tödlich und schwer erlitten und habe mich durch die Arbeit befreit, man braucht nicht zum Revolver zu greifen, sondern kann Vertrauen haben und hoffen" (Br., I [early in 1919], 47). He claimed that each of his characters incorporated a part of himself. " . . . Ich empfinde, seit je und immer mehr, die Einheit von Schöpfer und Geschaffenem," he wrote in 1931; "das Gewordene ist die andere Gestalt des Schöpfers, seine Phasen, sein Spiegelbild. . . ." (Br., II [Feb. 8, 1931], 169).

His grotesqueness was therefore not stylistic, as was the case with many Expressionists, not consciously superimposed, but inherent in his world. Everything, he claimed, is expressible. But in the very act of expression, certain actualities appear grotesque. Barlach did not create a conscious "Zerrbild" of his vision; the vision itself was grotesque. As Christian Morgenstern expressed it: "Gottes materielle Erscheinungsform ist notwendig grotesk."[24]

Nor was there an appreciable conscious distortion of humanity to evoke a grotesque effect. Barlach was relatively unconcerned with creating an effect; instead he was drawn to these figures which appeared to him to be suffering under a natural distortion or deformation, as if they contained irrepressible, otherwordly forces which were seeking release. It can be said therefore that for Barlach grotesqueness was not a device but a characteristic of certain phenomena of nature. It was inherent in the manner in which the eternal—in the broadest sense—found expression in the world:

> Das Phänomen ist auf quälende Art von jeher als unheimliches Rätselwesen vor mir aufgestiegen. Ich sah am Menschen das Verdammte, gleichsam Verhexte, aber auch das Ur-Wesenhafte, wie sollte ich das mit dem landläufigen Naturalismus darstellen! . . . Ich musste also Mittel suchen darzustellen, was ich fühlte und ahnte, statt dessen, was ich sah, und doch, was ich sah, als Mittel zu benutzen. . . . Freilich scheint mir für die Plastik nur das Menschentum in Frage zu kommen, das ins Riesenhafte gesteigert ist, durch Schicksal erschüttert, oder durch Selbstvergessen ausser sich gebracht, kurz, irgendwie mit dem grossen Begriff ewig in Verbindung gesetzt, das bei aller Zeitbedingtheit aus der Misere seiner Zeit herausgewachsen ist, dessen Freud- und Leidausdruck von keiner Überlegenheit belächelt werden kann. [Br., II (Aug. 8, 1911), 61]

Thus for Barlach, the grotesque was a phenomenon through which the eternal and otherwise unexpressible manifested itself in the world.

A good example of the manner in which Barlach represented the divine in grotesque imagery is to be seen in his portrayal of the "Elendskind" in his drama ***Der Findling***. The setting of the play is one of pestilence, struggle, and starvation, reminiscent of the Thirty Years' War. A child is abandoned at the feet of a stonecutter, around whose fire starving people begin to cluster in the hope of getting some food. When the stonecutter shows them the child they are horror-stricken and cannot endure the nauseous sight: "Einen Borstenbart hats an der Backe, sein Haar ist mit ausgeschwitztem Horn verklebt. Wie Klumpen Kot stechen seine Gedärme aus dem Leib, fingerlanges Gewürm frisst an der faltigen Haut, sein Rücken ist ein Gerümpel von gebrochenen Knochenstücken" (p. 273-74). It is difficult to imagine a more ghastly description. With his usual heavy hand, no less than five times in the course of the play Barlach describes the wretched creature in great detail. But when at the end of the play the gentle Elise and her friend Thomas demonstrate their rebirth to a better humanity and accept the miserable child as their own, it is miraculously transformed into a beautiful child and emerges, as the stone-cutter had promised, as the new saviour. However, the child fulfils in the play yet another and more profound function that that of a mirror in which mankind sees itself and shudders, from which it flees in terror, or which it overcomes. With a sudden insight into the real significance and magnitude of the grotesque little creature, the young girl Elise calls him "ein Spiegel der Fratze eines verzweifelten Gottes . . . Gottes Greuelgestalt" (p. 281). The "Elendskind" is here no longer a symbol of mere human putrefaction, but reflects to human eyes the terror of a god in despair. That the god in question may, in Barlach's opinion, be *in* man is here of little consequence.

Barlach enjoyed a deep appreciation of beauty and harmony, and his apparent predilection for the coarse, the ugly, and the grotesque must not be misconstrued. As Ruskin had required, Barlach's grotesquery is a terribleness taken from life, reflecting a spectre which Barlach actually saw, not merely a creation of his mind intended to terrify. It is because there was in the mind of the artist the vision of something higher that the world appeared so miserable and distorted. Man is normally so deceived by the artificial façade of his "normal" world which obstructs his vision that he cannot see beyond. Thus, when the playwright allows the seeming disbeliever Calan in *Die Sündflut* to experience his epiphany while having his eyes gnawed out and his face eaten away by starving vermin fleeing before the flood, he is far from enjoying ghastliness. To pierce the barrier before the eternal calls for an all-out assault on man's normal standards and orientation. Barlach's grotesqueness was part of an attempt to reach through man beyond man, to tap the elemental, the visionary regions of man and the universe; in a word, to plumb "den grossen Begriff," which for Barlach was but another name for God.

Two of the most powerful depictions of an all-pervading grotesque nature are the carnival-like parades in *Der arme Vetter* and *Die echten Sedemunds*. Jennings observed that the carnival or circus often provides a suitable background in which the grotesque can manifest itself, for in these contexts the normal standards of proportion no longer apply. The carnival creates a fantastic world which departs radically from everyday experience, and thus in a sense is grotesque in itself. In *Die echten Sedemunds* Barlach has created just such a background. The scene is a "Schützenfest," an occasion when men don their courage with their green and parade it through the streets. As if to reflect this sham, Barlach has erected an admittedly unreal world in the form of an amusement park in the centre of the town, and here dwells the toothless old lion which even when dead and flayed terrifies the hypocritical townsfolk, the Gierhahns, Ehrbahns and the Sedemunds into a moment of truth and a confrontation with their consciences. Near the end of the drama, the old Sedemund pushes the crippled Sabine in her wheelchair, accompanied by the screeching music of the organ-grinder, around the ancient, decrepit church into which the townspeople have fled to escape the lion. They are joined soon by Mankmoos clutching tightly his sack of money and eventually the rest of the "eben entlarvten Spitzbuben aus der guten Gesellschaft,"[25] forming, in Barlach's words, "einen Zug, der langsam, halb als Karnevalzug, halb als Leichenparade im Raum kreist" (p. 248). Once the deceit has been discovered, the old Sedemund leads this "Schar der

Hölle Entsprungenen. . . . die des Löwen lachen" (p. 252) out of their refuge and into the graveyard; away from their terrifying encounter with conscience, back to their familiar, accustomed milieu and their existence as corpses. Only when threatened from without and within did they really come to life.

In *Der arme Vetter,* Captain Pickenpack, who functions in rather a detached role similar to that of the stonecutter in *Der Findling,* emerges like Charon out of the darkness and fog of the Elbe with his ship of fools and looses his charges into the tavern of the inn already occupied by the principals of the play. As the demonic element (in a Goethian sense), "Frau Venus," a veterinarian masquerading as the goddess of love, and his motley *entourage* disembark from the little steamer "Primus" and force their way into the quiet, ordered life, bringing with them chaos and disorder, upsetting even the simplest social norms they encounter. But the effect is not entirely negative. The dissolute group functions as a catalyst upon the individuals, forcing each—through a crass inversion of all value and proportion—to recognize himself and his situation. But none can prevent the grisly prostitution of everything that Iver, the principal character, holds sacred. However, through this inversion both Iver and Fräulein Isenbarn see more clearly their spiritual relationship and the contrast between their vision of a higher realm and the baseness of that which they must leave behind. For Iver it is but a confirmation; for Miss Isenbarn it is an awakening and a recognition of the true face of things.

Having fulfilled its "demonic" function, the masquerade disappears again into the darkness. But the masquerade has another symbolic intent, as is demonstrated by the presence throughout of "der schöne Emil," a life-size, straw-stuffed doll which is hauled out of the attic into the midst of the motley group and is treated entirely as an equal. The border between the human and the non-human realms disintegrates as the straw doll takes on a truly spectral life and is pushed from table to table. "Frau Venus" makes little differentiation between man and doll in dealing out ridicule and abuse. When seated at Miss Isenbarn's table, Emil sits as if in leering mockery not only of Siebenmark, whom he replaces, but also of the aspirations of Miss Isenbarn to a higher form of life. The grotesqueness is even enhanced as the doll is shuttled about the inn and handled in much the same manner as is Iver. Clearly, "Frau Venus" is the all-pervading, all-perverting influence, ominous and threatening enough to be interpreted by one critic as the God in the play.[26] But if "Frau Venus" is the symbol behind the distortion, "der schöne Emil" is the symbol of the distortion, a distortion which, paradoxically enough, is a closer representation of reality than the deceptive everyday mask usually presented.

In *Der arme Vetter* Iver represents man, inspired by the vision of a higher reality, but trapped in the mire of the world about him. To awaken within the audience a desperation for this divine component, Barlach forces them to participate in the basest aspects of man's normal, uninspired life. Normal bodily functions are exaggerated and paraded on the stage to the point where life itself appears repulsive and distorted. Nothing is spared in his effort to incite the audience to cry out for relief. Conjugal love is reduced to the basest of animal instincts. However, Barlach's play contains nothing of the "schöne Bestie" with which Wedekind was concerned. The middle-aged, coarse, and lecherous sailor Bolz and the slattern, dowdy Frau Keferstein copulate openly a few paces away from the "Höhenmensch" Iver. The relationship between the young couple Siebenmark and Miss Isenbarn is thus placed by association in a bad light, and in the course of the play indeed threatens to move in the same direction. Because they are an expression of the animal instinct for self-preservation, that is, preservation of a self unworthy of existence, not only sex but also eating and sleeping and habits such as drinking and smoking are made to appear as an intrusion of the animal into the spiritual realm of man. Thus a vantage point is established from which human life itself, as it is known in all its forms, appears degenerate and foreign to the better instincts of man. And because man is none the less part of the degeneracy and baseness, because it is his own world which has become distorted, the enlightened man must yearn for relief. To a man who has had the briefest glimpse of the divine, human endeavours appear not only base but also futile. But when some elemental kinship to that divinity is felt within and even this divine vestige is threatened with annihilation by its environment, life itself takes on an aspect of evil. In comparison with spiritual values, life appears degenerate and demented, as though through some demonic force man had been rejected and cast into the abyss of earth to rot. Barlach speaks often of the "Irrtum des Lebens" and expresses the feeling "dass wir hier in der Hölle sitzen oder im Zuchthaus, einem raffinierten Zuchthaus mit sehr verschiedenen Strafgraden" (Br., I [April 2, 1925], 64-65). In his conversation with Siebenmark in the attic of the inn, Iver too speaks of this sudden realization of banishment and impoverishment:

> *Iver:* Num gut, haben Sie nicht manchmal Momente, wo Sie verarmter Vetter den hohen Herrn in seinem Glanz vorüberfahren sehen? Das heisst: Sie spürens in sich, als käme Ihnen etwas nahe, von dem ein Verwandtes zu sein Ihnen wissbar wird. Und das Herz stockt Ihnen, Sie schnappen nach Luft, und Sie brüllen wie ein Vieh auf in Ihrem Elend. [p. 128]

Full of desire and a hope bordering on despair, Iver knows but one escape, and chooses it. For the other "Strohköpfe" Iver's theophany is madness and his prison a paradise. "Wieso, ist die Welt nicht schön?" jeers the enigmatic "Frau Venus." "Warum sollte sie besser sein—sind wir nicht alle seelenvergnügt?" To which Miss Isenbarn who is awakening spiritually can only reply: "Man könnte fragen, wie kann die Welt gut sein, wenn *Sie* seelenvergnügt sind" (p. 131).

The dilemma of Siebenmark in *Der arme Vetter* furnishes us with an excellent example of the manner in which one's accustomed conception of everyday reality can become distorted and threatened with collapse. Jennings has described as grotesque a situation where "the familiar structure of existence has been undermined and chaos seems imminent." The effect of a grotesque situation differs from that of a grotesque object, he contends, inasmuch as "the current of demonic fear expresses itself in this case not as the menace of a bogey, but as the collapse of a world."[27] He argues that any thorough violation of the basic norms of existence can create a grotesque situation. The violation may be that of a person's integrity or the stability of the environment, but must involve man and must appear to pose a real threat to man's orientation in his familiar world. Siebenmark lacks totally Miss Isenbarn's combination of childlike exuberance and metaphysical anguish at the contemplation of the transitory superfluity of nature around her. He marks simply the march of time in an essentially hostile universe against which he must constantly shield himself. There is even a certain amount of unwillingness in his apparent incapacity to understand his fiancée's metaphors. Miss Isenbarn describes the plashing of water as heard from within a ship as "das Ziehen und Sausen des Bluts in den Adern des grösseren Lebens um uns, in dem wir treiben" (p. 108). Siebenmark claims that this is quite incomprehensible to him, although he has previously described the same sound "wie das Getöse der grundlosen, ewig widerhaarigen Unvernunft, in der wir uns mühsam Weg und Steg suchen müssen" (p. 108). "Zwischen uns," he had told his fiancée, "entstehen gegenseitige zehn mitten im Chaos. Die zehn Gebote für mich vernageln mir die mystische Welt mit bestimmten Forderungen und Verheissungen—so kann ich mein Leben wie einen Raum ableuchten—er hat seine sicheren Grenzen und Weiten" (p. 108). During his discussion with Iver, Siebenmark becomes momentarily aware of the meanness of his own safe, well-defined world. It is then that he experiences for the first time an almost complete collapse of his self-deception.

One thinks here of Kayser's definition of the grotesque. Siebenmark's world is but a naïve, self-constructed extension of himself, and as he stumbles around on the beach, frothing at the mouth, this familiar world becomes monstrous and alien. "Wauwau, die ganze Welt ist hündisch geworden," he rants, and then continues in soliloquy his nightmare vision of his now inverted world:

> Ihr Name ist Siebenmark, verstehen Sie? Darum ist eben alles siebenmärkisch: Ihre Braut und die Verstellungen Ihrer Braut von ihrer Brautschaft und alles, alles! Wer schafft die siebenmärkische Welt aus der Welt: ein Preis wird angeboten! Wer macht die Braut Siebenmarks zur Braut ohne Siebenmark, aber wohlgemerkt, immer vorausgesetzt, dass ich—ich—ich, das heisst doch immer noch Siebenmark—also: zu was denn dann? Kommt dann noch etwas? [p. 168]

The bonds of the flesh have not been severed; he has not yet gained sufficient distance. Yet for a period he does succeed in escaping the confines of his narrow world, and he flees from it "wie ein Affenpinscher, der in einen Spiegel hineinbellt, und es heult ein Wolf heraus" (p. 172). For a moment at least he is no longer Siebenmark as he exclaims to another character: "Herrgottherrgott still, mir dämmert was—reden Sie nur nicht weiter, greulich, greulich—ich war ausgelöscht so lange, ein gut Stück Ewigkeit, aber die Lampe wacht—und wacht weiter" (p. 173). The vision which was for Iver a home-coming, a release from the torture of the present, is for Siebenmark more terrible than the endurance of his own barren existence. It is with profound relief that he abandons the state of higher awareness and slips back into his former state of slumber. "Für eine Schlafratze kann eine Stunde hundert Jahre im Bauch haben—ich will weiter schlafen" (p. 173). He symbolically sets down the lantern he has been holding and continues his plodding up and down the desolate beach, forever on the shore-line. He has experienced a glimpse through the chinks, but has fled in terror. The experience has been effectively buried and readily forgotten, quite unlike the sustained state of awareness which Iver eagerly sought to prolong. Once again Siebenmark has become what the young Sedemund, with reference to his uncle Waldemar, had called "die Pause, die Atem- und Schöpfungspause, die Höhlen des Nichts, die das herrliche Was gliedern . . . ein Schweigen im All, trotz der Munterkeit seines Mundwerks eine Pause . . ." (p. 228). But with Siebenmark we have at least heard the "Klagen," "Klingen," and "Klappern" which perhaps forecast something better.

There would appear therefore to be considerable reason for rejecting Edson M. Chick's interpretation of the play in which he proclaims Siebenmark the "hero" of the drama. He interprets the play as a representation of the struggle of the "Everyman" Siebenmark to maintain his identity and a middle position between the two polar attractions of Iver and Miss Isenbarn, that is, as a struggle against being overwhelmed by an exaggerated feeling for either "the endless minutiae of the earth" and a "total lack of time," on the one hand, or "eternity" and "limitless space" on the other.[28] In the course of the play, his naïve view of time and space is besieged by the very presence of Iver and Miss Isenbarn; it is then "Siebenmark's task to try to assert himself as a human being against the two extremes. But first he must be shocked into real awareness."[29] In view of his declared intention, "ich will weiterschlafen," Siebenmark's state of "real awareness" is quite open to dispute. It would also appear to be much more consistent to regard Siebenmark as one who had failed to free himself from the bonds of his normal, mundane way of looking at the world than as one who had succeeded in maintaining a mean. He is not one of those who were reborn, as the symbolism of the play implies. The maintenance of a mean or a status quo was of little concern to Barlach, as was the perpetuation of the "human being" as typified by Siebenmark. As he wrote in 1916, before the publication of the play:

Ich habe seit Jahren ein Drama liegen, das aus dem Bewusstsein aufgebaut ist,—na, sagen wir gleich, dass man eine Art misslungene Seitenlinie des Höheren darstellt. "Armer Vetter." Man ahnt das Bessere, Vornehmere (naturwissenschaftlich: das Zukünftige), man spürt in Sehnsucht über sich hinaus. Ob ein "Gott" über uns lebt oder mein Wille und Trieb zum vergleichsweise Gottgleichen gegen den Zustand der Gegenwart leitet, ist einerlei. Hier fängt der Bürger an zu versagen, sein Gott soll ihn "beglücken," Leben als Fernsein von Glück und Zufriedenheit als Höher-Züchtung (Züchtigung und Züchtung) zu betrachten, versagte sich ihm. [Br., II (Apr. 4, 1916), 82-83]

Barlach stated of course that there was a bit of himself and his world in each of his characters. Although Siebenmark's world was not the playwright's ideal, it was well known to him and its depiction occupies a good deal of his play. And while Siebenmark is not an especially sympathetic character in his narrow-mindedness and bigotry, his dilemma was none the less very real to Barlach and appears to have represented some aspects of his own character which he sought to overcome.

Finally, the first chapter of Barlach's autobiographical novel *Seespeck* contains some excellent examples of Barlach's use of the grotesque. It depicts the hero in a state of mental confusion. Because he has an eye for the manifestations of the eternal in man and his world, he is estranged from most of his fellow beings who do not. But Seespeck has not yet found his bearings in a world of his own. The opening lines of the novel introduce us to the hero all but succumbing to an overpowering virtigo: "Als Seespeck . . . in einer Postkutsche . . . auf Buxtehude zu fuhr . . . sass er mehrere Stunden in eines Mannes Gesellschaft, die seinen gewöhnlichen Zustand so sehr verkehrte, dass es ihm zu Mute war, als stände er ohne Halt auf einer hohen Leiter oder als fasste ihn für die ganze Zeit ein Schwindel, weil er in einen Spiegel hineinschaute, in dem sich alles bewegte, was draussen sonst ruhig lag und stand" (I, 337). The man who wields such uncanny power over Seespeck is quite an ordinary looking man, except for something about his countenance: "Etwas passte hier nicht zusammen. . . . Die Augen in diesem Gesichte waren so, wie sie durch die Augenlöcher einer Maske schauen" (I, 337). Seespeck meets the same man again the next day in the bar of a tiny steamer on the Elbe and strikes up a conversation. To avoid a drunken, leering Baker who makes a nuisance of himself, Seespeck and his companion attempt to go out on deck, but blocking their passage, the mighty, corpulent Baker cynically offers his hand as if in token of friendly reconciliation. Seespeck's newly found companion angrily refuses the dubious honour. "In diesem Augenblick schien es Seespeck, als sehe er abermals das Widersprechende in seinen Mienen, dasselbe Auge, das durch die Gucklöcher einer Maske lugte" (I, 339). The Baker takes the refusal as an insult, becomes equally enraged, and thus begins an almost demonic power struggle between the two opponents, each attempting to hold his ground and browbeat the other and so bring him within his power. "Seespeck war es wieder," writes Barlach, "als drehten sich um ihn alle Dinge, und er wusste nicht, wo oben und unten war" (I, 340). With the increasing dusk, the Baker appears to feel more sure of himself and begins to sing a strange song:

> Was für eine Art Singen es war, liesse sich schwer beschreiben; man könnte denken und sagen, es war das gesungene Porträt des Bäckers, wie er etwa, befreit von der Schwere seines fleischigen Überflusses, aber doch als Riese und Ungetüm leicht tänzelnd, mühelos hüpfend in grotesker Gewandtheit seiner Unförmlichkeit spottend durch Wald und Heide striche, seiner selbst entledigt und doch sein Selbst entfaltend, durchaus unähnlich dem Begriffe, den man nach den früheren Vorgängen von ihm haben konnte, und doch musste man denken, dass sich so, wie er sich nun zeigte, erst die rechte Anschauung seines Wesens ergab. [I, 340-41]

His opponent is seemingly unruffled. Placing his elbows on his knees and blowing smoke up past his eyes, he stares at the Baker:

> Er fasste das singende Ungetüm von Bäcker ins Auge, er zog sich fest an ihn, er schnitt in ihn hinein mit der gelassenen Sachlichkeit eines Operateurs. Seespeck wurde angst und bange. Aber da sah er schon, wie des Bäckers Gesicht, wie aus einer Dunstwolke auftauchend, sich dem andern zuwandte und wie ein Grinsen, dessen Deutung nicht versucht werden kann, dieses Gesicht überzog und wie die dicke Zunge zwischen seinen Lippen aus verborgener Hölle hervor auf den Betrachter zielte. Der Bäcker schnitt seine Grimasse, und der andre parierte diese Hiebe, die in ihrer Scheusslichkeit, wie Entleerungen von Unrat, schlimmer als Fausthiebe oder Schimpfworte waren, mit der geräuschlosen Tätigkeit seiner Augen, aber nicht ohne von dem Ekel des Kampfes ermüdet und verwundet zu werden. Man sah wie seine Schultern im Krampf des Ringens nach Atem sich hoben und senkten. [I, 341]

Barlach explains that although an average man "von üblicher Betrachtungsweise" (I, 341) might have considered the actions of the Baker those of a madman, Seespeck's attitude was different. He sought an explanation beyond the normal human realm:

> Aber was war das auch für ein Wesen, das diese Verzerrungen, diese Entladungen, diese Selbstbehauptungen von unheimlichem Grunde wie stinkende Blasen aus dem Sumpf in Gebärden und Grimassen heraufquellen machte! Ein Mensch? Wenn ein Mensch so seine Fesseln sprengen kann, wenn er so Rasendes, Vulkanisches in sich hat, dann war es ein Mensch. Man konnte sich einbilden, den Widerhall vom Gebell von hunderttausend Dämonen zu hören, die sich gegen Gott empören. . . . Pfui Teufel, war das ein Menschenmund, der sich dazu hergab, ein ekelhaft ausgebildetes Ausgussloch zwischen ein Paar Hinterbacken zu werden? Kot und allerlei seelischen Unrat leerte [jener] gelassen aus, wobei es ihm recht darauf ankam, den Vorgang

unmissverständlich sein zu lassen; er verschob die untere Hälfte des Gesichts so weit, dass die Augen aus dem ordentlichen Zusammenhang gequetscht schienen, er bog den Kopf in den Nacken und misshandelte die Lippen zu einem lächelnden Ausdruck eines schweinischen Behagens; aber dies wenige und tausenderlei anderes gleichzeitig mit blitzschnell vorübergleitenden Variationen von Offenbarungen der Verblödung und der Selbstzerstückelung, der Verunehrung und Ableugnung alles Heiligen und überhaupt des menschlich Würdigen, Graden und Ganzen. Und das Schlimme schien, dass dies alles in getroster Verfassung stattfand, dass auf diese mit Verzweiflung geruhig noch einmal gespuckt, dass die Entwürdigung mit Prahlerei gesalzen wurde. [I, 342]

The Baker's opponent finds it impossible to resist such a complete assault on the norms of the world from which he launched his defence, and surrenders his will to the Baker.

Barlach here demonstrates his familiarity with the manner in which play with forces beyond man's normal ken can suddenly become inverted and lose its lightness in a most terrifying manner. This is essentially the phenomenon of which Kayser speaks when he defines certain grotesque representations as a playing with the absurd: "Es kann in Heiterkeit und fast in Freiheit begonnen werden. . . . Es kann aber auch mitreissen, dem Spielenden die Freiheit rauben und ihn mit allem Grauen vor den Geistern erfüllen, die er leichtfertig gerufen hat."[30] Seespeck finds himself witnessing a struggle similar to the one in which he himself would later be engaged when striving to overcome the power which majesty in any form exercises over those who are aware of and sensitive to it. As Barlach formulates it:

> Was aber Seespeck bald heraus hatte, war, dass der Sporn all dieser Anstalten zu guter Letzt so etwas war wie eine frevelhafte, bis zur Selbstausschaltung gehende Neugierde, eine ungehörige Begierde, die wie ein wollustartiger Krampf sich an Fremdes und Anderes wie an Besseres hingibt und verliert. Und über allem leuchtete der Schein eines Leidens, wie es einen Menschen zerfleischen kann, der im Jähzorn sein Kind misshandelt und dabei sein eigenes Gefühl vergewaltigt. [I, 343]

Seespeck can endure the situation no longer. "Ein Mensch, der das ansieht und sich nicht beteiligt fühlt, hört auf, ein anständiger Mensch zu sein," he later exclaims in justification for his intervention on behalf of the Baker's opponent. Seespeck calls out for light to break the spell, for it has become so dark, "dass die Fettleibigkeit des stumm rasenden Bäckers zur Gespensterhaftigkeit wurde" (I, 344). But that which "in der Dämmerung lebendig geworden war, starb unter der Lampe ab" (I, 344). It is clear that for Seespeck the Baker has become a grotesque phenomenon. It is as though he were a being of some other realm and that any manifestation of his true power and majesty must of necessity become grotesque in the eyes of man. The Baker comes into his own in proportion as man's world fades into darkness and becomes undifferentiated, for the two are incompatible and mutually destructive: "Was," dachte Seespeck, "ist dieser Klumpen von einem Bäcker ein Verdammter, der hier einmal seine Qual und seine Schuld herausgemimt hat? Hat diese Masse leiblicher Unsauberkeit das klare Bewusstsein seiner unsauberen Geistigkeit? Aber was für ein Fürst von einem Übeltuer!" (I, 344).

Seespeck plays the good Samaritan only to fall himself victim, and he knows full well that he is no match for this giant from some higher, foreign sphere now threatening his equilibrium. "Einen Augenblick blitzten die Grimassen des Kolosses im Dämmerlicht an seinen Augen vorüber. Er hatte die Vision eines Ungetüms, eines boshaften, schädlichen, unheimlich mächtigen und dabei spottlustigen Riesen" (I, 347). Seespeck knows only one defence. In a fit of rage he lands a well-placed kick in the middle of the monster's stomach. Since even the Baker cannot ignore completely his prison of flesh, he cringes in pain and the seance is over. But all this has not resolved anything for Seespeck. These manifestations of the grotesque have given him a greater insight not into the insanity of man but into the unknown depths of the universe from which phenomena such as the Baker find their way to earth. But his own world has not ceased to spin. As Seespeck returns home later that evening, once again it seems to him "als ginge er an einer langen Planke entlang und fände nirgends einen Ausgang, die Planke aber hatter er im Verdacht, dass sie im Kreise liefe und er mit ihr. Wie er aber hineingekommen, war ein Geheimnis" (I, 356).

Not even in his sleep does Seespeck find peace or stability for his spinning world. In his dreams that night he rides again in a coach, and again the world seems grotesque. He accompanies a woman and a young girl on a cross-country trip. On the seat next to her and across from Seespeck, the young girl puts down a package she has been carrying, a ham wrapped up in paper. This supposedly lifeless object continually leaps around in the coach as if possessed by a will of its own. "Damit er [the ham] nicht fortwährend vom Sitz sprang, stemmte Seespeck, der gegenüber sass, seinen Fuss dagegen, konnte aber niemals darüber klar werden, ob das Springen des Schinkens vom Poltern und Stossen des alten Rumpelkastens kam oder ob der Schinken sich aus eigenen Kräften bewegte" (I, 371). But not only does the inanimate appear to take on life, all logical orientation in Seespeck's own life also seems to decay. He sits facing the back of the coach, but thinks it nothing amiss when through the back window he sees a church steeple approaching. In his dreams, his encounter with the Baker also takes on a new dimension. The Baker not only retains his monstrous proportions, but also assumes the magnitude of some deranged divinity; he becomes man's creator, but a creator against whom man must fight to defend himself.

> In dieser Nacht träumte er nun wirklich allerlei Krauses. Er war in Hass und Todfeindschaft verklammert mit jemand, der zugleich niemand war, mit seinem Erschaffer, der sein Vernichter werden wollte. . . . Er stieg durchs Fenster und geisterte zu Menschen hinein, die ihn mit Entsetzen gewahrten. [I, 370]

In Chapters 5 and 6 of the novel, Barlach deals with Däubler by name and not in the guise of the Baker, but he is portraying essentially the same phenomenon, the same threat of overpowering domination to the integrity of the "Ich." Although Seespeck feels the same strong need as before to seek his own way and assert his own individuality against the threat, there is little doubt that he, as earlier Siebenmark, is doing so in conscious and desperate defence of his own insignificance.

The last chapter of the novel is reminiscent of *Die echten Sedemunds*. A circus has erected its tents in Güstrow, displaying a motley assortment of wild beasts and birds crowded miserably into small cages. The beasts are depicted as roaring, as if despairing in their misery. Following a whim of the moment, Seespeck spreads the rumour that a lion is loose, hoping thereby to instil fear in a public intent otherwise only on tormenting the beasts and ignorant of the majesty and nobility of the animal when free. However, while observing the confrontation of a child and an old man, both frightened by the allegedly escaped lion, Seespeck gains a new insight. He perceives that the suffering of man in his earthly bonds is similar to the suffering of the beasts in their cages:

> Wir sind ja alle Menagerietiere, dachte er, aus unserer freien Wildnis sind wir in den Käfig des Menschentums gebracht und hier . . . im Menschsein werden wir schlimmer zugerichtet als Eisbären, Kondoren, Affen und Löwen, die ja bloss blind und mottig werden. Aber wo sollen wir hin? Wenn wir ausbrechen, gehts uns wie den Bestien, wir werden doch wieder eingefangen. [I, 481-82]

For the early Barlach, man is trapped to the point of suffocation in the prison of his earthly exile. Each man is, as it were, a latent Däubler in miniature, potentially a god, forgotten in his exile. Only when his habitual, limited orientation is shattered does his true state become evident. As Barlach wrote in the description of the chaos perpetrated by the lion: "Die Welt wird frei, gross, kühn, wenn sie in Brand, in Not, in Wut gerät" (I, 480). But man in his puniness has no eye for greatness and shuts it out or flees from it in terror. His chief concern is but the maintenance of a comfortable and familiar status, not the experiencing of the divine. " . . . Für das Höchste," Barlach wrote, " . . . [hat] der Mensch kein Augenmass . . . wie er mit dem körperlichen Auge ja auch nicht den unendlichen Raum als Tiefe erfasst, sondern als Fläche, die letzten Sterne scheinen neben den nächsten zu stehen" (Br., II [Oct. 18, 1932], 178). As Iver remarked to himself as he raised his little lantern high into the star-filled sky before crawling into the dunes to die, "Es ist nicht zu leugnen, vor meinen Augen ist die Latüchte heller als der Sirius, eine

Tranlampe überscheint ihn. Es muss eben jeder selbst sehen, wie ers macht, dass diese selbstige Funzel nicht alle himmlischen Lichter auslöscht." (p. 173)

In conclusion, we might observe that a grotesque object or personage loses its power to threaten and becomes ludicrous when distorted beyond the limits of credibility. Similarly, if a grotesque situation is sustained long enough that the mind ceases to attempt to reorient itself, the situation ceases to be grotesque and becomes absurd. A grotesque situation can never exist without a conflict between two orders, between a norm and an anti-norm, one prevailing, the other threatening. It is the intrusion of one order into the other, the partial overlapping of two incompatible and mutually destructive systems which produces the disorientation and frightening vertigo characteristic of the grotesque experience. But it is only when the mind ceases to *try* to discern some order in the apparent chaos and gives up in despair, only when it comes to a realization, founded or otherwise, that the world is bereft of any humanly ordering logic or principle, that the grotesque situation becomes absurd. Thus Kayser can speak of the grotesque as "ein Spiel mit dem Absurden," for as long as the mind is only playing with the absurd, it has not yet lost all orientation. It may concern itself with chaos and with the absurd, it may play a kind of Russian roulette with forces beyond its ken and may not differentiate between apparition and reality. The mind's ordering logic may be threatened, but as long as the mind maintains enough strength to regain stability and its familiar orientation, the limits of play have not been overstepped.

It may well be the case that man will always experience a degree of the grotesque in the breakup of any rational, well-defined Weltanschauung, for it can be presumed that the mind toys to at least some degree with new modes of thought before putting the torch to the old ones. Such was certainly the case with Barlach. His best grotesques were created in the period of his life when his inner conflicts appear to have been the greatest. In his later years, he became somewhat more resigned to a perpetual state of uncertainty and transition, and even came to esteem it as a way of life. In a fragment written in 1929 but published posthumously, Barlach attacks the "Unser der Sieg"—mentality which requires "eine gespickte und gepolsterte Wirklichkeit" (II, 402) to make life tolerable. Such a mentality is totally ignorant of that other reality, "eine . . . abgeschabte, unansehnliche, der als einziger Pomp und Pathos Selbstverständlichkeit und Notwendigkeit wortlos innewohnt" (II, 402). He continues:

> Kann man nun riskieren, von der Tragik des Seins überhaupt zu sprechen, dem Dämonischen einen Fingerzeig zu gönnen? . . . Ist die Tragik des Erliegens euch so unverständlich? Wisst ihr nichts von der ewigen Unbefriedigung des Seins? Dass es immer zerstört, um neu zu werden, sich seiner selbst entledigt, um seiner selbst im Besseren habhaft zu werden, immer wieder das Unmögliche will, um am Möglichen zu scheitern? Nein, ihr wisst es nicht. Ihr wollt in unverdrossener

> Selbstzufriedenheit was sein? Die ewig Gleichen, und ahnt nicht, dass das Gleiche immer verworfen ist, weil es mit seinem Anspruch den schöpferischen Trieb im Sturm des Weltgeschehens beleidigt. [II, 403]

As long as man is concerned primarily with *maintaining* his identity and with perpetuating his own trivial world, the grotesque will be his common experience. Barlach argues that man must attain a flexibility of mind which will allow him to accept life as meaningful, even when ultimates cannot be defined and neatly categorized. His Weltanschauung must be undogmatic, serving as a guide rather than as an authority. Unless man's epistemological limitations are recognized and provision is made in his world view for change both in man and in his concept of the universe, the discovery or fear of the unanticipated may easily disturb man's equanimity and threaten his orientation to the world. Man must be prepared for change, but he must also be prepared *to* change. As the mature Barlach expressed it: "Zum Werden verhilft einzig bereit sein in ehrlicher Unerschrockenheit und mit dem Willen keinerlei Dogmatik über sich Gewalt zu lassen" (Br., II [Oct. 18, 1932], 176). Accordingly, the grotesque will be a part of man's experience as long as he has not learned to live without an image and to take final responsibility for himself and his fellow men instead of passing it on to some deity. Boll, Celestine, and finally Heinrich, Graf von Ratzeburg, come to appreciate this, and the latter two choose to make the ultimate sacrifice rather than shirk their responsibility.

It does not follow from this that man must view the world as absurd. However, man must not deceive himself with facile solutions. Even in his pronouncing as absurd the primitive concept of God as entertained by Noah in *Die Sündflut* Barlach already envisions the possibility of something higher. It is not the totality of the universe which he declares absurd but only a narrow, restricted view of it. As his last plays demonstrate, the universe in its totality grew even more mysterious and incongruous for him than before, but it was no longer either grotesque or absurd. The old Barlach was not to be seduced by the comforts of what he called a "siebenmärkische Welt" but he never abandoned hope in the ultimate wisdom of the creation:

> So lebe ich in einem gewissen Zwiespalt meines Glauben und Ahnens [he wrote to Pastor Schwartzkopf] aber seien Sie versichert, nicht ungern, sondern in der Zuversicht, dass Zweifel und Unsicherheit nichts sind, als was ich einmal in einem sonst schlechten Gedicht das "Glück des Ungenügens" nannte. Ich muss bekennen, dass dieses Glück beseligend ist, beseligend durch die Erfahrung einer schöpferischen und unaufhaltsamen Ruhelosigkeit des absoluten Geschehens, vor dem weder eine religiöse noch philosophische Bestimmung Geltung beanspruchen kann. . . . [Br., II (Oct. 18, 1932), 178]

NOTES

[1] Clemens Heselhaus, *Deutsche Lyrik der Moderne, von Nietzsche bis Yvan Goll* (Düsseldorf, 1961), pp. 287-88.

[2] Reinhold Grimm, "Parodie und Groteske im Werke Friedrich Dürrenmatts," *Germanisch-romanische Monatsschrift,* N.F. 11 (1961), 449.

[3] George Santayana, *The Sense of Beauty* (New York, 1898), p. 257.

[4] Lee Byron Jennings, *The Ludicrous Demon, Aspects of the Grotesque in German Post-Romantic Prose,* University of California Publications in Modern Philology, 71 (Berkeley and Los Angeles, 1963), p. 16.

[5] John Ruskin, *The Works of John Ruskin,* ed. E. T. Cook and A. Wedderburn (London, 1904), XI, 151.

[6] Jennings, p. 16.

[7] Jennings, p. 14.

[8] Jennings, p. 17.

[9] Jennings, p. 27.

[10] Jennings, pp. 15-16.

[11] Wolfgang Kayser, *Das Groteske, seine Gestaltung in der Dichtung und Malerei* (Oldenburg, 1958), p. 219.

[12] Schweizer, p. 25.

[13] Schweizer, p. 12.

[14] Schweizer, pp. 17-18.

[15] Schweizer, p. 18.

[16] Kayser, pp. 198-99.

[17] *Ibid.*

[18] Kayser, p. 199.

[19] Heselhaus, pp. 287-88.

[20] Kayser, pp. 199, 201, 202 respectively.

[21] Kayser, p. 199.

[22] References to Barlach's works and correspondence are included in parenthesis in the text as follows: page references alone are to the volume *Dramen;* page numbers following the Roman numeral I or II refer to the volumes *Prosa* I and *Prosa* II respectively of the Piper edition, *Ernst Barlach, Das dichterische Werk in drei Bänden* (München, 1956-59); Br., I, and Br., II, followed by the date and page number, refer to the two editions of Barlach's letters, I, the small paperback selection, *Ernst Barlach, Aus seinen Briefen* (München, 1947), and II, letters not contained in the above edition, quoted from *Ernst Barlach, Leben und Werk in seinen Briefen* (München, 1952).

[23] Hellmut Krapp, "Der allegorische Dialog," *Akzente,* 1 (1954), 215.

[24] Cited without reference in Kayser, p. 221.

[25] Gerhard Lietz, *Das Symbolische in der Dichtung Barlachs* (Marburg, 1937), p. 61.

[26] Edson M. Chick, "Ernst Barlach's *Der arme Vetter:* a Study," *Modern Language Review,* 58 (1962), 376.

[27] Jennings, p. 18.

[28] Chick, p. 376.

[29] *Ibid.*

[30] Kayser, p. 202.

Alfred Werner   (essay date 1969)

SOURCE: "The Letters of Ernst Barlach," in *Art Journal,* Vol. XXIX, No. 2, Winter, 1969/70, pp. 200-01.

[*In the following review of* The Letters of Ernst Barlach, *Werner calls the letters invaluable because of the informal, honest picture they present of Barlach.*]

At one point in the last century, when the artist's alienation from society had reached its peak and the gap between the creative man and his potential public seemed unbridgeable, the ancient notion of the artist as a rather boorish, uncouth creature was revived. To this very day, artists are often thought of as individuals bound to seem fools as soon as they utter a word, let alone issue written statements. The fallacious idea that "artists say the silliest things" has, of course, been encouraged by members of the brotherhood who knowingly made absurd pronunciamentos to demonstrate their disdain for any over-intellectual approach to art.

The German sculptor and print-maker, Ernst Barlach (1870-1938) did not participate in this game of "épater le bourgeois." Nonetheless, even this unusual man, whose stupendous literary talent is evident in his plays, novel fragments, essays and memoirs, that, for the past few years, have been available in three substantial volumes, covering more than eighteen hundred pages, once in a while made rather puzzling remarks, as when he called himself a "barbarian," though he was one of the most well-read, most well-informed men of his period. In his **Briefe,** vol. I, now made accessible in a painstakingly annotated edition, one finds, for instance, the enigmatic assertion, "The barbaric is essential for me."

Yet this was not made as a challenge to aestheticians who might have misinterpreted him, since the letters were not written with an eye to publication; in all likelihood, "barbaric" stood for "unrestrained" and "unrefined" rather than "uncivilized" and "rude," as far as he was concerned.

Indeed, these letters—1591 that have survived, of which 601, all from the 1888 to 1924 period are presented in the first volume—are so valuable because, with very few exceptions, they are utterly informal, spontaneous, unpremeditated outpourings, comparable, perhaps, to his free charcoal drawings that have all the freshness, all the impulsiveness that, at times, was lost in the artist's translation of them into wood or clay (only in a few cases, where circumstances demanded it, is the diction formal, or the tone of the letters didactic). Like the initial drawings, most of these private letters are devoid of dexterity and finish. They are not always as sparkling, as is his other prose, nor as critically selective and tight. In fact, aesthetically speaking, most of the text will interest only those Central Europeans whose enthusiasm for Barlach comes close to idolatry, and who treasure every newly discovered scribble, every scrap of information on this many-faceted man whom they consider one of the greatest Germans of all time.

He may not have been the greatest German sculptor, print-maker or playwright even of his period, though this claim has been made. Yet that he was among the noblest men of all periods: always ready to help, always generous, never vindictive, never vain, can be gathered even from the vast stretches of rather trivial details that constitute the bulk of this book, and also of the second and final volume, we must assume. Perhaps some day a skillful compiler will select the gems of philosophical observation, of commentary on the visual arts, the theatre (especially Barlach's explanations of his own plays), and politics, and give us a scintillating volume of about two hundred pages, no more.

Yet, for the time being, we are most grateful for the unpruned *Briefe*. In a way, the trivia, too, is interesting: the constant complaints about illness, financial worries, litigations and so forth. Amazingly devoid of self-pity, they indicate the almost superhuman effort required to create the works that now grace museums like Hamburg's Barlach-Haus, or that still captivate theater-goers. They also allow us to watch his growth, his development. Barlach did not start out as a saint, yet, by the time of his death, at sixty-eight, he had come as close to a holy way of life as anyone could. The letters demonstrate how he struggled with, and conquered, his own chauvinism, anti-Semitism, egocentricity, bad taste. Above all, busy though he was with countless projects as sculptor and author, he found time for his duties towards his family: his widowed mother; his brothers who were quite unsuccessful in their business careers; his son, the fruit of an unfortunate interlude with a model (for years, he battled the authorities for custody of Nikolaus, who turned out to be a problem child) and his cousin Karl, whose gifts as a

painter and writer were quite limited, yet whom he tried to help through long, serious letters, filled with constructive criticism as well as exhortation.

But his concern for other people went beyond the confines of his family. Gradually, as Barlach became more widely known, he became deluged with letters requesting information about him and his work, with bulky manuscripts submitted for his expert opinion, with congratulations on all sorts of occasions, designed to elicit from the celebrated man some statement or other. Barlach conscientiously replied in epistles that ranged from brief acknowledgments to full-length essays. Late in life, when he felt that he no longer could afford to squander so many precious hours, he sent printed replies, regretfully explaining his inability to make personal statements (yet when young people approached him with their own problems and anxieties, he continued to sacrifice time and strength to set them as straight as he could).

The number of his correspondents is very large (unfortunately, their own letters are no longer extant, since Barlach detroyed in the Nazi period all letters written to him, so as to spare friends and acquaintances any troubles that might accrue from having been in touch with him, the "degenerate" artist). The majority of the letters in Volume One are addressed to relatives, or boyhood friends. Some went to collectors who wanted to buy his works, or to give him commissions. Barlach, gratefully loyal, referred such inquiries to Paul Cassirer, his dealer in Berlin (oddly, not a single letter to Cassirer is included here, though the two began their business association in 1907). Very few of his correspondents are well-known figures. Among these, the publisher Reinhold Piper, the sculptor August Gaul, the writer Arthur Moeller van den Bruck, and the musician Leo Kestenberg might be mentioned.

Born in a small town in Holstein, Barlach never felt at ease in any big city, neither Hamburg or Berlin, Paris or Florence. He was always, and perhaps wanted to be, an outsider, and yet he constantly complained about his loneliness, his isolation. He was a rebel as a young art student, at a time when Reinhold Begas reaped fame and financial success through huge monuments of emperors and statesmen that combine theatrical poses with insipidly faithful treatment of banal details. Thus, in a period of triumphant Naturalism the young man wanted to extract from what he saw "das Wirkliche und Wahrhaftige" (the real and the true), that is, the truths hidden by the accidentals of ordinary visual data.

Again, in 1911, when Kandinsky inaugurated the first break-through of Abstract Art, he opposed the new current, as indicated in his letter to Piper:

> . . . An abyss is gaping [between Barlach and Kandinsky] that could not be deeper. . . . My artistic mothertongue is, after all, the human figure or the milieu, the object through which or in which man lives, suffers, rejoices, feels, thinks. . . .

During his long sojourn in Paris, he did not fall in love with French ways, nor with French art, and found that his German soul could not be seduced by French charm and sensuality (unfortunately, it seems that no one called his attention to the revolutionary work of the Impressionists, and it is doubtful that the young Barlach ever saw one work by the man who later was to become one of his idols, Daumier). In Florence, he began to work in wood rather than, as one might expect, in marble, and while his letters reveal his infatuation with the Tuscan landscape, they also assert that he did not really feel contented until after he had turned his back to Italy and again had German soil under his feet.

He even pronounced Guestrow—the small, provincial city to which he had retreated—as equal to any city of Tuscany. He preferred the flat land of Mecklenburg, where he could walk across the fields, feel the enormous cloudy sky above him (he did develop a kinship to the vast steppe of the Ukraine and to its peasants, as we know from his plastic work and his diary, but there are no letters from Russia, only a brief reference to the trip and the "endless inspiration, or let us rather say, revelations" in a letter, written weeks after his return).

Barlach who ended up as a fervently anti-Nazi conservative, began as a nationalist, a patriot. He does not seem to have been an admirer of Emperor Wilhelm II for more than a fleeting moment, in his innocent, romantic youth. His enthusiasm for the cause of the Central Powers, awakened in him by World War I, was short-lived. His disillusionment with war and all it stood for was, in all probability, deepened by his own experience as a most awkward and inefficient soldier in a North Schleswig training-camp, at the age of forty-six. Frail and sickly, he was greatly relieved when he was quickly returned to civilian life, but his encounter with the military establishment was enough to turn him into a convinced pacifist (whose monuments in memory of the war-dead, executed in the 1920's, are, indeed, strong indictments of any sort of belligerency).

But he did not enthusiastically offer his services or, at least, his sympathy, to the Weimar Republic, as so many of his fellow-Expressionists did (by the way, the letters indicate that Barlach, so often grouped with the Expressionists, did not care to be regarded as one of them). While he voted for Walther Rathenau's Deutsche Demokratische Partei, he, the perennial outsider, sneered at the Social Democratic Party that was in power for several years: "God knows, man is too good to be a Social Democrat." Skeptically, he wrote Piper:

> Politically speaking I believe in a Communism of a high-ranking humanity. But the dictatorship of the proletariat? The Raeterepublic? [a reference to the Soviet Republic that emerged briefly in Bavaria] Altogether, the superstitious belief in happiness and justice, prosperity and contentment is suspicious to me.

He conceded that he felt closer to Buddhism, and the mysticism of Asia, than to 20th century European liberalism. He had his own ideas about God and religion—though brought up in a Protestant home and the grandson of a Protestant minister, he was not affiliated with any church. He was a mystic who drew his inspiration from the words of Christ, from the verse of Li Po, from the novels of Dostoievsky. He knew that he did not fit into any category, and he wanted to be considered nothing but a "plattdeutscher Bildhauer," a Low-German carver, struggling with the problems of the soul, reaching down into its depths and up into its heights, seeing the masks man wears, and trying to tear it off and view man as he is: tortured, puzzled, bewitched, damned, yet capable of redemption.

All this and more can be gathered from the six hundred letters. They will mean little to one who has never seen Barlach's plastic work, nor read his plays and other serious writings, though even one totally unaware of what Barlach actually stands for would be able to discern that the writer of these letters was an immensely sensitive, altruistic and sincere being. By the same token, those familiar with his work will emerge from the reading of the letters with better understanding of sculptures like *Moses* or *The Avenger,* or plays like *Die Suendflut* or *Der tote Tag* (in his letters, Barlach refers to his dramas more frequently than to his sculptures or prints). The first volume, incidentally, prepares one for the misfortunes to be mentioned in the second, covering the period from 1925 to the artist's death as an "Inner Emigrant," thirteen years later.

To be precise, during his lifetime Barlach was thoroughly accepted by only a small minority of Germans. Oddly, he, the mild-mannered, unaggressive man, had many adversaries. As early as 1912—as Barlach reports, more amused than angry—some of these reactionaries assailed him as a Russian Jew, so as to be able to condemn his work on racial grounds. And in 1924—the last year covered by this volume—*Der tote Tag,* staged in Aachen, was subjected to violent protest, and had to be closed after five performances. "I thought that I had written a pious and edifying thing . . . at most, I was afraid that people might yawn," he told a correspondent in great modesty. As if to compensate him for these acts of rejection, a committee, in the same year, awarded him the much-coveted Kleist-Prize for *Die Suendflut.* He was pleased, but would have liked to return the money, had this been possible, since the prize was meant to encourage young talents, while he, at the age of fifty-four, considered himself a "peevish old man." He was at the height of his artistic powers, at the peak of success, nevertheless. Yet when, in the last week of 1924, he wished a "Happy New Year" his friend Piper, he was not aware—how could he have been—of all the harassment that the years to come would bring. Germany was not yet prepared to accept him at his full value. To be able to do so, she would have to go through a purgatory, unparalleled in history.

Peter Meech (essay date 1973)

SOURCE: "The Frog and The Star: The Role of Music in the Dramatic and Visual Works of Ernst Barlach," in *Forum for Modern Language Studies,* Vol. IX, No. 1, January, 1973, pp. 24-34.

[*In the following essay, Meech examines the place of music in Barlach's plays and sculpture in order to assess "the expressive potential of the different media at his disposal."*]

Towards the end of 1971 was published the third volume, covering the drawings, of the **Ernst Barlach. Werkverzeichnis.**[1] Thus was completed the definitive catalogue of the visual works, compiled by the artist's friend Friedrich Schult, which has appeared over a period of thirteen years. Of more than 2000 drawings documented the vast majority are reproduced in miniature, from the derivative *Jugendstil* designs of the turn of the century through the sketches made on the decisively influential Russian journey of 1906 to the distinctive style of his artistic maturity. Together with its companion volumes[2] this recent publication confirms Barlach's status as an artist of exceptionally wide-ranging abilities. In the drama, in sculpture and graphic work, notably the woodcut and lithograph, his achievements are such that they claim attention from critics in each of these fields. In addition to which must be mentioned two volumes of narrative and descriptive prose, including two unfinished novels, and a correspondence as extensive as it is illuminating. Yet for all the wide formal range of his *œuvre,* there are striking coincidences of theme and intention which underlie the works in the various media and produce a fundamental unity in diversity.

As a recurring motif in Barlach's work, music appears relatively insignificant in comparison with others. Certainly it has received little attention from critics. And yet it is invaluable in that it provides an insight both into his *Weltanschauung* and, more important for this study, into his understanding of the expressive potential of the different media at his disposal. An ostensibly artless story told by Barlach to his son serves as a convenient starting-point for an analysis of these topics. According to the writer Hans Franck, the boy Nikolaus was puzzled one day as to how a frog and a (reflected) star could inhabit the same puddle. The child's curiosity prompted the following explanation from his father:

> Der Frosch im Wasser sah den Stern an Himmel und fragte: Ist es da oben schön? Der antwortete: Ja, schön! Spring doch herauf! Da sprang der Frosch hinauf, aber er fiel wieder herunter, und da sitzt er noch heut. Da fragte der Stern: Ist es im Wasser schön? Ja, schön! antwortete der Frosch, spring doch herunter! Da sprang der Stern herunter, und da sitzt er noch heut.[3]

Venturing beyond the simple surface, it is possible to interpret this fable as having a metaphysical significance. The puddle can be taken to represent the material world—the "vale of tears" in another aqueous metaphor—the frog stands as a cipher for mankind, and the reflection of the star becomes a representative in this world of a distant and inaccessible realm of perfection. Additional evidence to support what may appear at first sight to be a far-fetched interpretation is provided by Barlach himself in another, quite distinct context. Writing in 1923 to his publisher Reinhard Piper, he first confesses his antipathy to the work of Max Beckmann, then expresses his own contrasting attitude:

> Mich verlangt instinktiv, elementar nach dem Anzeichen, dass über diesem Pfuhl ein Himmel ist, möchte über dem Schauder einen Reflex der ewigen Harmonie spüren.[4]

In letters and in the diary written during his self-imposed isolation in the little Mecklenburg town of Güstrow he makes clear that he regarded Classical and sacred music as just such a reflection or hieroglyph. Listening to it, he was able to divert his attention from everyday concerns to the contemplation of the sublime, to merge his individual identity with something ineffably greater, supra-personal. Thus, he notes after a performance of Beethoven's Ninth Symphony in Güstrow Cathedral: "Das ist Segen, und der Fluch wird aufgehoben, aber leider—wieder aufgelegt."[5] Music of this kind can be seen to have fulfilled for Barlach a similar function to that of the reflected star in the fable, for which reason it will henceforward be referred to as "star-music". In contrast, other varieties, such as popular music, drinking songs and dancing will be classed as "frog-music", for reasons which will become clear. The distribution of these two aspects of the tonal art is of particular interest. While instances of "frog-music" are found in the dramas, the graphic work and drawings, examples of "star-music" feature almost exclusively in the visual media.

To take the former category first: from his second play **Der arme Vetter** (1918) onwards crude snatches of song or grotesque and tasteless dancing are employed to portray the depravity of a wholly egoistic, worldly outlook. In this work, which invites comparison in terms of developmental significance with Goethe's *Die Leiden des jungen Werthers,*[6] a young man, Hans Iver, escapes through suicide from a world that has become intolerable to him because of its crass materialism. But this neurotic idealist, while himself sinking ever deeper into an all-pervading gloom, nevertheless manages to bring about a spiritual awakening in one Fräulein Isenbarn, which culminates in her breaking off her engagement to the boorish Siebenmark in the presence of the corpse. In an earlier scene, a crowd of day-trippers awaiting the arrival of the steamer back to Hamburg comment as a chorus on highly emotional moments for the protagonists by breaking into songs of a nonsense character. On one occasion, when the couple are commanded to find a new partner each, Fräulein Isenbarn refuses Siebenmark's suggestion that they should leave to avoid any possible unpleasantness, adding: "Geh du—ich nicht".[7] This firm, unambiguous statement is picked up by the drunken crowd (referred to as a *Chor der Rache*) and, to the melody *Krambambuli,* distorted into the trivializing chant: "Geduichnicht—gedaichnicht—gedaichnicht—gedu—geda—geda—ich nicht". Shortly afterwards they behave again in a similar fashion, when to the tune of the Wedding March from Wagner's *Lohengrin* they sing: "Am Kattegatt, am Kattegatt—da ward de Katt dat Gad ver-er-gatscht—am Kattegatt usw",[8] thereby creating an atmosphere of ridicule for what is the first, though belated exchange of words between Iver and Fräulein Isenbarn. Dancing, too, is mentioned by Iver in this context. The first reference is in connection with his past life ("Gott, wenn ich bedenke, wo ich schon manchmal getanzt habe, es können nicht immer feine Lokale gewesen sein"),[9] and secondly, at the end of their tête-à-tête, alluding to Fräulein Isenbarn's future ("Sie müssen wohl noch einmal rumtanzen").[10] As used by Iver the verb *tanzen* is a metaphor for the kind of existence from which he seeks release, and in which, he implies, Fräulein Isenbarn must continue for a while longer. As before, the assembled company overhears and derides what it cannot comprehend. Appropriately, Siebenmark, whose earlier renderings of Negro spirituals have been considered out of place on an Easter Sunday by his sensitive fiancée,[11] chooses to dance round the corpse of her spiritual mentor, taunting her with a tactlessness that is both heavy-handed and savage.[12]

There are further examples of such dancing elsewhere in the dramas, reminiscent as they are of frogs leaping about in their murky pools. There is also an instance of another form of dance which, though apparently more civilized than the last, is in reality just as loathsome. Sibylle and Volrad in *Die gute Zeit* (1929), the nymphomaniac and the pansy, in dancing together[13] produce a sense of distaste in the reader or audience through such close contact between incompatible sexual types. A reaction of this kind is clearly Barlach's intention in viewing the frivolous, hedonistic community, of which they are members, as a whole. In this his last play he employs satirical means to criticize the utter sterility, the dead-end pleasure-seeking of a seemingly utopian society, wealthy enough to afford a claimed "Absolute Versicherung"[14] against all of life's risks. Later, after the catechizing of the residents of the society's commandments (performed by the Hugh Hefner-like Atlas, the establishment's director), music and dancing again take place.[15] On this occasion they serve to celebrate the ideal of self-satisfied contentment, acquired at considerable expense, that is boasted of in Atlas' valediction.

It will suffice to mention just two further examples of "frog-music" in the dramas. The figure of the organ-grinder in *Die echten Sedemunds* (1920) forms a link between the singing and dancing in this work, in which, through a bogus report that a lion has escaped from a menagerie, a North German provincial community is temporarily driven into a panic of soul-searching and self-criticism. The jangling notes of his instrument firstly lend emphasis to the sarcastic lyrics of a song

aimed at the local militia and the ensuing criticism of the entire community for their hypocrisy.[16] And later, as the leader of a grotesque, hysterical procession to the local cemetery—immediately before the discovery of the hoax allows the majority to resume their old identities—he is described as the "Musiktrabant der Höllenreise".[17] In this role he strengthens the character of the procession as an evocation of the medieval Dance of Death, expressive of human vanity and transience.[18]

The conclusion of this section is provided by Barlach's only drama to incorporate extensive verse passages, the mystery play ***Der Findling*** (1922). In this work the miraculous transformation of the deformed, diseased and deserted child of the title into an object of radiant beauty results from the love of a young couple, Elise and Thomas, the only ones to manifest an attitude of concern for others. The remaining characters, including their parents, are refugees in flight, but are presented as a totally unsympathetic group, scornful of youthful ideals and absorbed in their own predicament to the extent of indulging in cannibalism. At the end of the work, immediately following the mystical testimony of the *Beter,* the essence of which is that truth cannot be approached or expressed through language, Sauerbrei makes a final statement of his own attitude to life. Having enthused about the simple existence of the mole and scratched out a hole in the earth into which to put his head, he sings "ein Lied in der zufriedenen Maulwurfsweise".[19] This seven line song of praise, in being addressed to the *Muttererde* or *Mutterboden,* combines the ideas of the physical soil and the conventionally anthropomorphic Mother Earth (normally *Mutter Erde*). According to Sauerbrei, this composite object displays a maternal solicitude both for the living ("Sie nährt dich wie sie soll und kann") and for the dead ("Umfängt mit Liebesarmen den toten, / Mühselig müd gewordnen Mann").[20] But the comfort that he preaches *im Singsangton*[21] is only for those whose concerns are wholly worldly and physical, for whom in short there is no problem of reconciling the rival claims of the spirit. If God exists for Sauerbrei, then he is nothing but a *Gott der Würmer,*[22] as another character puts it, a chthonic entity to be sought in the ground underfoot rather than in contemplation of the firmament. Earlier, Thomas' father, the puppeteer Klinkerfuss, throws his puppets out, then climbs into their box. After uttering some particularly crude threats, he sings a song to the couple:

> Hähnchen hupft auf einem Beenchen,
> Lenchen säugt ihr süsses Söhnchen,
> O du liebe Luderliese,
> Lümpchen wackelt mit dem Stümpchen,
> Evchen hält ein Schäferschläfchen,
> O du liebe Luderliese,
> Hunger macht den fetter Vater junger,
> Liebe herzt ihn mit dem Hiebe,
> O du lose Luderliebe.[23]

What is noteworthy here is not the generally coarse tone, the proliferation of diminutives, the bad scansion in line 7, or even the crass alliteration of the apostrophized Elise ("O du liebe / lose Luderliese"), but the fact that the initial letters of the lines (HLOLEOHLO) can be read as an imperfect acrostic of the word *Hölle*. This, in conjunction with Klinkerfuss' reference to the box as his *Sarg*, demonstrates the mental and spiritual distance that separates him from Elise and Thomas, through whom the transfigured child begins a new life. Klinkerfuss' song and the blasphemous, gargantuan parody of the Lord's Prayer by the *Tenor* in the previous scene[24]—though not specifically *sung*—constitute what is arguably the ugliest instance in the dramas of "frog-music", that is, the singing and dancing expressive of unregenerate, complacent man.

In the visual media there are a number of equivalent examples of this phenomenon. *Die Wandlungen Gottes* (Sch. II. 164-167, 169-171), a cycle of seven woodcuts depicting the transformations that God undergoes at the hands of mankind, was produced in 1920-1 and published in 1922, the same year as **Der Findling**. Just as in the play Thomas and Elise are surrounded by abuse, so in the print entitled *Totentanz* (Sch. II. 167) a young couple walk hand in hand, shielding themselves with a blanket from a hostile crowd behind. This *verlästertes Paar*,[25] as Barlach himself described them, are taunted among others by two musicians, one playing a flute, the other a concertina. Here music functions as an agent of division, uniting one group in aggressive opposition to another, as in the case of many children's and soldiers' songs, and national anthems. Barlach's first three plays all appeared together with his own illustrations: 27 lithographs in the case of **Der tote tag** (1912), 34 lithographs for **Der arme Vetter** and 20 woodcuts for **Der Findling**. In the second of these series there is a print, entitled *Verzweifelter Abtanz* (Sch. II. 151), depicting the incident discussed above, in which Siebenmark performs a callous, if somewhat premature dance of triumph around the dead Hans Iver, his rival for the attentions of Fräulein Isenbarn. The clumsy inappropriateness of the dance is expressed in the print by the awkward stance of the figure. In particular, the left leg is drawn straight across the bent right leg and the elbows shown flung up and out to their limit, as each hand lifts a coat-tail. The overall angularity, its jagged outline, is a feature this graphic figure has in common with the sculpture *Tanzende Alte* (Sch. I. 223).[26] Although the tone here is more lighthearted, even comic, a similarly grotesque character is projected, here not unlike the Dame of traditional British pantomime. There is an exaggeration in the length of the toes and fingers, and a low centre of gravity emphasized by the solid support section between the feet. Of special interest are the suggestion of a centrifugal force at work, scattering areas of detail and interest (face, fingers, raised foot) out to the periphery, and the enclosed space on each side of the body, similar to the previous figure, resulting from the lateral movement of the arms. These features are distinctive for the group and contrast markedly with those of the "star-music" group of figures. Apart from the series of prints for his own plays, Barlach only published one other set of illustrations for a dramatic work:

the 20 woodcuts based on the "Walpurgisnacht" scene from Goethe's *Faust* (1923. Sch. II. 203-206 & 208-223). On the whole they interpret the literary text with a much greater licence than previous attempts, with Barlach's visual imagination creating often fantastic figures, as in the case of the bizarre *Reitender Urian* (Sch. II. 213), springing from the slightest of textual hints.[27] As regards *Faust, tanzend mit der Jungen* (Sch. II. 220), however, the print is a straightforward graphic realization of a stage direction.[28] A greater sense of movement, appropriate for the mood of lecherous abandon, is suggested here than in either *Verzweifelter Abtanz* or *Tanzende Alte*. Faust's cloak swirls round his shoulders. Feet, "frozen" in mid air and foreshortened in the case of the young witch, are emphasized by the contrasting white area alongside. The hatching on the naked female body, which continues across the background and appears too on the first fold of Faust's cloak, strengthens the diagonal and forward movement inherent in the composition as a whole. Another interesting feature is that, except for her legs which appear not without significance between Faust's, the outline of the woman's body is contained within his. Thus the line of her back continues into his right leg, while his left leg is an extension of her arm. The effect is to streamline the triangular form of their seemingly integrated torso, so throwing into sharper contrast the zig-zag configuration of their legs and feet. With this woodcut is concluded an examination of some examples from the dramatic and visual works that express a negative attitude of irresponsibility, vulgarity and self-satisfaction, the products, for Barlach, of a wholly secular outlook.

In turning to the topic of "star-music", it will be remembered that the star in the puddle was in reality simply a reflection of a star in the sky. One interpretation makes of this a symbol in the physical world of a sphere of perfection for ever beyond man's grasp; and evidence was adduced to suggest the analogous role of certain kinds of music in Barlach's works.[29] The contrasting category of "frog-music" has been shown to find expression in all fields, which distinguishes it further from "star-music", a feature almost entirely limited to the sculptures, woodcuts, lithographs and drawings. Here Barlach was faced by the perennial problem of rendering in visual and spatial terms something that is essentially abstract and temporal. In common with other artists, he attempts to realize in a metaphor of line and volume (though not of colour) his emotional response to a particular musical work or his conception of the symbolic, metaphysical character of music in general.[30] As might be expected, it is the figure of the singer or instrumentalist that is most frequently chosen to fulfil this function. On the other hand there are several examples too where the connection with music is far less overt. To the first group belongs the small figure of *Der singende Mann* (1928, Sch. I. 343), one of his best known bronzes. A strong rhythmic movement is created by a series of triangles in various planes, e.g. knee—feet—knee; shoulder—hands—shoulder, head—hands—waist. Bold vertical and horizontal forms hold in check the diagonal emphases, so that the work achieves a balance of expressive rhythms and overall restraint. The broad stylized folds of the drapery are arcs of concentric circles, whose centre is located in the figure's head. Similarly, the long straight arms lead the eye to the focal point of the work: the slightly reclining head with its closed eyes and open mouth, suggesting a complete absorption in the activity of singing. The vigour, coupled with self-control, with which the song is produced, in contrast to the impetuous dancing already discussed, reveals itself on the one hand in the flowing movements of the constituent parts, and on the other in a detail such as the modelling and set of the toes. Based on an original drawing of 1919/20 (Sch. III. 1366) is the bronze sculpture *Der Flötenbläser* (Sch. I. 469) made in 1936, two years before his death and one year before the infamous *Ausstellung der entarteten Kunst* in Munich, which included work by Barlach. So compelling did he find the earlier design of the rustic flautist during the period in which he fell victim to official Nazi censorship, that he produced in addition a teak (Sch. I. 470) and an oak version (Sch. I. 471) in the course of the same year. These works can be considered as at once an escape from current persecution into a timeless world of tranquillity and as an affirmation of a belief in the symbolic significance of music. A diagonal movement up to the head, whose eyes are once again closed, links them with *Der singende Mann.* But in contrast to the previous work, they exhibit a closed form, a fusion of individual parts, with no space between them. To this end, the knees are drawn towards each other and the flute itself held close to the chest. In addition, the outline is softly contoured, with the width of the shoulders reduced and the left arm and elbow minimized. Thus the calm, relaxed playing of the man, the source of whose inspiration seems to lie entirely within, finds its appropriate expression in a compact design of gentle, sweeping curves.

Perhaps more than any other sculptural work of Barlach's the clinker figure *Singender Klosterschüler* (also called *Der Sänger*) (Sch. I. 389) best represents the category of "star-music". This work, one of only three which were able to be completed by Barlach for the series *Die Gemeinschaft der Heiligen* (Sch. I. 355, 389, 411), was restored in 1947 to its original niche position on the facade of St. Katharine's Church, Lübeck, after a dozen years of concealment from unsympathetic and hostile forces.[31] Finished in a matt violet-grey and a little over life-size, the figure is of a simple construction, since its site requires it to be seen from afar and from below. With the exception of the hair, the work is almost perfectly symmetrical. As in the case of *Der Flötenbläser,* the form is of a closed variety, with the limbs contained within the overall shape of the garment. On this occasion, however, the standing figure thus composed is lent the compactness and concentrated strength of a pillar. Yet, despite this somewhat monumental character, the main quality that is projected is one of sublime composure. C. G. Heise, the erstwhile director of the Lübeck museum who instigated the original commission, conveys this in his description of the work: "Ein ganz in

sich ruhender, gottseliger Diener des Herrn steht gelassen da".[32] The collective name of the group to which it belongs, the site they occupy, and the title of the figure itself all suggest that it is a hymn that is being sung. Whether this is addressed directly to God as an act of worship, or sung in His praise to all men, it would appear that it has become so much a part of the singer that he need no longer refer to the score. Despite the general avoidance of specific characteristic detail, there is evidence on the brow and in the throat of the energy needed to project the voice. However, this does not substantially impair the serenity and control of the figure, exemplified by its symmetrical form. An extension of this attitude is to be found in the nine oak figures constituting the *Fries der Lauschenden* (1930-35, Sch. I. 351, 370, 371, 452, 456, 457, 460, 462). Originally planned as reliefs decorating the vase of a memorial bust of Beethoven (Sch. I. 314), they were eventually commissioned for a music room by the tobacco magnate Hermann Reemtsma, so that a musical context was always the intention. Once again, each figure is column-like, exhibiting little outward movement and a tendency to the symmetrical. They themselves do not sing or perform music, but are shown rather in the act of listening. This activity may concern itself simply with terrestrial music, or it may involve an extra sensory contact with the sublime, with God, through the agency of such music. The counsel that the ghost of Moses receives from the Christian ascetic Hilarion in the posthumous *Der Graf von Ratzeburg* (1951) provides a useful parallel:

> Hättest du gelernt, der Stille und ihrer Stimme zu
>   lauschen, so
> vernähmest du deutlich ihr Graben und Schaben
>   am Stein. Gottes
> Stille ist gewaltiger als Gottes Donner . . . [33]

The silent contemplation advocated by Hilarion is in marked contrast to the row in the *Wirtsstube* scene of *Der arme Vetter* and to the din of the shooting festival that provides the background for *Die echten Sedemunds.* C. S. Lewis' devil Screwtape might almost have been describing these scenes, when in his ironic way he writes:

> Noise, the grand dynamism, the audible expression
> of all that is exultant, ruthless, and virile. Noise
> which alone defends us from silly qualms, despairing
> scruples, and impossible desires. We will make
> the whole universe a noise in the end. We have
> already made great strides in this direction as
> regards the Earth. The melodies and silences of
> Heaven will be shouted down in the end.[34]

Barlach's reference to the figures of the *Fries der Lauschenden* as "Heiligen—und Andachtsgestalten"[35] suggests that, through their outward silence, they at least are in communion with the "melodies and silences of Heaven". In comparison with these melodies, even those of Bach and Beethoven lose their semblance of perfection, to reveal a relationship as of the reflection to the brilliant star.

In a letter of 1924 Barlach speaks for the first time of illustrating Schiller's ode *An die Freude,* adding: "Freude als Sinn, Zweck, Wesen der Welt, eine längst beliebte Vorstellung in meinen Gedanken über Zeit und Raum hinaus".[36] The resulting series of nine woodcuts (Sch. II. 271-9) was completed during the following winter, though not published till 1927. "Lied an die Freude", the title by which the series is referred to in his letters,[37] indicates Barlach's conception of this work as "musical" (in the "star-music" sense). An exemplary print from the series is *Engelreigen* (Sch. II. 273). Round a small, but intense light source, whose rays inform and enliven the whole picture, hover angelic figures in an arc formation. While those in the foreground are linked by the outstretched arms of one of them, the rest, who are made to appear to extend beyond the limits of the print, are depicted as separate, though contiguous. The floating figure, an abiding preoccupation of Barlach's in all the visual media, expressing a release from mundane concerns and anxieties, here finds its most vivid statement. All reference to the physical world, to the *Mutterboden* of Sauerbrei's song, is excluded. Instead, the myriad shafts of light radiating from the star-like source stress the other-worldly joy of the angels' song. Thus Barlach, in supplying a visual equivalent for Schiller's poetry and Beethoven's music, achieves a form of synthesis of the arts, which, since Romanticism, has been regarded as an expression of the unity of all creation.

Absolute perfection, whether of beauty, truth, goodness or love, is not confined by the limitations of time or space. In its unchanging condition it remains a sublime ideal which man can only aspire to, never attain. Acknowledging this, Barlach nevertheless recognized in music the closest approach to this ideal, through its being at the one time the most abstract of the arts and the one most able to express directly the emotions experienced in contemplating the absolute. However, even music cannot escape the category of time, but must continually unfold and develop in a sequence of elusive sounds. In sculpture, however, in addition to the other visual media, Barlach had a mode which permitted him to suggest at least a sense of "stasis", of removal from time, one of the qualities of the absolute. This he emphasizes, for instance, in the quoted examples of visual "star-music", by an anti-Realist avoidance of the particular and the characteristic in his figures, depersonalizing them both in form and title. In addition, he inclines, especially in his later years, towards representations of contemplative states in preference to depicting figures in action. Thus the inward experience of blissful self-forgetfulness through music lends itself particularly, for Barlach, to being realized visually in motionless figures of a generalized character. In contrast to the ideal of timeless perfection, the inherent imperfections of humanity manifest themselves above all in conflict and change. Individual traits of character or appearance, in reality unique constellations of imperfections, may be the features which distinguish human beings, giving them "personality", but this particularizing is also the source of tensions. These tensions, or dissonances, have been labelled "frog-music" and identified as such, especially in the dramas. Here the need for proper names and speech forms befitting the personality of the speaker serve to individualize and set apart one character from another. But these are merely the surface expressions of a deep-rooted aggressive instinct, which reveals itself in its most extreme form dramatically in murder, suicide and mutilation. Related, although less extreme, are the immoderate singing and impetuous dancing of the dramas and visual works, in the latter case performed by similarly individualized figures. Above all, the drama, being the art-form at Barlach's disposal that is dependent on chronological time, becomes the means to expression of the fundamental characteristic of the human condition: transience. The contrast with sculpture is clear.

Unlike his literary cousins in Aesop, La Fontaine or Luther, Barlach's fabulous frog acquires a self-knowledge that enables him to accept the patent inadequacies of his existence. Moral sustenance is provided by the stellar image, a constant reminder of a desired, but unattainable perfection. As has been shown, Classical music can be similarly sustaining, particularly for those who perceive in it a distant echo of the music of the spheres. Since this characteristic is at no time more conspicuous than in periods of tension and conflict, it is appropriate to conclude by quoting from a diary entry of 23 August 1914:

> [Ich] hörte aus der Nachbarschaft ein bisschen Musik, es schien echte Musik und erschütterte mich so stark wie die Kriegserlebnisse. Eine andere Welt zog mich unversehens an sich, da schaltete wie hier die höchste Gewalt mit den Seelen, und die Gewalt brach sich als Unendlichkeit im stillen Spiegel klarer Klänge, einfacher Töne. Wenig und Alles, wie das Stück Sternhimmel, in einer Pfütze gespiegelt, ebenso unermesslich ist wie der ganze Weltraum.[38]

NOTES

[1] *Ernst Barlach. Werkkatalog der Zeichnungen. Werkverzeichnis Band III.* Bearbeitet von Friedrich Schult, Hamburg, 1971. (Sch. III., followed by a figure, indicates the catalogue number of a drawing.)

[2] *Ernst Barlach. Das plastische Werk. Werkverzeichnis Band I.* Bearbeitet von Friedrich Schult, Hamburg, 1960 (Sch. I).

Ernst Barlach. Das graphische Werk. Werkverzeichnis Band II. Bearbeitet von Friedrich Schult, Hamburg, 1958 (Sch. II).

[3] Hans Franck, *Ernst Barlach. Leben und Werk,* Stuttgart, 1961, pp. 69 f.

[4] Ernst Barlach, *Die Briefe I* (1888-1924), Hrsg. von Friedrich Dross, Munich, 1968, pp. 694 f. (quoted as *Briefe I*).

[5] *Briefe I*, p. 629. This statement, augmented by the knowledge that Barlach had a deep affection for the cantatas of J. S. Bach (Herr Friedrich Schult in conversation, Güstrow, 7.8.1965), suggests that it was choral works in particular that produced this quasi-mystical state in him. It is as if in purely instrumental music the human element was insufficiently in evidence for someone whose own work in all the media was exclusively concerned with the human form and morality.

[6] Karl Graucob, *Ernst Barlachs Dramen,* Kiel, 1969, p. 39.

[7] Ernst Barlach, *Das dichterische Werk. Band I: Die Dramen,* Munich, 1959, p. 147 (*Dramen*).

[8] Ibid., p. 150.

[9] Loc. cit.

[10] Ibid., p. 151.

[11] Ibid., p. 107.

[12] *Dramen*, p. 177.

[13] Ibid., p. 461.

[14] Loc. cit.

[15] Ibid., p. 467.

[16] *Dramen*, p. 226.

[17] Ibid., p. 248.

[18] In 1923-24 Barlach returned to this theme in his illustrations to Goethe's poems. Cf. Sch. II. 229, 230, 231, and Sch. III. 1704, 1705, 1706.

[19] *Dramen*, p. 315. Cf. Sch. II. 303.

[20] Loc. cit.

[21] *Dramen*, p. 315.

[22] Loc. cit.

[23] Ibid., p. 284.

[24] Ibid., pp. 278 f.

[25] Ernst Barlach, Sch. II, p. 106.

[26] Scratched into the plinth of this plaster study (1920) for the subsequent limewood (Sch. I. 225) and bronze (Sch. I. 224) versions is the word *Kulegraaksch*. This was apparently the name of a Mecklenburg matron who used to arrive uninvited at weddings to entertain the guests with jokes and dancing. Ernst Barlach, Sch. I, p. 134). The fact that Barlach individualizes the work, in this case through the incised name, is characteristic of these examples from the visual media.

[27] "Verlangst du nicht nach einem Besenstiele?
    Ich wünschte mir den allerderbsten Bock."

Goethes Werke, Hamburger Ausgabe, vol. III, 7th edition, 1964, p. 121.

[28] Ibid., p. 129.

[29] That all music is in the final analysis a human product finds a possible parallel in the fable: the reflected star is as it were "created" from the perspective of the frog.

[30] As early as 1898/99 Barlach had drawn the ethereal *Sphärenklänge* (Sch. III. 124). Otherwise these works post-date the Russian journey.

[31] The troubled history of this work, the anxieties over finance, personal ill health and political reactions, can be followed in Barlach's correspondence from 1929. [Ernst Barlach, *Die Briefe II* (1925-1938)]. Hrsg. von Friedrich Dross, Munich, 1969 (*Briefe II*).

[32] C. G. Heise, *Ernst Barlach. Der Figurenschmuck von St. Katharinen zu Lübeck,* Stuttgart, 4th edn., 1964, p. 13.

[33] *Dramen*, p. 551.

[34] C. S. Lewis, *The Screwtape Letters,* London, 1944, p. 114.

[35] *Briefe II*, p. 634. That Barlach was conscious too of their musicality is shown by the extended musical metaphor contained in his request for the return of the first three figures to assist the completion of the remainder (*Briefe II*, p. 526).

[36] *Briefe I*, p. 73.

[37] *Briefe II*, pp. 42, 567, 637, for example, Beethoven's setting of the poem in the last movement of his Ninth Symphony clearly provided an additional source of inspiration.

[38] Ernst Barlach, *Das dichterische Werk. Band III: Die Prosa II,* Munich, 1959, p. 24.

Henry Hatfield (essay date 1974)

SOURCE: "Cave Matrem: The Battle of the Sexes in Ernst Barlach's *Der Tote Tag,*" in *Studies in the German Drama: A Festschrift in Honor of Walter Silz,* edited by Donald H. Crosby and George C. Schoolfield, The University of North Carolina Press, 1974, pp. 225-34.

[*In the following essay, Hatfield examines Barlach's use of the mythic "battle of the sexes" in* Der tote Tag.]

Barlach's *Der tote Tag* (1912) has been discussed rather often; remarkably often if one remembers that this is his first, and by no means his best play. Technically it is not even a passable drama; the third act consists of less than three pages (in the standard edition) relating the killing of the magic steed; the fourth and fifth act show a cast mainly composed of highly neurotic characters who re-hash in a more or less *tief* way what the reasonably intelligent reader or spectator has long since known. In general, critics who based themselves on an especially naive *Zeitgeist* theory have overrated Barlach's dramas because he is indeed a fine sculptor and graphic artist; *therefore,* they infer, he must be a fine writer. Others seem to value the plays because they are *teutsch und tief.* The latter criterion was of course used in praising the works of Erwin Guido Kolbenheyer and other heroes of that kidney. On the other hand, it should be noted that Thomas Mann's review of *Der tote Tag,* in the *Dial* of October, 1924, claims that Barlach's play was the boldest and most exciting drama of the Munich season. Mann does not tell us about the competition that year, but presumably it was not negligible.

The (largely extradramatic) appeal of *Der tote Tag* de-rives, I think, from Barlach's employment of several potent myths—a procedure which may well have been unconscious. Gnosticism, Christianity, the old "Amazo-nian" theme of the battle between the sexes (which agrees with certain psychoanalytical insights), all play a part. As we shall see, Barlach came to see his own struggle with the mother of his son Nikolaus in mythical terms.

Lacking complete evidence, one may surmise that Barlach assumed a Gnostic stance not from reading books or hearing lectures—he was hardly an "intellectual"—but from bitter personal experience and from the character-istic expressionistic devotion to *Geist* and the equally expressionistic scorn of mere empirical matter. Be this as it may, we do have in *Der tote Tag* devotion to *Geist* and opposition to matter. Etymologically, almost auto-matically, matter includes the female sex. *Materia, matrix, mater* are all Bad Things—which does not ex-clude an occasional grudging sympathy for the Mother in our drama. She is a frightful, vicious person, but very strong. Without any true ally, she defeats the various representatives of spirit until almost the end of the play. (It is very unexpressionistic that the father is exalted far above the mother. Here "The father is God, the son man, the mother anti-God."[1]) Throughout *Der tote Tag,* it is made clear that *Geist,* light, and God pertain to the male sex alone. This "sexist" attitude of Barlach's did not persist; in his next play, *Der arme Vetter* (1918) the heroine, Fräulein Isenbarn, offers herself to her unfortu-nate fiancé, Siebenmark, not because she loves him but because she feels that "mere" flesh is all he deserves. She becomes a sort of lay nun—a further rejection of the world. How far *Der tote Tag* is from any viable human or dramatic balance becomes especially clear if one briefly compares it—may Mozart forgive me!—with *Die Zauberflöte.* Here too light, reason, and the male prin-ciple are arrayed against the hysterical feminism of the Queen of the Night; but the work ends with forgiveness, reconciliation, and indeed a sacred marriage, a *hieros gamos.* Of course there are those who prefer the gloomi-est obfuscation to Enlightenment.

Appropriately enough, physical darkness or at best twi-light prevails throughout the play: the whole stage is one gigantic metaphor of spiritual gloom. As Edson Chick wittily puts it, this is literally Barlach's most obscure piece.[2] Beneath the large room, furnished in peasant style, lies the black cellar where carcasses are stored—the home of rats, particularly nasty insects, etc. Granted that it would be forcing things—given Barlach's antipathy to psychoanalysis—to equate the cellar with the unconscious, the contemporary reader can hardly help seeing the analogy. At any rate, without going beyond the play, we see the cellar as the epitome of blackness—and of lurking evil. After the killing of the magic steed Herzhorn, the sun averts its face; and the sun is clearly linked with the masculine principle and hence with the divine father of the hero or semihero of the drama. At this point we grasp the full force of the title: if the spirit is overthrown, the result is—death. The Mother, of course, incarnates the power of dark-ness, and tries in every sense to keep the Son in the dark. Kule's blindness is relevant here, as is the invis-ibility of the exceptionally grotesque gnome Steissbart. For an artist like Barlach, such a deprivation of seeing and light must have represented an ultimate horror.

Since Gnosticism had many bonds with Christianity, it is not surprising that a Christian element fits rather neatly into the play. It is supplied by the blind wanderer and prophet Kule—incidentally the only human charac-ter in *Der tote Tag* who has a name of his own. In literary terms Kule is a Tiresias figure, not to say a cliché: his wisdom seems to derive from his blindness. As he was the Mother's lover or husband before the god took her and begot the Son, he is also a Joseph figure. More importantly, it is his vocation to bear other people's burdens—symbolized by some remarkably vo-cal rocks which he totes about. He is even willing to assume the guilt for the murder of Herzhorn, but this self-sacrificing deception does not work for long. With his altruistic orientation, he is—though often a bore—the one admirable person in the drama.

In a fierce polemic against Richard Wagner, Paul Henry Lang charged that "the sun of Homer" does not shine on the inhabitants of his artistic world.[3] This is perhaps a bit harsh: is not Siegfried a sort of third-string Achilles? Certainly Homer's sun did not shine on Barlach—who did not profit as an artist from the sun of Paris or Flo-rence either—or on his creatures. Some touches in *Der tote Tag*—the gnomes, the generally "Northern" atmo-sphere, the occasional alliterations[4]—do suggest Wagner. And the Son is a sort of potential savior, like Siegfried, but he turns out to be pitifully weak.

To touch briefly on one of Barlach's own mythical in-ventions—the horse Herzhorn, sent by the distant, invisible Father (God, or at least the sun god) to encourage and liberate the Son—this is as obvious a phallic symbol as one is likely to find. "Herzhorn," Barlach tells us, was a place name associated in his mind with his father's life,[5] and as such, we may add, the use of the term is pro-male, anti-maternal. Very well; but why that particular place name? Both "Herz" and "Horn" are highly suggestive. When the Mother murders Herzhorn (the word is not too strong) she commits an act of symbolic castration,[6] and indeed the Son's modest powers are further reduced at this point. Thus there would seem to be a link between *Der tote Tag* and yet another myth—here the term is honorific—the creation of the Great Enlightener and Magician of Vienna. Almost certainly this connection has nothing to do with direct or conscious influence: Barlach reading Freud would seem at least as improbable an event as Hermann Hesse reading Voltaire.

A major component of *Der tote Tag* was furnished by Barlach's own life during the years when he was composing the play. He was engaged in a bitter struggle, which he eventually won, for the possession of his son Nikolaus. According to Barlach, Nikolaus' mother was a very dreadful person, but one never finds her side of the case stated. Indeed, I have never found her name, either in Barlach's writings or in the secondary literature—which seems to be evidence of a truly monumental hostility. Barlach writes with some pride that he has never called his former mistress "low" (*schlecht*), but goes on "Ich wollte ihm [dem Sohn im *Toten Tag*] in der Mutter alles geben, was abstösst und doch nicht loslässt."[7] At the same time, he had no intention of writing a bourgeois tragedy. His working titles were "Der Göttersohn," which may point back toward Wagner, and then—hardly an improvement—"Blutgeschrei."[8] *Der tote Tag* surely was a far happier solution.

Barlach had some trouble with his own mother, who struck him as possessive and emotionally parasitical, as we know from *Ein selbsterzähltes Leben.*[9] However, this problem was contained, if not resolved. There was nothing demonic about it, little to suggest the ferocious possessiveness of the Mother of Barlach's first tragedy, who is a Jungian *Magna Mater*[10] of the most man-eating sort. No, when Barlach talks about "the mother" in connection with the play, he means, exclusively or almost exclusively, the mother of his son.[11]

Barlach explains how the transition to the mythical world took place: "Die Mutter wollte den Knaben nicht hergeben. Auf diese Weise musste ich früher oder später notwendig Gott für ihn werden. [!] Das war der Anstoss. Unter den Händen wuchs die Idee von selber ins Mythische."[12]

In a letter to Dr. Julius Cohen,[13] Barlach remarked that his first drama probably owed more to his joy in scenes and pictures than to the desire to state convictions. One wonders: certain convictions could hardly be more emphatically stated; it sounds as if he were retreating in

the letter from fanatic anti-feminism. Disarmingly, he adds that it was perhaps arrogant to have built his drama on a mythical basis.[14]

Another letter to Dr. Cohen, written about a month later (22-28 April 1916), contains what is by far Barlach's most important statement on the play. The situation was a humorous one: psychoanalysis had discovered *Der tote Tag* and found—how could it not!—that the play was grist to its mill. Barlach protested that he had no thought of incest, which is certainly true, and that he had read only "little articles" about Freud.[15] With some heat he rejected any sexual interpretation: "Fort vom Mütterlichen, vom Schmeichelnden, Wohlberatenen, Sichaneinander-Genügenden und am Ende (in meinem Falle persönlich) weg von dem ewigen Sexuellen."[16]

"Away from sex!" has at least the virtue of originality, even in a decade supersaturated with slogans. But to denounce sexuality so vehemently does not mean that one is free of it. "When me ye flee, I am the wings," as Emerson wrote in a somewhat different context. In any case, the symbolic castration[17] (the killing of Herzhorn) harmonizes perfectly if painfully with "Away from sex!" After reading *Der tote Tag* Jung remarked that Barlach was more accessible in terms of Jungian psychology than of Freud's: Barlach dealt with a symbolic rather than a concrete mother figure.[18] All depends here on what Nikolaus' mother was really like; we do not know, and we cannot judge how 'real' the mythical Mother of Barlach is. We do know that Jung is more helpful with the Hermann Hesses; Freud with the Thomas Manns. In *Seelenprobleme der Gegenwart*[19] Jung quoted the last sentence of *Der tote Tag* to refute his former master: "Sonderbar ist nur, dass der Mensch nicht lernen will, dass sein Vater Gott ist." Probably this is the best line in the play, but one cannot imagine that Freud felt particularly crushed when he read it.

To turn to the text: the *Personen* comprise the archetypal figures Mother and Son; Kule, as blind prophet, is almost an archetype too; Steissbart "as voice,"[20] Besenbein, another gnome; and the *Alb,* a highly symbolic nightmare figure to whom we shall return. Three humans (if one may include the Mother) are balanced by three representatives of Northern mythology; to the best of my knowledge, Steissbart and Besenbein are Barlach's own inventions. The stage is dark, at least in part. We are in the joyless world of unaesthetic paganism.

ACT I

The word "unaesthetic" may seem to betray classicistic prejudice, but the first incident in the play confirms its rightness. The Mother arises from the cellar, like Wagner's Erda from the ground, and at once undertakes physically to determine Steissbart's sex. Yes, he indeed has the appropriate organs. Not unnaturally annoyed by her aggressive researches, he urinates on her. Both Barlach's vehement hatred of his son's mother and his utter scorn of decorum are here vividly and irrefutably illustrated. No one could be blamed, at this point, for throwing down the book and going back permanently to Racine, or at least to Goethe. Perhaps when Thomas Mann called Steissbart "filthy," he was referring to this episode.[21] As far as I know, no one has discussed this cloacal confrontation. This is all too understandable, but the episode is enlightening, especially for those who regard Barlach as a sort of Low German saint.

The incident strikes a note of gratuitous ugliness which is repeated throughout the play. A similar exploitation of the ugly is apparent in Ernst Toller's *Hinkemann,* in Brecht's early plays, and indeed in many dramas written after 1945.

Unhousebroken though he is, Steissbart is a rather important figure in the play. A male, he upholds the paternal principle; scorning the flesh, in Manichaean or Gnostic fashion, he maintains "Dass Männer von Männern herkommen" (14)[22] and that the Son knows too little of his father. Appropriately, the Son is the only one who can see Steissbart; the two seem to be mysteriously linked. Old Kule comes in with his staff and various oracular remarks; the Mother eventually recognizes him. Recalling that the Son's father is a god, he speaks of the Son as a hero—the Mother disagrees—as one who may be breaking out of the world like a bird from the egg. (18) One thinks of Hesse's *Demian.* Kule too believes that divine children do not come from mothers. The Mother admits that the God has announced to her in a dream that he is sending a steed to carry his son into the world.

> *Kule:* Zum Heil der Welt.

> *Mutter:* Zum Tode der Mutter. (20)

Almost immediately, the Son proclaims that the magic steed is there; he too has seen it in a dream. True to her emasculating role, the Mother compares it to a cow. (21) She is also fighting the battle of the generations: "Sohnes-Zukunft ist Mutter-Vergangenheit." (23) There follow a few pages of appropriately vague talk about the future—of course a typical expressionistic theme. Clearly revealing her own wish to make a baby of the Son, the Mother fashions a crude doll in his image; faithful little Steissbart knocks off its head. Shifting the image, the Mother truculently proclaims that she is no cradle: "Bin ich wie eine Wiege? Lass ich ein Kind in mich legen [*sic!*] und von mir nehmen wie aus einer Wiege? Mich zum Gerümpel stecken? Mein, mein, mein Sohn ist es gewesen und mein soll er bleiben." (28 f.)

As the act ends, the Son staunchly maintains that he is no longer a baby.

ACT II

This is the decisive part of the action, literally and symbolically. The night is only half-dark; but animal, largely unpleasant images set the tone: carrion, bear,

stag, rooster; also manure, mould, slime. Again, Steissbart is linked to a bit of gratuitous ugliness. (32)

Stcissbart is gagged because of his previous offense, but not before he warns the Son to guard his divine steed. He however prefers to engage in theological discourse with Kule. Apparently jealous, the Mother objects to their talking late:

> Und die Nacht betrügen, die heilige Nacht? (33)

While she is obviously a "night" figure in more senses than one, Novalis' words sound strange in her mouth. At this point the Son seems to be gradually developing in the direction of the expressionistic "new man"; he is fascinated with the life of the gods and aspires to it. Probably there are veiled references to Jesus, Siegfried, and Zarathustra—a peculiar triad.

Splitting wood hurriedly in the dark, a none too intelligent procedure, the Son cuts his hand. The Mother's sense of "triumph" at this is only half concealed; this is not sheer sadism, but is based on her correct calculation that the weaker he becomes, the more he must depend on her. She loves him in her own fashion, like a baby, or better, like a sexless doll.

When the *Alb* appears and the Son eventually battles with him, his wound is obviously a handicap. His curious opponent is a "guter Alb" who plagues men at night: "Weil es sie gut macht, wenn ich sie quäle." (38) The Son remarks that if the *Alb* were slain men would be no worse and still could sleep soundly at night. Essaying the role of hero, as a youth of divine origin, the Son would tear the creature's heart out, and the poor *Alb* would be only too happy to die, like Wotan toward the end of the *Ring.*

Probably the *Alb* is best viewed as the Christian conscience, seen in more or less Nietzschean terms: as a very powerful entity, well-meaning but obsolete and capable of causing great suffering. Of course we associate the idea of being pressed and oppressed with *Alb/Alp* and its compounds. Or it could be associated with remorse, as defined and rejected by Spinoza and Goethe. The two concepts are obviously interrelated; the general significance of the figure is fairly clear. One notes that the altruistic Kule is particularly plagued by the *Alb;* whereas Barlach himself had little use for orthodox religion.

Thus the Son engages in the classic ordeal of the heroes of myth. (Perhaps we may also think of Nietzsche assaulting the whole Christian tradition.) Weakened as he is—obviously we must take his injured hand symbolically—he makes little headway in his struggle. Though the son of a god, he calls on his mother; the *Alb* is amazed: "Mutter, rufst du—ein Göttersohn und rufst Mutter!" (43) Steissbart howls from the rafters, where he has been hung to accelerate his housebreaking. Remembering that he is completely on the masculine side, we tend to see the episode as the absolute victory of the maternal element, and it indeed proves decisive.

What are we to make of a mythical hero who fails in his very first ordeal? Such failure need not be final; Parzival, for instance, also got off to a bad start. The mother, however, will soon make it very sure that the youth will never have a second chance. One should remember also that relatively few "new men" in expressionistic literature really fulfill their potential. On the autobiographical level, Barlach may well have feared that his young son—and perhaps he himself—would fail to stand up to that all too human mother whom he so greatly hated and feared.

At the end of the act, the Mother plays with the idea of letting her son bleed to death; then she could never lose him to the Father. Even for her that would be a bit too much; she will attack Herzhorn instead; of course the steed is part of the Son, in a very real sense. The sun image at the end of the act is enlightening: "Ob ich den Mut hätte, die Sonne wie einen Topf zu Scherben zu schlagen?" (44 f.) she asks herself. Doubtless, Barlach knew *Ghosts:* "The sun! The sun!" It is more relevant, though, to remember that later in the play the sun will turn away from the foul world of ***Der tote Tag.*** In spiritually destroying her child, she has defeated the sun and the sun god—temporarily.

ACT III

This scene (only nominally an act) also is played on a very dark stage. The Mother enters slowly, knife in hand, a Barlachian Lady Macbeth. Of course she has killed Herzhorn. By threatening to put the blame on the helpful *Hausgeist* Besenbein, she forces him to drag in the carcass; it is to be stored—suppressed—in her ghastly cellar. He escapes. Blackmailing the harmless Besenbein is the Mother's lowest deed so far. Fortunately for her, Kule and the exhausted Son sleep through the entire act. Still hanging from the rafters, Steissbart *röchelt im Rauch;* only Wagnerian alliteration remains to him. Yet there is a hint of retribution: the Mother notices that her son is laughing in his sleep: "Sollte er noch immer vom Reiten träumen? Weh mir, wenn du vom Reiten träumst!" (48)

Perhaps the Father will send another magic steed.

ACT IV

The action takes place in a pale, livid *Morgendämmer*—possibly we should think of *Götterdämmerung,* for the quasi-divine Son has been defeated and is to be further humiliated. *Tot, sterben,* etc. function as leitmotifs. The act is retrospective and extremely talky: falling action with a vengeance. The grunts and groans of poor Steissbart, who is still being smoked like a ham, furnish a very Barlachian obbligato.

Kule has dreamt of the downfall of the quasi-hero. It is at this point that the sun averts its eyes; the day is like a child born dead, "ein toter Tag." (53) The redoubtable Mother launches a two-pronged strategy: Kule is to as-

sume the guilt for the equicide—or rather the disappearance of the horse, for of course she makes no explicit confession; the Son is to regress to being a small boy. Alas, she is largely successful. Not given to half measures, she strikes her son; he recalls that the *Alb* called him "Muttersohn."

While it is in line with Kule's altruism and his weakness that he refuses to deny his "guilt," this point seems dramatically useless: no one is fooled, and further evidence that the Mother is no lady is surely redundant. When Kule refuses to refute the charges against himself, the Son remarks: "Er hat wohl tiefe Keller in seiner Seele" (57), reminding us of the cellar where Herzhorn is lying, and perhaps also of psychoanalysis, but it is equally possible that no specific source is involved. There is a hint that the Son is a blood relation of the emphatically masculine Steissbart; the Son rightly feels that his Mother wishes to reduce him to the stature of a gnome. Equally strong indications suggest that the Mother is beginning to feel a sense of guilt after all; she becomes less of a monster, and we can almost sympathize with her.

Within three pages, at the end of the act, Kule launches an important prophecy *and* is grossly humiliated. One recalls Gundolf's words "tiefen Mangel an *Richtigkeit.*" Of course, prophecy and humiliation could be meaningfully counterpointed against each other, but such is not the case here. Kule prophesies that things will come to a good end; this is almost certainly untrue. Two pages later, the Son, following a hint given by the Mother, plays hobbyhorse, riding around on Kule's allegedly magic staff. Not content with this infantile regression, he breaks the staff to pieces, to use it for kindling wood. Obviously he has inherited the sadism of his Magna Mater. This is another Wagnerian touch: a greatly reduced Siegfried has broken the spear of a most unconvincing Wotan. The nasty word "castration" again comes to mind. With the breaking of the staff, with a whimper, the act ends.

ACT V

Again, the light is dim; again there is far more talk than dramatic development. Winter is approaching. The day is "a dead steed"; the Mother is full of *Angst*. Going out of doors, the Son at once is lost in a sudden fog, which he compares to the dying of a god, and again calls on his mother; he too is symbolically blind. Steissbart, the most intelligent of this remarkable group, realizes that the Mother has been lying. His manners, however, leave much to be desired: he repeatedly calls the Son a bed wetter (74, 86)—though the gnome is the last one who should use that term—and the poor boy is too beaten down to react.

To concentrate on Steissbart for a moment: he and his ancestors all had no mothers—an excellent thing from the point of view of this play—they had a form of second sight, and his father, though wingless, was able to rise vertically through the air. To be sure, breaking wind was necessary, to supply the necessary upward propulsion.

What is the function of all this ugliness in **Der tote Tag,** or is it all merely repulsive nonsense, alien corn? In addition to the examples already noted, we find at the end that the Mother has served up the horse: they have been eating Herzhorn unawares. Shades of Atteus and Thyestes! Is this what Barlach is really like? In calling the ugliness gratuitous, I meant that it serves no dramatic purpose, but it must have had a cathartic function. One might compare Goethe's so uncharacteristic nastiness in the *Venetian Epigrams.* Barlach rid himself of much black bile: there are many grotesque and cruel elements in his later plays, but he was not again to sink to these depths, except in **Der Findling.** This is a sick play by a sick man, but he was to recover.

Toward the end of the play, the Son finally calls on his father, twice. Turning at last against the Mother, he bitterly reproaches her for hiding the god from him. He believes that he has met someone in the fog—obviously the Father—but actually he has not left the house. Believing that a messenger awaits him, he tries to leave the room, utterly rejecting the Mother: "Euer Sehen ist mein Blindsein, euer Kopfschütteln mein Nicken." (94) She reacts with total war: she curses him, confesses her crimes, and stabs herself. After a few more speeches, the Son also kills himself. Like Fortinbras, Kule and Steissbart carry on: they will wander through the world, proclaiming the father principle. Steissbart has the last word: "Sonderbar ist nur, dass der Mensch nicht lernen will, dass sein Vater Gott ist." (95) It is one of the few really good lines in the play. How eccentric, however, to assign it to an invisible gnome with no doubt a squeaky voice.

CONCLUSION

It would appear that an otherwise inferior work of literature may be memorable if it contains a strong charge of genuine passion. Barlach's emotional struggle with his son's mother must have been more intense than one could infer from his letters and autobiography.[23] Although **Der tote Tag** is not one of the handful of truly satisfying German expressionistic plays, it deals with a universal theme: sexual hostility. Most of us overcome this aversion or at least contain it; but as a potential danger, the psychologists tell us, it lies within us all.

NOTES

[1] See Herbert Meier, *Der verborgene Gott* (Nuremberg: Glock & Lutz 1963), p. 16.

[2] Edson M. Chick, *Ernst Barlach* (New York: Twayne, 1967), p. 30.

[3] Paul Henry Lang, "Background Music for Mein Kampf," *Saturday Review of Literature,* 28/3 (20 Jan. 1945), 5.

[4] Wolfgang Paulsen, "Zur Struktur von Barlachs Dramen," *Aspekte des Expressionismus,* ed. Wolfgang Paulsen (Heidelberg: Stiehm, 1968), p. 121.

[5] See Karl Graucob, *Ernst Barlachs Dramen* (Münich: Insel-Bücherei, 1963), p. 14.

[6] Erich Neumann, *Ursprungsgeschichte des Bewusstseins* (Zürich: Rascher, 1949), pp. 186, 206.

[7] Quoted by Willi Flemming, *Ernst Barlach: Wesen und Werk* (Berne: Francke, 1958), p. 182, from letter to Julius Cohen, 23. IV. 1916.

[8] Graucob, p. 13.

[9] Barlach, *Ein selbsterzähltes Leben,* included in *Das dichterische Werk,* II (Münich: Piper, 1958), p. 42.

[10] Neumann, p. 183.

[11] For a different view, see Paulsen, p. 111.

[12] Cf. *Barlach im Gespräch,* ed. Friedrich Schult, (Munich: Insel-Bücherei, 1963), p. 32.

[13] Barlach, *Die Briefe, I: 1888-1924,* ed. Friedrich Dross (Munich: Piper, 1968), pp. 477 f. Letter of 23. III. 1916.

[14] *Ibid.*

[15] *Briefe,* I, 481.

[16] *Ibid.,* p. 480.

[17] See n. 6.

[18] See Dross, in the notes to *Briefe,* I, 798 f.

[19] C. G. Jung, *Seelenprobleme der Gegenwart* (Zurich: Rascher, 1931), p. 74; cited by Dross, *Briefe,* I, 800.

[20] Steissbart is visible only to the Son.

[21] Thomas Mann, "German Letter (October 1924)," *The Dial,* 77 (1924), 414-19.

[22] Page references in the text are to Ernst Barlach, *Das dichterische Werk, I: Die Dramen,* ed. K. Lazarowicz (München: Piper, 1956).

[23] See however the very bitter letter of 19. IX. 1907 (*Briefe,* I, 286) where he speaks of poisoning the boy's mother.

FURTHER READING

Criticism

Carls, Carl Dietrich. *Ernst Barlach.* New York: Frederick A. Praeger, 1931, 216 p.
    Comprehensive overview of Barlach's literary and

artistic career; illustrated with photographs of his sculptures, drawings, and woodcuts.

Chick, Edson M. "Ernst Barlach's *Der arme Vetter*: A Study." *Modern Language Review* LVII, No. 3 (July 1962): 373-84.
  Close examination of *Der arme Vetter*.

Hinderer, Walker. "Theory, Conception, and Interpretation of the Symbol," in *Perspectives in Literary Symbolism*, edited by Joseph Strelka, pp. 83-127. University Park: Pennsylvania State University Press, 1968.
  Examines the history of symbols and symbolism, using Barlach's dramas as examples.

Hooper, Kent W. *Ernst Barlach's Literary and Visual Art: The Issue of Multiple Talent*. Ann Arbor, Mich.: UMI Research Press, 1987, 185 p.
  Attempts to explore "interartistic relations between diverse means of expression," particularly in the expressionist mode in which Barlach worked.

Lucas, W. I. "Barlach's *Der blaue Boll* and the New Man." *German Life & Letters* XVI, Nos. 3-4 (April-July 1963): 238-47.
  Discusses Boll's conversion and the notion of spiritual rebirth in *Der blaue Boll*.

Synn, Ilhi. "The Language in Barlach's Dramas." *Revue des Langues Vivantes* XXXVII, No. 6 (1971): 723-30.
  Examines the problem of Barlach's protagonists explaining their "visions of the Absolute and the Infinite" through the imperfect and inadequate medium of language.

Willett, John. "Elemental Threats." *New Statesman* 61, No. 1574 (12 May 1961): 762-63.
  Brief overview of Barlach's plastic arts in anticipation of an exhibition of his sculptures at St. James Square.

Additional coverage of Barlach's life and career is contained in the following source published by Gale: *Dictionary of Literary Biography*, Vols. 56, 188.

John Erskine

1879-1951

American critic, essayist, novelist, poet, biographer, and autobiographer.

INTRODUCTION

During his lifetime, John Erskine was known for his irreverent fictional portrayals of classical icons and other models of the Western tradition. His most famous work, *The Private Life of Helen of Troy,* along with other popular novels such as *Galahad: Enough of His Life to Explain His Reputation,* offered thinly veiled depictions of contemporary fashions and mores. At the time of *Helen*'s publication, Erskine's presentation of its leading character as a self-centered creature of the 1920s constituted a deliciously scandalous departure from accepted tradition, and even seemed to align its author with the debunking forms of biography then being pioneered by Sigmund Freud, Lytton Strachey, and others. Erskine remained notable for his sensitive portrayals of women, but he was not a modernist; by the time of his death in 1951, his fiction and poetry were dismissed as the product of another era and another sensibility. Erskine's principal legacy emerged from his work as an educator, through which he exerted an influence on leading minds of the 1950s and afterwards, including Mortimer Adler, Kenneth Burke, Clifton Fadiman, and Carl Van Doren. Adler's development of the "Great Books" series would later be seen as an outgrowth of Erskine's teaching and critical writing, though in fact Erskine took exception to any efforts toward the use of the so-called Western canon as "an educational method for teaching all subjects." Erskine is better remembered for his criticism, essays, and work as an educator than for the novels which earned him popularity during his lifetime.

Biographical Information

The second of six children, Erskine was born the son of a silk manufacturer in New York City in 1879. He grew up in New York and Weehawken, New Jersey, where his father had a silk mill. His family influenced him through their Episcopalian faith and their abiding interest in music. Erskine, who would later work as a musician, music critic, and music educator, became involved at an early age in the music of his church. In 1893, at the age of fourteen, he entered Columbia Grammar School in New York City, where he was educated in Latin and Greek studies. Three years later he entered Columbia College, where he studied music with composer Edward MacDowell, and literature with W. P. Trent, who later coauthored

Great American Writers with Erskine. Other professors with a strong influence on his literary studies at Columbia included Brander Matthews and George E. Woodberry. Erskine received his A.B. degree in 1900, and his master's degree in 1901. Two years later, he earned his Ph.D. with a dissertation that became his first published book, *The Elizabethan Lyric.* This book and his prizewinning poem in a contest sponsored by *Century* magazine (the poem was later published as the title work in *Actaeon, and Other Poems*) earned the author a measure of fame and invitations to join the faculties of a number of institutions. Erskine chose to teach at Amherst College in Massachusetts, where he remained until 1909. That year he began teaching at his alma mater, by then renamed Columbia University; he remained there for the next fourteen years. In 1910 he married Pauline Ives, with whom he had two children. In 1913 he published his first significant essay, which was collected two years later as the title work in *The Moral Obligation to Be Intelligent, and Other Essays.* He also edited a four-volume publication of lectures given in Tokyo by Lafcadio Hearn. With the entrance of the United States into

World War I in 1917, Erskine was invited to develop a plan whereby Americans and other Allied soldiers would study at British and French universities after the end of the war. In 1919, Erskine returned to Columbia, where he began work on a course of study whereby his students would read "the best sellers of ancient times." This was the birth of the "Great Books" concept as interpreted by Erskine, who tended to be more pragmatic and empirical in his approach to literature than his more famous pupils later turned out to be. In this he was much like Hearn, who considered the reading of literature a primarily emotional rather than an intellectual experience. In the 1920s and 1930s, Erskine served as pianist with the New York Symphony Orchestra and as president of the Juilliard School of Music from 1928 to 1937. He wrote a number of critical works on music, a biography of composer Felix Mendelssohn, and songs and opera libretti. Erskine reached the peak of his fame in 1925 with the publication of his best-seller *The Private Life of Helen of Troy.* In seventeen novels that he wrote during the remainder of his life, he replicated the formula of *Helen* with varying degrees of success. He also continued to write criticism, and in his last years lectured throughout North and South America. In 1945, Erskine divorced his first wife and shortly thereafter married his longtime friend Helen Worden. He died in 1951. In subsequent years his reputation as a novelist faded. He is remembered chiefly for his work as an educator, through which he had an impact on some of the leading minds in twentieth-century American literary criticism.

Major Works

The great watershed of Erskine's writing career came in 1925, with the publication of *The Private Life of Helen of Troy;* prior to that time, he had written primarily poetry and nonfiction focused on a number of topics at the forefront in American intellectual life during the 1910s and 1920s, including "great books" and Prohibition. Like a number of other writers during that era, Erskine was concerned with the formation of uniquely American literary forms and with the American "experiment" in politics, social life, and art. His works in this vein include *Leading American Novelists*; *The Moral Obligation to Be Intelligent, and Other Essays,* devoted in part to the state of education in the New World; and *Democracy and Ideals,* an essay in which Erskine approached increasingly pressing questions regarding the foundations of the American political order. Then came *Helen,* in which the author employed a spare literary format, consisting chiefly of dialogue, to depict events that followed the return of Helen to her husband Mene-laus following the Trojan War. The worldly, licentious Helen finds herself at odds with her serious-minded daughter Hermione, a reversal of traditional roles that readers in the 1920s considered highly entertaining. Erskine's approach in *Helen,* which he attempted to replicate with his portrayal of King Arthur's famous knight in

Galahad: Enough of His Life to Explain His Reputation, made him seem a modernist. With diminishing degrees of success, he took on figures from the Bible in *Adam and Eve: Though He Knew Better*; Greek mythology in *Penelo-pe's Man: The Homing Instinct,* which concerned the return voyage of Odysseus; fairy tales in *Cinderella's Daughter, and Other Sequels and Consequences*; and American icons in *Uncle Sam in the Eyes of His Family.* Later critics found Erskine to be a traditionalist reacting to the spirit of the age with an eye toward the past, not the future. With *Unfinished Business* he brought his critique of modern times into a contemporary setting, and readers responded favorably, but critics cited his novel *Bachelor—Of Arts* as evidence that the author was out of touch with contemporary sensibilities. At the start of World War II, he published *Mrs. Doratt,* which resurrected his reputation as a novelist, but it was to be his last work of fiction. Thereafter Erskine confined himself to works of criticism and other nonfiction, most notably a series of autobiographical works that included *The Memory of Certain Persons* and *My Life in Music.*

PRINCIPAL WORKS

The Elizabethan Lyric (criticism) 1903
Actaeon, and Other Poems (poetry) 1907
Leading American Novelists (criticism) 1910
Great American Writers [with W. P. Trent] (criticism) 1912
The Moral Obligation to Be Intelligent, and Other Essays (essays) 1915
Democracy and Ideals (essay) 1920
The Kinds of Poetry, and Other Essays (criticism and essays) 1920
The Literary Discipline (criticism) 1923
The Private Life of Helen of Troy (novel) 1925
Sonata, and Other Poems (poetry) 1925
Galahad: Enough of His Life to Explain His Reputation (novel) 1926
Adam and Eve: Though He Knew Better (novel) 1927
The Delight of Great Books (criticism) 1928
Penelope's Man: The Homing Instinct (novel) 1928
Sincerity, a Story of Our Time (novel) 1929
Cinderella's Daughter, and Other Sequels and Consequences (sketches) 1930
Uncle Sam in the Eyes of His Family (novel) 1930
Unfinished Business (novel) 1930
Bachelor—Of Arts (novel) 1934
Song without Words: The Story of Felix Mendelssohn (biography) 1940
Mrs. Doratt (novel) 1941
The Complete Life (essay) 1943
The Memory of Certain Persons (autobiography) 1947
My Life as a Teacher (autobiography) 1948
My Life in Music (autobiography) 1950

CRITICISM

The Nation (essay date 1916)

SOURCE: A review of *The Moral Obligation to Be Intelligent*, in *The Nation*, New York, Vol. 103, No. 2664, July 20, 1916, pp. 63-4.

[*In the following essay, a review of* The Moral Obligation to Be Intelligent, *Erskine's views on American intellectual life are examined in light of Matthew Arnold's observations on "Hebraism" and "Hellenism."*]

This [*The Moral Obligation to Be Intelligent*] is a collection of four academic discourses, of which three, inspired by Phi Beta Kappa Societies and graduating classes, quite consistently praise the life of reason. Professor Erskine's point of view differs little from that taken by Matthew Arnold when he talked to the English people about Hebraism and Hellenism. He would commend conduct if he were not engrossed in enlightening conduct. If he attends rather to thought than to action, it is not that he loves the Hebrews less, but that he loves the Greeks more.

It ought to be said in passing that Arnold's distinction between the Hebrews and the Hellenes, based in great part on the difference between Plato and the Old Testament, is at present somewhat misleading. To many observers it is beginning to appear that the open, restless, curious, inquiring, penetrating mind of modern times is the Jewish mind; and the descendants of men who came over in the Mayflower may not infrequently be heard asking uneasily how long it will be before the Jews are doing the thinking for the country. When that day comes, we shall have a new pair of terms: Hebraism for the lovers of light, and Yankeeism for those who clamor for action and chant with set faces, "Right or wrong, my country."

Professor Erskine looks with a friendly eye upon the non-Teutonic immigrants in the United States, and upon the criticism of our unintellectual habits, which comes from them. The Anglo-Saxon and the Teutonic people generally, he holds, are predisposed to exalt will as compared with intelligence, and benevolence as compared with vision. English literature exhibits and fosters a kind of sentimental affection for amiable fools and well-intentioned blunderers. We profess faith in an orderly universe, but we applaud manifestations of miraculous influences, as in *The Passing of the Third Floor Back* and *The Servant in the House*. Commencement orators with childlike faith in the magical powers of a college course urge the young generation to go forth and reform the world. Mr. Erskine pleads for a more comprehensive scientific spirit, for a keener loyalty to the ideals and obligations of educated men; and, at the risk of being charged with preaching a gospel of selfishness, he argues that the true calling of an intelligent man in these days is to make himself still more intelligent.

For though he does not exactly say that there is no sin but ignorance, he believes that the most important moral and social problems of our day are to be solved by untraditional applications of intellect rather than by the old-fashioned unilluminated English virtues of courage and steadfastness. "We"—that is, the unregenerate Anglo-Saxons among us—"make a moral issue of an economic or social question, because it seems ignoble to admit it is simply a question for intelligence." The truth of this generalization is up to the intellectual radicals for demonstration.

With singular inconsistency Professor Erskine abandons the intelligence when he comes to explain the "mind of Shakespeare," and accounts for the dramatist's works by a kind of natural magic. There is no reason, he admits, why great intellect and great poetic faculty should not meet in the same person; "but it seems that they did not meet in Shakespeare." Those who consider Shakespeare's achievement rather better than tolerable are thus forced by Professor Erskine himself to conclude that intelligence is not so important after all. Those, on the other hand, who cling to intelligence as the supreme faculty are driven to conclude that Shakespeare was not so important after all. As neither conclusion appeals very strongly to common-sense, one is tempted to reject the account of Shakespeare's mind on which they are based.

J. W. Krutch (essay date 1923)

SOURCE: "Pseudo Classic," in *The Nation*, New York, Vol. 117, No. 3032, August 15, 1923, pp. 168-69.

[*In the following essay, a review of* The Literary Discipline, *Krutch faults Erskine for his conservative approach to the study of literature.*]

Disturbed by the vagaries of modern literature, Mr. Erskine [in *The Literary Discipline*] bases his criticism on a theory of limits—the limits of decency, the limits of naturalism, and the limits of originality. His doctrine, he says, is based upon the belief "that language as a medium of expression has certain limits which the writer must respect, and that the psychology of his audience limits him also in what he may say, if he would gain a wide hearing and keep it."

Now something of the sort may possibly be true. The absolute and unchangeable may exist in manners, morals, science, and art. It may be said, however, not at all in cheap personal mockery but as the enunciation of a critical doctrine, that if rules exist in the realm of literature Mr. Erskine does not know what they are. The story of art, like the story of morals and the story of science, is the story of the breakers of tablets, and the business of a writer is not to be constantly afraid of overstepping the limits set by his material. Instead he should do all in his power to break through them, for every really important piece of writing is, in some sense, a crashing through the limits of what it was formerly believed possible to make words say and readers understand. The old saying that in art rules exist only to be broken holds true for content as well as for form, and what Mr. Erskine believes to be the eternal rules of propriety, for instance, are no more eternal than the rule of the three unities. Before a great writer who felt the need of breaking them he would be as impotent and as absurd as Thomas Rymer before Shakespeare.

What passes with the school of conservative critics for the spirit of classicism is in reality only a sort of timidity. They are so thoroughly habituated to a certain kind of literature and a certain code of manners and morals that they feel uncomfortable at the thought that there may be others. They would rather say to literature and society "Thus far shalt thou go and no further" than to expose themselves to the discomfort inherent in making a readjustment. In the interest of their own peace of mind they would set limits upon the human spirit, and shutting themselves up within the confines of one sort of literature and one group of social conventions they would say to the world "This is all." In such an atmosphere, Alexandrian rather than classic, men may grow learned and polished and sterile, but creative spirits will know that there is something to be said, felt, and done beyond the limits of safe thinking, good manners, and respectable behavior.

As a reproach to the spirit and aims of modern literature Mr. Erskine does not hesitate to quote once more "saw life steadily and saw it whole." Platitude though the phrase is, it is false. Not Sophocles and not Mr. Erskine's revered Aristotle saw life whole, for such a vision is reserved alone for whatever gods may be. Of their knowledge and their experience, Sophocles and Aristotle made a synthesis more satisfactory, perhaps, than any which we moderns have achieved, but their task was simpler. Since their day the world has learned much and suffered much, penetrated many secrets, seen strange visions, and tossed through strange nightmares. Men of the younger times with their calm, complete art were happier perhaps than we, but we cannot return to them. And if we are to attain for ourselves a synthesis and a serenity we must win our own, not return to theirs. Romanticism is to art what experiment is to science—a gathering of the material from which synthesis is made. The over-particularity, the contemporaneity, the barbarous novelty which Mr. Erskine perceives in contemporary literature are there, but they must be there as the waste products of our experiment and we must suffer them. For us there is but one alternative—to experiment or to abandon all hope of putting the modern soul into literature and to rest content in the platitudes of a pseudo-classicism.

Ernest Boyd (essay date 1925)

SOURCE: "Readers and Writers," in *The Independent*, Vol. 115, No. 3941, December 12, 1925, p. 683.

[*In the following essay, a review of* The Private Life of Helen of Troy, *Boyd compares the book unfavorably with other interpretations of classical legends.*]

In *The Private Life of Helen of Troy* (Bobbs-Merrill), Mr. John Erskine gives us his version of Homer in modern dress. After having seen Mr. Horace Liveright's remarkable production of "Hamlet" in modern dress, and been enchanted by the humor, vitality, and humanity of the play stripped of unreal conventions, I turned to this book with pleasurable anticipations. I might not have done so had I not seen "Hamlet," but the skepticism with which I entered the theatre was soon dispelled by the notable acting of Messrs. Basil Sydney and Ernest Lawford and by the strength and freshness of the performance as a whole. I came expecting to see a mere "stunt" and remained to applaud the first production of "Hamlet" which has ever held me completely.

Let me confess at once that Mr. Erskine has not done as much for me with his re-creations of Helen, Menelaos, Hermione, Agamemnon, and Orestes. The temptation to interpret the great characters of classical legend has come to many authors, and with varying degrees of success they have allowed their fancy to evoke old scenes and incidents, or to imagine sequels to stories that have been handed down by tradition. Jules Lemaître did some beautiful sketches in his *En Marge des Vieux Livres,* and Maurice Baring's *Dead Letters* are sometimes effective. In recent times the happiest of all such efforts have been those reincarnations of Gaelic mythology by James Stephens which he has called *Deirdre* and *In the Land of Youth.* I might also mention Gabriel Miró's *Figures of the Passion of Our Lord,* which I discussed at length in this place when the English translation appeared. Whether people out of classical antiquity, out of Gaelic legend, or Holy Writ, these figures move and live as our fellow men and women at the direction of their modern creators.

Those of us who have a limited appetite for historical fiction are repelled by the weight of local detail and color with which even novels as great as "Salammbô" are burdened. That is the trap into which almost all writers of historical fiction fall. They immerse themselves in the subject, and then become so absorbed in it, or so anxious to prove their scholarship, or so determined to avoid anachronisms, that they can leave nothing out. Like so many productions of Shakespeare's plays, their stories become lost in piles of costumes and tons of paraphernalia supposed to add to the dignity and beauty of the occasion. We very naturally welcome any hope of escaping from that sort of thing, and rejoice whenever the author, by whatever means, succeeds in not getting entangled in his trappings.

The Private Life of Helen of Troy suffers from no embarrassment of local color or scholarly learning. Mr. Erskine refrains carefully from giving us any of the pictures which our reading of Homer may suggest to the imagination. All that we are supposed to know about those lives and times is elementary: the flight of Helen, the war of Troy, and the relationship between the central characters. "After Troy," he postulates, "Helen reestablished herself in the home. Apart from her divine beauty and entire frankness she was a conventional woman." On these premises he builds up his story of Helen's domestic career as the wife of her matter-of-fact husband, Menelaos, and the mother of a highly serious daughter, Hermione, who insists upon marrying Orestes rather than Pyrrhus, whom her mother admires, although Orestes has murdered Hermione's aunt, Clytemnestra, and her friend Ægisthus.

The novel is largely a series of conversations, in which are contrasted the philosophy of Helen and that of her daughter. Hermione, for instance, has tried before her mother's return from Troy to clear her name of scandal by spreading the story that Helen was carried off by force and that she did not go to Troy at all but remained with friends in Egypt, well chaperoned. As soon as Helen hears this story she sets out to deny it and to tell the real truth. She was perfectly happy to elope with Paris and to pay the penalty of death for her adventure, had Menelaos not refrained from killing her. She is a beautiful and passionate woman, who believes in love above every other prize in this world, and it is this attitude of hers which scandalizes Hermione and makes the lady somewhat of a trial to her husband. Men no sooner come in contact with her than she has her way with them. In the end Orestes begins to fall under her sway and has to be taken away by the cautious Hermione. In spite of Mr. Erskine's preliminary announcement of the fact, Helen was not, as he describes her, a "conventional woman."

Actually, Helen and Hermione cannot see things alike, for Helen is passionately instinctive, whereas her daughter is reflective and reasonable. If she were to elope, she would do so for a principle, in the approved modern feministic manner. Helen was an old-fashioned unconventional woman, whose theories of life—if any—are respectable, but whose conduct depends entirely upon whim and the impulse that fires her blood at a given moment. If the clash of these two points of view had been stimulating, I should have enjoyed the book; but the mere fact of knowing that the person into whose mouth certain words are placed is the famous Helen of Troy does not render that character interesting. Without their costumes the people in this play are not impressive.

What is the story in this form, without background or local color? It is simply the familiar situation of the flighty mother who has a serious and very sensible daughter. If the names of the characters were modernized and the setting contemporary, nothing would be added to or taken away from Mr. Erskine's invention. It is true, allusions to sacrificing one's mother might seem incongruous if Orestes were called Smith. But I regret to say that Orestes is Smith, so far as I can see him, and his vengeance on Clytemnestra simply does not fit into the picture. The penalty for putting these legendary

characters into modern dress is that one must then succeed in making them live as contemporaries. Mr. Erskine does not make me see Helen as a modern woman, but shows me a modern woman who is rehearsing a part in a Greek play for some college entertainment. She is neither for an age nor for all time.

I cheerfully grant that the aforesaid situation may interest many readers. I seem to recall that *The Second Mrs. Tanqueray* was regarded as the last word in excitement and novelty in my youth. The marrying of Hermione and the trials of a nice girl whose mother has been involved in a scandal are the legitimate material of fiction. But, since the Greek elements in the story are nothing, the names might just as well be modernized, too. Mrs. Tanqueray would not have seemed more real had Pinero told us that she was Helen, and that her face had launched a thousand ships. We should have known at once that it had not.

William S. Knickerbocker (essay date 1927)

SOURCE: "John Erskine: Enough of His Mind To Explain His Art," in *The Sewanee Review,* Vol. XXXV, 1927, pp. 154-74.

[*In the following essay, Knickerbocker examines* The Private Life of Helen of Troy *and* Galahad: Enough of His Life to Explain His Reputation *in light of moral concerns raised by Erskine's portrayals of his characters.*]

There was a time, not so very long ago, when John Erskine was known chiefly to those who had been students under him in Columbia and possibly to a few others who had read his poems and literary criticism; but now that he has published two novels which have had an unusual success, his name is conspicuous on all railroad news-stands throughout the country. "Translations [of *The Private Life of Helen of Troy* and of *Galahad: Enough of his Life to Explain his Reputation*] are now"—so runs the publisher's blurb—"appearing in one continental country after another." He has "surprised with a fine excess." A well-known rabbi of New York eloquently denounced *Helen of Troy* as one of the most immoral books of the time; and an eminent literary critic was moved almost to tears by Mr. Erskine's "sacrilegious" handling of the Greek story. Thus his "excess" has brought upon him a terrific critical assault from two different batteries: he has offended moralists by the immoral suggestions of his novels; and he has offended æstheticians by his unconventional use of traditional story material.

Now this is very strange: for John Erskine, as those who know him best are well aware, has well-defined notions of morality and equally well-defined notions of what constitutes beauty in art. He takes considerable pride in the fact that he is as conservative in literature as in some other activities of life. You may read John Erskine's poetry, or his literary criticism, and not at all suspect that he is the novelist who has been so soundly denounced by Rabbi Wise and Mr. Powys. *Ash Wednesday*—one of his most beautiful and best known poems—is an autobiographical fragment which reveals his pained sensibilities on hearing a devastating lecture by his then colleague, James Harvey Robinson, on primitive survivals in Christianity. Indeed, if you read *Actœon* or *The Poetic Bus-Driver* or *Youth Dying*, you will find the same poet who delighted the gentle soul of Clarence Edmund Stedman in the early years of this century; or if you read his essays in literary criticism, *The Moral Obligation to be Intelligent*, *The Kinds of Poetry*, or *The Literary Discipline*, you will find no cavalier naturalist defending sorties into the salacious. It is, I confess, a different Erskine you encounter in *The Private Life of Helen of Troy* and in *Galahad: Enough of his Life to Explain his Reputation*, and for all of my own admiration for them, I am forced to admit that their titles suffer the suspicion of bad taste because they so patently appeal to our tawdry weakness for backstairs gossip. Their very wording has alienated some cultivated and refined people: "sheer vulgarity," I heard some one describe the novels who had not even read them.

How, then, to explain a confessedly conservative professor of English literature indulging in such "insinuendoes" (as Humpty Dumpty might say), so frequent in *Helen* and *Galahad*? If John Erskine were merely "a flash in the pan" of the fiction market, the effort to understand him would hardly be worth the bother of reading or writing about him. But because he is not an accidental success in the literary world, because he has something to say which modern readers want to read, and because from critical essays of his which have apparently been forgotten we may get an intelligent understanding of his novels, it is appropriate now to review enough of his mind to understand his art.

II

We shall not appreciate the art until we know something of the man himself; something about the making of his mind.

When John Erskine was a Columbia undergraduate, the days of the æsthetic movement (late in reaching American shores) were in the yellow leaf; the cloying, impersonal, embroidered melodies of the British æsthetes, particularly of Wilde and Swinburne, were filling the ears of susceptible young lovers of beauty with haunting echoes. In the English department at Columbia was George Edward Woodberry, himself the disciple of Lowell and heir of the fine Harvard memories of the elegant eighties. To Columbia he brought some rich ideas and inspired a group of young men there to the career of poetry. John Erskine was among them; he has never forgotten those days. Woodberry inspired him to live intensely with the choir invisible; his daily ghostly companions were Homer, Dante, Shakespeare, Milton, Wordsworth, Shelley, and Keats. So vividly did John Erskine live in this phantom world of loveliness in the

unlovely days of William McKinley that he has never wholly escaped it. Sometimes when you see him striding grandly down the street at Columbia, with the gaping whale's mouth of the famous colonnaded library for a background, you think that he is stalking Ariel. He has a distant look in his eyes. This is the mark of Woodberry upon him. How appropriate, therefore, is his simple dedication of *The Literary Discipline*, "to George Edward Woodberry." In the preface he magnificently says: "I have offered this book in my dedication to our one poet-critic in America who has spent his genius in the service of literature as art, and as art alone. . . . I must bear witness to his leadership among all in this country who in my lifetime have known how to prize the immortal things in great books—imagination, ideal humanity, beauty, and the kind of truth that is beauty. . . . Twenty-five years ago he taught us to love the masters in poetry. . . . We have still to acquire his hospitality toward the future, to look on with his good humor and sympathy while the immature in the world of art, as elsewhere, try to rearrange the universe, not knowing that it has been here for some time and is set in its ways."

Those were halcyon days when John Erskine sat under Professor Woodberry. In the fervor of new spiritual excitements, he became a poet and wrote *Actœon*, an exquisite thing. It immediately attracted wide attention and established in some measure his reputation; he was launched on the career of the poet. For the next ten or fifteen years he continued to practise his art, rigidly keeping himself within the bounds of technique which marked his first effort, disdaining to join the experimentalists in 1912 who started the "Imagiste" and "Vers Libre" schools on the course which has now, alas! ended in contortionism. His work revealed only too clearly his acquiescence in the Gildered world of his formative days. Working diligently, ransacking the past, strenuously studying the secrets of the Elizabethan lyricists, he emerged from pupilage only to become a teacher of English; for a short time at Amherst, and then in his own *alma mater*. He was engaged as a professor; he professed to teach. Really, he was an artist disguised as a pedagogue.

His lectures, when I heard him as an undergraduate, were provocative, marked by a studied finesse. I think, however, that his influence as a teacher reached its zenith in the college generation just before my own. He had stimulated a group of enterprising youths to publish a literary monthly in which may now be found some of the earlier efforts of Randolph Bourne. The business manager was a young undergraduate named Alfred A. Knopf. Bourne's tragic death in 1918 cut short a promising career in criticism; yet he, unlike his teacher who so greatly influenced him, was "a literary radical". On one or two occasions, a year or two before Bourne died, we talked about Erskine; I recall vividly Bourne's high tribute, though he confessed to some disagreement with Erskine in point of approach and in matters of taste.

Bourne, in his *History of a Literary Radical,* a landmark in American criticism, has given a glimpse of his experiences in college, with some very pertinent allusions to Professor Erskine. In his character study, "The Professor", we have a choice portrait of Dr. Erskine:

> The Professor's inspiring influence upon his students, however, is not confined to his courses. He has formed a little literary society in the college, which meets weekly to discuss with him the larger cultural issues of the time. Lately he has been interested in philosophy. "In my day", he once told me, "we young literary men did not study philosophy". But now, professor that he is, he goes to sit at the feet of the great metaphysicians of his college. He has been immediately stirred by the social and moral awakening of recent years. . . . To be radical, he tells his boys, is a necessary part of experience. In professorial circles he is looked upon as a veritable revolutionist, for he encourages the discussion of vital questions even in the classroom. . . . We must above all, he says, teach our undergraduates to think.
>
> Although the Professor is thus responsive to the best radicalisms of the day, he does not let their shock break the sacred chalice of the past. He is deeply interested in the religious life of his college. A devout Episcopalian, he deplores the callousness of the present generation towards the immemorial beauty of ritual and dogma. The empty seats of the college chapel fill him with dismay. One of his most beautiful poems pictures his poignant sensations as he comes from a quiet hour within its dim, organ-hunted shadows out into the sunlight, where the careless athletes are running carelessly past him, unmindful of the eternal things.
>
> I think I like the Professor best in his study at home, when he talks on art and life with one or two respectful students. On the wall is a framed autograph of Wordsworth, picked up in some London bookshop; and a framed letter of appreciation from Richard Watson Gilder. On the table stands a richly-bound copy of "Ganymede" [*Actæon*] with some of the very manuscripts, as he has shown us, bound in among the leaves. His deep and measured voice flows pleasantly on in anecdotes of the Authors' Club, or reminiscences of the golden past. As one listens, the glamor steals upon one. This is the literary life, grave, respected, serene. All else is hectic rush, modern ideas a futile label. It is men like the Professor who hold true the life of the scholar and the gentleman as it was lived of old. In a world of change he keeps the faith pure.

In this passage, Bourne refers to John Erskine's lately having "become interested in philosophy". The essay was written sometime about 1911, and the statement probably bears a reference to a crucial moment in the novelist's intellectual life. I confess that I don't know when or how John Erskine came under the influence of George Santayana, but I guess that it was some time during the mid-course of his literary career. It is evident that it has since been the chief lunar influence on the

tides of his thought. "I must record my gratitude", he wrote in the preface of **The Literary Discipline**, "to two living philosophers . . . towers of strength to those of us who love books as works of art—George Santayana and Frederick J. E. Woodbridge. The first taught me through his books—are any books more beautiful than his written in English to-day?" Certainly anyone who has ever heard him lecture will know what I mean when I say that John Erskine in teaching literature has used the great classics to illustrate Santayana's doctrine that "the spiritual has a physical basis and the physical has a spiritual fulfilment"; an axiom never to be forgotten in reading Erskine's novels. And what is still more evident is that those whom John Erskine has most subtly touched—young scholars like Irwin Edman, author of *Human Traits* and *Richard Kane Looks at Life,* and John Herman Randall, Jr., author of *The Making of the Modern Mind*—have carried with them, with whatever modifications caused by other influences, the Santayana doctrine as a workable theory in the life of intelligence. Just as Erskine's poetry reflects his indebtedness to Woodberry, so does his criticism reflect Santayana.

III

I once heard Professor Erskine say something to this effect: "Novelists dissipate much of their inventive powers in creating new plots and situations. What folly! The old stories are still capable of yielding new possibilities of enjoyment by a fresh and original treatment." Did he have **The Private Life of Helen of Troy** in mind when he spoke? If he did, apparently he did not write it to document his theory. If he had done so then, it would probably have been a mere *tour-de-force.*

Then how did **Helen** come to be written?

I guess that the idea had been with him for a long time, for not only did I hear him make the remark at the head of this section, but in re-reading his **The Literary Discipline** (1923) recently, I ran across this pertinent paragraph:

> "Is it the business of art to discover new ideas, or indeed to busy itself much with any ideas, as separated from emotion and the other elements of complete experience? Is it the originality of genius to say something no one has ever thought of before, or to say something we all recognize as important and true? As for the mere question of priority, even stupid things have been said for the first time; do we wear the laurel for being the first to say them? . . . Excellence is the only originality that art considers. They understand these things better in France. There the young [writer] even of the most radical school will respect the bias of art towards continuity rather than toward novelty, toward the climax of a tradition rather than its beginning. . . . If the object of literature is still, as it was for the great writers, to portray human nature, then the only new thing the artist will look for is a greater success in his art. Human nature is old and unchangeable: he will hope to

make a better portrait than has yet been made—better, at any rate, for his own people and his own age, and if possible, better absolutely. . . . *Something remains to be told of each eternal theme.* [My italics.]

The story of how *Helen* came to be published, as I have it, explains how so unlikely a novel—unlikely from the publisher's usual marketing notions—"got across". Mr. Erskine had received a contract from the publishers to write a volume in the "How-to-Know" series to which, for instance, the late Stuart P. Sherman contributed a *How to Know Arnold.* John Erskine was to write a *How to Know Milton.* But for some reason the publishers decided to stop the series before the book was written, and were sufficiently generous, in cancelling the contract, to offer to publish whatever Mr. Erskine might submit to them in its place. Whether he thereupon wrote *The Private Life of Helen of Troy*, or had it in a complete form at that time, I do not know, but the story has it that he sent the publishers the manuscript of that novel. *Helen*'s immediate success was an "event" in the publishing world. Sophisticates read it and liked it; I myself, sitting in a street car beside a factory girl returning from work, saw her eagerly reading it.

Then, after *Helen*, came *Galahad*, with a similar technique re-interpreting through the comic spirit situations in a story which had long been familiar to us in the traditional form. Of course the thing seemed sacrilegious. Under the ægis of John Cowper Powys a number of people, until then inarticulate, wrote letters bordering on the hysterical to papers like *The Saturday Review,* protesting against the profanity of so mistreating classic stories, and *The Literary Digest* took up the matter, devoting an entire page to it. Beautifully silent remained John Erskine, for had he not already answered them in his literary manifesto, *The Literary Discipline*, published two years before *Helen*? He had anticipated every possible objection. Decency? The first chapter in *The Literary Discipline* was entitled, "Decency in Literature."

> The principle of literary decorum which applies to the representation of the body applies also to the allied theme of sex. The body is a fit subject for literature, but not in detail. Sex is a proper subject for literature, so long as it is represented as a general force in life, and particular instances of it are decent so long as they illustrate that general force and turn our minds to it; but sexual actions are indecent when they cease to illustrate the general fact of sex, and are studied for their own sake; like the ears in the portrait, they then assume an emphasis they do not deserve. This seems to be the decorum of the theme as the great writers have treated it, and this is the decorum which men instinctively adopt in discussion, if they have not been trained to think that all discussion of sex is naughty.

Degrading a familiar and beautiful story?

> If we could ask Tennyson, Morris, Browning, Arnold and Meredith each to write out a summary

of something we all know, we should have five criticisms, and five revelations of personality. And there are more personalities in the world than we may realize; only they waste themselves in the search for the original, when all that is needed is to be sincere.

Is he detached, impersonal, in his treatment of life; cold, objective, lacking in specific details of the natural? But read his arraignment of naturalism in the chapter, "The Cult of the Natural." Ought he to have done his *Helen* or his *Galahad* in a modern setting and with characters of other names?

> To say that in writing, even when our purpose is art, and not satire, we should express ourselves in terms of the life around us, is to lay down a formula which has been contradicted in practice by the influential writers of the world. To find a language already wide-spread and therefore intelligible, the artist will always draw to some extent on the past, even though he does so unconsciously, and how far back into the past will depend on what it is he wants to express. . . . If Homer were not Homer in English . . . how much Homer would the English or Americans know? Some bouquet of his time is gone, but perhaps we should not have liked it if it had remained. At least we have kept what we liked: we have suited our spiritual needs.

So he pronounced judgment on "The Cult of the Contemporary." But, howls the dreadful modern, neither *Helen* nor *Galahad* gives us a social document. John Erskine met the criticism before it was made.

> To have our novel appraised as a social document may seem to us a compliment, and we may be glad to escape the equivocal verdict that our picture of life is art. . . . But the fact remains that some books we are to read many times, and permanently, whereas others are for a season only.

These are bold words; they cross the currents of most contemporary literary notions. Yet for me, *Helen* and *Galahad* are concrete illustrations of Dr. Erskine's understanding of literature as an art. I have no brief for the theories, but in so far as they give enough of his mind to explain his art I am profoundly thankful. For the novels are much better than the theories on which they rest.

IV

There are, as I have already said, two main criticisms of *Helen* and *Galahad*: one is æsthetic; the other is ethical. Mr. Powys questioned the taste of the novelist in appropriating a beautiful story for unworthy ends. This is the æsthetic criticism. Rabbi Wise has condemned both novels as vulgar and immoral.

To avoid the moral indictment of *Helen* and *Galahad* is to evade the main problem in John Erskine's art. There are serious questions raised by speeches and incidents in both novels; no thoughtful reader can brush them lightly aside with the assertion that they are merely intended to heighten the comedy. They are worthy of discussion before they are categorically dismissed. To discuss them in detail now is not my purpose because to do so would lead me far afield from my main object, which is to consider the novels as works of art in the æsthetic terms of the artist.

Let me say candidly that I do not pretend to justify or even to understand some of the more apparent moral issues implied in **Helen** and **Galahad**. There seems to be in both novels enough concession to the present moral anarchy to make even a tolerant person wonder if the novelist approves of everything he writes. Both Helen and Guinevere are considerably ego-centric—too ego-centric, indeed, to win sympathy. They seem to justify their conduct solely on the grounds of holiness of their heart's affections. Unless the novelist wishes us to understand that he holds both ladies (as he draws their portraits) in high disdain, he misses fire. What I am saying may be thus summed up: if **Helen of Troy** and **Galahad** are gull's handbooks of morals, they are indeed highly questionable, if not downright bad. If, however, they are considered as works of art, they are no more immoral than Titian's *Sacred and Profane Love,* or *The Song of Solomon*. They do abound in ideas; but then, so do the plays of George Bernard Shaw and the novels of H. G. Wells. What takes one's breath away is that Dr. Erskine puts plain words into the mouths of Helen and of Elaine; such frankness staggers us, for the conventional lady of fiction is anything but candid. These ladies, however, love; and apparently are not ashamed of it. This is what shocks us. Yet in spite of our pained feelings, we do recognize the ladies as flesh and blood creatures; they are as vibrant as Meredith's *Diana* or Shaw's *Candida*. What shocks us, too, is that all of these ladies are so keenly aware of the primal forces of animal life as we live it; of sex, of beauty, of power.

Which at once sends us to Erskine's criticism of the great masters of fiction of the past; and for those who may not know it, I repeat here some of his comments:

> . . . . We might trace this valuation of intelligence through the English novel. We should see how often the writers have distinguished between intelligence and goodness, and have enlisted our affections for a kind of inexpert virtue. In Fielding or Scott, Thackeray or Dickens, the hero of the English novel is a well-meaning blunderer who in the last chapter is temporarily rescued by the grace of God from the mess he has made of his life. Unless he also dies in the last chapter, he will probably need rescue again. The dear woman whom the hero marries is, with a few notable exceptions, rather less intelligent than himself. . . .

> No less significant is the kind of emotion the English novelist invites toward his secondary or lower-class heroes. . . . These characters amuse us, and we feel pleasantly superior to them, but we agree with the novelist that they are wholly admirable in their station. Yet if a Frenchman— let us say Balzac—were presenting such types, he

would make us feel, as in *Père Goriot* or *Eugénie Grandet,* not only admirable for the stable, loyal nature, but also deep pity that such goodness should be so tragically bound in unintelligence or vulgarity.[1]

In his essay, **"The Moral Obligation to be Intelligent"**, Mr. Erskine pointed out the Anglo-Saxon tendency to divorce moral goodness from intelligence (remember the conclusion of **Galahad**: Lancelot in the monastery asks his confessor, "Cannot a man in a state of grace ask questions?") and has shown how English novelists have made "good" heroes eminently lacking in good sense, as though it were too bad that goodness were inevitably accompanied by stupidity. Mr. Erskine's implication is that the villains have intelligence, and points it out in Shakespeare's villains and in Milton's Satan. There are characters in both **Helen** and **Galahad** who have no unimpeachable morals but who do have intelligence; in them Mr. Erskine reverses the traditional treatment in fiction: he makes Helen and Lancelot admirable, not for their *morals* but for their intelligence.

A cardinal point in Erskine's philosophy is *sincerity,* which he developed at some length in **The Literary Discipline**. In a passage of **The Private Life of Helen of Troy**, he makes Helen illustrate the theme in her conference with Hermione:

> "Your facts are correct", Helen went on, "but some aspects of them you are too young to understand. I ought to have made you happy—one's child ought to be happy. But not one's lover; I deny any obligation there. If we only knew before hand, and accepted the obligations, that happiness is the last thing to ask of love! A divine realization of life, yes, an awakening to the world outside and to the soul within—but not happiness. Hermione, I wish I could teach you how that a man or a woman loved is simply the occasion of a dream. The stronger the love, as we say, the clearer and more life-like seems the vision. To make your lover altogether happy would be a contradiction of terms; if he's really your lover he will see in you far more than you really are, but if you prove less than he sees, he will be unhappy."

> "We have to build up the illusion [of love] before we can be disappointed."

Helen's sincerity almost touches the point of extreme cynicism; we can stand the cynicism, even if it is disturbing, provided it is sincere. But, the question arises as we consider Helen against the background of her experience, is *any* kind of conduct excusable on the ground that it is sincere? This question lies at the root of the ethical implications of Erskine's art. At this point enters the contemporary discussion of morals—especially as morals are related to the whole question of virtuous love and sexual propensities. Here, I confess, I find it impossible to follow the novelist; he is far too subtle for me. The question I would put to him is: Can there be *any* morality motivated by sincerity alone, apart from considerations of the effect of an action upon the character of him who does it? Or, to put the question in another form, is the term "character" interchangeable with "sincerity"; are we moral in our conduct if we can prove that we are sincere in it? Further, is he only sincere who is guided by intelligence, even if that intelligence inspires attitudes and actions abhorrent to others?

I am well aware that these questions have been partially answered by Professor Erskine's in **"The Moral Obligation to be Intelligent":**

> As a race we seem as far as possible from realizing that an action can intelligently be called good only if it contributes to a good end; that it is the moral obligation of an intelligent creature to find out as far as possible whether a given action leads to a good or bad end; and that any system of ethics that excuses him from that obligation is vicious. If I give you poison, meaning to give you wholesome food, I have—to say the least—not done a good act; and unless I intend to throw overboard all pretence to intelligence, I must feel some responsibility for that trifling neglect to find out whether what I gave you was food or poison.

In the face of that statement, we remember *Helen of Troy*.

Is *Helen* food or poison? The difficulty in reading the novel for its wholesome and moral implication is, it seems to me, that except as it is read as an effort in irony, we are asked to admire a bad woman because she is intelligent and to despise her husband, a courageous and good man, because he is stupid: so stupid, indeed, that his stupidity is heightened by its vivid contrast with Helen's cleverness. And cleverness is to Dr. Erskine a form of intelligence; he makes the distinction clear by his citing Kingsley's famous line:

> Be good, sweet maid, and let those who will be clever.

If Helen can be admirable because she is intelligent and clever, why could she not be admirable because she is good? Has the novelist fallen into the trap he has set; has he hoisted himself with his own petard? Helen's attractiveness to him whom it was unlawful for her to love may be a great tribute to her beauty, but her quickness in accommodating her mind to execrable actions leaves one aghast at the pattern of conduct which the author seems to hold up for our emulation.

I need raise no more questions concerning the superficial moral implications in the two novels; what I have asked is sufficient indication of the fact that I find some moral problems there and that I am not shutting my eyes to them. Yet I do insist that to those who can read with intelligence—those who hold the parts of a literary work in solution until the whole is encompassed—there is a moral criticism of life in *Helen* and *Galahad* which is not apparent to the factory girl who reads those novels. To her, of course, they are slightly risqué, and she probably reads them for their risqué elements. She may,

possibly, be edified by the grand moments in which both Helen and Lancelot, speaking out of a high ethical sense, condemn their follies with no uncertain voice, but long before she reaches these passages she has been titillated by the appeals to unused powers of her mind and emotion which stimulate a kind of admiration for the heroine or hero who are obviously so clever but who are also, alas! so obviously naughty.

The moral implications turn on whether you do or not admire Helen as a woman, or Lancelot as a man.

V

From these reflections, it ought to be obvious that I do not think that Rabbi Wise is "barking up the wrong tree". I shall, however, presently return to a reconsideration of more significant moral questions involved in *Helen* and *Galahad* with the conviction that some of Mr. Erskine's critics have not thoughtfully considered all of the moral implications of the novels.

But now I wish briefly to notice the æsthetic criticism that Mr. Erskine has used time-honored and familiar stories in unjustifiable ways. It is evident that what has offended Mr. Powys is that the novelist has taken two beautiful stories which everybody knows and loves and has used them as vehicles for his own purposes. Surely there is nothing new in this! And if Mr. Erskine sinned, so has Sir Harry Johnston who appropriated several of Dickens's characters for new rôles; and so has George Bernard Shaw who has helped himself to Joan of Arc, Napoleon, and Cæsar and Cleopatra for Shavian purposes. And only the other day Elinor Wylie did much worse: she rescued the body of Shelley from the Bay of Spezzia, and set him afoot for a series of adventures in the America of the eighteen-twenties! These borrowings have been tolerated because they served high purposes.

But what, it will be asked, was John Erskine's purpose? Was it merely to repeat Mark Twain's effort in *A Connecticut Yankee in King Arthur's Court*—to make the old world ridiculous in the eyes of the new? Unfortunately, John Erskine loves the old world much more than he does the new: he has too much, indeed, of the typical American condescension for things American. As I see it, his purpose was to bring into the stream of American thought a very old idea, and he did so deliberately because, as he believes, "the world has been here for some time and is set in its ways." If in a single phrase I were to suggest Mr. Erskine's purpose in *Helen* and *Galahad*, I doubt if I could do better than to fall back on the title of Titian's picture, "Sacred and Profane Love"; or, to take another which means the same, "The Marriage of Earth and Heaven." He wishes to reveal the true significance of an idealized passion rooted in physical experience; and does so by depicting the love experience under immoral conditions of two of the most famous lovers. The conditions are unquestionably immoral, but the love experience is beautiful. After all, the immorality was always there: the artist has stirred our intelligence to see it. An appeal to intelligence ought not to offend our æsthetic sense. If this be so, then the æsthetic criticism is fairly met. We may not like Mr. Erskine's pointing out so bluntly the essential immorality of Helen and Guinevere but we ought to concede to the artist his own way of working.

Both *Helen* and *Galahad* are motivated by the theme of love. This is so obvious that it hardly needs to be proved. What does need to be proved is my assertion that Mr. Erskine's theme in both novels is his contrast of sacred and profane love. If I attempt to prove this assertion, I do so merely to point out the climaxes of both novels in order to suggest a point of rest to which the whole of both narratives may be referred. In the light of these climaxes—climaxes of ideas rather than of situation—both novels should be read: they give meaning and order, to say nothing of morality, to the novels.

The climax of *Helen* may be found in Chapter 5 of Book IV. Helen is talking to Adraste who enjoyed precipitate love:

> We've talked about love, you know what I think of that, and how widely I've missed my ideal there. In sorrow, too, I've missed it. Any one who sees how wonderful and brief life is, would hope to know it, if not all of it, at least the high and deep things in it; the awful fate would be to be numb and sleepy, to rest in one's habits, to let the days simply pass. I wanted to know life down to the quick. Either it can't be done, or I never found out how. With me, life refuses to be known. It sets me apart, it makes me feel like a special case, and the normal fortunes I wanted—I'm convinced they are normal—seem dream-like.
>
> . . . I think I . . . know about life, but not in the right way—not through my own feelings. . . . Since I haven't felt experience deeply in myself, I could only study others, try to understand life, through them. When you learn to see human beings that way, and yourself, in spite of what they think, as just one more illustration of the common nature, you gain in charity, perhaps you acquire a more generous interest in your fellows, but the edge of sorrow is gone—indeed, of most passionate states. It isn't that you know too much; no one is too wise. But you forget how to cry, and you learn to smile at mankind, beginning with yourself. Love stays with us longer than sorrow, and pain stays longer; they both have somewhat to do with the body. But sorrow, the kind of heartache you have, seems all of the spirit. I'd rather my spirit had not been educated away from it.

The criticism of Helen is—does not the novelist plainly indicate it?—that she lives too much in her intelligence and not enough in her emotions. Her spirit has "been educated away from sorrow."

Now parallel with this Lancelot's frank talk with the innocent young Galahad, his son. The latter has just learned to his shame the truth concerning his birth:

"The relations men have with every kind of woman," said Lancelot, "are pretty much the same, everywhere and always. When you're older, you'll accept them as a fact of nature. But, in addition, there are more beautiful relations with exceptional women. You've got to see it as a whole, Galahad. You can't confine yourself to the spiritual ecstasies, and discard or ignore the bodily impulses out of which they grow. Love is a common thing, and it still rests on common facts when it becomes noble."

Similarities between the two novels are frequent; yet they reveal the same theme in different ways. Helen, who comes to see life as a comedy, lives too intensely in her intelligence and sees with pathetic apathy the tragedies which have followed her experiments. Lancelot, in his relations with Guinevere experiences the same ecstasy in the marriage of Earth and Heaven without the tragic consequences which followed Helen's acts. Yet there is a spiritual tragedy in his story, too; his rôle of lover completely shocked his son, Galahad, into a disgust for all of the physical aspects of love; to such an extent, indeed, that Galahad denies himself the great earthly experience of love by dedicating himself to the search for the Grail. There will be no women in his life.

VI

We are not asked to admire either Helen or Lancelot as characters: their experience as lovers provides the artist with his opportunity to make "a criticism of life in the terms of poetic truth and beauty". The final question to be asked of the artist is not, by what right has he taken beloved stories and stripped them of their romance, but has he succeeded in enlarging our appetite for life? Before this final question (even aware as I am of the many difficulties of technique and matter which I find in his novels), I can simply answer that he has.

Why? Because he has made a sacrament of love.[2]

To me, the significant feature of the Erskine novels is the absence of the Freudian, subjective element. In a day when it is thought that psychoanalysis offers the only sound interpretation and solution of the love-life, rooting love wholly in its animal aspects, it was a bold procedure to re-tell these two famous love stories without recourse to it. *Helen* and *Galahad* are objectively narrated; the author attempts no disquisitions on the subconscious or the unconscious of his characters. The chief characters may be immoral but they certainly are healthy. The novelist reveals them in the drama of dialogue, dispensing with all elaborate and provocative scenic effects which might stimulate sexual responses either of his characters or in his readers. To indicate what possibilities he had before him one might contrast his narrative strategy with Sienkewicz's in *Quo Vadis,* Van Vechten's in *The Blind Bow Boy,* or even, for that matter, with Keats's in *The Eve of Saint Agnes.* Yet, no doubt perfectly aware of what he could have done to produce similar reactions in his readers, Mr. Erskine centers attention on the speech rather than on the actions or on the concealed psychological processes of his characters. If his treatment of sex must have support from recognized thinkers on the subject, a closer parallel than Freud will be found in the discussions of Edward Carpenter and of Havelock Ellis. Carpenter's *Love's Coming of Age,* and Ellis's *Little Essays of Love and Virtue* point in the direction of the solution which Mr. Erskine suggests in his novels. This suggestion is, as I have indicated, shown in the fact that to the novelist love is an experience which has its basis in our animal nature but is realized only by an imaginative invasion which elevates the processes of sexual attraction into spiritual powers. To know love in its physical aspect alone ("wantonly to satisfy carnal lusts and appetites like brute beasts", as the Anglican Prayer Book has it) is to know only the satisfaction of completed animal desires while the total consummation is absent. Witness the incomplete love experience of the first Elaine who tricked Lancelot into his great betrayal. In his relations with Guinevere Lancelot has realized the fullest possibilities of love: if he enjoys them under immoral conditions, it is because, alas! the husband, King Arthur (no less than King Menalaos), has not discovered what Havelock Ellis calls "the play instinct in love".

And this leads us directly to the novelist's criticism of life. It is indeed unfortunate that he was compelled to appropriate two of the greatest of the world's love stories in order to make his meaning clear. Yet Mr. Erskine did not invent those stories or their situations. He selected them probably because they conveniently illustrated what others as well as he have learned about the relations of married men and women. If we *must* make his treatment of **Helen** and **Galahad** point a moral as well as adorn a tale, can we not suppose that the beauty of the love experience which Helen found in her relations with Paris, and Guinevere in hers with Lancelot, might have been possible under more estimable conditions had Arthur and Menalaos known as much of love technique as Paris and Lancelot did? Both took their wives for granted; neither discovered that the consummation of love in the married state is the development of the technique of the lover. After the fall of Troy, Menelaos had the opportunity of a second honeymoon. Did he seize it? He did not. He brought Helen back to Sparta and vainly attempted to resume his life with her at the very point and under the same intolerable conditions of bored understanding which Paris had interrupted ten years before. And, perversely enough, the novel ends with the prospect of another about to fall prey to Helen's beauty. Apparently, Menelaos has learned nothing from his experience. With the beginning of Helen's new *amour* with the young Telemachus going on right under his nose, Menelaos, blissfully indifferent to his wife's effect on the young visitor, pays more attention to his breakfast than to her.

Neither Arthur nor Menelaos learned that successful marriage is possible only on the condition of perpetual courtship within the wedded state. What Mr. Erskine has done is simply to make clear the defects of the husband as lover by developing in the terms of our modern respect for love what was always implicit in the two time-honored love stories. We have, to be honest, never before questioned the propriety of the immoral relations between Helen and Paris or of Guinevere and Lancelot. We have ignorantly loved their loves because they were true in spite of the fact that they were immoral. And they were immoral not only because of the infidelity of the wives to the husbands but also because of the criminal negligence of the husbands who, being married, permitted the love life to lapse while their wives sought love elsewhere. If this be so, we may see how both stories have sprung from the sincerest intentions of the novelist. He is clever, to be sure, but he is not merely clever. The elements of comedy and of irony need not blind us to the fact that the effect is edifying. And if edifying, then sincere. The novelist has not debased his materials; he has made explicit what was always implicit in them. By making love a sacrament, by fusing its physical and spiritual aspects, he has communicated through his art an interpretation of life which is at the core of his mind.

VII

This interpretation is intimately bound up with his religion. Ultimately, to appreciate his art, it is necessary to discern the difference between two irreconcilable attitudes toward life: the *mediatist* and the experimentalist. I am aware of the novelty of these terms, and it is therefore necessary to explain them. The mediatist is distinguished from the experimentalist in the use of symbols about which have gathered a vast collective experience. He has a deep and reverent sense of the continuity of experience which the symbols symbolize. He grows through his experience as these symbols communicate to him the larger organic experience of the race. Unlike the experimentalist, who is wholly contemporaneous in his attitude towards experience, he does not dissipate his nervous and emotional energies by the successive spiritual cataclysms of immediate experiments in the art of life. He conserves his powers in a cumulative progression, enriching thereby the life of intelligence.

For John Erskine, poet, critic, and novelist, is above all things a mediatist; he has saved his mind and his art from the extremities of contortion which have been the inevitable fate of many artists in our generation: a generation which prefers its experience "straight"; unmediated through symbols. To him, experimentalism is a form of the cult of the impulsive, and therefore he has little sympathy with it. We ought not to forget that he is a devout Churchman: an Episcopalian. And this means everything in the effort to understand him. Born and reared in the Episcopal Church, he remains steadfastly faithful to its traditions and discipline: particularly to its two chief tenets: decorum and the sacramental system. The great stories of the world—those about which the minds of peoples in different ages have played, leaving rich deposits in every interpretation—

are to him the sacraments or symbols of mediated experience. So the stories of **Helen** and of **Galahad**, familiar as they are to every schoolboy, become in his hands beautiful media for the communication of an eternally fresh—because eternally true—reading of experience. Through them he touches the essence of life with a delicate touch, and with a high decorum. Decorum! The one word which fits John Erskine's style. For he, like any decorous man, controls his instincts by the principle of good taste; he is not distinguished by extravagant displays of voluptuousness. Decorum motivated and sustained his intention.

There is only one hero in both novels; that hero is intelligence, discoverable in the total drift of the talk. Whatever drama is present is purely that of the accommodations and integrations of mind with mind in the effort towards the deliverance of self. In modern literature, the closest analogy is the novels of Anatole France. Dialogue in John Erskine's novels becomes the sacrament, as it is the mark of decorum, of the life of intelligence. Here, it seems to me, lies the reason for the calm, poised manner of both *The Private Life of Helen of Troy* and of *Galahad: Enough of his Life to Explain his Reputation*. The emotional and sexual concomitants which might have been only too painfully evident in both, had an experimentalist like James Joyce or Theo-dore Dreiser handled them, have been sluiced away by the mediated intelligence of the artist. In the high decorum of intelligence they move in a pure white light of gaiety which only partly conceals a ground-tone of a high morality, appealing partly to the intelligence, partly to the emotions. And the laughter which results is caused by the severe detachment of the artist; a laughter which is, in a Bergsonian sense, a moral and social corrective.

NOTES

[1] See also pp. 143-156, "The Moral Obligation to be Intelligent."

[2] To many, the idea of a sacrament seems merely ecclesiastical, but that is a misunderstanding. The word 'sacrament' is the ancient Roman name of a soldier's oath of military allegiance, and the idea, in the deeper sense, existed long before Christianity, and has ever been regarded as the physical sign of the closest possible union with some great spiritual reality.—Havelock Ellis, *Little Essays of Love and Virtue*, p. 69.

Melvin Cane (essay date 1957)

SOURCE: "John Erskine: An Appreciation," in *Columbia Library Columns*, Vol. VII, No. 1, November, 1957, pp. 4-12.

[In the following essay, an address given on the presentation of Erskine's papers to his widow, Helen Worden Erskine, Cane offers his personal reminiscences regarding the author.]

I am deeply mindful of the honor of being invited to speak on this occasion. It will, however, be an impossible task, within the imposed time limit, to do even scant justice to the rich and manifold personality we knew and remember as John Erskine. At best I can only sketch out and suggest the range of his interests and his durable impact on the life of our time.

John was, with one exception, my oldest friend. Our relationship covered 58 years. It was close from the start and never suffered the slightest lapse in warmth or depth. We first met in the fall of 1893, when we both entered Columbia Grammar School to gain the groundwork of a classical education. We continued as classmates and with common interests at Columbia College in the class of 1900, and from there with ever deepening intimacy we moved on together into maturity and the larger world, down the years, until his death in June, 1951.

John was one of the taller boys in our class at prep school, probably 5 feet 7 or 8, at the age of 14, and giving every promise of the towering, generous figure of his adult years. He was definitely serious, in essence the student type, but at the same time outgoing and popular. He laughed easily and heartily not only at other people's jokes but also at his own. His laugh grew, in the process of time, to the thunderous proportions we all remember as characteristic of him.

From the early days of our acquaintance I still recall an episode which may throw light, in different ways, on each of us. One day we were discussing poetry, already a bond between us, when John shocked me with the statement that he didn't think too well of Longfellow. To my uncritical mind which accepted all poets as equally divine and untouchable, this was not only heresy, it was sacrilege.

The grounds of his dissent are forgotten and unimportant. What stands out sharply for me is that at the age of fourteen John already had a mind of his own and was prepared to deliver independent judgments, however unorthodox. It was an augury of the future.

Columbia Grammar School in the Eighteen Nineties was situated on 51st Street, just off Madison Avenue. Around the corner, a block below, lay Columbia College. The times were tranquil and, except in the Balkans, warless. The tempo matched the speed of the ambling, passing horsecars. We boys were fortunate in enjoying the stimulation of teachers who loved teaching. Languages—Greek, Latin, French, German, English—took up the greater part of the curriculum; it may be truly said that our lifelong feeling for literature, John's certainly, was energized at this source. In 1896 we left Columbia Grammar to become freshmen in the College, the last class ever to register and attend at the old site.

That fall we were baptized in the clouded waters of politics. It was a presidential year. If Bryan, with his populistic heresies, should get in, the country, we were told, was headed for disaster. So, naturally, McKinley was our man. As patriots, John and I marched side by side up 5th Avenue in the Great Sound-Money Parade, huge gold-bugs of shining metal pinned to our blue-serge lapels. McKinley, partly through our support, won; the country was saved. The effect on either of us is conjectural. I can report only that John's later Republicanism did not prevent his voting for F. D. R. in 1932 and 1936, and that I, with reasonable regularity, prefer the Democrats.

John's strong interest, even as a child, was music. It remained so throughout his life. Like most of us of that era he learned to play the piano. Unlike most of us he dedicated himself to that instrument to the point where ultimately he was to perform professionally as a soloist with the leading orchestras of the country. But his enterprise was not confined to the piano. When only 13 years old, he took formal charge of the music at Grace Church, Weehawken, where the family then lived. There, for four years, he drilled the choir, selected the programs and presided regularly at the organ.

The part of John's life which was described in one of his autobiographical volumes, *My Life In Music*, would by itself make a full career for the average person.

In no small way John was also a composer. In our Senior year he not only wrote the complete score, to my lyrics, of the Columbia Varsity Show, **"The Governor's Vrouw,"** but he did the orchestration as well, a product of a course with Edward MacDowell. Following the method of Gilbert and Sullivan, whom we distantly resembled, I would hand on my lyrics to John who would then set them to music. Despite certain temperamental differences our friendship survived the strains of collaboration, which was not the case with G. and S.

In a larger area John was later to become a crusader for music as an essential element in our cultural life. To this end he lectured across the country, encouraging the formation of community groups to develop choral singing, chamber music, local orchestras, and even opera.

It seemed only natural therefore for John Erskine to have been selected above all others as the person signally qualified to organize and direct the Juilliard School of Music. He became its President in 1928, served it for eight devoted years and wisely laid the foundation for its eminence today.

John's literary career may be said to have started at Columbia Grammar in 1894 as editor of the school paper. He contributed prose and verse, but, chiefly verse, of adolescent seriousness and loftiness. In those school and college years I think of him first as a poet. At Columbia he was elected our class-day poet, and also poetry-editor of *Morningside,* a bright, saucy magazine of the period. At the same time I was running the more sedate *Lit,* its friendly rival. On occasion each would submit a poem to the other fellow's paper, with the attendant risk of rejection, but I can't recall that this ever happened. Naturally his quality steadily improved, and we were not too surprised to learn in 1901 that he had won youthful fame with his classical poem, **"Actaeon,"** for which he received the prize offered by *The Century* in an intercollegiate competition for students in the year after graduation. "This success," he reports, "opened doors for me. Mr. Gilder . . . continued to publish my work, and Bliss Perry, then editing *The Atlantic Monthly,* took some of my poems. But I had set a mark in 'Actaeon,' which for a long time I could not equal. Though I still had faith in myself, I began to doubt my talent for verses; if I were to go far, it might be in fiction or drama." Fiction rather than drama, as it turned out, proved to fulfil his prediction. Twenty-five years after "Actaeon" came *The Private Life of Helen of Troy.*

From time to time John would report progress as we lunched at the Columbia University Club. Particularly I remember one time when the book was nearing completion. It was at Briarcliff in June 1925 where we were holding our 25th class reunion. John and I and a third friend, already a best-selling novelist, were loafing in the shade, discussing the current state of belles-lettres, when John ventured to say he was making a try at fiction. He then went on to tell what his book was about. Our professional friend was unimpressed, if not actually scornful. Perhaps John's presentation was faulty; perhaps the advent of a possible rival was too much to be borne. I rather believe the man saw John only as a college professor forever doomed to write literary essays and to edit texts for high school boys. But John was not disturbed.

In *The Memory of Certain Persons* he sets forth in amusing detail how the idea of this novel had forced itself upon him. He had been committed to do a book on Milton for Bobbs-Merrill, but was too bored to get it going. Meantime, while reading widely for fresh legends for his graduate course on "Materials of Poetry," he fell captive to the seductions of the face that launched a thousand ships, and soon began to fantasy a myth of his own. "I was fascinated," he says, "by that period in Helen's career of which Homer gives one tantalizing glimpse in the Odyssey; after Troy, Menelaus took her back to Sparta, and for the rest of their lives they lived—how?"

"The war is over," he goes on. "Nothing to do now, but go home and meet each other daily at the breakfast table, like any other husband and wife. What did they talk about?"

A brief paragraph gives one a taste of how that question teased him.

"I began to imagine conversations in which Menelaus, having over-strained himself in the effort to forget the past, suddenly remembers it and picks on Helen; calm, controlled and as though her conscience were clear, she answers sweetly and reasonably, and in no time at all argues him off his feet."

The publishers sensibly accepted the book in lieu of the one under contract, but balked over the title. Wasn't it too frivolous? "Admitting the possibility," Erskine says, "I reminded them that it was Helen's public life which was scandalous; in private she was as I had represented her, a conventional woman, differing from her sisters only in looks and in brains. The brains were my gift to her. In Homer and the Greek dramatists Helen is inspiring to look at but not to listen to."

The publication of **Helen** made a stunning hit; it marked the start of a new career, that of the novelist. **Helen of Troy** has been translated into most of the European languages and Japanese, and as late as 1952, the year after John's death, it was dramatized and produced in Paris to a cheering audience by the French playwright André Roussin.

Helen and the two following books, **Galahad** and **Adam and Eve**, definitely established John Erskine as the innovator of a fresh genre in American fiction, that of the ironic commentary on human relationships, the characters derived from past history or legend, but reinterpreted in the light of our contemporary mores. As late as 1949 he was to repeat the formula effectively in his final novel, **Venus, The Lonely Goddess**.

Time will not permit more than a passing reference to Erskine's role as a distinguished scholar, editor and seminal force in the advancement of challenging ideas. One of his most noble pronouncements is to be found in his essay, **"The Moral Obligation To Be Intelligent,"** an American classic, and reprinted in a recent paperback collection of "Great Essays" of the English language from Francis Bacon to our present day. The theme appears in its title. Intelligence, in short, is not merely a cultural desideratum. "We really seek intelligence," Erskine says, "not for the answers it may suggest to the problems of life, but because we believe it is life; not for making the will of God prevail, but because we believe it is the will of God. We love it as we love virtue, for its own sake, and we believe it is only virtue's other and more precise name."

Here at Columbia John Erskine is remembered above all things as a great educator, an inspired teacher. From the moment of graduation, teaching was to form the main stream of his life. He started most fortunately in 1900 with the award of the Proudfit Fellowship in Letters, a grant to cover three years of preparation. Armed with a Ph.D. he was called to Amherst where he taught English literature for six years and took an active part in the life of the campus. Although I missed the satisfaction of hearing him lecture, I had the good luck to observe his popularity with his students. On John's invitation I visited Amherst twice to give talks on non-academic subjects. As soon as he entered the lecture-hall to introduce me, the boys crowded around him with affectionate

greetings and with unselfconscious intimacy. I might add for the record that my two subjects, at John's suggestion, were "Nonsense Verse and Parody" and English "Vers de Société," subjects which as undergraduates we had pursued with extracurricular relish.

In 1909 he was summoned back to Columbia and remained on the faculty until 1937. His effect on his hearers is best expressed by one of his most stimulating students and disciples, the late Irwin Edman: "The end of almost every lecture was punctuated by applause. . . . The incipient writers were best served by John Erskine. In his Elizabethan literature course he was a virtuoso lecturer who dramatized and illuminated every book he touched on. . . . He was a wonderful mentor and taught young writers the discipline of an art and the sense of and need for craftsmanship in writing. In a period when sentimental notions of the writer's function still flourished, he reminded us what we would make of our experiences and how we could look at our immediate world with the directness which Homer looked at his, how not to muse and dream nostalgically about Greece, but to write about New York City and Columbia University."

In 1917 he suggested a revolutionary step in the teaching of the humanities. Against stout resistance he battled for a new kind of course extending over the junior and senior years, in which the student was required to read and discuss a different classic each week. This eventually grew into "The Great Books" course; it enlisted the services of the younger instructors, Edman, Mark Van Doren, Mortimer Adler, Clifton Fadiman, Henry Morton Robinson, to name only a few. Its influence has spread nationwide through the liberal arts colleges, especially at the University of Chicago under Hutchins and Adler and at St. John's College, Maryland, under Stringfellow Barr.

Erskine's role as an administrator antedated his appointment at Juilliard by ten years. Perhaps his most valuable contribution as a citizen was his work in France at the end of World War I. Obtaining a leave of absence from the University, he assumed the prodigious task, with no precedent to guide him, of organizing and directing the American University at Beaune, France— an institution which with a hastily assembled faculty of 800, cared for 10,000 American boys during the months of delay before they were returned to this country and the pursuits of peace. For his patriotic services he received a special tribute from General Pershing, was decorated by both the French and American governments and was made an honorary citizen of the City of Beaune.

Undreamed of at the time, the Beaune experiment was to have far-reaching influence. Thirty years later, at the close of World War II, it became the model for similar army schools in Germany, Italy, France and England, sustaining morale in the perilous period of transition.

Despite the handicap of desperate illnesses and even the crippling infirmities of his later years, Erskine nevertheless continued unselfishly to answer every call to public service. In 1941, to cite but one instance, on the invitation of Secretary Cordell Hull and as the official representative of the State Department he sailed for South America on a mission to improve cultural and diplomatic relations. His visit proved both a personal and a diplomatic triumph. He lectured at the leading universities of Argentina and Uruguay, conferred with the heads of state, encouraged the exchange of scholars and even successfully brought about changes in one college curriculum through the introduction of courses in music at the University of Cordoba, a subject theretofore neglected.

This account is necessarily fragmentary and incomplete.

I hope you will in charity make allowances for the indulgences of friendship. For it is of John Erskine, my friend, that I have spoken, with admiration, respect and, first of all, affection. Others of greater and special competence have made and will continue to make more objective appraisals.

Whenever I think of John, the virtue I think of first is generosity. The generosity of the physical man, over six feet tall, broadly proportioned to match the height, wide-eyed, ample and strong of countenance, was the fitting repository for the spirit within. Generosity means largeness and liberality of spirit. To be generous is to live nobly, abundantly, freely, open-handedly. In defining the word the dictionary uses this illustration: "As a generous friend."

John was always the generous friend, unfailing in sympathy and support, encouraging with praise, strengthening with sharp but kindly criticism.

He was a lover of life—hearty, expansive, witty, caustic, ironic but uncynical over the frailties of mankind. Looking back on the Amherst days, when still under twenty-five, he once said: "I was already committed to the active life rather than the contemplative, so far as there is a mutually exclusive opposition between them." Time and maturity made such an exclusion unthinkable, for with the breadth of his interests came a correspondingly philosophic perspective, a basic sense of the meaning and aim of existence.

Scholar, artist, teacher, administrator, citizen of his country and of the world, John Erskine will be remembered as a twentieth-century humanist, a modern child of the Renaissance.

It gives me a personal pleasure to recall that eight years ago in this very place we each paid memorial tribute to George Edward Woodberry, our old teacher whose inspiration and idealism John was to carry forward into his own life and teaching. This was his final appearance at Columbia.

It was to Woodberry, our most popular professor, that we dedicated our senior year-book, the "Naughty Naughtian," with the following quatrain:

One who took manhood for his Art,
Taught it by manliness so rare,
We keep his lessons in our heart,
But first of all he entered there.

These lines, which are John's, I now rededicate to *his* memory.

Joan Shelley Rubin (essay date 1992)

SOURCE: "Classics and Commercials: John Erskine and 'Great Books'," in *The Making of Middle/Brow Culture*, The University of North Carolina Press, 1992, pp. 149-97.

[*In the following excerpt, Rubin chronicles Erskine's career, and explores the means by which his student Mortimer Adler developed the "Great Books" series.*]

In July 1915 Randolph Bourne, who had graduated from Columbia University two years earlier, contributed to the *New Republic* a sketch entitled "The Professor." Part of Bourne's call for a rebellion of youth against the genteel tradition, the essay depicted a figure who supplied his students with knowledge and inspiration but refused to commit himself openly to aesthetic or political judgments. In that tone of subtle, devastating sarcasm of which he was a master, Bourne described his subject's deepest experiences as literary ones, implicitly trivializing them as encounters that had no real consequences. Encapsulated in his study, the professor rejected the "futile babel" of "modern ideas" in favor of that serene, innocent, and, in Bourne's view, desiccated existence that the twentieth century was, he thought, eradicating none too soon.[1]

Bourne's sketch was a veiled portrait of John Erskine, poet, authority on the Elizabethan lyric, and enormously popular member of Columbia's English department. In the aftermath of "The Professor" episode, Bourne confessed to having grown "a little bashful about visiting Columbia in the daytime" while "mine ancient enemy" was "on the warpath." The following year, however, he did not hesitate to attack Erskine in a vituperative exchange of letters, at the end of which Bourne made clear the function Erskine played for him: "I am not unconscious," he wrote, "of the way I destroy the amenities of life when I have any bearing towards you. But this is only because of my need for a personal symbol for my intellectual bêtes noires. . . . I am quite sure that I perform this same office in a limited way for you."[2]

Yet, however useful Bourne found Erskine as a foil, his analysis of him was wrong on two counts. Despite Bourne's insistence that Erskine's way of life was dying, it was the teacher, rather than his student, who remained in the public eye for the next thirty years. In the era of World War I, Erskine proposed the first full-scale "great books" curriculum to the Columbia faculty; in the 1920s he not only implemented that curriculum but became a best-selling novelist, star of the lecture circuit, and president of the Juilliard School of Music. By the mid-1940s he had somewhat faded from sight but was not nearly as obscure as Bourne, whose death in 1918 had erased him from the memories of almost everyone but the avant-garde. More important, Erskine was not the stereotype of gentility Bourne imagined but rather, like Stuart Sherman, a figure whose Arnoldian commitments competed with a desire for self-expression and experience. Incapable of going as far as Sherman in renouncing prescriptions for character, he was less comfortably ensconced in the genteel tradition than Canby or Fisher. As such, his career adds a particularly rich biographical dimension to the effort to elucidate the middlebrow perspective.

A Genteel Childhood

Born in 1879, Erskine was actually only seven years senior to Bourne. He lived in New York until he was five but spent the rest of his youth in Weehawken, New Jersey. His father, James Morrison Erskine, a scholarly, man with a fondness for history and music, owned a silk factory that turned out decorative ribbons; his mother, Eliza Jane Hollingsworth Erskine, bore six children and ran the household. The genteel loyalties Bourne pilloried had their genesis in Erskine's upbringing. In terms of manners, his family preserved a set of rituals—morning recitations, afternoon study sessions, dressing for dinner, formal mealtime etiquette, piano recitals in the living room on leisurely afternoons—that bespoke the esteem in which it held both refinement and decorum. As a young boy, Erskine absorbed from his father and his "fastidious," well-read uncle William Hollingsworth the lesson that to attain culture meant to "know good books." On Sundays Erskine and his siblings attended Episcopal services at Grace Church, which his father had helped to found. In his autobiography, *The Memory of Certain Persons* (1947), he contrasted his own religious encounters with those some of his contemporaries had recorded: whereas it was "the fashion for American writers to describe their early contacts with religion as intellectually stultifying and spiritually depressing," his were "stimulating and happy." Socially, the Erskines were firmly allied with groups accustomed to enjoying prestige and exercising leadership in matters of taste. (In that way, his childhood was strikingly similar in atmosphere to Henry Seidel Canby's among the old Quaker families of Wilmington.) The Erskines' Weehawken neighbors, lined up in large estates along the palisades, had ties to the inhabitants of the mansions farther up the Hudson; their houses, decorated with walnut and marble, expressed their economic power. While Erskine's home and income were somewhat more modest, he nonetheless identified his boyhood surroundings as "aristocratic."[3]

For Erskine (as for Canby), that milieu had a number of positive aspects. Erskine's account of his first years conveys an ineffable feeling of belonging, of comforting stability. His aunts and uncles, for example, including two of his mother's sisters who lived with the Erskines, were always known by the babyish names the children had bestowed on them, as if to enshrine within the family circle the innocence and child-centeredness that financial security and social position permitted. The family's daily routine and its immersion in religion buttressed his sense of permanence. Erskine's father often told him that the beautiful and gracious neighborhoods of the Weehawken wealthy would "always contain the homes of those who like quiet and solitude"—that, in other words, those like the Erskines would endure against threats to their preeminence.[4] Moreover, Erskine's father initially personified the positive features of genteel self-reliance. As a man "affectionate but slightly reserved, always balanced and self-controlled," he seemed to embody substance and strength.[5]

By the late nineteenth century, however, it was clear that James Erskine's pronouncement about Weehawken was more wishful than prophetic. As Erskine recognized even as a child, the street on which he lived not only divided his township from the adjoining one of Union Hill but also demarcated the boundary between gentility and modern industrial America. Union Hill contained his father's factory, along with breweries and other mills; it was where the immigrants who worked for the elder Erskine lived. Before 1892 Erskine remained largely in the shelter of the past. "Perhaps the influence of all the Weehawken memories," he acknowledged, "kept me for years from observing real life, from seeing the America of the moment, which foretold the future."[6] That year, though, elements of "real life" became inescapable. In the mid-1880s James Erskine had invested in a second factory in central New York. In the economic downturn of the early 1890s, the venture proved a liability. Furthermore, changing fashions were eliminating the market for crafted ribbons and sashes. James Erskine's reaction was to pour money into the company, on the theory that his reversals were only temporary. Instead, he gradually spent most of his assets.[7]

As a witness, in adolescence, to his father's decline, Erskine acquired an impression of the human cost of commerce that cemented his allegiance to the genteel stance of alienation from the marketplace. In particular, James Erskine's predicament illustrated the fate of aesthetic impulses in the new industrial order. As Erskine explained retrospectively, "It was the artist in him who had succeeded, and when art was no longer desired in the business, he was through." Additionally, there is some evidence that Erskine connected the incursions of industrialization with the demands of women. The point is hard to document because, in his memoirs, he explicitly presented women as objects of adoration, recounting Eliza Hollingsworth Erskine's appearance at the dinner hour dressed in "flawless white" and reporting as his earliest recollection a visit to a dairy where women workers in "cool clean dresses" furnished pails of warm milk. Nevertheless, Erskine noted that his mother, the more "practical" of his parents, did not approve of his father's insistence on pursuing his artistic inclinations.

In light of that disagreement about what Erskine himself called "matters of such consequence," his cameo of his mother appears retouched, as if he needed to idealize her in order to avoid acknowledging the extent to which she contributed to his father's unhappiness.[8] In any case, by the 1890s James Erskine was less a representative of genteel self-reliance than of the sensitive misfits Van Wyck Brooks portrayed as victims of the "catchpenny realities" of American capitalism.[9] The balance and self-control he displayed, it appears, hid the fact that the defeats and disappointments of business had driven his energies inward, disrupting the correspondence between outward behavior and inner self.

Yet, in the world of Erskine's childhood, that discontinuity could also arise from a different source: the genteel tradition itself. More was involved than the imposition of parlor morality Brooks especially decried. The "dignified distance between himself and others" which, in Stow Persons's words, the gentleman "scrupulously preserved" could eventuate in a debilitating isolation.[10] In an atmosphere which rewarded conformity, restraint might turn into the stifling of feeling, refinement into a retreat from creative instincts. William Hollingsworth, a man successful in business but bored and miserable because of the compliance he was expected to exhibit, epitomized the consequences of those possibilities. In language that recalls descriptions of Stuart Sherman's distance and volatility, his young nephew remarked that his "iron self-control" seemed to conceal "a furnace or boiler, which might blow up at any minute." Although it is difficult to say how much Erskine as a child ascribed his uncle's turbulence to the genteel tradition gone sour—it is in the nature of repression, after all, to keep such perceptions buried—William Hollingsworth's uneasy combination of courtliness and rebellion was a portent of his own development. "If I introduce him here at length," he apologized in *The Memory of Certain Persons*, "it is because he influenced me greatly, and in some corners of my heart I need him to explain myself."[11]

Moreover, Erskine seems to have formed early on an incipient notion that women were at least exempt from, if not responsible for, the damages that gentility, as well as business pressures, could inflict on the self. His mother and aunt hovered over William Hollingsworth, worrying about his aversion to things "too safe to be interesting." At the same time, they appeared to Erskine as models of self-actualization. Whereas the men around him smoldered with emotional potential, Eliza Hollingsworth Erskine ignited: "She was an explosive reservoir of force—and of fun."[12] One episode in particular, one may speculate, must have intensified a sense that women were the unscathed perpetrators of a genteel attempt to hamper creativity. In 1898 Erskine's piano teacher announced that he had nothing more to teach his pupil and that a great musical career awaited him if his parents would send him to study in Europe. The thought of her son as a musician was more than his mother's conventional nature could bear, and she refused. "I think I would have been a composer," Erskine wistfully wrote

of the incident.[13] That decision, which, transmuted by denial, may have contributed toward his presentation of his mother as "flawless," left an aftertaste of bitterness toward women that one can detect in Erskine's writing forty years later.

Student and Teacher

Neither the challenge to genteel values the business world posed from without nor the capacity of those values to self-destruct from within, however, prevented Erskine from initially securing an education dedicated to instilling the liberal culture which marked the refined sensibility. His father sent him to Columbia Grammar School, where the idea of preparing students for "life" had not yet dislodged the nineteenth-century practice of preparing them for college by drilling them in Greek and Latin.[14] Nonetheless, the pursuit of liberal culture was growing more problematic at the school's parent institution. The rise of specialization had divided the Columbia College faculty since the late 1880s, setting the "university party" against the advocates of the liberal arts. By the time Erskine enrolled as a freshman in 1896, the specialists were in the majority, although the conflict between the two factions remained muted in the sense that the humanists continued to teach according to their point of view while their adversaries made policies in spite of them. There were enclaves, within certain departments, of genteel culture, untouched by new currents and expectations. But no one at Columbia during Erskine's undergraduate years could have failed to recognize the embattled position of those enclaves, even if, as Lionel Trilling suggested, the students on the whole were not very concerned with the college's long-range fortunes.[15] For Erskine, Columbia encompassed—and did not resolve—the dichotomy between Weehawken and Union Hill. Although not precisely the same thing, the contest between liberal study and specialization was a close enough variant of the tension between art and business as to make Columbia a stage for the second act of the drama he had begun witnessing at home.

Erskine first responded by gravitating toward the traditionalists. The composer and pianist Edward MacDowell occupied a special place in his affections. In actuality, Erskine's musical development, already thwarted by his mother, foundered under MacDowell's tutelage when MacDowell pronounced him a "good craftsman" rather than a "special talent." Yet the musician's devotion to creative expression for its own sake, without regard for either academic tradition or financial reward, made him seem the embodiment of "something ideal" and increasingly rare in the Columbia community. In that respect, MacDowell was a counterexample to James Erskine and William Hollingsworth. Erskine's description of him as an "authentic spirit" referred not only to the genuineness of his musical gifts but also to the consonance between his conduct and his nature. In the 1890s, when the mental illness that was to dominate MacDowell's last years was not much in evidence, and when his dealings with the Columbia administration were relatively untroubled, he appeared the picture not only of "energy and health" but also of self-reliance.[16]

The same qualities marked George Edward Woodberry, the poet and professor of literature to whom Erskine turned in his junior year when he began retreating from music. The greatest single influence on Erskine's career, Woodberry was born in Beverly, Massachusetts, in 1855. As a youth, he attended Emerson's last lecture and catalogued James Russell Lowell's library; in the same period, he studied at Harvard with Henry Adams and Charles Eliot Norton. Although his relations to the genteel tradition are more complex than that lineage suggests—for example, he wrote a disaffected essay on Bayard Taylor's verse—his critical categories derived essentially from Arnoldian and transcendentalist influences. Like MacDowell, Woodberry was an idealist, but in his case the term denoted a specific outlook as well as a dedication to principle: it referred to his conviction that the function of art was to illuminate the realm of the soul, which he conceived of as the primal, divine beauty common to all.[17]

In 1891, upon the recommendation of Lowell and Norton, Woodberry became a member of the English department at Columbia. From that position, he reassuringly addressed the dislocations of the late nineteenth century. For example, his lectures made the continuity of human nature the basis for literary understanding. Readers, Woodberry explained, profited most by examining literature in light of their own experience—experience which they shared with all people throughout history. In the face of ethnic diversity, class conflict, and anomie, Woodberry saw books as means of attaining what he called "the community of the soul."[18] Moreover, Woodberry's *Heart of Man,* which Erskine said "stirred" and "startled" the campus when it appeared in 1899, identified idealism as an instrument of intellectual order. The detection of universal laws and essential commonalities, Woodberry argued, organized the disparate and unsettling information that realism and science provided about the human condition. His own stance as a generalist within the university held the line against the danger that specialists would reduce knowledge to splinters, destroying faith and meaning.[19]

Woodberry's insistence that, instead of analyzing sources and symbols, individuals appropriate literature to foster "growth" and "self-development" freighted reading with a greater therapeutic function than his mentors assigned it. "Personality," he declared, "is the genius of life." Furthermore, Woodberry occasionally devalued aesthetic training in favor of business priorities. "Life is not long enough," he announced, for anyone "much occupied with many affairs" to read Shakespeare in a scholarly fashion. Similarly, his anti-rational bias—his democratically inspired claim that the "safest guide" to books was "the reader's instinct"—deviated from Arnoldian standards and severed the connections among cultivation, morality, and discipline.[20]

Yet, despite some kinship to modern advertisers and self-help crusaders, Woodberry largely rejected the therapeutic worldview. He commended reading not for the sake of building a malleable, other-directed self but rather to stir the "thousand susceptibilities" of the cultivated man that "never pass from his consciousness outward but are shut in his own silent world."[21] More important, Woodberry's conduct and temperament militate against the temptation to see him as primarily a purveyor of therapy in the guise of criticism. Sensitive and unworldly (Ferris Greenslet remarked that "his only outdoor sport was daydreaming"), Woodberry suggested by his visible rejection of efficiency, pragmatism, and skepticism the persistence of a romantic, confident cast of mind. Furthermore, his own life seemed to belie the need for a rehabilitation of the self. In Erskine's view, Woodberry's outstanding characteristic was unity—between belief and behavior, work and spirit. "He was the first teacher," Erskine remembered, "from whom I got the notion that the public life of the citizen is important as an expression . . . of his private aspirations, and that the business enterprises of a country cannot in the long run be separated from its essential religious or spiritual faith. Having learned from him that poetry is the flower of life but still an integral part of it, we went on to learn that all human activities are related, and—unless one is stupid or a hypocrite—must be harmonious." Erskine had seen, in his father's and uncle's cases, examples of the failure to join "business enterprises" with "spiritual faith." To be one of Woodberry's "boys" was to discover a second father, one who vindicated and realized the aspirations of the first.[22]

Woodberry's insistence on spirituality could be dismissed as tender-minded: William James observed of *Heart of Man* that the book lacked "that which our generation seems to need, the sudden word, the unmediated transition, the flash of perception that makes reasonings unnecessary."[23] For all his language about experience, Woodberry used the term as Emerson did when, in his essay of that title, he shunned "sensation" in favor of the "temperate zone . . . of thought, of spirit, of poetry." Seconding Emerson's remark that he was "content with knowing" rather than doing, Woodberry remained a poet and scholar whose encounters were mainly of the literary variety that Bourne disparaged.[24] Yet it was precisely its remoteness from a troubling present—its uncurdled gentility—that made Woodberry's outlook initially congenial to Erskine's social background, psychological requirements, and academic interests. "For boyhood," Erskine wrote (and he might have added "of a certain class and sensitivity"), "it was a thrilling vision, and in its power many who sat in Woodberry's classes have tried to live."[25]

In 1900 Erskine enrolled in the Columbia Graduate School to continue his work in English under Woodberry's direction.[26] At the same time, he began to build a reputation as a poet: Richard Watson Gilder selected Erskine's **"Actaeon"** as the winning entry in the *Century* magazine's 1901 poetry competition for recent college graduates. The reception of the poem, which perpetuated a vision of ideal beauty, reassuringly attested to the continuing power of Woodberry's philosophy. Similarly, Erskine's graduate training reinforced his conviction that a teaching career patterned on Woodberry's example offered a way of resisting the subordination of art to practicality. Although specialization had already placed Woodberry and his followers on the defensive, the appeal of idealism and the strength of Woodberry's popularity allowed Erskine to ignore that fact. It was as if, having conceded that his father's predicament signaled the demise of genteel culture in America at large, he turned with heightened urgency to the shelter of the university and, for a time, found what he was seeking.

Events at Columbia, however, soon challenged that institution's status as a refuge. The inauguration of Nicholas Murray Butler as president in 1902 entrenched the viewpoint of the "university" party. Butler represented everything that Woodberry was not: in place of reflective spirituality, he offered decisiveness and commitment to action. Woodberry's own circumstances were beclouded by an increasingly bitter relationship with his worldly, cynical colleague Brander Matthews. The feud between the two was more a matter of personal animosity than substantive disagreement, but whenever it spilled over into academic concerns, Butler favored Matthews. As a result, Woodberry came more and more to feel out of place at Columbia.[27]

Erskine regarded Woodberry's situation with mixed emotions; in fact, his remarks about his state of mind during 1902 and 1903 constitute a rare explicit reference to psychic conflict. Although his identification of Butler as a "supreme humanist" in "his own way" seems calculated to placate Butler (still living at the time *The Memory of Certain Persons* appeared), his subsequent expressions of confusion have a more genuine ring: "Our University would grow, its graduates would be legion, its endowment would become fabulous, its degrees would be well thought-of—but would it produce great personalities? Would there be a place on its staff for original minds? . . . On the other hand, is idealism really incompatible with practical sense? Why should not a poet like Woodberry be a man of action, competent in daily affairs? These questions, posed by swift changes at Columbia, filled my head almost as much as my studies."[28] Yet, despite such reservations, Erskine left graduate school with his image of himself as Woodberry's disciple intact. Appointed assistant professor of English at Amherst in 1903, he took up his teaching duties with the expectation that, regardless of the disturbing tendencies at Columbia, idealism would flourish in the atmosphere of the liberal arts college. The same year, he published a study of the Elizabethan lyric.

While on leave in 1904, Woodberry resigned from Columbia; a few months later MacDowell did the same, having clashed with Butler over the reorganization of the music department. Far from questioning the merits of Woodberry's case, Erskine responded to the turn of events at Columbia by helping to have Woodberry appointed a guest lecturer at Amherst for the spring of 1905, in the hope that he would stay permanently. Woodberry himself slipped into the pessimism that would characterize him until his death in 1930. As if he had awakened to the truth of James's observation, he felt increasingly at odds with the contemporary distaste for "the finer things" and depressed that he had been "passed by."[29] For Erskine, however, Woodberry's pedagogical premises remained inspiring. To his students (Bruce Barton among them), he stressed the connections between literature and life. Writing to his friend Melville Cane of his success, Erskine noted with pride, "I think you will see that I have something of a Woodberrian hold on the boys now; my work is extremely happy."[30]

Nevertheless, Erskine's cheerful identification with Woodberry masked anxieties which made his Amherst years psychologically turbulent ones. The immediate source of the turmoil was his uncertainty about his future as a poet. Henry Morton Robinson, a student of Erskine's in the 1920s and his most astute biographer, observed that reservations about his ability to meet the standard he had set in **"Actaeon"** began to plague Erskine after 1906. Although he eventually brought out two more volumes, self-doubt propelled him toward teaching and scholarship. Yet the crisis went deeper. As Robinson noted, Erskine's turn away from poetry resulted less from a considered judgment about his talents than from a reluctance fully to exercise his "poetic powers," as if to do so would invite an uncontrollable and isolating self-absorption. His declaration in 1907 that he would write not "for the pleasure of self-expression" but as a means of reaching "the largest possible audience" might be seen not only as a reflection of his Arnoldian sympathies but also as a flight from experience—that is, from the potentially painful unleashing of his emotions. Instead, on the one hand, Erskine remained wedded to the need for self-control shaped by his genteel upbringing. A less exuberant letter to Cane expressing the faith that it was not "unmanly" to pray for a "wise and an understanding heart" in order to "solve our own tangles" similarly revealed the power of the values with which he had been raised.[31]

Yet, on the other hand, his frustrations as a poet led him to reassess Woodberry's wraithlike spirituality. Unable, this time, to suppress the doubts he had first entertained as a graduate student, he seems to have admitted the possibility, in James's words, that "poor Woodberry" was "so high, so true, so good" yet ultimately "so ineffective."[32] His decision about his audience—which he implemented by lecturing to local women's clubs and students at Smith College—can also be read as a clue that Erskine hungered for *more* experience than Woodberry's contemplative pose provided. The same can be said of his resolve to make scholarship "creative." The social and intellectual aspects of his life in Amherst, moreover, fueled his dissatisfaction. The insular nature of a "country college" thwarted his cosmopolitan impulses; the white gloves and parlor conversation at faculty teas, while they added grace and charm to the Amherst social scene, sometimes seemed oppressive and even ridiculous. Furthermore, Amherst professors, for the most part, had few ambitions to publish research and resented anyone who did.[33] Interested in building a reputation as a scholar and concerned (if ambivalent) about being a "man of action," Erskine developed during his stint at Amherst a tension about his vocation and his genteel loyalties reminiscent of William Hollingsworth's restlessness—a tension that would reappear throughout the rest of his career. Although his writings from the period permit only speculation and inference, he appears to have broadened the questions he had formulated with respect to the future of Columbia: How could one preserve the unity Woodberry exemplified and be a "man of action" at the same time? How could one escape repression and plunge into the life that lay beyond the printed page without succumbing to the fragmentation that threatened to accompany the relinquishment of self-control?

Those dilemmas gave Erskine an affinity not only with Sherman but also—although both men would have shuddered at the comparison—with Bourne. Moreover, they were similar to the "longings for reintegrated selfhood and intense experience" Lears has described as rampant in late-nineteenth- and early-twentieth-century America.[34] Yet, although Erskine, like Sherman, resembled the antimodernists Lears has identified, he never made a thoroughgoing rejection of genteel values a prerequisite, as they did, for discovering an authentic self. Furthermore, he failed to join Bourne in attaching the search for experience to radical politics and only flirted with the prospect of therapeutic release. Erskine's way was different: to perpetuate the genteel tradition while accommodating his yearnings for freedom from restraint and control.

An invitation in 1909 to return to Columbia as associate professor in the English department promised to assuage some of Erskine's more tangible discontents. If going back to Columbia meant dealing with Butler, it also meant serving on a faculty with James Harvey Robinson, Charles Beard, John Dewey, and other distinguished scholars who made the institution in the pre-World War I period a center of extraordinary intellectual vitality. It offered as well virtually unlimited chances to extend the university's tradition of involvement with audiences outside its walls.[35]

At the height of his powers as a teacher, Erskine dazzled the Columbia undergraduates who flocked to his course on Elizabethan literature. Students like Lloyd Morris, Alfred Knopf, and Dixon Ryan Fox responded to his enthusiasm, erudition, and wit; they marveled at his analytical facility and wide-ranging interests. Yet Morris's description of him in this period suggests that Columbia could not, after all, provide Erskine with easy answers to the questions with which he seems to have grappled at Amherst. If Erskine was brilliant and dynamic in the classroom, Morris noted that he exhibited

as well a reticence and detachment which some interpreted as arrogance. "The professor would have been surprised, possibly displeased," Morris remembered, "to learn how thoroughly his students discussed him; how much he puzzled and attracted them; how often he was debated in fraternity houses, at lunch counters, or over nocturnal beers in Morningside saloons." Morris's observation might be chalked up simply to student curiosity were it not for its kinship with Erskine's own regretful portraits of his father and uncle—and its contrast with his admiring depiction of Woodberry. Erskine's "aloofness" and enigmatic formality, which Bourne misinterpreted as the ivory tower intellectual's willful and conscious withdrawal from political commitment, appear instead emblems of a divided sensibility; they hint that Erskine still contended with the difficulty of giving play to his desire for engagement without forfeiting self-reliance.[36] Erskine's marriage in 1910 to Pauline Ives, a conservative, duty-bound woman of high principle and little spontaneity with whom he was increasingly unhappy, pulled him back toward genteel repression, no doubt contributing to his distant manner.[37]

Erskine's most important essay from this period, **"The Moral Obligation to be Intelligent"** (1913), may be interpreted, on one level, as a translation of his personal struggles into philosophical terms. His argument, on the surface, was a plea for the consideration of intelligence as a virtue along with character and goodness.[38] Erskine understood his position as an attack on conventional morality, a substitution of new virtues for "obsolete" ones. In some respects, Erskine's view of himself as iconoclast was correct. In particular, although there is no evidence that he had anything more than a passing acquaintance with his colleague John Dewey, there are marked similarities between Erskine's outlook and the challenge pragmatism was then posing to idealist philosophy: the parts of **"The Moral Obligation to be Intelligent"** that deplore absolute definitions of good and evil and advocate attention to an action's consequences read like a pragmatist manifesto.

Nevertheless, as Lloyd Morris pointed out, the function of intelligence, as Erskine saw it, was "to dominate experience," to harness it in order to direct activity to ideal ends. Unwilling, like the pragmatists, to follow ideas wherever they might lead without prejudging their value, Erskine conceived of intelligence as a way of creating the same situation Woodberry had promised to foster: "the infinite order, wherein man, when he enters it, shall find himself." Despite his determination to break with the past, it was the "modern world," rather than the "old" one, that, in Erskine's terms, had "got into a kind of prison." The "key to the lock," it turned out, was to substitute intelligence for character within the familiar Emersonian framework of self-reliance and "moral obligation."[39] Thus, the essay neatly juggled freedom and control, while simultaneously invoking and rejecting genteel understandings.

"A Feeling of Peace All the Time"

Erskine's response to World War I, however, revealed the continuing lure of undomesticated experience in his own life. His involvement came on the civilian side, and when the end of the war was in view. Early in 1918, under the joint auspices of the YMCA and the army, he sailed for France to help design an educational program for American military personnel who would soon be demobilized. Assigned to *foyers* at the French front until the postwar planning could begin, he encountered firsthand the mud and the dampness of the trenches. Once he saw a nearly headless corpse dangling from an ambulance. After a few months, he moved to Paris and assumed charge of the planning commission. The following spring, having overseen the placement of American soldiers in French and British universities, he became educational director of the American University at Beaune. Within weeks, Erskine and his staff had transformed the hospital grounds there into a campus complete with a cadre of deans and streets named in honor of American colleges. The size and scope of the operation were impressive: at one point, there were close to ten thousand registered students, taught by almost eight hundred faculty members. Although several accounts have indicated that the curriculum at Beaune consisted of reading "great books," Erskine recalled that in fact the course offerings were traditional and widely varied, ranging from law to painting.[40]

Erskine reacted to his wartime activities in ways that reveal they meant more to him than simply the chance to serve the causes of education and patriotism. Until his death in 1951, he displayed pictures of the American University on the walls of his apartment and kept a folio of Beaune photographs close at hand. "Again and again," his second wife, Helen Worden, recalled, she and Erskine "looked at them together and as we looked, he described every detail of his exciting months" there. During his final illness, he made a nostalgic pilgrimage to the site of the campus, a journey he had talked about with Worden from the first day she met him. His treatment of the war occupies a radically disproportionate part of his autobiography, relegating his postwar years of public prominence to minor status in the narrative.[41] The tenaciousness of Erskine's memories—the way he sought to recapture and perpetuate them in a barrage of words and in his actions—argues that he derived from wartime service satisfactions that eluded him at other points in his life.

His letters from the front imply what those satisfactions were. Contrasting the taxing work he was doing with the "petty world" of Amherst and the prospect of "frittering myself away on small things" when he returned to Columbia, Erskine wrote his ailing mother in the spring of 1919, "I have sacrificed more in this war, I think, than some of the princes who have lost their thrones." In another letter to her, he averred, "If you were here for five minutes, you would see that this work is the moral and intellectual salvation of thousands of boys—hundreds of thousands." Constrained in those documents by his guilty awareness that his mother wanted him to return home, Erskine repeatedly proclaimed his desire only to be at her bedside. To his sister Rhoda, however, he was more candid: "The work here is enormous," he admitted. "I shall miss it if I go back."[42]

Such comments suggest that, for Erskine, World War I provided a version of the strenuous life: it was exhausting, debilitating, horrifying—yet more exhilarating than anything he had ever done before. Although Bourne actually could not have had Erskine in mind when he published his famous "The War and the Intellectuals" (1917), because Erskine had not yet joined the war effort, Bourne's description of the way the fighting assuaged the "craving for action" besetting university professors and "practitioners of literature" precisely matches Erskine's response to the conflict. Restless at Amherst, distant at Columbia, he found war a vehicle, in Bourne's phrase, for "doing something aggressive, colossal."[43] As Worden recalled, "He often said that his first trip to France in 1917 [*sic*] was a subconscious liberation. . . . How often he said, 'Remember to live! Be the active participant, not the onlooker!' . . . He preferred the Front. He said he found there the peace of decision, the calm that comes when you've made up your mind, when there is no turning back, when the die is cast." Nine years after the fact, a *New Yorker* profile similarly noted that the "qualities of swift and fervent living" he encountered with the army meant that "the professor in the war had a simply magnificent time." Erskine's remark in a letter home that, surrounded by war, he "had a feeling of peace all the time" corroborates the point.[44]

If he exemplified Bourne's liberated intellectual, however, his references to sacrifice make clear that he discovered in war a way of abandoning self-control that could be justified in terms of ideals of duty and self-discipline. As such, it furnished an escape from genteel repression under cover of genteel rhetoric. It was that comforting combination, one suspects, that fully accounted for Erskine's sense of peace. Similarly, his comment in his autobiography that the war passed "like a dream" encompassed several meanings: it connoted the serenity Bourne had in mind as well as the tranquillity Erskine ascribed to Woodberry; it was both a fantasy of unity between thought and behavior and the gratification of Erskine's desire for a more intense reality.[45]

Encouraged by the students' successes at Beaune, Erskine proposed a postwar continuation of the American University in the form of a mandatory national training program run by the army for eighteen-year-old men. Explicitly, he billed the idea as a mechanism for insuring that citizens (he especially meant immigrants) receive the vocational and liberal arts instruction necessary to maintain democracy; implicitly, he addressed his own problem of vocation, envisioning a kind of educational equivalent of war which extended to peacetime the vital role he had enjoyed in France. In fact, however, his "dream" ended with the demobilization. Although his correspondence from Beaune reveals some uncertainty about whether he would actually return to Columbia, he resumed his duties in the fall of 1919 and was soon caught up in the same routines—and the same controversies—that had absorbed him before his departure.[46]

"Great Books" as Curriculum and Ideology

In particular, Erskine tackled with renewed energy an issue which he had presented to the Columbia faculty in 1916, but about which he had begun thinking as early as 1908: the problematic relationship between American civilization and the tradition of classical and European thought. Arising out of curricular concerns, this preoccupation, in its narrowest formulation, eventuated in the central achievement of his academic career, the design of an undergraduate course devoted to the study of "great books." Yet because Erskine, for over twenty years, sought through magazines and the lecture circuit an off-campus forum for many of the same ideas he articulated at Columbia, it is possible to speak more broadly as well of a "great books" ideology that Erskine propounded both within and outside of the college classroom.

As curricular reform, Erskine's "great books" proposal was a response to the widespread conviction among his contemporaries in English departments throughout the country that current undergraduates, in contrast to their predecessors, were woefully ignorant of Western literature. In an article he wrote while still at Amherst, Erskine, reflecting Woodberry's influence, argued that the way to arrest the perceived decline was to devise courses that approached texts on their own terms, unencumbered by the baggage of scholarship and criticism. Noting that all books enshrined as "great" were at one time recent publications intended for wide audiences, Erskine urged professors of English to continue to treat them as such.[47] In fact, it was a work's susceptibility to reinterpretation by diverse readers—its capacity to function as a "mirror" of variable circumstances—that constituted Erskine's principal test of "greatness." As he put it in one of his later writings that carried his outlook beyond academia, *The Delight of Great Books* (1927), "The great books are those which . . . surprise us by remaining true even when our point of view changes. This is why we rank Homer and Virgil and Dante, Shakespeare, Chaucer, Cervantes, and Moliere so high—because they still say so much, even to peoples of an altogether foreign culture, a different past, an opposed philosophy." Such resilience, as Erskine saw it, enabled students to find joy and meaning in literature, provided their teachers would allow them simply to relate it to their own lives. Given that opportunity, they would emerge from college equipped with what "a [gentleman] should know of the recognized branches of knowledge and of the masterpieces . . . without which no education could be considered complete."[48]

To facilitate such an education, Erskine devised a list of around seventy-five works deemed "best" because they dealt with enduring human dilemmas or types. These he proposed students read in a course spanning two years. As Graff has pointed out, Erskine's "great books" curriculum was neither the first one in the United States nor solely his own invention. Nevertheless, he supplied a rationale, a system, a scope, and a commitment that distinguished his effort from its less formalized antecedents.[49] His syllabus concentrated on the Greeks in the first half-year, moving on to the Romans and Aquinas in the second semester. The third and fourth terms ranged over European history, literature, and philosophy, encompassing, among many others, Dante, Shakespeare, Voltaire, Milton, Goethe, Descartes, Mill, and Kant. Erskine's list was an obvious instance of the way in which the process of canon formation—as literary scholars have now made clear—has functioned to exclude writers who were not white males in the Western tradition. There were no women, black, or non-Western authors on the list. What is more, there were only four Americans: Josiah Royce, Santayana, William James, and Henry George. In addition, Erskine's canon entirely ignored literary modernism, although Erskine would have replied that it was premature to include such writers as Strindberg, Conrad, or Henry James.[50]

Yet the current interest in displaying those biases in the content of the "great books" program has obscured important features of its structure. Erskine's idea radically challenged a number of existing pedagogical practices. University English departments in the early twentieth century typically offered a sequence of courses organized mainly by period: a year on the Elizabethans, another on the eighteenth century, one or two more on the nineteenth century. Shakespeare usually merited separate study, and courses based on literary genres— the novel, the drama—provided alternative frameworks, but the limited focus prevailed. The standard mode of presentation was the lecture. Readings consisted exclusively of those by British and American authors, on the grounds that translations cheapened works to the point of worthlessness.[51] Even where philology competed with literary history, biography, and bibliography, the curriculum reflected the trend toward specialization, casting the professor as unveiler of linguistic mysteries, sharpening the divisions among English, foreign, and Greek and Latin texts, rewarding the acquisition of information, and discouraging the enrollment of students from other disciplines.

Erskine's sweeping survey, by contrast, implicitly legitimized the generalist. In its earliest version, his plan established similar, concurrent courses in history, philosophy, and scientific ideas. His syllabus for the first three of those courses (which he eventually modified but did not fundamentally alter) dismissed historical exegesis and philology as irrelevant, attempted interdisciplinary synthesis, cut across time and place, and accommodated translations. The format he devised was equally innovative. Although he at first retained a conventional schedule of biweekly lectures, Erskine subsequently called for small discussion groups meeting once a week under the guidance of two instructors, with each session focused on a different book. Moreover, the instructors were assigned Socratic roles: they were "not to lecture nor in any way to behave like professors" but only to keep ideas flowing by asking questions and prompting debate. In what would subsequently appear an odd convergence, given the animus between John Dewey and later proponents of the "great books" idea, that directive resembled Deweyite pronouncements about the student-centered curriculum. In addition, Erskine suggested that the course be open to all juniors and seniors and required for those who had not selected a major, on the assumption that there was a body of writing with which every recipient of a bachelor's degree ought to be acquainted.[52] Those latter two stipulations amounted to a frontal attack on the ethos of specialization, assailing as they did its exemplar, the professorial expert, and its curricular embodiment, the elective system.

Thus, while Richard Brodhead has observed that, at least in the case of American literature, the promulgators of the canon in the early twentieth century worked to "underwrite their own new cultural authority" by selecting texts so difficult as to require "expert assistance," the original "great books" ideology was predicated on precisely the opposite idea.[53] No doubt sensing that threat to their power, many of Erskine's colleagues objected to his plan when it came before them for debate late in 1916. Arguing that Erskine's curriculum would perpetuate superficiality at the expense of "true scholarship," they foresaw the sacrifice of "real understanding" as students galloped through the material. In addition, they were justifiably skeptical about the merits of reading in an intellectual and historical vacuum. The faculty nonetheless approved Erskine's scheme in principle in February 1917 but was diverted from instituting it by American entry into the war. When Erskine left for France, the matter was in abeyance, and, by his account, opposition persisted.[54]

In the long run, however, the war proved a boon to Erskine's campaign. Complying with a directive from the army, Columbia established an interdisciplinary course on "War Issues" to serve student recruits. That course in turn inspired the creation in 1919 of one devoted to "peace issues," or, as it became known, "Contemporary Civilization." Entailing discussion groups akin to those Erskine had advocated, it drew together faculty from diverse areas in the social sciences. More important, it acknowledged the college's responsibility to furnish its undergraduates with a thorough grounding in the liberal arts. Thus, in terms of organization and purpose, it smoothed the way for the sort of generalist venture Erskine had in mind. What is more, the sense that the war had imperiled the heritage of the West and revealed the human capacity for evil made educators wonder, as one of them wrote, "whether colleges actually did make students more fit to live the life of thoughtful and effective citizens" and "to enjoy the fruits of the [human] spirit."[55]

Hence, when Erskine renewed his request to act on his idea, it was in a climate modified by precedent and enough of a change in atmosphere to win him the necessary permission. Offered in 1920 as, ironically, an elective under the rubric "General Honors," and telescoped into a single interdisciplinary seminar, the course otherwise followed Erskine's design for the next nine years. In 1934, after a brief hiatus, it was reconstituted as "Colloquium on Important Books" and offered in that form well into the 1950s. Drawing once more on Erskine's innovation, Columbia also created a lower-level humanities course in 1937 which still survives today. As is well known, other institutions, notably the University of Chicago, Harvard, and Yale, subsequently devised similar programs in "General Education"—sometimes claiming to have invented them—but Erskine's role in preparing the ground for those efforts is indisputable.[56]

As an ideology of reading, Erskine's approach to "great books" moved beyond pedagogy and curriculum to address both his own emotional requirements and the priorities of an expanding consumer culture. Most significant, perhaps, Erskine's modification of Woodberry's outlook increased the extent to which reading the classics became an instrument of self-creation, by means that might be described as both centripetal and centrifugal. That is, on the one hand, Erskine's approach drew in toward individual readers' abilities and prerogatives that threatened to drift away from their control. In much the same way Sherman's reportorial stance reassigned authority from critic to audience, the primacy Erskine accorded the encounter with the text affirmed the ordinary person's capacity to understand literature. His basic message, like Woodberry's, was to trust one's own responses, or, as he put it in an unpublished manuscript that was to have introduced an **"Outline of Great Books,"** to "get yourself a comfortable chair and a good light—and have confidence in your own mind." In a situation "unmediated" by expertise, to borrow William James's word, readers would release their "zest" and "energy," qualities which would transform literary interpretation from a passive, mechanical process into one that was "human, natural, and direct." Thus, they would obtain "training in the acquisition of experience."[57] Those phrases, too, bolstered the self by arrogating more power to the individual.

On the other hand, those who delved in "great books" would, in Erskine's resonant phrase, "free [them]selves from the prison of egotism" and take part "in the complete citizenship of mankind."[58] Woodberry's emphasis on the universality of the classics had mapped that escape route from spiritual isolation, but Erskine actually embarked on it by specifying a particular body of literature which promised to create a visible community. To locate one's own reactions in a pattern—to recognize, for example, that Hamlet's tragedy was compelling to Elizabethans and New Yorkers alike—was to augment the self by spinning it outward. In this respect, reading "great books" carried out the recommendations of **"The**

Moral Obligation to be Intelligent" for self-discovery through a perception of "infinite order." Similarly, Erskine's hope, with regard to the curricular version of "great books," that the weekly discussion session would give students the basis for fellowship outside the classroom invested the meeting with the capacity to create not merely Woodberry's diffuse "community of the soul" but a real group of people who shared insights and interests. As Erskine later reflected, "Here would be, I believed, the true scholarly and cultural basis for human understanding and communication."[59]

Thus, Erskine's ideology encompassed self-transcendence as well as greater individualism. To shift the metaphor from modern to ancient science, it was as if Erskine imagined reading the classics as a kind of mental alchemy, whereby the reader's ample but leaden memories and feelings fused with the "golden accomplishments of the race" to produce a more complete person, one endowed with a richer understanding of life and a heightened ability to enjoy it.[60]

It is important to see that, for Erskine, that process functioned to intensify experience by adhering to a model of the self predicated on autonomy and (even though Erskine himself had devalued the word) reflective of character. If the self required more refurbishment than Woodberry had believed, it was in order to realize that ideal rather than to discard it in favor of cultivating personality. As Erskine explained in *The Delight of Great Books*, with respect to the merits of reading Sir Walter Scott: "To be steeped in his books, to be on familiar terms with the noble men and women who dwell in them, to share their courage, their zest in life, their self-reliance, their intellectual sincerity, until their outlook on life becomes our own—this would be a good protection against most of the romances which to-day it is our frailty rather than our fate to read, and against those social cure-alls which still offer to make us good and happy at low cost, with just a little rearranging of the environment."[61] In his invocation of self-reliance, his disparaging allusion to ease, and his moralistic expectations of literature, Erskine remained an heir of Emerson and Norton and a colleague of Canby and Fisher. Elsewhere, referring to the lessons of Aristotle, Erskine coupled "study" and "self-discipline" to his earlier preoccupation with "intelligence," urging that individuals apply those virtues to an examination of the wisdom of the past so as to "control" the "eternal forces of life."[62]

Similarly, to extrapolate from his later writings, even Erskine's expectation that readers would explore books socially rested on an ideal of "conversation" that owed more to Emerson than to Dale Carnegie. Although the term necessarily encompassed an element of public performance, nineteenth-century authors had typically defined that performance in terms of the revelation of inward "nobility." Surrounding "conversation" with stringent limits, they had attached restraint and lack of "egotism" to an encounter which supposedly had no goal larger than the exchange of ideas.[63] Erskine's own notion of conversational skill perpetuated those assumptions. At a time when other writers on the subject connected "conversation" with "self-assertion" and the arousal of "attraction" in order "to create an impression on the other man for social, business, or other purposes," Erskine counseled otherwise. "Conversation," he proposed, "aims at entertainment which subtly enlightens." Attainable "only so long as we remain unselfish," its "first rule" is that "all voices must be kept subdued. . . . [It is] suitable for groups which are sophisticated, thoughtful and refined." Read back into Erskine's "great books" design, such language suggests that even the features of his plan that involved intellectual display remained tied to the conservation of inner resources, contradicting the imperative to win approval by donning a series of "masks."[64]

Erskine's affirmation of autonomy made him more assured and less alienated than the figures who despaired, with Howells, that the self lacked a center. (Similarly, Erskine never concluded that Protestantism was vapid and insubstantial; rather, he sustained his childhood faith throughout his life, becoming a vestryman of Trinity Church in 1916.) Yet, drawing on that part of the Emersonian legacy that celebrated growth and self-transcendence, Erskine also invested his "great books" ideology with other possibilities. His emphasis on the release of "energy" perpetuated Woodberry's attraction to therapeutic modes of self-realization. More important, Erskine's identification with the literature of earlier eras offered not merely an escape from egotism into an ultimately ego-strengthening awareness of one's part in a well-ordered human drama but also the opposite outcome: the *loss* of autonomy. By reading "great books," one might surrender to the past so completely—drown in experience so enveloping—that the self ceased to exist as a separate entity. Such impulses, present in some "anti-modernists," gave Erskine an affinity with literary modernism as well—that is, with the very texts he rejected for inclusion in his "great books" list. It was that prospect of the "continual extinction of personality," for example, that T. S. Eliot welcomed in elevating "tradition" over the "individual talent." By seeking, along with self-reliance, what Daniel Bell has called the annihilation of "finitude," Erskine thus reflected "the deepest nature of modern man."[65]

To recognize those competing views of the self in Erskine's "great books" ideology is to see his effort at canon formation not as the expression of immutable, self-evident principles but, instead, as in part a projection of the psychic tensions his historical circumstances generated. In the pliability of his outlook, one feels the inexorable weight of Erskine's own history: his genteel background and loyalties, his impatience with genteel restraints, his persistent effort—fully but only temporarily realized in France—to accommodate and conjoin both attitudes.

At the same time, Erskine's approach to "great books" supplied a comforting answer to the question of whether

American consumer culture could sustain an adequate measure of "civilization." T. S. Eliot's directive that writers embrace "tradition" was feasible only if the historical record revealed that one existed. Both before and after World War I, as part of his attack on gentility, Van Wyck Brooks was among the loudest voices insisting that, in the United States, it emphatically did not. As Brooks observed in a well-known passage from "America's Coming-of-Age" (1915), American writers had no "genial middle ground of human tradition" on which to stand.[66] Although one might assume, because Brooks and Bourne together belonged to the Seven Arts coterie, that Erskine was the "ancient enemy" of both men, his postwar essays on American tradition so resembled Brooks's prewar efforts that they confound Bourne's determination to place his antagonist entirely outside the circle in which he traveled. In fact, Erskine's analysis seems derivative of Brooks's. His service in Europe had attuned him to the French reverence "for art, for scholarship, and for civilization." By contrast, Americans, having been uprooted from their original homes, lived without a life of the spirit, a sense of the "soil," or an awareness of cultural continuity. Erskine diagnosed the "cult of the contemporary" among his fellow literary critics as one symptom of that deprivation, but present-mindedness was pervasive. Emerson, Erskine's implicit model in other respects, was as guilty of it ("Why should we grope among the dry bones of the past?") as the pragmatists, whom, in this context, Erskine blamed for undermining tradition by rejecting the notion of unvarying truth.[67]

The American's disregard for history had devastating consequences for what Erskine called "taste." His statement of that conviction is worth quoting at length because it illuminates his relationship both to Brooks and company and to later figures who answered those writers' charges:

> The larger fabric of language, the racial memories to which an old country can always appeal, obviously do not exist in a land where every man is busy forgetting his past. . . . Without tradition there can be no taste, and what is worse, there can be little for taste to act upon. We have indeed some approaches, some faint hints and suggestions of a national poetry. The cartoon figure of Uncle Sam, for example, a great poet could perhaps push over into the world of art, but unless the poet soon arrives there will be few Americans left who can recognize in that gaunt figure the first Yankee, the keen, witty, audacious, and slightly melancholy type of our countrymen as they first emerged in world history.[68]

That gloomy assessment confirmed the fear that the United States would never achieve anything close to "civilization"; it implied that the nation seemed doomed to remain a bastion of clever but vulgar entrepreneurs.

Yet Brooks, Erskine, and others who addressed that prospect also provided various formulas for averting it.

Brooks (along with other cultural radicals) resolved the issue of whether tradition and consumer culture could coexist by freely conceding that the two were incompatible. They argued, instead, that true "civilization" could arise only when Americans shook off both their preoccupation with moneymaking and their loyalty to an Arnoldian insistence on "the best" in Western thought. In "Letters and Leadership" (1918), Brooks, echoing a complaint of Bourne's about "this tyranny of the 'best,'" claimed that Arnold's doctrine had permitted Americans to evade creating their own literature; it "conventionalized for them the spiritual experience of humanity, pigeon-holing it, as it were, and leaving them fancy-free to live 'for practical purposes.'" Harold Stearns, taking up the same cry, declared, "Whatever else American civilization is, it is not Anglo-Saxon." Instead, Brooks and Stearns alike placed their hopes in the creation of an American aesthetic heritage once a process of self-scrutiny had cleared away the debris of materialism.[69] Another response—that of Constance Rourke—proceeded from a similar view of America's distinctiveness but had no quarrel with the nation's practical bent. In fact, Rourke claimed, that trait had shaped an abundant basis for a unique "civilization" that only awaited discovery. Like Erskine, Rourke understood the artistic possibilities buried in the image of Uncle Sam but demonstrated that "great poets" had already arrived to incorporate that figure into their work.[70]

Erskine's approach to the reading of "great books" assuaged the same anxieties in a still different manner—one which did justify Bourne's sense of the disparity between himself and his "intellectual bete noire." His solution was simple and elegant. At exactly the moment Brooks issued "Letters and Leadership," Erskine reiterated the importance of heeding the standards Arnold had set. Moreover, instead of regarding America as exceptional, he asserted the continuity of American and European culture. Specifically, by contending that "great books" portrayed timeless, universal human situations, he permitted the conclusion that the classics of Western literature *were* the American heritage. That is, if Americans were really Romans under the skin, if they shared the same hopes and tragedies as Chaucer's pilgrims or Tennyson's knights—and if, to reverse the equation, the Greeks were like middle-class businessmen—then the troubling question of how America could reconcile art and materialism rested on a false dichotomy. All that was necessary (as Rourke also maintained) was that Americans possess the traditions that were already there. Erskine's translation of classical plots into modern language ("'Do you really mean,' [Lancelot] asks, 'that you want me to go back to my country and there marry somebody?'"), a technique he later perfected in his novels, not only fostered the self-transcendence described earlier but facilitated that comforting conflation of the United States and Europe.[71] So did Erskine's deliberate rejection of historical understanding as a prerequisite for critical insight. Without the bothersome intrusion of variations in time and place, Americans were free to see their own world as consonant with previous societies—and thus a "civilization" in its own right.

Erskine's vernacular style and ahistorical posture also helped him to carry out the Arnoldian mission of making tradition accessible to a wide audience. By presenting the classics in modern dress, and by emphasizing the primacy of feelings rather than training, Erskine assured his readers that culture was readily at hand. His description of the "great books" course as a setting for "intimate discussion," a phrase connoting warmth and easy exchange, rendered the encounter unintimidating and demanding of no special skills.[72] A similar sense of accessibility resulted from his insistence on minimizing the role of the literary expert. At the same time, his willingness to *function* as an expert—to tell readers which books were classics—alleviated the effects of expanded book production and the specialization of knowledge in much the same way the Book-of-the-Month Club board did. Although he was never dogmatic about the titles he included, his designation of writings ranging from Aristotle to Tolstoy as "great" brought a similarity and continuity to works which had in common neither form nor subject matter nor provenance. By amalgamating them in a single, ostensibly definitive list, Erskine added another dimension to the relationship between tradition and order—not the "infinite order" here, or even the abstract organizing principles Woodberry provided, but a palpable end to intellectual chaos.

As was true for his vision of the self, the primary effect of Erskine's depiction of the vitality and accessibility of the Western tradition was to carry Arnoldian values forward well into the twentieth century. Yet Erskine's reconciliation of a consumer culture with the ideal of "civilization" was as much capable of fortifying the former as of reinvigorating the latter. It was not simply that Erskine made his audience comfortable with their middle-class aspirations, thereby bolstering the self-congratulatory mood of the 1920s, although that was a large part of the story. Nor was it merely, as Brooks had so accurately understood, that in constructing a list of "great books" Erskine had assembled a ready-made tradition that conserved the American's time and energy for business. It was also that the list, by substituting information for aesthetics, once again increased the temptation to regard culture as a commodity. Two publishing ventures facilitated that outcome: the American Library Association's distribution in 1927, 1934, and 1935 of editions of the list as *Classics of the Western World* and the Encyclopedia Britannica's 1952 marketing of *Great Books of the Western World,* a set which Dwight Macdonald, making the same point, described in a review as "a hundred pounds of Great Books."[73]

Moreover, as Macdonald also noted, the phrase "great books," although underplayed in the initial course design and, in any event, hardly Erskine's invention, melded all too well with the propensity of advertisers to sell a product by touting it as "famous" or linking it to the testimonials of celebrities. To draw an analogy to another phenomenon of the early twentieth century, billing books as "great" could function as a literary equivalent of the star system, thrusting certain works into the spotlight as objects of pursuit and adulation on the basis of image and reputation alone. Likewise, however tightly Erskine himself clung to a different model, the social setting he devised was capable of absorbing a redefinition of conversation as an aid in winning "poise, charm, personality." Although he hardly meant to foster exchanges on the order of "Read any good books lately?," the fact that a 1936 conversation manual described Greek symposia as models of self-assertion is a reminder that Erskine's forum could serve the same end.[74]

The potential for accommodating that shift away from genteel premises was present as far back as Erskine's 1916 course proposal, which referred to furnishing "the average student with a body of cultural information, by requiring him to read certain famous books." Nevertheless, such implications, it should be stressed, were paradoxical in view of Erskine's avowed purposes. His recasting of the classics as recent publications fed the very "cult of the contemporary" he intended his advocacy of tradition to combat; the connotations of "great" undermined his attack on the proclivity of the modern magazine to be "a medium not for literature but for advertising," buying "reputations rather than writings." He also deplored the "journalistic tendency" in current books. Yet, despite his intentions, the headline introducing Erskine's *Delineator* articles revealed how susceptible his stance was to a radical revaluation of the nature and object of reading the classics. The banner proclaimed "There's Fun in Famous Books." This was a kind of literary "invasion of the body snatchers," in which the spirit of consumer culture appropriated the soul of the Arnoldian aesthetic, leaving only its outward form intact.[75]

The entanglements of genteel and consumer values in Erskine's understanding of both self and culture suggest an interpretation of the "great books" ideology, at least in its initial formulation, different from the one historians have customarily proposed in writing about its later manifestations. Its essence lay not in a one-sided assault on the dangers mass society and the fact-finding ethos of science posed to the preeminence of the refined individual, but rather in its capacity to provide familiar touchstones (self-reliance, character, Western civilization) in a changing world, while assenting to heightened demands for information, social performance, and personal growth.[76]

The debate today over the insistence of Allan Bloom and others on restricting the canon of "great books" to works by white men of European descent also makes it important to note a similar doubleness in the political ramifications of Erskine's program. Even more than Sherman and Canby, perhaps, Erskine was vulnerable to charges of elitism. To the extent that, as an academic curriculum, his plan challenged the elective system, it constituted, in Trilling's words, "a fundamental criticism of American democratic education." That is, while specialization could be construed as a type of democratization because it substituted diverse routes to education for a single body of knowledge, Erskine's innovation signaled a return to a less egalitarian policy: a fixed syllabus, handed down by the faculty and recommended for everyone regardless of aptitude, background, or vocational plans—to say nothing of gender, race, class, or ethnicity.[77]

Additionally, Erskine's assertion that immigrants ought to become familiar with "great books" barely concealed his dismay that they and their children comprised a rapidly increasing percentage of undergraduates in the postwar period. He had written to his mother in 1918, "When I see these boys [at Beaune] and realize that of the students at Columbia, many are those selfish immigrants who don't want to do anything for America, I feel as though I ought to stay here and work for the soldiers." In subsequently urging that "we [not] refuse to assume responsibility for the making of the foreign elements in the United States into a unified nation," lest we suffer the "ignorance, the disease and the discontent which in various ways menace our society," Erskine spoke as a Weehawken Episcopalian trying to keep the Union Hill workers within bounds. Thus, he made tradition serve order in one final respect: more urgently and explicitly than Woodberry, but along lines he had laid out, Erskine employed it to dispel the threat of class conflict and social disarray. "Great books" can be considered a type of "Americanization" program, with all of the antidemocratic characteristics associated with the term: the reassertion of white Anglo-Saxon Protestant superiority, the fear that foreigners (and, in the Columbia case, particularly Jews) would undermine that superiority, and the insistence that immigrants become acculturated to an existing white middle-class mold.[78]

Yet Erskine's conscious political commitments must not be discounted. Like the Progressives to whom his interest in "Americanization" connects him, Erskine sought order in the name of preserving democracy. At least publicly, beginning in 1919 and throughout the 1920s, he urged the university to open its doors to all members of American society. That position, which ran counter to a contemporary outcry against "mass education," impelled Erskine to take a more tolerant view of the curriculum than his emphasis on the centrality of "great books" might imply. If he advocated a return to a core of humanistic study, he also urged the university's collateral involvement in providing whatever technical or other training its constituency wanted. His worry was less that the academy might become an "'intellectual department store,'" a situation he actually welcomed, than that it might undervalue the abilities of its customers by failing to expose them to the "beauty" they were capable of perceiving. With respect to the "great books" design itself, moreover, his belief in the "resumption" of the "powers that for a while we delegated to the expert" may be seen, from one vantage point, as radically democratic.[79] The same is true of his equation of "greatness" with the ability of a book to tap every person's potential for exploring a shared human condition.

As the *New Republic* noted in a 1922 editorial on "The American College," the "abandonment of the aristocratic ideal [of culture] in fact brought about a great increase in the number of students able to enter college, while the retention of the ideal in name constituted a powerful inducement to them to do so. The college became one of those democratic institutions . . . whose function seemed to be to give exclusiveness to the masses."[80] Erskine's ambivalent political orientation meant that his "great books" idea could serve that purpose as well. Both within and outside of the classroom, his plan promised to deal equally well with two contradictory problems: how to shore up a shaky social structure and how to crack that structure to obtain, by firmly established means, a share of knowledge and prestige.

From Troy to Hollywood

Until the mid-1920s Erskine carried out the multiple mediations his "great books" scheme entailed largely behind the scenes and in an academic setting. Although he was a familiar name to lecture audiences and readers of the *Bookman, Outlook,* and *North American Review,* he exerted greatest influence in this period by teaching his "great books" course to a group of distinguished students, notably Mortimer Adler. In 1925, however, he moved to center stage by making his debut as a novelist.

Erskine's turn to fiction derived from several factors. Despite his pedagogical successes, Erskine was deeply troubled in the immediate postwar period. As Henry Morton Robinson observed, "Those who knew him between the fortieth and forty-fifth years of his life [1919-24] realized that he was undergoing a severe emotional crisis." Some of his distress arose from his relationship to the university. The implementation of "great books" at Columbia had not silenced his detractors on the faculty nor had it managed to undo the trend toward specialization. Feeling overworked and underappreciated, especially by Butler, he began to question once more the nature of his vocation. Robinson contended, moreover, that Erskine suffered from the suppression of the creative needs he had left unfulfilled in abandoning his career as a poet. Given Erskine's recurring preoccupation with self-reliance and experience, one might rephrase Robinson's perception in somewhat different terms: that Erskine's impulse to escape from genteel inhibitions and restore his wartime sense of wholeness and freedom was stronger than his ideology of reading could satisfy. His repressive marriage, now lacking any "decent friendship" and strained almost to the breaking point, added another element to his desire for release.[81]

In consequence, Erskine's interest slackened in his scholarly research project, a biography and anthology of Milton for which Bobbs-Merrill had contracted in 1921. He found one creative outlet by resuming the study of the piano, playing five or six hours a day in the summer of 1924 to prepare for his first public symphonic concert that August. Erskine's own description of that effort as a "crash[ing] through the barriers to expression in music" suggests the psychological function the performance served—the fundamental barrier having been, one recalls, his mother's restraint on his youthful ambitions.[82] He continued to play publicly until illness made it impossible.

That fall, however, he also discovered another form of expression when, prompted by a remark in the *Odyssey* and encouraged by a friend in the publishing business, he decided to write up his speculations about what happened when Menelaos took Helen home to Sparta after the Trojan War. The result was a novel, *The Private Life of Helen of Troy*, which he offered to Bobbs-Merrill in lieu of the Milton volume. Apart from extricating him from joyless scholarship, the fictional exercise enabled him to rebel against genteel attitudes by exploring a type of experience for which academic writing had been an inadequate vehicle: sex. In the novel, he portrayed Helen as unrepentant about having run off to Troy with Paris and anxious for her daughter Hermione to marry a man who exhibited the "love of life" she valued more than propriety. In overturning genteel morality, Erskine also removed classical figures from their pedestals. His aim, he later explained, was to make readers "see that Helen, instead of being a wicked villainness, was an almost conventional illustration of American life, even in the suburbs."[83] To that end, he sat the family across the dinner table from one another and spiced their dialogue with American colloquialisms. Many of the conversations counterposed Helen's wayward behavior to the steadfastness of the younger generation, a contrast that amusingly inverted the contemporaneous indictment of the flapper and other specimens of American youth. The combination of sex, topical interest, and iconoclasm gave the book a racy, urbane tone that helped to make it a stunning success. It was the best-selling American novel for 1926 and earned Erskine far wider recognition than had "great books" alone.

Much of that recognition took the shape of heralding Erskine's metamorphosis from sober professor to free spirit. The same *New Yorker* profile which described his heady reaction to World War I, for example, concluded that in the aftermath of war he relinquished a "Victorian" sensibility for a laudably less fettered, "more vulgar" point of view. In fact, to certain readers he was unrespectably unchained. Rabbi Stephen Wise attacked *Helen of Troy* in 1927 as "a bit of semi-Lombrosian Freudism [*sic*]," the "upshot" of which was "'go to it, young people; what you need is release; standards and self-respect are incompatibles.'"[84]

Those estimates, however, misgauged the extent of Erskine's transformation. It was true that the slick satire, sexual banter, and premium on shunning convention in *Helen of Troy* carried him much further away from gentility than had even the undercurrents in his "great books" design. Erskine himself saw writing the novel as a "liberation" that permitted him a "new development in sincerity."[85] His decision in 1926 to embark on a lengthy extramarital affair with a woman writer named Adelene Pynchon meant that the liberation spilled over into his personal life as well. Yet *The Private Life of Helen of Troy* was an updated version of an old tale not merely because it used ancient protagonists but also because it recapitulated many of the themes of Erskine's earlier career. The gimmick of endowing classical characters with the argot of the 1920s was essentially an embellishment of his premise that "great books" were contemporary literature; installing Helen in the suburbs was the logical extension of his belief that a common wellspring of feeling fed American and Greek civilizations. Moreover, in keeping with the maxim that there is no such thing as bad publicity, his irreverence toward the classics nonetheless kept them in the public eye, making Agamemnon, Clytemnestra, Orestes, and Menelaos household words to thousands of readers. As a painless expedition to ancient times, the book was less an assault on the past than a device for marketing it to an audience that wanted to combine culture and "fun." *The Private Life of Helen of Troy*, Erskine's student Clifton Fadiman noted, was popular because Americans between the wars relished the gentle mockery of hallowed figures—a pursuit very different from the wholesale rejection of them.[86]

Additionally, Erskine's sexual explorations, at least on paper, veered away from a genuine frankness toward the safety the classical plot provided; like a drapery covering a Greek statue, the placement of the action in the distant past made sexuality less immediate than in the work of writers like Fitzgerald or Dos Passos.[87] Nor, it almost goes without saying, did the structure and style of the novel come anywhere near the experimentations with form and language in which Erskine's avant-garde contemporaries were engaged. Thus, the book perfectly recapitulated the same tensions between competing sets of values that animated Erskine's role generally.

In the next few years, Erskine used the formula he had invented in *Helen of Troy* to produce novels featuring such characters as Galahad, Adam and Eve, and Tristan and Isolde, all of whom he made exemplify modern mores. Simultaneously, he published extensively on "great books," for a time turned out a monthly column for the *Century,* and wrote numerous other articles. The titles of some of these read like a catalogue of Emersonian virtues: **"Culture," "Taste," "Self-Reliance," "Integrity."** If it misinterpreted his development, the *New Yorker* caught his stance and outlook exactly when it pronounced him "instructor in genteel sophistication to the magazine readers of America." Erskine took a leave from Columbia in 1928 to embark on a nationwide lecture tour, speaking to admiring, overflow crowds on "the moral obligation to be intelligent" and on those classics he had adapted in writing fiction. Each performance ended with a piano recital, making the occasion a dramatic demonstration of his versatility—and, consequently, of the reassuring survival of the generalist. At the same time, one can see in Erskine's "elaborate show," as he called it, the display of personality his audiences sought to emulate. Newspapers, by his own account, began referring to him as "'the amazing Professor Erskine.'"[88]

Less enchanted, however, were his opponents within the university, several of whom now saw his novels as a further incursion against scholarship. As a result, even though he was being mentioned as a possible successor to Butler, with some misgivings he indefinitely extended his leave from Columbia at the end of the 1928 tour.[89] That summer he accepted an invitation to become the first president of the newly reorganized Juilliard School of Music. Erskine brought to that position not only his own musical talents but also the administrative skills he had developed at Beaune. In addition, his high profile and the institution's importance to New York's social and cultural scene worked to mutual advantage: Erskine was an ideal fund-raiser, and the Juilliard a good berth for someone who thrived on public trust. His philosophy as president paralleled the one he had voiced with reference to "great books." Music, he thought, ought to be accessible to and comprehensible by a broad audience, the training of which in listening and performing was as much a part of Juilliard's responsibilities as the cultivation of virtuosos.[90] That commitment to the popularization of music as well as literature drove him, beginning in the late 1920s, to speak and write on behalf of the musical amateur and, in 1935, to edit an American version of what was essentially a British "outline" book, *A Musical Companion*.

By 1930 Erskine had thus followed Sherman and Canby in adeptly reconstituting his authority outside the university. Subsequently, he added frequent radio appearances to his busy lecture schedule. Nevertheless, he continued to have difficulty sustaining in his personal life the equilibrium he achieved in his public stance. Echoing Robinson's observation about Erskine earlier in the decade, a tantalizing letter from Pynchon alludes to his "mental struggles between 1926 and 1931." Pynchon's remark may refer solely to Erskine's turbulent dealings with Columbia and with his wife, from whom he separated in 1927. Yet certain of his writings—notably the ones in which he abandoned the contrivance of the modernized ancient milieu—indicate that something else was going on: they convey a persistent anxiety about constructing a unified self. For example, his novel *Unfinished Business* (1931) featured a hero, Dick Ormer, who, at his death, is troubled by a number of unfulfilled intentions. In a fantasy that would seem an obvious representation of Erskine's own urge to join thought and behavior, Ormer, at the Golden Gates, receives a second chance at achieving a sense of integrity. Returning to earth, he revives a scheme to swindle his partner and almost rekindles a romance with a friend's wife. Afterward he reports to Saint Peter, who reiterates the lesson that, while the road to hell is paved with good intentions, completed plans—even immoral ones—mark the way to heaven. That theme, foreshadowed in Helen of Troy's injunction to live fully, and repeated in Erskine's other novels, reflected the same agitated concern with self-actualization that formed the basis for the Book-of-the-Month Club marketing campaign. It suggests that Erskine's expression in the various aspects of his career of his need to conjoin autonomy and intense

experience led him only to a kind of emotional halfway house, from which he was unable to go either forward or back to a stable psychic resting place.[91]

Erskine's personal history in the 1930s and 1940s supports that hypothesis. His involvement with Helen Worden, a lively, accomplished, yet conventionally "feminine" journalist whom he met in 1931 and married after finally obtaining a divorce in 1946, offset a good deal of his malaise, so much so that some of his old friends credited the relationship with turning him into a new person. Yet he still suffered from a sense of disappointment in himself and relied on Worden for "strength and hope." Then, while on a lecture tour late in 1935, he was seriously injured in an automobile collision, suffering multiple fractures. The accident elevated his mood of self-reproach about his shortcomings.[92] Although he taught himself to play again, it also deprived him of his former agility at the piano. Faced with enormous medical bills and short of assets because of losses in the stock market crash, Erskine spent the next several months recuperating, running Juilliard, and churning out essays and fiction. One of those pieces, a vitriolic book entitled *The Influence of Women—and Its Cure*, provides the best evidence that he held women primarily accountable for genteel repression. Depicting them as parasitic and manipulative, he accused the majority of middle-class women of denying sex, side-stepping evil, reducing religion to a drug, and emasculating the fine arts—all of which might be regarded as crimes against experience.[93] One does not have to push psychology very far to see in that portrait an alternative view of the mother he remembered only in "flawless white."

In February 1937, just over a year after the accident, Erskine suffered a stroke that paralyzed his right side. Interestingly, although he might plausibly have attributed the illness to residual effects from his skull fracture, he consistently described it as a "complete crack-up of nerves" or nervous breakdown. The reason for the collapse, Erskine thought, was exhaustion from overwork. Indeed, the previous December he had announced his decision to resign the Juilliard presidency, purportedly in order to free more time for writing. Yet Erskine's own disposition to ascribe his condition to emotional causes makes it tempting to interpret the episode as at least a metaphor for, if not the direct result of, a different kind of exhaustion: the ebbing of the psychic energy he had expended for so long in both sustaining and rebelling against genteel expectations.[94]

In any event, the illness signaled the beginning of a period of Erskine's life in which the manifestations of that struggle were particularly poignant. As the discussion below will explore, his association with "great books" diminished in inverse proportion to Mortimer Adler and Robert M. Hutchins's affiliation with the idea. Moreover, on the heels of his departure from Juilliard came an unsolicited and unwelcome letter from Butler designating him emeritus professor at Columbia. Adrift from both institutions, he floundered, in part because he needed to find other sources of income but also, one suspects, because (in the Columbia case) he had lost the connection which, even though attenuated after 1927, had furnished a context against which he had defined himself. As Trilling observed, although Erskine thought the university did "nothing but check and hamper him," it "served him better than he knew," providing him with "the antagonists he needed and the subjects and the disputes that brought out his strength." To a former colleague, he admitted "a constant yearning to be teaching again."[95] More than once, he considered trying to reanchor himself at Juilliard, but a financially acceptable offer was not forthcoming. As his paralysis abated, he resumed a heavy schedule of lectures, radio broadcasts, and writing, thereby sustaining his public role. (One of his activities in 1938 was a column on "men's furnishings" for a periodical called *Heywood Broun's Nutmeg.*) Some of his novels which today appear to have few redeeming features won surprising acclaim. After ten years, however, Erskine's formula had lost some of its sparkle, and even his best-received efforts also incurred judgments like "inconsequential" and "harmless but irrelevant."[96] Thus, having chosen to stake his identity largely on his literary endeavors, Erskine had then to contend with the limitations of his talent.

Overshadowed on the educational front and fading as a novelist, Erskine turned to an additional locus for his activities: Hollywood. He spent six weeks there in 1939 as master of ceremonies for a radio variety show that included performances by the Marx Brothers. On the same trip, he gathered material for a series his friend Fulton Oursler, the editor of *Liberty,* had commissioned. He returned in the early 1940s to do other articles and to discuss adapting some of his novels to the screen. Helen Worden even thought he might construct a more permanent relationship with the film industry by succeeding Will Hays as overseer of movie morals. However comic the juxtaposition of Erskine and Groucho, the idea that they should meet is not altogether startling. Rather, in that scenario one might see the culmination of Erskine's tendency to embrace the culture of personality by facilitating literary stardom. It was a fairly short step, after all, from Helen of Troy's "private life" to **"Clark Gable's Secret Wish."** Yet, his fascination with celebrity notwithstanding, Erskine's encounter with Hollywood appears strained and almost pathetic. Never really comfortable with glitter, he moved about sets and stars' residences unable to shake off his Weehawken background. Distinguishing between a "screen star" and a "good actress," his *Liberty* series blamed the star system's premium on "personality" for lowering the quality of American films by requiring performers to stick to type. He thereby merely transferred an Arnoldian preoccupation with upholding standards from one art form to another.[97]

In the same period, Erskine also issued his fullest statement of his own philosophy, *The Complete Life* (1943). As a compendium of advice not only on "great books" but also on such topics as gardening, cooksing, raising children, music, and art, the volume was a generalist's bible. Within that framework, Erskine's characteristic themes of experience and autonomy reasserted themselves. In the opening pages, he allied himself with an active, rather than a contemplative, life, explicitly contrasting "experience and the sideline attitude toward experience" and arguing for the former. Even more than his ideology of reading, *The Complete Life* bore traces of a therapeutic orientation: the "self-development" Erskine had in mind here contained only oblique references to the fulfillment of social or moral obligations and made growth its own reward. Yet one has only to compare the book to a contemporary advice manual such as Wiggam's *The Marks of an Educated Man* to appreciate the degree to which Erskine once again marshaled experience in the service of genteel commitments. Whereas Wiggam's concept of cultivation boiled down to mastering a series of mental "habits" that would insure practical success, Erskine's concern was with a program of study that would, echoing Emerson, increase the "power" of individuals to develop their "natural capacities." Distinguishing among opinions, information, and knowledge, Erskine urged the acquisition of the latter, although its attainment exacted "pain," because it alone derived from self-reliance. The conclusion of *The Complete Life* held out as a model an admittedly "old fashioned" conceit: the "self-made man," whose independence, genuineness, devotion to learning, and sense of responsibility for his own well-being firmly rooted him—and Erskine—in the values of an earlier age. Reviewers of the book unwittingly highlighted its anachronistic quality—its remoteness from the culture of personality—by expressing their wish that Erskine had written an autobiography instead.[98]

Nonetheless, Erskine's very preoccupation with completeness suggests the enduring incapacity of that older model to extinguish his own impulses toward a more vigorous version of experience, while it simultaneously prevented him from acting on them. As one examines his last years, the evidence of his divided sensibility mounts. He eventually produced not one autobiography but four, the titles of which are highly revealing. *My Life as a Teacher* (1948), *My Life in Music* (1950), and **"My Life in Literature"** (unfinished) are, taken together, a graphic representation of a fragmented (if impressively diverse) career; *The Memory of Certain Persons*, while playing to a curiosity about personality, kept the focus on others, as if to place a safe distance between his day-to-day encounters and an inner "boiler" that, like his father's and uncle's, remained hidden from sight. His letters to Worden, touching in their expression of the love and devotion he found with her, are likewise so utterly devoid of any antagonism that they point to the same buried repository of feeling, as does Worden's remark that she learned early in her marriage to Erskine never to criticize him.[99] Within *The Memory of Certain Persons*, Erskine's brand of "middleness" rose to the surface in the passages about Weehawken and Union Hill, Woodberry and Butler. Finally, always and pervasively at this time, there was the dream of

Beaune—the lengthy reminiscences, the clutching of photographs and plane tickets, the actual return in 1950 under the great hardship of a second stroke—in the hope of recovering the "peace" that, one senses, his awareness of disunity obstructed.

Adler, Hutchins, and "Great Books"

By that time, Erskine's student Mortimer Adler had reshaped his teacher's lessons to fit his own concerns. Although Adler's emergence as a popularizer occurred on the chronological margins of this study, the size of his following after 1945 demands a brief analysis of the ways in which he transformed Erskine's ideas. The process of appropriation had begun in 1921, when Adler took "General Honors" with Erskine. (Two years later, together with coleader Mark Van Doren, Adler in turn taught Clifton Fadiman.)[100] In 1926 Adler approached Scott Buchanan, a Columbia teaching fellow and assistant director of the People's Institute, a program of adult education based at Cooper Union, about the feasibility of offering "great books" seminars to the community. That fall, Adler, Fadiman, Buchanan, Richard McKeon (another Columbia instructor), and eight others led six groups modeled on "General Honors" for 134 participants.[101]

Erskine was only peripherally involved in the People's Institute undertaking—the group leaders consulted him occasionally—and was rather quickly alienated, it seems, from Adler's enthusiasms. Part of the reason for Erskine's detachment was that he and Adler were so utterly different temperamentally: Erskine, the reserved Trinity Church vestryman, must have seen in the zealous Adler, whom Fadiman dubbed a "lay Yeshiva *bucher,*" the realization of many of the fears that had impelled him to embrace "great books" in the first place.[102] The next year, when the community experiment expanded and, in response, the American Library Association brought out their "great books" list, Erskine did agree to supply an introduction to it. From that point on, however, except for a short collaboration in the mid-1940s, Adler and Erskine went their separate ways.

Thanks to a grant from the Carnegie Corporation, the People's Institute venture lasted until 1928, Adler inheriting Buchanan's job. As if to accentuate both the democratic and elitist potentialities inherent in Erskine's approach, Whittaker Chambers, already a member of the Communist party, ran a group with Adler; Fadiman, en route to a brief flirtation with the party himself, likewise attributed part of the leaders' motivation to a somewhat "starry-eyed" desire to bring culture to "ordinary people." Adler, by contrast, expressed a contempt for the popularization of knowledge which, by his own later admission, did not square with either the conception of the institute or his actual activities as a popularizer.[103] In keeping with that view, Adler soon retreated from his foray into the community. Instead, in October of 1929 he described his experiences as Erskine's disciple to Robert M. Hutchins, newly appointed president of the University of Chicago; Hutchins reacted by adding Adler to his faculty.

For the next decade, Adler's activities were less an aspect of the popularization of knowledge than of innovation within the academy. He and Hutchins implemented a "General Honors" seminar at Chicago in 1930, went on to reorganize the first two years of college studies around general education courses, and, between 1936 and 1942, sought to replace the entire undergraduate curriculum with "great books" courses rooted in the classical trivium and quadrivium. Those reforms, as Mark Van Doren pointed out, were "in one sense only an extension" of Erskine's because they rested on his premise that "great books are the best teachers." As such, they replicated the weekly "unmediated" discussion format he had devised as well as the use of two Socratic instructors with divergent outlooks. Adler also preserved his mentor's animus toward specialization, adopting Erskine's policy of proceeding like "debonair amateurs." Similarly, the Chicago version of "great books" retained Erskine's insistence on the centrality of the text and, concomitantly, the superfluousness of secondary sources; like the Columbia one, it measured "greatness" as the ability to remain accessible to contemporary readers. What is more, some of Hutchins's language bespeaks an unacknowledged debt to Erskine: his repudiation of "character" in favor of "intellect" recalls Erskine's paean to intelligence, while his similar rejection of "personality" echoes the dominant element in Erskine's vision of the self.[104]

Yet Hutchins and Adler, by transforming Columbia's single course into a comprehensive "Chicago Plan," launched a more sweeping assault on the elective system than Erskine had. Moreover, they made philosophy, rather than literature, the heart of their enterprise and went even further in formalizing what had been, back in Woodberry's time, a perspective rather than a system. Thus, paradoxically, they fostered their own brand of specialization. When they argued that only logic and metaphysics based on the teachings of Aristotle and Aquinas constituted education, they accentuated the antidemocratic implications of Erskine's approach; when they castigated science as destructive to culture because it exalted facts rather than values, they withdrew whatever overtures Erskine had made to pragmatism by lobbying for "intelligence"; when Hutchins, correctly perceiving the anti-intellectual streak in Erskine's position, announced, "If we want to give our students experiences, we should go out of business" because the "place to get experiences is in life," he rescinded a central goal of Erskine's design.[105]

Those aspects of Hutchins and Adler's program provoked an outcry from colleagues who saw the two Chicago "great books" proponents as medievalist enemies of positivism, democracy, and modernity. The controversy remained largely intramural until the mid-1930s, but two events subsequently made it an object of wider attention. The first was the 1935 publication of Hutchins's *The Higher Learning in America,* which summarized his view that universities ought to prescribe a course of study ordered by metaphysical principles and employing as texts "the greatest books of the Western world." The book sold 8,500 copies and drew loud rebuttal from highly visible defenders of scientific method, vocational learning, and democratic culture, notably Alfred North Whitehead and John Dewey. The second was the establishment of St. John's College in Annapolis, Maryland, in 1937. There Adler's old friend Stringfellow Barr and his companion from the People's Institute, Scott Buchanan, presided over a curriculum which consisted solely of reading "great books." The novelty of the experiment caught the public eye; in consequence, Dewey and Hutchins's quarrel became the subject of stories in such magazines as *Fortune*. Hutchins's office began receiving a steady stream of moving requests for his book list, many from people who had never had a college education and now sought its equivalent.[106]

The effect of the Chicago-St. John's expansion and systematization of "great books" was to steal the show from Erskine. Hutchins, for example, never even mentioned him in *The Higher Learning* and rubbed salt in the wound by citing Butler's view of the classics instead. Furthermore, Erskine's own misgivings about the curriculum his former students advocated contributed to his dissociation from the movement he had started. On sufficiently good terms with Buchanan to receive an invitation to visit St. John's in 1938, he nonetheless expressed dismay at the college's attempt to "turn what was essentially a reading course into a Medieval substitute for the study of science and other non-literary subjects." Perhaps because his disaffection had hardened over time, his description in *The Memory of Certain Persons* of the Chicago and St. John's endeavors even more forcefully attested to his skepticism and bitterness; there he called them "aberrations" and declared that with them he had "no sympathy whatever."[107]

Adler, however, enjoying the fanfare, was immune to Erskine's criticism. When Simon and Schuster published his *How to Read a Book* in 1940, he carried his ideas to a general audience, thereby rededicating himself to the old People's Institute premise that the clientele for "great books" was larger than the undergraduate population.[108] Although Adler's abrasiveness adds some incongruity to the term, the values underlying that document were in certain respects as genteel as Erskine's. *How to Read a Book* defined "great books" as classics that could "elevate our spirit" by addressing timeless human problems. Its vision of the reading process stressed discipline, while an inchoate model of self-reliance lay beneath the surface of a chapter on the efficacy of self-help. Urging readers to pursue knowledge rather than information, it repudiated the aim of supplying a formula for "'brilliant' conversation."[109]

Yet those assumptions existed within a matrix of maxims and precepts that interfered with Adler's Arnoldian message. Beginning with its title, which presumed a right and a wrong way to tackle a text, the volume reflected a rigidity that differentiated Adler from Erskine; it enjoined readers to "obey the rules," piled up distinc-

tions (as between a "theoretical" and a "practical" book), and insisted that real reading entailed executing an elaborate sequence of fixed tasks. Even though Adler, with European fascism in mind, appended a conclusion exploring the connection between liberal education and intellectual freedom, his dictates so predominated that they largely appeared as ends in themselves. Moreover, Adler's system countermanded the genteel emphasis on aesthetics by collapsing in the face of art. As Adler readily conceded, his approach basically worked only for nonfiction. In effect, he thus relinquished to the literary modernists he disdained the genteel critic's mantle as conservator of aesthetic standards.[110]

In addition, *How to Read a Book* perpetuated and sharpened Adler's and Erskine's double-edged approach to democracy and authority. On the one hand, it registered the voice of the diffident expert. Reiterating the principle that the "great books" could be "read by every man," it depicted active readers who extracted a work's meaning with no more equipment than the text and the "power" of their own minds. On the other hand, it repeatedly portrayed "great books" classes as dramas in which deluded students, confident that they had understood the assignment, discovered that they could not answer Adler's questions and then admitted that perhaps they had not read the book after all. The effect of that conception was to enhance Adler's stature as guardian of privileged insights and to heighten the reader's nervousness about obtaining access to them.[111]

Thus, despite his explicit commitments, Adler's reduction of the reading process to the anxious mastery of a table of rules actually went beyond Erskine in feeding the predilection for equating culture with information and products; here the rules themselves became an additional commodity. Similarly, his elevation of Erskine's remarks about conversation into the notion of a "Great Conversation" among all the writers—and readers—of "great books" led him to couch many of his directives in terms of the etiquette of social performance. Some of Adler's overtures to consumer values were no doubt intentional: his title, for instance, enabled him to cash in on the popularity, in the same period, of Dale Carnegie's and others' contributions to the how-to genre. His multiple appeals worked: *How to Read a Book* topped the bestseller list when it came out and still remains in print.

In 1943 Adler renewed his pursuit of a large extracurricular following by forming a "great books" discussion seminar for prominent Chicago executives. The group, nicknamed the "Fat Man's" class, drew so much publicity that it sparked the formation of nationwide seminars totaling twenty thousand people by the end of 1946. During the next two years, that number rapidly increased fourfold, resulting in the establishment of a Great Books Foundation independent of the university to handle the surge of interest.[112]

Although no systematic studies of the members' motivations exist for this period, contemporary observers—and subsequent historians—ascribed the phenomenon to a quest for permanence and meaning in a world rendered transient and confusing by the Second World War. As was the case after 1917, Americans regarded with new appreciation the recently endangered heritage of Western civilization; they looked upon it, with relief and protective pride, as a source of "enduring truths." Even though issues of selfhood and experience had receded from Adler's rhetoric, the "great books" ideology of the late 1940s still offered Erskine's lingering promise of a self made whole through a connection to tradition. Certainly many students voiced the belief that "great books" classes provided them with "riches of the mind and heart" that they could not procure in the marketplace. Some also sought the groups' congeniality as an antidote to anonymity, finding comfort in the fact, as one promotional announcement stated, that here "you will meet your minister, banker, . . . grocery clerk, and your neighbors." Such language kept alive Erskine's communal vision and underscored his message about the accessibility of culture. It took advantage as well, one may speculate, of a nascent Cold War preoccupation with glorifying the democratic nature of American life (while it also nourished dreams of upward mobility by giving the "grocery clerk" entrée into the "banker's" milieu).[113]

These groups both fostered literature and immeasurably enriched the lives of some of their members. (The "great books" phenomenon and, in some cases, the original postwar groups still survive today.) Yet, while Adler's vigilant Aristotelianism makes the point a bit harder to see, in reality the community "great books" programs of the late 1940s were hardly the sanctuaries from the business world that some of their adherents called them. For one thing, the greater the dissemination of Adler's rules, the more dogmatic they became. A 1946 training manual asserted, for example, that "it is absolutely essential that all the participants face each other, and that they have a table of some sort in front of them to lean on."[114] Such standardization made it even easier to view Adler's technique as prefabricated culture, as the same manual's unabashed discussion of analyzing the "market" for the "product" attests. Given that phrasing, it is not surprising that Adler wound up hawking his program in a downtown Chicago department store in 1948.

Furthermore, for all the program's strengths, one might argue that, at its worst, with friends like these, literature needed no enemies. Some people joined groups, in one commentator's words, "to shine among one's fellows by a parade of new-found knowledge." More than that, Adler's disregard for aesthetics, together with the lack of context and persistent drive for relevance he adopted from Erskine, combined in some groups to engender a quality of superficiality that was at the furthest remove from the concept of culture as inward. In the absence of guidance and background, some groups degenerated into "a muddle of blind-alley arguments, profitless repetitions, irrelevant remarks, silly opinions, and fundamental misunderstandings." The "great books" advocates' rejoinder that the purpose of the undertaking was not to study works exhaustively but rather to improve one's "ability to communicate by learning how to read, speak, and listen more effectively"—objectives worthy of Dale Carnegie—only revealed the extent to which the community movement could fulfill the potential for strengthening consumer values evident in Erskine's initial design. One participant, an advertising man, took advantage of that consonance between his occupation and his reading group by providing his classmates with slogans about the assigned books: he "packaged" Aristotle's *Ethics,* for example, as "'The rich don't know how to live, but they sure know where.'"[115]

Adler and Hutchins's permutation of the "great books" idea culminated in 1952 with the publication of the Encyclopedia Britannica's fifty-four volume *Great Books of the Western World.* The idea for the project had originated with William Benton, the former advertising whiz who, as Hutchins's vice-president for public relations, had acquired the encyclopedia for the University of Chicago. Benton approached Adler in 1943 about thinking up a "special idea" to help sell a companion set of classics. Adler seized the opportunity to create his ultimate system: the Syntopicon, or "Great Ideas," an index to the texts organized according to the topics they addressed, so that a reader could, in theory, trace throughout Western history a continuous line of thought on almost three thousand subjects. The scheme additionally included introductory essays to each of the 102 chapters into which the topics fell. Theoretically a way to highlight the underlying unity of the "great conversation," the Syntopicon could also work at cross-purposes to that aim by splintering works into isolated quotations. Called a "device" and an "invention," the term itself had a technological ring that promised the ability to solve practical problems with little effort.[116]

If the Syntopicon put Adler's stamp on the set as a whole, his priorities largely determined the choice of the individual works within it as well. The story of the selection process is instructive as an instance of canon formation even more visibly reflective of special interests than Erskine's construction of the original "great books" list. Adler, Barr, and Buchanan formed the core of an advisory board over which Hutchins presided. Together, they settled on inviting Mark Van Doren and two Chicago faculty members, Clarence Faust and Joseph Schwab, to join them. It was at this point that Erskine reentered Adler's orbit: as an afterthought, they added him to the board.[117]

From the outset, the board members were in tacit agreement about four assumptions. First, they were no more willing than Erskine to acknowledge the contributions of modernism—a stance that by the late 1940s was more willful and deliberate than it had been before World War I. For example, in response to the suggestion of Wallace Brockway, the Britannica editor (on loan from Simon and Schuster) working with the board, Hutchins wrote of *Ulysses,* "It is a monument of Irish wit; but I am not sure that this justifies its inclusion."[118] Freud, it is true, finally made it onto the list, but, because he was a writer of nonfiction, his presence dodged the issue of acknowledging the modernist aesthetic. Second, the board made no departure from Adler's emphasis on philosophy at the expense of novels, plays, and poetry; aside from the Greeks and Shakespeare, just eleven of the set's seventy-four authors were represented by writings in those categories. Third, it understood at the outset that American authors would occupy little space, although Erskine and Van Doren did labor unsuccessfully for Franklin, Emerson, Whitman, and Thoreau. The only Americans published in the set were the Founding Fathers, Melville, and William James. (Needless to say, the issue of representing women or blacks did not arise.) Fourth, in sharp contrast to modernist critics, who, as David Hollinger has described them, facilitated the canonization of the works they championed by insisting that the values they stood for had to remain elusive and mysterious in order to survive, the board had no hesitation about collectively issuing the definitive judgments that Erskine and Adler had been pronouncing for years.[119] The group also assented to two additional principles that Adler made explicit: one, that, in keeping with Erskine's bias against mediation, the texts would stand without explanatory or scholarly apparatus; the other, that, unlike the "Five-Foot Shelf," the set would include only works in their entirety. Under no circumstances was it to resemble an anthology.[120]

With so much consensus, one might conclude that *Great Books of the Western World* virtually assembled itself. Yet one controversy pervaded the deliberations throughout 1944: the question of whether, as participants in the "great conversation," all of the selections had to be thematically related to each other. Buchanan, Barr, and Van Doren approved that doctrine, which Adler called "the most important thesis we have."[121] Erskine and the others dissented, objecting that the project seemed to be endorsing a particular "philosophy of life." As Erskine queried, "Why not permit the world to use the masterpieces as it chooses, provided only that the masterpieces are read?" (In that respect, he deserves credit for anticipating the openness to diverse ways of reading that literary critics have recently explored.) To break the deadlock, Hutchins proposed the addition of new board members, among them Alexander Meiklejohn, who accepted, and Lionel Trilling, who declined. Outnumbered, Erskine lapsed into a posture that Brockway, whose sentiments Hutchins and Adler probably shared, called that of "a nice old uncle," adding, "But is that a recommendation?"[122] In the end, *Great Books of the Western World* represented exactly what Erskine had feared: a narrow, idiosyncratic embodiment of Adler's preferences.

The marketing for the set, which Benton oversaw, incorporated many of the tensions about the meaning and uses of culture that had been evident in the "great books" ideology from the start. Benton's strategies included consulting with Harry Scherman about direct-mail approaches, setting up a plan for corporate donations to nonprofit institutions, and using only an experienced book sales force. Adler, with his penchant for the limelight, was also an asset; although the two men later clashed, Benton once ventured that Adler was "America's top promotion man."[123] The key document of the campaign was an illustrated brochure. Concealing Adler's partisanship, one version assured purchasers that the board had based its selections only on the "ultimate criterion": which books were the "greatest"? Like *How to Read a Book,* the same document also disdained "intellectual ease." Allaying fears to the contrary, it told individuals that their awareness that the "best" was "hard to come by" would propel them actually to read the books. Even the primary pitch for the Syntopicon rested on an image of self-reliance: an analogue of the Book-of-the-Month Club's rhetoric of "service," it depicted the compilation as a guide to "help the reader help himself."[124] Those appeals reflected Benton's and his colleagues' belief in the continuing power of Arnoldian tenets for the set's prospective owners.

Yet the promoters were also cognizant of its audience's other needs and anxieties. At an advisory board meeting in 1944, Hutchins had impassively declared that "people would buy the books for display, and, in being sold them, would not have to be persuaded that they could understand them." Benton, schooled on Madison Avenue, went even further. Noting that "the thought of reading them [the books] would terrify many potential buyers who would perhaps fail to buy if they thought they were supposed to read them," he emphasized the attraction of the Syntopicon as a reference work supplying useful information. At one point, Benton urged the inclusion of an "index to the index"—an "Applied Course" that would point out "suitable subjects for discussion at your Christmas dinner or at Thanksgiving." Identifying with the consumer, he explained, "After all, I want to read the Great Books in order to be popular and successful—and what are the applications I would like to make of these Great Books that will help me and my child to become popular and successful?" Benton concluded, "This is actually the basic idea in Mortimer's index but it has never been expressed in this way before." Adler did not see things in quite that light; more concerned, to his credit, with the integrity of the texts, he threatened to resign if Benton carried out the "Applied Course." But Benton, as perceptive in his own way as Dwight Macdonald, was only trying to capitalize on the inherent potential of the Syntopicon to obviate reading, supply information, and serve practical ends.[125]

Even Adler was willing to exploit that potential in more subtle terms. In an interview with Clare Boothe Luce on Benton's showcase radio program "University of Chicago Round Table," he remarked that the "Great Ideas was created to save time" and explained that the reader "does not have to begin and read a whole book through, and then another book through" but could "go to the set" to learn about "taxation, government control of industry, sex, divorce," and so on. Similarly, the promotional brochure announced, "Without the Syntopicon to guide you, it would take, literally, years of reading . . . to find out what they [the "great books"] have to say." Raymond Rubicam, a veteran adman in his own right, laid bare the double nature of Benton and Adler's message when, in response to a solicitation offering him a sponsor's discount, he replied, "Great Ideas, or Syntopicon, is a fascinating idea. . . . Maybe we can just read the intro-.ductory essays in those two volumes and acquire a liberal education easily worth $500 (less 10 percent)."[126]

Great Books of the Western World made its formal debut on April 15, 1952, at a banquet for sponsors and friends in the Waldorf Astoria's Grand Ballroom. The rhetoric flowed as freely as the wine, the speakers celebrating the set's contributions to the survival of "tradition" and "Western civilization." But Erskine, who would have recognized such phrases as echoes of his own, was absent from the festivities; he had died the previous year. The incompleteness of the gathering reiterated the larger theme of his career. Erskine contributed the basis for one of the chief agencies of American middlebrow culture and indelibly colored the role of the middlebrow critic. Yet at his death he most resembled what, in describing Byron, he called the defeated romantic hero: "Failing ever to live completely, he carried with him to his grave the memory of much experience which he had yearned for, but which had escaped him."[127]

NOTES

[1] Bourne, "The Professor," pp. 91-97.

[2] *Letters of Randolph Bourne,* pp. 55-56, 136-38, 143, 188, 290-91, 340, 367-69.

[3] Erskine, *The Memory,* pp. 14, 18, 21, 43-46, 51.

[4] Ibid., p. 23.

[5] Persons, *Decline of American Gentility,* pp. 3, 6-7, 55; Bledstein, *Culture of Professionalism,* p. 146.

[6] Erskine, *The Memory,* pp. 21, 23.

[7] Ibid., pp. 47-48.

[8] Ibid., pp. 10, 45, 48.

[9] Brooks, "America's Coming-of-Age," p. 17.

[10] Persons, *Decline of American Gentility,* p. 43.

[11] Erskine, *The Memory,* p. 14.

[12] Ibid., pp. 12, 14.

[13] Erskine, *My Life in Music,* p. 9.

[14] Erskine, *The Memory,* pp. 63, 67.

[15] Trilling, "Van Amringe and Keppel Eras," pp. 19, 21.

[16] Erskine, *The Memory,* pp. 72-79; Erskine, *My Life in Music,* pp. 10-16; Erskine, "MacDowell, Edward," pp. 24-27.

[17] Spingarn, "Woodberry, George Edward," pp. 478-81.

[18] Woodberry, *Appreciation of Literature,* p. 2; Woodberry, *Heart of Man,* p. 209.

[19] Erskine, *The Memory,* p. 94; Woodberry, *Heart of Man,* pp. 121, 170.

[20] Woodberry, *Appreciation of Literature,* pp. 90, 107, 175, 193; Lewis Perry, *Intellectual Life,* p. 311.

[21] Woodberry, *Appreciation of Literature,* p. 53.

[22] Greenslet, *Under the Bridge,* p. 51; Erskine, *The Memory,* pp. 93-94; Trilling, "Van Amringe and Keppel Eras," p. 25.

[23] William James to Mrs. Henry Whitman, *Letters of William James,* 2:89.

[24] Whicher, *Selections from Ralph Waldo Emerson,* pp. 263-74.

[25] Erskine, *The Memory,* p. 94.

[26] Because Woodberry, in keeping with his generalist orientation, had been reappointed in comparative literature, Thomas R. Price became Erskine's official supervisor.

[27] Erskine, *The Memory,* pp. 101, 150-51; Morris, *Threshold,* pp. 81-84; Trilling, "Van Amringe and Keppel Eras," p. 24; Veysey, *American University,* pp. 426-27.

[28] Erskine, *The Memory,* pp. 110-11.

[29] Ibid., p. 151; Spingarn, "Woodberry, George Edward," p. 480.

[30] Erskine, *My Life as a Teacher,* p. 33; Erskine to Melville Cane, Apr. 15, 1907, Catalogued Correspondence, John Erskine Papers, Rare Book and Manuscript Library, Columbia University, New York, N.Y.

[31] Henry Morton Robinson, "John Erskine," p. 9; Erskine, *The Memory,* p. 182; Erskine to Cane, Oct. 3, 1906, Catalogued Correspondence, Erskine Papers.

[32] William James to Mrs. Henry Whitman, *Letters of William James,* 2:89.

[33] Erskine, *My Life as a Teacher,* pp. 32-49.

[34] Lears, "From Salvation to Self-Realization," p. 17; Lasch, *New Radicalism,* pp. 69-103; Blake, *Beloved Community,* pp. 63-75.

[35] Morris, *Threshold,* p. 80.

[36] Ibid., pp. 85-86.

[37] "Helen Worden Erskine and Melville Cane," Erskine Biographical File, Box 6, Folder Columbia 1900, pp. 11-12, Erskine Papers.

[38] Displeased by Theodore Roosevelt's presence at Butler's inauguration, Erskine may well have been responding to Roosevelt's habit during this time of labeling character, rather than intellect, the essential ingredient of civilization. Hofstadter, *Anti-Intellectualism,* pp. 207-8.

[39] Erskine, *Moral Obligation,* pp. 3, 12, 18, 24-25, 31; Morris, *Threshold,* p. 88.

[40] Erskine wrote to Scott Buchanan about an article Buchanan did on the history of the "great books" movement: "I was amused to see the legend of the A.E.F. University in Beaune growing steadily, and how like all legends it gets badly twisted. You seem to make the reading list the core of the army enterprise, though as far as my memory now serves, we had no selected reading list at Beaune." Erskine to Buchanan, Dec. 27, 1938, Box G-K, Folder "Great Books," Arranged Correspondence, Erskine Papers; Erskine, *The Memory,* p. 253; Graff, *Professing Literature,* p. 133.

[41] "The Reminiscences of Helen Worden Erskine," interview by Joan Pring, 1957, Columbia University Oral History Project, Butler Library, Columbia University, New York, N.Y., p. 161 (hereafter cited as Erskine, COHC); Erskine, *My Life in Music,* p. 113; Erskine, *The Memory,* pp. 256-337.

[42] John Erskine to Eliza Hollingsworth Erskine, Feb. 23, 1919, and Sept. 7, 1918, Box 1, 1975 Addition, Erskine Papers; John Erskine to Rhoda Erskine, July 16, 1918, Box 2, 1975 Addition, Erskine Papers.

[43] Bourne, "War and the Intellectuals," pp. 3, 11.

[44] Erskine, COHC, p. 113; Helen Huntington Smith, "Professor's Progress," p. 28; John Erskine to Eliza Hollingsworth Erskine, Mar. 18, 1918, Box 1, 1975 Addition, Erskine Papers.

[45] Erskine, *The Memory,* p. 329.

[46] Erskine, *Democracy and Ideals,* pp. 118-32; John Erskine to Eliza Hollingsworth Erskine, Feb. 23, 1919, Box 1, 1975 Addition, Erskine Papers.

[47] "Preliminary Report," p. 3; Erskine, "Teaching of Literature," pp. 202-5.

[48] Erskine, *Delight of Great Books,* pp. 21-22; "Abstract of the Discussion," p. 1.

[49] Graff, *Professing Literature,* pp. 133-36. Graff notes that—in addition to Woodberry—William Lyon Phelps,

Bliss Perry, and Charles Mills Gayley all contributed to the "great books" concept and that Gayley initiated a course with that title at Berkeley in 1901. One should add that Mortimer Adler did not invent the phrase "great books" either—despite his claim that it came to him in discussions with Robert Maynard Hutchins "at the end of the twenties." Perhaps Adler can be credited with devising (or, certainly, popularizing) the phrase "great books course." See Adler, *Philosopher-at-Large,* p. 55.

[50] "Preliminary Report," pp. 4-6; Moorhead, "Great Books Movement," pp. 688-89; Hollinger, "Canon and Its Keepers," pp. 74-91.

[51] Erskine, "English in the College Course," pp. 340-47.

[52] Erskine, *My Life as a Teacher,* p. 170; "Preliminary Report," p. 3.

[53] Brodhead, *School of Hawthorne,* p. 5.

[54] William W. Lawrence to Dean Frederick Keppel, Feb. 9, 1917, Box C, Arranged Correspondence, Erskine Papers; Erskine, *My Life as a Teacher,* p. 168; Erskine, "General Honors at Columbia," p. 13. Erskine's own memories of the sequence of events are at odds with the incomplete college records.

[55] Coss, introduction to *Five College Plans,* pp. 2-3.

[56] Trilling, "Van Amringe and Keppel Eras," pp. 44-47; Justus Buchler, "Reconstruction in the Liberal Arts," in *A History of Columbia College on Morningside,* pp. 48-54; Allen, *Romance of Commerce,* pp. 81-99; Barzun, *Teacher in America,* pp. 154-59.

[57] Erskine, "Outline of Great Books," p. 4, Uncatalogued Manuscripts, Helen Worden Erskine Papers, Rare Book and Manuscript Library, Columbia University, New York, N.Y.; Erskine, "Teaching of Literature," p. 203; Erskine, "My Life in Literature," p. 260, Uncatalogued Manuscripts, Helen Worden Erskine Papers.

[58] Erskine, *Prohibition and Christianity,* p. 250.

[59] Erskine, *The Memory,* p. 343.

[60] Erskine, *Prohibition and Christianity,* p. 255.

[61] Erskine, *Delight of Great Books,* p. 200.

[62] Erskine, *Democracy and Ideals,* pp. 82-83.

[63] Leland, *Art of Conversation,* p. 47.

[64] Wright, *Art of Conversation,* pp. 23, 38-40, 44-45; Erskine, *Complete Life,* pp. 145, 147; Erskine, *Prohibition and Christianity,* pp. 215-18.

[65] T. S. Eliot, "Tradition and the Individual Talent," pp. 13-22; Bell, "Beyond Modernism," pp. 214, 219.

[66] Brooks, "America's Coming-of-Age," p. 57.

[67] Erskine, *Democracy and Ideals,* pp. 42-44, 49-53, 62-63, 71.

[68] Ibid., p. 56.

[69] Brooks, "Letters and Leadership," in *Three Essays on America,* p. 135; Bourne, "Our Cultural Humility," p. 39; Stearns, *Civilization,* p. vii; Blake, *Beloved Community,* pp. 99-121.

[70] Rourke, *American Humor,* pp. 3-32.

[71] Erskine, *Delight of Great Books,* p. 66.

[72] Erskine, *My Life as a Teacher,* p. 169.

[73] Dwight Macdonald, "Book-of-the-Millennium Club," p. 171.

[74] Erskine, *My Life as a Teacher,* p. 169; Wright, *Art of Conversation,* pp. 117-19. On the "star system," see Boorstin, *The Image,* pp. 57, 154-68.

[75] "Preliminary Report," p. 4; Erskine, *American Character,* pp. 161-208; Erskine, "Spotlight or Fame?," pp. 449-51; Erskine, "Literature," p. 420. The inclusion of Erskine's "Literature" essay in *Century of Progress,* one of a series Charles A. Beard edited in order to grapple with the meaning of American civilization, symbolizes Erskine's involvement in that debate. Erskine, "There's Fun in Famous Books," pp. 14-15.

[76] Allen, *Romance of Commerce,* pp. 86-91. The idea that the impetus behind the later "great books" movement consisted solely of a rejection of "modern culture" has made its way into at least one American history textbook. See the discussion by Robert H. Wiebe in Bailyn et al., *Great Republic,* p. 1151.

[77] Trilling is quoted in Bell, *General Education,* p. 15; "American College," p. 208.

[78] John Erskine to Eliza Hollingsworth Erskine, May 5, 1918, Box 1, 1975 Addition, Erskine Papers; Erskine, *Democracy and Ideals,* pp. 128-29; Bell, *General Education,* p. 14.

[79] Erskine, *Democracy and Ideals,* pp. 110, 133-52; Erskine, *Prohibition and Christianity,* pp. 236-42; Erskine, "Twilight of the Specialist," p. 231.

[80] "American College," p. 208.

[81] Henry Morton Robinson, "John Erskine," p. 9; Erskine, COHC, pp. 146-47; Erskine, *My Life in Music,* p. 163; John Erskine to Hugh Guiler, Dec. 9, 1930, Box 10, Folder Anais Nin-Hugh Guiler, Biographical File, Erskine Papers.

[82] Erskine, *The Memory,* p. 347.

[83] Erskine, *Private Life,* pp. 70-76; Erskine, "My Life in Literature," p. 29.

[84] Helen Huntington Smith, "Professor's Progress," p. 28; "Helen and Galahad under Fire," p. 26.

[85] Erskine, "My Life in Literature," p. 32.

[86] Clifton Fadiman, interview with author, Apr. 1984, Santa Barbara, Calif.

[87] Erskine was somewhat aware of this, admitting that he had set his stories in the past "to make it easier for Mrs. Grundy." Erskine, *Complete Life,* p. 303.

[88] Erskine, *My Life as a Teacher,* pp. 206-11; Erskine, *My Life in Music,* pp. 81-82, 110.

[89] Erskine, *My Life in Music,* p. 163; Erskine, *My Life as a Teacher,* p. 209; Henry Morton Robinson, "John Erskine," p. 10.

[90] Erskine, "Adult Education in Music," pp. 647-53.

[91] Adelene Pynchon to Fulton Oursler, Aug. 21, 1951, Box 4, Folder Adelene [Atwater] Pynchon, Biographical File, Erskine Papers; Erskine, *Unfinished Business.*

[92] Erskine, COHC, p. 121; John Erskine to Helen Worden, May 12, 1933, May 16, 1933, Uncatalogued Correspondence, Helen Worden Erskine Papers; Erskine, *My Life in Music,* pp. 162-63.

[93] Erskine, *Influence of Women,* pp. 18-19, 87, 112-13.

[94] John Erskine to Curtis Walker, Dec. 15, 1937, Uncatalogued Correspondence, Helen Worden Erskine Papers; Erskine, *The Memory,* p. 402; Erskine, *My Life in Music,* pp. 176-80. He did make a connection between the accident and a second stroke in 1949. *My Life in Music,* p. 269.

[95] Erskine, *My Life in Music,* p. 173; Trilling, "Van Amringe and Keppel Eras," p. 28; John Erskine to F. J. E. Woodbridge, Sept. 28, 1937, Box 5, 1975 Addition, Erskine Papers.

[96] Fadiman, "Two Lives," pp. 81-82; "Democracy's Poet," p. 57; Theodore Purdy, "Snows of Yesteryear," p. 11.

[97] Helen Worden to John Erskine, n.d., Folder H. W. Erskine—Letters to John Erskine, Helen Worden Erskine Papers; Erskine, "Mickey Mouse," p. 11; Erskine, "Why Films Have So Many Authors," p. 13; Erskine, "Hollywood Stars," pp. 14-15; Erskine, "Clark Gable's Secret Wish," p. 14.

[98] Erskine, *Complete Life,* pp. 3, 11-12, 336-38; Roberts, "Personal Preferences," p. 8; Sugrue, "Civilized Man's Guide," p. 9.

[99] For example, John Erskine to Helen Worden Erskine, July 5, 1946, Uncatalogued Correspondence, Helen Worden Erskine Papers; Erskine, COHC, p. 128.

[100] Allen, *Romance of Commerce*, p. 86. Others associated with the course in its first year, either as instructors or students, included Jacques Barzun, Lionel Trilling, Irwin Edman, Rexford Tugwell, and Raymond Weaver. In their subsequent careers, some of those figures (the literary critics Weaver and Trilling) remained largely identified with "high" culture, but, in addition to Fadiman and Adler, Edman followed Erskine's lead as a popularizer, while Barzun and, to an extent, Van Doren combined academic stature with efforts to reach a wide audience.

[101] Moorhead, "Great Books Movement," p. 122.

[102] Fadiman interview.

[103] Ibid.; Adler, *Philosopher-at-Large*, pp. 106-7.

[104] Allen, *Romance of Commerce*, pp. 83-85; Mark Van Doren, *Autobiography*, p. 175; Adler, *Philosopher-at-Large*, pp. 56, 58; Hutchins, *Higher Learning*, pp. 67-78; Hutchins, *No Friendly Voice*, pp. 29-30. For a biography of Hutchins, see Ashmore, *Unseasonable Truths*.

[105] Mark Van Doren, *Autobiography*, p. 175; Hutchins, *No Friendly Voice*, p. 38.

[106] Allen, *Romance of Commerce*, pp. 85-86, 88, 92-93; Adler, *Philosopher-at-Large*, pp. 177-78; for example, Joseph G. Becht to Robert Maynard Hutchins, Dec. 28, 1938; Paul Dunaway to Robert Maynard Hutchins, June 23, 1944, Robert M. Hutchins Papers, University Archives, University of Chicago.

[107] Scott Buchanan to John Erskine, Dec. 16, 1938, and John Erskine to Robert E. Spiller, Mar. 5, 1942, Box G-K, Arranged Correspondence, Erskine Papers; John Erskine to John S. Kieffer, Dec. 29, 1948, Miscellaneous Additions, Erskine Papers; Erskine, *The Memory*, p. 343.

[108] Adler had kept the idea alive in the 1930s by leading occasional alumni discussion groups and, at the end of the decade, by having Chicago's extension division offer a "great books" seminar. Allen, *Romance of Commerce*, p. 99.

[109] Adler, *How to Read a Book*, pp. 35, 101-16, 328-35, 354-57.

[110] Ibid., pp. 102-10, 138, 147-53, 266-68; Hollinger, "Canon and Its Keepers," pp. 85-86.

[111] Adler, *How to Read a Book*, pp. 27, 62, 199.

[112] Ibid., p. 236; Allen, *Romance of Commerce*, p. 106.

[113] Redman, "No: Not without Socrates," pp. 32, 34; Allen, *Romance of Commerce*, p. 106; John D. Hill, "Business Man Views the Classics," p. 167.

[114] "Manual for Discussion Leaders," pp. 131, 137, Box 17, Folder 5, Hutchins Papers.

[115] Redman, "No: Not without Socrates," pp. 33, 35; "Manual for Discussion Leaders," p. 126; Mayer, "Great Books," p. 8.

[116] Adler, *Philosopher-at-Large*, pp. 237-38; "The University of Chicago Roundtable: The Great Ideas" (no. 637, June 11, 1950), p. 1, Box 35, Folder 2, Presidents' Papers ca. 1925-45, University Archives, University of Chicago.

[117] "Memo on the Britannica Project," Box 12, Folder 2, Presidents' Papers.

[118] Robert Maynard Hutchins to Wallace Brockway, Oct. 3, 1945, Box 34, Folder 6, Presidents' Papers.

[119] Hollinger, "Canon and Its Keepers," p. 64.

[120] This remained one of Adler's inviolable principles, even though, in practice, the community reading groups routinely read excerpts in order to accommodate their busy schedules. Redman, "No: Not without Socrates," p. 33; "Manual for Discussion Leaders," p. 126.

[121] "Report of the Encyclopedia Britannica Great Books Advisory Board meeting, Aug. 30, 1944," p. 3, Box 34, Folder 5, Presidents' Papers. Buchanan later rejected the doctrine. Adler, *Philosopher-at-Large*, p. 251.

[122] John Erskine to Robert Maynard Hutchins, Feb. 29, 1944, Box 34, Folder 5, Presidents' Papers; Lionel Trilling to Robert Maynard Hutchins, Sept. 19, 1944, Presidents' Papers; Wallace Brockway to Robert Maynard Hutchins, Apr. 19, 1945, Box 34, Folder 6, Presidents' Papers. Trilling refused out of misgivings about the esoteric, unedited nature of the set and about the board itself.

[123] William Benton to Mortimer J. Adler, Sept. 19, 1946, Presidents' Papers.

[124] "The Wisdom of Thirty Centuries," pp. 4, 7-8, Box 12, Folder 3, Presidents' Papers. This appears to be a near-final draft of the brochure.

[125] "Report of the Encyclopedia Britannica Great Books Advisory Board meeting, Aug. 30, 1944," p. 13; William Benton to Robert Maynard Hutchins, Oct. 18, 1949, Box 35, Folder 1, Presidents' Papers; Mortimer J. Adler to Robert M. Hutchins, Oct. 22, 1949, Presidents' Papers.

[126] "The University of Chicago Round Table: The Great Ideas," pp. 1, 6-7; "The Wisdom of Thirty Centuries," p. 21; Raymond Rubicam to Robert Maynard Hutchins, Apr. 24, 1950, Box 11, Folder 3, Presidents' Papers.

[127] Adler, *Philosopher-at-Large*, p. 216; Erskine, *Delight of Great Books*, p. 220.

FURTHER READING

Criticism

Aiken, Conrad. "Divers Realists." *The Dial* LXIII (18 November 1917): 453-55.
    Comparative review, including Erskine's *The Shadowed House,* notable both for the famous reviewer and for the fact that the list of then-current books under review includes T. S. Eliot's *Prufrock and Other Observations.*

Brickell, Herschel. "The Literary Landscape." *North American Review* 238, No. 2 (August 1934): 188.
    Short and scathing review of *Bachelor—Of Arts.*

Marble, Annie Russell. "John Erskine." In *A Study of the Modern Novel: British and American since 1900,* pp. 290-92. New York: D. Appleton, 1928.
    Brief overview of Erskine's career and major works.

Mencken, H. L. "Poetry." *The American Mercury* VI, No. 22 (19 October 1925): 251-54.
    Review of Erskine's *Sonata and Other Poems* and a score of volumes by others.

Payne, William Morton. "Recent Poetry." *The Dial* XLIII, No. 508 (16 August 1907): 90-94.
    Review maintains *Actaeon, and Other Poems* is "wholly derivative in merit, and of slight significance."

Van Doren, Mark. "Concerning Poetry." *The Nation* 112, No. 2901 (February 1921): 241.
    A review of several works of criticism, including Erskine's *The Kinds of Poetry.*

William Alexander Percy

1885-1942

American poet and autobiographer.

INTRODUCTION

William Alexander Percy's literary reputation rests principally on his autobiography, *Lanterns on the Levee,* a work which preserves the rapidly disappearing texture of the agrarian South. Although his fame has long since been eclipsed by that of his young cousin Walker Percy, whom he helped raise after the latter was orphaned, the elder Percy is remembered as a contributor to the development of the Agrarian and Fugitive movements in Southern literature. He did not associate closely with leading figures in these movements—Percy earned a living as an attorney, not as a writer or teacher—yet his work embodies many of the same values as those espoused by Robert Penn Warren, Cleanth Brooks, John Crowe Ransom, and others. Among those values are an appreciation for the Southern agricultural tradition coupled with a rejection of Northern liberalism and industrialization, attitudes almost inevitably tied, in the eyes of a later generation at least, with racism. Nonetheless it is important to note that Percy's views on race were benign and paternalistic rather than violent or malevolent; an aspect of his family history in which he took great pride, recounting the particulars in *Lanterns on the Levee,* was his senator father's longstanding feud with the Ku Klux Klan and the segregationist legislator James K. Vardaman. In his poetic works, Percy celebrated the ancient world. He was a classicist unwilling to accept modernity, a man who, as critic Willard Thorp wrote, "deliberately stood aside from the poetic movements of his time."

Biographical Information

Percy was born in 1885 in Greenville, Mississippi, to LeRoy and Camille Percy. His father, a lawyer, served in the United States Senate from 1910 to 1913 after defeating the race-baiter Vardaman. Senator Percy distinguished himself by making a stand against the Ku Klux Klan, no ordinary act in Mississippi in the 1910s, and his son would carry on this opposition. Percy was raised as a Catholic and studied at a convent school run by the Sisters of Mercy, but when it came time to continue his education at the age of fifteen, his father sent him to his Episcopalian alma mater, the University of the South at Sewanee, Tennessee. He had planned to enroll in the preparatory school, but because he passed the college entrance examinations, Percy was enrolled in a course of higher education. In 1904 he earned his A.B., thus ending a period that he later characterized as "idyllic" and "pastoral." Percy then spent a year in Paris, after which he enrolled in law school at Harvard University. He earned his LL.B. in 1908, and began practicing law in his hometown later that year. It was during this time that he began to write poetry seriously, perhaps seeking in his celebration of the classical age a refuge from the increasingly confusing world of Mississippi politics which dominated his family life. In Percy's view, blacks were not a dangerous political force; poor, embittered racist whites—people who supported Vardaman and the Klan—were. When war broke out overseas in 1914 Percy, who would later say that "The North destroyed my South; Germany destroyed my world," quickly became involved. He went to Belgium to serve under Herbert Hoover in the Commission for Relief, and when the United States entered the conflict in 1917, he returned to America to join the army. In Texas he received training as an infantry officer, and though he was underweight and small, Percy distinguished himself as a fighting man in France, service for which he was awarded the Croix de Guerre in 1918. After his return to Mississippi, Percy was again embroiled in opposition to the Klan, and he continued his relief work following the 1927 Mississippi flood, a vast natural disaster which he described as "a torrent ten feet deep the size of Rhode Island." Following the death of his parents in 1919, he inherited Trail Lake, an enormous cotton plantation that had belonged to them. Later, in *Lanterns on the Levee,* Percy would describe Trail Lake at length, and defended sharecropping as a form of profit-sharing. During the 1920s, he had published several volumes of poetry, but after he adopted his cousin Walker Percy and the boy's two brothers when their parents died, he appears to have given up verse almost entirely. Publisher Alfred A. Knopf suggested that Percy write his autobiography, and the result, after a decade's work, was *Lanterns on the Levee.* Percy, who never married, died a year after its publication.

Major Works

The poetry collections *Sappho in Levkas, In April Once,* and *Enzio's Kingdom* reflect Percy's idiosyncratic tastes. In them one will find little suggestion that he was writing at the same time as Eliot or Yeats; nor does the character of his verses suggest that their author came from the same region as Faulkner, Warren, and other writers soon to emerge on the national scene. Rather, Percy's settings are classical, either Greek or Roman; and his heroes and heroines are figures of restraint, often modelled after one of Percy's own heroes, the Stoic emperor-philosopher Marcus Aurelius. Perhaps most notable of Percy's poems is the title work in *Enzio's Kingdom,* the story of a prince in medieval Sardinia who mourns the death of his father King Frederick, a figure possibly modelled on Percy's own father. Given the fact that it stood largely outside of any literary movement, and failed to spawn significant imitators, Percy's poetic writing received a surprising amount of critical attention during his lifetime; since then, however, interest in his work has been minimal. *Lanterns on the Levee,* by contrast, remains a minor classic of personal and public history in which the author records for posterity his impressions of a rapidly fading world. Percy's model was Marcus Aurelius's *Meditations.* As in *Enzio's Kingdom,* Percy pays tribute to his father and provides a richly textured portrait of life in Mississippi from the 1880s to the 1930s. The book is, as its subtitle indicates, the "Recollections of a Planter's Son," and it includes events and phenomena such as the 1927 flood and his family's ongoing conflict with the Klan.

PRINCIPAL WORKS

Sappho in Levkas, and Other Poems (poetry) 1915
In April Once (poetry) 1920
Enzio's Kingdom, and Other Poems (poetry) 1924
Lanterns on the Levee: Recollections of a Planter's Son
   (autobiography) 1941
Of Silence and of Stars (poetry) 1953

CRITICISM

William Faulkner (essay date 1920)

SOURCE: "Books and Things," in *William Faulkner: Early Prose and Poetry,* Jonathan Cape, 1963, pp. 71-3.

[*In the following essay, originally published in the University of Mississippi student paper, a young Faulkner gives* In April Once *a generally favorable review.*]

We are presenting this week a review by William S. [*sic*] Falkner of *In April Once* by W. A. Percy, Yale University Press; later we shall give a discussion of some of the poets who are representative of the spirit of the present in the form and content of their verse.

In April Once by W. A. Percy

Mr. Percy is a native Mississippian, a graduate of the University of the South and of the Harvard Law School. He was a member of the Belgian Relief Commission in the early days of the war, then served as a lieutenant attached to the 37th Division. He now lives in Greenville.

Mr. Percy—like alas! how many of us—suffered the misfortune of having been born out of his time. He should have lived in Victorian England and gone to Italy with Swinburne, for like Swinburne, he is a mixture of passionate adoration of beauty and as passionate a despair and disgust with its manifestations and accessories in the human race. His muse is Latin in type—poignant ecstasies of lyrical extravagance and a short lived artificial strength achieved at the cost of true strength in beauty. Beauty, to him, is almost like physical pain, evident in the simplicity of this poem which is the nearest perfect thing in the book—

> I heard a bird at break of day
>   Sing from the autumn trees
> A song so mystical and calm,
>   So full of certainties,
> No man, I think, could listen long
>   Except upon his knees.
> Yet this was but a simple bird
>   Alone, among dead trees.

The influence of the frank pagan beauty worship of the past is heavily upon him, he is like a little boy closing his eyes against the dark of modernity which threatens the bright simplicity and the colorful romantic pageantry of the middle ages with which his eyes are full. One can imagine him best as a violinist who became blind about the time Mozart died, it would seem that the last thing he saw with his subjective intellect was Browning standing in naive admiration before his own mediocrity, of which Mr. Percy's **"Epistle from Corinth"** is the fruit. This is far and away the best thing in the book, and would have been better except for the fact that Mr. Percy, like every man who has ever lived, is the victim of his age.

As a whole, the book sustains its level of lyrical beauty. Occasionally it becomes pure vowelization, for it is not always the word that Mr. Percy seeks, but the sound. There is one element that will tend more than anything else to help it oblivionward, this is the section devoted to war poems. How many, many, many reams of paper that have been ruined with poetry appertaining to the late war no one, probably, will ever know, yet still the nightingales wear swords and Red Cross brassards.

Mr. Percy has not written a great book,—there is too much music in it for that, he is a violinist with an inferior instrument—yet (and most unusual as modern books of poetry go) the gold outweighs the dross. How much, I would not undertake to say, for he is a difficult person to whom to render justice; like Swinburne, he obscures the whole mental horizon, one either likes him passionately or one remains forever cold to him.

John Crowe Ransom (essay date 1924)

SOURCE: "Mississippian Is Rated Best Poet of Entire South," in *The Nashville Tennessean,* May 11, 1924.

[*In the following essay, Ransom—critical of Percy in other contexts—praises* Enzio's Kingdom.]

The third volume of poems [*Enzio's Kingdom*] to be issued by Mr. Percy, who lives at Greenville, Mississippi, will reinforce the opinion that here is the foremost of the Southern poets of this time. The honor was already widely conceded him by the reading public and the poets themselves.

And yet how to define him? No undertaking tries the critic so much as fixing the rare and fugitive flavor of certain poetry.

Of course there are some strains that have a quality much more obvious than that of others; these represent the poets that are willing to harp on one string only, that depend on certain tricks and dodges for their quick effects, that are in reality more violent and startling than they are poetical. Such poetry constitutes a great deal of the work of the present generation. The governing motive of American poets today, if one may risk a generalization, is to arrive by hook or by crook at the point of being "different."

Definition of a Poem.

Other poets, however—poets who are becoming increasingly rare in these days—are more sensible of the subtle resources of the delicate instrument poetry, and their work is more difficult to define. They understand that a poem is a very intricate play by which the right tones and the right words evoke a harmonious procession of ideas and emotions from the deeply guarded secret places of the heart. These tones and these words come only out of ripe and chastened poets, and they operate only upon kindred spirits. The poets are like musicians, who can play orchestra harmonies on our strings without making discord; they are like psychologists, who know what emotions their words will start within us, and also how quickly the wrong word will drive our shy responses to cover again. It is the finest and most difficult of the arts.

Mr. Percy, then, has no patent short-cuts, no sensational themes nor methods, no modernisms to limit the timeless poetic quality which he properly has aspired to realize. He is a Southern poet without anything specifically Southern in his work. His is a full spirit pouring itself out, and commending itself to those of us who may have organized the background of our experience something like as richly and as delicately as he has.

Verses Reach "Home."

He realizes that it is the fate of any poet to find a limited circle of understanding hearers: he says so in his key-poem on the first page:

> I seek an amaranth
> More lovely than its name,
> For me a very heart's rue,
> For your heart's not the same

It blows above the blue
Far-vistaed Paphian sea,
Or so the woman said
Whose green eyes sorcelled me.

> Joy to you in your meadows,
> But I'll search mine alone
> And find an amaranth—
> Or else a quiet stone.

The meadows through which Mr. Percy searches contain winter and sun, birds and flowers, mad maidens and then, some old-world scenes from Capri and Brittany, and glimpses of the Mississippi Delta; they are perfectly familiar territory to the lovers of poetry.

A tender philosophy is implicit in his pictures. See the fine poem, **"A Canticle,"** from which a stanza may in conclusion be quoted:

> Who lifteth in the eastern sky
>   the dark, gold moon?
> Who painteth green and purple
>   on the blackbird's throat?
> What hand of rapture scattereth
>   sunshine through the rain
> And flingeth round the barren
>   boughs of spring returned
> Dim fire? Who stenciled with
>   caught breath the moth's wide wing
> And lit the ruby in his eyes?
>   Whose ecstasy
> Set silver ripples on the racing
>   thunder-cloud
> And flared the walls of storm
>   with terrible dead green?
> What dreamer fretted dew
>   upon the flat-leafed corn
> And twined in innocence
>   of useless perfect art
> The morning-glory with its
>   bubble blue, soon gone?
> Was there no hand that braided
>   autumn branches in
> Their solemn breed and stained them
>   with a somber rust?
> Was there no love conceived the
>   one-starred, rivered evening.
> And dipped in crocus fire the
>   grey horns of the moon?

George Herbert Clarke (essay date 1925)

SOURCE: A review of *Enzio's Kingdom and Other Poems*, in *The Sewanee Review*, Vol. 33, No. 1, January-March, 1925, pp. 105-11.

[*In the following excerpt, Clarke appraises* Enzio's Kingdom *and finds it lacking in certain respects, but nonetheless judges it a competent poetic offering.*]

Mr. Percy's collection [*Enzio's Kingdom, and Other Poems*] is his third. Three of the poems he has included have already appeared in the *Sewanee Review,* the most notable one being *A Letter From John Keats to Fanny Brawne*. It is a moving document, many of whose pathetic verses linger in the memory. *Enzio's Kingdom*, another and much longer poem in blank verse, is a dramatic monologue of no inconsiderable power. Frederick II, of the Hohenstaufens, is its hero. He was the grandson of Frederick Barbarossa, and son of the German Emperor, Henry VI. His mother was the daughter of Roger I, the Norman King of Sicily, and Frederick was born in the march of Ancona, at Jesi, in December, 1194. Inheriting the kingdom of the Two Sicilies, he was elected Emperor of Germany in 1211 through the support of Innocent III, and was crowned by Honorius III in 1220. Thereafter his life was a struggle to retain and extend his power. He was excommunicated several times by Gregory IX and Innocent IV, the latter Pope eventually convening a council at Lyons to depose Frederick, who, after fighting a gallant but downhill fight, died on December 13, 1250, at his castle of Fiorentino. He was a man of tremendous courage, of high resolve, of proud and enduring will, whose lusts and cruelties were always made secondary to his vision of peace firmly based on capable absolutism. He promoted culture at his court (Michael Scott the Aristotelian and Leonard of Pisa were there, and his favorite adviser, Pietro delle Vigne, is said to have written the first sonnet), establishing the University of Naples and enlarging the medical school at Salerno. His own learning was various and curious, he spoke six languages, was a remarkably independent thinker, and was called *Stupor mundi et immutator mirabilis*. His government of Sicily was progressive, his Code of Laws, 1231, showing skill and sagacity. He had five children, three of them—Hensius or Enzio, Frederick and Manfred—being illegitimate. Of all his children, chivalric Enzio was the best loved, and he was made King of Sardinia. Enzio followed and fought for the policies of his father to the best of his power, but was at last taken prisoner by the Bolognese at the Battle of Fossalta, 1249, and was made a hostage, living in detention until his death twenty-two years after.

Mr. Percy imagines Enzio (in a rather harsher prison than that which he actually occupied) receiving from one Berard the news of Frederick's death, and begging the old follower of the Emperor to remain for a little that Enzio may free his memory and so ease the hearts of both. Enzio reviews with sorrowful pride the course of his father's life, in camp, in battle and at court; in the moment of splendid defiance of his enemies and in the after-moment of defeated hope and uncompleted vision. He justly appreciates his father's true character, in strength and weakness alike, and through all his utterance runs the unbreakable thread of a son's loyal love and a comrade-spirit's understanding fidelity. At times, perhaps, the emotional suggestion is overdone, as in the too frequent word and phrase repetitions on pages 133-136; yet the monologue as a whole is penetrated by much imaginative sympathy. Among its memorable verses are these:—

The multitudinous slow flight of stars.

So through the ebbing smoke-drifts of the room
I looked out on the lowlands and the moonlight
And watched the ravelled cloud-banks floating
    past,
The spindrift of a sunset's storm of color. . . .

A moon misshapen stumbled down the sky,
Bloody and sick. . . .

An old moon, blue with cold, limps up the east,
Thin as the new. . . .

And there are noble passages recounting the story of the son of Helios; the silent vigil of Enzio with Frederick (as of David with Browning's Saul) after darkness threatens; and the discovering of Pietro's treachery.

Technically, Mr. Percy is a little careless with his measures, sometimes permitting an unnecessary extra foot. Two lines appear uncompensatingly lame, namely—

Justice peace, and the young future teems . . .

Fools, fools, and serious fools who die . . .

And we find something objectionable in the use of such words as *rile* and *jarred,* and in the too frequent instances of split infinitive. "Death's purple-raftered house" is so good a phrase that the poet may be forgiven for using it more than once. As a whole, the humanity of this poem is amply authentic and its power real.

Among the lyrics and shorter reflective pieces there are several of unusual loveliness, as in the rhymeless poems, *Autumn Wisdom*, *A Debussy Serenade*, *October*, *A Canticle*, and *Winds of Winter*; the Shelleian *Courage*; the delicate lament, *Beth Marie*; the twin *Compensation* and *Autumn Song*; the tender *Portrait*; and the first part of *Rain Patter*. *Wonder and a Thousand Springs* uses too many identical vowel-values in its rhyme-scheme; and *The Delta Autumn* is more—and less—than the good sonnet it might have been. Mr. Percy's writing shows nearly always a really fine sensitiveness, but its craftsmanship sometimes stumbles below the level of its inspiration. We are grateful, indeed, for the much felicity in his work, for its manly sincerity, and for its constant hunger and thirst after the higher beauty that its author will yet win. Its very dissatisfactions tell its endowments and foretell its conquests.

Llewellyn Jones (essay date 1929)

SOURCE: A preface to *Selected Poems: William Alexander Percy*, Yale University Press, 1929, pp. v-ix.

[*In the following essay, a preface to* Selected Poems, *Jones briefly examines Percy's career as a poet.*]

Mr. Percy's first volume, *Sappho in Levkas*, was published in 1915 and from the copyright notice we may see that he was publishing as early as 1911. That fact almost sets him apart from all other contemporary American poets, for it was soon after the turn of the century that American poets learned to advertise, to lecture, and to write manifestoes. None of these things has Mr. Percy ever done, and from his group, **"In New York,"** we may discover that he does not appreciate that lively, up-to-date, self-assertive policy that has done so much, temporarily, for so many poets. For having visited New York and listened to its conversation:

> I once knew men as earnest and less shrill

he decided to go home:

> Back to the more of earth, the less of man,
> Where there is still a plain simplicity,
> And friendship, poor in everything but love,
> And faith, unwise, unquestioned, but a star. . . .

But the suffrages of those who do not have poetry thrust upon them but find it have always been Mr. Percy's and will be in increasing measure, I am sure, now that this volume of his own selections from his previous works— *Sappho in Levkas*, *In April Once* (1920), and *Enzio's Kingdom* (1924)—together with his new poems enables us to read his work in perspective.

The four lines quoted above suggest but do not limit the range of Mr. Percy's work. The visible world appeals to him as sensuously and as compellingly as it did to Keats but even in verses of a Keatsian "sweetness" he is conscious of a monitory daemon. From the sensuous world he can gather as much as any living poet. His work abounds with gracious figures:

> The pendent blue that bears
> No cloud except the daylight moon.

and:

> The unsilvering hour before dew warms to musk.

But the daemon is always with him, and in **"Girgenti"** we have one version of the argument:

> So many here have struggled, fought the fight!

And to what avail?:

> Did their names less profoundly plumb
>   The chasms of oblivion
> Than theirs who never fought,
> But, lightly submissive, spread
> The purple for their summer hearts
>   Within the garden's cool,
> Called for the golden cups, the snowy wine,
>   The honey-comb, and Aphrodite's flutes?

But the argument, and in purely human terms, goes against the

> Guzzlers against the fertile breasts of life.

even though the result be a splendid defeat for those who will not acquiesce.

For Mr. Percy, admiring a faith, "unwise, unquestioned," does not uncritically adopt one. His two longest poems, indeed, are both tragedies of faith betrayed by facts. They are laid in a period which has always engaged his sympathies, the thirteenth century. And here he finds in sharp conflict the sensuousness and the faith which we saw opposed in **"Girgenti."** In the first of these two to be written, **"In April Once,"** we have a tragic drama of the conflicting loyalties of the Middle Ages. Guido, once a page of the Holy Roman Emperor Frederick the Second—whose tragedy is to be unfolded for us in **"Enzio's Kingdom"**—brought up in a culture that anticipates the pagan joyousness of the Renaissance, is now imprisoned near Florence and has made friends with his gaoler, David. When their elders are away David lets his captive out of his cell. On this last and fated occasion he also lets out—that his friend may talk to them—the heretic Serle de Lanlarazon and a pirate. In the tense interviews that follow, Guido, pagan at heart and nominally a Roman Catholic, learns of the horrors that followed the Children's Crusade; and David, whose faith in God had been killed by his own participation in that sublime lunacy, learns that faith in God is yet possible, even though horror seems triumphant.

The reader who might judge from the early **"Page's Road Song"** or from the tenderly humorous **"St. Francis to the Birds"** that Mr. Percy's interest in the thirteenth century was decorative or sentimental may judge from this and from **"Enzio's Kingdom"** how thoroughly he has entered into the spirit of that time. In the latter poem, however, his interest is focussed not so much in the age as in the dream—a dream that might be of any age—of Frederick, Barbarossa's successor, who would build a united world. We are told the story, after Frederick's death, by his natural son, Enzio, though much of his story is given in direct quotation from his father. It is the old dream of the far-seeing and essentially benevolent imperialist who would give happiness, on his own level, to the common man, and freedom to the soaring spirit. And in the light of this aim, values are trans-valued, and as Frederick tells his vacillating lieutenant, Pietro:

> There's not a lie too great, a crime too gross
> I'll not be guilty of, if so thereby
> I may establish it and fix the lines
> Of the quivering vision I intend the world.

And Frederick is able to do this and to retain his magnanimity. For it is not any activity consciously engaged in that endangers a man's nobility. It is underground water only that tears away foundations, and the beginning of Frederick's disintegration is subtly shown us as springing from his righteousness rather than from his ignoring of this or that precept:

> He fought on with a difference that grew. . . .
> How do we hate iniquity and thrive,

But, hating them that are iniquitous,
Harden and grow ourselves somehow attaint
With the venom hoarded for the unrighteous foe?
Unjust dilemma! We cannot grip an evil
Fleshless, abstract, not cased in him or her
On whom we may lay hands of wrath and ruin!
To not hate wrong rubs out man's one distinction:
Ably to hate it saps the root of reason.

To deal with the pageant of the past is a temptation to any poet with a sense of the picturesque. To deal with the inwardness of the past is a challenge which few poets can successfully meet. But Mr. Percy has done it successfully.

In the later poems we find a continuation of Mr. Percy's interest in the evocation of the past—as he began his work with the story of Sappho's love for Phaon so he brings it to the present point with a beautiful retelling of the story of Castor and Pollux, and in the lyrics we meet more frequently the theme of the victorious acceptance of defeat—most tellingly phrased, perhaps, in **"Recompense."** But at once the most personal and the most generalized expression of Mr. Percy's point of view is given us in a series of fourteen untitled sonnets. Here imagery is with unusual success subordinated to poetic thought and we are given a sober magnificence that is the mark of poetic maturity. The sonnets beginning, "what disputations doth my spirit hold, . . ." "though we be breasted shallowly, to hold . . ." "with what unyielding fortitude of heart . . ." and "not the blue flagstones of eternal space, . . ." are notable examples of that rare poetry which is a reading—not a criticism—of life: of poetry which states, with finality, our ultimate human situation.

Clifton Fadiman (essay date 1941)

SOURCE: "Eskimos and Aristocrats," in *The New Yorker,* Vol. XVII, No. 5, March 15, 1941, pp. 71-3.

[*In the following excerpt, Fadiman takes a skeptical look at the romanticization of the agricultural South in* Lanterns on the Levee.]

From Castiglione's "The Courtier" to William Alexander Percy's *Lanterns on the Levee*, books by and about gentlemen have always made me a trifle uneasy. Garden-variety citizens like myself were taught somewhere or other, it seems to me, that the true gentleman is practically unaware of his status, does not need to insist on it, and never stoops—for that is an intellectual, not a gentlemanly, gesture—to analyze it. Mr. Percy, descendant of a long line of Southern gentlemen and, of course, gentlewomen, takes the situation with humor and grace—which cannot be said of that ineffable smug bore Castiglione—but even he cannot prevent the homiletic note from creeping in.

This said, let me add that it does not spoil his book, which is quite frankly a sentimental elegy on a way of life now dead, or if alive, alive only as an art consciously cultivated by such men—and they are regrettably few—as Mr. Percy himself. Without illusions, he writes, "Behind us a culture lies dying, before us the forces of the unknown industrial world gather for catastrophe."

Here, then, you will find a sweet-tempered defence, touched with tears, of the planter aristocracy, particularly as it developed in Mr. Percy's own country, the Mississippi delta. The author was born in 1885, son of a gallant father who served as a United States senator before the first World War. The tradition of the Percy family is consistently opposed to the new demagogic Southernism of such men as Talmadge, Bilbo, and Huey Long. The Percys fought the Klan (at the risk of their lives), had an unremitting sense of civic responsibility—the chapter on the 1927 flood is the most moving in the book—and they and men like them, if only there were enough of them, could certainly do more to solve the race problem than the Fascist-minded super-"poor whites" who now unfortunately dominate so much of the deep South's thinking.

Lanterns on the Levee is the record of a serene and philosophic defeatist. It has the Marcus Aurelius touch; indeed, much of the book is modelled on the "Meditations," especially those early chapters in which Mr. Percy pays eloquent tribute to his forebears and to his teachers, gentle and simple, black and white. It has charm, Southern charm, perhaps even too much of it for our frosty Northern hearts. It is single-minded, sentimental, humorous, and liberal in a manner very different from the programmatic economic-political liberalism of the Northeast. Whether Mr. Percy makes out an airtight case for the feudal regime whose tradition he inherited is questionable, but that he makes out a case for the sort of person he is himself is not.

William Jay Gold (essay date 1941)

SOURCE: "Southern Autobiography," in *The Saturday Review of Literature,* Vol. XXIII, No. 24, April 5, 1941, pp. 24, 26.

[*In the following essay, Gold offers a positive review of* Lanterns on the Levee, *assessing it as an accurate portrayal of the South and its problems.*]

William Alexander Percy was born in Greenville, on the Mississippi Delta, in 1885. That was one year before Henry W. Grady made his famous speech called "The New South"—a phrase used many times since to mean many different things. Grady pleaded for an end to sectional hatred and asked the South to look ahead rather than backward and he argued that the South's agricultural economy ought to be leavened with industry so that the region could end its colonial dependence on the manufacturing North. Men still find it necessary to beg for realism and a balanced economy in the South.

If we are to judge by his autobiography, Mr. Percy seems to have been born with the foreknowledge that he would have to live in a fading twilight. The South he knew still showed vestiges of what was once America's most gracious civilization, but the dark was falling fast in a world that had become "poor in spirit and common as hell." The corruption of defeat was in the very air that he breathed, and his was the bitter knowledge that his quarrel was with an enemy who would not give battle.

It was not only the old South that had perished, leaving nothing but ignoble heirs; it was, he soon discovered, the whole world: "The North destroyed my South; Germany destroyed my world." "In our brave new world a man of honor is rather like the Negro—there's no place for him to go." From Greenville he has looked out on the world, and everywhere found the "bottom rail on top."

But before full dark come the glories of sunset, and the story told in *Lanterns on the Levee* of a little boy growing up to be a Southern gentleman is full of charm. He recalls for us the robust people who were his ancestors: colorful and tempestuous and beautiful people who moved with sureness of step and certainty of conviction through a tradition they knew and helped form. A small boy living in rural Mississippi and Virginia learned all kinds of country lore from Negro playmates. For additional schooling there were private tutors, rugged and earnest individuals, from whom one could get a love of nature as well as a grounding in literature. There were steamboats and Negroes, the river and its levees, political gatherings with mint julep and high talk, and family dinners with food and stories. It was proper for the well bred to be poor and to own land, to love and care for the Negro but to distrust and scorn the uncouth rednecks and pecker-woods who were filtering into the Delta and making a farce of white supremacy.

Mr. Percy's formal schooling was accomplished at the University of the South, popularly called Sewanee ("because it was fairly near and healthy and genteel and inexpensive"), where his love of nature and poetry deepened and his formerly steadfast Catholic faith vaguely dissipated. There followed a year spent abroad, and then three years at Harvard Law School. Back in Greenville, Mr. Percy practised law with his father and began to write poetry in earnest. (Four volumes of his poetry have been published, but *Lanterns on the Levee* does not speak of them except in passing.) He campaigned with his father in a losing fight for reëlection to the United States Senate; with his father he fought the Ku Klux Klan in Greenville and saw it defeated at the polls; in the disastrous flood of 1927 he was chairman of the town's relief headquarters. A number of times he traveled abroad, and he was with the A. E. F. overseas during the war.

After his father's death he took over the management of Trail Lake, the plantation which employed nearly six hundred people. He has now retired from the practice of law as well as from the active management of the plan-

tation; his chief interest is his garden. But in Greenville he is still the one to whom white and black, rich and poor, come for advice, encouragement, money, and wisdom in living.

All through *Lanterns on the Levee* there runs a note of nostalgia, a longing not only for the old South, but for a time remembered only in legend and dream, when nobleness walked the earth and grandeur invested the hills and valleys, when majesty was man's everyday garment. He, too, has heard far off the horn of Roland in the passage of Spain, and has grieved that we do not hear it today. A great many of Mr. Percy's poems, it is worth noting, have thirteenth century themes. Small wonder that he has watched the passing scene with sorrow if not with scorn, small wonder that he has found today's battles mean and bemeaning. The single exception is his experience during the World War; then, although he hated the war, he says "That short period of my life spent in the line is the only one I remember step by step—as if it moved *sub specie aeternitatis.*"

Lanterns on the Levee is a beautifully written book; Mr. Percy's prose has dignity and vigor and style; and in every sentence he writes his own character is manifest. The book is rich in anecdotes well told and in people well portrayed. As autobiography it has few equals in recent books. It gives voice forthrightly to the faith of its author, and no one who wants to understand the conflicts in the South today can afford to neglect reading it.

As a commentary on the Southern scene the book will certainly be quoted in many places as giving the proper retort to those who believe with President Roosevelt that the South is Economic Problem No. 1, and that the sharecropper system is "infamous."

Willard Thorp (essay date 1943)

SOURCE: "William Percy's Collected Poems," in *The New York Times Book Review,* September 5, 1943, pp. 4, 12.

[*In the following essay, a review of* The Collected Poems, *Thorp treats Percy's verse as an artifact of another time.*]

This volume [*The Collected Poems of William Alexander Percy*] brings under one cover all the verse which the late William Alexander Percy published in his lifetime: *Sappho in Levkas* (1915), *In April Once* (1920), *Enzio's Kingdom* (1924) and *Selected Poems* (1930). No poem has been omitted or revised.

Though its imprint is 1943, much of the book is anachronistic. What could a reviewer say of "This Side of Paradise" if it were put into his hands and he were told it had just come from the press? This analogy is not farfetched. Percy considered himself a poet; what he wrote in verse seemed to him more essentially himself than anything he said or did. Yet he deliberately stood aside from the poetic movements of his time.

In his autobiography, *Lanterns on the Levee* (1941), whose popular success was deserved because it so attractively revealed the life and heart of a Southern patrician, Percy told how, after the war, he turned his back on the cosmopolitanism of the North and went back to the Mississippi delta where he was born. There he spent the remainder of his life (tragically cut short in 1942) as lawyer and plantation owner by inheritance, and, by choice, as poet and keeper of the conscience of the delta region.

Though he traveled widely and was always aware of the movements in art and thought of his time, his moral standards and artistic values he intended to work out for himself, with such help as he could get from the aristocratic tradition of the South. His effort to conserve what was best in this tradition, this constant return and re-valuation and the consequent exclusion of much that contemporary poets and philosophers were discovering, form the clues to Percy's life. He says, in **"Home"**:

> Back where the breakers of deep
>   sunlight roll
> Across flat fields that love and
>   touch the sky;
> Back to the more of earth, the
>   less of man,
> Where there is still a plain sim-
>   plicity,
> And friendship, poor in every-
>   thing but love,
> And faith, unwise, unquestioned,
>   but a star.

Percy's immersion in the past of his people and his own efforts to make music for himself in a discordant world explain the anachronistic quality of his verse. You would not guess from his poetry that Hopkins was discovered in the Twenties or that there has been an Eliot fashion and a Yeats cult. As you turn these pages you seem to be living again in those bright and expectant days when Fitzgerald spoke for the younger generation and the college literary magazines were deserting Rupert Brooke for Housman and the more disciplined of the Imagists. Until the publication of the "New Poems" in the 1930 volume we find little change or advance beyond his earliest work, when Swinburne, Browning and Gilbert Murray were his teachers.

In saying this I do not intend to imply that a poet must be in fashion, that Percy's verse would have been improved by a dash of Hart Crane and a pinch of Mac-Leish. The issue is deeper than the question of mere contemporaneity. Each generation evolves its own proper modes of expression. Often these are worked out by the advance guard of poets and other artists. At first the new modes baffle and seem ridiculous; those who invent them are called sensationalists and self-advertisers. But gradually, if they are really suitable, they are accepted.

Eventually even the unlettered comprehend by means of them. Movie-goers respond to symbolism without knowing the term, and those to whom cubism is still a laughing-word take in by means of it the vital messages of the four-color ad.

It would seem to be in the nature of things that a poet must learn to speak the new language of his time, modifying it for his peculiar purposes. Otherwise, to whom does he speak? Not to the past, surely; nor to the future, which can be spoken to only through what is permanent in the words of the present. To whom, then, are these poems of Percy's addressed? A good many of them, it must be admitted, to those who stopped reading poetry in 1915.

There would have been another way out, of course, for a poet like Percy who shut his ears to the poetic "voices shouting to be heard" in his own time. He might so perfect his own mode of speaking that his voice would be one of the few voices heard clearly above the din. Frost is this kind of poet. Some of Percy's poems make us believe that he might have been another such lone-goer if he had not been handicapped by his attitude toward poetry itself.

He belonged to the breed for whom the writing of poetry is primarily consummation or release. In *Lanterns on the Levee* he spoke of his poems as gushing up "almost involuntarily like automatic writing." The difficulty lay in "keeping the hot gush continuous and unself-conscious while at the same time directing it with cold intellect. I could never write in cold blood." Poetry was for him a way of stanching the bleeding, when wounded with anguish; a means of prolonging the moment, when struck with delight.

At this late date no one needs to point out the likelihood that a poet who holds these views may confuse the power of the emotion remembered with its incomplete expression in his verse. The reader of Percy's poetry will suspect that he made less effort than he imagined to direct into form the "hot gush" of feeling. His unrhymed cadences, not disciplined by the formal devices of the best free verse but modeled loosely on the choruses of "Samson Agonistes," were too easy for him. His verse plays and dramatic monologues permitted him to substitute the description of action for the precision of image. Even in his more carefully built stanzas the gear slips frequently: a line drops to bathos or its rhythm stumbles. He was capable of perfection when using simple forms (often the Emily Dickinson stanza) which compelled him to be faultless. His much-anthologized **"Overtones"** is as good a poem as it was in 1920.

Paradoxically Percy's best work belies his theory of poetry and his idea of himself as a poet. It is to be found in the group of "New Poems" first published in the *Selected Poems* of 1930. There is so much here that speaks eloquently to us that we must regret that though he loved poetry all his life he did not, save in these poems, take it seriously.

In spite of his disparagement of Donne, many of these last poems weld thought and emotion as poets have been doing since the metaphysical revival shook them out of their post-romantic dreaming of beauty. We know from his autobiography that Percy's life was fully lived, emotionally and intellectually. We should not know this from his early poems where his allegiance to the obsolete notion that poetry is reserved for one's moments of rapture prevented him from speaking from the mind as well as the heart. Here, at last, he came round to the belief—possibly never consciously formulated—that a divided sensibility enfeebles the artist as it does the man. That he should, while scorning to be a poet of his generation, have begun to write lines like these from **"Stirrup Cup"** makes one believe in the Time Spirit:

> We have seen stars and sunsets,
> We have heard birds and thunder,
> Many have been the travelers,
> We have had noble companions.
> Perhaps again (but the end is soon)
> We will see, and hear, and hold
>   lofty converse.

Whence came such fine (and modern) images as these, from **"Medusa"**?

> But I knew one who turned to stone
>   with terror
> Of facing quietly a flawless mirror.

Or these from the brave and moving **"At Sea"**?

> Break but the shackles and the
>   quailing sound is heard
> Of anchor chains that break.
>   The harbors of the past,
> Silted, have grown too shallow
>   for our deepening keels,
> Or we have lost the star that
>   guided to their entrance.

We to whom Mr. Knopf's sumptuous volume is presented must wish there were more poems like **"On an Antique Littoral."**

> Beauty gone, and beauty gone,
>   And gallant wisdom lost—
> Crowns the race so hardly won,
>   Twines of phantom frost!
>
> Sappho and Empedocles,
>   Time's kleptomaniac clan
> Coffer their gold where golden sleep
>   Knossos and Yucatan.
>
> Dreams that found their way in stone,
>   Cool mesmerists of peace,
> Or flushed to plumage in a song,
>   Or crimsoned Parian Greece.
>
> Loveliness dissuaded from
>   The locked and stubborn air—
> What rifling of the golden urn,
>   Our ransom from despair!

> Learn again, and lose again,
>   Create, and then destroy—
> For knowledge is the race's game
>   And loveliness its toy.

Walker Percy (essay date 1973)

SOURCE: An introduction to *Sewanee,* by William Alexander Percy, Frederic C. Beil, 1982, pp. vii-xv.

[*In the following essay, an introduction to his cousin's* Sewanee, *Percy offers his personal recollections of the man who raised him from the age of fourteen.*]

I remember the first time I saw him. I was thirteen and he had come to visit my mother and me and my brothers in Athens, Georgia, where we were living with my grandmother after my father's death.

We had heard of him, of course. He was the fabled relative, the one you liked to speculate about. His father was a United States senator and he had been a decorated infantry officer in World War I. Besides that, he was a poet. The fact that he was also a lawyer and a planter didn't cut much ice—after all, the South was full of lawyer-planters. But how many people did you know who were war heroes and wrote books of poetry? One had heard of Rupert Brooke and Joyce Kilmer, but they were dead.

The curious fact is that my recollection of him even now, after meeting him, after living in his house for twelve years, and now thirty years after his death, is no less fabled than my earliest imaginings. The image of him that takes form in my mind still owes more to Rupert Brooke and those photographs of young English officers killed in Flanders than to a flesh-and-blood cousin from Greenville, Mississippi.

I can only suppose that he must have been, for me at least, a personage, a presence, radiating that mysterious quality we call charm, for lack of a better word, in such high degree that what comes to mind is not that usual assemblage of features and habits which make up our memories of people but rather a quality, a temper, a set of mouth, a look through the eyes.

For his eyes were most memorable, a piercing gray-blue and strangely light in my memory, as changeable as shadows over water, capable of passing in an instant, we were soon to learn, from merriment—he told the funniest stories we'd ever heard—to a level gray gaze cold with reproof. They were beautiful and terrible eyes, eyes to be careful around. Yet now, when I try to remember them, I cannot see them otherwise than as shadowed by sadness.

What we saw at any rate that sunny morning in Georgia in 1930, and what I still vividly remember, was a strikingly handsome man, slight of build and quick as a youth. He was forty-five then, an advanced age, one would suppose, to a thirteen-year-old, and gray-haired besides, yet the abiding impression was of a youthfulness—and an exoticness. He had in fact just returned from the South Seas—this was before the jet age and I'd never heard of anybody going there but Gauguin and Captain Bligh—where he had lived on the beach at Bora Bora.

He had come to invite us to live with him in Mississippi. We did, and upon my mother's death not long after, he adopted me and my two brothers. At the time what he did did not seem remarkable. What with youth's way of taking life as it comes—how else can you take it when you have no other life to compare it with?—and what with youth's incapacity for astonishment or gratitude, it did not seem in the least extraordinary to find oneself orphaned at fifteen and adopted by a bachelor-poet-lawyer-planter and living in an all-male household visited regularly by other poets, politicians, psychiatrists, sociologists, black preachers, folk singers, itinerant harmonica players. One friend came to seek advice on a book he wanted to write and stayed a year to write it. It was, his house, a standard stopover for all manner of people who were trying to "understand the South," that perennial American avocation, and whether or not they succeeded, it was as valuable to me to try to understand them as to be understood. The observers in this case were at least as curious a phenomenon as the observed.

Now belatedly I can better assess what he did for us and I even have an inkling what he gave up to do it. For him, to whom the world was open and who felt more at home in Taormina than in Jackson—for though he loved his home country, he had to leave it often to keep loving it—and who in fact could have stayed on at Bora Bora and chucked it all like Gauguin (he told me once he was tempted), for him to have taken on three boys, age fourteen, thirteen, and nine, and raised them, amounted to giving up the freedom of bachelorhood and taking on the burden of parenthood without the consolations of marriage. Gauguin chucked it all, quit, cut out and went to the islands for the sake of art and became a great painter if not a great human being. Will Percy not only did not chuck anything; he shouldered somebody else's burden. Fortunately for us, he did not subscribe to Faulkner's precept that a good poem is worth any number of old ladies—for if grandmothers are dispensable, why not second cousins? I don't say we did him in (he would laugh at that), but he didn't write much poetry afterwards and he died young. At any rate, whatever he lost or gained in the transaction, I know what I gained: a vocation and in a real sense a second self, that is, the work and the self which, for better or worse, would not otherwise have been open to me.

For to have lived in Will Percy's house, with "Uncle Will" as we called him, as a raw youth from age fourteen to twenty-six, a youth whose only talent was a knack for looking and listening, for tuning in and soaking up, was nothing less than to be informed in the deepest sense of the word. What was to be listened to,

dwelled on, pondered over for the next thirty years was of course the man himself, the unique human being, and when I say unique I mean it in its most literal sense: he was one of a kind: I never met anyone remotely like him. It was to encounter a complete, articulated view of the world as tragic as it was noble. It was to be introduced to Shakespeare, to Keats, to Brahms, to Beethoven—and unsuccessfully, it turned out, to Wagner whom I never liked, though I was dragged every year to hear Flagstad sing Isolde—as one seldom if ever meets them in school.

"Now listen to this part," he would say as Gluck's *Orfeo* played—the old 78s not merely dropped from a stack by the monstrous Capehart, as big as a sideboard, but then picked up and turned over by an astounding hoop-like arm—and you'd make the altogether unexpected discovery that music, of all things, can convey the deepest and most unnameable human feelings and give great pleasure in doing so.

Or: "Read this," and I'd read or, better still, he'd read aloud, say, Viola's speech to Olivia in *Twelfth Night:*

> Make me a willow cabin at your gate,
> And call upon my soul within the house;
>
>   . . . . .
>
> And make the babbling gossip of the air
> Cry out "Olivia!"

You see? he'd as good as say, and what I'd begin to see, catch on to, was the great happy reach and play of the poet at the top of his form.

For most of us, the communication of beauty takes two, the teacher and the hearer, the pointer and the looker. The rare soul, the Wolfe or Faulkner, can assault the entire body of literature single-handedly. I couldn't or wouldn't. I had a great teacher. The teacher points and says *Look;* the response is *Yes, I see.*

But he was more than a teacher. What he was to me was a fixed point in a confusing world. This is not to say I always took him for my true north and set my course accordingly. I did not. But even when I did not follow him, it was usually in *relation* to him, whether with him or against him, that I defined myself and my own direction. Perhaps he would not have had it differently. Surely it is the highest tribute to the best people we know to use them as best we can, to become, not their disciples, but ourselves.

It is the good fortune of those who did not know him that his singular charm, the unique flavor of the man, transmits with high fidelity in **Lanterns on the Levee** (1941), which includes the chapter "Sewanee," published herewith. His gift for communicating, communicating himself, an enthusiasm, a sense of beauty, moral outrage, carries over faithfully to the cold printed page, although for those who did not know him the words cannot evoke—or can they?—the mannerisms, the quirk of mouth, the shadowed look, the quick Gallic shrug, the inspired flight of eyebrows at an absurdity, the cold Anglo-Saxon gaze. (For he was this protean: one time I was reading *Ivanhoe,* the part about the fight between Richard and Saladin, and knowing Richard was one of Uncle Will's heroes, I identified one with the other. But wait: wasn't he actually more like Saladin, not the sir-knight defender of the Christian West but rather the subtle easterner, noble in his own right? I didn't ask him, but if I had, he'd have probably shrugged: both, neither. . . .)

It should be noted that despite conventional assessments of *Lanterns on the Levee* as an expression of the "aristocratic" point of view of the Old South, Will Percy had no use for genealogical games, the old Southern itch for coats of arms and tracing back connections to the English squirearchy. Indeed if I know anything at all about Will Percy, I judge that in so far as there might be a connection between him and the Northumberland Percys, they, not he, would have to claim kin. He made fun of his ancestor Don Carlos, and if he claimed Harry Hotspur, it was a kinship of spirit. His own aristocracy was a meritocracy of character, talent, performance, courage, and quality of life.

It is just that, a person and a life, which comes across in *Sewanee*. And about him I will say no more than that he was the most extraordinary man I have ever known and that I owe him a debt which cannot be paid.

Walker Percy (essay date 1973)

SOURCE: An introduction to *Lanterns on the Levee: Recollections of a Planter's Son,* by William Alexander Percy, Louisiana State University Press, 1973, pp. vii-xviii.

[*In the following essay, an introduction to* Lanterns on the Levee, *Percy's famous relative expands on the comments he made in his introduction to* Sewanee, *portions of which constitute the first part of this essay.*]

I remember the first time I saw him. I was thirteen and he had come to visit my mother and me and my brothers in Athens, Georgia, where we were living with my grandmother after my father's death.

We had heard of him, of course. He was the fabled relative, the one you liked to speculate about. His father was a United States senator and he had been a decorated infantry officer in World War I. Besides that, he was a poet. The fact that he was also a lawyer and a planter didn't cut much ice—after all, the South was full of lawyer-planters. But how many people did you know who were war heroes and wrote books of poetry? One had heard of Rupert Brooke and Joyce Kilmer, but they were dead.

The curious fact is that my recollection of him even now, after meeting him, after living in his house for twelve years, and now thirty years after his death, is no less fabled than my earliest imaginings. The image of him that takes form in my mind still owes more to Rupert Brooke and those photographs of young English officers killed in Flanders than to a flesh-and-blood cousin from Greenville, Mississippi.

I can only suppose that he must have been, for me at least, a personage, a presence, radiating that mysterious quality we call charm, for lack of a better word, in such high degree that what comes to mind is not that usual assemblage of features and habits which make up our memories of people but rather a quality, a temper, a set of mouth, a look through the eyes.

For his eyes were most memorable, a piercing gray-blue and strangely light in my memory, as changeable as shadows over water, capable of passing in an instant, we were soon to learn, from merriment—he told the funniest stories we'd ever heard—to a level gray gaze cold with reproof. They were beautiful and terrible eyes, eyes to be careful around. Yet now, when I try to remember them, I cannot see them otherwise than as shadowed by sadness.

What we saw at any rate that sunny morning in Georgia in 1930, and what I still vividly remember, was a strikingly handsome man, slight of build and quick as a youth. He was forty-five then, an advanced age, one would suppose, to a thirteen-year-old, and gray-haired besides, yet the abiding impression was of a youthfulness—and an exoticness. He had in fact just returned from the South Seas—this was before the jet age and I'd never heard of anybody going there but Gauguin and Captain Bligh—where he had lived on the beach at Bora Bora.

He had come to invite us to live with him in Mississippi. We did, and upon my mother's death not long after, he adopted me and my two brothers. At the time what he did did not seem remarkable. What with youth's way of taking life as it comes—how else can you take it when you have no other life to compare it with?—and what with youth's incapacity for astonishment or gratitude, it did not seem in the least extraordinary to find oneself orphaned at fifteen and adopted by a bachelor-poet-lawyer-planter and living in an all-male household visited regularly by other poets, politicians, psychiatrists, sociologists, black preachers, folk singers, itinerant harmonica players. One friend came to seek advice on a book he wanted to write and stayed a year to write it. It was, his house, a standard stopover for all manner of people who were trying to "understand the South," that perennial American avocation, and whether or not they succeeded, it was as valuable to me to try to understand them as to be understood. The observers in this case were at least as curious a phenomenon as the observed.

Now belatedly I can better assess what he did for us and I even have an inkling what he gave up to do it. For him, to whom the world was open and who felt more at home in Taormina than in Jackson—for though he loved his home country, he had to leave it often to keep loving it—and who in fact could have stayed on at Bora Bora and chucked it all like Gauguin (he told me once he was tempted), for him to have taken on three boys, age fourteen, thirteen, and nine, and raised them, amounted to giving up the freedom of bachelorhood and taking on the burden of parenthood without the consolations of marriage. Gauguin chucked it all, quit, cut out and went to the islands for the sake of art and became a great painter if not a great human being. Will Percy not only did not chuck anything; he shouldered somebody else's burden. Fortunately for us, he did not subscribe to Faulkner's precept that a good poem is worth any number of old ladies—for if grandmothers are dispensable, why not second cousins? I don't say we did him in (he would laugh at that), but he didn't write much poetry afterwards and he died young. At any rate, whatever he lost or gained in the transaction, I know what I gained: a vocation and in a real sense a second self, that is, the work and the self which, for better or worse, would not otherwise have been open to me.

For to have lived in Will Percy's house, with "Uncle Will" as we called him, as a raw youth from age fourteen to twenty-six, a youth whose only talent was a knack for looking and listening, for tuning in and soaking up, was nothing less than to be informed in the deepest sense of the word. What was to be listened to, dwelled on, pondered over for the next thirty years was of course the man himself, the unique human being, and when I say unique I mean it in its most literal sense: he was one of a kind: I never met anyone remotely like him. It was to encounter a complete, articulated view of the world as tragic as it was noble. It was to be introduced to Shakespeare, to Keats, to Brahms, to Beethoven—and unsuccessfully, it turned out, to Wagner whom I never liked, though I was dragged every year to hear Flagstadt sing Isolde—as one seldom if ever meets them in school.

"Now listen to this part," he would say as Gluck's *Orfeo* played—the old 78s not merely dropped from a stack by the monstrous Capehart, as big as a sideboard, but then picked up and turned over by an astounding hoop-like arm—and you'd make the altogether unexpected discovery that music, of all things, can convey the deepest and most unnameable human feelings and give great pleasure in doing so.

Or: "Read this," and I'd read or, better still, he'd read aloud, say, Viola's speech to Olivia in *Twelfth Night:*

> Make me a willow cabin at your gate,
> And call upon my soul within the house;
>
>   . . . . .
>
> And make the babbling gossip of the air
> Cry out "Olivia!"

You see? he'd as good as say, and what I'd begin to see, catch on to, was the great happy reach and play of the poet at the top of his form.

For most of us, the communication of beauty takes two, the teacher and the hearer, the pointer and the looker. The rare soul, the Wolfe or Faulkner, can assault the entire body of literature single-handedly. I couldn't or wouldn't. I had a great teacher. The teacher points and says *Look;* the response is *Yes, I see.*

But he was more than a teacher. What he was to me was a fixed point in a confusing world. This is not to say I always took him for my true north and set my course accordingly. I did not. Indeed my final assessment of *Lanterns on the Levee* must register reservations as well as admiration. The views on race relations, for example, diverge from my own and have not been helpful, having, in my experience, played into the hands of those whose own interest in these matters is deeply suspect. But even when I did not follow him, it was usually in *relation* to him, whether with him or against him, that I defined myself and my own direction. Perhaps he would not have had it differently. Surely it is the highest tribute to the best people we know to use them as best we can, to become, not their disciples, but ourselves.

It is the good fortune of those who did not know him that his singular charm, the unique flavor of the man, transmits with high fidelity in *Lanterns on the Levee.* His gift for communicating, communicating himself, an enthusiasm, a sense of beauty, moral outrage, carries over faithfully to the cold printed page, although for those who did not know him the words cannot evoke—or can they?—the mannerisms, the quirk of mouth, the shadowed look, the quick Gallic shrug, the inspired flight of eyebrows at an absurdity, the cold Anglo-Saxon gaze. (For he was this protean: one time I was reading *Ivanhoe,* the part about the fight between Richard and Saladin, and knowing Richard was one of Uncle Will's heroes, I identified one with the other. But wait: wasn't he actually more like Saladin, not the sir-knight defender of the Christian West but rather the subtle easterner, noble in his own right? I didn't ask him, but if I had, he'd have probably shrugged: both, neither. . . .)

There is not much doubt about the literary quality of *Lanterns on the Levee,* which delivers to the reader not only a noble and tragic view of life but the man himself. But other, nonliterary questions might be raised here. How, for example, do the diagnostic and prophetic dimensions of the book hold up after thirty years? Here, I think, hindsight must be used with the utmost circumspection. On the one hand, it is surely justifiable to test the prophetic moments of a book against history itself; on the other hand, it is hardly proper to judge a man's views of the issues of his day by the ideological fashions of another age. Perhaps in this connection it would not be presumptuous to venture a modest hope. It is that *Lanterns on the Levee* will survive both its friends and its enemies, that is, certain more clamorous varieties of each.

One is all too familiar with both.

The first, the passionate advocate: the lady, not necessarily Southern, who comes bearing down at full charge, waving *Lanterns on the Levee* like a battle flag. "He is right! The Old South was right!" What she means all too often, it turns out, is not that she prefers agrarian values to technological but that she is enraged at having to pay her cook more than ten dollars a week; that she prefers, not merely segregation to integration, but slavery to either.

The second, the liberal enemy: the ideologue, white or black, who polishes off *Lanterns on the Levee* with the standard epithets: racist, white supremacist, reactionary, paternalist, Bourbon, etc., etc. (they always remind me of the old Stalinist imprecations: fascist, cosmopolitan, imperialist running dog).

Lanterns on the Levee deserves better and of course has better readers. Its author can be defended against the more extreme reader, but I wonder if it is worth the effort. Abraham Lincoln was a segregationist. What of it? Will Percy was regarded in the Mississippi of his day as a flaming liberal and nigger-lover and reviled by the sheriff's office for his charges of police brutality. What of that? Nothing much is proved except that current categories and names, liberal and conservative, are weary past all thinking of it. Ideological words have a way of wearing thin and then, having lost their meanings, being used like switchblades against the enemy of the moment. Take the words *paternalism, noblesse oblige,* dirty words these days. But is it a bad thing for a man to believe that his position in society entails a certain responsibility toward others? Or is it a bad thing for a man to care like a father for his servants, spend himself on the poor, the sick, the miserable, the mad who come his way? It is surely better than watching a neighbor get murdered and closing the blinds to keep from "getting involved." It might even beat welfare.

Rather than measure *Lanterns on the Levee* against one or another ideological yardstick, it might be more useful to test the major themes of the book against the spectacular events of the thirty years since its publication. Certainly the overall pessimism of *Lanterns on the Levee*, its gloomy assessment of the spiritual health of Western civilization, is hard to fault these days. It seems especially prescient when one considers that the book was mostly written in the between-wars age of optimism when Americans still believed that the right kind of war would set things right once and for all. If its author were alive today, would he consider his forebodings borne out? Or has the decline accelerated even past his imaginings? Would he see glimmerings of hope? Something of all three, no doubt, but mainly, I think, he'd look grim, unsurprised, and glad enough to have made his exit.

Certainly nothing would surprise him about the collapse of the old moralities, for example, the so-called sexual revolution which he would more likely define in less polite language as alley-cat morality. I can hear him now: "Fornicating like white trash is one thing, but leave it to this age to call it the new morality." Nor would he be shocked by the cynicism and corruption, the stealing, lying, rascality ascendant in business and politics—though even he might be dismayed by the complacency with which they are received: "There have always been crooks, but we've not generally made a practice of re-electing them, let alone inviting them to dinner." All this to say nothing of the collapse of civil order and the new jungle law which rules the American city.

Nothing new here then for him: if the horrors of the Nazi holocaust would have dismayed him and the moral bankruptcy of the postwar world saddened him, they would have done so only by sheer dimension. He had already adumbrated the Götterdämmerung of Western values.

But can the matter be disposed of so simply: decline and fall predicted, decline and fall taking place? While granting the prescience of much of *Lantern on the Levee*'s pessimism, we must, I think, guard against a certain seductiveness which always attends the heralding of apocalypse, and we must not overlook some far less dramatic but perhaps equally significant counterforces. Yes, Will Percy's indictment of modern life has seemed to be confirmed by the holocaust of the 1940s and by American political and social morality in the 1970s. But what would he make of some very homely, yet surely unprecedented social gains which have come to pass during these same terrible times? To give the plainest examples: that for the first time in history a poor boy, black or white, has a chance to get an education, become what he wants to become, doctor, lawyer, even read *Lanterns on the Levee* and write poetry of his own, and that not a few young men, black and white, have done just that? Also: that for the first time in history a working man earns a living wage and can support his family in dignity. How do these solid social gains square with pronouncements of decline and fall? I ask the question and, not knowing the answer, can only wonder how Will Percy would see it now. As collapse? Or as contest? For it appears that what is upon us is not a twilight of the gods but a very real race between the powers of light and darkness, that time is short and the issue very much in doubt. So I'd love to ask him, as I used to ask him after the seven o'clock news (Ed Murrow: *This*—is London): "Well? What do you think?"

The one change that would astonish him, I think, is the spectacular emergence of the South from its traditional role of loser and scapegoat. If anyone had told him in 1940 that in thirty years the "North" (i.e., New York, Detroit, California) would be in the deepest kind of trouble with race, violence, and social decay while the South had become, by contrast, relatively hopeful and even prosperous, he would not have believed it. This is not to say that he would find himself at home in the new Dallas or Atlanta. But much of *Lanterns on the Levee*— for example, the chapter on sharecropping—was written from the ancient posture of Southern apologetics. If his defense of sharecropping against the old enemy, the "Northern liberal," seems quaint now, it is not because there was not something to be said for sharecropping— there was a good deal to be said—and it is not because he wasn't naive about the tender regard of the plantation manager for the helpless sharecropper—he was naive, even about his own managers. It is rather because the entire issue and its disputants have simply been bypassed by history. The massive social and technological upheavals in the interval have left the old quarrel academic and changed the odds in the new one. It is hard, for example, to imagine a serious Southern writer nowadays firing off his heaviest ammunition at "Northern liberals." Not the least irony of recent history is that the "Northern liberal" has been beleaguered and the "Southern planter" rescued by the same forces. The latter has been dispensed by technology from the ancient problem, sharecroppers replaced by Farmall and Allis-Chalmers, while the former has fallen out with his old wards, the blacks. The displaced sharecroppers moved to the Northern cities and the liberals moved out. The South in a peculiar sense, a sense Will Percy would not necessarily have approved (though he could hardly have repressed a certain satisfaction), may have won after all.

So Will Percy's strong feelings about the shift of power from the virtuous few would hardly be diminished today, but he might recast his villains and redress the battle lines. Old-style demagogue, for example, might give way to new-style image manipulator and smooth amoral churchgoing huckster. When he spoke of the "bottom rail on top," he had in mind roughly the same folks as Faulkner's Snopeses, a lower-class, itchy-palmed breed who had dispossessed the gentry who had in turn been the true friends of the old-style "good" Negro. The upshot: an unholy hegemony of peckerwood politicians, a white hoi polloi keeping them in office, and a new breed of unmannerly Negroes misbehaving in the streets. But if he—or Faulkner for that matter—were alive today, he would find the battleground confused. He would find most members of his own "class" not exactly embattled in a heroic Götterdämmerung, not exactly fighting the good fight as he called it, but having simply left, taken off for the exurbs where, barricaded in patrolled subdivisions and country clubs and private academies, they worry about their kids and drugs. Who can blame them, but is this the "good life" Will Percy spoke of? And when some of these good folk keep *Lanterns on the Levee* on the bed table, its author, were he alive today, might be a little uneasy. For meanwhile, doing the dirty work of the Republic in the towns and cities of the South, in the schools, the school boards, the city councils, the factories, the restaurants, the stores, are to be found, of all people, the sons and daughters of the poor whites of the 1930s and some of those same uppity Negroes who went to school and ran for office, and who together are not doing so badly and in some cases very well indeed.

So it is not unreasonable to suppose that Will Percy might well revise his view of the South and the personae of his drama, particularly in favor of the lower-class whites for whom he had so little use. In this connection I cannot help but think of another book about the South, W. J. Cash's *The Mind of the South,* published oddly enough the same year by the same publisher as *Lanterns on the Levee*. Cash's book links Southern aristocrat and poor white much closer than the former ordinarily would have it. Both books are classics in their own right, yet they couldn't be more different; their separate validities surely testify to the diversity and complexity of this mysterious region. Yet in this case, I would suppose that Will Percy would today find himself closer to Cash in sorting out his heroes and villains, that far from setting aristocrat against poor white and both against the new Negro, he might well choose his present-day heroes—and villains—from the ranks of all three. He'd surely have as little use for black lawlessness as for white copping out. I may be wrong but I can't see him happy as the patron saint of Hilton Head or Paradise Estates-around-the-Country Club.

For it should be noted, finally, that despite conventional assessments of *Lanterns on the Levee* as an expression of the "aristocratic" point of view of the Old South, Will Percy had no more use than Cash for genealogical games, the old Southern itch for coats of arms and tracing back connections to the English squirearchy. Indeed if I know anything at all about Will Percy, I judge that in so far as there might be a connection between him and the Northumberland Percys, they, not he, would have to claim kin. He made fun of his ancestor Don Carlos, and if he claimed Harry Hotspur, it was a kinship of spirit. His own aristocracy was a meritocracy of character, talent, performance, courage, and quality of life.

It is just that, a person and a life, which comes across in *Lanterns on the Levee.* And about him I will say no more than that he was the most extraordinary man I have ever known and that I owe him a debt which cannot be paid.

Richard H. King (essay date 1977)

SOURCE: "Mourning and Melancholia: Will Percy and the Southern Tradition," in *The Virginia Quarterly Review,* Vol. 53, No. 2, Spring, 1977, pp. 248-64.

[*In the following essay, King examines* Lanterns on the Levee *as a historical document that preserves for posterity the South of the early twentieth century.*]

Capping as they did a decade of intense regional introspection, the early 1940's saw a remarkable proliferation of works by Southerners about the South. In 1942 William Faulkner published his last great work, *Go Down Moses,* an extended effort at moral and historical analysis. But the year preceding was perhaps even more fruitful, at least in quantity, for it had seen three unique, even idiosyncratic attempts to encompass the Southern present and past: W. J. Cash's *The Mind of the South,*

James Agee's *Let Us Now Praise Famous Men,* and William Alexander Percy's *Lanterns on the Levee.*

Of these four works Percy's has received the least attention. I would, therefore, like to examine *Lanterns on the Levee* and the man, Will Percy, whose autobiographical remembrance it is, in the hope that both the book and the man can be placed in proper context.

What the Vanderbilt Agrarians advanced as a relatively untroubled defense of the Southern tradition against the onslaughts of modernity was by 1941 to become in Percy's *Lanterns on the Levee* a melancholic reflection on a time out of joint, an elegy for a lost ethos by a son who mourned the loss of a father and a tradition of the Fathers. Ultimately the Agrarian vision was an academic one, a stance rather than a rooted position. Percy was a serious man, whatever else he was, and attempted to live by a tradition that had been created by the Civil War and destroyed by the First World War; or, perhaps as accurately, destroyed by the Civil War and re-created by the First War. Therein lies the difference and the greater authenticity which Percy embodied.

As a "last gentleman," Percy himself has become rather a monumental figure to be conjured with by those who knew him and by those who seek to understand the varieties of historical consciousness exhibited by Southern writers and intellectuals of the 1930's, particularly that form of memory which mourned the loss of a way of life. To his friends and admirers, Percy was something of a saint, a man of "fastidiousness and delicacy of manner," to quote his fellow Greenvillian and intimate friend, David Cohn. Hodding Carter, whom Percy helped persuade to come to Greenville, Mississippi, and found the *Delta Democrat,* remembered Percy's "giving of self," his willingness to aid those in distress. All remember his capacity for suffering fools. An outsider to the South and to the Delta, anthropologist Hortense Powdermaker, wrote of Percy's kindness in facilitating her access to Indianola, where she studied race relations in the 1930's. John Dollard consulted with Percy while researching his famous study of race and class; and while Percy took strong exception to Dollard's conclusions and would never comment on the substance of Miss Powdermaker's study, he was unfailingly courteous to them when called upon for aid.

II

Will Percy was not a happy man. Walker Percy remembers that his "uncle's" eyes were "shadowed by sadness" and wonders in his *The Message in the Bottle* (1975) "why he was sad from 1918 to 1941 even though he lived in as good an environment as man can devise . . . ?" Cohn struck much the same note when he wrote that Will Percy "was the loneliest man I have ever known." If the message of *Lanterns on the Levee* is any clue, it is no wonder that Will Percy was possessed by melancholy: the prophet of decline can hardly be expected to exhibit rising spirits. Yet the most apocalyptic of voices

may privately be joyful and the comic jests of the humorist underlain, as is well known, with private sadness. Still, in Percy's case, the private man did seem to reflect the essential pessimism of the cultural critic. Where the Agrarians had sought to re-evoke (even re-instate) a past cultural ethos, Percy had no confidence that the old order could be restored nor did he try to suggest a way of doing so. He was the melancholic Roman to the end—rarely the joyous and tragic Greek—and found a provisional solace only in the Stoic maxims of Marcus Aurelius and the ethical precepts of the Gospels. And though he presided over his own small realm in the Delta, he felt no more sense of freedom in the world at large than that experienced by the other great Stoic, the slave Epictetus.

Thus *Lanterns on the Levee* seems to present the Will Percy whom his friends knew and cherished. According to Cohn, Percy had begun his autobiographical reflections in the late 1930's, but he had put the manuscript aside when several friends discouraged him from completing it. Cohn found the fragments scattered throughout the Percy living room and upon reading them urged his friend to continue. *Lanterns on the Levee* was published in 1941; and not long thereafter, in January of 1942, Percy died of a cerebral hemorrhage. Percy had never been physically robust, and his memoirs reflect his own impending mortality. It is then a work in which personal fate, cultural vision, and historical development coalesce to produce a work in which death and the intimations of mortality preside.

Despite its melancholy tone, *Lanterns on the Levee* is anything but depressing: it is often charming, ironical, and informed by a winning self-deprecation. Despite his own angle of vision, W. J. Cash thoroughly enjoyed the book and forgave Percy his biases, while James Agee was fond of reading aloud to his friends those portions of *Lanterns on the Levee* which had to do with Sewanee. If the South's fate boded forth a "sideshow Götterdämmerung," as Percy suggested, it was a twilight of the Gods—and the quite mortal man, Will Percy, full experienced and contemplated it with the equanimity of a man who knew that he and his vision would surely die. But never is it morbid or whining. Not for nothing did Percy consider himself a Stoic.

Nor did Will Percy seclude himself to await his inevitable end. To Walker Percy, his uncle was the best teacher imaginable, introducing him and his brothers to the rich cadences of Shakespeare and the heavy mournful strains of Brahms and Wagner. And just as Walker Percy paid homage to his adoptive father as a teacher, so is *Lanterns on the Levee,* particularly in its early pages, a remembrance of those who had guided his own *Bildung.* What Will Percy seemed to remember from his various mentors, most of them lonely and eccentric in their way, was a way of living with loneliness, a quiet valor which provided an heroic but ultimately futile protest against an unfeeling world and death which presided over it.

Much of the moving power of *Lanterns on the Levee* and its elegiac ambience, which verges on but rarely succumbs to self-pity, lies in the barely suggested inner conflicts and the reticences which make themselves felt throughout the book. Though Will Percy has been scored, and rightly so, for his paternalism and racism, his own social and racial views were not without ambiguity and a sense of ambivalence beneath the surface. In *Lanterns on the Levee*, he returns repeatedly to the racial theme, as though he had to try to tell it again, so as to convince outsiders such as Powdermaker and Dollard and perhaps even himself. He laughs outwardly, but not inwardly, when his factotum, Ford, for whom Percy shows a quite condescending but real affection, informs him that the tenants on his "Trail Lake" plantation consider Percy's automobile as "us car." When Percy asks him what they mean by this odd phrase, Ford replies that they think the car belongs to them, since it is their labor which has paid for it. That Percy would include such an incident in his book shows something of his inner doubts.

On sharecropping Percy had opinions which jar against our more enlightened sensibilities. It is, he says, a form of "profit sharing . . . the most moral system under which human beings can work together . . . I am convinced that if it were accepted in principle by capital and labor, our industrial troubles would be over. . . . Sharecropping is one of the best systems ever devised to give security and a chance for profit to the simple and the unskilled." Yet he admits as well that the "organic" relationship of planter and cropper is often, even generally, an occasion for rank exploitation and, in truth, depends upon the character of the planter. One suspects that even Percy knew that the personal factor had ceased to play a role, if it ever had, and that the system was exploitative as such.

When discussing race directly, Percy marvels at the existing peace and amicability between the races in the South, since, he claims, they are centuries apart in intellectual and moral development. Yet this rather hackneyed judgment by the Delta aristocrat is balanced by the cogent observation that to live "habitually as a superior among inferiors . . . is a temptation to dishonesty and hubris and deterioration," an observation which shorn of its racial bias offers a truth that critics of colonialism have echoed. More than that, Percy states quite openly another home truth which those of more liberal promptings, then and now, hear reluctantly: "the sober fact is we understand one another not at all." Again, though the important insight is compromised by the racial assumptions, such comments indicate that Percy was not quite the undivided self on race that we would have him be. This is not to say that Percy was a liberal *malgré lui,* only that he was sensitive to certain aspects of class and racial domination which others downplayed or ignored.

About the "poor whites," however, he was neither reticent nor was his opinion marked by conflicting insights

which signalled doubt or inner division. In *Lanterns on the Levee*, Percy rendered no lip service to the egalitarian ideals of the 1930's; and, unlike Cash, Agee, and some of the Agrarians, he saw no virtue in the common whites, past or present. Reflecting in part the peculiar demography of the Delta, Percy divided his South and that of his ancestors into three categories: the aristocracy, the poor whites, and the blacks. The poor whites were "intellectually and spiritually . . . inferior to the Negro." They were the corrupters of "civil" society, the mob, *Demos,* whose emergence into the public realm heralded the decline of quality not only in the South, but in Italy, Germany, and Russia. His unmitigated animus against the common whites reflected not only the traditional attitudes of his class; it was given added bite by his experience in his father's bitter Senatorial campaign of 1911 against the champion of the poor whites, James K. Vardaman.

Thus Percy's protest against the world he never made assumed the following shape in his autobiography. First, he equated manners with morals; indeed he went so far as to elevate the former over the latter. The style was the man and the culture: "while good morals are all important between the Lord and his creatures, what counts between one creature and another is good manners." Manners were not, however, the exclusive property of the upper class but could be found throughout the social system. This nod toward equality was only apparent, since manners were those habitual attitudes and actions which preserved the order of things and guaranteed that the bottom rail remained on bottom. Percy, not surprisingly, felt that economics should mirror the social and political hierarchy, and his defense of sharecropping was part of a larger distaste for the cash nexus of capitalism and the levelling impulses of socialism. What was important was that the rational pursuit of profit be incorporated into an ethos of organic solidarity among the classes. Finally, Percy held that politics was an affair among gentlemen to whom the common whites should defer for enlightened guidance. Blacks were excluded altogether from the public realm and to be governed by the time-honored precepts of family relationships as the "younger brother(s)" which he claimed they were. About women he felt much the same.

More generally Percy's cultural vision embodied the "Delta ideal" and was linked in imagination with the early Virginia aristocracy and the feudal order of medieval Europe. The mood suffusing *Lanterns* was one of cultural pessimism. He felt that he was presiding over the closing time of civilized life; most had forgotten that it "is given to man to behold beauty and worship nobility." "A tarnish," Percy wrote, "has fallen over the bright world; dishonor and corruption triumph; my own strong people are turned into lotus-eaters; defeat is here again, the last, the most abhorrent."

III

How then can we characterize Percy and his vision of the Southern tradition? In his introduction to the paperback edition of *Lanterns on the Levee*, Walker Percy castigates present-day critics for calling his adoptive father a "racist, white supremacist, reactionary, paternalist, Bourbon" and goes so far as to claim that in the Mississippi of the 1930's and 1940's "Uncle" Will was considered a "flaming liberal" and a "nigger lover." Though one can agree in the abstract with Walker Percy's animadversions against facile name-calling, he seems guilty here of uncharacteristic obtuseness in rejecting these labels for his uncle. If it matters, Will Percy was all that his critics have claimed. But, more important, all of the above labels can be subsumed under a wider rubric to which we will now turn.

To understand Will Percy as a cultural type, we must see him against the background of the modernization of the South. If America was the first modern nation, then the South has historically been a partial exception to the tradition of Locke in politics and Franklin in the marketplace, at least, that is, in its cultural ambitions. In the post Civil War period, the "New South" movement was the cutting edge of the ideology of modernization in the South, but it disguised its full impact by diverting attention toward the glories of the ante-bellum past. By the 1930's, the South stood uneasily between past and future, and it was that decade which saw the emergence of a critical intelligentsia in the region whose divisions can be understood best in terms of various responses to modernization.

At one extreme stood modernizers such as Howard Odum and the University of North Carolina Regionalists, who saw the South's necessary course to lie in agricultural diversity, industrial development, and the maximum exploitation of natural and human resources. Left behind would be the irrationalities of the past; racial dogmas were ever so gently questioned; and political demagoguery, whether from the classes or the masses, was decried. It would be too much to call Odum and his colleagues "technocrats" or to group them with conventional "New South" advocates; still their essential vision was one of a South, rationalized and hence increasingly rational. Once accomplished in its essentials, modernization would see the fading of peripheral problems such as racial and religious intolerance and a turn away from the past toward the future.

At the other extreme were those such as the Vanderbilt Agrarians and Will Percy to whom Barrington Moore's label "Catonist" could well apply. The Catonist or reactionary response to modernization has appeared in every European nation, especially in Germany, and, as Moore's rubric indicates, has a history tracing back at least to the Roman Republic. Prototypically, Catonism is the ideological response of a landed upper class which is economically and politically on the defensive. Alien values intrude, and commercial, impersonal forces are seen as disrupting an aristocratic, hierarchical, and organic order held together by ties of family, status, tradition, and, sometimes, race. The Catonist fears the "people" politically, though he may often celebrate the supposed unity of all the classes. Further, according to Moore, the "sterner virtues" such as "militarism, contempt for decadent foreigners, and anti-intellectualism" are embraced. The Catonist takes the collapse of his own world—an historical fact—as the end of virtue and excellence generally—a metaphysical fact.

Aside from such intellectuals as T. S. Eliot and Henry Adams, the South has clearly been the *locus classicus* of Catonist intellectuals. Pessimistic about the future, the Catonist looks with longing toward a past heroic age. In Nietzsche's terms, he is a despairing "monumentalist." This vision has been relatively rare in America, whose dominant form of cultural nostalgia has been either Jeffersonian, a yearning for the return of a yeoman republic, or a hallowing of the Founding Fathers, who, for all their Roman posturings, were not very good Catonists themselves. But the South has had in its cultural imaginings a period of aristocratic domination, a heroic war, and an unjust occupation. Never discredited, but only defeated, the planters were a fit subject for 20th century monumentalizing on the part of Southern intellectuals. And though it would be unfair to call Percy an unqualified champion of militarism and anti-intellectualism, in most respects he fits the Catonist image quite well. With him, recollection led to a desire for repetition of the past. At the same time, he realized that such a repetition was impossible.

To understand the inner, psychological dynamic of Percy's Catonism, it is necessary to examine Percy's relationship with his father and his family, since for him, as for so many Southern writers of the 1930's, the father and the family became the mediating symbols by which they understood themselves and their past. Percy came from an old Mississippi family (though, as is always the case in such matters, not that old), dating back to the 1830's. On the maternal side were French blood and the Catholic faith, while the paternal line reputedly traced back to the Percys of Northumberland. Thus he was a member of the segment of Delta and Black Belt planter class with Catholic or high-church Episcopal connections. Such families summered in the Virginia mountains or more often on Monteagle Mountain near Sewanee or the north Alabama resort of Mentone. Typically, their sons would be sent, as was Percy, to a school like Sewanee, where the Confederacy and Episcopalianism vied for top place, and then on to legal finishing school at the University of Virginia or Harvard. After graduation, the sons would return to take over the family holdings or help their fathers until they relinquished the reins. Occasionally, one of the returning sons would be infected with advanced ideas while "abroad" and acquire a reputation as the local liberal because he subscribed to *The New Republic* or *The American Mercury* and, like Faulkner's Gavin Stevens, mouthed the traditional pieties in moderate tones. It might even happen that a returned son would choose the maverick's role, joining and perhaps even constituting the American Civil Liberties Union in the area or in the entire state. The lawyer portrayed by Jack Nicholson in *Easy Rider* is such a type, an alcoholic radical tolerated by family and friends in much the same way as the town looney or the crazy old lady who brandished her shotgun at children who trampled her flowers.

Implicit in this pattern, the staple of much Southern literature but nevertheless quite real, was the gradual decline in energy and will as generation gave way to generation. As Florence King has sardonically suggested, each Southern scion was urged by his mother to "be half the man your daddy was," and the son unhappily took her injunction to heart. The upshot was that, after three generations or so, the heroic age of the grandfathers who had fought the Yankees and driven out the carpetbaggers had given way to grandsons who had become pale copies of their fathers and fallen prey to brooding, drink, or other destructive impulses. Colonel John Sartoris gives way to young Bayard Sartoris, hell-bent on self-destruction; General Compson and Thomas Sutpen are followed by the psychotic Quentin Compson.

Though lacking the dramatic flourishes, this pattern was at work in the Percy family; at least Will Percy felt it to be. All his life he felt small and physically unprepossessing beside his virile father and grandfather. Where they were resolute and heroic public men, he was a private versifier and belletristic trifler. It was too much to live up to. Will Percy had to live in the shadow of a father he considered "the only great person I ever knew." "It was hard having such a dazzling father," he wrote of the man whose personal courage in facing down mobs and leading the fight against the Klan in the early 1920's was legendary in the Delta, "no wonder I longed to be a hermit."

Such admissions come relatively rarely in *Lanterns*. Clearly, however, the burden of being his father's son weighed heavily on Will Percy. Near the end of his memoirs Percy prefaces a discussion of the heroic efforts of his paternal grandfather—"Fafar" to Will Percy and "The Grey Eagle" or "Old Colonel Percy" to his acquaintances, a John Sartoris figure if there ever was one—in restoring white supremacy to Mississippi with the relieved comment that his great-grandfather, whose portrait also hung in the Percy house, had not been such a "demanding ancestor." This detail, almost a throwaway observation, is crucial and reveals some of the inner strain from which Will Percy must have suffered. Earlier, Percy admits that he and his father had not been close during his childhood and writes of the fun he had fishing with one of his uncles in Virginia: "You walked along carrying the empty fish-basket and felt easy and liked his grumpiness." But then he follows with: "Of course he wasn't comparable to Father. . . . "

IV

Never quite a hermit but always an outsider, Will Percy felt homeless where he should have felt most secure; and his constant travel throughout his life betrayed his essential lostness and failure to gain purchase on a con-genial reality. After college at Sewanee, he had no clear sense of what he wanted to do and backed into Harvard Law after a lonely year in Europe. Then after law school, he was again at loose ends; and Percy wonders in retrospect if his father hadn't yearned then for the younger son who had died early; he had been "all boy, all sturdy, obstreperous charm," everything which Will Percy felt he wasn't. And though he enjoyed teaching a term at Sewanee, he eventually returned to Greenville to join his father's law firm and take up his bachelor's existence as sometime poet and full-time assistant to his father.

Only with the onset of the Great War and his service in combat did Will Percy for a time feel necessary. Out from under his father and family, some of his essential despair and isolation were alleviated, and he came alive. Thinking back on his war experience, he writes: "Although you felt like a son of a bitch, you knew you were a son of God. A battle is something you dread intolerably and for which you have always been homesick . . . it somehow had meaning and daily life hasn't. . . . " Thus the First War had great personal meaning to Percy and many Southern young men, for it represented a chance to prove themselves the equals of their heroic grandfathers and fathers—real and symbolic—who had risked their lives in the only war that had really counted. It became the great repetition, the chance to mirror the monumental deeds of the founders of the Southern tradition. Daily life, the keeping of accounts and making of a living, were tedium itself. Even the cultivated and sensitive Percy was later to recall the contempt and irrelevance which he had felt for art and conventional notions of beauty on the eve of facing death in battle. What he desired was not a moral equivalent of war but something close to a military equivalent of culture.

The War did not last forever, and Percy returned to Greenville to resume his place in his father's shadow. He went through the Klan battles of the early 1920's with him, but the central event of the decade for our purposes was the flood of 1927. Will Percy had been named chairman of local relief efforts and found agreement from his committee that the black population should be moved from the levee to better and safer quarters in Vicksburg. The problem was that local planters feared that should their cheap black labor be evacuated, it would be lured north and never return to the plantation. As Percy relates it, his father agreed that he should not be intimidated but did suggest that Will poll his committee again to make certain that there was still general agreement to remove the blacks. When the group re-convened, Percy was astounded to find that each member had changed his mind and recommended to a man that the black labor force be maintained on the Greenville levee.

Later Percy discovered that his father had gone behind his back and personally persuaded the committee members to change their votes. Will Percy's authentic paternalism, uncomfortable as it may make us feel, had proved powerless before the commercial considerations of his father's kind of people. Even more startling—and telling—is that Will Percy cannot bring himself to register the hurt and sense of betrayal he must have felt at the contempt his father had shown him.

The extraordinary reticence here only reminds us of Will Percy's absorption in the "family romance." Why the subtitle "Recollections of a Planter's Son" unless to remind us of his status as a latecomer, a minor planet in his father's orbit? In fact, Will Percy was every bit as much the planter as his father, who was primarily a corporation lawyer. Nothing points so much to the distorted view of his family's place in the Southern tradition as the continued reference to his father as a planter. In other circumstances, a mother might have supplied the psychic and emotional resources for opposing the father and the collective weight of the tradition. But in the Percy family she did not or could not. Percy's mother remains a shadowy figure in *Lanterns on the Levee*, never really there for us, the readers, nor, one suspects, for Will Percy. We get a bare hint of his deep hurt only when Percy continues his description of the smile of his "undemanding" great-grandfather: it was "very shadowy and knowing, a little hurt but not at all bitter."

With his parents' death in the late 1920's, Will Percy's "life seemed superfluous." He took over the running of the family property and, as mentioned, became the man to see in Mississippi, an explainer of the region to outsiders. He lived the rest of his days travelling, reading, gardening, listening to his favorites, Brahms and Wagner, and providing an education for the three adopted sons who had been rendered homeless by their parents' suicide. Sharing himself generously with his sons, he became perhaps the father which he would have liked to have had.

Will Percy was also a poet, something one would scarcely learn from his autobiography. During his lifetime, three volumes appeared—*Sappho in Levkas and Other Poems* (1915), *In April Once* (1920), and *Enzio's Kingdom* (1924)—but after the mid-twenties the muse apparently departed him. His was a minor poetic gift, though his poetry is not without interest, since it allows us a glimpse of his more private concerns, however refracted they may be by their expression in verse. The setting is generally in the past—medieval or ancient Europe and the Mediterranean; the mode is pastoral and bucolic; the tone, not surprisingly, elegiac. Blues, violets, and lilacs are the dominant colors of settings often populated by fawns, nightingales, and shepherds. There is little sweat or toil, and of his own time or region Percy speaks little.

Three themes run throughout the poetry: the pathos of unrequited love, the deep conflict between physical desire and spiritual love, and the loyalty of son to father. The title poem of his first volume revolves around the love of Sappho for a "Slim, brown shepherd boy with windy eyes / and spring upon his mouth!" and how this carnal love for a mortal cuts her off from Zeus: "And meeting him lost Thee!" Sappho's love is not without social and intellectual condescension as when she observes of the object of her chaste desire that "His thoughts [were] the thoughts of shepherds." And though she dreams of kissing and being comforted by him, sexual passion is considered a form of "grossness." Still she desires him. The conflict of the spiritual and sexual is thematized again in **"To Lucrezia,"** where Percy writes more strikingly and with less reticence of "some young god, / With blown, bright hair and fillet golden, came / And stretching forth the blossoming rod of beauty / Upon me wrought a pagan spell." The poem **"Sublimation"** in his second volume talks of locking "your sin in a willow cage / . . . Outside your good deeds cluck and strut / But small's the joy they bring."

In **"Enzio's Kingdom"** the central theme is the loyalty of son to father, a concern which obviously reflects the sense of beleagueredness which Will Percy and his father experienced during the fight against the Klan and earlier against Vardaman. Enzio's father, Frederick II, has led a revolt against the Catholic Church and other European monarchs in the hopes of establishing a reign of universal peace in which the masses will be kept content, while the chosen few pursue the search for truth. Once his followers learn of his hard vision, Frederick is deserted and condemned. His father now dead, Enzio recalls their mighty plans and then how both grew as brutal and calloused as the enemy they had been fighting. The climax comes when he exclaims: "There is no certain thing I can lay hold on / And say, 'This, this is good! This will I worship!' / Except my father."

A consideration of Percy's poetic concerns leads one back to *Lanterns on the Levee*. In writing of his year in Paris, Percy remembers how he was repulsed by a leering hermaphroditic statue in the Louvre and how he later learned that at one time the Greeks had "practised bi-sexuality honestly and openly. . . . It's a grievous and a long way you travel to reach serenity and the acceptance of facts without hurt or shock. . . . By that time you are too old to practice your wisdom. . . . " And near the end of the book Percy casts back over his past to recall several fleeting and apparently unfulfilled homoerotic encounters. Thus, sexually, Percy depicts himself, albeit fleetingly, as a man divided within himself and unable to express openly his essential desires.

Not only in love, if his poetry hints rightly, but in his family Percy came to accept without self-pity that he "was never first place in any life." *Lanterns on the Levee* ends as Percy imagines his final confrontation with death, the "High God." "Who are you?" asks Death. Writes Percy: "The pilgrim I know should be able to straighten his shoulders, stand his tallest, and to answer defiantly: 'I am your son.'"

V

In a decaying patriarchal tradition such as the South's in the 1930's, cultural criticism had to begin with the father and culminate in a critique of the Fathers, the tradition. The real and symbolic aspects were too intimately connected to be avoided. Will Percy was in some fundamental way unmanned by his father and by the tradition; and this foreclosed, I suspect, the full expression of his intellectual and creative capacities. The tensions and ambivalences which he so obviously experienced were never quite fully explored. Percy knew that something was wrong, but he could never quite put his finger on exactly what it was and who was responsible.

The block in his way was his father who loomed over everything he did. Percy gave fulsome and authentic praise to his father and the tradition of the Fathers, yet if we know anything, it is that such over-valuations conceal resentments and bitterness. How else explain the rueful hints of awareness? And, more deeply, why the explicit association of his father with death itself? Why else the forging of a life which was diametrically opposed to his father's style, if not partly by way of revenge as well as veneration? With his father's presiding presence always at hand, he could only blame himself—as weak and disappointing; or blacks—as irresponsible and inferior; or poor whites—as envious and barbarians—for the decline which had set in.

Finally we can see in Percy what might be called a form of "cultural melancholia," a notion which subsumes the Catonist label and the psychological relationship with his father. As with the melancholic, Percy could only blame himself for what in truth he should have directed at his father with whom he had so closely identified yet under whose hold he surreptitiously chafed. This is not to claim that all reactionary protests against the modern world are the issue of sons who have been overwhelmed by strong fathers and publicly bemoan what they unconsciously welcome. But in Percy's case, there was something like that at work. Overcome by the anxiety of his father's influence and the influence of a tradition which was so strong precisely at the moment of its demise, Percy could only obliquely register his protest. Set beside the moral as well as artistic achievement of Cash, Agee, and particularly Faulkner, Percy's life and artistic efforts represent an important and fascinating failure. Indeed Faulkner, in his review of *In April Once*, noted that Percy was "like a little boy closing his eyes against the dark of modernity." This is perhaps too strong. Still Will Percy could only yearn for a world which was irretrievable, if it ever had existed, and which stood now under the sign of the father and of death.

Lewis A. Lawson (essay date 1980)

SOURCE: "William Alexander Percy, Walker Percy, and the Apocalypse," in *Another Generation: Southern Fiction since World War II,* University Press of Mississippi, 1980, pp. 122-43.

[*In the following essay, Lawson explores the use of apocalyptic imagery—a specific array of symbols dat-* *ing back to Joachim of Flora in Medieval times—in the works of both William Alexander Percy and Walker Percy.*]

In 1924 William Alexander Percy published his third volume of poetry, *Enzio's Kingdom and Other Poems*. The time for its writing had been snatched from a life that was otherwise given over to public demands. For Percy and his father, former Senator LeRoy Percy, were among those who had been occupied during the past several years in a furious battle to keep the Ku Klux Klan from establishing its control over Mississippi.[1]

Will Percy describes in his autobiography, *Lanterns on the Levee* (1941),[2] the onset of the Klan threat and the decision made by Greenville community leaders that LeRoy Percy should lead the defense, just as LeRoy's father had spoken for the town during Reconstruction times (*LL*, 274). Their community had not welcomed the original, postwar Klan, even though it had the Confederate cavalry tradition for cachet, and the new Klan was not about to be accepted. The Greenvilleans and others around the state were astonishingly successful in denying public acceptability to the Klan during those confused years, so that while the *New York Times* frequently detailed Klan activities in the South, and in the North (even on Long Island!), it remained silent about Mississippi.

Which is not to say that the Klan was totally frustrated in its Mississippi campaign. At first the citizens did rally to LeRoy Percy, who became a national anti-Klan leader. He spoke at rallies, some as far away as Chicago, and warned a national audience about "The Modern Ku Klux Klan" in the July 1922, *Atlantic Monthly*. His opponents were learning, though, to use the money they were accumulating through initiation and regalia fees and to use the advantages of secrecy and hierarchical organization. LeRoy Percy was forced to warn, in a letter to the *New York Times,* on June 18, 1924, that the Mississippi delegation to the upcoming national Democratic convention had been chosen by a Klan-dominated state convention. Some of the delegates might not be Klan members, he acknowledged, but because of the unit rule the Klan would control the delegation.

The enemy may have been thrown off the walls and driven through the skirts of Greenville, but the local victory was, to a man of Will Percy's temperament, destined to be lost in the general defeat. LeRoy himself might take comfort in a skirmish worn—but Will was one to think always of the entire campaign. The son could eat his greens only if they had vinegar on them; commenting upon his father's success in winning a Senate seat, Will observes, "Nothing is so sad as defeat, except victory" (*LL*, 145). Everything is sad, therefore, because nothing is absolute.

Even during the grand moments of '22 and '23, then, when LeRoy was speaking, in Greenville, then elsewhere, Will would have seen his father not as one man among a group of equal size and density, striving toward some attainable goal, but as one fully realized man against a background of smaller, insubstantial figures, who were merely a part of "the sorrowful pageant of the race" (*LL*, 234).[3] During those most rhetorical days, LeRoy became linked in Will's mind with Frederick II of Sicily (1194-1250), the Sun King, the "Stupor Mundi"; for, as he wrote to John Chapman,[4] he saw many a resemblance between his father and the Emperor, whose presence he must have felt intensely during his several visits to Sicily and Italy in the previous twenty years. Dissatisfied with the unpoetic possibilities of his own time, Will cast his father as Frederick II, in an extended narrative that ostensibly recounts Frederick's failure to attain his vision, but addresses as well his father's own inevitable failure.

The speaker of **"Enzio's Kingdom"**[5] is the thirty year old natural son of Frederick. King of Sardinia, Enzio had been his father's first child, remained a favorite, developed into a dependable and able military leader. But he had been captured by the Bolognese, who refused to accept ransom for him, despite Frederick's entreaties. He has languished a year in captivity, therefore, despairing to hear of the disaffections among his father's followers, of illnesses that sap his father's strength, of unaccustomed defeats for his father's armies.

As the poem begins, Berard, Archbishop of Palermo, his father's oldest and most trusted friend, has entered Enzio's cell to tell him of his father's death. Enzio acknowledges the fatigue of his visitor, but wishes nevertheless to speak of his memories of his father. In Enzio's recollection, Frederick assumes a very specific character. Rather than possessing the outlook expected of a ruler of his time, he transcends history: Frederick's goal is not merely to increase his wealth or the size of his state, but to accomplish a grand design: " . . . after peace I shall enchant the world / Into a universal Sicily . . ." (*CP*, 311). He has in mind, in short, nothing less than the accomplishment of the millennium, that thousand years of peace prophesied in Revelations XX, the beginnings of which had been awaited in Europe since before 1000 A.D., when the expectation had become virtually universal.

Frederick is so captivated by the vision that he alone can realize that he prefaces a statement to his lieutenant, Pietro da Vigna, with an assurance: "When we have built the new Jerusalem . . ." (*CP*, 317). He alludes, of course, to that holy city which Revelations XXI prophesies will come down from God at the apocalypse. Frederick is mindful that he is claiming divinity for himself; in the same breath, he, like Jesus, puns upon the name of his chief subordinate, celebrating his rocklike role. The pun is not Percy's poetic fancy, but rather relies on history.[6] Both in history and in the poem, then, Frederick is to be perceived as a secular leader, who claims that his person, incarnating a divine presence, is to make a decisive, radical change in the unfolding history of the world.

With such a purpose, " . . . today in the great staggering world / The only godlike, all-inclusive scheme / Of hope and betterment . . . ," Frederick feels justified in excluding himself from the laws which govern mere men: "Peace. Peace. The great prerequisite, / The race's single chance to reach its stature . . . / There's not a lie too great, a crime too gross / I'll not be guilty of, if so thereby / I may establish it and fix the lines / Of the quivering vision I intend the world . . ." (*CP*, 311)

There is yet another likeness to Jesus which Frederick implies: just as He had chosen those who would be His intimate associates in spreading the Word, so does Frederick identify a "flashing-eyed minority, / The Enzios of the world, the sons of light" (*CP*, 312), to be turned "free-pinioned on an earth / That they would make august and radiant!" He will "concede the masses to the Pope: / Their stultified obedience makes for peace" (*CP*, 314). But he will not give his "eaglets to his cage: / For them there shall be freedom if it takes / The very toppling down of Peter's throne."

The freedom of which Frederick speaks is intellectual freedom: the inference to be drawn from all of his speech is that he intends to combat his enemies by making the truth established by empirical investigation the world's telling criterion. He therefore has already established his academy, in which the intellectual elite will be taught to govern with benevolence, within the limits of rationality and firmness: " . . . the young future teams / To Naples and Salerno where my schools / Are aids and urgers to the starrier way" (*CP*, 312-313).

History dictates the outcome of Percy's narrative. Frederick was excommunicated, anathematized, and deposed by the Council of Lyons, on July 17, 1235. All of Frederick's tributaries were freed of their allegiance to him, all legitimacy attached to his rule was denied. Percy pictures a scene in which Frederick attempts to combat the reawakened subservience of his followers to Papal domination by proclaiming the dawn of a revolutionary secular era. As Enzio recalls: "He dignified them with the truth," "As if they could partake of visioning" (*CP*, 327). But "they chilled: and slipped vague glances at their neighbors." Afterwards, Frederick tells Enzio what is inevitable: "The end. Darkness ahead. Darkness ahead" (*CP*, 329).

Like Jesus, Frederick is betrayed by his Petrus. Then, separated from his scattered sons, he dies a strangely muted death, of a broken heart, Enzio feels. In a sense, then, Frederick has given his life for his vision. Enzio will not allow himself to consider an alternative meaning: "I cannot see by what integrity / High Heaven annihilated so his efforts! / Unless there be no heaven— and that I'll grant / Sooner than that his vision's fate was just! . . ." (*CP*, 341) Either an evil god or a godless universe—Enzio prefers the latter. If someday a divinity does appear, Enzio is confident that he will be "minded, willed, and souled" (*CP*, 342) like his father. Even though he will not be alive to see him, Enzio knows that in the coming of the avatar, Frederick will be resurrected.

In the Epilogue, Enzio reveals what has happened while he has talked through the night. In the short term, Enzio's senses have given him no information but the dispiriting; yet for the long term, now that he thinks about it, his intuition gives him a conviction of utter optimism—his father will return, someday, to fulfill his dream. So he concludes: "Some sky is in my breast where swings a hawk / Intemperate for immortalities / And unpersuaded by the show of death. / I am content with that I cannot prove." (*CP*, 343)

Enzio thus convinces himself that his father had *really* defeated his two hateful enemies, the Papal institution, then still a major political force, and the Italian bourgeoisie, just beginning to realize its potential. Such seemingly unlikely allies were joined in the Guelph party; the merchants could lend great amounts of money at high interest to the Pope, who, not being threatened by their rise could bless their activity. The Emperor and his lords constituted the Ghibelline party; for all of his apparent openness to novelty Frederick actually represented the old order, which derived its wealth from land.[7]

Seeing Frederick II in these partisan terms enables us to understand why Will Percy really associates his father with Frederick. Senator Percy's enemies were the various groups—usually satirically portrayed by Will as eccentric mobs—that attacked the traditional Mississippi squirearchy. Certainly Will did not intend to suggest that his father made any kind of eschatological claims for himself or justified his own behavior by announcing himself an exception, but rather to celebrate his father as one of those leaders who are defeated in the ever recurring victory of darkness.

It is impossible to tell from **"Enzio's Kingdom"** what Will Percy may have known of the legends of Frederick that blew across Europe after his death. But even if they were totally unknown, those legends have a bearing here, insofar as they inform us of the tradition of Will Percy and help to explain why Walker Percy, Will's adopted son, has reacted so strongly and so repeatedly to his parent's code.[8]

After the death, in 1929, of LeRoy Pratt Percy, the father of Walker and his two brothers, Will Percy, LeRoy Pratt's cousin, invited the boys to live with him and, after the death of LeRoy Pratt's wife, adopted them. Thereafter, as Walker Percy has written,[9] Will Percy did not write much more poetry. No doubt he was too busy being a father—without the help of a wife or even the support of good health. He was a good father—we have Walker Percy's testimony to that. Indeed he was so conscientious a father that he struggled even in his poor health to pass on to his sons a sense of their tradition. Published in 1942, the year before his death, his memoir, *Lanterns on the Levee*, was dedicated to them. It is a thoughtful book. Every person of his tradition, Will

Percy implies, has carried a lantern on the levee, helped in the communal effort to guard against the great external force which might at any time sweep away the results of man's work. The subtitle, "Recollections of a Planter's Son," grounds the tradition in local history.

Within the book, Will is at pains to spell out his views to his sons. Immediately he appears to be tracing his own life, but ultimately he is identifying those experiences which matter to him: his community, his family, his class, education, culture, activism. Very late he has a chapter, "For the Younger Generation," in which he distills his experience into a code for his sons: follow the ethics of Jesus and the stern inner summons of Marcus Aurelius. There are certain absolute values that are impervious to the pressures of irrational religion and base leveling. "Love and compassion, beauty, and innocence will return. It is better to have breathed them an instant than to have supported inequity a millennium. Perhaps only flames can rouse man from his apathy to his destiny" (*LL*, 313).

Having reached an apocalyptic climax in his peroration, Will then lessens the tension of his argument, to talk first of the failure of a philosophizing Christianity, which persists in its attempt to attribute divinity to Jesus, to promise eternal life, to split hairs about the Godhead. Then he talks of the anesthetic value to be derived from Aurelius' *Meditations*. From the two models can be extracted man's limit/opportunity: to respect himself, to respect others, to be open to the idea of a God—"it is given to man to behold beauty and to worship nobility (*LL*, 320). The best of all places to perform one's reverential gazing? "I think if one would sit in the Greek theater above Taormina with the wine-dark sea below and Aetna against the sunset, and if there he would meditate on Jesus and the Emperor, he would be assured a god had made earth and man." An allusion to Keats completes the paragraph: "And this is all we need to know."

Yet despite the force and clarity of his Stoic message, Will admits that many (and the implication is that some are nearby) still trouble their hearts "with foolish doubts and unwise questionings—the fear of death, the hope of survival, forgiveness, heaven, hell." He can only reply:

> Death, Heaven or Hell, Rewards or Punishments, Extinction or Survival, these are epic troubles for the epic Mind. Our cares are fitted to our powers. Our concern is here, and with the day so overcast and short, there's quite enough to do.

> So I counsel the poor children. But I look for the seer or saint who sees what I surmise—and he will come, even if he must walk through ruins. (*LL*, 321)

And so we are back to that yearning for the apocalypse that lurks beneath the apparent iron control of the immanentist.

The legend of Frederick II, the tradition in which that legend stands as a principal beginning, and the influence of that tradition upon modern political movements have been of particular interest since World War II. For there has been a rather wide recognition that the roots of Nazism lay in the tradition of which I speak, so that a tracing of the history of the tradition might account for the incredible ferocity with which adherents accepted Hitler *and* remained faithful to him to the bitter end. Still, though, one might object that Nazism is worthy of historical interest, no doubt, but of no more urgency than many another topic. On the contrary, as the analysts of the tradition point out, the same basic set of ideas that underlay Nazism provides the motive force for Marxism. When we read Eric Voegelin's *The New Science of Politics* (1952), or Norman Cohn's *The Pursuit of the Millennium* (1961), or Marjorie Reeves's *The Influence of Prophecy in the Later Middle Ages* (1969), then, we are struck not by the dated, "historical" nature of the reality being described, but rather by the frightening ease with which we can use descriptions of "medieval fanaticism" to deepen our understanding of today's headlines.

I refer specifically to the historical process which Voegelin describes as the redivinization of modern political mass movements.[10] Historians are agreed that the idea owes its basic stimulus to Joachim of Flora (1145-1202).[11] About 1190 Joachim, an Italian abbot, after years of isolated Scriptural study, conceived an idea whose time had come. While Scripture had always been interpreted for edifying purposes, Joachim discerned meanings that commented upon the current world situation and even forecast the plan according to which the future would be unfolded. His vision in all its intricacy Joachim called the "everlasting gospel," *evangelium aeternum,* in reference to Revelations XIV, 6. Fundamental to his scheme was the division of history into three stages, each presided over by a Person of the Trinity. The Father inspired the time of the Old Testament; the Son, the New Testament; and the Spirit would inhabit the millennium.[12]

By Joachim's calculations the third stage would begin sometime between 1200 and 1260. During the immediately preceding transitional period, certain actions must occur. There must be a new religious order to preach the new gospel; from this new order of spiritual men would emerge twelve patriarchs who would convert the Jews and a *novus dux* who would inspire the world to turn from materialistic to spiritual considerations. Exactly three and one half years before the fulfillment of the third dispensation, the Antichrist, the Last World Emperor, would destroy the corrupt and worldly Church, which presumed to place itself between man and God. Then with the destruction of the Church and the overthrow of the Antichrist, the millennium would commence.

Even at the moment of his birth, Frederick II was the object of eschatological expectation, for there already was a legend of the Emperor who would preside over the Last Days. As he matured, he and his lieutenants apparently believed in his divine destiny. Needless to say, the Pope and his party were of a different mind. Thus Frederick developed two legendary personalities, exactly opposed. To his German supporters he was to be the Emperor who would usher out the last secular age by conquering the real Antichrist, the Pope, then become the *novus dux* who would usher in the new world in which his lieutenant, Pietro da Vigna, would be the new Pope, his earthly representative. The new world would be free of institutions (and their attendant quarrels) because all activity would be subsumed to *one* institution. To his Italian opponents, he was the Beast of the Apocalypse who must be fought not merely as a secular, but as a demonic, threat, with every resource available. Frederick, in short, sets in the European imagination the legend of the secular leader who comes in the fullness of a known scheme; who commands absolute obedience; who in order to fulfill his destiny must purge his people of their traditional institutions (so that his personality, the only institution, will expand to its possibility and) so that they can respond to the truths of their blood; who will lead them to victory if they are worthy or to destruction (the very fact of which would be proof that they had not risen to his visionary demands).

If the figure of Frederick was not stripped of its eschatological promise by his death, neither was Joachitic thought discredited by the eventual decline of the Frederick myth. On the contrary, the basic features of the Joachitic scheme have continued to assert themselves in European political philosophies for seven hundred years. Eric Voegelin was particularly interested in the phenomenon, for he saw it as the modern manifestation of gnosticism, a religious stance that has always appealed to those weak in the faith. Disagreeing with those who had argued that modern political mass movements were neopagan, he countered that such movements, because of Joachim, actually represented a rejoining of the secular and sacred streams of history that St. Augustine had separated. Such movements as Nazism and Marxism and such philosophies of history as those of Condorcet, Turgot, Comte, Hegel, and Marx reflect, therefore, a vision in which God (especially the Redemptive Christ) has been replaced by History.[13] These various visions are generally agreed upon their "aggregate of symbols which govern the self-interpretation of modern political society": (1) the sequence of three ages; (2) the exalted leader; (3) the prophet of the new age (who is sometimes also the leader); and (4) the brotherhood of autonomous persons, who are the apparat of the prophet and the leader.[14]

All four of Voegelin's case symbols are to be observed in **"Enzio's Kingdom."** Most are directly stated: it is laboring the obvious to remind the reader that Frederick is an autocrat (2), that he as leader has himself for ideologue (3), that he employs his sons (and by extension all those bright young technocrats in his schools are his "sons") to vanquish the old so as to realize the new (4). Only the three-ages concept (1) must be inferred, but there are several data to support that inference. There is, for one thing, Frederick's repeated reference to the nearness of the millennium. Corollary to his belief in the millennium is his rejection of Christianity: " . . . I see the thing that calls itself / Christ's Church a noble detriment, a dream / Once valid, but in the dawning old and evil" (*CP*, 314). Percy imputes to Frederick a belief in the "hidden god" known to the gnostics[15]: "Three is enough: yet not enough, I know. . . . / Jesus, Mahomet, Abraham—good men / Guessing! I read their words with reverence / And know that still the ultimate word's not written . . ." (*CP*, 314).

Granted, Frederick did not destroy the Church or achieve the millennium—in his *first* life. But he will return, in the "guise" of others, "minded, willed, and souled like him." There is also the implied sequence of time-spirits in the poem: Frederick himself was born into the Age of the Father, in which fear and servitude have dominated the experience of life; Enzio represents the Age of the Son—his attitude toward his father reveals his faith and filial submission. Frederick had hoped to lead his youth, "the sons of light," in the Third Age, the Age of the Spirit, in which he "would change all this: and for imperial boon/Grant freedom to the spirits of the free" (*CP*, 312). Although the age of the Spirit has not been reached, at the end of the poem, yet it is ever about to be reached, for at any time, Enzio feels, a return of Frederick's spirit may occur.

Will Percy's apocalyptic imagination is further revealed in *Lanterns on the Levee*. The most striking evidence of it is the arrangement of three scenes that conveys Will's conception of history as a sequence of ages. First in the series is the description of Will's grandfather, "Fafar," who had led the community during the reestablishment of white supremacy. He had been so sure of the rightness of his view that he had broken mere laws to accomplish it. Percy's father, LeRoy, "considered Fafar superior to any human being he had ever known: he insisted he had a finer mind, a greater gusto, a warmer love of people, and a more rigid standard of justice than any of his sons" (*LL*, 274). Second in the series Will Percy describes LeRoy's leadership of the community in repelling the invasion of the Klan (*LL*, 225-251). LeRoy's conduct in the Klan episode was without reproach, was representative of his life: small wonder that Will worshipped him as LeRoy worshipped "Fafar." Those men, the fathers, belong, in Will's mind, "on the west portal of Chartres with those strong ancients, severe and formidable and full of grace, who guard the holy entrance" (*LL*, 74). The third scene—in which Will Percy was called upon in 1927 to lead the community through the crisis of the great Mississippi flood—marks the decline. Honest enough to describe himself as having done a creditable job, Will nevertheless has to distinguish his behavior from that of his legendary fathers. Like Enzio at the knee of Frederick, Will had listened to his father (*LL*, 75), but somehow the moves that he made did not fully accomplish the wisdom that he had heard. He includes in the story an account of his having made what

in retrospect he sees as a mistake and his father's having perpetrated a gentle subterfuge in order to allow him to save face. Will feels compelled, too, to admit that he became so exhausted that he had to resign his position, to go to Japan for a vacation. Further, he must say that "the two really great contributions made to the Delta by the Red Cross had been made without me and without my connivance" (*LL*, 269). There is, then, a tendency to see a radical hiatus between his fathers and himself, even as he tended to see each crisis in his own life not as an opening toward possibility, but a continued drift toward chaos.

The Age of the Son will not be a time of joy or victory. Writing in 1941, Will Percy sees Frederick's scorned "masses" everywhere triumphant: "in Russia, Germany, and Italy Demos, having slain its aristocrats and intellectuals [read "fathers"] and realizing its own incompetence to guide or protect itself, . . . submitted to tyrants" (*LL*, 312), while in the Western democracies Demos had grown bloated and corrupt. "We of my generation have lost one line of fortifications after another, the old South, the old ideals, the old strengths" (*LL*, 313): the end of the age is bound, undoubtedly, to be destruction.

Which will, of course, to a practiced apocalyptist, be man's salvation: "Perhaps only flames can rouse man from his apathy to his destiny" (*LL*, 313). But how can man be prepared to fulfill his destiny? The failed son must pass on to his sons the tradition of the fathers and the advice that his sons can only endure stoically until the new age commences: "So I counsel the poor children. But I long for the seer or saint who sees what I surmise—and he will come, even if he must walk through ruins" (*LL*, 321). Thus William Alexander Percy left a legacy that one son, Walker, has described as Southern Stoicism.[16]

Walker Percy's first novel, *The Moviegoer* (1961),[17] is dedicated "in gratitude to W.A.P." It would have looked, then, to anyone who knew of the relationship between the two men that Walker was emulating the behavior of his adoptive father. And it could have been assumed that the content of the book would be inspired by the older Percy's code. A reading would have confirmed that assumption, for there is a character, Aunt Emily, who is clearly modeled after Uncle Will, who walks, like Uncle Will and his Stoic models, as she ponders the decline of the old tradition.

The relationship of the statement of *The Moviegoer* with the code of Will Percy, though, is not finally a comparison, but a contrast. To be sure, there have been readers who have dismissed the protagonist as merely a weak, feckless young man of the modern persuasion and who have thought that Aunt Emily was intended to speak the author's piece in her great broad-sword-swinging speech toward the end of the novel (*M*, 219-227). But the statement of the novel, less eloquent, less obvious, is that one must reject the grimly satisfying pessimism about the present, the reveries about a legendary past, and the utterly baseless hankering after a post-apocalyptic paradise (*M*, 231). The old tradition must, in other words, be rejected. It can be respected as a good-faith effort in its time, but its present use would be indefensible. In that first novel Walker Percy is quite restrained in describing its baneful effects upon his protagonist (perhaps because of his recognition of its value in its original context), and even after the old code is rejected, the protagonist remains on good terms with its spokesman, Aunt Emily, in fact stands in her good graces, so that the unwary reader might be tempted to think that Binx Bolling has finally come to his senses and accepted the rightness of his aunt's code.

Walker Percy is not so temperate in his second novel, *The Last Gentleman* (1966).[18] The protagonist, Will Barrett, suffers from several disabilities, both physical and mental, that derive from his complicated linkage to the past. The novel traces his return to the South, even as he seeks deeper within himself to discover the cause of his distress. Thus he comes finally to his hometown, to approach the domain of his father by way of the levee:

> Here he used to walk with his father and speak of the galaxies and of the expanding universe and take pleasure in the insignificance of man in the great lonely universe. His father would recite "Dover Beach," setting his jaw askew and wagging his head like F.D.R.:
>
> > for the world which seems
> > To lie before us like a land of dreams,
> > So various, so beautiful, so new,
> > Hath really neither joy, nor love, nor light,
> > Nor certitude, nor peace, nor help for pain—

or else speak of the grandfather and the days of great deeds . . . (*LG*, 309-310)

Then Will approaches the house, to recall those dangerous times when his father had confronted and defeated a Klan-like organization. He remembers the night when the police came to tell his father that the intruders had left: " . . . there was a dread about this night, the night of victory. (Victory is the saddest thing of all, said the father)" (*LG*, 331). He had pleaded for his father not to leave him, but the father had gone upstairs and killed himself. For, according to the logic of the apocalyptist, if there is to be no apocalypse, then suicide is the only deliverance from everydayness. In *The Moviegoer* Percy had not openly asserted the eventual self-destructiveness of the apocalyptist; he had used only a shadowy father, who had grandly volunteered to fight in World War II, succeeding "not only in dying but in dying in Crete in the wine dark sea" (*M*, 157). His death, if not by his own hand, was nevertheless a suicide. In *The Last Gentleman* Percy does not dodge: separated from the legendary assurance of the fathers, the father turns ironic enough to kill himself and leave a horrified son. But Will must reject the stance of the lost son: he may grieve over his father's decision, but he does not have to honor it. The father was wrong, simply wrong. Freed of

the ghost by even breathing such an antipatriarchical idea, Will is ready to go forth to build his own life.

Tom More, in the third novel, *Love in the Ruins* (1971),[19] sees himself precisely as Uncle Will's "seer or saint who will walk through the ruins.[20] His mind is dominated by the gnostic tendency to devise schemes of time. He breaks the continuity of American history into century-chunks, for example. The year is 1983, hard upon the *annus apocalypsis* prophesied by George Orwell. From the present he works backward, to 1883, to 1783, to 1683, to . . . Eden (*LR*, 57). Destroyed by the white man's mistreatment of the black man and the red man, the American Eden can be restored—if Tom More uses his miracle, the lapsometer, the last word in technology. It will thus be the American spirit which becomes the Third Rome and brings universal peace. Whoever really believed the eschatological myth of Russia as the Third Rome? "And as for Russia and the Russian Christ who was going to save Europe from itself: ha ha" (*LR*, 58).[21] On the contrary, it will be a Louisiana Christ; appropriately, Tom More ignores the religious significance of Christmas Eve in order to gloat over his scientific breakthrough.

There is yet another scheme of time: while Tom does not acknowledge it, he must, as an American and a Southerner, recognize the significance of the first four days in July. In the first age, 1776, those days marked the completion and announcement of the American testament, the Declaration of Independence; surely 1776 was the time of the fathers, the Founding Fathers. In the second age, 1863, the defeat at Gettysburg and the surrender of Vicksburg on July 4 determined the ultimate destruction of the South; this must certainly be the age of the sons, as Lincoln recognized in "The Gettysburg Address." But even though the Union endured, the rending of the American fabric occurred, so that by 1983 every aspect of American life is polarized. Only Tom More has the technology, that body of knowledge that constitutes immanent man's chief glory, to resolve the tensions and usher in the millennium—or, if the apocalypse occurs, lead the survivors into a new Eden, such as is prefigured by the Honey Island experiment.

Except that—Tom More causes mischief rather than good. His machine, that is to say, all technology, further alienates by exaggerating, rather than diminishing the fragmentation of the human community. His Faustian dream is burlesqued by the appearance of a wacky Mephistopheles. The idea that Tom could cure the world when he cannot even cure himself! He had hoped to supplant his symbolic father: whereas Saint Thomas More had only planned a Utopia, Tom had visions of using the old American know-how (and Japanese subcontractors) to make it. Rather he must call on Saint Thomas to protect him; he still needs a father, after all. And in the Epilogue, he has a father, Father Smith. It is Christmas Eve and time for confession. Tom has been chastened from secular time schemes back to the Christmas event, the Incarnation. The novel is truly a comedy, in that all is concluded in a state of bliss; but the great fun provided by Walker Percy's glorious imagination should not cause us to forget his deadly serious theme, that modern man is ever a prey to his own gnostic longings.

It is soon apparent in Percy's fourth novel, *Lancelot* (1977),[22] that he is still concerned with the fatal ease with which the Southern ideal becomes a gnostic nightmare. In ordinary time the year is 1976; for the protagonist it is one year after the apocalypse. For Lance Lamar had literally walked through the ruins the previous year; at that time he had revealed the bitchery of his wife (and therefore all women), had executed her lover (and in the doing killed three other people, his wife included), and had experienced the explosion of his ancestral home. Miraculously uninjured, he had walked into the charred ruins to retrieve his weapon, a Bowie knife, which to him symbolizes the "broadsword tradition" which had inspired his past behavior and also the "sharp two-edged sword" of Revelations with which he will accomplish his future project. Even though he is at present confined to a "Center for Aberrant Behavior."

The initial situation of the novel thus bears an uncanny resemblance to that of **"Enzio's Kingdom."** The protagonist is a captive, who begins to spin out for a visitor an account of the events that led to his being where he is. There is one significant difference between Enzio and Lancelot, though: whereas Enzio is submissive to his fate, understands that he will die a prisoner, can only await the father-like seer who will come (return), Lancelot, convinced that his survival is a genuine miracle, must be thereby assured that he is destined to be the seer.

As he begins to talk to his silent visitor (like Berard a priest) Father John, an intimate friend from childhood, Lancelot describes his life in the years that they have been separated.[23] He had grown up in the Southern tradition, had excelled as an extrovert, had married his virgin, Lucy. He had, in other words, thrived in an immanent world, while maintaining what his tradition identified as the romantic ideal.

Then Lucy died, wasted away, as illusions do. Lance had lived on at Belle Isle with his mother, becoming more and more of a drunken recluse, marking time as a small town lawyer with a light caseload. When he met Margot Reilly, costumed as a Southern belle, but soon revealed as a wanton Texan, Lance thinks that he can have it both ways. As his wife, she can provide the cold cash to restore his estate and the warm flesh to reawaken his manhood.

The marriage eventually lapses into habit, though; Margot restores the house and becomes bored; Lance no longer finds her novel and is bored. She becomes restive, and he lapses back into his everydayness, drunkenness, TV watching, and ever more frequent occasions of impotence. In time he discovers her infidelity. It should

be clear that the severity of Lance's response to Margot's behavior is not just caused by his sense of betrayal by or jealousy of another human being. He never makes a single effort to speak to Margot—rather he reacts with such cold, obsessive fury because he had cast a role for her in his personal allegory. Her defection announces her escape from his mind into autonomy, tears apart his absolutist distinctions between ideal and real. Thus he feels that the apocalypse must come: all is darkness, evil, filth, bitchery, buggery, betrayal.

Lance systematically sets out to create the "flames." There is natural gas seeping to the surface in the cellar of his house; Lance plans to use it to create his ball of fire. So he pipes it into the ventilation system; then, armed with that legendary weapon, the Bowie knife, he goes forth to wreak vengeance, an insane man acting with monstrous cruelty in emulation of the legendary decisiveness associated with his patriarchical ancestors.

The novel is a brilliant, bitter comment upon the danger of acting in response to the appeal of a mythic past. For the past, as we retrieve it, undergoes simplification, fabrication, distortion: but even if we could know it in all its complexity, we would still be grotesque fools to imitate a past action, for that action was appropriate only to its own context. But there is more: the mythic past serves in the novel as the ground out of which a malicious vision of the future can grow. After all, millennial blueprints turn out to be the architect's conception of lost Eden.

Lance is so emboldened by his successful action, by which he has leaped the actuality of his father—a provincial poetaster, who conspired in his own betrayal—to behave with all the righteous force of his ideal father, that is, the legendary father, that he now intends to apply his purging wrath to the entire country. He *knows* now that the Third Age is beginning. The First Age lasted from 1776 to 1861, the Second Age from 1861 to 1976 (*L*, 157); the Fathers conceived of a grand idea, the Sons allowed it to perish in materialism. Did not his own father accept a bribe? Would one of his patriarchs have done that?

It will be up to Lance, then, to publicize his full understanding of the coming age. And so he gradually, over the several days that he speaks to Father John, amplifies his daydreams into a vision into a philosophy. And himself to act upon his knowledge. He recognizes the dread dissociation of sensibility in the modern world, knowledge severed from will. But he, acting both as seer and as leader, possesses "both the conviction and the freedom" to "start a new order of things" (*L*, 156), to be accomplished by his brotherhood of autonomous persons. Walker Percy has thus consciously satisfied Voegelin's criteria for gnostic self-representation in his creation of the character of Lancelot.[24]

Lancelot, then, is among other things a total rejection of **"Enzio's Kingdom."** William Alexander Percy had asserted that it is noble to dream of a millennial state which would be the restitution of the mythic world of the fathers. Walker Percy, no doubt with sadness, must counter that it is ultimately insane to dream of an immanent millennial state, for the dream sooner or later entices the dreamer to think of himself as God. Our sense of alienation is the only proof that we need to convince us that we are not God. Thus we *must* experience the loss of the father, then go forward in faith, toward the only paradise, our communion with the transcendent Father.

The loss of the father is precisely the theme that haunts Percy's latest novel, *The Second Coming* (1980).[25] It turns out that Will Barrett (of *The Last Gentleman*) had soon concluded that Sutter Vaught, the alienated physician, was an unfit father-figure. Thus he had returned from the apocalyptic Southwest to settle down in the secular city. There in New York he prospered as a lawyer and husband to a wealthy woman. Almost before he knew it, she had died and he had retired to the southern mountains—the Sewanee locale always recalls lost Eden in Percy's work.

There he plays golf, in Percy a game that both exercises and apotheosizes. Except that he has been beset by falling; it is no wonder that he has developed a bad slice. And at the same time he has begun to be bothered once more by the mystery of why his father had tried to kill him and why he had, on a second attempt, killed himself. As befits a self-conscious Hamlet, Will keeps a toy of desperation in his glove compartment.

If his life had remained perfect, he probably would have killed himself. His present bores, and his past either cannot be faced (his father's ghost) or cannot be retrieved (the high school cheerleader whom only now he has begun to remember). But then his condition deteriorates to the point that he wanders off the fairway, leaves the right of way, crosses a zone.

In an abandoned greenhouse, Will meets Allie Huger, who should be named "Grace"—*alleluia!* She, it turns out, is Kitty Vaught's daughter: Will is to have a second chance at life, a second coming into the world. In midlife, then, flagging Will is to be lifted by Allie, who is a "hoister." Not that Will has sense enough simply to accept his good fortune; who among God's stubborn children does? Deciding to put God to the test, Will hides himself in a cave, to see if He will come after him (for all the "adult" seriousness about the gamble, there is a certain ludentic air about it, as when a child hides in the closet—to be found, for otherwise the game is no fun). But nothing more numinous than a toothache nudges him out of the cave—not into a contemplation of Plato's distant Sun, but plop into the greenhouse, born again.

There Allie cares for him and accepts his love, becoming that miracle who both mothers and mates. Together they share a consciousness and build a world, get as close to Heaven as it is possible in North Carolina. Then

Will can finally throw those haunted weapons into the abyss, transcend the susceptibility to depression he has in his blood. Lifting up his eyes to the hills, he organizes a group of rest home relics as a construction company. Although he found love in the ruins, he now wants to build anew, as a man will when he has faith in the future. There will be no apocalypse, but rather the second coming that has occurred for Will and Allie, now sexual and spiritual, but prefiguring a Communion that transcends even those ecstasies.

NOTES

[1] Richard H. King, "Mourning and Melancholia: Will Percy and the Southern Tradition," *Virginia Quarterly Review,* 53 (Spring 1977): 248-264, explores Will Percy's relationship with the tradition of the fathers. He does not deal, though, with Will Percy's inclination toward the apocalypse or with Walker Percy's response to his adoptive father.

[2] William Alexander Percy, *Lanterns on the Levee* (Baton Rouge: Louisiana State University Press, 1973), 225-241. Hereafter, references are included in the text as *LL.*

[3] The last paragraph of *LL* confirms Will Percy's conception of history as frieze: "Here among the graves in the twilight I see one thing only, but I see that thing clear. I see the long wall of a rampart sombre with sunset, a dusty road at its base. On the tower of the rampart stand the glorious high gods, Death and the rest, insolent and watching. Below on the road stream the tribes of men, tired, bent, hurt, and stumbling, and each man alone. As one comes beneath the tower, the High God descends and faces the wayfarer. He speaks three slow words: 'Who are you?' The pilgrim I know should be able to straighten his shoulders, to stand his tallest, and to answer defiantly: 'I am your son.' (*LL,* 348)

[4] Phinizy Spalding, "A Stoic Trend in William Alexander Percy's Thought," *Georgia Review,* 12 (Fall 1958): 248.

[5] The text of the poem herein used is in *The Collected Poems of William Alexander Percy,* foreword by Roark Bradford (New York: Alfred A. Knopf, 1943). Hereafter, references are included in the text as *CP.*

[6] See Ernst H. Kantorowicz, *Frederick the Second, 1194-1250* (New York: Frederick Ungar Publishing Company, 1957), 511-513.

[7] Thomas Caldecot Chubb, *Dante and his World* (Boston: Little, Brown and Company, 1966), 105-112.

[8] In "Walker Percy's Southern Stoic," *Southern Literary Journal,* 3 (Fall 1970): 5-31, I explore Walker Percy's reaction in his first two novels to Will Percy's Stoicism. In "*The Moviegoer* and the Stoic Heritage," in *The Stoic Strain in American Literature,* ed. Duane J. MacMillan (Toronto: University of Toronto Press, 1979), 179-191,

I trace the Stoic tradition in Southern history in a very cursory way.

9 Walker Percy provides an "Introduction," vii-xviii, to the LSU Press reprint of *LL* being cited in this paper.

10 Eric Voegelin, *The New Science of Politics* (Chicago: The University of Chicago Press, 1952), 107.

11 Majorie Reeves, *The Influence of Prophecy in the Later Middle Ages* (Oxford: Clarendon Press, 1969) is a full-length treatment of Joachim.

12 Norman R. C. Cohn, *The Pursuit of the Millennium* (New York: Harper and Row, 1961), 99-123.

13 Voegelin, 111-112.

14 Voegelin, 112.

15 See discussions of the "hidden god" in Hans Jonas, *The Gnostic Religion* (Boston: Beacon Press, 1958), 42-43, and in Robert McQueen Grant, *Gnosticism and Early Christianity* (New York: Columbia University Press, 1966), 97-119.

16 Walker Percy, "Stocism in the South," *Commonweal*, 64 (6 July 1956):342-344.

17 Walker Percy, *The Moviegoer* (New York: Noonday Press, 1967). Hereafter references to *The Moviegoer* are included in the text as *M*.

18 Walker Percy, *The Last Gentleman* (New York: Farrar, Straus and Giroux, 1966). Hereafter references to *The Last Gentleman* are included in the text as *LG*.

19 Walker Percy, *Love in the Ruins* (New York: Farrar, Straus and Giroux, 1971). Hereafter references to *Love in the Ruins* are included in the text as *LR*.

20 In his early essay "The Man on the Train" (1956) Percy discusses the alienated man's hankering after "the old authentic thrill of the Bomb and the Coming of the Last Days. Like Ortega's romantic, the heart's desire of the alienated man is to see vines sprouting through the masonry." "The Man on the Train" is included in *The Message in the Bottle* (New York: Farrar, Straus and Giroux, 1975), and is the text herein cited, 84. Also "Notes for a Novel about the End of the World," obviously an essay bearing upon the apocalypse, is included in Percy's collection of essays.

21 Voegelin, 114-115, discusses the tradition of Russia as the Third Rome.

22 Walker Percy, *Lancelot* (New York: Farrar, Straus and Giroux, 1977). Hereafter references to *Lancelot* are included in the text as *L*.

23 I speak to Lance Lamar's Southern background in "The Fall of the House of Lamar" in *The Art of Walker*

Percy: Stratagems for Being, ed. Panthea R. Broughton (Baton Rouge: Louisiana State University Press, 1979), 219-244.

24 Cleanth Brooks, "Walker Percy and Modern Gnosticism," *Southern Review,* 13 (Autumn 1977): 677, receives credit for first remarking upon similarities between Eric Voegelin and Walker Percy. In "The Gnostic Vision in *Lancelot*," *Renascence,* 32 (Autumn 1979): 52-64, I cite Percy's specific reference to *The New Science of Politics* and describe the way in which Percy uses Voegelin's analysis of modern gnosticism to create a psychology for Lance Lamar.

25 (New York: Farrar, Straus and Giroux, 1980).

Carolyn Holdsworth (essay date 1981)

SOURCE: "The Gorgon's Head and the Mirror: Fact versus Metaphor in *Lanterns on the Levee*," in *The Southern Literary Journal*, Vol. XIV, No. 1, Fall, 1981, pp. 36-45.

[*In the following essay, Holdsworth examines the interplay of metaphors in* Lanterns on the Levee.]

Thirty years ago Mark Schorer published an article emphasizing the importance of metaphor in the novel: "Yet a novel, like a poem, is not life, it is an image of life; and the critical problem is first of all to analyze the structure of the image."[1] Recently critics have expanded the bounds of metaphor study to include the analysis of autobiographies, for although the composition of an autobiography is an enumeration of facts, it is also an artistic process. This process does not necessarily distort the facts but rather weaves them together and gives them a unity lacking in a bare chronology. The nature of man, and especially of man as artist, compels him to seek order in a seemingly disordered world. Particularly does man seek order in his own life. By expanding Schorer's rationale, a reader or writer is justified in believing that an autobiography, like a novel or poem, is not life but "an image of life." In producing an autobiography, a writer may well use some device such as the alter ego, the epiphany, the juxtaposition of inner and outer worlds, or recurrent symbols. If the autobiographer concerns himself with shaping his life rather than just narrating it, he may also use metaphor to create in the "image" a unity lacking in the original.

Apropos of the theory that autobiography may be complete with a defined and contributing style, James E. Rocks has recognized the art in William Alexander Percy's autobiography, *Lanterns on the Levee: Recollections of a Planter's Son.* Diverging from standard critical opinion, which deals with Percy's personality, subject matter, or philosophy, Rocks states that Percy's art is one of "opposition and tension" and that Percy uses metaphors to define the tension.[2] That is, Rocks identifies thematic tension expressed in metaphors as the organizing motif of *Lanterns on the Levee*. He says, "Although there is no conscious artistic pattern in the ordering of the chapters in *Lanterns on the Levee*, there is a movement back and forth between different themes and settings which gives evidence of Percy's dualistic mode of regarding reality."[3]

While not disagreeing with the substance of Rocks' analysis, I believe that the metaphors themselves are the primary organizing motif of the volume. My thesis differs from Rocks' in degree rather than kind, for he discusses the metaphors of nature, war, music, levee, garden, and journey as expressions of tension in Percy's autobiography while I shall consider them as consciously and adroitly used organizing principles.

Lanterns on the Levee is, naturally, ordered by chronology, but Percy's primary stylistic device is the transmutation of actual experiences and ideas (chronology and philosophy) into metaphor (art). I use "metaphor" broadly to include a whole family of related tropes: metaphor proper, buried metaphor, simile, metonymy, synecdoche, symbol, and the like. Percy's metaphorical technique organizes his thoughts and experiences and gives them symbolic value. With just a few exceptions, each of the chapters of his autobiography contains some dominant metaphor as a loose framework in which he writes.

The title of the autobiography, *Lanterns on the Levee: Recollections of a Planter's Son*, is the reader's first indication that the chronological facts (the "recollections" of the subtitle) are subordinate to metaphors (the "lanterns" and the "levee" of the main title). Judging from its position in the title, the reader may infer that the levee is one of Percy's most significant metaphors. Although Rocks states that the levee represents "man's battle with nature,"[4] the levee may be interpreted more narrowly as a metaphor for tradition. As a staunch Southern aristocrat, Percy firmly believed in the erection and maintenance of tradition to keep in control not just general nature but also human nature—the nature of both the black and the white man. Percy's "lanterns" are his recollections; they are his means of shedding light upon his views, particularly upon his views on the nature of the Southern aristocrat, on the beauty of the Southern order, and on the philosophy of the Southern mind regarding racial relations. The traditional views of the planter's son are represented by the levee, the place Percy actually walked and thought and the position all good Southern aristocrats guarded. With more than literal meaning, Percy writes, "Each guard walks alone [on the levee], and the tiny halo of his lantern makes our fearful hearts stouter."[5]

As with any recurrent metaphor, other references to the levee may be interpreted as either literal or symbolic. For example, the replacement of the original levee built by the Southern Levee Board (of which Percy's father and Percy were members) by the new levee built and paid for by the federal government implies a loss of Southern control of the South's social mores. Similarly, the deterioration of the old levee seems significant, given Percy's pessimism about the erosion of Southern culture. However, when Percy describes the procedure for correcting "boils" in the levee, the reader may or may not wish to infer (depending on his imagination or tenacity) that Percy is signifying some minor breach of Southern tradition which, if uncorrected, could cause the whole structure to crumble. That is, the levee is an actual object in Percy's world, and it only takes on metaphorical value when linked to his philosophy.

As with the title, Percy also uses metaphors to add unity and meaning to the chapters of his work. There are exceptions to this statement, however, either because the subject of the chapter has enough significance in and of itself to require no additional symbolic significance or because Percy is purposely setting down unrefined chronology. Examples of significant literal subjects are Percy's discussions of his grandmother Mur and his nurse Nain in chapter 3 and of the flood of 1927 in chapter 20. Examples of purposely unrefined chronology are chapter 17, containing Percy's youthful war letters, and chapter 25, composed mainly of Percy's diary entries. The marked contrast between Percy's chapters that use metaphors to unify experience and those that deliberately chronicle facts underscores Percy's use of metaphor for artistic effect. After concluding his diary entries in chapter 25, Percy makes a statement explicitly indicating his choice of metaphor as artistic tool. He says, "It's getting too late for facts anyway and they have a way these days of looking like the Gorgon's head seen without the mirror Perseus used" (331). By comparing "facts" to the "Gorgon's head," Percy emphasizes the ugliness and destruction inherent in a bare chronology. To avoid "petrification" by unrefined facts, Percy believes that man needs a mirror such as Perseus used to protect himself from Medusa. This mirror was given to Perseus by Pallas Athena, goddess of wisdom. Percy's "mirror" (given to him by the wisdom of his years) is his use of metaphors by which he can view the facts without fear and create his own "image" of his life. Following his use of the Gorgon metaphor, Percy concludes his diary chapter by saying, "The garden's the place" (331). He moves from the Gorgon's head of fact (chapter 25) to the garden of metaphor (chapter 26). Appropriately, Rocks says Percy's garden is "a magical place, capable of transforming the apparently mundane into metaphor."[6]

Percy's garden chapter is his most lyrical and best executed example of metaphor. Although chapter 9, in which Percy uses a pastoral motif to compare Sewanee to Arcadia, is more punctilious in sustaining its metaphor, its "Centaurs," "Arcadians," "fauns," "flutes," "lyres," and "Pans" are cloying in comparison to the metaphor of chapter 26: the jackdaw in the garden. At the beginning of this chapter, Percy indulges in a series of garden analogies: acidic soil becomes the trials of life; hybrid plants signify miscegenation; the heart, like a plant, has a "climate"; people's qualities are like plants' colors; the environmental deprivation of plants represents the spiritual deprivation of people (333-334). Percy is rather too careful in explaining his analogies, and he follows them with several other hackneyed comparisons: garden as Ivory Tower, life as a climbing journey, death as the shady side of a mountain (334-335). However, in this chapter's title, Percy creates a metaphor so striking as to betray his predilection for poetry. He compares himself to a jackdaw in a garden and the treasures of his heart to the pickings of the jackdaw. His description of himself as a jackdaw continues the self-deprecatory attitude apparent throughout the autobiography, and his reference to his memories as "pickings" reveals his ever-present irony toward the noble futility of man. This metaphor is Percy's most apt and intricate one, for he continues by characterizing his jackdaw heart as a "kleptomaniac for bits of color and scraps of god-in-man" (336), thus emphasizing his impulsive search for even traces of beauty and character in man. Percy's compulsion to search for these traces is admirably evoked by the "thieving" impulse of the jackdaw to collect beautiful objects. Despite his efforts, Percy tells us that the best that can be found will be "glinting indeed, but of no worth" (336). Here Percy plays upon the "bright" quality of the pickings: literally, the objects may be shiny, thus attracting the jackdaw's attention; metaphorically, the objects may be "glinting" (i.e., they seem valuable), but Percy hints that they are of base, not precious, metal. Percy organizes the rest of the chapter around his metaphor: he says he will "spread my treasure out" (336), and there follows a series of reminiscences, his "bits of treasure" (337). In concluding the chapter, Percy returns to double-edged irony and his metaphor. Although he again hints at his memories' lack of value by calling them "tinsel hoardings," he also discloses their irreplaceable value to him. He says his memories "lose nothing of their luster in this time of doom" and that "the only treasure that's exempt from tarnish is what the jackdaw gathers" (343). "Luster" and "tarnish" continue Percy's play upon the bright quality of the pickings/memories. After contemplating Percy's chapter 26, one understands something of his skill with metaphors.

Many of Percy's other chapters contain similar organizing metaphors. The subject of chapter 1 is the Delta, and Percy organizes the chapter around the animated figure of the river: "the shifting unappeasable god of the country, feared and loved, the Mississippi" (4). Percy both begins and ends this chapter by discussing the river, and the river serves as a stable symbol with which the changing Delta life is compared. Similarly, chapter 2 details the people of the Delta, and Percy employs the metaphor of social fabric. He says, "Almost any American community, I suppose, has similar bright strands being woven into its texture. But the basic fiber, the cloth of the Delta population . . . is built of three dissimilar threads and only three" (19). Percy uses the remainder of the chapter to discuss the characteristics of his three threads: the aristocrats, the poor whites, and the Negroes. These three classes are the woof of the Southern social fabric while the soil is the warp because it is "the only means of livelihood" (24).

Because chapter 4 deals with Percy's maternal grandparents, Mère and Père, Percy cleverly employs the metaphor of the family tree to unify the first part of the chapter. Old maids and widows who conceal family scandals are "pruners of family trees" (38), and people like Percy, interested in scandals of the past, are "climbers in the family tree" (39). Percy sagely warns us, "Playing Tarzan in the family tree is hazardous business; there are too many rotten branches" (40). The second part of chapter 4 exemplifies Percy's technique of transmuting actual experience into metaphor. Percy describes Mère's quilt-making process as "my first lesson in color-consciousness" (43). Watching her sew together scraps of different colored materials, he learns, "Pink, of course, matched with blue or lavender or even light green, but never with red" (43). In concluding the chapter, Percy combines the idea of ancestral influence (Mère and Père) with the quilting process turned metaphor for prejudices of temperament:

> The color of our temperament, our chief concern, is nothing of our making. If we are pink, we can only hope that fate will not set us cheek by jowl with red. If we see the world through mauve glasses, there's no sort of sense in wishing they were white. We may only console ourselves by noting that a certain opalescence . . . is not without a loveliness denied the truer and cruder white noons of the desert. (45)

Percy's "color-consciousness," of course, has less to do with quilts than with races. He transmutes Mère's different colored scraps of material, an actual memory, into a metaphor for the multicolored components of Southern society. Like the pink scraps, which do not match the red scraps, the white aristocrats can only hope not to be placed "cheek by jowl" with the Negro Southerners in the Southern "quilt." Percy continues his metaphor by discussing not just color but also perception of color. His aristocrats' mauve glasses are cultural prejudices through which they view the Negroes. Percy implies that this perception cannot be changed, and that, perhaps, it should not be changed.

Like chapter 4, chapter 5 transmutes actual experiences into metaphor. At the beginning of the chapter, Percy recalls anecdotes of catching crawfish and playing games about buzzards causing the fiery destruction of the world. He then makes these anecdotes the basis of his metaphorical well-wishing to Skillet, his childhood friend. He says, "I like to imagine that Skillet . . . has a farm of his own and many little crawfishers—in fine, that the swooping dark wings continue for him to light on a chip" (49). "Little crawfishers" is a fine example of metonymy for the children of his crawfishing friend. "The swooping dark wings" that "light on a chip" is an admirable metaphor for Percy's hope that Skillet's life will turn out favorably even against the highest odds. In the remainder of this chapter, Percy discusses other childhood playmates. He turns experience into metaphor by first describing the woods in which the children played and then referring to A. E. Housman's symbolic woods: "We'll to the woods no more" (55). Percy and Housman, who share more than one affinity, both use the woods as a symbol for the lost happiness of youth.

Chapters 6 and 7 each contain one dominant metaphor connoting Percy's deep admiration for the Southern aristocrats. Chapter 6 recounts, among other things, the deaths of Mère and Père. In connection with the deaths of these specific Southern aristocrats, Percy also mourns the death of the whole Southern aristocracy. He writes, "Under the southern Valhalla the torch has been thrust, already the bastions have fallen. . . . A side-show Götter-dämmerung perhaps, yet who shall inherit our earth, the earth we loved?" (63). Percy's allusion to Valhalla, a hall in the home of the mythological Norse gods, makes clear his comparison of the Southern aristocrats to gods. The allusion also makes clear the connection between the Southern and the Norse philosophies: each culture believes in fighting for the good cause, even though each well knows that victory is impossible. In the next chapter Percy catalogues his other childhood heroes, and the dominant metaphor of chapter 7 is that of the protagonists and plot of the Southern play. Percy emphasizes that the Southern men themselves, the "protagonists," are more important than the specific political issues of the day, the "plot" of the play. He agrees with the Delta men who believed that "no system of government was good without good men to operate it" (73).

The metaphor of chapter 10 is one of autumn. This chapter deals with Percy's year abroad, during which he was very lonely. The relative starkness of this metaphor contrasts effectively with the lushness of the pastoral motif of the preceding chapter about Sewanee. Percy refers to "men with the pathos of autumn in their souls" (109) and to "the autumn-hearted" (110), thus using the metaphor of autumn to describe his experiences during that particular autumn in France. Similarly, in chapter 11 Percy uses the metaphor of coldness to evoke his experiences while enrolled in the Harvard Law School. He says, "Yet when I lit in their midst I did feel a drop in the temperature" (115). Percy uses the literal coldness of the North to exemplify the metaphorical coldness of the people he met there. In describing his feelings at a Northern dance, for example, he says, "I feel the way a banana plant looks after a frost" (116). He also contrasts the Northern "cold logic" with his own, which "works only above boiling-point" (122). He is not completely condemnatory of the North, however, for in referring to the friends he made at law school, he says, "I had taken hostages against the long cold" (124). He thus broadens the implications of the "cold" not only to mean the alienation he often experienced in the North but also to mean the alienation he felt from all society.

Percy returns to his theme of cultural alienation in chapter 12, which concerns his return to Greenville, Missis-

sippi, in 1909. The metaphor of acting in this chapter recalls the "play" metaphor of chapter 7, but this time Percy himself is on stage. Life to him is "an arena," and he does not know "the animals' names" (125). He questions "what role" he should play and meanwhile discovers that "the curtain was up and I on stage" (126). To him life is a "show," and he says, "[But] of the plot I still know so little that I can't swear whether it's been tragedy or comedy" (127). Percy devotes the remainder of this chapter to recalling the person who helped him during his lonely years, Caroline Sterne.

Percy's alienation in Greenville is, in part, a result of his own nature, but it also results from the political practices he encountered. "The Bottom Rail on Top" is Percy's metaphor for the corruption of Southern politics, and it serves as his title for chapter 12. His disillusionment with Southern politics originated in his dismay at his father's defeat in the re-election campaign for the Senate. Within this metaphorical framework, Percy uses many comparisons to express his disgust with the corruption of the "bottom rail." He says James K. Vardaman "looked like a top-notch medicine man" and that his oratory was "bastard emotionalism and raven-tressed rant" (143). He also labels Vardaman "a pool-room wit" and "an exhibitionist playing with fire" (144). Huey Long he denounces as "a moral idiot of genius" (144). Enraged by attacks on his father's character, Percy describes a supposed bribe-taker as "vomiting his own infamy," and publishers he calls "professional lovers of carrion" (148). Percy's disdain encompasses not only the corrupt politicians but also the ignorant public that elects them. He describes the public as a "herd" that is "on the march" (153).

In Rocks' essay he says of the next four chapters, 14-17, "War itself in this section is a metaphor of life."[7] In chapter 15, particularly, Percy's writing displays the joining of form and content, for Percy often uses metaphors of war to describe his preparation for war at an officer's training camp. He says, "I was as proud as if I had captured a machine-gun nest" (173); "A buddy is as necessary as a rifle" (175); " . . . I was strewn on my bunk, three-fourths corpse . . ." (175); during inspection, a feather under his bunk looks "as big as a battleship" (176); "Sam's departure was our first casualty" (177); Peewees were the officers' "natural prey" (181); "Emmet and I in our squad stumbled along blindly, as proud as if we'd been presented with a helmet full of D.S.C.'s" (182). In this section on war, chapter 17 provides an interesting contrast of writing styles. The younger Percy's war letters to his mother conspicuously lack figurative language, while the older Percy's recollections about the war are more metaphorical.

Percy fought another kind of war when he arrived home, and he organizes his experiences by using a particular war metaphor. Chapter 18 concerns the Ku Klux Klan's attempted takeover of Greenville's politics. Percy's attitude toward the Klan is summarized by his repeated comparison of the Klan to the Nazis. He describes various Klan practices as "fifth-column tactic[s] before there was a Hitler" (232); "Nazi propaganda before there were Nazis" (233); "only less absurd than the Nazi principles of Aryan superiority and lebensraum" (235). He compares the Klansmen to spies and adds, "Like German parachute jumpers, they appeared disguised as friends" (237).

Chapters 21-23 share a unity of subject because all deal with topics related to Negroes: sharecropping, race relations with a particular Negro named Fode, and race relations with Negroes in general. Although these three chapters have no dominant metaphor, a partial survey of Percy's metaphorical references to Negroes throughout *Lanterns on the Levee* will illuminate his Southern aristocrat's point of view. On the "positive" side, Percy's similes show that he regards the Negroes as inept and delightful children who "wear idleness like a perfume and an allurement" (23), who can laugh "like a celesta playing triplets" (26), who have smiles "like the best brand of sunshine" (287), and who "thieve like children and murder ungrudgingly as small boys fight" (305). Percy's kindly feelings towards the Negroes are, therefore, just as condescending as his more open prejudices by which he expresses both derogation of them and his own sense of superiority. His use of synecdoche in referring to "the many black mouths" dependent on the slave-holders (5) reduces the Negroes to hungry liabilities. His use of simile in "a library was as portable as a slave" (7) and his use of metaphor in referring to a servant as "an elegant human fire-screen" (30) demonstrate his attitude that Negroes are property. Likewise, Percy's metaphors of "the dark feudal community" (10) and of "the lord of the manor among his faithful retainers" (291) convey his sense of superiority and ownership. At his best, Percy allows himself to be amused by the Negroes; at his worst, he regards them as racial inferiors, not quite human. Perhaps the metaphor best expressing his perplexing attitude toward the Negroes is the one in which he admits a lack of understanding of them: "To make it more bewildering, the barrier is of glass; you can't see it, you only strike it" (299).

In chapter 24 Percy outlines his philosophy for the younger generation. He does so by using light as a metaphor for understanding. After mentioning some of the problems facing the young people, Percy says, "But out of my own darkness . . . I try to point out to them the pale streak I see which may be a trail" (316). He continues his prescription for curing our ethical darkness by saying that the Gospels shed "more light than darkness" and that they are "drenched in a supernal light" (316). Nevertheless, he seems unsure about the perfectibility of man's understanding. He says, "Only the faintest wavering glimmer of the shouting light of creation penetrates our dark diminutive cell" (317). At the end of the chapter, Percy characterizes his time as an "overcast" day and counsels members of the younger generation to concern themselves with improving the present instead of worrying about the future (321).

Percy's last chapter, chapter 27, considers the subject of impending death. The chapter is entitled "Home," and this word is Percy's metaphor for death. He calls the family cemetery a "home of the dead" (345) and states, "It would be a chilly world without this refuge with its feel of home" (346). If the cemetery is one's destination (one's home), then it follows that life is a journey toward that home. Commenting on the autobiography's final chapter, Rocks has said, "As he sits in the cemetery, Percy thinks of himself as a traveler on the journey or road of life. This is the principal metaphor which informs the whole book and, like all the other metaphors he uses, it is a very traditional and conventional one."[8]

Rocks' dismissal of Percy's metaphors as "conventional" does not do justice to the artistry of *Lanterns on the Levee*. Although Percy's use of such metaphors as the pastoral motif, light, stage, and journey are conventional, his use of other modified or invented metaphors is not in the least conventional. Percy cleverly modifies the older metaphors of social fabric and family tree to illustrate certain parts of his autobiography. Moreover, his levee, Gorgon's head of fact, jackdaw in the garden, quilt of consciousness, and bottom rail on top are all vivid and evocative metaphors. In addition to their poetic quality, the metaphors of *Lanterns on the Levee* organize Percy's chapters around central concepts. Thus, Percy's metaphors give his autobiography both meaning and form. As the work of a Southerner, Percy's autobiography has been judged important for its subject; as the work of an artist, it is also important for its style.

NOTES

[1] Mark Schorer, "Fiction and the 'Analogical Matrix,'" *Kenyon Review,* 11 (Autumn 1949), 539.

[2] James E. Rocks, "The Art of *Lanterns on the Levee,"* *The Southern Review,* 12 (Autumn 1976), 815.

[3] Rocks, p. 817.

[4] Rocks, p. 821.

[5] William Alexander Percy, *Lanterns on the Levee: Recollections of a Planter's Son* (Baton Rouge: La. State Univ. Press, 1968), p. 247. All further references to this work appear parenthetically in the text.

[6] Rocks, p. 822.

[7] Rocks, p. 818.

[8] Rocks, p. 822.

Philip Castille (essay date 1983)

SOURCE: "East Toward Home: Will Percy's Old World Vision," in *Southern Literature in Transition: Heritage and Promise,* edited by Philip Castille and William Osborne, Memphis State University Press, 1983, pp. 101-09.

[*In the following essay, Castille explores the ideological ramifications of* Lanterns on the Levee.]

William Alexander Percy wrote his autobiography in Greenville, Mississippi, during the bad years of the Depression and the onset of World War II. During its composition, his health failed and he knew he was dying. His sole prose work, *Lanterns on the Levee: Recollections of a Planter's Son* was published by Knopf in 1941, shortly before Percy's death. Somewhat surprisingly, given the somber circumstances of its inception and preparation, the book is best remembered for its charming and wistful view of the bygone plantation world of the Mississippi Delta. Always a steady seller and now available in paperback reprint, *Lanterns on the Levee* remains today one of the South's favorite books.

However, despite the attention paid to southern manners in *Lanterns on the Levee*, Percy's intentions are more ideological than regional. The real strength of this autobiography lies not, as has often been claimed, in its pastoral treatment of the South. Unlike the Vanderbilt Agrarians, Percy writes less to celebrate the land than to eulogize the landowning class and the hierarchic society founded upon ownership of land, as in Europe. Percy extols the preindustrial civilization of the southern planter class only to insist that its extinction is but part of a larger destruction of Old World culture. Similarly, he decries the mass psychic impoverishment of contemporary urban life and solemnly predicts a new industrial Dark Age.

But, despite his misgivings, Percy does not counsel despair or cynicism. The active intent of Percy's autobiography is to guide his spiritual heirs toward moral and social commitment. While the prevailing mood of *Lanterns on the Levee* is regret for the overthrow of the ideals and authority of the southern plantocracy, its practical purpose is to use the remembered past to dispel the modernist sentiment that life has no meaning. Percy invokes the entire western cultural heritage both to assert the possibility of a good life founded on a firm sense of humane values and to encourage adherence to traditional standards of courage and dignity.

In Percy's vision, the Old World cultural tradition, sprung from biblical and classical roots, had crossed the Atlantic and flourished in the Old South in general and in Greenville, Mississippi, in particular. It had survived the military defeat of the Civil War and extended into the postbellum era of his father. By linking his little Delta town with such ancient cultural sources, Percy commits himself to a vision of historical continuity in which "General Lee and Senator Lamar would have been at ease, even simpatico, with Pericles and Brutus and Sir Philip Sidney."[1] While such a claim risks tendentiousness, it is not idle:

> The South—as well as other American colonies founded by Spain, Portugal, and France—was socially a scion of the seigneurial class of Europe.

Ideologically it was a scion of the Italian Renaissance; and, as England was under the spell of such culture more than Spain or Portugal, this was truer of the English Southern colonies than of the Latin-American colonies.[2]

When Percy, whose paternal line had its origins in Northumberland, compared southern planters to Old World models, he was in full earnest. To be sure, Will Percy's patrician qualities were often attested to, notably in character sketches by David Cohn, Hodding Carter, and Jonathan Daniels. And even a southern skeptic like W. J. Cash was impressed enough to write, "Percy is that exceedingly rare thing, a surviving authentic Southern aristocrat, as distinguished from pretenders to the title."[3] But more impressively, a fineness of spirit shines through *Lanterns on the Levee*; and while it may be "impossible to convey to anyone who did not know him the peculiar charm and uniqueness of his gifts . . . the tone of *Lanterns on the Levee* comes as close as the written word can."[4]

The structure of Percy's autobiography falls into three sections, unified by the developing personality of the author. The first twelve chapters are given over to background and schooling, the effort of the child and youth to learn the traditional values and standards of Old World culture. In the middle section (Chapters XIII-XXIII), Percy recounts his effort as a young man to confront the twentieth-century issues of war, race, and economics and to live up to the example of his distinguished father. In the closing section (Chapters XXIV-XXVIII), he describes his attempt to be a father and instruct his adopted sons, as he had been instructed, in the tenets of the classically-minded, hierarchical plantation world of the Old South.

Although he does not "enter" the book until Chapter III, Percy imprints his stamp on the two introductory chapters. He describes the geographical locus of the book, the Mississippi Delta, and the origins of its dynastic culture. But, while evoking the spirit of the past, he keeps a firm rein on the imposing reality of the present, "a new order unsure of itself and without graciousness" [p. 9]. Contemporary instability is set off against the abiding presence of the river, which figures throughout as a symbol of eternity. Under mounting pressure from American mass society, the old agrarian hierarchy is tottering. "Behind us a culture lies dying," he laments, "before us the forces of the unknown industrial world gather for catastrophe" [p. 24]. Among the victims of this onslaught will be his father, Senator LeRoy Percy, in whom Will Percy saw the embodiment of the Old World tradition of personal probity and public responsibility.[5] The sociodrama that his father lived through and that Will Percy (born in 1885) inherited is the defeat of the southern plantocracy, not by the Civil War, but by a new urban-industrial class, ignorant of its cultural past, "poor in spirit and common as hell" [p. 62]. Before its tide, not only is the southern tradition helpless, but also the entire cultural tradition of western civilization: "Under the Southern Valhalla the torch has been thrust, already the bastions have fallen. . . . A side-show Götterdämmerung perhaps, yet who shall inherit our earth, the earth we loved?" [p. 63]. Percy's insistence here, and throughout the book, is on the large-scale implications of the collapse of southern plantation civilization: the southern apocalypse provides but local testimony to the global disappearance of the landholding class and its aristocratic institutions.

Looking backward from the aspect of maturity, it thus appeared to Percy that the underlying principle of his life had been his "doomed" vocation as a planter's son, the descendant of a classical, agrarian Old World tradition now almost extinguished. But as a boy and young man, he did not perceive himself or his mission as such. Chapters VIII-XII recount his student years and ambitions. He graduated in 1904 from the University of the South at Sewanee, Tennessee, where he later taught English. He studied at the Sorbonne and in 1908 received his law degree from Harvard. In Chapter XII he touches upon his "first" career—not as a planter's son but as a poet. During his lifetime, four volumes of poetry were printed: *Sappho in Levkas* (1915), *In April Once* (1920), *Enzio's Kingdom* (1924), and *Selected Poems* (1930). Also, he served as editor of the Yale Series of Younger Poets, in 1923 and 1925 and from 1927 to 1931.[6] However, after 1924, Percy turned away from writing poetry to assume the public responsibilities of his hometown and the Delta. Although briefly describing this literary aspect of his life, Percy states flatly that *Lanterns on the Levee* "is not an account of my poetry nor of me as a poet" [p. 131]. With this declaration, Percy effectively closes the first section of his autobiography.

In the middle section of the book (Chapters XIII-XXIII), Percy records the crises of adult life and his effort to measure up to the standards of the past. In a pivotal chapter, "The Bottom Rail on Top" (XIII), he recounts his father's resounding defeat in 1912, losing his Senate seat. His victorious opponent was James K. Vardaman, who was nicknamed "Great White Father" for his racist policies. Vardaman was joined in the fight by Theodore G. Bilbo, another folk hero who in 1911 narrowly had escaped expulsion from the state senate on bribery charges. Percy saw his father voted out by "the sort of people that lynch Negroes, that mistake hoodlumism for wit, and cunning for intelligence, that attend revivals and fight and fornicate in the bushes afterwards" [p. 149]. His father's crushing defeat was the turning point of Will Percy's life, for it presaged the disintegration of the plantation way of life. Further, Percy foresaw that the displacement of the southern plantocracy was cause for far more than regional alarm: "today Mississippi is like the rest of the South and the South is like the rest of the nation. . . . The voters choose their representatives in public life, not for their wisdom or courage, but for the promises they make" [p. 153]. While Vardaman might seem only a backwater menace, to Percy he was an ominous forerunner of a new breed of cultural bar-

barians whose rise signalled the collapse of humanism, not only in America but also in Europe:

> In Russia, Germany, and Italy Demos, having slain its aristocrats and intellectuals and realizing its own incompetence to guide or protect itself, had submitted to tyrants who laughed at the security virtues and practiced the most vile of the survival virtues with gangster cynicism. In the democracies Demos had been so busy providing itself with leisure and luxury it had forgotten that hardihood and discipline are not ornaments but weapons. [p. 312]

The onset of World War I confirmed Percy's suspicions that humanism was dying not only in Mississippi and America but the world over. Unable to live in the lost world and unwilling to live in the new one, Percy somewhat to his astonishment found grateful relief from his alienation in the common cause of the war. His years of soldiering (Chapters XIV-XVII) were, by his own admission, the only time in his life when he had any fun. Also, he distinguished himself in action in northeastern France and was awarded the Croix de Guerre in 1918. But in 1919, returning to Greenville and its heritage of defeat, his pessimism for the twentieth century was renewed by the rebirth of the Ku Klux Klan (Chapter XVIII). "The most poisonous thing the Klan did to our town," he recalls, "was to rob its citizens of their faith and trust in one another. . . . from Klansmen you could expect neither frankness nor truth nor honor, and you couldn't tell who was a Klansman" [p. 237]. The fragmentation of Greenville seemed total, neighbor against neighbor in an ugly atmosphere of suspicion and violence. Years of rancor followed until, suddenly, in 1927 planters and river-rats, Catholics and Klansmen, blacks and poor whites were united in disaster by the great Mississippi flood (Chapter XIX). Joined in common subjection to the river, invoked earlier as the presiding deity of the Delta, these diverse elements once again came together in an order resembling that fostered by the old plantocracy. Percy himself served as state chairman of the Disaster Relief Committee of the Red Cross. But this enforced return to the old ways of getting along with one another was short lived; enmity and mistrust soon reasserted themselves. Percy's point is clear: the old planter kingdom is in disarray, and not even the mighty river can restore it.

Chapter XX and the three that follow present Percy's effort to vindicate himself and the tradition by which he has lived from "Northern liberal" criticism. In "Planters, Share-Croppers, and Such" (XXI), he marshals facts and statistics to explain to an industrial world an outdated agricultural system. Percy's voice turns uncharacteristically tinny in this vain effort, lashing out at "Knights of the Bleeding Heart" while disclosing little about why the southern economy has done badly in relation to northern urban-industrialism. However, in "Fode" (XXII), he writes movingly of the plight of his chauffeur and tries to depict the appeal and tragedy of southern blacks. Percy cuts through the abstractions and rhetoric to present concretely the human aspect of the problem and its great measure of personal involvement. Ford is a reality, not a theory, and Percy admits there are no easy answers to the problems of race and economics, and perhaps no way out at all. In Chapter XXIII, he makes his uncertainty explicit: "It is true in the South that whites and blacks live side by side, exchange affection liberally, and believe they have an innate and miraculous understanding of one another. But the sober fact is we understand one another not at all" [p. 299]. Ending on this plaintive note, Percy implies that blacks will fare no better, and perhaps far worse, in the urban ghettoes of the industrial North (and New South) than they did on the plantations of the Old South.[7]

These observations close the middle section of the book, eleven chapters devoted to Percy's attempts to confront the issues of adult life in the spirit of his father and in the tradition of the landowning class. With the death of Senator Percy in 1929, Will Percy assumed responsibility for running Trail Lake, the family plantation, and seemed to be confirmed in lifelong bachelorhood. However, two years later he found himself responsible for rearing three young cousins, orphaned by the deaths of their parents. He sensed a profound alteration in a life already settled into middle age. "Just as his maturity had begun when he learned from the past generation," writes Lewis Lawson, "so now he is obligated to become the past generation for his sons and provide them with the philosophy that will insure their successful maturity."[8]

Percy's effort to hand down the planter ideal begins in "For the Younger Generation" (Chapter XXIV), in which *Lanterns on the Levee* reaches its climax. Faced with educating his young charges, Percy is driven to a defense of the precepts by which he has lived. But in so doing, he must wrestle with the issue of whether his teachings are adequate in the modern world. Should he teach them an Old World creed which he still holds but which he suspects has been superannuated, or should he

> teach deceit, dishonor, ruthlessness, bestial force to the children in order that they survive? Better that they should perish. It is sophistry to speak of two sets of virtues, there is but one: virtue is an end in itself. . . . Honor and honesty, compassion and truth are good even if they kill you, for they alone give life its dignity and worth. [p. 313]

The values and ideals of the spiritual good life remain, and the culture of preindustrial western civilization abides even in the modern world. Classical in its origins and humanistic in its values, Percy's Old World vision is both the mainspring of *Lanterns on the Levee* and its legacy: "there is but one good life and men will yearn for it and will again practice it. . . . Love and compassion, beauty and innocence will return. It is better to have breathed them an instant than to have supported iniquity a millennium" [p. 313].

Though the bottom rail is everywhere on top, Old World ideals never die completely and never change at all. In brief, therein lies the theme of the book: standards of

competence and courage that we measure ourselves by, and ideals of right thinking and clean living that we follow—these have not been improved upon by the present age. Only by recourse to the past—the cultural continuity of western civilization—can the deficiencies of our own time be exposed and perhaps, in the total picture, corrected. The passive, survivalist virtues count for very little; only an unswerving commitment to classical styles of bravery and beauty can give grace and meaning to life and lift it above brutality and confusion.

The concluding chapter of *Lanterns on the Levee*, "Home," is set in the Greenville cemetery, but its spiritual locus lies far away. On the last page of his autobiography, Percy's thoughts drift eastward from his "tiny outpost" [p. 347] in Mississippi. In this ultimate vision, an Old World fortress rises before him where godlike forms pace the ramparts. They do not look southern. Below them, Will Percy, having discharged his duty to the younger generation, cries for admission, seeking at last his spiritual "true" home.

More than forty years after its appearance, *Lanterns on the Levee* thus stands as something of an oddity. Perhaps readers will continue to find in it an idyllic portrayal of a vanished South, and some may link it to the Agrarian movement of the twenties and thirties. But Percy seems a doubtful southern chauvinist. Though his sense of civic commitment is strong (and he is careful to stress the importance of community), Percy's motivation in writing *Lanterns on the Levee* is only incidentally regional. From Greenville to Moscow, the landholding class appeared doomed. At basis Percy is more concerned with the worldwide disappearance of hierarchic social structures than with fading images of the cotton kingdom, and more dedicated to the preservation of classical values than of sharecropping. Will Percy's main intention in his autobiography is to hand down to his descendants the heritage of a planter civilization whose antecedents stretched eastward toward the dynastic preindustrial culture of the Old World. By appreciating the frankly ideological nature of the book, we can come to understand better Will Percy's impassioned defense of his life, his homeland, and his class, and perhaps come more to admire his success in extending the tradition he memorializes.

NOTES

This essay, in slightly altered form, was presented at the Annual Convention of the Modern Language Association in Los Angeles, California, on 28 December 1982.

[1] *Lanterns on the Levee: Recollections of a Planter's Son* (1941; rpt. Baton Rouge: Louisiana State University Press, 1973), pp. 62-63.

[2] Raimondo Luraghi, *The Rise and Fall of the Plantation South* (New York: New Viewpoints, 1978), p. 33. In this Marxist perspective, the southern planter, along with his Canadian, West Indian, Brazilian, and Latin

American counterparts, is seen as the legitimate heir of a "seigneurial" Old World culture in sharp ideological opposition to mercantile and industrial capitalism.

[3] Review of *Lanterns on the Levee* in *Charlotte News*, 10 May 1941, rpt. in Joseph L. Morrison, *W. J. Cash: Southern Prophet* (New York: Knopf, 1967), p. 291.

[4] Letter received from Walker Percy, 17 November 1971.

[5] For a psychological examination of Will Percy's relationship with his father, see Richard H. King, "Mourning and Melancholia: Will Percy and the Southern Tradition," *Virginia Quarterly Review* 53 (Spring 1977): 248-264.

[6] For an account of Percy's career as a poet, see Benjamin Willis Dickey, "William Alexander Percy: An Alien Spirit in the Twentieth Century," M.A. Thesis, Auburn University, 1951.

[7] The question of Percy's alleged paternalistic or racist attitude toward blacks after all may be moot. For a discussion of the complexities of the larger issue, see Eugene D. Genovese, "Class and Race," *The World the Slaveholders Made* (New York: Vintage, 1971), pp. 103-113.

[8] "Walker Percy's Southern Stoic," *Southern Literary Journal* 3 (Fall 1970): 7.

William L. Andrews (essay date 1988)

SOURCE: "In Search of a Common Identity: The Self and the South in Four Mississippi Autobiographies," in *The Southern Review*, Vol. 24, No. 1, Winter, 1988, pp. 47-64.

[*In the following essay, Andrews subjects four Mississippi autobiographies—including* Lanterns on the Levee—*to a comparative study which takes into account a number of factors, most notably racial issues.*]

> "Your delta," he had said," "was not mine."
> —Willie Morris

An article of faith among the first generation of southern literary modernists, writes Lewis Simpson, is "the truth that man's essential nature lies in his possession of the moral community of memory and history." Much has been written, of course, about what an obsession with the past has done to mold southern novelists into a recognizable and distinctive group. But if, as Hugh Holman has stated, "the southerner is not really interested in an abstract past; he is interested in *his* past," and if, according to Faulkner, "it is himself that every Southerner writes about," then it is important to notice that southerners, especially since the Renaissance of the 1920s and '30s, have paid a substantial tribute to the

past in autobiography as well as fiction. While much southern fiction since mid-century has recorded a depletion of the mythic resources of *the* southern past, contemporary southern autobiographers have inscribed in their localized images of *a* southern past a sense of identity that invites our attention because of its social and existential, if not mythic, import. I propose, therefore, to investigate the extent to which recent southern autobiography has sought or signified a peculiar kind of selfhood and community, whether fashioned from individual or collective memory.

What follows in this essay is basically an intertextual reading of four well-known autobiographies: William Alexander Percy's *Lanterns on the Levee* (1941), Richard Wright's *Black Boy* (1945), Willie Morris's *North Toward Home* (1967), and Anne Moody's *Coming of Age in Mississippi* (1968). These works emanate from a common geocultural region, the Deep South in general, and Mississippi specifically; indeed, they all originate in the world of the Mississippi Delta, the locus of John Dollard's classic *Caste and Class in a Southern Town*. Even a cursory look reveals that the books may be compared in a variety of ways. Percy and Morris recount the tranquil growing-up experiences of two members of Mississippi's dominant caste and upper (in Morris's case upper-middle) classes. Wright and Moody record the bitter socialization of the children of those near the bottom class of the South's subordinate caste. Putting caste and class distinctions in abeyance, however, one can also see some commonness of purpose between these two generations of autobiographers. Acutely sensitized by the Depression and the world wars to the ravages of history, both Percy and Wright gravitated toward autobiography as a means of psychic survival, as a way of giving form and meaning to a sense of selfhood that the incoherence of modernity threatened. Galvanized by the Civil Rights Movement, Morris and Moody also came to autobiography at roughly the same time and with similar needs—to revaluate their personal histories in and evolving responsibilities to Mississippi in the throes of social upheaval. It is hard to imagine that Morris and Moody took up the form of first-person narrative ignorant of or indifferent to the example set by Percy and Wright, respectively. And yet, while one can easily point to thematic and stylistic echoes between the black- and white-authored autobiographies, the affinities between Morris and Wright and, to a lesser extent, between Moody and Percy, are probably more arresting because less expected. For instance, the aspirations of Wright and Morris take them out of Mississippi and, a bit later, the South itself on quests for intellectual fulfillment that eventually intersect in Paris in 1956. The narrators of *Lanterns on the Levee* and *Coming of Age in Mississippi,* by contrast, cannot abrogate the responsibility they feel to that sense of community that binds them to Mississippi. Percy and Moody make temporary forays outside their native state, but they always return to struggle with Mississippi's social problems and their own conflicting, sometimes desperate, feelings about the efficacy of their efforts.

Clearly, none of the obvious caste, class, generational, and gender differences among these autobiographers prevents them from sharing experiences, perspectives, and literary motives in common. But if we want to avoid simply reshuffling the deck of southern literature before we play out the familiar hands of genre criticism, our investigation of the communal identifications of these autobiographers needs to go deeper than the question of who's different from (or similar to) whom? We need to ask ourselves, foremost, what difference does difference make in the narrations of these writers and to a search for "a common identity" among black and white autobiographers of the modern South? What levels or modes of difference-making are fundamental to the process of *Bildung* that each of these autobiographers recounts and recreates in his or her text?

The concept of difference, of course, is crucial to southern notions of corporate identity. The feudal South fought the Civil War out of a conviction that it was a social, economic, and cultural entity different from the North and ought to be granted its political independence from Yankeedom as well. After that debacle, as Simpson has observed, southern white writers could be expected to make much of their region's spiritual differences from the rest of the Union, portraying Dixie as "a special redemptive community fulfilling a divinely appointed role in the drama of history." Black southerners inherited from their oppressed ancestors an image of themselves as a chosen people too, though it took a Martin Luther King, Jr., to make temporally viable the traditional black belief in a corporate apotheosis in the hereafter. George Brown Tindall reminds us that during times of national crisis in the twentieth century, southern blacks and whites have vied with each other for the right to proclaim themselves alone the guardians of true Americanism.

Caste and class difference has also been the key to southern social and economic structures throughout its history. The segregation system that evolved after the Civil War was founded on the assumption of essential genetic differences between whites and blacks and ineradicable social gradations among whites. The idea of Jim Crow was to regulate all dealings between the races so that the difference between white status and black status would be consistently attested and publicly confirmed. Caste solidarity was enforced among both whites and blacks, ostensibly out of each community's desire for self-preservation, but also because of fear and distrust of the racial other, into which each caste could project its fantasies and/or its repressed negative imagery of itself. Each caste tended to interpret any member's deviations from prescribed behavior simply as a sign of caste disloyalty: thus, white individualists could be impugned as "nigger lovers" for a wide range of social infractions, while individualistic blacks were condemned, often by both castes, for "trying to be white." Southern behavior exhibited many characteristics of what Erik Erikson has called the "ideological mind," typical of a people preoccupied, as an adolescent is, by peer approval and confirmation of one's worth by creeds and rituals that simultaneously furnish assurance that what is different is alien and inimical.

The autobiographies of Percy, Wright, Morris, and Moody suggest that in the mid-twentieth-century Deep South, neither the black nor the white caste could sanction traditional American individualism, if by that we mean the attempt to differentiate oneself from others according to what Emerson would have called one's subjective "genius." Mississippi recognized selfhood not as a function of the subject but of the object, namely the racial other, whose looming presence dictated the need for self-differentiation according *to* the strictures of law and custom rather than in creative opposition to them. What happens, however, when the southern youth discovers that the law is not a single but a double standard? This introduces the problem, among black southerners especially, of how to identify with half a society without feeling oneself to be but half a person. Among modern white southern autobiographers, the problem of identity is similarly one of incompleteness, symbolized by a sense of unresolved conflict within the self over one's attitude toward blacks. What Thadious Davis has termed a "preoccupation with wholeness" and a need to achieve a "unified vision" of the self and the South do not characterize Faulkner alone. To a large extent these desires manifest the legacy of caste consciousness in white and black southern autobiography as well.

The fundamental difference that the southern system of social difference makes in much modern autobiography from the South is this: it makes the notion of individuation—the achievement of personal indivisibility—a persistent, though not always recognized or acknowledged, ideal. Robert Penn Warren's definition of selfhood (in *Democracy and Poetry*)—"in individuation, the felt principle of significant unity"—represents the ideal to which people like Percy, Wright, Morris, and Moody all aspire. All four of their autobiographies record quests, both physical and intellectual, for a mode of coherent selfhood that is comprised of at least three desiderata: identity, community, and history. All four must contend with a parodic model of selfhood, engendered by caste consciousness, that valorizes image, society, and myth as substitutes for identity, community, and history, respectively. Thus, instead of seeking an identity to and for which one can feel responsible, the southerner (black or white) is socialized to accept an image, an imitation of something assigned to him or her by another. Instead of asserting his existential worth in *communitas,* the southerner must demonstrate his functional value to society by playing a prescribed socioeconomic role. Instead of viewing himself or herself as a part of historical continuity and change, the southerner is encouraged to subscribe to a static world view of ahistorical myths.

Percy, Wright, Morris, and Moody articulate fairly clearly their goals of coherent selfhood and the place, outside and/or beyond the Mississippi Way of Life, where they hoped to realize their goals. Through the mists of ancient history, Percy descried his ideal in the stoic nobility of Marcus Aurelius and tried to serve as a mediator between his hero and alienated southern youth. In an idealized "place where everything was possible," located somewhere in "the North" in the hazy future, young Wright, only "part of a man" in the South, imagined the fulfillment of his hunger for an unbounded selfhood. To Morris, New York was the only place where he could engage "in a subtle interior struggle with himself" and emerge, once tested, an integrated self, liberated from fear and bigotry yet neither ashamed of nor alienated from the distinctively southern traditions that had shaped him. Moody hoped to find in the marginal, integrated community of the Civil Rights Movement an alternative to the role and destiny of the powerless, choiceless black woman that her mother symbolized to her. All four of these autobiographers share a common goal, therefore. Individualists all, they may be thought of as southern aristocrats—if we accept Percy's philosophical definition of the term, not one based on caste or class privilege, but rather on a sense of moral commitment: "Their distinguishing characteristic probably is that their hearts are set, not on the virtues which make surviving possible, but on those which make it worth while."

The key differences among these four autobiographers arise when we consider each one's understanding of the route that he or she must take to achieve psychological and moral coherence as a self, rather than settling for the image, role, and myths of a caste system fixated on mere survival. Each autobiographer conceived of his or her route to achieved selfhood differently, of course, but there is at least one basis for comparison of all four. None of these routes can afford to bypass the racial other. If Sander L. Gilman is right, the other is the projected image of the anxieties that a person or a group develops when their senses of internal order and external control are threatened. Thus to recover or attain coherence as a self, a person must confront the other. It is certainly possible to argue, as Percy, Wright, Morris, and Moody testify, that whites and blacks confronted each other daily under the Mississippi caste system. But if confrontation means literally a coming together face-to-face, how often did the etiquette of caste behavior permit someone to show his face to or look into the face of a member of the opposite caste? Narrated instances of this etiquette in action as well as examples of its circumvention or suspension can give us a sense of the quality and consequences of confrontation between castes in the experiences of these Mississippians.

Regardless of race or generation, all four autobiographers recall a time early in life when each viewed the racial other through the undifferentiated perspective of childhood. But only the two white Mississippians were privileged to grow up with a myth of a homogeneous past in which, insofar as a child could tell, there were no racial barriers to their access to the pleasures of life. Morris speaks for both whites in recalling the compla-

cent, quasi-proprietary attitude towards blacks that he grew up with: "The Negroes in the town . . . were *ours,* to do with as we wished." To a nostalgic Will Percy, the memory of the black companions of his childhood was a balm to be savored in his last weary years. During the carefree summers he spent among them in Virginia, the children of his Aunt Nana's cook introduced him to a wealth of rural sensual delights. But Skillet and Ligey and Friday, like "small satyrs and fauns," belong completely to the world of childhood summers and natural innocence. Of them in adulthood, Percy knows nothing. With all the other blacks of his youth, they are ensconced in a chapter entitled "Playmates," denoting the role that Percy considered most blacks best suited for in the caste-conscious South of his memory.

When Percy confronted blacks in his adulthood, he consistently assumed the role of benevolent paternalist. "The black man is our brother," he announces to the white reader of his autobiography—but not our equal, "a younger brother, not adult, not disciplined, but tragic, pitiful, and lovable; act as his brother and be patient." Percy could not see in black people more than the potential (in the distant future) for mature relationships with whites. His everyday dealings with blacks left him worrying, "Is the inner life of the Negro utterly different from ours?" Given Percy's aristocratic self-image, the reader of his autobiography is not surprised to find that his one sustained personal relationship with a Negro was structured by the traditional lord-and-vassal arrangement. In a chapter entitled "Fode," Percy recounts what he learned from a lengthy association with his young retainer, Ford. From the outset, he claims that "every [southern] white man worth calling white or a man is owned by some Negro, whom he thinks he owns, his weakness and solace and incubus." The pride and ruefulness of an aristocrat facing obsolescence in a modernizing society are apparent in this statement. Ford, Percy admits, owns him because of his weakness for the kind of solace that this bond to a dependent black man gives him. More than once in his autobiography, and particularly in his chapter on the flood of 1927, Percy acknowledges his failure to convince blacks as a group to follow his leadership. That Ford needs him helps to counterbalance the sense of impotence and irrelevance that dogs Percy's adulthood.

In keeping with his penchant for irony, however, the emphasis in "Fode" is not on what Percy teaches Ford but on the "bitter tutelage" the patron receives from his underling. Ford makes it possible for Percy to see himself as others, *the* other, see him, underneath the image, role, and myths that he wears like psychosocial armor. It is Ford who translates for Percy a statement he hears some of his sharecroppers make when he arrives in his car on settlement day at his plantation, "the lord of the manor among his faithful retainers." "Whose car is dat?" one black asks another; "Dat's *us* car," is the reply. Percy thinks it odd that these men don't recognize his car, but "Ford elucidated: 'He meant that's the car *you* has bought with *us* money. They [the sharecroppers] all knew what he meant, but you didn't and they knew you didn't. They wuz laughing to theyselves.'" Percy admits, "I laughed too, but not inside." This is not the only instance when Ford lets Percy see the gap between his self-image (in this case, the beloved lord among his tenants) and the image he projects to the other (the crass and selfish rich man lording it over the poor). As Percy reconstructs such incidents in his autobiography, he pictures himself as the *naïf* unprepared for and sometimes genuinely hurt by Ford's revelations. In this way, the narrator suggests that the other-perception that Ford gave him access to taught him a little salutary humility. But at the same time, there is little indication in ***Lanterns on the Levee*** that Percy felt that gaps between self- and other-perception in the South could be bridged. How could he defend himself, he asks rhetorically, against the image his black cook had of him as a man who wanted to return blacks to slavery? The woman's grotesque appearance, religious beliefs, and morality, as Percy indites them, rendered absurd any attempt to reason with her. And so throughout his discussion of race relations, Percy pictures himself frustrated and dis-empowered by a "bewildering" barrier, as "of glass," that alienates the races and seems inevitably to produce black misperceptions of himself and the caste system he stands for. However, one need not read Du Bois' use of the same plate-glass metaphor while analyzing the psychology of segregation in *Dusk of Dawn* (1940) to conclude that this barrier was as much Percy's protection as his vexation.

"That I have any dignity and self-respect is not because of but in spite of Ford," Percy remarks only half tongue-in-cheek. To show the extent to which Ford enjoyed undermining that self-respect, Percy recounts an episode in the bathroom when, discovering his master in the shower, Ford "observed dreamily: 'You ain't nothing but a little old fat man.'" Since he was "not in a position of dignity" and it was "no use attempting to be haughty," the best Percy could manage in riposte was "you damn fool." Narrating this episode, Percy grants Ford a certain victory of wit, but he also notes that as a result of this exchange he dismissed Ford from his service. The extent to which the emperor was genuinely offended by this observation about him unclothed is hard to measure, given Percy's frequent self-effacing irony as a narrator. It is clear that Percy was not so vain as to deny the truth of Ford's physical characterization of him. But could Percy accept the existential validity of Ford's image of his bare humanity, stripped of the caste signifier, bereft of all the accoutrements of his social dignity? And could Percy realize that Ford in this instance had played the fool no less aptly than Lear's, when he urgently queried his master, "Can you make no use of nothing, nuncle?"? These are difficult questions to resolve, especially when so much of what Percy recalls about blacks underlines one conclusion: that despite the comfortable southern pretense of harmony and a shared way of life between the races, "the sober fact is we understand one another not at all." If Percy believed he could not understand Ford, it is highly unlikely that he

thought that Ford could comprehend him. And so, even though Percy recounts opportunities when he could have confronted his selfhood through the agency of the other, his autobiography leaves it to his reader to decide whether what he saw in these instances was an image reflected in, or an identity revealed through, the eyes of Ford.

As testimony to his reverence for his father, Percy subtitled his autobiography "Recollections of a Planter's Son." Had it not been for *his* father, Willie Morris's autobiography might well have been entitled "Reflections of a Planter's Son-in-Law." As a high school senior in Yazoo City a decade after Percy's death, Morris "had his heart set," he admits, "on entering Mississippi's educated landed gentry" by marriage to a majorette whose father was a plantation owner. But Morris's father (unlike Percy's) was determined that his son would not become a reflection, either of the planter class (from which Willie's mother came) or the yeomanry (from which he had sprung). He sent Willie west in search of *"opportunity"* at the University of Texas. This was the first of many "sharp breaks with the past" that Morris was to make on his way to precocious fame. But by the mid-1960s, like many thoughtful white southerners of his generation, he felt compelled by the social revolutions of that time to reassess himself in light of his past. Living in New York taught him, he writes, that "one's life, one's spanning of years and places, could never be of a piece, but rather were like scattered fragments of glass." Yet Morris was too much a southerner to accept being wholly alienated from his roots—or ashamed of them. He wrote *North Toward Home,* at least in part, out of a desire "to *understand* [his] origins, to discover what was distinctive and meaningful in them, to compare them with the origins of others, to give shape to them for the sake of some broader understanding of place and experience." It was particularly important to him to compare his origins to those of black southerners and to find bases for common understanding across the chasm of difference. In this way he could redeem his past and some of the most important qualities of southern distinctiveness that he had always identified with.

Morris's portrait of small-town Mississippi in the 1940s provides little evidence of commonality among blacks and whites. He acknowledges his own profound ambivalence toward blacks while he was growing up and pictures in brief vignettes acts of violence against blacks "as senseless and unpatterned later as they had been for me when they happened." But what Morris remembers best and what he concentrates on most in the racial sphere of his past are the moments in chance encounters when blacks and whites found a common ground of interest, if not understanding. A personal illustration of this appears in his description of a phase of his early teens when he and most of his white buddies in Yazoo City "went Negro"—i.e., aped black styles of speech and gesture—as a kind of unconscious tribute to the exotic other. It was all right for white boys to walk and talk black, and even to get together in sandlot football teams to compete against young blacks. But when the teams started to intermingle in these impromptu games, "the cops ordered us to break it up." Maybe the police sensed that the white youths, without being aware of it, were forgetting difference and experimenting with sameness. At any rate, Morris's mentioning it suggests that in "going Negro" he and his peers were acting out an unconscious resistance to the pervasive doubleness of their world. Southern whites, one might conclude from this and other evidence in Morris's picture of Mississippi, were not disposed by nature, as Percy believed, to differentiate themselves from blacks.

Morris carried with him to New York a rosy image of the delta of his boyhood, one that partially compensated for his lack of a sense of place in "the Big Cave," as he called it. But talking with black and white civil rights activists from his home state left him feeling "threatened and unsure" about nothing less than the validity of his cherished sense of the past. He could not reconcile the Mississippi he had known, or thought he knew, with the Mississippi the SNCC volunteers had experienced. Thus his myth of his homeland fissured, and in so doing, created a conflict within Morris between his loyalty to his sense of home and his need to be intellectually honest with himself. How he worked out this conflict is not made explicit in *North Toward Home*, but in the narrative's progression from this conflict to Morris's relationships with Richard Wright and Ralph Ellison, we gain some insight, perhaps, into the way that the white man salvaged something of his myth of the southern past.

Morris met Wright in Paris in 1957, while the younger man was in Europe as a Rhodes Scholar; he met Ellison in New York City at a *Paris Review* cocktail party in 1965. Despite the fact that Wright had once lived on a tenant farm not far from his hometown, Morris had a hard time talking to Wright. Wright, though admirable, "was so different from me in temperament and loyalty and experience that we had almost nothing in common." On the other hand, in conversation with William Styron and Ellison, Morris felt at once that he "probably had more in common" with these two southerners than with any other writer or intellectual at the party. It took Morris only one evening with Ellison to identify in the Oklahoman's social and storytelling manner, sense of the past, love of the tactile, and suspicion of the abstract a "distinctive *Southernness*" that was very similar to his own. "It would have been naive to ignore the differences" between the black man and the white, Morris notes, but it was the similarities—"temperamental, intellectual, imaginative—which interested me." They interested Morris so much, one suspects, because they confirmed an ideal that he very much needed confirmed—and which only a southern Negro could confirm—that beneath or beyond the racial differences, there is a core of southern experience and a fundamental southern view of life and of what is valuable in living that is shared by all raised in that milieu.

This ideal of southern wholeness, virtually antithetical to Percy's myth of a South alienated against itself by racial difference, is crucial to Morris's politics as a southern liberal and his strategy as a modern southern autobiographer. He is committed to integration, in the social fabric, in his personal life, and in the narrative persona he creates in *North Toward Home*. When Wright told Morris in Paris that he did not expect to return to the United States because "I want my children to grow up as human beings," the black Mississippian severely challenged the efficacy, in the American present and near future, of the white liberal's integrationist ideal. Not surprisingly then, Morris could see in Wright only difference. Even though the black man suggested they correspond, the young white man shied away. It is equally unsurprising that Morris found later in the congruence between Ellison and himself the confirmation he sought for his belief that an integrated, yet still "distinctively southern," identity could be reconstructed, transcending racial difference, out of the fundamental wholeness of what he and Ellison shared. But did Morris achieve that self-confirming sense of unity with Ellison by repressing the significance of that troubling otherness that he felt with Wright? If so, and it is hard to think differently, then we may conclude that the integrative ideal that Morris felt he shared with Ellison was probably less important to his realization of "distinctive *Southernness*" than the disintegrative skepticism that Morris associated with Wright. In any case, Morris's reactions to Ellison and Wright serve to warn white readers about the dangers of identifying as truly southern only those aspects of black experience that buttress, rather than destabilize, the totalizing tendencies of white integrative ideals.

In the quests for selfhood narrated by Wright and Moody, the discovery of difference comes early in childhood, creating a sense of disjunctiveness and unexplained mystery in the black child's most intimate world. As boys Percy and Morris perceived the world of blackness as different but not other, not outside the white boys' sphere of comprehension and control. By contrast, when Wright and Moody discover the difference that whiteness makes, the structure and order of all their relationships, with their families as well as their communities, are undermined. On a train ride to Arkansas, young Richard tries to understand what gives white people their special status in the railroad station and on the cars. The problem leads him to probe the significance of whiteness itself. He asks his mother whether his grandmother, who looks white to him, is a white woman. If so, then why does she associate with colored people like himself? Did she "become colored when she married Grandpa?" Is whiteness acquired or innate? Receiving no clear answers from his evasive, increasingly defensive mother, the boy tries to penetrate the mystery by tracing his grandmother's origins, but this only leads him to a blank, an unnamed and unknown white great-grandfather. Why does whiteness signify absence for some white people while conferring status on others? Who makes the decision, and why will "they" call him "a colored man" when he grows up, regardless of the whiteness in his own heritage? Concluding that his mother is trying to "shut [him] out of the secret," Richard, already troubled by a sense of alienation from his family, feels all the more alone and powerless. Without answers to the secret of the world's arbitrary, capricious, and repressive power over him, he barricades himself in the world of his own imagination and sustains himself on fantasies of violent reprisal against the motiveless malignity of whiteness. As narrator, Wright observes that the "emotional integrity" he developed as a child was an outgrowth of these fantasies. Eventually, though "I had never in my life been abused by whites," "at the mere mention of whites" "a vast complex of emotions, involving the whole of my personality, would be aroused," out of which young Richard created "a culture, a creed, a religion." In one sense *Black Boy* is the story of Wright's progress from his boyish fantasies of a desperate integrity based on rebellion against the terrible other to an ideal of selfhood liberated from an opposition to otherness as its negative *raison d' être*.

In *Black Boy* whiteness alone does not comprise the totality of repressive forces that Richard must resist. The first half of the book emphasizes the conformity that black authority, whether familial or institutional, demands from the black boy. Wright says he rejected the black males on whom he might have modeled himself because they seemed obsessed with forcing him to accept a place in a pecking order, rather than encouraging him to discover who he was. As a boy the only way Wright could express his desire for authenticity was through acts of verbal aggression, in which he persistently offended his elders' sense of dignity and propriety by speaking and writing "dirty words." As a teenager Wright encoded his resistance to white authority in speech acts that seemed to him unprovocative but were in fact just as much a profanation of the rituals of caste intercourse as the boy's obscenities were of his black elders' dignity. This is what his friend Griggs recognizes when he warns Wright, "You act around white people as if you didn't know that they were white. And they *see* it." Motivating all this offensive behavior toward others, Wright explains, was a fundamental need throughout his youth to view his world wholly, as a community, and to negotiate his world not through images and roles but as an authentic personality. "It was simply utterly impossible for me to calculate, to scheme, to act. . . . I would remember to dissemble for short periods, then I would forget and act straight and human again, not with the desire to harm anybody, but merely forgetting the artificial status of race and class. It was the same with whites as with blacks; it was my way with everybody."

It would be more accurate, in light of what is narrated in *Black Boy,* to say that this was Wright's *preferred* way with everybody. Very little in his description of his dealings with whites and blacks during his crucial last two years in the South suggests that he had any real hope of finding an alternative to the image and role of

"non-man" that the caste system expected of him. The extreme hostility and humiliation that he suffers while trying to "work his way up" in a Jackson, Mississippi, optical shop leaves him feeling profoundly "violated," "slapped out of the human race." Even though his boss, Mr. Crane, apparently sympathetic to the black youth, asks Wright to tell him what happened, Wright refuses. "There's no use of my saying anything." Gradually the youth whose principal weapon against the world had been words begins to fall silent, the ultimate sign, in Wright's case, of his alienation from his southern environment. The last chapters of *Black Boy* record his consistent refusal to talk to any whites, even to a solicitous Yankee like Falk, the bookish Irishman, "hated by the white Southerners," who might have shared much with Wright. While the black youth accepts the white man's library card, which gives him illicit access to the Memphis library, he spurns his benefactor's invitation to discuss with him his reactions to the works of Mencken, Dreiser, and other American realist novelists. "It would have meant talking about myself and that would have been too painful." There is no more despairing depiction of the inhibition of other-confrontation and self-revelation in modern southern autobiography than this.

Nevertheless, out of this seeming ratification of unbridgeable difference emerges, in the climax of *Black Boy,* the alienated black youth's discovery of new, potentially liberating ways of identifying himself as a writer, a southerner, and an American. The loss of the hope of community within the narrow boundaries of caste relationships, where so little can be spoken safely, provokes and actually facilitates Wright's search for "a world elsewhere" (to use Richard Poirier's phrase), not just in the magical land of "the North," but in the idealized unboundedness of the written word. Thus when young Wright encounters the combative literary style of *Prejudices,* he imagines himself, however doubtfully, as another Mencken, "using words as a weapon" against injustice. Through Dreiser's Carrie Meeber and Jennie Gerhardt, he recovers from the past "a vivid sense of my mother's suffering." After finishing *Main Street* and *Babbitt,* he no longer views his pretentious white boss, Mr. Gerald, as quite the implacable and inexplicable other. "I felt that I knew him" and could "identify him as an American type." In short, Wright's retreat into the world of literature does not seal his alienation; it liberates him from it by enhancing his powers of imaginative identification. He begins to recognize himself *in* and *through* others, even the ónce terrible other, by way of their common Americanness as revealed in the national perspective of the American realist novel. What he had been rebelling against in the South he understands as part of a larger "straitened American environment" that writers, indeed *white* writers, were trying to reshape "nearer to the hearts of those who lived in it." In this community the black man from the South believes he can become a self-wrighter.

Richard Wright acknowledges in the last paragraphs of *Black Boy* that he did not go north with an integral sense of the self he wanted to become. He went to Chicago "running more away from something than toward something." Anyone who reads *American Hunger* (1977), the posthumously published sequel to *Black Boy,* knows that Wright did not find the community, in personal, political, or artistic terms, that he vaguely imagined lay beyond his southern horizons in 1927. Wright's autobiographies testify eloquently to his hunger for an identity realized in community, but they do not picture his achievement of a communal identity in an historically locatable place and time. Wright's autobiographies send a double message, therefore, of optimism and skepticism about the possibility of the black southerner's achieving a fulfilling sense of identity and community in America. The experience of Richard Wright *within* history, as history is reconstructed in his autobiographies, justifies the skepticism that Morris reported in Wright's conversation with him—namely, that black children could not expect to grow up in America "as human beings." Yet the voice of Richard Wright as narrator in the timeless world of his text engages his American reader in a community of intimate discourse that is plainly intended to defy history, the very history that Wright claims to have personally experienced, in which all such efforts to engage the other in community are frustrated. As a result of the dialectical relationship of the voice of community and the experience of history in *Black Boy,* the reader is forced to make a choice of identification between one of two Richard Wrights.

Although Wright's southern experience places community and history at perpetual odds, it is important to notice that Anne Moody's does not. Unlike *Black Boy, Coming of Age in Mississippi* is punctuated by experiences of interracial community within history and within some of the most racially polarized sections of Mississippi. Like her famous literary predecessor, however, Moody begins her story by thrusting her reader abruptly into a black child's earliest impressions of a profoundly *dis*located world, one characterized by dread and devoid of that "sense of place" that has been traditionally regarded as a hallmark of southern literary consciousness. Percy and Morris, by contrast, usher their readers hospitably into childhood worlds that are easily locatable both spatiotemporally (note the well-developed family trees and thoroughly-mapped geographies) and psychologically (note the evocation of the past as a "paradise lost," consistent with many autobiographies of childhood). "We were always moving," Moody says of her childhood, "to a house on some white man's place." Living in close proximity to whites because her mother was a rural domestic, Moody, though fatherless and rootless like Wright, did not grow up viewing whites with the urban impersonality that characterized the young Wright's perspective. By the time she was seven she had been initiated into the reality of differences between whites and blacks, but at about the same time that her access to her white playmates was being restricted, her chance to associate with white adults expanded. She finds in Ola Johnson, the mother-in-law of Elmira Moody's employer, a kindly maternal figure who

nurtures her physically and intellectually, a stark contrast to the forbidding behavior of the grandmother in *Black Boy*. Mrs. Johnson is no white fairy godmother; Anne does "a hundred chores" for her and concludes from being around her that white women and black women differ in that the former need the latter to compensate for their laziness and incompetence in the kitchen. Still, despite all that the black girl sees that separates her status from that of the whites, she is not afflicted by the anxieties about her own worth, the persistent need to "redeem" herself, that haunt Wright throughout his growing up. White people like the Johnsons and later the Claibornes, for whom Moody worked in her late childhood, are singled out for praise in her autobiography because they treated her "like their equal," "always giving me things and encouraging me to study hard and learn as much as I could."

This is not to say that Moody does not credit her mother with encouraging her too, but her mother's support tends to be more selfish and less consistent than that which white women give her. Elmira Moody sees her daughter's success in school as a way to elevate her status in the eyes of her prospective mother-in-law, whose color-consciousness causes her to treat the dark-skinned Moodys with contempt. Moody associates her mother with powerlessness and dependency, the result of having too many mouths to feed and too little reliable male support. As she enters adolescence she refuses to identify with her mother's church, changes her name regardless of her mother's disapproval, and rejects the farm woman's life her mother leads. "Mrs. Claiborne had told me how smart I was and how much I could do if I just had a chance. I knew if I got involved in farming, I'd be just like Mama and the rest of them, and that I would never have that chance." Through her childhood and adolescence Moody studies diligently in school, proudly making straight A's, in the expectation of earning for herself a chance to escape the restrictions of the traditional black woman's role.

A week before she enters high school, Moody is violently initiated into history. The murder of Emmett Till in 1955 wrenches her out of her self-circumscribed world of schoolwork and housework and forces her to confront the reality of caste oppression in Mississippi. Her mother advises her to "just do your work like you don't know nothing," but Anne asks questions of her bigoted employer, Mrs. Burke, and of a teacher at her school. The ugly truths that she learns about white hate and black fear intensify her desire to flee her situation in Centreville. In the summers she goes to Baton Rouge in search of better-paying work; during the academic years she immerses herself in everything school has to offer, obsessively "keeping busy" so that she "won't have time to think" about the mounting violence against blacks throughout Mississippi in the late 1950s. Although Anne does not understand it at the time, the narrator of *Coming of Age in Mississippi* interprets this behavior as an attempt to "escape within myself," to separate herself from changes within and around her, thus reifying her image of herself as an individual in control of her own circumstances. What Moody is forced to recognize is that there can be no escape for her from the imperative of history and no refuge in an idea of individualism that feeds on the myth of self-sufficiency. Only when she becomes involved as a high school senior in the Civil Rights Movement does she find "something outside myself that gave meaning to my life."

Her growing dedication to the Movement in her college years forces Moody to move beyond the ideas of fulfilled selfhood that had been fixed in her mind for so long. Civil rights work gives a larger sense of purpose to her life than she had ever had, and it shows her that communality with whites is possible, but it does not provide coherence to her world or fulfillment of many of her personal needs. Her activism alienates her from most of her family, causes her almost to flunk out of college, puts her life in imminent peril, leads her to blaspheme the God of her childhood, and takes her to the brink of several nervous breakdowns. For every successful effort against the caste system, she can see a corresponding failure, often a humiliation, followed by doubts about the Movement, its leadership, its nonviolent methods, and the likelihood of its ever achieving its goals. In the last chapter of the book, Moody surveys the situation in Canton, Mississippi, the scene of so much of her effort apparently for naught, and declares, "I felt worse about everything than I had ever felt before." She boards a bus bound for Washington, D.C., where some of her fellow workers intend to testify before Congress as to "what Mississippi is all about." What a dispirited black community leader has told her, "We ain't big enough to do it by ourselves," vies with the song of a hopeful black youth on the bus, "We shall overcome," for Moody's anguished mind—and for the conclusion of her book. But she cannot foresee the fate of her community in history; she can only "wonder."

Moody's inconclusiveness at the end of her autobiography stems from her acknowledgement of the uncertain status of the community with which she has so unreservedly identified herself. Shall "we"—the oppressed blacks of Mississippi and their co-workers in freedom—ever overcome, she wonders, "by ourselves"? Or do the people of America, represented in and by the federal powers in Washington, have to identify themselves with this community to form a "we" that is "big enough" to achieve justice? Moody's wondering is as much about the disposition of her American reader to join this community and thereby determine history as it is about the ultimate outcome of the civil rights struggle. Having experienced and believed in the potential of interracial community to create, not just endure, history, Moody confronts her reader, particularly her white nonsouthern reader, with the opportunity to identify with *her* and thus fulfill in common their American destiny as a free and indivisible people.

The emphasis on unresolved (though by no means irresolute) selfhood in the conclusions of *Black Boy* and *Coming of Age in Mississippi* marks a striking contrast to the impression of defined or confirmed selfhood with

which Percy's and Morris's memoirs are designed to end. The last chapter of *Lanterns on the Levee*, entitled "Home," pictures Percy in the Greenville cemetery, pondering the significance of the deeds of the dead and assuaging his sense of "failure" with a deep assurance that he has lived "the good life" and has been faithful, to a fault perhaps, to himself. In the final scene of his autobiography, Morris, in the company of his son, surveys from the window of a departing jet the land of his birth and youth and feels the "easing of some great burden" as he is lifted "north toward home." Just before leaving Mississippi, he has gone with his mother and grandmother to the town cemetery in search of the graves of his illustrious Harper forebears. Significantly, he can find none of them. Although he does not say so, it is not hard to conclude that he felt more kinship with the *Harper's* of New York, of which he had become editor-in-chief, than with the dust of the Mississippi Harpers. At any rate, Morris, like Percy, closes his book with a distinct sense of the home where each belongs, the locus of coherence for, and confirmation of, the sense of selfhood that both men claim at the end of their autobiographies. For Wright and Moody, however, this sense of home remains on the horizon, potential but not realized. Their autobiographies end in scenes of transit in which both subjects are suspended somewhere between the South and the North, between an identity existentially *af*firmed and a sense of selfhood communally and historically *con*firmed. As rebels against the self-image that the black and white South would impress upon them, they affirm an alternative identity based on responsibility to the ideal of an individuated life and an indivisible people. The problem for them both, of course, is that the caste-conscious South (home for Percy) refuses to confirm this ideal, and the faraway North (Morris's home), or America in a larger sense, remains unaccounted for. Neither Wright nor Moody can be satisfied with realizing this ideal on an existential basis alone, which is why, ultimately, they must confront, through an autobiographical act, the otherness of the reader. Their open-ended stories call on the American reader to identify with the narrator in a national community of moral commitment so that together they can seize the pen of history and write the future in common.

Edward J. Dupuy (essay date 1991)

SOURCE: "The Dispossessed Garden of William Alexander Percy," in *The Southern Quarterly,* Vol. 29, No. 2, Winter, 1991, pp. 31-41.

[*In the following essay, Dupuy discusses "the garden," both as a physical reality and as a metaphor on several levels, in* Lanterns on the Levee.]

> It's getting too late for facts anyway and they have a way these days of looking like the Gorgon's head seen without the mirror Perseus used. The garden's the place.
>
> W. A. Percy, *Lanterns on the Levee*

Will Percy's garden was a busy place. It not only welcomed luminaries like William Faulkner, Carl Sandburg, Harry Stack Sullivan and Langston Hughes, but ladies from the garden club often dropped by to discuss their petunias (Baker 160). It was photographed by *National Geographic,* yet it provided Percy with the "best sort of Ivory Tower" (*Lanterns* 334). Important to his life, the garden is central to his autobiography as well. Percy had wanted to title his book "Jackdaw in the Garden" but was dissuaded by his editor (Baker 169). Like the lanterns on the levee after which he finally titled the work (and like the book itself), the garden is universal but local, public yet private, fact and metaphor (Hobson 273; Holdsworth; Rocks). "The garden's the place" (*Lanterns* 331), but it is also the man, for Will Percy wrestled continually with his "inner, poetic life and with the outer world" (Baker 62).

It was, of course, this outer world that Percy wished to address through *Lanterns on the Levee*. He hoped that his autobiography "would preserve the values of his community and inspire his readers to find similar values in theirs" (Baker 169). At the same time, he realized that his values were waning, if not already vanquished: "During my day I have witnessed a disintegration of that moral cohesion of the South which had given it its strength and its sons their singleness of purpose and simplicity. . . . Standards are in flux: there is no commonly accepted good way of life—and the hospitals can't hold the neurotics, the mental cripples, the moral anemics, the blasted who strove to build a pattern because none existed" (74).

Like Faulkner, Percy claimed affiliation with no "school" of writers, yet he shared many of the concerns of both Faulkner and the Agrarians—especially that of rekindling a sense of memory and history (Walker Percy, "Introduction"; Gulledge). Through his personal "recollections," Percy wished to offer the world a sense of memory and history that, like the lanterns he carried, would provide "stays against the darkness of the modern age that [he] saw engulfing not only the American south but Western civilization in its entirety" (Hobson 273). His garden was his "substitute for things preferred but denied" (332). As Lewis Simpson might say, Percy feared the dispossession of his garden by the forces of modernity (1-2).

Simpson believes that the evolution of both New England and southern literature can be understood in light of settlers' desires to maintain their respective gardens—in the North, the garden of the covenant, a pleasure garden for God's habitation; in the South, the garden of the chattel, based on a paradisiacal relationship with the fecund earth (2). Both gardens tried to provide stays against the advent of the modern age, but they were ultimately "dispossessed" by it. *Lanterns on the Levee* can be read as the record of a man dispossessed of his garden—public and private, universal and local—for things preferred, lost or denied provide thematic underpinnings of the entire work. Pastoral simplicity, represented by the "gardens" of youth, aristocracy and stoicism, wanes in the face of modernity. Furthermore, the garden of Percy's selfhood undergoes a similar dispossession, placing *Lanterns on the Levee* at the nexus of the southern literary tradition.

Percy opens his autobiography with a reflection on the Mississippi Delta and its people—those elements that cultivated and shaped his garden of youth. His sense of place cannot be mistaken or ignored. The Mississippi River provided him an ever-present reminder of the vicissitudes of his land. Order and change, freedom and control, giving and taking—all part of the warp and woof of his autobiography—were with him during his childhood by the river's simple presence (Rocks). While the "gods on their thrones are shaken and changed . . . it abides, aloof and unappeasable" (14). Percy bemoans the loss of the "gallant companies" and the "glamour" of the steamboat era, but he is haunted by a sound similar to theirs: "And still there is no sound in the world so filled with mystery and longing and unease as the sound at night of a river-boat blowing for the landing—one long, two shorts, one long, two shorts" (14). It is as though Will Percy is himself that boat adrift on the river, blowing for his landing.

During his youth, Percy sought moorings in his family and friends. He admits of having "no single memory of [my parents] dating from the first four years of [my] life" (26). Instead, he recalls being nurtured by Nain, his black "nanny," and Mur, his paternal grandmother. Percy experienced the first hints of his dispossessed garden of youth under their tutelage. From Nain's singing, he learned "not so much how lonely I could be as how lonely everybody could be, and I could not explain." And Mur's readings prepared him, he said, for "life as it should be," not necessarily for life as it is (27, 34).

Loneliness and the ideal life both reflect a type of dispossession. Seeking moorings in people, Percy discovered his inexplicable loneliness and separateness from them. Seeking an entrance into life through stories, he found an unattainable ideal. Later, Percy would find it necessary to befriend loneliness, and his struggle to live his preferred life, the "good life," never left him (Cohn). Mur's death when Percy was very young marked for him still another aspect of his dispossessed garden of youth.

Although he writes that he had "never been so close to any living creature since [Mur]" (34), Percy recalls fondly his maternal grandparents, Mère and Père, and the playmates of his youth. With his childhood friends he discovered the wonders of the living earth—hornets' nests, eels, leeches, frogs, crawfish, trees. With Mère and Père he came to know something of the ugliness of death. Reflecting on their painful deaths, he writes: "No wonder we hate [death] so unforgivingly: his ways are humiliating and his approaches brutal. His indignities we fear, not him" (63). Death, a veritable perennial in Percy's garden of youth, denied him that to which he would have preferred to cling. Neither could he maintain his childhood delight in the living earth. It was not forgotten, but neither was it to be recaptured. After a powerful description of playing in the aspen woods as a child, Percy writes: "That must have been the very wood old Housman had in mind when he sang 'We'll to the woods no more'" (55).

If the loss of Mère and Père taught the young Percy something of the ugliness of death, it taught him also something of his "caste." Percy recalls Mère's heroism in the face of her impending doom: "Mère gasped: 'C'est la mort.' Mother leaned to her and whispered: 'Tu n'as pas peur?' Mère steadied herself on the arms of her chair and said distinctly and firmly: 'Non.' So death took her" (64). It is not by accident that this scene closes the chapter Percy entitled "A Side-Show Götter-dämmerung." The twilight of the gods Percy envisioned focused on the loss of his garden of aristocracy, a garden composed of a "caste which, though shaken and scattered, refuses to call itself Demos" (60). W. J. Cash, in his review of *Lanterns on the Levee*, called Percy "a surviving authentic Southern aristocrat" (Hobson 274). Mère's unflinching stare toward death made him happy to be of such a class.

Percy's garden of aristocracy was formed not only by Mère's example. He recalls sitting on the front porch of his home and listening to his father discuss politics and affairs of the levee board with men of the town. These men were leaders of the people, "not elected or self-elected, but destined, under the compulsion of leadership because of their superior intellect, training, character, and opportunity" (69). They were the young Percy's heroes, above reproach, and embodying every characteristic of his preferred life.

All was not well in Paradise, however. Percy recalls the time when public money was pilfered from the levee board's funds. One of his father's friends, General Ferguson, was suspected of taking it. Ferguson, of course, denied the charges, and other members of the board supported him. When Ferguson fled Greenville for South America, the "Demos" had their field day. Will's father and his friends were removed from the levee board and were replaced by men of the people's choosing. "Commoners" had begun their march, and Percy's garden of aristocracy began to slip through his fingers.[1]

The march did not stop anytime soon. Years later, it would overtake him completely. Will recounts his father's (LeRoy's) battle for the senate seat left vacant by the death of Senator McLaurin. LeRoy's opponent, James K. Vardaman, was one of the "Demos" Percy's father and his cohorts despised—a man who "stood for all [LeRoy] considered vulgar and dangerous" (144). In the Percy's opinion, Vardaman and his followers represented the Snopeses of politics: "They were the sort of people that lynch Negroes, that mistake hoodlumism for wit, and cunning for intelligence, that attend revivals and fight and fornicate in the bushes afterwards" (149).

Although LeRoy was elected by the state legislature to finish Senator McLaurin's term, it was a bitter struggle. Vardaman accused Percy of buying votes, and though that charge was later proved false, when time for reelection came, election by the people, Vardaman won overwhelmingly.

Percy realized when he wrote *Lanterns on the Levee* that his garden of aristocracy was already lost. It was Vardaman's victory that sealed his conviction: "It was a turning point in my life. . . . Since then I haven't expected that what should be would be and I haven't believed that virtue guaranteed any reward except itself. . . . When I first saw defeat as the result of a man's best efforts, I didn't like the sight, and it struck me that someone had bungled and perhaps it wasn't man" (143, 154). The dispossession of the garden of aristocracy heightened the conflict Percy felt between his inner self and the outer world. The world he knew crumbled around him, evidenced not only in Mississippi but in the events of his contemporary Germany and Italy. Percy looked to the ancient Greeks and Romans for the roots of his garden of stoicism. It is significant that after his father's defeat, the Percys journeyed to Greece.

Perhaps no other element of Percy's writing—in both poetry and prose—has been commented upon as much as his espousal of the Stoic philosophy.[2] Phinizy Spalding writes: "This amazingly pliant philosophy remained quite popular in the agricultural South long after it had been discarded as *passé* by the other areas of our country" (242). Will Percy's association with the Greeks and Romans had begun during his private tutoring as a youth. It was reinforced by his listening to the conversations of LeRoy and his friends on his front porch. He once heard his father say: "I guess a man's job is to make the world a better place to live in, so far as he is able—always remembering the results will be infinitesimal—and to attend to his own soul." Will took these words as his philosophy of life—the "steady simple wisdom of the South" (75)—and created his garden of stoicism.

Spalding points out the similarities in thought and pattern between *Lanterns on the Levee* and the *Meditations* of the Great Stoic, the Emperor Marcus Aurelius: "The [similarities in thought are] of considerable interest, for from Aurelius, Percy adopted his concept of 'the good life' where man, fighting for a something beyond his ken, is defeated, but attains victory over the powers of darkness by virtue of the battle nobly fought" (242). Percy had learned this lesson well from the defeat of his father, but he did not submit to a stoical cynicism, as did Faulkner's Jason Compson. Instead, he felt that convictions should be molded into something practical, possible and above all, workable, on the local level, by a series of small acts (Spalding 246-47). Only through these small acts, Percy believed, could progress be made. He had little patience for the "Northern abstractors," who would provide a grand design for eliminating the world's troubles.

Will Percy had ample opportunity to practice his little way. His participation in World War I, his fight against the Ku Klux Klan in his hometown of Greenville, his work on the relief committee during the flood of 1927 and his inheritance of Trail Lake plantation after LeRoy's death all gave him the chance to help rekindle the values he held in highest esteem. Despite the disintegration he saw in the world around him, and despite his feeling "superfluous" after the death of his parents, the garden of stoicism was tried, and it apparently prevailed. As Richard King writes: "He was the melancholic Roman to the end" ("Mourning" 250).

Percy's garden of stoicism had its greatest trial after he adopted his Alabama cousins, LeRoy Pratt Percy's three sons—Walker, LeRoy and B. Phinizy. Their youthful energy cheered him, and "they offered [him] a sense of continuation, an assurance that the Percy family had replenished itself" (Baker 152). At the same time, Will wondered how best to educate his new heirs: "The old Southern way of life in which I had been reared existed no more and its values were ignored or derided. . . . I had no desire to send these youngsters of mine into life as defenseless as if they wore knights' armor and had memorized the code of chivalry. But what could I teach them other than what I myself had learned?" (312).

So he began his instructions of the "unassailable wintry kingdom of Marcus Aurelius" (313). The *Meditations* of the Emperor "convince a man he never need be less than tight-lipped, courteous, and proud, though all is pain" (316). But he also sent his sons to church. Percy believed that the language of the church was "a beautiful dead language" (315), but that their gospels offered "a supernal light" from which ethical precepts could be gleaned. The gospels and the *Meditations,* then, provided Will the roots with which to steady his new sons.

His sons, although impressed by the magnanimity of their new father, did not always respond to his teachings. Walker, who called his adoptive father "Uncle Will," has said that Will Percy was "the most extraordinary man I have ever known" ("Introduction" xviii). He recalls Will's ability of "communicating enthusiasm for beauty . . . [and] the excitement of reading" (Lawson, *Conversations* 258). Nevertheless, Walker often "preferred *The Brothers Karamazov* to Will's recitations of Keats and Marcus Aurelius" (Baker 152).

Will Percy had seen, and eventually accepted, the demise of his gardens of youth and aristocracy, but he never relinquished his stoic view. In fact, the fall of southern aristocracy bolstered it. But the stoic stance was ultimately dispossessed. With great finesse and respect, and without ever mentioning his adoptive father, Walker Percy writes: "[The stoic's] most characteristic mood was a poetic pessimism which took a grim satisfaction in the dissolution of its values—because social decay confirmed one in his original choice of the wintry kingdom of self. . . . For the Stoic there is no real hope. His finest hour is to sit tight-lipped and ironic while the

world comes crashing down around him" ("Stoicism" 343-44). Walker Percy rejects his mentor's garden of southern stoicism for the more hopeful path of Christianity: "The Christian is optimistic precisely where the Stoic is pessimistic" ("Stoicism" 344). In Walker's novels, Will's stoic stance is embodied in several characters, and his protagonists often go through the painful struggle, like Walker himself, of overcoming it. Lewis Lawson writes: "Only by recognizing how personal and how painful Walker Percy's rejection of Southern Stoicism had to be . . . can one really understand how fully committed he is to its alternative" ("Southern Stoic" 14). Will Percy's stoicism had been dispossessed in the South with the rise of the "Demos." It was dispossessed in the Percy line through the writings of his adopted son.

When Percy invites us into his garden in Greenville, he invites us into his "backward looks and questionings" (334) which are the jackdaw pickings of his memory and history. He invites us into the garden of his selfhood. As Walker Percy writes, "It is just that, a person and a life, that comes across in *Lanterns on the Levee*" ("Introduction" xviii). The garden is a place for self-reflection: "You sit there and think of the trip you have made, fifty-five years of trips, and you wonder what it means and what it totals up to" (*Lanterns* 334).

It is obvious by now that Percy's journey was carried on in the southern tradition. His attitudes toward his land and his people, especially blacks, were formed by his aristocratic and stoic upbringing. And although at times he gives the aristocratic and stoic sense of unflinching conviction—hence, the sense of a totally possessed person—he was nevertheless a wanderer and pilgrim. He maintained his dignity and manners but, like the riverboats he recalls, he sought a secure landing. *Lanterns on the Levee* does reveal a man, and many times it is a man in conflict with himself and his tradition.

King has pointed out "the barely suggested inner conflicts and the reticences which make themselves felt throughout the book" ("Mourning" 251). One such conflict is Percy's recounting of the time he and Ford, his black factotum, drove up to Trail Lake plantation and the workers there called Percy's automobile "us car" (291), indicating that it was through their labor that Percy had bought the car. King maintains that Percy would not have included this incident had he not had some "inner doubts" about his sharecropping enterprise ("Mourning" 251). When Percy extols sharecropping as the "most moral system under which men can work together" (278), yet admits that, without an honest planter, it offers an occasion for exploitation, King writes: "One suspects that even Percy knew that the personal factor had ceased to play a role, if it ever had, and that the system was exploitative as such" ("Mourning" 252).

King sees a much more profound and central conflict emerge in Percy's relation to his father. Recalling the oft-quoted southern injunction for male children to be "half the man your daddy was," King writes: "All his life [Percy] felt small and physically unprepossessing beside his virile father" (257). According to King, Percy's entire autobiography was written in light of his father, in the southern tradition of fathers. Why else would Percy subtitle the book "Recollections of a Planter's Son"? King believes that Percy showed great reticence during the flood of 1927, when as chairman of the local relief committee he had decided to deport the black labor force. LeRoy did not think Will's decision very wise, and he convinced the board to vote against it. King concludes that Percy was "unmanned" by his father in this incident and throughout his life and that "Will cannot bring himself to register the hurt and sense of betrayal he must have felt at the contempt his father had shown him" ("Mourning" 260).

While King's evaluation of *Lanterns on the Levee* may be too steeped in the psychoanalytic tradition—a bias he admits (*Renaissance* viii)—his contention that Percy felt "unprepossessing" is most helpful. It fits the schema from which this author has approached the book—the dispossessed garden. Percy's entire life can be seen as the movement from dispossession to dispossession. The "stays" he set up against the modern world—family, aristocracy, stoicism—were all part of the larger garden of his selfhood. As these stays crumbled around him, he "dug in" and became more "tight-lipped and courteous" than ever; he never lost his dignity. One wonders, though, how much of Percy is embodied in the sunlight-starved plants of his garden, "those unhappy things rooted against their will in the shade. . . . Branches die so that the remnant whole may survive" (334).

Will Percy's guiding lights had faded, and the branches from which he gained his sustenance had waned. His only remaining garden seemed to be "the cypress grove to which you know you are going" (335). Fred Hobson observes: "The author of *Lanterns on the Levee* cannot at the end see—does not want to see—beyond the grave: the death not only of an individual but of a way of life" (285). It is a strange twist of coincidence, if indeed it is coincidence, that a year after he completed *Lanterns on the Levee* Will Percy died.[3] He had set up his garden against modernity, had seen it—and himself—dispossessed, but held to his "wintry kingdom" nonetheless. His legacy is as noble as it is tragic (Walker Percy, "Introduction" xii).

By way of postscript, briefly consider Simpson's analysis in *The Dispossessed Garden*. Simpson sees two great periods in the history of twentieth-century southern literature (70-71). The first encompasses the literary genius of William Faulkner and Allen Tate who struggled to "comprehend the nature of memory and history," and in so doing, curb their disintegration. They cultivated the garden which provided the major concern of southern writers in the 1920s and 1930s. The second period, from the 1950s on, accepts the disintegration of the garden of memory and history—it cannot be stopped—and sets as its main concern "a struggle between a gnostic society and the existential self" (90). William Alexander Percy's recollections fall at the nexus of these two great periods. Like the Agrarians, he saw the old order—the pastoral, paradisiacal South—fading. Unlike the Agrarians, he realized the old order could not be reinstated. Moreover, like his literary heirs, he saw the individual self as alone in a patternless world, adrift on the river of time. Percy's own moorings no longer held him, his self, fast. One of his literary heirs, Walker Percy, uses his adoptive father as a bridge of sorts. While he rejects Will's southern stoicism, Walker makes man "lost in the cosmos," man orbiting the earth seeking reentry, his central subject. He addresses the predicament Will Percy attributed to others but also felt inchoately—the problem of living in a patternless world. In this sense, Walker has kept alive some remnants of the lanterns of William Alexander Percy.

NOTES

[1] William F. Holmes writes of the levee board scandal in more detail. Holmes denies that the men who replaced Percy's father and his friends were "inferior" in any way.

[2] See Allen, Castille, Hobson, King, Lawson, Spalding.

[3] Fred Hobson, writing of the southern "truth-tellers," reminds us of the connection between death (especially suicide) and the "rage to explain" (8).

WORKS CITED

Allen, William Rodney. *Walker Percy: A Southern Wayfarer.* Jackson: UP of Mississippi, 1986.

Baker, Lewis. *The Percys of Mississippi.* Baton Rouge: Louisiana State UP, 1983.

Castille, Philip. "East Toward Home: Will Percy's Old World Vision." *Southern Literature in Transition.* Ed. Philip Castille and William Osborne. Memphis: Memphis State UP, 1983. 101-09.

Cohn, David L. "Eighteenth-Century Chevalier." *Virginia Quarterly Review* 31 (1955): 561-75.

Gulledge, Jo. "William Alexander Percy and the Fugitives: A Literary Correspondence, 1921-23." *Southern Review* 21 (1985): 415-27.

Hobson, Fred. *Tell About the South.* Baton Rouge: Louisiana State UP, 1983.

Holdsworth, Carolyn. "The Gorgon's Head and the Mirror: Fact versus Metaphor in *Lanterns on the Levee.*" *Southern Literary Journal* 14 (1981): 36-45.

Holmes, William F. "William Alexander Percy and the Bourbon Era in the Yazoo-Mississippi Delta." *Mississippi Quarterly* 26 (1972-73): 71-88.

King, Richard H. "Mourning and Melancholia: Will Percy and the Southern Tradition." *Virginia Quarterly Review* 53 (1977): 248-64.

———. *A Southern Renaissance.* New York: Oxford UP, 1980.

Lawson, Lewis A. "Walker Percy's Southern Stoic." *Southern Literary Journal* 3 (1970): 5-31.

Lawson, Lewis A., and Victor A. Kramer, eds. *Conversations with Walker Percy.* Jackson: UP of Mississippi, 1985.

Percy, Walker. "Introduction to *Lanterns on the Levee.*" Baton Rouge: Louisiana State UP, 1973.

———. "Stoicism in the South." *Commonweal* 64 (6 July 1956): 342-44.

Percy, William Alexander. *Lanterns on the Levee.* 1941. Baton Rouge: Louisiana State UP, 1973.

Rocks, James E. "The Art of *Lanterns on the Levee.*" *Southern Review* 12 (1976): 814-23.

Simpson, Lewis P. *The Dispossessed Garden.* Athens: U of Georgia P, 1975.

Spalding, Phinizy. "A Stoic Trend in William Alexander Percy's Thought." *Georgia Review* 12 (1958): 241-51.

FURTHER READING

Bibliography

Dollarhide, Louis. "Selected Bibliography." In *Mississippi Heroes,* edited by Dean Faulkner Wells and Hunter Cole, pp. 156-57. Jackson: University Press of Mississippi, 1980.
    A list of Percy's first editions, along with writings about him by Walker Percy, Hodding Carter, and others.

Biography

"Will Percy: Poet, Author, Lawyer." *New York Times* (22 January 1942): 17.
    Percy's obituary, which quotes liberally from a 1941 *New York Times* review of *Lanterns on the Levee* by Herschel Brickell.

Wyatt-Brown, Bertram. "Kate Ferguson, Scandal, and Percy Mythmaking." In *The Literary Percys: Family History, Gender, and the Southern Imagination,* pp. 35-55. Athens: University of Georgia Press, 1994.
    The story of a little-known Southern writer who crossed paths with Percy and the rest of his family in what Wyatt-Brown calls "a poignant and melancholy exercise."

Criticism

Carter, Hodding. "Foreword." In *Of Silence and of Stars* by William Alexander Percy, n.p. Greenville, Miss.: Levee Press, 1953.
    A short appreciation of Percy by Carter, who recalls the numerous letters he received after he published a tribute in *Reader's Digest* a decade earlier.

Clarke, George Herbert. Review of *In April Once.* *Sewanee Review* 30, No. 1 (January-March 1922): 95-7.
    Generally favorable review which notes "minor defects in a volume containing . . . work of decided excellence."

———. Review of *Selected Poems,* by William Alexander Percy. *Queen's Quarterly* XXXVII, No. 3 (Summer 1930): 603-07.
    Favorable review of Percy's *Selected Poems.*

Firkins, O. W. "Tale-Tellers and Lyricists." *The Nation* 102, No. 2656 (25 May 1916): 565-66.
    Review of *Sappho in Levkas* and works by others. Firkins describes Percy's work as "compass[ing] nothing but coldness and sparkle," and compares a reading of his poetry to "passing through my fingers handfuls of fragments of porphyry and jade and onyx and lapis-lazuli."

Gorman, Herbert S. "A Crop of Spring Verse." *The Bookman,* New York, LIX, No. 4 (June 1924): 467-69.
    A review of *Enzio's Kingdom,* along with works by Edwin Arlington Robinson and others, in which Gorman notes that Percy "is crude and he overwrites"; nonetheless, when time, place, and technique come together, "he is apt to produce more distinguished matter than many a more finished poet."

Untermeyer, Louis. "Seven Against Realism." *Yale Review* 14 (1925): 791-97.
    A critical review of *Enzio's Kingdom,* along with works by Edwin Arlington Robinson, Archibald MacLeish, and John Crowe Ransom.

Weaver, Raymond. "What Ails Pegasus?" *The Bookman,* New York, LII, No. 1 (September 1920): 57-66.
    A favorable review of *In April Once,* along with works by others, in which Weaver observes that Percy "tastes in some degree of the divine madness of Keats."

Sri Ramana Maharshi

1879-1950

(Born Venkataraman) Indian spiritual teacher and poet.

INTRODUCTION

Sri Ramana Maharshi is regarded by Hindus as one of the holiest individuals of the twentieth century. He eschewed duality and the concept of death as the end of life in favor of the immortal and universal nature of the self, which for him was the spiritual essence of all humans. Following his spiritual transformation in his mid-teenage years, Ramana Maharshi became the religious center of the ashram at Arunachala, where he practiced the renunciation of worldly concerns and focused on defining the universal self through an intensive method of self inquiry. His simple explanations of the complex religious and philosophic concepts of Hindu Advaitic tradition earned him widespread influence that extended from South India to the West. Ramana Maharshi wrote very little, and many of the writings attributed to him are actually transcriptions made by those he counseled. These poems, translations, hymns, statements, and aphorisms are collected in *Teachings of Ramana Maharshi: An Anthology,* which includes *Upadesa Saram* (*Essence of Teaching*), *Ulladu Narpadu* (*Forty Verses on Reality*), and other selections.

Biographical Information

Ramana Maharshi was born in Tiruchuzhi, a small village near Madura, South India. He was the second son a of law court solicitor. He was an uninspired student at the various schools he attended, which included elementary schooling in Tiruchuzhi and Dindigul, as well as Scott's Middle School, Madura, and the American Mission High School. The most notable aspect of his childhood was his ability to sleep deeply as if in a trance, not awakening even if carried far distances or physically abused. His father died when he was twelve, and at the age of fourteen, Ramana Maharshi was impressed by an uncle's description of his visit to Arunachala, a hill in nearby Tiruvannamalai believed to embody the spirit of the God Siva. Ramana Maharshi later immersed himself in the *Periyapuranam*, a compendium of the life stories of sixty-three saints from the South Indian Tamil culture who were devoted to Siva. In 1896 Ramana Maharshi experienced a powerful realization and fear of his own mortality, which resulted in his devising his belief that the "Self" of an individual exists separate from his or her corporeal being. While the body will die and decay, a person's self is immortal. Shortly after this epiphany, Ramana Maharshi abandoned his studies, and wrote a letter to his family: "I have, in search of my Father and in obedience to His command, started from here. This is only embarking on a virtuous enterprise. Therefore, none need grieve over this affair."

He traveled to Arunachala where he imposed a voluntary vow of silence upon himself, and experienced a vision of blinding white light that obscured the material aspects of the natural world. Describing this experience as an actual death in which his heart stopped beating, he stated that he witnessed the physical decay of his own body: "I was also conscious of my hands and feet getting chill, and the stopping of the beats of my heart, but I had no fear in me. The flow of my thoughts and the consciousness of the Self were not lost. . . . Suddenly energy permeated throughout my body." The experience transformed him. He abandoned his vow of silence to answer all spiritual questions posed to him in the ashram, a religious community, that developed around him. His reputation attracted the Hindu scholar Ganapathi Muni, who recommended to his own followers that they join him as a disciple of Ramana Maharshi, whom he renamed the honorific Bhagavan Sri Ramana Maharshi; "Bhagavan" meaning "Swami" or "God," which combined with "Maharshi" denotes the most godlike of Hindu sages. The remainder of his life was spent meditating and counseling disciples and spiritual seekers, including Somerset Maugham, who used recollections of the experience as the basis for his novel *The Razor's Edge*. Other visitors from the West included Paul Brunton, Henri Cartier-Bresson, and Thomas Merton. Ramana Maharshi frequently experienced a deep meditative state known as Samadhi, where he derived his most profound spiritual insights. When he attained Maha-samadhi (death) in 1950, many witnesses, including Cartier-Bresson, observed a long, glowing trail in the night sky that disappeared behind Arunachala. His last words were, "I am not going away. Where could I go? I am here."

PRINCIPAL WORKS

The Collected Works of Ramana Maharshi (philosophy and poetry) 1968
*Teachings of Ramana Maharshi: An Anthology (philosophy and poetry) 1990

*Includes the works *Upadesa Saram* (*Essence of Teaching*) and *Ulladu Narpadu* (*Forty Verses on Reality*).

CRITICISM

Arthur Osborne (essay date 1968)

SOURCE: A preface to *The Collected Works of Ramana Maharshi,* edited by Arthur Osborne, Sri Ramanasraman Tiruvannamalai, 1968, pp. i-ix.

[*The following preface to* The Collected Works of Ramana Maharshi, *Osborne explains Ramana Maharshi's concepts of identity, non-duality, and oneness.*]

When the Maharsi, Bhagavan Sri Ramana, realized the Self he was a lad of seventeen in a middle-class Brahmin family of South India. He was still going to High School and had undergone no spiritual training and learnt nothing of spiritual philosophy. Normally some study is needed, followed by long and arduous training, often lasting a whole lifetime, more often still incomplete at the end of a lifetime. As the Sages say, it depends on the spiritual maturity of a person. It can be compared to a pilgrimage, and a day's journey on it to a lifetime: a person's attaining the goal, or how near he comes to it, will depend partly on the energy with which he presses forward and partly on the distance from it at which he wakes up and begins his day's journey. Only in the rarest cases is it possible, as with the Maharsi, to take a single step and the goal is reached.

To say that the Maharsi realized the Self does not mean that he understood any new doctrine or theory or achieved any higher state or miraculous powers, but that the 'I' who understands or does not understand doctrine and who possesses or does not possess powers became consciously identical with the Atman, the universal Self or Spirit. The Maharsi himself has described in simple, picturesque language how this happened.

> 'It was about six weeks before I left Madura for good that the great change in my life took place. It was quite sudden. I was sitting alone in a room on the first floor of my uncle's house. I seldom had any sickness, and on that day there was nothing wrong with my health, but a sudden violent fear of death overtook me. There was nothing in my state of health to account for it, and I did not try to account for it or to find out whether there was any reason for the fear. I just felt "I am going to die" and began thinking what to do about it. It did not occur to me to consult a doctor or my elders or friends; I felt that I had to solve the problem myself, there and then.
>
> The shock of the fear of death drove my mind inwards and I said to myself mentally, without actually framing the words: "Now death has come; what does it mean? What is it that is dying? This body dies." And I at once dramatized the occurrence of death. I lay with my limbs stretched out stiff as though *rigor mortis* had set in and imitated a corpse so as to give greater reality to the enquiry. I held my breath and kept my lips tightly closed so that no sound could escape, so that neither the word "I" nor any other word could be uttered. "Well then," I said to myself, "this body is dead. It will be carried stiff to the burning ground and there burnt and reduced to ashes. But with the death of this body am I dead? Is the body I? It is silent and inert but I feel the full force of my personality and even the voice of the "I" within me, apart from it. So I am Spirit transcending the body. The body dies but the Spirit that transcends it cannot be touched by death. That means I am the deathless Spirit" All this was not dull thought; it flashed through me vividly as living truth which I perceived directly, almost without thought-process. "I" was something very real, the only real thing about my present state, and all the conscious activity connected with my body was centred on that "I". From that moment onwards the "I" or Self focused attention on itself by a powerful fascination. Fear of death had vanished once and for all. Absorption in the Self continued unbroken from that time on. Other thoughts might come and go like the various notes of music, but the "I" continued like the fundamental *sruti* note that underlies and blends with all the other notes.[1] Whether the body was engaged in talking, reading, or anything else, I was still centred on "I". Previous to that crisis I had no clear perception of my Self and was not consciously attracted to it. I felt no perceptible or direct interest in it, much less any inclination to dwell permanently in it'.

Such an experience of Identity does not always, or even normally, result in Liberation. It comes to a seeker but the inherent tendencies of the ego cloud it over again. Thence-forward he has the memory, the indubitable certainly, of the True State, but he does not live in it permanently. He has to strive to purify the mind and attain complete submission so that there are no tendencies to pull him back again to the illusion of limited separative being. 'However, the Self-oblivious ego, even when once made aware of the Self, does not get Liberation, that is Self-realization, on account of the obstruction of accumulated mental tendencies. It frequently confuses the body with the Self, forgetting that it is itself in truth the Self'. The miracle was that in the Maharshi's case there was no clouding over, no relapse into ignorance; he remained thenceforward in constant awareness of identity with the One Self.

For a few weeks after this awakening he remained with his family, leading outwardly the life of a schoolboy although all outer values had lost their meaning for him. He no longer cared what he ate, accepting with like indifference whatever was offered. He no longer stood up for his rights or interested himself in boyish activities. So far as possible he conformed to the conditions of life and concealed his new state of consciousness, but his elders saw his lack of interest in learning and all worldly activities and resented it.

There are many holy places in India, representing different modes of spirituality and different types of path. The holy hill of Arunachala with the town of Tiruvannamalai at its foot is supreme among them in that it is the centre of the direct path of Self-enquiry guided by the silent influence of the Guru upon the heart of the devotee, the secret and sacred Heart-Centre of Siva, wherein He always abides as a Siddha (Great One).

It is the seat of Siva who, identified as Daksinamurti, teaches in Silence as was exemplified in the life of Bhagavan.

It is the centre and the path where physical contact with the Guru is not necessary but the silent teaching speaks direct to the heart. Even before his Realization it had thrilled the Maharsi and drawn him like a magnet.

'Hearken; It stands as an insentient[2] Hill. Its action is mysterious, past human understanding. From the age of innocence it had shone within my mind that Arunachala was something of surpassing grandeur,[3] but even when I came to know through another that it was the same as Tiruvannamalai I did not realize its meaning. When it drew me up to it, stilling my mind, and I came close, I saw it (stand) unmoving.'[4]

Now, seeing that his elders resented his living like a *sadhu* while enjoying the benefits of home life, he secretly left home and went as a *sadhu* to Tiruvannamalai. He never left there again. He remained for more than fifty years as Daksinamurti, teaching the path of Self-enquiry to all who came, from India and abroad, from East and West. An Ashram grew up around him. His name of Venkataraman was shortened to Ramana, and he was also called the Maharsi, that is the Maha Risi or Great Sage, a title traditionally given to one who inaugurates a new spiritual path. However his devotees mostly spoke of him as Bhagavan. In speaking to him also they addressed him in the third person as Bhagavan. Self-realization means constant conscious awareness of identity with Atman, the Absolute, the Spirit, the Self of all; it is the state which Christ expressed when he said: 'I and my Father are One'. This is a very rare thing. Such a one is habitually addressed as Bhagavan, which is a word meaning 'God'.

On Bhagavan's first arrival at Tiruvannamalai there was no question of disciples or teaching. He discarded even apparent interest in the manifested world, sitting immersed in that experience of Being which is integral Knowledge and ineffable Bliss, beyond life and death. Whether the body continued to live was indifferent to him, and he made no effort to sustain it. Others sustained it by bringing him daily the cup of food that was needed for its nourishment; and when he began to return gradually to a participation in the activities of life it was for the spiritual sustenance of those who had gathered around him.

The same applies also to his study of philosophy. He did not need the mind's confirmation of the resplendent Reality in which he was established, only his followers required explanations. It began with Palaniswami, a Malayali attendant who had access to books of spiritual philosophy only in Tamil. He had great difficulty in reading Tamil, so the Maharsi read the books for him and expounded their essential meaning. Similarly he read other books for other devotees and became erudite without seeking or valuing erudition.

There was no change or development in his philosophy during the half century and more of his teaching. There could be none, since he had not worked out any philosophy but merely recognized the expositions of transcendental Truth in theory, myth, and symbol when he read them. What he taught was the ultimate doctrine of Nonduality or Advaita in which all other doctrines are finally absorbed: that Being is One and is manifested in the universe and in all creatures without ever changing from its eternal, unmanifest Self, much as, in a dream, the mind creates all the people and events a man sees without losing anything by their creation or gaining anything by their re-absorption, without ceasing to be itself.

Some found this hard to believe, taking it to imply that the world is unreal, but the Maharsi explained to them that the world is only unreal as world, that is to say as a separate, self-subsistent thing, but is real as a manifestation of the Self, just as the events one sees on a cinema screen are unreal as actual life but real as a shadowshow. Some feared that it denied the existence of a Personal God to whom they could pray, but it transcends this doctrine without denying it, for ultimately the worshipper is absorbed back into Union with the Worshipped. The man who prays, the prayer, and the God to whom he prays all have reality only as manifestations of the Self.

Just as the Maharsi realized the Self with no previous theoretical instruction, so he attached little importance to theory in training his disciples. The theory expounded in the following works is all turned to the practical purpose of helping the reader towards Self-Knowledge—by which is not meant any psychological study but knowing and being the Self which exists behind the ego or mind. Questions that were asked for mere gratification of curiosity he would brush aside. If asked about the posthumous state of man he might answer: 'Why do you want to know what you will be when you die before you know what you are now? First find out what you are now.' Thus he was turning the questioner from mental curiosity to the spiritual quest. Similarly he would parry questions about *samadhi* or about the state of the *Jnani* (the Self-realized man): 'Why do you want to know about the *Jnani* before you know about yourself? First find out who you are.' But when questions bore upon the task of self-discovery he had enormous patience in explaining.

The method of enquiry into oneself that he taught goes beyond philosophy and beyond psychology, for it is not the qualities of the ego that are sought but the Self standing resplendent without qualities when the ego ceases to function. What the mind has to do is not to suggest a reply, but to remain quiet so that the true reply can arise. 'It is not right to make an incantation of "Who am I?" Put the question only once and then concentrate on finding the source of the ego and preventing the occurrence of thoughts.' 'Finding the source of the ego' implies concentration on the spiritual centre in the body, the heart on the right side, as explained by the Maharsi. And, so concentrating, 'to prevent the occurrence of thoughts'. 'Suggestive replies to the enquiry, such as "I am Siva", are not to be given to the mind during meditation. The true answer will come of itself. No answer the ego can give can be right. These affirmations or auto-suggestions may be of help to those who follow other methods but not in this method of enquiry. If you keep on asking the reply will come.' The reply comes as a current of awareness in the heart, fitful at first and only achieved by intense effort, but gradually increasing in power and constancy, becoming more spontaneous, acting as a check on thoughts and actions, undermining the ego, until finally the ego disappears and the certitude of pure Consciousness remains.

As taught by the Maharsi, Self-enquiry embraces *karma-marga* as well as *jnana-marga,* the path of action as well as that of Knowledge, for it is to be used not only as a meditation but in the events of life, assailing the manifestations of egoism by asking to whom is good or bad fortune, triumph or disaster. In this way, the circumstances of life, far from being an obstacle to *sadhana,* are made an instrument of *sadhana.* Therefore those who asked whether they should renounce the life of the world were always discouraged from doing so. Instead they were enjoined to perform their duties in life without self-interest.

It embraces the path of love and devotion also. The Maharsi said: 'There are two ways: either ask yourself, "Who am I?" or submit.' On another occasion he said: 'Submit to me and I will strike down the mind.' There were many who followed, through love, this path of submission to him. It led to the same goal. He said: 'God, Guru, and Self are not really different but the same.' Those who followed the path of Self-enquiry were seeking the Self inwardly, whereas those who strove through love were submitting to the Guru manifested outwardly. But the two were the same. That is more than ever clear to his devotees now that the Maharsi has left the body and become the Inner Guru in the heart of each one of them.

It was thus a new and integral path that the Maharsi opened to those who turn to him. The ancient path of Self-enquiry was pure *jnana-marga* to be followed in silent meditation by the hermit and had, moreover, been considered by the Sages unsuited to this *kali-yuga,* this spiritually dark age in which we live. What Bhagavan did was not so much to restore the old path as to create a new one adapted to the conditions of our age, a path that can be followed in city or household no less than in forest or hermitage, with a period of meditation each day and constant remembering throughout the day's activities, with or without the support of outer observances.

The Maharsi wrote very little. He taught mainly through the tremendous power of Spiritual Silence. That did not mean that he was unwilling to answer questions when asked. So long as he felt that they were asked with a sincere motive and not out of idle curiosity, he answered fully whether in speech or writing. However it was the silent influence upon the heart that was the essential teaching.

Nearly everything that he wrote was in response to some request, to meet the specific needs of some devotee, and therefore a short note is given at the beginning of the various items explaining their genesis. This is for the interest of the reader, but the particular need that evoked them does not in any way impair the universality of their scope.

NOTES

[1] The monotone persisting through a Hindu piece of music, like the thread on which beads are strung, represents the Self persisting through all the forms of being.

[2] The adjective also bears the meaning 'eradicating objective knowledge'.

[3] To view Chidambaram, to be born in Tiruvarur, to die in Benares, or merely to think of Arunachala is to be assured of Liberation.' This couplet is commonly known in the Brahmin households of South India.

[4] *Alternatively:* I realized that It meant Absolute Stillness.

[5] Sadhu Arunachala (Major A. W. Chadwick).

Paul Brunton (essay date 1970)

SOURCE: "In a Jungle Hermitage," in *A Search in Secret India,* Rider & Company, 1970, pp. 277-95.

[*In the following essay, Brunton recounts his personal visit to Ramana Maharshi, focusing heavily on the biographical details of his life.*]

There are moments unforgettable which mark themselves in golden figures upon the calendar of our years. Such a moment comes to me now, as I walk into the hall of the Maharishee.

He sits as usual upon the magnificent tiger-skin which covers the centre of his divan. The joss-sticks burn slowly away on a little table near him, spreading the penetrating fragrance of incense around the hall. Not today is he remote from men and wrapped up in some trance-like spiritual absorption, as on that strange occasion when I first visited him. His eyes are clearly open to this world and glance at me comprehendingly as I bow, and his mouth is stretched in a kindly smile of welcome.

Squatting at a respectful distance from their master are a few disciples; otherwise the long hall is bare. One of them pulls the punkahfan, which flaps lazily through the heavy air.

In my heart I know that I come as one seeking to take up the position of a disciple, and that there will be no rest for my mind until I hear the Maharishee's decision. It is true that I live in a great hope of being accepted, for that which sent me scurrying out of Bombay to this place came as an absolute command, a decisive and authoritative injunction from a supernormal region. In a few words I dispose of the preliminary explanations, and then put my request briefly and bluntly to the Maharishee.

He continues to smile at me, but says nothing.

I repeat my question with some emphasis.

There is another protracted pause, but at length he answers me, disdaining to call for the services of an interpreter and expressing himself directly in English.

"What is all this talk of masters and disciples? All these differences exist only from the disciple's standpoint. To the one who has realized the true self there is neither master nor disciple. Such a one regards all people with equal eye."

I am slightly conscious of an initial rebuff, and though I press my request in other ways the Maharishee refuses to yield on the point. But in the end he does say:

"You must find the master within you, within your own spiritual self. You must regard his body in the same way that he himself regards it; the body is not his true self."

It begins to voice itself in my thoughts that the Maharishee is not to be drawn into giving me a direct affirmative response, and that the answer I seek must be found in some other way, doubtless in the subtle, obscure manner at which he hints. So I let the matter drop and our talk then turns to the outward and material side of my visit.

I spend the afternoon making some arrangements for a protracted stay.

2

The ensuing weeks absorb me into a strange, unwonted life. My days are spent in the hall of the Maharishee, where I slowly pick up the unrelated fragments of his wisdom and the faint clues to the answer I seek; my nights continue as heretofore in torturing sleeplessness, with my body stretched out on a blanket laid on the hard earthen floor of a hastily built hut.

This humble abode stands about three hundred feet away from the hermitage. Its thick walls are composed of thinly plastered earth, but the roof is solidly tiled to withstand the monsoon rains. The ground around it is virgin bush, somewhat thickly overgrown, being in fact the fringe of the jungle which stretches away to the west. The rugged landscape reveals Nature in all her own wild uncultivated grandeur. Cactus hedges are scattered numerously and irregularly around, the spines of these prickly plants looking like coarse needles, Beyond them the jungle drops a curtain of scrub bush and stunted trees upon the land. To the north rises the gaunt figure of the mountain, a mass of metallic-tinted rocks and brown soil. To the south lies a long pool, whose placid water has attracted me to the spot, and whose banks are bordered with clumps of trees holding families of grey and brown monkeys.

Each day is a duplicate of the one before. I rise early in the mornings and watch the jungle dawn turn from grey to green and then to gold. Next comes a plunge into the water and a swift swim up and down the pool, making as much noise as I possibly can so as to scare away lurking snakes. Then, dressing, shaving, and the only luxury I can secure in this place—three cups of deliciously refreshing tea.

"Master, the pot of tea-water is ready," says Rajoo, my hired boy. From an initial total ignorance of the English language, he has acquired that much and more, under my occasional tuition. As a servant he is a gem, for he will scour up and down the little township with optimistic determination in quest of the strange articles and foods for which his Western employer speculatively sends him, or he will hover outside the Maharishee's hall in discreet silence during meditation hours should he happen to come along for orders at such times. But as a cook he is unable to comprehend Western taste, which seems a queer distorted thing to him. After a few painful experiments I myself take charge of the more serious culinary arrangements, reducing my labour by reducing my solid meals to a single one each day. Tea, taken thrice daily, becomes both my solitary earthly joy and the mainstay of my energy. Rajoo stands in the sunshine and watches with wonderment my addiction to the glorious brown brew. His body shines in the hard yellow light like polished ebony, for he is a true son of the black Dravidians, the primal inhabitants of India.

After breakfast comes my quiet lazy stroll to the hermitage, a halt for a couple of minutes beside the sweet rose bushes in the compound garden, which is fenced in by bamboo posts, or a rest under the drooping fronds of palm trees whose heads are heavy with coconuts. It is a beautiful experience to wander around the hermitage garden before the sun has waxed in power and to see and smell the variegated flowers.

And then I enter the hall, bow before the Maharishee, and quietly sit down on folded legs. I may read or write for a while, or engage in conversation with one or two of the other men, or tackle the Maharishee on some point, or plunge into meditation for an hour along the lines which the sage has indicated, although evening usually constitutes the time specially assigned to meditation in the hall. But whatever I am doing I never fail to become gradually aware of the mysterious atmosphere of the place, of the benign radiations which steadily percolate into my brain. I enjoy an ineffable tranquillity merely by sitting for a while in the neighbourhood of the Maharishee. By careful observation and frequent analysis I arrive in time at the complete certitude that a reciprocal inter-influence arises whenever our presences neighbour each other. The thing is most subtle. But it is quite unmistakable.

At eleven I return to the hut for the midday meal and a rest and then go back to the hall to repeat my programme of the morning. I vary my meditations and conversations sometimes by roaming the countryside or descending on the little township to make further explorations of the colossal temple.

From time to time the Maharishee unexpectedly visits me at the hut after finishing his own lunch. I seize the opportunity to plague him with further questions, which he patiently answers in terse epigrammatic phrases, clipped so short as rarely to constitute complete sentences. But once, when I propound some fresh problem, he makes no answer. Instead, he gazes out towards the jungle-covered hills which stretch to the horizon and remains motionless. Many minutes pass, but still his eyes are fixed, his presence remote. I am quite unable to discern whether his attention is being given to some invisible psychic being in the distance or whether it is being turned on some inward preoccupation. At first I wonder whether he has heard me, but in the tense silence which ensues, and which I feel unable or unwilling to break, a force greater than my rationalistic mind commences to awe me until it ends by overwhelming me.

The realization forces itself through my wonderment that all my questions are moves in an endless game, the play of thoughts which possess no limit to their extent; that somewhere within me there is a well of certitude which can provide me with all the waters of truth I require; and that it will be better to cease my questioning and attempt to realize the tremendous potencies of my own spiritual nature. So I remain silent and wait.

For almost half an hour the Maharishee's eyes continue to stare straight in front of him in a fixed, unmoving gaze. He appears to have forgotten me, but I am perfectly aware that the sublime realization which has suddenly fallen upon me is nothing else than a spreading ripple of telepathic radiation from this mysterious and imperturbable man.

On another visit he finds me in a pessimistic mood. He tells me of the glorious goal which waits for the man who takes to the way he has shown.

"But, Maharishee, this path is full of difficulties and I am so conscious of my own weaknesses" I plead.

"That is the surest way to handicap oneself," he answers unmoved, "this burdening of one's mind with the fear of failure and the thought of one's failings."

"Yet if it is true—?" I persist.

"It is not true. The greatest error of a man is to think that he is weak by nature, evil by nature. Every man is divine and strong in his real nature. What are weak and evil are his habits, his desires and thoughts, but not himself."

His words come as an invigorating tonic. They refresh and inspire me. From another man's lips, from some lesser and feebler soul, I would refuse to accept them at such worth and would persist in refuting them. But an inward monitor assures me that the sage speaks out of the depths of a great and authentic spiritual experience, and not as some theorizing philosopher mounted on the thin stilts of speculation.

Another time, when we are discussing the West, I make the retort:

"It is easy for you to attain and keep spiritual serenity in this jungle retreat, where there is nothing to disturb or distract you."

"When the goal is reached, when you know the Knower, there is no difference between living in a house in London and living in the solitude of a jungle," comes the calm rejoinder.

And once I criticize the Indians for their neglect of material development. To my surprise the Maharishee frankly admits the accusation.

"It is true. We are a backward race. But we are a people with few wants. Our society needs improving, but we are contented with much fewer things than your people. So to be backward is not to mean that we are less happy."

3

How has the Maharishee arrived at the strange power and stranger outlook which he possesses? Bit by bit, from his own reluctant lips and from those of his disciples, I piece together a fragmentary pattern of his life story.

He was born in 1879 in a village about thirty miles distant from Madura, which is a noted South Indian town possessing one of the largest temples in the country. His father followed some avocation connected with law and came of good Brahmin stock. His father appears to have been an extremely charitable man who fed and clothed many poor persons. The boy eventually passed to Madura to carry on his education, and it was here that he picked up the rudiments of English from some American missionaries who were conducting a school.

At first young Ramana was fond of play and sport. He wrestled, boxed and swam dangerous rivers. He betrayed no special interest in religious or philosophical concerns. The only exceptional thing in his life at the time was tendency to somnambulism or sleep-walking, and to a condition of sleep so profound that the most disturbing interruptions could not awaken him. His schoolmates eventually discovered this and took advantage of it to sport with him. During the daytime they were afraid of his quick punch, but at night they would come into his bedroom, take him into the playground, beat his body and box his ears, and then lead him back to bed. He was quite unconscious of these experiences and had no remembrance of them in the mornings.

The psychologist who has correctly understood the nature of sleep will find in this account of the boy's abnormal depth of attention, sufficient indication of the mystical nature which he possessed.

One day a relative came to Madura and, in answer to Ramana's question, mentioned that he had just returned from a pilgrimage to the temple of Arunachala. The name stirred some slumbering depths in the boy's mind, thrilling him with peculiar expectation which he could not understand. He enquired as to the whereabouts of this temple and ever after found himself haunted by thoughts of it. It seemed to be of paramount importance to him, yet he could not even explain to himself why Arunachala should mean anything more to him than the dozens of other great temples which are scattered over India.

He continued his studies at the mission school without showing any special aptitude for them, although he always evinced a fair degree of intelligence in his work. But when he was seventeen, destiny, with swift and sudden strokes, got into action and thrust its hands through the even tenor of his days.

He suddenly left the school and completely abandoned all his studies. He gave no notice to his teachers or to his relatives, and told no one before the event actually occurred. What was the reason of this unpromising change, which cast a cloud upon his future worldly prospects?

The reason was satisfying enough to himself, though it might have seemed mind-perplexing to others. For life, which in the ultimate is the teacher of men, set the young student on another course than that which his school-teachers had assigned him. And the change came in a curious way about six weeks before he dropped his studies and disappeared from Madura for ever.

He was sitting alone one day in his room when a sudden and inexplicable fear of death took hold of him. He became acutely aware that he was going to die, although outwardly he was in good health. The thing was a psy-chological phenomenon, because there was no apparent reason why he should die. Yet he became obsessed with this notion and immediately began to prepare for the coming event.

He stretched his body prone upon the floor, fixed his limbs in the rigidity of a corpse, closed his eyes and mouth, and finally held his breath. "Well, then," said I to myself, "this body is dead. It will be carried stiff to the burning ground and then reduced to ashes. But with the death of the body, am *I* dead? Is the body *I?* This body is now silent and stiff. But I continue to feel the full force of my self apart from its condition."

Those are the words which Maharishee used in describing the weird experience through which he passed. What happened next is difficult to understand though easy to describe. He seemed to fall into a profound conscious trance wherein he became merged into the very source of selfhood, the very essence of being. He understood quite clearly that the body was a thing apart and that the *I* remained untouched by death. The true self was very real, but it was so deep down in man's nature that hitherto he had ignored it.

Ramana emerged from this amazing experience an utterly changed youth. He lost most of his interest in studies, sports, friends, and so on, because his chief interest was now centred in the sublime consciousness of the true self which he had found so unexpectedly. Fear of death vanished as mysteriously as it came. He enjoyed an inward serenity and a spiritual strength which have never since left him. Formerly he had been quick to retaliate at the other boys when they had chaffed him or attempted to take liberties, but now he put up with everything quite meekly. He suffered unjust acts with indifference and bore himself among others with complete humility. He gave up old habits and tried to be alone as much as possible, for then he would sink into meditation and surrender himself to the absorbing current of divine consciousness which constantly drew his attention inwards.

These profound changes in his character were, of course, noticed by others. One day his elder brother came into the room when the boy was supposed to be doing his homework and found him sunk in meditation with closed eyes. The school books and papers had been tossed across the room in disgust. The brother was so annoyed at this neglect of studies that he jeered at him with sharp words:

"What business has a fellow like you here? If you want to behave like a Yogi, why are you studying for a career?"

Young Ramana was deeply stung by these words. He immediately realized their truth and silently decided to act upon them. His father was dead and he knew that his uncle and other brothers would take care of his mother. Truly he had no business there. And back into his mind there flashed the name which had haunted him for nearly a year, the name whose very syllables fascinated him, the name of the temple of Arunachala. Thither would he go, although why he should select that place he was quite unable to say. But an impelling urgency arose within him and formed the decision for him of its own accord. It was entirely unpremeditated.

"I was literally charmed here," said the Maharishee to me. "The same force which drew you to this place from Bombay, drew me to it from Madura."

And so young Ramana, feeling this inner pull within his heart, left friends, family, school and studies, and took the road which eventually brought him to Arunachala and to a still profounder spiritual attainment. He left behind a brief farewell letter, which is still preserved in the hermitage. Its flourishing Tamil characters read as follows:

"I have, in search of my Father and in obedience to His command, started from here. This is only embarking on a virtuous enterprise. Therefore none need grieve over this affair. To trace this out, no money need be spent."

With three rupees in his pocket and in utter ignorance of the world, he set out on the journey into the interior of the South. The amazing incidents which marked that journey prove conclusively that some mysterious power was protecting and guiding him. When at last he arrived at his destination, he was utterly destitute and among total strangers. But the emotion of total renunciation was burning strong within him. Such was the youth's scorn for all earthly possessions, at the time, that he flung his robe aside and took up his meditative posture in the temple precinct quite nude. A priest observed this and remonstrated with him, but to no purpose. Other shocked priests came along, and, after vehement efforts, forced a concession from the youth. He consented to wear a semi-loincloth, and that is all he has ever worn to this day.

For six months he occupied various spots in the precinct, never going anywhere else. He lived on some rice which was brought him once a day by a priest who was struck by the precocious behaviour of the youth. For Ramana spent the entire day plunged in mystical trances and spiritual ecstasies so profound that he was entirely oblivious of the world around him. When some rough Moslem youths flung mud at him and ran away, he was quite unaware of the fact until some hours later. He felt no resentment against them in his heart.

The stream of pilgrims who descended on the temple made it difficult for him to obtain the seclusion he desired, so he left the place and moved to a quiet shrine set in the fields some distance from the village. Here he continued to stay for a year and a half. He was satisfied with the food brought by the few people who visited this shrine.

Throughout this time he spoke to no one; indeed, he never opened his lips to talk until three years passed since his arrival in the district. This was not because he

had taken a vow of silence, but because his inner monitor urged him to concentrate all his energy and attention upon his spiritual life. When his mystic goal was attained the inhibition was no longer necessary and he began to talk again, though the Maharishee has remained an extremely taciturn man.

He kept his identity a complete secret, but by a chain of coincidences, his mother discovered his whereabouts two years after his disappearance. She set out for the place with her eldest son and tearfully pleaded with him to return home. The lad refused to budge. When tears failed to persuade him she began to upbraid him for his indifference. Eventually he wrote down a reply on a piece of paper to the effect that a higher power controls the fate of men and that whatever she did could not change his destiny. He concluded by advising her to accept the situation and to cease moaning about it. And so she had to yield to his obstinacy.

When, through this incident, people began to intrude on his seclusion in order to stare at the youthful Yogi, he left the place and climbed up the Hill of the Holy Beacon and made his residence in a large cavern, where he lived for several years. There are quite a few other caves on this hill and each one shelters holy men or Yogis. But the cave which sheltered young Ramana was noteworthy because it also contained the tomb of a great Yogi of the past.

Cremation is the usual custom of the Hindus in disposing of their dead, but it is often prohibited in the case of a Yogi who is believed to have made the highest attainment, because it is also believed that the vital breath or unseen life-current remains in his body for thousands of years and renders the flesh exempt from corruption. In such a case the Yogi's body is bathed and anointed and then placed in a tomb in a sitting posture with crossed legs, as though he were still plunged in meditation. The entrance to the tomb is sealed with a heavy stone and then cemented over. Usually the mausoleum becomes a place of pilgrimage. There exists still another reason why great Yogis are buried and not cremated, and that is because of the belief that their bodies do not need to be purified by fire since they were purified during their lifetimes.

It is interesting to consider that caves have always been a favourite residence of Yogis and holy men. The ancients consecrated them to the gods; Zoroaster, the founder of the Parsee faith, practised his meditations in a cave, while Muhammed received his religious experiences in a cave also. The Indian Yogis have very good reasons for preferring caves or subterranean retreats when better places are not available. For here they can find shelter from the vicissitudes of weather and from the rapid changes of temperature which divide days from nights in the tropics. There is less light and noise to disturb their meditations. And breathing the confined atmosphere of a cave causes the appetite to diminish markedly, thus conducing to a minimum of bodily cares.

Still another reason which may have attracted Ramana to this particular cave on the Hill of the Holy Beacon was the beauty of its outlook. One can stand on a projecting spur adjoining the cave and see the little township stretched out flat in the distant plain, with the giant temple rising as its centre-piece. Far beyond the plain stands a long line of hills which frontier a charming panorama of Nature.

Anyway, Ramana lived in this somewhat gloomy cavern for several years, engaged in his mysterious meditations and plunged in profound trances. He was not a Yogi in the orthodox sense, for he had never studied any system of Yoga and he had never practised under any teacher. The inner path which he followed was simply a track leading to self-knowledge; it was laid down by what he conceived to be the divine monitor within him.

In 1905 plague appeared in the locality. The dread visitant was probably carried into the district by some pilgrim to the temple of Arunachala. It devastated the population so fiercely that almost everyone left the little township and fled in terror to safer villages or towns. So quiet did the deserted place become that tigers and leopards came out of their lurking dens in the jungle and moved openly through the streets. But, though they must have roamed the hill-side many times, for it stood in their path to the township, though they must have passed and repassed the Maharishee's cave, he refused to leave, but remained as calm and unmoved as ever.

By this time the young hermit had involuntarily acquired a solitary disciple, who had become very much attached to him and persisted in staying by his side and attending to his needs. The man is now dead, but the legend has been handed down to other disciples that each night a large tiger came to the cave and licked Ramana's hands, and that the tiger was in return fondled by the hermit. It sat in front of him throughout the night and departed only at dawn.

There is a widespread notion throughout India that Yogis and faqueers who live in the jungles or on the mountains, exposed to danger from lions, tigers, snakes and other wild animals are unharmed and untouched if they have attained a sufficient degree of Yogic power. Another story about Ramana told how he was once sitting in the afternoon outside the narrow entrance to his abode when a large cobra came swishing through the rocks and stopped in front of him. It raised its body and spread out its hood, but the hermit did not attempt to move. The two beings—man and beast—faced each other for some minutes, gaze meeting gaze. In the end the snake withdrew and left him unharmed, although it was within striking distance.

The austere lonely life of this strange young man closed its first phase with his firm and permanent establishment in the deepest point of his own spirit. Seclusion was no longer an imperative need, but he continued to live at the cave until the visit of an illustrious Brahmin

pundit, Ganapati Shastri, proved another turning-point of his outer life, which was now to enter on a more social period. The pundit had recently come to stay near the temple for study and meditation. He heard by chance that there was a very young Yogi on the hill and out of curiosity he went in search of him. When he found Ramana, the latter was staring fixedly at the sun. It was not at all uncommon for the hermit to keep his eyes on the dazzling sun for some hours till it disappeared below the western horizon. The glaring light of the rays of an afternoon sun in India can hardly be appreciated by a European who has never experienced it. I remember once, when I had set out to climb the steep ascent of the hill at a wrong hour, being caught without shelter by the full glare of the sun at midday on my return journey. I staggered and reeled about like a drunken man for quite a time. So the feat of young Ramana in enduring the merciless glare of the sun, with face uplifted and eyes unflinching, may therefore be better evaluated.

The pundit had studied all the chief books of Hindu wisdom for a dozen years and had undergone rigorous penances in an endeavour to reach some tangible spiritual benefit, but he was still afflicted by doubts and perplexities. He put a question to Ramana and after fifteen minutes received a reply which amazed him with its wisdom. He put further questions, involving his own philosophical and spiritual problems, and was still more astounded at the clearing-up of perplexities which had troubled him for years. As a result he prostrated himself before the young hermit and became a disciple. Shastri had his own group of followers in the town of Vellore and he went back later and told them that he had found a Maharishee (Great Sage or Seer), because the latter was undoubtedly a man of the highest spiritual realization whose teachings were so original that the pundit had found nothing exactly like them in any book he had read. From that time the title of Maharishee began to be applied to young Ramana by cultured people, although the common folk wanted to worship him as a divine being when his existence and character became better known to them. But the Maharishee strongly forbade every manifestation of such worship in his presence. Among themselves and in private talk with me, most of his devotees and people in the locality insist on calling him a god.

A small group of disciples attached themselves to the Maharishee in time. They built a wooden frame bungalow on a lower spur of the hill and persuaded him to live in it with them. In different years his mother had paid him short visits and became reconciled to his vocation. When death parted her from her eldest son and other relatives, she came to the Maharishee and begged him to let her live with him. He consented. She spent the six years of life which were left to her at his side, and finished up by becoming an ardent disciple of her own son. In return for the hospitality which was given her in the little hermitage, she acted as cook.

When the old lady died, her ashes were buried at the foot of the hill and some of the Maharishee's devotees built a small shrine over the place. Here, ever-burning sacred lamps glow in memory of this woman, who gave a great sage to mankind, and little heaps of scented jasmines and marigolds, snatched from their stalks, are thrown on a tiny altar in offering to her spirit.

The efflux of time spread the reputation of the Maharishee throughout the locality, so that pilgrims to the temple were often induced to go up the hill and see him before they returned home. Quite recently the Maharishee yielded to incessant requests and consented to grace the new and large hall which was built at the foot of the hill as a residence for him and his disciples.

The Maharishee has never asked for anything but food, and consistently refuses to handle money. Whatever else has come to him has been voluntarily pressed upon him by others. During those early years when he tried to live a solitary existence, when he built a wall of almost impenetrable silent reserve around himself whilst he was perfecting his spiritual powers, he did not disdain to leave his cave with a begging bowl in hand and wander to the village for some food whenever the pangs of hunger stirred his body. An old widow took pity on him and thenceforth regularly supplied him with food, eventually insisting on bringing it up to his cave. Thus his venture of faith in leaving his comfortable middle-class home was, in a measure, justified, at any rate to the extent that whatever powers there be have ensured his shelter and food. Many gifts have since been offered him, but as a rule he turns them away.

When a gang of dacoits broke into the hall one night not long ago and searched the place for money, they were unable to find more than a few rupees, which was in the care of the man who superintended the purchase of food. The robbers were so angry at this disappointment that they belaboured the Maharishee with stout clubs, severely marking his body. The sage not only bore their attack patiently, but requested them to take a meal before they departed. He actually offered them some food. He had no hate towards them in his heart. Pity for their spiritual ignorance was the sole emotion they aroused. He let them escape freely, but within a year they were caught while committing another crime elsewhere and received stiff sentences of penal servitude.

Not a few Western minds will inevitably consider that this life of the Maharishee's is a wasted one. But perhaps it may be good for us to have a few men who sit apart from our world of unending activity and survey it for us from afar. The onlooker may see more of the game and sometimes he gets a truer perspective. It may also be that a jungle sage, with self lying conquered at his feet, is not inferior to a worldly fool who is blown hither and thither by every circumstance.

4

Day after day brings its fresh indications of the greatness of this man. Among the strangely diversified company of human beings who pass through the hermitage, a pariah stumbles into the hall in some great agony of soul or circumstance and pours out his tribulation at the Maharishee's feet. The sage does not reply, for his silence and reserve are habitual; one can easily count up the number of words he uses in a single day. Instead, he gazes quietly at the suffering man, whose cries gradually diminish until he leaves the hall two hours later a more serene and stronger man.

I am learning to see that this is the Maharishee's way of helping others, this unobtrusive, silent and steady outpouring of healing vibrations into troubled souls, this mysterious telepathic process for which science will one day be required to account.

A cultured Brahmin, college-bred, arrives with his questions. One can never be certain whether the sage will make a verbal response or not, for often he is eloquent enough without opening his lips. But to-day he is in a communicative mood and a few of his terse phrases, packed with profound meanings as they usually are, open many vistas of thought for the visitor.

A large group of visitors and devotees are in the hall when someone arrives with the news that a certain man, whose criminal reputation is a byword in the little township, is dead. Immediately there is some discussion about him and, as is the wont of human nature, various people engage in recalling some of his crimes and the more dastardly phases of his character. When the hubbub has subsided and the discussion appears to have ended, the Maharishee opens his mouth for the first time and quietly observes:

"Yes, but he kept himself very clean, for he bathed two or three times a day!"

A peasant and his family have travelled over one hundred miles to pay silent homage to the sage. He is totally illiterate, knows little beyond his daily work, his religious rites and ancestral superstitions. He has heard from someone that there is a god in human form living at the foot of the Hill of the Holy Beacon. He sits on the floor quietly after having prostrated himself three times. He firmly believes that some blessing of spirit or fortune will come to him as a result of this journey. His wife moves gracefully to his side and drops to the floor. She is clothed in a purple robe which flows smoothly from head to ankles and is then tucked into her waist. Her sleek and smooth hair is glossy with scented oil. Her daughter accompanies her. She is a pretty girl whose ankle-rings click in consort as she steps into the hall. And she follows the charming custom of wearing a white flower behind her ear.

The little family stay for a few hours, hardly speaking, and gaze in reverence at the Maharishee. It is clear that his mere presence provides them with spiritual assurance, emotional felicity and, most paradoxical of all, renewed faith in their creed. For the sage treats all creeds alike, regards them all as significant and sincere expressions of a great experience, and honours Jesus no less than Krishna.

On my left squats an old man of seventy-five. A quid of betel is comfortably tucked in his cheek, a Sanskrit book lies between his hands, and his heavy-lidded eyes stare meditatively at the bold print. He is a Brahmin who was a station-master near Madras for many years. He retired from the railway service at sixty and soon after his wife died. He took the opportunity thus presented of realizing some long-deferred aspirations. For fourteen years he travelled about the country on pilgrimage to the sages and saints and Yogis, trying to find one whose teachings and personality were sufficiently appealing to him. He had circled India thrice, but no such master had been discoverable. He had set up a very individual standard apparently. When we met and compared notes he lamented his failure. His rugged honest face, carved by wrinkles into dark furrows, appealed to me. He was not an intellectual man, but simple and quite intuitive. Being considerably younger than he, I felt it incumbent on me to give the old man some good advice! His surprising response was a request to become his master! "Your master is not far off," I told him and conducted him straight-away to the Maharishee. It did not take long for him to agree with me and become an enthusiastic devotee of the sage.

Another man in the hall is bespectacled, silken-clad and prosperous-looking. He is a judge who has taken advantage of a law vacation to pay a visit to the Maharishee. He is a keen disciple and strong admirer and never fails to come at least once a year. This cultured, refined and highly educated gentleman squats democratically among a group of Tamils who are poor, naked to the waist and smeared with oil, so that their bodies glisten like varnished ebony. That which brings them together, destroys the insufferable snobbishness of caste, and produces unity, is that which caused Princes and Rajahs to come from afar in ancient times to consult the forest Rishees— the deep recognition that true wisdom is worth the sacrifice of superficial differences.

A young woman with a gaily attired child enters and prostrates herself in veneration before the sage. Some profound problems of life are being discussed, so she sits in silence, not venturing to take part in intellectual conversation. Learning is not regarded as an ornament for Hindu women and she knows little outside the purlieus of culinary and domestic matters. But she knows when she is in the presence of undeniable greatness.

With the descent of dusk comes the time for a general group meditation in the hall. Not infrequently the Maharishee will signal the time by entering, so gently as occasionally to be unnoticed, the trance-like abstraction wherein he locks his senses against the world outside. During these daily meditations in the potent neighbourhood of the sage, I have learnt how to carry my thoughts inward to an ever-deepening point. It is impossible to be in frequent contact with him without becoming lit up inwardly, as it were, mentally illumined by a sparkling ray from his spiritual orb. Again and again I become conscious that he is drawing my mind into his own atmosphere during these periods of quiet repose. And it is at such times that one begins to understand why the silences of this man are more significant than his utterances. His quiet unhurried poise veils a dynamic attainment, which can powerfully affect a person without the medium of audible speech or visible action. There are moments when I feel this power of his so greatly that I know he has only to issue the most disturbing command and I will readily obey it. But the Maharishee is the last person in the world to place his followers in the chains of servile obedience, and allows everyone the utmost freedom of action. In this respect he is quite refreshingly different from most of the teachers and Yogis I have met in India.

My meditations take the line he had indicated during my first visit, when he had tantalized me by the vagueness which seemed to surround many of his answers. I have begun to look into my own self.

Who am I?

Am I this body of flesh, blood and bone?

Am I the mind, the thoughts and the feelings which distinguish me from every other person?

One has hitherto naturally and unquestioningly accepted the affirmative answers to these questions, but the Maharishee has warned me not to take them for granted. Yet he has refused to formulate any systematic teaching. The gist of his message is:

> "Pursue the enquiry "Who am I?' relentlessly. Analyse your entire personality. Try to find out where the I-thought begins. Go on with your meditations. Keep turning your attention within. One day the wheel of thought will slow down and an intuition will mysteriously arise. Follow that intuition, let your thinking stop, and it will eventually lead you to the goal."

I struggle daily with my thoughts and cut my way slowly into the inner recesses of mind. In the helpful proximity of the Maharishee, my meditations and self-soliloquies become increasingly less tiring and more effective. A strong expectancy and sense of being guided inspire my constantly repeated efforts. There are strange hours when I am clearly conscious of the unseen power of the sage being powerfully impacted on my mentality, with the result that I penetrate a little deeper still into the shrouded borderland of being which surrounds the human mind.

The close of every evening sees the emptying of the hall as the sage, his disciples and visitors, adjourn for supper to the dining-room. As I do not care for their food and will not trouble to prepare my own, I usually remain alone and await their return.

However, there is one item of the hermitage diet which I find attractive and palatable, and that is curds. The Maharishee, having discovered my fondness for it, usually asks the cook to bring me a cupful of the drink each night.

About half an hour after their return, the inmates of the hermitage, together with those visitors who have remained, wrap themselves up in sheets or thin cotton blankets and retire to sleep on the tiled floor of the hall. The sage himself uses his divan as a bed. Before he finally covers himself with the white sheets, his faithful attendant thoroughly massages his limbs with oil.

I take up a glazed iron lantern when leaving the hall and set out on my lonely walk to the hut. Countless fireflies move amongst the flowers and plants and trees in the garden compound. Once, when I am two or three hours later than usual and midnight is approaching, I observe these strange insects put out their weird lights. Often they are just as numerous among the thick growths of bush and cactus through which I have later to pass. One has to be careful not to tread on scorpions or snakes in the dark. Sometimes the current of meditation has seized me so profoundly that I am unable and unwilling to stop it, so that I pay little heed to the narrow path of lighted ground upon which I walk. And so I retire to my modest hut, close the tightly fitting heavy door, and draw the shutters over glassless windows to keep out unwelcome animal intruders. My last glimpse is of a thicket of palm trees which stands on one side of my clearing in the bush, the silver moonlight coming in streams over their interlaced feathery tops.

Arthur Osborne (essay date 1973)

SOURCE: *Ramana Maharshi and the Path of Self-Knowledge,* Samuel Weiser, 1973, 207 p.

[*In the following excerpt, Osborne presents a detailed overview of the life and teachings of Ramana Maharshi, and includes a glossary of Hindu terminology.*]

EARLY YEARS

Arudra Darshan, the day of the 'Sight of Siva', is observed with great devotion by Saivites, for it commemorates the occasion when Siva manifested himself to his devotees as Nataraja, that is in the cosmic dance of creation and dissolution of the universe. On this day in 1879 it was still dusk when Siva's devotees in the little town of Tiruchuzhi in the Tamil land of South India left their houses and padded barefoot along the dusty roads to the temple tank, for tradition demands that they should bathe at daybreak. The red glow of sunrise fell upon the brown torsos of the men, clad only in a *dhoti*, a white cotton cloth wrapped round the body from the waist down, and flashed in the deep reds and golds of the women's saris as they descended the stone steps of the large square tank and immersed themselves in the water. There was a nip in the air, for the festival fell in December, but they are hardy folk. Some few changed under trees or in houses near the tank but most waited for the rising sun to dry them and proceeded, dripping as they were, to the little town's ancient temple, hymned long ago by Sundaramurthi Swami, one of the sixty-three Saivite poet-saints of the Tamil land.

The image of Siva in the temple was garlanded with flowers and taken in procession throughout the day and night, with noise of drum and conch and chanting of sacred song. It was one o'clock at night when the processions ended, but still Arudra Darshan because the Hindu day stretches from dawn to dawn, not from midnight to midnight. The idol of Siva re-entered the temple just as the child Venkataraman, in whom Siva was to be manifested as Sri Ramana, entered the world in the house of Sundaram Ayyar and his wife Alagammal. A Hindu festival varies with the phase of the moon, like the Western Easter, and in this year Arudra Darshan fell on December 29th, so that the child was born a little later, both in time of day and year, than the divine child of Bethlehem nearly two thousand years before. The same coincidence marked the end of earthly life also, for Sri Ramana left his body on the evening of April 14th, a little later in time and date than Good Friday afternoon. Both times are profoundly appropriate. Midnight and the winter solstice are the time when the sun is beginning to bring back light to the world, and at the spring equinox day has equalled night and is beginning to exceed it.

After starting life as an accountant's clerk on the salary, ridiculously small even for those days, of two rupees a month, Sundaram Ayyar had set up for himself as a petition writer and then, after some years, obtained permission to practise as an uncertified pleader, that is a sort of rural lawyer. He had prospered and had built the house[1] in which the child was born, making it commodious enough for one side to be reserved for guests. It was not only that he was sociable and hospitable, but also because he took it on himself to house official visitors and new-comers to the town—which made him a person of civic importance and doubtless reacted favourably on his professional work.

Successful as he was, a strange destiny overhung the family. It is said that a wandering ascetic once stopped to beg food at the house of one of their forebears and, on being refused, turned on him and pronounced that thenceforth one out of every generation of his descendants would wander and beg his food. Curse or blessing, the pronouncement was fulfilled. One of Sundaram Ayyar's paternal uncles had donned the ochre robe and left home with staff and water-pot; his elder brother had gone ostensibly to visit a neighbouring place and from there slipped away as a *sanyasin,* renouncing the world.

There seemed nothing strange about Sundaram Ayyar's own family. Venkataraman grew up a normal, healthy boy. He was sent for awhile to the local school and then, when he was eleven, to a school in Dindigul. He had a brother, Nagaswami, two years his senior. Six years after him came a third son, Nagasundaram, and two years later a daughter, Alamelu. A happy, well-to-do, middle-class family.

When Venkataraman was twelve, Sundaram Ayyar died and the family was broken up. The children went to live with their paternal uncle, Subbier, who had a house[2] in the nearby city of Madura. Venkataraman was sent first to Scott's Middle School there and then to the American Mission High School. There was no sign of his ever becoming a scholar. He was the athletic, out-of-doors type of boy and it was football, wrestling, swimming, that appealed to him. His one asset, so far as school goes, was an amazingly retentive memory which covered up laziness by enabling him to repeat a lesson from hearing it once read out.

The only unusual thing about him in his boyhood years was his abnormally deep sleep. Devaraja Mudaliar, a devotee, relates in his diary how he described it in a conversation at the Ashram many years later on seeing a relative entering the hall.

> "Seeing you reminds me of something that happened in Dindigul when I was a boy. Your uncle, Periappa Seshayyar, was then living there. Some function was going on in the house and everyone attended it and then in the night went to the temple. I was left alone in the house. I was sitting reading in the front room, but after a while I locked the front door and fastened the windows and went to sleep. When they returned from the temple no amount of shouting or banging at the door or window would wake me. At last they managed to open the door with a key from the house opposite, and then they tried to wake me up by beating me. All the boys beat me to their heart's content, and your uncle did too, but without effect. I knew nothing about it till they told me in the morning. . . . The same sort of thing happened to me in Madura also. The boys didn't dare touch me when I was awake but if they had any grudge against me they would come when I was asleep and carry me wherever they liked and beat me as much as they liked and then put me back to bed and I would know nothing about it till they told me next morning."

Sri Bhagavan attributed no significance to this except sound health. Sometimes also he would lie in a sort of half-sleep at night. It may be that both states were foreshadowings of the spiritual awakening: the deep sleep as the ability, albeit still dark and negative, to abandon the mind and plunge deep beyond thought, and the half-sleep as the ability to observe oneself objectively as a witness.

We have no photograph of Sri Bhagavan in his boyhood years. He has told us in his usual picturesque style, full of laughter, how a group photograph was taken and he was made to hold a heavy tome to look studious, but a fly settled on him and just as the photograph was taken he raised his arm to brush it off. However, it has not been possible to find a copy of this and presumably none remains.

The first premonition of dawn was a foreglow from Arunachala. The schoolboy Venkataraman had read no religious theory. He knew only that Arunachala was a very sacred place, and it must have been a presentiment of his destiny that shook him. One day he met an elderly relative whom he had known in Tiruchuzhi and asked him where he was coming from. The old man replied, "From Arunachala." And the sudden realization that the holy hill was a real, tangible place on earth that men could visit overwhelmed Venkataraman with awe so that he could only stammer out: "What! From Arunachala? Where is that?"

The relative, wondering in his turn at the ignorance of callow youth, explained that Arunachala is Tiruvannamalai.

Sri Bhagavan referred to this later in the first of his *Eight Stanzas to Arunachala.*

> "Hearken! It stands as an insentient hill. Its action is mysterious, past human understanding. From the age of innocence it had shone in my mind that Arunachala was something of surpassing grandeur, but even when I came to know through another that it was the same as Tiruvannamalai I did not realize its meaning. When it drew me up to it, stilling the mind, and I came close I saw it stand unmoving."

This took place in November 1895, shortly before his sixteenth birthday by European computation, his seventeenth by Hindu. The second premonition came soon after. This time it was provoked by a book. Again it was a wave of bewildering joy at perceiving that the Divine can be made manifest on earth. His uncle had borrowed a copy of the Periapuranam, the life-stories of the sixty-three Tamil Saints. Venkataraman picked it up and, as he read, was overwhelmed with ecstatic wonder that such faith, such love, such divine fervour was possible, that there had been such beauty in human life. The tales of renunciation leading to Divine Union inspired him with awe and emulation. Something greater than all dreamlands, greater than all ambition, was here proclaimed real and possible, and the revelation thrilled him with blissful gratitude.

From this time on the current of awareness which Sri Bhagavan and his devotees designate 'meditation' began to awaken in him. Not awareness of anything by any one, being beyond the duality of subject and object, but a state of blissful consciousness transcending both the physical and mental plane and yet compatible with full use of the physical and mental faculties.

Sri Bhagavan has told with characteristic simplicity how this awareness began to awaken in him during his visits to the Meenakshi Temple at Madura. He said, "At first I thought it was some kind of fever but I decided, if so it is a pleasant fever, so let it stay."

AWAKENING

This current of awareness, fostered by continual effort, grows ever stronger and more constant until finally it leads to Self-realization, to *sahaja samadhi,* the state in which pure blissful awareness is constant and uninterrupted and yet without impeding the normal perceptions and activities of life. It is rare indeed for this consummation to be attained during the life on earth. In the case of Sri Bhagavan it occurred only a few months later and with no quest, no striving, no conscious preparation. He himself has described it.

> "It was about six weeks before I left Madura for good that the great change in my life took place. It was quite sudden. I was sitting alone in a room on the first floor of my uncle's house. I seldom had any sickness, and on that day there was nothing wrong with my health, but a sudden violent fear of death overtook me. There was nothing in my state of health to account for it, and I did not try to account for it or to find out whether there was any reason for the fear. I just felt 'I am going to die' and began thinking what to do about it. It did not occur to me to consult a doctor or my elders or friends; I felt that I had to solve the problem myself, there and then.
>
> The shock of the fear of death drove my mind inwards and I said to myself mentally, without actually framing the words: 'Now death has come; what does it mean? What is it that is dying? This body dies.' And I at once dramatized the occurrence of death. I lay with my limbs stretched out stiff as though *rigor mortis* had set in and imitated a corpse so as to give greater reality to the enquiry. I held my breath and kept my lips tightly closed so that no sound could escape, so that neither the word 'I' nor any other word could be uttered. 'Well then,' I said to myself, 'this body is dead. It will be carried stiff to the burning ground and there burnt and reduced to ashes. But with the death of this body am I dead? Is the body I? It is silent and inert but I feel the full force of my personality and even the voice of the 'I' within me, apart from it. So I am Spirit transcending the body. The body dies but the Spirit that transcends it cannot be touched by death. That means I am the deathless Spirit.' All this was not dull thought; it flashed through me vividly as living truth which I perceived directly, almost without thought-process. 'I' was something very real, the only real thing about my present state, and all the conscious activity connected with my body was centred on that 'I'. From that moment onwards the 'I' or Self focused attention on itself by a powerful fascination. Fear of death had vanished once and for all. Absorption in the Self continued unbroken from that time on. Other thoughts might come and go like the various notes of music, but the 'I' continued like the fundamental *sruti* note that underlies and blends with all the other notes.[3] Whether

the body was engaged in talking, reading or anything else, I was still centred on 'I'. Previous to that crisis I had no clear perception of my Self and was not consciously attracted to it. I felt no perceptible or direct interest in it, much less any inclination to dwell permanently in it."

Thus simply described, without pretention or verbiage, the state attained might seem no different from egotism, but that is due only to the ambiguity in the words 'I' and 'Self'. The difference is brought out by the attitude towards death, for one whose interest is centred in the ego, the 'I' as a separate individual being, has a dread of death which threatens the dissolution of the ego, whereas here the fear of death had vanished for ever in the realization that the 'I' was one with the universal deathless Self which is the Spirit and the Self of every man. Even to say that he knew he was One with the Spirit is inadequate, since it suggests a separate 'I' who knew this, whereas the 'I' in him was itself consciously the Spirit.

Years later the difference was expounded by Sri Bhagavan to Paul Brunton, a Western seeker.[4]

> BRUNTON: What exactly is this Self of which you speak? If what you say is true there must be another self in man.
>
> SRI RAMANA: Can a man be possessed of two identities, two selves? To understand this matter it is first necessary for a man to analyse himself. Because it has long been his habit to think as others think, he has never faced his 'I' in the true manner. He has not a correct picture of himself; he has too long identified himself with the body and the brain. Therefore I tell you to pursue this enquiry, 'Who am I?'
>
> You ask me to describe this true Self to you. What can be said? It is That out of which the sense of the personal 'I' arises and into which it will have to disappear.
>
> BRUNTON: Disappear? How can one lose the feeling of one's personality?
>
> SRI RAMANA: The first and foremost of all thoughts, the primeval thought in the mind of every man, is the thought 'I'. It is only after the birth of this thought that any other thoughts can arise at all. It is only after the first personal pronoun, 'I', has arisen in the mind that the second personal pronoun, 'you', can make its appearance. If you could mentally follow the 'I' thread until it led you back to its source you would discover that, just as it is the first thought to appear, so it is the last to disappear. This is a matter which can be experienced.
>
> BRUNTON: You mean that it is possible to conduct such a mental investigation into oneself?
>
> SRI RAMANA: Certainly. It is possible to go inwards until the last thought, 'I', gradually vanishes.

BRUNTON: What is then left? Will a man then become quite unconscious or will he become an idiot?

SRI RAMANA: No; on the contrary, he will attain that consciousness which is immortal and he will become truly wise when he has awakened to his true Self, which is the real nature of man.

BRUNTON: But surely the sense of 'I' must also pertain to that?

SRI RAMANA: The sense of 'I' pertains to the person, the body and brain. When a man knows his true Self for the first time something else arises from the depths of his being and takes possession of him. That something is behind the mind; it is infinite, divine, eternal. Some people call it the Kingdom of Heaven, others call it the soul and others again Nirvana, and Hindus call it Liberation; you may give it what name you wish. When this happens a man has not really lost himself; rather he has found himself.

Unless and until a man embarks on this quest of the true Self, doubt and uncertainty will follow his footsteps through life. The greatest kings and statesmen try to rule others when in their heart of hearts they know that they cannot rule themselves. Yet the greatest power is at the command of the man who has penetrated to his inmost depth. . . . What is the use of knowing about everything else when you do not yet know who you are? Men avoid this enquiry into the true Self, but what else is there so worthy to be undertaken?

This whole *sadhana* took barely half an hour, and yet it is of the utmost importance to us that it *was a sadhana,* a striving towards light, and not an effortless awakening; for a Guru normally guides his disciples along the path that he himself has trod. That Sri Bhagavan completed within half an hour not merely the *sadhana* of a lifetime but, for most *sadhakas,* of many lifetimes, does not alter the fact that it was a striving by Self-enquiry such as he later enjoined on his followers. He warned them that the consummation towards which it leads is not normally attained quickly but only after long striving, but he also said that it is "the one infallible means, the only direct one, to realize the unconditioned, absolute Being that you really are" (**Maharshi's Gospel,** Part II). He said that it immediately sets up the process of transmutation, even though it may be long before this is completed. "But the moment the ego-self tries to know itself it begins to partake less and less of the body in which it is immersed and more and more of the consciousness of Self."

It is also significant that, although knowing nothing of the theory or practice of *sadhana,* Sri Bhagavan did in fact use *pranayama* or breath-control as an aid to concentration. So also he did admit of it as a legitimate help towards attaining thought-control, although he discouraged its use except for that purpose and never actually enjoined it.

"Breath-control is also a help. It is one of the various methods that are intended to help us attain one-pointedness. Breath-control can also help to control the wandering mind and attain this one-pointedness and therefore it can be used. But one should not stop there. After obtaining control of the mind through breathing exercises one should not rest content with any experience that may accrue therefrom, but should harness the controlled mind to the question 'Who am I?' till the mind merges in the Self."

This changed mode of consciousness naturally produced a change in Venkataraman's sense of values and habits of life. Things that had formerly been valued lost all attraction, conventional aims in life became unreal, what had been ignored exercised a strong compulsion. The adaptation of life to this new state of awareness cannot have been easy in one who was still a schoolboy and who lacked all theoretical training in spiritual life. He spoke to no one about it and for the time being remained in the family and continued to go to school; in fact he made as little outer change as possible. Nevertheless, it was inevitable that his family should notice his changed behaviour and resent some features of it. This also he has described.

"The consequences of this new awareness were soon noticed in my life. In the first place, I lost what little interest I had in my outer relationship with friends and relatives and went through my studies mechanically. I would hold an open book in front of me to satisfy my relatives that I was reading, when in reality my attention was far away from any such superficial matter. In my dealings with people I became meek and submissive. Formerly if I was given more work than other boys I might complain, and if any boy annoyed me I would retaliate. None of them would dare make fun of me or take liberties with me. Now all that was changed. Whatever work was given, whatever teasing or annoyance there was, I would put up with it quietly. The former ego that resented and retaliated had disappeared. I stopped going out with friends to play games and preferred solitude. I would often sit alone, especially in a posture suitable for meditation, and become absorbed in the Self, the Spirit, the force or current which constituted me. I would continue in this despite the jeers of my elder brother who would sarcastically call me 'sage' or 'yogi' and advise me to retire into the jungle like the ancient Rishis.

Another change was that I no longer had any likes or dislikes with regard to food. Whatever was given to me, tasty or insipid, good or bad, I would swallow with like indifference.

One of the features of my new state was my changed attitude to the Minakshi Temple.[5] Formerly I used to go there very occasionally with friends to look at the images and put the sacred ash and vermilion on my brow and would return home almost unmoved. But after the Awakening I went there almost every evening. I used to go alone and stand motionless for a long time before an image of Siva or Minakshi or Nataraja and the sixty-three Saints, and as I stood there waves of emotion overwhelmed me. The soul had given up its hold on the body when it renounced the 'I-am-the-body' idea and it was seeking some fresh anchorage; hence the frequent visits to the temple and the outpouring of the soul in tears. This was God's play with the soul. I would stand before Iswara, the Controller of the universe and of the destinies of all, the Omniscient and Omnipresent, and sometimes pray for the descent of His Grace upon me so that my devotion might increase and become perpetual like that of the sixty-three Saints. More often I would not pray at all but silently allow the deep within to flow on and into the deep beyond. The tears that marked this overflow of the soul did not betoken any particular pleasure or pain. I was not a pessimist; I knew nothing of life and had not learnt that it was full of sorrow. I was not actuated by any desire to avoid rebirth or seek Liberation or even to obtain dispassion or salvation. I had read no books except the Periapuranam, the Bible and bits of Tayumanavar or Tevaram. My conception of Iswara[6] was similar to that found in the Puranas; I had never heard of Brahman,[7] *samsara*[8] and so forth. I did not yet know that there was an Essence or Impersonal Real underlying everything and that Iswara and I were both identical with it. Later, at Tiruvannamalai, as I listened to the Ribhu-Gita and other sacred books, I learnt all this and found that the books were analysing and naming what I had felt intuitively without analysis or name. In the language of the books I should describe the state I was in after the awakening as *Suddha Manas* or *Vijnana* or the intuition of the Illumined."

It was quite different from the state of the mystic who is transported into ecstasy for a brief unaccountable while, after which the gloomy walls of the mind close round him again. Sri Bhagavan was already in constant, unbroken awareness of the Self and he has said explicitly that there was no more *sadhana,* no more spiritual effort, after this. There was no more striving towards abidance in the Self because the ego, whose opposition it is that causes strife, had been dissolved and there was none left with whom to strive. Further progress towards continuous, fully conscious Identity with the Self, established in fully normal outer life and radiating Grace upon those who approached him, was henceforth natural and effortless; and yet that there was such progress is indicated by Sri Bhagavan's saying that the soul was still seeking a fresh anchorage. Things such as emulation of the Saints and concern as to what his elders would think still show a remnant of practical acceptance of duality which was later to disappear. There was also a physical sign of the continuing process. A constant burning sensation was felt in the body from the time of the Awakening until the moment when he entered the inner shrine of the temple at Tiruvannamalai.

ADVAITA

Sri Bhagavan was not a philosopher and there was absolutely no development in his teaching. His earliest expositions, *Self-Enquiry* and *Who Am I?,* are no different in doctrinal theory from those he gave verbally in his last years. When, as a lad of sixteen, he realized his identify with the Absolute, with That which is Pure Being underlying all that is, it was formless, intuitive knowledge of which the doctrinal implications were recognized only later. "I did not yet know that there was an Essence or Impersonal Real underlying everything and that God and I were both identical with it. Later, at Tiruvannamalai, as I listened to the Ribhu Gita and other sacred books, I learnt all this and found that they were analysing and naming what I had felt intuitively without analysis or name." It was no question of opinions but of Truth recognized; that is to say that he was not convinced by what he read but simply recognized its conformity with what he already intuitively knew.

All modes and levels of doctrine are comprised within Hinduism, all of them legitimate and corresponding to the various modes of approach required by people of varying temperament and development. The approach through love and worship of a Personal God exists, as it does in the Western or Semitic religions. So also does the approach through service, seeing God manifested in all His creatures and worshipping Him by serving them. However, the recognition of Pure Being as one's Self and the Self of the universe and of all beings is the supreme and ultimate Truth, transcending all other levels of doctrine without denying their truth on their own plane. This is the doctrine of Advaita, Non-duality, taught by the ancient Rishis and pre-eminently by Shankaracharya. It is the simplest as well as the most profound, being the ultimate truth beyond all the complexities of cosmology.

Non-duality means that only the Absolute is. The entire cosmos exists within the Absolute, having no intrinsic reality but merely manifesting the Absolute which, however, remains eternally unchanged and unmanifest, as the people and events in a man's dream exist within him and have no reality apart from him and yet add nothing to him by their creation and subtract nothing from him by their disappearance. This means that the Absolute is the Self of the cosmos and of every being. Therefore by seeking his self, by the constant investigation 'Who am I?' it is possible for a man to realize his identity with Universal Being. It was the purest Advaita that Sri Bhagavan taught.

Some may fear that the doctrine of the One Self deprives them of a Personal God to Whom they can pray, but there is no need for such fear, because as long as the reality of the ego who prays endures so long does the reality of the God to Whom he prays; so long as a man accepts his ego as a reality, the world outside it and God above it are also realities for him. This is the level of a dualistic religion and a Personal God. It is true but not the ultimate Truth. "All regions postulate the three fundamentals: individual, God and world. It is only so long as the ego endures that one says either, 'The One manifests Itself as the three' or, 'The three are really three'.

The supreme state is to inhere in the Self, the ego extinguished" (*Forty Verses on Reality,* V. 2).

Some people also revolt against the conception of the world as unreal, even while admitting the reality of the Spirit, but that is because they have not understood in what sense it is unreal. Sri Bhagavan often explained this, and nowhere more concisely than in the following statement recorded by S. S. Cohen:

> "Shankaracharya has been criticized for his philosophy of Maya (illusion) without understanding his meaning. He made three statements: that Brahman is real, that the universe is unreal, and that Brahman is the universe. He did not stop with the second. The third statement explains the first two; it signifies that when the universe is perceived apart from Brahman that perception is false and illusory. What it amounts to is that phenomena are real when experienced as the Self and illusory when seen apart from the Self."

The teaching of Sri Bhagavan was intensely practical. He expounded theory only in answer to the specific needs and questions of devotees and as a necessary basis for practice. When reminded once (in *Maharshi's Gospel*) that Buddha had refused to answer questions about God, he replied with approval, "In fact Buddha was more concerned with directing the seeker to realize Bliss here and now than with academic discussions about God and so forth." So also, he himself would often refuse to gratify curiosity, turning the questioner instead to the need for *sadhana* or effort. Asked about the posthumous state of man, he might reply: "Why do you want to know what you will be when you die before you know what you are now? First find out what you are now." A man is now and eternally the deathless Self behind this and every other life, but to be told so or to believe it is not enough; it is necessary to strive to realize it. Similarly, if asked about God he might reply: "Why do you want to know about God before you know yourself? First find out what you are."

The process by which this is to be done is described in a later chapter, but since the next chapter already recounts Sri Bhagavan's instructions to devotees, reference is made to it and to his teaching here.

That his teaching was not 'philosophy' in the usual sense of the term may be seen from the fact that (as will appear in his replies to Sivaprakasam Pillai in the next chapter) he did not instruct his devotees to think out problems but to eliminate thought. This may sound as though the process is stupefying, but, as he explained to Paul Brunton in the conversation quoted in Chapter Two, the reverse is true. A man is identical with the Self, which is pure Being, pure Consciousness, pure Bliss, but the mind creates the illusion of a separate individuality. In deep sleep the mind is stilled and a man is one with the Self, but in an unconscious way. In *samadhi* he is one with the Self in a fully conscious way, not in darkness but in light. If the interference of the mind is stilled, the consciousness of Self can, by the Grace of the Guru, awaken in the heart, thus preparing for this blissful Identity, for a state that is not torpor or ignorance but radiant. Knowledge, pure I-am-ness.

Many may recoil from the idea of destruction of the mind or (what comes to the same thing) of the separate individuality and find it terrifying, and yet it happens to us daily in sleep and, far from being afraid to go to sleep, we find it desirable and pleasant, even though in sleep the mind is stilled only in an ignorant way. In rapture or ecstasy, on the other hand, the mind is momentarily absorbed and stilled in a fragmentary experience of the bliss that is its true nature. The very words indicate the transcending of the individuality, since 'rapture' means etymologically being carried away and 'ecstasy' standing outside oneself. The expression 'it is breath-taking' really means 'it is thought-taking', for the source of thought and breath is the same, as Sri Bhagavan explained when speaking of breath-control. The truth is that the individuality is not lost but expanded to Infinity.

The elimination of thoughts is for the purpose of concentrating on the deeper awareness that is behind and beyond thought. Far from weakening the mind, it strengthens it, for it teaches concentration. Sri Bhagavan frequently confirmed this. It is the weak and uncontrolled mind that is constantly distracted by irrelevant thoughts and harassed by unhelpful worries; the mind that is strong enough to concentrate, no matter on what, can turn its concentration to the elimination of thoughts in quest of the Self, and conversely, the effort to eliminate thoughts in the manner prescribed gives strength and power of concentration. When the quest is achieved the faculties of the mind are not lost: Sri Bhagavan illustrated this by comparing the mind of the Gnani to the moon in the sky at midday—it is illuminated but its light is not needed in the greater radiance of the sun which illuminates it.

THE WRITTEN WORKS

The entire writings of Sri Bhagavan are very small in bulk, and even of them nearly all were written to meet the specific needs of devotees. Devaraja Mudaliar records in his diary how Sri Bhagavan remarked on this when speaking about a visiting poet.

> "All this is only activity of the mind. The more you exercise the mind and the more success you have in composing verses the less peace you have. What use is it to acquire such accomplishments if you don't acquire peace? But if you tell such people this it doesn't appeal to them; they can't keep quiet. They must be composing songs. . . . Somehow, it never occurs to me to write a book or compose poems. All the poems I have made were on the request of someone or other in connection with some particular event. Even *Forty Verses on Reality,* of which so many commentaries and translations now exist, was not planned as a

book but consists of verses composed at different times and afterwards arranged as a book by Muruganar and others. The only poems that came to me spontaneously and compelled me, as it were, to write them without any one urging me to do so are the *Eleven Stanzas to Sri Arunachala* and the *Eight Stanzas to Sri Arunachala*. The opening words of the *Eleven Stanzas* came to me one morning and even though I tried to suppress them, saying 'What have I to do with these words?' they would not be suppressed till I composed a song bringing them in; and all the words flowed easily, without any effort. In the same way the second stanza was made the next day and the succeeding ones the following days, one each day. Only the tenth and eleventh were composed the same day."

He went on to describe in his characteristically vivid way how he composed the *Eight Stanzas.*

"The next day I started out to go round the hill. Palaniswami was walking behind me and after we had gone some way Aijasami seems to have called him back and given him a pencil and paper, saying, 'For some days now Swami has been composing poems every day. He may do so today as well, so you had better take this paper and pencil with you.'

I learnt about this only when I noticed that Palaniswami was not with me for a while but caught me up later. That day, before I got back to Virupaksha, I wrote six of the eight stanzas. Either that evening or the next day Narayana Reddi came. He was at that time living in Vellore as an agent of Singer & Co. and he used to come from time to time. Aijasami and Palani told him about the poems and he said, 'Give them to me at once and I will go and get them printed.' He had already published some books. When he insisted on taking the poems I told him he could do so and could publish the first eleven as one form of poem and the rest, which were in a different metre, as another. To make up the required quota I at once composed two more stanzas and he took all the nineteen stanzas with him to get them published."

Many poets composed songs to Sri Bhagavan in various languages, outstanding among them being Ganapati Sastri in Sanskrit and Muruganar in Tamil. Although, in the conversation quoted above, Sri Bhagavan deprecated the writing of poetry as a dissipation of energy that could be turned inwards to *sadhana,* he listened graciously and showed interest when poems were sung before him. Prose books and articles about him were also written, and he would often have them read out and translated so that all could understand. One was struck by the extraordinary impersonality of his interest, the childlike innocence of it.

There are two prose books which one might say were written by Sri Bhagavan. During the early years at Virupaksha, when he was still maintaining silence, he wrote out instructions on various occasions for Gam-

biram Seshayyar, and after Seshayyar's death these were arranged and published as a book under the title *Self-Enquiry.* Similarly, his replies given at the same period to Sivaprakasam Pillai were amplified and arranged in book form as *Who Am I?* The other prose books that the Ashram has published were not written by him but are records of verbal expositions that he gave in answer to questions and are therefore all in the form of dialogue.

His poems fall into two groups: those which express rather the approach through *bhakti,* that is through love and devotion, and those which are more doctrinal. The first group is composed of the *Five Hymns to Sri Arunachala* all written during the Virupaksha period. The element of devotion in them does not imply any abandonment of Advaita but is perfectly fused with Knowledge. They were written from the standpoint of the aspirant or devotee, even though he who wrote them was in fact established in the supreme Knowledge, in the Bliss of Union not the pain of longing; and it is for this reason that they appeal so powerfully to the heart of the devotee.

Mention has already been made of two of them, the *Eight Stanzas* and the *Eleven Stanzas.* In the latter Sri Bhagavan not only wrote as an aspirant but actually used the words, "One who has not attained the Supreme Knowledge." Desiring an explicit confirmation, one of the devotees, A. Bose, asked him why he wrote so, whether it was from the standpoint of the devotees and for their sake, and Sri Bhagavan admitted that it was so.

The last of the *Five Hymns* Sri Bhagavan wrote first in Sanskrit and then translated into Tamil. The story of its writing is astounding. Ganapati Sastri asked him to write a Sanskrit poem, and he replied, laughing, that he did not know the fundamentals of Sanskrit grammar or any Sanskrit metres. Sastri explained a metre to him and implored him to try. The same evening he created five perfect verses in Sanskrit. They have been rendered into English as follows:

Ocean of nectar, full of Grace, engulfing the universe in Thy Splendour, Oh Arunachala, the Supreme! Be Thou the Sun and open the lotus of my heart in Bliss.

Oh Arunachala! in Thee the picture of the universe is formed, abides and is dissolved. In this enigma rests the miracle of Truth. Thou art the Inner Self Who dancest in the hearts as 'I'. 'Heart' is Thy name, Oh Lord!

He who turns inward with untroubled mind to search where the consciousness of 'I' arises realizes the Self and rests in Thee, Oh Arunachala! as a river when it merges in the Ocean.

Abandoning the outer world, with mind and breath controlled, in order to meditate on Thee within, the Yogi sees Thy Light, Oh Arunachala! and finds his delight in Thee.

He who dedicates his mind to Thee and, seeing
Thee, always beholds the universe as Thy form,
who at all times glorifies Thee and loves Thee as
none other than the Self, he is the Master without
peer, being one with Thee, Oh Arunachala! and
lost in Thy Bliss.

These stanzas are more doctrinal than the other four
hymns, epitomizing as they do the three main *margas* or
approaches to realization. Speaking about them later,
Sri Bhagavan explained: "The third stanza deals with
the *Sat* aspect (Being), the fourth with *Chit* (Consciousness) and the fifth with *Ananda* (Bliss). The *Gnani* becomes one with the *Sat* or Reality like a river merging
in the ocean; the Yogi sees the light of *Chit;* the *bhakta*
or karma yogin is immersed in the flood of *Ananda*."

However, the most moving and beloved of the *Five
Hymns* is the **"Marital Garland of a Hundred and
Eight Verses to Sri Arunachala,"** commonly known in
English by its refrain, 'Arunachala Siva'. During the
early years of Sri Bhagavan's abode at Virupaksha,
Palaniswami and others used to go into town to beg food
for the small group of devotees, and one day they asked
Sri Bhagavan for a devotional song to sing as they went.
He replied that there were plenty of sublime songs composed by the Saints, many of them neglected, so there
was no need to compose a new one. However, they continued to urge him and some days later he set out on
pradakshina round the hill, taking a pencil and paper
with him, and, on the way, composed the hundred and
eight verses.

Tears of ecstasy streamed down his face as he wrote,
sometimes blinding his eyes and choking his voice. The
poem became the great devotional inspiration of the
devotees. All the pain of longing and all the bliss of
fulfilment are mirrored in its glowing symbolism. The
perfection of Knowledge is combined with the ecstasy of
devotion. And yet this most heart-felt of poems was
composed from the standpoint of the devotee, of one
who is still seeking. It is also an acrostic, its hundred
and eight verses beginning with the successive letters of
the Tamil alphabet. Nevertheless, no poem could be
more spontaneous. Some devotees asked Sri Bhagavan
the interpretation of some of the verses and he replied:
"You think it out and I will too. I didn't think while I
was composing it; I just wrote as it came."

There is an ancient legend that a party of Rishis or
Sages, living with their families in a forest, were practising karmas, that is ritualistic and devotional acts and
incantations, by which they had attained supernatural
powers and hoped eventually to obtain the supreme
Deliverance. In this, however, they were mistaken. In
order to convict them of their error, Siva appeared before them as a mendicant, accompanied by Vishnu in
the guise of Mohini, a beautiful lady. All the Rishis fell
in love with Mohini and their wives with Siva, with the
result that their equanimity was disturbed and their
powers began to wane. Seeing this, they decided that

Siva must be an enemy and conjured up serpents, and a
tiger and elephant that they sent against him. Siva, however, merely took the serpents for a garland and, slaying
the tiger and elephant, used the skin of the former as a
loincloth and of the latter as a shawl. The Rishis thereupon, recognizing his greater power, bowed down before
him and besought him to give them *upadesa* or guidance. Only then did Siva explain to them their error,
teaching that action cannot bring release from action, that
karma is the mechanism, not the cause of creation, and
that it is necessary to go beyond action to contemplation.

The poet and devotee Muruganar wrote this story in
Tamil verse, but when he reached the point where Siva
gives instruction to the Rishis he besought Bhagavan,
who was Siva Incarnate, to write it. Thereupon Bhagavan composed the **Upadesa Saram** or **Instruction in
Thirty Verses** in which, beginning with devout and disinterested activity, he explains that, beneficent as this
is, incantations are more effective, silent incantations
again more effective than those uttered aloud, and more
effective still contemplation. Sri Bhagavan translated
the Thirty Verses into Sanskrit and the Sanskrit version
is regarded as a scripture in that it was chanted daily
before Sri Bhagavan together with the Vedas and is now
so chanted before his tomb.

The doctrine taught by Sri Bhagavan is enunciated the
most comprehensively in this poem and in the **Ulladu
Narpadu** or **Forty Verses on Reality** together with its
'Supplement' of a second forty verses.

Many translations have been made of the **Forty Verses
on Reality** and commentaries written on it. It has a
universality and a condensed wisdom that demands
commentary. And yet, as Sri Bhagavan remarked in the
conversation quoted above, it was not written as a continuous poem but the verses were composed from time to
time as occasion arose. Some of the supplementary forty
were not even composed by Sri Bhagavan himself, but
culled from other sources, for when an adequate verse
existed elsewhere he saw no need to write a new one.
Nevertheless, the whole is the most complete and profound enunciation of his doctrine.

Apart from these two groups there are a few short poems
also. Humour is not lacking among them. One contains
instructions for *sadhana* under the symbolism of a
recipe for making *poppadum,* a favourite South Indian
savoury. The mother of Sri Bhagavan was making it one
day and asked him to help, and he thereupon spontaneously wrote the symbolical recipe for her.

The poet Avvayar once wrote a complaint against the
stomach: "You will not go without food even for one
day, nor will you take enough for two days at a time.
You have no idea of the trouble I have on your account,
Oh wretched stomach! It is impossible to get on with you!"

One day there had been feasting at the Ashram and all
were feeling more or less uneasy, and Sri Bhagavan

parodied Avvayar's stanza. "You will not give even an hour's rest to me, your stomach. Day after day, every hour, you keep on eating. You have no idea how I suffer, Oh trouble-making ego! It is impossible to get on with you."

It was in 1947 that Sri Bhagavan wrote his last poem. This time it was not in response to any request, and yet it had something of the appearance of a *tour de force,* since he wrote it first in Telugu, but to a Tamil metrical form, and then translated it into Tamil. It was called **Ekatmapanchakam** (*Five verses on the Self*).

> Forgetting the Self, mistaking the body for the Self, going through innumerable births and finally finding and being the Self—this is just like waking up from a dream of wandering all over the world.
>
> He who asks 'Who am I?' although existing as the Self, is like a drunken man who asks about his own identity and whereabouts.
>
> When in fact the body is in the Self, to think that the Self is within the insentient body is like thinking that the cinema screen on which a figure is projected is inside the figure.
>
> Has the ornament any existence apart from the gold (of which it is made)? Where is the body apart from the Self? The ignorant mistake the body for the Self, but the *Gnani,* knower of the Self, perceives the Self as the Self.
>
> That one Self, the Reality, alone exists for ever. If even the Primal Guru (Adi-Guru, Dakshinamurthi) revealed it in silence, who can convey it in speech?

There are also a few translations, mainly from Shankaracharya. A visitor to Virupaksha Cave once left there a copy of Shankaracharya's *Vivekachudamani.* After looking through it, Sri Bhagavan recommended Gambiram Seshayyar to read it. He, however, did not know Sanskrit, so he wanted it in Tamil. Palaniswami obtained a loan of a Tamil verse rendering and Seshayyar, seeing it, wrote to the publishers for a copy but was told that it was out of print. He therefore asked Sri Bhagavan to make a simple rendering in Tamil prose. Sri Bhagavan began to write one but before he had got far with it Seshayyar received the verse edition he had ordered, so he left the work uncompleted. A few years later, on the earnest request of another devotee, he took up the work again and finished it. Only then did the devotee say that his purpose in pressing for its completion had been to get it published. Hearing this, Sri Bhagavan wrote a preface saying that a free prose version might be of use even though a Tamil verse rendering already existed. The preface itself contains an epitome of the book and a concise exposition of doctrine and the path.

The last thing he ever wrote was a Tamil translation of Shankaracharya's *Atma Bodha.* It had been with him in Virupaksha in the very early days but he had never thought of translating it. In 1949 a Tamil translation, perhaps not a very perfect one, was sent to the Ashram, and shortly afterwards Sri Bhagavan himself felt the urge to make one. For some days he ignored it, but the words of the translation rose up before him, verse by verse, as though already written, so he asked for paper and pencil and wrote them down. So completely effortless was the work that he said, laughing, that he was afraid some other author might come along and claim that the work was really his and had been copied.

Also among the works of Sri Bhagavan is a compilation of forty-two verses from the *Bhagavad Gita* which, on the request of a devotee, he selected and rearranged to express his teaching. This has been translated into English under the name **The Song Celestial.**

GLOSSARY

Abheda. No-otherness (see bheda).

Adi-Guru. The ancient or primordial or original Guru. The Divine Source from which the power of initiation and guidance descends to a line of Gurus. An epithet of Sri Shankaracharya and sometimes also of Dakshinamurthi.

Adina-Guru. The founder of a line of Gurus. Except in the case of the founder of a new path, initiation (like ordination) is valid only when given by one who is duly authorized and whose authorization goes back in an unbroken chain to the founder of his line.

Advaita. Non-duality, the doctrine that nothing exists apart from the Spirit, but everything is a form assumed by the Spirit. . . .

The principle doctrinal division among the Hindus is between the schools of Advaita and Dvaita. The Dvaitists or Dualists worship a Personal God separate from the worshipper. The Advaitists, while recognizing the truth of this conception on its own plane, go beyond it to the conception of the Absolute in which a man is absorbed back into That which is his Source and real Self, surviving in the pure Bliss and boundless Consciousness of Being.

Agnana. Ignorance. The prefix 'a' (as in abheda) is a negative, so the word literally means 'lack of knowledge'.

The first 'n' is pronounced almost like the 'ni' in 'onion'.

Ananda. Bliss, beatitude.

Anugrabam. Grace.

Arudra Darshan. The Day of the Sight of Siva. . . .

Arunachaleswar. God in the form of Arunachala, a contraction of Arunachala-Iswara.

Ashram. The establishment or colony that grows up around a Sage or Guru; sometimes mistranslated as 'monastery'.

Ashtavadhana. The ability to attend to eight different matters simultaneously.

Asramam. The Tamil form of 'ashram'.

Asuric. Diabolical, evil.

Atma or *Atman.* The Spirit or Self.

Atmaswarupa. Literally the 'form of the Spirit'; a term used for the universe to indicate that the universe has no intrinsic reality but exists only as a manifestation of the Spirit.

Avatar. An incarnation or manifestation of Vishnu, that is of God as the Preserver and Sustainer of the universe. Within the manvantara or cycle stretching (according to Christian symbolism) from the Earthly Paradise (the state of Adam before the fall) to the Heavenly Jerusalem (the consummation after the second coming of Christ) there are ten Avatars. The seventh is Rama, commemorated in the *Ramayana,* a Sanskrit epic; the eighth is Krishna, commemorated in the *Bhagavad Gita;* the ninth is described as the non-Hindu Avatar and is identified as Buddha or Christ or both; the tenth is Kalki, the destroyer of sin with whose coming the kali-yuga or dark age is to be ended. He is still to come and is equivalent to the second coming of Christ awaited by the Christians and Muslims and the Maitreya Buddha of the Buddhists.

Sometimes the term Avatar is used more loosely to indicate a divine manifestation.

Ayurveda. The traditional Hindu system of medicine.

Bhagavad Gita. Literally the 'Divine Song' or, more correctly, 'God-Song', since 'Bhagavad' is a noun used adjectivally. The scripture of Sri Krishna, the eighth Avatar, probably the most widely studied and followed Hindu scripture. It occurs as an episode in the Sanskrit epic, the *Mahabharata.*

Bhagavan. The same word as 'Bhagavad' with a different case-ending; the commonly used word for 'God'. Terms such as Iswara, Brahma, Vishnu, Siva and names for the various Aspects of God are more technical or philosophical. In ordinary conversation a man says either 'Bhagavan' (God) or 'Swami' (the Lord).

The term 'Bhagavan' is used by general consent of those few supreme Sages who are recognized as being completely One with God.

Both the B and the g are aspirated. The middle vowel is slurred over and scarcely heard.

Bhakta. Devotee. Also one who approaches God through love and devotion.

Bhakta-marga. The approach to God through love and devotion.

Bhakti. Love or devotion.

Bheda. Otherness. The difference between bheda and abheda is substantially the same as that between dvaita and advaita. The exponent of bheda regards himself as 'other than God', whereas the exponent of abheda regards God as the Absolute or Infinite apart from which there can be no other.

Bhiksha. An offering of food to the Guru or to a sanyasin. In the case of Bhagavan this came to mean providing an ashram meal, since he would accept nothing that was not shared by all.

Brahma. The highest and ultimate conception is Brahman (the neuter form of 'Brahma'), the Absolute, about Which nothing can be postulated, since any assertion would be a limitation. The first stage in the manifestation of Brahman is Iswara, the Personal God. Iswara is then conceived of under the threefold aspects of Brahma, the Creator, Vishnu, the Preserver, and Siva, the Destroyer. There are temples to Vishnu and Siva but not to Brahma, as man is concerned with God as Preserver or God as Destroyer of forms in the Bliss of Union rather than with God as Creator.

The h in Brahma is either not pronounced or pronounced after the m, as 'Bramha'.

Brahman. See Brahma.

Brahmin. The Hindus were divided traditionally into four castes, of whom the Brahmins were the highest, being devoted to a life of spirituality and study. Next came the Kshatriyas, who were the rulers, warriors and administrators. The Vaishas were the middle classes and the Shudras the labourers. The castes were not at first exclusively hereditary, but since each caste married within itself even the law of heredity made them so practically. In course of time they became strictly so and also subdivided into hereditary sub-castes, largely on a professional basis, like Mediaeval guilds in Europe. Also they tended to abandon their caste functions and engage in those of other castes. Today caste has little functional meaning. The Indian Government is trying to destroy it.

The h is not pronounced in Brahmin.

Chakra. The yogic and tantric paths (see marga) unfurl the spirit-force in man (kundalini) from its latency at the base of the spine and cause it to ascend through a series of spiritual centres in the body. Each of these is called a wheel or chakra. Each represents a different stage of development which is franchised as the kundalini attains it.

Chila. Disciple.

Chit. Consciousness. (See Satchitananda.)

Daivic. Godlike or Divine. An English adjectival form from deva, meaning angel or holy spirit.

Dakshinamurthi. Siva manifested in ancient times as a youth who taught in silence, initiating and guiding his disciples by direct transmission of the Spirit. He is particularly associated with Arunachala, the centre of silent and purely spiritual initiation and guidance, and therefore also with Sri Bhagavan, who was Siva teaching in silence.

Darshan. Literally 'sight'. Since one speaks of a holy man giving darshan, it could best be translated as 'silent audience'. To have darshan of a Sage could be translated as to enjoy the grace of his presence.

Dharma. Harmony, harmonious life or action. Also a man's role in life, since what is harmonious conduct for one (say, a soldier) may not be so for another (say, a priest).

Dhoti. A white cotton cloth that Hindu men in South India wear. It is wound round the waist and hangs down like a skirt from waist to ankles.

Diksha. Initiation.

Giripradakshina. Pradakshina is the circuit that is made of any holy place, walking round with one's right side inward, that is from south to west. Giri is a hill; so giripradakshina is used for circuit of Arunachala.

Gnana. Knowledge, Divine Wisdom or Understanding. Spiritual Enlightenment. The correct transliteration would be 'jnana' but 'gnana' is more phonetic, the first letter being pronounced like a hard g and the second like the ni in onion.

Gnana-marga. The Path of Knowledge. This does not mean a path requiring great theoretical elaboration but one based on intuitive knowledge or spiritual understanding. (See Marga. For pronunciation see Gnana.)

Gnani. A man of Knowledge. It may be used to mean one who follows the Gnana-marga, but in its correct meaning it is one who has attained complete Enlightenment and is established in the Absolute Knowledge which is Liberation from all illusion of duality. It thus means the same as Mukta, the liberated or perfectly realized man. (For pronunciation see Gnana.)

Guru. Spiritual guide or Master. . . .

Iswara. The Personal God. (See under Brahma.) Sometimes also transliterated as Ishvara.

Japa. Invocation or incantation.

Jayanthi. Birthday.

Kali-Yuga. The Dark Age, equivalent to the Iron Age of Graeco-Roman traditions, said to have begun in 3101 B.C. with the Battle of Kurukshetra, that is with the teaching of Sri Krishna recorded in the *Bhagavad Gita,* and to be now approaching its end. (See Yuga.)

Karma. The destiny that a man makes for himself by the law of cause and effect. There are three kinds of karma: prarabdha, or that which is to be worked out in this life, sanjitha, or that which existed at the beginning of this life but is held over, and agamya or the new karma which is accumulated in this life and added to the sanjitha. . . . The law of karma combines the two theories of predestination and cause and effect, since a man's present actions cause or predestine his future state.

Karma also means action. It is sometimes used to mean ritualistic actions performed as a marga or path to salvation.

Just as karma is accumulated by a man's actions and desires, so it can be destroyed by divine love and knowledge and by renunciation of desires. Therefore it is said that karma is like a mountain of gunpowder that can be burnt up by a single spark of Gnana (Divine Knowledge).

Karma-marga. The approach to God through harmonious and disinterested actions, that is, as is said in the *Bhagavad Gita,* by acting without being attached to the fruits of one's actions, doing one's duty simply because it is one's duty, not for profit or ambition, and not being deflected from it by fear or favour. This is normally accompanied by ritualistic acts.

Kavyakanta. One whose speech is like poetry. A brilliant improvisor of poetry.

Krishna. The eighth Avatar. The Divine Teacher whose doctrine is contained in the *Bhagavad Gita.*

Kumbhabhishekam. Consecration.

Lingam. An upright pillar of stone often used to represent Siva or the Absolute on the grounds that any image or idol is limiting and therefore misleading. The word comes from linga, to get absorbed, and the root meaning is 'that in which all beings are absorbed'.

Maharshi. Maha Rishi, the Great Rishi or Sage. The name is used for one who opens a new path to Realization. It is also a name of Vishnu as the fountain-head of initiation and paths to Realization.

Mahasamadhi. The great or final or complete samadhi or absorption in the Self or Spirit. The term is sometimes used for the physical death of a great Saint, but for the Maharshi even this is inappropriate since he was already in Mahasamadhi while wearing a body, and the body's death made no difference to him.

Mantapam. A shrine or bare stone hall, with or without the image of a God inside.

Mantra. A sacred formula used as an incantation.

Mantradhyana. Meditation or spiritual awareness induced or supported by the use of incantations.

Marga, Mode of approach in the spiritual quest. Basically, there are three margas: the Gnana-marga, bhakti-marga and karma-marga.

Gnana-marga is the approach through Knowledge or understanding, by which is meant not mental but spiritual knowledge. Physical knowledge is direct, as when you burn your finger and know pain; mental knowledge is indirect, as when you know that fire burns; spiritual knowledge is again direct, though quite different.

Bhakti-marga is the approach through love and devotion.

Karma-marga is the approach through harmonious and disinterested activity.

The three margas are not mutually exclusive. There can be no spiritual knowledge without love. Also, love and devotion to God leads to understanding and to Union, which is Knowledge. For activity to be perfectly harmonious and disinterested it must be inspired by love and understanding. Gnana-marga leads to disinterested activity free from the thought: 'I am the doer of this and should have the praise or reward for it.'

Bhakti-marga leads to dedicated activity, seeing God manifested in all his creatures and serving him by serving them.

Nevertheless, although the margas merge and all lead to the same goal, they start from different points and their methods are different in practice.

Apart from the three basic margas, there are two less direct and more elaborate developments of Bhakti-marga, that is the yogic and tantric paths. They are very far from the teaching of Bhagavan and need not be described here.

Math. A private temple or shrine, something like the chantries of Mediaeval England.

Matrubhateswara. God (Iswara) in the form of the Mother.

Maulvi. (Arabic.) A Muslim learned in Islamic doctrine and law. The Islamic equivalent of a pandit.

Moksha. Liberation or Deliverance. Salvation is generally used in a dualistic sense to mean the salvation of a purified soul in the presence of God; Moksha is used in the complete and ultimate sense of liberation from all ignorance and duality through realization of identity with the Self.

Mouna. Silence.

Mouna diksha. Initiation through silence. . . .

Mouni. One who has taken a vow of silence.

Mount Meru. The mountain which, in Hindu mythology, is the Spiritual Centre of the universe. Bhagavan affirmed that Arunachala is Mount Meru.

Mukta. One who has attained Moksha or Deliverance. One who attains Moksha during the life on earth is sometimes called Jivan-Mukta, that is 'Mukta while living'.

Mukti. Deliverance; the same as Moksha.

Muni. Sage.

Nataraja. A name for Siva. Siva in the cosmic dance of creation and destruction of the universe.

Nirvikalpa samadhi. Samadhi in a state of trance, with suspension of the human faculties.

Nishkamyakarma. Action without attachment to the outcome, that is without egoism. Action which does not create new karma.

OM. The supreme mantra, representing the substratum of creative sound which sustains the universe. It is written with the three letters AUM but pronounced OM.

Pandit. One learned in the Hindu scriptures, doctrines and law. Sometimes transliterated 'pundit'.

Paramatman. The Supreme Atma or Spirit. Actually, the word Atma itself is often used in this sense and was so used by Bhagavan.

Parayanam. Singing or chanting.

Pial. A raised platform or stone or concrete couch often built outside a Hindu house or in the porch of it.

Pradakshina. See Giripradakshina.

Prana. Breath or vital force.

Pranayama. Breath-control, either regulating or suspending breathing.

Prarabdha. See karma.

Prarabdhakarma. See karma.

Prasadam. Some object given by the Guru as a vehicle of his Grace. When food is offered to the Guru it is usual for him to return a part of it as prasadam.

Puja. Ritualistic worship.

Pujari. One who performs puja.

Purana. Mythological scriptural story carrying a symbolical meaning.

Purusha. The Spirit. Atma is used in the pure sense of Spirit, whereas Purusha is used more in the masculine sense where Spirit is contrasted or coupled with Substance (Prakriti). In common speech it can be used for 'man' or 'husband'.

Rishi. Sage, literally Seer.

Rudra. A name for Siva as He who proclaims himself aloud.

Rupa. Form.

Sadhaka. Spiritual aspirant or seeker.

Sadhana. Spiritual quest or path. The technique of spiritual effort.

Sadhu. This word should correctly mean one who has attained the Goal of sadhana but is in fact used for one who has renounced home and property in the quest, whether there is attainment or not.

Sahaja Samadhi. Continuous samadhi not requiring trance or ecstasy but compatible with full use of the human faculties. The state of the Gnani.

Saivite. From the point of view of Siva. A devotee of Siva. The main division in Hinduism is between Saivism and Vaishnavism, the standpoints represented by Siva and Vishnu respectively. This corresponds to the difference between Advaita and Dvaita, since the devotees of Vishnu stop short at duality, while Saivism is the doctrine of non-duality. It also corresponds to the difference between Gnana-marga and Bhakti-marga, since the Advaitist proceeds by spiritual understanding and the Dvaitist by love and devotion to God.

These differences are not similar to those between Christian sects, since both paths are recognized as legitimate and a man follows whichever suits his temperament.

Sakti. The Force, Energy or Activity of a Divine Aspect or Principal. In Hindu mythology a Divine Aspect or Principle is represented as a God and its Energy or Activity as the Wife of the God.

The form 'Shakti' is often used in transliteration.

Samadhi. (1) Absorption in the Spirit or Self, with or without trance and suspension of the human faculties.

(2) The tomb of a Saint. Sometimes any tomb is so described.

(3) A euphemism for death. Instead of saying that someone died it is customary to say that he attained samadhi.

Samatva. The practice of treating all equally, with like consideration, seeing all alike as manifestations of the Spirit.

Sambhu. A name of Siva; Siva as the Bounteous.

Samsara. The endless chain of births and deaths to be broken only by Self-realization. Human life. The cares and burdens of life. Commonly used in Tamil to mean 'wife'.

Sankalpas. Inherent tendencies, desires and ambitions.

Sanyasin. One who has renounced home, property, caste and all human attachments in the spiritual quest. The renunciation is permanent and definitive, whereas a sadhu is free to return to family life. A sanyasin wears the ochre robe as a badge of renunciation, whereas a sadhu wears a white dhoti.

Sari. The normal attire of women in most parts of India. The lower half is wound round the body like a skirt and the upper half taken up and draped over the left shoulder.

Sarvardhikari. Master or ruler.

Sastraic. Based on or in accordance with the Sastras. The Sastras are scriptural rules governing conduct, art, science, government, etc.

Sat. Pure Being. (See Satchitananda).

Satchitananda. Literally Being-Consciousness-Bliss. A term for the Divine State, since spiritually to know is to be, and to know or be the Self is pure Bliss.

Sat-Guru. The Guru of Divine power as distinguished from guru in a more limited sense. . . .

Sometimes transliterated 'Sad-Guru' though the pronunciation is more 'Sat-Guru'.

Sattvic. The universe is brought into being and maintained in equilibrium by the combined action of the three gunas (stresses, tensions or tendencies), sattva, rajas and tamas. Tamas is the movement downwards from Spirit to matter, from Unity to multiplicity; rajas is the expansion outwards into activity and multiplicity; sattva is the ascent to the Spirit.

Cosmically, the gunas are neither good nor evil but simply the mechanism of manifestation; however, in a human being tamas is the tendency to evil, malice and ignorance; rajas is the tendency to outer activity; sattva is the tendency to spirituality, involving freedom from worldly passions and attachments. 'Sattvic' and 'unsattvic' are English adjectival forms used respectively of anything that aids or impedes spiritual effort.

Sattya-Yuga. The golden age. (See Yuga.)

Shahada. (Arabic.) The Islamic creed: La ilaha ill' Allah, 'there is no god but God'.

Siddha. This may mean one who has attained Self-realization but is commonly used to mean one who has supernatural powers whether or not he has spiritual attainment.

Siddha Purusha. A Sage (embodied or disembodied) possessing supernatural powers.

Siddhi. Supernatural powers.

Siva. In the simple theoretical sense Siva may be regarded (see under Brahma) as an aspect of Iswara (the Personal God). However, to his devotees Siva is the Destroyer of the prison walls in which the Spirit in man is held, the Destroyer of the ego, of the duality of man and Iswara, of all limitations, leaving only Absolute Being, which is perfect Knowledge and pure Bliss. Therefore Siva is the Absolute personified, containing Iswara and all the gods and worlds as a dream within himself.

Sivaswarupa. The form of Siva; a name sometimes given to the universe to indicate that it has no intrinsic reality but exists only as a form assumed by Siva.

Sri. Blessed or beatific. In modern times it is often used as a form of address, almost equivalent to 'Mr.'; however, it is still applied in its true sense to a Saint.

Sruti. Scriptural text.

Suddha Manas. Purified, sattvic mind.

Swami. Lord. It is used to mean 'the Lord' in speaking of God; also for a spiritual master or teacher whether or not he has attained any higher state; sometimes also as a mere sign of respect.

Swarupa. One's true form.

Taluq. (Urdu.) A local governmental district.

Tao. In Chinese teaching 'Tao' is used both for the path (sadhana) and the Goal, that is the Self or Absolute (Atma).

Tapas. Penance or austerity. . . .

Tirtha. Sacred tank.

Unsattvic. See sattvic.

Upadesa. The instruction or guidance given to a disciple by his Guru.

Vairagya. Dispassion, detachment.

Vasanas. Latencies or tendencies inherent in a man, resulting from his actions in a previous life and governing those in this life unless overcome by tapas or by the Grace of his Guru.

Vedas. The earliest Hindu scriptures, revealed to the ancient Rishis.

Vichara. Discrimination. The path of Self-enquiry taught by Sri Bhagavan, since this path implies discrimination between the Real and the unreal, the Self and the ego.

Vignana. Specialized knowledge. Knowledge of the Self and also of the outer world.

Vishnu. God in His Aspect of Preserver and Sustainer of the universe.

Yoga. Literally 'Union'. An indirect approach (see Marga) which starts from the standpoint of duality and seeks to develop a man's latent powers by very technical means, with the final object of attaining Divine Union.

Yogi. One who follows or has mastered the path of yoga.

Yuga. Age. According to Hindu, as to Graeco-Roman and Mediaeval, teaching there are four ages in the manvantara or cycle from the 'Earthly Paradise' of Adam before the fall to the 'Heavenly Jerusalem' or consummation after the tenth Avatar (see Avatar). They are called the Sattya Yuga (Age of Truth or Purity), Dwapara Yuga (Second Age), Tretya Yuga (Third Age) and Kali Yuga (Dark Age). Their duration is said to be in the proportion of 4, 3, 2, 1, so that the Kali Yuga is one-tenth of the entire manvantara.

NOTES

[1] This house has now been acquired by the Ashram. Daily *puja* (ritualistic worship) is performed there and it is kept open as a place of pilgrimage for devotees.

[2] This is the house in which Sri Bhagavan attained realization. It has been acquired by the Ashram and a portrait of Sri Bhagavan installed there. It is kept as a place of pilgrimage for devotees.

[3] The monotone persisting through a Hindu piece of music, like the thread on which beads are strung, represents the Self persisting through all the forms of being.

[4] This and the other quotations from Paul Brunton given in this book are based on his *A Search in Secret India*, published by Rider & Co., London, and reproduced by the Ashram with his permission.

[5] The great temple at Madura.

[6] Iswara, the Supreme Being, corresponds to the Western conception of a Personal God.

[7] Brahman is the Impersonal Reality underlying Personal God, universe and man.

⁸ Samsara is the succession of births and deaths terminated only by the Liberation of Self-realization.

T. M. P. Mahadevan (essay date 1977)

SOURCE: *Ramana Maharshi: The Sage of Arunacala,* George Allen & Unwin Ltd., 1977, pp. 81-116.

[*In the following essay, Mahadevan explains the origins and meanings of many of Ramana Maharshi's poems, hymns, and philosophical teachings.*]

SELF-ENQUIRY
(*VICARA-SANGRAHAM*)

This work which is in Tamil prose consists of forty questions with the answers, covering the entire range of disciplines required for gaining the spiritual goal of Self-realisation. About the year 1900, there was a municipal overseer at Tiruvannamalai, Gambhiram Seshayya by name, who was an ardent devotee of God in the form of Rama, and also a student of yoga-practice. He used to read the lectures of Svami Vivekananda that had just then been published, as also some classical texts on *Yoga.* While reading these books some doubts would arise in his mind and he found some difficulties in understanding it all. From time to time, he used to climb the hill and approach Sri Ramana who was then living in a cave, for the purpose of getting his doubts and difficulties resolved. As Sri Ramana was not talking then, not because of any vow taken but because he was not inclined to talk, he wrote out his answers on bits of paper. These writings over the period 1900-2 were later copied into a notebook by Seshayya. The material thus gathered came to be published as **Vicara-sangraham** which literally means *A Compendium of Self-enquiry*

A study of the instructions given in the answers reveals that they are based on Sri Ramana's own plenary experience as confirmed by the sacred texts which were brought to his notice by the early devotees and which he read in order to clear the doubts that arose in their minds. In the course of his instructions he employs such expressions as 'the scriptures declare', 'thus say the sages' and so on; he also cites passages from texts like the *Bhagavad-gita* and the *Viveka-cudamani,* and once mentions by name the *Ribhu-gita.* But it is quite clear that these citations are offered only to confirm the truth discovered by Sri Ramana himself in his own experience.

The basic teaching offered in his work, as in all the others, is that of Advaita-Vedanta. The plenary experience of the non-dual Self is the goal; enquiry into the nature of the Self is the means. When the mind identifies the Self with the not-self (the body, etc.), there is bondage; when this wrong identification is removed through the enquiry 'Who am I?' there is release. Thus, Self-enquiry is the direct path taught by Sri Ramana. The 'I'-experience is common to all. Of all thoughts, that of the 'I' is the first to arise. What one has to do

is to enquire into the source of the 'I'-thought. This is the reverse process of what ordinarily happens in the life of the mind. The mind enquires into the constitution and source of everything else which, on examination, will be found to be its own projection; it does not reflect on and trace itself to its source. Self-discovery can be achieved by giving the mind an inward turn. This is not to be confused with the introspection of which psychologists speak. Self-enquiry is not the mind's inspection of its own contents, but tracing its first mode, the 'I'-thought, to its source which is the Self. When there is proper and persistent enquiry, this 'I'-thought also ceases and there is the wordless illumination of the form 'I'-'I' which is the pure consciousness. This is release, freedom from bondage. The method by which this is accomplished, as has been shown, is enquiry which, in Vedanta, is termed *jnana,* knowledge. True devotion (*bhakti*), meditation (*dhyana*), and concentration (*yoga*) are identical therewith. As Sri Ramana makes it perfectly clear, not to forget the plenary Self-experience is real devotion, mind-control, knowledge and all other austerities. In the language of devotion, the final goal may be described as the resolution of the mind in its source which is God, the Self; in that of technical *yoga,* it may be described as the dissolution of the mind in the Heart-lotus. These are only different ways of expressing the same truth.

The path of Self-enquiry is found difficult by those who have not acquired the necessary competence for it. The mind should first be rendered pure and one-pointed. This is done through meditation, etc. So the various paths, in their secondary sense, are auxiliaries to the direct path which is Self-enquiry. In this context, Sri Ramana refers to three grades of aspirants, the highest, the medium and the lowest. For the highest type, the path prescribed is Vedanta enquiry; through it, the mind becomes quiescent in the Self and finally ceases to be, leaving the pure Self-experience untarnished and resplendent. The path for the medium type is meditation on the Self and consists in directing a continuous flow of the mind towards the same object. There are several modes, the best being that which has the form 'I am the Self', and it eventually culminates in Self-realisation. For the lowest grade of aspirants, the discipline that is useful is breath-control which in turn results in control of the mind.

Sri Ramana explains the difference between the paths of knowledge (*jnana-yoga*) and meditation (*dhyana-yoga*) thus: *inana* is like subduing a self-willed bull by coaxing it with a sheaf of green grass, while *dhyana* is like controlling it by using force. Just as there are eight limbs for *dhyana-yoga,* there are eight for *jnana-yoga.* The limbs of the latter are closer to the final stage. For instance, while the *pranayama* of technical yoga consists in regulating and restraining breath, that of *jnana-yoga* relates to rejecting the world of name-and-form which is not real, and realising the Real which is Existence-Consciousness-Bliss.

Realisation of the Self can be gained in this life, for it is not something which is to be gained afresh. We are already the Self, it alone is. It is ignorance that makes us imagine that we have not realised it. When this ignorance is removed through Self-knowledge, we realise our eternal Self-nature. One who has gained this realisation is called a *jivan-mukta* (liberated while living). To others, he may appear to continue to tenant a body. For the benefit of those others it is stated that the body will continue so long as the residue of the *prarabdha-karma* (that *karma* of the past which has begun to fructify in the shape of the present body) lasts, and that when the momentum is spent it will fall and the *jivan-mukta* will become a *videha-mukta* (liberated from the body). But from the standpoint of the absolute truth, there is no difference in liberation. What needs to be understood is that *mukti* or release is the inalienable nature of the Self.

Thus, in the Self-enquiry we have the quintessence of Advaita-Vedanta taught by Sri Ramana as early as in the years 1900-2.

WHO AM I?
(*NAN YAR?*)

Like the **Self-enquiry,** this is also in the form of questions and answers. The questions were put to Sri Ramana by one M. Sivaprakasam Pillai.[1] He was a graduate in philosophy employed in the Revenue Department of the South Arcot Collectorate. During his official visit to Tiruvannamalai in 1902, he went to the cave where Sri Ramana was then living, and met him. Pillai sought from the Master spiritual guidance, and solicited answers to questions relating to Self-enquiry. The Master answered the questions put to him by gestures, and when the teaching was not understood he wrote the replies on the floor or on a slate. As recollected and recorded by Sivaprakasam Pillai, there were fourteen questions with answers given by Sri Ramana. This record was first published by himself, stating how the Master's grace operated in his case by dispelling his doubts and by saving him from a crisis in life. **Who am I?** has been published several times subsequently. We find thirty questions with answers in some editions and twenty-eight in others.

Along with **Self-enquiry, Who am I?** constitutes the first set of instructions in the Master's own words, and are the only pieces of prose among his works. They set forth clearly the central teaching that the direct path to liberation is Self-enquiry. The particular mode in which the enquiry is to be made is described lucidly in **Who am I?** The mind consists of thoughts, and the 'I' thought is the first to arise in it. When the enquiry 'Who am I?' is persistently pursued, all other thoughts are destroyed and finally the 'I' thought itself vanishes leaving the supreme non-dual Self alone. The false identification of the Self with the phenomena of non-self such as the body and the mind thus ends, and there is illumination. The process of enquiry, of course, is not an easy one. As one enquires 'Who am I?', other

thoughts will arise; but as these arise, one should not yield by following them, but ask 'To whom do they arise?' In order to do this, one has to be vigilant. Through constant enquiry one should make the mind stay in its source, without allowing it to wander away and get lost in the mazes of thought created by itself. All other disciplines such as breath-control and meditation on the forms of God should be regarded as auxiliary practices. They are useful in so far as they help the mind to become quiescent and one-pointed. For the mind that has gained skill in concentration, Self-enquiry becomes comparatively easy. It is by ceaseless enquiry that the thoughts are destroyed and the Self realised—the plenary Reality in which there is not even the 'I' thought, the experience which is referred to as 'Silence'.

A BUNCH OF INSTRUCTIONS
(*UPADESA-MANJARI*)

This is an anthology of questions and answers collected and arranged topically by an early devotee, Natanananda. The topics cover the entire range of Vedantic teaching, with emphasis on the practical disciplines. There are seventy questions, with Sri Ramana's answers. It is interesting to note that some of the questions are about the same length as or even longer than the answers. For instance:

Question: What is the reason for some great ones gaining knowledge without the guidance of a preceptor?

Reply: To a few mature persons the Lord reveals the truth, remaining within as the light of knowledge.

Question: Is it possible for all to know directly, without room for the least doubt, what the exact nature of one's true Self is?

Reply: That it is possible, there is no need to doubt.

QUINTESSENCE OF THE TEACHING
(*UPADESA-UNDIYAR, UPADESA-SARAM*)

This is a compendium of the teaching of Vedanta. The circumstance that led to its being written is the following:

Muruganar, an ardent devotee and eminent Tamil poet, put into verse the legendary story of how the ritualists of the Daruka-forest received instruction from the Lord Siva. They were believers in the independent efficacy of ritual in gaining for man the ends he desires. Siva in the guise of a mendicant went to Daruka. He was so resplendently handsome that the wives of the ritualists were attracted to him against their will. The ritualists were angry. But they soon fell in the same way when later the Lord Visnu, the aspect of Godhead responsible for protecting the world, came in the guise of an entrancingly beautiful woman. The ritualists thought that the mendicant was at the bottom of all this mischief. They performed sacrifices to destroy Siva, but found that they could not harm him. In the end they realised their mistake and discovered the identity of their saviour, Visnu. At this stage Muruganar felt unable to put into verse the teaching of Siva to the ritualists and implored Sri Ramana to do so for him. In response, the Master composed thirty verses setting forth the truth of Vedanta and the path that leads to the realisation of the truth. This poem is known as **Upadesa-vundiyar.** Sri Ramana later translated it into Sanskrit, Telugu, and Malayalam verse, with the title **Upadesa-saram.**

In the thirty couplets that constitute the **Upadesa-saram,** Sri Ramana gives the quintessence of Vedanta. The unique value of his teaching is that it was not the result of a formal study of the texts; it came out of his direct Self-experience, thus providing an independent contemporary confirmation of the plenary Vedantic truth. The poem opens with a criticism of the view that *karma,* the stock of one's past deeds, is all, and that there is no need to postulate a God behind the scene.

(1) How can *karma* which is inert yield any fruit of its own accord? It is by the command of God that *karma* functions and leads to its appropriate reward.

(2) If actions are performed for selfish ends, then they bring in those ends as commanded by God. Such actions, however, keep the soul in bondage which continues to wallow in transmigration.

(3) But if one's duties are done in a spirit of dedication to God, and without any selfish desire, they will purify one's mind and pave the way for release. The technique of unselfish dedicated action is called *karma-yoga.*

(4) Action is three-fold: pertaining to the body, speech, and mind. Worship *(puja)* is an act done with the body; muttering the sacred name *(japa)* is an act of speech, and meditation *(cintana)* of the mind. Of these, each succeeding act is superior to the preceding one, as it is subtler and takes one nearer the final goal.

(5) The highest form of worship is to serve the world in its eight modes (the five elements, the sun, the moon, and the souls) as an expression of God.

(6) *Mantra* repetition has three modes, repeating the *mantra* in a low tone is better than uttering it aloud, while the best mode is silent, mental *japa.*

(7) Meditation is directing a continuous flow of thought towards the Supreme and it is better to do so uninterruptedly like the flow of oil or of a river.

(8) One may meditate on God, imagining that he is different, an Other, but superior to this is the meditation which does not involve difference.

(9) When there is contemplation of the non-dual Self, then all thoughts vanish, and one is established in that supreme Reality. This is the highest devotion *(bhakti).*

(10) The culmination of the disciplines of *karma, bhakti, yoga,* and *jnana* is reached when the mind is made to rest in the Heart. It is thus that the mind becomes non-mind and the Self is realised.

(11) How is this to be accomplished? The control of breath is the first step. As one catches birds with nets, so one can restrain the mind by controlling the breath.

(12) The mind and breath spring from the same source. They rise in Heart which is the seat of the self-luminous Self, and they function as based thereon.

(13) And so, it is possible to control the mind through the breath. But control is not the same as destruction. The mind should not only be controlled, but also destroyed.

(14) This latter objective is gained by meditating on the One, Non-dual Reality.

(15) The supreme *yogi* is he whose mind has been destroyed. He rests in the Self and for him there is no *karma.*

(16) When the mind has been turned back from the objects of sense, and when it beholds the Self, it realises the Truth.

(17) The direct path to the supreme goal is the path of Self-enquiry. Let one enquire: what is this thing called mind? What is its nature? Such an enquiry will reveal that there is no such thing.

(18) 'Mind' is but a name for thoughts. Of all thoughts, that of 'I' is the support. Therefore, what is called 'mind' is truly the thought 'I'.

(19) One should enquire whence the 'I' thought arises, and then the 'I' vanishes.

(20) Where the 'I' thought has vanished, there the true Self shines as 'I', 'I' in the Heart.

(21) The 'I' thought, the pseudo-'I' is inconstant but the real 'I' is always there, it is eternal. In sleep, for instance, where thoughts are not, the 'I' stands as the witness, it never loses its reality.

(22) The physical body, the sense-organs, the vital principle, the mind, nescience—these are inert and inconstant. They are not 'I', these are unreal.

(23) The 'I', the Self, alone is real. As there is no other consciousness to know it, it is consciousness. The 'I' is consciousness.

(24) The distinction of 'God' and 'soul' is not real. They are but masks projected by ignorance. The pure Self is non-dual.

(25) When the masks are removed, there is Self-knowledge which is the knowledge of God.

(26) To know the Self is to be the Self, because

there are not two Selves. Here, knowing is being. Consciousness is existence.

(27) When the mental modes have been destroyed and nescience has been removed, the Self shines alone. With reference to it, both mental knowledge and ignorance have no meaning. There is no knower apart from it.

(28) When the Self is realised, it is that which has no decay and no thought, and which is the plenary consciousness and bliss.

(29) One who has the requisite divine heritage gains, while yet living, the supreme Reality which is beyond bondage and release, which is the final Beatitude, the plenary Bliss.

(30) This is the teaching of Sri Ramana—the teaching which shows the path to Self-realisation through the destruction of the pseudo-'I'. To follow it is the greatest of austerities—the enquiry that leads to wisdom.

FORTY VERSES ON EXISTENCE
(ULLADU-NARPADU)

This is a poem of forty verses on the nature of Existence. The Tamil *ulladu,* like the Sanskrit *sat,* means what exists, or existence and reality which are the same in Vedanta. When the Vedanta speaks of existence as reality, it does not mean brute existence, but one that is consciousness and bliss. It is this existence-consciousness-bliss *(sat-cit-ananda)* that is the non-dual Absolute, the one without a second. All distinctions such as 'I' and 'thou' are but appearance. The Self alone is.

Sri Ramana's **Ulladu-narpadu** is an authentic exposition of the Advaita-experience. In the form of these forty verses, the Sage of Arunacala transmits to us the plenary experience of Advaita.

The manner in which this work assumed its final shape has been explained by the Master himself:

'It was some time in 1928. Muruganar (an ardent devotee and Tamil poet) said, one day, that some odd verses composed by me now and then on various occasions should not be allowed to lapse, but should be collected together and some more added to bring the total to forty, and so make a book with an appropriate title. He accordingly gathered about thirty odd verses and asked me to compose ten more. In accordance with his wish, I wrote some more verses on different occasions, and as the mood came upon me. When the number totalled forty, Muruganar deleted one after another of the old collection on the ground that they were not quite germane to the subject or otherwise not quite suitable, and then requested me to make up the number. When this process was completed and there were forty verses, it was found that only two of the original collection had been included. So, the forty

verses were not made according to any set scheme, nor at a stretch, nor systematically. I composed different verses on different occasions, and Muruganar and others arranged them afterwards in some order according to the thoughts expressed in them to give a semblance of connected and systematic treatment of the subject, Reality.'

There was now the problem of what to do with the rejected verses, of which there were no less than forty. So, Sri Ramana had to write a few more, some being Tamil translations from other sources such as the *Yoga-vasistha.* The supplementary forty verses came thus to be added to the forty on **Existence.**

FIVE VERSES ON THE ONE SELF
(EKATMA-PANCAKAM)

This short poem had for its theme the One Self. Sri Ramana composed it in 1947—originally in Telugu, but set to a Tamil metre and later translated it into Tamil. It is well known that Sankara, the great consolidator of Advaita, besides writing extensive commentaries, had expounded the truth in single verses, in pentads, in decads, etc. Sri Ramana in only five verses teaches here lucidly the truth on non-duality.

(1) The Self is the only reality and the body is not real. On account of ignorance, one identifies oneself with the body and imagines that one is reborn and dies repeatedly. But when one realises the non-dual Self, one shakes off ignorance which is the root of evil. This is like waking up from a wandering dream.

(2) While being the Self, we ask 'Who am I? Who am I?', not knowing that we are that Self. This is just like a drunken man enquiring about who and where he is.

(3) Which is correct: the Self is in the body, or the body is in the Self? Certainly, the latter. The Self is all-inclusive and transcendent. To reverse the order and speak of the Self as being in the body is like saying that the canvas on which a picture is painted is contained in the picture.

(4) As the ornament is not apart from the gold, the body is not apart from the Self. The ignorant ones mistake the body for the Self; the sage knows that the Self alone is real.

(5) What exists always is that One Self alone. If the First Teacher, Daksinamurti, taught in silence the nature of that Reality, who can expound it in words?

Writing about the grandeur of this hymn Muruganar says: 'In these five verses, which Guru Ramana has sung, he who is of the nature of the One Self that is wisdom, has enabled devotees to realise the truth of the One Self and has destroyed their sense of identification of the body with the Self.'

FIVE HYMNS TO ARUNACALA
(*ARUNACALA-PANCAKAM*)

If Sri Ramana was attached to anything, it was to the holy hill, Arunacala, which to him was God Himself, the visible expression of the supreme Self. He used to say that it was 'the top of the spiritual axis of the earth; there must', he said, 'be another mountain corresponding to Arunacala exactly at the opposite side of the globe, the corresponding pole of the axis'.[2] He also stated that the hill with its caves and hollows is all light. Sages and Gods reside there and it is even Siva Himself. Although from the standpoint of the absolute Reality—the non-dual Self—there is no hill, no hollow, no one residing there, the analogy is meaningful. Concluding his explanation of the significance of the holy hill, the Master once said: 'Everything is within one's Self. To see the world, there must be a spectator. There could be no world without the Self, which is all-comprising. In fact the Self is all, there is nothing besides it.'[3]

Sri Ramana has sung the praise of Arunacala in **Five Hymns** to help the aspirants who are devotionally inclined. It is to be noted that even in these hymns it is the truth of non-duality that is presented as the goal.

A Muslim professor from the north once asked:

'I have been reading the **Five Hymns.** I find that they are addressed to Arunacala by you. You are an Advaitin. How do you then address God as a separate Being?'

Master: 'The devotee, God and the Hymns are all the Self.'

Professor: 'But you are addressing God. You are specifying this Arunacala Hill as God.'

Master: 'You can identify the Self with the body. Should not the devotee identify the Self with Arunacala?'[4]

The **Five Hymns** are inspired lyrical poems. They were composed on separate occasions and under different circumstances:

(1) *THE MARITAL GARLAND OF LETTERS FOR ARUNACALA*
(*ARUNACALA-AKSARA-MANA-MALAI*)

This was the first of the **Five Hymns** composed by Sri Ramana. While the sage was living on the hill at Virupaksa cave, the devotees asked him to compose a song which they could sing while they begged for food in the town. He did not agree, saying that there were many extant songs sung by the Saiva saints which would serve the purpose. Subsequently, however, when the Master was walking round the hill, with the devotees, the litany *Arunacala-aksara-mana-malai* welled forth from his heart, spontaneously and divinely inspired. He himself said that the poem was not the result of any premeditation or conscious thought, but that it came out of his heart unexpectedly and spontaneously.

The title of this hymn, *Arunacala-aksara-mana-malai,* means 'The marital garland of letters for Arunacala'. *Mana-malai,* in Tamil, means the wedding-garland which symbolises the union of the bride with the groom. It may also be taken to mean 'sweet-scented garland'. The poem is called *aksara-malai* (garland of letters) because the initial letters of its verses are in alphabetical order. The word *aksara* means letter and also the immutable Self. If it is understood in the latter sense, the title of the hymn would mean 'The garland that serves as the insignia of marriage with the immutable Lord'. The title also contains the name of the sage if the two middle words are split as *aksa-ramana.* There are 108 verses— a number that is held to be sacred.

From these verses it becomes evident that, according to Sri Ramana, the goal of bridal mysticism is the experience of non-duality. In this form of mysticism the devotee considers himself to be the bride of God. He employs the intimate language of love in conversing with his Lord. All the processes connected with carnal love take place between the devotee-soul and the bridegroom, except the carnality. The devotee pines for, cringes, cajoles, chides and quarrels with the beloved. There are courtship, union, separation and reunion. In this phase of mysticism the devotee revels in love-play with the Divine. It culminates, however, in the realisation of non-duality. Love cannot be fulfilled so long as the dualistic consciousness lasts. Where there are two, there is no true love, for love is one. Where duality is, there is fear, which is the antithesis of love. It is when the truth of non-duality is realised that there is unmixed love, plenary happiness, complete fearlessness. This is clearly taught in Sri Ramana's love-litany. Even in the first verse of the hymn he speaks of the 'I-am-Arunacala' experience. When love matures and realises itself, there is nothing but Arunacala, the supreme Self. Arunacala is all; all is Arunacala.

That non-duality is the purport of this hymn is evident, and is expressly so stated in several of the verses, two of which may be cited in translation:

> (92) O Arunacala! Making me the target, Thou hast released the weapon of grace at me, and hast devoured me alive.

> (99) O Arunacala! Grant me graciously the essential truth of the Veda which shines in the Vedanta as Reality with no distinctions.

The refrain of this most moving poem which is recited after each verse is:

> arunacala-siva arunacala-siva
> arunacala-siva arunacala,
> arunacala-siva arunacala-siva
> arunacala-siva arunacala

Arunacala-siva is the *mantra,* the sacred formula, the holy utterance. 'Siva' is the most auspicious name of God, for it means 'The Auspicious'. Siva, the formless, appears in many forms in order to bestow His grace on the devotees. At Tiruvannamalai, the form that He has assumed is *Arunacala* which is Light and Fire—the Light that reveals the truth, the Fire that burns away all impurities, all ignorance and its brood.

(2) *THE NECKLET OF NINE GEMS FOR ARUNACALA (ARUNACALA-NAVA-MANI-MALAI)*

This is a hymn of nine verses in Tamil set in different metres. The theme is devotion for Arunacala, the un-moving radiant Self, which leads the devotee to the final liberation through developing detachment, inner purification, and the dawn of wisdom.

In the second verse, the significance of the three syllables in the name *Aruna* is explained. *A-ru-na* stands for existence-consciousness-bliss *(sat-cit-ananda)* which is the non-dual *Brahman,* the supreme Self. It also signifies the supreme Self, the individual soul, and their non-duality as the absolute Spirit—the truth which is taught in the Upanisadic text *tat-tvam-asi* (That thou art). *Arunacala* is a compound word: *aruna+acala.* Having explained the meaning of *a-ru-na,* Sri Ramana points out that *acala* signifies 'perfection'. The very thought of Arunacala has the power to liberate the devotee from bondage.

In the last two verses, there are references to the nativity of Sri Ramana and to the manner in which he was saved by Arunacala. 'Born of the pious couple, Sundara and Alagu (names which both mean "Beauty") in the sacred place, Tirucculi,' says Sri Ramana, 'the Lord of the Earth (Bhuminatha, one of Siva's names) rescued me from the misery of earthly life and raised me to His State of eternal perfection. It is the same Lord, as Arunacala, that drew me to Himself, preventing me from falling into the deep sea of delusion.'

(3) *THE ELEVEN VERSES ON ARUNACALA (ARUNACALA-PADIGAM)*

This hymn and the next one, *The Eight Verses,* were not written at the request of anyone. As Sri Ramana himself said:

'The only poems that came to me spontaneously and compelled me, as it were, to compose them, without anyone urging me to do so, are the **Eight Verses on Arunacala** and the **Eleven Verses on Arunacala.** The opening words of the **Eleven Verses** suddenly came to me one morning, and even if I tried to suppress them, saying: "What have I to do with these words?" they would not be suppressed until I had composed a song beginning with them, and all the words flowed easily without any effort. The second stanza was composed in the same way on the next day and the remainder successively one each day except for the tenth and eleventh which came together. The next day I started to go round the hill. Palanisvami was walking behind me, but after we had gone some way Ayyasvami seems to have called him back and given him a pencil and paper saying: "For some days now Svami has been composing poems every day. He may do so today as well, so you had better take this paper and pencil with you." That day, before I returned to Skandasramam, I wrote six of the eight stanzas in the *Astakam.* Either that evening or the next day Narayana Reddi came. He was at that time living in Vellore as an agent of Singer & Co., and he used to come from time to time. Ayyasvami and Palani told him about the poems and he said: "Give them to me at once and I will go and print them." He had already published some books about me. When he insisted on taking the poems, I told him that he could do so and could publish the first eleven as *padi-gam* and the rest, which were in a different metre, as *astakam.* To make up the *astakam* I at once composed two more stanzas and he took all the nineteen with him to get them published.'[5]

The eleven verses are now in what is called *antadi,* in which each subsequent verse begins with the last words of the previous one. For instance, the eighth verse ends with the word *parane* (O the Supreme One!); the ninth begins with *parama,* which is the same word.

Some of the terms by which the Lord Arunacala is addressed in this poem are: Love in the shape of the Hill; the Sun of Suns; Form of Grace; Ocean of Grace; Blazing Pillar of Light; Expanse of Grace; the Pure One; Transcendent Self taking the form of Arunacala; Arunacala, the Supreme Itself; the Lodestone of Lives; the magnificent Arunacala that shines within the Heart. From these expressions it is clear that for Sri Ramana, Arunacala is the non-dual Self, Reality which is one only, without a second.

In the last verse, Sri Ramana recalls how Arunacala had rescued him while he was yet a boy, and recommends like-minded people to surrender to the Supreme Lord:

'How many there may be who, like me, got lost considering this Hill as Supreme! Whose of you who, wishing to give up attachment to this life because of the misery it spreads, wander about thinking of a device to give up this body! Know that this Hill is, in this world, a precious medicine which, if you contemplate it, kills you without killing.'

(4) *THE EIGHT VERSES ON ARUNACALA (ARUNACALA-ASTAKAM)*

This poem too is an *antadi.* In its eight verses, the truth of Advaita is set forth clearly in the guise of devotional adoration of Arunacala. The Hill is a representation of the South-facing Siva, Dassinamurti, who imparts wisdom through silence. Without movement and speech, it absorbs the individual soul into itself. No one can say: 'I see it' or 'I do not see it', for where is the seer apart from it? Formlessness is its form. To search for a glimpse of it is like travelling throughout the earth for tracing out and looking at space. The soul's attempt to know the Absolute, Arunacala, only ends in its own dissolution, like the fate of a doll made of sugar when it enters the sea of sugar-cane juice. Arunacala is *Brahman* which is of the nature of consciousness-bliss. To look for a God other than this is like going with a lamp to look for darkness. There is nothing other than Arunacala; the soul is not different from it. Arunacala reveals the soul's nature as the non-dual consciousness-bliss. After a film has been exposed to the sun, it cannot receive any impressions or images. When there is the blazing Aruna Hill, how can there be anything apart from it? In the boundless ocean of Grace and Effulgence that is Arunacala, there are no dualities, no change or mutation. That is the origin and end of all phenomena. That is the destiny and the final goal of the soul.

(5) *FIVE VERSES ON ARUNACALA (ARUNACALA-PANCARATNAM)*

This is the only one of the five hymns to Arunacala to be written by Sri Ramana in Sanskrit. Kavyakantha Ganapati Sastri, the great scholar and devotee, requested Sri Ramana one day in 1917 to compose a poem in Sanskrit. Ramana replied with a smile that he knew little Sanskrit and less of its prosody. But the Kavyakantha was not willing to leave the matter there. He explained to the sage the technique of one of the Sanskrit metres called *arya,* and repeated his request. That evening, the poem was ready for him in exquisite Sanskrit, expressing in five short verses addressed to Arunacala the entire teaching of Vedanta.

This hymn consists of five gem-like verses on Arunacala; hence the name **Arunacala-pancaratnam.** In the first two verses the nature of Reality is shown from two levels, *svarupa* (essential) and *tatastha* (accidental). In the remaining three verses the paths to perfection are sketched in outline. Thus, in this short poem, Ramana has given us the quintessence of Vedanta, as also the distinctive points of emphasis that are to be found in his teachings. It was translated into Tamil by Ramana himself for the benefit of Tamil-knowing aspirants. This was done in 1922 in response to a request from a devotee who wanted to add it to the four other poems in Tamil on Arunacala written by the sage, and to publish the collection under the title **Arunacala-pancakam.**

In the first two verses of the **Arunacala-pancaratnam,** as we have said, the nature of Reality is indicated. The Upanisads describe this nature in two ways; in itself Reality is existence-consciousness-bliss *(sat-cit-ananda)* yet its accidental qualification is the causality of the world. The former definition is of the essential nature of *Brahman,* and the latter is its definition *per accidens.* The Real in itself is attributeless *(nirguna)* and unconditioned *(nirupadhika).* On account of *maya,* it appears as the cause of the world. In the first verse, Ramana refers to Arunacala, the Supreme Self *(paramat-man),* that is unconditioned and unqualified existence-consciousness-bliss. It is supernal light and the ocean of bliss. In it there is no plurality, no world. In the second

verse, Arunacala is described as the world-ground, as God who is the source and the goal of the universe. Creation, however, is not real, it is an illusory appearance. This is the implication of the picture-analogy. As Ramana himself once explained to an inmate of Ramanasramam, 'the universe is like a painting on a screen—the screen being the Red Hill, Arunacala. This which rises and sinks is made up of what it rises from. The finality of the universe is the God Arunacala.' Thus, the world is an appearance *(vivarta)* of Arunacala-Brahman; it has no reality in itself. For the purpose of meditation on Arunacala, a location is assigned in the body—that of the 'heart', not the physical one which is in the left side of the chest, but the spiritual heart which is in the right side. Arunacala itself may be referred to as the 'Heart', since it is the centre and core of all things.

In the third verse, the sage teaches the path of Self-enquiry. This is the same as *jnana-marga* (the path of knowledge). According to Advaita-Vedanta, knowledge is the direct means to release. *Moksa* (release) is not something to be newly accomplished. It is the eternal nature of the Self. On account of ignorance *(avidya)* it remains unrecognised. What will make us recognise it is the true knowledge of the Self. Ramana's formulation of the path of knowledge is well known. It takes the form of the enquiry: 'Who am I?' Although all can take this path to gain sure and quick success they must possess a pure and one-pointed mind. The aids that make the mind fit to pursue the path of enquiry are meditation *(dhyana),* devotion *(bhakti),* and action *(karma).* In the fourth and fifth verses, Ramana mentions those disciplines. Selfless service *(karma-yoga)* removes all impurities from the mind. Devotion to God *(bhakti-yoga)* and meditation *(dhyana-yoga)* impart one-pointedness to it. When the pure mind turns within and enquires into its source, it ceases in that source which is the supreme Self, Arunacala. This is the final goal of all spiritual discipline—the plenary experience which is existence-consciousness-bliss.

OCCASIONAL VERSES

Off and on, Sri Ramana used to embody in verse the teaching that he gave in response to requests from aspirants, or as prompted by certain occasions. In the early years, many of these were lost because there was no one to record them, but some of the later ones have been published. Here, we shall refer to two, in order to show that the one theme of even the occasional verses is Advaita, the truth of the Absolute Self.

(1) *THE SONG OF APPALAM (APPALAP-PATTU)*

Appalam is a thin round cake made of black gram flour, which is fried crisp before it is served as a meal. One day when the Master's mother, Alagammal, was making these delicate thin cakes at Skandasramam, she called her son to help. Sri Ramana did not respond to her call. Instead he composed a song, giving the recipe for making spiritual *appalam.*

'Do make *appalam,* and see—satisfy your desire by eating it.' This is the refrain of the song.

For making this *appalam,* one need not go hither and thither, gathering the necessary ingredients. One cannot find the recipe in cookery books. The instruction is to be found in the silent teaching of the Master conveying the truth: 'That thou art.' The principal ingredient is black gram. The black gram for the spiritual *appalam* is grown in the field which is the body-mind complex. The roller-mill in which the gram is to be broken and powdered is the enquiry: 'Who am I?' The flour is to be mixed with the juice of the vine called *pirandai.* Here, the juice is the company of the good. The spices that are to be added are mind-control and restraint of the senses. The paste is to be seasoned with the salt which is indifference to the world of phenomena. The dough is to be placed on the stone of mind and beaten with the heavy strokes of 'I-I', delivered with the pestle of a mind turned within. Then the cake is to be placed on the vessel of endless silence which is kept heated by the fire of knowledge. The melted butter used is the supreme Self *(Brahman).* The frying is in the form of 'I am that'. It is this *appalam* that Sri Ramana asks us to eat.

(2) *THE SCIENCE OF THE SELF (ANMA-VIDDAI)*

Once a devotee gave the Master a piece of paper on which he had written that Self-knowledge was the easiest thing, and asked the Master to write a poem having that as the theme. The present song was in response to that request.

'O Sir, very easy is the Science of the Self—indeed, very easy.'

This is the refrain of the song set, like the previous one, to a popular tune.

The sage teaches in this song that there is nothing more evident than the self-luminous Self. The example that is usually given for a thing that is clear, distinct, and certain is the myrobalan fruit held in the open palm. The Self is far clearer than this fruit. It shines as the Siva within the Heart. It is the all-pervading Reality. The false appearance of the body and the world veil the Self. As soon as the veil is lifted, it reveals itself. Then, the darkness disappears, all obstacles are removed, and unexcellable bliss is gained. The thought that 'I am the body' is the basic error wrought by ignorance. On it are strung all other thoughts. When, through the enquiry, 'Who am I?', the true 'I' is discovered as shining in the Heart, one reaches the goal which is the highest good. There is no point in knowing anything except the Self, for nothing other than it is real. When the Self is realised as oneself, as the nondual Reality in the so-called individual selves, then there is no more sorrow, no more travail, caused by the phenomenal world. The ego commits suicide in the Self; and there shines the One Self as the Bliss Supreme—the Transcendent Arunacala.

TRANSLATIONS AND SELECTIONS

Even as most of the original works we have considered were written by Sri Ramana in response to requests from aspirants, so also his translations were made in order to help seekers to understand the truth. It will be noted that many of the translations are of the works of Sankara, the great consolidator of Advaita. Since Sankara wrote in Sanskrit, most of the Tamil devotees found it difficult to understand them. Yet there could be no more authentic or lucid expositions of Advaita than his. Hence, when the devotees gave to their Master the texts with requests for explanation, he explained and sometimes translated them into Tamil.

(1) THE CREST-JEWEL OF WISDOM (*VIVEKACUDAMANI*)

While Sri Ramana was living in the Virupaksa cave, he was given the Vivekacudamani, a metrical manual of Advaita written by Sankara. The Master felt that a prose paraphrase of the manual in Tamil would be useful for a large number of aspirants, and so he wrote one himself.

The salient points are lucidly brought out in his Tamil introduction. There is the universal desire for happiness and for freedom from misery: 'Let my sorrow be removed; let me be happy': this is the wish of every one. The goal sought is the complete removal of sorrow and the gain of unexcellable bliss. An analysis of experience reveals that sorrow comes from the objects of sense, and that the seat and centre of happiness is the Self. In the absence of all objects in deep sleep, there is happiness. The soul does not know this, because it is in the grip of ignorance. It imagines that happiness comes from outside, and so is caught in the round of transmigration. It was to show the aspirant the right royal road to happiness that Sankara, who was an incarnation of the Lord Siva, wrote his commentaries on the *Upanisads,* the *Bhagavad-gita* and the *Brahma-sutra.* They are, however, difficult to understand as they presume, besides other qualifications, a high level of scholarship. So Sankara wrote independent manuals like the *Vivekacu-damani* for all those who are intent on reaching the goal which is release *(moksa).*

Sri Ramana, then, lists the various topics expounded in the manual, covering the entire range of Vedantic teaching. The work is in the form of a dialogue between preceptor and pupil.

The *Vivekacudamani* ends with this note: For those who are afflicted by wandering aimlessly on the burning desert sands of transmigration, it is the blessed and victorious voice of Sankara that brings the good tidings that the comforting ocean of nectar which is *Brahman* is within easy reach.

(2) THE DISCRIMINATION BETWEEN THE SEER AND THE SEEN (*DRG-DRSYA-VIVEKA*)

This too is a metrical work on Vedanta ascribed to Sankara. Here, the technique of enquiry explained is that of distinguishing the Self from the not-self, the subject from the object, the seer from the seen. The Self, however, is not an individual subject as against the objective world. The world of objects, including the body-mind complexes called individuals, is an illusory manifestation. The reality is the Self which is non-dual and may be referred to as the subject with a capital *S*.

Sri Ramana has translated the *Drg-drsya-viveka* into Tamil prose, with an introduction and an invocation to Sankara. In the introduction, the central question in Advaita is posed and answered. If *Brahman,* the supreme Self, alone is real, why is it not evident to us, and why does the non-real world appear? The answer is: it is *maya* or *avidya* (nescience) that is responsible for veiling the true and projecting the untrue. Just as a movie picture cannot be seen either in sunlight or in the dark, but only in a focus of light in the midst of darkness, so also in *Brahman* there is no world of phenomena, nor in the state of deep sleep. The world-play takes place when in nescience there is the reflected light of the Self taking the form of thought. The primal thought is the ego or the individual soul. Under the influence of ignorance, it is caught in the matrix of the world-show. When, through enquiry, this bewitchment is broken, the light of truth dawns, and there is liberation.

Sri Ramana's invocatory verse reads in translation: 'The divine Sankara, the Seer, who taught that the discrimination between the seer and the seen arises in the mind, destroying its perverse view of (the duality of) the seer and the seen, and shining as the Light which is the non-dual Siva.'

(3) SELF-KNOWLEDGE (*ATMA-BODHA*)

Atma-bodha is another work of Sankara's consisting of sixty-eight couplets in Sanskrit. In it the great Master expounds the truth of Vedanta in a lucid manner with the help of familiar and apt analogies. Analogies may not convince the adversary; but they are very useful in instructing the disciple. Among the Vedantic manuals, the *Atma-bodha* occupies a pre-eminent place.

Sri Ramana translated this manual into Tamil verse in what is known as *venba* metre, which he then changed into *kalivenba.*

How he happened to teach one of the basic tenets of Advaita by explaining one of the verses in the second stanza of *Atma-bodha,* was described by Sri Ramana in one of his letters:

> 'We all started to go to the summit of the Arunacala hill, with all necessary things for cooking and eating our food. By the time we reached the Edudonalu (Seven Ponds) it was rather hot. So, we bathed and then wanted to cook our food. We took out the utensils and the foodstuffs such as dhal, salt and ghee, built a fire and then found that we had not brought the most important thing of all, the matches. The cave was too far away to

go and fetch a box. Moreover it was very hot and everyone was terribly hungry. Some tried to make fire by striking two pieces of flint together, but without success. Some tried to rub one piece of wood against another as they do in *yajnas* to light the sacrificial fire, but that too was a failure. The second stanza in *Atma-bodha* came to my mind. 'I read it out, explained the meaning and kept them all in good humour. It means that just as you cannot cook whatever you may have unless you have fire, so too you cannot attain liberation *(moksa)* unless you have *jnana* (knowledge).'[6]

In a prefatory stanza added to the translation of the *Atma-bodha,* Sri Ramana says: 'Is the Teacher Sankara, who grants the knowledge of the Self, other than the Self? Remaining in my heart as the Self, he who repeats the Tamil today—who is he other than that one himself?'

(4) HYMN TO DAKSINAMURTI (*DAKSINAMURTI-STOTRAM*)

This is Sankara's hymn to the south-facing Siva, the first preceptor, who taught the truth of non-duality through silence. The Creator-God Brahma, one member of the Hindu Trinity, created first from his mind four sons to assist him in the task of creation. But those sons were intent on pursuing the path of renunciation and knowledge. They sought the presence of the south-facing deity, Lord Siva, who was seated beneath the scared banyan tree, and learned from Him the truth in silence. This is indicated by what is known as the *cin-mudra* (sign of knowledge), which is made by the thumb and the index finger touching each other, and represents the identity of the individual soul and the supreme Self.

For the benefit of those aspirants who cannot understand the language of silence, Sri Sankara composed the *Hymn* setting forth the plenary truth of Advaita. The substance of what is taught in it is that, when the truth is realised, the world, the observer and the observed are all dissolved, leaving only the non-dual Self which is Daksinamurti. The goal is the realisation of All-Selfhood *(sarvatmatva),* without the least trace of duality.

Sri Ramana once explained the purpose and the structure of Sankara's hymn thus:

> 'Silence is the true, the perfect instruction, but it is suited only for the most advanced seeker. The others are not able to draw full inspiration from it. They require words explaining the Truth, but the Truth is beyond words. It does not admit of explanation. All that can be done is to indicate it. How?
>
> People are under an illusion. If the spell is removed, they will realise the Truth. If they are told to realise the falsity of the illusion, they will try to escape its snares, and the spirit of detachment will result. People will enquire into the Truth and seek the Self. That will make them abide as the Self. Sri Sankara, being an incarnation of Siva, was full of compassion for fallen beings and wanted all of them to realise their blissful Self. Since he could not reach them all with his

silence, he composed the *Daksinamurti-stotra* in the form of a hymn so that people might read it and understand the Truth.

The first four stanzas deal with the world. It is shown to be the same as the Master whose Self is also that of the seeker, or as the Master to whom the seeker surrenders himself. The second four stanzas deal with the individual whose Self is shown to be that of the Master. The ninth stanza deals with Isvara (God) and the tenth with realisation *(siddhi)*.

Such is the scheme of the *Hymn to Daksinamurti.*[7]

Sri Ramana translated Sankara's hymn into Tamil verse adding an annotation and an invocatory verse, which reads: 'That Sankara who came as Daksinamurti to grant peace to the great ascetics, who revealed his true state of silence, and who has expounded the nature of the Self in this Hymn, abides in me.'

(5) A PRAYER TO THE GURU *(GURU-STUTI)*

Some accounts of the life of Sankara include the story of how the Master took over the body of a dead king and lived in his palace for a while. Before leaving his own body in the care of his disciples, he asked them, if necessary, to go to the place and remind him that it was time to return. As anticipated by the Master this actually happened. The disciples went to the palace, and sang a song embodying the truth of non-duality. When Sankara heard this, it is said that he left the body of the king and re-entered his own.

The song called 'A Prayer to the Guru' *(Guru-stuti)* consists of eight verses, each of which ends with the exhortation: 'That thou art, O king!' Sri Ramana's translation is also in verse.

(6) THE HYMN OF HASTAMALAKA *(HASTAMALAKIYA)*

In the course of his tour of India, Sri Sankara visited the village of Sri-vali on the west coast of the southern peninsula. A father brought his thirteen-year-old son to the Master and submitted that the boy had been dumb from birth and took no interest in the affairs of the world. Recognising the enlightened soul that was dwelling in the boy's frame, Sankara put the usual questions, knowing full well what the answer would be. He asked: 'Who are you? Whose son are you? Where are you going? What is your name? Whence have you come?' Not only did the boy begin to speak, but he did not give the conventional answers. Instead, he declared his identity with the supreme Self which is not to be confused with the body, the sense organs, the mind, etc. He did this in the form of a set of verses, ending each one with the affirmation: 'I am the Self which is of the nature of eternal consciousness.' The Master was delighted. He admitted the boy to his fold, giving him *sannyasa* and the name Hastamalaka, which means 'one whose knowledge is as clear as a myrobalan fruit placed on one's palm'. This work of Hastamalaka's has the unique distinction of having a commentary written by the Master himself. It is called the *Hastamalak-iya-bhasya.* Sri Ramana translated the hymn in metrical Tamil, giving an account of the circumstances under which it was composed.

(7) OTHER TRANSLATIONS

The Essence of the Bhagavad-gita (Bhagavad-gita-saram)

The *Bhagavad-gita* is one of the basic texts of the Vedanta. It occurs in the Mahabharata in the form of a dialogue between Arjuna, the hero of the Epic, and Sri Krsna, the incarnation of God. The quintessence of Vedanta is taught by Sri Krsna in its seven hundred verses.

One day, a devotee made a submission to Sri Ramana. The *Bhagavad-gita* is rather long, so could the Master select one verse from it, which contained the essence of its teaching? The sage said that verse 20 of chapter X might serve the purpose. In it, the Lord Sri Krsna declares: 'I am the Self, O Arjuna, staying in the heart of all beings; I am the beginning, the middle, and the end of all beings.' It is significant that Sri Ramana selected this as the key verse in the *Bhagavad-gita,* for it proclaims the truth that God is not an entity apart, but the inner Self of all beings. There is nothing apart from the Self, which is the Alpha and Omega of all things. In short, the Self is non-dual.

Subsequently, Sri Ramana selected forty-two verses from the *Bhagavad-gita* and arranged them in an order which brings out the non-dualist teaching of the text. Some modern scholars while agreeing with Sankara that non-duality *(advaita)* is what is taught in the *Bhagavad-gita,* differ from him and say that the truth of non-duality may be realised through the path of selfless action *(karma-yoga),* and not necessarily through the path of knowledge *(jnana-yoga).* It is clear that Sri Ramana does not agree with this view. Once, when an aspirant remarked: 'The *Gita* was taught for action,' the Master replied:

> 'What does the *Gita* say? Arjuna refused to fight. Krsna said: "So long as you refuse to fight, you have the sense of a doer. Who are you to refrain or to act? Give up the notion of doing. Until that sense disappears you are bound to act. You are being manipulated by a Higher Power. You are admitting it by your refusal to submit to it. Instead, recognise the Power and submit as a tool. Or, to put it differently, if you refuse you will be forcibly drawn into it. Instead of being an unwilling worker, be a willing one. Rather, be fixed in the Self and act according to nature without the thought of being a doer. Then the results of action will not affect you. That is manliness or heroism. Thus 'inheritance in the Self' is the sum and substance of the *Gita*'s teaching".[8]

On another occasion, a questioner remarked: 'The *Gita* seems to emphasise action *(karma),* for Arjuna is persuaded to fight. Sri Krsna himself set the example by an active life of great exploits.'

Thereupon Sri Ramana replied: 'The *Gita* starts by saying that you are not the body, that you are not therefore the doer.'[9]

When asked to comment on the passage in the *Gita*, 'The whole cosmos forms a particle of Me,' Sri Ramana explained:

'It does not mean that a small particle of God separates from Him and forms the universe. His *Sakti* (power) is acting; as a result of one phase of such activity the cosmos has become manifest. Similarly, the statement in *Purusasukta*, "All beings form His one foot *(padosya visva bhutani)*" does not mean that *Brahman* is in four parts.

So the fact is that *Brahman* is all and remains indivisible. It is ever realised. Man, however, does not know it, although he must. Knowledge means the overcoming of obstacles which obstruct the revelation of the Eternal Truth that the Self is the same as *Brahman*. The obstacles create your idea of separateness as an individual. Therefore the present attempt will result in the truth being revealed that the Self is not separate from *Brahman*.'[10]

It is obvious how completely Sri Ramana accepts Sankara's interpretation of the *Bhagavad-gita*. This is reflected in his selection and arrangement of forty-two verses from the *Bhagavad-gita*.

In the invocatory couplet that Sri Ramana has added to his section, he says: 'May the gracious Lord, who, seated in Arjuna's chariot, removed his distress, by His good Word, protect (us)!'

(b) *Jnanacara-vicaram (The Enquiry into Knowledge and Conduct)*

Besides the *Vedas*, which are the basic scriptures of Hinduism, there are the sacred texts known as the *Agamas* which are equally authoritative. The three main Hindu sects of Saivism, Saktism, and Vaisnavism, have their respective *Agamas* on which they base their doctrines and beliefs. Temple construction, worship in the temples, the training of the priests, the details of ritual, and so on, are governed by the *Agamas*. There are also expositions of philosophical principles in these texts.

Then there are subsidiary *Agamas (Upagamas)*. One of these belonging to the Saiva tradition is the *Devikalottaram*, in which Lord Siva instructs His consort Parvati. In one of the sections, *Jnanacara-vicara*, the truth of non-duality and the means to realise it are clearly explained. Sri Ramana has rendered this section into Tamil verse.

In the invocatory verse prefixed to the translation, Sri Ramana says: 'The Self is witness to the bliss that is the silence of gracious non-duality—the divine nectar resulting from the wisdom contained in the *Devikallottaram*, uttered by the sacred mouth of the Lord in the ear of His Consort.'

(c) *Atma-saksatkaram (Self-realisation)*

A section from another subsidiary *Agama*, *Sarva-jnanottaram*, has also been turned into Tamil verse by Sri Ramana. It has for its theme Self-realisation.

Sri Ramana's invocatory verse reads thus: 'This work, *Atma-saksatkaram*, which was graciously vouchsafed to Subrahmanya by the Lord who is the Self, is now rendered in Tamil by Him who is the Primal Supreme One, abiding in me.'

(d) *Vicara-mani-malai (Garland of Gems of Enquiry)*

There is a work on Advaita in Hindi by Sadhu Niscaladasa, which has been translated into Tamil. A devotee once showed this translation to Sri Ramana, and complained that he was not able to understand it. With a view to helping him, the Master made a summary of the work, calling it *Vicara-mani-malai*.

(e) *Selections from Sankara's Hymn to Siva (Sivanandalahari)*

We shall end this Part by referring to Sri Ramana's selections from Sankara's poem, the *Sivanandalahari*, which has one hundred verses. The Master chose ten of them and added a mnemonic verse indicating the initial letters of the verses selected and their order in the selection:

> *am-bhak-jana-ghato-vaksah*
> *nara-guha-gabhi-vatuh,*
> *adya-dasa sivanandalahari-*
> *sloka-sucika.*

The ten verses are 61, 76, 83, 6, 65, 10, 12, 9, 11 and 91. (61) They define devotion with apt analogies. Devotion is constant contemplation of God. (76) When devotion fills the mind, life becomes worthwhile and fruitful. (83) There is no point in being devoted to what is finite and limited; the object of true devotion is the Infinite Reality, God. (6) Logic cannot be a substitute for devotion. Skill in the art of arguing will not yield happiness, but will only result in weariness of the mind. (65) The devotee has no such bitterness. He gains the supreme happiness, conquering death. Even the gods adore him. (10) What is important is devotion. Other considerations and conditions of life are of no consequence. (12) One may live anywhere and follow any mode of discipline but true *yoga* is devotion to God. (9) Devotion does not consist in mere external offering of flowers, etc., to God; it is the gift of the heart that is true devotion. (11) One may be a devotee in any stage of life; if one surrenders oneself to God, He is ready to take on all the burdens. (91) The end of devotion is *moksa* (release). Devotion to God removes the darkness of ignorance by shedding the light of wisdom.

NOTES

[1] Sivaprakasam Pillai wrote in a note-book: 'I met the Maharshi for the first time in the year 1902 . . . I put to him questions relating to Self-enquiry. He taught me the techniques of making Self-enquiry' (translation of the note in Tamil).

[2] Sadhu Arunacala (A. W. Chadwick) *A Sadhu's Reminiscence of Ramana Maharshi* (Sri Ramanasramam, Tiruvannamalai, 1961), p. 34.

[3] *Talks with Sri Ramana Maharshi*, 4th edn (Sri Ramanasramam, Tiruvannamalai, 1968), p. 125.

[4] *Ibid.*, p. 228.

[5] *Day by Day with Bhagavan, op. cit.* (1957), pp. 8-9.

[6] *Letters from Sri Ramanasramam*, pp. 349-50.

[7] *Talks with Sri Ramana Maharshi*, pp. 528-9.

[8] *Talks with Sri Ramana Maharshi*, pp. 65-6.

[9] *Ibid.*, p. 599.

[10] *Ibid.*, p. 611.

Dr. Arvind Sharma (essay date 1984)

SOURCE: "Predetermination and Free Will in the Teaching of Ramana Maharshi (1879-1950)," in *Religious Studies*, Vol. 20, No. 3, September, 1984, pp. 615-26.

[*In the following essay, Sharma argues that Ramana Maharshi's stand on predeterminism was not as immutable as previously interpreted.*]

I

Ramana Maharsi is one of the lesser lights of modern Indian thought but a major figure in the context of modern Advaitic thought in Hinduism. Modern Indian thought in general is distinguished by a robust confidence in the efficacy of effort as an expression of free will, a confidence it shares with the temper of the West in general and which it may have imbibed by coming in contact with it. Modern Advaitic thought, as represented by its popular modern exponents such as S. Radhakrishnan and T. M. P. Mahadevan, shares this confidence. Ramana Maharsi, however, strikes, at least at first glance, a somewhat discordant note. The purpose of this paper is to present his view on the time-honoured debate between predeterminism and free will and to analyze its philosophical implications.

II

One may begin by stating that Ramana Maharsi seems to come out clearly on the side of predetermination so far as conventional existence in the present life is concerned. The *locus classicus* in this respect, in the literature on Ramana Maharsi, is his written response to his mother, when she wanted him to return home with her. He was observing silence *(mauna)* at the time and was induced by a devotee to respond in writing to her importunities. He wrote:

> The Ordainer controls the fate of souls in accordance with their *prarabdhakarma* (destiny to be worked out in this life, resulting from the balance-sheet of actions in past lives). Whatever is destined not to happen will not happen, try as you may. Whatever is destined to happen will happen, do what you may to prevent it. This is certain. The best course, therefore, is to remain silent.[1]

He also saw his own life in these terms. When he suggested to an interlocutor that renunciation was not necessary for Realization he was asked: 'Why did you leave your home in your youth.' His answer: 'That is my *prarabdha* (destiny). One's course of conduct in this life is determined by one's *prarabdha*. My *prarabdha* lies this way; yours lies that way.'[2] In a hymn in praise of the Arunacala, the mountain where he resided, he says: 'If spurned by Thee, alas! what rests *(sic)* for me but the torment of my *prarabdha?*'[3]

How comprehensive in scope, it may be asked, was Ramana Maharsi's doctrine of predetermination? There are two ways in which the blow could be softened, so to say: (1) that predetermination only applied to the *major* events of life and not to its minor details and (2) that it implied a given pattern which could be *altered* by effort in this life. And such effort, of course, would be such as could be undertaken of one's own free will.

It turns out that Ramana Maharsi was quite 'uncompromising in his teaching that whatever is to happen will happen, while at the same time he taught that whatever happens is due to *prarabdha*, a man's balance-sheet of destiny acting according to so rigorous a law of cause and effect that even the word "justice" seems too sentimental to express it'.[4]

The following conversation indicates that he saw a single life as predetermined in exquisite, perhaps even excruciating detail:

> I: Are only the important events in a man's life, such as his main occupation or profession, predetermined, or are trifling acts also, such as taking a cup of water or moving from one part of the room to another?
>
> B: Everything is predetermined.
>
> I: Then what responsibility, what free will has man?
>
> B: Why does the body come into existence? It is designed for the various things that are marked out for it in this life.[5]

Ramana Maharsi also ruled out the possibility that predetermined patterns in one life may be amenable to Karmic effort in that life (effort which itself is not predetermined):

> If Karma be your lot according to *prarabdha,* it will surely be done whether you will it or not; if Karma be not your lot, it will not be done even if you intently engage in it.[6]

Thus Ramana Maharsi's commitment to the doctrine of predetermination seems to be total. One of the texts which upholds the doctrine of free will vigorously is the Yogavasistha (II: 4-9). When faced with the passage Ramana Maharsi did not acknowledge its force. I am no doubt arguing by silence here, which is usually suspect, but in this case, because of the massive evidence on his position on the issue, it may be given some credence. The concerned passage was referred to him by a visitor on the 4th of April 1947 in the course of conversation and Ramana Maharsi in effect said: 'find out who is asking the question'.[7]

Ramana Maharsi's commitment to the doctrine of predetermination also emerges in his adaptation and translation of Vivekacudamani wherein the present life is seen as the working out of *prarabdha* through the assumption of the body (verse 459).

The position of Ramana Maharsi on this point can be elaborated by developing two illustrations suggested by his works. An individual's present life could be compared to a movie. Just as, once the movie has started, it must run its course, so does one's life. Moreover, like the movie our life is also fully scripted. Once the picture show starts all that is to happen is already in there in the reel inside the projector. All that remains for it is to unfold. Such according to Ramana Maharsi is the life of ordinary mortals. Once we are born *all* that is to happen, as in the case of the movie, is already spelled out and will merely unfold as we proceed. Another illustration is provided by a dramatic performance. Once the play starts all the roles that are to be played out, what is to be said and done by whom to whom, is already determined, all that remains is its enactment. The life of ordinary mortals is also similarly scripted and fully so. There is no room for extemporaneous utterances, no scope for 'ad-libbing'. In this sense the movie is a better example than the play, as there isn't even that chance of changes occurring at all in the case of the movie.

III

A further study of the life, talks and writings of Ramana Maharsi, however, lead one to reassess the pre-deterministic severity of his position in at least four ways.

Although I have not succeeded in actually identifying an utterance of Ramana Maharsi to that effect, some of his statements suggest the possibility of alteration of karma in the sense of *prarabdha* either through transfer or prayer. 'Mrs Taleyarkhan, a Parsi devotee, besought

him: "Bhagavan! Give this sickness to me instead. Let me bear it!" And he replied, "And who gave it to me?"'[8] Again: 'A Swedish sadhu had a dream in which the afflicted arm opened and he saw there the head of a woman with grey hair dishevelled. This was interpreted to mean that it was the karma of his mother that he [Ramana Maharsi] assumed when he gave her *Moksha,* but others saw the woman to signify all mankind or Maya itself.'[9] Another case relates to his mother. When she fell ill Ramana Maharsi composed verses in honour of Arunacala, the sacred mountain he was residing at. These verses which 'he composed during her sickness are the only instance known of any prayer of his to influence the course of events'.[10] She recovered.

The next two points are perhaps even more significant. Ramana Maharsi seems to allow for the fact that our actions in this life may affect our future lives. In other words, although this life, once it has commenced, is predetermined, future lives, till they are in turn commenced, are not so. This gives us what I like to call the look back doctrine of karma. Our present life is predetermined by past lives, and our future life is predetermined by the past and present lives. In order to see the chain of causation one must look one step backwards, over the shoulder, so to say. Its practical implication is that future lives can be affected by actions performed in the present life. An illustration might help. Although the car may move from place to place, its mudguard will always remain ahead of the rest of the car. The mudguard is *prarabdha,* the driver at the steering wheel is *kriyamana* or present karma and the petrol is *sancita* or accumulated karma. Thus our *prarabdha* as mudguard must *always* be one step ahead of us, yet the location of the car can be altered. It could be argued that this understanding of karma in Ramana Maharsi is identical with the traditional one. This is so to a large extent but there is a wrinkle. In some accounts of the doctrine not *all* of the present life is seen as predetermined. It is so on Ramana Maharsi's account.

Thirdly, Ramana Maharsi seems to imply that while our *physical* destiny is predetermined, including the external events of our lives, our *mental* life is capable of modification in one life. Thus he said: 'All the activities that the body is to go through are determined when it first comes into existence. It does not rest with you to accept or reject them. The only freedom you have is to turn your mind inward and renounce activities there.'[11] This point may appear similar to the next one as it is not always easy to distinguish between the mental and the spiritual. But the distinction is important. Is it possible for a person to aim at mental improvement *in itself,* without regarding it as a propaedeutic to salvation? I have assumed this to be the case.

Finally, Ramana Maharsi clearly concedes the existence of free will in some passages:

> Has man any free will or is everything in his life predetermined?

Free will exists together with the individuality. As long as the individuality lasts, so long is there free will. All the scriptures are based on this fact and advise directing the free will in the right channel.[12]

On closer examination it turns out that these remarks apply to spiritual aspiration, especially the aspiration for salvation. Thus when asked what freedom there was in view of his predeterministic stance he said: 'As for freedom, a man is always free not to identify himself with the body and not be affected by the pleasures and pains consequent on its (i.e. the body's) activities.'[13] Moreover, according to him, as was pointed out earlier, 'All the activities that the body is to go through are determined when it first comes into existence. It does not rest with you to accept or reject them. The only freedom you have is to turn your mind inward and renounce activities there.[14]

Even more significantly, while the *futility* of effort in changing our *worldly* destiny in the course of one life is emphasized; its *utility* in affecting our *spiritual* destiny is recognized.[15] Thus when a devotee asked: 'If, as is said, everything happens according to destiny, even the obstacles that retard and prevent one from successfully carrying out the meditation may have to be considered insuperable, as being set up by such irrevocable destiny. How, then, can one ever hope to surmount them?' Ramana Maharsi replied: 'That which is called "destiny", preventing meditation, exists only to the externalized and not to the introverted mind. Therefore he who seeks inwardly in quest of the Self, remaining as he is, does not get frightened by any impediment that may seem to stand in the way of carrying on his practice of meditation. The very thought of such obstacles is the greatest impediment.'

Self-realization is the ultimate focus of the teachings of Ramana Maharsi. He, therefore, viewed the issue of predestination and free will in that light. The full text of the passage on the association of free will and individuality cited earlier may be reviewed here. It runs as follows: The question was put by Mr Das of Allahabad University.

> D: Has man any Free-Will or is everything in his life pre-destined and pre-ordained?
>
> M: Free-Will holds the field in association with individuality. As long as individuality lasts so long there is Free-Will. All the *sastras* are based on this fact and they advise directing the Free-Will in the right channel. Find out to whom Free-Will or Destiny matters. Abide in it. Then these two are transcended. That is the only purpose of discussing these questions. To whom do these questions arise? Find out and be at peace.[16]

On another occasion Ramana Maharsi observed:

> Free-will and destiny are ever-existent. Destiny is the result of past action; it concerns the body. Let the body act as may suit it. Why are you concerned with it? Why do you pay attention to it? Free-will and Destiny last as long as the body lasts. But wisdom *(Jnana)* transcends both. The Self is beyond knowledge and ignorance. Should anything happen, it happens as the resultant of one's past actions, of divine will and of other factors.[17]

The second passage is in the same spirit as the first, except that towards the end Ramana Maharsi seems to change his tune and allows for three factors as determining a happening: (1) one's past actions, (2) divine will and (3) other factors. The third is a catch all category. Thus the field is left wide open. However, while he leaves room for speculation on the factors underlying predeterminism he does not seem to question the fact of predeterminism itself.

IV

Ramana Maharsi's position on the question of predetermination and free will raises some very important conceptual issues, which do not seem to have been fully resolved in his teachings.

(1) By implicitly if not explicitly accepting the influence of transfer or prayer on karma, even in the context of a single life, the immutability of karma is compromised. The chief intellectual attraction of the doctrine of karma is its logical rigour, which in general is accepted by Ramana Maharsi himself. How, then, is this mitigation to be suitably explained? Either it is *que sera sera* as the song says, or it is not. It does not seem very consistent to emphasize that there are no exceptions to the rule and then add the comment 'but there are a few exceptions'.

(2) If it is accepted that during a single life the *jiva* can generate *genuinely* new karma, a premise which must be accepted if the future life is seen influenced by the actions performed in present life (which is itself pre-determined), then the question arises: how is this possible? One explanation could be that *spiritual* effort, (which is exempted from the vicious circle of effort itself having to be predestined) could lead to the modification of *samskaras* or mental impressions and through them of karma. This may be implied, but is not stated. Besides, should one not draw the conclusion that so far as worldly existence is concerned one is hopelessly trapped in the karmic cycle *not* in the sense that all actions produce results but in the sense that no genuinely new action is possible? The fact that the ordinary *jiva* presumably has led numerous previous lives so that his stock of karma to be worked out is pretty large lends some credence to this position, but it does not seem to have been confirmed by Ramana Maharsi. He does say: 'Pain and pleasure is the result of past *karma* and not of the present *karma*'[18] but then does not explain how such *past karma* is possible if life then too was predetermined.

(3) The psycho-physical nature of the human personality makes one wary of stipulating a Cartesian mind/matter dichotomy. Yet to indicate the one way in which karmic

change can be wrought in Ramana Maharsi's world-view one must not only make some such a distinction but also assume a mind-over-matter position. If '*samsara* is *samskara*' then the former is changed by changing the latter. However, Ramana Maharsi also discusses the question of dietic purity on the ground that it is conducive to spiritual development. This is a matter-over-mind situation. Given this interpretation of the physical and the mental it is not entirely clear whether for Ramana Maharsi the relation was unilateral or bilateral. It will be seen that this issue has a clear bearing on the issue of how, if all is predetermined, 'new' karma is to be accounted for.

(4) Ramana Maharsi acknowledges the role of God in the karmic mechanism. It is true that such a role of God is accepted in traditional Advaita but many schools of Indian thought, both *astika* and *nastika,* see no need for God. Its inclusion, therefore, calls for some justification. The inclusion of God in the scheme of predetermination is easier to justify if one believes in predestination *without* believing in rebirth. For then predestination can be explained in terms of God's will instead of one's own past karma. But Ramana Maharsi believed in rebirth. The explanation he offers thus is not metempsychotic but metaphysical. His position is summarized in the first three verses of his Upadesasaram:

> 1. Karma must ever yield its proper fruit,
> For thus it is ordained by God, Himself,
> Supreme Creator. Then is Karma God?
> No, for it is itself insentient.
>
> 2. Of Karma the results must pass away,
> Yet it leaves seeds, which in their turn sprout forth
> And throw the actor back into the flood
> Of Karma's ocean. Karma cannot save.
>
> 3. But acts performed without attachment's urge
> And solely for the service of the Lord
> Will cleanse the mind and indicate the way
> Which leads at length unto the final goal.[19]

The dilemma in this respect was articulated by a young girl of 9 or 10 at the Asrama in the course of the following dialogue with Ramana Maharsi. She asked: 'Why is there misery on Earth?' 'Due to karma.' 'Who makes Karma bear fruits?' 'God.' 'God makes us do karma and gives bad fruits for bad karma. Is it fair?'[20] A dialogue with one Mrs Piggott, obviously a more mature person, went like this. 'Why then is *samsara* . . . so full of sorrow and evil?' 'God's will.' 'Why does God will it so?' 'It is inscrutable. . . .'[21]

Ramana Maharsi also answered questions relating to free will and God's omnipotence without mediating the response directly through karma. He was asked: '*(a)* Is omnipotence of God consistent with ego's free-will? *(b)* Is omniscience of God consistent with God's free-will?' He replied: 'Yes. Free-will is the present appearing to a limited faculty of sight and will. That same ego sees its past activity as falling into a course of "law" or rules—its own free-will being one of the links in that course of law.

Omnipotence and omniscience of God are then seen by the ego to have acted through the appearance of his own free-will. So he comes to the conclusion that the ego must go by appearances. Natural laws are manifestations of God's will and they have been laid down.'

On these various points just discussed the answers to be found in Ramana Maharsi's teaching are either not clear or unsatisfactory. It may be said in extenuation that the issue of free will or predestination, however pressing it may be for us, was not one with which Ramana Maharsi himself was centrally concerned. Thus he may not have tied up all the loose ends neatly as it were. He would also have discouraged excessive speculation on the issue as his central concern was with self-realization. It must be added, though, that two points, on which he was frequently questioned, he did try to meet. The first was the obvious one—if everything is predetermined why make any effort at all? He answered the question at two levels. At the conventional level he argued, as Krsna did with Arjuna, that even the effort is pre-determined. Or else, as Arthur Osborne points out, 'The man who says "Everything is predestined, therefore I will make no effort" is intruding the false assumption "and I know what is predestined".'[22] At the spiritual level he was even more forthright. Once he was asked: 'But human effort is said to be useless; so what incentive has a man to improve himself?' At this point, Osborne writes: 'I asked where it was said that you should make no effort or that effort was useless; and the visitor pointed to the passage in "Who am I?" where it says that, since the indefinable power of the Lord ordains, sustains and controls everything, we need not worry what we shall do. I pointed out that what is deprecated there is not human effort but the feeling "I am the doer". I asked Bhagavan whether my explanation was not right and he approved of it.'[23]

The other question relates to helping others through public service which emerges as a particularly, though not solely, European concern. Ramana Maharsi's consistent response can be summed up thus: 'Helping yourself you help the world' though he often adds the more stratospheric statement: 'You are the world'.

Notwithstanding some loose ends Ramana Maharsi's teaching on the question of predestination and free will is reasonably clear. So far as the *jiva* bound in the realm of *samsara* is concerned (that's us) committed to leading an ordinary conventional existence any particular life is predetermined, by 'call it Iswara' (God) 'or call it karma'.[24] Such predetermination assumes that one does 'take things as they come in accordance with one's traditions' for 'If all people close their eyes and sit still saying if food comes, we eat, how is the world to get on?'[25] That is, a normal psychological life style is assumed. If it is recognized, however, even while leading such a predetermined life, that 'Things happen automatically in accordance with samskaras (the fruits of the actions of previous births)' and that 'the feeling that the doer is "I" is itself bondage' then one's spiritual ascent begins.

V

What is the significance of Ramana Maharsi's views on the question of predetermination and free will? Its historical significance has already been hinted at. Ramana Maharsi is one of the few modern Hindu figures who is clear and firm in his acceptance of predetermination, which he regards fully consistent with the search for salvation. A partial parallel to this position may be found in Mahatma Gandhi who believed in the supremacy of God's will. But although Mahatma Gandhi accepted a divinity presiding over earthly destinies and saw man as both ontologically and teleologically dependent on God, Ramana Maharsi saw this dependence as more mechanistic in nature. Although Ramana Maharsi approved of karma yoga and of its practise by Mahatma Gandhi, he was himself a follower of Jnana yoga. Among the important figures of modern Hinduism Ramana Maharsi is virtually unique in the degree and extent of his acceptance of predetermination. This being so, the philosophical significance of his position may be developed in the light of Advaitic philosophy, Hindu philosophy and the comparative philosophy of religion.

In the context of Advaita, Ramana Maharsi's uncompromising predeterminism does *not* affect his stand on the question of the nature of *jivanmukti*. The usual description regarding the state of *jivanmukti* runs as follows: '*Moksa* may be realized during one's life and when so realized one is a *jivanmukta*. All the accumulated action which has not yet borne fruit *(samcita-karman)* and all action which would otherwise take place in the future *(agami-karman)* is obliterated; action done in the past which has already begun to bear fruit *(prarabdha-karman)* must, however, be carried out. The *jivanmukta* carries this out through without its affecting him, for he is unattached to it.'[26] This seems to imply that the *jivanmukta* works out his *prarabda,* so to say. This would seem to be quite consistent with Ramana Maharsi's position on *prarabdha.* It turns out, however, that such is not the case. As soon as Realization dawns all *three* forms of karma *(prarabdha, sancita* and *agami)* are fully accounted for, according to Ramana Maharsi. He explained:

> Karma is posited as past *karma,* etc., *Prarabdha, Agami* and *Sanchita.* There must be *kartritva* (doership) and *karta* (doer) for it. *Karma* (action) cannot be for the body because it is insentient. It is only so long as *dehatma buddhi* ('I am the body idea') lasts. After transcending *dehatma buddhi* one becomes a *jnani.* In the absence of that idea *(buddhi)* there cannot be either *kartritva* or *karta.* So a *jnani* has no karma. That is his experience. Otherwise he is not a *jnani.* However an *ajnani* identifies the *jnani* with his body which the *jnani* does not do. So the *ajnani* finds the *jnani* acting, because his body is active, and therefore he asks if the *jnani* is not affected by *prarabdha.*

> The scriptures say that *jnana* is the fire which burns away all karma *(sarvakarmani).* *Sarva* (all) is interpreted in two ways: (1)

to include *prarabhda* and (2) to exclude it. In the first way: if a man with three wives dies, it is asked, 'Can two of them be called widows and the third not?' All are widows. So it is with *prarabdha, agami* and *sanchita.* When there is no karta none of them can hold out any longer.

> The second explanation is, however, given only to satisfy the enquirer. It is said that all karma is burnt away leaving *prarabdha* alone. The body is said to continue in the functions for which it has taken its birth. That is *prarabdha.* But from the *jnani's* point of view there is only the Self which manifests in such variety. There is no body or karma apart from the Self, so that the actions do not affect him.[27]

Ramana Maharsi takes the same position in his adaptation and translation of the verses of Vivekacudamani bearing on the relationship between these three kinds of karma to *jivanmukti.*

It is true that the two positions, those adopted in the tradition and by Ramana Maharsi, are quite close but they are not close enough to be identical and there is an important difference, though of degree; so important in fact that in one of the texts frequently referred to by Ramana Maharsi, the doctrine that all the three kinds of karma are immediately dissolved on self-realization is held with such conviction as to lead to the suggestion that the *prarabdha* of the *mukta* falls to the share of those around him: 'His detractors share the demerits, and his devotees the merits.'[28]

In the context of Hindu philosophy in general Ramana Maharsi's view of predetermination is capable of a striking extension. Ramana Maharsi approves of karma yoga but makes no original contribution to its understanding. If, however, his view that ordinary empirical life is totally predetermined is accepted then it becomes possible to suggest that such wholehearted acceptance could result in the attainment of such a degree of mental equipoise as might render self-realization accessible. This suggestion has in fact been made by one of his disciples. 'He said explicitly: "All the actions that the body is to perform are already decided upon at the time it comes into existence: the only freedom you have is whether or not to identify yourself with the body." If one acts a part in a play the whole part is written out beforehand and one acts as faithfully whether one is Caesar who is stabbed or Brutus who stabs, being unaffected by it because one knows one is not that person. In the same way, he who realizes his identity with the deathless Self acts his part on the human stage without fear or anxiety, hope or regret, not being touched by the part played. If one were to ask what reality one has when all one's actions are determined, it would lead only to the question: Who, then, am I? If the ego that thinks it makes decisions is not real and yet I know that I exist, what is the reality of me? This is only a preparatory, mental version of the quest that Sri Bhagavan prescribed, but it is an excellent preparation for the real quest.'[29]

The suggestion is not unprecedented in Hindu thought.[30]

In the context of the comparative philosophy of religion the views of Ramana Maharsi on free will and predestination are capable of making a contribution in two directions.

His views on the ego provide an interesting point of intersection with Buddhist thought. Ramana Maharsi denies the ego but not the *atman;* the Buddhists deny the *atman* as well as the ego and in fact do not seem to distinguish between the two. But the mode of their respective denials constitute an interesting parallel. Ramana Maharsi's views on the ego in the context of free will and predestination parallel the Buddhist argument as presented in the Abhidharma-Kosa as a quotation from the Milindapanha.[31]

In the broader context of the comparative philosophy of religion the manner in which Ramana Maharsi reconciles the competing claims of free will and predestination are of some interest, especially in the context of Islamic thought. We may restrict ourselves here to a consideration of the positions developed in orthodox Islam and modern Qur'anic scholarship. The 'ultimate, scholastic, *Ash'*arite statement' denies that 'man possesses any action at all' and the 'orthodox difficulty was rather with man's consciousness of freedom'. 'Thus man is an automaton, although part of his machinery is that he believes himself free.'[32] This view, inasmuch as it lurches towards an full-fledged and unabashed predeterminism, comes close to Ramana Maharsi's own. In fairness it must be added that the *Ash'*arite position is not the only one to be found in Islam nor is Ramana Maharsi's the only one to be found in Hinduism. There is also a difference though between the two positions. While in the A*sh'*arite case the implication is 'that on the psychological level man continues to act as if he were free . . . though in reality acting of necessity',[33] in the case of Ramana Maharsi while this is accepted, the further statement is made that man has the genuine freedom to dissociate himself from such action even while performing it.

Modern Qur'anic scholarship seems to arrive at the conclusion best represented by Montgomery Watt's statement that 'In the end, then, the Qur'an simply holds fast to the complementary truths of God's omnipotence and man's responsibility without reconciling them intellectually. This is basically also the position of the Bible, though many western Christians have placed the chief emphasis on man's responsibility where most Muslims would have placed it on God's omnipotence.'[34] It has been further suggested that the reconciliation is practical, not intellectual. The Muslims have believed that everything happens according to God's will but act as if they are responsible for what they do.

This brief discussion provides three paradigmatic positions on the question of free will and predestination: (1) that paradoxically both genuinely exist and cannot be intellectually reconciled; (2) that they can be reconciled by accepting predetermination in theory or belief and free will in practise or action; (3) that they can even be theoretically reconciled by *(a)* free will being related to *moral* and spiritual responsibility and predetermination to an *ontological* basis of activity or by *(b)* free will being related to human *psychological* awareness of it and predetermination to an *existential* givenness. It has to be admitted that *(a)* and *(b)* overlap to some extent, though it is useful to distinguish between the two.

Ramana Maharsi's teachings seem to fit in best with (3) *(b)* in the context of worldly existence and with (3) *(a)* in the context of spiritual aspiration.

NOTES

[1] See Arthur Osborne, *Ramana Maharshi and the Path of Self-Knowledge* (New York: Samuel Weiser Inc., 1971) p. 42. Also see Arthur Osborne, ed., *The Teachings of Bhagavan Sri Ramana Maharshi in His Own Words* (London: Rider and Company, 1962) p. 66, wherein he adds: 'He sometimes also made such statements to devotees.' For a poetic rendering see Arthur Osborne, ed., *The Collected Works of Ramana Maharshi* (London: Rider & Company, 1972), p. 95.

[2] Arthur Osborne, ed., *The Teachings of Bhagavan Sri Ramana Maharshi in His Own Words,* p. 84.

[3] Arthur Osborne, ed., *The Collected Works of Ramana Maharshi,* p. 55.

[4] Arthur Osborne, *op. cit.* p. 42.

[5] Arthur Osborne, ed., *The Teachings of Bhagavan Sri Ramana Maharshi in His Own Words,* p. 66. B. stands for Bhagavan = Ramana Maharsi.

[6] *Talks with Sri Ramana Maharshi,* infra, p. 55. Note that enough free will to *try* to engage in karma even when it is not one's lot is conceded.

[7] D. S. Sastri, tr., *Letters from Sri Ramansramam* Volumes I & II by Suri Nagamma (Tiruvannamalai: Sri Ramanasramam, 1970), pp. 225-6.

[8] Arthur Osborne, *op. cit.* p. 185.

[9] *Ibid.*

[10] Arthur Osborne, *op. cit.* p. 70.

[11] Arthur Osborne, ed., *The Teachings of Bhagavan Sri Ramana Maharshi in His Own Words,* p. 66.

[12] *Ibid.* p. 67.

[13] *Ibid.* p. 66.

[14] *Ibid.*

[15] Arthur Osborne, *op. cit.* p. 43-4.

[16] *Talks with Sri Ramana Maharshi* (Tiruvannamalai: Sri Ramanasramam, 1963), p. 476. 'M' stands for Maharsi.

[17] *Ibid.;* see pp. 15, 187, 312, 379, etc. Also see *Sat-Darshana Bhasya and Talks with Maharshi by K* (Tiruvannamalai: Sri Ramanasramam, 1968) pp. 76-8.

[18] *Talks with Sri Ramana Maharshi,* pp. 624-5.

[19] *Upadesa Saram of Bhagwan Raman Maharshi* (Bombay: Central Chinmaya Mission Trust, no year) pp. 1-3.

[20] *Talks With Sri Ramana Maharshi,* p. 406.

[21] *Ibid.* p. 38.

[22] Arthur Osborne, *op. cit.* p. 44.

[23] Arthur Osborne, ed., *The Teachings of Bhagavan Sri Ramana Maharshi in His Own Words,* p. 73.

[24] D. S. Sastri, tr., *op. cit.* Vol. 1, p. 240; also see pp. 46, 103, etc.

[25] *Ibid.* p. 239.

[26] Eliot Deutsch and J. A. B. van Buitenen, *A Source Book of Advaita Vedanta* (Honolulu: The University Press of Hawaii, 1971), p. 312.

[27] *Talks with Sri Ramana Maharshi,* pp. 421-2. The statement made at the beginning of the passage that 'Karma is posited as past *karma,* etc., *Prarabdha, Agami* and *Sanchita*' is not strictly correct as *agami karma* 'is the coming *karma* which includes also *karma* that is being gathered at present' (T. M. P. Mahadevan, *Outlines of Hinduism* (Bombay: Chetana Limited, 1971) p. 60). In terms of the analogy of *prarabdha* being the arrow shot by an archer, *sancita* being those in the quiver, *agami* again is 'one he is about to send forth from his bow' (*ibid.* p. 60), the fact that Ramana Maharsi regards even *agami karma* as tied to past here karma indicates the thoroughgoing nature of his predeterminism.

[28] Swami Ramanananda Saraswathi, tr., *Kaivalya Navaneeta* (Tiruvannamalai: Sri Ramanasramam, 1974) p. 22. Also see Section II. Also see *Talks With Sri Ramana Maharshi,* p. 293. But also see D. S. Sastri, tr., *op. cit.* Vol. 1, pp. 254-5.

[29] Arthur Osborne, *op. cit.* p. 42-3.

[30] In the Adhyatma Ramayana for instance; see Louis Renou, ed., *Hinduism* (New York: Washington Square Press Inc., 1963) pp. 172-3.

[31] See Theodore Stcherbatsky, *The Soul Theory of the Buddhists* (Varanasi: Bharatiya Vidya Prakashan, 1970) pp. 45-7.

[32] See H. A. R. Gibb and J. H. Kramers, *Shorter Encyclopedia of Islam* (Leiden: E. J. Brill, 1974) p. 200.

[33] H. A. R. Gibb, 'Islam', in R. C. Zaehner, ed., *The Concise Encyclopedia of Living Faiths* (Boston: Beacon Press, 1959) p. 200.

[34] W. Montgomery Watt, *Bell's Introduction to the Qur'an* (Edinburgh University Press, 1970) p. 149.

FURTHER READING

Biography

Maharshi, Ramana. *Teachings of Ramana Maharshi: An Anthology.* Madras: Affiliated East-West Press, 1990, 174 p.

> Collection of works by Ramana Maharshi that features commentary by translator and disciple A. R. Natarajan.

Otto Weininger

1880-1903

Austrian nonfiction writer.

INTRODUCTION

Weininger is remembered for the only book he published during his lifetime–*Geschlecht und Charakter* (1903; *Sex and Character*), a vitriolic psychological tract in which he expounded on the animal nature of women and Jews and suggested that the ideal human being possesses only masculine traits. Weininger's book has been both excoriated and embraced by a wide variety of thinkers including Sigmund Freud, Ford Madox Ford, and Germaine Greer and was in its time a sensation in the European and American intellectual communities, due in part to its author's dramatic suicide four months after the book's publication.

Biographical Information

Weininger was born in Vienna in 1880. A precocious child, he learned seven languages by the age of sixteen. At that time he attempted to publish his first essay, an etymological paper on Homeric adjectives; the essay was rejected by the philological journal to which Weininger sent it. Weininger graduated from high school in 1898 and enrolled at the University of Vienna in the philosophy program, against his father's wishes that he study languages. At the University Weininger was known for his moodiness and brooding as well as his ability to engage others in heated debate. Although he was a Jew, Weininger never felt at home with the religion–eventually, in *Sex and Character*, he wrote that Judaism was a loathsome religion and that Jews had the "female" essence he despised so much. In 1900 he expressed his wish to convert to Protestantism, but was discouraged by his father. Nonetheless, Weininger converted in 1902. In 1903 Weininger published *Sex and Character*, which was an expanded version of his doctoral thesis. Four months later, distraught by the initial lack of response to his treatise, Weininger shot himself.

Major Works

In *Sex and Character* Weininger attempted to explain the effect of gender on fundamental character. Arguing that pure maleness and pure femaleness are polar opposites, Weininger concluded that the essence of woman is her basic non-existence–her complete lack of identity, character, or individuality–and that femaleness consists of nothing more than the image reflected from maleness, which he postulates as being ultimately and unquestionably superior. Weininger then went on to equate Jews with femaleness. In order to be able to

remove himself from the Judaism into which he was born, he decided that Judaism was neither a religious creed nor a racial makeup but instead a state of mind based entirely upon individual psychology. Because of this subjectivity, Weininger held that Jews possessed the female essence; like women, Jews represented negativity and mediocrity and did not therefore exist as the Aryan–with whom Weininger identified maleness—did. According to Weininger, both women and Jews are the result of guilt and therefore both are sick conditions of the soul.

Critical Reception

Recent psychoanalytic review of Weininger's life and work has led many critics to believe that Weininger was a homosexual who was deeply disturbed by his family's Judaism. Many critics posit that this is the reason for his violent misogyny and anti-Semitism. But while most of Weininger's ideas are dismissed today, *Sex and Character* received much attention in the years following his suicide. Weininger found supporters in August Strindberg, Ford Madox Ford, and William Carlos Williams, among others, all of whom believed that Weininger had at last solved the "woman problem." Sigmund Freud—although he disagreed with Weininger's theories—acknowledged the potential of Weininger's thought and regarded his suicide as a loss to the intellectual community. Today Weininger is credited with adding an interesting debate to fin de siècle European culture.

PRINCIPAL WORKS

Geschlecht und Charakter [*Sex and Character*] (nonfiction) 1903
Über die letzten Dinge (essays and fragments) 1904
Die Liebe und das Weib (essay) 1917

CRITICISM

W. I. Thomas (essay date 1906)

SOURCE: A review of *Sex and Character*, in *The American Journal of Sociology*, Vol. II, July, 1905-May, 1906, pp. 843-6.

[*In the following review of* Sex and Character, *Thomas admits Weininger's genius and calls the book well worth reading for the unique point of view it brings to the discussion of gender, but also points out that it is uneven in quality, concluding that Weininger's treatise is a "remarkable jumble of insane babble and brilliant suggestion."*]

No men who really think deeply about women retain a high opinion of them; men either despise women or they have never thought seriously about them. (P. 236.)

Woman is neither high-minded nor low-minded, strong-minded nor weak-minded. She is the opposite of all these. Mind cannot be predicated of her at all; she is mindless. (P. 253.)

Women have no existence and no essence; they are not, they are nothing. Mankind occurs as male or female, as something or nothing. Woman has no share in ontological reality, no relation to the thing-in-itself, which in the deepest interpretation is the absolute, is God. Man in his highest form, the genius, has such a relation, and for him the absolute is either the conception of the highest worth of existence, in which case he is a philosopher; or it is the wonderful fairyland of dreams, the kingdom of absolute beauty, and then he is an artist. Both views mean the same. Woman has no relation to the idea, she neither affirms nor denies it; she is neither moral nor anti-moral; mathematically speaking, she has no sign; she is purposeless, neither good nor bad, neither angel nor devil, never egotistical (and therefore has often been said to be altruistic); she is as non-moral as she is non-logical. But all existence is moral and logical existence. So woman has no existence. (P. 286.)

The woman of the highest standard is immeasurably beneath the man of the lowest standard. (P. 302.)

I have shown that logical and ethical phenomena come together in the conception of truth as the ultimate good, and posit the existence of an intelligible ego or soul, as a form of being of the highest super-empirical reality. In such a being as the absolute female there are no logical and ethical phenomena, and, therefore, the ground for the assumption of a soul is absent. The absolute female knows neither the logical nor the moral imperative, and the words law and duty, duty toward herself, are words which are least familiar to her. The inference that she is lacking in super-sensual personality is fully justified. The absolute female has no ego. (P. 186.)

A psychological proof that the power of making judgments is a masculine trait lies in the fact that woman recognizes it as such, and that it acts on her as a tertiary sexual character of the male. A woman always expects definite convictions in a man, and appropriates them; she has no understanding of indecision in a man. She always expects a man to talk, and a man's speech is to her a sign of his manliness. It is true that woman has the gift of speech, but she has not the art of talking; she converses (flirts) or chatters, but she does not talk. She is most dangerous, however, when she is dumb, for men are only too inclined to take her quiescence for silence. (P. 195.)

The absolute female, then, is devoid not only of the logical rules, but of the function of making concepts and judgments which depend on them. As the very nature of the conceptual faculty consists in posing subject against object, and as the subject takes its fullest and deepest meaning from its power of forming judgments on its objects, it is clear that woman cannot be recognized as possessing even the subject. (P. 195.)

I must add to the exposition of the non-logical nature of the female some statements as to her non-moral nature. The profound falseness of woman, the result of the want in her of a permanent relation to the idea of truth or the idea of value, would prove a subject of discussion so exhaustive that I must go to work another way. There are such endless imitations of ethics, such confusing copies of morality, that women are often said to be on a moral plane higher than man. I have already pointed out the need to distinguish between the non-moral and immoral, and I now repeat that with regard to women we can talk only of the non-moral, or the complete absence of a moral sense. . . . I am not arguing that woman is evil and anti-moral; I state that she cannot be really evil; *she is merely non-moral.* (Pp. 195-97.)

A mother makes no difference in arranging a marriage for her own daughter and for any other girl, and is just as glad to do it for the latter if it does not interfere with the interests of her own family; it is the same thing, match-making throughout, and there is no psychological difference in making a match for her own daughter and doing the same thing for a stranger. I would even go so far as to say that a mother is not inconsolable if a stranger, however common and undesirable, desires and seduces her daughter. (P. 255.)

We may now give with certainty a conclusive answer to the question as to the giftedness of the sexes: there are women with undoubted traits of genius, but there is no female genius, and there never has been one (not even amongst the masculine women of history which were dealt with in the first part) *and there never can be one.* . . . How could a soulless being possess genius? The possession of genius is identical with profundity; and if anyone were to try to combine woman and profundity as subject and predicate, he would be contradicted on all sides. A female genius is a contradiction in terms, for genius is simply intensified, perfectly developed, universally conscious maleness. (P. 189.)

Mr. Weininger's serious and ambitious study is the most remarkable jumble of insane babble and brilliant suggestion that it has been my fortune to consider seriously. The author takes himself and his subject seriously, and while he is obviously prepared for his work neither on the psychological, biological, nor yet the ethnological side, yet he is almost prepared in all of these fields, and brings to the subject a most astonishing originality. There is exhibited the most acute and subtle mental play throughout, but the whole argument is characterized by downright unreasonableness. The man (he was almost a boy) was a genius, a German genius, and the volume is remarkable, not as a contribution to science but as a work of the imagination, and an exhibition of what fantastic antics the human mind is capable of. The form also is as bizarre as the content. There are parts so poor, obscure, illogical, and stupid that they would not be accepted in a college boy's essay, and other parts worthy of Kant or Schopenhauer.

We almost feel that such a mind is detached from its environment and is creating a world of its own, but that this is not and cannot be so is shown in a most interesting manner by the fact that in the concrete illustrations which he uses to illustrate the traits of womankind in general (as he thinks) he is really speaking always of German Gretchen or her mother. He falls into the same error as Karl Vogt who some years ago, in a description of the mental traits of women students at Zurich, denied woman in general the ability to understand certain subjects in which American university women were already confessedly conspicuously proficient. So Weininger reflects—vaguely, indeed, and fantastically, as a dream reflects reality—the character of the German woman. The American woman, however, is quite a different thing, and presents characters the very opposite of what Weininger claims are and must be the characters of woman universally and in perpetuity. It has not even, seemingly, occurred to him that the status of woman, as of the lower races, is in a measure dependent on the run of habit in her group and the limited range of her attention.

But impossible and extra-phenomenal as the book certainly is, it is yet worth the while. Jevons has remarked that the greatest inventor is the one whose mind is visited by the largest number of random guesses. Anything which brings more points of view into the case is valuable, and this book is rich in this respect. That no one is either completely male or completely female is for instance, a good thesis, and the bearing of this view on the phenomena of sexual inversion is very suggestively stated and argued. And two other of the writer's main propositions amount essentially to this, namely, that the male is more highly differentiated than the female, and that the female is more completely sexually saturated and her interests more sexually limited than in the case of male. These are probably truths, though not new ones, and it would have been fortunate if he had substituted a simple and sane exposition of them for such extravagant statements as I have quoted above.

Janko Lavrin (essay date 1935)

SOURCE: "Sex and Eros," in *Aspects of Modernism: From Wilde to Pirandello,* Books for Libraries Press, Inc., 1968, pp. 141-59.

[*In the following essay, which was originally published in 1935, Lavrin discusses the writings of the Russian thinker Vassily Rozanov and Weininger's* Sex and Character, *observing the influence of both on D. H. Lawrence.*]

I

Among the pioneers of the erotic trek in recent European literature two writers can be mentioned who are so conspicuous as private "cases" that they cannot help arousing a general interest. One of them is the Russian thinker and publicist, Vassily Rozanov; and the other—the Jewish renegade Otto Weininger whose book, *Sex and Character* (as well as his subsequent suicide at the age of twenty-four), had caused a considerable stir at the beginning of the century.

What surprises one, at the very outset, in the work of Rozanov and Weininger is their all-absorbing scrutiny of the deeper aspects of sex. Both writers regard sex—whether rightly or wrongly—as the cardinal problem of man. Yet the final attitudes at which they arrive are irreconcilable. Their quest—a quest equally sincere in both and, with all that, leading to such a difference in conclusions—makes a comparison between the two seekers the more tempting and interesting. This interest is enhanced by the light the comparison itself can shed on certain dilemmas of modern consciousness in general. Moreover, in contrast to the cold and "clinical" explorations of sex on the part of Marcel Proust, the passionate metaphysical propensities of Rozanov and of Weininger make one think of D. H. Lawrence whose query can best be approached through these two men.

II

Rozanov, some of whose writings have already appeared in English, was a fragmentary, self-centred and self-contradictory individual, displaying a thousand masks, and also a peculiar capacity for mixing even sincere reverence with a cynical chuckle. Endowed with a rare psychological insight, he felt at ease only when rummaging in the most complicated shades of man's subconscious and half-conscious inner chaos. And the deeper he dived in its mazes, the more eager was he to dwell with gusto on what might be called (for lack of a better expression) psychic and spiritual underwear. He wallowed in it, examined it almost with a microscope, and at the same time delighted in unfolding it before his audience with a vocabulary full of winks, grimaces, suggestive stutters and smiles.

His very language has thus brought a unique *personal* accent into modern Russian literature. This accent is increased by the "naive" impudence with which he exhibits his own inner deformities. Never bothering about the distance between himself and his readers, he is usually anxious to catch his ideas on the wing, and to present them while they still trepidate with the most intimate personal experience.

This may perhaps explain the apparent unconcern with which Rozanov tackles the riskiest themes during his excursions into the essence of sex, of morality, or of the voluptuous aspects of asceticism—exposed with great penetration in such works of his as *The Dark Image* and *The People of Moonlight*. The curious point however is that the farther he ventures in his analysis the less one feels that his daring is the result of inner courage. On the contrary, the final impression is that he goes to extreme limits owing to a kind of inertia on the part of his own prying inquisitiveness. Like Proust, he is a past master at peeping through the keyholes. And he is too weak to stop, to restrain himself, or even to wait until his own observations should settle and cool down. With Rozanov depth itself is due to the line of least resistance. So is his jerky soliloquizing bravado, his exhibitionism, and his continuous urge to "confess" in order to relieve the pressure of his own chaos.

An additional interest is attached to Rozanov by the fact that in many ways he is the Russian counterpart of D. H. Lawrence. The ideas about love and sex, made current in this country by Lawrence, had been expressed by Rozanov long before him—with the same emphasis, but often with a greater, serpent-like subtlety. For he, too, had found his "mission" in preaching a renewal of life through Sex made innocent again and imbued with that mystery which would confer upon its functions a religious depth and significance. Like Lawrence, he hated asceticism as much as he hated the vulgar sexual licence. Finally, he made the same mistake as Lawrence with regard to the solution of the dilemma itself. That is why an analysis of Rozanov is bound to elucidate at least a few aspects of D. H. Lawrence as well.

III

There were two basic features in Rozanov the interaction of which can explain his attitude towards sex, and also towards Christianity. One of them was his much too little disciplined passion for the irrational; and the other, his much too warped love of life. As a profoundly irrational religion Christianity attracted him. It also appealed to his feminine passivity, to his yearning for inner warmth and for a metaphysical surrender. But Christianity as a religion which has driven joy out of life became repellent to him.

It was largely due to his interest in Christian asceticism that he reacted by embracing the opposite ideal of life. And in doing this he was confronted first of all by the problem of Sex in its physical, moral, spiritual and social significance. He became engrossed with this problem, even obsessed by it. As a result, he arrived at a kind of mystical pan-sexuality which was very unlike that of Freud, and from which he expected a renewal of man and of life.

Yet in spite of his violent reaction against the ascetic ideals, Rozanov still remained a Christian by instincts—an "atavistic" trait which he shares with Nietzsche. But whereas Nietzsche increased the vigour of his anti-Christian utterances in proportion as he became aware of the spiritual temptations on the part of his own latent Christianity, Rozanov adopted a much more cowardly strategy. He attacked mainly from behind the ambush, and always kept ready an emergency exit—in case a retreat should be necessary. The way he combined his anti-Christian attitude towards "flesh" with a continuous reluctance to abandon Christianity was truly astonishing. On the other hand, had he been endowed with a stronger will and character, his field of psychological self-observation would have been much smaller, perhaps, than it was. For Rozanov developed his acuteness while exploiting his own weaknesses and inner contradictions, the "literary" advantages of which he realized, time and again, only too well. No wonder that he refused to abandon the comfortable maternal lap of the Russian Church even during the years of his most scathing attacks—attacks directed against the evils of asceticism, in the detection of which more than once he proved deeper than any of his contemporaries.

IV

The principal feature which Rozanov shares with Lawrence is his hatred of the Christian "spiritualization" of love for the sake of a bloodless and self-lacerating ascetic ideal. It was Christianity he incriminated with that gulf between the sex-less Love and the love-less Sex which is responsible for one of the most painful cleavages in man's nature. Rozanov hated this cleavage all the more because he himself was perhaps only too familiar with it. And not unlike Lawrence, he sought for an escape in that undifferentiated pre-Christian unity between Sex and Love which is typical of an earlier, fresher and more "savage" stage of human consciousness.

In his desire for such a unity (which he considered no less essential for the integration of life than Lawrence did) Rozanov, too, was attracted by various "primitives", particularly by those patriarchical races in whose healthy and spontaneous affirmation of sex he saw an eloquent contrast to Christian ideals. His pets in this respect were not Lawrence's Mexicans with their "dark gods", but the ancient Egyptians, Babylonians, and the Old Testament Jews, on whose culture he threw some valuable gleams.

As for Jews, he was so fascinated by them that his fascination often turned into its own opposite: the Catullian hatred through love—*odi et amo*—so typical of a "womanly" nature. The more he admired them by instinct, the more he attacked them through his frequent and positively nauseating political anti-Semitism.

This duality which is not unlike his ambiguous attitude towards the Russian Church, stuck to him to the end of his life. He had an organic need, as it were, of such inner contrasts and paradoxes. And their very piquancy seemed to be one of his creative stimuli. After all, it was not for nothing that Rozanov was among the first modern admirers and commenters of Dostoevsky.[1] Yet what attracted him in the Jewish race was above all the feature he himself entirely lacked: the wholeness and wholesomeness of its sexual life. Brought up as a gloomy Christian, Rozanov could not help admiring the Old-Testamental pre-moral harmony and matter-of-factness in this respect. He admired them through envy, and envied through admiration. That was why after each of his anti-Semitic fits he usually hurried to praise Judaism, taken in its positive, life-affirming quintessence. And he paid the greatest compliment to it in his last work, *The Apocalypse of our Times,* written shortly before his death in 1919.

V

In contrast to Rozanov's yearning for sexual wholeness, Otto Weininger represents and also advocates the greatest *conscious* cleavage between Sex and Love; between what he calls the sensuous "lower" life on the one hand, and the life of Spirit on the other. His point of departure thus becomes extremely Christian. No Christian could go further in his dualism than Weininger goes, when affirming that "the lower life is merely a projection of the higher on the world of the senses, a reflection of it in the sphere of necessity, as a degradation of it, or its Fall. And the great problem is how the eternal, lofty idea came to be bound with earth. This problem is the guilt of the world. . . . It is the riddle of the universe and of life; the bonding of the unlimited in the bonds of space, of the eternal in time, of the spirit with matter. It is the relation of freedom to necessity, of something to nothing, of God to the devil. The dualism of the world is beyond comprehension; it is the plot of the story of man's Fall, the primitive riddle. It is the binding of eternal life in a perishable being, of the innocent in the guilty."[2]

It was out of such an attitude towards the world that arose Weininger's Manichaean valuation of life, and of love. In love, more than anywhere else, he saw a manifestation of cosmic dualism, expressed in the antinomy between Sex as such and what he calls Eros. While identifying Eros with the idea of the de-sexualized Christian-Platonic *caritas,* he insists—often with an almost hysterical vehemence—that the awakening of Eros as something different from (and utterly opposed to) Sex, is one of the inevitable and most important stages of man's inner development. He never tires of pointing out that Eros and Sex, or love and desire, are "two unlike, mutually exclusive, opposing conditions, and during the time a man really loves, the thought of physical union with the object of his love is insupportable. The more erotic a man is the less he will be troubled with his sexuality, and vice versa. . . . That person lies, or has never known what love is, who says he loves a woman whom he desires. . . . Then there is the 'Platonic love', which the professors of psychology have such a poor opinion of. I should say rather, there is only 'Platonic love', because any other so-called love belongs to the kingdom of the senses: it is the love of

Beatrice, the worship of Madonna. The Babylonian woman is the idol of sexual desire."

It was the feature which Rozanov admired in the Jews—the spontaneous undifferentiated sexual life on the "biological" plane, as well as the glow of physical contact (so dear to Lawrence)—that Weininger detested as "low" and unworthy of human beings. Although a Jew by birth, he therefore rejected the "sensual" Judaism and embraced Christianity, in whose sexless Madonna worship he thought he had discovered the highest expression of Eros.

What is important in Weininger's case is not so much the question whether his solution is right or wrong, but the fact that he refused to look backwards, or to "solve" the conflict by seeking for shelters in a wholeness which is in essence more primitive than the conflict itself. He must have realized that the call of the wild to the sexual state which existed before the cleavage is as futile as Rousseau's naive return to Nature with which it is analogous in more than one respect.

The truth is that no "return" of the sort can ever succeed. In trying to eliminate the gulf between Love and Sex by forcing ourselves into a past stage of consciousness, we do not come to real harmony or integration, but only to that rather messy *mixture* of the two planes, the mixture of biology and metaphysics, which is well known to the readers of Rozanov, and also to those of D. H. Lawrence.

VI

Otto Weininger was the man in whom the differentiation between Sex and Love must have reached a tension verging on madness. Such at least is the impression left by his *Sex and Character,* by his Diaries, and by some of those interesting fragments and essays of his which were published, after his death, under the title *On Ultimate Things* (*Ueber die letzten Dinge*).

In Central Europe there exists an entire literature about Weininger. Still, the sensation once caused by his work was out of proportion with its actual merit. Not a few pages of his unpleasant *opus magnum* are now out of date. The book remains however a valuable personal document whose very aberrations can throw much light upon the mentioned inner conflict.

The acuteness of that conflict was responsible not only for Weininger's rancorous tone, but also for his biassed attitude towards women and the Jews, both of whom he considered representative of the "sexual" principle devoid of Eros. What else could he do but denounce them—for metaphysical and moral reasons! And the vehemence of his attacks was all the stronger the more he was aware of the sensuous "Jew" and the "Woman" within himself.

That is why his notorious *Sex and Character* represents one of the most anti-feminist and at the same time anti-Jewish documents in European literature. But in essence it is a disguised self-attack. It is also a frantic attempt on the part of a spiritually expatriated Semite to take root in the values of a religious mentality which still may seem somewhat alien to his race.

It certainly is amusing to see how Weininger denounces that very sympathy and spontaneous warmth in human intercourse which was so much praised, as well as aimed at, by Rozanov and Lawrence. He was the last person to be impressed by the expansive gregarious propensities of the Jews, and by their "pairing instinct" (as he calls it). Instead of seeing in either of these two tendencies a virtue, he denounced them as vices, typical of both Jews and women. According to him, "like women, Jews tend to adhere together, but they do not associate as free independent individuals mutually respecting each other's individuality. . . . The pairing instinct is the great remover of limits between individuals; and the Jew, *par excellence,* is the breaker down of such limits. He is the opposite pole from aristocrats, with whom the preservation of the limits between individuals is the leading idea. The Jew is an inborn communist. The Jew's careless manners in society and his want of social tact turn on this quality, for the reserves of social intercourse are simply barriers to individuals."

To make his generalizations even more sweeping, he asserts that women and Jews are not individualities enough to know all the inner contradictions of the "Aryan" man. And so, "greatness is absent from the nature of the woman and the Jew, the greatness of morality, the greatness of evil. In the Aryan man the good and bad principles of Kant's religious philosophy are ever present, ever in strife. In the Jew and the woman, good and evil (i.e., Eros and Sex) are not distinct from one another."[3]

VII

Unlike Lawrence and Rozanov, Otto Weininger saw in Sex as such the primeval dark power by means of which Nature opposes the process of individualization and tries to reduce all separate selves to a premoral and pre-individual "Dionysian" welter. Absolute Sex he therefore identified with the absolute negation of both morality and individuality.

A return to the undifferentiated sexual "monism" *à la* Rozanov was therefore considered by him a regression, a fall, even a spiritual suicide, which he would never contemplate. Unwilling to go "back to Sex", and yet unable to overcome the cleavage by a higher balance or synthesis, he saw one solution only: a ruthless suppression of Sex in the name of Eros. Hence the Puritanic fury with which he attacked anything that reminded him of Sex. But like all Puritans, he denounced in everybody the very thing from which he himself suffered and of which he was all the time afraid.

Failing to overcome the antithesis of his own dilemma, Otto Weininger thus could not help thinking mainly in

antitheses. Eros and Sex, Man and Woman, Mother and Prostitute, "Aryans" and Jews—these are some of his dogmatic contrasts. Barricaded behind his moral principles, he refused any compromise, any pourparlers, with the fiend within himself. He rejected wholesale the healthy "non-moral" (as distinct from immoral) sexuality of the same Old Testament which was so much relished by his Russian antipodes, Rozanov. The only salvation he saw was in an unswerving submission to the ascetic ideals of Plato, of the Gospels, and of Kant's "Categorical Imperative".

In his frantic attempts to suppress Sex at any price, Weininger would not even think of Eros as a creative sublimation of Sex—a sublimation which turns our "libido" into an æsthetic and spiritual experience. He refused to see that in true Eros the division between physical and spiritual disappears not because one of them has been suppressed for the sake of the other, but simply because the cleavage itself has been balanced and left behind. This new unity is however poles apart from that pre-moral wholeness in which the cleavage has not even begun to take place. Eros certainly does transcend Sex as such, but for this very reason it also includes and ennobles it. Whenever it fails to do so, Sex has the tendency to turn against Eros, to grow at its expense, and therefore at the expense of the individual.

VIII

Weininger's tragedy was due not so much to the acuteness of his inner conflict as to his own inability to transcend it. In essence he was an over-sexed individual who hated sex because he was only too well aware of his helplessness before it. And so he summoned all his hatred, his "philosophy", his Kant and his logic (often based on false premises) to stay off the enemy. In his moral self-defence he went so far as to turn, eventually, against love of any kind—even against the "higher" Platonic love. In order to discard his own obsession or obsessions, he compared all love with murder. These are some of his conclusions:

"Since Novalis first called attention to it, many have insisted on the association between sexual desire and cruelty. All that is born of woman must die. Reproduction, birth and death are indissolubly associated; the thought of untimely death awakens sexual desire in its fiercest form, as the determination to reproduce oneself. And so sexual union, considered ethically, psychologically, and biologically, is allied to murder. . . . Ordinary sexuality regards the woman only as a means of gratifying passion or of begetting children. The higher eroticism, however, is merciless to the woman because it requires her to be the vehicle of a projected personality, or the mother of psychic children.[4] Such love is not only anti-logical, as it denies the objective truth of the woman and requires an illusory image of her, but it is anti-ethical with regard to her. . . . Madonna worship itself is fundamentally immoral, inasmuch as it is a shutting of the eyes to truth. The Madonna worship of the great artist is a destruction of woman, and is possible only by a complete neglect of the women as they exist in experience; a replacement of actuality by a symbol; a re-creation of woman to serve the purpose of man, and a murder of woman as she exists."

It would be impossible to imagine a greater contrast to the views of Lawrence or of Rozanov, and yet the dilemma with which they both were trying to cope was the dilemma of Weininger. The contrast becomes more than evident when one compares their religious exaltation of sex with such passages of Weininger as these: "The rejection of sexuality is merely the death of the physical life, to put in its place the full development of the spiritual life. . . . The only true goal is divinity and the union of humanity with Godhead; that is the real choice between good and evil, between existence and negation."

Thus the Jew, Otto Weininger, surpasses even the most ardent Christian fanatics of asceticism. In his final conclusion he not only agrees with aged Tolstoy and his *Kreutzer Sonata,* but becomes even more radical and more stern than the sage of Yasnaya Polyana. We know, however, that at the bottom of Tolstoy's Puritanism there was a fight against his half-suppressed lust. A similar fight, and hardly less intense than in Tolstoy, was the secret of Weininger also. But instead of Tolstoy's biological horror of death, Weininger was haunted by a metaphysical horror comparable to that of August Strindberg (during his last phase) or, recently, of Franz Kafka, the author of *The Castle.*

IX

Only an inveterate sensualist, grimly struggling against his own latent sensuality, could have written such an ultra-Puritanic book as *Sex and Character.* In this respect Otto Weininger could almost be defined as D. H. Lawrence from the other end. For D. H. Lawrence suffered from the opposite fault: from too much Puritanism, inherited and innate Puritanism, which he was anxious to eliminate by a forced affirmation of senses and of Sex.[5] But like Lawrence who remained, with all his anti-Puritanism, a disguised self-righteous Puritan to the end of his days, Weininger remained a disguised voluptuary.

It is even possible that Weininger's suppressed sensuality was of a perverted kind—a thing of which Rozanov more than suspected him when writing in *Fallen Leaves* (Wishart): "From every page of Weininger's there is heard the shout 'I love men'. 'Well, you're a sodomite then', and with that you may close the book. . . . He speaks of *all women* as if they were his rivals, just with the same irritation. . . . His jealousy of women (for men) made him hate 'women-rivals'. And along with this he is full of the most profound moral nostalgia; and thereby revealed the moral nature of women, which he in his jealousy denies."

If Rozanov be right (and there are factors supporting his suspicion), then Weininger's tragedy becomes all the more confused and poignant. His eventual suicide may even have been prompted to him by *moral* reasons—by the fear he would not be strong enough to resist the perverted temptations of "flesh" which threatened to hurl him down from his ascetic pinnacles.

Facing the choice between the physical and the spiritual death (or what he considered as such), he preferred the former. He sacrificed his life to his intense moral will. In this way his end is so different from that of Rozanov. For even in his death Rozanov took the line of least resistance. Peacefully reconciled, he died in the warm lap of that very Church whose ascetic spirit he had been fighting for years.

NOTES

[1] Rozanov's first wife—his senior by some twenty years—was the one-time mistress of Dostoevsky, Mlle. Suslova. Paulina in Dostoevsky's "Gambler" is supposed to be her portrait.

[2] This and other quotations are from the English edition of *Sex and Character.* (Heinemann.)

[3] The nonsensical and utterly dilettantish "Aryan" twaddle in Hitlerite Germany is due, not only to *Gobineau* (via Houston Chamberlain, faked Nietzsche, and Spengler), but partly also to the pathologic and purely personal outbursts of the Jew, Otto Weininger.

[4] He means Dante's love in *Vita Nuova* and *Divine Comedy.* J.L.

[5] This tendency was tinged and complicated in him by his strong "mother-complex", and probably also by a hidden fear of losing (through consumption or some physical defect) his virility. His vehemence, reminiscent at times of a "hot-gospeller", is not a proof of real strength, but only of a yearning for it.

Leon Katz (essay date 1978)

SOURCE: "Weininger and *The Making of Americans,*" in *Twentieth Century Literature,* Vol. 24, No. 1, Spring, 1978, pp. 8-26.

[*In the following essay, Katz explains Gertude Stein's initial encounters with and eventual assimilation of Weininger's theories and the ways in which they affected her writing and her views of character and gender.*]

It is a significant mistake that [Gertrude] Stein remembered starting *The Making of Americans* in 1906 and finishing it in 1908.[1] As with many of her inaccurate reflections, this one was patently false and yet bore a kind of truth that explains its error. For from the spring of 1906, when she took up work on the novel in earnest, she pursued her original purpose of showing "the old world in the new or more exactly the new world all made out of the old"; but in the summer of 1908 the book suddenly began to develop explicitly and in earnest the understanding of personality first used in *Melanctha,* and which had implied, when it was being used most authentically in *Melanctha,* a contradiction of the fictional form itself. When this understanding of character description was brought to its logical conclusion in the last chapter of *The Making of Americans,* Stein had moved outside the conventions of communicative literary art—a development in her writing which, because its continuity has not been apparent, has come to symbolize the capricious and irresponsible side of twentieth-century art.

The transition from the realistic and thoroughly conventional first novel to the unique manner of the second followed inevitably from the fixed allure that psychological schematizing held for her, but the catalyst that led to so sudden and dramatic a change in the novel's purpose and method in the summer of 1908 was a book that fell into her hands during the previous winter.

It was probably Leo Stein who first picked up a copy of Otto Weininger's **Sex and Character**[2] in a bookshop, though, as in the case of buying pictures, it is a debatable question whether Leo himself or he and Gertrude together first came across the book and bought it.[3] In any case, they were among the first of their acquaintances to read it, and for the rest of the winter until they set off for Florence in May of 1908, the book was the center of violent discussion. After the first enthusiasm, they sent copies to everyone, even to old friends in America.[4] Leo felt that Weininger was an example of pure genius, and since he was meeting regularly with Roché about once a week during that winter for hours-long discussions of set subjects, they used Weininger's book for a while as their focus, and as Leo adumbrated, Roché interlarded his copy of the book with Leo's notes and comments. Leo responded for a time to Weininger's antifeminism, and at the peak of his interest in him, declared that if one could take women's minds off their wombs, they might be helped to some kind of development after all.[5] But his interest in this project passed, and he returned soon to his more comfortable preoccupations with questions of consciousness and of art.

Gertrude's response to Weininger left more permanent impress on her; the book confirmed and extended a variety of her own current beliefs, but most importantly of all, prodded her toward emulating Weininger's systematization of psychology. From the beginning, she avoided Leo's invitations to point-by-point discussion of the book, and though she shared his enthusiasm for it entirely, she felt that once Weininger started his premises rolling, the rest of his elaborate argument followed normally and without surprise, needing neither discussion nor elaboration.[6] Regarding the book as a major contribution to the study of character, she felt Weininger's work corroborated her own. He clarified problems of description and explanation on which she had been foundering and suggested almost limitless descriptions of relations among the mass of people she was using for the character studies in her notebooks. The surge of renewed speculation finally broke the confines of the fictional frame to which she was still clinging in the novel, and to use up the new possibilities, and the quantities of notes that were accumulating, she started several studies of characters, the most important of which were *A Long Gay Book, Many Many Women,* and a work published as *Two: Gertrude Stein and Her Brother,* but which is in fact an analysis not of Gertrude but of her sister-in-law Sarah Stein and of Leo.[7]

Weininger's book was ostensibly nothing more than a violent antifeminist tract basing its argument on a definition of the psychological differences between "maleness" and "femaleness," and pushing its argument into the outer reaches of the absurd by equating the highest individual possible with the "total male" and the lowest with the "total female."[8] Except for a noticeable change in Stein's tone in analyzing men and women after reading Weininger—she adopted his vocabulary and his animus against women freely during the early months of his influence on her writing[9]—and her tentative borrowing of Weininger's basic distinction between male and female for the basic distinction used for her own system,[10] this part of Weininger's animadversions had little permanent interest for her. His book was fundamentally concerned, however, with much more interesting and useful matters, and these Stein either availed herself of for the first time or used to bolster the direction in which her own views and interests had already been tending.

The nature of his influence must be carefully defined, since Stein's way of absorbing influence was aberrant and unusual. That the book was of major importance in the framing of the "system" Stein organized at this time is evident, but there is little point in looking for logical extensions of Weininger's notions in her work, or even for the presence of his ideas in their own logical context. Her relations with books and ideas were neither disciplined nor conscientious. Unlike Leo, whose reading in philosophy and psychology kept abreast with his interests in art and in letters, Stein appears to have read little but narrative during these years, with almost the single exception of Weininger's book; nor was she habituated to precise comprehension of close philosophic reasoning. It is even possible to suspect that her reading Weininger at all is largely a reflection on the blunt, dogmatic, unshaved, and unqualified clarity of his reasoning. Stein would easily have been held by his flamboyant way of sweeping aside, in compact and violently lucid paragraphs, centuries of common belief. The very qualities of his writing that caused him to be dismissed and laughed at (Freud thought he was mad) would have been the ones to awaken startled interest in her, and a host of tangential ruminations.

Tangential rumination was her way. Leo's and Roché's cognition over and burrowing through the connective tissue of Weininger's elaborate thesis was avoided by Stein, who was interested in new suggestions only if they could be woven into the fabric of her own beliefs. The evidence of the extent to which she carried such assimilation does her no credit. Though she speaks of Weininger as a genius in the notebooks[11] and quotes fragments of his book at length,[12] she actually writes in one entry, "That thing of mine of sex and mind and character all coming together seems to work absolutely."

The aspect of Weininger's thesis that would have struck her immediately was his orientation toward the problem of a science of psychology. Like Nietzsche, Weininger believed psychology to be the "queen of the sciences," but experimental psychology as he knew it in Germany and Austria, and as Stein had known it in America at the Harvard Psychological Laboratory, was for Weininger not merely a superficial but an irrelevant approach to true psychological inquiry.

> If anything is to be gained in the future there must be a demand for a really psychological psychology, and its first battle-cry must be: "Away with the study of sensations."[13]

> This unlimited science of character . . . will be more than a sort of polity of the motor and sensory reactions of the individual, and in so far will not sink so low as the usual "results" of the modern experimental psychologists, which, indeed, are little more than statistics of physical experiments. . . . The two most intelligent of the empirical psychologists of recent times, William James and R. Avenarius, have felt almost instinctively that psychology cannot really rest upon sensations of the skin and muscles, although, indeed, all modern psychology does depend upon study of sensations.[14]

Stein, having come to the same conclusion about experimental psychology in the course of her work at Harvard, had already anticipated Weininger's substitute for it: a "broad and deep characterology," at the heart of which would *not* be "a complex system of coordinate lines" signifying the "particular determinants" for the description of each individual, for this would only result in, as Weininger put it, "a mosaic psychology"—a psychology which defines character by a mosaic of typifying adjectives. It is true that both Weininger and Stein, in their separate but wholly parallel endeavors in creating a characterology, expended a good deal of energy in trying to "determine the exact point occupied by an individual on the line between two extremes, and multiply this determination by discovering it for a great many characters"; still, beyond this preliminary charting of terms, the essence of Weininger's search lies in the attempt to discover and describe "the single and simple existence" in a man, his "character" in this "unlimited" sense, which "is not something seated behind the thoughts and feeling in the individual, but something revealing itself in every thought and feeling." "This existence, manifest in every moment of the psychical life, is the object of characterology."[15] Stein had already, both in *Melanctha* and in *QED,* attempted to describe the operation of a "ruling force"—not *in* character, but *of* char-

acter—the sense in which the "whole man is manifest in every moment of the psychical life, although, now one side, now the other, is more visible";[16] she had already attempted to inform her string-of-adjectives descriptions of her characters in those works with some principle of wholeness which she thought of as their pulse, their "timing," their rhythm. Weininger was now to make her goal explicit for her: to achieve a synoptic vision of the ego of each character so inclusive that the character's every act and sensation could be observed in its whole relevance to the complete field of his ego. The observer, passing beyond the need to separate one "aspect" of personality from another—a separation which he can accomplish only by the trick of abstraction—would seize on his wholeness, and in that way know in each character "the last touch of [his] human being."

This was precisely the intention Stein first fully recognized in herself during her wrestlings with Annette Rosenshine's woes, and Weininger's fixing of the problem—coming as it did in the midst of her work with Annette—became a kind of call to action in both her messianic psychological activity and her writing.[17] Weininger certainly did not have the effect of changing her intention in her writing, but rather of suppressing all others—all general themes, all ethical precepts, all plans for the narrative, in favor of this single pursuit.

There was no further writing done of any other kind; all of *The Making of Americans* written after 1908, and all of the portraits and short works written through 1911, are "characterological" and nothing else, either diagramming relations among many or setting down synoptic visions of one.

Weininger's psychology, beginning as it does from philosophic premises, is itself not worked out in *Sex and Character,* but merely anticipated.[18] His explosion is *toward* a psychology of character, and lays the basis for both the fundamental typology through which distinctions of character may be described and the ultimate conception of the nature of character which transcends the "mosaic" of typologies.

The typology itself begins with a basic distinction between male and female, as representing, not "types" in human being, but factors. He posits bisexuality in all human beings, whereby the basic sexual nature of a single human being is made up of maleness and femaleness in varying proportions. Human relations in love, in friendship, in hostility, are predicated on the basis of instinctive pairing of opposite "types"—that is, those whose sexual natures complement one another (producing love) and those whose sexual components are similar (producing hostility or indifference).

The opacity and mathematical rigidity of this system is extraordinary. Weininger even went so far as to express his "Laws of Sexual Attraction" in formulae such as

$$A = \frac{K}{a-b} f^t$$

where f is an empirical or analytical function of the period during which it is possible for the individuals to act upon one another, what may be called the "reaction-time"; whilst K is the variable factor in which we place all the known and unknown laws of sexual affinity [etc., etc.].[19]

But Weininger's naïve scientism is a little mitigated by his detailed enumeration of the factors either belonging to or attending on the two sexual natures, although his violent dogmatism is given even more free play in these enumerations: everything good is male, everything bad is female.

It is important to understand the distinction, though, that some of these characteristics are *components* of the sexual bases, while others are merely attendant on them. Further, some "factors" that contribute to the description of human being are not present at all in one of the ideal types. "Femaleness," for example, not being capable of conceiving of the good, cannot be spoken of as either ethical or unethical; it is merely nonethical. Nor can it be spoken of in terms of lying and telling the truth, for it cannot conceive the truth.[20]

The descriptive attributes of male and female are further particularized in relation to the categories of mind, religion, ethics, existence, individuality,[21] and so on. All these categories are subsequently mirrored in Stein's system; even when she breaks away from the basic separation of types into male and female, her own two basic types continue to be examined in relation to Weininger's categories.

A further problem concerning sex in relation to character is elucidated by Weininger and in turn provides matter for Stein's own system. Since no ideal male or female exists, in a proper psychology both must be treated merely as fictions, valuable as descriptive terms but not to be confused with the actual facts of human being. The error of psychology has always been, says Weininger, that it has been diverted into endless attempts to describe such unrealities as ideal types, but a true characterology must describe actual human beings and the relations among them, not the relations of descriptive terms to one another. Experimental psychology fails in this task because the observations it makes through experimental and statistical methods can never be better than the descriptive categories within which it is making them, and not being grounded in a thoroughly and conscientiously explored philosophy of character, it endlessly confuses even its primitive, unsophisticated descriptive terms with observable instances of human being.[22]

The characterology to which Weininger is looking forward, then, is to meet the practical problem of description with greater refinement of terms and a more precise elaboration of its philosophic justification than had ever before been attempted. And since his own book is merely a preliminary excursion into the philosophy of psychology, and far from a model exercise in psychologizing itself, he confesses that the refinement of psychological terms will have to be far greater than he himself provides in his own work. Nevertheless, he offers examples in his book of the kind of categorizing that is to be done.

Beginning with the assertion that the male-female component in each human being is at the base of his character, the problem of description is that of working out the precise relation of a man's "temperament" and "mind" to his sexual base. To do this intelligibly, various "ideal" combinations of maleness and femaleness must be used as categories. Weininger uses common and recognizable character roles to name artificially fixed points along the line of gradation from total male to total female and matches up these "ideal" fixed points for man and woman by pairing "roles" that are equivalent for each of them. The female prostitute, for example, is equivalent to the male politician; both, as sexual types, are located near the extreme of total femaleness, exhibiting the same self-negating urges of servility, lack of memory, and moral apathy.[23] Since the book is an antifeminist tract, Weininger concentrates on enumerating female roles to attack woman; men's roles are named sparsely.

Stein's system is noticeably afflicted by this imbalance in her source. Her names for female roles include all of Weininger's suggestions, and her additional terms are consistent in kind with his originals. His enumerated female roles are prostitute, mother, servant, saint, and masculine woman.[24] Stein's variations on these are prostitute, "mother of all," servant girl, and "genuine masculine."[25] Weininger's "saint" disappears as a group in her system except for a single instance: Alice Toklas is called by either her own name or St. Theresa's, though the original significance of "saint" is gone. In Weininger, saints exemplify hysteria in women; in Stein, "St. Theresa" is an instance of self-effacing devotion akin to, and allied to, the femininity of the prostitute.[26] Stein adds four women's roles to Weininger's: the "lady," the "mistress," the "sister," and the "spinster." These are juxtaposed in subgroups and combinations such as the "mistress prostitute," the "lady masculine," the "pseudo-masculine,"[27] and so on.

In establishing male groups—finding little to go on in Weininger—her inability to cope for long with a logical scheme betrays her. After striking obvious parallels to some of Weininger's female groups, she adds whimsical and privately suggestive names for male groups that are inconsistent as classification with the other terms and among themselves. They are unhappily as consistently banal, too, as the names she inherited. The list runs: "Bazarofian," man-of-the-world, Anglo-Saxon, masculine prostitute, adolescent, old tabby, fanatic, and primitive soul. One additional large group—idealist—is divided into four subgroups, depending upon what one is being idealistic about: intellect, beauty, romance, or power.[28]

But more significant than any of the terms and categories that Stein took from Weininger—and the aspect of his work that apparently struck her most forcibly—was his immensely pertinent resolution of her original twin problem: the conscious feeling of dissociation from the cosmos (in her phrase, the loss of the "feeling of ever-lasting") and that contemporary description of men as bundles of "factors" and causative patterns which leads to a loss of one's sense of uniqueness (in her phrase, that "each one is one").[29]

Since Weininger's interests are fundamentally ethical and metaphysical, his psychology of "character" moves unswervingly toward the definition of "ultimate" human being, which is defined in terms of consciousness. Ultimate self-consciousness embraces absolute memory, absolute self-comprehension, and truth; and ultimate cosmic consciousness embraces absolute identification and unqualified relation of the self with the universal and the eternal. For Weininger, therefore, the completed individual is one whose consciousness—and therefore whose true existence—has moved outside of time and has thereby conquered it.[30]

The importance of this notion for Stein can hardly be overestimated. It appears at length in her work first in the portrait of David Hersland, but later in her work—in her speculative writing of the 1930s—this notion of the "completed individual" continued to be the basis of her repeated attempts to lay to rest her nineteenth century dilemmas concerning loss of uniqueness and "everlasting." The concept of the completed individual, "outside of time," became in fact the unifying locus of her thought from the beginning to the end of her writing.

William James's *The Will to Believe* was merely a disappointment to her hope that it, at least, might mitigate her large metaphysical desperations.[31] Whatever logic exists in her speculative writing rests on her denial of pragmatism and her conscientious attempt to shore up against its ruins minimal certainties on the basis of Weininger's Kantian idealism. The whole incrustation of Stein's ideas and feelings in her writings from 1908 to the end of her life derives from Weininger's envisioning of the highest "type" of human being—the only true individuality—in terms of his achieving the promise of immortality by escaping from the contingency of time. Her later discussions of human nature as opposed to the human mind, of genius, of memory, of the hopelessness of "human nature" (for her, the "diagrammed" aspects of human being) achieving "entity" out of itself, and her notion that the "human mind" alone and of itself can effect and know its own "entity"—all these discussions elaborate the basic definition in Weininger of the steps whereby the ultimately human redeems itself from the "mosaic" of factors currently accounting for human existence. And Stein follows Weininger's system of values to its end by insisting that this victory over time is achieved only by means of those qualities and capabilities of mind and spirit that belong to the genius or to the saint alone. In her writing of the 1920s and 1930s, the relevance of saints to her thought, the meaning of works such as "Saints and Singing," the meaning, in *The*

Mother of Us All, of Susan B. Anthony's "You may be married to the past one, no one can be married to the present one, the one, the one, the present one,"[32] the rationale of her insistence on her own genius (apart from its basis in personal idiosyncracy), may be looked for in her emulation of Weininger's unqualified and unlimited individuality, incapable of being known to others but capable only of being self-known, and the consequence to human being of such a creature coming to fruition.

Her enthusiasm for this new conception was first expressed in her revision and enlargement of the portrait of David Hersland in the novel. In the first version of the novel, he was to be merely "singular" as a Westerner—and in terms of the first version, that was eminence enough. Now, in the 1908 notes for revision, his "singularity" is given Weiningerian dimensions. Make "David completed individual," she instructs herself, and further, "must realise my hero by making him go through my development."[33] Understood in this light, does this mean that David was to be the "genius" of Weininger's description? No, he was to be merely the character in the book who might have been, the only character of whom one might properly say that he should have been, and failed. None of the other characters have sufficient "being" to be worthy of such a failure—neither their success nor their failure is on a par with his. As in the original plan of the book, he remains a defeated man, trapped by his longing for death.

To give his failure further distinction, Stein added her own imagined characterization of Weininger himself, when she made the shocking discovery of his suicide.[34] After that discovery, everything fitted anew: her own "sense of failure" at twenty-nine (that is, in 1903, her desperate "suicidal" year after the abortive May Bookstaver affair); Leon Solomon's "suicide" when he "chose" cancer and, more verifiably, chose to undergo a fatal operation at the age of twenty-nine; and finally Weininger's suicide after his brilliant achievement, especially relevant since that achievement rested so largely on the intellectual comprehension and expression of the victory the "singular" individual is capable of winning over death. Weininger, a Jew, could be understood, then, to have suffered from what Stein thought of as the inevitable failure of Jews: that they "run themselves by their minds."[35] And David, in the 1908 revision, so acquired one of his subtlest dimensions. Beyond his longing to discover why he should be alive—a cripplingly laborious activity in itself—he "runs" himself and his inquiry "by his mind," and so shares in the tragic mistakes of Weininger the man; but all the while he is making this error as a man, he is moving toward the discovery of and in part becoming the embodiment of, the individual envisioned by Weininger the philosopher.

The abrupt change in the style as well as in the subject matter of the novel occurred in the summer of 1908, when everything in her writing was subordinated to the double inquiry recommended by Weininger. During the winter of 1907-08, when the new endeavor was gradually sharpening in focus, Gertrude's conversation appears to have taken on a new intensity and seriousness, and her "studies" of friends became so all-consuming an activity that she thoroughly lost interest in everything else. Nothing mattered now but classification of everybody and unique illumination of test cases.

During the winter, the assimilation of Weininger into her own already vaguely forming system was at first awkward and tentative, for in one crucial respect, her own insight remained at variance with his. Not until she made the discovery on her own of Weininger's central proposition concerning character was she able to incorporate satisfactorily his terms and values into her own; when this was accomplished, the assimilation of Weininger and the enlargement of her own psychological system proceeded with a rush, and with abandon.

The crucial obstacle lay in Weininger's positing of a one-to-one relation between sex and character. "Sex" for him was simply the degree of masculinity or femininity in any given case, not so much a "bottom layer" of personality as a pervasive control of all character manifestations, the most significant being the degree of "consciousness" attained by a human being—another way of saying the degree of masculinity he possessed.[36] But Gertrude's whole interest in character was centered in its dynamic—and for her it was dynamic in two senses. She "saw" character in the thrust and withdrawal, the attack and resistance, the fight and surrender, the campaigning skill or ineptitude of human beings; from the days of her earliest writing, and her first analyses of May Bookstaver and Mabel Haynes, characters became clarified for her, became "themselves" in fact, when they were in motion, struggling, winning, and losing in their endless war for power over one another. But it was "dynamic" in another sense, too: *within* a human being, there were complex, uncharted motions of separate nuclei of being which moved in characteristic and increasingly habitual and recognizable ways—characteristically appearing and disappearing from view, habitually colliding and collaborating with one another—tending toward "harmony" if the separate motions and divagations were consistent with one another, and toward "shipwreck" if they contradicted each other.[37] But this whole interior solar system of delicate ruptures and delicate balances had two aspects that were of primary interest to her. The first was that each one had a constant of some kind that guaranteed the uniqueness and consistency of character throughout one's life.[38] The second was that, from the point of view of the observer, there was some sort of order—an "arrangement" of facets of character—through which order the whole character was gradually to be seen and ultimately to be understood.[39] It is these two convictions concerning the nature and the understanding of character that remained with Stein to the end of her "struggle" with her problem. Through each of the shifts of her growing psychological conception, she retained always, as her central curiosity, the observing of character's "drama of emergence." What was "emerg-

ing" in the course of her study of Annette—going on concurrently with the discovery of Weininger—was a profoundly felt but descriptively useless conception of "bottom being." For however abstractly formulaic might be Weininger's conception of the role of sexuality in the revelation of character, it was nevertheless, compared to Stein's mystique about bottom being, precision and clarity itself. To make use of either notion in her own system, it was necessary for Stein to adopt some kind of conceptual precision into her image of all the loosely circulating "beings" within character so that one character could be made comparable to another. The problem of clarifying what she was talking about led her off course: she attempted to stratify facets of character into "layers" on the assumption that if there was a "bottom" there necessarily was a "top," and probably some sort of middle as well. The attempt was rendered doubly foolish when she adopted as the names for her three strata the distinctions Weininger most persistently employed, of sex and character and intellect.

In the fall of 1907 Stein first began recording the new "system" in several notebooks, the most important of which she labeled "The Diagram Book."[40] She begins the record of the system with a note on the triple division she was borrowing tentatively from Weininger: a long, wavering line is drawn down the first page of "The Diagram Book" with the word "top" scrawled at the top of it, and halfway down, "middle," and at the bottom, "what it comes from."[41] Valiantly, in the first months of recording the system, she tries to hold to this triple division and names the levels "sex" for the bottom one and variously "temperament" or "character" for the second and "ideals" or "mind" or "intellect" for the first.

But in point of fact these terms do not mirror her notion of the layers of being at all. Her genuine allegiance was to the notion of repetition in being, and in terms of this notion, "layers" could not signify different aspects of being, but the same ones at various removes from the observer and from the character's consciousness. Nor was it consistent for her to speak of sex as the bottommost level of being, since her real concept of "bottom being" was in no sense monistic. To discover the "bottom" level of character was not to find the secret explanation and the driving impulse of character; for character was a "system" of interrelated impulses and habits, and the "bottom" was simply the range of such interrelations furthest removed from consciousness. Rather than a single force impelling behavior fundamentally, it was itself a "system" of impulses, both reflecting and reflected in all the others. There was, then, no single "secret" of character other than the "secret" of the unique organization in each individual of a whole complex operation.

Her unsettled feeling that she was not describing what she intended to describe can be traced through the notes on the system during the fall and winter of 1907-08, but the problem is finally laid to rest to her satisfaction. In the course of a conversation during the winter, she suddenly realized the use to which she could put Weininger's divisions to create a sufficient and consistent range of terms to describe the dynamic operation within character without violating her feeling that each "level" repeated aspects of personality. "That epoch-making—for me—conversation with Harriet about Sally," she recalls in the notebooks, was one in which Harriet Levy described Sarah Stein, according to Gertrude, accurately; but as in the case of Annette, Gertrude found her accurate only generally—"all but the bottom." In her rejoinder to Harriet, she apparently felt that she took "the bottom" into account, and, doing so, found herself with an explanation of Sally's "success" as a human being that gave her the clue she needed: Sally, she explained, exhibited a sexual "type and temperament and ideal all flowing together to a perfect harmony."[42] The value, then, of Weininger's sexual types was that one could elicit from them, according to his analysis, their counterparts in terms of "character" and "intellect." But Stein preserves her sense of the uniqueness of each individual arrangement of elements by supposing that these triple groupings are by no means inevitably yoked in a single personality. On the contrary, their occurrence in harmony is exceptional, and signifies, when it does occur, the "success" of a personality. The pure prostitute, for example, ought ideally to have no interest in "running herself by her mind" because she has none, damned, according to Weininger, by her lack of all memory, all consciousness, and all sense of ethical distinction. But, in fact, the most frequent failure of this type, as Stein reiterated for a considerable number of women, lay in the very mistake of using their intellects as their chief weapon in their struggle for power, for security, and for self-esteem. Assuming that both the prostitute sexual nature and the mistaken use of the intellect are not at different "levels," but at the same one in a given character, it becomes further possible for the bottommost level of the same character to exhibit a different sexuality altogether, and at this level an altogether different relation between sexuality and intellect may be operating. Without enumerating further variations, it is clear that the possibilities of scrutinizing permanent success and failure of personality, intermittent success and failure, and contradictory success and failure at different "levels" of being are almost endless. Weininger's "whole" person becomes merely a single level of Stein's. The relations within a single person, therefore, become almost as various as the relations among people.[43]

Having supplanted Weininger's notion of sexuality as the fixed base of character, Stein was free also to dispense with "sexuality" as the basis for dividing personalities into types and to develop as her fundamental distinction in character one that came more naturally to her and one that has been fundamental to her own sense of character from the beginning. By the time she concluded "The Diagram Book" and the notebooks written concurrently, "attack" and "resistance," not Weininger's "maleness" and "femaleness," are used as the alpha and omega of her classification.[44] The central division of her whole system, then, reflects the two chief human activities on which she dwelled most largely during the early years when her psychological interests were becoming fixed: fighting and loving. Alternatively, her two basic types are also those who need to love and those who need to be loved. These two complementary needs—reflecting the complementary roles of maleness and femaleness in Weininger, but no longer intending the same distinction—overlap but do not everywhere coalesce with the notions of attack and resistance. They overlap because the two "needs" are thought of simply as the controlling factors in the choice of weapons in human relations: always, Stein thought of human relations, with cold consistency, in terms of battle.

Enormously elaborate and unaccountably fascinating though Stein's subsequent immense proliferations of her system may be, it is not the business of this essay to explore them, restricted as it is to an account of Stein's way to the threshold of her book rather than to her even more astonishing adventures when she crossed it. She had found a profoundly stimulating new dedication for her work because of Weininger, and found in him further a multiplicity of suggestions which, when they stopped confusing her, impelled the enlargement of her observation and reference.

To be sure, the whole bent of her writing had been tending in the direction marked out by Weininger from the beginning of her work, and assuredly her instinctive sense of "character" would have become increasingly articulate without Weininger's help. The difference his book made was in the complete, undivided absorption with which she turned to the composition of a systematic psychology of human relations, building on the philosophic justification and the preliminary lines so clearly drawn by him.

With his corroboration and detailed guidance, she undertook in all seriousness the heroic labor of describing all the possible kinds of human being and built her system with the ultimate hope that there would grow out of its terminological network sufficient bases for her to grasp in the end the goal set by him—evincing the "last touch" of human being. And during the years that were to follow, when the monotonous and often discouraging labor was under way, with small daily increments of new observations, connections, and expansions gathered into the notebooks and rephrased for use in current writing on the novel and the smaller peripheral works, she held on to the philosophic justification of her impossible undertaking and stood up successfully under the criticism before which she had previously demurred—her brother Leo's. When he became aware of what she was doing, he took violent exception to both its method and its goal, and commented, as a good Jamesian, that classifying human beings in this arbitrary way was simply creating another "teleology"—of less than no use to science or to general knowledge. His comment fixed her purpose—and certainly started the break with him and with her own past intellectual loyalties. The break was a bold, startling, and immensely difficult step for her; and as it turned out, it was also the beginning of her settling knowingly into creative loneliness.

> When Leo said that all classification was teleo-logical I knew I was not a pragmatist. I do not believe that, I believe in reality as Cézanne or Caliban believe in it. I believe in repetition. Yes. Always and always write the hymn of repetition. Sterne gave me the feeling of it.[45]

The "reality" she is talking about is not merely Weininger's suggested "system." It is the reality of what she "heard with her ears" as it was coming out of Maurice Sterne—his talk repeating its own pattern and also the pattern, to use Weininger's phrase, of the "single and simple existence" of the man "revealing it-self in every thought and feeling." Her own insight wedded to Weininger's projected psychology fired the vision that clearly overwhelmed her. Each man repeat-ing himself, each man being of a "kind," and in an endless multiplicity of relations, through the compo-nents of being that all men share with all other "kinds"—, this panoramic vision of endless human repetition was now to be hymned in full.

NOTES

[1] Title page, *The Making of Americans* (Paris: Contact Editions, 1925). All subsequent complete editions are offsets of this edition. *The Making of Americans* will hereafter be abbreviated as *MA.*

[2] Otto Weininger, *Sex and Character* (London: William Heinemann; New York: G. P. Putnam's Sons, 1906).

[3] Alice B. Toklas, interviews, and Henri Pierre Roché, interview. From November of 1952 to February of 1953 Toklas adumbrated and orally annotated the "Note-books" out of her store of memories for about eight hours a day, four days a week. See footnote 9 for a history of the "Notebooks." For information on Roché see *The Autobiography of Alice B. Toklas* (New York: Harcourt, Brace and Co., 1933), pp. 54-55, 123.

[4] Letters, E. L. Erving to GS, December 14, 1908, and May 3, 1909; Marion Walker to GS, 1909. All letters referred to in this article are part of the Gertrude Stein Collection, the Yale Collection of American Literature, the Beinecke Rare Book and Manuscript Library, Yale University.

[5] Roché, interview.

[6] Toklas, interviews.

[7] Gertrude Stein, *Two: Gertrude Stein and Her Brother, and Other Early Portraits (1908-1912)* (New Haven: Yale Univ. Press, 1951). *A Long Gay Book* and *Many Many Women* were published in *Matisse Picasso and Gertrude Stein* (Paris: Plain Edition, 1933).

[8] Weininger, pp. 5-10.

[9] See especially *NB*-DB, passim. It was Thornton Wilder who warned Gertrude Stein in 1936 to get her unpublished manuscripts into the safekeeping of the Yale Library be-cause of the danger of another world's war breaking out on French soil. Charmed by the notion that all her work was to be safely harbored for later publication and study, Stein packed several cases of material consisting of manu-scripts, letters, and miscellany and sent them off. The packing was done with characteristic Steinian abandon: neatly piled manuscripts were dumped into crates, and correspondence, carefully alphabetized and filed at the end of each year by Stein's amanuensis, Alice Toklas, was pulled out in drawerfuls and overturned into boxes. Fi-nally, all the scraps of paper that Stein never threw away, budget lists, garage attendants' instructions about the Fords she owned, forgotten old bills, were tossed in, too. Toklas remonstrated about their inclusion, but Stein used every hoarder's excuse: "You can never tell whether some laundry list might not be the most important thing."

Two packages in brown wrapping paper at the bottom of the armoire, lying among chunks of manuscript of the novel, *The Making of Americans,* fell into the crates along with the other papers. Stein had forgotten what they contained, and Toklas had never seen them, and merely assumed they were part of the manuscript. When they were opened at Yale some time later, they revealed a mound of copybooks small enough to push into one's pocket, and one or two school-children's notebooks. Sheets that had been torn out of the little books were found in the original manuscripts of *The Making of Americans* and the other works concurrent with it. When the small pads, the large copybooks, and the scat-tered scraps were all assembled, they made up a star-tling continuity of discourse that may be regarded (with her letters) as Stein's only remaining unpublished work, her "Notebooks." The penciled scrawls were the writing notes and comments she made to herself, never intended to be seen by anyone and so recorded without any self-conscious concern for the bluntness of their style or the injudicious nature of their content. They were the notes from which she worked directly for most of her writing from 1902 to 1911. At the time of transcription of the "Notebooks," this author numbered and lettered the manuscript booklets. Hereafter the "Notebooks" will be cited as *NB* followed by an identifying code.

[10] *NB*-DB, p. 16.

[11] *NB*-A, pp. 15, 16; *NB,* 'Note #49.

[12] Weininger's quotation from Kant's *Anthropology,* p. 161, is in turn quoted by GS in an unassigned fragment. Two other unassigned notes quote passages from *Sex and Character.*

[13] Weininger, p. 83.

[14] Ibid., pp. 81-82.

[15] Ibid., p. 83.

[16] Ibid.

[17] Gertrude's and Sarah Stein's sessions with Annette Rosenshine, during which they alternately attempted to cure their patient of her neuroses (Sarah with Christian Science and Gertrude with her own aggressive brand of psychological analysis), is recounted in Annette Rosenshine's unpublished memoirs, "Life's Not a Paragraph," deposited in the Bancroft Library, University of California at Berkeley.

[18] Weininger, p. ix.

[19] Ibid., pp. 37-38, 195.

[20] Ibid., p. 130.

[21] Ibid., Ch. IX.

[22] Ibid., pp. 82, 84.

[23] Ibid., p. 228.

[24] Ibid., pp. 8, 17, 214-35, 272, 277.

[25] The concurrent *NB*s, *NB*-DB and *NB*-C, detail these types.

[26] *NB*-D, pp. 4, 6, 8, 9, 10, 15; *NB*-E, p. 11.

[27] *NB*-DB, *NB*-B, *NB*-C, and *NB*-J.

[28] *NB*-DB, pp. 8, 9, 10, 11, 13, 17, 18; Note #45.

[29] Refrain used in *Many Many Women,* published in *Matisse Picasso and Gertrude Stein,* pp. 119-98.

[30] Weininger, pp. 136-37:

> Memory only fully vanquishes time when it appears in a universal form, as in universal men.
>
> The genius is thus the only timeless man—at least, this and nothing else is his ideal of himself; he is, as is proved by his passionate and urgent desire for immortality, just the man with the strongest demand for timelessness, with the greatest desire for value. . . . His universal comprehension and memory forbid the annihilation of his experiences with the passing of the moment in which each occurred; his birth is independent of his age, and his work never dies.

[31] The most considerable misunderstanding involves the importance of the influence of William James. (The influence of William James's "practical and radical empiricism" is thoroughly argued by Frederick J. Hoffman, *Gertrude Stein,* Univ. of Minnesota, Pamphlets on American Writers, No. 10 [Minneapolis: Univ. of Minnesota, 1961].) Gertrude, during the writing of *The Making of Americans,* was in full flight from James and from pragmatism. Her personal admiration for James

and her continuing interest in him is evident in several notebook entries: *NB*-A, p. 1; *NB*-B, p. 1; *NB*-H, p. 3; *NB*-J, pp. 12, 13, 15; but her revolt from his teaching is one of the important bases of the whole book. After so many repetitions of the notion that what Gertrude called the "prolonged present" of *The Making of Americans* was borrowed and renamed from James's chapter "The Sense of Time" in *The Principles of Psychology,* it is difficult to argue that they are in no way related. But the "prolonged present" Gertrude later spoke of as expressing "the sense of time" in *The Making of Americans* does not even exist in her novel. Hoffman, pp. 36-37, illustrates the tendency to impose an explicit philosophy of time on the meaning of *MA:* "*The Making of Americans* is in a sense a book about time, about history, particularly about American history. . . . The repetition of characteristics of human being makes a constant intermingling of universal and particular. . . . The conflict between the two, once formulated, is the most one can make of time and history." Her own contribution to this understanding of her work appears principally in her lecture *Composition as Explanation* (London: The Hogarth Press, 1926), in which she explains that her use of "beginning again and again," participial constructions and so on being based, as she says, on the inevitable contemporary "way of seeing," led to narration that was "serial" and "listic" and that "distributed time" over a composition (see pp. 17-19, 27-30).

But a close comparison of the notebooks and the first draft with the finished novel shows that there is nothing unconventional or exceptional about Gertrude's "use of time" in *MA,* and that "beginning again and again" has nothing to do with the representation of time in the narrative. The repeated "beginning" is the inadvertent effect of two of her practical problems in narration. There was, first, the problem of writing separate histories for each of the Hersland children, and what was originally projected as the parenthetical "past action." Since each of these histories was to go back to the beginning of the story, she had simply to overcome without confusing her reader the practical difficulty involved in repeatedly lurching him back to that beginning. Second, there was the problem of moving from the past to the present action and of keeping clear the differences in time between them. Consequently the reiterated "beginning again and again" is the result of Gertrude's attempt to keep absolutely clear for the reader that she is momentarily interrupting and freezing her narrative lest he suppose that the story is flowing on when it is not. Further, the novel is heavily sprinkled with narrative digressions in which the events of a certain period of time are reviewed from an angle tangential to narration as such. Gertrude repeatedly resumes the significance of events from slightly varying analytic positions after the simple narration has been given. From this point of view the repeated "beginnings" are merely the inadvertent effect of Gertrude's not being able to shut her narrator's mouth in order to get on with her story. Her reasons for composing her novel of digressions may later have seemed to her to be bound up with Jamesian definitions of the consciousness of time. But when the novel was being written, the urgency to digress from the story was motivated by considerations that would have shocked and annoyed James—if he had been subject to intellectual shock—as they did in fact shock and annoy his more orthodox disciple, Leo Stein. See Leo Stein, *Journey into the Self* (New York: Crown, 1950), pp. 60-61.

[32] "Saints and Singing, A Play," published in *Operas and Plays* (Paris: Plain Edition, 1932); "The Mother of Us All," in *Last Operas and Plays* (New York: Rinehart & Co., 1949), p. 75.

[33] *NB-MA*, p. 23.

[34] Toklas, interviews.

[35] *NB-A*, p. 1.

[36] Weininger, pp. 100-02.

[37] *NB*, Note #45.

[38] *MA*, pp. 388-93.

[39] Example of use of this assumption: *MA*, pp. 382-83.

[40] See note 33 above.

[41] *NB-DB*, p. 1.

[42] *NB-10*, pp. 4, 9.

[43] Question resolved—with explicit contradiction of sexuality as "bottom nature"—in *MA*, p. 154.

[44] Distinction first appears in *NB-DB*, pp. 16-17.

[45] *NB-D*, p. 8.

Gisela Brude-Firnau (essay date 1979)

SOURCE: "A Scientific Image of Woman?: The Influence of Otto Weininger's *Sex and Character* on the German Novel," in *Jews & Gender: Responses to Otto Weininger,* edited by Nancy A. Harrowitz and Barbara Hyams, translated by Barbara Hyams and Bianca Philippi, Temple University Press, 1995, pp. 171-82.

[*In the following essay, originally published in 1979, Brude-Firnau discusses Weininger's influence on the modern German novel.*]

Otto Weininger's *Sex and Character* still incites as much disgust and fascination in today's readers as when it was first published in 1903. Its significance is due largely to the history of its reception. Its large circle of readers included such illustrious names as Sigmund Freud, Ludwig Wittgenstein, Oswald Spengler, and James Joyce as well as numerous German-speaking au-

thors who have by no means all been identified. The most well known are the authors of major novels from the first half of this century: Franz Kafka, Hermann Broch, Robert Musil, Heimito von Doderer, Stefan Zweig, Karl Kraus, and Franz Blei.[1] Weininger's work, stresses Heinz Politzer, "left a distinct mark on Kafka's generation, especially on those who, like Kafka, had learned to sympathize with the rampant misogyny of August Strindberg and were stimulated by Sigmund Freud's ardor to observe the mechanisms at work below the threshold of consciousness" (Politzer 1966, 197).[2] Even Günter Grass describes the six-hundred-page opus as "the devil's work" and "a stroke of genius" *(Geniestreich)* (Grass 1989, 202).[3]

Along with those who carried on an earnest debate with Weininger, other critics took neither the book nor its author seriously. An anonymous reviewer of 1904 wrote: "It is a despicable book that has been set in front of us. Even if Strindberg's influence is unmistakable, no rational person would write a book such as *Sex and Character.* Had Weininger placed himself under the care of a psychiatrist in time, the German publishing industry would have been spared from such a disgrace, and the author would have been spared the bullet. It is incredible that there are people who still sing Weininger's praises despite his impudent book."[4]

How did this highly lauded yet "despicable book" come to be? The first part, regarded as positivistic and scientific, was presented as a doctoral dissertation to the faculty of the philosophy department at the University of Vienna. A year later the twenty-three-year-old author published it as a monograph, now expanded to include a psychological-speculative section. A few months later Weininger took his life. This contributed to *Sex and Character*'s status as a best seller for decades: the twenty-sixth German edition came out in 1926, the twenty-eighth in 1947 (Kohn 1962, 46), and there were numerous translations (Blomster 1969, 124).

The book struck the "nerve of the times"; it belonged to a kind of "philosophical journalism" (Lukács 1962, 88) that provided the bourgeoisie with a *Weltanschauung* until World War II. Weininger was quoted and reviewed. Accordingly, Georg Lukács included Weininger's work in the philosophy of life he considered to be the "ruling ideology of the entire imperialistic period in Germany" (Lukács 1962, 88). Weininger belongs among the early propagators of the irrational *völkisch* tradition: with a fanatical disdain for all materialism and everything "Jewish," he, like them, preaches a Germanic-Christian salvation myth. It is hardly surprising that his work was later appropriated by the Nazis and incorporated into their propaganda machine (Centgraf 1943).[5]

Last but not least, *Sex and Character* must also be understood as a reaction to the women's movement at the turn of the century, which threatened to bring about shifts in the social structure.[6] Yet, as we shall see, Weininger's ideas go far beyond the antifeminism of his time.

Under these auspices—the success of a best seller and the work's relation to its time—the influence of *Sex and Character* on the German novel and its portrayal of women is almost predictable. A comprehensive study of the broad spectrum of literary-historical Weininger reception has not yet been written. The present essay merely attempts to bring one aspect into sharper focus and to allude to others.

Since providing proof of Weininger's direct influence on other authors is more difficult and to some extent impossible because of his eclecticism, we shall begin by outlining the content of *Sex and Character:* Weininger's basic concern is an ethical one. His book is a confused attempt to construct a portrait of humanity that even outshines Kant's categorical imperative. Weininger sees the central problem of all ethics in the relationship between the sexes. For him it is once again woman who is the cause of the problem; she embodies sexuality. Therefore, it is also she who impedes the ethical salvation of humanity and indeed the process of becoming authentically human altogether.

Given these premises, the question that runs throughout *Sex and Character* is: What is woman? How can she be defined in a biological, psychological, and ethical sense? In these terms, Weininger's work can be read as an early attempt to formulate a scientific understanding of woman. As hardly ever before, the entire conceptual and epistemological apparatus of contemporary science as well as examples from cultural history are employed to arrive at a complete definition of woman. The point of departure for this attempt is the thesis that all human beings have bisexual inclinations; in reality, neither "man" nor "woman" exists, but instead "all sorts of intermediate conditions between male and female—sexual transitional forms (Weininger 1906, 7).[7]

For heuristic purposes, the author erects two opposing constructs: an ideal man *("M")* and an ideal woman *("W").* Using a far-reaching catalogue of examples encompassing religious history, the writings of the church fathers, and nineteenth-century philosophers, Weininger begins to give the terms *M* and *W* qualitative definition. Yet he does not spurn occasional recourse to such banal sayings as "the longer the hair, the smaller the brain" (Weininger 1906, 68).[8] Collectively, such popular sayings only support one firmly established a priori conclusion: all negative human characteristics belong fundamentally to type *W.* If they also show up as empirically verifiable traits in a man, this can be attributed to the share of *W* in the man's character. All ethical, creative, and intellectual values belong essentially to type *M.* The author is obviously as unconscious of the sophomoric arbitrariness of this definition as he is of the groundlessness of his further conclusions, for he makes hardly any distinctions between speculation and description. Instead he indulges in leaps of logic between the methodologically weak definition of type *W* and instances of real women. One would be tempted to suspect a logical sleight of hand if it were not one's obligation to impute

ethical honesty to the author. However, the noncritical reader may hardly notice that the premise of a sentence frequently is based on the abstraction *W,* yet the sentence concludes with a statement about *das Weib,* that is to say, empirical women.

Weininger then measures and evaluates the definition of woman derived in this manner in relation to Kant's ethics, and concludes that in both thought and action woman is determined exclusively by her sexuality. Therefore she is, in the sense of a Kantian ethical absolute, thoroughly reprehensible. Since she is determined entirely by instinct, she also lacks any kind of distinct consciousness. However, in Weininger's view this very thing—distinct consciousness—is the fundamental precondition for genius, and thus something to which woman cannot lay a single claim. Since he considers genius to be the highest form of human consciousness and existence, woman is ultimately excluded from being human. Countless talents and other abilities that constitute human identity for Weininger are also incompatible with being a woman, namely logic, memory, and awareness of ethical responsibility. And, like Palström, he "astutely concludes that that which isn't permitted cannot possibly exist";[9] in the ethical-philosophical sense, woman is the undetermined one, a formless nothingness.

True to his initial query regarding the relationship between the sexes, Weininger now attempts to explain how woman, who is "without values," can inspire love in man. He decides—entirely caught in a web of compulsive conclusions—that man projects the values to which he aspires onto woman and loves only his own ideals in woman; that is, he loves only himself. According to Weininger, man completely ignores empirical woman, who functions solely as a means. In this way, profane love commits the harshest offense against the categorical imperative. In Weininger's judgment, "Love is murder" (Weininger 1906, 249).[10]

In a courageous metaphysical upswing, Weininger offers a solution to this moral entanglement: in the cosmic order of things, woman is relegated to an object for man, from whom she expects definition and meaning. She is her own impediment to becoming truly human because of her reliance upon instinct. For this reason, man must annihilate *das Weib.* By means of asceticism he must kill that which is female in woman, for only then can divine salvation be achieved in this world. As Weininger summarizes: "The question is not merely if it is possible for woman to become moral. It is this: is it possible for woman really to wish to realize the problem of existence, the conception of guilt? Can she really desire freedom? This can only happen by her being penetrated by an ideal, brought to the guiding star. It can happen only if the categorical imperative were to become active in woman—only if woman can place herself in relation to the moral idea, the idea of humanity. In that way only can there be an emancipation of woman" (Weininger 1906, 348-49).[11]

The ductus of the language and the stringent demands that nullify any comforting thoughts make one suspect that Weininger adhered to this absurdly extreme ethos as his own personal law. He could only resolve his Kantian conflict by means of self-obliteration.

As archaic and nonsensical as the message of *Sex and Character* may appear today, all the more telling is its literary reception. If we trace its course by way of representative authors, the following points emerge as indicators of Weininger's influence:

> 1. Positivistic proof directly in text or in correspondence of familiarity with Weininger's work
>
> 2. A rather consistently applied combination of those characteristics that Weininger designated as female appearing in a fictitious female character
>
> 3. The use of Weininger quotes, paraphrases, or otherwise unmistakable analogies.[12]

Two of these indicators are found in Kafka's work. Heinz Politzer was the first to discover that Kafka's female figures, above all in *The Trial,* are sketched as if according to Weiningerian formulas (Politzer 1966, 200).[13]

Heimito von Doderer can only be mentioned in passing as having "become acquainted [with Weininger] through Hermann Swoboda" (Wolff 1969, 275; cf. Doderer 1958, 190, 269, 274-75). However, the misogyny of both authors had to have deeper roots. It was merely articulated by Weininger and subsequently reverberated with greater intensity by Doderer.

Hermann Broch's understanding of Weininger was fundamentally determined by the ongoing debate of *Sex and Character* in *Der Brenner,* which was less concerned with the definition of woman than with the ethical-philosophical aspect of the book. Of all of Weininger's critics, Broch employed the most emphatic superlative when he apostrophized Weininger in August 1914 as the "most passionate moral philosopher since Kant" (Broch 1914, 689).[14]

Fifteen years later, the intensity of Broch's Weininger reception becomes fully evident in *The Sleepwalkers.* In Broch's trilogy, the conceptual foundation in the relationship between man and woman is Weiningerian, albeit not without critical or ironic refraction.

This is true for four couples. The "little whore" Ruzena, as Broch describes her (Broch 1957, 21), is reduced to Weininger's formula, which defines woman's existence in its entirety: she lacks the will and intentionality to make any decisions outside the realm of the erotic. Elizabeth von Baddensen seems to escape Weininger's terminological guillotine, but her image in Pasenow's consciousness is determined by Weininger: Pasenow uses her like a screen to conjure up a Madonna for himself. The concept of purely spiritual, salvational love is clearly seminal to his ethical-religious imagination.

Only the reader is aware of the ironic-critical relativity of these hopes.

Broch defines the most important female character in *Esch* in a manner that sounds very much like a paraphrase of Weininger: "Mother Hentjen is for her part 'without values' and 'autonomous' right from the beginning, just as 'the feminine' or 'nature' as such is always without values."[15] Purged of all sentimental glorification, she embodies the Weiningerian definition of motherhood: mindless, inert, oriented toward possession and materialism, determined and ruined by man. Weininger's thesis, according to which there is a latent whore in every mother, can be seen in Hentjen's indifferent surrender to Huguenau during the chaotic events at the end of the war.

The fatal chapter 13 of *Sex and Character* in which the Jew is equated with the conceptual abstraction of "woman" and condemned accordingly plays a decisive part in Broch's differentiation from Weininger. With the ridiculous claim to being "scientific" Weininger hardly differentiates himself from other anti-Semitic pamphlet writers of his time. Moreover, his personal point of departure as a converted Jew is disconcerting. As Theodor Lessing writes, explaining this "Jewish self-hatred," woman and Jew signified for Weininger "two different names for the ground of nature [*Naturgrund*] that he feared and avoided" (Lessing 1930, 91). Lessing fittingly labeled Weininger a "Jewish Oedipus."

Broch attempts to effect a resolution to Weininger's Judeo-Christian antagonism and ethical salvation myth by poetic means at the end of the trilogy as, in a kind of mythical union, the Jew Nuchem and the Christian Marie are bound as man and wife in spiritual love. Broch himself later criticizes the unreality of such gender metaphysics: "If I think back, on the first level it was an imperative to the Jew Nuchem: 'Do not let yourself be led astray by any fables, but stay true to the abstract book, remain a Jew, and stay true to your Torah.' On the second level, however, it is an imperative to the poet: 'Do not allow yourself to be seduced by the promise of salvation: Poetry cannot confer grace; rather, the path to grace is through knowledge.'"[16]

Broch's individual psychological debate with Weininger in *The Sleepwalkers* is translated into the sociopolitical dimension in the original 1935-36 version of *The Spell*[17] and leads to a decisive refutation. One can already see the signs of Broch distancing himself from Weininger in his 1914 essay "Ethics," in which he stresses that Weininger's Kant ethos is whipped "into dogmatism" (Broch 1914, 689) and thereby turns into unethical rigor. This dialectical reversal of values is the intellectual scaffolding of the 1935-36 edition of *The Spell:* "We are to live a chaste life so that the world may get better," is the postulate with which the wanderer Marius tries to make himself popular in the mountain village of Kuppron. His demand for asceticism, together with his aggressively antifemale and by extension anti-Semitic stance, proves him to be a figure largely inspired by Weininger (Broch 1987, 8).[18]

Broch only indirectly employs Weininger's pejorative equation of the Jew with woman: Wetchy, the commercial agent and sole non-Catholic of the village, conforms in virtually every detail to the literary caricature of the Jew indelibly drawn by Wilhelm Heinrich Riehl, Gustav Freytag, and Wilhelm Raabe, and described by George L. Mosse as follows: "It held the Jew to be without a soul, without the humble German virtues, and consequently uprooted. . . . In contrast to the German soul, which acted as a filter between man and cosmos, the soul of a Jew was an insensitive, materialistic thing" (Mosse 1964, 126-27). Marius attempts to press Wetchy into this stereotype—in which Broch substitutes urban ways for Jewishness—in order to direct the villagers' hatred and dissatisfaction toward him. Marius's diatribes read like *völkisch*/National Socialist propaganda; the antifeminist component evokes Weininger: "They insinuate themselves and tempt us with their wheeling and dealing like women, yes, like women, for they only pose as men, and though they still may manage to grow beards, those beards cannot hide the womanly greed staring from their flaccid faces." (Broch 1988, 351).[19]

Discrimination against Wetchy and his exile from the village are subplots with concrete and timely significance. Marius's confrontation with Mother Gisson, which takes on cosmic dimensions with the death of the old peasant woman, remains in the foreground. This cosmic conflict between a perverted male principle and an idealized female principle must be seen as the actual myth that is functioning behind the scenes of the peasant milieu of the novel. Until now it has proved difficult to identify one myth running through the work: is it about Demeter or the earth mother, about an affirmed or a negated "mysticism of the soil" *(Bodenmystik)?* The diverse, so eclectically assembled mythological allusions become comprehensible if viewed as set pieces that are meant to conceal Broch's ongoing reckoning with Weininger's salvation myth, for Weininger had recently "elevated male-female dichotomy into a cosmic principle," as Mosse stresses (Mosse 1964, 215).[20] In the ritualized murder of Irmgard, Broch shows the murderous consequences of Weininger's postulates made absolute. The abstruse doctrine of purity and salvation that Marius preaches like a madman in a trance or a demagogical agitator of the masses shows how very far Broch distances himself from Weininger. At this juncture he refers to the totalitarian potentiality that is inherent in every form of dogmatism.

Unfortunately, this interpretation loses credibility through Broch's cliché-strewn conception of the female characters: Mother Gisson's death bears an embarrassing resemblance to the Assumption. Agatha is exclusively the naive pregnant woman caught up in her dreams. Irmgard remains the weak-willed, loving victim. Even the pediatrician Barbara, clearly intended as a counterweight, is too good to be true. There is an overabundance of female virtues, virtues that coat the women like a shiny varnish. The women enter into battle against a metaphysical principle, indeed not one corresponding to the Weiningerian *M* ideal, but rather to the historical and sociological consequences that ensued from Weininger's doctrines about male superiority. Another reason why Broch's female characters are far removed from reality is that historically the majority of German women most certainly did not oppose the National Socialist movement.

As we gain distance over time, we are able to see a greater parallel between Broch's *The Sleepwalkers* and Robert Musil's *The Man Without Qualities* than their authors were once willing to acknowledge. One of the—thus far scarcely examined—analogies between the works lies in the influence of Otto Weininger on Musil's monumental novel.[21]

If we read **Sex and Character** alongside *The Man Without Qualities,* we find in Musil's work a more peripheral, less conceptually fundamental confrontation with Weininger; the conceptual mechanisms of the young rigorist, and Musil, with his "gliding logic of the soul," were completely different forms of thought. Therefore, in Musil's novel Weininger's conceptual patterns are merely integrated as representative time-bound material into the consciousness of particular characters. This is demonstrated in the first short episode of *The Man Without Qualities,* for it is conceived like a fictional paraphrase of Weininger: a not precisely identified "lady" and her "escort" happen upon the scene of a traffic accident. The contrast between their respective observations of the same event demonstrates the difference between male and female spheres of thought and experience. This difference is first portrayed through particular narrative modes: the "lady's" reactions—pity, indecisiveness, and relief—are presented through indirect discourse. The discourse of her "escort"—technical explanations, statistical details, and original observations—is expressed exclusively as direct speech. The narrator's irony-laden offer of identification stands in contrast to the neutral information about the "escort." This contrastive technique as well as the willful ignorance of the "lady," who gratefully accepts her male counterpart's interpretation and valuation of the experience, is characteristic of Weininger's analysis of "male and female consciousness," which he analyzes in Chapter Three: female consciousness consists of inarticulate, feeling-bound complexes of thought, whereas male consciousness shows "greater decisiveness in . . . judgments." Weininger stresses that "wherever a new judgment is to be made (not merely something already settled to be put into proverbial forms), it is always the case that the female expects from the man the clarification of her data, the interpretation of her henids" (Weininger 1906, 101).[22]

The attentive gaze with which the "lady" responds to the decisive quality of male consciousness finds its explanation in Weininger: "A psychological proof that the power of making judgments is a masculine trait lies in the fact that the woman recognizes it as such, and that it acts on her as a tertiary sexual character of the male. A woman always expects definite convictions in a man, and appropriates them" (Weininger 1906, 195).[23] This definition of supposedly gender-specific consciousness is a determining factor for various female characters in Musil's novel, which is similar to Weininger's work in theme but not in its ethical judgments.

Above all, Musil's psychological profile of the charming, man-hungry society matron Bonadea corresponds to Weininger's definitions, as she continually fluctuates between the poles of "whore" and "mother." Now and then, a societally imposed feeling for "manners and morals" awakens in her a sporadic attack of conscience: "For the woman unfaithfulness is an exciting game, in which the thought of morality plays no part, but which is controlled only by the desire for safety and reputation," as Weininger pronounces in a corresponding passage (Weininger 1906, 221).[24]

Almost the entire retinue of negative female characteristics described by Weininger comes to life in Bonadea's unsuccessful attempt to seduce Ulrich in Chapter 63. The narrator makes the following comment on the pretext she uses as an entrée to Ulrich: "She always believed many things at once, and half truths made it easier for her to tell lies" (Musil 1979, vol. 1, 307).[25] In Weininger's logistic terminology, the same sentence appears as: "A creature that cannot grasp the material exclusiveness of A and not A has no difficulty in lying; more than that, such a creature has not even any consciousness of lying, being without a standard of truth" (Weininger 1906, 149).[26]

The basic constellation of the scene is also compatible with Weininger's theories: "The female principle is, then, nothing more than sexuality; the male principle is sexual and something more" (Weininger 1906, 90).[27] *M* possesses—as Ulrich demonstrates—the ability to distance himself from both his mental as well as his physical urges, whereas Bonadea is entirely at their mercy.

Even Bonadea's interest in the Collateral Campaign, a mere pretext for her singular objective of winning Ulrich for herself, is in keeping with Weininger's assertion that "when the female occupies herself with matters outside the interests of sex, it is for the man she loves or by whom she wishes to be loved. She takes no real interest in the things for themselves" (Weininger 1906, 89-90).[28]

Both the far-reaching "devaluation of sexuality"[29] in *The Man Without Qualities* and the way in which female characters are mirrored in Ulrich's consciousness frequently bring Weininger's formulations to mind. Yet *Sex and Character*'s importance for Musil should not be overestimated: as Corino's work on Musil and psychoanalysis makes very clear, his underlying childhood experiences and family constellation were of greater significance. For Musil, like Kafka, Weininger may only

have had the function of raising his awareness and of confirming preformulated ideas.

Musil's differentiation from Weininger is most obvious when Weiningerian values show up in his novel as time-bound judgments and preconceived notions, such as in the letter in which Professor Hagauer replies to Agathe's request for a divorce. In it he categorizes her as an intellectually and consequently morally deficient type, for "the irregular form of behaviour manifest in his wife could be associated with a fairly general type of inferiority that was simply feminine, in other words, it could be termed 'social imbecility'" (Musil 1979, vol. 3, 338).[30] For Weininger, the purported "connection between logic and ethics" is the fundamental link that holds his case against women together. Thus he does not view her as immoral but simply as amoral: "Woman resents any attempt to require from her that her thoughts should be logical. She may be regarded as logically insane" (Weininger 1906, 150).[31] Lindner also receives prompts from Weininger when he resolves to concern himself "solely" with Agathe's ethical improvement. He explains unctuously "that I serve you as a brother, wishing at the same time to awaken in woman herself the antidote against woman,"[32] which corresponds to Weininger's plea for the "emancipation of the female from the female" (Weininger 1906, 343).[33]

In these and similar cases, the woman is judged and condemned in the realm of commonly held truisms, that is, in the narrow compound of socially accepted standards. The corresponding phrases are often tellingly introduced with "people say" *(man sagt)*. Ulrich alone transcends this level with the insight that "definite rules were contrary to the essential nature of morality" (Musil 1979, vol. 3, 154).[34]

Agathe reacts to Hagauer's written diagnosis much as a noncritical female reader would react to Weininger's book: she allows herself to be defined within the categories of her judge, for "her behaviour struck her now as so entirely that of someone who was really not quite responsible for her actions" (Musil 1979, vol. 3, 340).[35] She appears to have accepted her own condemnation right down to her choice of words when she asks, "So what it does come to is that I'm a moral imbecile?" (Musil 1979, vol. 3, 349).[36] And as Ulrich appears to confirm this, her self-esteem collapses, and she decides to take her life. Musil thus demonstrates clearly how an external judgment turns into self-condemnation.

"She [woman] possesses no personal value, she is devoid of man's sense of value of his own personality for itself" (Weininger 1906, 202)[37]—as *Sex and Character* synopsizes the seldom articulated presupposition of those who believe in male superiority. Agathe's intention to commit suicide demonstrates how in individual cases, such generally and silently accepted propositions can ultimately degenerate into hardened roles, and finally into murderous, obsessive compulsions. If the author had not needed the character of Agathe later in the novel, she would have become, next to Broch's Irmgard, the second literary offering to Weininger.

Musil's reckoning with Weininger occurs through the character Clarisse, in whose mind "the contents of the times had gotten all mixed up." Her obsessive demand for "pure love" appears to be the ironic counterpart to Weininger's metaphysically exorbitant postulate demanding an end to sexuality altogether, for "there is no possibility of establishing the kingdom of God on earth" (Weininger 1906, 343).[38] Clarisse echoes this in a secularized form: "And the world will never get any better until there are such lovers!" (Musil 1979, vol. 3, 291).[39]

Above all, the imagery connected with Clarisse, who becomes ever more overtly schizophrenic, points to Weininger: "every person has an animal that he inwardly resembles,"[40] she proclaims analogously to Weininger's claim that "certain people embody specific animal-like possibilities."[41]

In his **"Animal Psychology"** Weininger sees close parallels between women and birds "physiognomically as well as characterologically," while for him worm and snake "are related to the hunchbacked criminal."[42] In a similarly abstruse and forced relationship, Clarisse sees a blackbird and "a fat caterpillar that it was devouring": remembering her earlier conversation about Moosbrugger, she experiences at the sight of it "an ineffable correspondence of interior and exterior experience" (Musil 1979, vol. 3, 308).[43] "Every form of life in nature corresponds to a human quality. Every possibility in human beings corresponds to something in nature,"[44] wrote Weininger, who had suffered similarly from schizophrenia in the last few months of his life (cf. Abrahamsen).

As the examples have clearly shown, Musil takes a number of stances toward Weininger in his fiction. The character Bonadea shows that several of Weininger's claims were based on his observations of women in the Viennese leisure class of his time. Insofar as Musil interprets Bonadea's "one-sided" behavior in the final analysis as "ambition" (Musil 1979, vol. 3, 263; 1970, 889), he illustrates, in contrast to Weininger, that it had not so much to do with an existential standard of behavior as with a psychosexual potency that lacked any other means of expression because of the social conditions for women in those times. Musil thereby rejects Weininger's primitive, generalizing conclusions. Through Hagauer, Agathe, and to some extent Ulrich, however, he shows how these views belonged to an unreflected *opinio communis* prior to World War I and how they reified into ruinous, obsessive compulsions. By integrating Weininger's imagery into Clarisse's consciousness, which moves increasingly into a reality of its own, he emphasizes the insane elements in this paradigm.

Weininger and the consequences are with us to this day. Even in Günter Grass's *Dog Years,* which was written sixty years after *Sex and Character,* the book figures as a document of German anti-Semitism (Grass 1989, 36-37, 109-10, 202-4, 216, 262). And in 1976 *Sex and Character* was translated into French as an example—however eccentric—of German philosophizing (Amery 1976, 429). By virtue of the sheer number of novels in which Weininger's influence may be ascertained, there is a danger of overestimating the intellectual significance of his work. A more realistic evaluation is possible only if we first become cognizant of the biographical and historical conditions in which *Sex and Character* was created: Weininger gave eloquent expression to his family-influenced and pubescent animosity toward women, which he stylized into scientific knowledge with the help of some examples from cultural history and data from the natural sciences. In so doing, he articulated subliminal fears to which his epoch was quite susceptible. His work remains a "singularly grandiose error"[45] that made history.

NOTES

[1] On the Freud-Weininger relationship and Freud's accusation of plagiarism, see Abrahamsen (1946, 43), Fliess (1906), and Freud (1955, 5; 1953, 135); on the influence of Weininger on James Joyce refer to Ellmann (1959, 477). I would like to thank John E. Woods, who gave me this reference during the Amherst Colloquium. For Karl Kraus, see Kraft (1956, 73-94); also see Blei (1903), Goldmann (1971, 68), and Kohn (1961).

[2] Politzer (1965, 288-89): "prägte sich der Generation Kafkas ein, besonders jenen Zeitgenossen, die sich für die Weiberfeindschaft August Strindbergs empfänglich gezeigt hatten oder von Sigmund Freuds Ehrgeiz angefeuert waren, die unterschwelligen Mechanismen des Seelenlebens zu beobachten."

[3] The phrases "Brain child" and "stroke of genius" *(Geniestreich)* in reference to Weininger's work appear as early as p. 36 of Grass's novel. See Blomster (1969).

[4] Anonymous (1904). Quoted in a forty-eight-page prospectus of *Sex and Character* provided by the publisher Wilhelm Braumüller as a supplement to the twelfth edition: "Es ist ein niederträchtiges Buch, das wir vor uns haben. Mag auch der Einfluss Strindbergs unverkennbar sein, ein Buch wie *Geschlecht und Charakter* schreibt kein vernünftiger Mensch. Hätte Weininger sich rechtzeitig in die Behandlung eines Psychiaters gegeben, so wäre der deutsche Büchermarkt vor einer solchen Schande und der Verfasser vor dem Revolver bewahrt geblieben. Unbegreiflich aber ist es, wie es Leute gibt, die Weininger trotz seines frechen Buches noch Loblieder singen."

[5] Weininger's critique of Judaism was used as late as 1939 in an anti-Semitic German radio broadcast (cf. Abrahamsen 1946, 122).

[6] On Weininger's significance for the women's movement, see Klein (1946, 53-70).

[7] Weininger (1910, 9): "unzählige Abstufungen zwischen Mann und Weib."

[8] Weininger (1910, 84): "Je länger das Haar, desto kürzer der Verstand."

[9] Morgenstern (1965, 263): "schliesst er messerscharf, dass nicht sein kann, was nicht sein darf."

[10] Weininger (1910, 334): "Liebe ist Mord."

[11] Weininger (1910, 472): "Nicht die Frau heilig zu machen, nicht darum kann es so bald sich handeln. Nur darum: kann das Weib zum Problem seines Daseins, zum Begriff der Schuld redlich gelangen? Wird es die Freiheit wenigstens wollen? Allein auf die Durchsetzung des Ideales, auf das Erblicken des Leitsternes kommt es an. Bloss darauf: kann im Weib der kategorische Imperativ lebendig werden? Wird sich das Weib unter die sittliche Idee, unter die Idee der Menschheit, stellen? Denn einzig das wäre Frauen-Emanzipation."

[12] "Unmistakable analogies" are a contestable point, since frequently used sources, such as the works of Nietzsche, Schopenhauer, or the earlier writings of Freud, may be equally pertinent. For this reason, I will apply this indicator only to the imagery in *The Man Without Qualities*.

[13] In contrast to Politzer, see Bödecker (1974, 104-5).

[14] For other reviews, see Dallago (1912) and Ebner (1919). On Broch's Weininger reception, see Durzak (1968, 11-23) and Lützeler (1973, 36-37).

[15] Broch (1957, 26): "Mutter Hentjen, die ihrerseits von allem Anbeginn 'wertfrei' und 'autonom' ist, wie eben das 'Weibliche' oder die 'Natur' als solche immer wertfrei ist."

[16] Broch (1957, 348): "Denke ich zurück, so steht auf der ersten Ebene eine Aufforderung an den Juden Nuchem: 'Lass dich von keiner noch so zarten Legendenhaftigkeit verführen, sondern bleib beim abstrakten Buch, bleib ein Jud, bleib bei deiner Thora.' Auf der zweiten Ebene jedoch ist es eine Aufforderung an den Dichter: 'Lass dich nicht vom Heilversprechen verführen: Dichtung vermittelt dir keine Gnade, vielmehr liegt der Gnadenweg in der Erkenntnis.'"

[17] See Broch (1988). Only the first version of the novel, except as noted by its translator, H. F. Broch de Rothermann, is available in English. Cf. Broch de Rothermann's "Brief Genesis of the Novel" and "Translator's Note" in Broch (1988, 387-91).

[18] Marius is specifically called a "foe of mothers" (Broch 1987, 67); he attacks Agatha publicly as a "witch."

[19] Broch (1969, 405): "Wie die Weiber schmeicheln sie sich heran mit ihren Geschäften, ja, wie die Weiber, denn sie tun ja nur so, als ob sie Männer wären, weil ihnen der Bart im Gesicht hängt, aber die Weiberhabsucht in ihrem weichen Gesicht können sie damit nicht verdecken."

[20] The doctor/narrator's passive complicity in the murder of Irmgard has been interpreted in various ways. Furthermore, the narrator's susceptibility to demagogic seduction—analogous to a criticism often levied against Weininger—is related to his youthful fanaticism for chastity. Cf. the second version of Broch (1969, 16).

[21] I would like to thank Professor Ingo Seidler for pointing out during the Amherst Colloquium that Weininger is mentioned a number of times in Musil's unpublished manuscripts. Sporadic reference to Weininger also appears in the following secondary literature on Musil: Roth (1972, 57), Appignanesi (1973, 84), and Corino (1973, 154, 177).

[22] Weininger (1910, 129): "wo immer ein neues Urteil zu fällen, und nicht ein schon lange fertiges einmal mehr in Satzform auszusprechen ist, dass in solchem Falle stets W von M die Klärung ihrer dunklen Vorstellungen . . . erwartet."

[23] Weininger (1910, 252): "Ein psychologischer Beweis für die Urteilsfunktion ist dieser, dass das Urteilen vom Weibe als männlich empfunden wird, und wie ein (tertiärer) Sexualcharakter anziehend auf dasselbe wirkt. Die Frau verlangt vom Manne stets bestimmte Überzeugungen, die sie übernehme."

[24] Weininger (1910, 289): "Für die Frau ist der Ehebruch ein kitzelndes Spiel, in welchem der Gedanke der Sittlichkeit gar nicht, sondern nur die Motive der Sicherheit und des Rufes mitspielen."

[25] Musil (1970, 258): "Sie glaubte immer mehreres gleichzeitig, und halbe Wahrheiten erleichterten ihr das Lügen."

[26] Weininger (1910, 193-94): "Ein Wesen [i.e., die Frau], das nicht begreift oder nicht anerkennt, dass A und non-A einander ausschliessen, wird durch nichts mehr gehindert zu lügen; vielmehr gibt es für ein solches Wesen gar keinen Begriff der Lüge, weil ihr Gegenteil, die Wahrheit, als das Mass, ihm abgeht." Ulrich muses correspondingly over Agathe: "but she hasn't the slightest idea what Truth means!" ("aber sie weiss doch gar nicht, was Wahrheit bedeutet!" [Musil 1970, 1797]).

[27] Weininger (1910, 113): "W ist nichts als Sexualität, M ist sexuell und noch etwas darüber."

[28] Weininger (1910, 112-13): "W befasst sich . . . mit aussergeschlechtlichen Dingen nur für den Mann, den sie liebt, oder um des Mannes willen, von dem sie geliebt sein möchte. Ein Interesse für diese Dinge an sich fehlt ihr vollständig."

[29] Corino (1973, 132): "Abwertung der Sexualität."

[30] Musil (1970, 952): "ziehen sittliche Mängel nach sich, spricht man doch von moralischem Blödsinn."

[31] Weininger (1910, 192): "Die Frau erbittert die Zumutung, ihr Denken ausnahmslos von der Logik abhängig zu machen. Ihr mangelt das intellektuelle Gewissen. Man könnte bei ihr von 'logical insanity' sprechen!"

[32] Musil (1970, 1353): "dass ich Ihnen brüderlich dienen, gleichsam im Weibe selbst das Gegengewicht gegen das Weib . . . erwecken möchte."

[33] Weininger (1910, 463): "Emanzipation des Weibes vom Weibe."

[34] Musil (1970, 797): "feste Regeln dem innersten Wesen der Moral widersprächen."

[35] Musil (1970, 954): "ihr Verhalten kam ihr so sehr wie das eines wirklich nicht zurechnungsfähigen Wesens vor."

[36] Musil (1970, 961): "Es bleibt also dabei, dass ich moralisch schwachsinnig bin?"

[37] Weininger (1910, 261): "So kann sie [die Frau] eben keinen Wert an sich selbst besitzen, es fehlt ihr der Eigenwert der menschlichen Persönlichkeit."

[38] Weininger (1910, 466): "es ist keine Möglichkeit für eine Aufrichtung des Reiches Gottes auf Erden, eh dies nicht geschehen ist."

[39] Musil (1970, 912): "Und die Welt wird sich nicht eher bessern, als es solche Liebende gibt!"

[40] Musil (1970, 1473): "jeder Mensch hat ein Tier, dem er innen ähnlich sieht."

[41] Weininger (1907, 126): "dass gewisse Menschen spezielle Tier-Möglichkeiten verwirklichen."

[42] Weininger (1907, 128): "zum buckligen Verbrecher Beziehungen [aufweisen]."

[43] Musil (1970, 926): "eine unaussprechliche Übereinstimmung des inneren Geschehens mit dem äusseren." Clarisse views Rachel as a "gazelle and queen of snakes" (Musil 1970, 1473).

[44] Weininger (1907, 114): "Jeder Daseinsform in der Natur entspricht eine Eigenschaft im Menschen. Jeder Möglichkeit im Menschen entspricht etwas in der Natur."

[45] Brann (1924, 26): "ein einziger grandioser Irrtum."

Ralph Robert Joly (essay date 1982)

SOURCE: "Chauvinist Brew and Leopold Bloom: The Weininger Legacy," in *James Joyce Quarterly*, Vol. 19, No. 2, Winter, 1982, pp. 194-8.

[*In the following essay, Joly briefly explicates James Joyce's use of Weininger's ideas regarding women and Jews in his characterization of Leopold Bloom in* Ulysses.]

In his splendid biography of Joyce, Ellmann convincingly unearths myriad prototypes and seminal influences for the realization of Leopold Bloom. Among the latter is Otto Weininger, whom Ellmann informs us looms as a source for the effeminacy of Joyce's hero (*JJ* 477). Nonetheless, Ellmann's brief treatment of Weininger's role belies the immensity of his contribution to Bloom's characterization.

Himself an apostate Jew, Weininger was a Viennese psychologist given to a prodigious flow of acid commentary on women and Jews in *Geschlecht und Charakter,* initially published in May 1903, and in its twenty-second edition when Joyce completed *Ulysses*.[1] It is probable that Joyce discovered Weininger through Italo Svevo, a mainstay for much of the Jewish lore in *Ulysses*. Italian literary historian Attilio Momigliano notes that critics were often comparing the characters of *Una Vita* (1893) and *As a Man Grows Older* (1898) to Weininger's conception of the Jew in *Geschlecht und Charakter*.[2]

Weininger held that "Judaism [was] saturated with femininity" (*Weininger* 306). Jews were womanly men, or fastidiously vain, passively dependent, materially and romantically self-centered (*Weininger, et passim*). Accordingly, Bloom makes his initial formal appearance in the kitchen, where he prepares breakfast. Later in the novel, and as Ellmann has pointed out (*JJ* 477), Joyce applies Weininger's phrase, "womanly man" (*Weininger* 56) directly to Bloom (*U* 493) and assigns him the middle name, "Paula" (*U* 723). In "Cyclops," the narrator dismisses Bloom's masculinity when he castigates Bloom as "One of those mixed middlings. . . . Lying up in the hotel . . . once a month with headache like a totty with her courses" (*U* 338). Earlier in "Aeolus," Bloom's office cohorts mock his walk as they watch from a window, one of them doing a mazurka in "caricature" (*U* 130) of his gait. Bloom's effeminacy extends even to his physical movements, fulfilling Weininger's dictum that there are some men who "because of the female element in them . . . are coquettish in gait and manner" (*Weininger* 56).

Similarly, Joyce renders his hero fastidious about his appearance. Weininger had said that "there are 'men' who go out walking with the sole object of displaying their faces like the faces of women, hoping that they will be admired, after which they return contentedly home. The ancient 'Narcissus' was a prototype of such persons. These persons are naturally fastidious about the dressing of their hair, their apparel, shoes and linen; they are concerned as to their personal appearance at all times and the minutest details of their toilet . . ." (*Weininger* 56). In *Ulysses,* Bloom pays ubiquitous heed to his appearance, whether in pressing his pants, shining his shoes, bathing his body, or in slicking down his carefully combed hair with hair oil.

In "Circe," Joyce consummates his vision of Bloom as "womanly man" with Weininger a primary source for much of the episode material. Here Bloom fantasies himself as a woman, admits to impersonating a female in a high school play, and to trying on women's clothing (*U* 535-36). Weininger had said that Jews were possessed of a "slavish disposition" (*Weininger* 313) and thus their predilection for legal codes such as the Ten Commandments. He requires, like women, "the rule of exterior authority" (*Weininger* 313). In "Circe," Bloom pledges himself a bondslave to Bello, brothel madam now male in this scene of sexual reversal (*U* 530-44).

Bloom's own metamorphosis into literal woman in the episode is analogous with Weininger's belief that "it is possible for him (i.e., the Jew) to attain to the loftiest heights, or to sink to the lowest depth; he can become like animals, or plants, or even like women . . ." (*Weininger* 188). Though Joyce's main source here was Sacher-Masoch's *Venus im Pelz* (*JJ* 380), whose central character, Severin, proves servile before his mistress, there can be little doubt the metamorphosis aspect, *not* found in Sacher-Masoch, fitted in well with the bewitching trickery of Homer's Circe and Joyce's plans for a passive, womanly Jew.

So exacting is Joyce's employment of Weininger that when Bloom is asked his profession by the nightwatch in "Circe," he replies: "I follow a literary occupation. Author-journalist" (*U* 458). Weininger had contended that Jews had a feminine bent in their talent for journalism though, paradoxically, they lacked in originality like their female counterparts (*Weininger* 320). Thus in "Circe," Beaufoy, the short story writer (*U* 68-9), appears in a fantasy to denounce Bloom as "A plagiarist. A soapy sneak masquerading as a literateur. It's perfectly obvious that with the most inherent baseness he has cribbed some of my bestselling books . . ." (*U* 458).

Beyond the episode, there exist other Weiningerian elements upholding the consanguinity of women and Jews. Weininger believed, for example, that women were essentially non-religious, preferring the practical and material dimensions of life. Attempting an affinity of sensibility, Weininger asserted that the Jewish predilection for reducing life's issues to materialist paradigm was evidenced in the Old Testament, which offers no view of immortality. In short, "the Jew is eminently the unbeliever" (*Weininger* 320).

In *Ulysses,* this tenet proves central to Bloom's characterization in juxtaposition to that of Stephen Daedalus.

In almost every way, Bloom is Stephen's opposite—in race, in age, in outlook. Married and practical, he leans to the science and business areas (unlike the philosophical Stephen, lover of the arts). This differential extends even to the language patterns of the two. Stephen's is largely abstract in character, frequently polysyllabic, usually involving extended syntax and, almost always, resounding with eloquence. Bloom's, on the other hand, is replete with nouns, rare in adjectives, limited in syntax, prosaic in rhythm, befitting a man of earthly appetites.

In "Eumaeus," Bloom informs Stephen that Jews "are practical and are proved to be so" (*U* 644), then follows with a chimerical program of economic well-being synonymous with the good life. It had been Weininger's assertion that because Jews are atheistic, they resort to material consolations. Earlier in the episode, Bloom tells Stephen that "it's a horse of quite another colour to say you believe in the existence of a supernatural God" (*U* 634).

Now in all of this, it would be an oversight not to touch on Bloom's sexual preoccupations, so central to the novel's concerns. Even here, Joyce was substantially indebted to Weininger, who held that women are fundamentally concerned with being "desired physically" and "taken possession of like . . . new property" (*Weininger* 292). Thus Molly yearns to be possessed by a real man (*U* 754). But Bloom, too, from the "moving hams" of the girl in the butcher shop of the early pages to the later "Nausicaa" and "Circe" episodes in particular, is concerned with sexual capacity and the reciprocation of desire. It is a preoccupation that confused the early guardians of public morals. Joyce employed it to reiterate story theme. In Judaism, the home is a place where sexuality is commanded, the act of physical union honored. After all, one may just father the Messiah. As Weininger put it, "On no other supposition can we account for the long persistence of the Jewish race which has outlived so many other peoples. Their tradition to increase and multiply is connected with this vague hope, that out of them shall come the Messiah" (*Weininger* 329).

Weininger had noted that family plays a significant role among Jews. As he stated it, "The fusion, the continuity of the members of the family reaches its highest point among the Jews. It is only among the Jews that the son feels deep rooted in the family and is fully at one with his father." In *Ulysses,* Bloom is ever conscious of family origins, and nearly always from a perspective that is Jewish. Thoughts of a dead friend, Paddy Dignam, trigger memories of a deceased father: "Poor papa, with his hagadah book, reading backwards with his finger to me. Pessach. Next year in Jerusalem" (*U* 122).

Pangs of guilt in the brothel of Bella stir recall of a father's love and concern, and if alive, his words of probable remonstrance:

> What you making down this place? Have you no soul? [Weininger—313—had said Jews were without

soul.] . . . Are you not my son Leopold, the grandson of Leopold . . . who left the house of his father and left the god of his fathers Abraham and Jacob? (*U* 437)

Late in the novel, Bloom recalls the aftermath of his father's suicide, an act in keeping with Weininger's contention that Jews were given to self-destructive tendencies, though Weininger ironically took his own life (*Weininger* 286, 292, 313, 321). Earlier in the novel, Bloom contemplates suicide (*U* 152). Here, he remembers his father's material legacy:

> An ancient hagadah book in which a pair of horn-rimmed convex spectacles inserted marked the passage of thanksgiving in the ritual prayers for Pessach . . . an envelope addressed *To my Dear Son Leopold* (*U* 723).

Remorseful, Bloom regrets "he had treated with disrespect certain beliefs and practices" (*U* 724).

In retrospect, Joyce found Weininger a confirming source for attitudes he had previously formed and a stimulus for new ones to be shaped in effecting theme. Weininger had written that "the Jew is always more absorbed by sexual matters than the Aryan, although he is notably less potent sexually." In the "Circe" episode Bello exclaims to Bloom, "What else are you good for, an impotent thing like you? . . . Can you do a man's job?" (*U* 541). It is in Bello's challenge that we discover why Joyce employed an anti-Semite misogynist for the characterization of Bloom. Joyce was certainly neither anti-Jewish nor anti-woman as seasoned Joyceans know and as *Ulysses* so eloquently confirms in "Cyclops" where Bloom emerges the winner of our esteem—and our hearts—in his confrontation with the bigots of his time. If there is to be salvation for the Bloomian household, then our hero must yield his womanly ways and do a "man's job." As in *The Odyssey,* action, not passivity, is life's key.

NOTES

[1] See Otto Weininger, *Sex and Character* (London: William Heinemann, and New York: G.P. Putnam's Sons, n.d.). Hereafter referred to in the text as *Weininger.*

[2] For Momigliano's observation, see Edouard Roditi, "A Note on Svevo," in Italo Svevo, *As a Man Grows Older,* trans., Beryl De Zoete (New York: New Directions, 1949), pp. xv-xvii.

Lech Sokól (essay date 1987)

SOURCE: "The Metaphysics of Sex: Strindberg, Weininger and S. I. Witkiewicz," in *Theatre Research International,* Vol. 12, No. 1, Spring, 1987, pp. 39-51.

[*In the following essay, Sokól examines misogynist elements in Weininger, Strindberg, and S. I. Witkiewicz.*]

'Otto Weininger sent me his *Geschlecht und Charakter,* a terrific book that seems to solve the most difficult of all problems. He pronounces clearly what I only managed to utter. Voilà un homme!' These words, from Strindberg's article 'Idolatry, Gynolatry' are meant as an homage to Otto Weininger (1880-1903) who was barely twenty-three years old when he committed suicide. Strindberg's article was published by the famous Vienna periodical *Die Fackel* which played an important part in defending and propagating Weininger and his book.[1] Weininger's extraordinary and scandalous work, the full title of which is *Geschlecht und Charakter. Eine prinzipielle Untersuchung (Sex and Character. A Fundamental Investigation;* English edition—1906) was published in June 1903. It was a revised version of his doctoral thesis presented at Vienna University in June 1902. Outstanding as the book is, it also possesses some disturbing features and it did not receive the welcome its author had expected. This poor reception, or rather the lack of any serious response, was an important factor in the author's suicide on 4 October 1903. The book became the subject of critical interest only after its author's death: suicide turned out to be a good advertisement.

Strindberg also expressed his profound admiration for Weininger in letters of 22 October and 8 December 1903, to Arthur Gerber, a friend of the Viennese philosopher. He had earlier addressed a letter to Weininger in which he expressed his thanks for a copy of *Geschlecht und Charakter* in the following terms: 'You have saved me by giving us the final solution to the problem of women. Please, do accept my deepest gratitude and admiration.'[2] Strindberg's own copy of *Sex and Character* is covered with his remarks and underlinings which testify to very careful reading.

Strindberg was interested both in Weininger's work and in his life. He saw a parallel between Weininger's and his own biography. In his letter to Gerber of 22 October he compares Weininger's suicide to a situation from his own past and quotes a fragment of his *Diary.* About 1880 he was ready to commit suicide; he comments that the pessimistic view of life which justifies such a step is not just an opinion, but an objective discovery similar to the unquestionable discoveries of science.[3] Strindberg also quotes a fragment of Emil Schering's letter to himself, in which his German translator wrote: 'Weininger's suicide sealed his faith.' Strindberg meant that the suicide of the author was the proof and verification of the authenticity of the ideas expressed in his book.

Weininger aroused Strindberg's interest not only as a man and author, but also as a 'brotherly soul', almost an embodiment of his own personality, as someone putting his own thoughts into words. We are dealing here with a frequent occurrence in Strindberg's life: his interest in somebody's life and work leads him to identification with the given author. In the second letter to Gerber (8 December 1903) the parallel between Weininger and Strindberg is even clearer:

[Weininger was] born in a state of guilt, like myself, who was born into this world with remorse, fear of everything, fright of life and people, I actually believe I must have done something wrong before my birth [. . .]. I too became religious so as not to become a monster. I too worship Beethoven and even founded a club in which only his music was played [Weininger committed suicide at 5 Schwarzspanierstrasse where his favourite composer Beethoven died] [. . .]. And Weininger's life? Did he reveal the secrets of Gods? Did he steal fire? Was cynical life too cynical for him? The fact that he quitted life proves to me that he had superior consent to do so. Otherwise, all these things would have never happened.[4]

Strindberg writes about Weininger with ostentatious solemnity, almost exaltation. Weininger, in turn, had considered Strindberg to be the most remarkable mind of his times. Although he devotes more attention to Ibsen, Ibsen stands to some extent as an example of attitudes characteristic of a bygone period. On the whole *Sex and Character* owes much more to Strindberg, but the degree of dependence is slightly obscured by the fact that Weininger's and Strindberg's misogyny derives from the same sources: Schopenhauer, Eduard von Hartmann and Nietzsche. Scandinavia in general aroused Weininger's keen interest: he knew Swedish and Norwegian among other foreign languages and visited Norway where he met Hamsun.

In 'Idolatry, Gynolatry' Strindberg says that the extraordinary feature of Weininger's book is its author's courage in speaking out on things which, though obvious, are always left unsaid, i.e. the inferiority of women. This evident fact is generally ignored because of a vast conspiracy to deny it. In Strindberg's opinion the conviction expressed by Weininger that 'woman is placed between child and man in the evolution series' is unquestionable: generally speaking 'woman is man in his rudimentary stage, despite some exceptions' which confirm the rule. The male is the sole creator of culture, both intellectually and materially. Although it is said that women have some potential for culture, they are in fact mediocre talents, re-creative rather than creative, or else simply bogus.

It is extraordinary, Strindberg says, that this fundamental truth, known, in fact, since the obscure beginnings of our history, still needs discovery. Anyone who ventures to speak out about it takes a tremendous risk, as if the secret had to be kept in order not to make the sexual act impossible. Man, in order to unite with woman, has to court her. His courtship is based on a 'sweet illusion' accompanying the erotic or divine folly, so perfectly described by Socrates in *The Symposium*. This subjection of man is a tribute paid to love. Man's role of wooer, according to Strindberg, is to be found only in Western civilization and is completely unknown in the East. *The Talmud*, for example, puts a curse on the man who gives way to the woman. What a woman really wants is to be confronted with man's will, or rather with

the mental energy that she does not possess herself. That is why a woman in love desires the man's humiliation and degradation, that is why she wants to dominate him—only then can she consider herself superior. In the physical sense all she seeks in man is 'the spark of life that will provide her with progeny. The love of a woman is 50% lust and 50% hatred. It may seem strange but it is true', says Strindberg; and he adds: 'When a woman loves a man she hates him because she feels subdued and inferior to him. The course of her love is not permanent, it frequently changes and continuously oscillates between the extremes.' It is precisely in this mutability and oscillation that the negative and passive nature of woman is expressed, whereas man is all positiveness and activity. According to Strindberg, the essence of Weininger's 'virile' book is to have revealed the generally known, but never divulged, secret of femininity and love. Such revelation brought about the author's death, and he merits our admiration for being a 'virile and fearless thinker'.[5]

Strindberg thus recognized in Weininger the thinker who presented in discursive language the very ideas he himself had expressed in literary form. Weininger is in a sense his disciple since he applied the knowledge he had gained from Strindberg's dramas: but he is also his partner, if not his master, in the domain of the metaphysics of sex, since he managed to express clearly what Strindberg hardly 'managed to utter'.

Direct references to Strindberg are scarce in Weininger: *The Father* is mentioned in the course of his discussion of 'telegony' (impregnation at a distance) and of the belief that what a pregnant woman sees influences the foetus. Weininger held that mothers-to-be should look at beautiful people and objects, a view shared by various scientific authorities, as well as by Goethe *(Elective Affinities),* Schopenhauer, and Ibsen *(The Lady from the Sea). The Father* depicts 'the deplorable illusion of fatherhood': what is fatherhood if another man can shape the child even when the woman remains faithful? Therefore, Weininger agrees with Strindberg that 'it is only women who have children'. *Creditors,* in turn, supports Weininger's thesis that 'the absolute woman has no ego'.[6] That woman is without a continuous ego, that she lacks a soul, is a very old belief, shared by the ancient Chinese, by Mahomet and Aristotle; the same conviction was shared by Ibsen (who, in contrast to most critics, was considered by Weininger to be a misogynist, which is not altogether unreasonable), as well as by Strindberg in *Creditors*.[7]

I shall now discuss the issues of fatherhood as presented in *The Father,* and deal with the play's direct parallels with Weininger's thesis. The Captain's doubts about his fatherhood lead to total disaster. Trying desperately to find out the truth, he opens a whole line of reasoning resulting only in the impossibility of certainty. He rediscovers the principle expressed in Roman Law: 'Mater semper certa est, pater, quem nuptiae demonstrant'. For him, however, the guarantee of fatherhood normally associated with matrimony has no value, since his wife herself hints at the possibility of her having been unfaithful. The Captain tortures himself: he draws on biological arguments in his conversation with the Doctor, he cites Homer and Ezekhiel, and remarks on the life of Pushkin in order to demonstrate that 'it is impossible to prove who is the father'. His reasoning resembles Weininger's remark: 'fatherhood is an illusion; it has to be shared with things and people, whereas the right of the mother is natural and physical. White women who have once had children with a Black later often give birth to children of evidently negroid features, though their fathers are white'.[8] Weininger alludes here both to the phenomenon of the influence of former pregnancies upon later progeny (a view which is still current among some dog breeders!) and to the belief in telegony. Other common points between Strindberg and Weininger may be explained by the convergence of their basic ideas: the fundamental opposition between man and woman, the inferiority of woman, who does not cease to be dangerous in spite of her inferior position, and finally the implacable struggle of the sexes.

The man-woman opposition which is common to both writers may be placed against the background of a more general tradition. Jacques Le Rider points to the fact that the greatest contribution to this way of thinking was made by German Romantic writers who, in opposing the abstract idea of the equality of human beings as present in the philosophy of the Enlightenment, introduced the polarization of man and woman. Man was opposed to woman in the same way as the Spirit was opposed to Nature and consciousness to subconsciousness. The goal of both sexes was considered to be the state of androgyny, a happy unity, putting an end to the opposition. Johann Wilhelm Ritter said that man is a god for woman, whereas woman is nature for man; when united god and nature create the world. A writer like, for example, Lorenz Oken, placed woman on an inferior level of development thus anticipating Strindberg and Weininger. And Friedrich de la Motte Fouqué in *Undine* has created a character who announces both Wedekind's Lulu, and Giraudoux's Ondine: the type of woman-child who brings destruction and death. Undine is mentioned by Weininger as embodying the 'Platonic idea of Woman'. If we seek to sum up Weininger's position with regard to the inheritance of the nineteenth century, we may observe that in the works of Schopenhauer, Nietzsche, von Hartmann, Wagner, Ibsen and Strindberg the opposition of the sexes has a tragic dimension. Weininger brought this opposition to an extreme Manichean vision which divides humanity into two races, two cultures, two completely unconnected fates.[9] And strictly speaking, the term 'human being' can be attributed only to man.

Weininger used *Creditors* to prove that woman has no soul. Thekla is a vampire; her ideas, her writings, everything she is in the spiritual sense, comes from men—from her former and present husbands. Therefore Gustav is right when he says: 'The woman is the man's

child and if she does not become one, then he himself becomes the woman's child, but the world is all wrong then', and later he adds: 'After all you have no soul'. Not possessing all the qualifications to become a complete being, woman does not exist as an individual. The notorious secret of femininity lies in the fact that 'women do not have this or that quality; their quality consists in possessing no qualities at all; here is the whole complexity and the secret of woman; hence arises her domination and evasiveness in front of man, who, as he has always done, tries to find her permanent essence'.[10]

The trap that woman sets upon man is based upon the force of inertia that can drag him down from the spiritual and intellectual heights to the level of Nature, Biology, Body, and Unconsciousness. She also opposes him actively in the implacable 'mortal struggle' that is spoken of by Laura in *The Father,* where the conflict is not so much between two individual characters as between two opposing forces. The failure is that of a man who is virile *par excellence,* being a military man and a scientist, and who represents physical strength, willpower and the power of intellect. He loses because he turns out to be the weaker; he has qualms of conscience, he fights openly and observes fair play. The woman has no principles. All she cares for is her goal—victory. The loser in *The Father* is Man with a capital 'M', and what is defeated in his person is Consciousness, Intellect, and Will. Victory is with Nature, with Biology, with Schopenhauer's 'will of the species' as opposed to the individual's goals, for Weininger woman represents above all the force of sexuality. The way she adopts to lead man towards his humiliation and destruction is the way of sex. Man satisfies woman's desire best when he is just a phallus. For a man, sexual intercourse can never be a cognitive or inspirational experience. It is an animal-like act, desired, in fact, by the woman, but signifying only failure for the man.

Wanting to prove the general inferiority of woman Weininger even deprives her of the beauty of her body: 'a living naked woman can no longer be considered beautiful, since the sexual drive impedes the objective contemplation which is essential for the consideration of beauty'. All we can truly admire are statues of beautiful women, since there is no lust in such a contemplation. 'The sexual impulse, driving to a union with a woman, destroys her beauty; once a woman has been touched and possessed, she can no longer be worshipped for her beauty.'[11] The beauty of a woman's body is also questioned in *Creditors* by Gustav: 'It is a young boy, only with the breasts, an unfinished man, a child that grew too quickly but stopped its development, chronically anaemic, losing blood regularly thirteen times a year.'

Weininger's vision of the world is made up of sets of oppositions: spirit—body, virile—feminine, conscious—subconscious, freedom—sexuality, morality—materiality.[12] Most of the oppositions can be easily applied to Strindberg's vision of the world; only the dualism of morality and materiality (the slavery imposed by the material world) does not always appear in a distinct way. Similar oppositions, though in a slightly different sense, turn out to construct the relation between man and woman in the dramatic works and novels of the Polish author and playwright Stanislaw Ignacy Witkiewicz (1885-1939).[13]

Witkiewicz was a great admirer of Strindberg; he knew Weininger's *Sex and Character* and he had a vast knowledge of the works of Schopenhauer and Nietzsche. He also knew the Polish writers most obsessed by the problem of demonic femininity and the struggle of the sexes like Stanislaw Przybyszewski (1868-1927) and Tadeusz Micinski (1873-1918).[14] Witkiewicz read Strindberg and Weininger mainly in Polish. Translations of Strindberg's plays appeared in 1890 and were first staged in Poland in 1905.[15] Direct allusions to Weininger, even if his name is not mentioned, are quite numerous in Witkiewicz's work, but what is important are the dramatist's general concepts: the idea of the struggle of the sexes, and the essence and the role of woman and man.[16]

In Witkiewicz's play *Gyubal Wahazar, or Along the Cliffs of the Absurd* (1921) Wahazar, the hero, is head of a totalitarian state. He is addressed as His Uniqueness and he combines the features of a grotesque absolute monarch with those of a modern dictator. His goal is to create a new society of totally mechanized individuals—a world of ultimate happiness. This commendable purpose is to become real only in a distant and unspecified future; for the time being (and for the duration of the play) Wahazar's state is a playground for bureaucratic madness and for the cruelty of those in power. The police and the military as well as the biologist/'metabiologist' who serve the regime are busy preparing people for their future life in a new society.

Wahazar's political programme takes care of other means of social education by providing for a proper upbringing of children which are 'voluntarily' given over to the state by their mothers. Special research has been carried out to enable the authorities to classify women according to their usefulness to the new society. The most valued is the type of 'mechanical mother'. Demonic women are to be totally eliminated; they are useless as they do not fulfil the purposes of the species (we observe here a distant echo of Schopenhauer's views). Moreover, demonic women do not obey the dictator's political directions and are a threat to political stability. If, according to Plato, the unsupervised evolution of a style in music may bring about the fall of a government, what is to be said of uncontrolled sex as a danger for Wahazar's ideal of mechanization? Sex is a domain which by its nature is ruled by demonic women and not by political leaders or their deputies. In Act II, two women undergo an extraordinary examination carried out by the 'Commission for Supernatural Selection' whose task is to seek out and eliminate demonic women. The overall results are as follows: Donna Scabrosa Macabrescu is 30% woman, 65% 'masculette', 5% 'unimportant psychic refuse' and Donna Lubrica Terramon

is 43% woman, 55% 'masculette', 2% 'unimportant psychic refuse'.

The examination is an evident parody of Weininger's theory presented in the first volume of *Sex and Character;* it is the theory of the bisexuality of every human being. There are no sexually uniform types, both men and women possess small fractions of the qualities of the opposite sex. Weininger worked out an algebraic formula of femininity and virility as well as the law of sexual attraction: 'Sexual unity is aimed at by a complete Man (M) and a complete Woman (W), although these two types are shared in various proportions between couples of different individuals'.[17] Witkiewicz obviously changed the elements of Weininger's sexual algebra and enriched it with an element of his own invention by adding the notions of 'masculette' (his version of androgyne) and of 'psychic refuse'. He applies percentages in the place of fractions, but Weininger is unquestionably the source of the concept.

Despite its parodistic presentation the man-woman relation constitutes the fundamental issue of Witkiewicz's works and takes a key position in his system of metaphysics which can also be described as the 'metaphysics of sex'. The term is taken from Schopenhauer's 'die Metaphysik der Geschlechtsliebe', but Witkiewicz was able to develop the concept in quite an original way. It should be borne in mind that he distinguished himself not only as playwright and novelist but also as an author of treatises on philosophy and aesthetics.

Witkiewicz's heroes are never united through love in its exalted sense, a love that would resemble Christian concepts as, for example, in saint Paul, *I Letter to the Corinthians;* there appears no reciprocal affection and there are no psychological gradations or shades. Nor do we come across friendship between representatives of the opposite sexes, nor among one sex. Human relationships are determined by aggression and lust, by the desire to dominate the fellow man and reduce him to the role of an object. Let us formulate here a provisional conclusion: the world of Witkiewicz's protagonists is not fully human, since too great a role is played in it by the animalistic factor. Rather than talk about humanity one is inclined to use the term 'human fauna'.

The problem of the relationship, or in fact of the conflict between the sexes appears already in Witkiewicz's first work *The 622 Falls of Bungo, or the Demonic Woman,* a novel written in 1910-11, but published only years after the author's death in 1972. The novel is an autobiographical *roman à clef* in which the young author presents himself and the circle of his friends. Witkiewicz is obviously Bungo and it is quite easy to recognize other slightly disguised characters like Bronislaw Malinowski, the future anthropologist, or Leon Chwistek, the future painter, writer and professor of logic, or Witkiewicz's admired master, Tadeusz Micinski, who appears as Childeric the Magus. *Bungo* is a novel of adolescence (*Bildungsroman,* or *Entwick-*

lungsroman) and it may also be termed an artist novel *(Künstlerroman);* the latter genre was as popular in Poland between 1900 and 1918 as it was in the rest of Europe. Joyce's *Portrait of the Artist,* although published in 1916, was written a few years earlier and is almost contemporary with Witkiewicz's 'self-portrait'. As to the comparison between the two novels, Daniel Gerould seems to have the final word when he says:

> Whereas in the usual 'Künstlerroman' we witness the young artist's struggles against the traditions and values of an uncomprehending family and a hostile bourgeois society, in *Bungo* the themes of art and sex are developed virtually to the exclusion of all others, as if in a vacuum. The conflicts are all interior, of an aesthetic or existential nature, between different conceptions of art and its relation to reality: as a self-sufficient absolute or as a tool of ulterior purposes. The hero is not isolated, but is a member of a group of kindred spirits. These young characters are not fighting against a crass philistine world, they have no financial worries, and their sexual adventures are not protests against bourgeois mores, nor are they judged adversely by society. Religion and the social, political, and national background—the other two motifs which occupy such an important position in Joyce's portrait of Stephen Daedalus—are non-existent in Witkacy's novel.[18]

The very title of the novel is significant as it opposes the hero who 'falls' and the demonic woman who is the cause of his fall. Bungo, the main character, is a young artist, an exquisite aesthete, and the demonic woman is his most dangerous and ultimately victorious enemy who diverts him from his glorious vocation and reduces him to the role of sexual aid. Bungo faces the choice between ascetic life, exclusively devoted to art, and sexual life which is mere subjection to the body. There emerges a certain model of the man-woman relationship that inevitably calls to mind Strindberg and Weininger. There is an opposition of values which can be presented by the following pairs: man vs. woman; art and intellect vs. sexual pleasure; consciousness vs. corporality. Consciousness is here identified with a metaphysical experience, with the awareness of the 'strangeness of existence', which is Witkiewicz's term for the wonder, or astonishment as the starting point for any philosophy. This very experience constitutes the humanity of a given individual: those ignorant of it are men only in a nominal sense; they can neither create nor perceive art or philosophy.

The quality referred to as corporality determines the human being as a member of the animal world, the representative of the species and therefore one of the elements of the earthly fauna. According to Pomian, whose conclusions I am applying here to a great extent, corporality is best summed up and expressed in the impulses of sex and aggression, since they combine its two fundamental components: the drive of the body to be in contact with another and the need to find an outlet for spontaneity.[19]

Yet, apart from corporality, man is also endowed with a need to constitute himself as an individual, to stop being just a bundle of impulses. Consciousness as opposed to corporality is characterized by the aspiration to break out of the imprisonment of animalistic existence, and to make manifest the fact that one is a conscious being. It can be and it is a means to escape from the animality of the world and to pass to the sphere of higher culture.

The human being is always torn between corporality and consciousness. If consciousness is missing, man is incomplete, not essentially different from an animal. Yet, man is characterized by what Witkiewicz calls metaphysical insatiability, which is a more or less distinct aspiration to find one's way out of the sphere of everyday life, a thirst for something external, metaphysical. The insatiability, or rather the desire for satiety is the prime motive in the activity of Witkiewicz's protagonists. Their acts are determined either by the choice of superior values or by the satisfaction of corporeal impulses; in other words, they choose between consciousness and corporality. Spiritual aspirations lead them to seek contact with the intellectuals who are representatives of consciousness; on the other hand, the desire to satisfy their impulses brings them into woman's bed. Woman is nothing but corporality, therefore relationships with her must be viewed as a fall. As woman is corporality, an incomplete, animalistic creature, and thus has no soul, she is not a full human being. Witkiewicz, though using a different language, and moving within his own metaphysics, meets here with Strindberg and Weininger.

The animality of the woman is stressed by her corporeal perfection; woman is a 'beautiful animal' (Joseph de Maistre's 'bel animal'), whereas man devoted to the intellect is sometimes lame (in Witkiewicz's novel *Insatiability* (1930) the artist Tengier is a cripple and the intellectual Bazyli is impotent). The intellectual milieu is exclusively composed of man, a congregation of solitaries who want to bring into life the ancient myth of a world without women, which was revived in European literature at the turn of the nineteenth century. Such an exclusively male group offers a certain resemblance to the army, which recalls Strindberg (The Captain in *The Father* and in *The Dance of Death*).

The solitude of intellectuals is the essential condition of their creativity; having a wife and a family would make creation extremely difficult if not impossible. A similar obstacle is presented by sexual relations with women who entangle man in corporeal and animal dependence and stimulate his aggression. Moreover, woman tries to bring man down to the level of subhumanity. The heroines of Witkiewicz's novels and plays follow one and the same course—they insist on destroying any kind of feelings in their sexual partners, including the very love that they have for them. Without love men are left in a state of animal-like desire which revives again and again after being satisfied; women aim at making men dependent and transforming them into mere instruments of sexual pleasure. Reduced to such a state man betrays his mission and passes temporarily or permanently under the rule of corporality. This pattern is clearly presented in *The 622 Falls of Bungo* by the couple Bungo and Acne, and later in *Insatiability* by Genezyp and The Duchess, or in the play *The Shoemakers* (1927-34) by The Prosecutor and The Duchess; the pattern works from the very beginning to the very end of Witkiewicz's creative life. The principle of the demonism of his heroines is to make another human being an instrument to satisfy their own needs.

Pomian points to an issue which is essential for our purpose: *The 622 Falls of Bungo* and *Insatiability* are novels in which woman appears before the eyes of an inexperienced youth as a combination of mother and mistress. In the course of their relationship affection disappears and pure sexuality takes over; the mistress kills the mother and love is killed by sex.[20] Strindberg's madonna and courtesan or Weininger's motherly type and harlot, are the set of references for Witkiewicz's conception. The relationship between man and woman turns into that of victim and executioner, eroticism becomes inseparable from sado-masochism, as may be clearly seen in Witkiewicz's last play, *The Shoemakers*.

By succumbing to the corporality man falls under the power of the species, the needs of which are served by woman. If, instead, he chooses consciousness, he remains an individual at the price of fighting the domination of the species, of opposing society and corporality embodied in woman. Only by taking such a course is he able to pursue art, philosophy or religion. These are the only aspirations and pursuits that reflect the consciousness of the individual and enable him to experience what Witkiewicz calls the Mystery of Being. In this way the notion of the metaphysics of sex expands into the central notion of Witkiewicz's metaphysical system as presented in his novels and plays. The notion of the metaphysics of sex applies to Witkiewicz in a paradoxically inverted way: in contrast to the characters of many other writers, his heroes do not experience anything metaphysical at the climax of sexual intercourse. The keys to the Mystery of Being are to be found by transcending carnality.

Witkiewicz's presentation of the relationship between man and woman is determined in fact by the struggle for domination and power. The protagonists of his plays and novels frequently define the mutual relationship of the sexes by referring to animal pre-copulative rites. Their situation makes the comparison totally justified. They declare themselves partisans of corporality and thus pass into the world of biology, even if they occupy the highest position on the scale of evolution. Talking about what once was supposed to be love and about what became, in fact, pure sexuality in their decaying world of disintegrating values, they explicitly mention the habits of insects—the Praying Mantis in *The Shoemakers,* or vampires feeding on human blood.

The motif of the mantis (omophagia) is a particularly emphatic means of presenting the relation between man and woman as reduced to a purely biological phenomenon and at the same time of stressing the cruelty of the human female; it may also serve as an expression of another motif—that of vampirism. The illustrative examples from the life of insects (spiders, scorpions and, above all, the mantis) were taken by Witkiewicz from Jean-Henri Fabre's *Souvenirs entomologiques* which are explicitly mentioned by one of the characters in *The Independence of Triangles* as his favourite reading. The mantis mythology which has been summarized in the well-known essay of Roger Caillois *La Mante religieuse* must, consequently, be supplemented by including Witkiewicz. His fullest contributions may be found in the following lines spoken by The Duchess in *The Shoemakers:*

> Doctor Scurvy, your utter helplessness excites me to perfect madness. I'd like you to have watched me while I was—you know?—doing it—but there's a really divine lieutenant in the blue hussars, someone from my own class or social sphere, too, and there's a certain actor, too . . . Your doubts are a reservoir for me of the choicest, female, straight-from-the-guts-insect-style sensuality—I'd like to be like the female praying mantis—near the climax they devour their partners from the head down and despite that, he keeps on doing it—you know, heehee.[21]

The reference to the ways and habits of insects seems to be the best, or perhaps even the only way of briefly presenting what has happened in the world of Witkiewicz: human relationships of the animal type. The vicious circle closes here, as it did for Strindberg and Weininger, with one essential difference: beyond the struggle of the sexes as perceived by Witkiewicz—the specialist and authority on the subject of demonic women—lies the/province of Witkiewicz—the intellectual, philosopher and art reformer. The struggle of the sexes is only one of the elements, though admittedly an important one, in the construction of his system.

NOTES

[1] I quote Strindberg's article from Jacques Le Rider, *Le cas Otto Weininger. Racines de l'antiféminisme et l'antisémitisme* (Paris, Presses Universitaires de France, 1982), p. 137. In volume 54 of the standard Swedish edition of Strindberg's works this article is published as *Weininger. An Obituary Notice/Weininger. Eftermäle;* the above words are omitted from the article (cf. *Samlade skrifter av August Strindberg.* Femtiofjärde delen. Suplementdel I: *Efterslater,* Stockholm: Bonniers, 1920, pp. 412-14).

[2] Cf. J. Le Rider, *Le cas Otto Weininger,* pp. 151-2.

[3] Cf. Marthe Robert, 'Strindberg et Weininger', in: *Obliques,* 1972, no. 1: *Strindberg,* p. 72.

[4] Ibidem.

[5] cf. Le Rider, op. cit., pp. 40-1.

[6] Otto Weininger, *Plec i charakter. Rozbiór zasadniczy,* Polish translation by Ostap Ortwin, Warszawa: Biblioteka Dziel Naukowych, 1926, vol. II, p. 6.

[7] Ibidem, p. 7.

[8] Ibidem, p. 96.

[9] Cf. J. Le Rider, op. cit., pp. 121-5.

[10] O. Weininger, op. cit., p. 216.

[11] Ibidem, p. 113.

[12] Cf. Le Rider, op. cit., pp. 168-9.

[13] Krzysztof Pomian, *Powiesc jako wypowiedz filozoficzna (Próba strukturalnej analizy 'Nienasycenia'),* in: *Studia o Stanislawie Ignacym Witkiewiczu.* Edited by Michal Glowinski and Janusz Slawinski, Wroclaw: Ossolineum, 1972, pp. 9-31.

[14] Stanislaw Przybyszewski published an essay in *Die Fackel* (1907) entitled 'Das Geschlecht' ('The Sex') dedicated to 'Weininger's shadows'. In 1906 Felicja Nossig published *Man and Woman. A Psychological Study Based on Weininger's Work 'Geschlecht und Charakter'.* In 1911, Leo Belmont published *Otto Weininger; Genius and Enemy of Woman;* Adam Zielenczyk wrote an article in *Sfinks* on the metaphysics of sex, from Plato to Schopenhauer and Weininger; Ostap Ortwin published the first edition of his translation of *Sex and Character.*

[15] Witkiewicz, then director of the Formist Theatre, Zakopane, presented the Polish première of *The Ghost Sonata* in 1926.

[16] In Witkiewicz's *Dainty Shapes and Hairy Apes, or The Green Pill (Beelzebub Sonata, Plays, Essays and Documents).* Edited and translated by Daniel Gerould and Jadwiga Kosicka, New York: Performing Arts Journal Publications, 1980, p. 113) the innocent and virginal Tarquinius, expert in erotic theory, states: 'I know the *Kamasutra* and Weininger, Freud and the Babylonian sexologists.'

[17] O. Weininger, op. cit., vol. I, p. 56.

[18] Daniel Gerould, *Witkacy. Stanislaw Ignacy Witkiewicz as an Imaginative Writer,* Seattle and London: University of Washington Press, 1981, pp. 35-6.

[19] K. Pomian, op. cit., p. 15.

[20] Ibidem, p. 19.

[21] S. I. Witkiewicz, *The Madman and the Nun and Other Plays,* translated and edited by Daniel Gerould and C. S. Durer (Seattle and London: University of Washington Press, 1968) pp. 232-3.

Barbara Z. Schoenberg (essay date 1987)

SOURCE: "'Woman-Defender' and 'Woman-Offender', Peter Altenberg and Otto Weininger: Two Literary Stances vis-à-vis Bourgeois Culture in the Viennese 'Belle Epoque'," in *Modern Austrian Literature,* Vol. 20, No. 2, 1987, pp. 51-69.

[In the following essay, Schoenberg discusses the social and psychic implications of the paradoxical images of women in late-nineteenth-century Viennese bourgeois culture and the contrasting viewpoints of Weininger and Peter Altenberg.]

During the second half of the nineteenth century the "femme bourgeoise," a central figure in much of eighteenth-century drama, claims her place in narrative fiction as well. In order to illustrate the widespread manifestation of and interest in this type of woman one need only recall a few of the narrative masterpieces of latter nineteenth-century European fiction such as Flaubert's *Madame Bovary* (1857), Tolstoi's *Anna Karenina* (1887), and Fontane's *Effi Briest* (1895). These works not only served to highlight the "femme bourgeoise" but, more importantly, enabled their authors to express some of the more subtle and effective criticisms of bourgeois culture through the vehicle of sensitive female characterizations.

While there is no equivalent masterpiece in Austrian narrative literature other than perhaps Schnitzler's *Frau Bertha Garlan* (1901), which might reflect as well as these other European models both the tragic role of the "femme bourgeoise" and the author's critical stance towards bourgeois society, it is also true that with rare exception the female bourgeois characters who populate the narrative fiction of the Viennese "belle époque" are similarly and consistently portrayed as hapless victims of an extremely deleterious social order. Furthermore, only in the Viennese "belle époque" does one encounter writers who focus *exclusively* on "woman" as a primary vehicle for criticism of bourgeois mores and institutions.

Certainly most of the major Austrian writers of the period such as Schnitzler, Bahr, Hofmannsthal, Beer-Hofmann, and even Kraus at times used "woman" as a means of pointing out the flaws in their society. But none did this so exclusively, with such persistence, nor with such absolute, almost obsessive determination to improve their bourgeois world thereby as did two of the "belle époque's" more controversial figures, the prose poet Peter Altenberg, who preferred the company of whores to "femmes bourgeoises," and the young philosopher who equated the two, Otto Weininger.

Altenberg and Weininger are also of interest for two additional reasons. First, they represent two extremes in attitude toward women in Austrian literature—protective, romantic idolatry ("Frauenlob") as expressed by Altenberg on the one hand and aggressive hostility ("Frauenhass") as uncovered in the work of Weininger on the other. Second and most important, at times misunderstood or misclassified by critics, their single-minded efforts to expose the foibles of their bourgeois society through the vehicle "Woman" frequently overlooked or left unexplored, an examination of their work provides us with some of the most severe and overt criticism of the "femme bourgeoise" in particular and bourgeois culture in general as it has been confronted in "belle époque" literature to date.

PETER ALTENBERG

While there have been numerous articles on Peter Altenberg, the majority of these concentrate on his earliest of twelve volumes, *Wie ich es sehe* (1896), and on his aestheticism, a tendency which has led some critics to judge him quite negatively, viewing Altenberg as little more than an "esoterischen Stilkunst-Poeten," a "dekadenten Kaffeehausliteraten," or "bindungslosen Snob und Impressionisten."[1] With the exception of Gisela Wysocki's monograph (1979), a "selbstpoetisches Konstrukt" which at times misinterprets and tends to mystify Altenberg and his work,[2] and Camillo Schaefer's biography (1980), which provides next to no textual analyses and is hardly more than a restatement of earlier contemporary appraisals of Altenberg's life and literary production,[3] since Altenberg's death in 1919 there has been no longer "comprehensive stylistic study" and no detailed thematic analysis of Altenberg's *total* oeuvre.[4] The seemingly haphazard manner of his writing and the numerous superficial inconsistencies and contradictions in his work[5] have not aided scholars and may have dissuaded even the most positive and astute of such recent critics as Andrew Barker from justifying or attempting to find "formal cohesion" in any but Altenberg's first volume.[6] Through a study of his "feminine awareness" and particularly an examination of the "femme bourgeoise" and her female entourage, as presented in his poetic world, however, not only Altenberg's extreme modernity, but also the unity of purpose and overall artistic consistency of *all* his work,—the total and uncompromising commitment to the amelioration of his bourgeois society—are to be found.

It is commonplace today to see the substitution of such words as "chairperson" for "chairman," "layperson" for "layman," and the inclusion of the female alternate pronouns in general statements, such as "If one is sick, *he* or *she* must make up *his* or *her* work." It is not without some astonishment, however, that we note as early as the first two decades of this century in, of all places, patriarchal absolutist Austria the following statement where the writer provides the feminine alternate form "jede" in a generalization which would have been implied or understood without it: *"Jeder und Jede finden ihren eigenen Vorteil darin."*[7] This unusual formulation is found as early as 1908 in a prose sketch by Altenberg, a literary novelty which continues with greater frequency in his later works, particularly in *Vita ipsa, Mein Lebensabend* and in the *Nachlass,* a posthumous compilation of earlier unpublished pieces.[8] In these works we find several alternate feminine forms for us to consider. Usually associated with Altenberg's criticism of the artificiality of bourgeois norms, at times these feminine-gender inclusions appear as isolated occurrences, while elsewhere, as in the following, they are more consistent, crowded together in a single passage. Here, for example, they are noticeably linked to Altenberg's censure of his bourgeois world—a society which he feels is so caught up in itself and its superficial values as to exclude the possibility for any real or permanent relationship:

> Aber da sind so viele Hindernisse, Missverständnisse, Komplikationen jeglicher Art, dass man stets blöderweise auf *irgend Einen, irgend Eine* hofft . . . *Jeder, jede* ist mit den eigenen Komplikationen direkt emsigst pathologisch beschäftigt . . . Infolgedessen gibt es auch keine reelle Freundschaft, sondern nur gefährliche Gespräche über dieselbe! . . . Jeder sucht hingegen sein armseliges . . . Persönchen *dem anderen, der anderen* aufzudrängen. *Jeder, jede* wehrt sich *seiner, ihrer* Haut. . . . Freundschaft ist eine allertiefste, allerweiseste Erkenntnis! Wer hat sie?!? Niemand! (LA 335-336)

Further example of Altenberg's "feminine awareness" can be discovered in an analysis of his metaphorical language, where, although not as overwhelming in their frequency as are the images which refer to high capitalism, disease, decay, and death allusions to exclusively feminine activities such as childbirth, post-natal care, and motherhood abound. While the contexts in which these images appear concern relationships and emotional ties which have little to do with childbirth or maternal love, for example, the bond between an artist and his art, or "Naturempfinder" and natural setting, they are nevertheless related in Altenberg's mind. We read references to "Wöchnerinnenkost," "kranke Wöchnerin," and "Wochenbettfrau"[9] in pieces where Altenberg advocates a simpler diet for his overindulged bourgeois contemporaries, and we encounter numerous similes which refer to the relationship between mother and child—"wie eine Mama an ihrem Baby" (P 51); "wie wenn ein Baby . . . ruhig an der Mutterbrust schliefe" (ML 136)—in sketches treating a variety of subjects. In an aphorism Altenberg compares a passive interest in politics, for example, with "verblendete Mütter, die alle scheusslichen Ungezogenheiten ihrer Lieblinge bewundern,"[10] and in "Natur" he links together maternal feelings and "nature appreciation": "Naturempfinden ist wie die Mutterliebe eine ewige rastlose Emotion . . . Es muss ein 'Nervenrausch' sein, sonst ist es nichts, nichts! Es darf keinerlei Zweck haben für die werte Gesundheit, es muss von selbst wirken und beglücken, *wie das Antlitz der jungen Mutter, die sich über die Wiege des soeben erwachten Kindchens beugt.*"[11]

Some of the literary works which Altenberg advocates reading shed additional light on his pro-feminine position, for Altenberg seems captivated by works which are either written by women or treat of female characterizations and feminine sensibilities. He advocates reading "Feierabend" by Ilka Maria Unger, whose poems he greets with a "Hymne, eine Fanfare der Begeisterung" (ML 209). Also he repeatedly praises the "Bücher der 'Bibliothèque rose" by "Madame de Ségure (sic) née Rostopshine" (ML 159), and refers to these same works as his "Lebensbibeln" (V 91), relating that he .reread them often, particularly in his later years: "Ich las heute fünf Stunden lang in meinem Zimmerchen: Hermann Bahr . . . Egon Friedell . . . les petites filles modèles (F 156).[12]

In Pròdrômôs, however, Altenberg's pro-feminine stance is underscored by a reference to one of the leading feminists of his day, the Swedish writer Ellen Key.[13] In "Buchbesprechung," for example, Altenberg praises Ellen Key's insights concerning love and marriage with the words "Menschen' von Ellen Key . . . der Dichterin Elisabeth Barrett Liebe und Ehe. Ich habe für eine teure Dame das Buch zusammengestrichen . . . Auf diesen Seiten erlebt man das märchenhafteste des Daseins . . ." (P 152). Not only does Altenberg praise Ellen Key's interpretation of the poetess Browning's life and work, but, as if reciprocally, Ellen Key in turn lavishes the highest praise upon Altenberg, "der ganz begreift, was die Frau will," and who describes Woman in "tausend Tonarten." In Über Liebe und Ehe, one of her most comprehensive feminist works, Key evaluates the then current feminist viewpoints concerning the woman question and alludes to Altenberg in this context: "Aber nicht nur in der Frauenliteratur wird die neue Liebe verkündigt. Schon jetzt gibt es Männer, die ganz begreifen, was die Frau willl . . . Unter den Älteren hat . . . Ibsen . . . es teilweise verstanden . . . Ein anderer ist Peter Altenberg."[14]

An examination of the women in Altenberg's poetic world shows at once his great love and rare understanding of the female soul and correspondingly his deep-seated aversion to the bourgeois world of which these women are a part. Altenberg's total oeuvre is a compendium of the mores and empty life-styles of the bourgeoisie, a rich and varied "Gesamtbild"[15] of Viennese society in the "belle époque." For Altenberg this world produced two types of woman which he describes in his prose sketches: one a "fallen" woman, not really a prostitute of the kind he was known to befriend and occasionally write about,[16] but nevertheless one "lost" or "sold," given to the demands and mercantile preoccupations of the bourgeois social strata; and the other a young innocent, still savable because untainted by the bourgeois way of life.

Ever contrasted in Altenberg's work are the older woman, usually unhappily married, "die sich in Sorge um einen zu meist wertlosen Mann und Haushalt . . . täglich verbraucht . . . die . . . zur gegebenen Zeit den Stier [nimmt], kalbt . . . Milch [gibt]" (BL 152) and the young maiden who is still pure and who possesses a "künftige Seele"—the woman who is interested only in "Commissionen machen" or the "Dame," whose face

is "verwittert und bleich" because she will "niemand mehr Freude geben, Licht und Wärme," vis-à-vis the "Mädchen," whose face is by contrast radiant with hope and who possesses "eine tiefe Schönheit."[17] Compared are simply dressed young innocents who play in parks and meadows, or scantily clad Ashantee maidens, primitively housed in temporary huts in the "Wiener Thiergarten," with bourgeois matrons who are consumed by a desire for possessions and concerned only with externals. These overindulged women by contrast brag of richly decorated homes which a modern architect like "Herr A. L. [Adolf Loos] eingerichtet [hat]" (F 31) and are attracted by luxury items such as cuff links, furs, plumes, "aparte Frisuren," and designer clothing, thinking always that "man müsse bei Goldmann und Salatsch ausstaffiert werden, bei Wunderer seine Dessous beziehen und bei Helene von Zimmerauer . . . seine Photographien" (LA 133; 137).

In Altenberg's poetic world (except for P. A. himself, of course!) fairytale princes of the romantic past have been transformed into fat bank directors—"Sie war die Schönste. Sie erregte Neid. Sie glaubte, ein Prinz werde kommen oder etwas Ähnliches, z.B. ein Bankdirektor. Was hätte sie anderes sich erträumen können, in gelben Musselin-Rüschen?" (S 109)—and men are concerned with bourgeois aspirations, hoping to become "Sektionsrath" or "Hofrat" while their wives, the bourgeois matrons, are nothing more than commodities, "erstehenswerte preiswürdige Ware" (ML 228), interested only in materialistic pursuits. Altenberg's interest in the plight of the female seems to emerge most strongly, however, in prose pieces in which he defends the young, still unblemished members of his bourgeois world—those fragile existences who have been spared because they are still too young to have succumbed to the bourgeois life-style,[18]—and in sketches which treat of maidservants or other female members of the working classes, those who have been victimized, as Altenberg sees it, or abused outright by the comfort and pleasure-seeking, often ruthless, bourgeoisie.

Thus the objects of attention in the initial sketches of Altenberg's first volume, Wie ich es sehe (1896), are still innocent females aged nine to eleven, and the subject of the first sketch he ever wrote, "Lokale Chronik," was a fifteen-year-old neophyte, who had fallen prey to the bourgeois world of busy time-schedules and superficial activities and had disappeared, swallowed up in the "Wirbel des Grossstadtmeeres": "Dieses junge Mädchen begann er zu lieben, von ganzer Seele . . . Sie verwandelte sich in das 'gehetzte Reh,' er sah die 'brechenden Augen.' Überhaupt, sie entsprach seinem Ideale" (A 204). Furthermore, the titles of Wie ich es sehe show Altenberg's interest in women, for the numbered titles, "Neun und Elf," "Zwölf," "Siebzehn bis Dreissig," "Fünfundzwanzig," and "Fünfunddreissig," suggest the progression in age from young girl to married woman, and the content of these pieces focuses almost exclusively on female subjects.

On the underside of the corrupt, morally bankrupt, leisurely way of life of the bourgeoisie, which, paradoxically, Altenberg paints with great charm and allure[19] yet never fails to attack, is the suppression and exploitation of the lower classes, who work almost ceaselessly to make this exalted world possible. Without exception the "Woman-Defender" Altenberg champions their rights and pleads their case: "Hinter den erleuchteten Fenstern spürt man arbeitsmüde Menschen. Besonders die Mädchen, die ihre wenigen Jahre da verarbeiten" (V 237), as he demonstrates keen insight into the desperation of their predicament, and notes passionately the "Verzweiflung hysterischer,[20] überbürdeter, arbeitsbelasteter armer junger Mütter, die ihrem eigenen Schicksale trostlos und die Welt verfluchend gegenüber stehen" (ML 95). In a letter to the "Arbeiter-Führer" Viktor Adler, for example, Altenberg addresses the question of bourgeois exploitation and seduction of the working-class female but offers a rather naive solution to the problem: the "Reorganisation der Volks-Tracht der armen Mädchen, der Arbeiterinnen," so that they "dem bürgerlichen Putze und elenden Tand einen auffälligen Protest entgegensetzen."[21]

Whenever it is a matter of Altenberg's perception of the social injustices inherent in his world, he consistently expresses through the vehicle of "Woman" the most severe indictments against his bourgeois society. Correspondingly, the females in Altenberg's work most often suffer and bear the brunt of social inequality and injustice. Altenberg repeatedly points up the outrageous manner in which young female servants are treated and taken advantage of by the idle bourgeoisie: "Die Bonne sass schweigend da . . . bedrückt von der miserablen Behandlung, die man ihr von allen Seiten angedeihen liess" (BL 92). He commiserates with this exploited class which is subjected to indignities and which is constantly at the beck and call of its bourgeois mistresses, ever scapegoats to the latter's discontent and whims, as suggested in the following statements: "Die Dame kam aus der Oper und zankte dennoch mit ihrem Stubenmädchen" (P 184); "Ich war sehr streng gegen meine Dienstboten, aber seit ich Karl kenne, bin ich ungeheuer milde mit ihnen" (P 176); "Sie heirateten, gebaren, wurden sehr nervös, und malträtierten infolgedessen ihre armen Dienstboten" (BL 12).

Along with the many attractive scenes depicting feminine purity and innocence and the various criticisms concerning the exploitation of the servant class by the bourgeoisie are also several sketches which treat of child abuse (always a female child!), tales of battered and mistreated children, who, according to Altenberg, also owe their sufferings directly to the exploitations and excessive ambitions of the bourgeoisie. Altenberg contrasts, for example, the purity and serenity of nature, where exploitation or mistreatment of children does not occur, with the aspirations of bourgeois culture, where by implication such atrocities abound: "Hier werden keine kleinen Kinder malträtiert. Hier wünscht niemand Sektionsrath zu werden."[22] So aware was Altenberg of the injustices and atrocities rampant in his society and so committed to combating the evils attributable to the bourgeois social structure that, even though he was reduced to accepting gifts from benefactors and friends such as Karl Kraus and Adolf Loos[23] to sustain himself, Alten-berg nevertheless frequently shared his meager profits with the "Kinderschutz- und Rettungs-gesellschaft." In "Zeug-nisse" we encounter three letters dated within two months of each other, one from a benefactor, Ludwig Domansky, inviting Altenberg to "Souper," enabling the former "einem österreichischen Dichter sein nicht allzu sorgen-freies Dasein erleichtern zu können," and the other two from officials of the Kinderschutz- und Rettungs-Gesellschaft thanking Altenberg for "die uns gütigst übermittelte Spende" (NF 329-331).

In Altenberg's work, therefore, we not only find impressionistic prose poems with the most lavish of color schemes and sensual depictions, but we are made to observe as well a series of "Gerichtsverhandlungen,"[24] sketches treating of abused female children, prose pieces which relate cruelties suffered by young daughters at the hands of equally mistreated mothers, women who often had been victims of abuse themselves: "Soll sie's besser haben als mir, warum?!"[25] In relating the facts of a "Gerichtsverhandlung" dated 3 May 1907 Altenberg tells of the brutal slaying of an illegitimate female child by a mother who had covered its body with burning coals and who had been subsequently set free since "die Geschworenen fanden, dass das Kind nicht direkt an den Brandwunden gestorben sei" (ML 187)! These horridly realistic depictions of lower class violence illustrate that there was something very rotten in Altenberg's Vienna. By including these sordid, starkly realistic texts among his more poetic sketches of muted colors, "fauteuils," house-balls and "soirées" Altenberg suggests that "Neid, Sehnsucht nach sogenannten basseren Verhältnissen, Eifersucht in äusserlichen Dingen, Verführtwerden wegen elender Fetzen, Hüten und scheusslichen Schmuckes,"[26] that observed acts of violence and brutality were unavoidable reactions to hunger, poverty, and injustice which the lower-class females had to endure at the hands of the idle pleasure-seeking bourgeoisie. Altenberg, who perceived these inconsistencies and injustices and who was ready to rally to the defense of victimized women, can perhaps today be viewed as an "avant-garde-feminist," a "Woman-Defender," whose pro-feminine orations were often heard echoing down deserted streets and across tables in the night spots of Vienna. Moreover, Altenberg's defense of woman extends far beyond the probing into the soul of some of his female characters, which the feminist Ellen Key had so appreciated; it is apparent in the many prose poems dedicated to and concerned with young girls, and it is manifested equally strongly in the numerous socially engaged sketches involving the bourgeois matron and the often tragic lives of her *female* entourage—her acquaintances, her sisters and daughters, and in particular her servants.

OTTO WEININGER

While praising Altenberg's sensitivity and concern for the woman question, the Swedish feminist Ellen Key also mentions *Geschlecht und Charakter* (1903) by Otto Weininger, a work which seemingly provides an entirely different viewpoint of Woman. Key likens Weininger to two of the greatest "Frauenschmäher" of her time, Nietzsche and Strindberg, since Weininger "in der Frau ein sehr tief stehendes Wesen sieht."[27]

In the initial chapters of *Geschlecht und Charakter,* a sensationally successful work with twenty-five editions in twenty years but still controversial today,[28] Weininger's extreme misogyny[29] appears to be presented under the guise of the utmost "philosophische Gründlichkeit"[30] with the detached authority and objectivity of the scientist. At times Weininger attempts either to excuse or soften his cynicism, "Es kommt mir nicht in den Sinn, die Männer zu idealisieren, um die Frauen leichter in der Schätzung herabdrücken zu können,"[31] or to lend his work the aura of objectivity by apologizing for his presentation of "allem Schlechtem und Garstigem, das ich den Frauen nachgesagt habe" (W 281). But for the most part Weininger's work is saturated with extremely negative anti-feminine and anti-feminist viewpoints which are highly subjective in nature. In contrast to Altenberg's stance as "Woman-Defender" his pro feminine arguments and his feminine-gender inclusions, by which he had attempted to give "equal time" and consideration to women: ("Jeder und Jede," "Mancher und Manche"), Weininger's generalizations seem initially to achieve the opposite effect and appear to negate woman's role altogether, rendering her senseless, "un-sinnig," and devoid of meaning, "ein hohles Gefäss . . . das Symbol des Nichts" (W 346; 404), "oder sogar . . . noch weniger."[32] While I concur with Nike Wagner who unmasks Weininger's extreme subjectivity hidden beneath the guise of scientific investigation,[33] I also share Norbert Leser's view that Weininger's misogyny might be mainly a "front," an anti-feminist means to a profeminine end. Leser warns in defense of Weininger that one ought not to label him a "Frauenfeind" nor take his "anti-feministische Auslassungen für bare Münze,"[34] indicating that Weininger's misogyny was only "Schocktherapie" used to arrive at a new and heightened plan for an improved relationship between the sexes. In addition to these two views I would like to add yet another explanation for Weininger's anti-feminine stance, suggesting in the following that Weininger's misogyny may have been a "front" or "cover" for a quite different antagonism: Weininger vis-à-vis his bourgeois culture.

Throughout *Geschlecht und Charakter* Weininger expresses a deep-seated hatred for woman as well as all activities involving women. He has nothing but contempt for women writers and in contrast to Altenberg, for example, considers Elizabeth Barrett Browning unimportant: "in der Tat gehört sehr viel Milde und Laxheit dazu, um Frauen wie . . . Elisabeth Barrett Browning . . . auch nur ein Titlechen von Bedeutung

beizulegen" (W 85). His offensive against women includes a denunciation of the Women's Movement, which he belittles as being more "Dirnen-Emanzipation als Frauen-Emanzipation" (W 454), an anti-feminist position criticized by Ellen Key but especially objectionable to the Viennese feminist Rosa Mayreder. Often bordering on the absurd, Weininger states unequivocally that women are stupid, preoccupied with sex, have no fantasy or genius, and in addition lack a great many exclusively masculine attributes: They are neither heroic nor tragic, they lack piety, memory, logic, morality, regard for the law, duty and judgment. They have no sense of truth, since "Verlogenheit . . . sämtliche Frauen [charakterisiert]" (W 371), no sense of reality, no sense of self or self-worth, no soul, no freedom, no character, or will: "So ist denn ein ganz umfassender Nachweis geführt, dass "W" seelenlos ist, dass es kein Ich und keine Individualität, keine Persönlichkeit und keine Freiheit, keinen Charakter und keinen Willen hat" (W 269). "W" also has no heart and thus can never know, understand, or be capable of love or friendship. She cannot know faithfulness, since fidelity is, according to Weininger, an exclusively masculine trait, "der ganz und gar männliche Gedanke der Treue" (W 289). Further, "W" lacks modesty and chastity, and all her ostensible prudery is just a fake, a "Verleugnung und Abwehr der eigenen Unkeuschheit" (W 372).

In addition to his misogynous offensive, in which Weininger enumerates woman's many faults, his presentation of woman's capabilities is again totally negative. "W" is envious, anti-social, apolitical, dishonest, covetous and larcenous. She is easily impressed, superstitious, extremely brutal, and insensitive to another's pain, for, Weininger argues, it is "Frauen . . . die . . . am meisten Härte beweisen" (W 295).

Weininger's "W" comes in two shapes or sizes only, mothers, who are particularly odious to him and summarily dismissed: "Ich kann . . . in die allgemeine bewunderung der Mutterliebe nicht einstimmen" (W 297), and prostitutes. While Altenberg, whose prose poems contained numerous similes presenting maternal love as the highest bond in contrast to Weininger's negative view of motherhood, idealizes and idolizes young maidens, Weininger insists "Die Jungfrau, die gibt es nicht" (W 285) because to his way of thinking all virgins are hysterics and all hysterics are only suppressed prostitutes.[35] To Weininger some women may be mothers, some may be prostitutes, but all are "im Dienste der Idee des Koitus" (W 353) and all are panderers, since "jedes Weib . . . kuppelt" (W 352).

Were we to overlook some of Weininger's more subjective observations, where he gives vent to his antipathy for two peoples, the Jews and the British, who he perceives as being akin to Woman, or where he includes the perception that youths not twenty years of age are attracted to women thirty-five years or older, or that mothers want to see their sons married "ganz ohne Rücksicht auf die individuelle Eigenart des Sohnes" (W

347), a closer look at the passages of his most blatant misogyny would nevertheless suggest a very definite bias—for they are based almost exclusively upon one type of woman only, the bourgeois matron or "Ehefrau." Weininger makes a sweeping generalization that "W" is a panderer ever enthralled by the sexual act. But how does he substantiate this generalization? He draws from personal experience, relating the actions of a personal acquaintance, a *bourgeois matron:*

> Ich habe eine längst verheiratete Hausfrau gekannt, die ihr Dienst mädchen, das den Liebhaber eingelassen hatte, zuerst lang in groâer Anteilnahme vor der Tür behorchte, ehe sie hineingegangen, ihm seine Stellung zu kündigen. Die Frau hatte also den ganzen Vorgang innerlich bejaht, um dann das Mädchen . . . hinauszuwerfen (W 350).

As further testimony of "W"'s predilection for "Kuppelei" Weininger draws another example from his bourgeois milieu. "Eine verheiratete Dame, die für geistreich und mannigfach talentiert gelten konnte . . . hörte ich einmal über ihre unschöne und ältliche italienische Lehrerin sich lustig machen, weil diese wiederholt betont habe . . . sie sei noch eine Jungfrau" (W 457).

The passages which treat of marriage disclose even more clearly that Weininger's "W" is a specific type of woman and that his projectiles are aimed not only at her, but also at bourgeois institutions in general. Some of these statements make Weininger's kinship with Altenberg readily discernible; the latter's gynolatry ("Frauenlob") and the former's misogyny ("Frauenhaâ") are related, like two edges of a sword hurled at the same target, the bourgeois social structure. We encounter statements which disclose that "W" will readily marry "einen ungeliebten Mann" (W 267), phrases which tell of "ohne Liebe Heiratenden" (W 49), of "bloâer Geld-heirat" (W 51), and words which deny emphatically that love exists in marriage: "Darum wird es auch fast immer als eine Heuchelei empfunden, wenn einer von Liebe in der Ehe spricht" (W 319).

We find repeatedly that Weininger's "W" is not really "W" in general: she is never a member of the working class nor a peasant girl but is rather immediately recognizable as "das bürgerliche Mädchen" or "die Ehefrau," the epitome of the bourgeois female. Quite similar to Altenberg's negative characterizations of married women caught up in the superficialities of the bourgeois lifestyle, Weininger's models of "W," the objects of his bitter hatred, wear "Krinoline" and "Mieder" (W 259), measure their worth by the dances they attend, the "Zahl, Gröâe und Preis der Bouquets" (W 158), the value of their "Geld und Gut," and the "Rang ihrer Loge im Theater" (W 261). Furthermore, "W" is concretely presented as a woman of leisure cuddling her lap dog-a woman totally committed to the "Pflege und Kleidung von Mann und Kind, in Besorgung oder Aufsicht von Küche und Haus, Garten und Feld" (W 297), absorbed with petty jealousies and the idle pursuits of "einer geschmackvolleren Toilette oder Frisur" (W 356).

Finally, at the close of his huge misogynous treatise, but with momentary ambivalence and quite contradictory emotion, Weininger confides that the bourgeois woman is indeed the focal point of his interest. In a passage strikingly similar to those where Altenberg expresses concern for the female members of his bourgeois world and where he demonstrates equally engaged poetic pleadings for sexual abstinence[36] Weininger argues that only through woman's reeducation and paradoxically through her lack of reproduction(!) can his society be saved:

> Hiemit erst, aus dem höchsten Gesichtspunkte des Frauen- als des Menschheitsproblems, ist die Forderung der Enthaltsamkeit für beide Geschlechter gänzlich begründet . . . Die Verneinung der Sexualität tötet bloâ den körperlichen Menschen und ihn nur, um den geistigen erst das volle Dasein zu geben . . . Also widerspricht der Koitus in jedem Falle der Idee der Menschheit . . . Und wer nicht verstehen kann, was mit dieser Kantischen Idee der Menschheit gemeint ist, der mag es sich zum Bewuâtsein bringen, daâ es *seine Schwestern, seine Mutter, seine weiblichen Verwandten sind, um die es sich handelt:* um unser selbst willen sollte das Weib als Mensch behandelt, geachtet werden, und nicht erniedrigt (W 469-470; italics mine).

A closer look at Weininger's misogynous theories and a review of his inveterate hatred for woman, his contempt for the English, the Jews, and ultimately himself (since he admits to being "selbst jüdischer Abstammung" [W 412]) point up how the vast majority of his conclusions have a subjective rather than an objective scientific character, garbed and colored by his time and by his own very personal relationship to his surroundings. The "W" Weininger presents us with is not really "W" in her purest form; she is much more an alloy, "W" tainted by the bourgeois lifestyle and cast by Weininger into a specifically bourgeois mold. Consequently it may not be "W" whom Weininger despises—she is perhaps only a metaphor for his time, for his bourgeois world, the symbol of a universe and an era which for him was odious, corrupt, and diseased to the core, as he stated in one of the most emotionally charged passages of his diagnostic arguments. Here the young man, whom Kraus deemed a "frustrated poet,"[37] sums up the ills-run-rampant of his time in a diatribe reminiscent of both Nietzsche's philosophical writings and the poetry of Ecclesiastes. While restating his grievances against Impressionism, anarchism, the superficiality, impiousness and excessive sexuality, the "Ödigkeit" of his age—all of which he subsumes as "emale"—Weininger, like the prophet of old, demonstrates his malaise, his extreme discontent and disillusionment with living in this particularly despicable time:

> Unsere Zeit, die nicht nur die jüdischste, sondern auch die weibischste aller Zeiten ist; die Zeit, für welche die Kunst nur ein Schweiâ—tuch ihrer Stimmungen abgibt, die den künstlerischen Drang aus den Spielen der Tiere abgeleitet hat; die Zeit des leichtgläubigsten Anarchismus, die Zeit ohne

Sinn für Staat und Recht . . . die Zeit, der Geschichte, Leben, Wissenschaft, alles nur mehr Ökonomie und Technik ist; die Zeit, die das Genie für eine Form des Irrsinns erklärt hat, die aber auch keinen einzigen groâen Philosophen mehr besitzt, die Zeit der geringsten Originalitätshascherei; die Zeit, die an die Stelle des Ideals der Jung-fräulichkeit den Kultus der demi-Vierge gesetzt hat; diese Zeit hat auch den Ruhm, die erste zu sein, welche den Koitus nicht nur bejaht und angebetet, sondern wie zur Pflicht erhoben hat . . . nicht um sich zu vergessen, wie der Römer . . . im Bacchanal, sondern um sich zu finden und der eigenen Ödigkeit erst einen Inhalt zu geben (W 452).

In early twentieth-century Vienna, whether one took the stance of "Woman-Defender" or "Woman-Offender," one thing was certain: the role and psyche of the bourgeois woman was of paramount interest and primary concern to both Altenberg and Weininger. Each took "woman" as a vehicle for expressing his discontent with bourgeois customs and institutions. Each in his own way turned his attention to the flaws in his society in an attempt to change his culture, a culture so concerned with superficiality and transient values as to neglect and often harm the more helpless of its members. Significantly and perhaps because of similar concerns—while Freud's formulation of the Oedipus complex, arrived at "anhand der Analyse von Männern,"[38] originated in the same Vienna of the woman-oriented Altenberg and Weininger—the most important tragedy that emerges at this time and place does not take Oedipus as its subject at all. Instead it concerns itself with his female counterpart, "Elektra" (Hofmannsthal, 1903), an often hysterical, compulsively chaste—("Pfui, die's denkt, pfui, die's mit Namen nennt!")[39]—and ineffectual young woman, whose consuming desire for justice and refusal to follow the norms set by her shallow society, cause her extreme isolation and ultimate destruction, as Altenberg notes: "Die Begriffe: Mutter, Schwester . . . Bräutigam, Erfüllung, Mütterlichkeit, Glück, Glück, Frieden, werden hinweggeschwemmt . ." (P 118).

Thus because of the predicament of "woman" in his society Altenberg, a living paradox of his time, unable to tear himself away from his beloved Vienna yet ever remaining an "erbitterter outsider,"[40] at once fascinated and repelled by his bourgeois surroundings, was able to derive meaning out of contradiction and devise a *premise* from *paradox*. Escaping through the medium of his gynolatrous poetic sketches, he devoted his entire life to opposing his bourgeois culture in defense of the abused and victimized, the women of his bourgeois world. Weininger's misogynous *premise,* however, his bitter offensive against woman, derived from opposition to and extreme revulsion for the *same* bourgeois reality, led him directly to the *ultimate paradox*—the salvation of woman through her extinction—a paradox from which he, unlike Altenberg, could find no escape but in tragic suicide.

NOTES

[1] Jost Hermand, "Peter Spinell," *Modern Language Notes,* 79 (1964), 440-441.

[2] Gisela Wysocki, *Peter Altenberg* (München: Hanser, 1979), p. A.

[3] Camillo Schaefer, *Peter Altenberg. Ein biographischer Essay* (Wien: Freibord, 1980).

[4] D. S. Low, "Peter Altenberg: A Case of Neglect," *Trivium* 4 (1969), 31-32. In his initially sympathetic article Low regrets the reluctant acceptance of Altenberg's work by scholars and stresses that "his work still awaits a comprehensive stylistic study, although it is now almost fifty years since his death." Low, however, then weakens what positive effects his article may have had on scholarship when he adds his own negative reactions, stating that Altenberg's neglect may be due to the "sub-literary quality" in the "formal sense" of Altenberg's prose. While there have been next to no longer works dedicated to Altenberg, there have been numerous recent editions such as the excellent latest edition by Hans Christian Kosler, ed. *Peter Altenberg: Leben und Werk in Texten und Bildern* (München: Matthes und Seitz, 1981).

[5] Altenberg was known to have contradicted himself frequently, as a diary entry of Schnitzler's on 20 March 1897 would indicate: "Im Imperial mit . . . Altenberg . . . Als er sich einmal in wenigen Minuten auffallend widersprach, machte ich ihn darauf aufmerksam." Cited in Kurt Bergel, *Arthur Schnitzlers unveröffentlichte Tragikomödie "Das Wort"* (Chapel Hill: University of North Carolina Press, 1963), p. 8.

[6] Andrew Barker, "Die weiseste Ökonomie bei tiefster Fülle"—Peter Altenberg's *Wie ich es sehe,"* *Studies in Nineteenth Century Austrian Literature,* B. O. Murdoch and M. G. Ward, eds. (Glasgow: Scottish Papers in Germanic Studies, 1983), pp. 77-101. Barker states that his essay is an attempt to demonstrate that "*in his early work at least* Altenberg is able to achieve formal cohesion." P. 82, italics mine.

[7] Peter Altenberg, *Märchen des Lebens* (Berlin: S. Fischer, 1924), p. 112, italics mine. Hereafter all references to this work will appear immediately following the citation in the text proper in abbreviated form (ML).

[8] Peter Altenberg, *Vita ipsa* (Berlin: S. Fischer, 1919); *Mein Lebensabend* (Berlin: S. Fischer, 1919); *Der Nachlaâ* (Berlin: S. Fischer, 1925). Hereafter all references to these works will appear immediately following the citation in the text proper in abbreviated form: *Vita ipsa* (V), *Mein Lebensabend* (LA), *Der Nachlaâ* (NL). Italics in cited texts are mine.

[9] Peter Altenberg, *Prodrômôs* (Berlin: S. Fischer, 1906), p. 57; *Fechsung* (Berlin: S. Fischer, 1916), p. 58;

Bilderbogen des kleinen Lebens (Berlin: Eric Reiss, 1909), p. 24. Hereafter all references to these works will appear immediately following the citation in the text proper in abbreviated form: *Pròdrômôs* (P), *Fechsung* (F), *Bilderbogen des kleinen Lebens* (BL).

[10] Peter Altenberg, *Nachfechsung* (Berlin: S. Fischer, 1916), p. 165. Hereafter all references to this work will appear immediately following the citation in the text proper in abbreviated form: (NF).

[11] *Semmering* (Berlin: S. Fischer, 1913), p. 199, hereafter referred to in the text proper with the abbreviation (S). Italics mine.

[12] Madame de Ségur wrote a series of children's books which appeared in a collection called "La Bibliothèque Rose" and contained stories of escapades of French "well-to-do" children growing up. In addition to *Les Petites Filles Modèles* cited here one of the most popular of these was *Les Malheurs de Sophie* which Altenberg cites in *Was der Tag mir zuträgt* (Berlin: S. Fischer, 1902), p. 47, hereafter referred to in the text proper with the abbreviation (WT). Other references to Madame de Ségur can be found on page 58 of the same volume, as well as in (ML 159), (F 156), (V 91; 275) and *Ashantee* (Berlin: S. Fischer, 1897), p. 201, hereafter referred to in the text proper with the abbreviation (A).

[13] Ellen Key (1849-1926); Swedish writer who wrote essays as well as longer works on sociological, literary, and pedagogical problems. She is considered a "Vorkämpferin in der Frauensache" as presented in Helene Lang and Gertrud Baumer, eds., *Die Geschichte der Frauenbewegung in den Kulturländern* (Berlin: W. Moeser, 1901), p. 326. Rosa Mayreder, a Viennese contemporary of Altenberg's, took issue with certain aspects of Ellen Key's feminism, arguing that Key's viewpoints concerning love and marriage were too conservative and still conformed to the ideology of the male bourgeois. The Viennese audience, however, met Ellen Key's lectures and literary works with "Begeisterungsstürmen," according to Nike Wagner in *Geist und Geschlecht* (Frankfurt/Main: Suhrkamp, 1982), p. 89.

[14] Ellen Key, *Über Liebe und Ehe* (Berlin: S. Fischer, 1906), p. 461.

[15] Egon Friedell, *Ecce Poeta* (Berlin: S. Fischer, 1912), pp. 168-171. In this work, which to date provides one of the finest analyses of Altenberg's philosophical, social and literary stance, Friedell states that Altenberg's work will perhaps be better understood and referred to by future generations, who may recognize in it an accurate and valuable guide to the Viennese "belle époque."

[16] Schnitzler confirms Altenberg's preference for prostitutes in a diary entry of 25 May 1896, where he writes somewhat critically: "Richard E., der ein Buch herausgegeben unter Peter Altenberg . . . derselbe Richard E., dem man früher Ähnlichkeiten mit mir zuschrieb . . . verkehrt meist in Hurenkaffeehäusern, Neigung—Pose—Gewohnheit, fast schon echt—verliebt sich meistens in Dirnen (à drei fl.)." In addition Altenberg describes the inhabitants of a bordello in quite vivid detail, suggesting first-hand information, in his sketch entitled "In einem Wiener 'Puff'" (ML 164).

[17] Peter Altenberg, *Wie ich es sehe* (Berlin: S. Fischer, 1922), pp. 7;30-31. Hereafter all references to this work will appear in the text, abbreviated as (WS).

[18] This type of young innocent, "die hilflosen Frauen und präpubertären kleinen Mädchen, die das Werk Peter Altenbergs in gradezu obsessioneller Manier durchziehen" (Wagner, *Geist und Geschlecht*, p. 139), is explained by the architect Adolf Loos in an essay on ladies' fashions as an example of the latest fad in Modernism. In his essay entitled "Damenmode" Loos writes concerning the newest rage in fashion design: "Bald darauf wurde volle üppigkeit, reife weiblichkeit durch die kleidung scharf zum ausdruck gebracht. Wer sie nicht besass musste sie vortäuschen: le cul de Paris. Dann trat die reaktion ein. Der ruf nach jugend erscholl. Das weibkind kam in mode. Man lechzte nach unreife. Die psyche des mädchens wurde ergründet und besungen: Peter Altenberg," in Adolf Loos, *Sämtliche Schriften*, Franz Glück, ed. (Wien: Herold, 1962), pp. 159-160.

[19] Karl Kraus suggests that the bourgeois standards and code of behavior caused Altenberg's ambivalence and paradoxical stance vis-à-vis his environment. He excuses the latter's frequent use of the paradox and his paradoxical world view with the words, "Sein Paradoxon war nur unsere Welt," in Karl Kraus, ed., *Peter Altenberg: Auswahl aus seinen Büchern* (Zürich: Atlantis, 1963), p. 8.

[20] Unlike Freud and Breuer, who in their "Studien über Hysterie" of 1892, view hysteria as the result of the repressive elements in bourgeois culture, Altenberg attributes the causes of hysteria to the excesses rather than to the repressions, to the exploitations and seductions engaged in by the hedonistic bourgeoisie, rather than to any self-control or abstinence. Hence derives Altenerg's advocacy rather than criticism of sexual containment, his pleas of celibacy for men and chastity for women. In "Das Gespräch von der Keuschheit" he suggests that the sole possibility for true happiness is through abstinence: happiness is achievable only if woman has "nie das Gift der Sexualität in sich eingesogen," in Egon Friedell, ed., *Das Altenbergbuch* (Wien: Wiener Graphische Werkstätte, 1921), p. 423.

[21] Egon Friedell, ed., *Das Altenbergbuch*, p. 295.

[22] Other examples of Altenberg's equating the ambitions of bourgeois culture with deleterious effects upon children can be seen in the following examples: "Hier werden keine kleinen Kinder malträtiert, hier wünscht niemand Hofrat zu werden" (F 109); "Hier werden keine

kleinen Kinder malträtiert, hier ersehnt niemand sich Reichtümer und Ehrenämter" (ML 30).

[23] Altenberg reports, for example, that Adolf Loos gave him a gift of snowshoes (S 47), and a silk suit (LA 168) and alludes to less important "Gönner" in (ML 51), (ML 123), (F 153-54), (NF 248), (NF 313), and (LA 292), to list a few.

[24] Ironically, Kraus urges securing the realms of poetry and philosophy from contamination by the medical and legal professions when he states that it was high time "aus einer Welt, die den Denkern und Dichtern gehört, die Juristen und die Mediziner hinauszujagen," in *Die Fackel,* Nr. 300, 1910, p. 28; reprinted in 12 volumes with "Personenregister" by Franz Ögg (München: Kösel, 1977). And yet both Kraus and Altenberg refer to the legal profession, to judgments and trials, in their works. Kraus's polemic was waged against the entire legal system, however, and does not focus only upon those cases involving child abuse, which seem to have attracted Altenberg's special attention.

[25] Peter Altenberg, *Neues Altes* (Berlin: S. Fischer, 1911), p. 53.

[26] Peter Altenberg, "Brief an Viktor Adler" in Egon Friedell, ed., *Das Altenbergbuch,* p. 295.

[27] Ellen Key, *Über Liebe und Ehe,* p. 470.

[28] Nike Wagner, *Geist und Geschlecht,* p. 69. Not only does Karl Kraus acknowledge the impact Weininger made on him, "Ein Frauenverehrer stimmt den Argumenten ihrer Frauenverachtung mit Begeisterung zu" (cited in Wagner, p. 159), but several writers of the time, including Altenberg, (though examples of his misogyny are extremely rare and the reasons for it explained above) take up a similar "hue and cry" against "woman," echoing Weininger's "Hetzjagd auf das Weib," as one of the chapters in Kraus's *Sittlichkeit und Kriminalität* is appropriately entitled. In *Otto Weininger. Werk und Wirkung,* Jacques Le Rider and Norbert Leser, eds. (Wien: Österreichischer Bundesverlag, 1984), Norbert Leser ("Otto Weininger und die Gegenwart") indicates that Weininger's work continues to be a "sensational" success because of the great disparity in reactions of contemporary critics to Weininger's misogyny, ranging from "Kritik und Abrechnung" or "Huldigung" to fascination and the highest admiration. For a detailed account of Weininger reception to date refer to the "Literatur- und rezeptions-geschichtliche Essays" in this volume.

[29] Weininger is referred to as "der grösste Theoretiker der Misogynie," in Nike Wagner, *Geist und Geschlecht,* p. 153.

[30] Rosa Mayreder (1858-1938), Viennese feminist and contemporary of Altenberg, *Zur Kritik der Weiblichkeit* (Jena: Eugen Diederichs, 1907), p. 240. Mayreder here discusses a feminist's reactions to Weininger.

[31] Otto Weininger, *Geschlecht und Charakter* (Wien: Wilhelm Braumüller, 1918), p. 409. Hereafter all references to this work will appear immediately following the citation, in the text proper abbreviated as (W). Except for a volume of aphorisms, *Über die letzten Dinge,* this is the only work of Weininger, who died prematurely in 1903, at 23 years of age.

[32] E. M. Cioran, "Brief an Jacques Le Rider," in *Otto Weininger. Werk und Wirkung,* p. 31.

[33] Nike Wagner, *Geist und Geschlecht,* p. 158.

[34] Norbert Leser, *O. W. Werk und Wirkung,* p. 26.

[35] The influence of Freud's theories, especially the "Studien über Hysterie," is obvious here. For further discussion on Freud and Weininger see Paul Laurent Assoun, "Die perverse Diskurs über die Weiblichkeit," in *Otto Weininger. Werk und Wirkung,* op. cit, pp. 181-196.

[36] Cf. Note 20.

[37] William M. Johnston, *The Austrian Mind* (Berkeley: University of California Press, 1972), p. 161.

[38] Nike Wagner, *Geist und Geschlecht,* p. 75.

[39] Hugo von Hofmannsthal, "Elektra" in *Dramen II* (Wien: S. Fischer, 1954), p. 20. Although Nike Wagner discusses the origin and impact of Drs. Breuer and Freud's "Studien über Hysterie" as well as the conception of woman as "femme fatale" and "femme fragile" in the "Zeitgeist" of the "belle époque," she ignores Hofmannsthal's "Elektra" (1903) in her analyses, a character whose personality traits in matters sexual, whose instinctive reactions, differing in degree from those of her sister and mother, not only reveal striking parallels to Freud's studies on hysteria in particular and to Weininger's and Altenberg's theories as well but also serve as an example of the prevalent attitudes of and about woman at that time.

[40] Egon Friedell, *Ecce Poeta,* p. 118.

Gerald Stieg (essay date 1987)

SOURCE: "Kafka and Weininger," in *Jews & Gender: Responses to Otto Weininger,* edited by Nancy A. Harrowitz and Barbara Hyams, translated by Barbara Hyams, Temple University Press, 1995, pp. 199-206.

[In the following essay, which was originally published in 1987, Stieg analyzes Franz Kafka's interpretation in The Castle *of Weininger's theories.]*

Nowadays decency would seem to forbid mentioning the names Kafka and Weininger in one breath, but historical truth forces one to commit such a sacrilege. In certain respects, the differences between the two are vast:

Franz Kafka "had the ability to transform himself into the most insignificant man,"[1] and for that reason was "the greatest expert on power,"[2] whereas Otto Weininger's texts provide a philosophical directive whose swaggering surpasses Zarathustra in content if not in tone. Kafka was haunted by suicidal thoughts his whole life and wanted to take his life's work with him to the grave, even though it is what kept him alive, whereas Weininger masterfully orchestrated his posthumous fame—so that his book **Sex and Character** could live, he shot himself in a "consecrated place," the house in which Beethoven had died. He did not delude himself: Indeed, his book became the philosophical best seller of the first third of the century, and if many of his ideas had not taken on terrible political gestalt in 1933, it would most certainly have had many more printings and popular editions (!) (Le Rider 1985).

Yet Kafka did not delude himself either. On January 28, 1922, shortly before he began writing *The Castle,* he made the following note to himself about his position in the world: he describes himself as having "been forty years wandering from Canaan" in the desert, where he was the "most insignificant and timid of all creatures," as he had been in the patriarchal-bourgeois Canaan. Thus he sees himself in every context as the "most insignificant," but he also knows that in contrast to Canaan, in the *desert* "it is possible even for the humblest to be raised to the heights as if with lightning speed." (He would not be himself if he did not also immediately append, "though they can be crushed forever as if by the weight of the seas" (Kafka 1949, 213-14; 1954, 564f.).

Both Kafka and Weininger underwent "a kind of Wandering in the Wilderness in reverse": instead of seeking the land, or even remaining in the land "where milk and honey flows," they used desert monks as their models. Consequently, each of them has something of the stylite about him. In this endeavor they are by no means alone. The Benedictine-Occidental *ora et labora* is shattered: intent upon remaining in Kafka's and Weininger's purview, Ludwig Wittgenstein (the most monk-like of all), Karl Kraus, Trakl, and Rilke bear witness to it. For all of them, writing is their "form of prayer," for them, prayer and work are one.

This monkish sacralization of writing is a constitutive trait of Viennese modernism that is *truly* deserving of the name. The process has something heart-wrenching about it: appearing long before *Dialectic of Enlightenment,* which used World War II as illustrative material, it was nothing more and nothing less than a lament over the bankruptcy of the Enlightenment. The apparently unstoppable and irrevocable secularization process of the eighteenth century that Sigmund Freud still wishes to validate in *The Future of an Illusion* in 1927 has culminated in a powerful movement of *resacralization.*

The "sacrifices for the dead" that Weininger and Kafka concocted for themselves and their work are probably the most astonishing attestations to this process. By comparison the diverse aesthetic cults that arose in the aftermath of George seem simply ridiculous, although from a purely historical perspective, something comparable is being played out. (Moreover, Kafka, like Karl Kraus, was thoroughly receptive to the gospel of the "stern master" George [Kafka 1958b, 301 (September 1921)].

So the poets formed a gallery of "stylites." Weininger and Kafka (in a very particular sense, one can look at Karl Kraus as the connecting link between them) are exemplary *monks.* They share a radicalness of experience in the world that is dictated to them by *angst:* they are afraid of the *others.* Their *others* are first of all women. On a more abstract plane, the *others* are the intermediaries who disturb the *praying man* in his solitude. Weininger believed that in his urge toward monkhood he had compre-and appre-hended once and for all the identity of these interlopers: the women *and* the Jews. His thinking becomes murderous: the salvation of the world depends on "overcoming" *the* woman and *the* Jew. It results—one can formulate this without applying rhetorical brakes—in a demand for the suicide of all mankind, in which both fascistic Papini and friendly Cioran followed his lead (cf. Le Rider 1985; Le Rider and Leser 1984). In the face of such grand projects, one must look at Kafka's assessment of his private situation, written on January 31, 1922: "Hence it is a defensive instinct in me that won't tolerate my having the slightest degree of lasting ease and smashes the marriage bed, for example, even before it has been set up" (Jan. 31, 1922) (Kafka 1949, 217).[3]

In such sentences Kafka appears as a Weininger in private, as a private monk in a negative theological undertaking that proposes to "treat" Weininger's philosophical claim on a "world scale." This total disavowal and condemnation of the "pleasure principle" becomes a violent drive in Weininger's case to compress the manifold, i.e., anti-monkishness (the monk is the "monachos" who easily confuses "alone" with "singular") into a higher unity. Kafka's urge to "smash the marriage bed" is terrible but harmless, because he is only thinking of this for himself, as opposed to Weininger's demand to "do away with" women and Jews in the name of the (holy) *spirit.*

The biographical material indicates that the Jews Kafka and Weininger suffered equally from their Jewishness and their sexuality. The "monkish" aspirations of both only take on their full import when one confronts them with their "temptations."

In 1923 Karl Kraus, who had been Weininger's highly conscious advocate against defamation by the liberal bourgeois Viennese press and as such had influenced Kafka, published the following poem by the nineteen- (or twenty-one)-year-old Weininger:

> Filled with longing and carefully hidden,
> Stealing my way through the darkest night,

I laugh at all that your law has bidden,
Burning, voluptuous, yet full of fright.

This is the road I have often wandered
To her, the Goddess who knows no shame,
The road desire bade me to follow,
And I was weeping when home I came.

May darkness reign on the road I follow;
May God turn day into darkest night,
Make the windows and mirrors empty, hollow,
Leave not a shimmer, no trace of light.

And, scornful still, the ancient terror
Steals darkly ahead of the dear delight.
Oh, redden the cheeks of Sinful Error
That I may serve him, free of fright
                    (Abrahamsen 1946, 84).[4]

The third stanza is a great *poem of prayer*. It corresponds to the following in Kafka's diary and letters:

Coitus as punishment for the happiness of being together. Live as ascetically as possible, more ascetically than a bachelor, that is the only possible way for me to endure marriage. But she? (Kafka 1948, 296 [August 14, 1913]).[5]

And as it was then, so it has always remained. My body, sometimes quiet for years, would then again be shaken to the point of not being able to bear it by this desire for a small, a very specific abomination, for something slightly disgusting, embarrassing, obscene, even in the best that existed for me there was something of it, some small nasty smell, some sulphur, some hell. This urge had in it something of the eternal Jew, being senselessly drawn, wandering senselessly through a senselessly obscene world (Kafka 1953, 164 [letter to Milena concerning the "first night," August 9, 1920]).[6]

It is beyond question that such texts are treating something besides the private sphere and that the epoch itself is being heard. The fact that the "sexuality-Judaism" syndrome could be concentrated in such a private form may help us of the present generation to understand what an overwhelming influence Weininger had on his own. The uncanny part is that in such writings the most dreadful aspects of the political propaganda of National Socialism seem to present themselves in the most private sphere, internalized to the point of self-torture. It is not a Jewish "family matter" that is at stake but rather a kind of historical humus. Consider that Weininger's thinking exercised the strongest of influences upon Lanz von Liebenfels's periodical "for blonds and masculinists," *Ostara,* which started in Vienna in 1905. Weininger was the most ardent—but by no means the only— disavower of two emancipation movements: those for *Jews* and *women.* He could tolerate them in one single form: as emancipation *from* Judaism and *from* femaleness.

From a critical point of view, what I have said up to this point belongs in the broad realm of analogies and asso-

ciations that are convincing in themselves, but do not necessarily carry the strength of *proof.*

A weighty argument contradicts my enterprise: in Kafka studies, whose gigantic proportions are legendary, Weininger plays a completely subordinate role. There are standard works (Brod 1937; Emrich 1958; Sokel 1964; Wagenbach 1964) in which he is purely and simply ignored; Binder (1966) takes him more seriously, but is too caught up in his biographical puzzles. He is only taken truly seriously by Politzer (1965), who personally experienced Weininger's milieu. Yet strangely enough, Politzer confines his analysis to the figure of Leni in *The Trial.* Politzer was Max Brod's collaborator, and therefore Brod's strategy to stifle the name of Weininger thoroughly must be taken as an act of repression.[7]

My thesis, then, is that Weininger's possible "influence on Kafka," or the "parallel" between Weininger and Kafka, fully unfolds for the first time in *The Castle,* which is a novel about Judaism *and* sexuality. In this essay I do not intend to discuss both aspects in their reciprocal relationship to one another, but rather to put the accent on the pole of sexuality. Since it is well known that the dear Lord lurks in the details, I will begin with a textual explication of *The Castle* in which both poles appear to be nearly inseparable.

After his first futile attempt to enter the Castle under his *own* steam, the Land-Surveyor K. is drawn into the magnetic field (one may certainly speak in terms of "elective affinities") of Barnabas's family. People suggest to him that this is where he belongs. But he does not believe it, does not *want* to believe it, and prefers to go to the Herrenhof Inn. He goes there on the arm of the Jewish whore, Olga, in the belief that he is heading toward a *higher* goal. (In his plot scheme, Kafka made a very telling "Freudian slip": at first he wrote *Castle* instead of *Herrenhof* [Kafka 1982, 82].) Although she arrived on K.'s arm, the whore is left to her usual fate: Klamm's servants will relish her in the stables. There is a lot to be said about Olga's story that actually has less to do with sexuality than would at first seem to be the case. (She is the little coin with which the Barnabas family tries to buy its freedom. The fact that this "coin" correlates to the equation of Jew with woman turns Olga into a Weiningerian paradigm.) Yet Olga has a sister, Amalia, the paragon and incarnation of nunlike chastity. Amalia is the embodiment of the Weiningerian ideal of pure self-abnegation and emancipation *from* sexuality. K.—the monk—is her utopian bridegroom. (One also could say that: Amalia represents emancipation *from* Judaism, insofar as it refers to those particular clichés that were considered "typically" Jewish.)

Aside from a letter of April 1921 that contains a comment that presupposes Kafka's acquaintance with Weininger's work but provides no substantive leads (Kafka 1958b, 276), our attempt to connect the two is confined to weaving a tapestry of *associations and analogies* so tightly that the speculative character of our hypothesis can claim great probability. This process has to do with a kind of "securing of clues" that has already been achieved with respect to the same topic as it relates to Elias Canetti's *Auto-da-Fé* (Pöder 1985, 57ff.). Therefore, I am excluding from my analysis the wide-meshed concluding chapters of *Sex and Character* from which the book's fatal posthumous fame stems. Since these two chapters—"Judaism," Chapter XIII; "Woman and Mankind," Chapter XIV—can be taken as the spiritual common property of the era, the fact that *The Castle* is also infected by them requires no extensive proof. What I am endeavoring to do is to tighten the net of analogies to a measurable degree of possibility by limiting the field of observation and comparison to Weininger's posthumously published work *Über die letzten Dinge* (On Last Things),[8] and the subplot of "Frieda" in Kafka's *The Castle.*

Weininger's *Über die letzten Dinge* first appeared in 1904 and was reprinted in 1907, 1912, 1918, 1919, 1920 and 1980. It is noteworthy that *Geschlecht und Charakter* not only went through an astonishing numbering of printings, but that in the years immediately following World War I, the rate of new printings for both works is almost the same. (*Geschlecht und Charakter* appeared in 1918, 1919, 1920 in two printings, and 1921.) Kafka's sole reference to Weininger is apparently the result of this "boom." Nevertheless, it would be incorrect to limit ourselves to this period. Naturally, Kafka was familiar with Weininger's thought by way of the "Fackel," and I'd also like to refer at this point to another source of Kafka's Weininger reception: Max Brod and Kafka met in Riva with Carl Dallago, who was prominently involved in the intensive Weininger debate that commenced in the journal "Der Brenner" in 1912.[9]

These brief references to Weininger reception have been made to demonstrate

> · that there was extremely intensive interest in his work immediately following the publication of Kraus's *The Last Days of Mankind;*

> · that this phenomenon was also true for Weininger's *Über die letzten Dinge.* This posthumous work is distinctive because here Weininger has completely forsaken the dissertation genre of *Sex and Character* in favor of more *literary and radicalized* forms of thought.

His more literary approach is shown in Weininger's more and more frequent use of the *aphorism* to express his thoughts. His radicalization manifests itself everywhere, but especially in two areas: (1) intensified interest in the Wagner cult, as seen through his use of Wagner's *Parsifal* in his discussions; (2) heightened involvement of the morality cult in his series of aphorisms "On the One-Directionality of Time and Its Ethical Significance." The common thread is Weininger's masculine ideal of the restless Faustian seeker.

The Castle can be read as a variation on the Faust or Parsifal myth. Mythical substrates are present everywhere in Kafka's novel in an extended state of decay (e.g., in the beer-drinking god Klamm and Bürgel, who embodies the Greek god Chios). If *The Castle* is read in this way—that is, as a novelistic fable about "seeking" and "pathfinding,"—then the story of Frieda takes on a meaning that far exceeds the biographical coffeehouse framework of the "Herrenhof" and refers to a philosophical-cultural context in which Weininger is its figurehead.

These claims are intended to be made plausible on the strength of the following three examples:

> · Weininger's interpretation of sexuality in *Parsifal*

> · Weininger's thoughts about the one-directionality of time

> · Weininger's comments on the "spatialization" of consciousness.

1. WEININGER'S INTERPRETATION OF *PARSIFAL*

Weininger's interpretation of Wagner's *Parsifal* seems significant from the outset because this work belongs to the tradition of great myths about seeking and pathfinding to which *The Castle* belongs. As such, one parallel comes immediately to our attention: Parsifal is portrayed as the "pure fool," and K. is treated again and again as a *child* or a *simpleton* by the *experienced* characters in the novel. Parsifal's search for the Grail and K.'s search for the Castle are also easy comparisons. During his search for the Grail, Parsifal meets an obstacle, the seductive woman Kundry.

Weininger's commentaries go as follows: "Man's morality understands sexual intercourse as sin";[10] "Woman is no longer meaningful when man is chaste";[11] "Kundry *in* Parsifal (it's *yearning* that prevents him from reaching the Grail, i.e., the moral, the divine) . . .";[12] "To be sure, Kundry would have to die already in Act II, since Parsifal resists her."[13]

Thus, Weininger sees Kundry—the W(oman) principle itself—as present in the heroic M(an); however, this principle is constructed by Weininger to be *surmountable.*

Weininger's condemnation of Goethe's *Faust,* which he rates far below *Parsifal* because it concludes with "Woman, eternally,/shows us the way" (Goethe 1984, 305),[14] must be seen in this context as well. For him—and Kafka stands very close to him in this respect—the opposite is true: the feminine pulls man down into the *obscenity* that was discussed above. The union between K. and Frieda is consummated in garbage.

Weininger expresses the same idea on a less metaphysical plane when he writes: "'Gander, find your goose' means *get married,* but then don't set the Kingdom of God as your goal."[15] It is a monk's turn of phrase that played an underground role in Kafka's attempts to marry. There is, however, a qualitative difference between Kafka and Weininger, since Kafka held marriage (at least theoretically) quite high in the hierarchy of *ethical goods,* while Weininger appears to address it as a primitive nod to convention, indeed, as a bestial stage in the development of humanity. Yet, in Kafka's life as well as *The Castle,* marriage, or more precisely the matrimonial strategies themselves prove to be an obstacle on the path to the Castle, a *losing one's way and a wrong track* that leads away from the goal that, for Kafka, is often identical with the "sacralization" of writing.

It is only hesitantly that I dare include in this context one of Weininger's most bizarre utterances, which seems to be echoed in *The Castle:* "Kundry's laughter crosses over into Judaism. The metaphysical sin of the Jew is to smile over God."[16] Thus for Weininger, Kundry embodies the negative twice over: as woman *and* Jewess. Now the story of Frieda is set from its very beginning under the law of *laughter and smiling.* It begins with the laughter of the Jewess Olga (a paradigmatic Kundry figure) over K.'s question about Frieda's relationship to Klamm. (At this moment, Klamm is still Frieda's [false] god). The subject of God and Eros is handled most ironically of all in the episode with *Klamm's brandy.* The drink, which purports to be a heavenly essence, transforms itself through actual enjoyment into something "fit for a coachman" *(kutschermässiges),* that is, into something that everyone possesses, regardless of the higher expectations that they have attached to it. This scene clearly shows the proximity of Freud, the greatest ironist that God and religion have encountered in the twentieth century. In *The Castle,* the Jewish sin of "smiling over God" is omnipresent as the Freudian "Ecclesia supra cloacam."

Weininger's "unethical" woman appears in two forms that emerge in *The Castle:* (1) the *human* (i.e., the whore), and (2) the *bestial* (i.e., the mother). The significance of prostitute and mother figures (among them, the enigmatic Madonna-like girl from the Castle) is clear, as well as is the meaning of the unusual role of the "female monk" *(Mönchin)* Amalia. (I am consciously employing Trakl's androgynous term, for there is relatively great certainty about his relationship to Weininger. See Doppler 1971, 43-54). She is the true anti-Kundry. K.'s path is ambivalent in contrast to that of his heroic bride, Amalia. K. will come closer to the ascetic ideal: Frieda leaves him, and he himself throws the assistants out of the temple.[17]

2. ON THE ONE-DIRECTIONALITY OF TIME AND ITS ETHICAL SIGNIFICANCE

Weininger's discussion of *Parsifal* is complemented by his complex of considerations on the problem of the human experience of time, which is integrated in his series of aphorisms collected under the title **"On the One-Directionality of Time and Its Ethical Significance."**[18]

Weininger's thinking on this question can be summarized as follows: TIME passes in one direction *(Einsinnigkeit),*[19] that is, it flows toward a GOAL. The *ethical* person is duty-bound to obey this law of time and therefore to be constantly SEEKING. (The Faust and Parsifal themes are closely tied to the theme of time.) The greatest temptation that threatens mankind (man?), according to Weininger, is belief in the CIRCULARITY OF LIFE, the eternal repetition. For Weininger, sexuality belongs exclusively to the drive toward repetition, which assumes eternal sameness. The ethical man-person breaks out of this circle in order to have a goal toward which he can strive.

A few of Weininger's considerations on this issue can be employed directly for an interpretation of *The Castle,* especially the Frieda theme. In order to do this, a bit of textual interpretation is necessary.

Weininger hates circular motion, even in the galaxy. Circular motion and retrograde motion are ethically unbearable for him. He looks for "vulgar" analogies to planetary circular motion and finds the following example: "Spinning around in a circle is senseless, purposeless; someone who spins around on his tiptoes has a self-satisfied, ridiculously vain, commonplace nature."[20] In *The Castle* there is an extreme example of this in the miserable smugness of Momus (i.e., the *sense*less scoffer), the tip of whose tongue runs in a circle round "his slightly parted lips" in the chapter, "Waiting for Klamm" (Kafka 1974, 134; 1968, 90). With this allegorical mouth gesture, Momus's "return" is converted by Kafka into his *own* regressive "reason" *(Vernunft),* which has not allowed itself to be thrown off track by K.'s "foolishness." The apparently "enlightening" impulse of this antagonism toward the "disturber of the peace" is completely devaluated by the gesture and reduced to what it really is: an expression of the self-complacency of the completely hermetic, controlled course of events that sees itself as impervious to every interruption of the circle. K., however, interrupts the *circles.*

In Weininger's case, such reflexion on time culminates almost compulsively in the following type of observation: "Dance is female motion, and indeed, it is above all the motion of prostitution."[21] In contrast to this "female" motion, which becomes a gestalt through the roundelay ring of peasants around Olga, Weininger posits the "male" attitude toward time, which is that of the WANDERER, he who travels toward his goal, driven by unexplicit yearning for a higher ethical good (e.g., Gralsburg).

In opposition to the "senseless" and directionless circling of sexuality, Weininger juxtaposes the never-abating strivings of human will:

The *one-directionality of time* is thus identical to the fact that the human being is a deeply willing being. *The ego as will is time.*

The realized ego would be God: the ego on the *path* to self-realization is will.

Will is something between non-being and being; its *path* goes from non-being to being (for all will is the will to freedom, to value, to the absolute, to being, to idea, to God).[22]

It goes without saying that sexuality is assigned to Platonic non-being. As abstract as this approach may sound, it could be K.'s approach during his search for access to the Castle. In the same context, Weininger says something about time that applies to Kafka's *Castle* not only thematically but also aesthetically:

"Life is a kind of journey through the realm of the innermost ego, a journey, to be sure, from the narrowest interior regions to the most comprehensive, freest overview of the universe."[23]

This *spatialization* of consciousness and those forms of it that are manifested through time are *the* essential artistic method that Kafka uses in *The Castle*.

By comparing the previously mentioned aspects of Weininger's thinking about time and sexuality, we obtain an important key to *The Castle*. To document this convincingly, we must take a very precise look at the "love scene" at the Herrenhof.

3. ". . . FRIEDA HAD TURNED OUT THE ELECTRIC LIGHT"

A kind of interrogation and hide-and-seek precedes the famous passage from *The Castle*, "Frieda had turned out the electric light" (Kafka 1974, 53),[24] in which Kafka gave up on first-person in favor of third-person narrative. The landlord would like to oust the *stranger* from the inn; Frieda plays along in order keep the *stranger* there, no matter what the cost. The controlling authority, who is uncertain about K.'s presence and apparently fears it, has scarcely left the room when the *light* goes out.

Frieda consummates a conscious exchange: Klamm's passive mistress becomes a lover, K. her beloved. She exchanges the position, respect, and protection that Klamm had provided for free love with K. She yields fully to this love, this "rapture," this unconscious and timeless swooning ("time must have seemed endless to her in the prospect of her happiness" [Kafka 1974, 53]);[25] she is thus freed from the one-directionality of time and therefore is nothing more than a vessel for the blissful moment. She is also *speechless:* "she sighed rather than sang some little song or other."[26]

The antigrammatical zeugma of singing and sighing corresponds perfectly to Frieda's deteriorating consciousness. K. doesn't immediately follow Frieda in her path to unconsciousness: he remains "absorbed in thought," that is, conscious. Frieda starts up at this, for indeed K.'s manner is at absolute odds with her condition. She "began to tug at him like a child,"[27] which once again offers a grammatical interference: who is the object, who the subject, i.e., who is the child? (The zeugma is never innocent.) That which follows eradicates the difference, for K. and Frieda become a couple ("embraced each other").[28] This course of events is portrayed as K.'s transition to a reflective position in a rolling (circular) motion, which is perceived as a "state of unconsciousness" and ends with K.'s Grail-like search for the Castle being degraded to a "thud" on the forbidden door. In the act of love K. loses consciousness—consciousness of the path that he wants to pursue. Instead of the proper path, there is a sense- and goal-less circular motion. This circular motion is not merely senseless but obscene; it is consummated in puddles of beer and refuse.

Weininger's and Kafka's assessments of coitus are absolutely identical. Another passage in *The Castle*, the episode about Klamm's *brandy*, may serve to corroborate this finding:

"the perfume was so sweet, so caressing, like praise and good words from someone whom one likes very much, yet one does not know clearly what they are for and has no desire to know and is simply happy in the knowledge that it is one's friend who is saying them" (Kafka 1974, 132).[29]

This is where Kafka *defines* the essence of love as the negation of knowledge. If the promises of the perfume become reality, then the drink "burns" (just as Frieda's body *burned*), and the "heavenly" *(himmlische)* drink becomes something "fit for a coachman" *(kutschermässigen)*.

In this passage, there is not only an exemplary presentation of a *disappointment* following "delusion" *(Blendung)*, but the context sheds a telling light on the Frieda chapter and gives Pepi's brandy—she has "no other" (!) than bestial sexuality—its true significance.

K.'s encounter with Frieda (it is carried out through glances, whereas when Pepi seduces K., he closes his eyes!) is clearly marked off from the animalistic sexuality of the locale (where the bestial roundelay, into which Frieda is nearly drawn, takes place). Here the scene is set for something apparently quite different, namely, individual love. Yet in Kafka's use of images the act of love itself is hardly differentiated from what happens in the stables. "Obscenity," "puddles of beer," "stables," and "drink fit for a coachman," supplement one another to draw a (Swine)ingerian picture of sexuality.

K. spends quite distinctive time *there,* i.e., at the obscene site. Kafka invented brilliant sentences to describe it. (Something comparable can only be found in the starkly contrasting vision of isolation at the end of the chapter, "Waiting for Klamm").

There hours went past, hours in which they breathed as one, in which their hearts beat as one, hours in which K. was haunted by the feeling that he was losing himself or wandering into a strange country, farther than ever man had wandered before, a country so strange that not even the air had anything in common with his native air, where one might die of strangeness, and yet whose enchantment was such that one could only go on and lose oneself further (Kafka 1974, 54).[30]

In this sentence, the most violent oppositions are teamed: "breathed as one, in which their hearts beat as one," are expressions of the greatest familiarity, of a complete sense of being at home. Yet in the same sentence homeland transforms itself into the most foreign, most suffocating Other. Intimacy becomes the farthest outpost, love that promises hearth and home becomes the most senseless, pathless enticement. I do not hesitate to draw upon etymology: sexuality is *sense*-less, and therefore *path*-less and *goal*-less, perversion, as Kafka formulated it in his description of intercourse: "it had in it something of the eternal Jew, being senselessly drawn, wandering senselessly through a senselessly obscene world."[31]

Love, or at least consummated sexual union, proves to be the wrong path. "Strangeness" and "losing himself" are the key words of the sentence. If one considers that the entire novel is a tremendous variation on the *path* theme, this judgment takes on enormous significance. The fusion of extreme hope and extreme hopelessness— losing one's way approaches *insanity (Irrsinn)*—in a sentence about love makes it the sum and substance of *The Castle*. In the face of such sum and substance, in which an extremely reactive consciousness creates language, that which follows may seem almost trivial.

From the *rapture of love* there is a gradual return to the everyday consciousness from which K. and Frieda had cut all ties. Frieda admits to this (senseless?) break; she exchanges Klamm for the Land Surveyor. K., on the other hand, sees Frieda's body by the dawning light as a now worthless pawn in his possession. The first glimmer of morning makes it obvious to K. that he had lost his way in the night. He believes that he has lost something; Frieda thinks that she has won him. In the present context, one can also note that

· The assistants who were sent by Galater were also on hand during the act of love.

· Olga returns from the stables, she says to K., "Why did you not *come home* with me?"[32] It is a terrible sentence, for it connotes 1) that K. sent Olga into the stables, and 2) that instead of "going home," K. cast himself through his night of love with Frieda into nothing but *strange country,* while the path back to Olga's house offered him a *homeland.*

· In the morning K. does not proceed with Frieda's bundle on his search for the Castle, but takes it instead to the originating point of the journey, the

"Bridge Inn," Frieda's "womb," the foremother Gardena. The *bed* will be the predominant object in his place of residence.

· In this bed, the instrument of mothers and whores, the lost Parsifalistic and Faustian seeker K. *wastes* the entire day sleeping.

The Castle is a novel about the path to the holy. The path quickly proves itself to be a labyrinth. Sexuality is consciously used by Kafka as one of the labyrinthine paths. In the process, Kafka makes an almost transparent reference to Weininger and Wagner, or Weininger's interpretation of Wagner's *Parsifal* and *Tristan*. K.'s and Frieda's "night of love" is an obvious parody of *Tristan*. In the construction of the novel, the detour/path through Eros seems like a wrong way à la Weininger, indeed even more than that, like a *regression*. For the lost way of the night that led to false quarters ends with a return to the point of origin, to the great mother in the Bridge Inn who will give her all to throw obstacles in K.'s *path* (progress?). He has her to thank for a day lost to sleeping. Woman robbed him of sleep in the night, woman robs him of the day.

We cannot rule out the possibility that the analogies presented here rest only on coincidence. Even if that were the case, coincidence would provide a not-so-insignificant key to one of the innumerable doors of the Castle. Why shouldn't coincidence for once bear the name of Weininger instead of Bürgel?

NOTES

[1] Canetti (1982b, 49): "dem es gegeben war, sich ins Kleine zu verwandeln."

[2] Canetti (1969, 86): "der grösste Experte der Macht."

[3] Kafka (1954, 568): "Darum ist es ein Abwehrinstinkt, der die Herstellung des kleinsten dauernden Behagens für mich nicht duldet und zum Beispiel das Ehebett zerschlägt, ehe es noch aufgestellt ist."

[4] Sieh mich gebeugt mit lockerm Schritte

> In Mauernähe ängstlich gehn,
> Verhöhnend dein Gebot der Sitte.
> Nach Füsschen und nach Busen spähn.
>
> Das ist der Weg, der längst bekannte,
> Zu ihr, der Göttin ohne Scham,
> Den ich so oft zu gehen brannte
> Und reuig weinend wiederkam.
>
> O Gott, in alle Spiegel schlage
> Vernichtend deine Faust hinein,
> Das klare Licht entzieh dem Tage,
> Dem Bache nimm den Widerschein!
>
> —Und höhnisch schleicht das alte Bangen
> Der heissbegehrten Lust voran.—
> O!!! Gib dem Laster rothe Wangen,
> Dass ich ihm angstlos fröhnen kann
>
> (Weininger 1923, 158).

[5] Kafka (1954, 315): "Der Coitus als Bestrafung des Glücks des Beisam-menseins. Möglichst asketisch leben, asketischer als ein Junggeselle, das ist die einzige Möglichkeit für mich, die Ehe zu ertragen. Aber sie?"

[6] Kafka (1983, 197f.): "Und so wie es damals war, blieb es immer. Mein Körper, oft jahrelang still, wurde dann wieder geschüttelt bis zum Nichtertragen-Können von dieser Sehnsucht nach einer kleinen, nach einer ganz bestimmten Abscheulichkeit, nach etwas leicht Widerlichem, Peinlichem, Schmutzigem; noch in dem Besten, was es hier für mich gab, war etwas davon, irgendein kleiner schlechter Geruch, etwas Schwefel, etwas Hölle. Dieser Trieb hatte etwas vom ewigen Juden, sinnlos gezogen, sinnlos wandernd durch eine sinnlos schmutzige Welt."

[7] I am not afraid to compare this silencing to religious practices of suppressing the name of God or the devil.

[8] Passages are cited from Weininger (1904); English translations are by Barbara Hyams.

[9] For more on this point, see Stieg (1976).

[10] Weininger (1904, 89): "Die Moralität des Mannes empfindet den Geschlechtsverkehr als Sünde."

[11] Weininger (1904, 89): "Das Weib hat keinen Sinn mehr, wenn der Mann keusch ist."

[12] Weininger (1904, 89): "Kundry in Parsifal (das Sehnen ist's, das ihn verhindert, zum Gral, d.i. zum Sittlichen, Göttlichen zu kommen)."

[13] Weininger (1904, 89): "Kundry müsste freilich schon im II. Akt sterben, da Parsifal ihr widersteht."

[14] Cf. Weininger (1904, 89): "All of that places Wagner far above Goethe, whose last words, after all, were only about the 'Eternal Feminine,' the salvation of man through woman." ("Das alles stellt Wagner hoch über Goethe, dessen letztes Wort doch nur das vom 'Ewig-Weiblichen,' die Erlösung des Mannes durch das Weib war")

[15] Weininger (1904, 91): "'Suche dir Gänser die Gans' heisst heirate, aber dann steck dir nicht das Reich Gottes zum Ziel."

[16] Weininger (1904, 91): "Das Lachen der Kundry geht aufs Judentum. Die metaphysische Schuld des Juden ist Lächeln über Gott."

[17] The role of the assistants deserves in-depth consideration. It would be meaningful to see the circumstance of their being sent by Galater as directly connected to the Epistle of Saint Paul to the Galatians. In *The Castle,* they represent the "Galatian principle" (i.e., "pleasure principle") that was severely condemned by Paul. I believe that taking biblical "sign" names seriously (Barnabas, Galater) leads us quite a bit closer to our goal.

[18] Weininger (1904, 93-109): "Über die Einsinnigkeit und ihre ethische Bedeutung."

[19] Translator's note: There is no single English translation for "Einsinnigkeit." Weininger constructed the noun to express his interpretation of teleology. "Ein," of course, refers to oneness, to singularity, and "sinnig" ranges in meaning from "ingenious, clever," to an ironic "appropriate, apt," to a poetic "thoughtful, delicate." "Sinnigkeit," then, can mean "ingenuity, cleverness," ironic "appropriateness, aptness," or "thoughtfulness, delicacy" (Springer 1974, vol. 2, 1406). Gerald Stieg italicizes the root "Sinn," which encompasses the five senses, mind, wits, consciousness, sexual desires, thought, feeling, sense, meaning, significance, and direction—in short, a veritable complex unto itself of matters that preoccupied Weininger.

[20] Weininger (1904, 97): "Sich im Kreis zu drehen ist sinnlos, zwecklos; jemand, der sich auf der Fussspitze herumdreht, selbstzufriedener, lächerlich eitler, gemeiner Natur."

[21] Weininger (1904, 98): "Der Tanz ist eine weibliche Bewegung, und zwar vor allem die Bewegung der Prostitution."

[22] Weininger (1904, 104):

"Die *Einsinnigkeit der Zeit* ist sonach identisch mit der Tatsache, dass der Mensch zutiefst ein wollendes Wesen ist. *Das Ich als Wille ist die Zeit.*

Das realisierte Ich wäre Gott: das Ich auf dem *Wege* zur Selbstrealisierung ist Wille.

Der Wille ist etwas zwischen Nichtsein und Sein; sein *Weg* geht vom Nichtsein zum Sein (denn aller Wille ist Wille zur Freiheit, zum Wert, dem Absoluten, zum Sein, zur Idee, zu Gott)."

[23] Weininger (1904, 108): "Das Leben ist eine Art Reise durch den Raum des inneren Ich, eine Reise vom engsten Binnenlande freilich zur umfassendsten, freiesten Überschau des Alls."

[24] Kafka (1968, 37): "Schon hatte Frieda das elektrische Licht ausgedreht"

[25] Kafka (1968, 37): "die Zeit war wohl unendlich vor ihrer glücklichen Liebe."

[26] Kafka (1968, 37): "sie seufzte mehr als sang irgendein kleines Lied."

[27] Kafka (1968, 37): "fing an wie ein Kind ihn zu zerren."

[28] Kafka (1968, 37): "umfassten einander."

[29] Kafka (1968, 89): "der Geruch war so süss, so schmeichelnd, so wie man von jemand, den man sehr

lieb hat, Lob und gute Worte hört und gar nicht genau weiss, worum es sich handelt, und es gar nicht wissen will und nur glücklich ist in dem Bewusstsein, dass er es ist, der so spricht."

[30] Kafka (1968, 38): "Dort vergingen Stunden, Stunden gemeinsamen Atems, gemeinsamen Herzschlags, Stunden, in denen K. immerfort das Gefühl hatte, er verirre sich oder er sei so weit in der Fremde, wie vor ihm noch kein Mensch, einer Fremde, in der selbst die Luft keinen Bestandteil der Heimatluft habe, in der man vor Fremdheit ersticken müsse und in deren unsinnigen Verlockungen man doch nichts tun könne als weiter gehen, weiter sich verirren."

[31] Cf. Kafka's letter to Milena of August 9, 1920 (Kafka 1953, 164).

[32] "Warum bist du nicht mit mir nach Hause gegangen?"

Reiner Stach (essay date 1989)

SOURCE: "Kafka's Egoless Woman: Otto Weininger's *Sex and Character*," in *Reading Kafka: Prague, Politics, and the Fin de Siècle,* edited by Mark Anderson, Schocken Books, 1989, pp. 149-69.

[*In the following essay, Stach examines Kafka's characterization of women in his fiction and the extent to which it was influenced by Weininger.*]

With the idea of myth, the Feminine gained entry into the realm of theory—but only as another myth. The familiar images of woman as natural being, primal mother, vampire, sphinx, or the promise of happiness, were not disavowed but rather conceptualized into theory. However, the very continuity of these cultural projections allows us to decode prevalent sexual myths in their theoretical, largely affirmative reformulations. Besides psychoanalysis, the most influential attempt to develop a theory of sexuality was Otto Weininger's dissertation, which was published under the title *Sex and Character* in 1903.[1] The extent to which the struggle between the sexes had become the subject of scholarly research can be gauged by the case with which Weininger refers at central points in his argument to everyday erotic phenomena such as cosmetics, fashion, coquetry, and prostitution, apparently assuming that such discussions would not cause his examiners to question the seriousness of his work. Even his completely unfounded aesthetic and moral invectives against women escaped academic censure.[2]

Today it is difficult to comprehend the enormous success of his work, although traces of its influence can be found throughout the century. Fed by the sensational suicide of its twenty-three-year-old author (a convert from Judaism to Christianity), interest in the work increased steadily through the 1920s, but was eventually suppressed under pressure of anti-Semitic cultural poli-

tics in Germany and Austria. The twenty-fifth edition of *Sex and Character* appeared in 1923, and translations were published in eight languages. In 1926 and 1932 there even appeared popular "folk editions" with fewer notes; a collection of quotations for salon society also found a market.[3] What might appear to be merely a "popular" reception is misleading, though, for the book had a strong influence on contemporary writers and intellectuals, especially in Austria, but also in Italy, for example, where for a time a Weininger cult raged.[4] The popular topoi "genius" and "insanity" around the turn of the century served to further Weininger's notoriety and interest in his fate. As late as 1949, Gottfried Benn counted the author of *Sex and Character* among the three Jewish geniuses he had encountered; Kafka he praised merely as a "talent of the first order."[5]

The extent of Weininger's influence indicates a strong need for such theories, a need that undoubtedly originated in the incipient breakdown of traditional sex roles. To bourgeois men, it seemed incomprehensible that women, who had begun to enter the spheres of production and culture, could or would want to abandon their previously well-protected positions. As fear of feminine domination spread, Weininger promised complete enlightenment, a solution to these mystifying developments. In Kafka's case one must also add his curiosity (perhaps as a result of his own fear of sexuality) about theories positing an inherent polarity between the sexes or, more generally, the conflictual nature of sexuality—as his interest in psychoanalysis suggests.

There is no direct documentation available to establish how and at what point Kafka became acquainted with Weininger's theories.[6] It seems inconceivable, however, that he could have ignored such a well-known and controversial theory, especially one whose appeal derived from its claim to liberate men, through analysis, from their fear of femininity and simultaneously excuse this fear as an entirely natural *horror vacui*.[7] But here the biographical question of influence is secondary, and in any case an answer would require an exact, methodological definition of "influence." More important is the profound similarity between Weininger's theoretical description and Kafka's aesthetic projection of femininity, a similarity indicating that both authors shared a common fund of social and cultural experience.

This similarity is by no means readily apparent, and requires interpretation as well as methodological discrimination. Before discussing the function of the female figures in Kafka's texts, it is essential to clarify the female characterology they embody, either implicitly or explicitly. In Weininger's *Sex and Character* one can distinguish between his model of the feminine and his moral judgments, which constantly influence his explication of the model. Explication is for Weininger always "deduction," and his concept of "woman" an attempt to use a pure Kantian category, without regard for the history of women in society. Even when introduced as the logical consequence of the model, his moral judgments are thinly, if ontologically, disguised polemics and invectives, which today make the book unbearable; as a result, its cultural significance has been underestimated.[8] Contemporary readers dismissed his vehemently misogynist rhetoric as youthful excess, while devoting much attention to those sections of the book that—by comparison—seemed to be analytical. Karl Kraus's message to Weininger is characteristic: "An admirer of women concurs with the arguments of your contempt for women."[9]

Weininger begins with a grand thesis and devotes much space to establishing its scientific foundation: the fundamental bisexuality of human life and the existence of a graduated scale of intermediate sexual forms between male and female. More exactly, there are *only* intermediate forms, mixtures of the two "types" of "ideal man" (M) and "ideal woman" (W), which exist only in theory. Bisexuality, formerly a mild variant of homosexual perversion, is advanced to the status of an anthropological constant: "The fact is that males and females are like two substances combined in different proportions, but with neither element ever wholly missing. We find, so to speak, never either a man or a woman, but only the male condition or the female condition" (8).

Someone unfamiliar with the history of male projections of femininity might believe that such an acknowledgment of fluid sexual boundaries is progressive per se because it questions rigid sex roles and undercuts the logic for stereotypes which degrade and marginalize women. The opposite, however, is true. With his tactic of "sexual mixtures," Weininger avoids two old methodological difficulties of misogynist theories without altering their repressive nature. The first concerns the epistemological justification of male judgments about the female psyche: How can the (male) observer gain access to those emotional fluctuations that, as is well known, the woman never discloses? Weininger answers: Through introspection, since each man carries a portion of femininity within himself.[10] The second difficulty is the sheer impossibility of proving empirically the inferiority of women. After all, more than a few men displayed "female" characteristics such as passivity, sentimentality, and conceptual weakness, whereas women were already being recognized for their scientific and artistic achievements. Weininger responds that the "mixture coefficient" of these men and women tends in each case to the opposite sexual pole, as is evident in their external features: the feminine is by definition passive, whereas active women are simply masculinized women.

Such maneuvers, long known as the hypostatization of femininity, find their purest and most perverse expression in Weininger's work: he does not theorize about empirical women but about the typological *ideal* of womanhood, about "W," the "Feminine," "woman." This hypostatization protects his theory from social reality: as an "investigation of principles"—this is Weininger's subtitle—the work remains impervious to empirical observation or experience. However, his subject matter is empirical, and the ethical, cultural, and political consequences of his theory of femininity affect real women, not femininity.

Characteristic of this manner of specious rationalism, which dominated the discussion of femininity around the turn of the century, is the brutally systematic approach with which Weininger believes himself able to specify every aspect of that puzzling substance W. One learns that the purely Feminine is a negative syndrome, a syndrome of defects and deficiencies: essentially, it is defined by what it is not.[11] Positive (male) traits of differentiation, such as individuality and personality, are weak in W. Weininger claims the existence of a central empty core: "The absolute woman has no ego" (186). And insofar as Weininger understands the "self" as the stronghold of regulative, strictly conceptual ideas—the result of his psychologized reception of Kant—he merely needs to develop a complete canon of these rules in order to arrive at an equally complete negative canon for W.

Accordingly, in his view, woman has no conception of *truth*. She can relate to this concept neither affirmatively nor negatively, to say nothing of critically. If she speaks truth, then it is not for the sake of truth; if she lies, it is not for the sake of lying: thus, "the woman always lies, even if, objectively, she speaks the truth" (287). Weininger continues in this vein, to the point of complete nonsense, speaking of an "ontological untruthfulness of women" (264).

Among the analogous defects, woman suffers with respect to a concept of morality and guilt, which has the interesting consequence that a woman cannot sin. Weininger solves the old problem of why woman, traditionally the embodiment of sin, is statistically underrepresented in all categories of crime: "I am not arguing that woman is evil and anti-moral; I state that she cannot be really evil; *she is merely non-moral*" (197). For the same reason—a claim with important implications for *The Trial*—she also knows no self-doubt: "Women are convinced of their own integrity without ever having sat in judgment on it" (196). In this tone he traverses the firmament of ideas about bourgeois emancipation. W has no sense of beauty as such, only the effect of attractiveness on men, the "social currency" of beauty. Freedom, necessity, and causality are unknown to women; thus, they lack not only all insight into their own "destiny" (to be a woman), but also the capacity to arrive at such an insight through analytical, logical thinking. Finally, Weininger denies women the capacity to conceive of property—private, of course—as a genuine quality of the self, thus providing himself with an excellent explanation of female kleptomania (205-206).[12]

To understand the social behavior of W, it is essential to note that, since W is itself undifferentiated, it has no access to concepts of individuality and subjectivity. Women can relate to themselves only as things; they are without dignity. For women, self-consciousness, pride, and vanity depend only upon external qualities—an unblemished bodily appearance, fashionable attire, and so on (210-12). Women measure the significance of all others according to the same criteria. Since the subjectivity of others, as well as their own, is beyond their comprehension, women remain excluded from meaningful social achievement. "W is at most in love; M loves," Weininger claims. "Female friendship means merely sticking together" (288).

For Weininger the woman is a cheat of nature, who becomes sphinxlike because man does not wish to admit that there is nothing to discover:

> Women can appear everything and deny everything, but in reality they are never anything. Women have neither this nor that characteristic; their peculiarity consists in having no characteristics at all; the complexity and terrible mystery about women come to this; it is this which makes them above and beyond man's understanding—man, who always wants to get to the heart of things. (294)

Weininger deals in this passage only with the static aspect of the Feminine, affirming that W is without structure. Actual women in society, however, are not simply diffuse, amorphous, ungovernable creatures. They are neither fully passive nor malleable at will; goal-oriented, "active" women also exist. What, then, takes the place of male "ideas"?

Here Weininger invokes the ancient myth of woman as sexuality incarnate—to provide support for his rigid, formal model. Sexual desire is the incomprehensible, vital, regulating factor of all female thought, volition, and behavior. The woman is formless matter, is nothing, but sexuality colors this nothingness, which shines forth from every female action.

Female social activity is the atrophied, but sexually charged vestige of male sociality—its caricature, in fact. The female, who knows no self, and thus no "Thou," can perceive and acknowledge neither herself nor an other as a unique, defined, and differentiated being. Her longing is directed not at man, but at a particular man's masculinity; therefore, her sexuality is always reifying and instrumental. She encroaches upon the male ego, destroys it, dissolves its boundaries; his ego, however, is capable of mixing with an other (without destroying it). The woman wants the couple, wants to couple.[13]

Female interaction is thus always a form of sexual reification. Female desire, which is never anything other than sexual, is directed entirely toward the condition of mixing and merging, which it tries to achieve without exception in each physical, psychological, and social action. Not only love or coitus offer women the possibility of fulfillment; the extending of sympathy, caring, mothering, touching other and touching herself, as well as participation in the coitus of others through gossip and matchmaking, also provide this fulfillment.[14]

Two apparently irreconcilable and radical forms of this kind of desire appear in society—motherhood and prostitution. It is perhaps Weininger's most popular thesis that these two boundaries mark the spectrum for the "empirical" character of all women. Each feminine display of affection is at once erotic and maternal. Yet these components are compatible since both "types" represent both the desire to merge as well as the deindividualized arbitrariness of this desire: on the one hand, "absolute mother" whose love is independent of the personality of her child or the husband she has accepted as a child, and on the other, the "absolute whore," whose promiscuity is likewise indiscriminate. Despite their completely different status in society, these two variants always appear together and in a nearly inextricable ambiguity.

It quickly becomes clear that this schematization of female deficiency is a theoretical system with striking similarities to the practice of Kafka's literary characterization of women. Heinz Politzer has noted that at least two women in *The Trial,* the usher's wife and Leni, correspond entirely to Weininger's mother-whore type; in particular, their offers of help display "an exemplary mix of the maternal and the whorish."[15] This approach can lead much further, however, to reveal a profound affinity between Kafka's portrayal of the Feminine and Weininger's model of female deficiency, which, because of his typology, I will henceforth refer to as the "feminine type."[16] [. . .]

Perhaps as a result of the passive core of their constructions, Kafka's female characters act entirely as variations on Weininger's feminine type—not with respect to their narrative function but instead on the level of a feminine characterology. Several figures appear who clearly represent the model in toto, while others illustrate in varying degrees certain aspects of the model such as egolessness and passive activity. Therefore, an approach is required that is not simply descriptive or chronological; rather, we must establish correspondences between Kafka's female protagonists *through* the model of the feminine type, and thereby show the figures in a series extending beyond individual characters in individual works.

Weininger deserves credit for having formulated with previously unparalleled directness two characteristics of antifeminine resentment. First, that masculinity is law, measure, rule, territory—entities that are threatened by, and antagonistic to, whatever is without order, exceptional, unbounded. The feminine draws the masculine beyond its own limits and is, in the language of Deleuze and Guattari's *Anti-Oedipus,* the agent of "deterritorialization" itself. Second, that antifeminine resentment is totalitarian and paranoid. The more it braces itself against the hated exception, the more reason it has to fear contamination. To those under the spell of this resentment, any discussion or compromise appears as a dangerous blurring of boundaries, as "destruction." Since only a single form of confrontation is imaginable without redefining boundaries—namely, the systematic and complete destruction of the other—Weininger's line of reasoning devolves into fantasies of annihilation that throw a grim light on the motives behind his brutal system: the essence of woman, the substratum of the feminine, must be obliterated.[17]

However, this directness has been achieved with a degree of abstraction that can hardly be imitated in aesthetic terms. Strindberg, who was a devoted follower of Weininger in later years, made this clear with a series of entirely schematic and bloodless thesis-characters that depart from the traditional portrayal of femininity, but only manage to reproduce the negative canon partially, and out of context at that: his women sponge off others, lie, squander, and speak stupidities.[18]

Admittedly, for Weininger, women have at their disposal a broad palette of social graces—tactics which, on the one hand, make them dangerous and, on the other, allow them to correspond to male projections. However, the inner point where all these threads meet is presumed to be simply an emptiness, a barren nothingness dominated by an uncontrolled sexual appetite. Weininger initially avoids the precipice of women's unconstrained sexuality by separating the concept of feminine nature from any specific cases of individual psychology, thus making the problem ontological.[19] In contrast, the dramatist must work with a particular individual, whom he can of course invent, but cannot reduce to a bare concept. His character can never be transparent, she remains open to interpretation and unfolds sensual, gestural, and discursive qualities which the spectator is free to make sense of. The difficulty for the misogynist author, which Strindberg clearly did not resolve, would be to compose a believable female character whose interpretation and reconstruction *reveal* this inner nothingness.

In his prose Kafka developed a number of characterization techniques that achieve this requirement. Conclusions about his model of the feminine and its moral consequences can be drawn only very indirectly, as will become clear. Yet one must see that he held on to such deindividualizing techniques even when the results became grotesque. This is already apparent in an early and still relatively rough effort, the figure of Brunelda in *Amerika,* upon whose sensual abundance the chapter "The Refuge" focuses. There are two linked processes here that amount to a virtual emptying of the female ego—reification of the body and psychic regression.

Brunelda's body, bathed in harsh light, appears as a monstrous, inanimate object, whose particular movements we learn about in the neutral tone of an instruction manual, and whose distinguishing features are primarily mass and inertness. Brunelda is almost entirely immovable and is not able to undress or wash herself (A 211). "Although she's so fat, she's very delicate" (A 215), and therefore spends her days lying on the sofa. When she must vacate her apartment, it takes her male companions hours to carry her down the steps. She eats and smacks her lips, breathes heavily, and while sleeping, sighs and snorts like a machine so that the whole room is filled with the sound of her breathing. Her very being, it seems, robs other occupants of the "refuge" of space and air. Delamarche, Robinson, and Karl crowd around Brunelda; they lack even the freedom of movement needed to clean the room. When she forces the young but strong Karl against the balcony railing, he cannot avoid a tender hug by her "soft, fat little hands that immediately crush everything" (A 236).

Brunelda's sexuality is radically externalized in her bodily appearance, in pure passivity, uncontrollable states and theatrical posturings. Inexplicable attacks of feverishness are apparently characteristic—"I can't bear this heat, I'm burning, I must take off my clothes" (A 210)—as is her repeated spreading of her legs "so as to get more room for her disproportionately fat body" (A 210-11). A diffuse shamelessness, with no identifiable goal, appears as the expression, even as the demand, of her bodily mass. And as if reification were not carried far enough, Kafka illuminates this figure with the colors of bordello eroticism; the room is suffused with "dim red lighting" (A 239); of her many possessions, she prefers a red dress, which "suits her far the best of them all," and which is mentioned repeatedly in the text (A 214-15). When she meets Delamarche, she is dressed in white and carrying a red parasol, with which she points out to her new lover the way to her apartment. Kafka's use of color signals is extraordinarily precise here: in a fragment [not translated in the English edition] he has Brunelda run "her fat red tongue back and forth between her lips"; her "very loose dress" is nevertheless now only "pale pink," an indication of her diminishing sexual powers. In fact, another fragment assumes that her friend Delamarche has taken off or been put in jail, so that her only remaining means of survival is prostitution (for which she, oddly enough, is already officially registered). While she has Karl cart her to "Enterprise Number 25," she covers herself with a *gray* cloth.[20]

This monster in apparent decline has established a tortuous tyranny, but is not really dangerous. Brunelda is not erotically attractive; her body is too strictly circumscribed by its animal needs. Her atrophied psyche, barricaded within her like a vestigial organ, does not lead one to look for a communicative ego or the "heart of things" denied women by Weininger. Here we find pure regression: willful desires (such as that for perfume) appear suddenly, are enforced by laments and crying, and disappear a moment later when some new bodily need occurs to her. Brunelda sits in her bathtub and hits the water with her fists, she drums on the sofa with her hands and screams senselessly until she passes out. No doubt a somatic willpower is at work here, as if the body knows nothing but its own corporeality. Brunelda throws her weight around against Karl and threatens Delamarche that she will run naked in the street. Only in one passage does this animalistic and infantile behavior reflect a threatening authoritarianism where it sharpens to an aggressive, asocial gesture. When Brunelda's former husband, disdained but still slavish, leaves her a luxurious present made of porcelain, she breaks it and urinates on it.

We will not learn from Brunelda herself who or what she really is. There is no "herself." There is a body, whose lament sounds to the world like a poorly tuned instrument.[21] We get everything else—her experiences and opinions—third hand, but nevertheless are forced to accept their legitimacy. It is characteristic that everything Karl explains to himself about Brunelda must be pedantically completed by Robinson: "Sometimes she actually does what she says, but mostly she lies on the couch the same as before and never moves" (A 213). And when Brunelda cries for help, "she doesn't mean it." Kafka describes the feminine as a discontinuous, illogical being, approximating here the technique of Strindberg, who both shows the woman and interprets her at the same time.

Certainly this is one of the reasons that Brunelda has received little scholarly attention. The reader's curiosity receives little nourishment from this figure, whereas the women in *The Castle* are supposed to be more profound and difficult. If one ignores the simple narrative function of these figures—Brunelda is of course conceived as a contrast to Karl's innocence—one can indeed perceive an increasing refinement in Kafka's characterization skill. The crude portrayal of the body, which stands out in *Amerika* (1912) in high relief, has already been replaced in *The Trial* (1914) by subtler signals that render the body less material, thus freeing it as a surface of projections.[22]

An analysis of the usher's wife and the erotic disruptions in the courtroom in *The Trial* (chapter two; A 37-48) provides all the static and dynamic elements of Weininger's feminine "type": prominent, above all, is the diffusion of traits denounced by him as "egolessness" and experienced by the hero K., who searches for the "inner core" of things, as a bottomless surge in the ocean. The usher's wife is passive insofar as she seeks her "consummation as object." She offers herself to the gaze and grasp of the judge, the student, and K. Only when she disappears does K. notice her body. This body is constantly present when they sit together, as the unnoticed center of language, gesture, and promise, with the ambiguous suggestion that it is both the promise and what is promised. K.'s subliminal wishes and projections, which gradually spin out of control, anticipate the woman's sexual advances, indeed, actually initiate them. The feminine nothingness that produces this appeal does not, as in Brunelda's case, stem from regression or a lack of psychological acuity. The nothingness of the usher's wife is not revealed through the narrator's instructive interventions but through her own numerous meaningful ambiguities, her persistently vague mode of expression.

In accordance with the logic of *The Trial*—the logic of a failure whose cause becomes more apparent with each

repetition—the episode with the usher's wife is repeated in another seduction that follows a similar course and leads to similar results. Leni, the nurse and lover of the lawyer Huld, is a character no less puzzling than the usher's wife—even if her function with respect to the accused is more clearly marked, as critics have not failed to emphasize. Her offer of help, expressed in her gesture of covering K.'s hands with her own, appears alternately erotic or motherly. Her diffuse opportunism, which demands K.'s subjugation; her naïve coquetry ("But you didn't like me at first and you probably don't like me even now" [T 107]); her little lies and deceptions—these are all repetitions. In addition, her relation to the similarly accused salesman Block also oscillates between solicitude and sadism. Finally, she has an ambiguous relationship to Huld, exchanging secret caresses with K. in order to "entertain" Huld later, behind K.'s back, with details of this liaison.

It is worth noting that Kafka's narrative technique now supports the woman's reifying and reified self-presentation by breaking down her bodily image into a series of isolated features which are fraught with symbolism. Leni's "two great, dark eyes" have apparently impressed K.—as well as Kafka the narrator—since he later recognizes her by the "dark, somewhat protuberant eyes" (T 99). The sight of her face, which seems to have no expression, intimates the nature of his opponent:

> K. was still glaring at the girl, who turned her back on him . . . she had a doll-like, rounded face; not only were her pale cheeks and her chin quite round in their modeling, but her temples and the line of her forehead as well. (T 99-100)

Again we encounter that same fragmenting gaze, which paralyzes its object. The notion here of a doll elicits similar threatening associations by indicating a danger that is both supraindividual and oblivious to direct communication. This threat closes in on K. when Leni shows him her "pretty little paw" (T 110), two webbed fingers connected by skin, like an amphibian. Adorno noted rightly that this detail is more important than, for example, the excursus about the law, because such a concrete detail contains much experience that has been lost in conceptual language and even more so in the discourse between the sexes.[23] Benjamin had the same thing in mind when he spoke of the "bog" of unsettling experiences in Kafka, out of which climb "swamp creatures like Leni."[24]

Such images of the body, borrowed from dream symbolism, can be integrated only with difficulty into a naturalistic representation. Their frequency gives rise to moments of abstraction and deindividuation, as if primal, not yet individualized forces were breaking in upon the everyday play of personal relations:

> Now that she was so close to him she gave out a bitter exciting odor like pepper; she clasped his head to her, bent over him, and bit and kissed him on the neck, biting into the very hairs of his head. (T 110)

Here Leni appears completely banished from the level of aesthetic characterology. A dense net of material ciphers covers the text, leading Walter Sokel, for example, to draw the conclusion of Leni's pure functionality within the narrative. One might object, however, that Kafka's abstract manner of characterization follows entirely the logic of the feminine type: if the female is a generic being, then no feminine individual can be more precisely characterized than through the supraindividual, feminine "essence" it shares. Viewed positively, abstraction is the sole means of characterization appropriate to the feminine character and to feminine nonindividuality. And indeed, the tendency of Kafka's abstract characterization corresponds to a precise ideological premise that puts the coded female body into an empty ego. Her body is her essence.

The shift from the usher's wife to Leni does not negate psychological realism in favor of a strict narrative economy, but instead orders and compresses experience through repetition. K.'s seduction of Leni proceeds more quickly, but its completion has a compulsive and mechanical quality. The woman herself no longer speaks of her body, the author does. Seduction and subjugation no longer need to be painstakingly deciphered from her obscure, slow language. The struggle is conducted in the open: Leni's attributes are preverbal, but all the more direct.

The necessity for this compression is well founded. On the one hand, in the text itself, K. is already worn down. He has recognized that he has to stand trial but that, emerging from his isolation, he will barely be able to endure it. He is now more susceptible to offers of help and attention, even openly sexual ones, than he was immediately after his arrest; that saves the woman words and digressions. Furthermore, the reader has been prepared for their encounter. The outcome of the struggle over reciprocal instrumentalization is already known. Only in a superficial sense does K. achieve more with Leni than with the wife of the court usher. His defeat is not, as he first believes, that at the last moment the woman chooses the bed of someone more powerful than himself; rather, his defeat is the sober realization that the woman, whether before or after coitus, is neither inclined nor able to keep her promise. Thus, tormented by the estrangement and senselessness of these love affairs, K. is more distracted and fragmented than before, and even further removed from his trial. In her vampiric, depersonalized obtrusiveness, Leni remains incomprehensible to him; the motherly care he receives from her (the most personal treatment he experiences in the novel) is not exclusively his. Kafka's text doubly and firmly disavows the ludicrous male turn of phrase to "possess" a woman. Leni is indeed "to be had," but she is nevertheless—as K. finds out in passing, and too late—innocently promiscuous. She likes all accused men. This "dirty creature" only gains human traits of trustworthiness and intimacy in the dim glow of the courtroom. Just as the unattainable body of the usher's wife is suddenly "illuminated" in the courtroom, so

Leni's flickering femininity takes on a calmer, more definite form, her individual features combining into a beautiful whole when K. sees her in the distance, close to her lover, Huld: "Then Leni, displaying the fine lines of her taut figure, bent over close to the old man's face and stroked his long white hair" (T 193).

The figure of Leni with her openly declared sexual availability seems to mark a limit in Kafka's works. The ideal form of the feminine type is tangibly near. Feminine nullity and voraciousness are covered by a social veneer so thin that further abstraction would lead either to a completely automated woman or to a pornographic scenario—neither of which the author has in mind, since his texts deliberately leave such matters in obscurity. Nevertheless, in *The Trial* one encounters figures that clearly announce the author's intention to portray if not the source, at least the phenomenology of such matters with extreme precision. These are the girls of the court, whom K. meets when he climbs the long stairway to the painter Titorelli's atelier. Here Kafka has found the way out: he prevents any individuation of the feminine by using multiple figures, similar to his frequent use of pairs or triads of characters; but he manages to depict their characteristic gestures by plucking a single protagonist indiscriminately from the crowd:

> "Does a painter called Titorelli live here?" The girl, who was slightly hunchbacked and seemed scarcely thirteen years old, nudged him with her elbow and peered up at him knowingly. Neither her youth nor her deformity had saved her from being prematurely debauched. She did not even smile, but stared unwinkingly at K. with shrewd, bold eyes. "I want him to paint my portrait," he said. "To paint your portrait?" she repeated, letting her jaw fall open, then she gave K. a little slap as if he had said something extraordinarily unexpected or stupid, lifted her abbreviated skirts with both hands, and raced as fast as she could after the other girls. (T 141-42)

Here Kafka achieves the most extreme compression; in two sentences he presents the entire litany of female seduction techniques: the girl's look, flirtatious touch, and display of legs. At the same time, her "handicap" evokes again the radical, threatening strangeness and autonomy of her body, which lend her coquetry a shade of obscenity. But this concretization of erotic terror lasts only a second; then the girl sinks back into the feminine horde, of which she is the leader:

> They stood lined up on either side of the stairway, squeezing against the walls to leave room for K. to pass, and smoothing their skirts down with their hands. All their faces betrayed the same mixture of childishness and depravity which had prompted this idea of making him run the gauntlet between them. (T 142)

This gauntlet, which might be the memory of a bordello experience (see D 458-59), creates the atmosphere of an entirely abstract threat, no longer tied to coitus. No external attack actually threatens K. here—what could happen if he took the begging girls into Titorelli's room? He is faced rather with the fragmentation, degradation, and painful dissipation of his male ego. Something alive and insect-like, without consciousness or visible individuation, incites in K. mortal dread, perhaps also the fear of a previously unknown desire for self-dissolution. Kafka uses subtle means to make the feminine approximate animalistic and even blindly vegetative forces. The girls' erotic play—one of them already uses lipstick—is harmless compared to their abstract presence, which literally seeps in through the cracks in Titorelli's room. They quiet down for a while in front of the door, but "one of them had thrust a blade of straw through a crack between the planks and was moving it slowly up and down" (T 150). When K. takes off his coat, he provokes renewed commotion: "he could hear them crowding to peer through the cracks and view the spectacle for themselves" (T 156). And when, panic-stricken because of the unbearable warmth, K. tries to get past the door, almost fleeing, the girls begin to scream, a childish squeaking to be sure, less ill-natured than Brunelda's but still enough to terrify him: "K. felt he could almost see them through the door" (T 162).

It is difficult to understand how critics have consistently overlooked the gender-related aspects of this nightmare; Emrich and Politzer even concentrate exclusively on the relation of the girls to the "artist" Titorelli. The analysis of female figures in terms of their feminine characteristics, including the male reactions they provoke, points in a different direction. The usher's wife, Leni, and the girls at court form a chain which links narrative and characterological aspects. We will discuss the significance of this chain later, but here it is worth noting the women's increasing proximity to the court: the usher's wife flirts with revolt, Leni demands K.'s confession of guilt, the girls "belong" to the court. This increasing proximity, which K. perceives as a growing animosity toward him, corresponds to a mental and social reduction of the narrative. The figures become more and more abstract; an amoral, unconscious, sexually aggressive entity progressively emerges in their place, and not only at the cost of their discursive and social dimension, but of their human individuality as well. At the end of the chain their individuality is entirely done away with and femininity expresses itself only in gestures and in the collective practice of the horde.

The idea of the feminine type, which leads not to an empirical but to an essentialist portrait of the feminine, is doubly reinforced by this transition to the collective. First, in the text the horde of girls represents the biographical lineage of women. Out of this "bog" of non-individuality will be recruited the next generation of court mistresses. The transition is the biographical commentary on the giddy promiscuity of the Usher's wife. Moreover, the girls at court provide an image of the essential origin of femininity itself. In contrast to Leni and the Usher's wife, who already possesses the complex social techniques of flirting and a sort of façade-

self, the court girls reveal the feminine in its elemental, not yet socialized form. The historical, fearful question of essence—What is woman *before* her socialization?—is replicated here in an image whose clarity omits nothing: corporeality, lust for life, sexual aggression, animalistic collectivity.

"She did not even smile" (T 142), we read of the hunchbacked girl whom K. looks in the eye. The traps of erotic hypnotism designed to overcome the male's guardedness have not yet been set. Even the moral camouflage of the female desire for sexual merging is not invoked: the girls show—rare for Kafka—not the slightest trace of motherliness. In place of social grace they show intensity, in place of social role-playing they band together freely. Deleuze and Guattari are on target when they remark that the court girls are not a childhood memory but a childhood block, that is, the fear of the return of a greater, antifamilial, emotional intensity. One must add, however, that this intensity only returns in order to congeal into the form of the feminine.

Only in *The Trial* does Kafka use the horde as a narrative technique of feminine depersonalization to this degree of radical, almost archaicizing stylization. The reason may be that this tendency toward dramatic dialogue, which emerges with increasing clarity in his work, resists such diffuse, incommunicable elements. With the court girls, as well as with Brunelda, no understanding is possible; language as the medium of figuration, which even in its misuse and decay would allow for moments of truth, has been omitted. The double or multiple figure will not admit distinct, individual voices. When his assistants speak for the first time *not* in chorus, the Land Surveyor K. in *The Castle* says: "You're already trying to dissociate yourselves from each other" (C 26).

This formal conflict is even more complicated in the case of Kafka's female voices, since they are not centered on an individual ego but, rather, on a general and transsubjective entity: feminine language is the language of the body. In his treatment of the girls in *The Castle,* Kafka is reluctant either to let the discursive incompetence of women speak for itself—which would appear as the paradoxical utterance "I am mute"—or to let it persist in its silence. The nameless girls, whom K. treats (like his assistants) as an indistinguishable pair, work as maids in the inn, where they share a room, bed, and blanket. For his quarters K. is given a miserable, cramped room, still in the squalid condition the maids left it in. Two days later K., who in the mean-time has gotten together with Frieda, wants to change to a supposedly better place to stay, and an odd scene takes place: just as he and Frieda are about to move out, the maids appear at the door with packed bags, ready to reclaim their room: "'You're surely in a hurry,' said K., who this time was very pleased with the maids, 'did you have to push your way in while we're still here?'" (C 125). The critical edition of *The Castle* reveals three different continuations to this passage:

(1) "Embarrassed, they gathered their bags together and said . . ."

(2) "They didn't answer. K. appeared. . . ."

(3) "They didn't answer and fidgeted in embarrassment with their bags, from which K. saw the familiar dirty rags protruding. . . ."

The gesture that is supposed to be reinforced by their verbal answer in (1) completely replaces it in (3). The maids remain mute. K. is still not satisfied:

> "You probably have never washed your things," said K. He didn't say it angrily but with a certain tenderness. They noticed it, opening their hard mouths at the same time, displayed their beautiful, strong, animal-like

(1) teeth, and laughed silently.

(2) teeth and red gums high above the teeth, and laughed silently.

(3) teeth and laughed silently.[25]

One cannot mistake Kafka's intention here not only to depersonalize the women but to shift them into an intermediate realm between humans and animals. His hesitation concerns only the degree of characterization: the "had mouths" and the teeth, reinforced with three strong adjectives, are united in a vulturelike grimace (2); but this accentuation proves unnecessary for the already grotesque image and is deleted.

Kafka clearly had difficulty in balancing the doubleness of his characters: their deindividualized nature is pushed to an inhuman extreme. Yet the last step must be taken by the reader: only in one's imagination does the range of associations elicited by the female characters' corporeality and inscrutable psychology overlap with the idea of animality, an ambiguity which is both traditional in Western culture and problematic from a moral standpoint.

The motif of filth that commonly clings to Kafka's female characters as a sign of the asociality is effective as well in rendering them animalistic. Brunelda, the Usher's wife, and the "filthy creature" Leni all feel quite at home in unclean surroundings. The court girls mess up "every corner" (T 144) of Titorelli's atelier. The maids' room is reminiscent of a stall, "filthy and stuffy." The bed has no sheets, merely a horsehair blanket, the table is encrusted with dust, their few belongings are in a "filthy pile" (C 115).

This persistent accumulation of filth around marginal figures, each of whom takes up hardly more than a page of print, is profoundly alienating. The maids serve no recognizable purpose in the world surrounding the castle.[26] They remain foreign bodies, external elements that disappear like apparitions from the text without in the slightest changing the dramatic situation, the relations between characters, or K.'s consciousness. They

remain without depth and without the possibility of developing further. Exemplars of a certain phenomenology of the feminine, their presence in the text can only be explained by their thematic function as women, not as characters important for the narrative.

This view can be proven. In the dialogue from his diary (DF 339-42), dated the end of 1920, Kafka sketched a female couple that must be seen as a variation or even, because of verbal correspondences as a draft for the maids at the inn, who were conceived a year later.[27] These women appear to represent ironic, puppetlike versions of the single feminine type. Unrestrained by a narrative context (the dialogue has a self-reflexive quality), the text offers an entire arsenal of depersonalizing techniques and achieves a degree of stylization that depicts the female body as a mythical force breaking into quotidian life. Above all, one notes Kafka's technique of doubling, which aims (as with the maids) not at differentiation but at unidentifiability. The women have names, Alba and Resi, but the man with whom they live cannot tell them apart and does not need to, since "jealousy is entirely foreign to them." Their bodily fullness, which causes them to breathe heavily, reminds us of Brunelda, to whom they are also related by their insatiable eating and all-day lounging around on the sofa. Although they are "very receptive to reasonable discussion"—an ironic example is given of their being persuaded to do nothing—their corporeality clearly dominates the scene, though as animalistic immediacy rather than erotic promise. They run around "almost naked," "laugh with throaty noises" (the first such reference), and are sexually unrestrained: "they storm in, hot, with torn shirts and the stinging smell of their breath." If visitors are expected, they clear away their "filthy rags." Otherwise, they save their energies during the day for their long private cult of evening coitus, which, as always with Kafka, takes place on the floor, in filth: "For instance, they think they clean the apartment well, and yet it is so dirty that it disgusts me to step over the threshold. . . ."

"A foreigner," Kafka himself says, "could be frightened by it." By what? It is not only the *horror vacui* that these texts elicit; that would be comprehensible, if Kafka, as Weininger continually claims, had natural history on his side. But Weininger's ontological conclusion that women represent nothingness because they are without an ego too clearly bears the marks of a self-placating rationalization. His conclusion covers over the fact that women's "amorphousness," which supposedly fills the gap left by the lack of feminine identity, is more frightening than a presumed feminine nothingness ever could be. Kafka's female characters show that the male figures must ward them off as if in flight from something that is too strong, too ubiquitous, completely *different*. The feminine horde and aggressive female corporeality transform the woman into something suprapersonal and natural by destroying her identity: the feminine no longer appears as a tangible adversary, nor as a simple deficiency, but as an engulfing, viscous medium that the male ego can no more avoid than a swimmer can avoid water. This is the meaning of the symbolism of water, fire, and light that is so consistently attached to the feminine in European literature. In its opulent illumination of formlessness, this symbolism reinforces the impotence of merely formal representation. The theft of feminine identity avenges itself: whatever is without form can adopt any form and gains new power from its previous lack.

The animalization of women—likewise an ancient topos that has survived most obviously in present-day advertising—fits itself seamlessly into these transformations. Its purpose is not the slick hypostasis of danger—which wouldn't be very convincing, since Brunelda, for example, is more pig than predator—but rather the further embedding of the feminine in nature, or even (as Spengler claimed) in the cosmic universe.[28] From these spheres, however, the feminine returns as a danger of a higher order, an eternal residue of civilization, and an avenging spirit for the abomination committed against nature. Nietzsche, who himself remains caught in this ideology, was also the first to give it precise formulation. His commentary, metaphorically naïve, just barely misses camouflaging his own projection:

> That in woman which inspires respect and fundamentally fear is her *nature,* which is more 'natural' than that of the man, her genuine, cunning, beast-of-prey suppleness, the tiger's claws beneath the glove, the naïveté of her egoism, her ineducability and inner savagery, and how incomprehensible, capacious and prowling her desires and virtues are. . . .[29]

The important quality here is woman's uncontrollable elusiveness, her amorphousness and omnipresence. Nothing stays "pure," her animal nature intrudes everywhere. The leitmotiv and source of this paranoid stream of images is, as one would guess, sexuality as a destructive principle. One similarly finds in Kafka that women bond into sibling groups and series, which prefigure the mingling of the sexes, the liquefaction of all form, dissolution and decline. Kafka's erotic fantasies reveal that he, like Weininger, feared this dissolution of boundaries as something irreversible and deadly.

NOTES

[1] Except for occasional emendations, all references are to *Sex and Character* (New York: AMS Press, 1975 [reprint of 6th edition, 1906, London: W. Heinemann; New York: Putnam]).

[2] Two examples: That women are fascinated by an erect penis, which represents "the most unpleasant thing of all," is for Weininger the "most decisive proof that women want from love not beauty, but rather—something else." On the relationship of the genius to his own sexuality, Weininger explains: "For there will never be, can never be, a truly significant person who sees in coitus more than an animalistic, piggish, disgusting act, or who would find in it the most profound divine mystery."

[3] Otto Weininger, *Gedanken Über Geschlechtsprobleme,* ed. Robert Saudek (2nd ed.: Berlin, 1907).

[4] The influence of Weininger on, among others, Arnold Schönberg, Ludwig Wittgenstein, Georg Trakl, Karl Kraus, August Strindberg, Gottfried Benn, Cioran . . . and Mussolini, is well established. Elias Canetti attests that in the twenties in Vienna *Sex and Character* was still to be counted among the most talked about books (*The Torch in My Ear* [New York: Farrar, Straus and Giroux, 1982], trans. by Joachim Neugroschel). On its reception, see J. Le Rider and N. Leser (eds.), *Otto Weininger. Werk und Wirkung* (Vienna: Österreichischer Bundesverlag, 1984). Further, Hans Mayer, *Outsiders: A Study in Life and Letters* (Cambridge, Mass.: The MIT Press, 1982).

[5] Gottfried Benn, "Doppelleben," *Prosa und Autobiographie* (Frankfurt a.M., 1984), p. 397. The American edition of Benn's work *Primal Vision* (New York: New Directions), includes only excerpts from "A Double Life."

[6] The only document about Kafka's lasting interest in Weininger is a letter from the year 1921, in which he asks the writer Oskar Baum for the manuscript of his lecture on Weininger (L 276). The few surviving letters from Kafka's student years provide only sparse information about his participation in contemporary cultural currents. His notebooks from that time are lost. Nevertheless, around 1903 Kafka was very active in the literary section of the "Reading and Discussion Group of German Students in Prague," a liberal fraternity. Its well-stocked library, which he often consulted, subscribed to the most important literary journals, for example, Karl Kraus's *Die Fackel,* which devoted great space to the Weininger case.

[7] "Fear of woman is fear of senselessness . . . of the alluring abyss of nothingness" (*Sex and Character,* p. 298).

[8] Ernst Bloch writes of "the devaluation of woman here into a hetaira." "Weininger proceeded in this direction with total obsession . . . the most vehement misogyny known to history, a single anti-utopia of woman, in the middle of the Secession period" (*The Principle of Hope,* trans. Neville Plaice, Stephen Plaice, and Paul Knight [Cambridge, Mass.: The MIT Press, 1986], vol. II, pp. 593-94).

[9] *Die Fackel,* no. 229 (July 1907), p. 14: "One can imagine someone who abhors Weininger's conclusions (about the inferiority of women) and who cheers his premises (the otherness of women)" (*Die Fackel,* vol. 169 [November 1904], p. 7n. Freud found Weininger's work only "rather unconsidered."

[10] It is remarkable that this argument, stripped of polemical force, is today the basis for a possible sublation of sexual alienation: universal bisexuality as the basis for the communicability of sexual experiences. Cf.

Christian David, "On Male Mythologies of Femininity," in J. Chasseguet-Smirgel (ed.), *Psychoanalyse der weiblichen Sexualität* (Frankfurt a.M., 1974), p. 71.

[11] Apparently, negation seems particularly obvious to Weininger's audience as the most concise formulation of patriarchal claims to power. With Robert Musil, femininity as an abstract deficiency is still a fact of general psychological formation: "he . . . sometimes sensed almost bodily the feminine nature of her deficiency as one among other sexual differences," *The Man Without Qualities.*

[12] Weininger does not mention the quality of material generosity that would have to follow here from this defect.

[13] Cf. pp. 287-88.

[14] Cf. pp. 288-89.

[15] Heinz Politzer, *Parable and Paradox* (Ithaca, N.Y.: Cornell University Press, 1962), pp. 197-200.

[16] "Sexual Types" is the title of the main section of *Sex and Character.* The concept of *type* is one of the frequent categories in the debate abut femininity at the turn of the century. Apparently, its ideological function is to sterilize and dull erotic experience, and is comparable to the medical nomenclature of sexual deviance. Max Brod noted correctly that the type "woman" corresponds to the type "ladies' man" ("Der Frauen-Nichtkenner," *Über die Schönheit hässlicher Bilder* [Leipzig, 1913], p. 24). Kafka used the word with extreme reluctance.

[17] Weininger writes: "And if all femininity is immoral, women must stop being women and become men." "Not affirmation and not denial, but the negation, the overcoming of femininity is what matters." "Women must fervently and truly and completely renounce coitus, which means, however: woman is doomed."

[18] See, for example, Bertha in *Comrades* (1886), Laura in *The Father* (1887), Thekla in *The Believers* (1888), Henriette in *Intoxication* (1899), the mother in *The Pelicans* (1907).

[19] "Woman is nothing; therefore, and only therefore, she can become everything, while man can only remain what he is" (294).

[20] Originally Brunelda was a singer, a private erotic allusion which refers to a medical lecture that Kafka attended in Jungborn in 1912. There, a doctor asserted "that breathing from the diaphragm contributes to the growth and stimulation of the sexual organs, for which reason female opera singers, for whom diaphragm breathing is requisite, are so immoral" (L 81; see also D 477).

[21] In the work of Franz Jung one finds a startling formulation which most concisely characterizes this terrible somatic dominance: a woman screams "coldly, as if from behind any core of humanity" (*Das Trottelbuch* [Berlin, 1918], p. 23).

[22] In a fragment to *The Trial,* a female figure (whose corporeality recalls Brunelda's, though in more subdued tones) appears and disappears—Helene, who for several weeks was the lover of state attorney Hasterer. "She was a fat female of uncertain age with yellowish skin and dark curls clustering round her forehead. At first K. never saw her except in bed, shamelessly sprawling, reading a serial novel. . . . Only when it was getting late, she would stretch and yawn or even throw one of her serial numbers at Hasterer if she could not attract his attention in any other way." "It was only misery and not malice which made her lean across the table, exposing her bare, fat, rounded back, in order to bring her face into close proximity with K.'s and force him to look at her" (243). This figure also reflects Kafka's voyeuristic interest in prostitutes. On November 19, 1913, about a year before writing this fragment, he notes in his diary: "I intentionally walk through the streets where there are whores. . . . I want only the stout, older ones, with outmoded clothes that have, however, a certain luxuriousness because of various adornments. One woman probably knows me by now" (D 238). This unusual "uniform," as it is described by Kafka, is also worn by Helene in *The Trial:* "generally in a dress which she doubtless thought highly becoming and stylish, actually an old ball-dress bedizened with trimmings and draped with several rows of conspicuously unsightly fringes. K. had no idea what this dress really looked like, for he could hardly bring himself to glance at her . . ." (243).

[23] Theodor Adorno, "Notes on Kafka," *Prisms,* trans. Samuel and Shierry Weber (Cambridge, Mass.: The MIT Press, 1981).

[24] Walter Benjamin, "Some Reflections on Kafka," *Illuminations,* ed. H. Arendt (New York: Schocken Books, 1969). See also the recent article on the connection between Leni and the Lilith of Jewish legend: Robert Kauf, "A Lilith Figure in Kafka's *Prozess?*" *Monatshefte,* 73 (1981), no. 1, pp. 63-66.

[25] All quotes are from *Das Schloss,* edited by M. Pasley (Frankfurt a.M.: Fischer, 1982), p. 154. See also p. 237 in the accompanying critical volume.

[26] The maids' disruptive function is interesting as a textual strategy. Kafka first writes: "There was hardly any peace and quiet in the room at all, the assistants. . . ." Here he apparently notices that the assistants already caused a commotion three sentences above; he then crosses out "the assistants" and continues: "often the maids came stomping in with their men's boots."

[27] Here, and subsequently, the dating of fragments and short texts follows the conclusions of M. Pasley and K. Wagenbach: "Datierung sämtlicher Texte Franz Kafkas,"

in *Kafka-Symposion,* ed. J. Born et. al. (2nd ed.: Berlin, 1966). Kafka presumably began writing *The Castle* at the end of January 1922; cf. Hartmut Binder, *Kafka. Der Schaffensprozess* (Frankfurt a.M., 1983), p. 306f.

[28] Oswald Spengler, *The Decline of the West,* abridged edition by Helmut Werner (New York: The Modern Library, 1962), trans. Charles Francis Atkinson: "The feminine stands closer to the Cosmic. It is rooted deeper in the earth and it is immediately involved in the grand cyclic rhythms of Nature" (p. 354).

[29] Nietzsche, *Beyond Good and Evil,* trans. and ed. Walter Kaufmann (New York: Vintage Books/Random House, 1966), p. 169.

Robert Byrnes (essay date 1990)

SOURCE: "Bloom's Sexual Tropes: Stigmata of the 'Degenerate' Jew," in *James Joyce Quarterly,* Vol. 27, No. 2, Winter, 1990, pp. 303-23.

[*In the following essay, Byrnes examines James Joyce's use of stereotypes related to Jews, particular those found in Weininger's* Sex and Character.]

In 1923 Joyce drew a pencil sketch of Leopold Bloom and wrote beside it the Greek for "Tell me, Muse, of the man of many devices, who over many ways" . . . (*JJII* 482ff.). We can assume he understood the semantic range of *polytropos:* many tricks, many rhetorical turns, devices of every kind. And we can assume he exploited some interlingual ambiguity because when he sent his abject hero on his travels he armed him not only with devices but with vices, not only with tropes but with perversions. Hence the sexual abominations Joyce credits Bloom with in "Circe." As Stanley Sultan pointed out years ago, Bloom's hallucinatory Odyssey through Nighttown rehearsed the stages of male perversion that Richard von Krafft-Ebing documented in *Psycopathia Sexualis.* Sultan conflates numerous case studies into a formula ("from passivity to masochism to feminization") and finds that this pattern matches the sequence of Bloom's abasement in "Circe": first his passive "submission to Molly," then his masochistic surrender to Bella's abuse, finally his transformation into a woman.[1] And of course Joyce has festooned Bloom with fetishes and nauseating fixations he garnered from cases in the *Psycopathia.* This might well look like straightforward comedy, but Bloom's sexual tropes have always seemed more an embarrassment than a joke.

Maurice Samuel, writing in the Jewish journal *Reflex,* thought Joyce had resurrected the "medieval tradition of the Jew-monster, half-comical, half-horrible, wholly grotesque," in order to "work an immortal classic around it" as Shakespeare had done with Shylock.[2] Bloom's odious obsessions in "Circe" reminded him of Krafft-Ebing and he ascribed these to an "implacable malice," apparently against Bloom as stereotypical Jew:

By the time the scene closes the worst that can be revealed concerning human beings, the most loathsome, has been unfolded about the figure of Bloom. . . . For the character of Bloom, the Jew, Joyce harbours a mad, insatiable hatred. As he sees into the soul of Stephen with great love, he sees into the soul of Bloom with the mercilessness of hate. . . . Perhaps it would be stupid to use the word anti-Semitism in this connection: but I am compelled to wonder what complex in the mind of Joyce explains this cosmic loathing for the little Jew, Bloom.[3]

Ellmann aggravated the embarrassment when he traced Bloom's Jewishness and androgyny to Otto Weininger's *Geschlecht und Charakter* (*Sex and Character*), an anti-feminist, anti-Semitic work which, after assigning character and intelligence to men and will-less mental vacuity to women, lumps all Jews, male and female, with the intellectually disenfranchised women (*JJI* 477-78). Bloom's appalling penchants were now not simply ornamental and confined to "Circe" but organic and constitutional. Bloom was feminized and therefore, via Krafft-Ebing, perverse by nature rather than by Joycean artifice alone. He inhabited an anti-Semitic stereotype as well as a Greek epic.

And so the misprision of Joyce's comedy persisted. Robert Adams, rather more subtle than Maurice Samuel, has suggested that a "sizable element of anti-Semitism in Joyce himself" may well have emerged in his portrait of Bloom as an exercise in "masochistic self-loathing."[4] In this reading, Joyce would have projected his own femininity, perversity, and sometime ineffectuality onto his stereotypical Jew and then enjoyed the humiliations he heaped upon him.

Neither Ellmann nor Sultan nor Adams pressed his remarks very far, but an alarm bell sounded deep in the Joycean sentimental consciousness, and excursions have been made to save both Bloom and *Ulysses* from such a compromised heritage. Marilyn Reizbaum, addressing herself to the anti-Semitism Joyce's use of Weininger seems to imply, argues that Joyce allowed *Sex and Character* to supervise his portrait of Bloom not to sustain Weininger's argument but to expose it. Since Weininger, a Jew, committed suicide as soon as his book came out, Reizbaum can distinguish his despairing reaction to anti-Semitic stereotypes from Bloom's affirmative one. Whereas "Weininger exorcised his fears by theorizing and dying," Bloom, she insists, "exorcises his fears through imaginative action and by emerging with a sense of who he is, an acceptance of that self, and with a son, symbol of the continuation of life."[5]

Suzette Henke, seizing on general remarks Krafft-Ebing makes in his introduction, exculpates Bloom from the character of "impotent onanist" by pointing out that he is not, in Krafft-Ebing's language, "morose, peevish, egotistical, narrow-minded, devoid of energy, self-respect and honor," traits Krafft-Ebing derived from masturbation. The flagrant evidence of "Circe" notwithstanding, she finds that "Joyce's modern hero seems to possess all the traits antithetical to those delineated by Krafft-Ebing."[6]

Each kind of reading, sentimental and anti-Semitic, impoverishes *Ulysses* in a different way. The sentimental reading irons out all of Bloom's fascinating kinks, flattens him into a schlemiel or a generic humanist saint. It drains him of all his potent bad blood, leaves him to wander anemically through Dublin without the resource of his odd and messy proclivities. How, for example, would he ever have had the tactical imagination to engineer his wife's infidelity (however obliquely) if not impelled to it by his masochism? When he hears Boylan's "bold hand" will visit Molly that afternoon he makes sure she knows he will stay away late at the Gaiety.

The anti-Semitic reading deprives *Ulysses* of depth in another way by taking Bloom out of his proper characterological context—the psychiatric theories dominant in European medicine just before Freud reinvented psychiatry—and by forgetting that Joyce wrote a comedy. By the turn of the century Krafft-Ebing had become the dean of European psychiatry and his widely read textbooks promulgated a theory of nervous degeneracy and sexual pathology that Joyce takes pains to make Bloom fit. Writing shortly after Krafft-Ebing died, Weininger elaborated a theory of gender and Jewish degeneration that Joyce adopted as his template for Bloom. Why would Joyce seize upon these anachronistic theories to adumbrate the portrait of a perverted Jew?

In the interests of high comedy. Between the 1904 in which Joyce set *Ulysses* and the 1914 in which he sat down to write it, the psychiatric model of degenerate heredity and sexuality had been largely superseded by the psychoanalytic revolution. Joyce was well aware of both Freud and Jung, of course. He had read an early version of Ernest Jones's Freudian analysis of Hamlet; he had obtained a copy of Jung's *The Significance of the Father in the Destiny of the Individual* (*Die Bedeutung des Vaters dur das Schicksal des Einzelnen,* 1909), and as Ellmann notes, he must have discussed Freud with Ettore Schmitz (Italo Svevo), uncle to Dr. Edoardo Weiss who in 1910 brought psychoanalysis to Italy (*JJII* 340n.). By 1914 the works of both Krafft-Ebing and Weininger had lost their status as science and had come to look like ingenious reinventions of humoral psychology. Krafft-Ebing's taxonomies of degenerates in various stages of effemination and perversion were comically Linnaean; Weininger's sliding scale of androgyny and Jewish degeneracy had long since been acknowledged as inspired quackery. Ludicrously spatchcocked one upon the other they made for a Rube Goldberg contraption of invalidated medicine and passé pop psychology, prime material for a comedy of the epic abject. If we take Krafft-Ebing's *Psycopathia* and Weininger's *Sex and Character* together (Weininger wrote under the stimulus of Krafft-Ebing) we recognize a program for Bloom's character that needs as much exposition as the Odyssean parallels.

Joyce's constitutive comic trope for *Ulysses,* then, is not so much to counterpoint an *homme moyen sensuel* with the Odyssean paradigm of epic heroism (the sentimental reading) as to inscribe Bloom within a counter-myth of racial and physiological degeneration, to plot against Ulysses' heroic apotheosis the terminal declension of an *homme sensuel dégénéré.* From the beginning, then, Bloom inhabits two matrices, one mythic, the other medical, morbid. It takes historical and imaginative sympathy to understand how Joyce could transubstantiate the stereotypes of anti-Semitism into the stuff of redemptive comedy, but to dispel critical anesthesia on this subject returns to Bloom much of the relish the "curiously, kindly" (*U*4.21) sentimental favorite of the last sixty-five years has lost.

Degeneration theory first appeared, manufactured out of nearly whole cloth, twenty-odd years before Krafft-Ebing sat down to write the first edition of his *Psycopathia.* It was fathered by Benedict-Augustin Morel in two treatises that appeared successively in 1857 and 1860: the *Traité des Dégénérescences Physiques, Intellectuelles et Morales de L'Espèce Humaine* and the *Traité des Maladies Mentales.*[7] Morel, a psychiatrist, had noticed that his patients' nervous complaints were often associated with what we now call substance abuse, particularly alcoholism. Other toxins also seemed involved, however, including lead, arsenic, and various industrial chemicals the urban proletariat worked with in mines and factories. Morel thought he noticed, moreover, that nervous ailments ran in families and in fact increased in their virulence in successive generations. From this he hypothesized two principles that remained with degeneration theory at least through Krafft-Ebing. According to the first principle, toxins precipitate a nervous degeneration that appears, in the person first exposed, as general irritability and tendencies to violence. According to the second principle, that of "progressivity," degeneration intensifies from one generation to the next; in some Lamarkian manner the germ of degeneration, the primal wound, passes via sperm and ovum to produce progeny yet further debilitated.

The decline usually lasted the Biblical four generations. The "tainted" second generation was vulnerable to specifically neurological complaints: hysteria, epilepsy, cerebral hemorrhages. Third generation victims, as their neurological degradation raced toward extinction, became prey to manias and insanity. Members of the fourth generation, if they survived gestation and infancy at all, were likely to be weak, sterile, dwarfish, and imbecilic.[8]

In psychiatry the short twenty years between Morel's work and Krafft-Ebing's marked a revolution. The whole theory slowly reoriented itself around what one has learned to think of as especially Freudian axioms; the theory now deemphasized toxins as the precipitants of nervous degeneracy and emphasized specifically nervous traumas themselves. Degeneracy was triggered either by the new stresses of civilized city living or by "venereal excess," whether too much heterosexual congress or the debilitating practices of masturbation and coitus interruptus. Either excess could seriously undermine the nervous constitution and provoke neurasthenia and assorted perversions. The abuser weakened his germ plasm and passed the nervous defect on to his progeny. As Krafft-Ebing began issuing early versions of what eventually became the monumental *Psycopathia* (expanded through twelve editions between 1880 and 1903) he could assume a consensus in the European medical community as to the model's theoretical adequacy.

Further, Joyce's templating of Bloom on Krafft-Ebing resonates with wider historical obsessions than critical memory may appreciate. Degeneracy theory had quickly emerged from its medical context to invade the social sciences and to infuse culture criticism. For a number of reasons it found ready soil to grow in. In part the model of hereditary taint was consistent with the social determinism the European academy had inherited from Comte. In part its argument seemed congruent with that of Darwin's *Origin of Species;* degenerate lines, willless and perverse, would presumably extinguish themselves. But the model clearly appealed to the larger European imagination as a metaphor for its own intensifying cultural malaise. Political radicalism, sexual perversion, aesthetic decadence seemed to pass via the very seed of the elders into more virulent expression in their young.

By the 1890s the degenerate had become a very round character, two generations of psychiatry having filled out the list of his "stigmata," morbid deviations from type that betrayed, quite literally in the imagination of the time, a subspecies, an *Untermensch.* Max Nordau, in his 1895 *Degeneration,* synthesized a portrait from a number of medical authorities. Physical stigmata included stunted growth, multiple deformities, over-large ears, squinting eyes, harelips, flat or pointed palates, webbed fingers, and perceptible asymmetry in the face or cranium. Mental stigmata revealed a parallel asymmetry, some faculties being morbidly developed while others atrophied. The degenerate is egotistical, impulsive and emotional, easily exhilarated and dejected by turns. When not reverberating to aesthetic quavers beyond the insensitivity of the Philistine (Valentin Magnan had introduced the concept of morbid oversensitivity in the *dégénéré supérieur*) he plunges into bottomless abulia, embraces pessimistic philosophies, and remains torpid, incapable of stirring either hand or foot until some trifle rouses his over-labile nervous system to new accesses of hysterical delirium.[9] When neither neurasthenic nor hysterical, he inhabits a twilight mood of logical incoherence and random impressionability that sounds like nothing so much as a psychological profile of Leopold Bloom:

> With the incapacity for action there is connected the predilection for inane revery. The degenerate is not in a condition to fix his attention long, or indeed at all, on any subject, and is equally incapable

of correctly grasping, ordering, or elaborating into ideas and judgments the impressions of the external world conveyed to his distracted consciousness by his defectively operating senses. It is easier and more convenient for him to allow his brain-centers to produce semi-lucid, nebulously blurred ideas and inchoate embryonic thoughts, and to surrender himself to the perpetual obfuscation of a boundless, aimless, and shoreless stream of fugitive ideas; and he rarely rouses himself to the painful attempt to check or counteract the capricious, and, as a rule, purely mechanical associations of ideas and succession of images, and bring under discipline the disorderly tumult of his fluid presentations.[10]

Nordau was a journalist and rose to fortune and honor on a flood of his own near hysterical hyperbole. But he was also a physician, and he did believe that civilization was succumbing to nervous degeneracy; his widely translated book simply popularized a theory that had already captured the intellectual imagination of his time. The metaphorical potential of the model was one of its chief attractions. Its loose Lamarkism permitted an easy transition from the rigor of medical diagnosis to the rhetoric of moral and political diatribe. It could underwrite ascriptions of degeneracy to sex, to aesthetics, to city living, and to race. With anti-Semitism reaching its own hysterical delirium in Europe after 1871, especially in German-speaking countries, with Nietzsche chanting the advent of the *Ubermensch* (with whom Stephen is identified—*U*1.708), it is no wonder that the discourse of anti-Semitism immediately absorbed the medical model of degeneration and demoted the Jew to its most abject echelons.

Not that the Jews had never been accused of degeneracy before. In fact the new theory simply culminated a history of pseudo-scientific inquiry into Jewish medical deviation. In 1792 F. L. de La Fontaine had surveyed Polish Jews and found them more diseased and more prone to disease than their Christian neighbors. He blamed their predisposition on early marriages—ages thirteen, fourteen, fifteen—which sapped the young parents of their precious bodily fluid *(Lebenssaft)* and left them vulnerable to medical accidents from conjunctivitis to syphilis. Venereal excess not only distinguished the Jew from the Christian but degraded him physically as well.[11]

In 1863 M. Boudin had reported in the *Bulletins de la Société d'Anthropologie de Paris* that German census statistics indicated higher rates of psychopathology among German Jews than either German Protestants or Catholics. Boudin traced Jewish idiocy and alienation to inbreeding; locked up in their ghettoes, constrained to genetic exclusivity by their refusal to assimilate, Jews were breeding psychopaths by marrying blood relatives. Incest (Jewish uncles could marry nieces), the sign, in Christian terms, of moral depravity, had become the seed of physical degeneration as well. Thus both medical opinion and popular prejudice had long been prepared for authoritative "diagnoses" of Jewish moral and physical pathology.[12]

In 1888 Jean Martin Charcot, the Paris psychiatrist under whom Krafft-Ebing, Freud, and Nordau all interned, ordained pseudo-science into science in his *Tuesday Lesson* for October 23: Jews had so weakened their nervous systems through inbreeding, he had concluded, as to become particularly susceptible to hysteria, neurasthenia, and all other nervous complaints.[13] By the 1890s standard textbooks had all adopted Charcot's analysis. Krafft-Ebing, in his *Textbook of Insanity,* represents the consensus:

> Statistics have been collected with great care to show the percentage of insanity in the various religious sects, and it has been shown that among the Jews and certain sects the percentage is decidedly higher. This fact stands in relation with religion only in so far as it constitutes a hindrance to marriage among those professing it; the more when its adherents are small in number, and there is consequent insufficient crossing of the race and increased inbreeding.[14]

Anti-Semitic pseudo-science had, for the moment, carried the citadels of respectable medical opinion as well.

Oddly enough, even Jewish authorities anxious to defend their race from the diagnosis of hereditary taint began by accepting the statistics on Jewish psychopathology. The censuses from which the data came were misleadingly explicit. Since most Jews lived in cities—where psychopathology was more likely to be noticed and treated—the higher incidence was more apparent than real. But the defenders were as statistically unsophisticated as their anti-Semitic antagonists; they responded not by discrediting the statistics but by searching for less disquieting explanations.

In *Anti-Semitism and the Jews in the Light of Modern Science,* Cesare Lombroso, himself a Jew, attributed Jewish nervous ailments to both the stresses of urban life and the trauma of anti-Semitism itself. His sensitive argument became the model for apologies within the Jewish community. The Viennese Zionist Martin Englander extended Lombroso's analysis in his 1902 *The Evident Most Frequent Appearances of Illness in the Jewish Race.* Englander dismissed the argument about inbreeding by pointing to America, where neurasthenia was endemic in its large cities despite exogamous marriage. The Jews suffered from the "American illness," neurasthenia provoked by big-city hurry rather than heredity.[15]

Thus within both the pseudo-science of anti-Semitism and the psychiatric explanations accepted by Jewish physicians themselves, the Jewish race bore a stigma of degeneration that could be interpreted but not interpreted away. For the anti-Semite the degeneration, because hereditary, was ineradicable—another of the signs of Cain—making the Jew a permanent *Untermensch* as well as an eternal wanderer. For the Jewish apologist degeneracy simply rehearsed the Jew's tragic destiny again in the new arena of the urban wilderness. For the

gentile imagination generally, anti-Semitic or not, the Jew had come to figure the essential urban degenerate. It was to this new mythos of abjection that Joyce turned for his counterpoint to Hellenic heroism.

Although Bloom's kinks derive from Krafft-Ebing's degenerate, he moves and has his being within a penumbral characterology Joyce absorbed from Otto Weininger's theory of sexual intermediacy. There are no pure men or women, Weininger insisted, but men-women with male and female characteristics that run along a continuum. Maleness and Femaleness inhere in the "Idioplasm" (what we would call genes), and its proportion in any organism is determined by the proportion of the Weiningerian inventions "Arrhenoplasm" (male plasm) and "Thelyplasm" (female plasm). Just as there are physiologically intermediate forms (the various hermaphrodites) so too there were psychologically intermediate forms, manly women and womanly men.[16]

Although Weininger wrote in 1903 when the medical establishment was abandoning the theory of degeneration, he preserved an essential feature of it by seeing male nervous pathologies in terms of a declension toward the feminine. Male psychology was of course privileged altogether; it had analytical and moral clarity backed up by an imperial will. Females suffered from hazy, associative mental processes, a vacuous, vacillating will and a lack of moral fiber. Weininger derived a "law of sexual attraction" (from his model: "For true sexual union it is necessary that there come together a complete male (M) and a complete female (F), even although in different cases the M and F are distributed between the two individuals in different proportions" (29). A womanly man had best marry a manly woman, for example, or a pure male a pure female. Where sexual attraction is greatest, Weininger argued, the offspring will be robust and fertile. If mismatches occur, the progeny will be nervous, feeble, and infertile. Most will die quickly (43-44).

We might plot *Ulysses'* characters within Weininger's characterology like this:

Stephen
(androgynous artist)
(Ubermensch)

(F) Molly   Boylan (M)

Bloom
(womanly man)
(Untermensch)

Sexual attraction is greatest between Molly and Boylan, the vessels of pure F and M. Molly and Bloom are mismatched, their sexual formulas adding up to one-and-a-half F and only half an M. Hence Rudy will be born unviable and die early. Stephen, who wishes to fly by the nets of family, race, country, sees himself as transcending, via androgyny, the limitations of either sex; he aspires to the divinity of the artist, the status of

Ubermensch. Bloom, in the comic perspective we must adopt toward him, has simply degenerated.

Weininger also dabbled in race psychology. In his notorious chapter on "Judaism" he first convicts Jewish males of having, as a group, fairly well succumbed to the femininity of their culture and then of bearing in both their culture and their genes the essential decadence of European civilization. As he puts it in lines that might well have been appreciated by Hitler:

> Judaism is the spirit of modern life. . . . Our age
> is not only the most Jewish but the most feminine.
> It is a time when art is content with daubs . . . the
> time of superficial anarchy, with no feeling for
> Justice and the State; a time of communistic ethics,
> of the most foolish of historical views, the
> materialistic interpretation of history. (329)

Indeed, as easy as it is today to dismiss Weininger's virtually unreadable pseudo-science as the ravings of a self-torturing Jewish anti-Semite, his obsessions resonated with political and metaphysical issues that dominated his age. He concludes his chapter on Judaism with an invocation that is horrifically prophetic and publishes his book less than twenty years before Hitler staged his Munich putsch:

> But from the new Judaism the new Christianity
> may be pressing forth; mankind waits for the new
> founder of religion, and, as in the year one, the
> age presses for a decision. The decision must be
> made between Judaism and Christianity, between
> business and culture, between male and female,
> between the race and the individual, between
> unworthiness and worth, between the earthly and
> the higher life, between negation and the God-
> like. Mankind has the choice to make. There are
> only two poles, and there is no middle way. (330)

If Joyce was not interested in the political or metaphysical angles in Weininger, he was certainly attracted to his ideas on Jews, femininity, and pathologies of the will, especially as they were congruent with Krafft-Ebing's. Bloom is Jewish, feminine, will-less, and intellectually fuzzy, one supposes, because Joyce had read Weininger's *Sex and Character.* But Bloom is a degenerate too because Joyce wanted a comic counter-myth to that of the *Odyssey.* Krafft-Ebing's work had suffered the most useful deflation and therefore could be worked for comedy. As Pound implied when he called the Homeric scaffolding an "affaire de cuisine,"[17] one might never notice that *Ulysses* had been structured upon the *Odyssey;* the "ironic perspective" enters the deliberations of critics more than the experience of the reader as he or she flounders through Bloom's stream of consciousness. But without Weininger and Krafft-Ebing there would be no Bloom, no *Untermensch,* no comic characterology at all. They provide far more constitutive paradigms for Bloom (if not for *Ulysses*) than does Homer.

Krafft-Ebing's account of sexual degeneracy begins with heredity. Perverts almost invariably come from "tainted" or "neurasthenic" families. Parents, grandparents, siblings, and cousins will generally have been afflicted with various perversions and mental deficiencies, often culminating in insanity or suicide. The "degenerate" is so called because he is understood to have inherited a weakened nervous system with specifically disabled nervous centers in brain, spinal erection centers, and genitals. The hereditary disability sometimes begins in the first few weeks of fetal development. The fetus, rather than evolving quickly into either male or female, gets caught somewhere between and is born a gynecomast (man-woman). In the male, for example, testicles remain stunted while breasts develop during puberty. Defective genitals and other organic malformations are frequent.

The degenerate usually inherits a specific perversion or a pronounced tendency to develop it if circumstances permit. Krafft-Ebing taxonomizes the basic perversions into four categories: 1) Anaesthesia Sexualis (no sexual feeling whatever); 2) Hyperaesthesia (excessive sexual affect that makes a subject vulnerable to various perversions. The hyperaesthesia is understood as a nervous "irritable weakness" rather than a strength); 3) Paraesthesia (a tendency to develop the three basic perversions: sadism, masochism, fetishism); 4) Antipathetic sexual instinct—homosexuality—which divides into various subcategories: psychical hermaphroditism (bisexuality with one sexual predisposition stronger than the other), eviration or defemination (in which physiological and character changes lead a subject to identify with the opposite sex) and finally the ultimate antipathetic psychosis, the delusion that one has actually changed sex.

Masturbation accompanies all of these degeneracies and exacerbates the symptoms, usually precipitating the turn toward specific perversion. It does so by further weakening the already debilitated nervous system. Masturbation leads to a number of lesser characterological debilities as well, including timidity, awkwardness, loss of memory, diminished intellectual capacity, and, on occasion, insanity.[18]

At Bloom's trial for indecency, Joyce has a panel of sexologists diagnose Bloom with Krafft-Ebing's taxonomy:

DR MULLIGAN

> *(in motor jerkin, green motorgoggles on his brow)*
> Dr Bloom is bisexually abnormal. He has recently
> escaped from Dr Eustace's private asylum for
> demented gentlemen. Born out of bedlock hereditary
> epilepsy is present, the consequence of unbridled
> lust. Traces of elephantiasis have been discovered
> among his ascendants. There are marked symptoms
> of chronic exhibitionism. Ambidexterity is also latent.
> He is prematurely bald from selfabuse, perversely
> idealistic in consequence, a reformed rake, and has
> metal teeth. In consequence of a family complex he
> has temporarily lost his memory and I believe him
> to be more sinned against than sinning. I have

made a pervaginal examination and, after application of the acid test to 5427 anal, axillary, pectoral and public hairs, I declare him to be *virgo intacta*.

(Bloom holds his high grade hat over his genital organs.)

DR MADDEN

Hypsospadia is also marked. In the interest of coming generations I suggest that the parts affected should be preserved in spirits of wine in the national teratological museum.

DR CROTTHERS

I have examined the patient's urine. It is albuminoid. Salivation is insufficient, the patellar reflex intermittent.

DR PUNCH COSTELLO

The *fetor judaicus* is most perceptible.

DR DIXON

(reads a bill of health) Professor Bloom is a finished example of the new womanly man. (*U*15.1774-99)

In the way of hereditary taint Bloom has inherited defective genitals ("hypsospadia"), epilepsy (a form of nervous degeneracy), and intellectual incapacity ("lost his memory"). His "selfabuse" has culminated in insanity ("Dr Eustace's private asylum"). Altogether he suffers from general gynecomastia (bisexuality, vagina, and ultimate diagnosis as "new womanly man").

Details from elsewhere in "Circe" confirm the diagnosis. His family line is contaminated at its source, where Noah begat his progenitor "Eunuch" (*U*15.1855). His genitals are further compromised by the offside testicles (*U*15.1301). Three accusers confirm his chronic masturbation: the first, "in the cattlecreep behind Kilbarrack" (*U*15.1873-74), implies the crime against fertility carried forward from "Oxen of the Sun"—masturbation empties the barracks by killing soldiers before they are conceived. His masochism appears in his submission to Bella's brutality and his fetishism in his predilection for shoes and feet (his dream to work as "a shoefitter in Manfield's"— *U*15.2814), and various articles of female attire, drawers and corsets (*U*15.2973-82), etc. His idiosyncratic version of antipathetic perversity (change of sex delusion) emerges when he bears children (*U*15.1821ff.) and when he metamorphoses into a female as Bella becomes Bello (*U*15.2834-35). In retrospect it seems clear that all this came latent in his very name: Leopold from Leopold von Sacher-Masoch, the novelist after whom Krafft-Ebing named masochism, Paula (gynecomastia), and Bloom from Virag ("flower" in Hungarian but virago, "masculine woman," in English—Bloom's state after his sex change).

Joyce has drawn on three Krafft-Ebing cases in particular for the Bella/Bloom fantasy. Case #129, the longest reported in the *Psycopathia,* recounts a "stage of transition to change of sex delusion" (the subject feels as if transformed into a woman both physically and psychically while remaining sanely aware he is still a man). Case #133 records a change of sex delusion in which the subject became fully convinced of a physiological change to female estate. Case #130 recounts a delusive change in the opposite direction, a woman who felt herself developing male physical characteristics. Details from these cases, as we will see, inform Joyce's history of Bloom's antecedents as well as his characterization of Bloom.

Case #129 was born in Hungary (like Bloom's father) into an hereditarily tainted family: "numerous nervous and mental diseases." Except for a brother who was born late, all children in the family died of "general weakness." Women and schoolchildren found the subject feminine in behavior and, when they discovered a girl whose features resembled his, began to call them by each other's names. The subject exacerbated his predisposition by masturbation, and when he eventually engaged in coitus, wished he could take the part of the woman and exchange his penis for his correspondent's vagina. He began to stay awake at night having hallucinations, both visual and auditory, in which he "was with both the living and the dead." The subject reported that such hallucinations persisted as a "habit of mind." Eventually the subject married into a family "in which female government was rampant."

One day after taking a quadruple dose of hashish and lying down in a hot bath he suddenly felt himself transformed into a woman, with broadened pelvis, swollen breasts, and an accompanying feeling of shrunken testicles. Thereafter he experienced his penis as a clitoris and his scrotum as labia majora, a vulva. His anus as well, he reported, felt feminine, and only religious conviction kept him from becoming a "passive pederast." Every month from that time on he felt menstrual discomfort for five days. Occasionally his menses did not arrive and he felt pregnant until they returned. He suffered from irregular bowels from time to time that brought on "all the symptoms of female constipation." His progressive eviration led to a loss of will power (*PS* 200-13).

Case #133 extends the fantasy of sex change into delusion. The subject, already institutionalized for paranoia, masturbated himself into effemination, eventually becoming convinced he was a woman. He felt pregnant on occasion and demanded to be moved to a lying-in hospital. His feeling of pregnancy was presumably precipitated by a combination of tenesmus (painful desire to evacuate) and cystospasm (bladder spasm) probably associated with the prenatal breaking of the waters (*PS* 218-21).

Since it was Joyce's way to derive his own text from numerous sources, to position details of narrative and character within a matrix of parallel and allusion that gave depth to the superficies of his own chronicle, we would be claiming too much if we were to match points in these slender anecdotes with moments in *Ulysses* and insist they had determined them. Bloom's first name, for example, was probably determined in part by numerous sources besides Leopold von Sacher-Masoch. There was an edition of the Swan of Avon's works called the *Leopold Shakespeare;* Joyce was fond of telling an anecdote (sexual) about Leopold II of Belgium; several Austro-Hungarian emperors were named Leopold. No single source for anything ever satisfied Joyce's mania for reticulation. But if we can trace a great many congenialities between Krafft-Ebing's cases and important dimensions of Bloom's character both within and without "Circe," then the argument that the cases constitute a reliable analytic venue (at the very least) may be assumed to have been made. And in fact the similarities, both in the larger dimensions of Bloom's character and in the details, saturate both "Circe" and the novel as a whole.

In the first climax of "Circe," Bloom's abasement before Bella, the similarities are explicit. The womanly man transforms into a woman as the manly woman transforms into man (Bello). Krafft-Ebing cases #129 and #130 confront each other in the fantasy. Bella sprouts a mustache and wears phallic "eardrops" (*U*15.2748) while Bloom evolves a vulva (*U*15.3089). The Fan accuses Bloom of having married into "Petticoat government" (*U*15.2759-60). He confesses hereditary nervous taint in the form of glutear sciatica (*U*15.2782) and cystospasm (*U*15.3020), associated in Case #131 with the delusion of pregnancy. Bello reminds him that he used to pose in front of a mirror looking at his "udders" (*U*15.2992) and that, in a fantasy of passive pederasty, he "clipped off [his] backgate hairs and lay swooning . . . across the bed as Mrs Dandrade about to be violated by lieutenant Smythe-Smythe" and others (*U*15.3000-02). The hallucination of shrinking genitals in case #129 reappears perhaps as Bello inspects Bloom for his wherewithal: "Up! Up! Manx cat! What have we here? Where's your curly teapot gone to or who docked it on you, cockyolly?" (*U*15.3129-30). "My willpower!" Bloom cries nostalgically at fantasy's end as the transformation deprives him of psychical as well as physical masculinity (*U*15.3215).

Echoes of these cases reverberate throughout *Ulysses* as well. In "Cyclops" the Citizen accurately diagnoses Bloom's gynecomasty and retails a perhaps not apocryphal story of Bloom's menses: "One of those mixed middlings he is. Lying up in the hotel Pisser was telling me once a month with headache like a totty with her courses" (*U*12.1658-60). Bloom himself calls the "stitch" in his side an "awful cramp" and attributes it to his "Monthly" (*U*15.199, 207, 210). In "Lotus Eaters" we find Bloom lying in a hot bath. His "floating flower" may be taken (via "Virag") to recall the delusive transformation of male to female genitals under the same stimulus in case #129, but even if we do not take it so, the "limp father of thousands" covertly introduces a witty sexual ambiguity. The phrase invokes the *Saxifraga*

stolonifera, ordinarily called the "mother of thousands" because it spreads by sending out innumerable runners.[19] Bloom's genitals are symbolically ambiguous, hermaphroditic (*U*5.571-72).

More generally, Bloom's family line shows symptoms of hereditary nervous and sexual degeneracy. Lipoti Virag, for all his sexual sophistication, had only one son, Rudolph. Rudolph in turn left only the womanly man Leopold before he committed suicide, the usual end, besides insanity, of exacerbated neurasthenia. Bloom, as the hereditary degeneracy increased, fathered no son strong enough to live (cf. the "general weakness" that killed case #129's siblings). He produces only a female (Milly) and himself turns progressively feminine and perverse, withdrawing, after Rudy's death, from "complete intercourse." Onanism in its nineteenth-century construction referred, of course, not so much either to the sin of Onan (coitus interruptus) or to masturbation but to any nonreproductive sexual expression. Krafft-Ebing's attitude is typical for his time and represents the context in which we must view Bloom's masturbation and coitus interruptus: "With opportunity for the natural satisfaction of sexual instinct, every expression of it that does not correspond with the purpose of nature—i.e., propagation—must be considered as perverse" (*PS* 53).

As for masochism, the other explicit perversion in the Bella/Bloom fantasy, it derives not only from Krafft-Ebing but from Joyce's reading of Sacher-Masoch's *Venus im Pelz* upon which title Molly puns when she says to Boylan, "I'm in my pelt" (*U*15.3770). Most of the specific details of Bloom's masochism seem to originate in Krafft-Ebing, while the "French triangle" in which Bloom involves himself derives rather directly from Sacher-Masoch.

Krafft-Ebing defines masochism first in terms of will and contrasts it with sadism. Whereas "sadism arises from the pathological intensification of the masculine character" (by which Krafft-Ebing means will, aggression, cruelty—*PS* 133), masochism represents "the pathological growth of specific feminine mental habits" (by which he means, among others, "inclination to subordination"—*PS* 130). Krafft-Ebing is at pains to point out that an intensification of either sadism in men or masochism in women is not necessarily abnormal, whereas sadism in women or masochism in men is quite perverse. In a male masochist the "unlimited subjection of the will" (*PS* 133) to a woman enacts his ultimate phylogenetic degradation. The degenerate ends by exciting himself with the drama of his own willed but willless abjection.

Since Bloom is fully aware that Molly and Boylan will consummate their adulterous flirtation sometime after four o'clock, we realize he is conspiring to cuckold himself, may even have scripted the drama, however tacitly. We may check our suspicion against *Venus in Furs,* where the protagonist announces that "Nothing more fully excites my passion than the tyranny, the cruelty and especially the infidelity of a beautiful woman."[20] His mistress conspires with him, for his own satisfaction, by using him as an intermediary between herself and other lovers. Though Bloom's role in his own cuckolding is less active, his masochistic intent seems clear.

But if the general contours of the masochistic triangle seem derived from Sacher-Masoch, the innumerable nuances of masochism throughout *Ulysses* and the phantasmagoria of masochistic fantasy and fetish in "Circe" come straight from Krafft-Ebing. One of Krafft-Ebing's most famous case studies, nicknamed "Erotic Horse," clearly incited several moments in "Circe." A part of the case study, reported in the patient's own words, goes like this:

> Being of tall stature, both hands braced on a chair, I made my back horizontal, and she mounted astride, after the manner of a man. I then did the best I could to imitate the movements of a horse, and loved to have her treat me like a horse, without consideration. She could beat, prick, scold, or caress me, just as she felt inclined. I could carry on my back persons weighing from sixty to eighty kilos for half or three-quarters of an hour, without interruption. . . . When time and circumstances allowed it, I did this three or four times in succession. It sometimes happened that I practiced it both in the morning and afternoon. . . . When possible, I like best to bare my trunk, that I might feel the riding-whip more sharply. (*PS* 102)

In Joyce's rewriting the fantasy is triggered by an accidental reference to Throwaway, the winning horse in the afternoon's race:

BELLO

> . . . (*he throws a leg astride and, pressing with horseman's knees, calls in a hard voice*) Gee up! A cockhorse to Banbury cross. I'll ride him for the Eclipse stakes. (*he bends sideways and squeezes his mount's testicles roughly, shouting*) Ho! Off we pop! I'll nurse you in proper fashion. (*he horserides cockhorse, leaping in the, in the saddle*) The lady goes a pace a pace and the coachman goes a trot a trot and the gentleman goes a gallop a gallop a gallop a gallop. (*U*15.2940-49)

Krafft-Ebing makes much of certain kinds of fetishes related directly to masochism. Shoe fetishes derive from a previous foot fetish provoked by the desire to be trod upon: "Yes. Walk on him! I will," Zoe says (*U*15.2918). This is masochism by synecdoche. In a similar manner, certain of Bloom's unsavory predilections derive from fantasies in which coprolagnia and urine drinking culminate the masochist's abasement (*PS* 123-30). The whole fantasy appears in one of Bello's threats:

BELLO

> You will make the beds, get my tub ready, empty the pisspots in the different rooms, including old

Mrs Keogh's the cook's, a sandy one. Ay, and rinse the seven of them well, mind, or lap it up like champagne. Drink me piping hot. (*U*15.3072-76)

Bloom at one point seems to have reversed roles with the sadist in that he is accused of having urinated in a bucket of porter:

THE GAFFER

> (*crouches, his voice twisted in his snout*) And when Cairns came down from the scaffolding in Beaver street what was he after doing it into only into the bucket of porter that was there waiting on the shavings for Derwan's plasterers. (*U*15.583-87)

As Bloom defends himself the fantasy shades (via Glauber salts, a cathartic) into an intimation that he wished to inflict his own feces on the unsuspecting plasterers as well:

THE LOITERERS

> Jays, that's a good one. Glauber salts. O jays, into the men's porter. (*U*15.595-96)

But Bloom's "SINS OF THE PAST" include moments of synecdochic masochism:

> By word and deed he frankly encouraged a nocturnal strumpet to deposit fecal and other matter in an unsanitary outhouse attached to empty premises. . . . Did he not lie in bed, the gross boar, gloating over a nauseous fragment of well-used toilet paper presented to him by a nasty harlot, stimulated by gingerbread and a postal order? (*U*15.3027-40)

Even the chocolates Bloom carries with him into Nighttown (*U*15.143) may best be interpreted, if Krafft-Ebing is correct about the "consumption of confects" that resemble feces, as synecdoche for coprolagnia (*PS* 128). They are certainly an aphrodisiac for Bloom, as he implies by asking "Aphrodisiac?" and taking one just before Bella appears (*U*15.2736). The chocolate in fact triggers the entire Bello/Bloom fantasy. Does the "mucksweat" Bella complains of (*U*15.2750) imply both feces and urine? Her final sadistic threat (to suffocate Bloom in a cesspool—*U*15.3207-11) would symmetrically bracket this fantasy if it did.[21]

The degeneration hypothesis clarifies several otherwise odd moments in the text as well. There is the question of Bloom's impossibly narrow chest as recorded in measurements he compiled while exercising with Eugene Sandow's *Physical Strength and How to Obtain It*. Hugh Kenner has argued that Joyce, exhausted by the twelve-hour days he spent proofreading "Ithaca," had copied the abnormally modest measurements (with incidental emendations) from a testimonial printed at the back of the book, but alas without noting that the dimensions had been sent by a Mr. Thos. A Fox who described himself as "small of stature, being only five feet in height and seven stone in weight." This makes Mr. Fox, as Kenner points out, the "classic ninety-eight pound weakling," and makes Joyce's adoption of his measurements a simple error occasioned by fatigue and haste.[22]

But if Joyce were intent on degrading Bloom to *Untermensch,* the pattern of his emendations makes a great deal of sense. For chest, biceps, and forearms, he simply shaves an inch off Fox's "Before" figures to make Bloom physically tinier than his prototype. Bloom's gains are correspondingly more modest than Fox's. For Bloom's legs though—thigh and calf—he goes to a great deal of trouble to make sure that the "After" measurements are identical at twelve inches, giving him the ludicrously skinny and unproportioned "stork's legs" of "Calypso" (*U*4.384):

Such numerological fastidiousness in the emendations indicates malice prepense; Joyce was diminishing Bloom deliberately, inflicting on him the physiology of a ninety-eight pound degenerate.

Again, Molly has always seemed to have spoken with inexplicable callousness when she refused to mourn for Rudy because, as she asks herself, "what was the good in going into mourning for what was neither one thing nor the other?" (*U*18.1307-08). What could she possibly mean? That the child was neither dead nor alive? Hardly; it survived for eleven days, more than enough to make a normal mother grieve for a normal child. Molly reacts as if Rudy were unviable in some more fundamental sense, and surely the hints Joyce lets drop suggest a being far from normal.

In "Hades" Bloom remembers Rudy in painfully odd flashes with "A dwarf's face, mauve and wrinkled" and with a "Dwarf's body, weak as putty" (*U*6.326-27). Bloom is not simply being fanciful, remarking some curious similarity between newborn infants and grown dwarfs. The child is clearly defective: "Meant nothing. Mistake of nature" (*U*6.328-29). Rudy resembles the dwarfish, imbecilic degenerates of Morel's fourth generation of decline. Given his Weiningerian paternity he was probably born hermaphroditic as well—"neither one thing nor the other"—a Lamarkian organic declension from the androgynous "womanly man" Bloom to a physically bisexual degenerate, the last unviable scion of a "tainted" line. Bloom accepts his biological guilt for Rudy's pathology, in any case: "If it's healthy it's from the mother. If not from the man" (*U*6.329).

In a famous telegram sent from Paris to his aging master at Medan, a follower assured Zola that "Naturalism isn't dead. [Strong] letter to follow."[24] But naturalism, having pursued its positivist premises into fathomless pessimism, was moribund. Zola had begun his great chronicle of the Empire after having read Claude Bernard's theories of heredity and Morel's of degeneration. He had traced both healthy and tainted lines of the

Rougon-Macquart family through twenty-odd novels and exhausted not only the patience of his European readers but the resources of medical determinism. Except for faint echoes, as in Ibsen's *Ghosts,* European literature had abandoned the medical model of degeneration which incited it.

In Leopold Bloom, Joyce resurrected it. Despite his novel's title, Joyce found much not only of his *prima materia* in Weininger and Krafft-Ebing but much of his prime inspiration as well. Joyce had been a medical student no less than three times, and he must have read the *Psycopathia,* at least, with reasonable faith in its status as medical science. And according to Ellmann he was quite persuaded by Weininger on the subjects of both femininity in Jewish men and the general organic disenfranchisement of women. But the medical naturalism he eventually writes transvalues the determinist pessimism of his precursors and the animus of Weininger's heavily drawn metaphysical moral. Joyce tropes naturalism by taking the tragic premises of determinism and degeneration and, in a Nietzschean reversal of polarity, treating them as comic. Degeneration theory, having suffered its deflation by 1914, probably modeled the inversion for him. Disenfranchised as psychiatry, it was reissued in the popular imagination as a sort of humoral psychology. Discarded by medicine, it became available for comic exploitation. This is why neither Joyce nor the degenerate Bloom needs defending; his degeneracy is meant to be comic, not realistic. We do not protect Bloom by sentimentalizing him—we just undernourish him. Bloom is a great character because of his perversities, not in spite of them. There is no question of Joyce's compassion for Bloom but neither should there be any about Bloom's characterological contumacy. To insist that Joyce's portrait of Bloom is entirely compassionate, to see in him only a kindly, curious *homme moyen* who, though despicable in his penchants, ungainly in his gait, ineffectual as a man and ridiculous in the eyes of all Dublin, nevertheless rises above the degraded matter of his composition, transcends the limits of the human, becomes a saintly version of Everyman, an Elijah, a light unto the Gentiles, is not only to sentimentalize him but to miss all the fun. Bloom is Charlie Chaplin but he is a nitwit and a pervert as well. Given the ironic times in which Joyce wrote, anyone less diminished simply could not carry the weight of his epic comedy.

NOTES

[1] Stanley Sultan, *The Argument of "Ulysses"* (Columbus: Ohio State Univ. Press, 1964), p. 317.

[2] Maurice Samuel, "Bloom of Bloomusalem," *Reflex,* 4 (January 1929), 11.

[3] Samuel, 14-16.

[4] Robert Martin Adams, *Surface and Symbol: The Consistency of James Joyce's "Ulysses"* (New York: Oxford Univ. Press, 1962), p. 104n.

[5] Marilyn Reizbaum, "The Jewish Connection, Cont'd," in *The Seventh of Joyce*, ed. Bernard Benstock (Bloomington: Indiana Univ. Press, 1982), p. 232.

[6] Suzette Henke, "Joyce and Krafft-Ebing," *JJQ*, 17 (Fall 1979), 86.

[7] Eric T. Carlson, "Medicine and Degeneration: Theory and Praxis," in *Degeneration: The Dark Side of Progress*, ed. J. Edward Chamberlin and Sander L. Gilman (New York: Columbia Univ. Press, 1985), pp. 121-22.

[8] Carlson, p. 122.

[9] Max Nordau, *Degeneration* (1895; rpt. New York: Howard Fertig, 1968), pp. 16-20.

[10] Nordau, p. 21.

[11] Sander L. Gilman, "Jews and Mental Illness: Medical Metaphors, Anti-Semitism and the Jewish Response," *Journal of the History of the Behavioral Sciences*, 20 (1984), 151.

[12] Gilman, pp. 151-52.

[13] Cited in Gilman, p. 153.

[14] Richard von Krafft-Ebing, *Textbook of Insanity* (Philadelphia: F.A. Davis Company, 1905), p. 143.

[15] Cited in Gilman, p. 154.

[16] Otto Weininger, *Sex and Character* (London: W. Heinemann, 1906), p. 16. Further references are cited parenthetically in the text.

[17] Ezra Pound, "James Joyce et Pecuchet," *Mercure de France*, CLVI (June 1, 1922), 307-20, reprinted in *Pound/Joyce*, ed. Forrest Read (New York: New Directions, 1967), pp. 200-11. Translated into English in *Shenandoah*, 3 (Autumn 1952), 9-20.

[18] Richard von Krafft-Ebing, *Psycopathia Sexualis*, trans. Franklin S. Klaf (New York: Stein and Day, 1965), see Ch. 4. Subsequent references will be cited parenthetically in the text as *PS*.

[19] Don Gifford and Robert J. Seidman, *Notes for Joyce* (New York: Dutton, 1974), p. 77.

[20] Leopold von Sacher-Masoch, *La Venus a la Fourrure*, trans. Aude Willm (Paris: Editions de Minuit, 1967), p. 154, my translation.

[21] Since writing this article I have come upon a sentence in Fritz Senn's *Joyce's Dislocations* (Baltimore: Johns Hopkins Univ. Press, 1984) that anticipates the connection I have made between "tropes" and "perversions." It appears in the chapter "Book of Many Turns," and reads: "Among [Circe's] polymorphic turns are the deviate turns of the psyche, with such authorities as Krafft-Ebing being responsible for parts of the script," p. 131.

[22] Hugh Kenner, *"Ulysses"* (London: George Allen and Unwin, 1980), pp. 164-65.

[23] See Kenner, pp. 164-65.

[24] Lilian R. Furst and Peter N. Skrine, *Naturalism* (London: Methuen, 1971), p. 31.

Misha Kavka (essay date 1995)

SOURCE: "The 'Alluring Abyss of Nothingness': Misogyny and (Male) Hysteria in Otto Weininger," in *New German Critique*, Vol. 66, Fall, 1995, pp. 123-45.

[*In the following essay, Kavka discusses the ways in which Weininger's virulent misogyny and anti-Semitism appear to have been symptoms of widespread male "hysteria" over the nature and place of women in fin de siècle European society.*]

In May 1903 there appeared in Vienna a study entitled *Sex and Character* [*Geschlecht und Charakter*] by an unknown 23-year old, Otto Weininger, who could not be immediately placed either as a sexologist, biologist, empirical psychologist, or philosopher. In the preface to the work, the author undertakes to "place the relations of the sexes in a new and decisive light" and thus to go beyond the common scientific categorizations "to the heart of psychology," but a psychology understood from a "purely philosophical" standpoint.[1] Weininger claims nothing less than to have worked out a system of existential philosophy upon the "single principle" of sexual difference. Three pages into the preface, however, he feels the need to apologize to the philosophical reader who may feel the awkwardness of treating the "highest questions" in the service of "a special problem of no great dignity": the "problem" of sexual difference. Elaborating philosophy through the vehicle of sexuality is for Weininger an uncomfortable mixing of the high and low registers. He considers his approach necessary and yet, like the reader he imagines, finds the very necessity "unpleasant." Clearly, the issue of sexual difference carries a taint—a taint which turns out to be the unavoidable presence in the formula of woman herself.

Sex and Character now stands as one of the most blatant examples of misogynist and anti-Semitic writing to come out of turn-of-the-century Austria and Germany. Drawing on biology, physiology, psychology, Kantian philosophy, literature, and Christian mysticism, Weininger develops a lengthy expostulation on the morally, logically, aesthetically, ethically, and emotionally bankrupt nature of woman, which he then, in a notorious chapter on Judaism, applies wholescale to the feminine nature of the Jew. One is almost pressed to admire his dogged consistency: nowhere in some 500 pages does he allow woman any quality or characteristic of value. In fact, the chapter entitled "The Nature of Woman and Her Significance in the Universe" begins with a determined and all-encompassing denunciation of her worth: "The deeper the analysis goes in the estimation of woman, the more we must deny her all that is lofty and noble, great and beautiful" (*SC* 344). Although Weininger alleges that his larger goal is to develop a philosophy of being, he takes as his immediate project the unmasking of turn-of-the-century woman, who, as he phrases it, has herself managed to convince an entire culture that she is one of two things: either chaste, virtuous, and soulful, or strong, intelligent, and equal in capacity to men. On both counts, Weininger insists, woman's claim to esteem is fraudulent. In the first case, she is imitating men; in the second, she is at best already biologically constituted as a man.

In making this onslaught on the self-presentation of "woman," Weininger is clearly attacking cultural constructions of femininity (as domestic angel, as emancipated woman), but he does so by blaming "the woman" herself, claiming to expose a fraud which she, albeit unknowingly, commits on society at large. I purposefully retain Weininger's use of the singular to denote women (he refers to *das Weib,* a grammatically neutral term translated as "the female") in order to stress the tension between the utter passivity of women as he characterizes them and the syntactical agency of the singular term. This usage pulls "the female" in two different directions: "she" as the nominative singular term has the agency to create a mask for herself, in essence to create her own projected persona, while as the characterization of the feminine "she" has no ego, no judgment, nor any ideas that are not borrowed from a man. Though the preface claims that ultimately the blame for woman's duplicitous nature lies with men—"in the end the investigation turns against the man and assigns to him the greatest actual guilt" (*SC* vii)—"the female" as agent means that at the syntactic level the text insists that women are at fault. It means, too, that woman's most frightening characteristic, her duplicity, is actually produced by the text at the same time as it operates as the object of Weininger's consideration.

In undertaking to expose the duplicitous psychology of woman as only a man can, Weininger intentionally sets himself at odds with accepted limits of misogyny and even revels in his oppositionality.[2] The question thus arises whether *Sex and Character* can be read as representative of a cultural moment, or whether we must understand it as an individual deviation from the intellectual and social milieu. There have been enough patho-biographies of Weininger written, certainly, to argue that in *Sex and Character* Weininger has written only his own case history for discerning psychologists. Nonetheless, the very impact of Weininger's work, and not only in German-speaking countries, indicates that his extremist formulations of femininity and Jewishness resonated profoundly with existing ideological conditions. This is not to say, simply, that anti-feminism and anti-Semitism were alive and well at the turn of the century; that much is clear even without the help of Otto Weininger. Rather, the impact of Weininger's study suggests that a large, implicitly male intellectual audience identified with Weininger's hatred of women, and, through the vehicle of misogyny, his hatred of Jews. His many readers participated strongly though ambivalently in his defenses against the feared collapse of sexual difference, that is, against the collapse of manhood into the nothingness of femininity.

An overview of publishing statistics reveals that *Sex and Character* went through 28 editions between the years 1903 and 1947—twelve editions in the first seven years after publication, with four in 1904 alone.[3] Beginning in 1906 it was translated into English, Italian, Polish, Hungarian, Russian, Danish, Norwegian, and Swedish, as well as, less predictably, into Yiddish and Japanese. Clearly, this work excited a great deal of interest, not only in Vienna, but also in England, Italy, Scandinavia, and central Europe.[4] The statistics are somewhat misleading, though, since the book actually failed to attract much attention upon its first appearance. What catapulted it suddenly onto Vienna's bestseller list was the "scandal" of Otto Weininger's suicide, staged in the house of Beethoven's death by the 23-year old barely four months after the publication of his masterwork. The impetus behind his suicide remains a mystery, as such a gesture must, but with his suicide Weininger undoubtedly made himself into an artifact of turn-of-the-century Anglo-European intellectual culture; thereafter, it became difficult to distinguish the individual from the text. By taking his life so dramatically directly after publication, Weininger ensured not only his readers' fascination with himself and his work, but also the inseparability of his philosophical treatise from a psychological case history. It is this fascination with the intellectually extreme and the psychologically borderline which drove Weininger's masterwork into multiple editions and translations.

Most posthumous studies of Weininger approach his works through the lens of his suicide, deciphering a particular pathology out of *Sex and Character,* his few letters, and *About the Last Things* [*Über die letzten Dinge*], a collection of essays and aphorisms published posthumously. Ferdinand Probst, responsible for the first study which concentrates on Weininger the man rather than on his work, published *The Case of Otto Weininger* [*Der Fall Otto Weininger*] in 1904 in direct response to the public interest fomented by Weininger's suicide. As a psychiatrist Probst sees Weininger simply as a "highly interesting figure, for whom a lasting place in the annals of psychiatry will be made."[5] Though otherwise silent on the work of Otto Weininger, Freud refers to him briefly in 1909, to mark him by comparison with Little Hans as a case of neurosis arising from unresolved castration anxiety. The first full-scale study of Weininger, published in 1946 by David Abrahamsen, MD, is actually a psychobiography; the study painstakingly collects and arranges biographical material in order to prove that, in fact, Weininger suffered from schizophrenia.[6] This range of publications, each insisting narrowly on the "truth" of Weininger's special malady, returns us to the text as a marker of individual deviation and exposes the problem involved in reading Weininger as a self-produced case history. On the one hand, one cannot simply replace the absent/dead psyche with a published text and perform a psychoanalysis of the latter as a reputable stand-in for the former. On the other hand, it would be mistaken to assume that the author here is dead to his text; particularly in *Sex and Character* one constantly feels the lurking presence of the writer's psyche, for whose glorification and defense the philosophical system seems constructed.

Despite the inextricability of Weininger's work from his suicide, the intellectual claims of *Sex and Character* hardly went unnoticed. Even more than providing fodder for psychiatry, Weininger became a touchstone for turn-of-the-century male intellectual culture as the representative voice of anti-feminism. This voice attracted readers as much as it discomfited them. On the one hand, Weininger had a wide readership, as a number of editions and translations of *Sex and Character* shows; on the other hand, traces of his influence tend to appear as oblique echoes and resonances rather than actual references. In Anglo-European intellectual circles during the first decades of the twentieth century, everyone would have been familiar with the content of the work, yet only Karl Kraus and August Strindberg were unequivocal defenders of *Sex and Character*.[7] (Ironically, two physicians, P.J. Möbius and Wilhelm Fliess, loudly denounced Weininger for plagiarism, which itself amounts to an unequivocal, if antagonistic, form of agreement.[8]) Most reviews treated Weininger with radical ambivalence: they exalted a "learned and gifted author" while distancing themselves from his project. One reviewer praises him for treating "from all standpoints a huge philosophical question of natural and cultural history," then asks with concern what the author actually wishes to accomplish by his work.[9] Another claims the book to be so prodigious that "one gazes spellbound . . . at the heights of thought and moral courage" in the work; the reviewer recommends it to all "thinking people," though he does rue the fact, on behalf of women, that the "greater majority" of them will not belong to its reading circle.[10] A third prophesizes that the work will have a difficult birth into the cultural history of Vienna—"one will first be silent about it, then one will destroy it . . . it will be destroyed very, very often"—but praises the worthiness of this fate as appropriate to very few books.[11]

These reviews participate in and mark a recurring tone of contemporary responses to Weininger. A reviewer on the one hand marvels at Weininger's ability to push his thoughts to their furthest conclusions and to keep himself free of bitterness in the face of such dreadful conclusions, while on the other hand he declares "our" indignation at the tenor of these conclusions.[12] As with the reviewer who "gazes spellbound . . . at the heights

of thought and moral courage" in Weininger's work, there is again and again in these responses a sense of fascination, of being drawn to a "learned and gifted" intellect, which is then complicated by a distancing gesture of criticism or disagreement as though agreeing outright with Weininger were not possible in a public forum. The extravagance of the reviewers' appreciation, itself extravagantly contradicted rather than muted by defensive disagreement, suggests that *Sex and Character* located its (male) reviewers and readers in a relationship of antagonistic identification to the text. Such is the rhythm of textual fascination: the readers both identified with Weininger's misogyny and sought to distance themselves from its extreme formulation by reading it as pathological, as an individual deviation. By committing suicide after publication, Weininger himself conveniently marked his misogyny as pathological, yet *Sex and Character* also made uncomfortable reading precisely because it threatened to expose the centrality of misogyny to the turn-of-the-century ideological complex—at least to the Anglo-European cult(ure) of educated masculinity—and to expose it, moreover, as a cultural pathology. Thus Weininger was both celebrated and castigated as a genius. As the banner-holder of *fin-de-siècle* anti-feminism, he spoke in the voice of the cultural moment, but, by association with his suicide, he posthumously dubbed the culture's most cherished tenets as pathological. We might say, given Weininger's interest in using the concept of hysteria to mark sexual difference, that *Sex and Character* held up a mirror to turn-of-the-century cultural male hysteria.

DIVERSITY VERSUS TYPES

Sex and Character consists of three parts: the empirically psychological, the philosophical, and what today we might call the cultural, although Weininger tellingly separates the work only into two sections, "Sexual Diversity" and "Sexual Types." In order to bridge what he considers to be the inhibitive disjunction between the physical sciences and the humanities, Weininger has recourse first to biology, then to Kantian philosophy, and finally to his own brand of cultural psychology. As Nike Wagner points out, the progression of methodologies is no coincidence: each new "scientific" approach is meant to surpass and replace the former, with philosophy taking up the conclusions of biology and compensating for its methodological limitations, and cultural psychology extending and completing the conclusions of Kantian philosophy.[13] Clearly, the conclusions drawn from the final and thus most encompassing methodology are meant to be the most expansive and the most "true," but these claims about women and Jews establish instead a law of cultural stereotypes carried to the point of philosophical absurdity. What is often overlooked in a reading of *Sex and Character* is that the first section of the study, ostensibly limited by the demands of positivistic rigor, in fact allows for a diversity of sexualities and sexual orientations which surpasses the liberalism of even the most open-minded sexologist.[14] The question arises, then, how the relation between theories of biological polymorphousness and social stereotyping produces uncompromisingly rigid formulations of masculinity and femininity.

The first section, "Sexual Diversity," takes as its starting point the (even then) little-respected theory of idioplasm (SC 26), which claimed that all cells in a body carry the body's specific race characteristics (idioplasm seemed to function in much the same way as our layman's understanding of DNA). Weininger transfers this onto the sexual register in order to claim gender character for each cell of the body. Not only is each cell either male or female, but in fact maleness and femaleness are embodied in separate plasmas which appear together in certain amounts in every cell, though these amounts are by no means uniform in all cells across the body. This results in a theory of bisexuality at the biological level, so that sexual difference comes to mean a spectrum of sexual mixing that ranges from ideal maleness to ideal femaleness, whereby one's sexuality is ultimately decided by the sum total of the sexuality of the body's cells. The sheer complexity of this system precludes the possibility of any ideal type appearing in biological reality; therefore, there can be no ideal male or female, only women with degrees of masculinity and men with degrees of femininity. Thus, Weininger effectively rejects the idea of a normative polarized gender system. Recourse to biochemistry "proves" that every person is ultimately bisexual, in a unique ratio of maleness to femaleness.

In this model, sexual attraction works according to reciprocal completion, which means that maximum sexual suitability is achieved when two people make up between them a complete male and a complete female. The positivist in Weininger cannot resist authorizing his law with formulas, often to absurd degrees, so that the law of attraction includes specific variables for "reaction time," distance of separation between the parties, and "all the known and unknown laws of sexual affinity" (SC 44). Despite this "mathematical" grounding, the experimental proof for Weininger's law of sexual affinity consists in showing photographs of "aesthetically beautiful" women to his friends and predicting which one they would find attractive. Since the answer "invariably" matches his prediction, and since he finds in "almost every couple on the street" new proof of his law, he considers himself scientifically vindicated. This method of "proof," obviously, allows social conventions to seep back into his scientific and mathematical law, thereby betraying his dependence on cultural norms. Moreover, the method displays a conventional tendency to define a woman's attractiveness in scopic terms, not to mention defining her sexual role simply in terms of aesthetic objectification. This, too, is an eruption of cultural assumptions into the field of hard science, but it is also a scopocentric sexual attitude which will resurface when Weininger confronts what is, for him, the difficult issue of erotics and aesthetics: why men find women attractive at all.

The "law" of sexual attraction has important implications for homosexuality. "Sexual inversion," to Weininger, is neither acquired nor hereditary; its etiology is unimportant since the homosexual falls onto the same spectrum of sexuality as the heterosexual, although somewhere near the middle, meaning that the homosexual either has as much femaleness as maleness or even more of the gender opposite to the genital indicator. "Inverts" choose their complement according to the same law as heterosexuals. Thus the complement to the male invert would be—no, the answer is not what we might expect. Weininger ultimately shies away from letting men pair up together, even the more "masculine" man with the more "feminine." He demands a more stringent heterosexual basis for formulas of attractions. And since two people must make up one ideal man and one ideal woman, the male invert's complement is supposedly the most man-like woman, the lesbian (SC 60). Only at the end of the chapter does Weininger mention that a male invert's complement may actually be a very male woman or a very female man. The model is unable to explain why homosexuals as well as heterosexuals should make a genital choice in the process of making an object choice based on sexual complementarity. More to the point, Weininger is unwilling to think anything but a heterosexual genital complementarity. Though he derides the practice of deciding sexuality at birth based on genitality, his law of attraction depends on homophobic genital classification while it silences this dependence under the cover of mathematical formulas.

The maleness/femaleness ratio extends as well to mental qualities, which leads Weininger to establish a science of "characterology," in essence a psychology of gender rationing. Despite his insistence on the bisexual status of human beings, however, he claims that they are always "one or the other," either male or female. The passage is notable for its sudden unequivocal reversal of the previous argument: "about human beings it can be said with full psychological certainty that one is first and foremost . . . necessarily either a man or a woman" (SC 97-98; original emphasis). "Full certainty," "first and foremost," "necessarily"—this is the point at which Weininger telescopes the study of sexual diversity into a study of two sexual types with a rhetorical insistence which leaves no room for ambiguity. The shift allows him to develop not a characterology of individuals, but a characterology of the true male and the true female. The female principle, as he defines it, consists of nothing more than sexuality; in fact, because the woman is only sexuality, only an object, she has no subjectivity by which to recognize this about herself. The male, on the other hand, is sexual and "something [read: everything] more." He is a subject who can take himself as its object, and thus has access to the full range of self-knowledge. The female consciousness consists of thought always tainted by feeling, a cloudy sense which Weininger dubs the Henide. Male consciousness, on the other hand, consists of clear, distinct thoughts. Weininger extends the notion of the Henide to establish that the female principle is unconsciousness, linked with the body and sexuality, while the male principle is consciousness, linked with ego and rationality. The woman, moreover, receives clarity and ideas only from the man, so that Weininger ends up with a rather perverse prototype of the claim that Freud makes for the function of psychoanalysis. Weininger writes, "the function of making the unconscious conscious is the sexual function of the man" (*SC* 130). Rather than Freud's "where it [id] was, I [ego] shall be" [*wo es war, soll ich werden*], we have "where woman was, there man shall be." The notion that the female unconsciousness can and is to be masculinized, however, will prove to be the very problem of femininity for Weininger.

This basic differentiation between man and woman is superimposed onto and extended at the philosophical level. Since woman cannot think, she cannot think conceptually; she can neither make judgments, nor desire "truth." She easily loses touch with reality if it stands in the way of her wishes. As a result, her speech consists of lies and errors, but since her very being is a "profound falseness," incapable of conceiving truth and separate from any moral standard, her lies are the measure of her amorality rather than her immorality. Woman can thus feel no "true" guilt. She has no free will, no ego, and, transposing philosophical value into religious value, no soul. A woman's pride is her body; instead of operating from and through her ego, she operates through her body. Nonetheless, having no moral subjectivity, she is devoid of any sense of personal value, so that she constantly demands admiration of her body from the outside, specifically from men. Since woman has no ego, she is always in a state of fusion with everyone she knows; she practices no self-sufficiency, understands no privacy, and is therefore shameless and immodest (the evidence for which supposedly lies in the fact that women undress freely amongst one another, while men seek to cover their nakedness before each other [*SC* 258]). And since a woman has no free will and no boundaries to her individual ego, she is eminently suggestible, taking her ideas and indeed the form of all her conscious thought from man.

Anyone who has read Weininger recognizes the above litany. A parody of Weininger's characterization of woman can only be written as a comic catalogue of lack: she has no ego, no soul, no morality, no thought, *ad nauseum*. Indeed we can afford to laugh, since the catalogue applies only to the absolute female, the "type" which the first section of **Sex and Character** assures us is only an ideal, unrelated to real women. The chapter on "Male and Female Psychology" which generates this catalogue, however, opens with a quiet warning. There is in fact a limitation to the assertions of sexual diversity in the first part of the work, and that limitation applies only to women. Do what she might, the woman (*die Frau* this time, the real woman rather than the female type) *"can never become a man"* (*SC* 241; original emphasis). While it is possible for anatomical men to be psychically either men or women, anatomical women can psychically be *only* women (*SC* 242). For

the woman in Weininger's psychology, anatomy is destiny and the destiny ain't pretty. What begins as a field of biological, psychical, and sexual possibilities closes down around the woman, leaving her with the choice, as posed by Weininger, either of acting out her worthlessness in the field limited to her, the field of sexuality, or of wearing the mask of a moral system not her own and falling ill to the punishment for constitutional female duplicity: hysteria.

THE FEMALE HYSTERIC

In the fall of 1901 Weininger took his nearly completed doctoral dissertation, then entitled *Eros and Psyche*, to the psychologist he most admired, Sigmund Freud. According to Freud, this early version of *Sex and Character* contained "no depreciatory words about the Jews and much less criticism of women" as well as "consideration to my views on hysteria."[15] This "consideration" Freud refers to elsewhere angrily as material written *ad captandam benevolentiam mean,* that is, purely for the gain of his benevolence.[16] And indeed, though Weininger by no means parrots Freud, he does refer in glowing terms to *Studies on Hysteria* and accepts the view laid out there that hysteria is a battle between two "natures," the conscious and the unconscious. He adopts as well Freud's claim that the unconscious is the site of sexual desire, repressed because of its unacceptability to the conscious mind.

From this it is not yet clear why Freud was so angered by Weininger's "tribute" rather than claiming him as a willing disciple. But Weininger, though he describes hysteria as a "continuous alternation between [two] different voices" (*SC* 362), accepts only one of these voices as the real "nature" of the woman. Since the female principle is nothing but sexuality, and woman's own purpose is nothing aside from sexual union, the real nature of woman is revealed in unconscious sexual desire. What struggles against this desire is an artificial moral voice, a slavish imitation of a value system which is "real" only to the man. The woman is so profoundly false, however, that she cannot know her own duplicity; she has no way of distinguishing between self and imitation. Being all body, she can only incorporate [*einverleiben*, literally to take into the body] man's "ethically negative evaluation of sexuality" (*SC* 361), and being all falseness, she takes it for her own and then perceives the "desire for the sexual act" as a "foreign body in her consciousness" (*SC* 360). Weininger says of Freud and Breuer that they were perceptive about the structure of hysteria, but were deceived in their characterization of the hysteric as an eminently moral person; they, in fact, "fell victim" to the hysteric's duplicity as much as she herself (*SC* 366). Hysteria, for Weininger, is not a mysterious functional disturbance with no physiological basis, but "the organic crisis of the organic untruthfulness of the woman" (*SC* 361). The organic nature of female duplicity proves both "how deep the lie sits" and that it does not sit deep enough, since it is powerless completely to repress the woman's true sexual nature, hence her hysteria.

Part of the reason for Freud's anger must surely have been the very closeness of Weininger's understanding of hysteria to his own. After all, Freud's theory of hysteria posits an unconscious sexual nature which is perceived by the hysteric as a foreign body, but is actually more "real" than, in the sense of primary to, the socialized system of reality testing which marks the boundaries of the conscious mind. The cure, moreover, requires that the unconscious sexual material be incorporated into the consciousness, just as Weininger could claim that the crisis of hysteria will end only once the hysteric realizes and accepts her sexual nature, thereby no longer lying to herself about her "organic" duplicity. For Freud, though, hysteria is a specific form of neurosis, whereas Weininger understands it as the crisis condition of *all* women. Nonetheless, if Freud indeed felt "slavishly imitated," then his usual pleasure in being emulated must have been brutally truncated by the realization that very little held his theory of female hysteria apart from Weininger's strident misogyny. The unstable dividing line between hysteria as a form of neurosis and hysteria as the condition of women, after all, approximates Freud's own repeated insistence that the structures of neurosis can be used to clarify the most "everyday" psychic operations.

Weininger invites his readers to consider the larger implications for women of his theory of hysteria. Since hysteria is the organic crisis of woman's natural untruthfulness, one must ask why every woman is not a hysteric. In response, Weininger claims that the hysterical condition arises out of the hysterical constitution, marked by the woman's "passive pliancy" which allows her "to accept simply the complex of male and social values" (*SC* 370). By contrast, the non-hysteric is the woman who lives true to her own sexual nature, who never attempts anything aside from the female tasks: mothering, prostitution, and matchmaking (that is, sexual union for the sake of a child, sexual union for the sake of personal pleasure, and sexual union for the sake of impersonal pleasure). Here we come to the crux of Weininger's characterization of femininity: any sincerity, love of truth, chastity, judgment, or strength of will in a woman is "a part of that pseudo-personality which the woman [*die Frau*] in her passivity has taken up to display before herself and the world" (*SC* 362). Paradoxically, sincerity and will are marks of the woman's untruthfulness and pliancy, and must therefore lead her, given any precipitation, into the hysterical condition of self-contradiction. Only the insincere woman lives out her nature, thereby avoiding hysteria. This, then, is Weininger's answer to women's demands for emancipation as well as to men who want to protect the Victorian image of the sensitive, moral woman. It is the conclusion to which Freud did not want his theory of hysteria taken. Weininger's conclusion must by its very theoretical proximity have threatened Freud's cherished claim that he himself was not in any way misogynistic, suggesting that Freud read in *Sex and Character* only too clearly the bitterly misogynistic potential, if not basis, of his own theories of hysterical women.

THE MALE HYSTERIC IN (SELF-)LOVE

In the chapter entitled "Erotics and Aesthetics," Weininger momentarily shifts his project from the psychology of women to the psychology of men, specifically of those men whom he expects to disagree with his characterization of the true woman. He forestalls the accusation of misogyny by reading it as a tactic of vindication undertaken by those who cannot or will not intellectually refute his arguments. This is, of course, a tried and true counter-defense, but Weininger adds polish to it by reading the accusation of misogyny itself as a pathological symptom of most *men:* "the huge majority of men . . . never *want* to see the woman clearly" (*SC* 315; original emphasis) because they cherish notions of woman's tenderness, sympathy, and virtue, that is, of her worthiness to be loved. By explaining the psychology of love, Weininger intends to provide what amounts to a curative service for these men, since if they only understood the reasons for their false beliefs, they too "would give due weight to the reality which so conflicts with their wishes" (*SC* 316). In other words, according to his own gender theory, Weininger's function here is to make the (male, heterosexual) unconscious conscious. In the process of performing this function, Weininger feminizes the "huge majority of men" to whom he writes (who are like women in that they need their unconscious wishes turned into conscious ideas) in tandem with his own emphatic masculinization (as the explicator who makes conscious). From this stance of superior knowledge and secure masculinity, however, the text begins to unravel and the fantasms behind Weininger's theory of female hysteria begin to appear. Love is a dangerous topic for Weininger, sliding irrevocably into questions of sexuality and desire. "Erotics and Aesthetics," ostensibly about men and idealized love, turns out to be about women and the sexual body, revealing a male hysterical anxiety about unstable genders and sexualities.

Weininger situates love, or what he calls eroticism, by distinguishing it emphatically from sexuality; love and sexuality in Weininger's understanding not only oppose one another, but are mutually exclusive. Love depends for its stimulation on separation and distance, while sexual desire depends on the opposite—physical intimacy. This means that "bodily union" is "fully unthinkable" (*SC* 319) when one loves, and love, by extension, has no part in the sexual act. Philosophically stated, the distance is necessary because it allows for the idealization of the object. And without idealizing her, Weininger implies, how could one imagine loving a woman?

> Who is the object of this love? The same woman who has here been described, without one quality to which value attaches, the woman without the will to attain value on her own account? Hardly—it is the transcendentally beautiful, the angelically pure woman, who is loved with this love. (*SC* 320)

At issue here is more than the idealization made possible by nearsighted vision. Though he does not state it explicitly, Weininger considers the woman permanently tainted by the touch of male sexual desire. Twice he lets slip reference to this taint, once in the context of the woman being ruined as a love object for the man who has desired her ("He who claims still to love a woman whom he has desired is either lying or has never known what love is" [*SC* 319]), and once in the context of her being ruined by this desire for any man to follow ("the woman who has been handled, possessed, will not be adored for her beauty by anyone again" [*SC* 323]). In both cases, once the woman has become the object of the sexual touch, even the metaphorical touch of desire, no man will see the idealized beauty necessary for loving her again. What has obviously come between love and its aesthetic object is *contact,* actual or imagined, with the woman. It is this fear of contact with the female sexual body, I contend, which lies at the heart of Weininger's misogynistic philosophy and makes of his putatively philosophical treatise a male hysterical narrative.

Despite the fact that Weininger insists all along that woman is synonymous with her body, the equivalence poses a peculiar problem for his aesthetics of love. A beautiful woman can be loved, but her body cannot be beautiful. The woman lends herself to aesthetic idealization, but the female body does not. As though he were in training for a Freudian case history, Weininger claims that the naked living woman, in contrast to an artistic image of woman, cannot be beautiful because she gives the impression "of something unfinished, of straining after something outside of her" (*SC* 321). This sense of something missing fills the male spectator with a feeling of aversion [*Unlust*] in the place of aesthetic/erotic pleasure. What Weininger misses in the spectacle presented by the living female body is, to put it bluntly, the penis. If this seems too tendentious or reductive a reading, then we need only look to the next sentence, which claims that this sense of "something unfinished" in the naked woman appears most strongly when she is standing, less so when she is lying down. And if that is still not convincing, the following paragraph declaims the ugliness of the female genitals outright. What Weininger wants to see on a woman, what will for him complete the scopic body beautiful, is a phallus.

This contemplation of the difference between the living woman and her representation can easily be read as the unveiling of Weininger's castration anxiety. Artistic representations of the naked woman, for Weininger, can be beautiful precisely because they leave veiled, if only by a hand, her nakedness and weakness [*Blösse*, meaning both]. The naked woman herself, on the other hand, reveals her lack, the "something missing," precisely at the spot where the something that causes visual pleasure should be. Given Weininger's fixation on "something missing," the lack which makes the female genitals ugly, it is tempting to argue that he suffers fear of castration at projected contact with the already-castrated woman and that this castration anxiety manifests itself in the guise of misogynistic aesthetic theory. But this would take us no further than Freud's footnote about

Weininger's unresolved castration complex. The challenge here is not to diagnose Weininger's individual pathology. More interesting is to consider the textual resonances around the representation of the (missing) phallus and to question particularly the desiring position which the phallus as fantasm articulates. I aim to read this passage not for the absence of the phallus on the woman (the basis for the castration anxiety narrative), but rather for its intrusive *presence* around and beyond her as a textually palpable desire. For the text does not so much agonize over the woman's lack as insist on her missing something in order to present her with a phallus from elsewhere. My point, then, is that Weininger's anxiety about the female sexual body stems from the fact that the woman's incompleteness, to the male gaze, suggests the actual object desired by this spectator: the phallic *male* body.

The passage here turns not on castration, but rather on a reified, *un*castratable phallus. The woman, as Weininger characterizes her, strives as her one goal to fill the space of the "something missing" with the phallus and thereby complete herself: "the phallus completely dominates the entire life of the woman [*die Frau*], though often only in the unconscious" (*SC* 341). Since she lacks the ethical capacity to be an aesthetic subject like the man, this desire is not a question of an aesthetic choice, or of any choice at all; it is so necessary, in fact, as to be characterized not as a desire but a destiny. The phallus is that "for which she has no name; it is her destiny, it is that which she cannot escape" (*SC* 341). She perceives it similarly to "the man seeing the Medusa's head, or the bird seeing the snake; it has a hypnotising, spellbinding, fascinating effect on her." The phallus—for the woman, but also as a textual effect—has the potency of a supernatural fetish, an object that simultaneously fascinates and terrifies. This is the phallus which clearly cannot brook castration. From the spellbound gaze of the woman cowering before her destiny, the phallus is identical with the man and with her desire. But in making this argument the text produces an affective remainder which disrupts precisely the rigorous separation between the male gaze and female object which the psychology of love is meant to uphold.

The woman who suffers "something missing" does not herself yearn for completion. Because she is unconscious and therefore not self-aware, she never perceives her incompleteness. This is left to the male spectator, who misses the phallus when he tries to fit the naked woman into a visual frame of pleasure. The text moves directly from claiming that something is missing from the woman as visual object to reifying the phallus as the completion of feminine subjectivity, but this quick transition elides the first and foremost function of the missing phallus: to make of the incomplete female body a desirable male body. This, in effect, is the desire of the male spectator as positioned in the text; only he can identify the woman's desire and thereby he finds himself identified *in* it. Homosexual desire surfaces as man's identification of woman's incompleteness. According to Weininger's philosophy of gender relations, the defining characteristic of the woman, her unconsciousness, means that the male spectator is required to make her incompleteness conscious: Where it ["the female"] was, I [the man] shall be, to paraphrase Freud. It is in this interstice between feminine unconsciousness and male mastery that homosexual desire threatens the entire system of rigidly separate gender stereotypes. Just as in the first section of *Sex and Character,* Weininger could conceive of the homosexual's desired object only in terms of heterosexual complementarity, so now homosexual desire surfaces cast in the terms of woman's heterosexual destiny.

Male homosexual desire can be expressed only as a detour through (heterosexual) femininity and, similarly, the detour through femininity bespeaks male homosexual desire. Weininger's theory of love—the answer to the question of how a man could love a woman at all—makes the same detour, but does so more visibly. Weininger in fact claims that man never loves the woman, because no woman can ever be worthy of his love; instead, he projects onto her the highest moral ideal of himself, and loves in her the self he wishes to become:

> *In all love, man loves only himself.* . . . He projects his ideal of an absolutely worthy being, which he is not capable of isolating in himself, onto another human being—this and nothing else is the meaning of his loving this being. (*SC* 324, 325; my emphasis)

Love, in other words, operates homo-narcissistically. The man loves his best self, that is, a masculine ideal (both an ideal of masculinity and an ideal that is male) in whom he misrecognizes the woman. Through her, he loves a(nother) man. Weininger does his best to refer to the object of this love as a "being" [*das Wesen*] and thereby to keep gender specification at bay, but the issue of gender resurfaces under the guise of a guilt which Weininger claims the man feels whenever he loves. This guilt has numerous sources as Weininger outlines them, but stems at bottom from the fact that love must detour through the woman. Love has its birth in guilt-consciousness [*Schuldbewusstsein*], because the male lover is fully dependent on the woman, his unequivocal inferior, in order to love the best in himself. Again, the rhetoric of this claim attempts to erase the woman by referring instead to *der Mensch:* "I want something from the person [*der Mensch*] whom I love . . . instead of searching and striving further, I want to take from the hand of the person next to me nothing less, nothing else, than myself" (*SC* 330). The hand of the "person" next to the man, though, is the female hand, which establishes him as dependent on the woman for his most transcendental emotion. Interestingly, the emphasis on guilt which Weininger links with the heterosexual love relation slowly becomes an obsession with love itself as a crime. Weininger ends the section on (self-)love by calling the lover a criminal. Surely this "crime" has at its base two competing sources of horror for Weininger:

one, that the male lover is dependent in his love on a woman and also that in a woman he loves a man.

The criminal is no abstract category for Weininger. In the months before his death, in his journals and aphorisms he returned again and again to the themes of guilt and crime, and their relation to suicide.[17] And in an earlier bout of suicidal depression, during which his friend Artur Gerber stayed up the night with him, Weininger accused himself of being not only a criminal, but a murderer (as we will see, Weininger claimed in his treatise not only that love is a crime, but that it amounts to murder).[18] From this one might spin biographical narratives about Weininger's own "crime" of homosexual love, particularly in relation to Artur Gerber, the one friend whom he trusted to comfort him in his bouts of depression. Yet what evidence exists for these narratives is couched in the metaphoric language of Weininger's increasingly incoherent philosophy. Not even in the personal correspondence to Gerber does Weininger discuss his own desire or sexuality. My point in reading the homosexual nuances of *Sex and Character* is therefore not to "out" Weininger as gay, since such a claim has little support and would be anachronistic at best. Rather, what I find important here is the way in which homosexual desire is produced *by* the text against the very heterosexual gender system it elaborates. Homosexuality as textual affect disrupts precisely that system which is meant to make it unthinkable. If, as I would suggest, we read *Sex and Character* as a project of masculinist self-understanding, a project whose misogyny is the necessary agent for the construction of a stable masculinity, then what is revealed by the production of disruptive homosexual affect is the very inadequacy of the terms available to Weininger for thinking masculinity. Ultimately, masculinity thus collapses into femininity, male self-love becomes self-hatred, and hysteria, even in Weininger's terms, no longer applies exclusively to the woman.

THE MALE HYSTERIC IN (SELF-)HATRED

Much has been written about Weininger and self-hatred in the context of his own Judaism.[19] A brief footnote to the anti-Semitic chapter in *Sex and Character,* which aligns Jews with femininity and then denounces them as an even worse form of woman's negative subjectivity, claims unobtrusively that the author himself comes from "a Jewish background" [*judenstämmig*]. In fact, Weininger's connection to Judaism is closer than he allows; he grew up in a Jewish household where he remained through the writing of his doctoral dissertation, converting to Protestantism barely one month after receiving his doctorate.[20] Weininger himself uses the term self-hatred and provides a definition for it. For him, love and hate function in the same way, through the mechanism of projection (*SC* 326). Whereas with love, one projects onto and loves in another those values which one cannot find in oneself, with hate one unconsciously isolates the intolerable in oneself, projects it onto another, and then hates it as something separate from oneself. (As an example of the projective mechanism of hatred, Weininger tellingly claims that anti-Semites are precisely the people who unconsciously recognize and hate the "psychological characteristics" of the Jew in themselves.) Whether it takes a positive or negative form, the mechanism is reflexive, so that one actually loves or hates oneself in a detour through the other. In *Sex and Character* these "others," Weininger's objects of love and hate, are clearly personified. Aside from the anti-Semitic chapter which reads Jews as worse forms of women, only two other characters people *Sex and Character:* the male genius and the worthless woman. The roles that each of these characters play should by now be clear; the genius represents the object of Weininger's self-love, his masculine ideal, while the woman—standing in also for the Jew—represents the object of his self-hatred, the fantasized crime he cannot escape.

Love is murder, Weininger bluntly claims (*SC* 334), because it commits cruelty to the woman by using her simply as a screen onto which higher values can be projected (*SC* 326). Her own individual attributes never appear, masked as they are by the projected masculine ideal. Love thus annihilates the woman in the very structure of loving. Weininger's sudden apparent compassion for the hitherto worthless woman should surprise us. As a writer who, for three hundred pages, has consistently denied the woman any characteristics but sexuality and corporeality, Weininger should invite our suspicion that he now is so concerned with the demise of a woman's "real attributes" (*SC* 334). I would agree that the woman, as Weininger constructs her, is murdered at the site of love, but not as an effect of love, as he claims, so much as an abjection which attempts to defend the male lover against a collapse into femininity. The "crime" of love, to the extent that it must detour through the woman, is that it feminizes the man; in loving a male ideal through her, his position collapses into that of the woman, the being who gives "the impression of something incomplete, of striving after something outside of herself" (*SC* 321). Both the man and the woman strive for something outside of themselves, he for the masculine ideal and she for a missing body part, but in so doing they are marked by the same phallic lack. If the collapse into femininity thus threatens the distanced relationship that is love, then it presses even more frighteningly in the sexual relationship, which requires that the man unite himself bodily with the woman's lack and desire what she desires, the actual phallus. It is here, where contact with the female sexual body and homosexual desire overlap, that the projective mechanism of hatred becomes inseparable from that of love. Loving the masculine ideal, then, means hating the woman, and through her hating oneself.

Love *is* murder. It sets Weininger into a frenzy and sends him into a series of hysterical attempts to contain the woman's influence, to control her existence, and finally to erase her altogether.

From at least a cipher onto which the male lover projects his ideal of masculinity, Weininger turns her into a nothing that needs to be said twice: "Women [*die Frauen;* note the plural] have no existence and no essence; they *are* nothing, they are *nothing*" (*SC* 388; original emphasis). Out of this nothing, she comes into being only through man's sexual desire for her:

> It is only when the man affirms his own sexuality, when he negates the Absolute, turning away from eternal life and to the lower life, that the woman [*das Weib*] receives her existence. *Only* when the something comes to nothing can the nothing come to *something* (*SC* 405; original emphasis).

Ultimately, man is responsible for bringing the woman into existence, but in doing so he threatens himself with his own annihilation (as "something comes to nothing"). Conversely, if men deny their sexuality, as Weininger advises, even pleads, then they deny women existence, since women take their single-faceted being only through repeated sexual concourse with men. Deny male sexuality, and the woman will simply disappear. And with her, so the fantasy implies, will disappear the Jew, whom she represents, and male homosexual desire, which detours through her. This is finally for Weininger the necessary condition of masculine stability: the refusal of sexual contact and even sexuality as such.

Weininger's theory of hysteria thus resurfaces as an unwitting analysis of the condition of unstable masculinity. Like the hysteric, the man struggles against a sexual nature which he perceives to be foreign to the moral and spiritual nature of the male conscious self. As with the hysteric, these two selves are not coded simply as natural and unnatural, but are gendered, so that man struggles against a sexuality coded as feminine by having recourse to the masculine code of morality, will, intelligence. Supposedly, sexuality represents the woman's "real" self, against which her morality is only an imitation of the masculine, while the man's moral sense is "real" whereas sexuality is a detour into femininity. But if Weininger can claim that man creates the woman by desiring her, if male sexual desire brings woman into being as its consequence, then that which is insistently coded as feminine—sexuality—must already be an aspect of masculinity. The demon of femininity, then, is within. The male hysteric ultimately hates the woman not because he is horrified by her castrated otherness, but because she is *already* inside him, internalized in the very process of masculine self-understanding. No amount of textual containment and control of the woman, therefore, can ever successfully eject her from masculinity as Weininger painstakingly elaborates it. Weininger's recommended social "cure," that men reject their sexual desire in order to refuse the woman being, is thus a desperate defensive attack against the collapse of masculinity into femininity. Increasingly, what Weininger most fears, his "criminality," is something he understands in terms of gender collapse: "the most stupid, the rawest" criminal, the criminal most worthy of contempt, is the man who becomes a woman (*SC* 404). Becoming a woman, he claims, is "that deepest fear in man: . . . the fear of the alluring abyss of nothingness" (*SC* 404). The profoundest criminal is thus the male version of the hysteric, the man in whom the feminine, sexual body exists in contradiction with his masculine ego. As the journals suggest, Weininger considered himself to be such a criminal. He berated himself for his criminality and finally gave in to the "alluring abyss of nothingness," choosing the nothingness of death over the nothingness of becoming feminine. If love indeed for Weininger means the murder of the woman, then his final act was to murder his own feminine identification.

The work of textual production, creating himself as the male philosophical voice which produces masculinist self-understanding, ultimately fails Weininger. His misogynistic approach positions the woman as the devalued object of a knowing male gaze in order to hold apart male and female "characters" and to inscribe himself in the masculine position of self-knowledge. Weininger attempts to produce a stable concept of masculinity into which he can write himself, thereby keeping his hysterical identifications at bay. But the theory of (female) hysteria produces, despite itself, the (male) hysterical text. From the early draft, *Eros and Psyche,* to **Sex and Character,** the defamation of women becomes more radical as the defensive strategy becomes more desperate while, as Weininger's late journals indicate, this strategy is accompanied by his own increasing sense of criminality. Unable to control the collapse of intellectual masculinity into bodily femininity, Weininger annihilates his own body in order to leave behind, in the form of his masterwork, the image of the masculine ideal—himself as genius. Such a violent separation, of course, cost him his life.

Ultimately, the importance of **Sex and Character** to early twentieth-century intellectual culture indicates that this is more than the narrative of one man's struggle with personal demons. Weininger's suicide, coming so quickly after the publication of his treatise, acts out the untenability of the turn-of-the-century masculinist position taken to the extreme. Weininger did not create an anti-feminine gender philosophy from pathological scratch; he distilled from available cultural material the misogyny whose terms he used to stabilize his own problematic sense of masculinity. Admittedly it is the extreme nature of his misogyny which makes him a simultaneously fascinating and disturbing figure, but we should be aware that his misogyny reflects contemporary cultural forms. Misogyny in its purest form operates, then as now, as a cultural fantasy. And precisely because it is a fantasy, one of many circulating in the cultural space, its terms are not by any means coherent, particularly at the Anglo-European turn of the century when gender and sexual relations were undergoing such violent social and political upheavals. One could say that Weininger's work was and remains fascinating because he translated the misogynistic fantasy of his period wholesale into a philosophical system. His masculinist philosophy thus manifests the incoherence of the cul-

tural fantasy, in that it shows the inadequacy of the terms available to this culture for thinking masculinity in a terrain of shifting gender relations. To its (male) readers, **Sex and Character** promised the consolation of stable masculinity, but Weininger's suicide, written into the margins of the text for the reader, simultaneously undermined this stability and warned that such an extremist position was untenable. Hence the double-edged fascination exerted so widely by Weininger's work: it made the "pleasures" of misogyny supremely available, but also suggested that the cultural fantasy of misogyny—and by extension of masculinity—could not be lived out.

NOTES

[1] Otto Weininger, *Geschlecht und Charakter,* 3rd ed. (Vienna and Leipzig: Wilhelm Braumüller, 1904) v. Also republished with the same page numbering as *Geschlecht und Charakter* (Munich: Matthes und Seitz, 1980). Further references to the former edition will be hereafter noted parenthetically in the article as *SC*. Translations mine.

[2] According to Weininger, only a man can describe women in such a way as to write their rigorous psychology: "If we grant that a woman could describe herself with the required sharpness, it does not necessarily follow that she would be interested in the things that most interest us; moreover, even if she could and would know herself fully—let us assume the case—we still have to ask ourselves if she could be brought to talk about herself" (*SC* 106-07).

[3] Jacques Le Rider, *Der Fall Otto Weininger: Wurzeln des Antifeminismus und Antisemitismus* (Vienna and Munich: Löcker, 1985) 221.

[4] Interestingly, *Sex and Character* was not translated into French until 1975. Since there was certainly communication (albeit often antagonistic) between the intellectual and professional circles of Vienna and Paris at the turn of the century, this indicates not a lack of opportunity for translation so much as a cultural barrier to translation.

[5] Ferdinand Probst, *Der Fall Otto Weininger. Eine psychiatrische* Studie, Grenzfragen des Nerven- und Seelenlebens, *Einzel-Darstellungen für Gebildete aller Stände* (Wiesbaden: J. F. Bergmann, 1904) xxxi.

[6] David Abrahamsen, *The Mind and Death of a Genius* (New York: Columbia UP, 1946).

[7] In England, scattered references to Weininger appear in Edward Carpenter's *The Intermediate Sex,* in Bram Stoker's *Lady Athlyne,* in Wyndham Lewis's *The Art of Being Ruled,* and in the journals of D.H. Lawrence. For the last, see Emile Delavenay, "D.H. Lawrence, Otto Weininger and 'rather raw philosophy,'" *D. H. Lawrence: New Studies,* ed. Christopher Heywood (Lon-

don: Macmillan, 1984). For responses from Kraus and Strindberg, see *Die Fackel,* 17 October 1903 and 23 November 1903.

[8] During Weininger's lifetime, P. J. Möbius published a review of *Sex and Character* which admits that there are "many good things in it" (quoted in Abrahamsen 137f), but attributes them all to plagiarism of his own work, *On the Physiological Feeble-Mindedness of Women,* which had appeared in 1900. Weininger responded by demanding that Möbius retract his accusation or face charges of slander, but the latter only extended his criticism and published it in pamphlet form in 1904, after Weininger's death (as *Geschlecht und Unbescheidenheit*). The second accusation of plagiarism, involving Freud's one-time friend Wilhelm Fliess, was more complicated. Fliess accused Weininger of having plagiarized the notion of human bisexuality from him, with Hermann Swoboda and Sigmund Freud acting as intermediaries (the former was a patient of Freud's at the time that Weininger was working on his dissertation). Though Freud quickly removed himself from this entanglement by ending his correspondence with Fliess a second time, Fliess considered the affront important enough to make the charges public in two separate texts both published in 1906 (*Der Ablauf des Lebens* and a monograph devoted entirely to the plagiarism affair, *In eigener Sache: gegen Otto Weininger und Hermann Swoboda*). Swoboda himself responded with a pamphlet in the same year (*Die gemeinnützige Forschung und der eigennützige Forscher*). Both these plagiarism cases and the lengths to which the affronted parties went to publicize their ownership of intellectual property indicate that Weininger was indeed taken seriously by members of the contemporary German scientific community.

[9] *Neues Wiener Tagesblatt* 14 June 1903.

[10] *Westen und Daheim* 2 Aug. 1903. The reviewer leaves it unclear whether women will not be Weininger's readers because they will be offended by him or because they simply will not be able to keep up with his "all-encompassing learning and scholarly expressions." In other words, the reviewer leaves his agreement with Weininger as to the abilities and character of women ambivalently unstated.

[11] *Die Wage* 29 Aug. 1903.

[12] *Die Wage* 29 Aug. 1903: "He thinks his thoughts to the most extreme results. We are indignant about these results, but we admire the relentlessness of the thinker."

[13] Nike Wagner, *Geist und Geschlecht: Karl Kraus und die Erotik der Wiener Moderne* (Frankfurt/Main: Suhrkamp, 1987) 70.

[14] In the opening years of the twentieth century, this "most open-minded sexologist" would best be represented by Freud in *Three Essays on Sexuality* (1905).

[15] Letter to David Abrahamsen, 11 June 1939, quoted in Abrahamsen 208.

[16] Abrahamsen 55.

[17] See Otto Weininger, *Taschenbuch und Briefe an einen Freund,* ed. Arthur Gerber (1919; Leipzig and Vienna: E.P. Tal, 1921).

[18] Artur Gerber, introduction, *Taschenbuch und Briefe an einen Freund,* by Otto Weininger 8.

[19] See Sander Gilman, *Jewish Self-Hatred* (Baltimore: Johns Hopkins UP, 1986) 244-47; Theodor Lessing, *Der jüdische Selbsthass* (1930; Munich: Matthes and Seitz, 1984); and Le Rider 189-219.

[20] Le Rider 33.

Nancy A. Harrowitz (essay date 1995)

SOURCE: "Weininger and Lombroso: A Question of Influence," in *Jews & Gender: Responses to Otto Weininger,* edited by Nancy A. Harrowitz and Barbara Hyams, Temple University Press, 1995, pp. 73-90.

[*In the following essay, Harrowitz examines possible cultural and literary influences on Weininger, particularly Cesare Lombroso.*]

To better understand Otto Weininger and the influence of his *Sex and Character,* we need to better comprehend both the cultural context in which Weininger and his book appeared and other texts that may have influenced him. This may seem to be an obvious and clear task, but the issues surrounding Weininger's text are anything but obvious and clear, and so the task becomes fraught with difficulties. The concerns that a reading of Weininger raises—the dynamics of self-hatred, the question of the importance of milieu and historical context, the relations between different kinds of prejudice, for example—are not only polemical but diabolically complex.

A familiarity with the work of Cesare Lombroso is important to the project of comprehending Weininger for several reasons.[1] The first is a question of sources, since Weininger makes direct reference to Lombroso's work on women in the footnotes to *Sex and Character.* The others have to do with similarities between the two authors that go beyond Weininger's indebtedness to Lombroso for certain of his theories. These similarities paved the way for the warm welcome that a generation of Italian intellectuals gave Weininger's theories in the early part of this century. Finally, an examination of the relation of Lombroso to Weininger illustrates the problem of how to consider influence, whether it is the influence of intertextuality or that of historical context.

Cesare Lombroso was a well known and highly influential Italian criminologist who also considered himself a (pre-Freudian) psychiatrist. Lombroso's attempts to standardize an approach to the criminal resulted in his categories of the physical signs of a criminal body. Lombroso was born in Turin in 1835 and died in 1909. Educated as a doctor, his main interests included psychiatry and anthropometry, and he describes himself in his 1894 text *L'antisemitismo e le scienze moderne* (Antisemitism and Modern Science) as a practitioner of psychiatry and experimental anthropology. Lombroso was generally considered the greatest prison reformer since Cesare Beccaria. Some of his ideas, such as indeterminate sentencing, parole, and juvenile court, are still widely used in the United States. Along with Lombroso's innovative ideas regarding the criminal mind and body came a whole set of categories governing what might be called the "management of cultural difference." According to this approach, if society can understand the physical as well as the moral dimensions of crime, it can better contain its criminal elements.

During his time, and for at least thirty years after his death, Lombroso's theories were taken very seriously by scientists and the general public alike. Leon Radzinowicz writes that "virtually every element of value in contemporary criminological knowledge owes its formulation to that very remarkable school of Italian criminologists who took pride in describing themselves as the 'positivists'" (quoted in Lombroso-Ferrero 1972, IX). According to Leonard D. Savitz, who wrote the introduction to the most current edition in translation of Lombroso's *Criminal Man,* there is a general consensus that Lombroso and the school of positivist criminology that resulted from his theories had a tremendous impact on the development of criminology, and the country in which his theories had the most influence was the United States.[2]

In the later stage of his career, Lombroso turned his attention to two cultural targets that were much closer to him than the world of the criminal: woman and the Jew. The choice of subject is not surprising, since scientists since Darwin had been trying to understand the place of the female in evolution, and racialist science had been studying the Jew in relation to some of the same questions raised by studies of women and other groups. What perhaps is surprising is that Lombroso waited so long to study these two groups. In 1893 he published (with his son-in-law Guglielmo Ferrero) *La donna delinquente, la prostituta e la donna normale* (The Criminal Woman, the Prostitute, and the Normal Woman), thus turning his attention to the "fairer" sex. Fairer on the outside, perhaps, but with an atavistic viciousness lying just under the surface of calm, serene, and idealized nineteenth-century womanhood. We note a distinct difference between Lombroso's treatment of the male criminal, set forth in his 1879 text *L'uomo delinquente* (Criminal Man), and the female. Lombroso, in identifying the *"criminale nato"* (born criminal), does not attempt to define what is particularly "male" about these criminals. He does connect criminal behavior with atavistic signs that link the criminal with a primitive, savage world. When Lombroso concentrates on the female of the criminal species, as it were, the focus of analysis changes as he attempts to define what is female, as if the question "What is female?" were as important as "What is the female criminal?" In fact, he ultimately conflates these two questions, making his interpretation of the identity of the prostitute a middle ground to facilitate this move between the identity of woman and that of the female criminal. Just what *is* female for Lombroso, in the "normative" sense he sets out to establish, is laid forth in the last section of this long text.[3] For Lombroso, the three terms "woman criminal," "prostitute," and "woman," were inseparable, and he theorizes this inseparability over and over.

Criminality becomes the model by which to understand woman, because, as Lombroso repeats many times, the normal woman is but a criminal whose immoral, criminal tendencies are kept in abeyance by maternal instincts and by society. These points are made repeatedly in *La donna delinquente,* as he refers to "that latent base of immorality that is found in every woman" and "that latent base of evil that is found in every woman."[4] Woman's salvation—and, it would appear, also her damnation—is physiology: "maternity is, we would almost say, itself a moral vaccination against crime and evil."[5] It appears that not only maternity but also culture and bourgeois society help to keep the criminal tendencies in women at bay. Culture, for the male, is instead his product, and thus the male criminal, criminal behavior, immorality, and the like are atavistic throwbacks. The "normal" male hence has no connection to atavism. There is the sense here that the male criminal is in fact ultimately not responsible for his condition, because of the compelling force of atavism. Women on the other hand are all potential criminals, and only the soothing forces of culture and their maternal physiology may or may not keep this criminality suppressed.

Women are continually described by Lombroso as "closer to nature" than men: more atavistic, closer to her ancestor, the female savage. The sexual nature of primitive woman provides another link to modern woman, as Lombroso asserts that "if primitive woman was only rarely an assassin, she was, as we have proved above [. . .], always a prostitute, and remained thus almost until the semicivilized epoch; so even atavistically one can explain that the prostitute must have more regressive traits than the female criminal."[6]

Lombroso goes to great lengths to explain both his conception of the prostitute and the history of prostitution, since he believes that this history will shed light on modern woman. Another important aspect of prostitutes is their virility, precisely that which, according to Lombroso, makes them less female. Certain physical characteristics mark them as virile; for example, he describes the masculine larynx he claims is often found on prostitutes—"one would say the larynx of a man. And thus in the larynx, as well as the face and the cranium, the characteristics particular to them come out: virility"—and notes as well the "virile distribution of hair" found in many prostitutes.[7] He then offers a theory of the mutability of the characteristics of the young prostitute as she ages:

> Even in the most beautiful criminals, however, their virile aspect—the exaggeration of the jaw, the cheekbones—is never missing, just as it is never missing in any of our great courtesans. Thus they all have a familial look which links the Russian sinners to those who pound the streets, whether they be gilded carriages or humble rags. When youth disappears, those jaws and plump rounded cheeks give way to prominent angles and makes the face completely virile, uglier than a man. Wrinkles deepen like a wound, and that once pleasing face shows the degenerate type which youth had hidden.[8]

We see in this description a discursive shifting from a scientific mode of observation ("the exaggeration of the jaw, the cheekbones") to a more poetic one ("wrinkles deepen like a wound"). This shifting ultimately ends in stereotyping: the image of the beautiful woman turns out to be but a façade, with an ugly wrinkled hag—a virile one in this case—lying just underneath the surface that youth provides. The underlying notion is of the woman as trickster and as falsification personified as she seduces her client through her youthful appearance, which hides the "man" underneath. The idea that a certain type of woman is really a man under the surface is compounded by what she does for a living, as it were. The fact that she sells sex, what is supposed to be specifically female sex, to her male clients, and that Lombroso is suggesting that she is not really female at all, casts an even more onerous light on the situation. What is being sold is pure artifice, then: not female, thus not female sex, but rather a kind of androgynous, falsified, and cheating substitution.

The contradiction in Lombroso's analysis of the prostitute is apparent: the "normal" woman is closer to nature, in other words more atavistic, than man. Primitive woman, as he states openly, equals prostitution. Yet the prostitute is figured as virile. So what is less female is at the same time more: more atavistic, i.e., more prostitute; more prostitute, less female. This confusion of categories is emblematic of Lombroso and provides a thematic link to the work of Weininger inasmuch as both attempt to theorize gender difference.

Lombroso, like some other nineteenth-century scientists, believed that women had much in common with children. They lie "naturally," he says, as if lying were part of their natures. At the beginning of the section of *La donna delinquente* entitled "Lie," Lombroso tells us that "to show that the lie is habitual and almost physiological to women would be superfluous because it is so widespread in popular legend." He then lists ten proverbs, such as "women always say the truth, but never in its entirety," and "women—says Dohm—use lies like the bull uses his horns."[9] He follows up the proverbs

with citations from Flaubert, Schopenhauer, Zola, Molière, and Stendhal, all claiming the purported propensity of women to untruth.

Lombroso makes no distinction between quotations from the literary creations of these authors and direct statements from the authors themselves regarding the subject. In his analysis of what is female (and how male culture can manage to live with the female), Lombroso often uses proverbs to back up his conclusions. His adoption of cultural expressions such as proverbs and sayings to make a "scientific" point is the most audacious part of his argument, and shows the irrefutable link between the cultural prejudices he draws upon as evidence and his own bias toward the subject. No distance is thus taken between the proverbs Lombroso cites, the cultural voices he quotes, and the personal opinions and conclusions he expresses regarding women and lying.

According to Lombroso, women are morally deficient, vengeful, and jealous. In his discussion of women criminals, he points out their shortcomings and excesses in the area of language, saying that "one understands how the chattering about the crime is more frequent in the woman than in the man, because she must supplement all those means that the male has to relive the image of the crime, like drawings and writing, that we see lacking in the woman. The woman speaks often of her crimes, just as the man draws them, writes about them, or sculpts them in vases, etc."[10]

It would seem that women criminals, in Lombroso's appraisal, talk too much and write too little. Elsewhere he tells us that women are lacking skills and development in the graphic area of the brain, which would explain their reluctance or inability to write at a very sophisticated level. He tells us also that women criminals quite literally cannot keep their mouths shut about their crimes, that they are compelled to tell someone about them and to brag about them. At the same time, they will stick to the most audacious lies, even when confronted with absolute proof of their ridiculousness. Lombroso concludes from this that women have a poor sense of reality when it comes to truth, that reality is actually estranged from them in some way. His pinpointing of language as a locus of attack is significant in that language is very often, in the discourse of bigotry, exactly that part of the culture of difference that is singled out as particularly threatening. The charge that women lie, are unreliable linguistically, are underdeveloped in this area, and do not understand the difference between truth and lies thus fits into a more general attack. If the language of difference can be made out as entirely unreliable, then it proves in some way that the difference is unreliable, threatening, and unstable as well, not part of culture, unacceptable because of the threat of the unknown that it poses. Sander Gilman's landmark study of antisemitism and the role that language plays in the establishment of categories of intolerance demonstrates this point (Gilman 1986).

Lombroso's views of women discussed above proclaim a correlation to Weininger's text and show why Lombroso's theories would have appealed to Weininger. We can go beyond the question of directly cited textual influence and look at Lombroso's views on women and Jews together: a juxtapositioning that pulls Lombroso and Weininger even closer together than the citation of a few footnotes would suggest. As a major proponent of an important part of that new science, the originator of the atavistic theory of the criminal, Lombroso was thought to be the scientist who could challenge the theoreticians of antisemitism on their scientific methodologies and overall merit. Lombroso did just this with his text of 1894, a purported defense of the Jews from the biologically based racism developing at the time.

Lombroso begins his text by explaining its origin in the requests he received to write it and the investigative urge that spurred him on. As he says of antisemitism, "I felt that disgust that seizes even the least impatient scientist when he has to study the most revolting human secretions. Deciding whether hatred between peoples can be justified, in our times, is certainly a difficult and sad enterprise, and it is not easy to get comfortable with it."[11] Lombroso insists in this introduction that the new methods available to him from psychiatry and experimental anthropology, and his own new method of scientific inquiry, "safeguarded me against the perils of partiality, so great in matters like this."[12] Later in the preface, after listing some of the materials and authors he has consulted in his study, he says that "the help of such assorted experts from the nations richest with antisemites and with philosemites was a token to me of the rectitude and the impartiality of my judgment, for he who doubts the instrument that I have handled for a short period of time."[13] Clinging to his role as dispassionate objective scientist, Lombroso does not tell us that he himself is Jewish. We see nonetheless three points of anxiety thus far in this short preface that would seem to be related to this fact: his concern over justifying antisemitism, his worry about impartiality, and his justification of himself as a competent author of such a study. Similar claims are not made, for example, in his book on women, and yet that analysis would seem to warrant corresponding concerns. The emphasis on impartiality can be read as the prevailing ideology of scientific methods, and as a claim to authority and mastery over the material. It can also be read as an expression of Lombroso's anxiety that he is perhaps too close to the subject.

The text is divided into short chapters that discuss different aspects of antisemitism. The first, entitled "Cause," attempts to analyze the general phenomenon of racial intolerance. At the end of a short historical sketch of antisemitism, Lombroso tacks on some reasons for antisemitism that he directly attributes to the nature of the Jewish community itself: "Segregation of habitation, the dissonance of the customs, the food, the languages, and the competition in business that breeds jealousy, increases real and apparent disparities, making their

vilification desirable and useful to individuals and even the state; finally the psychic epidemic that diffuses and multiplies hates and legends."[14]

Religious and cultural difference itself is vilified in Lombroso's analysis, as he blames the victim and in so doing leads us into his next chapter, entitled "Difetti degli ebrei" (Defects of the Jews). Beginning this chapter with the statement that "the character of those persecuted certainly contributed to their persecution" allows Lombroso to continue on the path he initiated at the end of the last chapter, that of blaming the victim for the sins of the perpetrator.[15] He continues with an explanation of how certain traits and cultural customs of the Jews have contributed to their persecution and prejudice. Lying and cleverness are mentioned immediately as two of the defects; the lying brings to mind the critique Lombroso made of women. The figure of the Jew that Lombroso draws in this chapter is similar to the stereotypes used by many racist theorists: the cheating merchant, the dual personality, the person capable of chameleon-like rapid changes as the situation necessitates, etc.

The thrust of Lombroso's attack lies in his critique of what we might call the singularity of the Jews: those customary practices that constitute their difference from Christian society. Lombroso chooses three major points of attack: the use of Passover matzoh, the wearing of *tefillin* (phylacteries), and the practice of circumcision. Passover matzoh comes under fire precisely because it is a mark of difference: "the stupid ritual of Passover matzoh, which, since it differs from usage among the local people, naturally stirs up ridicule and revulsion, which grows due to the exaggerated importance that the Orthodox attach to it."[16]

What is particularly interesting about Lombroso's text is his logic of what constitutes difference and how he analyzes and interprets that difference. Elsewhere in his text Lombroso again points out *"gergo"* (jargon) as another difference that, along with strange customs, marginalizes the Jew (Lombroso 1894). Difference is perceived most dramatically when it is visual or aural. Another way in which cultural difference is figured as problematic in the history of antisemitic intolerance is through language. Language has been a crucial site of attention in the history of antisemitism. According to the theorists of antisemitism, language was the vilifying mark of difference that set the Jews apart. In Jewish Self-Hatred: Anti-Semitism and the Hidden Language of the *Jews,* Gilman maintains that language in the history of antisemitism, and especially during the Renaissance, was overdetermined as the most important demarcation of the radical split between Christianity and Judaism. The language of the Jews was seen as the location of fundamental theological differences. These differences were immediately translated into social sign through a displacement of theology onto language. Gilman analyzes the ways in which the language of the Jews often became a point of attack for their enemies. Hebrew and then Yiddish were perceived as secret or hidden languages, with magical properties. The hidden language was thought to conceal from the Christian world a number of religious and social differences that denied Christianity. The language of the Jews was thus perceived as both a foreign language and a discourse; as Gilman says, "it is evident that the myth-building that surrounds the concept of a 'hidden' language of the Jews links both language and discourse in the stereotype of the Jew" (Gilman 1986, ix). The differences between the Christian world and the world of Judaism were summed up in antisemitic theory under the rubric of language, and so the language of the Jews came under attack. Lombroso's choice of language as a point of attack thus fits into a long tradition of antisemitism: a disquisition on discourse as that which distinguishes, yet ultimately confuses, Jewish culture and the theology of Judaism.

Both too atavistic and too modern, the Jews, become scapegoats for the modern age. The contradiction is obvious: Lombroso says repeatedly that the Jews do not sufficiently conform in either custom or dress to the country in which they live. How then could they bear the "wounds of modernity," as he claims elsewhere in his text (Lombroso 1894, p. 100), if in fact, as he suggests, they are living in a past age? The word that he uses for "wounds"—*piaga*—is a telling one, for it may also refer to stigmata.

Lombroso reads language and religious customs as primitive, yet the Jew is made to represent the worst of modernity. Finally he employs a Christian logic and vocabulary of relics, saints, and Jesus to analyze and then stigmatize difference. It is also revealing that Lombroso adopts the language of the scientists who had labeled the signs of hysteria "stigmata," a term that has a rich Christian significance. Not only do stigmata refer to the wounds of Jesus, but the verb "to stigmatize" has some interesting shades of significance. "To stigmatize" means to label in a negative way; the referent is both physical, as it refers to the wounds of Jesus left by the nails of the cross, and cultural, as it refers to that which is different and undesirable. A great irony is created by Lombroso's choice of the term "stigmata" in the particular context in which he uses it: Lombroso the Jewish scientist uses the word to refer to the marks of difference apparent on the bodies of criminals. In *La donna delinquente,* he also uses it metaphorically: "an important stigmata of degeneration is the lack of maternal affection in many female born criminals."[17] His own stigmatization as a Jew can thus be seen as displaced onto the even more unfortunate and stigmatized body of the criminal, the woman, and the all-so-distant figure of the Orthodox Jew.

The logic of cultural difference becomes a pretext for derision as Lombroso attempts to assign a logic to, and then make absurd, the practice of religious ritual. In this text, on the surface an objective scientific defense of the Jews, Lombroso adopts the logic of antisemitism in order to analyze the practice of cultural difference. He attacks the Jews for their cultural difference, for those practices that in fact make them Jewish, and he singles out their alleged attitudes toward language as the basis of this critique of difference. Purportedly an examination of the relationship between antisemitism and modern science, the text quickly changes direction. It soon becomes clear that it is not really a book on this topic at all, but rather one on two related subjects: who the Jews are and how Lombroso feels about that. The text would have been more accurately entitled "Antisemitism and the Modern Scientist"—the scientist, of course, being a Jewish one, represented by Lombroso himself.

Lombroso's conclusion is that assimilation is the answer to the problem of antisemitism; in other words, the solution is the total obliteration of difference. Lombroso employs a different kind of logic in his last assessment of cultural practices, as he explains the need for assimilation:

> It is time for the Jews to persuade themselves that many of their rituals belong to other epochs and that their useless strangeness (matzoh and circumcision, for example) make one suspect profane customs for which they themselves feel a maximum disgust. If all other religions have modified their essence, not only their dress, according to the times, why can't they [the Jews] modify at least a smattering? Why not renounce that savage wounding that is circumcision, those many fetishes of sacred writing or of some of their sentences, that they place around the house and even bind onto their bodies, just like amulets, thus conserving without knowing it that adoration of letters that the first discoverers had and that savages still have?[18]

Lombroso lists here just exactly what it is that bothers and frustrates him about the Jews: the dress, customs, and religious habits that separate them from other people. He goes further in his assessment of *tefillin* and *mezuzot,* calling them fetishes.[19] Lombroso's desire for Jews to give up their religious practices because they are outmoded, not reasonable, and the like is based on a logic of culture that becomes meaningless if applied to religion. The equivalent might be telling Catholics to give up the concept of the Virgin Mary because such a story is impossible medically or scientifically, and is based on a primitive story that modern science has proved untenable. Seen in this light, applying what Lombroso would call scientific logic to religion is nothing short of absurd. Once again, however, it must be noted that what Lombroso is attacking are differences that are strongly visual.

Unlike Weininger, Lombroso is attempting to save the Jews from something: the racist rhetoric of biologically based antisemitism. In so doing, Lombroso has adopted, wittingly or not, the racist logic of the erasure of difference. The topic of assimilation for the Jews in the late nineteenth century is a difficult and complicated one. The assimilationist movement was not always an attempt to leave Judaism behind and convert to Christianity, but rather in part an attempt to move away from Orthodoxy, although the ramifications of assimilation are every bit as serious as outright conversion.[20] Assimilation and a physical exodus to another place were both seen as potential ways to eliminate the uncomfortable status of marginality, two sides of the same coin. Theodor Herzl's solution was Zionism: a land where Jews would not be outsiders. Lombroso's solution was the obliteration of difference.[21]

Lombroso's defense of the Jews lies almost entirely in his criticism of the sense of proportion involved. To his credit, he does take on the most ferocious theorists of antisemitism, destroying their arguments in his discussion of the problem of biologically based racism. He does not believe that cultural differences, although they make for divisiveness and derision, are reason enough for the viciousness of antisemitism, and he posits extreme antisemitism as a disease in itself. He discusses the political scope of antisemitism, and how it has been used by political factions for their own ends. "Another epidemic bacillus" is how he describes that which propagates antisemitism, which he calls elsewhere "the germs of the illness."[22] Lombroso is using terms he can understand in a scientific framework of illness—an illness that then has a potential cure. However, his cure for the illness is the demise of the patient—no more germs, so no more epidemic. This is a haunting precursor of Weininger's solution of the extinction of the human race that he posits at the end of *Sex and Character*.

LOMBROSO, WOMEN, AND JEWS

Like Weininger, Lombroso ends up joining his analyses of women and Jews. Unlike Weininger, Lombroso's way of doing this is not overt. The intersection of women and Jews comes about almost, it would seem, by accident, when Lombroso is busy determining the "real" nature of woman. In *La donna delinquente*, Lombroso provides a short history of prostitution that is divided into sections, one of which is entitled "Sacred Prostitution" and deals with the history of prostitution within religious sects. It is here that Lombroso's prejudicial opinions regarding Jews and women are most clear: namely, when the two categories collide and the topic becomes Jewish women, which in turn becomes, in Lombroso's perspective, Jewish prostitutes. This collision—or collusion—creates a very great moment of tension in the text, as we will see presently.

At the beginning of the section dealing with religious prostitution, Lombroso states, "Among the Jews, before the definitive version of the Tablets of Law, the father had the right to sell the daughter to a man who would make her his concubine for a period of time established by the sales contract. The daughter sold in this way for the profit of her father did not gain anything from the forced abandonment of her body, except in the case where the man would engage her to his son and so would substitute her with another concubine. The Jews trafficked thus in the prostitution of their own daugh-

ters."[23] This shocking passage brings up not a few questions pertaining to its interpretation. Could this terrible accusation possibly have been true in any way? Could Lombroso have had some kind of source for this statement, even an untrue one? The answer to the first question is probably no, to the second probably yes.[24] The kinds of questions generated by this passage go well beyond any that are localized in the sense of looking at biblical history and its interpreters through the centuries to determine if Lombroso was right or wrong. What is important here is not so much proving that Lombroso either had a source or even made this up entirely out of his own prejudices to serve his own agenda, but rather that he gives the episode so much emphasis and that he frames certain questions within the context of this passage. Other forms of religious prostitution merit a paragraph here, a sentence there in this chapter. Three full pages are devoted to the role of the Jews in prostitution, and other references appear elsewhere in the text. In fact, it is clear from this section that Lombroso makes the connection between Jews and prostitutes just as often as he is able.

The question of the interpretation of the passage itself and the images that are embedded within looms large in this scenario. The first image is the stereotype of the greedy Jew who capitalizes on the body of his female child. This image is emphasized with the words "for the profit of her father." Even more insidious is the notion that somehow the daughter is being deprived of the profit she herself could have made! Lombroso is careful to point this out, as he says that "the daughter sold in this way . . . did not gain anything"—as if her profit from prostitution would have made the outcome positive and therefore fully acceptable. The second image is that of the Jewish woman as prostitute. Here the daughter is figured as a potential prostitute who is stymied by her father's insistence on making the profit himself. This last point is emphasized once again by the statement that "the Jews trafficked thus in the prostitution of their own daughters." The connection between Jews and prostitutes made in early modern culture has been analyzed by Sander Gilman in "'I'm Down on Whores': Race and Gender in Victorian London," as he says, "The relationship between the Jew and the prostitute also has a social dimension. For both Jew and prostitute have but one interest, the conversion of sex into money or money into sex" (Gilman 1990b, 161). This is an apt description of Lombroso's passage, as the two parties—father and daughter—are literally competing for the right to profit from her body.

There is something so intense about the intersection of women and Jews in Lombroso's text that it causes an outright derailing of his scientific methodology. This is even more noticeable in a text that obsessively cites its sources, whether they be physical measurements from studies or proverbs. Here instead Lombroso does not cite other scholars at all. There is a self-confidence about the material presented in this section that creates a different tone than found elsewhere in Lombroso's work. Usually in his texts there seems to be the assumption that citations from other experts, numbers from studies, measurements, and so on are required to support his statements, even if these "proofs" are specious. In this section, however, there is the sense that because he is dealing with a biblical text—in other words, with common cultural knowledge—and perhaps also because he himself is Jewish and these are his forebears whose behavior he is analyzing—he does not need to cite anyone else and is free to come up with these outrageous interpretations.

Already in this text we have seen Lombroso mingling the terms for the "normal" woman, the prostitute, and the criminal. When the figure of the Jewish father is introduced as another player in Lombroso's drama of cultural difference, the confusion level becomes so high that the potential for overt fictionalization is created. At best, we can view this as a confusion between different biblical laws regarding the legislation of slaves and marriage contracts. At worst, it is a deliberate misreading and misinterpretation of the story of the biblical Jews, designed to link them to cults of prostitution and to infer a connection between pernicious antisemitic stereotypes and biblical paradigms, as if the stereotype of Jew-as-profiteer is already imbedded in these first biblical Jews and thus is an inseparable part of what is Jewish. The identity of these biblical Jews would seem to furnish a key for Lombroso so that he may understand the identity of modern Jews. It is also noteworthy that he uses the term *Gesù Cristo* to refer to Jesus. The title "Christ," or Savior, implies belief in the tenets of Christianity.

What is at stake for an author like Lombroso, Jewish himself but first and foremost a scientist, when he confronts the issue of the identity of the Jews, both modern and biblical? Similar questions have been asked of Weininger, the converted Jew. Robert Oden, in "Religious Identity and the Sacred Prostitution Accusation," formulates related questions that are raised by what he calls the "accusations of sacred prostitution":

> Perhaps sacred prostitution ought to be investigated as an accusation rather than as a reality. Perhaps, then, this alleged practice belongs in the same category with cannibalism, sodomy, and abhorrent dietary and sexual practices generally—that is to say, in the category of charges that one society levels against others as part of that society's process of self-definition. . . . Viewed in this way, the accusation that other societies utilize religious personnel as part of sacred sexual rites surely tells us something about those who formulate and repeat the accusation. . . . The accusation may tell us little or nothing about those religions against which the charge is leveled (Oden 1987, 132-33).

Oden's double charge is well taken in the consideration of Lombroso's versions of biblical episodes and is pertinent to our comprehension of Weininger as well. The accusatory nature of Lombroso's agenda regarding Jew-ish women is better understood in the light of Oden's theory regarding the identity of the accuser in relation to the accusations that are made.

In his meditations on women, Lombroso sets up a misogynist model for the interpretation of female behavior that reinforces negative stereotypes about women and posits the female criminal as the woman who exemplifies the worst traits of his stereotypes, but who is typical of "normal" women in many ways. Fear of what is female is categorically structured in his text as we learn that the average woman is but a criminal waiting to strike and a prostitute waiting to be unleashed. Here and in his other works Lombroso marginalizes the notion of criminal through his attempts to measure and categorize the correlations between physical difference and behavior. He attempts to quantify difference as he reads physical signs of difference and links them to types. Lombroso finds himself concluding, as we have seen, that the female criminal quite often demonstrates male characteristics. He thus blurs the distinctions between men and women in his discussions of both the criminal and women.

This confusion is apparent as well in Lombroso's study of the Jews, who are at once too primitive and too modern. Another kind of distinction is also challenged as Lombroso mixes cultural categories through which he reads Jewish religious practice. His emphasis on the physical quantification of difference underscored the acceptability of biologically based theories of the inferiority of certain groups popular at the time, even though in his book on Jews he denied the racist theorists any validity as he maintained that the Jews were not a single race.

LOMBROSO AND WEININGER

These two theorists of difference, Lombroso and Weininger, share some distinct attributes. First, a theoretical similarity is found in their tendency to blur the very differences that they seek to stigmatize. Just as striking, however, is a dissimilarity in the reception of certain of their texts: Lombroso was a world-renowned criminologist, yet there are literally only a few lines in print about his text on antisemitism, while Weininger, a young student of philosophy and characterology, was hailed by many important figures of his day as a genius who understood both the nature of sexual difference and the nature of the Jews.

Both Weininger and Lombroso were Jewish, although Weininger converted to Christianity. Lombroso does not as easily fit the portrait of the antisemitic Jew: his Jewish background shows no sign of restlessness, no conversion, no abandonment of the faith. He did, however, write the very problematic text on Jews discussed here and an equally problematic one on women. Important for the study of Weininger reception in Italy, Lombroso's theories about women in part paved the way for the warm welcome that Weininger's text was later given. Through his influential theories and his attitude toward difference, Lombroso helped create an intellectual atmosphere in Italy that at the beginning of this century was receptive to Weininger and hostile to Freud.[25] In addition to the direct influence on Weininger that Allan Janik has demonstrated (Janik 1986), Lombroso's reading of the motives for antisemitism and the place of the Jews in culture provides a link to Weiningerian theories of cultural and sexual difference and ways in which those theories are interpreted. It is in part the confusion of category in Lombroso's work that would allow a future generation of Italian intellectuals such easy access to Weininger's blending of categories of difference. Lombroso's particular brand of cultural intolerance and its connections to Weininger reception in Italy furnish a link to the theories that informed the web of political and social distortions of the Holocaust; and Lombroso's theories were made to fit a later brand of racism and intolerance that provided the theoretical base for the Holocaust. Lombroso is the figure of the dispassionate scientist who banks on the impartiality of scientific method, who flinches in the face of difference, particularly his own, and then pulls out the measuring devices to show positively that difference does exist physically, even to the naked eye.[26]

Weininger's text is much more complicated than a simple diatribe against two groups, women and Jews, who at the time were often the target of abuse and attack. Weininger, in his insistence that he is talking about "qualities" or "tendencies" rather than "people," intrigued his intellectual generation and one or two subsequent generations by his formulation of women and Jews into recognizable groups of traits that are, however, largely disembodied. His description of Judaism and antisemitism provides a kind of road map for self-hatred: "I must however, make clear what I mean by Judaism; I mean neither a race nor a people nor a recognised creed. I think of it as a tendency of the mind, as a psychological constitution which is a possibility for all mankind, but which has become actual in the most conspicuous fashion only amongst the Jews. Antisemitism itself will confirm my point of view" (Weininger 1906, 303).

This is a circular argument, and it sets the stage for Weininger's description of antisemitism. If Judaism is a tendency of the mind and Jews are the only ones who have this tendency in a conspicuous fashion, then Jews are the only ones who are Jews, according to Weiningerian logic. There are also the "near-Jews," the only ones who are capable of hating the Jews:

> The purest Aryans by descent and disposition are seldom Antisemites, although they are often unpleasantly moved by some of the peculiar Jewish traits; they cannot in the least understand the Antisemite movement. . . . The aggressive Antisemites, on the other hand, nearly always display certain Jewish characters, sometimes apparent in their faces, although they may have no real admixture of Jewish blood. The explanation is simple. People love in others the qualities they would like to have but do not actually have in any great

degree; so also we hate in others only what we do not wish to be, and what notwithstanding we are partly (Weininger 1906, 304).

The connection between this statement and Weininger's own life is unmistakable, as Weininger the convert speaks about the dynamics of self-hatred as he sees them. The failure for Weininger of conversion from Judaism to anything else is made clear in his articulation of what is and what is not Jewish as simultaneously a racial issue, as he discusses elsewhere physical traits of Jews, and a psychic issue, as he defines Judaism as "tendencies"; Weininger has thus set up a paradox from which no conversion is possible. Judaism both is and is not racial, and is and is not a set of "tendencies" synonymous with "being" Jewish (i.e., found only among Jews). And antisemites (like Weininger) find themselves trapped within the same paradox. If they hate Jews, they must be to some degree Jewish in their psychic make-up; therefore, if they are self-hating Jews, there is absolutely no escape from this condition, whatever their new religious status.

Weininger also confuses other categories in his analysis of Jews and woman. Like the Jew, "woman" does not always refer to a human being but often to the quality of the female element: the abstract idea, as he calls it. To make direct comparisons between the Jew and woman, Weininger labels the Jew as womanly: "some reflection will lead to the surprising result that Judaism is saturated with femininity, with precisely those qualities the essence of which I have shown to be in the strongest opposition to the male nature." He takes us through this argument of comparison between the Jew and woman: they both lack a "real sense of landed property"; they both are "wanting in personality," which means they cannot grasp the "conception of a State"; they both lack dignity; they both are "non-moral" and more involved in "sexual matters" than are Aryan men (Weininger 1906, 306, 307, 309, 311). This last idea bears a strong resemblance to the way in which Lombroso assesses Jewish women as bearers of syphilis and as prostitutes sold by their greedy fathers.

At the end of the chapter on Judaism, Weininger lines up the opposing camps: Jewish and Christian, business and culture, female and male, race and individual. He states very emphatically that there are only two poles, no middle way, and that a decision must be made. Here he clearly departs from his stated intent of examining qualities, abstract ideas of Jewish and female, as he is now addressing real groups in what is a political as well as cultural agenda. In his last chapter he proposes that the only solution to the problem of woman is for woman to overcome her femaleness through an abandonment of her sexuality. Weininger views undesirable sexuality or religion as a state to be conquered. His "solution" calls for, quite simply, the end of the human race. The erasure of cultural, sexual, or religious difference Weininger advocates is a kind of total assimilation, not dissimilar to Lombroso's solution to antisemitism. Weininger's assimilation is, of course, much more radical.

In sum, it is clear that Weininger's theories about Jews and women have several major points of comparison to Lombroso's theories that cannot be ignored and that go far beyond some borrowing of Lombroso's theories regarding women. Both authors end up problematizing the relationship of the terms "Jew" and "woman." Their versions of this differ considerably: Weininger creates the womanly Jew; Lombroso, rather than overtly feminizing the male Jew, puts the terms "Jew" and "woman" together in an explosive combination resulting in the figure of the prostitute. His feminization of the Jew is limited to deprecatory remarks regarding the inability of the Jews to withstand the physical rigors of living in Palestine. Both authors clearly advocate assimilation as a solution to cultural or sexual difference, and both authors confuse definitions of woman and Jew to arrive at their solutions to difference.

The history of Weininger criticism is fraught with disagreements on how literally his text can or should be read, and how it should be contextualized. The disagreements themselves signal some evident dangers in interpreting a text like that of Weininger. First and foremost is the risk of creating a critical atmosphere that can function as a kind of apology. It is important to avoid the pitfall of reading writings like those of Lombroso or Weininger through a modern perspective that ignores contextualization and an understanding of the historical period that produced them, but it is equally important not to be blinded by the god of contextualization to the point where the pernicious content and influence of such texts are ignored or made less significant. There is a delicate middle ground between an overly apologetic stance toward the text, generated by perhaps too much sympathy for the historical conditions in which the author found himself and fostered as well by a certain blindness to the overt perniciousness of the text, and a naive horror that does not take into account at all the conditions that produced the writing.

As examination of Lombroso's work as a source for Weininger is, I believe, illustrative of the pitfalls involved in interpreting Weininger. Looking at Janik's useful assessment of Lombroso as a direct source for Weininger on the subject of women provides a key to a reading model I am proposing for both Lombroso and Weininger. Janik, in *How Not to Interpret a Culture: Essays on the Problem of Method in the* "Geisteswissenschaften," asserts the following:

> Even a cursory glance at Weininger's notes and references indicates that he was heavily indebted for his data about women to a work called *La Donna Delinquente e La Prostituta [sic]* by Cesare Lombroso, Professor of Forensic Medicine and father of modern criminology. . . . Not a little of the "empirical data" upon which Weininger based his reasoning is to be found in Lombroso's study of the female offender. For example two ideas which were to recur as central themes in *Geschlecht und Charakter,* namely that women are generally less sensitive to perceptual stimuli

and the notion that women are more prone to lying than men (for which he advances eight causes) are already central themes in Lombroso's work. In fact most of the things that we find obnoxious and repugnant in *Geschlecht und Charakter* today, can be found in *La Donna Delinquente* (Janik 1986, 40-41).

Janik's evidence for supposing that Lombroso had a major effect on Weininger's theories regarding women is indisputable. His and other scholars' emphasis on contextualizing Weininger within the cultural milieu of turn-of-the-century Vienna, including within the painful debates regarding assimilation that were taking place in the Jewish community, is crucial. What is much more arguable and pertinent to a meaningful discussion of influence is the tone and meaning of Janik's statement that "in fact most of the things that we find obnoxious and repugnant in *Geschlecht und Charakter* today, can be found in *La Donna Delinquente.*" An examination of Lombroso's work discloses, I believe, striking similarities between the two authors that go beyond the footnotes that Weininger allocates to Lombroso in his text. The question of influence, however, is not easily shunted off to a question of footnotes, nor is the perniciousness of Weininger's text explained or excused by its indebtedness to Lombroso. Reading Lombroso will provide some direction for reading Weininger, but not just in the interest of assigning blame. Is the purpose of tracking down sources and demonstrating that ideas have come from other thinkers to exculpate the one who has borrowed, on the excuse that those ideas were not original to that person anyway? Is there a notion of original sin floating around here? Is Weininger any less responsible for his text if he was not the author of all of its ideas? Does the demonstration of influence mean "not guilty"? To state that what we find obnoxious in Weininger is already in Lombroso, as if that were any kind of answer, is to displace a very important question. If what is implied in Janik's statement is that if these sentiments are already in Lombroso, then Weininger isn't such a "bad guy" after all, the essential question is still being ignored: why did Lombroso write these theories about Jews and women? A more detailed look at Lombroso within the context of the science practiced in his day demonstrates that his theories regarding women are not all original either, that they are a composite of misogynist proverbs, the theories of other scientific experts, and his own opinions.

A look at a model of analysis proposed by Saul Friedlander in his assessment of historical narratives regarding the Holocaust is useful here. Friedlander, in discussing what he calls "the basic narratives underlying the historical representations" of the Holocaust, specifies the differences between the "structuralist" approach to understanding the Holocaust, which is to cast it in terms of nineteenth-century development of racialist ideas, and the "liberal" approach, which attempts to assign responsibility through an analysis of German politics and policies in the Nazi era (Friedlander 1988, 67). Friedlander points out that the structuralist approach has the tendency to place responsibility for the event on so many sources that the notion of guilt itself can be dispersed: "in the structuralist view, there are many active and almost independent subgroups within the wide category of perpetrators; these subgroups interact with one another in such a way that it becomes extremely difficult to pinpoint where the responsibility lies (Friedlander 1988, 70). The model that is thus created would appear to be a binary one, either "many sources = displaced responsibility" or "single source = specific responsibility." Friedlander points out, however, that "both the liberal and the structuralist approach belong to a common consensus about basic responsibilities and basic victimization, notwithstanding the divergences just described" (Friedlander 1988, 71). We can use this useful model of divergencies sharing a common basis about what constitutes responsibility that Friedlander proposes to ponder both the question of influence regarding Lombroso and Weininger, and . . . the influence of Weininger on many other thinkers and writers. Considering the problem in this way, it becomes clear that we may fully appreciate the depth to which Weininger owed some of his beliefs about women to Lombroso without lessening the impact of those theories reformulated and represented a generation later. To acknowledge sources should not mean an automatic exculpation of the borrower.

Perhaps the notion of originality, when it comes to the expression of prejudice, is really not relevant at all. Plagiarism is, after all, the *modus operandi* of the dissemination of bigotry.

NOTES

[1] The readings of Lombroso in this essay are revised from my book on Lombroso and Serao (Harrowitz 1994a, chaps. 2-3).

[2] This edition was put together just before Lombroso's death by his daughter Gina Lombroso-Ferrero and is a summary of his theories. The volume was first published in 1911, two years after his death. Lombroso wrote the introduction, which provides a valuable contextualization of his theories within the discipline of criminology. Savitz points out that the issue of who was translated played an important role in which texts were influential in the development of American criminology. The Lombrosian school was quickly and frequently translated, while the French school was poorly represented in translation, and thus many of the latter texts remained unavailable to American criminologists, the majority of whom were unskilled in foreign languages.

[3] Lombroso and Ferrero ([1893] 1903). Although Lombroso did co-author this text with the young historian Guglielmo Ferrero, who later was to marry Lombroso's daughter Gina, Lombroso was very clearly the senior author with ultimate responsibility for the text, and he alone wrote the preface.

[4] Lombroso and Ferrero (1903, 490): "quel fondo d'immoralità che latente si trova in ogni donna"; "quel fondo di malvagità che è latente in ogni donna."

[5] Lombroso and Ferrero (1903, 499): "la maternità è—quasi diremmo—essa stessa un vaccino morale contro il delitto e il male."

[6] Lombroso and Ferrero (1903, 358): "ma se la donna primitiva non fu che di raro assassina, fu, come provammo sopra . . . sempre prostituta, e restò tale quasi fino all'epoca semi-barbara; quindi anche atavisticamente si spiega che la prostituta debba avere più caratteri regressivi della donna criminale."

[7] Lombroso and Ferrero (1903, 334, 330): "si direbbe la laringe di un uomo. E così nella laringe, come nella faccia, come nel cranio, spicca il carattere speciale a queste, la virilità"; "distribuzione virile del pelo."

[8] Lombroso and Ferrero (1903, 350): "Però, anche nelle ree più belle il carattere virile, l'esagerazione della mascella, degli zigomi, non manca mai, come non manca in nessuna delle nostre grandi cocottes, sicchè hanno tutte un'aria di famiglia che avvicina le peccatrici Russe a quelle che stancano le vie delle nostre città, sieno esse in cocchi dorati o in umili cenci. E fate che la giovinezza scompaia, e allora quelle mandibole, quegli zigomi arrotondati dall'adipe, sporgono gli angoli salienti e ne rendono il viso affatto virile, più brutto di un uomo, e la ruga si approfonda come una ferita, e quella faccia piacente mostra completamente il tipo degenerato che l'età nascondeva."

[9] Lombroso and Ferrero (1883, 133): "Dimostrare come la menzogna sia abituale e quasi fisiologica nella donna sarebbe superfluo, tanto è perfino nella leggenda popolare"; "le donne dicono sempre il vero, ma non lo dicono mai intero (Toscania)"; "le donne—dice il Dohm—si servono della bugia come il bue delle corna."

[10] Lombroso and Ferrero (1893, 465): "E si capisce come la chiacchiera del delitto sia più frequente nella donna che nell'uomo, perchè essa deve supplire a tutti quei mezzi usati dal maschio a ravvivare l'immagine del delitto, come il disegno e la scrittura, che vedemmo mancare alla donna. La donna parla spesso de' suoi delitti, come l'uomo li dipinge, o li scrive, o li scolpisce nei vasi ecc."

[11] Lombroso (1894, 5). "Ne provavo quel disgusto che coglie anche il meno impaziente scienziato quando deve studiare le più ributtanti secrezioni umane. Il decidere se un odio fra popoli possa essere giustificato, nei nostri tempi, è già certo un odioso e doloroso compito; e non è agevole acconciarvisi."

[12] Lombroso (1894, 6): "mi garantiva anche contro il pericolo, massimo in tali quistioni, della parzialità."

[13] Lombroso (1894, 7): "l'aiuto di tali mastri sorti nelle nazioni più ricche di antisemiti e di filosemiti mi era

nuova arra della rettitudine e dell'imparzialità del giudizio per chi dubitasse dello strumento che da poco tempo maneggio."

[14] Lombroso (1894, 12): "la segregazione dell'abitato, la dissonanza degli usi, dei cibi, dei dialetti, la concorrenza nei commerci che fomentava gelosie, aumentava disparità reali e apparenti, rendendo desiderabile ed utile ai privati, se non al paese, il loro avvilamento; e infine la epidemia psichica che diffonde e centuplica gli odi e le leggende."

[15] Lombroso (1894, 13): "certo contribuì pure alla persecuzione il carattere degli stessi perseguitati."

[16] Lombroso (1894, 14): "gli stupidi riti delle azime Pasquali; i quali, divergendo da tutti quelli in uso fra i popoli in cui vivono, destano naturalmente il ridicolo e la ripugnanza che cresce coll'esagerata importanza che gli ortodossi vi annettono."

[17] Lombroso and Ferrero (1903) "una stigmata grave di degenerazione è in molte criminali-nate la mancanza dell'affetto materno."

[18] Lombroso (1894, 107): "Agli ebrei a lor volta tocca persuadersi come molti dei loro riti ormai appartengono ad altre epoche e per le loro inutili stranezze (azime, p. es.; circoncisione) fanno sospettare ai profani di costumi di cui essi stessi hanno il massimo ribrezzo. Se tutte le religioni hanno modificato le loro essenza, non che la loro veste, a seconda dei tempi, perchè non dovrebbero modificarne essi almeno la vernice? perchè non rinunciare a quel vero ferimento selvaggio che è la circoncisione, a quei molteplici feticci della scrittura sacra o di alcuni dei suoi periodi, che essi spargono nelle proprie case e persino legano sopra il proprio corpo, precisamente come gli amuleti, conservando senza saperlo quell'adorazione delle lettere che ne ebbero i primi scopritori e che hannno ancora i selvaggi?"

[19] *Mezuzot* are small objects placed on the doorframe of houses where Jews live, containing an important prayer from the book of Deuteronomy.

[20] Even as famous and important a figure as Theodor Herzl, known as the father of Zionism, became an important protagonist in the debates regarding the favorability of assimilation. As Steven Beller asserts, "Herzl wanted to free the Jews from what he saw as the dehabilitating state of being outsiders in a hostile society, and hence make Jews normal as it were" (Beller 1989b, 208).

[21] Katz (1980, esp. 4-6) assesses various kinds of reactions to antisemitism in the second half of the nineteenth century on the part of the Jewish community.

[22] Lombroso (1894, 24, 26): "Un altro bacillo epidemico"; "i germi del morbo."

[23] Lombroso and Ferrero (1903, 223): "Presso gli Ebrei, prima della redazi. . . ."

Barbara Hyams (essay date 1995)

SOURCE: "Weininger and Nazi Ideology," in *Jews & Gender: Responses to Otto Weininger,* edited by Nancy A. Harrowitz and Barbara Hyams, Temple University Press, 1995, pp. 155-68.

[*In the following essay, Hyams explains how the theories in* Sex and Character *were eventually exploited by the Nazis.*]

Otto Weininger's popular scientific treatise of 1903, *Geschlecht und Charakter* (*Sex and Character*), lent itself in many ways to exploitation by *völkisch* and, slightly later, Nazi ideologues. Weininger, an apostate Viennese Jew who converted to Protestantism the day he became a doctor of philosophy in June of 1902, had attempted to define Jewish character in a single chapter of a work otherwise dedicated to defining male and female character and to suggesting a solution to the alleged moral depravity of the era. By drawing negative parallels between male Jews and "Aryan" women, Weininger appeared to fall victim to his contempt for women, who in his view were morally inferior beings driven either by a herdlike instinct to reproduce or by lasciviousness. Many people viewed his suicide at the age of twenty-three in the house in which a symbol of male "Aryan" genius, Beethoven, had died, as a desperate acknowledgment of unavoidable parallels between female character and Jewish male character.

Weininger's sensational suicide, the subsequent intellectual debate over his theories in Karl Kraus's influential periodical *Die Fackel* (The Torch) and elsewhere, and the popularity of his book, which went through twenty-five editions in roughly as many years, rendered Weininger for some a saint too ethical for this vile world and for others a tragic example of a Jew who could not overcome the ignobility of his race. Because *Sex and Character* was so popular in the first third of the century, *völkisch* and Nazi ideologues used him as a prime example of a tormented Jew who provided not just evidence but eloquent evidence of Jewish "inferiority."

Indeed, the Nazi view of Weininger was mostly a straightforward matter of exploiting the "Jewish self-hate" in a "racist classic."[1] However, Weininger proved to be a problematic figure for Nazi ideologues, because *Sex and Character*[2] was primarily about gender, not race, and its low opinion of women made manifest what was covert in Nazi ideology. As Annette Kuhn has demonstrated, "German fascism concealed its extreme antifeminism behind racist-biological rhetoric. Its *Weltanschauung* was overtly racist and implicitly antifeminist" (Kuhn 1988, 41).

As far as I can ascertain, *Sex and Character* was never banned during the Third Reich. Nazi men's reception of Weininger until 1943 tended to ignore his negative assessment of female character and motherhood while exploiting his condemnations of Jewish character. Their implicit point of agreement with Weininger's antifeminism was their belief that "superior" male intellect could analyze and control "Aryan" women's vulnerability to seduction by channeling it into socially desirable modes of behavior. The specific point of disagreement between Weininger and Nazi ideologues lay in their respective definitions of socially desirable behavior: for Weininger, it meant a spiritually motivated abstention from intercourse; for the Nazis, a racially motivated acceleration of selective breeding. Thus, since a number of Weininger's theses about women and motherhood contradicted some Nazi myths about the family, it eventually became opportune for Nazi men to discredit—by means other than censorship—Weininger's blatantly low assessment of women. Weininger's ideas were a point of contention between Nazi men and women, and Nazi men eventually attacked his specifically antifeminist ideas as a ruse to pacify "Aryan" women. Although it goes beyond the bounds of this article to discuss in detail Nazi women's motivations and experiences in creating and promoting a fascist state in "Greater Germany," the works of feminist historians such as Annette Kuhn, Claudia Koonz, Rita Thalmann, and Christina von Braun[3] provide a specific context within which to understand Weininger's reputation during the Third Reich.

However, one cannot understand Nazi women's and men's views of Weininger's treatment of the "woman question" without first addressing their views of his contribution to the "Jewish question." While Weininger sought to relativize his Jewish heritage in a footnote to the chapter on Judaism in *Sex and Character*—"The author notes at this juncture that he himself is of Jewish descent" (Weininger 1980, 406)—Nazi ideology and its precursors treated his conversion to Protestantism as an exemplary failure and prefaced all references to him with "the Jew." Most *völkisch* and Nazi Weininger reception falls under the rubric of "Jewish self-revelations" (*jüdische Selbstbekenntnisse*). Theodor Fritsch, the "creator of practical anti-Semitism,"[4] and Hans Jonak von Freyenwald (1941), for example, compiled anthologies of quotes taken out of context in which Jewish thinkers appear to support a blanket condemnation of Judaism and Jews.

Theodor Fritsch was a major contributor to the genre as both a writer and founder of the anti-Semitic Hammer publishing house in Leipzig. He quoted brief passages from Weininger under the heading "Jewish Character" in *Jüdische Selbstbekenntnisse* ([Jewish Self-Revelations], 1929). Other categories include "Masters of Perversity," "Judaism and Marxist Workers' Movement," "The Jew as Capitalist," "Jews as Rulers of Economic Life and Representatives of Shady Dealing," "Baptised Jews Remain Jews," "State Within a State," and "Complete World Domination." The 1919 and 1929 editions of Fritsch's book include fourteen identical quotes; however, the 1919 edition cites a passage from *Sex and Character* that is not reprinted in the later edition. It is Weininger's only quote that ties purported Jewish character to purported female character and thus is the truest

to his agenda in the chapter on Judaism: "The great talent of the Jews for journalism, the 'agility' of the Jewish spirit, the lack of a rooted and fundamental cast of mind—do these not hold true for Jews as well as women: they *are* nothing, and therefore they can *become* everything?" (Weininger 1903, 429). Fritsch's omission a decade later of this comparison between Jewish males and "Aryan" women is consistent with Nazi men's reception of Weininger until 1943.

Fritsch crafted the other fourteen quotations to exploit Weininger's self-hatred. The quotes focus on the following claims: that Jewish physical features have an apparent anthropological relatedness to Negroid and Mongolian features (Weininger 1903, 405; that "outstanding" people have been "almost always anti-Semitic" (Tacitus, Pascal, Voltaire, Herder, Goethe, Kant, Jean Paul, Schopenhauer, Grillparzer, and Wagner are cited [Weininger 1903, 406]); that the Jew excludes everything transcendent and has no feeling for mysteries, while the "Aryan" feels that the unfathomable lends life its meaning (Weininger 1903, 421); that Jews are only interested in the purely chemical aspect of medicine, not in the treatment of human beings as an organic whole (Weininger 1903, 422); that the Jew's ability to adapt to new requirements and host cultures is parasitic (Weininger 1903, 430); that the Jew believes in nothing and takes nothing and no one seriously (Weininger 1903, 431); that the Jew is frivolous and mocks piety (Weininger 1903, 431); that the Jew has no understanding of the concept of a state or citizenship (Weininger 1903, 410-11); that the notion that Jewish behavior is the product of historical misfortune is false (Weininger 1903, 413); that the Jew's belief in Jehovah and the teachings of Moses is merely belief in "the Jewish species and its vitality" (Weininger 1903, 416); that Jewish matchmaking is another proof of the Jews' lack of soul, since Jews more than any other people do not wed for love (Weininger 1903, 417); that since the "superior Aryan" wants to respect the Jew, anti-Semitism is not a pleasure nor an idle way of passing the time (Weininger 1903, 419); that the male Jew's total lack of humility explains his inability to understand grace and that his servile disposition leads to an immoral willingness to seek earthly affluence (Weininger 1903, 419-20); and that the Jew has no soul and therefore no belief in immortality, and that Judaism is not a religion of pure reason but of old wives' tales, materialism, slave consciousness, and impudence (Weininger 420-21).

Fritsch's quotation of the passage concerning the "superior Aryan" is particularly instructive, since it is lifted from a paragraph which, if cited in full, would attack the entire rationale for publishing "Jewish self-revelations" and challenge anti-Semites' refusal to accept apostate Jews as individuals. In fact, the ensuing paragraph in *Sex and Character* criticizes Fritsch himself in no uncertain terms: "The Jew's so crucial and so necessary recognition of the actual nature of *Jewishness* and *Judaism* would be the solution to one of the most difficult problems; Judaism is a much deeper riddle than many an Anti-Semitic Catechism believes, and ultimately it will never be completely dislodged from a certain inscrutability" (Weininger 1903, 419). Fritsch's *Handbuch der Judenfrage* (Handbook on the Jewish Question [1930, 1944]) was originally published in 1887 as *Der Antisemiten-Catechismus* (The Anti-Semitic Catechism).[5]

In *Sex and Character* Weininger explicitly confines himself to a discussion of the "singularity [*Eigenheit*] of Jewishness" as a state of mind. According to his definition, the most rabidly anti-Semitic "Aryan" exhibits "Jewishness," because part of "Jewishness" is a fixation on racial identity. By attempting to define "Jewishness" (*das Judentum* or *das Jüdische*) rather than "the Jews" (*die Juden),* he allows for the "triumph" of individuals over their racial heritage. However, as George L. Mosse points out, "As early as 1919 [Hitler] denied that anti-Semitism could be based upon one's feelings toward the individual Jew, unfavorable though this was bound to be. Instead, the evils for which the Jew stood were a 'fact' of his race."[6] While Weininger posited the Jew as a type, the non-believer, and consequently argued that, like Christ, one could *overcome* the Jew in oneself, the Nazi ideologue Alfred Rosenberg took advantage of Weininger's careless confusion of the Jew as a type, Jews as adherents of a religion, and Jews as a race. In his *Dietrich Eckart: Ein Vermächtnis* (Dietrich Eckart: A Legacy) of 1928, Rosenberg elaborated on the Jew's alleged lack of a soul. "To the Jew Weininger his own nation is like an invisible cohesive web of slime fungus (plasmodium), existing since time immemorial and spread over the entire earth; and this expansionism, as he correctly observes (without, of course, proving it), is an essential component of the idea, of the nature of Judaism."[7] In Rosenberg's view, Jews are by definition earth-centered, that is, incapable of overcoming themselves and ascending to spiritual heights. They thus exist as a counterweight to those peoples who are able to strive for salvation. As was often the case, Rosenberg expressed in pseudomystical terms that which Hitler stated baldly.

Most of the Weininger quotes in Hans Jonak von Freyenwald's *Jüdische Bekenntnisse aus allen Zeiten und Ländern* (Jewish Confessions from All Eras and Lands) of 1941 are identical to those in Fritsch's works, although they appear under a wider range of headings: "The Jewish People," "Race," "The Essence of Judaism," "Jewish Morality," "Assimilation and Baptism," "Anti-Semitism," "Marxism," "Means and Ways to Power," and "Messianism and World Rule."

In the section "on Jewish Morality," Von Freyenwald includes Weininger's enigmatic assertion about Jewish male sexuality, which comes as no surprise, since the book was published by Julius Streicher's Der Stürmer publishing house: "The Jew is always more lecherous, hornier, if also oddly enough, perhaps in connection with his not actually antimoral nature, sexually less potent, and certainly less capable of all great pleasure

than the Aryan man" (Freyenwald 1941, 417).[8] This odd balance of "more" and "less" serves a two-edged stereotype: the man who is driven by lustful designs yet who is physically[9] or morally incapable of the heights of feeling (a further indication of his lack of soul).

Weininger's brief discussion of the Jewish male's sexual appetite was by no means solely responsible for but added credence to the Nazi image of Jewish sexual insatiability: "In the popular culture and pornography of Germany, and Central Europe generally, the Jew often played a sexual role similar to that assigned the black male in the United States. He was presented as combining oversized genitals, insatiable appetites, and an irresistible approach" (Showalter 1982, 87). As Koonz (1987) and Braun (1990, 196ff.) point out, the male Jew was often portrayed as an economic bloodsucker *and* a seducer (the fat capitalist exploiting his secretary), and in caricatures his enormous nose symbolized a disproportionately large phallus. According to National Socialist ideology, Jewish lasciviousness had nothing in common with natural sensuality (Hahn 1978, 114). Ideologues like Rosenberg spread the misconception that the Talmud "obligates pious Jews to lead a sex life that is immoral, disgusting, and antisocial. The Jew is incapable of love. Since his physical urges are inseparable from his striving for power, his sexuality can only emerge as a deformation that plunges fellow human beings into torment and disaster."[10]

Two other Weininger quotes in Freyenwald's collection augment the themes in Fritsch's volumes: the Jew is someone who blurs the borders and categories between human beings *(Grenzverwischer)* and hence the "born Communist" (Freyenwald 1941, 417); and since "the spirit of modernity is Jewish," the present age is the highest point of Judaism since Herod (Freyenwald 1941, 440-41). Both of these additional quotes accentuate elements that Hitler made central to National Socialist ideology in *Mein Kampf.*

In his *Rassenkunde des jüdischen Volkes* (Racial Science of the Jewish People) of 1930, Hans F. K. Günther, who became one of the principal racial experts under the Nazi regime (Mosse 1964, 208, 302-3), explicated Weininger's statement that "the spirit of modernity is Jewish" as follows: Jews controlled the press and used the media to divert non-Jewish peoples from their spiritual values by substituting whatever values suited the needs of Judaism. Thus according to Günther, Weininger was a "highly gifted, perceptive critic of this spirit" (Günther 1930, 314). Günther also argued that modern city life in the West led to the assimilation that was corroding the biological safeguards that had traditionally protected the Jewish race. In a ploy to deliver a high-minded rationale for removing Jews from Western European societies, he concluded that Zionism was the one way to secure the future of Judaism, for only it could provide a means for Jews to turn their backs on the "modern spirit" and "individualism" and to emphasize family and *Volk,* eugenics and rural life (Günther

1930, 338). He recast Weininger's equation of the modern spirit with the Jewish spirit as a Nazi aversion to individualism. And, in a foregone conclusion, Günther speculated that the suicide of the "extraordinarily talented Jew" Weininger might have had something to do with his realization concerning the "dubiousness" of modern Judaism in the diaspora (Günther 1930, 320f.). The more brilliant Weininger could be made to appear, the more he posthumously condemned all Jews.

In a similar vein, Hitler's mentor Dietrich Eckart referred to Weininger as "the only decent Jew." Hitler recalled Eckart's remark during a conversation in December 1941 with Henry Picker in the Wolf's Lair: "Dietrich Eckart once told me that he had made the acquaintance of only one decent Jew, Otto Weininger, who took his life when he realized that the Jew lives from the destruction of other peoples" (Picker 1989, 79). In Eckart's posthumously published *Der Bolschewismus von Moses bis Lenin: Zwiegespräche zwischen Adolf Hitler und mir* (Bolshevism from Moses to Lenin: Conversations with Adolf Hitler), Weininger comes up in a discussion of the Old Testament. Eckart quotes Hitler as saying that "the Jew Weininger suspects that Christ too [i.e., in addition to Paul, whom Hitler has just described as a mass murderer] was originally a criminal, but my God, if a Jew says it a hundred times that doesn't necessarily mean that it has to be true" (Eckart 1923, 20). It is quite unlikely that Hitler ever bothered to read *Sex and Character.*

Using Weininger as a prime example, Nazi ideologues stressed the impossibility of Jews overcoming their "blood" through religious conversion. Georg von Schönerer had emphasized biological identity in 1885 (Weininger was five years old), adding a twelfth point to his hitherto non-anti-Semitic Linz Program of 1882: "The removal of Jewish influence from all sections of public life is indispensable for carrying out the reforms aimed at" (Pulzer 1988, 147). A 1942 article celebrating "One Hundred Years of Schönerer" credited Schönerer with "building the victorious road to Austria" for Hitler and for clearing up a false distinction between Jews and Christians: "What the Jew *believes* is all the same, in his *race* resides the dirty shame!" (Pichl 1942, 301-4). As Von Braun points out, Schönerer's portrayal of anti-Semitism as a "cleansing agent" made a great impression on Hitler.[11]

The Jewish theoretician Theodor Lessing had reinforced blood imagery in *Der jüdische Selbsthaß* (Jewish Self-Hatred) in 1930. No Jewish writer of the period did more to secure Weininger's reputation as a self-hating Jew than did Lessing in this famous book. Featured in one of six case studies, Weininger emerges as a "Jewish Oedipus" who cursed his mother's blood (Lessing 1930, 82). According to Lessing, Weininger became obsessed with the belief that spirit is superior to nature, such that "woman" and "Jew" became synonymous with the "depths of nature" he feared and avoided. While Lessing pointed correctly to the tragic effect of Weininger's

extremely polarized philosophy, he himself was caught up in the inflammatory racial rhetoric of his era. His most unfortunate pronouncement was that "no human being has ever freed himself from the constraints of his blood. No categorical imperative has ever obscured the voice of blood" (Lessing 1930, 91), which Nazi propagandists used to their best advantage (Kohn 1962; Janik 1987).[12]

Julius Streicher, editor of the notoriously anti-Semitic magazine for SA men, *Der Stürmer* (The Stormer), published from 1924 to 1945,[13] and Nazi *Gauleiter* of Nuremberg, popularized the racist eugenic belief that led to the criminalization of sex between "Aryans" and Jews: "A single act of intercourse between a Jewish man and an Aryan woman is enough to poison the woman's blood forever. Even if she marries an Aryan man, she will never bear pure Aryan children, but only bastards" (Westenrieder 1984, 31).[14] A lavishly illustrated text by Professor Theodor Pugel, a historian at the University of Vienna, expressed the same ideas somewhat less crudely in *Die arische Frau im Wandel der Jahrtausende: Kulturgeschichtlich geschildert* (The Aryan Woman in the Course of the Millennia) in 1936.[15]

In 1935, when *völkisch* notions about race were put into effect by Nazi laws such as the "Blood Protection Law" forbidding marriage and extramarital intercourse between non-Jewish and Jewish Germans, and the Marriage Health Law establishing hereditary biological standards for marriage between "Aryans" (Westenrieder 1984, 31), Robert Körber and Theodor Pugel edited *Antisemitismus der Welt in Wort und Bild* (The World of Anti-Semitism in Words and Pictures). In his concluding chapter, Körber, a popular anti-Semitic writer, stresses that one cannot adopt an ethnic identity or take it off "like a worn-out suit," insisting instead on "nationalism by blood only" *(Blutsvolkstum).* "Spare our people above all," he beseeches, "from the unfortunate figures of a Weininger and a Trebitsch, who could not overcome 'jewing' *(Judenzen)* despite their hating nothing more than their people of origin" (Körber and Pugel 1935, 316). Arthur Trebitsch (1880-1927) was an anti-Semitic Viennese Jew who published *Deutscher Geist und Judentum* (German Spirit and Judaism) in 1919 and also featured prominently in Lessing's study of Jewish self-hatred. As Sander Gilman notes, "Here was the Jew who bore witness to the truth of the accusation that it was the Jews who caused Germany's defeat [in World War I]" (Gilman 1986, 249). Between Lessing and the Nazis, the stereotypes of Weininger and Trebitsch as self-hating Jews were assured.

Houston Stewart Chamberlain's *Grundlagen des* 19. *Jahrhunderts (The Foundations of the Nineteenth Century)* of 1899 served as a mutual point of reference for Weininger and Nazi ideologues. Weininger had met Chamberlain at sessions of the Viennese Philosophical Society and was thoroughly familiar with his highly celebrated work, which was one of the main sources for his views on Judaism. Citing the fourth printing of *The Foundations* in 1903, Weininger notes that Chamberlain's attempts to solve the "anthropological question" of the origin of Judaism had recently met with a great deal of controversy. His observation reflects the fact that Chamberlain's book, although rejected by many contemporary scholars as the work of a dilettante, nonetheless enjoyed enormous popular success.[16]

It has often been observed that Weininger chose to convert to Protestantism in the midst of the predominantly Catholic culture of Vienna. His decision underscores the fact that he felt most at home intellectually in the Protestant philosophical tradition upon which Chamberlain drew. Weininger was clearly inspired by Chamberlain's reading of Kant as "the first perfect pattern of the absolutely independent Teuton who has put aside every trace of Roman absolutism, dogmatism and anti-individualism," and who "can—whenever we please—emancipate us from Judaism: not by bitterness and persecution, but by once for all destroying every historical superstition, every cabalisticism of Spinoza, every materialistic dogmatism" (Chamberlain 1913, vol. 3, 490).[17] In *Sex and Character* Weininger underscored his intentions: "I shall emphasize once again, although it ought to be obvious: in spite of my adverse evaluation of the actual Jew, the last thing I have in mind is—on the basis of these or the following observations—to play into the hands of theoretical, or even worse, practical persecution of the Jews" (Weininger 1903, 417-418). Weininger's reading of Christ as the symbol of hope that individual Jews could "put aside" or "emancipate" themselves from "Jewishness" is an impassioned answer to Chamberlain's argument—so necessary for Chamberlain's synthesis of Christianity and "Aryan" identity—that Jesus had not been a Jew by "blood."[18] However, the evidence shows repeatedly that *völkisch* and Nazi ideologues dismissed this aspect of Weininger's argument, preferring to focus on the (self-hating) ways in which he agreed with Chamberlain, such as his reference to a section of *The Foundations* called "Consensus Ingeniorum," in which Chamberlain recites a consensus of anti-Jewish judgments among Cicero, Frederik the Great, Bismarck, Mommsen, Herder, and Goethe (Chamberlain 1913, vol. 1, 344-46).

In *Das Lebenswerk Houston Stewart Chamberlains in Umrissen* (The Life's Work of Houston Stewart Chamberlain in Outline) a tribute to Chamberlain published in 1927, the year of his death, Georg Schott cites the "Weininger case" as evidence for Chamberlain's claim that the Jewish race is "a crime against the holy law of life" (Schott 1927, 38). Schott stresses the "race question," quoting Weininger and Benjamin Disraeli as Jews who attest to its importance. Schott goes so far as to call Weininger a "martyr to his conviction" (Schott 1927, 96-97), thereby manipulating a prevalent view of Weininger's ethical integrity among intellectuals. He praises Chamberlain as an "inexorable judge and avenger for truth" who must feel like "a sword piercing the soul" to "a Jew of Weininger's inner constitution." Lauded as a martyr, Weininger "cannot blame" but rather must admire Chamberlain for his relentless campaign against

Judaism—a campaign whose "high moral ground" Schott admonishes his fellow anti-Semites to emulate (Schott 1927, 109).

As a *völkisch* thinker, Oswald Spengler made a crucial distinction for later Nazi ideologues between culture and civilization, between a rooted (German) soul and (Jewish) rootlessness.[19] In Spengler's view, Jewish mysticism had produced "three more saints in the sense of Oriental Sufism—though to recognize them as such we have to see through a colour-wash of Western thought-forms" (Spengler 1928, 321). Weininger is the third of these saints, preceded by Spinoza and Baal Shem. Spengler labels Weininger's "moral dualism" and "death in a spiritual struggle [as] one of the noblest spectacles ever presented by a Late religiousness." Weininger's experience is said to be *Magian*, Spengler's term for those spiritual cultures in which man "belongs to himself alone, but something else, something alien and higher, dwells in him, making him with all his glimpses and convictions just a member of a consensus which, as the emanation of God, excludes error, but excludes also all possibility of the self-asserting Ego" (Spengler 1928, 235). The classification is only apparently problematic in relation to Weininger—Weininger's answer to Ernst Mach's "irretrievable self" being the restoration of Kant's "intelligible self"[20]—for Spengler cites a tradition of Magian fascination with Kant's thought.[21]

Spengler's respectful image of Weininger as a saint, albeit one whom Westerners could never fully understand, clashed with the flagrant anti-Semitism of the Weimar era. Like other *völkisch* and Nazi ideologues, Schott believed that Spengler's theories were not sufficiently anti-Semitic.[22] In his chapter "Spengler or Chamberlain?"—in which Chamberlain triumphs as the "Nordic" over the "Magian" character type—Schott classifies Weininger together with Spengler as "a Faustian spirit in a Magian soul." Such natures are "tragic," and their readers must learn to distinguish the "good" and "healthy" from the "insane" aspects of their genius (Schott 1927, 149).

When National Socialism came to power, some of the Nazi Party's female adherents attempted to exert influence (Koonz 1987), in spite of the party's explicit history of excluding women from its top ranks (Franz-Willing 1962, 80; Thalmann 1984, 74). Rita Thalmann pinpoints a decisive moment in Nazi ideology in which Hitler left it up to party theoreticians like Rosenberg to justify women's subordinate role and at the same time to ensure their enthusiastic participation as mothers in the eugenic design of the future Germanic state. While Rosenberg drew on the "cultural pessimism of a host of misogynist thinkers from Schopenhauer to Wagner, Nietzsche, Houston Chamberlain and up through Otto Weininger" in his *Mythus des 20. Jahrhunderts* (Myth of the Twentieth Century) of 1930, he had to reconcile the call in cultural pessimism for a "return to chastity" with the aims of National Socialism (Thalmann 1984, 75). Thus, he claimed that in world history the creative-constructive world of the Apollonian "fathers" had triumphed over the orgiastic-destructive chaos of the Dionysian "mothers," thereby creating a "new" place of honor through marriage for the woman *as mother* within the Nordic-Apollonian principle. Lydia Gottschewski, a Nazi youth organizer since the 1920s and first appointed head of the Women's Front in 1933, accused Hans F. K. Günther of borrowing his views on women from Weininger and chided Rosenberg for his theory that Nordic man was the sole inventor of marriage (Thalmann 1984, 84; Koonz 1987, 142-43, 157). However, in any case Rosenberg's abstractions were too difficult for the average German. Consequently, Hitler made sure that key party concepts were also communicated in simpler language by himself and others (Thalmann 1984, 75-76; Diehl 1932).

The anthropologist Pia Sophie Rogge-Börner, who had been writing on gender and race since the early 1920s, "accurately perceived the danger of an all-male elite turning women into breeding machines" but "exalted racial thinking as long as it did not diminish women's participation in the master race" (Koonz 1987, 113). Rogge-Börner and some of her women Nazi friends wrote letters to Hitler in March 1932 and January 1933, demanding that the German people be led by the best and brightest of both genders. She took issue with Weininger's famous assertion about the relative abilities of men and women at the beginning of his chapter on Judaism: "Just because a Weininger has claimed that even 'the lowliest man is immeasurably superior to the most remarkable woman,' that's no reason to conclude that the majority of men are better suited to leadership positions than are the majority of women" (Rogge-Börner 1934, quoted in Thalmann 1984, 84). Hitler never answered her letter.[23]

Yet the National Socialists eventually did respond in an oblique form after the disaster in Stalingrad, since the policy of total war included gestures to increase women's sense of comradeship with men. As we have seen, Nazi ideology had always implicitly concurred with Weininger's contempt for women, but it needed them to produce the next "Aryan" generation (Koonz 1987, 59-60). Hitler's refusal to tap women as a reserve work force until late in the war and Himmler's cynical *Lebensborn* program, which provided prenatal care for unwed "Aryan" mothers and included plans for SS officers to impregnate vast numbers of "Aryan" girls, were both based on a view of women as breeding machines for the Third Reich (cf. Lilienthal 1985). It was only after Stalingrad that Hitler's deputies were able to override his opposition to drafting women into war work (Koonz 1987, 398).[24]

In the fall of 1943, a thirty-two-page pamphlet by Dr. Alexander Centgraf, "Ein Jude treibt Philosophie" ("A Jew Tries His Hand at Philosophy"), was published in Berlin (Kohn 1962; Janik 1987). In the preface, which is dated the end of August 1943, Centgraf, "currently in Kiev," admits that "many will ask whether it is actually

necessary at this moment, when we are at the zenith of the greatest of all wars, to write a booklet of this kind. Who is still interested," he wonders, "in a twenty-three-year-old who has been dead for forty years [Weininger]— even if his book was a great success?" (Centgraf 1943) "Even if" is significant, for Weininger was apparently earmarked in the Nazi propaganda effort for the reasons I have stated above.

The "spiritual construction of Aryan culture," Centgraf explains, is a "fine weave" into which Weininger has smuggled a "Jewish thread." Centgraf sees a direct line between *Sex and Character,* Freud, and Magnus Hirschfeld, in all of whose writings "woman is branded as a person of low quality, and above and beyond that, is desecrated intellectually and spiritually. Above all today, when woman is employing her entire personality to fight with us for the political and spiritual conditions for a new Europe, we owe it to her as a comrade to thoroughly settle the score with *such a dangerous Jewish intellectual as Otto Weininger*" (Centgraf 1943 [emphasis added]).

Centgraf was probably relieved from active military duty in Kiev long enough to write this homage to German women because the Propaganda Ministry deemed it a good idea. He had studied journalism at the University of Berlin in the late 1930s. His doctoral dissertation, written under the direction of Professor Emil Dovifat (Benedikt 1986),[25] was published in 1940 as *Martin Luther als Publizist: Geist und Form seiner Volksführung* (Martin Luther as a Publicist: The Spirit and Form of His Leadership of the Volk).[26] As a friend of the Provostry of Berlin, he had also published a commemorative essay, *Luther und Berlin,* in 1939 for the four-hundredth anniversary of the Reformation.

The opening chapter of "A Jew Tries His Hand at Philosophy," entitled "A philosophical Prodigy," blasts Weininger's "dangerous definitions of women," which rob mothers of their dignity. Centgraf views Weininger's call to ban mothers from the pedagogical tasks of childrearing as the "first stages of Bolshevist collective thinking," while at the same time accusing him of preparing the ground for "unbridled individualism" (Centgraf 1943, 6). However, Weininger's call for celibacy at the cost of the extinction of the human race receives Centgraf's harshest criticism: Weininger's "complete negation of the human race" is "Jewish" (Centgraf 1943, 7).

The second chapter, "No One Has Ever Freed Himself from the Constraints of His Blood,[27] declares Weininger's death a catastrophe for assimilated Jews, who had set for themselves the impossible goal of slipping into the protective covering of another race (Centgraf 1943, 9). Since the Jews have a different "spirit," they can never become Germans. Centgraf invokes the expertise of Theodor Lessing regarding Jewish self-hatred after citing Weininger's own prejudices about Jewish character (Centgraf 1943, II). Weininger genuinely tried to become a Christian, Centgraf believes, but it was impossible for him to leave the "spiritual abyss of Jewishness" (Centgraf 1943, 13).

In Chapter Three, "The Demonic Nature of Sexuality: The Sexual Problem at the Core of Otto Weininger's Ideas," Centgraf explains that the Jew has deteriorated ontologically due to the demonic nature of sexuality; hence the predominance of Jews in sex research. Jews have less shame and less awe for the mysteries of life. Centgraf takes up the familiar theme of Jewish lasciviousness, then comes to the thrust of his argument: it is an outrage for a "Jewish philosophy" to place "Aryan" women on a par with the inferior Jewish race (Centgraf 1943, 17). In contrast, Centgraf praises the work of a Professor Mathilde Vaerting (1931) at the University of Jena on the psychology of the sexes, as "women must be consulted in order to gain a full picture of the psychology of the sexes" (Centgraf 1943, 20). Weininger's impertinent book, he laments, has done great damage to many immature young people in the first decades of the twentieth century by teaching them to undervalue women. Moreover, Bolshevism owes a great deal to its "apostle Weininger" for its view of woman as a "soulless machine" (Centgraf 1943, 21).

The fourth chapter, "A Jewish Prescription for Homosexuals of Both Sexes," is a homophobic attack on Weininger's theory of sexual gradations. Weininger, the "philosophical quack," has branded all famous women as lesbians and attempted to make "Aryan" heroes despicable by equating genius with homosexuality and perversion (Centgraf 1943, 24-25). Centgraf scoffs at Weininger's proposal to decriminalize homosexuality, and is alarmed by his suggestion that society mandate the pairing of contrasting "M" and "W" types, for the offspring would inherit their parents' imbalances (Centgraf 1943, 26). Weininger's "Jewish" agenda, he claims, is to corrupt and destroy "Aryan" morality (Centgraf 1943, 27).[28]

Centgraf's concluding chapter, "The Epistemological Cardinal Error in Dr. Weininger's *Sex and Character*: Truth Rather Than Jewish Arrogance," foresees the gradual emancipation of women and an accompanying increase in male objectivity toward women. He faults Weininger for his "one-sided" analysis of women. This, in and of itself, would be forgivable, Centgraf admits, since other psychologists and philosophers "have made the same mistake," but Weininger's "latent homosexual inclinations caused him to write a book that would violate woman's body and soul" (Centgraf 1943, 29). He rejects Weininger's argument that "man projects his own need for beauty and love onto soulless woman" as an idea borrowed from Islam (Centgraf 1943, 31): "When this incomparable war of destiny is behind us, should the European people degrade their women to soulless beings, to willing slaves to the desires of man, to slaves who can only hope to gain a soul from him? That would be poor thanks to all of the wives and mothers fighting as comrades side by side with men in

two great wars for a newer, better future for our continent" (Centgraf 1943, 31). Centgraf accuses Jewish speculators of keeping *Sex and Character* alive by artificial means in order to pave the way for "sexual anarchy" and to "pit man against woman and woman against man" (Centgraf 1943, 32).

Centgraf has contorted the usual Nazi argument to serve Nazi ends, for Nazi idealogues typically blamed "Jewish intellect" for advancing the cause of women's emancipation. Women's emancipation, according to the prevailing Nazi argument, upset the social order by blurring borders between sexual spheres. Hitler had claimed in his 1934 speech to the Nationalsozialistische Frauenschaft thatthe phrase "emancipation of woman" is the product of Jewish intellect, and its content is stamped with that same intellect. During those truly good times in German life the German woman never found it necessary to emancipate herself. She controlled exactly that which nature freely gave her as her due to administer and preserve—just as the man in good times did not have to fear that woman would oust him from his position. . . . It is not true—as Jewish intellect would have us believe—that mutual respect is based upon the overlapping of sexual spheres of activity. On the contrary, such respect demands that neither sex encroach upon the sphere of the other (Hitler 1934, 376-77).

However, in this instance, Centgraf blames Weininger for his "arrogant Jewish" rejection of equal social status for women and men. Centgraf's task was in fact to lie about the actual sexist premise of National Socialism, which aimed to exploit women as a "means to the selective production and reproduction of the fascist body" (Kuhn 1988, 41). Even if Centgraf was naive—or frightened—enough to believe his own statements,[29] his naiveté was surely and cynically exploited.

As late as January 1945, Weininger's name appears in a major channel of Nazi propaganda to invoke yet again the dangers of "the Jewish essence." The *WeltDienst: Die Judenfrage/Internationale Korrespondenz* (World Service: The Jewish Question/International Correspondence), which was published bi-weekly in twenty-one languages, cites "the Jew Weininger's" definition of the Jew as one who contains all possibilities without actually *being* anything.[30] Jews are likened to species of animals whose biological characteristics include the ability to adapt to host cultures. Even Zionism is viewed disparagingly as the Jews' attempt to adapt themselves to European nationalism. The *WeltDienst* takes up the familiar refrain from prefaces to "Jewish self-revelations" that Jews themselves admit that their bad traits are not the result of centuries of oppression, but are endemic: "Jews themselves confirm it, and not just a few individuals like Otto Weininger at the turn of the century, but official Jewish organs, newspapers geared specifically toward Jews, like the Yiddish 'Tog' that appears in New York, or the 'American Hebrew,' which seeks to promote 'better understanding between Jews and Christians'" (*WeltDienst* 1945, 10). In the final frenzy of their war against the Jews, Nazi ideologues continued to milk Weininger's critique of "Jewish character" after they had already murdered millions.

NOTES

[1] Mosse (1966, 76f) calls *Sex and Character* "a classic not only of Jewish self-hate but also of racist literature."

[2] Weininger's posthumously published *Über die letzten Dinge* (On Last Things) is never quoted by Nazi ideologues.

[3] Koonz (1987) has become a standard work on both National Socialist policy toward women and women's responses to life in the Third Reich. For a preliminary study on the European cultural history of hostility toward women and Jews, see Braun (1992, 1993). Also cf. Jakubowski (1991).

[4] See Fritsch (1887, 1919, 1929, 1943). A biographical note in his *Handbuch der Judenfrage,* first published in 1930, proudly refers to Fritsch as "der Schöpfer des praktischen Antisemitismus" (the creator of practical anti-Semitism). Fritsch also published under a number of pseudonyms such as Thomas Frey, Fritz Thor, and F. Roderich-Stoltheim.

[5] The *Handbuch* also contains an appendix of "Jewish Self-Revelations" in which two of the same quotations appear, also under the rubric "Jewish Character."

[6] See Mosse (1964, 302), who in turn cites Deuerlein (1959, 203).

[7] Rosenberg (1928, 214-19), quoted in "The Earth-Centered Jew Lacks a Soul" (Mosse 1966, 75-78). Also see Rosenberg (1930).

[8] The phrase "and certainly less capable of all great pleasure" did not appear in the first edition, but was added to subsequent editions.

[9] Another aspect of Weininger's portrayal of Jewish male sexuality has to do with body image. Cf. John M. Hoberman's essay in this volume (Chapter 9).

[10] Richard Wagner is the source of both Rosenberg's and Weininger's assertions. See Rosenberg (1933, 15), quoted in Koch (1986, 72).

[11] For an explication of the significance of blood imagery in anti-Semitism, see Braun (1990, 153).

[12] See Janik (1987, 80): "The simple fact about Theodor Lessing's account of Weininger in *Der jüdische Selbsthass* is that it is based upon a racism which is just as crude as anything that the most vulgar Nazi ideologues might have asserted. For Lessing Weininger's problem was rooted in hatred for his blood."

[13] Also see Bytwerk (1983).

[14] The same racist tone is appearing again in neo-Nazi publications; for example, "A vagina that has been sullied by a Jew remains a cesspool. No Aryan broom can sweep it clean," which appeared in an issue of the *Skinhead-Zeitung,* was quoted in "Bestie aus deutschem Blut" (Beast of German Blood), the cover story in *Der Spiegel* (50/1992) 30.

[15] See in particular Pugel's chapter "Die deutsche Frau im Kampfe gegen das Judentum und den Bolschewismus" (The German woman in battle against Judaism and Bolshevism).

[16] However, as Jacques Le Rider notes, it also impressed more subtle thinkers, such as Karl Kraus (Le Rider 1985, 23, 144, 190-91, 201, 217). Also see Rodlauer's (1990) discussion of Chamberlain and Weininger, and the abridged translation of the work in this volume (Chapter 3).

[17] On the Chamberlain-Kant connection cf. Mosse (1964, 94).

[18] Cf. Braun (1990, 157).

[19] See Mosse (1964, 6; 1970, 15, 36, 57, 162, 243 n. 68).

[20] See Beller (1989b, 222). Regarding the last months of Weininger's life, during which he rejected the Kantian self, see Kohn (1962, 41-42).

[21] Cf. Spengler in the passage on Jewish saints: Kant's "abstract kind of thought has always possessed an immense attraction for Talmudic intellects" (Spengler 1928, 321).

[22] Cf. Spengler (1928, 318): "But all this has nothing to do with the silly catchwords 'Aryan' and 'Semite' that have been borrowed from philology."

[23] Rogge-Börner also made a bid to become national director of women's affairs, but was disqualified because she was independent and charismatic (Koonz 1987, 140). Her journal, "Die deutsche Kämpferin" (The German Woman Fighter), was banned in 1937 when it was perceived as too critical of National Socialist policies toward women (Thalmann 1984, 85f).

[24] Also see, for example, Buresch-Riebe (1942), and articles in the *Völkischer Beobachter* (Berlin edition) such as Sachisthal (1943), "Berliner Mädel" (1943) and "Nationaler Ehrendienst (1943).

[25] Dovifat, who began his career in the Weimar era and ended it as a renowned professor at the Free University of Berlin and founding editor of the journal *Publizistik,* provides yet another example of "inner emigration" during National Socialism. Although his academic freedom was curtailed at the University of Berlin because

his loyalty to the state was under suspicion, he was allowed to teach, and he managed to inspire enthusiasm among young Nazis and fledgling critics of the regime alike. Benedikt reports that in 1982 one of Dovifat's former doctoral students, Elisabeth Noelle-Neumann, recalled his general principle that "the first and last three pages of a dissertation had to make National Socialist arguments, and that he referred to these pages among his trusted inner circle as 'wrapping paper'" (Benedikt 1986, 202). On the controversy surrounding Noelle-Neumann, see Bogart (1991) and Lederer (1993). Dovifat's most controversial publication during the Third Reich was a 1937 analysis of political orators and oratory in which he wrote of Hitler: "Just as he can explain with technical rationality the principles of leading the masses, so too does he vividly and warmly look beyond the primary substance of the masses for the *Volk,* which he wants to convince, to turn into a believer, and thereby transform. . . . Everything is folksy, eager to instruct, presented with tireless clarity, not speaking beyond the *Volk,* but rather of and for the *Volk*" (Dovifat 1937, 138). While it is easy to read such statements after the fact as veiled criticisms, Dovifat never openly resisted the Nazi state.

[26] Centgraf had the appropriate Nazi credentials to write a diatribe against Weininger. His dissertation topic, which casts Martin Luther in the light of a charismatic German leader who engaged in "propaganda for the masses" with his books and leaflets (Centgraf 1940, 5), is completely in line with Houston Stewart Chamberlain's view of the Reformation as "the most decisive of all political acts." Chamberlain's views served as the ideological foundation for subsequent *völkisch* interpretations of Luther (cf. Brosseder 1972, 98-101). Centgraf comments in a lengthy footnote on Luther's infamous treatise of 1543, "On the Jews and Their Lies": "Luther makes . . . practical suggestions on how to do battle with the Jews and shows himself *here especially to be the* innovative and path-breaking communicator of timeless importance *for and influence on the German nation*" (Centgraf 1940, 34f.).

[27] The title is a quote from Theodor Lessing's *Der jüdische Selbsthaâ* of 1930.

[28] Magnus Hirschfeld regularly came under attack for his sexual preference and for his scientific studies on homosexuality. *Der Stürmer,* for example, accused homosexuals like Hirschfeld of creating "a Jewish conspiracy to destroy marriage and the family" (Showalter 1982, 100).

[29] Centgraf continued to publish after the war, but under the pseudonym of N. Alexander Centurio. He devoted himself to the sixteenth-century prophetic visions of Nostradamus, a longstanding fascination he had in common with many prominent Nazi leaders, Goebbels among them. Centgraf/Centurio translated and interpreted the prophecies in the "first complete German edition" in 1953 as *Nostradamus, der Prophet der*

Weltgeschichte (Nostradamus, The Prophet of World History). The book is still available today in the Goldmann Verlag *Esoterik* series (Centurio 1991). Centgraf/Centurio defines National Socialism as "a strange mixture of romanticism and brutality" (Centurio 1991, 198). He mentions Jews only in the context of Nostradamus's biography, noting that Nostradamus's paternal ancestors were Sephardic Jews who fled religious persecution (Centurio 1991, 13), and in the context of the still unresolved Arab-Israeli conflict in the Middle East. According to Centgraf/Centurio's reading of 1,45, "Hitler did away with all parties that criticized the system. He set up concentration camps in which dogs were also set on the unfortunate victims. With ancient cruelty of a sadistic nature, the inmates of these camps were tortured and killed. As a result of the crimes of the Nazi Party, the world is thrust into division and despair" (Centurio 1991, 202). Interpreting Nostradamus's prophecies about the years 1942-45, in Verse 5,96, Centgraf/Centurio writes, "Hitler . . . spilled, for the sake of his insane goals, the blood of six million Germans. All opposition to the politics of violence was stifled by the Gestapo" (Centurio 1991, 211). While Centgraf/Centurio has no difficulty recalling that *Germans* were subject to National Socialist brutality, he apparently cannot face up to the mass murder of *European Jews* to which he contributed indirectly at the very least.

[30] This issue contains two anonymous essays, "Das jüdische Wesen" (The Jewish Essence) and "Juden zeichnen sich selbst" (Jews Portray Themselves), which refer in passing to Otto Weininger.

Chandak Sengoopta (essay date 1996)

SOURCE: "The Unknown Weininger: Science, Philosophy, and Cultural Politics in Fin-de-Siècle Vienna," in *Central European History,* Vol. 29, No. 4, 1996, pp. 453-93.

[*In the following essay, Sengoopta presents an overview of the* scientific, philosophical, and cultural background *of late-nineteenth-century Vienna into which Weininger was born.*]

Otto Weininger (1880-1903) is a notorious figure in European history.[1] A Jewish intellectual of Vienna, Weininger committed suicide at the age of 23 after publishing a single book based on his doctoral dissertation, **Geschlecht und Charakter** (**Sex and Character,** 1903).[2] The work was admired by some of the greatest intellects of our century—Franz Kafka, Ludwig Wittgenstein, James Joyce, Karl Kraus, August Strindberg. More recently, it has attained virtually legendary status among scholars as an exemplary text of European misogyny and antisemitism.[3] While **Geschlecht und Charakter** is certainly unrivaled as a compendium of turn-of-the-century prejudices, stereotypes, and anxieties, it is not simply a deranged thinker's chronicle of personal nightmares. This fact has been obscured due to the failure of recent scholars to situate Weininger and his work in the intellectual and cultural contexts of fin-de-siècle Central Europe. This paper demonstrates that *Geschlecht und Charakter* is an intensely personal analysis of intellectual, political, and cultural themes that were of central importance to contemporary Viennese intellectuals.[4]

Geschlecht und Charakter is lengthy and complex, but its fundamental objectives are clear: to understand the underlying nature of differences between masculinity and femininity and to use that knowledge to explain certain perceived cultural predicaments. Although the work of an academic philosopher, the text is far from purely academic. Weininger emphasizes that the central purpose of his work is to resolve the "woman question," which, for him, does not simply denote the demands of fin-de-siècle feminist activists but the whole debate they generated on woman's nature and her place in society and the world. Disregarding purely social or economic issues, Weininger concentrates on metaphysical and broadly political questions of female autonomy. Are women complete, autonomous individuals in an ontological sense? If not, then how could they even demand emancipation and equality?

Weininger addresses this question from numerous angles, drawing upon an enormous range of material from philosophical, biological, medical, and psychological discourses. This discursive polyphony of *Geschlecht und Charakter* has not been adequately analyzed and its use of science, in particular, has been ignored or ridiculed. Instead of dismissing Weininger as a pseudoscientist, as his recent biographer Jacques Le Rider has done, we need to explore how Weininger's use of scientific discourse is constantly and explicitly modulated by his ideological aim of resolving the woman question. While the ideologically motivated use of scientific metaphors or theories by non-scientists has hardly been uncommon in modern times, Weininger's use of science is unusual in its extraordinary discursive range and depth of engagement. Weininger does not simply refer to one theory or adopt a few metaphors: he takes numerous ideas from numerous scientific fields and integrates them into his larger political project according to different strategic principles. Which aspects of science, which texts, which specific notions does Weininger consider important? Which does he reject? And, more importantly, why? Is Weininger merely a prejudiced crank who raids the culturally neutral realm of science, grabs whatever he finds, and distorts whatever he uses? Or are his appropriations conditioned by definite requirements and principles?

Such questions, of course, are biographical as well as historical. My aim is to explore how *Geschlecht und Charakter* incorporates, reformulates, and responds to broad, historically specific issues in ways that are intensely personal and frequently idiosyncratic. Weininger's text is best approached as a set of complex interactions and mediations between an individual thinker and his densely—and unpredictably—populated discursive universe. The challenge of reading Weininger is to situate his work in its contexts without deriving it therefrom in a linear, simplistic manner.

THE EDUCATION OF OTTO WEININGER

Otto Weininger's biography is well known in its outlines. He was born on 3 April 1880 to a Jewish family of Vienna, the second child and oldest son of Leopold Weininger (1854-1922) and Adelheid Frey (1857-1912). His father was a famous goldsmith, a devotee of Richard Wagner's music, and a self-taught polyglot ambivalent about his Jewish identity.[5] Otto turned out to be a brilliant student, exhibiting a special flair for the humanities. Emotionally close to his father, he possessed Leopold's talent for languages and shared his passion for Wagner. At eighteen, he "knew Latin and Greek, spoke French, English, and Italian well, and was fluent in Spanish and Norwegian."[6] After graduating from the Gymnasium in 1898, he enrolled in the philosophical faculty of the University of Vienna, where he attended an eclectic range of courses on logic, experimental psychology, pedagogy, the history of philosophy, mathematics, physics, chemistry, botany, zoology, anatomy, physiology, histology, embryology, neurology, and psychiatry.[7] His primary intellectual interests, however, were philosophy and psychology, which he approached in the "critical positivist" spirit of physicist-philosopher Ernst Mach and the Swiss philosopher Richard Avenarius, a perspective he later disavowed.[8]

In 1900, Weininger's friend Hermann Swoboda began an analysis with Sigmund Freud, who, although not yet internationally famous, was a well-known figure among the Viennese intelligentsia.[9] During this period, Freud was working out the founding principles of psychoanalysis in an intense correspondence with his close friend, the Berlin otolaryngologist and biological theorist Wilhelm Fliess. This correspondence dealt with numerous issues, among which questions of sexuality were preeminent.[10] During Swoboda's analysis, Freud mentioned to him that all human beings were partly male and partly female or "bisexual." This was a topic that Fliess considered his own. Swoboda, apparently ignorant of this, reported Freud's observation to Weininger.[11] Excited by this notion, Weininger immediately began to work on a monograph on sexuality that, he was convinced, would produce salutary social effects. This project developed eventually into his doctoral dissertation and, then, into the monograph *Geschlecht und Charakter*.[12]

Weininger's dissertation has disappeared but two early outlines have recently been found in the archives of the Viennese Academy of Sciences.[13] Two vital points emerge from these drafts. First, Weininger, for reasons that are not clear, jettisoned his earlier allegiance to Mach and Avenarius around the middle of his university career.[14] Disenchanted with positivistic psychology, he now decided that speculation and introspection, guided by Kantian principles, were preferable routes to inner truth.[15] Second, Weininger developed the conviction that women and Jews were not truly autonomous individuals in the Kantian sense: they did not possess distinct, coherent, inner selves. The dissertation that resulted from this intellectual odyssey contained many idiosyncrasies. The examiners were critical of these but, on the whole, regarded it as an impressive work of scholarship that, after revisions, was worthy of publication.[16]

Immediately after obtaining his doctorate, Weininger converted to Protestantism.[17] He then suffered periods of deep depression but, nevertheless, began to revise his dissertation for publication and the renowned firm of Wilhelm Braumüller published it in June 1903.[18] The book aroused little interest at first and few reviews of any note were published before October. Still deeply depressed, Weininger now rented a room in the house where Ludwig van Beethoven had died, and, on the night of 3 October 1903, shot himself to death.[19] Weininger's decision to kill himself did not really surprise those who knew of his recent, severe bouts of depression. For those who knew of Weininger only through his work, however, the symbolic dimensions of his death were more noteworthy than its possible etiology. The sales of *Geschlecht und Charakter* soared and countless newspapers and magazines published reviews and appreciations, many of them portraying Weininger as a tragic genius. As Peter Gay has remarked, the suicide seemed to come as an appropriately "melodramatic end to an (at least inwardly) melodramatic life."[20]

WEININGER'S WORLDS: IDENTITY, PHILOSOPHY, AND POLITICS IN CENTRAL EUROPE

The personal melodrama of Weininger's life was related intimately to the dramas of his age. Some of the most significant intellectual and cultural currents of the time entered into his consciousness and *Geschlecht und Charakter* is essentially incomprehensible without some appreciation of contexts as different as Viennese traditions of cultural criticism, fin-de-siècle feminism, Ernst Mach's theories of the self, neo-Kantian philosophy, and the racial ideas of Richard Wagner. Each of these themes has been explored in great detail by historians. Surprisingly, however, that research seems to have made little impact on the literature on Weininger, which continues, by and large, to view the Viennese philosopher in splendid (and, all too often, psychotic) isolation from his epoch.

The Annihilation of the Self—Much has been written on fin-de-siècle Viennese culture, the crisis of Austrian liberalism, and the consequent retreat of liberal intellectuals into their own selves.[21] This inward turn did not necessarily lead, however, to outer quiescence. The diverse members of the Viennese avant-garde were virtually unanimous in their dissatisfaction with the cultural contradictions and spiritual emptiness of Viennese life.[22] Their outpourings, epitomized by the writings of Karl Kraus, amounted to a distinct genre of cultural criticism, the major theme of which was a quest for authenticity. Regardless of personal targets of criticism (newspaper-language for Kraus, ornate architecture for architect Adolf Loos, femininity for Otto Weininger), the avant-garde aimed to uncover the true identity of the self, of language, of races, of sexes, or of objects.[23]

The identity of the self was a crucial issue. The collapse of Viennese liberalism, Carl Schorske has argued, undermined traditional liberal faith in the autonomy of the rational, individual subject.[24] This crisis, however, was not exclusively political: the psychophysical theories of Ernst Mach, Professor of Philosophy at the University of Vienna, contributed greatly toward the demolition of the Enlightenment concept of a coherent self.[25] What people thought of as their distinct, unified "ego," said Mach, was simply a complex of sensations. Individual differences stemmed from differences in the configuration of these sensations. "The ego," Mach proclaimed, "is beyond salvage."[26] The intellectual elite of Vienna was electrified by this declaration. Essayist, critic, and perpetually fashionable intellectual Hermann Bahr (1863-1934) reminisced that with that one provocative statement of Mach's, "the last of the idols seemed to be smashed, the last refuge fallen, the highest freedom won, the work of annihilation completed. There really remained nothing else."[27] Some intellectuals and artists, such as Arthur Schnitzler, Hugo von Hofmannsthal, or Robert Musil, were stimulated or even exhilarated by Mach's demolition of the self. Others, such as Otto Weininger and Hermann Broch, felt deeply threatened.[28]

In the scientific field, Mach's ideas greatly influenced new, experimental approaches to psychology that were developed by, among others, Oswald Külpe (1862-1915) and Hermann Ebbinghaus (1850-1909).[29] Rejecting earlier philosophical versions of psychology, they swore allegiance to Mach, rejected mind-body dualism, and all mentalistic explanations in psychology.[30] Although eventually embraced by the majority of early twentieth-century psychologists, this rigorously positivistic and experimental approach was initially opposed as too extreme by many, including Wilhelm Wundt, who was himself an experimentalist, and the philosopher and historian Wilhelm Dilthey.[31] The new experimental psychology also opposed significant tenets of Kantian philosophy. Kant had taught that the moral center of the human individual was his noumenal self, which was inaccessible to empirical investigation and independent of space and time. Its existence could be philosophically deduced but never scientifically demonstrated: it was *intelligible,* not phenomenal. If the new experimentalists were right, however, that inner self simply did not exist.[32] *Geschlecht und Charakter* is, in part, an acerbic attack on experimental psychology in the name of Kant, proclaiming the reality of the Kantian noumenal self.

While Austrian academic philosophers never, as a group, came under the sway of Kant, Weininger's work needs to be placed in the neo-Kantian tradition of German philosophy, which had emerged after the collapse of Hegelianism in the mid-nineteenth century.[33] Two prominent centers of neo-Kantian thought were the Marburg school led by Hermann Cohen and Paul Natorp and the Heidelberg (or Baden or South-West German) school of Wilhelm Windelband and Heinrich Rickert. Both schools asserted that the proper object of philosophical investigation was the logical structure of knowledge and rejected all kinds of empiricism, biologism, historicism, and psychologism. For them, the rational *Geist* was beyond all external influence.[34] Weininger aligned himself wholeheartedly with this general program: his goal was to resurrect Kant's concept of the noumenal, undemonstrable, but intelligible self as the unchanging basis of psychological knowledge.[35]

Weininger's salvage of the self, however, applied only to male Aryans. Women and Jews, he conceded, are mere Machian bundles of sensations. The specifics of this argument were Weininger's own but its roots lay in the complex politics of gender and racial identity in turn-of-the-century Central Europe.

The Woman Question: Feminism as Apocalypse—The emergence of feminist movements in the late nineteenth century generated theoretically complex analyses of "the nature of woman" and new justifications for traditional ideas on gender roles. Although few feminist demands for equal intellectual, moral, and political rights were fulfilled during the period, the cultural and intellectual impact of early feminism far outstripped its numerical strength or political successes. The very fact that women were demanding equality was seen as apocalyptic by opponents.

Most male European intellectuals of the late nineteenth century subscribed to norms of gender that were firmly established only at the end of the eighteenth century but seemed, nevertheless, to be eternal, natural, and obvious.[36] Immanuel Kant, Otto Weininger's intellectual ideal and the prototypical German thinker of the Enlightenment, believed that women acted on inclination and needed to be governed by men, who acted according to reason. Morally, women could not be their own masters and, therefore, could not be full and active citizens.[37] This conviction was widely shared and, from the beginning of the nineteenth century, was expressed increasingly in biological and psychological terms. The body and mind of woman were now thought to be designed primarily to serve the reproductive needs of the species. The male, on the other hand, was biologically and psychologically designed for intellectual and cultural activity. The social inequality of the sexes, then, reflected a fact of nature and this made it acceptable to liberal political philosophy.[38]

"By the late nineteenth century," Theodore Roszak observes, "this supposedly marginal curiosity called the 'woman problem' had become one of the most earth-shaking debates in the Western world. . . . One would be hard-pressed to find many major figures of the period in any cultural field who did not address themselves passionately to the rights of women."[39] The voice of

science was heard with great respect in this scientific epoch; biologists and physicians were vociferous in their opposition to the "unnatural" imposition of sexual equality.[40] The psychiatrist Paul Julius Möbius claimed that women were naturally weak-minded: creative intelligence in a woman signified degeneration.[41] The Italian psychiatrist, anthropologist, and criminologist Cesare Lombroso believed that women's perceptual abilities were duller than men's, that women were liars by nature, and that prostitutes had no maternal feelings.[42] Möbius and Lombroso were far from alone. Innumerable cultural critics, artists, physicians, biologists, philosophers, social thinkers, and politicians of the time were tireless in discussing woman's nature and her place in the cosmic and social order.[43]

Much of this interest in women's issues was in direct response to growing feminist activism.[44] While I cannot rehearse the complexities of Central European feminist movements here, three salient features do require strong emphasis. First, feminists may have been in the minority but their number was not inconsiderable. Germany alone had 850 organizations with close to a million members campaigning for women's rights in 1900. Austria, too, had active women's organizations, although fewer than Germany.[45] While these organizations differed considerably in outlook and political commitment, male intellectuals of the time rarely noticed these differences. They regarded all feminists as members of one undifferentiated and, frequently, culturally threatening group.

The second crucial point about Central European feminism was its stress on the social, cultural, political, and metaphorical importance of motherhood. Women, the German feminists believed, were not just biological mothers but spiritual and social mothers as well.[46] Recently, historian Ann Taylor Allen has linked the successes of German feminists to this strategic deployment of motherhood, a womanly role and function that was honored even by the staunchest conservatives.[47] Some radical feminists—including Grete Meisel-Hess in Vienna—asserted that there was no better way to undermine the patriarchy than by exerting the ancient "mother-right" against fathers.[48]

The third point concerns female sexuality. Although feminists of the time certainly did not preach promiscuity and sexual abandon, *some* of their assertions may have suggested such advocacy to an ideological opponent. Take Helene Stöcker, for example. A romantic individualist greatly influenced by Nietzsche, she believed that women, although culturally trained to be sexually unexpressive, were innately no less sexual than men. Later, Stöcker came to see marriage itself as detrimental to the development of female individuality. While more conservative feminists argued for marriage based on a shared interest in "family values," Stöcker emphasized that sexual passion was the most important foundation for a happy marriage. This true sexual love of equals, she argued, was not possible in patriarchal society.[49] In Vienna, feminist theorist Rosa Mayreder declared that the best remedy against prostitution was to cultivate a freer social attitude toward premarital sex.[50]

Toward the end of the first decade of the new century, the German feminist movement retreated from its former radicalism, while antifeminism became increasingly strident. Antifeminists often equated feminism with defeminization.[51] The dramatist August Strindberg, for instance, described feminists as "hermaphrodites" and "half-women."[52] German sexologist Iwan Bloch agreed that homosexual (and therefore, according to the principles of contemporary medical sexology, masculine) women were prominent in the feminist movement; such women, said Bloch, craved spiritual contact with men and wished to change the current social order much more intensely than the average, truly feminine woman.[53] Even some radical feminists seem to have accepted this theory in its essence.[54]

The Man Question—Historian Jacques Le Rider discounts any feminist impact on the work of Weininger and other Viennese modernists. Instead, he attributes their antifeminist views to a psychoanalytically conceived crisis of masculine identity. He argues that the Viennese avant-garde felt threatened by perceptions of individual and cultural effeminacy rather than by the inroads of feminism.[55] There is a kernel of truth in this analysis. The Viennese literary critic Rudolf Lothar, for instance, declared in 1891 that "the female hypersensitivity to gaze, to pleasure, to thought, and to feeling, has been communicated to men and is taking them over."[56] Rosa Mayreder argued that the feminist movement did not aim to conquer the male world: men had already surrendered. Modernity had undermined old male "warrior values"; men had become passive and feminized, although they still chose to subscribe to archaic myths of virility. Mayreder quoted the mid-nineteenth-century literary critic Otto Ludwig's question: "Since men have turned into women . . . do women have any choice but to occupy the ground men have abandoned?"[57]

No careful reader of *Geschlecht und Charakter* could overlook the intense anxiety over masculinity that pervades the treatise. It is inadequate, however, to attribute that anxiety to a crisis of male identity alone. There was clearly a crisis of gender in turn-of-the-century Vienna but it was not solely a crisis of masculinity or femininity. It was a crisis of gender itself as a cultural category—a moment when the boundaries and norms of male and female shifted, disintegrated, and seemed to intertwine. Neither feminist activism nor any self-contained crisis of masculine identity was alone responsible for the situation: they were mutually constitutive, each dialectically reinforcing the other. Karl Kraus fulminated against the "vaginal age" as well as against suffragettes; Otto Weininger lamented the pervasive effeminacy of the epoch while condemning feminist activism. *The Jewish Question*—The Viennese crisis of gender was closely related to a crisis of Jewish identity.[58] It

is well known that the late nineteenth century saw an upsurge in political and cultural antisemitism in Central Europe.[59] Jews were no longer seen simply as ethnically distinct but also as lacking in such basic human traits as morality, love, and the desire for freedom. This so-called national character of the Jewish people, defined in what one could roughly describe as psychological and cultural, rather than biological terms, was not entirely an invention of antisemitic gentiles. Some of the strongest supporters of Jewish emancipation stressed that Jews had to transcend their "Jewishness" in order to become worthy of freedom.[60] Politically too, antisemitism followed no clear party lines and was integral to a specifically German tradition spanning the Left and the Right, which Paul Rose calls "German revolutionism."[61] This was a broadly political project for the renewal of German life on new moral, philosophical, and cultural principles, and colored the world views of such luminaries as Kant, Fichte, Herder, and later, Schopenhauer and Wagner. All of them were more or less antisemitic and considered Jewish and German national characters to be distinct and mutually opposed: the Jews were the major obstacles to the flight of the German spirit.[62]

In the late nineteenth century, Richard Wagner's views on German regeneration received a degree of acclaim and emotional support rarely accorded the political thought of an artist.[63] The greatest obstacle to social revolution, Wagner believed, was materialism: egoism, heartlessness, greed, and the "demonic idea of money." This materialism was symbolized by Jews.[64] Wagner's death in 1883 did not stop the triumphal progress of Wagnerism across Europe, which was presided over by his widow Cosima and a "magic circle" of true believers scattered over the continent. One leading member of the circle was the emigré Englishman Houston Stewart Chamberlain (1855-1927), whose love for Germanic culture and Wagner's music bordered on religious veneration. In 1889, Chamberlain moved to Vienna, which was second only to Bayreuth as a center of Wagnerism, and where Chamberlain quickly made a place for himself among the literati and the Pan-German nationalists.[65] Chamberlain was a prolific writer who, today, is remembered most often as the author of *The Foundations of the Nineteenth Century* (1900), a work with which Otto Weininger was deeply familiar.[66] In this immensely popular book, Chamberlain marshaled a wide array of arcane and apparently unrelated lore to portray the history of humanity as the history of struggles between different races. After the Roman Empire had collapsed in "racial chaos" induced by miscegenation, he argued, there arose two pure races: the Jews and the Teutons. The recent history of humanity was essentially the story of their combat.[67]

Jews and Viennese Culture: Assimilation and "Self-Hatred"—On arriving in Vienna in 1889, Houston Stewart Chamberlain wrote a joyous letter to a friend, praising the beauty of the architecture and "the pretty women of easy morals," but adding that the one unsavory feature of the city was the "enormous quantity of

Jews."[68] Since 1848, when the Government had allowed them to reside in the city, Jews from the eastern regions of the Habsburg Empire had been emigrating to Vienna in large numbers.[69] Middle and upper-class Viennese Jews were characterized by their sincere admiration for and assimilation to German culture. Jews were particularly conspicuous in institutions of higher education, the medical profession, and journalism.[70] Historian Norman Stone declared that "most of the twentieth-century intellectual world was invented" in Vienna by secularized Jews.[71] Stone's doctoral student Steven Beller has shown that in imperial Vienna, cultural innovators (ranging from Sigmund Freud to Gustav Mahler, from Ludwig Wittgenstein to Arthur Schnitzler) and their audiences were largely Jewish.[72] Even the scions of thoroughly assimilated families—such as Wittgenstein or Hugo von Hofmannsthal, both raised as Christians and steeped in classical German culture from childhood—were always conscious of their Jewish identity, which did not necessarily imply any interest in Judaism. Much of this identity was imposed, in fact, from without: it was due more to being perceived as a Jew by others than to any spontaneous feeling of "Jewishness."[73] But what, if anything, marked their diverse contributions as distinctly Jewish? Beller argues that for all the differences in specific content, the works of Jewish artists and intellectuals were related fundamentally to ethics and personal identity.[74] This was compatible with Judaism as well as with German Protestant culture, which many Viennese Jews deeply admired.[75] This liberal-Jewish-Protestant individualism led to a preoccupation with inner truth and the moral autonomy of the individual.[76]

Politically, assimilated Jews were overwhelmingly liberal, although later generations often turned away from liberalism in reaction to the many failures of Viennese liberal politics. Viennese liberalism, however, did not encourage the pursuit of ethnic separatism. For many Jews, being liberal meant purging themselves of Jewishness and becoming one with the German mainstream. Emancipation from the ghetto, many Jewish intellectuals argued, had to be succeeded by emancipation from Judaism. One popular path toward that second emancipation was immersion in German literature, philosophy, and science. Jews, by and large, ignored the ostentatious Catholic culture unique to Austria, looking up to Protestant Germany as the promised land of Kant and Goethe.[77] By the end of the nineteenth century, however, this assimilationist project had clearly failed. The rapid rise of antisemitism and the simultaneous collapse of liberalism evoked diverse responses from Jewish intellectuals.[78] Increasingly, many retreated into the self. For Arthur Schnitzler, this inward impulse was expressed in artistic creativity; for Sigmund Freud, in the elaboration of psychological theory; and for Otto Weininger, in the philosophical validation of the Kantian noumenal self.[79]

Some, of course, internalized antisemitism, developing an acute repugnance for their own Jewish identity, a phenomenon that Theodor Lessing called "self-hatred."[80] Weininger occupied a prominent position in Lessing's analysis, and continues to have a stellar presence in every study of the subject since then.[81] The nuances and contexts of his "self-hatred," however, are often ignored.[82] Steven Beller has demonstrated that Weininger's views on Jewishness shared much with liberal Jewish critiques of Jewishness.[83] More importantly, as Sigurd Paul Scheichl has recently shown, antisemitic language was omnipresent in Viennese discourse but its meanings differed according to speaker, intent, and context. Even Jewish socialists such as Victor Adler used antisemitic language against Jewish capitalists and the bourgeois press. But Adler and his associates were neither racists nor self-haters in any uncomplicated sense: they supported Dreyfus and Emile Zola while denouncing Dreyfus's supporters among Jewish financiers and journalists. Any critic of modernity in fin-de-siècle Vienna might use antisemitic rhetoric because of the widespread identification of Jews with capitalism. Such rhetorical convergence with antisemitic politicians or street thugs did not, however, indicate a convergence in goals. Kraus and Weininger, Scheichl points out, were against the persecution of Jews, did not espouse biological theories of race, had Jewish friends, and frequently emphasized the nonpolitical nature of their critiques.[84] To say this is not to "disinfect" Kraus or Weininger but to identify their historical personae with greater specificity than is possible with undifferentiated conceptions of antisemitism or self-hatred.

MAN, WOMAN, TEXT: THE STRUCTURE AND SUBSTANCE OF *GESCHLECHT UND CHARAKTER*

All the contexts I have enumerated are indispensable to any informed assessment of **Geschlecht und Charakter**. It is equally essential, however, to read the text—difficult and dense as it is—from beginning to end, including the long, dialogical endnotes. As Allan Janik points out, **Geschlecht und Charakter** has four reciprocally interactive analytic moments: the biology of sexuality, an idiosyncratic version of neo-Kantian ethics, Nietzschean cultural criticism, and a Diltheyan psychology of "lived experience."[85] The first "moment" is of greater importance in **Geschlecht und Charakter** than scholars have usually appreciated.

Geschlecht und Charakter is divided into two parts. The first, "preparatory" section entitled "Die sexuelle Mannigfaltigkeit" ("Sexual Diversity") contains six short chapters amounting to less than one hundred pages. The second, "main" section called "Die sexueller Typen" ("The Sexual Types") comprises fourteen longer chapters sprawling over some four hundred pages. While neither section is wholly devoted to any one of Janik's specific "moments," the first section is predominantly concerned with biological aspects of sexuality and the second with its metaphysical analysis.[86] The crucial differences between the two sections, however, lie less in their substance than in their style of argumentation. Weininger uses the discourse of science and medicine throughout his book, but in different ways and with quite different aims.[87] The first part of *Geschlecht* *und Charakter* consists of short, temperately phrased chapters commencing with facts or theories accepted by contemporary scientists. Original hypotheses are presented in relation to orthodox theories as suggestions, revisions, or potentially fruitful analogies. Each assertion in the text is supported by numerous references and copious endnotes. Wherever he disagrees with current scientific beliefs, Weininger tries to explain his reasons, citing similar critiques. He sometimes points out how the revision of current dogmas might have clear social or intellectual utility. *Stylistically,* the first part of *Geschlecht und Charakter* reads no differently than monographs on sexual subjects by contemporary scientists and physicians.

Deconstructing Gender: The Principle of Sexual Intermediacy—Weininger conceives of Male and Female as mutually opposed ideal types that do not really exist. In strictly biological terms, no individual belongs exclusively to one sex. Virtually every biologist of the time would have agreed with Weininger. By 1900, the biological boundaries between the sexes had been shown to be indistinct and fluid.[88] As Weininger points out, there was no fundamental biological difference separating *all* men from *all* women (p. 6). Anatomically, innumerable men possessed such "feminine" traits as a wide pelvis or full breasts, just as "masculine" women commonly possessed facial hair or a narrow pelvis. Moreover, as most embryologists of the time agreed, all human embryos developed into males or females from an initial, sexually undifferentiated condition (p. 7). Every individual, then, was situated on a spectrum extending between the two imaginary poles of absolute masculinity and absolute femininity. Some were closer to one pole and some to the other, but all were *intermediate* between the two. This "principle of sexual intermediacy" was used by contemporary physicians to explain phenomena ranging from hermaphroditism to homosexuality.

The organism, Weininger hypothesizes, is constructed of two basic components: a male plasma and a female one. This is an original speculation, complementary to theories of sexual intermediacy. Each cell, according to Weininger, is part male and part female, and the degree of masculinity or femininity differs among cells and cell-groups. Sexual intermediacy, then, is not just an overall feature of the individual: it is inherent in the building blocks of the organism. This notion is grounded in biological discourse and draws upon the work of the Danish zoologist Johannes Japetus Smith Steenstrup (1813-1897) and the Munich botanist, Carl Wilhelm von Nägeli (1817-1891). Steenstrup had argued in the mid-nineteenth century that the sex of an organism was not localized in any particular anatomical zone: each and every part of the organism was endowed with sex.[89] Having appropriated Steenstrup's conviction that sex was located everywhere in the organism, Weininger places it within Carl Wilhelm von Nägeli's late-nineteenth-century theory of the idioplasm. Nägeli was one of the foremost botanists of the nineteenth century and also made significant contributions to anatomy, cytol-

ogy, morphology, and systematics.[90] He believed that the protoplasm of each cell—and not just the germ-cells—possessed a special component carrying hereditary material, which he named "idioplasm."[91]

Weininger extracts two notions from Nägeli's theory of the idioplasm (p. 479). First, all biological differences between individuals are due to differences in their idioplasm. Second, each and every cell of the organism possesses a certain amount of idioplasm.[92] Weininger then postulates that the idioplasm could theoretically occur in two ideal-typical forms: male (arrhenoplasm) and female (thelyplasm). Absolute masculinity or femininity is unattainable at any level and the idioplasm of each cell is sexually intermediate: it is partly arrhenoplasmic and partly thelyplasmic. The proportions of the two plasmas, moreover, need not necessarily be identical in all cells in one individual (pp. 20-21). Each individual, then, is a mosaic of variably sexual cells. This explains why, for instance, a very masculine man may have a sparse beard or weak musculature or why an effeminate man may still have a full beard (pp. 21-22). Such localized sexual asymmetries, Weininger argues, could only be due to localized cellular variations. He emphasizes that these variations are primarily idioplasmic and not, as some scientists were beginning to suggest, determined by the secretions of the sex glands (p. 25).[93] In his pioneering treatise on reproductive physiology, Francis H. A. Marshall summarized Weininger's ideas on the arrhenoplasm and the thelyplasm, remarking:

> Weininger made no suggestion as to what it is that determines the differentiation of the original protoplasm into arrhenoplasm and thelyplasm, but his idea, though somewhat too morphologically conceived, is useful if only because it emphasises the fact that male and female characters coexist (though they are very unequally represented) in most if not in all dioecious individuals.[94]

Weininger uses the principle of universal sexual intermediacy to deconstruct the traditional assumption that each individual belongs to a certain sex, which can be "read off" the genitals. Sexual intermediacy, however, is not simply a static, morphological attribute of the adult individual: it also governs behavior and sexual choice. Mating, Weininger declares, is not a haphazard affair, nor, despite human illusions, one dependent solely on love. Weininger commences with the conventional wisdom that each individual is sexually drawn only to a certain kind of person and, conversely, repelled by certain other types (pp. 31-33). But what determines the complementarity of certain types? Can sexual affinity be predicted? Nature decrees, according to Weininger, that an ideal sexual match can occur only between one complete male and one complete female. The principle of sexual intermediacy, however, rules out the existence of completely male or female individuals. Weininger suggests, therefore, that in an ideal sexual relationship, the *total* masculinity and femininity of the two partners amount to 1 in algebraic terms. A male who is 3/4 masculine and 1/4 feminine would be ideally complemented by a woman who is 1/4 masculine and 3/4 feminine (pp. 34-37). This "law of nature," Weininger declares, was unknown prior to his work, except for the intuitive comments of Arthur Schopenhauer (pp. 32, 488).[95] Weininger then refines his "law" to include the strength of attraction between the partners. He imagines two hypothetical persons X and Y, whose masculine elements are indicated by M and feminine elements by W. X, Weininger assumes, possesses αM and $\alpha'M$, whereas Y has βW and $\beta'M$. Now, if A is the strength of attraction between the two, then

$$A = (K/\alpha - \beta) \; f(t)$$

where "k" is a factor including all known and unknown laws of sexual affinity, including those of race, species, and deformity and "f(t)" is a temporal function, indicating the period during which the two entities are in proximity to each other. When $\alpha = \beta$, A is infinite. This is the strongest and most elemental form of attraction.[96] Weininger's discussion of sexual affinity aims to establish that universal sexual intermediacy is not simply an ancient poetic metaphor but a biological fact. He shows that the concept of universal intermediacy explains why individuals mate only with particular individuals and argues that one could use the degree of intermediacy to predict a person's actual choice of mate. Weininger's Law of Sexual Affinity may be dismissed today as a piece of baroque pseudomathematics, but it is firmly grounded in the concept of universal sexual intermediacy, which was impeccably scientific by the standards of the time.

Naturalizing Male Homosexuality—Weininger illustrates his Law of Sexual Affinity by addressing male homosexuality, which was an important cultural issue in fin-de-siècle Europe. In the German-speaking areas, a homosexual emancipation movement gathered strength around the turn of the century. Physicians played a major role in this movement and the political program of the emancipationists influenced as well as borrowed from medical discourse on homosexuality.[97] According to prominent physicians and activists of the era, a homosexual orientation was neither a disease nor a vice but a prime example of sexual intermediacy. They believed that a male homosexual had been psychosexually feminized by an unknown intrauterine error of development. Hence, "he" could pair successfully only with a male. Weininger accepts this idea but denies that the feminization of the homosexual male originated in a developmental error. The concept of anomaly was integral to medical theories of homosexuality, even to those of the leading German homosexual emancipationist Magnus Hirschfeld.[98]

In his role as an activist, Magnus Hirschfeld challenged the idea that there was one, heterosexual, norm of development and portrayed the world as full of sexually intermediate organisms. As a physician, however, he believed that these intermediate forms had been created by

anomalous biological processes which needed to be understood.[99] Weininger, too, sees the world as full of sexual intermediates—but stops there.[100] It is a simple fact and not a pathological problem. He argues that the birth of feminized males is a statistical consequence of universal sexual intermediacy: if individuals are located on a spectrum stretching from absolute masculinity to absolute femininity, then there will, of course, be individuals located at the middle of the spectrum who are almost equally male and female. According to Weininger's Law of Sexual Affinity, a man who is 46 percent male needs a mate who is 54 percent male. Such a mate is more easily found among men than among women. Secondly, since all human beings are sexually intermediate to various degrees, everybody is both homosexual and heterosexual in different proportions. Those near the middle of the spectrum of intermediacy are predominantly (but not exclusively) homosexual, while those near either end of the spectrum are predominantly (but again, not exclusively) heterosexual (p. 57).

Weininger had not always been so radical. In an early draft of his dissertation, he had espoused the same theory of homosexuality but had included a section on the therapy of homosexuality under the slender pretext of enabling homosexuals to reproduce.[101] Here, Weininger had recommended that the male homosexual's weak innate masculinity should be augmented with sex-gland extracts. This was not simply a theoretical recommendation. Weininger, otherwise the archetypal armchair-theorist, had tested this idea in human experiments. In April 1901, he had sent this report to Hermann Swoboda:

> My agent to combat homosexuality seems to be successful!! Even though this only confirms my own theory, I have yet to recover from my amazement. If only I could be certain that no suggestion was involved . . . In any case, the doses must be continued . . . My patient is already preparing for his first coitus![102]

Although we have no unequivocal proof, it is strongly likely that this "patient" may well have been Weininger himself.[103] If so, this might explain much of the anxiety about masculinity that pervades *Geschlecht und Charakter*. In the absence of further evidence, however, speculation is futile. Biographical explanations, in any case, cannot be self-sufficient since similar tensions over masculinity marked the works of such emphatically heterosexual Viennese intellectuals as Karl Kraus.

Sexual Intermediacy and Social Reform: Differential Psychology and the Biology of Feminism—Physical sexual intermediacy, Weininger argues, is reflected in the psycho-behavioral realm: morphology and psychology should, therefore, be twin sciences (p. 71). It is not enough, he warns, to classify somebody as more feminine or more masculine; one must also assess the exact degree of masculinity and femininity in the individual and then determine whether specific deeds or thoughts stemmed from the male or the female element of an individual. By individualizing each human being, such an approach would provide a basis for the study of individual differences or "differential psychology" (pp. 62-63, 499) and eventually revolutionize pedagogy.[104] To educate all boys in one uniform way and all girls in another, says Weininger, is senseless because all boys are not equally masculine, nor all girls equally feminine. Teachers must acknowledge the differential psychology of individual students and nurture their particular abilities and inclinations (pp. 69-70).[105]

Weininger then suggests that the male and female elements of a person's character are not necessarily active at the same time. It is more likely, he says, that human beings oscillate between the male and female poles of their personality; this inherent sexual duality may be evident only in chronological succession, rather than simultaneously. The changes may be regular or irregular and the amplitude of oscillation toward one sex may be greater than the amplitude of oscillation toward the other (pp. 64-65). Weininger thus transforms sexual intermediacy from a static and morphological phenomenon into a potentially periodic event.[106] Surprisingly, however, he does not return to this concept in later sections of his book.

Weininger now applies the concept of sexual intermediacy to the central problem of his book: the "woman question." Defining emancipation as spiritual and moral freedom, he declares that a woman's desire for such freedom and her capacity to handle it responsibly are grounded in her masculine element (p. 80).[107] The feminine element does not require this inner freedom and is incapable of employing it. All women currently striving for emancipation, and all truly talented women across the ages, Weininger asserts, display numerous masculine traits, including anatomical ones (p. 80). Sappho, he declares, was a lesbian, and lesbianism, as an expression of masculinity, is a sign of distinction. Catherine II of Russia, Queen Christina of Sweden, and George Sand are other examples that Weininger deploys to support his equation of lesbianism with talent. Even heterosexual women desiring emancipation were unmistakably masculinized in their features and in their penchant for effeminate men (p. 82).

Weininger's proposed solution to the woman question is simple. Women whose genuine psychic and biological needs, frequently reflected in their physical attributes, drive them toward masculine occupations should be allowed to pursue their goals (p. 87). Full equality with men, however, is impossible. Even the most gifted woman, he explains, is only slightly more than 50 percent masculine and owes her achievements to this small excess over other women. Without disclosing how he calculated this figure, Weininger asserts that this modest additional amount of masculinity cannot even ensure the full equality of a talented woman with the average man, who, despite being sexually intermediate, possesses a much stronger masculine element (p. 88). Not one woman in history, he asserts, could even equal a fifth-rate male genius (p. 85).

Woman's lack of creativity, Weininger emphasizes, cannot be blamed on inadequate social freedom. Emancipated women have appeared in all ages, albeit not in equal numbers.[108] Demands for women's emancipation were prominent during the tenth, fifteenth, sixteenth, nineteenth, and twentieth centuries. This conviction is not Weininger's alone. He cites an expert on genealogy who had pointed out in 1898 that feminism did not flourish in ages that regarded masculine women as unattractive.[109] Weininger suggests that excessively masculine females or effeminate males are born more frequently during periods marked by movements for women's emancipation (p. 90).[110] He finds scientific evidence for such sexual variations in Charles Darwin's observation that older or sick female birds were masculinized more frequently during certain years than during others (p. 504).[111]

His own era, Weininger claims, is one of virilized women and feminized men. Weininger denounces the preponderance of tall, slender women with flat breasts and narrow hips in current "secessionist" art and the "monstrous increase" of fops (*Stutzertum*) and homosexuals in real life. All this, he states, could only be due to the "greater femininity" (*grösseren Weiblichkeit*) of the age (p. 91). Challenging the conventional belief that evolutionary progress leads inexorably to the greater differentiation of sexes, Weininger quotes biologist August Weismann's observation that sexual differentiation is greatest not in humans, but in lower animal species.[112] There is, then, no reason to believe that the human sexes are programmed to move further apart with time. Periods of lesser differentiation between men and women might well alternate with periods of greater sexual differentiation, when men are biologically more masculine and women more feminine. With the coming of those latter times, says Weininger, feminism would be negated by true femininity, which is antithetical to the idea of emancipation (p. 93).

Restricting Sexual Intermediacy: The Biology of Woman— The second part of **Geschlecht und Charakter,** entitled "The Sexual Types," commences with a "restriction" of the biological principle of sexual intermediacy. Although scientific discourse does not disappear from this part, it is incorporated differently into the larger argument and voiced with a new declamatory flamboyance. Weininger no longer writes as a protoscientist or scientistic social reformer. He still cites his scientific sources scrupulously but does not express his disagreements with moderation or even professional courtesy. Nor does he hesitate to change the content of scientific theories to fit his framework. Religious and metaphysical images abound in his language and the authorial voice takes on prophetic overtones.

This intellectual and stylistic transition is signaled by the assertion that despite biological intermediacy, every human being, *psychologically,* is either male or female, at least at one and the same time (pp. 97-98). After arguing in the first part of the treatise that no individual is solely masculine or feminine and that morphology and psychology are interrelated sciences, Weininger seems to contradict himself with the unqualified affirmation of psychological monosexuality. This would have been a logical point to emphasize his earlier notion that sexually intermediate forms need not be male and female at the same time; they could periodically oscillate between the two. Weininger, however, does not offer this argument and the transition between the two parts of his book is its point of greatest incoherence.

Weininger challenges the conventional opinion that all apparent mental and behavioral differences between men and women stem from the greater intensity of the male sex drive.[113] It is the female sex drive, he declares, that is the more intense, although it is less conspicuous because of its extraordinarily passive quality (pp. 110-11).[114] Woman, in fact, is completely and exclusively sexual—this is the fundamental argument of the second part of *Geschlecht und Charakter*—whereas Man is both sexual and concerned with war and play, scholarship and discussion, politics, religion, and art (p. 112). This argument, of course, recalls the views of Jean Jacques Rousseau, which, in turn, were characteristic of Enlightenment ideas on gender.[115] Interestingly, however, Weininger does not cite Rousseau here but Charles Darwin, who had observed that female animals "seldom offer remarkable secondary sexual characters" (p. 508).[116] In an astounding conceptual leap, Weininger infers from Darwin's statement that females must, therefore, be sexual throughout! Extrapolating to the human female, Weininger closes this section with one of his most frequently quoted aphorisms: "Man possesses the penis, but the vagina possesses the woman" (Der Mann hat den Penis, aber die Vagina hat die Frau, p. 116).

From Woman to Man and Back Again: Genius and the Dialectic of *Gender*—The next seven chapters of *Geschlecht und Charakter* address lofty themes that are not obviously related to gender: logic, ethics, genius, and the self. This cluster of chapters, however, plays an important role in the overall scheme of the treatise. It is in these seven arcane chapters that Weininger unveils his idea of masculinity, which is constantly and dialectically related to his idea of femininity. Weininger's Woman is constructed largely in biological terms, whereas his ideal-typical Man is a psychological and philosophical construct. In his analysis of masculinity, Weininger moves sharply away from biomedical discourse, turning instead to the philosophy of Kant, and framing his Kantian image of Man within a critique of contemporary "soulless" psychology.

Woman, Weininger claims, is capable only of feeling and cannot differentiate between feeling and thought.[117] Females have vague and unformed thoughts, which Weininger calls "henids." He acknowledges that every thought, whether in males or in females, begins in "a kind of half-thought," which undergoes clarification and refinement in Man but remains nebulous in Woman (p. 122). Then, embarking upon a meandering discussion of genius, Weininger states that a genius is "he who has

incomparably greater understanding of other beings than the average man."[118] The examplar of such genius is, of course, Goethe, who, Weininger reports, even understood every form of crime or criminal (p. 135). Supremely conscious and infinitely sensible, the genius unites innumerable contrasts and types within himself.[119] His thought is at the furthest remove from henids.

Genius, therefore, is perfected masculinity (*eine ideale, potenzierte Männlichkeit*): femininity and genius are antithetical qualities (p. 141, 144). The elevated consciousness of the genius implies perfect memory. The "absolute" genius can remember everything he has experienced: "his entire past, everything that he has ever thought or heard, seen or done, perceived or felt."[120] These memories are not stored discretely in the psyche: they comprise "in some mysterious way one great whole" (p. 157). Such continuity is rare in most people, but Woman lacks it completely. When she looks back on her life, a woman recollects only a few isolated moments related to her sexual experiences (p. 158).[121] The absolute genius, of course, is an ideal type: no real individual could possibly remember all his experiences. There are, then, different degrees of genius and—this is the vital point—"no male is quite without a trace of genius" (p. 147). To recapitulate Weininger's argument: females think in henids and, therefore, do not really have memories; all males possess a clearer consciousness and better memory than any female; a genius must have a near-perfect memory; hence, all males have some genius. Whatever the logician's verdict on this argument, there is no denying its importance in Weininger's model of masculinity.

Having argued that memory is intimately related to genius, Weininger claims that memory is also the basis of logical and ethical thought, "mankind's most peculiar qualities." Memory is indissolubly linked with morality because repentance is impossible without memory. A being without memory is necessarily mendacious. This mendacity is not immoral, since there can be no immorality in the absence of a standard of truth. Woman, who lies because she lacks memory, is not immoral but simply amoral (pp. 193-94).[122] The continuous memory that enables Man to be truthful and logical does not, however, directly engender the desire and need for truth. Those hail from a deeper source that is unchangeable and independent of time: the intelligible self of Kant, the existence of which can be philosophically deduced but never empirically verified (pp. 194-95).[123]

The Kantian concept of the intelligible self is pivotal to Weininger's analysis of masculinity and femininity. His exposition of Kant's concept is set within a critique of empirical psychology and Ernst Mach's concept of the self. The human ego, Weininger asserts, is not simply "a waiting-hall for perceptions" (*Wartesaal für Empfindungen*). All logical thought and ethical behavior originate in the intelligible ego, it follows that a consistently unethical or illogical being does not possess an intelligible self (pp. 198-99). Since Woman is such an amoral and alogical being, Weininger triumphantly concludes, she does not possess an intelligible self (pp. 239-40).[124]

Weininger now moves from Woman or the Absolute Female to individual women. He emphasizes that the sexually intermediate nature of individuals notwithstanding, most women resemble the Absolute Female very closely (p. 241). Men, on the contrary, are distinct individuals and do not necessarily embody all attributes of the ideal-typical Absolute Male. The Absolute Male possesses everything, including the potential for femininity: the individual man may choose to develop one or more of these qualities. If he chooses the lowest traits, he can easily reach the nadir of humanity, which explains the existence of feminine men. While men can acquire female attributes, however, the reverse possibility does not exist. "A woman," Weininger asserts, "can never become a man" (aber die Frau kann nie zum Manne werden). This impossibility represents his most important qualification of the notion of universal sexual intermediacy (p. 241).[125]

Hysteria: The Organic Mendacity of Woman—What, then, is the real nature of Woman and her ontological significance? Identifying "match-making" as an invariable propensity among women, Weininger argues that Woman is constantly preoccupied with sexuality: not simply with her own sexual urges, but with sexuality in general and in the most physical sense. "The transcendental function of Woman" is to bring about the physical union of male and female (p. 351). Women veil this from society by unconsciously acting out male ideas of female purity (pp. 352-54). This camouflage, Weininger argues, is removed in hysteria. Sigmund Freud and Josef Breuer, building upon standard psychiatric opinion of the time, had theorized that hysteria was caused by a split in the consciousness: the hysterical psyche comprised a genuine self and a sealed-off "foreign body" that was normally inaccessible to consciousness.[126] Weininger retains this framework but transposes the ontological meaning of the two selves. The true nature of Woman, according to Weininger, is pure sexuality, and this is what Freud and Breuer had mistakenly called the "foreign body." What they had regarded as the real self of women is actually foreign and false: a simulacrum developed to win the esteem of Man. This simulation is unconscious: Woman is so passive and so suggestible that she incorporates and responds to male signals without being conscious of them. In normal life, the outer, false self effectively hides the real, sexual self, but the false self is shattered by hysteria. Hysteria, then, is the crisis of the "organic mendacity of Woman."

The outer self is, of course, false and unworthy of any ontological notice. But the inner, purely sexual self of Woman, too, lacks ontological weight. Female sexuality is generalized desire—contrary to popular opinion, it is not directed at particular men. Such supraindividual desire cannot confer individuality and being (p. 397). Ontologically, the relationship between Man and Woman is the Aristotelian one of form and matter. To be formed

by Man is Woman's sole destiny and greatest fulfillment (pp. 391-96). Man, built in the image of God, represents Being, while Woman—including the feminine element in a male—is the symbol of Nothing (*das Symbol des Nichts*). Consequently, there is nothing so contemptible as the feminized man (p. 398). Her total lack of significance, says Weininger, is the cosmic significance of Woman. Woman exists, he points out, because of Man's immoral affirmation of his own sexuality and his denial of the Absolute. It is only male sexuality that creates and gives meaning to Woman. "Woman," therefore, "is the sin of Man" (p. 401).

The Political Physiology of Impregnation—Weininger acknowledges that critics will oppose his ethical and ontological demolition of femininity by pointing to the high moral status of Woman as Mother (p. 281). He is also aware that the Mother is the symbol of emancipated womanhood in contemporary feminist discourse. No serious and truly radical resolution of the woman question in contemporary Central Europe could ignore the political and moral dimensions of maternity. True to his style, Weininger approaches the issue typologically and divides femininity into two ideal types: Mother and Prostitute. (Mother and Prostitute, Weininger emphasizes, are ideal types like Man and Woman. Just as real individuals are partly male and partly female, all women are both Mother and Prostitute to different degrees.)[127] The distinction is highly original, despite its ancient terminology.

Weininger's Mother is not the saintly figure of tradition. Maternity, he argues, is as much an expression of Woman's pervasive sexuality as is prostitution. The Mother's sexuality is reproductive—her cosmic purpose is to perpetuate the species. She uses men—and is used by them—as a means to that end, and, as Kant had emphasized, using anybody as a means to any end is profoundly unethical. The Prostitute is different but ethically no worse: she uses men and is herself used as a means to sexual pleasure.[128] Prostitutes may, in fact, be ethically somewhat superior to Mothers when, by serving as muse to great men, they inspire the production of noble works of art or thought. Despite their differences of aim and expression, however, both types are wholly and exclusively sexual. Since sexuality, in Weininger's world, signifies ontological and ethical nullity, there is nothing admirable or politically emancipatory about motherhood.[129]

Weininger then argues that the very fact of women's impregnability rules out subjectivity and autonomy. His argument, as usual, is interwoven with biological and medical discourse. Uncharacteristically, however, he wholly rejects current theories, rather than building upon them or, as with hysteria, transforming their content. Employing a new strategy, he returns to theories of reproductive biology that, by 1903, were being progressively rejected by professional scientists. One of these older theories, that of "maternal impressions," held that the psychological experiences, fears, and desires of a pregnant woman could physically influence or deform the embryo.[130] Another was the theory of telegony, which held that a woman's first mate transformed her body permanently.[131] Herbert Spencer, Austin Flint, and Charles Darwin had believed that due to telegony, the children fathered by a woman's second or later mates physically resembled her first lover.[132] The idea also left its trace on the novels of Emile Zola (1840-1902) and on the plays of Henrik Ibsen (1828-1906) and August Strindberg (1849-1912).[133] Weininger quotes these and other authors in the belief that literature knew truths that science was forgetting to recognize. This is, of course, a desperate maneuver, but, given Weininger's antifeminist project, an unavoidable one. If Woman can be shown to be infinitely impressionable and modifiable by Man, then she obviously cannot claim ontological autonomy. Hysteria shows that, psychologically, Woman develops a false self under male influence. If telegony and maternal impressions do exist, then Woman is somatically impressionable too. Weininger's espousal of telegony is not due to ignorance: in his copious notes, he demonstrates his awareness of the obsolescence of these theories. For strategic reasons, however, he is compelled to incorporate them into his argument. Although continuing to be immersed in the discourse of science, he no longer speaks as its constructive critic, let alone as a participant. His only concern now is to use science to demonstrate the ontological nullity of Woman and thus expose the political futility of feminism.

Paternity and Its Viscissitudes—Weininger's analysis of motherhood is interwoven with his concerns over paternity. He expresses great admiration for August Strindberg's 1887 play, *The Father*, which hinges on its protagonist's doubts about the parentage of his daughter. These doubts are insinuated into his mind by his wife, who repeatedly insists that "no one can really know who the father of a child is." Ultimately, the father is driven insane by his doubts. At the end of the play, he declares: "A man has no children; only women have children."[134] Strindberg had written the play after reading an article by a Marxist sociologist arguing that while the patriarchal system had been established by the brutal overthrow of an earlier matriarchal civilization, its replacement by a new matriarchy would involve as many crimes and brutalities.[135] This remark gave Strindberg the idea of a plot portraying "the vast wheel of history turning backward, with women trying to gain ascendancy over men." Such new matriarchs would destroy men's faith in themselves by making them doubt the one essential feature of patriarchy: fatherhood.[136]

Weininger reiterates that the only natural, physical claim on the child is that of the mother: fatherhood is an illusion. Since Woman is completely and exclusively sexual, and since her sexuality is spread all over the body, any male who makes an impression on the Mother is at least partly the father of her child. There can, therefore, be no absolute certainty that any particular man is the real, exclusive father of a woman's children, and instead of yearning for biological heirs, men should

concentrate on producing "children of the spirit": great works of art or of knowledge (p. 307). Weininger's deconstruction of the subjectivity of Woman succeeds only at the cost of the deconstruction of the Father and the elevation of the Mother, which Strindberg had identified as the first step toward the reestablishment of a matriarchal civilization. Seeking to negate female subjectivity, Weininger, ironically, affirms the total power of Woman over the species.

The Gender of Jewishness—Weininger's analysis of "Jewishness" has often been seen as the predominant theme of *Geschlecht und Charakter*. Actually, however, it is subsidiary to and dependent upon his analyses of femininity and masculinity, and similar approximations of race and gender were common at the time.[137] Weininger's chapter on "Jewishness" commences with a problem related to gender. Why, Weininger wonders, do Jews approach the transcendent qualities of the Absolute Male only very rarely? It is this "psychical peculiarity of the Jewish race," rather than its racial origins or physical anthropology that Weininger strives to explain. Acknowledging his own Jewish descent at the outset, he defines Jewishness "only as a psychical tendency or constitution, which is a possibility for *all* humans but had reached its fullest expression among the Jewish people" (p. 406). Weininger emphasizes that many racial Aryans are psychologically more Jewish than many ethnic Jews and many of the latter are mentally more Aryan than some of the former (p. 407). He is concerned with all humans who express in themselves "the platonic idea of Jewishness," regardless of their racial origins (p. 409). After several vitriolic pages on this "platonic idea," Weininger points out that, despite his low opinion of Jewishness, he is wholly opposed to "any practical or theoretical persecution of Jews" (pp. 417-18). The true Aryan is seldom an antisemite, even though he might be repelled by aspects of Jewish culture. Aggressive antisemites, on the other hand, frequently possess Jewish traits: people hate in others what they hate in themselves. "Whoever detests the Jewish disposition detests it first of all in himself" (pp. 406-7).

What, however, is the Jewish disposition? Here is Weininger's own definition:

> The Jewish race (*Judentum*) is pervasively feminine. This femininity comprises those qualities that I have shown to be in total opposition to masculinity. The Jews are much more feminine than Aryans . . . and the manliest Jew may be taken for a female (p. 409).

Although Weininger is unwilling to argue for the complete identification of the Jew with Woman, he acknowledges that the two ideal types share many traits. Neither, for instance, understands the notion of personal property, and both show a marked preference for communism—not, however, for socialism, which Weininger identifies as Aryan (p. 410)![138] Zionism, Weininger concedes, expresses some of the noblest qualities of Jews but it is an impossible dream. Jewishness necessarily means the dispersion of Jews all over the world. The Jew cannot grasp the idea of the state: as deficient in personality as females, Jews cannot associate as free and equal individuals within a larger whole (p. 411). "To be capable of Zionism," Weininger asserts, "Jews must first overcome Jewishness." Each Jew must fight relentlessly against his own Jewish self (p. 418). Once that inner battle had been won, however, the former Jew would earn the right to be considered as an individual by Aryans, and not as the member of a certain race (p. 419). Jesus, according to Weininger, developed Christianity—which represents the complete negation of Judaism—by overcoming the Jew within himself (p. 439). Christ was "the greatest man because he conquered the greatest enemy" and Richard Wagner was the greatest man since Christ because he overcame the Jewish traits in his early music and eventually composed *Parsifal,* a work so Germanic that no Jew could ever comprehend its greatness (p. 440). This stress on transcendence and Weininger's own conversion to Christianity suggest obvious autobiographical subtexts for these passages.

Weininger surrounds these statements with assorted antisemitic observations. Examples: Jewish men are avid matchmakers and this is "the strongest similarity between femininity and Jewishness"; the Jew is "always more absorbed by sexual matters than the Aryan, although he is notably less potent sexually" (p. 417); Jewish acquisitiveness is not the consequence of centuries of oppression but an inborn tendency (p. 413); and finally, Jews are seldom actively immoral: they are feminine in their amorality. "Greatness," Weininger declares, "is absent from the nature of the Woman and the Jew, the greatness of morality, or the greatness of evil" (pp. 414-15). The Jew lacks an intelligible self, understands only matter, and attempts to reduce humanity to that level (p. 422).

"Ours Is Not Only the Most Jewish, But Also the Most Feminine of Ages"—From the last pages of the chapter on Jewishness until the end of *Geschlecht und Charakter,* Weininger speaks as a diagnostician of cultural malaise and as its healer. His criticism of modern culture, rooted in his ideas on femininity and Jewishness, is abrasive, antisemitic, and misogynistic. Nevertheless, not all is negative about these pages: Weininger also attempts to construct a future utopia, in which, he hopes, even women will become fully human.

Not since the age of Herod, Weininger declares, had Jews attained such power and influence as in contemporary times: "The spirit of modernity is Jewish." Sexuality pervades society and contemporary ethics affirm the glories of coitus. This sexualization of life reflects the influence of the Jew and the Woman, both obsessed with sex and determined to drag humanity down into the mire of sensuousness: "Ours is not only the most Jewish but also the most feminine of ages" (pp. 440-41). Contemporary men, influenced by Judaism, have accepted the new order. Male chastity is ridiculed and Woman is no longer regarded as the embodied sin of man. Sexual excess has become a symbol of status. Only the woman without a lover is a figure of shame (pp. 443-44). Revolted by this "modern coitus-culture," Weininger cries: "But this means there are no men left!"[139]

A "New Christianity," Weininger hopes, might still emerge from this "New Judaism" (p. 441). That regeneration, however, would depend on the male attribute of chastity. Woman encourages sensuality and opposes her own emancipation because she is enslaved to the phallus.[140] "The ultimate opponent of the emancipation of women is Woman" (p. 447). Kantian morality demands that Man refuse feminine blandishments and see Woman as a human being and respect whatever little individuality she possesses.[141] Women have the right to be regarded as free individuals, even if they "never prove worthy of such a lofty view."

Weininger's misogyny has sometimes been compared to that of Schopenhauer and Nietzsche. Their commonalities, however, are less striking than their differences. Both Schopenhauer and Nietzsche considered women to be intellectually negligible and advocated an "Asiatic" subordination of women in society.[142] Nietzsche also believed that women were driven by the biological urge for pregnancy.[143] Weininger contends that women lack reason and morality and are pervasively and exclusively sexual but, invoking the fundamental principles of Kantian ethics, repudiates the social oppression of women.

Moral relations with women, then, entail the avoidance of all sexual relations, since morality forbids the use of women as means to pleasure or children. Since femininity is amoral and all morality is masculine, "Woman must cease to be Woman and become Man" (p. 452). Weininger warns that he does not mean that women should try to *appear* masculine but, rather, they must masculinize their inner selves. Women should deny and transcend their femininity, which means that they must transcend sexuality itself (p. 453). They must sincerely demand and value male chastity. "Woman, as Woman, must disappear." Destroyed as a sexual being, she would then "rise rejuvenated from the ashes as a genuine human being" (p. 457). The woman question can be resolved only by the total negation of femininity.[144]

TEXT, DISCOURSES, AND MEANING

Geschlecht und Charakter is a heterogeneous, even bewildering text. Its goal, however, is unitary and ostensibly simple: to resolve the woman question. Weininger's text is so complicated because he does not focus on one or a few aspects of the woman question. Instead, he addresses the fundamental ontological questions of gender itself: What is male? What is female? What are their differences? Are those differences eternal and essential? Nothing if not thorough, and unhampered by professional specialization, Weininger plows through virtually every field of thought that addresses these issues. Since these fields are as different as zoology, epistemology, psychology, moral philosophy, and psychiatry, Weininger's study has a thematic and substantive diversity one rarely encounters in contemporary texts on the woman question.

Geschlecht und Charakter combines the languages of science and philosophy for specific ideological purposes. Historians need to analyze the diverse ways in which Weininger, guided by his ideological preferences, appropriates and combines these languages and then uses the resulting discourse to resolve issues, not so much of science or of philosophy, but of cultural politics. Weininger's definition and deconstruction of gender are grounded in the biological theories of his time, as is his analysis of female sexuality. His resolution of the woman question depends on his demonstration that Woman, ontologically, is not an autonomous subject. That metaphysical verdict follows, however, from Weininger's interpretation of medical theories of hysteria, maternal impressions, and telegony. His deployments of scientific arguments, to be sure, are not those of a professional scientist but of a well-informed, ideologically motivated intellectual. And that, precisely, is why Weininger's use of scientific discourse deserves historical analysis. A meticulous contextual analysis of **Geschlecht und Charakter** provides us with a detailed case study of the processes and contexts whereby scientific discourse was interwoven with philosophical and broader cultural discourses at a specific historical moment in order to resolve a pressing issue of cultural politics. To dismiss **Geschlecht und Charakter** as a pseudoscientific work unworthy of historical examination is to ignore the opportunity to make sense of a well-known but puzzling text, to delineate the processes of its construction, and to identify the intellectual, cultural, and political contexts it drew upon and sought to influence.

NOTES

[1] The two most useful biographies of Weininger are David Abrahamsen, *The Mind and Death of a Genius* (New York, 1946); and Jacques Le Rider, *Der Fall Otto Weininger: Wurzeln des Antifeminismus und Antisemitismus,* trans. Dieter Hornig (Vienna, 1985).

[2] The first edition of the work has recently been reprinted: Otto Weininger, *Geschlecht und Charakter: Eine prinzipielle Untersuchung* (Munich, 1980): all page references in this paper are to this edition. Quotations in English follow the anonymous translation, *Sex and Character* (New York, 1906) but rarely without significant revisions. All other translations, unless otherwise mentioned, are my own. After Weininger's death, his friends and literary executors published some of his drafts, aphorisms, and letters in two collections: Otto Weininger, *Über die letzten Dinge* (Vienna, 1904) and Weininger, *Taschenbuch und Briefe an einen Freund* (Leipzig, 1919). Although interesting, these drafts add

little of substance to the argument of *Geschlecht und Charakter* and I have ignored them in this paper.

[3] The reception of Weininger's work deserves a paper in itself. For an overview, see Chandak Sengoopta, "Sex, Science, and Self in Imperial Vienna: Otto Weininger and the Meanings of Gender" (Ph.D. diss., The Johns Hopkins University, 1996), 411-60. For examples of recent approaches to Weininger, see the essays in Nancy A. Harrowitz and Barbara Hyams, eds., *Jews and Gender: Responses to Otto Weininger* (Philadelphia, 1995); and Jacques Le Rider and Norbert Leser, eds., *Otto Weininger: Werk und Wirkung* (Vienna, 1984).

[4] Allan Janik has long been emphasizing these points. See his articles, "Therapeutic Nihilism: How Not to Write about Otto Weininger," in *Structure and Gestalt: Philosophy and Literature in Austria-Hungary and Her Successor States,* ed. Barry Smith (Amsterdam, 1981), 263-92; "Weininger and the Science of Sex: Prolegomena to Any Future Study," in *Decadence and Innovation: Austro-Hungarian Life and Art at the Turn of the Century,* ed. Robert B. Pynsent (London, 1989), 24-32; and "Writing about Weininger," in Janik, *Essays on Wittgenstein and Weininger* (Amsterdam, 1985), 96-115. See also A. Janik, "Must Anti-Modernism be Irrational?" in Janik, *How Not to Interpret a Culture: Essays on the Problem of Method in the Geisteswissenschaften* (Bergen, 1986), 66-84.

[5] Leopold Weininger died in 1922 and it is possible that he had left Judaism by then. His death was not registered by the Israelitische Kultusgemeinde of Vienna. See Abrahamsen, *Mind and Death,* 10.

[6] Abrahamsen, *Mind and Death,* 14. At age sixteen, he had written an etymological essay on certain Greek adjectives found only in Homer and attempted unsuccessfully to publish it in a leading philological journal of the time. A linguist has recently tried to reconstruct this lost essay on the basis of descriptions in Weininger's letters. See Manfred Mayrhofer, "Ein indogermanistischer Versuch Otto Weiningers," *Historische Sprachforschung (Historical Linguistics)* 104 (1991): 303-6.

[7] See Hannelore Rodlauer, "Fragmente aus Weiningers Bildungsgeschichte (1895-1902)," in *Otto Weininger, Eros und Psyche: Studien und Briefe 1899-1902,* ed. H. Rodlauer (Vienna, 1990), 13-53, here 16. Weininger's biomedical training critically influenced his approach to gender and sexuality in *Geschlecht und Charakter,* a fact that has not been adequately recognized by scholars. Allan Janik considers this to be the central deficiency of recent research on Weininger. See Janik, "Therapeutic Nihilism," and Janik, "Weininger and the Science of Sex."

[8] See Weininger's curriculum vitae in Rodlauer, ed., *Otto Weininger,* 210-11. On critical positivism, see Maurice Mandelbaum, *History, Man, and Reason: A Study in Nineteenth-Century Thought* (Baltimore, 1971), 10-20; and Leszek Kolakowski, *The Alienation of Rea-*

son: A History of Positivist Thought, trans. Norbert Guterman (New York, 1969), 101-28. Avenarius and Mach themselves denied that they were positivists. Avenarius coined the term "Empiriocriticism," derived from "empiricism" and "criticism," to describe his philosophy. See Friedrich Carstanjen, "Richard Avenarius and His General Theory of Knowledge, Empiriocriticism," trans. H. Bosanquet, *Mind* new ser. 6 (1897): 449-75.

[9] On Freud's early reputation within Central Europe, see Hannah S. Decker, *Freud in Germany: Revolution and Reaction in Science, 1893-1907* (New York, 1977); and Michael Worbs, *Nervenkunst: Literatur und Psychoanalyse im Wien der Jahrhundertwende* (Frankfurt am Main, 1983).

[10] See *The Complete Letters of Sigmund Freud to Wilhelm Fliess 1887-1904,* trans. and ed. Jeffrey Moussaieff Masson (Cambridge, Mass., 1985). This friendship has been "psychoanalyzed" by several commentators. See, for instance, Patrick Mahony, "Friendship and its Discontents," *Contemporary Psychoanalysis* 15 (1979): 55-109.

[11] After Weininger's death, the transmission of this idea (from Freud to Weininger through Swoboda) created a major controversy. The most cogent and well-informed overview of the episode is provided by Frank J. Sulloway, *Freud, Biologist of the Mind: Beyond the Psychoanalytic Legend* (New York, 1977), 223-29. See also Kurt R. Eissler, *Talent and Genius: The Fictitious Case of Tausk Contra Freud* (New York, 1971); and Peter Heller, "A Quarrel over Bisexuality," in *The Turn of the Century: German Literature and Art, 1890-1915,* ed. Gerald Chapple and Hans H. Schulte (Bonn, 1981), 87-115.

[12] Letter to Swoboda dated 14 February 1901, in Rodlauer, ed., *Otto Weininger,* 68. Weininger's own sexual "aberrations" may have conditioned his choice of subject but the evidence is too scanty to be useful. In any case, Viennese intellectuals and artists did not need to be sexually disturbed—not extraordinarily disturbed, at any rate—to develop a serious interest in the subject of sex. In fin-de-siècle Vienna, Edward Timms suggests, sexuality became a "symbolic territory" for debates on identity, reason, and irrationalism. David Luft adds that Viennese intellectuals were distinctive in combining biological approaches to sex with a Schopenhauerian irrationalism, which stressed the internal reality of feelings. *Geschlecht und Charakter* is one of the major representatives of this tradition. See Edward Timms, *Karl Kraus, Apocalyptic Satirist: Culture and Catastrophe in Habsburg Vienna* (New Haven, 1986), 28-29; and David S. Luft, "Science and Irrationalism in Freud's Vienna," *Modern Austrian Literature* 23 no. 2 (1990): 89-97.

[13] See Hannelore Rodlauer, "Von 'Eros und Psyche' zu 'Geschlecht und Charakter': Unbekannte Weininger-Manuskripte im Archiv der Österreichischen Akademie der Wissenschaften," *Österreichische* Akademie der Wissenschaften, philosophisch-historische Klasse: *Anzeiger* 124 (1987): 110-39, here 113. These outlines, entitled "Eros und Psyche" and "Zur Theorie des Lebens," are reprinted in Rodlauer, ed., *Otto Weininger.*

[14] At least two factors were important in his decision: a preoccupation with Henrik Ibsen's reflections on man's inner self in his play *Peer Gynt* and deeper acquaintance with Immanuel Kant's metaphysical and ethical analyses of the empirically undemonstrable noumenal self. Referring to Mach's conviction that the coherent, unified self was a fiction that could not be "salvaged," Weininger declared: "The self *is.* There is absolutely no need to 'salvage' it." See Otto Weininger, Letter to H. Swoboda dated 2 March 1902, in Rodlauer, ed., *Otto Weininger,* 107-8.

[15] Sigmund Freud, who read one version of Weininger's manuscript, exclaimed in exasperation: "The world wants evidence, not thoughts!" See O. Weininger, undated letter to H. Swoboda (probably October 1901), in ibid, 87.

[16] See the examiners' reports in ibid, 211-14.

[17] Steven Beller has shown that many Jewish intellectuals of Vienna converted to Protestantism rather than to the Habsburg state religion of Catholicism because of their strong identification with the Lutheran culture of northern Germany. See S. Beller, *Vienna and the Jews, 1867-1938: A Cultural History* (Cambridge, 1989), 153.

[18] Weininger seemed so depressed at this time that the friend, Artur Gerber, feared he might commit suicide immediately. See A. Gerber, "Ecce homo," in Otto Weininger, *Taschenbuch und Briefe an einen Freund* (Leipzig, 1919), 17-20.

[19] Sander Gilman points out that Beethoven was not simply a great artist to early-twentieth-century Central Europeans but "the quintessential German artist." Weininger's decision to kill himself in Beethoven's death chamber was obviously his last and most dramatic attempt to identify with the spirit of Germany. See Sander L. Gilman, *Jewish Self-Hatred: Anti-Semitism and the Hidden Language of the Jews* (Baltimore, 1986), 248.

[20] See Peter Gay, *Freud, Jews and Other Germans: Masters and Victims in Modernist Culture* (New York, 1978), 196.

[21] See the seminal essays by Carl Schorske in *Fin-de-Siècle Vienna: Politics and Culture* (New York, 1981).

[22] For an anecdotal but compelling portrait of this pervasive malaise, see Frederic Morton, *A Nervous Splendor: Vienna, 1888/1889* (Boston, 1979).

[23] See Dagmar Barnouw, "Loos, Kraus, Wittgenstein, and the Problem of Authenticity," in *The Turn of the Century,* ed. Gerald Chapple and Hans Schulte, 249-73; and Timms, *Karl Kraus, Apocalyptic Satirist.*

[24] Schorske, *Fin-de-Siècle Vienna,* 4. On the history of the concept of the self, see Charles Taylor, *Sources of the Self: The Making of the Modern Identity* (Cambridge, Mass., 1989).

[25] On Mach and his work, see John T. Blackmore, *Ernst Mach: His Work, Life, and Influence* (Berkeley, 1972); Judith Ryan, "Die andere Psychologie: Ernst Mach und die Folgen," in *Österreichische Gegenwart: Die moderne Literatur und ihr Verhältnis zur Tradition,* ed. Wolfgang Paulsen (Bern, 1980), 11-24; Friedrich Stadler, *Vom Positivismus zur "wissenschaftlichen Weltauffassung": Am Beispiel der Wirkungsgeschichte von Ernst Mach in Osterreich von 1895 bis 1934* (Vienna, 1982), esp. 13-132; and Patrizia Giampieri Deutsch, "Mach, Freud, Musil: Die Frage nach dem Subjekt," *Sigmund Freud House Bulletin* 14 no. 2 (1990): 47-56.

[26] See E. Mach, *Analyse der Empfindungen und das Verhältniss des Physichen zum Psychischen,* 4th ed. (Jena, 1903), 20. Mach's original sentence, "Das Ich ist unrettbar," was translated somewhat inadequately as "the ego must be given up" in E. Mach, *The Analysis of Sensations,* trans. C. M. Williams and S. Waterlow (New York, 1959), 17.

[27] Hermann Bahr, *Bilderbuch* (Vienna, 1921), cited and translated in Blackmore, *Ernst Mach,* 155.

[28] See Stadler, *Vom Positivismus,* 50-52.

[29] See Kurt Danziger, "The Positivist Repudiation of Wundt," *Journal of the History of the Behavioral Sciences* 15 (1979): 205-30.

[30] Danziger, "Positivist Repudiation of Wundt," 209-11. Külpe later turned into an outspoken opponent of Mach's psychological theories. See E. G. Boring, *A History of Experimental Psychology,* 2nd ed. (New York, 1957), 397, 409.

[31] See Danziger, "Positivist Repudiation of Wundt," 213-14; and Katherine Arens, *Structures of Knowing: Psychologies of the Nineteenth Century* (Dordrecht, 1989), 155-60. Dilthey, whom Weininger greatly admired as a psychological thinker, advocated that psychologists cease to imitate natural scientists and aim, instead, to comprehend the total "lived world" of human beings. Weininger cites Dilthey's work with approval in *Geschlecht und Charakter* (102, 501, 506) and condemns experimental psychology for its Machian disregard for the self. For general information on Dilthey, see Rudolf A. Makkreel, *Dilthey: Philosopher of the Human Studies* (Princeton, 1975).

[32] See K. Danziger, *Constructing the Subject: Historical Origins of Psychological Research* (Cambridge, 1990), 19-20; and C. Thomas Powell, *Kant's Theory of Self-Consciousness* (Oxford, 1990).

[33] On Neo-Kantianism in Germany, see Thomas E. Willey, *Back to Kant: The Revival of Kantianism in German Social and Historical Thought, 1860-1914* (Detroit, 1978); and Klaus Christian Köhnke, The Rise of Neo-Kantianism: German Academic Philosophy between *Idealism and Positivism* (Cambridge, 1991). For illuminating discussions of the Austrian situation, see Rudolf Haller, "Österreichische Philosophie," in R. Haller, *Studien zur österreichischen Philosophic: Variationen über ein Thema* (Amsterdam, 1979), 5-22; and R. Haller, "Wittgenstein and Austrian Philosophy," in Haller, *Questions on Wittgenstein* (London, 1988), 1-26.

[34] See Willey, *Back to Kant,* 102-52.

[35] See Allan Janik, "Philosophical Sources of Wittgenstein's Ethics," in Janik, *Essays on Wittgenstein and Weininger,* 74-95, here 94.

[36] For general discussions, see Lorenne M. G. Clark and Lynda Lange, eds., *The Sexism of Social and Political Theory: Women and Reproduction from Plato to Nietzsche* (Toronto, 1979); Ute Frevert, "Bürgerliche Meisterdenker und das Geschlechterverhältnis: Konzepte, Erfahrungen, Visionen an der Wende vom 18. zum 19. Jahrhundert," in *Bürgerinnen und Bürger: Geschlechterverhältnisse im 19. Jahrhundert,* ed. U. Frevert (Göttingen, 1988), 17-48; and Nancy Tuana, *The Less Noble Sex: Scientific, Religious, and Philosophical Conceptions of Woman's Nature* (Bloomington, 1993).

[37] See Immanuel Kant, *Anthropologie in pragmatischer Hinsicht,* in Kant, *Gesammelte Schriften,* ed. Königlich Preussische Akademie der Wissenschaften (Berlin, 1902), 7:305-6. For analyses of Kant's views on gender, see Heidemarie Bennent, *Galanterie und* Verachtung: Eine philosophiegeschichtliche Untersuchung zur *Stellung der Frau in Gesellschaft und Kultur* (Frankfurt am Main, 1985), 96-108; and Susan Mendus, "Kant: An Honest but Narrow-Minded Bourgeois?," in *Women in Western Political Philosophy: Kant to Nietzsche,* ed. Ellen Kennedy and Susan Mendus (Brighton, 1987), 21-43.

[38] See Ute Frevert, "Bürgerliche Meisterdenker und das Geschlechterverhältnis"; and Karin Hausen, "Die Polarisierung der 'Geschlechtscharaktere': Eine Spiegelung der Dissoziation von Erwerbs- und Familienleben," in *Sozialgeschichte der Familie in der Neuzeit Europas,* ed. Werner Conze (Stuttgart, 1976), 363-69. On the role of scientists in establishing this "natural" order of sexual inequality, and the necessity of such a basis for the justification of women's inferior status in liberal political philosophy, see Londa Schiebinger, *The Mind Has No Sex? Women in the Origins of Modern Science* (Cambridge, Mass., 1989), 215-16.

[39] Theodore Roszak, "The Hard and the Soft: The Force of Feminism in Modern Times," in *Masculine/Feminine: Readings in Sexual Mythology and the Liberation of Women,* ed. Betty Roszak and T. Roszak (New York, 1969), 87-104, here 87-88.

[40] See Susan Sleeth Mosedale, "Science Corrupted: Victorian Biologists Consider 'The Woman Question,'" *Journal of the History of Biology* 11 (1978): 1-55; Janet Sayers, *Biological Politics: Feminist and Anti-Feminist Perspectives* (London, 1982); Cynthia Eagle Russett, *Sexual Science: The Victorian Construction of Womanhood* (Cambridge, Mass., 1989); and Tuana, *The Less Noble Sex*. Almost all of these studies have an Anglo-American focus. The Central European discourse remains insufficiently explored, but see Claudia Honegger, *Die Ordnung der Geschlechter: Die Wissenschaften vom Menschen und das Weib, 1750-1850* (Frankfurt am Main, 1991).

[41] Paul J. Möbius, *Ueber den physiologischen Schwachsinn des Weibes* (Halle, 1912). On Möbius, see Francis Schiller, *A Möbius Strip: Fin-de-Siècle Neuropsychiatry and Paul Möbius* (Berkeley, 1982).

[42] See Cesare Lombroso and Guglielmo Ferrero, *Das Weib als Verbrecherin und Prostituierte: Anthropologische Studien gegründet auf eine Darstellung der Biologie und Psychologie des normalen Weibes*, trans. Hans Kurella (Hamburg, 1894). Weininger shared many of Lombroso's views: see Janik, "Weininger and the Science of Sex," 28; and Nancy A. Harrowitz, "Weininger and Lombroso: A Question of Influence," in *Jews and Gender*, eds. Harrowitz and Hyams, 73-90.

[43] See Terry R. Kandal, *The Woman Question in Classical Sociological Theory* (Miami, 1988), esp. 89-185; Silvia Bovenschen, Die imaginierte Weiblichkeit: Exemplarische Untersuchungen zu kulturgeschichtlichen und literarischen Präsentationsformen des *Weiblichen* (Frankfurt am Main, 1979); and Nike Wagner, *Geist und Geschlecht: Karl Kraus und die Erotik der Wiener Moderne* (Frankfurt am Main, 1981).

[44] See Richard J. Evans, *The Feminist Movement in Germany 1894-1933* (London, 1976); Harriet Anderson, *Utopian Feminism: Women's Movements in Fin-de-Siècle Vienna* (New Haven, 1992); Werner Thönnessen, *The Emancipation of Women: The Rise and Decline of the Women's Movement in German Social Democracy 1863-1933*, trans. Joris de Bres (London, 1973); Jean H. Quataert, *Reluctant Feminists in German Social Democracy, 1885-1917* (Princeton, 1979); and Edith Rigler, *Frauenleitbild und Frauenarbeit in Österreich vom ausgehenden 19. Jahrhundert bis zum Zweiten Weltkrieg* (Munich, 1976).

[45] See Gordon A. Craig, *Germany 1866-1945* (New York, 1978), 212; and Martha S. Braun *et al.*, eds., *Frauenbewegung, Frauenbildung und Frauenarbeit in Österreich* (Vienna, 1930).

[46] See Herrad U. Bessemer, "Bürgerliche Frauenbewegung und männliches Bildungsbürgertum 1860-1880," in *Bürgerinnen und Bürger: Geschlechterverhältnisse im 19. Jahrhundert*, ed. Ute Frevert (Göttingen, 1988), 190-205; and Irene Stoehr, "'Organisierte Mütterlichkeit': Zur Politik der deutschen Frauenbewegung um 1900," in *Frauen suchen ihre Geschichte: Historische Studien zum 19. und 20. Jahrhundert*, ed. Karin Hausen (Munich, 1983), 221-49.

[47] See Ann T. Allen, *Feminism and Motherhood in Germany, 1800-1914* (New Brunswick, N.J., 1991).

[48] See Anderson, *Utopian Feminism*, 190-91.

[49] See Amy Hackett, "Helene Stöcker: Left-Wing Intellectual and Sex Reformer," in *When Biology Became Destiny: Women in Weimar and Nazi Germany*, ed. Renate Bridenthal, Atina Grossmann, and Marion Kaplan (New York, 1984), 109-30.

[50] Anderson, *Utopian Feminism*, 72-73.

[51] See Evans, *Feminist Movement in Germany*, 145-205.

[52] See *Strindberg's Letters*, selected, edited, and translated by Michael Robinson, 2 vols. (London, 1992), 1:154; August Strindberg, *The Confession of a Fool*, trans. Ellie Schleussner (London, 1912), 252-53; and Strindberg, preface to *Miss Julie: A Naturalistic Tragedy*, trans. Helen Cooper (London, 1992), xvi. On Strindberg's complex relations with feminism, see Gail Finney, Women in Modern Drama: Freud, Feminism, and European Theater at *the Turn of the Century* (Ithaca, 1989), 207-26.

[53] See Iwan Bloch, *Das Sexualleben unserer Zeit in seinen Beziehungen zur modernen Kultur* (Berlin, 1907), 580-81; and Gudrun Schwarz, "'Viragos' in Male Theory in Nineteenth-Century Germany," trans. Joan Reutershan, in *Women in Culture and Politics: A Century of Change*, ed. Judith Friedlander et al. (Bloomington, 1986), 128-43.

[54] In a 1904 lecture at a gathering of homosexual emancipationists, feminist activist Anna Rüling, herself homosexual, declared that the lesbian did not imitate males: she *was* partly male, biologically unsuited for marriage and motherhood, and eminently well-equipped to be a professional or a university professor. Many prominent feminist leaders, Rüling declared, were indeed lesbians, and could easily be recognized as such by anybody with the slightest understanding of lesbian traits. See A. Rüling, "Welches Interesse hat die Frauenbewegung an der Lösung des homosexuellen Problems?," *Jahrbuch für sexuelle Zwischenstufen* 7 (1905): 129-51. As far as I know, however, Käthe Schirmacher was the only German feminist *leader* who was openly lesbian. See Ilse Kokula, *Weibliche Homosexualität um 1900* (Munich, 1981), 31.

[55] Jacques Le Rider. *Modernity and Crises of Identity: Culture and Society in Fin-de-Siècle Vienna*, trans. Rosemary Morris (New York, 1993). See also Bernd Widdig, *Mannerbunde und Massen: Zur Krise männlicher Identität in der Literatur der Moderne* (Opladen, 1992). Recently, there has been a remarkable prolifera-

tion of studies on American and British concepts of masculinity. For examples, see Michael Roper and John Tosh, eds., *Manful Assertions: Masculinities in Britain since 1800* (New York, 1991) and Michael S. Kimmel, *Manhood in America: A Cultural History* (New York, 1996).

[56] R. Lothar, "Kritik in Frankreich" (1891), in *Das junge Wien: Österreichische Literatur- und Kunstkritik, 1887-1902,* ed. Gotthart Wunberg, 2 vols. (Tübingen, 1976), 1:211.

[57] Rosa Mayreder, *Zur Kritik der Weiblichkeit: Essays* (Jena, 1910), 102-5.

[58] See Le Rider, *Modernity;* and Christina von Braun, "'Der Jude' und 'Das Weib': Zwei Stereotypen des 'Anderen' in der Moderne," *Metis* (Pfaffenweiler) 1 (1992): 6-28, esp. 6-9.

[59] There is an enormous literature on German and Austrian antisemitism. For an excellent survey, see Peter Pulzer, *The Rise of Political Anti-Semitism in Germany and Austria,* rev. ed. (Cambridge, Mass., 1988). For the specifically Viennese context, see John W. Boyer, *Political Radicalism in Late Imperial Vienna: Origins of the Christian Social Movement, 1848-1897* (Chicago, 1981); and Carl E. Schorske, "Politics in a New Key: An Austrian Trio," in Schorske, *Fin-de-Siècle Vienna.*

[60] Exactly *how* one could transcend it, however, was difficult to answer. Certainly, conversion to Christianity was not universally accepted as satisfactory. The Jewish character, critics argued, could not be "washed away" by baptismal water. Biological racism was a later innovation, and when grafted on to this earlier psychological/cultural racism, left absolutely no scope for the individual to transcend his "Jewishness," even if he desired to. See Paul Lawrence Rose, *Revolutionary Antisemitism in Germany from Kant to Wagner* (Princeton, 1990), xvi-xvii, 14-15.

[61] Ibid, xvi.

[62] Ibid, 12. Otto Weininger observes that among intellectuals, only Friedrich Nietzsche and dramatist Gotthold Ephraim Lessing were philosemitic. Weininger attributes Nietzsche's philosemitism to his opposition to Richard Wagner and Arthur Schopenhauer. As for Lessing, Weininger dismisses him curtly as "greatly overrated" (p. 586).

[63] See David C. Large and William Weber, eds. *Wagnerism in European Art and Politics* (Ithaca, 1984).

[64] See Richard Wagner, "Art and Revolution," in *Richard Wagner's Prose Works,* trans. William Ashton Ellis, 6 vols. (London, 1892-99), 1:59, 65 (1892); "The Artwork of the Future," ibid., 147, 177; "Judaism in Music," ibid, 3:79-82. On Wagner's antisemitism, see Marc A. Weiner, *Richard Wagner and the Anti-Semitic Imagination* (Lincoln, Neb., 1995).

[65] The Jewish-born Karl Kraus, for instance, published Chamberlain's articles in his journal and shared his conviction that Jews were the forces of mammon. See Timms, *Karl Kraus, Apocalyptic Satirist,* 238.

[66] See Geoffrey Field, *Evangelist of Race: The Germanic Vision of Houston Stewart Chamberlain* (New York, 1981), 168-277. Published in two volumes in 1990, the *Foundations* brought its author immediate fame and a following. One of his followers was Rudolf Kassner, a friend of Otto Weininger's. See Rodlauer, "Fragmente," 45.

[67] See Field, *Evangelist of Race,* 186; and H. S. Chamberlain, *The Foundations of the Nineteenth Century,* trans. John Lees, 2 vols. (London, 1913), 1:299-300. Chamberlain was far from unequivocal on the immutability of Jewishness. He wrote in the *Foundations* that "it is pointless to call the purest bred Israelite a Jew, if he has succeeded in throwing off the shackles of Ezra and Nehemiah and no longer acknowledges the law of Moses in his mind or despises others in his heart." Elsewhere, he almost contradicted himself by using quasi-biological arguments. This same equivocation was also characteristic of Wagner himself. See Field, *Evangelist of Race,* 155-56, 217-18. Otto Weininger cites Chamberlain frequently, though not always in agreement, in *Geschlecht und Charater,* 586, 588-91.

[68] See Field, *Evangelist of Race,* 95.

[69] See Marsha L. Rozenblit, *The Jews of Vienna, 1867-1914: Assimilation and Identity* (Albany, N.Y., 1983). In 1848, there had been, at most, 4000 Jews in Vienna. By the end of the century, the Jewish population had risen to 150,000, approximately nine percent of the total population of the city. Around 1900, only about 20 percent of all Jews living in the city had been born there, ibid., 18. The Jewish migration to Vienna was part of a larger European trend of Jewish migration to cities from outlying provinces, ibid, 15-16.

[70] See Steven Beller, *Vienna and the Jews, 1867-1938: A Cultural History* (Cambridge, 1989), 33, 52, 38-40; and Gary B. Cohen, "Ideals and Reality in the Austrian Universities, 1850-1914," in *Rediscovering History: Culture, Politics, and the Psyche,* ed. Michael S. Roth (Stanford, 1994), 83-101.

[71] Norman Stone, *Europe Transformed 1878-1919* (Cambridge, Mass., 1984), 404-11.

[72] See Beller, *Vienna and the Jews,* 3. For the relationship with Stone, see ibid., x. For Beller's views on the problematic question of how to define who was Jewish and who was not, see ibid., 11-13.

[73] Ibid., 73-78.

[74] Ibid., 102-3.

[75] Ibid., 106-13. Of all who left Judaism, as many as a quarter converted to Protestantism, including Victor Adler, Alfred Adler, Peter Altenberg, Arnold Schoenberg, and Otto Weininger. See ibid, 153.

[76] Ibid., 114-21.

[77] See Robert S. Wistrich, *The Jews of Vienna in the Age of Franz Joseph* (Oxford, 1989), 131-63.

[78] See ibid., 205-37; and Michael Pollak, "Cultural Innovation and Social Identity in Fin-de-Siècle Vienna," in *Jews, Antisemitism, and Culture in Vienna,* ed. Ivar Oxaal, M. Pollak, and Gerhard Botz (London, 1987), 59-74. On the most dramatic Jewish response to antisemitism, Theodor Herzl's Zionism, see Wistrich, *Jews of Vienna,* 421-93; and Steven Beller, *Herzl* (London, 1991).

[79] See Beller, *Vienna and the Jews,* 220-21.

[80] Theodor Lessing, *Der jüdische Selbsthass* (Munich, 1984). Lessing himself had been strongly antisemitic in his early years. See Lawrence Baron, "Theodor Lessing: Between Jewish Self-Hatred and Zionism," *Leo Baeck Institute Yearbook* 26 (1981): 323-40.

[81] For a recent, widely-read example, see Gilman, *Jewish Self-Hatred.* See also Michael Pollak, "Otto Weiningers Antisemitismus," in *Otto Weininger: Werk und Wirkung,* ed. Le Rider and Leser, 109-22.

[82] See Allan Janik, "Viennese Culture and the Jewish Self-Hatred Hypothesis: A Critique," in *Jews, Antisemitism, and Culture in Vienna,* ed. Oxaal, Pollak and Botz, 75-88.

[83] See Steven Beller, "Otto Weininger as Liberal?," in *Jews and Gender,* ed. Harrowitz and Hyams, 91-101.

[84] See S. P. Scheichl, "The Contexts and Nuances of Anti-Jewish Language: Were all the 'Antisemites' Antisemites?," in *Jews, Antisemitism and Culture in Vienna,* ed. Oxaal, Pollak, and Botz, 89-110.

[85] See Janik, "Weininger and the Science of Sex."

[86] In his preface, Weininger acknowledges the disjointed nature of his text. Describing the two parts as, respectively, "biological-psychological" and "psychological-philosophical," he concedes it might have been more appropriate to have published them as two separate works: one purely scientific and the other metaphysical (p. ix). He argues, however, that he had to "free" himself of biology before he could become a pure psychologist (pp. ix-x).

[87] There is no substantive separation of scientific and extra-scientific discourse between the first and second parts. As examples, one may cite chap. 6 of part 1, which deals with feminism, and chap. 12 of part 2,

dealing, among other issues, with medical views of hysteria. Such examples may be easily multiplied.

[88] Historians of science and medicine have not analyzed this issue in any detail. See, however, Sulloway, *Freud,* 158-60; Ornella Moscucci, *The Science of Woman: Gynaecology and Gender in England 1800-1929* (Cambridge, 1990), 13-22; and Gert Hekma, "'A Female Soul in a Male Body': Sexual Inversion as Gender Inversion in Nineteenth-Century Sexology," in *Third Sex, Third Gender: Beyond Sexual Dimorphism in Culture and History,* ed. Gilbert Herdt (New York, 1994), 213-39. Thomas Laqueur's contention that males and females have been seen in modern times as totally different underplays the tense interplay of notions of sexual similarity and difference in nineteenth and twentieth-century biomedical discourse. Lawrence Birken provides a more nuanced and useful analysis of this issue. See Thomas W. Laqueur, *Making Sex: Body and Gender from the Greeks to Freud* (Cambridge, Mass., 1990); and L. Birken, *Consuming Desire: Sexual Science and the Emergence of a Culture of Abundance, 1871-1914* (Ithaca, 1988).

[89] See J. J. S. Steenstrup, *Untersuchungen über das Vorkommen des Hermaphroditismus in der Natur,* trans. C. F. Hornschuch (Greifswald, 1846), 9-10. For an incisive critique of Steenstrup's ideas, see R. Leuckart, "Zeugung," in *Handwörterbuch der Physiologie,* ed. Rudolf Wagner, 4 vols. in 5 (Braunschweig, 1853), 4:707-1000, here 742-43.

[90] The most concise and comprehensive discussion of Nägeli's multifaceted career is still that of Erik Nordenskiöld, *The History of Biology: A Survey* (New York, 1928), 552-57.

[91] See Carl v. Nägeli, *Mechanisch-physiologische Theorie der Abstanmmungslehre* (Munich 1894); Gloria Robinson, *A Prelude to* Genetics, Theories of a Material Substance of Heredity: Darwin to *Weismann* (Lawrence, Kansas, 1979), 109-30; and Hans-Jörg Rheinberger, "Naudinn, Darwin, Nägeli: Bemerkungen zu den Vererbungsvorstellungen des 19. Jahrhunderts," *Medizinhistorisches Journal* 18 (1983): 198-212, esp. 206-11.

[92] Nägeli, *Mechanisch-physiologische Theorie,* 531.

[93] Weininger does not completely reject contemporary research on the internal secretions but he refuses to recognize them as the sole determinants of sex. This moderate skepticism was shared by many contemporary medical scientists, who believed that the internal secretions of the sex glands acted on a congenitally determined sexual soma. The role of the sex glands, they argued, was important but secondary. As late as 1910, the eminent physiologist Artur Biedl devoted many paragraphs to a careful discussion of this question in his classic textbook of endocrinology. See A. Biedl, *The Internal Secretory Organs: Their Physiology and Pathology,* trans. Linda Forster (London, 1913), 360-70.

[94] F. H. A. Marshall, *The Physiology of Reproduction,* 2nd ed. (London, 1922), 690. It is ironic that Marshall criticized Weininger's views as "somewhat too morphologically conceived" and did not mention Weininger's ideas on the role of the internal secretions. There was a simple reason for this. Marshall seems to have been familiar only with the English translation of *Geschlecht und Charakter.* Most of Weininger's endocrinological hypotheses were presented in long endnotes, all of which were omitted from the English version. Another British biologist, Edward A. Minchin, also found merits in Weininger's idioplasmic hypothesis of sex. See E. A. Minchin, "Protozoa," *Encyclopaedia Britannica,* 11th ed. (1911), 22:479-89, on 486.

[95] Weininger claims that he had not seen Schopenhauer's passage when he "discovered the law" in early 1901. Acknowledging Schopenhauer's partial priority, he quotes him at length (489): "In the first place, all sexuality is partiality. This partiality or one-sidedness is more decidedly expressed and present in a higher degree in one individual than in another. Therefore in every individual it can be better supplemented and neutralized by one individual of the opposite sex than by another, since every individual requires a one-sidedness, individually the opposite of his or her own. Accordingly, the most manly man will look for the most womanly woman and vice versa." See A. Schopenhauer, *The World as Will and Representation,* trans. E. F. J. Payne, 2 vols. (New York, 1966), 2:546. On Schopenhauer's analysis of sexuality, see Wolfram Bernhard, "Schopenhauer und die moderne Charakterologie," *Schopenhauer-Jahrbuch* 44 (1963): 25-133, on 74-85. For a discussion of Weininger's "law" in the context of Schopenhauer's observations, see ibid., 79-85.

[96] Surprisingly, Weininger does not emphasize his originality in framing human sexual attraction in algebraic terms. No biologist or medical sexologist of the time seems to have attempted anything similar. Ian Hacking has observed that in the nineteenth century, "the numbering of the world was occurring in every branch of human inquiry." Weininger's law and equations, of course, have less to do with numbers than with a more general urge for quantification and mathematical expression. Nevertheless, they fall within Hacking's definition of laws: "Any equations with some constant numbers in them. They are positivist regularities, the intended harvest of science." See Ian Hacking, *The Taming of Chance* (Cambridge, 1990), 60, 63.

[97] See Vern L. Bullough, *Homosexuality: A History* (New York, 1979); Jeffrey Weeks, *Sex, Politics, and Society: The Regulation of Sexuality since 1800,* 2nd ed. (London, 1989), 96-121; and Martin Bauml Duberman, Martha Vicinus, and George Chauncey, Jr., eds., *Hidden from History: Reclaiming the Gay and Lesbian Past* (New York, 1989). For the sake of convenience, I use the word "homosexuality" throughout as a generic term including homosexual acts, psychological orientation, and sexual preference. This does not reflect the complexities of nineteenth-century terminology and conceptualization, for a comprehensive review of which see Havelock Ellis, *Studies in the Psychology of Sex,* 2 vols. (New York, 1936), vol. 1, pt. 4 *(Sexual Inversion),* 310-17. On emancipationist movements, see John Lauritsen and David Thorstad, *The Early Homosexual Rights Movement (1864-1935)* (New York, 1974); James D. Steakley, *The Homosexual Emancipation Movement in Germany* (New York, 1975); and John C. Fout, "Sexual Politics in Wilhelmine Germany: The Male Gender Crisis, Moral Purity, and Homophobia," *Journal of the History of Sexuality* 2 (1992): 388-41. On homosexual subcultures in Weininger's Vienna, see Hanna Hacker and Manfred Lang, "Jenseits der Geschlechter, zwischen ihnen: Homosexualitäten im Wien der Jahrhundertwende," in *Das lila Wien um 1900: Zur Ästhetik der Homosexualitäten,* ed. Neda Bei et al. (Vienna, 1986), 8-18. On medical theories of homosexuality in Central Europe, see Sulloway, *Freud,* 277-319.

[98] Physicians found it easier to jettison the idea of disease than that of anomaly. The eminent British sexologist Havelock Ellis, for instance, accepted that homosexuals were not diseased but denied that they were so unpathological as to constitute "an anthropological human variety comparable to the Negro or the Mongolian man." Citing no less an authority than Rudolf Virchow, Ellis argued that any deviation from the norm was pathological, without necessarily being a disease. See Ellis, *Studies in the Psychology of Sex,* 1, pt. 4, 321. Ellis's distinction between *pathos* (an anomaly, i.e., any deviation from the norm) and *nosos* (disease) was drawn from R. Virchow, "Eröffnungsrede, xxv. Allgemeine Versammlung und Stiftungsfest der deutschen anthropologischen Gesellschaft in Innsbruck vom 24.-28. August 1894," *Correspondenz-Blatt der deutschen Gesellschaft für Anthropologie, Ethnologie und Urgeschichte* 25 (1894): 80-87, here 84.

[99] On this point, see Manfred Herzer, *Magnus Hirschfeld* (Frankfurt, 1992), 98-99.

[100] For a medical view approaching that of Weininger's, see A. Aletrino, "Uranisme et dégénérescence," *Archives d'anthropologie criminelle* 23 (1908): 633-67, esp. 649-53. According to Ellis (*Studies,* 1, pt. 4, 321), Aletrino's position was quite singular among physicians and I have found no evidence to question that assessment.

[101] See Rodlauer, ed., *Otto Weininger.* 173.

[102] "Mein Mittel zur Bekämpfung der Homosexualität scheint Erfolg zu haben!! Trotzdem es ja zu meiner Theorie nur stimmen würde, habe ich mich doch von meinem Staunen darüber noch nicht erholt. Wenn ich nur sicher wäre, dass keine Suggestion vorliegt! . . . Jedenfalls werden die Dosen fortgesetzt werden müssen . . . Mein Patient bereitet sich schon auf den ersten Koitus vor!" See ibid., 73.

[103] See Le Rider, *Der Fall Otto Weininger,* 25-26.

[104] Weininger's conception of "differential psychology" is his own, but he obtains the term from L. William Stern, *Psychologie der individuellen Differenzen,* Schriften der Gesellschaft für psychologische Forschung 12 (1900).

[105] Weininger would later argue that true psychology was not concerned with such empirical tasks. Here, however, he is still imbued with his initial conviction that the investigation of gender differences would lead to social reform.

[106] In his notes to these passages, Weininger heaps praise on Wilhelm Fliess and his 1897 monograph, *Die Beziehungen zwischen Nase und weiblichen Geschlechtsorganen.* Weininger remarks that Fliess's "extraordinarily original treatise," although inappropriately titled, contained the "most interesting and most stimulating" observations on periodic phenomena in human life, 499-500.

[107] This opinion would not have seemed outlandish to contemporary physicians. Weininger himself says that his analysis, although completely independent, parallels that of Arduin, "Die Frauenfrage und die sexuellen Zwischenstufen," *Jahrbuch für sexuelle Zwischenstufen* 2 (1900): 211-23. Arduin believed that many of the leaders of the women's emancipation movements were masculine and lesbian, ibid., 216. These masculine women were biologically driven to masculine occupations and should be permitted to do so, ibid., 220-21. Arduin was the pseudonym of the physiologist and psychologist K. F. Jordan. See Peter Gorsen, "Nachwort," in Jahrbuch für sexuelle Zwischenstufen: Auswahl aus den Jahrgängen *1899-1923,* 2 vols., ed. W. J. Schmidt (Frankfurt, 1984), 2: 257-84, here 259.

[108] Weininger quotes historian Jacob Burckhardt's statement that masculine intelligence and independence were prized features in women during the Renaissance, 88, 504. See Jacob Burckhardt, *Die Kultur der Renaissance in Italien,* ed. Horst Günther (Frankfurt am Main, 1989), 388, 434.

[109] Ottokar Lorenz, *Lehrbuch der gesammten wissenschaftlichen* Genealogie, Stammbaum und Ahnentafel in ihrer geschichtlichen, *sociologischen und naturwissenschaftlichen Bedeutung* (Berlin, 1898), 54-55.

[110] If feminist movements are really caused by the birth of masculine women and feminine women in higher numbers during specific periods, then, Weininger points out, it follows that the current women's movement would disappear spontaneously and reappear again after many years (p. 91).

[111] Charles Darwin, *The Variation of Animals and Plants under Domestication,* 2nd ed., 2 vols. (New York, 1897), 2:26.

[112] A. Weismann, *The Germ-Plasm: A Theory of Heredity,* trans. W. N. Parker and Harriet Rönnfeldt (New York, 1893), 363-64.

[113] It was standard medical teaching at the time that women had a weaker sex drive than men. Weininger cites Alfred Hegar (A. Hegar, *Der Geschlechtstrieb: Eine social-medicinische Studie* (Stuttgart, 1894), 5-6) for support but the idea had been expressed much more vigorously by Richard von Krafft-Ebing: "Woman . . . if physically and mentally normal, and properly educated, has but little sensual desire . . . Her need of love is greater, it is continual not periodical, but her love is more spiritual than sensual." See R. v. Krafft-Ebing, *Psychopathia Sexualis: A Medico-Forensic Study,* 12th ed., trans. anonymous (New York, 1939), 14.

[114] Weininger links his views on female sexual passivity with that of Aristotle, whose theory of reproduction assigned the active role to the male principle and the passive role to the female. Weininger laments that Aristotle, like all Greek authors except Euripides, restricted himself to the reproductive sphere while discussing female sexuality (p. 240, 537).

[115] "The male is only a male now and again, the female is always a female . . . everything reminds her of her sex." See J. J. Rousseau, *Émile,* trans. Barbara Foxley (London, 1992), 324. On the contexts of Rousseau's beliefs on gender, see Joel Schwartz, *The Sexual Politics of Jean-Jacques Rousseau* (Chicago, 1984).

[116] Charles Darwin, *On the Origin of Species by Means of Natural Selection,* 6th ed. (New York, 1876), 119.

[117] Weininger derives this argument from Havelock Ellis, who had suggested that women respond more readily to stimuli but men perceive stimuli with greater precision and intensity. Women were more "irritable," while men were more "sensible." Ellis had added that women might be less sensible because their senses are "habitually subject to a less thorough education." See H. Ellis, *Man and Woman: A Study of Human Secondary Sexual Characters* (London, 1904), 148-49. Weininger ignores Ellis's qualification.

[118] The difference between talent and genius, according to Weininger, is fundamental and qualitative. He rejects Cesare Lombroso's definition of genius as an extreme degree of talent (p. 521). See Cesare Lombroso, *The Man of Genius,* trans. anon. (London, 1891), viii.

[119] This protean ability, Weininger emphasizes, need not be simultaneous. Like masculinity and femininity in the same individual, the manifestations of genius might well be sequential.

[120] Here, Weininger launches into a caustic attack on experimental psychologists who use "letters, long rows of figures, unconnected words" to test memory. He finds such experiments worthless because they place their subjects, regardless of their individuality, under the same experimental conditions and "treat them merely as good or bad recording devices *(Registrierapparate).*" People remember only what interests them, and different

people are interested in different things. Psychologists who fail to take this elementary fact into account, Weininger suggests, do not really know anything about the mind (pp. 146-47).

[121] The lack of clear consciousness and perfect memory, according to Weininger, is also responsible for women's deficiencies in creative imagination. Men, says Weininger, have traditionally regarded women as more imaginative solely on account of the female preoccupation with sexual fantasies (p. 151). Women succeed only in those imaginative arts, where vague and unformed sentiments could produce some small effect, such as painting, poetry, and pseudomysticism (p. 152).

[122] Since she does not possess any moral sense whatever, Woman cannot be expected to act morally or be blamed when she did not (p. 252). Weininger reads the criminological literature of the late nineteenth century quite accurately and says that women commit fewer crimes than men. See Ellis, *Man and Woman.* 364-66; Lombroso and Ferrero, *Das Weib als Verbrecherin und Prostituierte,* 193-95. Many of Weininger's other beliefs on the relations between gender and criminality, however, are entirely his own. He says, for instance, that the male criminal never really feels his punishment is unjust. Criminals may be born with a "criminal drive" (*verbrecherischen Trieb*) but, despite all fashionable theories about moral insanity, male criminals are always conscious that they had demeaned themselves by their crime. Women criminals, on the other hand, are always convinced that they are in the right (p. 253).

[123] On Kant's views on the origin of morality, see Roger J. Sullivan, *Immanuel Kant's Moral Theory* (Cambridge, 1989), 126-29.

[124] Weininger reminds his reader that this is not a novel contention; he has merely discovered the philosophical foundations of an old truism. The Chinese, he points out, had denied women a soul in ancient times, and the prophet Mohammed had barred women from paradise on similar grounds. In the Western tradition, Aristotle had used the word "soul" only for the active masculine principle, thus indicating that females had no soul (p. 240).

[125] His anecdotal as well as confusing argument for this belief deserves to be quoted in full: "I know a large number of men who are psychologically almost completely female . . . I even know many women with masculine traits but not one woman who is not fundamentally female, even when this femininity is hidden by various means not just from others but also from the person herself. One is either man or woman, however many features of both sexes one might possess, and this 'Being' [*Sein*] . . . is determined by one's relationship with ethics and logic. While there are individuals who are anatomically men but psychologically women, there is no individual who is physically a woman but psychologically a man, regardless of external masculine traits" (p. 242).

[126] See Sigmund Freud and Josef Breuer, *Studies on Hysteria,* in *The* Standard Edition of the Complete Psychological Works of Sigmund *Freud,* ed. and trans. James Strachey (London, 1966), 2. On the history of medical concepts of hysteria, see Ilza Veith, *Hysteria: The History of a Disease* (Chicago, 1965); on the cultural contexts of medical concepts, see Mark S. Micale, *Approaching Hysteria: Disease and Its Interpretations* (Princeton, 1995); on the cultural importance of hysteria in Vienna, see Manfred Schneider, "Hysterie als Gesamtkunstwerk," in *Ornament und Askese im Zeitgeist des Wien der Jahrhundertwende,* ed. Alfred Pfabigan (Vienna, 1985), 212-29; and on the place of hysteria in Freud's work, see Ola Andersson, *Studies in the Prehistory of Psychoanalysis* (Stockholm, 1962). Little work has been done on Weininger's reading of hysteria, but see Marianne Schuller, "Weibliche Neurose' und Identität: Zur Diskussion der Hysterie um die Jahrhundertwende," in *Die Wiederkehr des Körpers,* eds. Dietmar Kamper and Christoph Wulf (Frankfurt am Main, 1982), 180-92.

[127] Nevertheless, he adds, more women come close to being "absolute" Prostitutes than "absolute" Mothers (pp. 286-87). Nobody who has seen how modern women move around on the streets in clinging, form-revealing clothes would, he avers, consider this an exaggeration (p. 312).

[128] Weininger dismisses all socioeconomic explanations of prostitution and follows Lombroso in attributing it to an innate disposition. In the extensive debates on prostitution in Central Europe around the turn of the century, most participants espoused either the biological perspective of Lombroso and Weininger or the sociological approach of the socialist leader August Bebel. See Nancy McCombs, *Earth Spirit, Victim, or Whore? The Prostitute in German Literature, 1880-1925* (New York, 1986), 44-49.

[129] David Abrahamsen suggested, without providing any concrete evidence, that Weininger's negative portrayal of the maternal type may have been influenced by his relationship with his own mother. See Abrahamsen, *Mind and Death,* 10-11. Again, the biographical context cannot be self-sufficient. The maternalist orientation of Central European feminism is clearly crucial to Weininger's project.

[130] This was an ancient idea, going back at least to Hippocrates. For a concise historical overview, see Ellis, *Studies in the Psychology of Sex,* 2, pt 1, *Erotic Symbolism, The Mechanism of Detumescence, The Psychic State in Pregnancy,* 218-27. See also Marie-Hélène Huet, *Monstrous Imagination* (Cambridge, Mass., 1993), 1-123; and Barbara Maria Stafford, *Body Criticism: Imaging the Unseen in Enlightenment Art and Medicine* (Cambridge, Mass., 1991). On the popularity of the idea among German-speaking physicians, see Hermann Heinrich Ploss and Max Bartels, *Das Weib in der Natur- und Völkerkunde: Anthropologische Studien,* 4th ed., 2 vols (Leipzig, 1895), 1:614.

[131] See Richard W. Burkhardt, Jr., "Closing the Door on Lord Morton's Mare: The Rise and Fall of Telegony," *Studies in History of Biology* 3 (1979): 1-21.

[132] See Darwin, *Variation*, 1:427-28, 432-33. Darwin's interest in telegony was part of his biological project of explaining the inheritance of variations. He attempted to explain telegony as well as other puzzling phenomena with his "provisional hypothesis of pangenesis." August Weismann coined the term "telegony" but dismissed the concept because it challenged his distinction between the germ-plasm and the soma. See A. Weismann, *Germ-Plasm,* 385. Herbert Spencer's attacks on Weismann's ultra-Darwinism incorporated a fervent defense of the reality of telegony. See H. Spencer, "The Inadequacy of 'Natural Selection,'" *Popular Science Monthly* 42 (1892-93): 799-812; 43 (1893): 21-28, 162-73; and "Professor Weismann's Theories," ibid., 43 (1893): 473-90. Weininger quotes Darwin and Spencer extensively.

[133] See Marvin Carlson, "Ibsen, Strindberg, and Telegony," *PMLA: Publications of the Modern Language Association of America* 100 (1985): 774-82. In an early novel by Zola, for example, a woman has a child who does not resemble her husband but her first lover. The narrator reflects: "[Jacques] left behind him . . . a young woman stamped for ever with the mark of his kisses, possessed to such a point that she was no longer merely mistress to his body, but in herself bore another being, those male essences which had completed her and in that new shape consolidated her. *It was a purely physical process at work . . .* She was shaped, fashioned by the male, for all time . . . Her husband possessed merely her heart. Her body was no longer to be given, she could only lend it." See Emile Zola, *Madeleine Férat,* in Zola, *Oeuvres complètes,* ed. Henri Mitterand, 15 vols. (Paris, 1966-70), 1:683-903, on 812-13. The quotation is slightly modified from *Madeleine Férat* trans. Alec Brown (London, 1957), 163-64, emphasis added.

[134] *The Father,* in August Strindberg, *Selected Plays,* trans. Evert Sprinchorn (Minneapolis, 1986), 163, 197. For an analysis of the personal and political motifs in the play, see Gail Finney, *Women in Modern Drama,* 207-26.

[135] This opinion was common enough in the wake of Johann Jakob Bachofen's treatise, *Das Mutterrecht: Eine Untersuchung über die* Gynaikokratie der alten Welt nach ihrer religiösen und rechtlichen *Natur* (Stuttgart, 1861). On the broader contexts of Bachofen's work, see Lionel Gossman, "Basle, Bachofen, and the Critique of Modernity in the Second Half of the Nineteenth Century," *Journal of the Warburg and Courtauld Institutes* 47 (1984): 136-85. Bachofen's work had influenced Friedrich Engels's 1884 work *The Origin of the Family, Private Property and the State* and much of later marxist theory. On Bachofen's influence on later social thought, see Harvey Greisman, "Matriar-

chate as Utopia, Myth, and Social Theory," *Sociology* 15 (1981): 321-36; Daniel Burston, "Myth, Religion, and Mother Right: Bachofen's Influence on Psychoanalytic Theory," *Contemporary Psychoanalysis* 22 (1986): 666-87; and Carolyn Fluehr-Lobban, "Marxism and the Matriarchate: One Hundred Years after *The Origin of the Family, Private Property, and the State,*" *Critique of Anthropology* 7 (1987): 5-14.

[136] See John Ward, *The Social and Religious Plays of Strindberg* (London, 1980), 47-57.

[137] For examples, see Le Rider, *Modernity and Crises of Identity,* 165, 186, 291-92.

[138] According to Weininger, communists, exemplified by Karl Marx, wish to abolish private property, whereas socialists encourage cooperation between individuals and recognize human individuality. Modern social democracy, Weininger complains, had retreated from the classical socialism of Owen, Carlyle, Ruskin, and Fichte due to Jewish influence (p. 410).

[139] The Jewishness and femininity of the epoch had led to pervasive cultural degradation. Art had degenerated into "daubs," and in literature, the cult of the madonna had been replaced by the cult of the whore. Anarchy was rampant in political and social life. Nobody believed in the state or in the rule of law. Beguiled by historical materialism, the most foolish of concepts, historians believed they could explain the evolution of science, scholarship, and culture by changes in political economy. Psychiatrists saw genius as a form of insanity and the age had not produced a single great artist or philosopher (p. 441).

[140] Sensuousness, Weininger clarifies, is not immoral because it is voluptuous. Asceticism, he emphasizes, is equally immoral. First, it takes a negative approach to the issue: a person is declared moral if he simply abandons the pursuit of pleasure. More importantly, the ascetic imperative comes from outside the individual, and is thus, in Kantian terms, heteronomous and not genuinely moral (p. 448).

[141] Weininger compares the emancipation of women to that of Jews and Blacks. "Undoubtedly," he says, "the principal reason why these people have been treated as slaves and inferiors is to be found in their servile dispositions; their desire for freedom is not as strong as that of the Indo-Germans." But, despite the low worth of these groups, Weininger insists that right is "on the side of the emancipators" (p. 449). No matter how morally worthless, Jews, Blacks, and women are human and one must respect this humanity (p. 450). Since there is no Absolute Woman, all individual women, Weininger points out, possess at least faint traces of an intelligible self. He immediately adds, however, that women cannot be allowed to share political power: they must be excluded for the same reasons that children, the mentally handicapped, and crimi-

nals are excluded. Female influence can only be harmful to public welfare (p. 450).

[142] See A. Schopenhauer, "Über Weiber," in *Arthur Schopenhauer: Sämtliche Werke,* ed. Arthur Hübscher, 7 vols. (Wiesbaden, 1972), 6:650-63; and F. Nietzsche, *Beyond Good and Evil,* trans. Walter Kaufmann, in *Basic Writings of Nietzsche,* ed. W. Kaufmann (New York, 1968), 356-57.

[143] See Nietzsche, *Beyond Good and Evil,* in *Basic Writings of Nietzsche,* ed. Kaufmann, 359; Carol Diethe, "Nietzsche and the Woman Question," *History of European Ideas* 11 (1989): 865-75; and David Booth, "Nietzsche's 'Woman' Rhetoric," *History of Philosophy Quarterly* 8 (1991): 311-25.

[144] In such an ethical utopia, there would, of course, be no reproduction, and the human species would soon be extinct. This objection, Weininger says, reveals a cowardly and irreligious lack of belief in individual immortality. Nobody with courage and true individuality, he says, could fear the loss of the body. Faith in the soul's immortality went hand in hand with individuality. "The rejection of sexuality," he explains, "leads merely to the physical death of humanity and gives full play to the spiritual element of life . . . It follows, therefore, that it is not an ethical duty to ensure the continuation of the species." Does anyone ever have coitus, he asks, out of concern for the future of the species?

FURTHER READING

Criticism

Hewitt, Andrew. "The Philosophy of Masculinism." In *Political Inversions: Homosexuality, Fascism, and the Modernist Imaginary*, pp. 79-129. Palo Alto, Calif.: Stanford University Press, 1996.
    Examines the ways in which Weininger fit into the homosexual "masculinist" subculture of the Weimar Republic in Germany.

Liptzin, Solomon. "Jewish Aryans." In *Germany's Stepchildren*, pp. 184-94. Philadelphia: The Jewish Publication Society of America, 1944.
    Discusses Weininger's anti-Semitism and the feelings of inferiority because of his Judaism that led to his suicide.

Mayer, Hans. "Excursus: Otto Weininger, *Sex and Character*." In *Outsiders: A Study in Life and Letters*, translated by Denis M. Sweet, pp. 97-104. Cambridge, Mass.: The MIT Press, 1982.
    Analyzes Weininger as a "reactionary thinker."

Wickham, Harvey. "Hermes and Aphrodite." In *The Impuritans*, pp. 34-83. New York: Lincoln MacVeagh/ The Dial Press, 1920.
    Examines Weininger's theory of sex and sexuality.

Twentieth-Century
Literary Criticism

Cumulative Indexes
Volumes 1-84

How to Use This Index

The main references

> **Calvino, Italo**
> 1923–1985 .... CLC 5, 8, 11, 22, 33, 39,
> 73; SSC 3

list all author entries in the following Gale Literary Criticism series:

BLC = *Black Literature Criticism*
CLC = *Contemporary Literary Criticism*
CLR = *Children's Literature Review*
CMLC = *Classical and Medieval Literature Criticism*
DA = *DISCovering Authors*
DAB = *DISCovering Authors: British*
DAC = *DISCovering Authors: Canadian*
DAM = *DISCovering Authors: Modules*
　　　DRAM: *Dramatists Module;* *MST*: *Most-Studied Authors Module;*
　　　MULT: *Multicultural Authors Module;* *NOV*: *Novelists Module;*
　　　POET: *Poets Module;* *POP*: *Popular Fiction and Genre Authors Module*
DC = *Drama Criticism*
HLC = *Hispanic Literature Criticism*
LC = *Literature Criticism from 1400 to 1800*
NCLC = *Nineteenth-Century Literature Criticism*
PC = *Poetry Criticism*
SSC = *Short Story Criticism*
TCLC = *Twentieth-Century Literary Criticism*
WLC = *World Literature Criticism, 1500 to the Present*

The cross-references

> See also CANR 23; CA 85-88;
> obituary CA116

list all author entries in the following Gale biographical and literary sources:

AAYA = *Authors & Artists for Young Adults*
AITN = *Authors in the News*
BEST = *Bestsellers*
BW = *Black Writers*
CA = *Contemporary Authors*
CAAS = *Contemporary Authors Autobiography Series*
CABS = *Contemporary Authors Bibliographical Series*
CANR = *Contemporary Authors New Revision Series*
CAP = *Contemporary Authors Permanent Series*
CDALB = *Concise Dictionary of American Literary Biography*
CDBLB = *Concise Dictionary of British Literary Biography*
DLB = *Dictionary of Literary Biography*
DLBD = *Dictionary of Literary Biography Documentary Series*
DLBY = *Dictionary of Literary Biography Yearbook*
HW = *Hispanic Writers*
JRDA = *Junior DISCovering Authors*
MAICYA = *Major Authors and Illustrators for Children and Young Adults*
MTCW = *Major 20th-Century Writers*
NNAL = *Native North American Literature*
SAAS = *Something about the Author Autobiography Series*
SATA = *Something about the Author*
YABC = *Yesterday's Authors of Books for Children*

Literary Criticism Series
Cumulative Author Index

See also CA 21-24R; CAAS 14; CANR 59; DLB
5; MTCW 1
Bell, W. L. D.
See Mencken, H(enry) L(ouis)
Bellamy, Atwood C.
See Mencken, H(enry) L(ouis)
Bellamy, Edward 1850-1898 .... NCLC 4
See also DLB 12
Bellin, Edward J.
See Kuttner, Henry
**Belloc, (Joseph) Hilaire (Pierre Sebastien Rene
Swanton)** 1870-1953 TCLC 7, 18; DAM
POET; PC 24
See also CA 106; 152; DLB 19, 100, 141, 174;
YABC 1
Belloc, Joseph Peter Rene Hilaire
See Belloc, (Joseph) Hilaire (Pierre Sebastien
Rene Swanton)
Belloc, Joseph Pierre Hilaire
See Belloc, (Joseph) Hilaire (Pierre Sebastien
Rene Swanton)
Belloc, M. A.
See Lowndes, Marie Adelaide (Belloc)
Bellow, Saul 1915-CLC 1, 2, 3, 6, 8, 10, 13, 15,
25, 33, 34, 63, 79; DA; DAB; DAC; DAM
MST, NOV, POP; SSC 14; WLC
See also AITN 2; BEST 89:3; CA 5-8R; CABS
1; CANR 29, 53; CDALB 1941-1968; DLB
2, 28; DLBD 3; DLBY 82; MTCW 1
Belser, Reimond Karel Maria de 1929-
See Ruyslinck, Ward
See also CA 152
Bely, Andrey .... TCLC 7; PC 11
See also Bugayev, Boris Nikolayevich
Belyi, Andrei
See Bugayev, Boris Nikolayevich
Benary, Margot
See Benary-Isbert, Margot
Benary-Isbert, Margot 1889-1979 .... CLC 12
See also CA 5-8R; 89-92; CANR 4, 72; CLR
12; MAICYA; SATA 2; SATA-Obit 21
Benavente (y Martinez), Jacinto 1866-1954
TCLC 3; DAM DRAM, MULT
See also CA 106; 131; HW; MTCW 1
Benchley, Peter (Bradford) 1940- CLC 4, 8;
DAM NOV, POP
See also AAYA 14; AITN 2; CA 17-20R; CANR
12, 35, 66; MTCW 1; SATA 3, 89
Benchley, Robert (Charles) 1889-1945 T C L C
1, 55
See also CA 105; 153; DLB 11
Benda, Julien 1867-1956 .... TCLC 60
See also CA 120; 154
Benedict, Ruth (Fulton) 1887-1948 TCLC 60
See also CA 158
Benedict, Saint c. 480-c. 547 .... CMLC 29
Benedikt, Michael 1935- .... CLC 4, 14
See also CA 13-16R; CANR 7; DLB 5
Benet, Juan 1927- .... CLC 28
See also CA 143
Benet, Stephen Vincent 1898-1943 . TCLC 7;
DAM POET; SSC 10
See also CA 104; 152; DLB 4, 48, 102; DLBY
97; YABC 1
Benet, William Rose 1886-1950 .... TCLC 28;
DAM POET
See also CA 118; 152; DLB 45
Benford, Gregory (Albert) 1941- ..... CLC 52
See also CA 69-72; CAAS 27; CANR 12, 24,
49; DLBY 82
Bengtsson, Frans (Gunnar) 1894-1954 T C L C
48
Benjamin, David
See Slavitt, David R(ytman)
Benjamin, Lois
See Gould, Lois
Benjamin, Walter 1892-1940 .... TCLC 39

See also CA 164
Benn, Gottfried 1886-1956 .... TCLC 3
See also CA 106; 153; DLB 56
Bennett, Alan 1934-CLC 45, 77; DAB; DAM
MST
See also CA 103; CANR 35, 55; MTCW 1
Bennett, (Enoch) Arnold 1867-1931 TCLC 5,
20
See also CA 106; 155; CDBLB 1890-1914;
DLB 10, 34, 98, 135
Bennett, Elizabeth
See Mitchell, Margaret (Munnerlyn)
Bennett, George Harold 1930-
See Bennett, Hal
See also BW 1; CA 97-100
Bennett, Hal .... CLC 5
See also Bennett, George Harold
See also DLB 33
Bennett, Jay 1912- .... CLC 35
See also AAYA 10; CA 69-72; CANR 11, 42;
JRDA; SAAS 4; SATA 41, 87; SATA-Brief
27
Bennett, Louise (Simone) 1919-CLC 28; BLC
1; DAM MULT
See also BW 2; CA 151; DLB 117
Benson, E(dward) F(rederic) 1867-1940
TCLC 27
See also CA 114; 157; DLB 135, 153
Benson, Jackson J. 1930- .... CLC 34
See also CA 25-28R; DLB 111
Benson, Sally 1900-1972 .... CLC 17
See also CA 19-20; 37-40R; CAP 1; SATA 1,
35; SATA-Obit 27
Benson, Stella 1892-1933 .... TCLC 17
See also CA 117; 155; DLB 36, 162
Bentham, Jeremy 1748-1832 .... NCLC 38
See also DLB 107, 158
Bentley, E(dmund) C(lerihew) 1875-1956
TCLC 12
See also CA 108; DLB 70
Bentley, Eric (Russell) 1916- .... CLC 24
See also CA 5-8R; CANR 6, 67; INT CANR-6
Beranger, Pierre Jean de 1780-1857 NCLC 34
Berdyaev, Nicolas
See Berdyaev, Nikolai (Aleksandrovich)
Berdyaev, Nikolai (Aleksandrovich) 1874-1948
TCLC 67
See also CA 120; 157
Berdyayev, Nikolai (Aleksandrovich)
See Berdyaev, Nikolai (Aleksandrovich)
Berendt, John (Lawrence) 1939- ...... CLC 86
See also CA 146
Beresford, J(ohn) D(avys) 1873-1947 T C L C
81
See also CA 112; 155; DLB 162, 178, 197
Bergelson, David 1884-1952 .... TCLC 81
Berger, Colonel
See Malraux, (Georges-)Andre
Berger, John (Peter) 1926- .... CLC 2, 19
See also CA 81-84; CANR 51; DLB 14
Berger, Melvin H. 1927- .... CLC 12
See also CA 5-8R; CANR 4; CLR 32; SAAS 2;
SATA 5, 88
Berger, Thomas (Louis) 1924-CLC 3, 5, 8, 11,
18, 38; DAM NOV
See also CA 1-4R; CANR 5, 28, 51; DLB 2;
DLBY 80; INT CANR-28; MTCW 1
Bergman, (Ernst) Ingmar 1918- CLC 16, 72
See also CA 81-84; CANR 33, 70
Bergson, Henri(-Louis) 1859-1941 TCLC 32
See also CA 164
Bergstein, Eleanor 1938- .... CLC 4
See also CA 53-56; CANR 5
Berkoff, Steven 1937- .... CLC 56
See also CA 104; CANR 72
Bermant, Chaim (Icyk) 1929- .... CLC 40
See also CA 57-60; CANR 6, 31, 57

Bern, Victoria
See Fisher, M(ary) F(rances) K(ennedy)
Bernanos, (Paul Louis) Georges 1888-1948
TCLC 3
See also CA 104; 130; DLB 72
Bernard, April 1956- .... CLC 59
See also CA 131
Berne, Victoria
See Fisher, M(ary) F(rances) K(ennedy)
Bernhard, Thomas 1931-1989 CLC 3, 32, 61
See also CA 85-88; 127; CANR 32, 57; DLB
85, 124; MTCW 1
Bernhardt, Sarah (Henriette Rosine) 1844-1923
TCLC 75
See also CA 157
Berriault, Gina 1926- . CLC 54, 109; SSC 30
See also CA 116; 129; CANR 66; DLB 130
Berrigan, Daniel 1921- .... CLC 4
See also CA 33-36R; CAAS 1; CANR 11, 43;
DLB 5
Berrigan, Edmund Joseph Michael, Jr. 1934-
1983
See Berrigan, Ted
See also CA 61-64; 110; CANR 14
Berrigan, Ted .... CLC 37
See also Berrigan, Edmund Joseph Michael, Jr.
See also DLB 5, 169
Berry, Charles Edward Anderson 1931-
See Berry, Chuck
See also CA 115
Berry, Chuck .... CLC 17
See also Berry, Charles Edward Anderson
Berry, Jonas
See Ashbery, John (Lawrence)
Berry, Wendell (Erdman) 1934- CLC 4, 6, 8,
27, 46; DAM POET
See also AITN 1; CA 73-76; CANR 50; DLB 5,
6
Berryman, John 1914-1972 CLC 1, 2, 3, 4, 6, 8,
10, 13, 25, 62; DAM POET
See also CA 13-16; 33-36R; CABS 2; CANR
35; CAP 1; CDALB 1941-1968; DLB 48;
MTCW 1
Bertolucci, Bernardo 1940- .... CLC 16
See also CA 106
Berton, Pierre (Francis Demarigny) 1920-
CLC 104
See also CA 1-4R; CANR 2, 56; DLB 68; SATA
99
Bertrand, Aloysius 1807-1841 .... NCLC 31
Bertran de Born c. 1140-1215 .... CMLC 5
Beruni, al 973-1048(?) .... CMLC 28
Besant, Annie (Wood) 1847-1933 .... TCLC 9
See also CA 105
Bessie, Alvah 1904-1985 .... CLC 23
See also CA 5-8R; 116; CANR 2; DLB 26
Bethlen, T. D.
See Silverberg, Robert
Beti, Mongo ... CLC 27; BLC 1; DAM MULT
See also Biyidi, Alexandre
Betjeman, John 1906-1984 CLC 2, 6, 10, 34,
43; DAB; DAM MST, POET
See also CA 9-12R; 112; CANR 33, 56; CDBLB
1945-1960; DLB 20; DLBY 84; MTCW 1
Bettelheim, Bruno 1903-1990 .... CLC 79
See also CA 81-84; 131; CANR 23, 61; MTCW
1
Betti, Ugo 1892-1953 .... TCLC 5
See also CA 104; 155
Betts, Doris (Waugh) 1932- ...... CLC 3, 6, 28
See also CA 13-16R; CANR 9, 66; DLBY 82;
INT CANR-9
Bevan, Alistair
See Roberts, Keith (John Kingston)
Bey, Pilaff
See Douglas, (George) Norman
Bialik, Chaim Nachman 1873-1934 TCLC 25

Bickerstaff, Isaac
  See Swift, Jonathan
Bidart, Frank 1939- .... **CLC 33**
  See also CA 140
Bienek, Horst 1930- .... **CLC 7, 11**
  See also CA 73-76; DLB 75
Bierce, Ambrose (Gwinett) 1842-1914(?)
  **TCLC 1, 7, 44; DA; DAC; DAM MST; SSC
  9; WLC**
  See also CA 104; 139; CDALB 1865-1917;
  DLB 11, 12, 23, 71, 74, 186
Biggers, Earl Derr 1884-1933 .... **TCLC 65**
  See also CA 108; 153
Billings, Josh
  See Shaw, Henry Wheeler
Billington, (Lady) Rachel (Mary) 1942- **C L C
  43**
  See also AITN 2; CA 33-36R; CANR 44
Binyon, T(imothy) J(ohn) 1936- .... **CLC 34**
  See also CA 111; CANR 28
Bioy Casares, Adolfo 1914-1984**CLC 4, 8, 13,
  88; DAM MULT; HLC; SSC 17**
  See also CA 29-32R; CANR 19, 43, 66; DLB
  113; HW; MTCW 1
Bird, Cordwainer
  See Ellison, Harlan (Jay)
Bird, Robert Montgomery 1806-1854**NCLC 1**
  See also DLB 202
Birney, (Alfred) Earle 1904-1995**CLC 1, 4, 6,
  11; DAC; DAM MST, POET**
  See also CA 1-4R; CANR 5, 20; DLB 88;
  MTCW 1
Bishop, Elizabeth 1911-1979 **CLC 1, 4, 9, 13,
  15, 32; DA; DAC; DAM MST, POET; PC
  3**
  See also CA 5-8R; 89-92; CABS 2; CANR 26,
  61; CDALB 1968-1988; DLB 5, 169;
  MTCW 1; SATA-Obit 24
Bishop, John 1935- .... **CLC 10**
  See also CA 105
Bissett, Bill 1939- .... **CLC 18; PC 14**
  See also CA 69-72; CAAS 19; CANR 15; DLB
  53; MTCW 1
Bitov, Andrei (Georgievich) 1937- ... **CLC 57**
  See also CA 142
Biyidi, Alexandre 1932-
  See Beti, Mongo
  See also BW 1; CA 114; 124; MTCW 1
Bjarme, Brynjolf
  See Ibsen, Henrik (Johan)
Bjoernson, Bjoernstjerne (Martinius) 1832-
  1910 .... **TCLC 7, 37**
  See also CA 104
Black, Robert
  See Holdstock, Robert P.
Blackburn, Paul 1926-1971 .... **CLC 9, 43**
  See also CA 81-84; 33-36R; CANR 34; DLB
  16; DLBY 81
Black Elk 1863-1950 **TCLC 33; DAM MULT**
  See also CA 144; NNAL
Black Hobart
  See Sanders, (James) Ed(ward)
Blacklin, Malcolm
  See Chambers, Aidan
Blackmore, R(ichard) D(oddridge) 1825-1900
  TCLC 27
  See also CA 120; DLB 18
Blackmur, R(ichard) P(almer) 1904-1965
  CLC 2, 24
  See also CA 11-12; 25-28R; CANR 71; CAP 1;
  DLB 63
Black Tarantula
  See Acker, Kathy
Blackwood, Algernon (Henry) 1869 1951
  TCLC 5
  See also CA 105; 150; DLB 153, 156, 178
Blackwood, Caroline 1931-1996**CLC 6, 9, 100**

See also CA 85-88; 151; CANR 32, 61, 65; DLB
  14; MTCW 1
Blade, Alexander
  See Hamilton, Edmond; Silverberg, Robert
Blaga, Lucian 1895-1961 .... **CLC 75**
  See also CA 157
Blair, Eric (Arthur) 1903-1950
  See Orwell, George
  See also CA 104; 132; DA; DAB; DAC; DAM
  MST, NOV; MTCW 1; SATA 29
Blais, Marie-Claire 1939-**CLC 2, 4, 6, 13, 22;
  DAC; DAM MST**
  See also CA 21-24R; CAAS 4; CANR 38; DLB
  53; MTCW 1
Blaise, Clark 1940- .... **CLC 29**
  See also AITN 2; CA 53-56; CAAS 3; CANR
  5, 66; DLB 53
Blake, Fairley
  See De Voto, Bernard (Augustine)
Blake, Nicholas
  See Day Lewis, C(ecil)
  See also DLB 77
Blake, William 1757-1827. **NCLC 13, 37, 57;
  DA; DAB; DAC; DAM MST, POET; PC
  12; WLC**
  See also CDBLB 1789-1832; CLR 52; DLB 93,
  163; MAICYA; SATA 30
Blasco Ibanez, Vicente 1867-1928 **TCLC 12;
  DAM NOV**
  See also CA 110; 131; HW; MTCW 1
Blatty, William Peter 1928-**CLC 2; DAM POP**
  See also CA 5-8R; CANR 9
Bleeck, Oliver
  See Thomas, Ross (Elmore)
Blessing, Lee 1949- .... **CLC 54**
Blish, James (Benjamin) 1921-1975. **CLC 14**
  See also CA 1-4R; 57-60; CANR 3; DLB 8;
  MTCW 1; SATA 66
Bliss, Reginald
  See Wells, H(erbert) G(eorge)
Blixen, Karen (Christentze Dinesen) 1885-1962
  See Dinesen, Isak
  See also CA 25-28; CANR 22, 50; CAP 2;
  MTCW 1; SATA 44
Bloch, Robert (Albert) 1917-1994 .... **CLC 33**
  See also CA 5-8R; 146; CAAS 20; CANR 5;
  DLB 44; INT CANR-5; SATA 12; SATA-Obit
  82
Blok, Alexander (Alexandrovich) 1880-1921
  TCLC 5; PC 21
  See also CA 104
Blom, Jan
  See Breytenbach, Breyten
Bloom, Harold 1930- .... **CLC 24, 103**
  See also CA 13-16R; CANR 39; DLB 67
Bloomfield, Aurelius
  See Bourne, Randolph S(illiman)
Blount, Roy (Alton), Jr. 1941- .... **CLC 38**
  See also CA 53-56; CANR 10, 28, 61; INT
  CANR-28; MTCW 1
Bloy, Leon 1846-1917 .... **TCLC 22**
  See also CA 121; DLB 123
Blume, Judy (Sussman) 1938- ... **CLC 12, 30;
  DAM NOV, POP**
  See also AAYA 3, 26; CA 29-32R; CANR 13,
  37, 66; CLR 2, 15; DLB 52; JRDA;
  MAICYA; MTCW 1; SATA 2, 31, 79
Blunden, Edmund (Charles) 1896-1974 **C L C
  2, 56**
  See also CA 17-18; 45-48; CANR 54; CAP 2;
  DLB 20, 100, 155; MTCW 1
Bly, Robert (Elwood) 1926-**CLC 1, 2, 5, 10, 15,
  38; DAM POET**
  See also CA 5-8R; CANR 41; DLB 5; MTCW
  1
Boas, Franz 1858-1942 .... **TCLC 56**
  See also CA 115

Bobette
  See Simenon, Georges (Jacques Christian)
Boccaccio, Giovanni 1313-1375 ... **CMLC 13;
  SSC 10**
Bochco, Steven 1943- .... **CLC 35**
  See also AAYA 11; CA 124; 138
Bodel, Jean 1167(?)-1210 .... **CMLC 28**
Bodenheim, Maxwell 1892-1954 .... **TCLC 44**
  See also CA 110; DLB 9, 45
Bodker, Cecil 1927- .... **CLC 21**
  See also CA 73-76; CANR 13, 44; CLR 23;
  MAICYA; SATA 14
Boell, Heinrich (Theodor) 1917-1985 **CLC 2,
  3, 6, 9, 11, 15, 27, 32, 72; DA; DAB; DAC;
  DAM MST, NOV; SSC 23; WLC**
  See also CA 21-24R; 116; CANR 24; DLB 69;
  DLBY 85; MTCW 1
Boerne, Alfred
  See Doeblin, Alfred
Boethius 480(?)-524(?) .... **CMLC 15**
  See also DLB 115
Bogan, Louise 1897-1970. **CLC 4, 39, 46, 93;
  DAM POET; PC 12**
  See also CA 73-76; 25-28R; CANR 33; DLB
  45, 169; MTCW 1
Bogarde, Dirk .... **CLC 19**
  See also Van Den Bogarde, Derek Jules Gaspard
  Ulric Niven
  See also DLB 14
Bogosian, Eric 1953- .... **CLC 45**
  See also CA 138
Bograd, Larry 1953- .... **CLC 35**
  See also CA 93-96; CANR 57; SAAS 21; SATA
  33, 89
Boiardo, Matteo Maria 1441-1494 .... **LC 6**
Boileau-Despreaux, Nicolas 1636-1711. **LC 3**
Bojer, Johan 1872-1959 .... **TCLC 64**
Boland, Eavan (Aisling) 1944- .. **CLC 40, 67,
  113; DAM POET**
  See also CA 143; CANR 61; DLB 40
Boll, Heinrich
  See Boell, Heinrich (Theodor)
Bolt, Lee
  See Faust, Frederick (Schiller)
Bolt, Robert (Oxton) 1924-1995 ..... **CLC 14;
  DAM DRAM**
  See also CA 17-20R; 147; CANR 35, 67; DLB
  13; MTCW 1
Bombet, Louis-Alexandre-Cesar
  See Stendhal
Bomkauf
  See Kaufman, Bob (Garnell)
Bonaventura .... **NCLC 35**
  See also DLB 90
Bond, Edward 1934- **CLC 4, 6, 13, 23; DAM
  DRAM**
  See also CA 25-28R; CANR 38, 67; DLB 13;
  MTCW 1
Bonham, Frank 1914-1989 .... **CLC 12**
  See also AAYA 1; CA 9-12R; CANR 4, 36;
  JRDA; MAICYA; SAAS 3; SATA 1, 49;
  SATA-Obit 62
Bonnefoy, Yves 1923-... **CLC 9, 15, 58; DAM
  MST, POET**
  See also CA 85-88; CANR 33; MTCW 1
Bontemps, Arna(ud Wendell) 1902-1973**C L C
  1, 18; BLC 1; DAM MULT, NOV, POET**
  See also BW 1; CA 1-4R; 41-44R; CANR 4,
  35; CLR 6; DLB 48, 51; JRDA; MAICYA;
  MTCW 1; SATA 2, 44; SATA-Obit 24
Booth, Martin 1944- .... **CLC 13**
  See also CA 93-96; CAAS 2
Booth, Philip 1925- .... **CLC 23**
  See also CA 5-8R; CANR 5; DLBY 82
Booth, Wayne C(layson) 1921- .... **CLC 24**
  See also CA 1-4R; CAAS 5; CANR 3, 43; DLB
  67

Borchert, Wolfgang 1921-1947 .... **TCLC 5**
See also CA 104; DLB 69, 124
Borel, Petrus 1809-1859 .... **NCLC 41**
Borges, Jorge Luis 1899-1986 **CLC 1, 2, 3, 4, 6,
8, 9, 10, 13, 19, 44, 48, 83; DA; DAB; DAC;
DAM MST, MULT; HLC; PC 22; SSC 4;
WLC**
See also AAYA 26; CA 21-24R; CANR 19, 33;
DLB 113; DLBY 86; HW; MTCW 1
Borowski, Tadeusz 1922-1951 .... **TCLC 9**
See also CA 106; 154
Borrow, George (Henry) 1803-1881 **NCLC 9**
See also DLB 21, 55, 166
Bosman, Herman Charles 1905-1951 **T C L C
49**
See also Malan, Herman
See also CA 160
Bosschere, Jean de 1878(?)-1953 ... **TCLC 19**
See also CA 115
Boswell, James 1740-1795 . **LC 4; DA; DAB;
DAC; DAM MST; WLC**
See also CDBLB 1660-1789; DLB 104, 142
Bottoms, David 1949- .... **CLC 53**
See also CA 105; CANR 22; DLB 120; DLBY
83
Boucicault, Dion 1820-1890 .... **NCLC 41**
Boucolon, Maryse 1937(?)-
See Conde, Maryse
See also CA 110; CANR 30, 53
Bourget, Paul (Charles Joseph) 1852-1935
TCLC 12
See also CA 107; DLB 123
Bourjaily, Vance (Nye) 1922- .... **CLC 8, 62**
See also CA 1-4R; CAAS 1; CANR 2, 72; DLB
2, 143
Bourne, Randolph S(illiman) 1886-1918
TCLC 16
See also CA 117; 155; DLB 63
Bova, Ben(jamin William) 1932- ...... **CLC 45**
See also AAYA 16; CA 5-8R; CAAS 18; CANR
11, 56; CLR 3; DLBY 81; INT CANR-11;
MAICYA; MTCW 1; SATA 6, 68
Bowen, Elizabeth (Dorothea Cole) 1899-1973
**CLC 1, 3, 6, 11, 15, 22; DAM NOV; SSC 3,
28**
See also CA 17-18; 41-44R; CANR 35; CAP 2;
CDBLB 1945-1960; DLB 15, 162; MTCW
1
Bowering, George 1935- .... **CLC 15, 47**
See also CA 21-24R; CAAS 16; CANR 10; DLB
53
Bowering, Marilyn R(uthe) 1949- .... **CLC 32**
See also CA 101; CANR 49
Bowers, Edgar 1924- .... **CLC 9**
See also CA 5-8R; CANR 24; DLB 5
Bowie, David .... **CLC 17**
See also Jones, David Robert
Bowles, Jane (Sydney) 1917-1973 **CLC 3, 68**
See also CA 19-20; 41-44R; CAP 2
Bowles, Paul (Frederick) 1910-1986 **CLC 1, 2,
19, 53; SSC 3**
See also CA 1-4R; CAAS 1; CANR 1, 19, 50;
DLB 5, 6; MTCW 1
Box, Edgar
See Vidal, Gore
Boyd, Nancy
See Millay, Edna St. Vincent
Boyd, William 1952- .... **CLC 28, 53, 70**
See also CA 114; 120; CANR 51, 71
Boyle, Kay 1902-1992 **CLC 1, 5, 19, 58; SSC 5**
See also CA 13-16R; 140; CAAS 1; CANR 29,
61; DLB 4, 9, 48, 86; DLBY 93; MTCW 1
Boyle, Mark
See Kienzle, William X(avier)
Boyle, Patrick 1905-1982 .... **CLC 19**
See also CA 127
Boyle, T. C. 1948-

See Boyle, T(homas) Coraghessan
Boyle, T(homas) Coraghessan 1948- **CLC 36,
55, 90; DAM POP; SSC 16**
See also BEST 90:4; CA 120; CANR 44; DLBY
86
Boz
See Dickens, Charles (John Huffam)
Brackenridge, Hugh Henry 1748-1816 **N C L C
7**
See also DLB 11, 37
Bradbury, Edward P.
See Moorcock, Michael (John)
Bradbury, Malcolm (Stanley) 1932- **CLC 32,
61; DAM NOV**
See also CA 1-4R; CANR 1, 33; DLB 14;
MTCW 1
Bradbury, Ray (Douglas) 1920- **CLC 1, 3, 10,
15, 42, 98; DA; DAB; DAC; DAM MST,
NOV, POP; SSC 29; WLC**
See also AAYA 15; AITN 1, 2; CA 1-4R; CANR
2, 30; CDALB 1968-1988; DLB 2, 8; MTCW
1; SATA 11, 64
Bradford, Gamaliel 1863-1932 ...... **TCLC 36**
See also CA 160; DLB 17
Bradley, David (Henry, Jr.) 1950- .. **CLC 23;
BLC 1; DAM MULT**
See also BW 1; CA 104; CANR 26; DLB 33
Bradley, John Ed(mund, Jr.) 1958- .. **CLC 55**
See also CA 139
Bradley, Marion Zimmer 1930- **CLC 30; DAM
POP**
See also AAYA 9; CA 57-60; CAAS 10; CANR
7, 31, 51; DLB 8; MTCW 1; SATA 90
Bradstreet, Anne 1612(?)-1672 **LC 4, 30; DA;
DAC; DAM MST, POET; PC 10**
See also CDALB 1640-1865; DLB 24
Brady, Joan 1939- .... **CLC 86**
See also CA 141
Bragg, Melvyn 1939- .... **CLC 10**
See also BEST 89:3; CA 57-60; CANR 10, 48;
DLB 14
Brahe, Tycho 1546-1601 .... **LC 45**
Braine, John (Gerard) 1922-1986 **CLC 1, 3, 41**
See also CA 1-4R; 120; CANR 1, 33; CDBLB
1945-1960; DLB 15; DLBY 86; MTCW 1
Bramah, Ernest 1868-1942 .... **TCLC 72**
See also CA 156; DLB 70
Brammer, William 1930(?)-1978 .... **CLC 31**
See also CA 77-80
Brancati, Vitaliano 1907-1954 .... **TCLC 12**
See also CA 109
Brancato, Robin F(idler) 1936- .... **CLC 35**
See also AAYA 9; CA 69-72; CANR 11, 45;
CLR 32; JRDA; SAAS 9; SATA 97
Brand, Max
See Faust, Frederick (Schiller)
Brand, Millen 1906-1980 .... **CLC 7**
See also CA 21-24R; 97-100; CANR 72
Branden, Barbara .... **CLC 44**
See also CA 148
Brandes, Georg (Morris Cohen) 1842-1927
TCLC 10
See also CA 105
Brandys, Kazimierz 1916- .... **CLC 62**
Branley, Franklyn M(ansfield) 1915- **CLC 21**
See also CA 33-36R; CANR 14, 39; CLR 13;
MAICYA; SAAS 16; SATA 4, 68
Brathwaite, Edward Kamau 1930- . **CLC 11;
BLCS; DAM POET**
See also BW 2; CA 25-28R; CANR 11, 26, 47;
DLB 125
Brautigan, Richard (Gary) 1935-1984 **CLC 1,
3, 5, 9, 12, 34, 42; DAM NOV**
See also CA 53-56; 113; CANR 34; DLB 2, 5;
DLBY 80, 84; MTCW 1; SATA 56
Brave Bird, Mary 1953-
See Crow Dog, Mary (Ellen)

See also NNAL
Braverman, Kate 1950- .... **CLC 67**
See also CA 89-92
Brecht, (Eugen) Bertolt (Friedrich) 1898-1956
**TCLC 1, 6, 13, 35; DA; DAB; DAC; DAM
DRAM, MST; DC 3; WLC**
See also CA 104; 133; CANR 62; DLB 56, 124;
MTCW 1
Brecht, Eugen Berthold Friedrich
See Brecht, (Eugen) Bertolt (Friedrich)
Bremer, Fredrika 1801-1865 .... **NCLC 11**
Brennan, Christopher John 1870-1932 **T C L C
17**
See also CA 117
Brennan, Maeve 1917-1993 .... **CLC 5**
See also CA 81-84; CANR 72
Brent, Linda
See Jacobs, Harriet A(nn)
Brentano, Clemens (Maria) 1778-1842 **N C L C
1**
See also DLB 90
Brent of Bin Bin
See Franklin, (Stella Maria Sarah) Miles
(Lampe)
Brenton, Howard 1942- .... **CLC 31**
See also CA 69-72; CANR 33, 67; DLB 13;
MTCW 1
Breslin, James 1930-1996
See Breslin, Jimmy
See also CA 73-76; CANR 31; DAM NOV;
MTCW 1
Breslin, Jimmy .... **CLC 4, 43**
See also Breslin, James
See also AITN 1; DLB 185
Bresson, Robert 1901- .... **CLC 16**
See also CA 110; CANR 49
Breton, Andre 1896-1966 **CLC 2, 9, 15, 54; PC
15**
See also CA 19-20; 25-28R; CANR 40, 60; CAP
2; DLB 65; MTCW 1
Breytenbach, Breyten 1939(?)- . **CLC 23, 37;
DAM POET**
See also CA 113; 129; CANR 61
Bridgers, Sue Ellen 1942- .... **CLC 26**
See also AAYA 8; CA 65-68; CANR 11, 36;
CLR 18; DLB 52; JRDA; MAICYA; SAAS
1; SATA 22, 90
Bridges, Robert (Seymour) 1844-1930 **T C L C
1; DAM POET**
See also CA 104; 152; CDBLB 1890-1914;
DLB 19, 98
Bridie, James .... **TCLC 3**
See also Mavor, Osborne Henry
See also DLB 10
Brin, David 1950- .... **CLC 34**
See also AAYA 21; CA 102; CANR 24, 70; INT
CANR-24; SATA 65
Brink, Andre (Philippus) 1935- **CLC 18, 36,
106**
See also CA 104; CANR 39, 62; INT 103;
MTCW 1
Brinsmead, H(esba) F(ay) 1922- .... **CLC 21**
See also CA 21-24R; CANR 10; CLR 47;
MAICYA; SAAS 5; SATA 18, 78
Brittain, Vera (Mary) 1893(?)-1970 . **CLC 23**
See also CA 13-16; 25-28R; CANR 58; CAP 1;
DLB 191; MTCW 1
Broch, Hermann 1886-1951 .... **TCLC 20**
See also CA 117; DLB 85, 124
Brock, Rose
See Hansen, Joseph
Brodkey, Harold (Roy) 1930-1996 .... **CLC 56**
See also CA 111; 151; CANR 71; DLB 130
Brodskii, Iosif
See Brodsky, Joseph
Brodsky, Iosif Alexandrovich 1940-1996
See Brodsky, Joseph

See also AITN 1; CA 41-44R; 151; CANR 37; DAM POET; MTCW 1

Brodsky, Joseph 1940-1996 **CLC 4, 6, 13, 36, 100; PC 9**
See also Brodskii, Iosif; Brodsky, Iosif Alexandrovich

Brodsky, Michael (Mark) 1948- .... **CLC 19**
See also CA 102; CANR 18, 41, 58

Bromell, Henry 1947- .... **CLC 5**
See also CA 53-56; CANR 9

Bromfield, Louis (Brucker) 1896-1956 **T C L C 11**
See also CA 107; 155; DLB 4, 9, 86

Broner, E(sther) M(asserman) 1930- **CLC 19**
See also CA 17-20R; CANR 8, 25, 72; DLB 28

Bronk, William 1918- .... **CLC 10**
See also CA 89-92; CANR 23; DLB 165

Bronstein, Lev Davidovich
See Trotsky, Leon

Bronte, Anne 1820-1849 .... **NCLC 71**
See also DLB 21, 199

Bronte, Charlotte 1816-1855 **NCLC 3, 8, 33, 58; DA; DAB; DAC; DAM MST, NOV; WLC**
See also AAYA 17; CDBLB 1832-1890; DLB 21, 159, 199

Bronte, Emily (Jane) 1818-1848 **NCLC 16, 35; DA; DAB; DAC; DAM MST, NOV, POET; PC 8; WLC**
See also AAYA 17; CDBLB 1832-1890; DLB 21, 32, 199

Brooke, Frances 1724-1789 .... **LC 6**
See also DLB 39, 99

Brooke, Henry 1703(?)-1783 .... **LC 1**
See also DLB 39

Brooke, Rupert (Chawner) 1887-1915 **T C L C 2, 7; DA; DAB; DAC; DAM MST, POET; PC 24; WLC**
See also CA 104; 132; CANR 61; CDBLB 1914-1945; DLB 19; MTCW 1

Brooke-Haven, P.
See Wodehouse, P(elham) G(renville)

Brooke-Rose, Christine 1926(?)- .... **CLC 40**
See also CA 13-16R; CANR 58; DLB 14

Brookner, Anita 1928- **CLC 32, 34, 51; DAB; DAM POP**
See also CA 114; 120; CANR 37, 56; DLB 194; DLBY 87; MTCW 1

Brooks, Cleanth 1906-1994 **CLC 24, 86, 110**
See also CA 17-20R; 145; CANR 33, 35; DLB 63; DLBY 94; INT CANR-35; MTCW 1

Brooks, George
See Baum, L(yman) Frank

Brooks, Gwendolyn 1917- **CLC 1, 2, 4, 5, 15, 49; BLC 1; DA; DAC; DAM MST, MULT, POET; PC 7; WLC**
See also AAYA 20; AITN 1; BW 2; CA 1-4R; CANR 1, 27, 52; CDALB 1941-1968; CLR 27; DLB 5, 76, 165; MTCW 1; SATA 6

Brooks, Mel .... **CLC 12**
See also Kaminsky, Melvin
See also AAYA 13; DLB 26

Brooks, Peter 1938- .... **CLC 34**
See also CA 45-48; CANR 1

Brooks, Van Wyck 1886-1963 .... **CLC 29**
See also CA 1-4R; CANR 6; DLB 45, 63, 103

Brophy, Brigid (Antonia) 1929-1995 **CLC 6, 11, 29, 105**
See also CA 5-8R; 149; CAAS 4; CANR 25, 53; DLB 14; MTCW 1

Brosman, Catharine Savage 1934- ..... **CLC 9**
See also CA 61-64; CANR 21, 46

Brossard, Chandler 1922-1993 .... **CLC 115**
See also CA 61-64; 142; CAAS 2; CANR 8, 56; DLB 16

Brother Antoninus
See Everson, William (Oliver)

The Brothers Quay
See Quay, Stephen; Quay, Timothy

Broughton, T(homas) Alan 1936- ..... **CLC 19**
See also CA 45-48; CANR 2, 23, 48

Broumas, Olga 1949- .... **CLC 10, 73**
See also CA 85-88; CANR 20, 69

Brown, Alan 1950- .... **CLC 99**
See also CA 156

Brown, Charles Brockden 1771-1810 **N C L C 22**
See also CDALB 1640-1865; DLB 37, 59, 73

Brown, Christy 1932-1981 .... **CLC 63**
See also CA 105; 104; CANR 72; DLB 14

Brown, Claude 1937- **CLC 30; BLC 1; DAM MULT**
See also AAYA 7; BW 1; CA 73-76

Brown, Dee (Alexander) 1908-.. **CLC 18, 47; DAM POP**
See also CA 13-16R; CAAS 6; CANR 11, 45, 60; DLBY 80; MTCW 1; SATA 5

Brown, George
See Wertmueller, Lina

Brown, George Douglas 1869-1902 **TCLC 28**
See also CA 162

Brown, George Mackay 1921-1996 **CLC 5, 48, 100**
See also CA 21-24R; 151; CAAS 6; CANR 12, 37, 67; DLB 14, 27, 139; MTCW 1; SATA 35

Brown, (William) Larry 1951- .... **CLC 73**
See also CA 130; 134; INT 133

Brown, Moses
See Barrett, William (Christopher)

Brown, Rita Mae 1944- **CLC 18, 43, 79; DAM NOV, POP**
See also CA 45-48; CANR 2, 11, 35, 62; INT CANR-11; MTCW 1

Brown, Roderick (Langmere) Haig-
See Haig-Brown, Roderick (Langmere)

Brown, Rosellen 1939- .... **CLC 32**
See also CA 77-80; CAAS 10; CANR 14, 44

Brown, Sterling Allen 1901-1989 **CLC 1, 23, 59; BLC 1; DAM MULT, POET**
See also BW 1; CA 85-88; 127; CANR 26; DLB 48, 51, 63; MTCW 1

Brown, Will
See Ainsworth, William Harrison

Brown, William Wells 1813-1884 ... **NCLC 2; BLC 1; DAM MULT; DC 1**
See also DLB 3, 50

Browne, (Clyde) Jackson 1948(?)- .... **CLC 21**
See also CA 120

Browning, Elizabeth Barrett 1806-1861 **NCLC 1, 16, 61, 66; DA; DAB; DAC; DAM MST, POET; PC 6; WLC**
See also CDBLB 1832-1890; DLB 32, 199

Browning, Robert 1812-1889 **NCLC 19; DA; DAB; DAC; DAM MST, POET; PC 2; WLCS**
See also CDBLB 1832-1890; DLB 32, 163; YABC 1

Browning, Tod 1882-1962 .... **CLC 16**
See also CA 141; 117

Brownson, Orestes Augustus 1803-1876 **NCLC 50**
See also DLB 1, 59, 73

Bruccoli, Matthew J(oseph) 1931- ... **CLC 34**
See also CA 9-12R; CANR 7; DLB 103

Bruce, Lenny .... **CLC 21**
See also Schneider, Leonard Alfred

Bruin, John
See Brutus, Dennis

Brulard, Henri
See Stendhal

Brulls, Christian
See Simenon, Georges (Jacques Christian)

Brunner, John (Kilian Houston) 1934-1995

CLC 8, 10; DAM POP
See also CA 1-4R; 149; CAAS 8; CANR 2, 37; MTCW 1

Bruno, Giordano 1548-1600 .... **LC 27**

Brutus, Dennis 1924- **CLC 43; BLC 1; DAM MULT, POET; PC 24**
See also BW 2; CA 49-52; CAAS 14; CANR 2, 27, 42; DLB 117

Bryan, C(ourtlandt) D(ixon) B(arnes) 1936- **CLC 29**
See also CA 73-76; CANR 13, 68; DLB 185; INT CANR-13

Bryan, Michael
See Moore, Brian

Bryant, William Cullen 1794-1878 . **NCLC 6, 46; DA; DAB; DAC; DAM MST, POET; PC 20**
See also CDALB 1640-1865; DLB 3, 43, 59, 189

Bryusov, Valery Yakovlevich 1873-1924 **TCLC 10**
See also CA 107; 155

Buchan, John 1875-1940 ..... **TCLC 41; DAB; DAM POP**
See also CA 108; 145; DLB 34, 70, 156; YABC 2

Buchanan, George 1506-1582 .... **LC 4**
See also DLB 152

Buchheim, Lothar-Guenther 1918- .... **CLC 6**
See also CA 85-88

Buchner, (Karl) Georg 1813-1837 . **NCLC 26**

Buchwald, Art(hur) 1925- .... **CLC 33**
See also AITN 1; CA 5-8R; CANR 21, 67; MTCW 1; SATA 10

Buck, Pearl S(ydenstricker) 1892-1973 **CLC 7, 11, 18; DA; DAB; DAC; DAM MST, NOV**
See also AITN 1; CA 1-4R; 41-44R; CANR 1, 34; DLB 9, 102; MTCW 1; SATA 1, 25

Buckler, Ernest 1908-1984 .... **CLC 13; DAC; DAM MST**
See also CA 11-12; 114; CAP 1; DLB 68; SATA 47

Buckley, Vincent (Thomas) 1925-1988 **CLC 57**
See also CA 101

Buckley, William F(rank), Jr. 1925- **CLC 7, 18, 37; DAM POP**
See also AITN 1; CA 1-4R; CANR 1, 24, 53; DLB 137; DLBY 80; INT CANR-24; MTCW 1

Buechner, (Carl) Frederick 1926- **CLC 2, 4, 6, 9; DAM NOV**
See also CA 13-16R; CANR 11, 39, 64; DLBY 80; INT CANR-11; MTCW 1

Buell, John (Edward) 1927- .... **CLC 10**
See also CA 1-4R; CANR 71; DLB 53

Buero Vallejo, Antonio 1916- ..... **CLC 15, 46**
See also CA 106; CANR 24, 49; HW; MTCW 1

Bufalino, Gesualdo 1920(?)- .... **CLC 74**
See also DLB 196

Bugayev, Boris Nikolayevich 1880-1934 **TCLC 7; PC 11**
See also Bely, Andrey
See also CA 104; 165

Bukowski, Charles 1920-1994 **CLC 2, 5, 9, 41, 82, 108; DAM NOV, POET; PC 18**
See also CA 17-20R; 144; CANR 40, 62; DLB 5, 130, 169; MTCW 1

Bulgakov, Mikhail (Afanas'evich) 1891-1940 **TCLC 2, 16; DAM DRAM, NOV; SSC 18**
See also CA 105; 152

Bulgya, Alexander Alexandrovich 1901-1956 **TCLC 53**
See also Fadeyev, Alexander
See also CA 117

Bullins, Ed 1935- **CLC 1, 5, 7; BLC 1; DAM DRAM, MULT; DC 6**

Author Index

See also CA 5-8R; 41-44R; CANR 8, 59; DLB
    77; MTCW 1
Crebillon, Claude Prosper Jolyot de (fils) 1707-
    1777 .... **LC 28**
Credo
    See Creasey, John
Credo, Alvaro J. de
    See Prado (Calvo), Pedro
Creeley, Robert (White) 1926-**CLC 1, 2, 4, 8,**
    11, 15, 36, 78; DAM POET
    See also CA 1-4R; CAAS 10; CANR 23, 43;
    DLB 5, 16, 169; DLBD 17; MTCW 1
Crews, Harry (Eugene) 1935- **CLC 6, 23, 49**
    See also AITN 1; CA 25-28R; CANR 20, 57;
    DLB 6, 143, 185; MTCW 1
Crichton, (John) Michael 1942-**CLC 2, 6, 54,**
    90; DAM NOV, POP
    See also AAYA 10; AITN 2; CA 25-28R; CANR
    13, 40, 54; DLBY 81; INT CANR-13; JRDA;
    MTCW 1; SATA 9, 88
Crispin, Edmund .... **CLC 22**
    See also Montgomery, (Robert) Bruce
    See also DLB 87
Cristofer, Michael 1945(?)- .... **CLC 28; DAM**
    DRAM
    See also CA 110; 152; DLB 7
Croce, Benedetto 1866-1952 .... **TCLC 37**
    See also CA 120; 155
Crockett, David 1786-1836 .... **NCLC 8**
    See also DLB 3, 11
Crockett, Davy
    See Crockett, David
Crofts, Freeman Wills 1879-1957 .. **TCLC 55**
    See also CA 115; DLB 77
Croker, John Wilson 1780-1857 .... **NCLC 10**
    See also DLB 110
Crommelynck, Fernand 1885-1970 .. **CLC 75**
    See also CA 89-92
Cromwell, Oliver 1599-1658 .... **LC 43**
Cronin, A(rchibald) J(oseph) 1896-1981**C L C**
    32
    See also CA 1-4R; 102; CANR 5; DLB 191;
    SATA 47; SATA-Obit 25
Cross, Amanda
    See Heilbrun, Carolyn G(old)
Crothers, Rachel 1878(?)-1958 ...... **TCLC 19**
    See also CA 113; DLB 7
Croves, Hal
    See Traven, B.
Crow Dog, Mary (Ellen) (?)- .... **CLC 93**
    See also Brave Bird, Mary
    See also CA 154
Crowfield, Christopher
    See Stowe, Harriet (Elizabeth) Beecher
Crowley, Aleister .... **TCLC 7**
    See also Crowley, Edward Alexander
Crowley, Edward Alexander 1875-1947
    See Crowley, Aleister
    See also CA 104
Crowley, John 1942- .... **CLC 57**
    See also CA 61-64; CANR 43; DLBY 82; SATA
    65
Crud
    See Crumb, R(obert)
Crumarums
    See Crumb, R(obert)
Crumb, R(obert) 1943- .... **CLC 17**
    See also CA 106
Crumbum
    See Crumb, R(obert)
Crumski
    See Crumb, R(obert)
Crum the Bum
    See Crumb, R(obert)
Crunk
    See Crumb, R(obert)
Crustt

See Crumb, R(obert)
Cryer, Gretchen (Kiger) 1935- .... **CLC 21**
    See also CA 114; 123
Csath, Geza 1887-1919 .... **TCLC 13**
    See also CA 111
Cudlip, David 1933- .... **CLC 34**
Cullen, Countee 1903-1946**TCLC 4, 37; BLC**
    1; DA; DAC; DAM MST, MULT, POET;
    PC 20; WLCS
    See also BW 1; CA 108; 124; CDALB 1917-
    1929; DLB 4, 48, 51; MTCW 1; SATA 18
Cum, R.
    See Crumb, R(obert)
Cummings, Bruce F(rederick) 1889-1919
    See Barbellion, W. N. P.
    See also CA 123
Cummings, E(dward) E(stlin) 1894-1962**CLC**
    1, 3, 8, 12, 15, 68; DA; DAB; DAC; DAM
    MST, POET; PC 5; WLC 2
    See also CA 73-76; CANR 31; CDALB 1929-
    1941; DLB 4, 48; MTCW 1
Cunha, Euclides (Rodrigues Pimenta) da 1866-
    1909 ....
TCLC 24
    See also CA 123
Cunningham, E. V.
    See Fast, Howard (Melvin)
Cunningham, J(ames) V(incent) 1911-1985
    CLC 3, 31
    See also CA 1-4R; 115; CANR 1, 72; DLB 5
Cunningham, Julia (Woolfolk) 1916-**CLC 12**
    See also CA 9-12R; CANR 4, 19, 36; JRDA;
    MAICYA; SAAS 2; SATA 1, 26
Cunningham, Michael 1952- .... **CLC 34**
    See also CA 136
Cunninghame Graham, R(obert) B(ontine)
    1852-1936 ....
TCLC 19
    See also Graham, R(obert) B(ontine)
        Cunninghame
    See also CA 119; DLB 98
Currie, Ellen 19(?) .... **CLC 44**
Curtin, Philip
    See Lowndes, Marie Adelaide (Belloc)
Curtis, Price
    See Ellison, Harlan (Jay)
Cutrate, Joe
    See Spiegelman, Art
Cynewulf c. 770-c. 840 .... **CMLC 23**
Czaczkes, Shmuel Yosef
    See Agnon, S(hmuel) Y(osef Halevi)
Dabrowska, Maria (Szumska) 1889-1965**CLC**
    15
    See also CA 106
Dabydeen, David 1955- .... **CLC 34**
    See also BW 1; CA 125; CANR 56
Dacey, Philip 1939- .... **CLC 51**
    See also CA 37-40R; CAAS 17; CANR 14, 32,
    64; DLB 105
Dagerman, Stig (Halvard) 1923-1954 **T C L C**
    17
    See also CA 117; 155
Dahl, Roald 1916-1990**CLC 1, 6, 18, 79; DAB;**
    DAC; DAM MST, NOV, POP
    See also AAYA 15; CA 1-4R; 133; CANR 6,
    32, 37, 62; CLR 1, 7, 41; DLB 139; JRDA;
    MAICYA; MTCW 1; SATA 1, 26, 73; SATA-
    Obit 65
Dahlberg, Edward 1900-1977 .. **CLC 1, 7, 14**
    See also CA 9-12R; 69-72; CANR 31, 62; DLB
    48; MTCW 1
Daitch, Susan 1954- .... **CLC 103**
    See also CA 161
Dale, Colin .... **TCLC 18**
    See also Lawrence, T(homas) E(dward)
Dale, George E.
    See Asimov, Isaac

Daly, Elizabeth 1878-1967 .... **CLC 52**
    See also CA 23-24; 25-28R; CANR 60; CAP 2
Daly, Maureen 1921- .... **CLC 17**
    See also AAYA 5; CANR 37; JRDA; MAICYA;
    SAAS 1; SATA 2
Damas, Leon-Gontran 1912-1978 .... **CLC 84**
    See also BW 1; CA 125; 73-76
Dana, Richard Henry Sr. 1787-1879**NCLC 53**
Daniel, Samuel 1562(?)-1619 .... **LC 24**
    See also DLB 62
Daniels, Brett
    See Adler, Renata
Dannay, Frederic 1905-1982 . **CLC 11; DAM**
    POP
    See also Queen, Ellery
    See also CA 1-4R; 107; CANR 1, 39; DLB 137;
    MTCW 1
D'Annunzio, Gabriele 1863-1938**TCLC 6, 40**
    See also CA 104; 155
Danois, N. le
    See Gourmont, Remy (-Marie-Charles) de
Dante 1265-1321 .... **CMLC 3, 18; DA; DAB;**
    DAC; DAM MST, POET; PC 21; WLCS
d'Antibes, Germain
    See Simenon, Georges (Jacques Christian)
Danticat, Edwidge 1969- .... **CLC 94**
    See also CA 152
Danvers, Dennis 1947- .... **CLC 70**
Danziger, Paula 1944- .... **CLC 21**
    See also AAYA 4; CA 112; 115; CANR 37; CLR
    20; JRDA; MAICYA; SATA 36, 63, 102;
    SATA-Brief 30
Dario, Ruben 1867-1916 .... **TCLC 4; DAM**
    MULT; HLC; PC 15
    See also CA 131; HW; MTCW 1
Darley, George 1795-1846 .... **NCLC 2**
    See also DLB 96
Darrow, Clarence (Seward) 1857-1938**T C L C**
    81
    See also CA 164
Darwin, Charles 1809-1882 .... **NCLC 57**
    See also DLB 57, 166
Daryush, Elizabeth 1887-1977 ...... **CLC 6, 19**
    See also CA 49-52; CANR 3; DLB 20
Dasgupta, Surendranath 1887-1952**TCLC 81**
    See also CA 157
Dashwood, Edmee Elizabeth Monica de la Pas-
    ture 1890-1943
    See Delafield, E. M.
    See also CA 119; 154
Daudet, (Louis Marie) Alphonse 1840-1897
    NCLC 1
    See also DLB 123
Daumal, Rene 1908-1944 .... **TCLC 14**
    See also CA 114
Davenport, Guy (Mattison, Jr.) 1927-**CLC 6,**
    14, 38; SSC 16
    See also CA 33-36R; CANR 23; DLB 130
Davidson, Avram 1923-
    See Queen, Ellery
    See also CA 101; CANR 26; DLB 8
Davidson, Donald (Grady) 1893-1968**CLC 2,**
    13, 19
    See also CA 5-8R; 25-28R; CANR 4; DLB 45
Davidson, Hugh
    See Hamilton, Edmond
Davidson, John 1857-1909 .... **TCLC 24**
    See also CA 118; DLB 19
Davidson, Sara 1943- .... **CLC 9**
    See also CA 81-84; CANR 44, 68; DLB 185
Davie, Donald (Alfred) 1922-1995 . **CLC 5, 8,**
    10, 31
    See also CA 1-4R; 149; CAAS 3; CANR 1, 44;
    DLB 27; MTCW 1
Davies, Ray(mond Douglas) 1944- ... **CLC 21**
    See also CA 116; 146
Davies, Rhys 1901-1978 .... **CLC 23**

See De Voto, Bernard (Augustine)
Gilbert, W(illiam) S(chwenck) 1836-1911
TCLC 3; DAM DRAM, POET
See also CA 104; SATA 36
Gilbreth, Frank B., Jr. 1911- .... **CLC 17**
See also CA 9-12R; SATA 2
Gilchrist, Ellen 1935-**CLC 34, 48; DAM POP;**
SSC 14
See also CA 113; 116; CANR 41, 61; DLB 130;
MTCW 1
Giles, Molly 1942- .... **CLC 39**
See also CA 126
Gill, Eric 1882-1940 .... **TCLC 85**
Gill, Patrick
See Creasey, John
Gilliam, Terry (Vance) 1940- .... **CLC 21**
See also Monty Python
See also AAYA 19; CA 108; 113; CANR 35;
INT 113
Gillian, Jerry
See Gilliam, Terry (Vance)
Gilliatt, Penelope (Ann Douglass) 1932-1993
CLC 2, 10, 13, 53
See also AITN 2; CA 13-16R; 141; CANR 49;
DLB 14
Gilman, Charlotte (Anna) Perkins (Stetson)
1860-1935 ....
TCLC 9, 37; SSC 13
See also CA 106; 150
Gilmour, David 1949- .... **CLC 35**
See also CA 138, 147
Gilpin, William 1724-1804 .... **NCLC 30**
Gilray, J. D.
See Mencken, H(enry) L(ouis)
Gilroy, Frank D(aniel) 1925- .... **CLC 2**
See also CA 81-84; CANR 32, 64; DLB 7
Gilstrap, John 1957(?)- .... **CLC 99**
See also CA 160
Ginsberg, Allen 1926-1997**CLC 1, 2, 3, 4, 6, 13,**
36, 69, 109; DA; DAB; DAC; DAM MST,
POET; PC 4; WLC 3
See also AITN 1; CA 1-4R; 157; CANR 2, 41,
63; CDALB 1941-1968; DLB 5, 16, 169;
MTCW 1
Ginzburg, Natalia 1916-1991**CLC 5, 11, 54, 70**
See also CA 85-88; 135; CANR 33; DLB 177;
MTCW 1
Giono, Jean 1895-1970 .... **CLC 4, 11**
See also CA 45-48; 29-32R; CANR 2, 35; DLB
72; MTCW 1
Giovanni, Nikki 1943-**CLC 2, 4, 19, 64; BLC**
2; DA; DAB; DAC; DAM MST, MULT,
POET; PC 19; WLCS
See also AAYA 22; AITN 1; BW 2; CA 29-32R;
CAAS 6; CANR 18, 41, 60; CLR 6; DLB 5,
41; INT CANR-18; MAICYA; MTCW 1;
SATA 24
Giovene, Andrea 1904- .... **CLC 7**
See also CA 85-88
Gippius, Zinaida (Nikolayevna) 1869-1945
See Hippius, Zinaida
See also CA 106
Giraudoux, (Hippolyte) Jean 1882-1944
TCLC 2, 7; DAM DRAM
See also CA 104; DLB 65
Gironella, Jose Maria 1917- .... **CLC 11**
See also CA 101
Gissing, George (Robert) 1857-1903**TCLC 3,**
24, 47
See also CA 105; 167; DLB 18, 135, 184
Giurlani, Aldo
See Palazzeschi, Aldo
Gladkov, Fyodor (Vasilyevich) 1883-1958
TCLC 27
Glanville, Brian (Lester) 1931- .... **CLC 6**
See also CA 5-8R; CAAS 9; CANR 3, 70; DLB
15, 139; SATA 42

Glasgow, Ellen (Anderson Gholson) 1873-1945
TCLC 2, 7
See also CA 104; 164; DLB 9, 12
Glaspell, Susan 1882(?)-1948 .... **TCLC 55**
See also CA 110; 154; DLB 7, 9, 78; YABC 2
Glassco, John 1909-1981 .... **CLC 9**
See also CA 13-16R; 102; CANR 15; DLB 68
Glasscock, Amnesia
See Steinbeck, John (Ernst)
Glasser, Ronald J. 1940(?)- .... **CLC 37**
Glassman, Joyce
See Johnson, Joyce
Glendinning, Victoria 1937- .... **CLC 50**
See also CA 120; 127; CANR 59; DLB 155
Glissant, Edouard 1928- . **CLC 10, 68; DAM**
MULT
See also CA 153
Gloag, Julian 1930- .... **CLC 40**
See also AITN 1; CA 65-68; CANR 10, 70
Glowacki, Aleksander
See Prus, Boleslaw
Gluck, Louise (Elisabeth) 1943-**CLC 7, 22, 44,**
81; DAM POET; PC 16
See also CA 33-36R; CANR 40, 69; DLB 5
Glyn, Elinor 1864-1943 .... **TCLC 72**
See also DLB 153
Gobineau, Joseph Arthur (Comte) de 1816-
1882 .... **NCLC 17**
See also DLB 123
Godard, Jean-Luc 1930- .... **CLC 20**
See also CA 93-96
Godden, (Margaret) Rumer 1907- ... **CLC 53**
See also AAYA 6; CA 5-8R; CANR 4, 27, 36,
55; CLR 20; DLB 161; MAICYA; SAAS 12;
SATA 3, 36
Godoy Alcayaga, Lucila 1889-1957
See Mistral, Gabriela
See also BW 2; CA 104; 131; DAM MULT;
HW; MTCW 1
Godwin, Gail (Kathleen) 1937- **CLC 5, 8, 22,**
31, 69; DAM POP
See also CA 29-32R; CANR 15, 43, 69; DLB
6; INT CANR-15; MTCW 1
Godwin, William 1756-1836 .... **NCLC 14**
See also CDBLB 1789-1832; DLB 39, 104, 142,
158, 163
Goebbels, Josef
See Goebbels, (Paul) Joseph
Goebbels, (Paul) Joseph 1897-1945**TCLC 68**
See also CA 115; 148
Goebbels, Joseph Paul
See Goebbels, (Paul) Joseph
Goethe, Johann Wolfgang von 1749-1832
NCLC 4, 22, 34; DA; DAB; DAC; DAM
DRAM, MST, POET; PC 5; WLC 3
See also DLB 94
Gogarty, Oliver St. John 1878-1957**TCLC 15**
See also CA 109; 150; DLB 15, 19
Gogol, Nikolai (Vasilyevich) 1809-1852**NCLC**
5, 15, 31; DA; DAB; DAC; DAM DRAM,
MST; DC 1; SSC 4, 29; WLC
See also DLB 198
Goines, Donald 1937(?)-1974**CLC 80; BLC 2;**
DAM MULT, POP
See also AITN 1; BW 1; CA 124; 114; DLB 33
Gold, Herbert 1924- .... **CLC 4, 7, 14, 42**
See also CA 9-12R; CANR 17, 45; DLB 2;
DLBY 81
Goldbarth, Albert 1948- .... **CLC 5, 38**
See also CA 53-56; CANR 6, 40; DLB 120
Goldberg, Anatol 1910-1982 .... **CLC 34**
See also CA 131; 117
Goldemberg, Isaac 1945- .... **CLC 52**
See also CA 69-72; CAAS 12; CANR 11, 32;
HW
Golding, William (Gerald) 1911-1993**CLC 1,**
2, 3, 8, 10, 17, 27, 58, 81; DA; DAB; DAC;

DAM MST, NOV; WLC
See also AAYA 5; CA 5-8R; 141; CANR 13,
33, 54; CDBLB 1945-1960; DLB 15, 100;
MTCW 1
Goldman, Emma 1869-1940 .... **TCLC 13**
See also CA 110; 150
Goldman, Francisco 1954- .... **CLC 76**
See also CA 162
Goldman, William (W.) 1931- .... **CLC 1, 48**
See also CA 9-12R; CANR 29, 69; DLB 44
Goldmann, Lucien 1913-1970 .... **CLC 24**
See also CA 25-28; CAP 2
Goldoni, Carlo 1707-1793**LC 4; DAM DRAM**
Goldsberry, Steven 1949- .... **CLC 34**
See also CA 131
Goldsmith, Oliver 1728-1774**LC 2; DA; DAB;**
DAC; DAM DRAM, MST, NOV, POET;
DC 8; WLC
See also CDBLB 1660-1789; DLB 39, 89, 104,
109, 142; SATA 26
Goldsmith, Peter
See Priestley, J(ohn) B(oynton)
Gombrowicz, Witold 1904-1969**CLC 4, 7, 11,**
49; DAM DRAM
See also CA 19-20; 25-28R; CAP 2
Gomez de la Serna, Ramon 1888-1963**CLC 9**
See also CA 153; 116; HW
Goncharov, Ivan Alexandrovich 1812-1891
NCLC 1, 63
Goncourt, Edmond (Louis Antoine Huot) de
1822-1896 ....
NCLC 7
See also DLB 123
Goncourt, Jules (Alfred Huot) de 1830-1870
NCLC 7
See also DLB 123
Gontier, Fernande 19(?)- .... **CLC 50**
Gonzalez Martinez, Enrique 1871-1952
TCLC 72
See also CA 166; HW
Goodman, Paul 1911-1972 ...... **CLC 1, 2, 4, 7**
See also CA 19-20; 37-40R; CANR 34; CAP 2;
DLB 130; MTCW 1
Gordimer, Nadine 1923-**CLC 3, 5, 7, 10, 18, 33,**
51, 70; DA; DAB; DAC; DAM MST, NOV;
SSC 17; WLCS
See also CA 5-8R; CANR 3, 28, 56; INT CANR-
28; MTCW 1
Gordon, Adam Lindsay 1833-1870 **NCLC 21**
Gordon, Caroline 1895-1981**CLC 6, 13, 29, 83;**
SSC 15
See also CA 11-12; 103; CANR 36; CAP 1;
DLB 4, 9, 102; DLBD 17; DLBY 81; MTCW
1
Gordon, Charles William 1860-1937
See Connor, Ralph
See also CA 109
Gordon, Mary (Catherine) 1949-**CLC 13, 22**
See also CA 102; CANR 44; DLB 6; DLBY
81; INT 102; MTCW 1
Gordon, N. J.
See Bosman, Herman Charles
Gordon, Sol 1923- .... **CLC 26**
See also CA 53-56; CANR 4; SATA 11
Gordone, Charles 1925-1995**CLC 1, 4; DAM**
DRAM; DC 8
See also BW 1; CA 93-96; 150; CANR 55; DLB
7; INT 93-96; MTCW 1
Gore, Catherine 1800-1861 .... **NCLC 65**
See also DLB 116
Gorenko, Anna Andreevna
See Akhmatova, Anna
Gorky, Maxim 1868-1936**TCLC 8; DAB; SSC**
28; WLC
See also Peshkov, Alexei Maximovich
Goryan, Sirak
See Saroyan, William

Gosse, Edmund (William) 1849-1928TCLC 28
See also CA 117; DLB 57, 144, 184
Gotlieb, Phyllis Fay (Bloom) 1926- .. CLC 18
See also CA 13-16R; CANR 7; DLB 88
Gottesman, S. D.
See Kornbluth, C(yril) M.; Pohl, Frederik
Gottfried von Strassburg fl. c. 1210- C M L C
10
See also DLB 138
Gould, Lois .... CLC 4, 10
See also CA 77-80; CANR 29; MTCW 1
Gourmont, Remy (-Marie-Charles) de 1858-
1915 .... TCLC 17
See also CA 109; 150
Govier, Katherine 1948- .... CLC 51
See also CA 101; CANR 18, 40
Goyen, (Charles) William 1915-1983CLC 5, 8,
14, 40
See also AITN 2; CA 5-8R; 110; CANR 6, 71;
DLB 2; DLBY 83; INT CANR-6
Goytisolo, Juan 1931- . CLC 5, 10, 23; DAM
MULT; HLC
See also CA 85-88; CANR 32, 61; HW; MTCW
1
Gozzano, Guido 1883-1916 .... PC 10
See also CA 154; DLB 114
Gozzi, (Conte) Carlo 1720-1806 .... NCLC 23
Grabbe, Christian Dietrich 1801-1836N C L C
2
See also DLB 133
Grace, Patricia 1937- .... CLC 56
Gracian y Morales, Baltasar 1601-1658LC 15
Gracq, Julien .... CLC 11, 48
See also Poirier, Louis
See also DLB 83
Grade, Chaim 1910-1982 .... CLC 10
See also CA 93-96; 107
Graduate of Oxford, A
See Ruskin, John
Grafton, Garth
See Duncan, Sara Jeannette
Graham, John
See Phillips, David Graham
Graham, Jorie 1951- .... CLC 48
See also CA 111; CANR 63; DLB 120
Graham, R(obert) B(ontine) Cunninghame
See Cunninghame Graham, R(obert) B(ontine)
See also DLB 98, 135, 174
Graham, Robert
See Haldeman, Joe (William)
Graham, Tom
See Lewis, (Harry) Sinclair
Graham, W(illiam) S(ydney) 1918-1986C L C
29
See also CA 73-76; 118; DLB 20
Graham, Winston (Mawdsley) 1910- CLC 23
See also CA 49-52; CANR 2, 22, 45, 66; DLB
77
Grahame, Kenneth 1859-1932TCLC 64; DAB
See also CA 108; 136; CLR 5; DLB 34, 141,
178; MAICYA; SATA 100; YABC 1
Grant, Skeeter
See Spiegelman, Art
Granville-Barker, Harley 1877-1946TCLC 2;
DAM DRAM
See also Barker, Harley Granville
See also CA 104
Grass, Guenter (Wilhelm) 1927-CLC 1, 2, 4, 6,
11, 15, 22, 32, 49, 88; DA; DAB; DAC;
DAM MST, NOV; WLC
See also CA 13-16R; CANR 20; DLB 75, 124;
MTCW 1
Gratton, Thomas
See Hulme, T(homas) E(rnest)
Grau, Shirley Ann 1929- . CLC 4, 9; SSC 15
See also CA 89-92; CANR 22, 69; DLB 2; INT
CANR-22; MTCW 1

Gravel, Fern
See Hall, James Norman
Graver, Elizabeth 1964- .... CLC 70
See also CA 135; CANR 71
Graves, Richard Perceval 1945- .... CLC 44
See also CA 65-68; CANR 9, 26, 51
Graves, Robert (von Ranke) 1895-1985 C L C
1, 2, 6, 11, 39, 44, 45; DAB; DAC; DAM
MST, POET; PC 6
See also CA 5-8R; 117; CANR 5, 36; CDBLB
1914-1945; DLB 20, 100, 191; DLBD 18;
DLBY 85; MTCW 1; SATA 45
Graves, Valerie
See Bradley, Marion Zimmer
Gray, Alasdair (James) 1934- .... CLC 41
See also CA 126; CANR 47, 69; DLB 194; INT
126; MTCW 1
Gray, Amlin 1946- .... CLC 29
See also CA 138
Gray, Francine du Plessix 1930- ..... CLC 22;
DAM NOV
See also BEST 90:3; CA 61-64; CAAS 2;
CANR 11, 33; INT CANR-11; MTCW 1
Gray, John (Henry) 1866-1934 ...... TCLC 19
See also CA 119; 162
Gray, Simon (James Holliday) 1936- CLC 9,
14, 36
See also AITN 1; CA 21-24R; CAAS 3; CANR
32, 69; DLB 13; MTCW 1
Gray, Spalding 1941-CLC 49, 112; DAM POP;
DC 7
See also CA 128
Gray, Thomas 1716-1771LC 4, 40; DA; DAB;
DAC; DAM MST; PC 2; WLC
See also CDBLB 1660-1789; DLB 109
Grayson, David
See Baker, Ray Stannard
Grayson, Richard (A.) 1951- .... CLC 38
See also CA 85-88; CANR 14, 31, 57
Greeley, Andrew M(oran) 1928- ..... CLC 28;
DAM POP
See also CA 5-8R; CAAS 7; CANR 7, 43, 69;
MTCW 1
Green, Anna Katharine 1846-1935 TCLC 63
See also CA 112; 159; DLB 202
Green, Brian
See Card, Orson Scott
Green, Hannah
See Greenberg, Joanne (Goldenberg)
Green, Hannah 1927(?)-1996 .... CLC 3
See also CA 73-76; CANR 59
Green, Henry 1905-1973 .... CLC 2, 13, 97
See also Yorke, Henry Vincent
See also DLB 15
Green, Julian (Hartridge) 1900-
See Green, Julien
See also CA 21-24R; CANR 33; DLB 4, 72;
MTCW 1
Green, Julien .... CLC 3, 11, 77
See also Green, Julian (Hartridge)
Green, Paul (Eliot) 1894-1981CLC 25; DAM
DRAM
See also AITN 1; CA 5-8R; 103; CANR 3; DLB
7, 9; DLBY 81
Greenberg, Ivan 1908-1973
See Rahv, Philip
See also CA 85-88
Greenberg, Joanne (Goldenberg) 1932- C L C
7, 30
See also AAYA 12; CA 5-8R; CANR 14, 32,
69; SATA 25
Greenberg, Richard 1959(?)- .... CLC 57
See also CA 138
Greene, Bette 1934- .... CLC 30
See also AAYA 7; CA 53-56; CANR 4; CLR 2;
JRDA; MAICYA; SAAS 16; SATA 8, 102
Greene, Gael .... CLC 8

See also CA 13-16R; CANR 10
Greene, Graham (Henry) 1904-1991CLC 1, 3,
6, 9, 14, 18, 27, 37, 70, 72; DA; DAB; DAC;
DAM MST, NOV; SSC 29; WLC
See also AITN 2; CA 13-16R; 133; CANR 35,
61; CDBLB 1945-1960; DLB 13, 15, 77,
100, 162, 201; DLBY 91; MTCW 1; SATA
20
Greene, Robert 1558-1592 .... LC 41
See also DLB 62, 167
Greer, Richard
See Silverberg, Robert
Gregor, Arthur 1923- .... CLC 9
See also CA 25-28R; CAAS 10; CANR 11;
SATA 36
Gregor, Lee
See Pohl, Frederik
Gregory, Isabella Augusta (Persse) 1852-1932
TCLC 1
See also CA 104; DLB 10
Gregory, J. Dennis
See Williams, John A(lfred)
Grendon, Stephen
See Derleth, August (William)
Grenville, Kate 1950- .... CLC 61
See also CA 118; CANR 53
Grenville, Pelham
See Wodehouse, P(elham) G(renville)
Greve, Felix Paul (Berthold Friedrich) 1879-
1948
See Grove, Frederick Philip
See also CA 104; 141; DAC; DAM MST
Grey, Zane 1872-1939 .. TCLC 6; DAM POP
See also CA 104; 132; DLB 9; MTCW 1
Grieg, (Johan) Nordahl (Brun) 1902-1943
TCLC 10
See also CA 107
Grieve, C(hristopher) M(urray) 1892-1978
CLC 11, 19; DAM POET
See also MacDiarmid, Hugh; Pteleon
See also CA 5-8R; 85-88; CANR 33; MTCW 1
Griffin, Gerald 1803-1840 .... NCLC 7
See also DLB 159
Griffin, John Howard 1920-1980 ..... CLC 68
See also AITN 1; CA 1-4R; 101; CANR 2
Griffin, Peter 1942- .... CLC 39
See also CA 136
Griffith, D(avid Lewelyn) W(ark) 1875(?)-1948
TCLC 68
See also CA 119; 150
Griffith, Lawrence
See Griffith, D(avid Lewelyn) W(ark)
Griffiths, Trevor 1935- .... CLC 13, 52
See also CA 97-100; CANR 45; DLB 13
Griggs, Sutton Elbert 1872-1930(?)TCLC 77
See also CA 123; DLB 50
Grigson, Geoffrey (Edward Harvey) 1905-1985
CLC 7, 39
See also CA 25-28R; 118; CANR 20, 33; DLB
27; MTCW 1
Grillparzer, Franz 1791-1872 .... NCLC 1
See also DLB 133
Grimble, Reverend Charles James
See Eliot, T(homas) S(tearns)
Grimke, Charlotte L(ottie) Forten 1837(?)-1914
See Forten, Charlotte L.
See also BW 1; CA 117; 124; DAM MULT,
POET
Grimm, Jacob Ludwig Karl 1785-1863NCLC
3
See also DLB 90; MAICYA; SATA 22
Grimm, Wilhelm Karl 1786-1859 .... NCLC 3
See also DLB 90; MAICYA; SATA 22
Grimmelshausen, Johann Jakob Christoffel von
1621-1676 .... LC 6
See also DLB 168
Grindel, Eugene 1895-1952

See also AAYA 25; BEST 90:1; CA 123; CANR
50; DLB 145; HW

Hikmet, Nazim 1902(?)-1963 .... **CLC 40**
See also CA 141; 93-96

Hildegard von Bingen 1098-1179 . **CMLC 20**
See also DLB 148

Hildesheimer, Wolfgang 1916-1991 .. **CLC 49**
See also CA 101; 135; DLB 69, 124

Hill, Geoffrey (William) 1932- **CLC 5, 8, 18,
45; DAM POET**
See also CA 81-84; CANR 21; CDBLB 1960
to Present; DLB 40; MTCW 1

Hill, George Roy 1921- .... **CLC 26**
See also CA 110; 122

Hill, John
See Koontz, Dean R(ay)

Hill, Susan (Elizabeth) 1942- .... **CLC 4, 113;
DAB; DAM MST, NOV**
See also CA 33-36R; CANR 29, 69; DLB 14,
139; MTCW 1

Hillerman, Tony 1925- . **CLC 62; DAM POP**
See also AAYA 6; BEST 89:1; CA 29-32R;
CANR 21, 42, 65; SATA 6

Hillesum, Etty 1914-1943 .... **TCLC 49**
See also CA 137

Hilliard, Noel (Harvey) 1929- .... **CLC 15**
See also CA 9-12R; CANR 7, 69

Hillis, Rick 1956- .... **CLC 66**
See also CA 134

Hilton, James 1900-1954 .... **TCLC 21**
See also CA 108; DLB 34, 77; SATA 34

Himes, Chester (Bomar) 1909-1984 **CLC 2, 4,
7, 18, 58, 108; BLC 2; DAM MULT**
See also BW 2; CA 25-28R; 114; CANR 22;
DLB 2, 76, 143; MTCW 1

Hinde, Thomas .... **CLC 6, 11**
See also Chitty, Thomas Willes

Hindin, Nathan
See Bloch, Robert (Albert)

Hine, (William) Daryl 1936- .... **CLC 15**
See also CA 1-4R; CAAS 15; CANR 1, 20; DLB
60

Hinkson, Katharine Tynan
See Tynan, Katharine

Hinton, S(usan) E(loise) 1950- **CLC 30, 111;
DA; DAB; DAC; DAM MST, NOV**
See also AAYA 2; CA 81-84; CANR 32, 62;
CLR 3, 23; JRDA; MAICYA; MTCW 1;
SATA 19, 58

Hippius, Zinaida .... **TCLC 9**
See also Gippius, Zinaida (Nikolayevna)

Hiraoka, Kimitake 1925-1970
See Mishima, Yukio
See also CA 97-100; 29-32R; DAM DRAM;
MTCW 1

Hirsch, E(ric) D(onald), Jr. 1928- .... **CLC 79**
See also CA 25-28R; CANR 27, 51; DLB 67;
INT CANR-27; MTCW 1

Hirsch, Edward 1950- .... **CLC 31, 50**
See also CA 104; CANR 20, 42; DLB 120

Hitchcock, Alfred (Joseph) 1899-1980 **CLC 16**
See also AAYA 22; CA 159; 97-100; SATA 27;
SATA-Obit 24

Hitler, Adolf 1889-1945 .... **TCLC 53**
See also CA 117; 147

Hoagland, Edward 1932- .... **CLC 28**
See also CA 1-4R; CANR 2, 31, 57; DLB 6;
SATA 51

Hoban, Russell (Conwell) 1925- . **CLC 7, 25;
DAM NOV**
See also CA 5-8R; CANR 23, 37, 66; CLR 3;
DLB 52; MAICYA; MTCW 1; SATA 1, 40,
78

Hobbes, Thomas 1588-1679 .... **LC 36**
See also DLB 151

Hobbs, Perry
See Blackmur, R(ichard) P(almer)

Hobson, Laura Z(ametkin) 1900-1986 **CLC 7,
25**
See also CA 17-20R; 118; CANR 55; DLB 28;
SATA 52

Hochhuth, Rolf 1931- .. **CLC 4, 11, 18; DAM
DRAM**
See also CA 5-8R; CANR 33; DLB 124; MTCW
1

Hochman, Sandra 1936- .... **CLC 3, 8**
See also CA 5-8R; DLB 5

Hochwaelder, Fritz 1911-1986 **CLC 36; DAM
DRAM**
See also CA 29-32R; 120; CANR 42; MTCW 1

Hochwalder, Fritz
See Hochwaelder, Fritz

Hocking, Mary (Eunice) 1921- .... **CLC 13**
See also CA 101; CANR 18, 40

Hodgins, Jack 1938- .... **CLC 23**
See also CA 93-96; DLB 60

Hodgson, William Hope 1877(?)-1918 **TCLC
13**
See also CA 111; 164; DLB 70, 153, 156, 178

Hoeg, Peter 1957- .... **CLC 95**
See also CA 151

Hoffman, Alice 1952- ... **CLC 51; DAM NOV**
See also CA 77-80; CANR 34, 66; MTCW 1

Hoffman, Daniel (Gerard) 1923- **CLC 6, 13, 23**
See also CA 1-4R; CANR 4; DLB 5

Hoffman, Stanley 1944- .... **CLC 5**
See also CA 77-80

Hoffman, William M(oses) 1939- ...... **CLC 40**
See also CA 57-60; CANR 11, 71

Hoffmann, E(rnst) T(heodor) A(madeus) 1776-
1822 .... **NCLC 2; SSC 13**
See also DLB 90; SATA 27

Hofmann, Gert 1931- .... **CLC 54**
See also CA 128

Hofmannsthal, Hugo von 1874-1929 **TCLC 11;
DAM DRAM; DC 4**
See also CA 106; 153; DLB 81, 118

Hogan, Linda 1947- ... **CLC 73; DAM MULT**
See also CA 120; CANR 45; DLB 175; NNAL

Hogarth, Charles
See Creasey, John

Hogarth, Emmett
See Polonsky, Abraham (Lincoln)

Hogg, James 1770-1835 .... **NCLC 4**
See also DLB 93, 116, 159

Holbach, Paul Henri Thiry Baron 1723-1789
LC 14

Holberg, Ludvig 1684-1754 .... **LC 6**

Holden, Ursula 1921- .... **CLC 18**
See also CA 101; CAAS 8; CANR 22

Holderlin, (Johann Christian) Friedrich 1770-
1843 ....
NCLC 16; PC 4

Holdstock, Robert
See Holdstock, Robert P.

Holdstock, Robert P. 1948- .... **CLC 39**
See also CA 131

Holland, Isabelle 1920- .... **CLC 21**
See also AAYA 11; CA 21-24R; CANR 10, 25,
47; JRDA; MAICYA; SATA 8, 70

Holland, Marcus
See Caldwell, (Janet Miriam) Taylor (Holland)

Hollander, John 1929- .... **CLC 2, 5, 8, 14**
See also CA 1-4R; CANR 1, 52; DLB 5; SATA
13

Hollander, Paul
See Silverberg, Robert

Holleran, Andrew 1943(?)- .... **CLC 38**
See also CA 144

Hollinghurst, Alan 1954- .... **CLC 55, 91**
See also CA 114

Hollis, Jim
See Summers, Hollis (Spurgeon, Jr.)

Holly, Buddy 1936-1959 .... **TCLC 65**

Holmes, Gordon
See Shiel, M(atthew) P(hipps)

Holmes, John
See Souster, (Holmes) Raymond

Holmes, John Clellon 1926-1988 ...... **CLC 56**
See also CA 9-12R; 125; CANR 4; DLB 16

Holmes, Oliver Wendell, Jr. 1841-1935 **TCLC
77**
See also CA 114

Holmes, Oliver Wendell 1809-1894 **NCLC 14**
See also CDALB 1640-1865; DLB 1, 189;
SATA 34

Holmes, Raymond
See Souster, (Holmes) Raymond

Holt, Victoria
See Hibbert, Eleanor Alice Burford

Holub, Miroslav 1923- .... **CLC 4**
See also CA 21-24R; CANR 10

Homer c. 8th cent. B.C.- ... **CMLC 1, 16; DA;
DAB; DAC; DAM MST, POET; PC 23;
WLCS**
See also DLB 176

Hongo, Garrett Kaoru 1951- .... **PC 23**
See also CA 133; CAAS 22; DLB 120

Honig, Edwin 1919- .... **CLC 33**
See also CA 5-8R; CAAS 8; CANR 4, 45; DLB
5

Hood, Hugh (John Blagdon) 1928- **CLC 15, 28**
See also CA 49-52; CAAS 17; CANR 1, 33;
DLB 53

Hood, Thomas 1799-1845 .... **NCLC 16**
See also DLB 96

Hooker, (Peter) Jeremy 1941- .... **CLC 43**
See also CA 77-80; CANR 22; DLB 40

hooks, bell .... **CLC 94; BLCS**
See also Watkins, Gloria

Hope, A(lec) D(erwent) 1907- .... **CLC 3, 51**
See also CA 21-24R; CANR 33; MTCW 1

Hope, Anthony 1863-1933 .... **TCLC 83**
See also CA 157; DLB 153, 156

Hope, Brian
See Creasey, John

Hope, Christopher (David Tully) 1944- **CLC
52**
See also CA 106; CANR 47; SATA 62

Hopkins, Gerard Manley 1844-1889 .. **NCLC
17; DA; DAB; DAC; DAM MST, POET;
PC 15; WLC**
See also CDBLB 1890-1914; DLB 35, 57

Hopkins, John (Richard) 1931- .... **CLC 4**
See also CA 85-88

Hopkins, Pauline Elizabeth 1859-1930 **TCLC
28; BLC 2; DAM MULT**
See also BW 2; CA 141; DLB 50

Hopkinson, Francis 1737-1791 .... **LC 25**
See also DLB 31

Hopley-Woolrich, Cornell George 1903-1968
See Woolrich, Cornell
See also CA 13-14; CANR 58; CAP 1

Horatio
See Proust, (Valentin-Louis-George-Eugene-)
Marcel

Horgan, Paul (George Vincent O'Shaughnessy)
1903-1995 .... **CLC 9, 53; DAM NOV**
See also CA 13-16R; 147; CANR 9, 35; DLB
102; DLBY 85; INT CANR-9; MTCW 1;
SATA 13; SATA-Obit 84

Horn, Peter
See Kuttner, Henry

Hornem, Horace Esq.
See Byron, George Gordon (Noel)

Horney, Karen (Clementine Theodore
Danielsen) 1885-1952 .... **TCLC 71**
See also CA 114; 165

Hornung, E(rnest) W(illiam) 1866-1921
TCLC 59
See also CA 108; 160; DLB 70

59; DLB 157

King, Francis (Henry) 1923-CLC **8, 53; DAM NOV**
  See also CA 1-4R; CANR 1, 33; DLB 15, 139; MTCW 1

King, Kennedy
  See Brown, George Douglas

King, Martin Luther, Jr. 1929-1968 CLC **83; BLC 2; DA; DAB; DAC; DAM MST, MULT; WLCS**
  See also BW 2; CA 25-28; CANR 27, 44; CAP 2; MTCW 1; SATA 14

King, Stephen (Edwin) 1947-CLC **12, 26, 37, 61, 113; DAM NOV, POP; SSC 17**
  See also AAYA 1, 17; BEST 90:1; CA 61-64; CANR 1, 30, 52; DLB 143; DLBY 80; JRDA; MTCW 1; SATA 9, 55

King, Steve
  See King, Stephen (Edwin)

King, Thomas 1943- ... CLC **89; DAC; DAM MULT**
  See also CA 144; DLB 175; NNAL; SATA 96

Kingman, Lee .... CLC **17**
  See also Natti, (Mary) Lee
  See also SAAS 3; SATA 1, 67

Kingsley, Charles 1819-1875 .... NCLC **35**
  See also DLB 21, 32, 163, 190; YABC 2

Kingsley, Sidney 1906-1995 .... CLC **44**
  See also CA 85-88; 147; DLB 7

Kingsolver, Barbara 1955-CLC **55, 81; DAM POP**
  See also AAYA 15; CA 129; 134; CANR 60; INT 134

Kingston, Maxine (Ting Ting) Hong 1940-CLC **12, 19, 58; DAM MULT, NOV; WLCS**
  See also AAYA 8; CA 69-72; CANR 13, 38; DLB 173; DLBY 80; INT CANR-13; MTCW 1; SATA 53

Kinnell, Galway 1927- CLC **1, 2, 3, 5, 13, 29**
  See also CA 9-12R; CANR 10, 34, 66; DLB 5; DLBY 87; INT CANR-34; MTCW 1

Kinsella, Thomas 1928- ....CLC **4, 19**
  See also CA 17-20R; CANR 15; DLB 27; MTCW 1

Kinsella, W(illiam) P(atrick) 1935- . CLC **27, 43; DAC; DAM NOV, POP**
  See also AAYA 7; CA 97-100; CAAS 7; CANR 21, 35, 66; INT CANR-21; MTCW 1

Kipling, (Joseph) Rudyard 1865-1936 T C L C **8, 17; DA; DAB; DAC; DAM MST, POET; PC 3; SSC 5; WLC**
  See also CA 105; 120; CANR 33; CDBLB 1890-1914; CLR 39; DLB 19, 34, 141, 156; MAICYA; MTCW 1; SATA 100; YABC 2

Kirkup, James 1918- .... CLC **1**
  See also CA 1-4R; CAAS 4; CANR 2; DLB 27; SATA 12

Kirkwood, James 1930(?)-1989 .... CLC **9**
  See also AITN 2; CA 1-4R; 128; CANR 6, 40

Kirshner, Sidney
  See Kingsley, Sidney

Kis, Danilo 1935-1989 .... CLC **57**
  See also CA 109; 118; 129; CANR 61; DLB 181; MTCW 1

Kivi, Aleksis 1834-1872 .... NCLC **30**

Kizer, Carolyn (Ashley) 1925-CLC **15, 39, 80; DAM POET**
  See also CA 65-68; CAAS 5; CANR 24, 70; DLB 5, 169

Klabund 1890-1928 .... TCLC **44**
  See also CA 162; DLB 66

Klappert, Peter 1942- .... CLC **57**
  See also CA 33-36R; DLB 5

Klein, A(braham) M(oses) 1909-1972CLC **19; DAB; DAC; DAM MST**
  See also CA 101; 37-40R; DLB 68

Klein, Norma 1938-1989 .... CLC **30**
  See also AAYA 2; CA 41-44R; 128; CANR 15, 37; CLR 2, 19; INT CANR-15; JRDA; MAICYA; SAAS 1; SATA 7, 57

Klein, T(heodore) E(ibon) D(onald) 1947-CLC **34**
  See also CA 119; CANR 44

Kleist, Heinrich von 1777-1811 NCLC **2, 37; DAM DRAM; SSC 22**
  See also DLB 90

Klima, Ivan 1931- .... CLC **56; DAM NOV**
  See also CA 25-28R; CANR 17, 50

Klimentov, Andrei Platonovich 1899-1951
  See Platonov, Andrei
  See also CA 108

Klinger, Friedrich Maximilian von 1752-1831 NCLC **1**
  See also DLB 94

Klingsor the Magician
  See Hartmann, Sadakichi

Klopstock, Friedrich Gottlieb 1724-1803 NCLC **11**
  See also DLB 97

Knapp, Caroline 1959- .... CLC **99**
  See also CA 154

Knebel, Fletcher 1911-1993 .... CLC **14**
  See also AITN 1; CA 1-4R; 140; CAAS 3; CANR 1, 36; SATA 36; SATA-Obit 75

Knickerbocker, Diedrich
  See Irving, Washington

Knight, Etheridge 1931-1991CLC **40; BLC 2; DAM POET; PC 14**
  See also BW 1; CA 21-24R; 133; CANR 23; DLB 41

Knight, Sarah Kemble 1666-1727 .... LC **7**
  See also DLB 24, 200

Knister, Raymond 1899-1932 .... TCLC **56**
  See also DLB 68

Knowles, John 1926- . CLC **1, 4, 10, 26; DA; DAC; DAM MST, NOV**
  See also AAYA 10; CA 17-20R; CANR 40; CDALB 1968-1988; DLB 6; MTCW 1; SATA 8, 89

Knox, Calvin M.
  See Silverberg, Robert

Knox, John c. 1505-1572 .... LC **37**
  See also DLB 132

Knye, Cassandra
  See Disch, Thomas M(ichael)

Koch, C(hristopher) J(ohn) 1932- .... CLC **42**
  See also CA 127

Koch, Christopher
  See Koch, C(hristopher) J(ohn)

Koch, Kenneth 1925- ..... CLC **5, 8, 44; DAM POET**
  See also CA 1-4R; CANR 6, 36, 57; DLB 5; INT CANR-36; SATA 65

Kochanowski, Jan 1530-1584 .... LC **10**

Kock, Charles Paul de 1794-1871 . NCLC **16**

Koda Shigeyuki 1867-1947
  See Rohan, Koda
  See also CA 121

Koestler, Arthur 1905-1983CLC **1, 3, 6, 8, 15, 33**
  See also CA 1-4R; 109; CANR 1, 33; CDBLB 1945-1960; DLBY 83; MTCW 1

Kogawa, Joy Nozomi 1935- .. CLC **78; DAC; DAM MST, MULT**
  See also CA 101; CANR 19, 62; SATA 99

Kohout, Pavel 1928- .... CLC **13**
  See also CA 45-48; CANR 3

Koizumi, Yakumo
  See Hearn, (Patricio) Lafcadio (Tessima Carlos)

Kolmar, Gertrud 1894-1943 .... TCLC **40**
  See also CA 167

Komunyakaa, Yusef 1947-CLC **86, 94; BLCS**
  See also CA 147; DLB 120

Konrad, George
  See Konrad, Gyoergy

Konrad, Gyoergy 1933- .... CLC **4, 10, 73**
  See also CA 85-88

Konwicki, Tadeusz 1926- .... CLC **8, 28, 54**
  See also CA 101; CAAS 9; CANR 39, 59; MTCW 1

Koontz, Dean R(ay) 1945- ..... CLC **78; DAM NOV, POP**
  See also AAYA 9; BEST 89:3, 90:2; CA 108; CANR 19, 36, 52; MTCW 1; SATA 92

Kopernik, Mikolaj
  See Copernicus, Nicolaus

Kopit, Arthur (Lee) 1937-CLC **1, 18, 33; DAM DRAM**
  See also AITN 1; CA 81-84; CABS 3; DLB 7; MTCW 1

Kops, Bernard 1926- .... CLC **4**
  See also CA 5-8R; DLB 13

Kornbluth, C(yril) M. 1923-1958 .... TCLC **8**
  See also CA 105; 160; DLB 8

Korolenko, V. G.
  See Korolenko, Vladimir Galaktionovich

Korolenko, Vladimir
  See Korolenko, Vladimir Galaktionovich

Korolenko, Vladimir G.
  See Korolenko, Vladimir Galaktionovich

Korolenko, Vladimir Galaktionovich 1853-1921 .... TCLC **22**
  See also CA 121

Korzybski, Alfred (Habdank Skarbek) 1879-1950 .... TCLC **61**
  See also CA 123; 160

Kosinski, Jerzy (Nikodem) 1933-1991CLC **1, 2, 3, 6, 10, 15, 53, 70; DAM NOV**
  See also CA 17-20R; 134; CANR 9, 46; DLB 2; DLBY 82; MTCW 1

Kostelanetz, Richard (Cory) 1940- .. CLC **28**
  See also CA 13-16R; CAAS 8; CANR 38

Kostrowitzki, Wilhelm Apollinaris de 1880-1918
  See Apollinaire, Guillaume
  See also CA 104

Kotlowitz, Robert 1924- .... CLC **4**
  See also CA 33-36R; CANR 36

Kotzebue, August (Friedrich Ferdinand) von 1761-1819 ....
  NCLC **25**
  See also DLB 94

Kotzwinkle, William 1938- ..... CLC **5, 14, 35**
  See also CA 45-48; CANR 3, 44; CLR 6; DLB 173; MAICYA; SATA 24, 70

Kowna, Stancy
  See Szymborska, Wislawa

Kozol, Jonathan 1936- .... CLC **17**
  See also CA 61-64; CANR 16, 45

Kozoll, Michael 1940(?)- .... CLC **35**

Kramer, Kathryn 19(?)- .... CLC **34**

Kramer, Larry 1935-CLC **42; DAM POP; DC 8**
  See also CA 124; 126; CANR 60

Krasicki, Ignacy 1735-1801 .... NCLC **8**

Krasinski, Zygmunt 1812-1859 .... NCLC **4**

Kraus, Karl 1874-1936 .... TCLC **5**
  See also CA 104; DLB 118

Kreve (Mickevicius), Vincas 1882-1954T CLC **27**

Kristeva, Julia 1941- ....CLC **77**
  See also CA 154

Kristofferson, Kris 1936- ....CLC **26**
  See also CA 104

Krizanc, John 1956- ....CLC **57**

Krleza, Miroslav 1893-1981 .... CLC **8, 114**
  See also CA 97-100; 105; CANR 50; DLB 147

Kroetsch, Robert 1927-CLC **5, 23, 57; DAC; DAM POET**
  See also CA 17-20R; CANR 8, 38; DLB 53;

NCLC 23
See also DLB 39

Lentricchia, Frank (Jr.) 1940- .... **CLC 34**
See also CA 25-28R; CANR 19

Lenz, Siegfried 1926- .... **CLC 27**
See also CA 89-92; DLB 75

Leonard, Elmore (John, Jr.) 1925-**CLC 28, 34, 71; DAM POP**
See also AAYA 22; AITN 1; BEST 89:1, 90:4; CA 81-84; CANR 12, 28, 53; DLB 173; INT CANR-28; MTCW 1

Leonard, Hugh .... **CLC 19**
See also Byrne, John Keyes
See also DLB 13

Leonov, Leonid (Maximovich) 1899-1994
CLC 92; DAM NOV
See also CA 129; MTCW 1

Leopardi, (Conte) Giacomo 1798-1837**NCLC 22**

Le Reveler
See Artaud, Antonin (Marie Joseph)

Lerman, Eleanor 1952- .... **CLC 9**
See also CA 85-88; CANR 69

Lerman, Rhoda 1936- .... **CLC 56**
See also CA 49-52; CANR 70

Lermontov, Mikhail Yuryevich 1814-1841
NCLC 47; PC 18

Leroux, Gaston 1868-1927 .... **TCLC 25**
See also CA 108; 136; CANR 69; SATA 65

Lesage, Alain-Rene 1668-1747 .... **LC 28**

Leskov, Nikolai (Semyonovich) 1831-1895
NCLC 25

Lessing, Doris (May) 1919-**CLC 1, 2, 3, 6, 10, 15, 22, 40, 94; DA; DAB; DAC; DAM MST, NOV; SSC 6; WLCS**
See also CA 9-12R; CAAS 14; CANR 33, 54; CDBLB 1960 to Present; DLB 15, 139; DLBY 85; MTCW 1

Lessing, Gotthold Ephraim 1729-1781 . **LC 8**
See also DLB 97

Lester, Richard 1932- .... **CLC 20**

Lever, Charles (James) 1806-1872 **NCLC 23**
See also DLB 21

Leverson, Ada 1865(?)-1936(?) ...... **TCLC 18**
See also Elaine
See also CA 117; DLB 153

Levertov, Denise 1923-1997**CLC 1, 2, 3, 5, 8, 15, 28, 66; DAM POET; PC 11**
See also CA 1-4R; 163; CAAS 19; CANR 3, 29, 50; DLB 5, 165; INT CANR-29; MTCW 1

Levi, Jonathan .... **CLC 76**

Levi, Peter (Chad Tigar) 1931- .... **CLC 41**
See also CA 5-8R; CANR 34; DLB 40

Levi, Primo 1919-1987 . **CLC 37, 50; SSC 12**
See also CA 13-16R; 122; CANR 12, 33, 61, 70; DLB 177; MTCW 1

Levin, Ira 1929- .... **CLC 3, 6; DAM POP**
See also CA 21-24R; CANR 17, 44; MTCW 1; SATA 66

Levin, Meyer 1905-1981 . **CLC 7; DAM POP**
See also AITN 1; CA 9-12R; 104; CANR 15; DLB 9, 28; DLBY 81; SATA 21; SATA-Obit 27

Levine, Norman 1924-........................ **CLC 54**
See also CA 73-76; CAAS 23; CANR 14, 70; DLB 88

Levine, Philip 1928-... **CLC 2, 4, 5, 9, 14, 33; DAM POET; PC 22**
See also CA 9-12R; CANR 9, 37, 52; DLB 5

Levinson, Deirdre 1931- .... **CLC 49**
See also CA 73-76; CANR 70

Levi-Strauss, Claude 1908- .... **CLC 38**
See also CA 1-4R; CANR 6, 32, 57; MTCW 1

Levitin, Sonia (Wolff) 1934- .... **CLC 17**
See also AAYA 13; CA 29-32R; CANR 14, 32; CLR 53; JRDA; MAICYA; SAAS 2; SATA

4, 68

Levon, O. U.
See Kesey, Ken (Elton)

Levy, Amy 1861-1889 .... **NCLC 59**
See also DLB 156

Lewes, George Henry 1817-1878 ... **NCLC 25**
See also DLB 55, 144

Lewis, Alun 1915-1944 .... **TCLC 3**
See also CA 104; DLB 20, 162

Lewis, C. Day
See Day Lewis, C(ecil)

Lewis, C(live) S(taples) 1898-1963**CLC 1, 3, 6, 14, 27; DA; DAB; DAC; DAM MST, NOV, POP; WLC**
See also AAYA 3; CA 81-84; CANR 33, 71; CDBLB 1945-1960; CLR 3, 27; DLB 15, 100, 160; JRDA; MAICYA; MTCW 1; SATA 13, 100

Lewis, Janet 1899- .... **CLC 41**
See also Winters, Janet Lewis
See also CA 9-12R; CANR 29, 63; CAP 1; DLBY 87

Lewis, Matthew Gregory 1775-1818**NCLC 11, 62**
See also DLB 39, 158, 178

Lewis, (Harry) Sinclair 1885-1951 . **TCLC 4, 13, 23, 39; DA; DAB; DAC; DAM MST, NOV; WLC**
See also CA 104; 133; CDALB 1917-1929; DLB 9, 102; DLBD 1; MTCW 1

Lewis, (Percy) Wyndham 1882(?)-1957**TCLC 2, 9**
See also CA 104; 157; DLB 15

Lewisohn, Ludwig 1883-1955 .... **TCLC 19**
See also CA 107; DLB 4, 9, 28, 102

Lewton, Val 1904-1951 .... **TCLC 76**

Leyner, Mark 1956- .... **CLC 92**
See also CA 110; CANR 28, 53

Lezama Lima, Jose 1910-1976**CLC 4, 10, 101; DAM MULT**
See also CA 77-80; CANR 71; DLB 113; HW

L'Heureux, John (Clarke) 1934- .... **CLC 52**
See also CA 13-16R; CANR 23, 45

Liddell, C. H.
See Kuttner, Henry

Lie, Jonas (Lauritz Idemil) 1833-1908(?)
TCLC 5
See also CA 115

Lieber, Joel 1937-1971 .... **CLC 6**
See also CA 73-76; 29-32R

Lieber, Stanley Martin
See Lee, Stan

Lieberman, Laurence (James) 1935- **CLC 4, 36**
See also CA 17-20R; CANR 8, 36

Lieh Tzu fl. 7th cent. B.C.-5th cent. B.C.
CMLC 27

Lieksman, Anders
See Haavikko, Paavo Juhani

Li Fei-kan 1904-
See Pa Chin
See also CA 105

Lifton, Robert Jay 1926- .... **CLC 67**
See also CA 17-20R; CANR 27; INT CANR-27; SATA 66

Lightfoot, Gordon 1938- .... **CLC 26**
See also CA 109

Lightman, Alan P(aige) 1948- .... **CLC 81**
See also CA 141; CANR 63

Ligotti, Thomas (Robert) 1953-**CLC 44; SSC 16**
See also CA 123; CANR 49

Li Ho 791-817 .... **PC 13**

Liliencron, (Friedrich Adolf Axel) Detlev von 1844-1909 .... **TCLC 18**
See also CA 117

Lilly, William 1602-1681 .... **LC 27**

Lima, Jose Lezama
See Lezama Lima, Jose

Lima Barreto, Afonso Henrique de 1881-1922
TCLC 23
See also CA 117

Limonov, Edward 1944- .... **CLC 67**
See also CA 137

Lin, Frank
See Atherton, Gertrude (Franklin Horn)

Lincoln, Abraham 1809-1865 .... **NCLC 18**

Lind, Jakov .... **CLC 1, 2, 4, 27, 82**
See also Landwirth, Heinz
See also CAAS 4

Lindbergh, Anne (Spencer) Morrow 1906-
CLC 82; DAM NOV
See also CA 17-20R; CANR 16; MTCW 1; SATA 33

Lindsay, David 1878-1945 .... **TCLC 15**
See also CA 113

Lindsay, (Nicholas) Vachel 1879-1931 **TCLC 17; DA; DAC; DAM MST, POET; PC 23; WLC**
See also CA 114; 135; CDALB 1865-1917; DLB 54; SATA 40

Linke-Poot
See Doeblin, Alfred

Linney, Romulus 1930- .... **CLC 51**
See also CA 1-4R; CANR 40, 44

Linton, Eliza Lynn 1822-1898........ **NCLC 41**
See also DLB 18

Li Po 701-763 .... **CMLC 2**

Lipsius, Justus 1547-1606 .... **LC 16**

Lipsyte, Robert (Michael) 1938-**CLC 21; DA; DAC; DAM MST, NOV**
See also AAYA 7; CA 17-20R; CANR 8, 57; CLR 23; JRDA; MAICYA; SATA 5, 68

Lish, Gordon (Jay) 1934- ... **CLC 45; SSC 18**
See also CA 113; 117; DLB 130; INT 117

Lispector, Clarice 1925(?)-1977 .... **CLC 43**
See also CA 139; 116; CANR 71; DLB 113

Littell, Robert 1935(?)- .... **CLC 42**
See also CA 109; 112; CANR 64

Little, Malcolm 1925-1965
See Malcolm X
See also BW 1; CA 125; 111; DA; DAB; DAC; DAM MST, MULT; MTCW 1

Littlewit, Humphrey Gent.
See Lovecraft, H(oward) P(hillips)

Litwos
See Sienkiewicz, Henryk (Adam Alexander Pius)

Liu, E 1857-1909 .... **TCLC 15**
See also CA 115

Lively, Penelope (Margaret) 1933- ..**CLC 32, 50; DAM NOV**
See also CA 41-44R; CANR 29, 67; CLR 7; DLB 14, 161; JRDA; MAICYA; MTCW 1; SATA 7, 60, 101

Livesay, Dorothy (Kathleen) 1909-**CLC 4, 15, 79; DAC; DAM MST, POET**
See also AITN 2; CA 25-28R; CAAS 8; CANR 36, 67; DLB 68; MTCW 1

Livy c. 59B.C.-c. 17 .... **CMLC 11**

Lizardi, Jose Joaquin Fernandez de 1776-1827
NCLC 30

Llewellyn, Richard
See Llewellyn Lloyd, Richard Dafydd Vivian
See also DLB 15

Llewellyn Lloyd, Richard Dafydd Vivian 1906-1983 ....

CLC 7, 80
See also Llewellyn, Richard
See also CA 53-56; 111; CANR 7, 71; SATA 11; SATA-Obit 37

Llosa, (Jorge) Mario (Pedro) Vargas
See Vargas Llosa, (Jorge) Mario (Pedro)

Lloyd, Manda

See Mander, (Mary) Jane

Lloyd Webber, Andrew 1948-
See Webber, Andrew Lloyd
See also AAYA 1; CA 116; 149; DAM DRAM;
SATA 56

Llull, Ramon c. 1235-c. 1316 .... **CMLC 12**

Lobb, Ebenezer
See Upward, Allen

Locke, Alain (Le Roy) 1886-1954 . **TCLC 43;
BLCS**
See also BW 1; CA 106; 124; DLB 51

Locke, John 1632-1704 .... **LC 7, 35**
See also DLB 101

Locke-Elliott, Sumner
See Elliott, Sumner Locke

Lockhart, John Gibson 1794-1854 .. **NCLC 6**
See also DLB 110, 116, 144

Lodge, David (John) 1935- .... **CLC 36; DAM
POP**
See also BEST 90:1; CA 17-20R; CANR 19,
53; DLB 14, 194; INT CANR-19; MTCW 1

Lodge, Thomas 1558-1625 .... **LC 41**
See also DLB 172

Lodge, Thomas 1558-1625 .... **LC 41**

Loennbohm, Armas Eino Leopold 1878-1926
See Leino, Eino
See also CA 123

Loewinsohn, Ron(ald William) 1937-**CLC 52**
See also CA 25-28R; CANR 71

Logan, Jake
See Smith, Martin Cruz

Logan, John (Burton) 1923-1987 .... **CLC 5**
See also CA 77-80; 124; CANR 45; DLB 5

Lo Kuan-chung 1330(?)-1400(?) .... **LC 12**

Lombard, Nap
See Johnson, Pamela Hansford

London, Jack . **TCLC 9, 15, 39; SSC 4; WLC**
See also London, John Griffith
See also AAYA 13; AITN 2; CDALB 1865-
1917; DLB 8, 12, 78; SATA 18

London, John Griffith 1876-1916
See London, Jack
See also CA 110; 119; DA; DAB; DAC; DAM
MST, NOV; JRDA; MAICYA; MTCW 1

Long, Emmett
See Leonard, Elmore (John, Jr.)

Longbaugh, Harry
See Goldman, William (W.)

Longfellow, Henry Wadsworth 1807-1882
**NCLC 2, 45; DA; DAB; DAC; DAM MST,
POET; WLCS**
See also CDALB 1640-1865; DLB 1, 59; SATA
19

Longinus c. 1st cent. - .... **CMLC 27**
See also DLB 176

Longley, Michael 1939- .... **CLC 29**
See also CA 102; DLB 40

Longus fl. c. 2nd cent. - .... **CMLC 7**

Longway, A. Hugh
See Lang, Andrew

Lonnrot, Elias 1802-1884 .... **NCLC 53**

Lopate, Phillip 1943- .... **CLC 29**
See also CA 97-100; DLBY 80; INT 97-100

Lopez Portillo (y Pacheco), Jose 1920-. **C L C
46**
See also CA 129; HW

Lopez y Fuentes, Gregorio 1897(?)-1966**C L C
32**
See also CA 131; HW

Lorca, Federico Garcia
See Garcia Lorca, Federico

Lord, Bette Bao 1938- .... **CLC 23**
See also BEST 90:3; CA 107; CANR 41; INT
107; SATA 58

Lord Auch
See Bataille, Georges

Lord Byron

See Byron, George Gordon (Noel)

Lorde, Audre (Geraldine) 1934-1992**CLC 18,
71; BLC 2; DAM MULT, POET; PC 12**
See also BW 1; CA 25-28R; 142; CANR 16,
26, 46; DLB 41; MTCW 1

Lord Houghton
See Milnes, Richard Monckton

Lord Jeffrey
See Jeffrey, Francis

Lorenzini, Carlo 1826-1890
See Collodi, Carlo
See also MAICYA; SATA 29, 100

Lorenzo, Heberto Padilla
See Padilla (Lorenzo), Heberto

Loris
See Hofmannsthal, Hugo von

Loti, Pierre .... **TCLC 11**
See also Viaud, (Louis Marie) Julien
See also DLB 123

Louie, David Wong 1954- .... **CLC 70**
See also CA 139

Louis, Father M.
See Merton, Thomas

Lovecraft, H(oward) P(hillips) 1890-1937
TCLC 4, 22; DAM POP; SSC 3
See also AAYA 14; CA 104; 133; MTCW 1

Lovelace, Earl 1935- .... **CLC 51**
See also BW 2; CA 77-80; CANR 41, 72; DLB
125; MTCW 1

Lovelace, Richard 1618-1657 .... **LC 24**
See also DLB 131

Lowell, Amy 1874-1925 .... **TCLC 1, 8; DAM
POET; PC 13**
See also CA 104; 151; DLB 54, 140

Lowell, James Russell 1819-1891 .... **NCLC 2**
See also CDALB 1640-1865; DLB 1, 11, 64,
79, 189

Lowell, Robert (Traill Spence, Jr.) 1917-1977
**CLC 1, 2, 3, 4, 5, 8, 9, 11, 15, 37; DA; DAB;
DAC; DAM MST, NOV; PC 3; WLC**
See also CA 9-12R; 73-76; CABS 2; CANR 26,
60; DLB 5, 169; MTCW 1

Lowndes, Marie Adelaide (Belloc) 1868-1947
TCLC 12
See also CA 107; DLB 70

Lowry, (Clarence) Malcolm 1909-1957**T CLC
6, 40; SSC 31**
See also CA 105; 131; CANR 62; CDBLB
1945-1960; DLB 15; MTCW 1

Lowry, Mina Gertrude 1882-1966
See Loy, Mina
See also CA 113

Loxsmith, John
See Brunner, John (Kilian Houston)

Loy, Mina .... **CLC 28; DAM POET; PC 16**
See also Lowry, Mina Gertrude
See also DLB 4, 54

Loyson-Bridet
See Schwob, Marcel (Mayer Andre)

Lucas, Craig 1951- .... **CLC 64**
See also CA 137; CANR 71

Lucas, E(dward) V(errall) 1868-1938 **T C L C
73**
See also DLB 98, 149, 153; SATA 20

Lucas, George 1944- .... **CLC 16**
See also AAYA 1, 23; CA 77-80; CANR 30;
SATA 56

Lucas, Hans
See Godard, Jean-Luc

Lucas, Victoria
See Plath, Sylvia

Ludlam, Charles 1943-1987 .... **CLC 46, 50**
See also CA 85-88; 122; CANR 72

Ludlum, Robert 1927-**CLC 22, 43; DAM NOV,
POP**
See also AAYA 10; BEST 89:1, 90:3; CA
33-36R; CANR 25, 41, 68; DLBY 82;

MTCW 1

Ludwig, Ken .... **CLC 60**

Ludwig, Otto 1813-1865 .... **NCLC 4**
See also DLB 129

Lugones, Leopoldo 1874-1938 .... **TCLC 15**
See also CA 116; 131; HW

Lu Hsun 1881-1936 .... **TCLC 3; SSC 20**
See also Shu-Jen, Chou

Lukacs, George .... **CLC 24**
See also Lukacs, Gyorgy (Szegeny von)

Lukacs, Gyorgy (Szegeny von) 1885-1971
See Lukacs, George
See also CA 101; 29-32R; CANR 62

Luke, Peter (Ambrose Cyprian) 1919-1995
CLC 38
See also CA 81-84; 147; CANR 72; DLB 13

Lunar, Dennis
See Mungo, Raymond

Lurie, Alison 1926- .... **CLC 4, 5, 18, 39**
See also CA 1-4R; CANR 2, 17, 50; DLB 2;
MTCW 1; SATA 46

Lustig, Arnost 1926- .... **CLC 56**
See also AAYA 3; CA 69-72; CANR 47; SATA
56

Luther, Martin 1483-1546 .... **LC 9, 37**
See also DLB 179

Luxemburg, Rosa 1870(?)-1919 ..... **TCLC 63**
See also CA 118

Luzi, Mario 1914- .... **CLC 13**
See also CA 61-64; CANR 9, 70; DLB 128

Lyly, John 1554(?)-1606**LC 41; DAM DRAM;
DC 7**
See also DLB 62, 167

L'Ymagier
See Gourmont, Remy (-Marie-Charles) de

Lynch, B. Suarez
See Bioy Casares, Adolfo; Borges, Jorge Luis

Lynch, David (K.) 1946- .... **CLC 66**
See also CA 124; 129

Lynch, James
See Andreyev, Leonid (Nikolaevich)

Lynch Davis, B.
See Bioy Casares, Adolfo; Borges, Jorge Luis

Lyndsay, Sir David 1490-1555 .... **LC 20**

Lynn, Kenneth S(chuyler) 1923- .... **CLC 50**
See also CA 1-4R; CANR 3, 27, 65

Lynx
See West, Rebecca

Lyons, Marcus
See Blish, James (Benjamin)

Lyre, Pinchbeck
See Sassoon, Siegfried (Lorraine)

Lytle, Andrew (Nelson) 1902-1995 ... **CLC 22**
See also CA 9-12R; 150; CANR 70; DLB 6;
DLBY 95

Lyttelton, George 1709-1773 .... **LC 10**

Maas, Peter 1929- .... **CLC 29**
See also CA 93-96; INT 93-96

Macaulay, Rose 1881-1958 .... **TCLC 7, 44**
See also CA 104; DLB 36

Macaulay, Thomas Babington 1800-1859
NCLC 42
See also CDBLB 1832-1890; DLB 32, 55

MacBeth, George (Mann) 1932-1992**CLC 2, 5,
9**
See also CA 25-28R; 136; CANR 61, 66; DLB
40; MTCW 1; SATA 4; SATA-Obit 70

MacCaig, Norman (Alexander) 1910-**CLC 36;
DAB; DAM POET**
See also CA 9-12R; CANR 3, 34; DLB 27

MacCarthy, Sir(Charles Otto) Desmond 1877-
1952 .... **TCLC 36**
See also CA 167

MacDiarmid, Hugh**CLC 2, 4, 11, 19, 63; PC 9**
See also Grieve, C(hristopher) M(urray)
See also CDBLB 1945-1960; DLB 20

MacDonald, Anson

See Heinlein, Robert A(nson)
Macdonald, Cynthia 1928- .... **CLC 13, 19**
See also CA 49-52; CANR 4, 44; DLB 105
MacDonald, George 1824-1905 .... **TCLC 9**
See also CA 106; 137; DLB 18, 163, 178;
MAICYA; SATA 33, 100
Macdonald, John
See Millar, Kenneth
MacDonald, John D(ann) 1916-1986 **CLC 3,
27, 44; DAM NOV, POP**
See also CA 1-4R; 121; CANR 1, 19, 60; DLB
8; DLBY 86; MTCW 1
Macdonald, John Ross
See Millar, Kenneth
Macdonald, Ross .... **CLC 1, 2, 3, 14, 34, 41**
See also Millar, Kenneth
See also DLBD 6
MacDougal, John
See Blish, James (Benjamin)
MacEwen, Gwendolyn (Margaret) 1941-1987
CLC 13, 55
See also CA 9-12R; 124; CANR 7, 22; DLB
53; SATA 50; SATA-Obit 55
Macha, Karel Hynek 1810-1846 .... **NCLC 46**
Machado (y Ruiz), Antonio 1875-1939**T C L C
3**
See also CA 104; DLB 108
Machado de Assis, Joaquim Maria 1839-1908
TCLC 10; BLC 2; SSC 24
See also CA 107; 153
Machen, Arthur .... **TCLC 4; SSC 20**
See also Jones, Arthur Llewellyn
See also DLB 36, 156, 178
Machiavelli, Niccolo 1469-1527**LC 8, 36; DA;
DAB; DAC; DAM MST; WLCS**
MacInnes, Colin 1914-1976 .... **CLC 4, 23**
See also CA 69-72; 65-68; CANR 21; DLB 14;
MTCW 1
MacInnes, Helen (Clark) 1907-1985 **CLC 27,
39; DAM POP**
See also CA 1-4R; 117; CANR 1, 28, 58; DLB
87; MTCW 1; SATA 22; SATA-Obit 44
Mackay, Mary 1855-1924
See Corelli, Marie
See also CA 118
Mackenzie, Compton (Edward Montague)
1883-1972 .... **CLC 18**
See also CA 21-22; 37-40R; CAP 2; DLB 34,
100
Mackenzie, Henry 1745-1831 .... **NCLC 41**
See also DLB 39
Mackintosh, Elizabeth 1896(?)-1952
See Tey, Josephine
See also CA 110
MacLaren, James
See Grieve, C(hristopher) M(urray)
Mac Laverty, Bernard 1942- .... **CLC 31**
See also CA 116; 118; CANR 43; INT 118
MacLean, Alistair (Stuart) 1922(?)-1987**C L C
3, 13, 50, 63; DAM POP**
See also CA 57-60; 121; CANR 28, 61; MTCW
1; SATA 23; SATA-Obit 50
Maclean, Norman (Fitzroy) 1902-1990 **C L C
78; DAM POP; SSC 13**
See also CA 102; 132; CANR 49
MacLeish, Archibald 1892-1982**CLC 3, 8, 14,
68; DAM POET**
See also CA 9-12R; 106; CANR 33, 63; DLB
4, 7, 45; DLBY 82; MTCW 1
MacLennan, (John) Hugh 1907-1990 **CLC 2,
14, 92; DAC; DAM MST**
See also CA 5-8R; 142; CANR 33; DLB 68;
MTCW 1
MacLeod, Alistair 1936-**CLC 56; DAC; DAM
MST**
See also CA 123; DLB 60
Macleod, Fiona

See Sharp, William
MacNeice, (Frederick) Louis 1907-1963**C L C
1, 4, 10, 53; DAB; DAM POET**
See also CA 85-88; CANR 61; DLB 10, 20;
MTCW 1
MacNeill, Dand
See Fraser, George MacDonald
Macpherson, James 1736-1796 .... **LC 29**
See also Ossian
See also DLB 109
Macpherson, (Jean) Jay 1931- .... **CLC 14**
See also CA 5-8R; DLB 53
MacShane, Frank 1927- .... **CLC 39**
See also CA 9-12R; CANR 3, 33; DLB 111
Macumber, Mari
See Sandoz, Mari(e Susette)
Madach, Imre 1823-1864 .... **NCLC 19**
Madden, (Jerry) David 1933-........**CLC 5, 15**
See also CA 1-4R; CAAS 3; CANR 4, 45; DLB
6; MTCW 1
Maddern, Al(an)
See Ellison, Harlan (Jay)
Madhubuti, Haki R. 1942-**CLC 6, 73; BLC 2;
DAM MULT, POET; PC 5**
See also Lee, Don L.
See also BW 2; CA 73-76; CANR 24, 51; DLB
5, 41; DLBD 8
Maepenn, Hugh
See Kuttner, Henry
Maepenn, K. H.
See Kuttner, Henry
Maeterlinck, Maurice 1862-1949 ... **TCLC 3;
DAM DRAM**
See also CA 104; 136; DLB 192; SATA 66
Maginn, William 1794-1842 .... **NCLC 8**
See also DLB 110, 159
Mahapatra, Jayanta 1928- .... **CLC 33; DAM
MULT**
See also CA 73-76; CAAS 9; CANR 15, 33, 66
Mahfouz, Naguib (Abdel Aziz Al-Sabilgi)
1911(?)-
See Mahfuz, Najib
See also BEST 89:2; CA 128; CANR 55; DAM
NOV; MTCW 1
Mahfuz, Najib .... **CLC 52, 55**
See also Mahfouz, Naguib (Abdel Aziz Al-
Sabilgi)
See also DLBY 88
Mahon, Derek 1941- .... **CLC 27**
See also CA 113; 128; DLB 40
Mailer, Norman 1923-**CLC 1, 2, 3, 4, 5, 8, 11,
14, 28, 39, 74, 111; DA; DAB; DAC; DAM
MST, NOV, POP**
See also AITN 2; CA 9-12R; CABS 1; CANR
28; CDALB 1968-1988; DLB 2, 16, 28, 185;
DLBD 3; DLBY 80, 83; MTCW 1
Maillet, Antonine 1929- .... **CLC 54; DAC**
See also CA 115; 120; CANR 46; DLB 60; INT
120
Mais, Roger 1905-1955 .... **TCLC 8**
See also BW 1; CA 105; 124; DLB 125; MTCW
1
Maistre, Joseph de 1753-1821 .... **NCLC 37**
Maitland, Frederic 1850-1906 .... **TCLC 65**
Maitland, Sara (Louise) 1950- .... **CLC 49**
See also CA 69-72; CANR 13, 59
Major, Clarence 1936-**CLC 3, 19, 48; BLC 2;
DAM MULT**
See also BW 2; CA 21-24R; CAAS 6; CANR
13, 25, 53; DLB 33
Major, Kevin (Gerald) 1949-..**CLC 26; DAC**
See also AAYA 16; CA 97-100; CANR 21, 38;
CLR 11; DLB 60; INT CANR-21; JRDA;
MAICYA; SATA 32, 82
Maki, James
See Ozu, Yasujiro
Malabaila, Damiano

See Levi, Primo
Malamud, Bernard 1914-1986**CLC 1, 2, 3, 5,
8, 9, 11, 18, 27, 44, 78, 85; DA; DAB; DAC;
DAM MST, NOV, POP; SSC 15; WLC**
See also AAYA 16; CA 5-8R; 118; CABS 1;
CANR 28, 62; CDALB 1941-1968; DLB 2,
28, 152; DLBY 80, 86; MTCW 1
Malan, Herman
See Bosman, Herman Charles; Bosman, Herman
Charles
Malaparte, Curzio 1898-1957 .... **TCLC 52**
Malcolm, Dan
See Silverberg, Robert
Malcolm X .... **CLC 82; BLC 2; WLCS**
See also Little, Malcolm
Malherbe, Francois de 1555-1628 .... **LC 5**
Mallarme, Stephane 1842-1898 **NCLC 4, 41;
DAM POET; PC 4**
Mallet-Joris, Francoise 1930- .... **CLC 11**
See also CA 65-68; CANR 17; DLB 83
Malley, Ern
See McAuley, James Phillip
Mallowan, Agatha Christie
See Christie, Agatha (Mary Clarissa)
Maloff, Saul 1922- .... **CLC 5**
See also CA 33-36R
Malone, Louis
See MacNeice, (Frederick) Louis
Malone, Michael (Christopher) 1942-**CLC 43**
See also CA 77-80; CANR 14, 32, 57
Malory, (Sir) Thomas 1410(?)-1471(?)**LC 11;
DA; DAB; DAC; DAM MST; WLCS**
See also CDBLB Before 1660; DLB 146; SATA
59; SATA-Brief 33
Malouf, (George Joseph) David 1934-**CLC 28,
86**
See also CA 124; CANR 50
Malraux, (Georges-)Andre 1901-1976**CLC 1,
4, 9, 13, 15, 57; DAM NOV**
See also CA 21-22; 69-72; CANR 34, 58; CAP
2; DLB 72; MTCW 1
Malzberg, Barry N(athaniel) 1939- ... **CLC 7**
See also CA 61-64; CAAS 4; CANR 16; DLB
8
Mamet, David (Alan) 1947-**CLC 9, 15, 34, 46,
91; DAM DRAM; DC 4**
See also AAYA 3; CA 81-84; CABS 3; CANR
15, 41, 67, 72; DLB 7; MTCW 1
Mamoulian, Rouben (Zachary) 1897-1987
CLC 16
See also CA 25-28R; 124
Mandelstam, Osip (Emilievich) 1891(?)-1938(?)
TCLC 2, 6; PC 14
See also CA 104; 150
Mander, (Mary) Jane 1877-1949 ... **TCLC 31**
See also CA 162
Mandeville, John fl. 1350- .... **CMLC 19**
See also DLB 146
Mandiargues, Andre Pieyre de .... **CLC 41**
See also Pieyre de Mandiargues, Andre
See also DLB 83
Mandrake, Ethel Belle
See Thurman, Wallace (Henry)
Mangan, James Clarence 1803-1849**NCLC 27**
Maniere, J.-E.
See Giraudoux, (Hippolyte) Jean
Mankiewicz, Herman (Jacob) 1897-1953
TCLC 85
See also CA 120; DLB 26
Manley, (Mary) Delariviere 1672(?)-1724 **L C
1**
See also DLB 39, 80
Mann, Abel
See Creasey, John
Mann, Emily 1952- .... **DC 7**
See also CA 130; CANR 55
Mann, (Luiz) Heinrich 1871-1950 ... **TCLC 9**

See also CA 106; 164; DLB 66
Mann, (Paul) Thomas 1875-1955 **TCLC 2, 8, 14, 21, 35, 44, 60; DA; DAB; DAC; DAM MST, NOV; SSC 5; WLC**
See also CA 104; 128; DLB 66; MTCW 1
Mannheim, Karl 1893-1947 .... **TCLC 65**
Manning, David
See Faust, Frederick (Schiller)
Manning, Frederic 1887(?)-1935 ... **TCLC 25**
See also CA 124
Manning, Olivia 1915-1980 .... **CLC 5, 19**
See also CA 5-8R; 101; CANR 29; MTCW 1
Mano, D. Keith 1942- .... **CLC 2, 10**
See also CA 25-28R; CAAS 6; CANR 26, 57; DLB 6
Mansfield, Katherine **TCLC 2, 8, 39; DAB; SSC 9, 23; WLC**
See also Beauchamp, Kathleen Mansfield
See also DLB 162
Manso, Peter 1940- .... **CLC 39**
See also CA 29-32R; CANR 44
Mantecon, Juan Jimenez
See Jimenez (Mantecon), Juan Ramon
Manton, Peter
See Creasey, John
Man Without a Spleen, A
See Chekhov, Anton (Pavlovich)
Manzoni, Alessandro 1785-1873 .... **NCLC 29**
Mapu, Abraham (ben Jekutiel) 1808-1867 **NCLC 18**
Mara, Sally
See Queneau, Raymond
Marat, Jean Paul 1743-1793 .... **LC 10**
Marcel, Gabriel Honore 1889-1973 . **CLC 15**
See also CA 102; 45-48; MTCW 1
Marchbanks, Samuel
See Davies, (William) Robertson
Marchi, Giacomo
See Bassani, Giorgio
Margulies, Donald .... **CLC 76**
Marie de France c. 12th cent. - **CMLC 8; PC 22**
Marie de l'Incarnation 1599-1672 ...... **LC 10**
Marier, Captain Victor
See Griffith, D(avid Lewelyn) W(ark)
Mariner, Scott
See Pohl, Frederik
Marinetti, Filippo Tommaso 1876-1944 **TCLC 10**
See also CA 107; DLB 114
Marivaux, Pierre Carlet de Chamblain de 1688-1763 .... **LC 4; DC 7**
Markandaya, Kamala .... **CLC 8, 38**
See also Taylor, Kamala (Purnaiya)
Markfield, Wallace 1926- .... **CLC 8**
See also CA 69-72; CAAS 3; DLB 2, 28
Markham, Edwin 1852-1940 .... **TCLC 47**
See also CA 160; DLB 54, 186
Markham, Robert
See Amis, Kingsley (William)
Marks, J
See Highwater, Jamake (Mamake)
Marks-Highwater, J
See Highwater, Jamake (Mamake)
Markson, David M(errill) 1927- .... **CLC 67**
See also CA 49-52; CANR 1
Marley, Bob .... **CLC 17**
See also Marley, Robert Nesta
Marley, Robert Nesta 1945-1981
See Marley, Bob
See also CA 107; 103
Marlowe, Christopher 1564-1593 **LC 22; DA; DAB; DAC; DAM DRAM, MST; DC 1; WLC**
See also CDBLB Before 1660; DLB 62
Marlowe, Stephen 1928-
See Queen, Ellery

See also CA 13-16R; CANR 6, 55
Marmontel, Jean-Francois 1723-1799 .. **LC 2**
Marquand, John P(hillips) 1893-1960 **CLC 2, 10**
See also CA 85-88; DLB 9, 102
Marques, Rene 1919-1979 ..... **CLC 96; DAM MULT; HLC**
See also CA 97-100; 85-88; DLB 113; HW
Marquez, Gabriel (Jose) Garcia
See Garcia Marquez, Gabriel (Jose)
Marquis, Don(ald Robert Perry) 1878-1937 **TCLC 7**
See also CA 104; 166; DLB 11, 25
Marric, J. J.
See Creasey, John
Marryat, Frederick 1792-1848 .... **NCLC 3**
See also DLB 21, 163
Marsden, James
See Creasey, John
Marsh, (Edith) Ngaio 1899-1982 **CLC 7, 53; DAM POP**
See also CA 9-12R; CANR 6, 58; DLB 77; MTCW 1
Marshall, Garry 1934- .... **CLC 17**
See also AAYA 3; CA 111; SATA 60
Marshall, Paule 1929- .. **CLC 27, 72; BLC 3; DAM MULT; SSC 3**
See also BW 2; CA 77-80; CANR 25; DLB 157; MTCW 1
Marshallik
See Zangwill, Israel
Marsten, Richard
See Hunter, Evan
Marston, John 1576-1634 **LC 33; DAM DRAM**
See also DLB 58, 172
Martha, Henry
See Harris, Mark
Marti, Jose 1853-1895 **NCLC 63; DAM MULT; HLC**
Martial c. 40-c. 104 .... **PC 10**
Martin, Ken
See Hubbard, L(afayette) Ron(ald)
Martin, Richard
See Creasey, John
Martin, Steve 1945- .... **CLC 30**
See also CA 97-100; CANR 30; MTCW 1
Martin, Valerie 1948- .... **CLC 89**
See also BEST 90:2; CA 85-88; CANR 49
Martin, Violet Florence 1862-1915 **TCLC 51**
Martin, Webber
See Silverberg, Robert
Martindale, Patrick Victor
See White, Patrick (Victor Martindale)
Martin du Gard, Roger 1881-1958 **TCLC 24**
See also CA 118; DLB 65
Martineau, Harriet 1802-1876 .... **NCLC 26**
See also DLB 21, 55, 159, 163, 166, 190; YABC 2
Martines, Julia
See O'Faolain, Julia
Martinez, Enrique Gonzalez
See Gonzalez Martinez, Enrique
Martinez, Jacinto Benavente y
See Benavente (y Martinez), Jacinto
Martinez Ruiz, Jose 1873-1967
See Azorin; Ruiz, Jose Martinez
See also CA 93-96; HW
Martinez Sierra, Gregorio 1881-1947 **TCLC 6**
See also CA 115
Martinez Sierra, Maria (de la O'LeJarraga) 1874-1974 ....
TCLC 6
See also CA 115
Martinsen, Martin
See Follett, Ken(neth Martin)
Martinson, Harry (Edmund) 1904-1978 **CLC 14**

See also CA 77-80; CANR 34
Marut, Ret
See Traven, B.
Marut, Robert
See Traven, B.
Marvell, Andrew 1621-1678 ... **LC 4, 43; DA; DAB; DAC; DAM MST, POET; PC 10; WLC**
See also CDBLB 1660-1789; DLB 131
Marx, Karl (Heinrich) 1818-1883 . **NCLC 17**
See also DLB 129
Masaoka Shiki .... **TCLC 18**
See also Masaoka Tsunenori
Masaoka Tsunenori 1867-1902
See Masaoka Shiki
See also CA 117
Masefield, John (Edward) 1878-1967 **CLC 11, 47; DAM POET**
See also CA 19-20; 25-28R; CANR 33; CAP 2; CDBLB 1890-1914; DLB 10, 19, 153, 160; MTCW 1; SATA 19
Maso, Carole 19(?)- .... **CLC 44**
Mason, Bobbie Ann 1940- **CLC 28, 43, 82; SSC 4**
See also AAYA 5; CA 53-56; CANR 11, 31, 58; DLB 173; DLBY 87; INT CANR-31; MTCW 1
Mason, Ernst
See Pohl, Frederik
Mason, Lee W.
See Malzberg, Barry N(athaniel)
Mason, Nick 1945- .... **CLC 35**
Mason, Tally
See Derleth, August (William)
Mass, William
See Gibson, William
Master Lao
See Lao Tzu
Masters, Edgar Lee 1868-1950 **TCLC 2, 25; DA; DAC; DAM MST, POET; PC 1; WLCS**
See also CA 104; 133; CDALB 1865-1917; DLB 54; MTCW 1
Masters, Hilary 1928- .... **CLC 48**
See also CA 25-28R; CANR 13, 47
Mastrosimone, William 19(?)- .... **CLC 36**
Mathe, Albert
See Camus, Albert
Mather, Cotton 1663-1728 .... **LC 38**
See also CDALB 1640-1865; DLB 24, 30, 140
Mather, Increase 1639-1723 .... **LC 38**
See also DLB 24
Matheson, Richard Burton 1926- ..... **CLC 37**
See also CA 97-100; DLB 8, 44; INT 97-100
Mathews, Harry 1930- .... **CLC 6, 52**
See also CA 21-24R; CAAS 6; CANR 18, 40
Mathews, John Joseph 1894-1979 .. **CLC 84; DAM MULT**
See also CA 19-20; 142; CANR 45; CAP 2; DLB 175; NNAL
Mathias, Roland (Glyn) 1915- .... **CLC 45**
See also CA 97-100; CANR 19, 41; DLB 27
Matsuo Basho 1644-1694 .... **PC 3**
See also DAM POET
Mattheson, Rodney
See Creasey, John
Matthews, Greg 1949- .... **CLC 45**
See also CA 135
Matthews, William (Procter, III) 1942-1997 **CLC 40**
See also CA 29-32R; 162; CAAS 18; CANR 12, 57; DLB 5
Matthias, John (Edward) 1941- .... **CLC 9**
See also CA 33-36R; CANR 56
Matthiessen, Peter 1927- **CLC 5, 7, 11, 32, 64; DAM NOV**
See also AAYA 6; BEST 90:4; CA 9-12R;

Author Index

See Slade, Bernard
See also CA 81-84; CANR 49; DAM DRAM

Newby, P(ercy) H(oward) 1918-1997 **CLC 2, 13; DAM NOV**
See also CA 5-8R; 161; CANR 32, 67; DLB 15; MTCW 1

Newlove, Donald 1928- .... **CLC 6**
See also CA 29-32R; CANR 25

Newlove, John (Herbert) 1938- .... **CLC 14**
See also CA 21-24R; CANR 9, 25

Newman, Charles 1938- .... **CLC 2, 8**
See also CA 21-24R

Newman, Edwin (Harold) 1919- .... **CLC 14**
See also AITN 1; CA 69-72; CANR 5

Newman, John Henry 1801-1890 .. **NCLC 38**
See also DLB 18, 32, 55

Newton, Suzanne 1936- .... **CLC 35**
See also CA 41-44R; CANR 14; JRDA; SATA 5, 77

Nexo, Martin Andersen 1869-1954 **TCLC 43**

Nezval, Vitezslav 1900-1958 .... **TCLC 44**
See also CA 123

Ng, Fae Myenne 1957(?)- .... **CLC 81**
See also CA 146

Ngema, Mbongeni 1955- .... **CLC 57**
See also BW 2; CA 143

Ngugi, James T(hiong'o) .... **CLC 3, 7, 13**
See also Ngugi wa Thiong'o

Ngugi wa Thiong'o 1938- .. **CLC 36; BLC 3; DAM MULT, NOV**
See also Ngugi, James T(hiong'o)
See also BW 2; CA 81-84; CANR 27, 58; DLB 125; MTCW 1

Nichol, B(arrie) P(hillip) 1944-1988 **CLC 18**
See also CA 53-56; DLB 53; SATA 66

Nichols, John (Treadwell) 1940- .... **CLC 38**
See also CA 9-12R; CAAS 2; CANR 6, 70; DLBY 82

Nichols, Leigh
See Koontz, Dean R(ay)

Nichols, Peter (Richard) 1927- **CLC 5, 36, 65**
See also CA 104; CANR 33; DLB 13; MTCW 1

Nicolas, F. R. E.
See Freeling, Nicolas

Niedecker, Lorine 1903-1970 .... **CLC 10, 42; DAM POET**
See also CA 25-28; CAP 2; DLB 48

Nietzsche, Friedrich (Wilhelm) 1844-1900 **TCLC 10, 18, 55**
See also CA 107; 121; DLB 129

Nievo, Ippolito 1831-1861 .... **NCLC 22**

Nightingale, Anne Redmon 1943-
See Redmon, Anne
See also CA 103

Nightingale, Florence 1820-1910 ... **TCLC 85**
See also DLB 166

Nik. T. O.
See Annensky, Innokenty (Fyodorovich)

Nin, Anais 1903-1977 **CLC 1, 4, 8, 11, 14, 60; DAM NOV, POP; SSC 10**
See also AITN 2; CA 13-16R; 69-72; CANR 22, 53; DLB 2, 4, 152; MTCW 1

Nishida, Kitaro 1870-1945 .... **TCLC 83**

Nishiwaki, Junzaburo 1894-1982 .... **PC 15**
See also CA 107

Nissenson, Hugh 1933- .... **CLC 4, 9**
See also CA 17-20R; CANR 27; DLB 28

Niven, Larry .... **CLC 8**
See also Niven, Laurence Van Cott
See also AAYA 27; DLB 8

Niven, Laurence Van Cott 1938-
See Niven, Larry
See also CA 21-24R; CAAS 12; CANR 14, 44, 66; DAM POP; MTCW 1; SATA 95

Nixon, Agnes Eckhardt 1927- .... **CLC 21**
See also CA 110

Nizan, Paul 1905-1940 .... **TCLC 40**
See also CA 161; DLB 72

Nkosi, Lewis 1936- .... **CLC 45; BLC 3; DAM MULT**
See also BW 1; CA 65-68; CANR 27; DLB 157

Nodier, (Jean) Charles (Emmanuel) 1780-1844 **NCLC 19**
See also DLB 119

Noguchi, Yone 1875-1947 .... **TCLC 80**

Nolan, Christopher 1965- .... **CLC 58**
See also CA 111

Noon, Jeff 1957- .... **CLC 91**
See also CA 148

Norden, Charles
See Durrell, Lawrence (George)

Nordhoff, Charles (Bernard) 1887-1947 **TCLC 23**
See also CA 108; DLB 9; SATA 23

Norfolk, Lawrence 1963- .... **CLC 76**
See also CA 144

Norman, Marsha 1947- **CLC 28; DAM DRAM; DC 8**
See also CA 105; CABS 3; CANR 41; DLBY 84

Normyx
See Douglas, (George) Norman

Norris, Frank 1870-1902 .... **SSC 28**
See also Norris, (Benjamin) Frank(lin, Jr.)
See also CDALB 1865-1917; DLB 12, 71, 186

Norris, (Benjamin) Frank(lin, Jr.) 1870-1902 **TCLC 24**
See also Norris, Frank
See also CA 110; 160

Norris, Leslie 1921- .... **CLC 14**
See also CA 11-12; CANR 14; CAP 1; DLB 27

North, Andrew
See Norton, Andre

North, Anthony
See Koontz, Dean R(ay)

North, Captain George
See Stevenson, Robert Louis (Balfour)

North, Milou
See Erdrich, Louise

Northrup, B. A.
See Hubbard, L(afayette) Ron(ald)

North Staffs
See Hulme, T(homas) E(rnest)

Norton, Alice Mary
See Norton, Andre
See also MAICYA; SATA 1, 43

Norton, Andre 1912- .... **CLC 12**
See also Norton, Alice Mary
See also AAYA 14; CA 1-4R; CANR 68; CLR 50; DLB 8, 52; JRDA; MTCW 1; SATA 91

Norton, Caroline 1808-1877 .... **NCLC 47**
See also DLB 21, 159, 199

Norway, Nevil Shute 1899-1960
See Shute, Nevil
See also CA 102; 93-96

Norwid, Cyprian Kamil 1821-1883 **NCLC 17**

Nosille, Nabrah
See Ellison, Harlan (Jay)

Nossack, Hans Erich 1901-1978 .... **CLC 6**
See also CA 93-96; 85-88; DLB 69

Nostradamus 1503-1566 .... **LC 27**

Nosu, Chuji
See Ozu, Yasujiro

Notenburg, Eleanora (Genrikhovna) von
See Guro, Elena

Nova, Craig 1945- .... **CLC 7, 31**
See also CA 45-48; CANR 2, 53

Novak, Joseph
See Kosinski, Jerzy (Nikodem)

Novalis 1772-1801 .... **NCLC 13**
See also DLB 90

Novis, Emile
See Weil, Simone (Adolphine)

Nowlan, Alden (Albert) 1933-1983 **CLC 15; DAC; DAM MST**
See also CA 9-12R; CANR 5; DLB 53

Noyes, Alfred 1880-1958 .... **TCLC 7**
See also CA 104; DLB 20

Nunn, Kem .... **CLC 34**
See also CA 159

Nye, Robert 1939- .. **CLC 13, 42; DAM NOV**
See also CA 33-36R; CANR 29, 67; DLB 14; MTCW 1; SATA 6

Nyro, Laura 1947- .... **CLC 17**

Oates, Joyce Carol 1938-**CLC 1, 2, 3, 6, 9, 11, 15, 19, 33, 52, 108; DA; DAB; DAC; DAM MST, NOV, POP; SSC 6; WLC**
See also AAYA 15; AITN 1; BEST 89:2; CA 5-8R; CANR 25, 45; CDALB 1968-1988; DLB 2, 5, 130; DLBY 81; INT CANR-25; MTCW 1

O'Brien, Darcy 1939-1998 .... **CLC 11**
See also CA 21-24R; 167; CANR 8, 59

O'Brien, E. G.
See Clarke, Arthur C(harles)

O'Brien, Edna 1936- **CLC 3, 5, 8, 13, 36, 65; DAM NOV; SSC 10**
See also CA 1-4R; CANR 6, 41, 65; CDBLB 1960 to Present; DLB 14; MTCW 1

O'Brien, Fitz-James 1828-1862 ..... **NCLC 21**
See also DLB 74

O'Brien, Flann .... **CLC 1, 4, 5, 7, 10, 47**
See also O Nuallain, Brian

O'Brien, Richard 1942- .... **CLC 17**
See also CA 124

O'Brien, (William) Tim(othy) 1946- . **CLC 7, 19, 40, 103; DAM POP**
See also AAYA 16; CA 85-88; CANR 40, 58; DLB 152; DLBD 9; DLBY 80

Obstfelder, Sigbjoern 1866-1900 ... **TCLC 23**
See also CA 123

O'Casey, Sean 1880-1964**CLC 1, 5, 9, 11, 15, 88; DAB; DAC; DAM DRAM, MST; WLCS**
See also CA 89-92; CANR 62; CDBLB 1914-1945; DLB 10; MTCW 1

O'Cathasaigh, Sean
See O'Casey, Sean

Ochs, Phil 1940-1976 .... **CLC 17**
See also CA 65-68

O'Connor, Edwin (Greene) 1918-1968**CLC 14**
See also CA 93-96; 25-28R

O'Connor, (Mary) Flannery 1925-1964 **C L C 1, 2, 3, 6, 10, 13, 15, 21, 66, 104; DA; DAB; DAC; DAM MST, NOV; SSC 1, 23; WLC**
See also AAYA 7; CA 1-4R; CANR 3, 41; CDALB 1941-1968; DLB 2, 152; DLBD 12; DLBY 80; MTCW 1

O'Connor, Frank .... **CLC 23; SSC 5**
See also O'Donovan, Michael John
See also DLB 162

O'Dell, Scott 1898-1989 .... **CLC 30**
See also AAYA 3; CA 61-64; 129; CANR 12, 30; CLR 1, 16; DLB 52; JRDA; MAICYA; SATA 12, 60

Odets, Clifford 1906-1963**CLC 2, 28, 98; DAM DRAM; DC 6**
See also CA 85-88; CANR 62; DLB 7, 26; MTCW 1

O'Doherty, Brian 1934- .... **CLC 76**
See also CA 105

O'Donnell, K. M.
See Malzberg, Barry N(athaniel)

O'Donnell, Lawrence
See Kuttner, Henry

O'Donovan, Michael John 1903-1966**CLC 14**
See also O'Connor, Frank
See also CA 93-96

Oe, Kenzaburo 1935- **CLC 10, 36, 86; DAM NOV; SSC 20**

13, 33
See also CA 85-88; DLB 40
Porter, William Sydney 1862-1910
See Henry, O.
See also CA 104; 131; CDALB 1865-1917; DA;
DAB; DAC; DAM MST; DLB 12, 78, 79;
MTCW 1; YABC 2
Portillo (y Pacheco), Jose Lopez
See Lopez Portillo (y Pacheco), Jose
Post, Melville Davisson 1869-1930 **TCLC 39**
See also CA 110
Potok, Chaim 1929- ... **CLC 2, 7, 14, 26, 112;
DAM NOV**
See also AAYA 15; AITN 1, 2; CA 17-20R;
CANR 19, 35, 64; DLB 28, 152; INT CANR-
19; MTCW 1; SATA 33
Potter, (Helen) Beatrix 1866-1943
See Webb, (Martha) Beatrice (Potter)
See also MAICYA
Potter, Dennis (Christopher George) 1935-1994
CLC 58, 86
See also CA 107; 145; CANR 33, 61; MTCW 1
Pound, Ezra (Weston Loomis) 1885-1972
**CLC 1, 2, 3, 4, 5, 7, 10, 13, 18, 34, 48, 50,
112; DA; DAB; DAC; DAM MST, POET;
PC 4; WLC**
See also CA 5-8R; 37-40R; CANR 40; CDALB
1917-1929; DLB 4, 45, 63; DLBD 15;
MTCW 1
Povod, Reinaldo 1959-1994 .... **CLC 44**
See also CA 136; 146
Powell, Adam Clayton, Jr. 1908-1972**CLC 89;
BLC 3; DAM MULT**
See also BW 1; CA 102; 33-36R
Powell, Anthony (Dymoke) 1905-**CLC 1, 3, 7,
9, 10, 31**
See also CA 1-4R; CANR 1, 32, 62; CDBLB
1945-1960; DLB 15; MTCW 1
Powell, Dawn 1897-1965 .... **CLC 66**
See also CA 5-8R; DLBY 97
Powell, Padgett 1952- .... **CLC 34**
See also CA 126; CANR 63
Power, Susan 1961- .... **CLC 91**
Powers, J(ames) F(arl) 1917-**CLC 1, 4, 8, 57;
SSC 4**
See also CA 1-4R; CANR 2, 61; DLB 130;
MTCW 1
Powers, John J(ames) 1945-
See Powers, John R.
See also CA 69-72
Powers, John R. .... **CLC 66**
See also Powers, John J(ames)
Powers, Richard (S.) 1957- .... **CLC 93**
See also CA 148
Pownall, David 1938- .... **CLC 10**
See also CA 89-92; CAAS 18; CANR 49; DLB
14
Powys, John Cowper 1872-1963**CLC 7, 9, 15,
46**
See also CA 85-88; DLB 15; MTCW 1
Powys, T(heodore) F(rancis) 1875-1953
TCLC 9
See also CA 106; DLB 36, 162
Prado (Calvo), Pedro 1886-1952 ... **TCLC 75**
See also CA 131; HW
Prager, Emily 1952- .... **CLC 56**
Pratt, E(dwin) J(ohn) 1883(?)-1964 **CLC 19;
DAC; DAM POET**
See also CA 141; 93-96; DLB 92
Premchand .... **TCLC 21**
See also Srivastava, Dhanpat Rai
Preussler, Otfried 1923- .... **CLC 17**
See also CA 77-80; SATA 24
Prevert, Jacques (Henri Marie) 1900-1977
CLC 15
See also CA 77-80; 69-72; CANR 29, 61;
MTCW 1; SATA-Obit 30

Prevost, Abbe (Antoine Francois) 1697-1763
LC 1
Price, (Edward) Reynolds 1933-**CLC 3, 6, 13,
43, 50, 63; DAM NOV; SSC 22**
See also CA 1-4R; CANR 1, 37, 57; DLB 2;
INT CANR-37
Price, Richard 1949- .... **CLC 6, 12**
See also CA 49-52; CANR 3; DLBY 81
Prichard, Katharine Susannah 1883-1969
CLC 46
See also CA 11-12; CANR 33; CAP 1; MTCW
1; SATA 66
Priestley, J(ohn) B(oynton) 1894-1984**CLC 2,
5, 9, 34; DAM DRAM, NOV**
See also CA 9-12R; 113; CANR 33; CDBLB
1914-1945; DLB 10, 34, 77, 100, 139; DLBY
84; MTCW 1
Prince 1958(?)- .... **CLC 35**
Prince, F(rank) T(empleton) 1912- .. **CLC 22**
See also CA 101; CANR 43; DLB 20
Prince Kropotkin
See Kropotkin, Peter (Aleksieevich)
Prior, Matthew 1664-1721 .... **LC 4**
See also DLB 95
Prishvin, Mikhail 1873-1954 .... **TCLC 75**
Pritchard, William H(arrison) 1932-**CLC 34**
See also CA 65-68; CANR 23; DLB 111
Pritchett, V(ictor) S(awdon) 1900-1997 **C L C
5, 13, 15, 41; DAM NOV; SSC 14**
See also CA 61-64; 157; CANR 31, 63; DLB
15, 139; MTCW 1
Private 19022
See Manning, Frederic
Probst, Mark 1925- .... **CLC 59**
See also CA 130
Prokosch, Frederic 1908-1989 ...... **CLC 4, 48**
See also CA 73-76; 128; DLB 48
Prophet, The
See Dreiser, Theodore (Herman Albert)
Prose, Francine 1947- .... **CLC 45**
See also CA 109; 112; CANR 46; SATA 101
Proudhon
See Cunha, Euclides (Rodrigues Pimenta) da
Proulx, Annie
See Proulx, E(dna) Annie
Proulx, E(dna) Annie 1935-... **CLC 81; DAM
POP**
See also CA 145; CANR 65
**Proust, (Valentin-Louis-George-Eugene-)
Marcel** 1871-1922 **TCLC 7, 13, 33; DA;
DAB; DAC; DAM MST, NOV; WLC**
See also CA 104; 120; DLB 65; MTCW 1
Prowler, Harley
See Masters, Edgar Lee
Prus, Boleslaw 1845-1912 .... **TCLC 48**
Pryor, Richard (Franklin Lenox Thomas) 1940-
CLC 26
See also CA 122
Przybyszewski, Stanislaw 1868-1927**TCLC 36**
See also CA 160; DLB 66
Pteleon
See Grieve, C(hristopher) M(urray)
See also DAM POET
Puckett, Lute
See Masters, Edgar Lee
Puig, Manuel 1932-1990**CLC 3, 5, 10, 28, 65;
DAM MULT; HLC**
See also CA 45-48; CANR 2, 32, 63; DLB 113;
HW; MTCW 1
Pulitzer, Joseph 1847-1911 .... **TCLC 76**
See also CA 114; DLB 23
Purdy, A(lfred) W(ellington) 1918-**CLC 3, 6,
14, 50; DAC; DAM MST, POET**
See also CA 81-84; CAAS 17; CANR 42, 66;
DLB 88
Purdy, James (Amos) 1923-**CLC 2, 4, 10, 28,
52**

See also CA 33-36R; CAAS 1; CANR 19, 51;
DLB 2; INT CANR-19; MTCW 1
Pure, Simon
See Swinnerton, Frank Arthur
Pushkin, Alexander (Sergeyevich) 1799-1837
**NCLC 3, 27; DA; DAB; DAC; DAM
DRAM, MST, POET; PC 10; SSC 27;
WLC**
See also SATA 61
P'u Sung-ling 1640-1715 .... **LC 3; SSC 31**
Putnam, Arthur Lee
See Alger, Horatio, Jr.
Puzo, Mario 1920-**CLC 1, 2, 6, 36, 107; DAM
NOV, POP**
See also CA 65-68; CANR 4, 42, 65; DLB 6;
MTCW 1
Pygge, Edward
See Barnes, Julian (Patrick)
Pyle, Ernest Taylor 1900-1945
See Pyle, Ernie
See also CA 115; 160
Pyle, Ernie 1900-1945 .... **TCLC 75**
See also Pyle, Ernest Taylor
See also DLB 29
Pyle, Howard 1853-1911 .... **TCLC 81**
See also CA 109; 137; CLR 22; DLB 42, 188;
DLBD 13; MAICYA; SATA 16, 100
Pym, Barbara (Mary Crampton) 1913-1980
CLC 13, 19, 37, 111
See also CA 13-14; 97-100; CANR 13, 34; CAP
1; DLB 14; DLBY 87; MTCW 1
Pynchon, Thomas (Ruggles, Jr.) 1937-**CLC 2,
3, 6, 9, 11, 18, 33, 62, 72; DA; DAB; DAC;
DAM MST, NOV, POP; SSC 14; WLC**
See also BEST 90:2; CA 17-20R; CANR 22,
46; DLB 2, 173; MTCW 1
Pythagoras c. 570B.C.-c. 500B.C. . **CMLC 22**
See also DLB 176
Q
See Quiller-Couch, SirArthur (Thomas)
Qian Zhongshu
See Ch'ien Chung-shu
Qroll
See Dagerman, Stig (Halvard)
Quarrington, Paul (Lewis) 1953- ..... **CLC 65**
See also CA 129; CANR 62
Quasimodo, Salvatore 1901-1968 ..... **CLC 10**
See also CA 13-16; 25-28R; CAP 1; DLB 114;
MTCW 1
Quay, Stephen 1947- .... **CLC 95**
Quay, Timothy 1947- .... **CLC 95**
Queen, Ellery .... **CLC 3, 11**
See also Dannay, Frederic; Davidson, Avram;
Lee, Manfred B(ennington); Marlowe,
Stephen; Sturgeon, Theodore (Hamilton);
Vance, John Holbrook
Queen, Ellery, Jr.
See Dannay, Frederic; Lee, Manfred
B(ennington)
Queneau, Raymond 1903-1976 **CLC 2, 5, 10,
42**
See also CA 77-80; 69-72; CANR 32; DLB 72;
MTCW 1
Quevedo, Francisco de 1580-1645 .... **LC 23**
Quiller-Couch, SirArthur (Thomas) 1863-1944
TCLC 53
See also CA 118; 166; DLB 135, 153, 190
Quin, Ann (Marie) 1936-1973 .... **CLC 6**
See also CA 9-12R; 45-48; DLB 14
Quinn, Martin
See Smith, Martin Cruz
Quinn, Peter 1947-............................. **CLC 91**
Quinn, Simon
See Smith, Martin Cruz
Quiroga, Horacio (Sylvestre) 1878-1937
TCLC 20; DAM MULT; HLC
See also CA 117; 131; HW; MTCW 1

51; DAM NOV; SSC 21
See also CA 25-28R; 85-88; CANR 35, 62;
CDBLB 1945-1960; DLB 36, 117, 162;
MTCW 1

Ribeiro, Darcy 1922-1997 .... **CLC 34**
See also CA 33-36R; 156

Ribeiro, Joao Ubaldo (Osorio Pimentel) 1941-
CLC 10, 67
See also CA 81-84

Ribman, Ronald (Burt) 1932- .... **CLC 7**
See also CA 21-24R; CANR 46

Ricci, Nino 1959-................................. **CLC 70**
See also CA 137

Rice, Anne 1941- .... **CLC 41; DAM POP**
See also AAYA 9; BEST 89:2; CA 65-68; CANR
12, 36, 53

Rice, Elmer (Leopold) 1892-1967 **CLC 7, 49;**
DAM DRAM
See also CA 21-22; 25-28R; CAP 2; DLB 4, 7;
MTCW 1

Rice, Tim(othy Miles Bindon) 1944- **CLC 21**
See also CA 103; CANR 46

Rich, Adrienne (Cecile) 1929-**CLC 3, 6, 7, 11,**
18, 36, 73, 76; DAM POET; PC 5
See also CA 9-12R; CANR 20, 53; DLB 5, 67;
MTCW 1

Rich, Barbara
See Graves, Robert (von Ranke)

Rich, Robert
See Trumbo, Dalton

Richard, Keith .... **CLC 17**
See also Richards, Keith

Richards, David Adams 1950- **CLC 59; DAC**
See also CA 93-96; CANR 60; DLB 53

Richards, I(vor) A(rmstrong) 1893-1979**C L C**
14, 24
See also CA 41-44R; 89-92; CANR 34; DLB
27

Richards, Keith 1943-
See Richard, Keith
See also CA 107

Richardson, Anne
See Roiphe, Anne (Richardson)

Richardson, Dorothy Miller 1873-1957**TCLC**
3
See also CA 104; DLB 36

Richardson, Ethel Florence (Lindesay) 1870-
1946
See Richardson, Henry Handel
See also CA 105

Richardson, Henry Handel .... **TCLC 4**
See also Richardson, Ethel Florence (Lindesay)
See also DLB 197

Richardson, John 1796-1852**NCLC 55; DAC**
See also DLB 99

Richardson, Samuel 1689-1761**LC 1, 44; DA;**
DAB; DAC; DAM MST, NOV; WLC
See also CDBLB 1660-1789; DLB 39

Richler, Mordecai 1931-**CLC 3, 5, 9, 13, 18, 46,**
70; DAC; DAM MST, NOV
See also AITN 1; CA 65-68; CANR 31, 62; CLR
17; DLB 53; MAICYA; MTCW 1; SATA 44,
98; SATA-Brief 27

Richter, Conrad (Michael) 1890-1968**CLC 30**
See also AAYA 21; CA 5-8R; 25-28R; CANR
23; DLB 9; MTCW 1; SATA 3

Ricostranza, Tom
See Ellis, Trey

Riddell, Charlotte 1832-1906 .... **TCLC 40**
See also CA 165; DLB 156

Riding, Laura .... **CLC 3, 7**
See also Jackson, Laura (Riding)

Riefenstahl, Berta Helene Amalia 1902-
See Riefenstahl, Leni
See also CA 108

Riefenstahl, Leni .... **CLC 16**
See also Riefenstahl, Berta Helene Amalia

Riffe, Ernest
See Bergman, (Ernst) Ingmar

Riggs, (Rolla) Lynn 1899-1954 ..... **TCLC 56;**
DAM MULT
See also CA 144; DLB 175; NNAL

Riis, Jacob A(ugust) 1849-1914 ..... **TCLC 80**
See also CA 113; 168; DLB 23

Riley, James Whitcomb 1849-1916**TCLC 51;**
DAM POET
See also CA 118; 137; MAICYA; SATA 17

Riley, Tex
See Creasey, John

Rilke, Rainer Maria 1875-1926**TCLC 1, 6, 19;**
DAM POET; PC 2
See also CA 104; 132; CANR 62; DLB 81;
MTCW 1

Rimbaud, (Jean Nicolas) Arthur 1854-1891
NCLC 4, 35; DA; DAB; DAC; DAM MST,
POET; PC 3; WLC

Rinehart, Mary Roberts 1876-1958**TCLC 52**
See also CA 108; 166

Ringmaster, The
See Mencken, H(enry) L(ouis)

Ringwood, Gwen(dolyn Margaret) Pharis
1910-1984 .... **CLC 48**
See also CA 148; 112; DLB 88

Rio, Michel 19(?)- .... **CLC 43**

Ritsos, Giannes
See Ritsos, Yannis

Ritsos, Yannis 1909-1990 .... **CLC 6, 13, 31**
See also CA 77-80; 133; CANR 39, 61; MTCW
1

Ritter, Erika 1948(?)- .... **CLC 52**

Rivera, Jose Eustasio 1889-1928 ... **TCLC 35**
See also CA 162; HW

Rivers, Conrad Kent 1933-1968 .... **CLC 1**
See also BW 1; CA 85-88; DLB 41

Rivers, Elfrida
See Bradley, Marion Zimmer

Riverside, John
See Heinlein, Robert A(nson)

Rizal, Jose 1861-1896 .... **NCLC 27**

Roa Bastos, Augusto (Antonio) 1917-**CLC 45;**
DAM MULT; HLC
See also CA 131; DLB 113; HW

Robbe-Grillet, Alain 1922-**CLC 1, 2, 4, 6, 8, 10,**
14, 43
See also CA 9-12R; CANR 33, 65; DLB 83;
MTCW 1

Robbins, Harold 1916-1997 ..... **CLC 5; DAM**
NOV
See also CA 73-76; 162; CANR 26, 54; MTCW
1

Robbins, Thomas Eugene 1936-
See Robbins, Tom
See also CA 81-84; CANR 29, 59; DAM NOV,
POP; MTCW 1

Robbins, Tom .... **CLC 9, 32, 64**
See also Robbins, Thomas Eugene
See also BEST 90:3; DLBY 80

Robbins, Trina 1938- .... **CLC 21**
See also CA 128

Roberts, Charles G(eorge) D(ouglas) 1860-1943
TCLC 8
See also CA 105; CLR 33; DLB 92; SATA 88;
SATA-Brief 29

Roberts, Elizabeth Madox 1886-1941 **T C L C**
68
See also CA 111; 166; DLB 9, 54, 102; SATA
33; SATA-Brief 27

Roberts, Kate 1891-1985 .... **CLC 15**
See also CA 107; 116

Roberts, Keith (John Kingston) 1935-**CLC 14**
See also CA 25-28R; CANR 46

Roberts, Kenneth (Lewis) 1885-1957**TCLC 23**
See also CA 109; DLB 9

Roberts, Michele (B.) 1949-............... **CLC 48**

See also CA 115; CANR 58

Robertson, Ellis
See Ellison, Harlan (Jay); Silverberg, Robert

Robertson, Thomas William 1829-1871**NCLC**
35; DAM DRAM

Robeson, Kenneth
See Dent, Lester

Robinson, Edwin Arlington 1869-1935**T C L C**
5; DA; DAC; DAM MST, POET; PC 1
See also CA 104; 133; CDALB 1865-1917;
DLB 54; MTCW 1

Robinson, Henry Crabb 1775-1867**NCLC 15**
See also DLB 107

Robinson, Jill 1936- .... **CLC 10**
See also CA 102; INT 102

Robinson, Kim Stanley 1952-............ **CLC 34**
See also AAYA 26; CA 126

Robinson, Lloyd
See Silverberg, Robert

Robinson, Marilynne 1944- .... **CLC 25**
See also CA 116

Robinson, Smokey .... **CLC 21**
See also Robinson, William, Jr.

Robinson, William, Jr. 1940-
See Robinson, Smokey
See also CA 116

Robison, Mary 1949- .... **CLC 42, 98**
See also CA 113; 116; DLB 130; INT 116

Rod, Edouard 1857-1910 .... **TCLC 52**

Roddenberry, Eugene Wesley 1921-1991
See Roddenberry, Gene
See also CA 110; 135; CANR 37; SATA 45;
SATA-Obit 69

Roddenberry, Gene .... **CLC 17**
See also Roddenberry, Eugene Wesley
See also AAYA 5; SATA-Obit 69

Rodgers, Mary 1931-........................... **CLC 12**
See also CA 49-52; CANR 8, 55; CLR 20; INT
CANR-8; JRDA; MAICYA; SATA 8

Rodgers, W(illiam) R(obert) 1909-1969**CLC 7**
See also CA 85-88; DLB 20

Rodman, Eric
See Silverberg, Robert

Rodman, Howard 1920(?)-1985 .... **CLC 65**
See also CA 118

Rodman, Maia
See Wojciechowska, Maia (Teresa)

Rodriguez, Claudio 1934- .... **CLC 10**
See also DLB 134

Roelvaag, O(le) E(dvart) 1876-1931**TCLC 17**
See also CA 117; DLB 9

Roethke, Theodore (Huebner) 1908-1963**CLC**
1, 3, 8, 11, 19, 46, 101; DAM POET; PC 15
See also CA 81-84; CABS 2; CDALB 1941-
1968; DLB 5; MTCW 1

Rogers, Samuel 1763-1855 .... **NCLC 69**
See also DLB 93

Rogers, Thomas Hunton 1927- .... **CLC 57**
See also CA 89-92; INT 89-92

Rogers, Will(iam Penn Adair) 1879-1935
TCLC 8, 71; DAM MULT
See also CA 105; 144; DLB 11; NNAL

Rogin, Gilbert 1929-........................... **CLC 18**
See also CA 65-68; CANR 15

Rohan, Koda .... **TCLC 22**
See also Koda Shigeyuki

Rohlfs, Anna Katharine Green
See Green, Anna Katharine

Rohmer, Eric .... **CLC 16**
See also Scherer, Jean-Marie Maurice

Rohmer, Sax .... **TCLC 28**
See also Ward, Arthur Henry Sarsfield
See also DLB 70

Roiphe, Anne (Richardson) 1935- .. **CLC 3, 9**
See also CA 89-92; CANR 45; DLBY 80; INT
89-92

Rojas, Fernando de 1465-1541 .... **LC 23**

Sadoff, Ira 1945- .... **CLC 9**
See also CA 53-56; CANR 5, 21; DLB 120
Saetone
See Camus, Albert
Safire, William 1929- .... **CLC 10**
See also CA 17-20R; CANR 31, 54
Sagan, Carl (Edward) 1934-1996**CLC 30, 112**
See also AAYA 2; CA 25-28R; 155; CANR 11,
36; MTCW 1; SATA 58; SATA-Obit 94
Sagan, Francoise .... **CLC 3, 6, 9, 17, 36**
See also Quoirez, Francoise
See also DLB 83
Sahgal, Nayantara (Pandit) 1927- .... **CLC 41**
See also CA 9-12R; CANR 11
Saint, H(arry) F. 1941- .... **CLC 50**
See also CA 127
St. Aubin de Teran, Lisa 1953-
See Teran, Lisa St. Aubin de
See also CA 118; 126; INT 126
Saint Birgitta of Sweden c. 1303-1373**CMLC 24**
Sainte-Beuve, Charles Augustin 1804-1869
NCLC 5
Saint-Exupery, Antoine (Jean Baptiste Marie
Roger) de 1900-1944**TCLC 2, 56; DAM NOV; WLC**
See also CA 108; 132; CLR 10; DLB 72;
MAICYA; MTCW 1; SATA 20
St. John, David
See Hunt, E(verette) Howard, (Jr.)
Saint-John Perse
See Leger, (Marie-Rene Auguste) Alexis Saint-Leger
Saintsbury, George (Edward Bateman) 1845-1933 .... **TCLC 31**
See also CA 160; DLB 57, 149
Sait Faik .... **TCLC 23**
See also Abasiyanik, Sait Faik
Saki .... **TCLC 3; SSC 12**
See also Munro, H(ector) H(ugh)
Sala, George Augustus .... **NCLC 46**
Salama, Hannu 1936- .... **CLC 18**
Salamanca, J(ack) R(ichard) 1922-**CLC 4, 15**
See also CA 25-28R
Sale, J. Kirkpatrick
See Sale, Kirkpatrick
Sale, Kirkpatrick 1937- .... **CLC 68**
See also CA 13-16R; CANR 10
Salinas, Luis Omar 1937- ...... **CLC 90; DAM MULT; HLC**
See also CA 131; DLB 82; HW
Salinas (y Serrano), Pedro 1891(?)-1951
TCLC 17
See also CA 117; DLB 134
Salinger, J(erome) D(avid) 1919-**CLC 1, 3, 8, 12, 55, 56; DA; DAB; DAC; DAM MST, NOV, POP; SSC 2, 28; WLC**
See also AAYA 2; CA 5-8R; CANR 39; CDALB
1941-1968; CLR 18; DLB 2, 102, 173;
MAICYA; MTCW 1; SATA 67
Salisbury, John
See Caute, (John) David
Salter, James 1925- .... **CLC 7, 52, 59**
See also CA 73-76; DLB 130
Saltus, Edgar (Everton) 1855-1921 . **TCLC 8**
See also CA 105; DLB 202
Saltykov, Mikhail Evgrafovich 1826-1889
NCLC 16
Samarakis, Antonis 1919- .... **CLC 5**
See also CA 25-28R; CAAS 16; CANR 36
Sanchez, Florencio 1875-1910 .... **TCLC 37**
See also CA 153; HW
Sanchez, Luis Rafael 1936- .... **CLC 23**
See also CA 128; DLB 145; HW
Sanchez, Sonia 1934-.. **CLC 5; BLC 3; DAM MULT; PC 9**
See also BW 2; CA 33-36R; CANR 24, 49; CLR

18; DLB 41; DLBD 8; MAICYA; MTCW 1;
SATA 22
Sand, George 1804-1876**NCLC 2, 42, 57; DA; DAB; DAC; DAM MST, NOV; WLC**
See also DLB 119, 192
Sandburg, Carl (August) 1878-1967**CLC 1, 4, 10, 15, 35; DA; DAB; DAC; DAM MST, POET; PC 2; WLC**
See also AAYA 24; CA 5-8R; 25-28R; CANR
35; CDALB 1865-1917; DLB 17, 54;
MAICYA; MTCW 1; SATA 8
Sandburg, Charles
See Sandburg, Carl (August)
Sandburg, Charles A.
See Sandburg, Carl (August)
Sanders, (James) Ed(ward) 1939- .... **CLC 53**
See also CA 13-16R; CAAS 21; CANR 13, 44;
DLB 16
Sanders, Lawrence 1920-1998**CLC 41; DAM POP**
See also BEST 89:4; CA 81-84; 165; CANR
33, 62; MTCW 1
Sanders, Noah
See Blount, Roy (Alton), Jr.
Sanders, Winston P.
See Anderson, Poul (William)
Sandoz, Mari(e Susette) 1896-1966 .. **CLC 28**
See also CA 1-4R; 25-28R; CANR 17, 64; DLB
9; MTCW 1; SATA 5
Saner, Reg(inald Anthony) 1931- .... **CLC 9**
See also CA 65-68
Sannazaro, Jacopo 1456(?)-1530 .... **LC 8**
Sansom, William 1912-1976 **CLC 2, 6; DAM NOV; SSC 21**
See also CA 5-8R; 65-68; CANR 42; DLB 139;
MTCW 1
Santayana, George 1863-1952 .... **TCLC 40**
See also CA 115; DLB 54, 71; DLBD 13
Santiago, Danny .... **CLC 33**
See also James, Daniel (Lewis)
See also DLB 122
Santmyer, Helen Hoover 1895-1986 **CLC 33**
See also CA 1-4R; 118; CANR 15, 33; DLBY
84; MTCW 1
Santoka, Taneda 1882-1940 .... **TCLC 72**
Santos, Bienvenido N(uqui) 1911-1996 . **CLC 22; DAM MULT**
See also CA 101; 151; CANR 19, 46
Sapper .... **TCLC 44**
See also McNeile, Herman Cyril
Sapphire 1950- .... **CLC 99**
Sappho fl. 6th cent. B.C.- ...... **CMLC 3; DAM POET; PC 5**
See also DLB 176
Sarduy, Severo 1937-1993 .... **CLC 6, 97**
See also CA 89-92; 142; CANR 58; DLB 113;
HW
Sargeson, Frank 1903-1982 .... **CLC 31**
See also CA 25-28R; 106; CANR 38
Sarmiento, Felix Ruben Garcia
See Dario, Ruben
Saro-Wiwa, Ken(ule Beeson) 1941-1995**CLC 114**
See also BW 2; CA 142; 150; CANR 60; DLB
157
Saroyan, William 1908-1981**CLC 1, 8, 10, 29, 34, 56; DA; DAB; DAC; DAM DRAM, MST, NOV; SSC 21; WLC**
See also CA 5-8R; 103; CANR 30; DLB 7, 9,
86; DLBY 81; MTCW 1; SATA 23; SATA-Obit 24
Sarraute, Nathalie 1900-**CLC 1, 2, 4, 8, 10, 31, 80**
See also CA 9-12R; CANR 23, 66; DLB 83;
MTCW 1
Sarton, (Eleanor) May 1912-1995**CLC 4, 14, 49, 91; DAM POET**

See also CA 1-4R; 149; CANR 1, 34, 55; DLB
48; DLBY 81; INT CANR-34; MTCW 1;
SATA 36; SATA-Obit 86
Sartre, Jean-Paul 1905-1980**CLC 1, 4, 7, 9, 13, 18, 24, 44, 50, 52; DA; DAB; DAC; DAM DRAM, MST, NOV; DC 3; SSC 32; WLC**
See also CA 9-12R; 97-100; CANR 21; DLB
72; MTCW 1
Sassoon, Siegfried (Lorraine) 1886-1967**CLC 36; DAB; DAM MST, NOV, POET; PC 12**
See also CA 104; 25-28R; CANR 36; DLB 20,
191; DLBD 18; MTCW 1
Satterfield, Charles
See Pohl, Frederik
Saul, John (W. III) 1942-**CLC 46; DAM NOV, POP**
See also AAYA 10; BEST 90:4; CA 81-84;
CANR 16, 40; SATA 98
Saunders, Caleb
See Heinlein, Robert A(nson)
Saura (Atares), Carlos 1932- .... **CLC 20**
See also CA 114; 131; HW
Sauser-Hall, Frederic 1887-1961 ...... **CLC 18**
See also Cendrars, Blaise
See also CA 102; 93-96; CANR 36, 62; MTCW
1
Saussure, Ferdinand de 1857-1913 **TCLC 49**
Savage, Catharine
See Brosman, Catharine Savage
Savage, Thomas 1915- .... **CLC 40**
See also CA 126; 132; CAAS 15; INT 132
Savan, Glenn 19(?)- .... **CLC 50**
Sayers, Dorothy L(eigh) 1893-1957 **TCLC 2, 15; DAM POP**
See also CA 104; 119; CANR 60; CDBLB 1914-
1945; DLB 10, 36, 77, 100; MTCW 1
Sayers, Valerie 1952- .... **CLC 50**
See also CA 134; CANR 61
Sayles, John (Thomas) 1950- . **CLC 7, 10, 14**
See also CA 57-60; CANR 41; DLB 44
Scammell, Michael 1935- .... **CLC 34**
See also CA 156
Scannell, Vernon 1922- .... **CLC 49**
See also CA 5-8R; CANR 8, 24, 57; DLB 27;
SATA 59
Scarlett, Susan
See Streatfeild, (Mary) Noel
Schaeffer, Susan Fromberg 1941- **CLC 6, 11, 22**
See also CA 49-52; CANR 18, 65; DLB 28;
MTCW 1; SATA 22
Schary, Jill
See Robinson, Jill
Schell, Jonathan 1943- .... **CLC 35**
See also CA 73-76; CANR 12
Schelling, Friedrich Wilhelm Joseph von 1775-
1854 ....
NCLC 30
See also DLB 90
Schendel, Arthur van 1874-1946 ... **TCLC 56**
Scherer, Jean-Marie Maurice 1920-
See Rohmer, Eric
See also CA 110
Schevill, James (Erwin) 1920- .... **CLC 7**
See also CA 5-8R; CAAS 12
Schiller, Friedrich 1759-1805 . **NCLC 39, 69; DAM DRAM**
See also DLB 94
Schisgal, Murray (Joseph) 1926- .... **CLC 6**
See also CA 21-24R; CANR 48
Schlee, Ann 1934- .... **CLC 35**
See also CA 101; CANR 29; SATA 44; SATA-
Brief 36
Schlegel, August Wilhelm von 1767-1845
NCLC 15
See also DLB 94
Schlegel, Friedrich 1772-1829 .... **NCLC 45**

Sommer, Scott 1951- .... **CLC 25**
See also CA 106

Sondheim, Stephen (Joshua) 1930- .**CLC 30, 39; DAM DRAM**
See also AAYA 11; CA 103; CANR 47, 68

Song, Cathy 1955- .... **PC 21**
See also CA 154; DLB 169

Sontag, Susan 1933-**CLC 1, 2, 10, 13, 31, 105; DAM POP**
See also CA 17-20R; CANR 25, 51; DLB 2, 67; MTCW 1

Sophocles 496(?)B.C.-406(?)B.C. ... **CMLC 2; DA; DAB; DAC; DAM DRAM, MST; DC 1; WLCS**
See also DLB 176

Sordello 1189-1269 .... **CMLC 15**

Sorel, Julia
See Drexler, Rosalyn

Sorrentino, Gilbert 1929-**CLC 3, 7, 14, 22, 40**
See also CA 77-80; CANR 14, 33; DLB 5, 173; DLBY 80; INT CANR-14

Soto, Gary 1952- **CLC 32, 80; DAM MULT; HLC**
See also AAYA 10; CA 119; 125; CANR 50; CLR 38; DLB 82; HW; INT 125; JRDA; SATA 80

Soupault, Philippe 1897-1990 .... **CLC 68**
See also CA 116; 147; 131

Souster, (Holmes) Raymond 1921-**CLC 5, 14; DAC; DAM POET**
See also CA 13-16R; CAAS 14; CANR 13, 29, 53; DLB 88; SATA 63

Southern, Terry 1924(?)-1995 .... **CLC 7**
See also CA 1-4R; 150; CANR 1, 55; DLB 2

Southey, Robert 1774-1843 .... **NCLC 8**
See also DLB 93, 107, 142; SATA 54

Southworth, Emma Dorothy Eliza Nevitte 1819-1899 ....

NCLC 26

Souza, Ernest
See Scott, Evelyn

Soyinka, Wole 1934-**CLC 3, 5, 14, 36, 44; BLC 3, DA; DAB; DAC; DAM DRAM, MST, MULT; DC 2; WLC**
See also BW 2; CA 13-16R; CANR 27, 39; DLB 125; MTCW 1

Spackman, W(illiam) M(ode) 1905-1990**C L C 46**
See also CA 81-84; 132

Spacks, Barry (Bernard) 1931- .... **CLC 14**
See also CA 154; CANR 33; DLB 105

Spanidou, Irini 1946- .... **CLC 44**

Spark, Muriel (Sarah) 1918-**CLC 2, 3, 5, 8, 13, 18, 40, 94; DAB; DAC; DAM MST, NOV; SSC 10**
See also CA 5-8R; CANR 12, 36; CDBLB 1945-1960; DLB 15, 139; INT CANR-12; MTCW 1

Spaulding, Douglas
See Bradbury, Ray (Douglas)

Spaulding, Leonard
See Bradbury, Ray (Douglas)

Spence, J. A. D.
See Eliot, T(homas) S(tearns)

Spencer, Elizabeth 1921- .... **CLC 22**
See also CA 13-16R; CANR 32, 65; DLB 6; MTCW 1; SATA 14

Spencer, Leonard G.
See Silverberg, Robert

Spencer, Scott 1945- .... **CLC 30**
See also CA 113; CANR 51; DLBY 86

Spender, Stephen (Harold) 1909-1995**CLC 1, 2, 5, 10, 41, 91; DAM POET**
See also CA 9-12R; 149; CANR 31, 54; CDBLB 1945-1960; DLB 20; MTCW 1

Spengler, Oswald (Arnold Gottfried) 1880-1936 **TCLC 25**

See also CA 118

Spenser, Edmund 1552(?)-1599**LC 5, 39; DA; DAB; DAC; DAM MST, POET; PC 8; WLC**
See also CDBLB Before 1660; DLB 167

Spicer, Jack 1925-1965 **CLC 8, 18, 72; DAM POET**
See also CA 85-88; DLB 5, 16, 193

Spiegelman, Art 1948- .... **CLC 76**
See also AAYA 10; CA 125; CANR 41, 55

Spielberg, Peter 1929- .... **CLC 6**
See also CA 5-8R; CANR 4, 48; DLBY 81

Spielberg, Steven 1947- .... **CLC 20**
See also AAYA 8, 24; CA 77-80; CANR 32; SATA 32

Spillane, Frank Morrison 1918-
See Spillane, Mickey
See also CA 25-28R; CANR 28, 63; MTCW 1; SATA 66

Spillane, Mickey .... **CLC 3, 13**
See also Spillane, Frank Morrison

Spinoza, Benedictus de 1632-1677 .... **LC 9**

Spinrad, Norman (Richard) 1940- ... **CLC 46**
See also CA 37-40R; CAAS 19; CANR 20; DLB 8; INT CANR-20

Spitteler, Carl (Friedrich Georg) 1845-1924 **TCLC 12**
See also CA 109; DLB 129

Spivack, Kathleen (Romola Drucker) 1938-**CLC 6**
See also CA 49-52

Spoto, Donald 1941- .... **CLC 39**
See also CA 65-68; CANR 11, 57

Springsteen, Bruce (F.) 1949- .... **CLC 17**
See also CA 111

Spurling, Hilary 1940- .... **CLC 34**
See also CA 104; CANR 25, 52

Spyker, John Howland
See Elman, Richard (Martin)

Squires, (James) Radcliffe 1917-1993**CLC 51**
See also CA 1-4R; 140; CANR 6, 21

Srivastava, Dhanpat Rai 1880(?)-1936
See Premchand
See also CA 118

Stacy, Donald
See Pohl, Frederik

Stael, Germaine de 1766-1817
See Stael-Holstein, Anne Louise Germaine Necker Baronn
See also DLB 119

Stael-Holstein, Anne Louise Germaine Necker Baronn 1766-1817 .... **NCLC 3**
See also Stael, Germaine de
See also DLB 192

Stafford, Jean 1915-1979**CLC 4, 7, 19, 68; SSC 26**
See also CA 1-4R; 85-88; CANR 3, 65; DLB 2, 173; MTCW 1; SATA-Obit 22

Stafford, William (Edgar) 1914-1993 **CLC 4, 7, 29; DAM POET**
See also CA 5-8R; 142; CAAS 3; CANR 5, 22; DLB 5; INT CANR-22

Stagnelius, Eric Johan 1793-1823 . **NCLC 61**

Staines, Trevor
See Brunner, John (Kilian Houston)

Stairs, Gordon
See Austin, Mary (Hunter)

Stannard, Martin 1947- .... **CLC 44**
See also CA 142; DLB 155

Stanton, Elizabeth Cady 1815-1902**TCLC 73**
See also DLB 79

Stanton, Maura 1946- .... **CLC 9**
See also CA 89-92; CANR 15; DLB 120

Stanton, Schuyler
See Baum, L(yman) Frank

Stapledon, (William) Olaf 1886-1950 **T C L C 22**

See also CA 111; 162; DLB 15

Starbuck, George (Edwin) 1931-1996**CLC 53; DAM POET**
See also CA 21-24R; 153; CANR 23

Stark, Richard
See Westlake, Donald E(dwin)

Staunton, Schuyler
See Baum, L(yman) Frank

Stead, Christina (Ellen) 1902-1983 **CLC 2, 5, 8, 32, 80**
See also CA 13-16R; 109; CANR 33, 40; MTCW 1

Stead, William Thomas 1849-1912 **TCLC 48**
See also CA 167

Steele, Richard 1672-1729 .... **LC 18**
See also CDBLB 1660-1789; DLB 84, 101

Steele, Timothy (Reid) 1948- .... **CLC 45**
See also CA 93-96; CANR 16, 50; DLB 120

Steffens, (Joseph) Lincoln 1866-1936 **T C L C 20**

See also CA 117

Stegner, Wallace (Earle) 1909-1993**CLC 9, 49, 81; DAM NOV; SSC 27**
See also AITN 1; BEST 90:3; CA 1-4R; 141; CAAS 9; CANR 1, 21, 46; DLB 9; DLBY 93; MTCW 1

Stein, Gertrude 1874-1946**TCLC 1, 6, 28, 48; DA; DAB; DAC; DAM MST, NOV, POET; PC 18; WLC**
See also CA 104; 132; CDALB 1917-1929; DLB 4, 54, 86; DLBD 15; MTCW 1

Steinbeck, John (Ernst) 1902-1968 **CLC 1, 5, 9, 13, 21, 34, 45, 75; DA; DAB; DAC; DAM DRAM, MST, NOV; SSC 11; WLC**
See also AAYA 12; CA 1-4R; 25-28R; CANR 1, 35; CDALB 1929-1941; DLB 7, 9; DLBD 2; MTCW 1; SATA 9

Steinem, Gloria 1934- .... **CLC 63**
See also CA 53-56; CANR 28, 51; MTCW 1

Steiner, George 1929- ... **CLC 24; DAM NOV**
See also CA 73-76; CANR 31, 67; DLB 67; MTCW 1; SATA 62

Steiner, K. Leslie
See Delany, Samuel R(ay, Jr.)

Steiner, Rudolf 1861-1925 .... **TCLC 13**
See also CA 107

Stendhal 1783-1842**NCLC 23, 46; DA; DAB; DAC; DAM MST, NOV; SSC 27; WLC**
See also DLB 119

Stephen, Adeline Virginia
See Woolf, (Adeline) Virginia

Stephen, SirLeslie 1832-1904 .... **TCLC 23**
See also CA 123; DLB 57, 144, 190

Stephen, Sir Leslie
See Stephen, SirLeslie

Stephen, Virginia
See Woolf, (Adeline) Virginia

Stephens, James 1882(?)-1950 .... **TCLC 4**
See also CA 104; DLB 19, 153, 162

Stephens, Reed
See Donaldson, Stephen R.

Steptoe, Lydia
See Barnes, Djuna

Sterchi, Beat 1949- .... **CLC 65**

Sterling, Brett
See Bradbury, Ray (Douglas); Hamilton, Edmond

Sterling, Bruce 1954- .... **CLC 72**
See also CA 119; CANR 44

Sterling, George 1869-1926 .... **TCLC 20**
See also CA 117; 165; DLB 54

Stern, Gerald 1925- .... **CLC 40, 100**
See also CA 81-84; CANR 28; DLB 105

Stern, Richard (Gustave) 1928- .... **CLC 4, 39**
See also CA 1-4R; CANR 1, 25, 52; DLBY 87; INT CANR-25

Sternberg, Josef von 1894-1969 .... **CLC 20**

Swift, Augustus
See Lovecraft, H(oward) P(hillips)
Swift, Graham (Colin) 1949- ...... **CLC 41, 88**
See also CA 117; 122; CANR 46, 71; DLB 194
Swift, Jonathan 1667-1745 **LC 1; DA; DAB; DAC; DAM MST, NOV, POET; PC 9; WLC**
See also CDBLB 1660-1789; CLR 53; DLB 39, 95, 101; SATA 19
Swinburne, Algernon Charles 1837-1909 **TCLC 8, 36; DA; DAB; DAC; DAM MST, POET; PC 24; WLC**
See also CA 105; 140; CDBLB 1832-1890; DLB 35, 57
Swinfen, Ann .... **CLC 34**
Swinnerton, Frank Arthur 1884-1982**CLC 31**
See also CA 108; DLB 34
Swithen, John
See King, Stephen (Edwin)
Sylvia
See Ashton-Warner, Sylvia (Constance)
Symmes, Robert Edward
See Duncan, Robert (Edward)
Symonds, John Addington 1840-1893 **N C L C 34**
See also DLB 57, 144
Symons, Arthur 1865-1945 .... **TCLC 11**
See also CA 107; DLB 19, 57, 149
Symons, Julian (Gustave) 1912-1994 **CLC 2, 14, 32**
See also CA 49-52; 147; CAAS 3; CANR 3, 33, 59; DLB 87, 155; DLBY 92; MTCW 1
Synge, (Edmund) J(ohn) M(illington) 1871-1909 ... **TCLC 6, 37; DAM DRAM; DC 2**
See also CA 104; 141; CDBLB 1890-1914; DLB 10, 19
Syruc, J.
See Milosz, Czeslaw
Szirtes, George 1948- .... **CLC 46**
See also CA 109; CANR 27, 61
Szymborska, Wislawa 1923- .... **CLC 99**
See also CA 154; DLBY 96

T. O., Nik
See Annensky, Innokenty (Fyodorovich)
Tabori, George 1914- .... **CLC 19**
See also CA 49-52; CANR 4, 69
Tagore, Rabindranath 1861-1941**TCLC 3, 53; DAM DRAM, POET; PC 8**
See also CA 104; 120; MTCW 1
Taine, Hippolyte Adolphe 1828-1893 . **N C L C 15**
Talese, Gay 1932- .... **CLC 37**
See also AITN 1; CA 1-4R; CANR 9, 58; DLB 185; INT CANR-9; MTCW 1
Tallent, Elizabeth (Ann) 1954- .... **CLC 45**
See also CA 117; CANR 72; DLB 130
Tally, Ted 1952- .... **CLC 42**
See also CA 120; 124; INT 124
Tamayo y Baus, Manuel 1829-1898 **NCLC 1**
Tammsaare, A(nton) H(ansen) 1878-1940 **TCLC 27**
See also CA 164
Tam'si, Tchicaya U
See Tchicaya, Gerald Felix
Tan, Amy (Ruth) 1952-**CLC 59; DAM MULT, NOV, POP**
See also AAYA 9; BEST 89:3; CA 136; CANR 54; DLB 173; SATA 75
Tandem, Felix
See Spitteler, Carl (Friedrich Georg)
Tanizaki, Jun'ichiro 1886-1965**CLC 8, 14, 28; SSC 21**
See also CA 93-96; 25-28R; DLB 180
Tanner, William
See Amis, Kingsley (William)
Tao Lao
See Storni, Alfonsina

Tarassoff, Lev
See Troyat, Henri
Tarbell, Ida M(inerva) 1857-1944 . **TCLC 40**
See also CA 122; DLB 47
Tarkington, (Newton) Booth 1869-1946**TCLC 9**
See also CA 110; 143; DLB 9, 102; SATA 17
Tarkovsky, Andrei (Arsenyevich) 1932-1986 **CLC 75**
See also CA 127
Tartt, Donna 1964(?)- .... **CLC 76**
See also CA 142
Tasso, Torquato 1544-1595 .... **LC 5**
Tate, (John Orley) Allen 1899-1979**CLC 2, 4, 6, 9, 11, 14, 24**
See also CA 5-8R; 85-88; CANR 32; DLB 4, 45, 63; DLBD 17; MTCW 1
Tate, Ellalice
See Hibbert, Eleanor Alice Burford
Tate, James (Vincent) 1943- ..... **CLC 2, 6, 25**
See also CA 21-24R; CANR 29, 57; DLB 5, 169
Tavel, Ronald 1940- .... **CLC 6**
See also CA 21-24R; CANR 33
Taylor, C(ecil) P(hilip) 1929-1981 .... **CLC 27**
See also CA 25-28R; 105; CANR 47
Taylor, Edward 1642(?)-1729 ..... **LC 11; DA; DAB; DAC; DAM MST, POET**
See also DLB 24
Taylor, Eleanor Ross 1920- .... **CLC 5**
See also CA 81-84; CANR 70
Taylor, Elizabeth 1912-1975 ..... **CLC 2, 4, 29**
See also CA 13-16R; CANR 9, 70; DLB 139; MTCW 1; SATA 13
Taylor, Frederick Winslow 1856-1915 **T C L C 76**
Taylor, Henry (Splawn) 1942- .... **CLC 44**
See also CA 33-36R; CAAS 7; CANR 31; DLB 5
Taylor, Kamala (Purnaiya) 1924-
See Markandaya, Kamala
See also CA 77-80
Taylor, Mildred D. .... **CLC 21**
See also AAYA 10; BW 1; CA 85-88; CANR 25; CLR 9; DLB 52; JRDA; MAICYA; SAAS 5; SATA 15, 70
Taylor, Peter (Hillsman) 1917-1994**CLC 1, 4, 18, 37, 44, 50, 71; SSC 10**
See also CA 13-16R; 147; CANR 9, 50; DLBY 81, 94; INT CANR-9; MTCW 1
Taylor, Robert Lewis 1912- .... **CLC 14**
See also CA 1-4R; CANR 3, 64; SATA 10
Tchekhov, Anton
See Chekhov, Anton (Pavlovich)
Tchicaya, Gerald Felix 1931-1988 .. **CLC 101**
See also CA 129; 125
Tchicaya U Tam'si
See Tchicaya, Gerald Felix
Teasdale, Sara 1884-1933 .... **TCLC 4**
See also CA 104; 163; DLB 45; SATA 32
Tegner, Esaias 1782-1846................... **NCLC 2**
Teilhard de Chardin, (Marie Joseph) Pierre 1881-1955 ....
TCLC 9
See also CA 105
Temple, Ann
See Mortimer, Penelope (Ruth)
Tennant, Emma (Christina) 1937-**CLC 13, 52**
See also CA 65-68; CAAS 9; CANR 10, 38, 59; DLB 14
Tenneshaw, S. M.
See Silverberg, Robert
Tennyson, Alfred 1809-1892 ... **NCLC 30, 65; DA; DAB; DAC; DAM MST, POET; PC 6; WLC**
See also CDBLB 1832-1890; DLB 32
Teran, Lisa St. Aubin de .... **CLC 36**

See also St. Aubin de Teran, Lisa
Terence 195(?)B.C.-159B.C. **CMLC 14; DC 7**
Teresa de Jesus, St. 1515-1582 .... **LC 18**
Terkel, Louis 1912-
See Terkel, Studs
See also CA 57-60; CANR 18, 45, 67; MTCW 1
Terkel, Studs .... **CLC 38**
See also Terkel, Louis
See also AITN 1
Terry, C. V.
See Slaughter, Frank G(ill)
Terry, Megan 1932- .... **CLC 19**
See also CA 77-80; CABS 3; CANR 43; DLB 7
Tertullian c. 155-c. 245 .... **CMLC 29**
Tertz, Abram
See Sinyavsky, Andrei (Donatevich)
Tesich, Steve 1943(?)-1996 .... **CLC 40, 69**
See also CA 105; 152; DLBY 83
Teternikov, Fyodor Kuzmich 1863-1927
See Sologub, Fyodor
See also CA 104
Tevis, Walter 1928-1984 .... **CLC 42**
See also CA 113
Tey, Josephine .... **TCLC 14**
See also Mackintosh, Elizabeth
See also DLB 77
Thackeray, William Makepeace 1811-1863 **NCLC 5, 14, 22, 43; DA; DAB; DAC; DAM MST, NOV; WLC**
See also CDBLB 1832-1890; DLB 21, 55, 159, 163; SATA 23
Thakura, Ravindranatha
See Tagore, Rabindranath
Tharoor, Shashi 1956- .... **CLC 70**
See also CA 141
Thelwell, Michael Miles 1939- .... **CLC 22**
See also BW 2; CA 101
Theobald, Lewis, Jr.
See Lovecraft, H(oward) P(hillips)
Theodorescu, Ion N. 1880-1967
See Arghezi, Tudor
See also CA 116
Theriault, Yves 1915-1983 .... **CLC 79; DAC; DAM MST**
See also CA 102; DLB 88
Theroux, Alexander (Louis) 1939-**CLC 2, 25**
See also CA 85-88; CANR 20, 63
Theroux, Paul (Edward) 1941- **CLC 5, 8, 11, 15, 28, 46; DAM POP**
See also BEST 89:4; CA 33-36R; CANR 20, 45; DLB 2; MTCW 1; SATA 44
Thesen, Sharon 1946- .... **CLC 56**
See also CA 163
Thevenin, Denis
See Duhamel, Georges
Thibault, Jacques Anatole Francois 1844-1924
See France, Anatole
See also CA 106; 127; DAM NOV; MTCW 1
Thiele, Colin (Milton) 1920- .... **CLC 17**
See also CA 29-32R; CANR 12, 28, 53; CLR 27; MAICYA; SAAS 2; SATA 14, 72
Thomas, Audrey (Callahan) 1935-**CLC 7, 13, 37, 107; SSC 20**
See also AITN 2; CA 21-24R; CAAS 19; CANR 36, 58; DLB 60; MTCW 1
Thomas, D(onald) M(ichael) 1935- . **CLC 13, 22, 31**
See also CA 61-64; CAAS 11; CANR 17, 45; CDBLB 1960 to Present; DLB 40; INT CANR-17; MTCW 1
Thomas, Dylan (Marlais) 1914-1953**TCLC 1, 8, 45; DA; DAB; DAC; DAM DRAM, MST, POET; PC 2; SSC 3; WLC**
See also CA 104; 120; CANR 65; CDBLB 1945-1960; DLB 13, 20, 139; MTCW 1; SATA 60

Thomas, (Philip) Edward 1878-1917 . **T C L C 10; DAM POET**
See also CA 106; 153; DLB 19

Thomas, Joyce Carol 1938- .... **CLC 35**
See also AAYA 12; BW 2; CA 113; 116; CANR 48; CLR 19; DLB 33; INT 116; JRDA; MAICYA; MTCW 1; SAAS 7; SATA 40, 78

Thomas, Lewis 1913-1993 .... **CLC 35**
See also CA 85-88; 143; CANR 38, 60; MTCW 1

Thomas, Paul
See Mann, (Paul) Thomas

Thomas, Piri 1928- .... **CLC 17**
See also CA 73-76; HW

Thomas, R(onald) S(tuart) 1913- **CLC 6, 13, 48; DAB; DAM POET**
See also CA 89-92; CAAS 4; CANR 30; CDBLB 1960 to Present; DLB 27; MTCW 1

Thomas, Ross (Elmore) 1926-1995 ... **CLC 39**
See also CA 33-36R; 150; CANR 22, 63

Thompson, Francis Clegg
See Mencken, H(enry) L(ouis)

Thompson, Francis Joseph 1859-1907 **TCLC 4**
See also CA 104; CDBLB 1890-1914; DLB 19

Thompson, Hunter S(tockton) 1939- **CLC 9, 17, 40, 104; DAM POP**
See also BEST 89:1; CA 17-20R; CANR 23, 46; DLB 185; MTCW 1

Thompson, James Myers
See Thompson, Jim (Myers)

Thompson, Jim (Myers) 1906-1977(?)**CLC 69**
See also CA 140

Thompson, Judith .... **CLC 39**

Thomson, James 1700-1748 ... **LC 16, 29, 40; DAM POET**
See also DLB 95

Thomson, James 1834-1882 **NCLC 18; DAM POET**
See also DLB 35

Thoreau, Henry David 1817-1862**NCLC 7, 21, 61; DA; DAB; DAC; DAM MST; WLC**
See also CDALB 1640-1865; DLB 1

Thornton, Hall
See Silverberg, Robert

Thucydides c. 455B.C.-399B.C. .... **CMLC 17**
See also DLB 176

Thurber, James (Grover) 1894-1961. **CLC 5, 11, 25; DA; DAB; DAC; DAM DRAM, MST, NOV; SSC 1**
See also CA 73-76; CANR 17, 39; CDALB 1929-1941; DLB 4, 11, 22, 102; MAICYA; MTCW 1; SATA 13

Thurman, Wallace (Henry) 1902-1934**T C L C 6; BLC 3; DAM MULT**
See also BW 1; CA 104; 124; DLB 51

Ticheburn, Cheviot
See Ainsworth, William Harrison

Tieck, (Johann) Ludwig 1773-1853 **NCLC 5, 46; SSC 31**
See also DLB 90

Tiger, Derry
See Ellison, Harlan (Jay)

Tilghman, Christopher 1948(?)- .... **CLC 65**
See also CA 159

Tillinghast, Richard (Williford) 1940-**CLC 29**
See also CA 29-32R; CAAS 23; CANR 26, 51

Timrod, Henry 1828-1867 .... **NCLC 25**
See also DLB 3

Tindall, Gillian (Elizabeth) 1938- ...... **CLC 7**
See also CA 21-24R; CANR 11, 65

Tiptree, James, Jr. .... **CLC 48, 50**
See also Sheldon, Alice Hastings Bradley
See also DLB 8

Titmarsh, Michael Angelo
See Thackeray, William Makepeace

Tocqueville, Alexis (Charles Henri Maurice Clerel Comte) 1805-1859 ... **NCLC 7, 63**

Tolkien, J(ohn) R(onald) R(euel) 1892-1973
CLC 1, 2, 3, 8, 12, 38; DA; DAB; DAC; DAM MST, NOV, POP; WLC
See also AAYA 10; AITN 1; CA 17-18; 45-48; CANR 36; CAP 2; CDBLB 1914-1945; DLB 15, 160; JRDA; MAICYA; MTCW 1; SATA 2, 32, 100; SATA-Obit 24

Toller, Ernst 1893-1939 .... **TCLC 10**
See also CA 107; DLB 124

Tolson, M. B.
See Tolson, Melvin B(eaunorus)

Tolson, Melvin B(eaunorus) 1898(?)-1966
CLC 36, 105; BLC 3; DAM MULT, POET
See also BW 1; CA 124; 89-92; DLB 48, 76

Tolstoi, Aleksei Nikolaevich
See Tolstoy, Alexey Nikolaevich

Tolstoy, Alexey Nikolaevich 1882-1945**T C L C 18**
See also CA 107; 158

Tolstoy, Count Leo
See Tolstoy, Leo (Nikolaevich)

Tolstoy, Leo (Nikolaevich) 1828-1910**TCLC 4, 11, 17, 28, 44, 79; DA; DAB; DAC; DAM MST, NOV; SSC 9, 30; WLC**
See also CA 104; 123; SATA 26

Tomasi di Lampedusa, Giuseppe 1896-1957
See Lampedusa, Giuseppe (Tomasi) di
See also CA 111

Tomlin, Lily .... **CLC 17**
See also Tomlin, Mary Jean

Tomlin, Mary Jean 1939(?)-
See Tomlin, Lily
See also CA 117

Tomlinson, (Alfred) Charles 1927-**CLC 2, 4, 6, 13, 45; DAM POET; PC 17**
See also CA 5-8R; CANR 33; DLB 40

Tomlinson, H(enry) M(ajor) 1873-1958**TCLC 71**
See also CA 118; 161; DLB 36, 100, 195

Tonson, Jacob
See Bennett, (Enoch) Arnold

Toole, John Kennedy 1937-1969 **CLC 19, 64**
See also CA 104; DLBY 81

Toomer, Jean 1894-1967**CLC 1, 4, 13, 22; BLC 3; DAM MULT; PC 7; SSC 1; WLCS**
See also BW 1; CA 85-88; CDALB 1917-1929; DLB 45, 51; MTCW 1

Torley, Luke
See Blish, James (Benjamin)

Tornimparte, Alessandra
See Ginzburg, Natalia

Torre, Raoul della
See Mencken, H(enry) L(ouis)

Torrey, E(dwin) Fuller 1937- .... **CLC 34**
See also CA 119; CANR 71

Torsvan, Ben Traven
See Traven, B.

Torsvan, Benno Traven
See Traven, B.

Torsvan, Berick Traven
See Traven, B.

Torsvan, Berwick Traven
See Traven, B.

Torsvan, Bruno Traven
See Traven, B.

Torsvan, Traven
See Traven, B.

Tournier, Michel (Edouard) 1924-**CLC 6, 23, 36, 95**
See also CA 49-52; CANR 3, 36; DLB 83; MTCW 1; SATA 23

Tournimparte, Alessandra
See Ginzburg, Natalia

Towers, Ivar
See Kornbluth, C(yril) M.

Towne, Robert (Burton) 1936(?)- ..... **CLC 87**
See also CA 108; DLB 44

Townsend, Sue .... **CLC 61**
See also Townsend, Susan Elaine
See also SATA 55, 93; SATA-Brief 48

Townsend, Susan Elaine 1946-
See Townsend, Sue
See also CA 119; 127; CANR 65; DAB; DAC; DAM MST

Townshend, Peter (Dennis Blandford) 1945-
CLC 17, 42
See also CA 107

Tozzi, Federigo 1883-1920 .... **TCLC 31**
See also CA 160

Traill, Catharine Parr 1802-1899 .. **NCLC 31**
See also DLB 99

Trakl, Georg 1887-1914 .... **TCLC 5; PC 20**
See also CA 104; 165

Transtroemer, Tomas (Goesta) 1931-**CLC 52, 65; DAM POET**
See also CA 117; 129; CAAS 17

Transtromer, Tomas Gosta
See Transtroemer, Tomas (Goesta)

Traven, B. (?)-1969 .... **CLC 8, 11**
See also CA 19-20; 25-28R; CAP 2; DLB 9, 56; MTCW 1

Treitel, Jonathan 1959- .... **CLC 70**

Tremain, Rose 1943- .... **CLC 42**
See also CA 97-100; CANR 44; DLB 14

Tremblay, Michel 1942- **CLC 29, 102; DAC; DAM MST**
See also CA 116; 128; DLB 60; MTCW 1

Trevanian .... **CLC 29**
See also Whitaker, Rod(ney)

Trevor, Glen
See Hilton, James

Trevor, William 1928- . **CLC 7, 9, 14, 25, 71; SSC 21**
See also Cox, William Trevor
See also DLB 14, 139

Trifonov, Yuri (Valentinovich) 1925-1981
CLC 45
See also CA 126; 103; MTCW 1

Trilling, Lionel 1905-1975 ...... **CLC 9, 11, 24**
See also CA 9-12R; 61-64; CANR 10; DLB 28, 63; INT CANR-10; MTCW 1

Trimball, W. H.
See Mencken, H(enry) L(ouis)

Tristan
See Gomez de la Serna, Ramon

Tristram
See Housman, A(lfred) E(dward)

Trogdon, William (Lewis) 1939-
See Heat-Moon, William Least
See also CA 115; 119; CANR 47; INT 119

Trollope, Anthony 1815-1882**NCLC 6, 33; DA; DAB; DAC; DAM MST, NOV; SSC 28; WLC**
See also CDBLB 1832-1890; DLB 21, 57, 159; SATA 22

Trollope, Frances 1779-1863 .... **NCLC 30**
See also DLB 21, 166

Trotsky, Leon 1879-1940 .... **TCLC 22**
See also CA 118; 167

Trotter (Cockburn), Catharine 1679-1749**L C 8**
See also DLB 84

Trout, Kilgore
See Farmer, Philip Jose

Trow, George W. S. 1943- .... **CLC 52**
See also CA 126

Troyat, Henri 1911- .... **CLC 23**
See also CA 45-48; CANR 2, 33, 67; MTCW 1

Trudeau, G(arretson) B(eekman) 1948-
See Trudeau, Garry B.
See also CA 81-84; CANR 31; SATA 35

Trudeau, Garry B. .... **CLC 12**
See also Trudeau, G(arretson) B(eekman)
See also AAYA 10; AITN 2

Wallace, Irving 1916-1990 **CLC 7, 13; DAM NOV, POP**
See also AITN 1; CA 1-4R; 132; CAAS 1; CANR 1, 27; INT CANR-27; MTCW 1

Wallant, Edward Lewis 1926-1962**CLC 5, 10**
See also CA 1-4R; CANR 22; DLB 2, 28, 143; MTCW 1

Walley, Byron
See Card, Orson Scott

Walpole, Horace 1717-1797 .... **LC 2**
See also DLB 39, 104

Walpole, Hugh (Seymour) 1884-1941**TCLC 5**
See also CA 104; 165; DLB 34

Walser, Martin 1927-........................ **CLC 27**
See also CA 57-60; CANR 8, 46; DLB 75, 124

Walser, Robert 1878-1956 **TCLC 18; SSC 20**
See also CA 118; DLB 66

Walsh, Jill Paton .... **CLC 35**
See also Paton Walsh, Gillian
See also AAYA 11; CLR 2; DLB 161; SAAS 3

Walter, Villiam Christian
See Andersen, Hans Christian

Wambaugh, Joseph (Aloysius, Jr.) 1937-**CLC 3, 18; DAM NOV, POP**
See also AITN 1; BEST 89:3; CA 33-36R; CANR 42, 65; DLB 6; DLBY 83; MTCW 1

Wang Wei 699(?)-761(?) .... **PC 18**

Ward, Arthur Henry Sarsfield 1883-1959
See Rohmer, Sax
See also CA 108

Ward, Douglas Turner 1930- .... **CLC 19**
See also BW 1; CA 81-84; CANR 27; DLB 7, 38

Ward, Mary Augusta
See Ward, Mrs. Humphry

Ward, Mrs. Humphry 1851-1920 .. **TCLC 55**
See also DLB 18

Ward, Peter
See Faust, Frederick (Schiller)

Warhol, Andy 1928(?)-1987 .... **CLC 20**
See also AAYA 12; BEST 89:4; CA 89-92; 121; CANR 34

Warner, Francis (Robert le Plastrier) 1937-**CLC 14**
See also CA 53-56; CANR 11

Warner, Marina 1946- .... **CLC 59**
See also CA 65-68; CANR 21, 55; DLB 194

Warner, Rex (Ernest) 1905-1986 ...... **CLC 45**
See also CA 89-92; 119; DLB 15

Warner, Susan (Bogert) 1819-1885 **NCLC 31**
See also DLB 3, 42

Warner, Sylvia (Constance) Ashton
See Ashton-Warner, Sylvia (Constance)

Warner, Sylvia Townsend 1893-1978 **CLC 7, 19; SSC 23**
See also CA 61-64; 77-80; CANR 16, 60; DLB 34, 139; MTCW 1

Warren, Mercy Otis 1728-1814 ..... **NCLC 13**
See also DLB 31, 200

Warren, Robert Penn 1905-1989**CLC 1, 4, 6, 8, 10, 13, 18, 39, 53, 59; DA; DAB; DAC; DAM MST, NOV, POET; SSC 4; WLC**
See also AITN 1; CA 13-16R; 129; CANR 10, 47; CDALB 1968-1988; DLB 2, 48, 152; DLBY 80, 89; INT CANR-10; MTCW 1; SATA 46; SATA-Obit 63

Warshofsky, Isaac
See Singer, Isaac Bashevis

Warton, Thomas 1728-1790 ..... **LC 15; DAM POET**
See also DLB 104, 109

Waruk, Kona
See Harris, (Theodore) Wilson

Warung, Price 1855-1911 .... **TCLC 45**

Warwick, Jarvis
See Garner, Hugh

Washington, Alex
See Harris, Mark

Washington, Booker T(aliaferro) 1856-1915 **TCLC 10; BLC 3; DAM MULT**
See also BW 1; CA 114; 125; SATA 28

Washington, George 1732-1799 .... **LC 25**
See also DLB 31

Wassermann, (Karl) Jakob 1873-1934**TCLC 6**
See also CA 104; DLB 66

Wasserstein, Wendy 1950- ... **CLC 32, 59, 90; DAM DRAM; DC 4**
See also CA 121; 129; CABS 3; CANR 53; INT 129; SATA 94

Waterhouse, Keith (Spencer) 1929- . **CLC 47**
See also CA 5-8R; CANR 38, 67; DLB 13, 15; MTCW 1

Waters, Frank (Joseph) 1902-1995 .. **CLC 88**
See also CA 5-8R; 149; CAAS 13; CANR 3, 18, 63; DLBY 86

Waters, Roger 1944- .... **CLC 35**

Watkins, Frances Ellen
See Harper, Frances Ellen Watkins

Watkins, Gerrold
See Malzberg, Barry N(athaniel)

Watkins, Gloria 1955(?)-
See hooks, bell
See also BW 2; CA 143

Watkins, Paul 1964- .... **CLC 55**
See also CA 132; CANR 62

Watkins, Vernon Phillips 1906-1967 **CLC 43**
See also CA 9-10; 25-28R; CAP 1; DLB 20

Watson, Irving S.
See Mencken, H(enry) L(ouis)

Watson, John H.
See Farmer, Philip Jose

Watson, Richard F.
See Silverberg, Robert

Waugh, Auberon (Alexander) 1939- .. **CLC 7**
See also CA 45-48; CANR 6, 22; DLB 14, 194

Waugh, Evelyn (Arthur St. John) 1903-1966 **CLC 1, 3, 8, 13, 19, 27, 44, 107; DA; DAB; DAC; DAM MST, NOV, POP; WLC**
See also CA 85-88; 25-28R; CANR 22; CDBLB 1914-1945; DLB 15, 162, 195; MTCW 1

Waugh, Harriet 1944- .... **CLC 6**
See also CA 85-88; CANR 22

Ways, C. R.
See Blount, Roy (Alton), Jr.

Waystaff, Simon
See Swift, Jonathan

Webb, (Martha) Beatrice (Potter) 1858-1943 **TCLC 22**
See also Potter, (Helen) Beatrix
See also CA 117

Webb, Charles (Richard) 1939- .... **CLC 7**
See also CA 25-28R

Webb, James H(enry), Jr. 1946- .... **CLC 22**
See also CA 81-84

Webb, Mary (Gladys Meredith) 1881-1927 **TCLC 24**
See also CA 123; DLB 34

Webb, Mrs. Sidney
See Webb, (Martha) Beatrice (Potter)

Webb, Phyllis 1927-........................... **CLC 18**
See also CA 104; CANR 23; DLB 53

Webb, Sidney (James) 1859-1947 .. **TCLC 22**
See also CA 117; 163; DLB 190

Webber, Andrew Lloyd .... **CLC 21**
See also Lloyd Webber, Andrew

Weber, Lenora Mattingly 1895-1971 **CLC 12**
See also CA 19-20; 29-32R; CAP 1; SATA 2; SATA-Obit 26

Weber, Max 1864-1920 .... **TCLC 69**
See also CA 109

Webster, John 1579(?)-1634(?) ... **LC 33; DA; DAB; DAC; DAM DRAM, MST; DC 2; WLC**
See also CDBLB Before 1660; DLB 58

Webster, Noah 1758-1843 .... **NCLC 30**

Wedekind, (Benjamin) Frank(lin) 1864-1918 **TCLC 7; DAM DRAM**
See also CA 104; 153; DLB 118

Weidman, Jerome 1913- .... **CLC 7**
See also AITN 2; CA 1-4R; CANR 1; DLB 28

Weil, Simone (Adolphine) 1909-1943**TCLC 23**
See also CA 117; 159

Weininger, Otto 1880-1903 .... **TCLC 84**

Weinstein, Nathan
See West, Nathanael

Weinstein, Nathan von Wallenstein
See West, Nathanael

Weir, Peter (Lindsay) 1944- .... **CLC 20**
See also CA 113; 123

Weiss, Peter (Ulrich) 1916-1982**CLC 3, 15, 51; DAM DRAM**
See also CA 45-48; 106; CANR 3; DLB 69, 124

Weiss, Theodore (Russell) 1916-**CLC 3, 8, 14**
See also CA 9-12R; CAAS 2; CANR 46; DLB 5

Welch, (Maurice) Denton 1915-1948**TCLC 22**
See also CA 121; 148

Welch, James 1940- ..... **CLC 6, 14, 52; DAM MULT, POP**
See also CA 85-88; CANR 42, 66; DLB 175; NNAL

Weldon, Fay 1931- . **CLC 6, 9, 11, 19, 36, 59; DAM POP**
See also CA 21-24R; CANR 16, 46, 63; CDBLB 1960 to Present; DLB 14, 194; INT CANR-16; MTCW 1

Wellek, Rene 1903-1995 .... **CLC 28**
See also CA 5-8R; 150; CAAS 7; CANR 8; DLB 63; INT CANR-8

Weller, Michael 1942-.................. **CLC 10, 53**
See also CA 85-88

Weller, Paul 1958- .... **CLC 26**

Wellershoff, Dieter 1925- .... **CLC 46**
See also CA 89-92; CANR 16, 37

Welles, (George) Orson 1915-1985**CLC 20, 80**
See also CA 93-96; 117

Wellman, John McDowell 1945-
See Wellman, Mac
See also CA 166

Wellman, Mac 1945- .... **CLC 65**
See also Wellman, John McDowell; Wellman, John McDowell

Wellman, Manly Wade 1903-1986 .... **CLC 49**
See also CA 1-4R; 118; CANR 6, 16, 44; SATA 6; SATA-Obit 47

Wells, Carolyn 1869(?)-1942 .... **TCLC 35**
See also CA 113; DLB 11

Wells, H(erbert) G(eorge) 1866-1946**TCLC 6, 12, 19; DA; DAB; DAC; DAM MST, NOV; SSC 6; WLC**
See also AAYA 18; CA 110; 121; CDBLB 1914-1945; DLB 34, 70, 156, 178; MTCW 1; SATA 20

Wells, Rosemary 1943-...................... **CLC 12**
See also AAYA 13; CA 85-88; CANR 48; CLR 16; MAICYA; SAAS 1; SATA 18, 69

Welty, Eudora 1909- **CLC 1, 2, 5, 14, 22, 33, 105; DA; DAB; DAC; DAM MST, NOV; SSC 1, 27; WLC**
See also CA 9-12R; CABS 1; CANR 32, 65; CDALB 1941-1968; DLB 2, 102, 143; DLBD 12; DLBY 87; MTCW 1

Wen I-to 1899-1946 .... **TCLC 28**

Wentworth, Robert
See Hamilton, Edmond

Werfel, Franz (Viktor) 1890-1945 ... **TCLC 8**
See also CA 104; 161; DLB 81, 124

Wergeland, Henrik Arnold 1808-1845**NCLC 5**

Wersba, Barbara 1932-...................... **CLC 30**

INT CANR-25; SATA 78

Williams, Shirley
See Williams, Sherley Anne

Williams, Tennessee 1911-1983 **CLC 1, 2, 5, 7, 8, 11, 15, 19, 30, 39, 45, 71, 111; DA; DAB; DAC; DAM DRAM, MST; DC 4; WLC**
See also AITN 1, 2; CA 5-8R; 108; CABS 3; CANR 31; CDALB 1941-1968; DLB 7; DLBD 4; DLBY 83; MTCW 1

Williams, Thomas (Alonzo) 1926-1990 **CLC 14**
See also CA 1-4R; 132; CANR 2

Williams, William C.
See Williams, William Carlos

Williams, William Carlos 1883-1963 **CLC 1, 2, 5, 9, 13, 22, 42, 67; DA; DAB; DAC; DAM MST, POET; PC 7; SSC 31**
See also CA 89-92; CANR 34; CDALB 1917-1929; DLB 4, 16, 54, 86; MTCW 1

Williamson, David (Keith) 1942- ...... **CLC 56**
See also CA 103; CANR 41

Williamson, Ellen Douglas 1905-1984
See Douglas, Ellen
See also CA 17-20R; 114; CANR 39

Williamson, Jack .... **CLC 29**
See also Williamson, John Stewart
See also CAAS 8; DLB 8

Williamson, John Stewart 1908-
See Williamson, Jack
See also CA 17-20R; CANR 23, 70

Willie, Frederick
See Lovecraft, H(oward) P(hillips)

Willingham, Calder (Baynard, Jr.) 1922-1995 **CLC 5, 51**
See also CA 5-8R; 147; CANR 3; DLB 2, 44; MTCW 1

Willis, Charles
See Clarke, Arthur C(harles)

Willy
See Colette, (Sidonie-Gabrielle)

Willy, Colette
See Colette, (Sidonie-Gabrielle)

Wilson, A(ndrew) N(orman) 1950- ... **CLC 33**
See also CA 112; 122; DLB 14, 155, 194

Wilson, Angus (Frank Johnstone) 1913-1991 **CLC 2, 3, 5, 25, 34; SSC 21**
See also CA 5-8R; 134; CANR 21; DLB 15, 139, 155; MTCW 1

Wilson, August 1945- **CLC 39, 50, 63; BLC 3; DA; DAB; DAC; DAM DRAM, MST, MULT; DC 2; WLCS**
See also AAYA 16; BW 2; CA 115; 122; CANR 42, 54; MTCW 1

Wilson, Brian 1942- .... **CLC 12**

Wilson, Colin 1931- .... **CLC 3, 14**
See also CA 1-4R; CAAS 5; CANR 1, 22, 33; DLB 14, 194; MTCW 1

Wilson, Dirk
See Pohl, Frederik

Wilson, Edmund 1895-1972 **CLC 1, 2, 3, 8, 24**
See also CA 1-4R; 37-40R; CANR 1, 46; DLB 63; MTCW 1

Wilson, Ethel Davis (Bryant) 1888(?)-1980 **CLC 13; DAC; DAM POET**
See also CA 102; DLB 68; MTCW 1

Wilson, John 1785-1854 .... **NCLC 5**

Wilson, John (Anthony) Burgess 1917-1993
See Burgess, Anthony
See also CA 1-4R; 143; CANR 2, 46; DAC; DAM NOV; MTCW 1

Wilson, Lanford 1937- **CLC 7, 14, 36; DAM DRAM**
See also CA 17-20R; CABS 3; CANR 45; DLB 7

Wilson, Robert M. 1944- .... **CLC 7, 9**
See also CA 49-52; CANR 2, 41; MTCW 1

Wilson, Robert McLiam 1964- .... **CLC 59**
See also CA 132

Wilson, Sloan 1920- .... **CLC 32**
See also CA 1-4R; CANR 1, 44

Wilson, Snoo 1948- .... **CLC 33**
See also CA 69-72

Wilson, William S(mith) 1932- .... **CLC 49**
See also CA 81-84

Wilson, (Thomas) Woodrow 1856-1924 **TCLC 79**
See also CA 166; DLB 47

Winchilsea, Anne (Kingsmill) Finch Counte 1661-1720
See Finch, Anne

Windham, Basil
See Wodehouse, P(elham) G(renville)

Wingrove, David (John) 1954- .... **CLC 68**
See also CA 133

Wintergreen, Jane
See Duncan, Sara Jeannette

Winters, Janet Lewis .... **CLC 41**
See also Lewis, Janet
See also DLBY 87

Winters, (Arthur) Yvor 1900-1968 **CLC 4, 8, 32**
See also CA 11-12; 25-28R; CAP 1; DLB 48; MTCW 1

Winterson, Jeanette 1959- **CLC 64; DAM POP**
See also CA 136; CANR 58

Winthrop, John 1588-1649 .... **LC 31**
See also DLB 24, 30

Wiseman, Frederick 1930- .... **CLC 20**
See also CA 159

Wister, Owen 1860-1938 .... **TCLC 21**
See also CA 108; 162; DLB 9, 78, 186; SATA 62

Witkacy
See Witkiewicz, Stanislaw Ignacy

Witkiewicz, Stanislaw Ignacy 1885-1939 **TCLC 8**
See also CA 105; 162

Wittgenstein, Ludwig (Josef Johann) 1889-1951 **TCLC 59**
See also CA 113; 164

Wittig, Monique 1935(?)- .... **CLC 22**
See also CA 116; 135; DLB 83

Wittlin, Jozef 1896-1976 .... **CLC 25**
See also CA 49-52; 65-68; CANR 3

Wodehouse, P(elham) G(renville) 1881-1975 **CLC 1, 2, 5, 10, 22; DAB; DAC; DAM NOV; SSC 2**
See also AITN 2; CA 45-48; 57-60; CANR 3, 33; CDBLB 1914-1945; DLB 34, 162; MTCW 1; SATA 22

Woiwode, L.
See Woiwode, Larry (Alfred)

Woiwode, Larry (Alfred) 1941- .... **CLC 6, 10**
See also CA 73-76; CANR 16; DLB 6; INT CANR-16

Wojciechowska, Maia (Teresa) 1927- **CLC 26**
See also AAYA 8; CA 9-12R; CANR 4, 41; CLR 1; JRDA; MAICYA; SAAS 1; SATA 1, 28, 83

Wolf, Christa 1929- .... **CLC 14, 29, 58**
See also CA 85-88; CANR 45; DLB 75; MTCW 1

Wolfe, Gene (Rodman) 1931- **CLC 25; DAM POP**
See also CA 57-60; CAAS 9; CANR 6, 32, 60; DLB 8

Wolfe, George C. 1954- .... **CLC 49; BLCS**
See also CA 149

Wolfe, Thomas (Clayton) 1900-1938 **TCLC 4, 13, 29, 61; DA; DAB; DAC; DAM MST, NOV; WLC**
See also CA 104; 132; CDALB 1929-1941; DLB 9, 102; DLBD 2, 16; DLBY 85, 97; MTCW 1

Wolfe, Thomas Kennerly, Jr. 1930-

See Wolfe, Tom
See also CA 13-16R; CANR 9, 33, 70; DAM POP; DLB 185; INT CANR-9; MTCW 1

Wolfe, Tom .... **CLC 1, 2, 9, 15, 35, 51**
See also Wolfe, Thomas Kennerly, Jr.
See also AAYA 8; AITN 2; BEST 89:1; DLB 152

Wolff, Geoffrey (Ansell) 1937- .... **CLC 41**
See also CA 29-32R; CANR 29, 43

Wolff, Sonia
See Levitin, Sonia (Wolff)

Wolff, Tobias (Jonathan Ansell) 1945- . **C L C 39, 64**
See also AAYA 16; BEST 90:2; CA 114; 117; CAAS 22; CANR 54; DLB 130; INT 117

Wolfram von Eschenbach c. 1170-c. 1220 **CMLC 5**
See also DLB 138

Wolitzer, Hilma 1930- .... **CLC 17**
See also CA 65-68; CANR 18, 40; INT CANR-18; SATA 31

Wollstonecraft, Mary 1759-1797 .... **LC 5**
See also CDBLB 1789-1832; DLB 39, 104, 158

Wonder, Stevie .... **CLC 12**
See also Morris, Steveland Judkins

Wong, Jade Snow 1922- .... **CLC 17**
See also CA 109

Woodberry, George Edward 1855-1930 **TCLC 73**
See also CA 165; DLB 71, 103

Woodcott, Keith
See Brunner, John (Kilian Houston)

Woodruff, Robert W.
See Mencken, H(enry) L(ouis)

Woolf, (Adeline) Virginia 1882-1941 **TCLC 1, 5, 20, 43, 56; DA; DAB; DAC; DAM MST, NOV; SSC 7; WLC**
See also CA 104; 130; CANR 64; CDBLB 1914-1945; DLB 36, 100, 162; DLBD 10; MTCW 1

Woolf, Virginia Adeline
See Woolf, (Adeline) Virginia

Woollcott, Alexander (Humphreys) 1887-1943 **TCLC 5**
See also CA 105; 161; DLB 29

Woolrich, Cornell 1903-1968 .... **CLC 77**
See also Hopley-Woolrich, Cornell George

Wordsworth, Dorothy 1771-1855 .. **NCLC 25**
See also DLB 107

Wordsworth, William 1770-1850 .. **NCLC 12, 38; DA; DAB; DAC; DAM MST, POET; PC 4; WLC**
See also CDBLB 1789-1832; DLB 93, 107

Wouk, Herman 1915- **CLC 1, 9, 38; DAM NOV, POP**
See also CA 5-8R; CANR 6, 33, 67; DLBY 82; INT CANR-6; MTCW 1

Wright, Charles (Penzel, Jr.) 1935- **CLC 6, 13, 28**
See also CA 29-32R; CAAS 7; CANR 23, 36, 62; DLB 165; DLBY 82; MTCW 1

Wright, Charles Stevenson 1932- ... **CLC 49; BLC 3; DAM MULT, POET**
See also BW 1; CA 9-12R; CANR 26; DLB 33

Wright, Jack R.
See Harris, Mark

Wright, James (Arlington) 1927-1980 **CLC 3, 5, 10, 28; DAM POET**
See also AITN 2; CA 49-52; 97-100; CANR 4, 34, 64; DLB 5, 169; MTCW 1

Wright, Judith (Arandell) 1915- **CLC 11, 53; PC 14**
See also CA 13-16R; CANR 31; MTCW 1; SATA 14

Wright, L(aurali) R. 1939- .... **CLC 44**
See also CA 138

Wright, Richard (Nathaniel) 1908-1960 **C L C**

1, 3, 4, 9, 14, 21, 48, 74; BLC 3; DA; DAB; DAC; DAM MST, MULT, NOV; SSC 2; WLC
See also AAYA 5; BW 1; CA 108; CANR 64; CDALB 1929-1941; DLB 76, 102; DLBD 2; MTCW 1

Wright, Richard B(ruce) 1937- .... CLC 6
See also CA 85-88; DLB 53

Wright, Rick 1945- .... CLC 35

Wright, Rowland
See Wells, Carolyn

Wright, Stephen 1946- .... CLC 33

Wright, Willard Huntington 1888-1939
See Van Dine, S. S.
See also CA 115; DLBD 16

Wright, William 1930- .... CLC 44
See also CA 53-56; CANR 7, 23

Wroth, LadyMary 1587-1653(?) .... LC 30
See also DLB 121

Wu Ch'eng-en 1500(?)-1582(?) .... LC 7

Wu Ching-tzu 1701-1754 .... LC 2

Wurlitzer, Rudolph 1938(?)- .... CLC 2, 4, 15
See also CA 85-88; DLB 173

Wycherley, William 1641-1715 LC 8, 21; DAM DRAM
See also CDBLB 1660-1789; DLB 80

Wylie, Elinor (Morton Hoyt) 1885-1928
TCLC 8; PC 23
See also CA 105; 162; DLB 9, 45

Wylie, Philip (Gordon) 1902-1971 ... CLC 43
See also CA 21-22; 33-36R; CAP 2; DLB 9

Wyndham, John .... CLC 19
See also Harris, John (Wyndham Parkes Lucas) Beynon

Wyss, Johann David Von 1743 1818 NCLC 10
See also JRDA; MAICYA; SATA 29; SATA-Brief 27

Xenophon c. 430B.C.-c. 354B.C. ... CMLC 17
See also DLB 176

Yakumo Koizumi
See Hearn, (Patricio) Lafcadio (Tessima Carlos)

Yanez, Jose Donoso
See Donoso (Yanez), Jose

Yanovsky, Basile S.
See Yanovsky, V(assily) S(emenovich)

Yanovsky, V(assily) S(emenovich) 1906-1989
CLC 2, 18
See also CA 97-100; 129

Yates, Richard 1926-1992 .... CLC 7, 8, 23
See also CA 5-8R; 139; CANR 10, 43; DLB 2; DLBY 81, 92; INT CANR-10

Yeats, W. B.
See Yeats, William Butler

Yeats, William Butler 1865-1939 TCLC 1, 11, 18, 31; DA; DAB; DAC; DAM DRAM, MST, POET; PC 20; WLC
See also CA 104; 127; CANR 45; CDBLB 1890-1914; DLB 10, 19, 98, 156; MTCW 1

Yehoshua, A(braham) B. 1936- .. CLC 13, 31
See also CA 33-36R; CANR 43

Yep, Laurence Michael 1948- .... CLC 35
See also AAYA 5; CA 49-52; CANR 1, 46; CLR 3, 17; DLB 52; JRDA; MAICYA; SATA 7, 69

Yerby, Frank G(arvin) 1916-1991 . CLC 1, 7, 22; BLC 3; DAM MULT
See also BW 1; CA 9-12R; 136; CANR 16, 52; DLB 76; INT CANR-16; MTCW 1

Yesenin, Sergei Alexandrovich
See Esenin, Sergei (Alexandrovich)

Yevtushenko, Yevgeny (Alexandrovich) 1933-·
CLC 1, 3, 13, 26, 51; DAM POET
See also CA 81-84; CANR 33, 54; MTCW 1

Yezierska, Anzia 1885(?)-1970 .... CLC 46
See also CA 126; 89-92; DLB 28; MTCW 1

Yglesias, Helen 1915- .... CLC 7, 22
See also CA 37-40R; CAAS 20; CANR 15, 65;

INT CANR-15; MTCW 1

Yokomitsu Riichi 1898-1947 .... TCLC 47

Yonge, Charlotte (Mary) 1823-1901 TCLC 48
See also CA 109; 163; DLB 18, 163; SATA 17

York, Jeremy
See Creasey, John

York, Simon
See Heinlein, Robert A(nson)

Yorke, Henry Vincent 1905-1974 ...... CLC 13
See also Green, Henry
See also CA 85-88; 49-52

Yosano Akiko 1878-1942 .... TCLC 59; PC 11
See also CA 161

Yoshimoto, Banana .... CLC 84
See also Yoshimoto, Mahoko

Yoshimoto, Mahoko 1964-
See Yoshimoto, Banana
See also CA 144

Young, Al(bert James) 1939- CLC 19; BLC 3; DAM MULT
See also BW 2; CA 29-32R; CANR 26, 65; DLB 33

Young, Andrew (John) 1885-1971 ...... CLC 5
See also CA 5-8R; CANR 7, 29

Young, Collier
See Bloch, Robert (Albert)

Young, Edward 1683-1765 .... LC 3, 40
See also DLB 95

Young, Marguerite (Vivian) 1909-1995 C L C 82
See also CA 13-16; 150; CAP 1

Young, Neil 1945- .... CLC 17
See also CA 110

Young Bear, Ray A. 1950- ...... CLC 94; DAM MULT
See also CA 146; DLB 175; NNAL

Yourcenar, Marguerite 1903-1987 CLC 19, 38, 50, 87; DAM NOV
See also CA 69-72; CANR 23, 60; DLB 72; DLBY 88; MTCW 1

Yurick, Sol 1925- .... CLC 6
See also CA 13-16R; CANR 25

Zabolotsky, Nikolai Alekseevich 1903-1958
TCLC 52
See also CA 116; 164

Zamiatin, Yevgenii
See Zamyatin, Evgeny Ivanovich

Zamora, Bernice (B. Ortiz) 1938- .. CLC 89; DAM MULT; HLC
See also CA 151; DLB 82; HW

Zamyatin, Evgeny Ivanovich 1884-1937
TCLC 8, 37
See also CA 105; 166

Zangwill, Israel 1864-1926 .... TCLC 16
See also CA 109; 167; DLB 10, 135, 197

Zappa, Francis Vincent, Jr. 1940-1993
See Zappa, Frank
See also CA 108; 143; CANR 57

Zappa, Frank .... CLC 17
See also Zappa, Francis Vincent, Jr.

Zaturenska, Marya 1902-1982 ...... CLC 6, 11
See also CA 13-16R; 105; CANR 22

Zeami 1363-1443 .... DC 7

Zelazny, Roger (Joseph) 1937-1995 . CLC 21
See also AAYA 7; CA 21-24R; 148; CANR 26, 60; DLB 8; MTCW 1; SATA 57; SATA-Brief 39

Zhdanov, Andrei Alexandrovich 1896-1948
TCLC 18
See also CA 117; 167

Zhukovsky, Vasily 1783-1852 .... NCLC 35

Ziegenhagen, Eric .... CLC 55

Zimmer, Jill Schary
See Robinson, Jill

Zimmerman, Robert
See Dylan, Bob

Zindel, Paul 1936- CLC 6, 26; DA; DAB; DAC;

DAM DRAM, MST, NOV; DC 5
See also AAYA 2; CA 73-76; CANR 31, 65; CLR 3, 45; DLB 7, 52; JRDA; MAICYA; MTCW 1; SATA 16, 58, 102

Zinov'Ev, A. A.
See Zinoviev, Alexander (Aleksandrovich)

Zinoviev, Alexander (Aleksandrovich) 1922-
CLC 19
See also CA 116; 133; CAAS 10

Zoilus
See Lovecraft, H(oward) P(hillips)

Zola, Emile (Edouard Charles Antoine) 1840-1902 TCLC 1, 6, 21, 41; DA; DAB; DAC; DAM MST, NOV; WLC
See also CA 104; 138; DLB 123

Zoline, Pamela 1941- .... CLC 62
See also CA 161

Zorrilla y Moral, Jose 1817-1893 .... NCLC 6

Zoshchenko, Mikhail (Mikhailovich) 1895-1958
TCLC 15; SSC 15
See also CA 115; 160

Zuckmayer, Carl 1896-1977 .... CLC 18
See also CA 69-72; DLB 56, 124

Zuk, Georges
See Skelton, Robin

Zukofsky, Louis 1904-1978 CLC 1, 2, 4, 7, 11, 18; DAM POET; PC 11
See also CA 9-12R; 77-80; CANR 39; DLB 5, 165; MTCW 1

Zweig, Paul 1935-1984 .... CLC 34, 42
See also CA 85-88; 113

Zweig, Stefan 1881-1942 .... TCLC 17
See also CA 112; DLB 81, 118

Zwingli, Huldreich 1484-1531 .... LC 37
See also DLB 179

Literary Criticism Series
Cumulative Topic Index

This index lists all topic entries in Gale's *Classical and Medieval Literature Criticism, Contemporary Literary Criticism, Literature Criticism from 1400 to 1800, Nineteenth-Century Literature Criticism,* and *Twentieth-Century Literary Criticism.*

Topic Index

Topic Index

Twentieth-Century Literary Criticism
Cumulative Nationality Index

ISBN 0-7876-2742-9

90000